BRITISH HISTORY

VOLUME II
M TO Z
INDEX

BRITISH HISTORY

VOLUME II
M TO Z
INDEX

DAVID LOADES, EDITOR

FITZROY DEARBORN
New York   London

Published in 2003 by

Fitzroy Dearborn
29 West 35th Street
New York, NY 10001-2299
www.routledge-ny.com

Published in Great Britain by
Fitzroy Dearborn
11 New Fetter Lane
London EC4P 4EE
www.routledge.co.uk
Fitzroy Dearborn is an imprint of the Taylor & Francis Group.

10   9   8   7   6   5   4   3   2   1

Printed on acid-free, 250-year-life paper
Manufactured in the United States of America

Library of Congress Cataloging-in-Publication Data

Reader's guide to British history / David Loades, editor.
     p. cm.
Includes bibliographical references and index.
  ISBN 1-57958-242-7 (set : alk. paper) — ISBN 1-57958-426-8 (v. 1 : alk. paper) —
ISBN 1-57958-427-6 (v. 2 : alk. paper)
  1. Great Britain—History—Encyclopedias. I. Loades, D. M.
  DA34.R43 2003
  941′.007′2—dc21

                                                           2003001083

CONTENTS

M

Macbeth d. 1057
King of Scotland

Anderson, Alan Orr, "Macbeth's Relationship to Malcolm II",
Scottish Historical Review, 25 (1928): 377

Barrow, G.W.S., "Macbeth and Other Mormaers of Moray"
in *The Hub of the Highlands: The Book [of] Inverness and
District: The Centenary Volume of Inverness Field Club,
1875–1975*, edited by L. Maclean, Edinburgh: Albyn Press,
1975

Chadwick, Nora K., "The Story of Macbeth: A Study in
Gaelic and Norse Tradition", *Scottish Gaelic Studies*, 6
(1949): 189–211; 7 (1951): 1–25

Cowan, Edward, "Historical Macbeth" in *Moray: Province
and People*, edited by W.D.H. Sellar, Edinburgh: Scottish
Society for Northern Studies, 1993

Crawford, Barbara E., *Scandinavian Scotland*, Leicester:
Leicester University Press, and Atlantic Highlands, New
Jersey: Humanities Press, 1987

Hudson, Benjamin T., "Cnut and the Scottish Kings", *English
Historical Review*, 107/423 (1992): 350–60

Hudson, Benjamin T., *Kings of Celtic Scotland*, Westport,
Connecticut: Greenwood Press, 1994

MacBeth, John, *Macbeth: King, Queen, and Clan*, Edinburgh:
W.J. Hay, 1921

MacMillan, Somerled, *A Vindication of Macbeth and His
Claims*, Ipswich, Massachusetts: Edward B. McMillan,
1959 (private publication)

The popular fame of Macbeth, correctly Mac bethad mac
Findláech, rests less on the career of the historical monarch
than on the notoriety of his literary namesake. Although
Shakespeare's drama *Macbeth* was not the only element in the
evolution of the fictional character for whom the name was
borrowed, much modern historical interest in Macbeth has
revolved around perceptions of the eponymous theatrical figure.
The image of Macbeth as a personification of evil has been
vigorously attacked by a variety of individuals, who have
installed in its place the equally false and simplistic figure of a
highland patriot. Most of these accounts compensate with
enthusiasm for what they lack in scholarship, and MACBETH
and MACMILLAN are typical of these partisan commentators.
Both writers immediately and honestly state their intention to
"rescue" Macbeth's reputation from what they feel is the unjust
portrait given in works from the late Middle Ages to their own
time. John Macbeth gives a useful survey of the literature to his
day with many accurate critical comments. His effort to write
a biography of the 11th-century prince is hampered by his interest in establishing a lineage that extends to his own family.
MacMillian also uses a genealogical approach both to justify
Macbeth's claim to the kingship and to place him within an
historical context. Unfortunately, neither writer demonstrates
more than a slight understanding of the culture, institutions,
or political situation of the mid-11th century.

The career of the real Macbeth was only slightly less compelling than that of his fantasy copy. HUDSON (1994) assembles
the known materials, and argues that Macbeth was an important innovator who understood the benefits he could gain from
the world outside the Gaelic-speaking lands. He was the first
sole king of all the Scots and was the first Scottish monarch who
is known to have made a pilgrimage to Rome. With his queen,
Gruoch, a distant relative of his predecessor Duncan I, they were
benefactors of the church, while Macbeth was a patron of literature who commissioned a poem on the legendary history of the
Picts. Far more influential was his political triumph, brief as it
was, which would lay the foundations for the later medieval
kingdom. At the same time, his success owed something to his
broad view, and Macbeth deliberately looked to the continent,
especially Francia, for new ideas. His use of Norman mercenaries, together with his pilgrimage and diplomatically astute
marriage, reveal a sophisticated mind determined to hold power
by any means possible.

Macbeth's reign was welcomed by many of his subjects, and
he was generally seen as a good monarch. A contemporary view
of him is given in the *Prophecy of Berchán*, which combines
an eyewitness description of his appearance (he was slender
with blond hair and a ruddy complexion – not a description of
beauty by Celtic standards) with a glowing report of his reign,
in contrast with the unfavourable comments of later writers.
ANDERSON suggests that he might have been a kinsman of
Malcolm II, which is mentioned by several, late, records, and
that this could partly explain his success as well as imply a
dynastic aspect to his "usurpation". HUDSON (1992) argues
that whatever were, or were not, his family connections with
Malcolm II, there were political ties that are visible in his
attendance on that king for the famous meeting with Cnut. The
identification of Macbeth as a king by English records shows
that he was the ruler of his home territory by 1031, and almost
certainly by 1029 when he would have succeeded his cousin.
BARROW sees the rivalry between Macbeth's dynasty and that
of his successor but one, Malcolm "Canmore", as spanning
several centuries. He considers that part of Macbeth's success

was due to the secure position enjoyed by his family in his native area of Moray, and that his career should not be considered in isolation, but as part of a much longer competition between noble families. The contest would not end until the 13th century, when the literary transformation of Macbeth into a tormented villain began, a process studied by CHADWICK. She traces the development of the legend in which, by the end of the Middle Ages, even a diabolical parentage was not too fantastic to find its way into the 15th-century versified history of Andrew of Wyntoun.

Only recently has one important source of information about Macbeth been given its due: the Scandinavian sagas. The tentative identification of Macbeth as the Karl Hundasson of the *Orkneyinga Saga* was convincingly argued by CRAWFORD, who accepts the historical basis of the saga and shows how it forces a reassessment of the political situation in northern Scotland. She notes that the true importance of Karl's battles with the saga's hero Thorfinn of the Orkneys was a fight for control of northern Scotland. Linking the Norse with Gaelic sources, COWAN shows how Macbeth's career demonstrates what an able monarch he was. Forced to fight on two fronts – in the north against the Orkney jarl Thorfinn and in the south against the Northumbrian earl Siward – Macbeth's defeats were due less to incompetence than a lack of resources. His successor and stepson Lulach was unable to hold together the kingdom in the face of hostility coupled with the installation of Malcolm Canmore south of the Highlands, whence he led his ultimately successful campaign.

The hold of literature on the popular (as well as learned) imagination ensures that, for a long while yet, Macbeth is doomed to be a captive of the image of a cruel fiend, regardless of how many scholarly, or semi-scholarly, studies argue otherwise. This is unfortunate, for the reign of the historical Macbeth is important for understanding not just his Scottish kingdom, but also for his influence throughout Britain.

BENJAMIN HUDSON

See also Duncan I; Edward "the Confessor"; Malcolm II; Malcolm III

MacDonald, (James) Ramsay

1866–1937

Labour politician, statesman, and prime minister

Barker, Bernard (editor), *Ramsay MacDonald's Political Writings*, London: Allen Lane, and New York: St Martin's Press, 1972

Elton, Godfrey, *The Life of James Ramsay MacDonald (1866–1919)*, London: Collins, 1939

Hamilton, Mary Agnes, *J. Ramsay MacDonald*, London: Jonathan Cape, 1929; reprinted, Freeport, New York: Books for Libraries Press, 1971

"Iconoclast" [M.A. Hamilton], *The Man of To-morrow: J. Ramsay MacDonald*, London: Parsons, 1923; as *J. Ramsay MacDonald, the Man of To-morrow*, New York: Seltzer, 1924

"Iconoclast" [M.A. Hamilton], *J. Ramsay MacDonald (1923–1925)*, London: Parsons, and New York: Seltzer, 1925

Lyman, Richard W., *The First Labour Government, 1924*, London: Chapman and Hall, 1957; reprinted, New York: Russell and Russell, 1975

Marquand, David, *Ramsay MacDonald*, London: Jonathan Cape, 1977; with new introduction, London: Richard Cohen, 1997

Morgan, Austen, *J. Ramsay MacDonald*, Manchester: Manchester University Press, 1987

Morgan, Kenneth O., *Labour People: Leaders and Lieutenants from Hardie to Kinnock*, Oxford and New York: Oxford University Press, 1987; revised edition, 1992

Mowat, C.L., "Ramsay MacDonald and the Labour Party" in *Essays in Labour History 1886–1923*, edited by Asa Briggs and John Saville, London: Macmillan, and Hamden, Connecticut: Archon Books, 1971

Sacks, Benjamin, *J. Ramsay MacDonald in Thought and Action*, Albuquerque: University of New Mexico Press, 1952

Skidelsky, Robert, *Politicians and the Slump: The Labour Government of 1929–1931*, London: Macmillan, 1967

Tanner, Duncan, entry on MacDonald in *Biographical Dictionary of British Prime Ministers*, edited by Robert Eccleshall and Graham Walker, London and New York: Routledge, 1998

Tiltman, H. Hessell, *James Ramsay MacDonald: Labour's Man of Destiny*, London: Jarrolds, 1929; as *J. Ramsay MacDonald: Labor's Man of Destiny*, New York: Stokes, 1929

Tracey, Herbert, *From Doughty Street to Downing Street: The Rt. Hon. J. Ramsay MacDonald, M.P., A Biographical Study*, London: Marlowe Savage, 1924

Weir, L. MacNeill, *The Tragedy of Ramsay MacDonald: A Political Biography*, London: Secker and Warburg, 1938

Wrigley, Chris, "James Ramsay MacDonald 1922–1931" in *Leading Labour: From Keir Hardie to Tony Blair*, edited by Kevin Jefferys, London and New York: I.B. Tauris, 1999

Both in his lifetime and since, the reputation of Ramsay MacDonald has fluctuated more widely than that of most other figures in British public life. Before 1914 he was a Labour MP who acted as the leading theoretician of his party; in World War I he was traduced for his lack of support for the war and lost his parliamentary seat in 1918; regaining the leadership of his party, he became prime minister in the minority Labour governments of 1924 and 1929–31; and in the economic crisis of 1931 he deserted his party to lead the National Government, an action that many on the left regarded as treachery. He continued as the prime minister of a Conservative-dominated administration until 1935, and, as lord president of the council, remained in the cabinet until 1937. Earlier biographical studies, coloured by the political sympathies of their authors, reflect this trajectory.

A Labour Party publicity officer, TRACEY, celebrated the advent of MacDonald's premiership in a book titled to emphasize its subject's rise from obscurity to fame (a genre then common in labour biography). Two books by a Labour Party activist, HAMILTON, writing under the pen-name "Iconoclast", gave a sympathetic yet not sycophantic account of the period up to the end of the first Labour government; in 1929 a revised single-volume version of these books appeared under her own name. In that year, TILTMAN somewhat journalistically portrayed MacDonald in a favourable light in a book that quoted extensively from his speeches. After 1931 memoirs and journalism emanating from the left were coloured by antipathy towards MacDonald. The most bitter and sustained criticism was that of a Labour MP, WEIR, who denounced not only the apostasy of 1931 but also the whole of MacDonald's career. This large and powerfully written book exerted an influence for many years; by comparison ELTON's life, written by a supporter of the National Government with the assistance of MacDonald's politician son, Malcolm, and ending in 1919, made little impact, not least as the projected second volume never appeared. Elton also contributed a lengthy and favourable assessment to the *Dictionary of National Biography*. The outbreak of war in 1939 and the search for those culpable led to the grouping of MacDonald among the "guilty men" who had seemingly failed to prepare national defences against the threat of fascism.

By the 1950s there was, if not a rehabilitation of MacDonald's reputation, a greater willingness to approach his career without rancour. SACKS, an American academic, compiled a positive biography in 1952, while another American scholar, LYMAN, in 1957 provided a balanced account of the first minority Labour government. By the time of the centenary of MacDonald's birth in 1966, a number of more sympathetic articles had appeared. It was accepted that, in his rejection of revolutionary socialism in favour of reformist policies, MacDonald represented an intrinsic feature of the Labour Party, an argument developed by SKIDELSKY in his study of the second minority Labour government and by BARKER in his introduction to a selection of his writings. Similarly in an authoritative essay MOWAT argued that in the crisis of 1931 MacDonald was helpless, while for the Labour Party to condemn him amounted to a condemnation of itself, for the party had chosen and retained him as its leader.

These revisionist publications anticipated part of the case made in the major study of MacDonald, MARQUAND's biography of 1977. Written by a right-of-centre Labour MP at the invitation of Malcolm MacDonald, and drawing extensively on hitherto unavailable family papers, it contained much new material. Most reviewers were warm in their praise. Asa Briggs, for example, described it as "an outstanding contribution to historical understanding" that swept away the old myths to give a rounded portrait (*Guardian*, 3 March 1977). In the words of A.J.P. Taylor, "Marquand does not conceal MacDonald's faults and failures, but he also does justice to MacDonald's great achievements" (*Observer*, 6 March 1977). Max Beloff wrote: "it is the best and best-written biography we now have of any 20th-century British statesman" (*Daily Telegraph*, 2 March 1977). Although in his preface Marquand discussed the need to avoid the traps of hindsight and apologia, his study has been criticized for an approach that shares similar principles of social democracy to those of MacDonald. Forty years after his death, there were some who continued to echo the charge that MacDonald's vanity and arrogance had led him to betray his

party. It is perhaps also the case that access to an extensive amount of primary material led to a relative neglect of the findings of other historians. This was emphasized when in 1997 a second edition of the biography consisted of the unrevised text of 1977 together with a short introduction of a general nature. However, the stature of Marquand's book means that it has cast a shadow over subsequent work on MacDonald and the Labour politics of his time. This was recognized by Austen MORGAN in his book-length study. Although writing from an avowedly Marxist position, Morgan acknowledged that Marquand's "is the one and only serious book on MacDonald". His own conclusion is that the failings of later Labour governments make any judgement of MacDonald's policies appear less unfavourable. The starting-point for Kenneth MORGAN, too, is Marquand's biography, although in a brief but characteristically shrewd assessment he takes a more critical position regarding the crisis of 1931, yet allows also for the broader inadequacies of the Labour Party. Two recent chapter-length surveys of MacDonald's political record – those by TANNER and WRIGLEY – while citing more recent work and including other insights also show their debt to Marquand.

DAVID E. MARTIN

See also Citrine; Depression; Henderson; Independent Labour Party; Morrison; Snowden

Macmillan, Harold, Earl of Stockton

1894–1986

Conservative politician, statesman, and prime minister

Aldous, Richard and Sabine Lee (editors), *Harold Macmillan and Britain's World Role*, London: Macmillan, and New York: St Martin's Press, 1996

Aldous, Richard and Sabine Lee (editors), *Harold Macmillan: Aspects of a Political Life*, London: Macmillan, and New York: St Martin's Press, 1999

Booker, Christopher, *A Looking-Glass Tragedy: The Controversy over the Repatriations from Austria in 1945*, London: Duckworth, 1997

Davenport-Hines, Richard, *The Macmillans*, London: Heinemann, 1992

Fisher, Nigel, *Harold Macmillan: A Biography*, London: Weidenfeld and Nicolson, 1982

Gearson, John P.S., *Harold Macmillan and the Berlin Wall Crisis, 1958–1962: The Limits of Interest and Force*, London: Macmillan, and New York: St Martin's Press, 1998

Horne, Alistair, *Macmillan*, 2 vols, London: Macmillan, 1988–89; as *Harold Macmillan*, 2 vols, New York: Viking, 1989

Hughes, Emrys, *Macmillan: Portrait of a Politician*, London: Allen and Unwin, 1962

Lamb, Richard, *The Macmillan Years 1957–1963: The Emerging Truth*, London: John Murray, 1995

Macmillan, Harold, *Winds of Change 1914–1939*, London: Macmillan, and New York: Harper and Row, 1966

Macmillan, Harold, *The Blast of War 1939–1945*, London: Macmillan, 1967; New York: Harper and Row, 1968

Macmillan, Harold, *Tides of Fortune 1945–1955*, London: Macmillan, and New York: Harper and Row, 1969

Macmillan, Harold, *Riding the Storm 1956–1959*, London: Macmillan, and New York: Harper and Row, 1971

Macmillan, Harold, *Pointing the Way 1959–1961*, London: Macmillan, 1972

Macmillan, Harold, *At the End of the Day, 1961–1963*, London: Macmillan, and New York: Harper and Row, 1973

Ritschel, Daniel, *The Politics of Planning: The Debate on Economic Planning in Britain in the 1930s*, Oxford: Clarendon Press, and New York: Oxford University Press, 1997

Sampson, Anthony, *Macmillan: A Study in Ambiguity*, London: Allen Lane, and New York: Simon and Schuster, 1967

Tolstoy, Nikolai, *The Minister and the Massacres*, London: Hutchinson, 1986

Turner, John, *Macmillan*, London and New York: Longman, 1994

Tratt, Jacqueline, *The Macmillan Government and Europe: A Study in the Process of Policy Development*, London: Macmillan, and New York: St Martin's Press, 1996

Following his early retirement in 1963, MACMILLAN set out to shape his own historical image with a massive six-volume autobiography, published between 1966 and 1973. A well-researched and highly engaging work of historical self-validation, it painted a romantic portrait of a difficult but ultimately rewarding political life. Macmillan depicted his decision to enter politics after World War I as that of a one-nation Tory radical, determined to serve those who had so courageously followed his orders as a young officer during the war. It was the strength of this paternalistic commitment that led him to incur the wrath of his own Conservative Party leadership with his pioneering advocacy of Keynesian recovery policies during the slump-ridden inter-war years. His isolation was only compounded by his early and vocal opposition to appeasement. However, his bold stance of principled dissent was finally rewarded during the war, when he rose to prominence under Churchill's patronage, and thoroughly vindicated afterwards, when his party's unexpected defeat in 1945 persuaded it to embrace his brand of progressive Toryism for its own. Macmillan himself ascended rapidly through the ranks, reaching the pinnacle of 10 Downing Street in 1957. After rescuing his party from the debacle of Suez and winning convincingly in the 1959 general election, he confidently steered the country through the stormy waters of the Cold War into a graceful retreat from the empire. At home, he remained true to his early ideals by protecting the welfare state against critics within his own cabinet and presiding over the unprecedented affluence of the late 1950s. While the original meaning of the famous phrase may have been much misunderstood, the autobiography clearly conveyed Macmillan's firm conviction that Britain had "never had it so good".

Macmillan's highly successful attempt to write his own myth was later sustained by popular nostalgia for his era, kindled in no small measure by his severe scolding of Thatcherism in the 1980s. Historians have certainly found it remarkably difficult to resist the seductive romance of his well-crafted self-portrait. Though early biographers such as HUGHES, SAMPSON, and

FISHER drew attention to the fact that Macmillan's political success owed as much to his enlightened ideas as it did to his ruthless ambition, cynical scheming, and a highly artificial public persona of an Edwardian grandee, they clearly failed to dislodge his original narrative of paternalistic virtue rewarded.

HORNE's official biography served mostly to reinforce the authorized image. Horne was criticized for his over-reliance on the autobiography and extensive interviews with Macmillan himself, at the expense of research in either official or private papers. Although he provided a highly compelling picture of Macmillan's personality, including a very candid first-time account of the miseries of his private life, and shed a less than flattering light on some of the darker recesses of Macmillan's career, such as his about-face during the Suez crisis, Horne was less effective in assessing his subject's public record as a politician and statesman.

When it finally arrived, the revisionist challenge to Macmillan's flattering image was appropriately dramatic. The most explosive was TOLSTOY's loud accusation that, in his wartime role as minister resident in the Mediterranean, Macmillan had been directly responsible for the deaths of thousands of pro-German White Russians, who had surrendered to the British in Yugoslavia but were handed over to the Soviets in 1945. While Macmillan's formal role in authorizing the transfer is clear, a lengthy libel trial and BOOKER's more recent scholarly analysis have conclusively laid to rest Tolstoy's charge of moral culpability in what was ultimately a very difficult decision to honour the Yalta agreement and preserve peaceful relations with wartime allies.

DAVENPORT-HINES wrote a highly entertaining, if also very unauthorized, romp through some of the more salacious anecdotes in the Macmillan family saga, climaxing with a flamboyant psycho-historical deconstruction of its most prominent member. Denied by the family the right to use any of Macmillan's private or published words, Davenport-Hines took his revenge with a detailed account of the emotionally crippling role played by Macmillan's domineering mother, intimations of early homosexuality, and gossipy tales of illegitimacy and dysfunctionality within the Macmillan clan.

More recent studies have been less diverting, though also perhaps more balanced and scholarly. RITSCHEL's examination of the dissident economic debate in the 1930s rejects the accepted image of Macmillan as a progressive Keynesian, noting instead the heavily corporatist nature of the business ideology of "capitalist planning" which dominated his economic thought for much of the inter-war period. Macmillan's embrace of Keynesianism shortly before the war is shown to have come about less as an ideological conversion to a more progressive economic agenda than as the pragmatic by-product of his search for a politically attractive domestic platform to unite the disparate opponents of appeasement. It thus served as an early premonition of Macmillan's opportunistic use of Keynesian demand management for electoral benefit in the 1950s.

TURNER's and LAMB's books represent the first extensive studies of Macmillan's governments since the public records for all of his years in power became available under the 30-year rule. Though both writers show considerable sympathy for Macmillan and the constraints he faced, they tend to be highly critical of his record. Both conclude that Macmillan wasted an opportunity to modernize Britain's industrial base by opting for politically rewarding but economically damaging consumerism. His chronic manipulation of the economy for electoral purposes aggravated the widening trade gap and inflationary tendencies building up in the postwar economy. Similarly, Macmillan's Quixotic efforts to preserve Britain's declining world power status are shown to have seriously undermined his vacillating attempts to join the European Economic Community (EEC), while his pursuit of the largely mythical "special relationship" with the United States failed to provide Britain with a clear alternative role. His handling of decolonization was similarly plagued by indecision and a profound failure to envision a workable alternative to imperial government.

The most recent studies by GEARSON, TRATT, and ALDOUS & LEE have focused mainly on the foreign policy dimension of the Macmillan era. Benefiting from access to Macmillan's large collection of private papers, recently made available at the Bodleian Library in Oxford, these works offer much valuable detail, but alter surprisingly little in the basic picture drawn by Turner and Lamb.

DANIEL RITSCHEL

See also Baldwin; Consensus in the Postwar Period; Decolonization; Eden; Keynes; Suez Crisis

Magna Carta 1215

Holt, J.C., *Magna Carta*, 2nd revised edition, Cambridge and New York: Cambridge University Press, 1992

McKechnie, William Sharp, *Magna Carta: A Commentary on the Great Charter of King John*, Glasgow: Maclehose, 1905; 2nd revised edition, Glasgow: Maclehose, and New York: Franklin, 1914

Norgate, Kate, *John Lackland*, London and New York: Macmillan, 1902

Powicke, Frederick Maurice, *Stephen Langton: Being the Ford Lectures Delivered in the University of Oxford in Hilary Term 1927*, Oxford: Clarendon Press, 1928; New York: Barnes and Noble, 1965

Warren, W. Lewis, *King John*, London: Eyre and Spottiswoode, and New York: Norton, 1961

West, Francis, *The Justiciarship in England, 1066–1232*, Cambridge: Cambridge University Press, 1966

From the 17th to the early 20th century, Magna Carta has been seen as the assertion of law against a king who, in McKECHNIE's words, abused his power for selfish ends. As a lawyer, McKechnie was chiefly concerned, in his commentary on its 63 clauses – its length being the reason the charter is called "Great" by contrast with the "Little" charter of forest law and customs – to show how they became the common law of England. In doing so he did not consider the political and social context in which they were framed. By implication Magna Carta was a document of fundamental importance in the protection of English liberty, especially parliamentary consent to taxation and the right to trial by jury. NORGATE, however, had already argued that the Great Charter was a feudal document, the barons who forced it on the king being concerned with specific feudal issues and being unable to rise to the lofty conception of a contract between king and people to secure equal rights to every class and individual in the nation. Many later writers accepted her views, not allowing that even a few of the barons might have been "statesman-like".

Any lofty principles, it followed, must have come from a man of principle: Stephen Langton. A leading theologian in the schools of Paris, made a cardinal by Innocent III, in 1206 Langton was elected archbishop by the monks of Christ Church, Canterbury in the presence of the pope; King John's refusal to accept him led to the papal interdict of 1208. In 1213 the penitent king received Langton into England at a time when the northern barons were refusing overseas service in his expedition to Poitou. POWICKE gave Langton the credit for using Henry I's coronation charter of liberties as the keystone of his insistence that the king judge men according to the just judgement of his court when John proposed to take vengeance on the northern barons who had refused service in Poitou. Powicke connected this to the "Unknown Charter", the first written legal commentary on the king's oath to do good justice since Langton's return, which had a clause limiting service to Normandy and Brittany. But he did not accept that all the barons were incapable of statesmanship in the resistance which followed John's military failure in Poitou and Normandy. Not all barons joined the rebels, even though some, parting company with Langton, were prepared, as a group bound by oath and formally renouncing their fealty, to use force against the king in 1215.

This view of Langton as a man of principle with a practical turn of mind, contrasted with the "greedy passions" of leading baronial opponents of the king, was accepted by WARREN. Hotheads might fly to arms, provoke the king, inflate their demands when he offered concessions, but their fathers, together with the bishops headed by Langton, formed the middle party which negotiated the Magna Carta settlement between John and the rebels at Runnymede.

In a scholarly and exhaustive account of what led to the charter, of its contents, and its quality, HOLT did not accept that Langton was an originator. He held Magna Carta to be a failure: it was intended as a peace but provoked a war; it pretended to state customary law but promoted disagreement and contention. It was valid for only three months, then annulled by the pope. When it was reissued in 1216 and 1217 disputed clauses were deleted. Still further amended, the reissue of 1225 was the version which became law. In June 1215, the text bristled with the technicalities of feudal law: reliefs, wardships, escheats, marriages, dower, widows, debts, aids, ransom, knight service, assizes, amercements, court pleas, and good justice. Nevertheless, in what survived in later reissues, the charter was a grant to the kingdom or community: to the church through free election of bishops and abbots; to all free men who might not be taken, imprisoned, exiled or ruined except by the lawful judgement of peers. It took non-baronial interests into account in limiting the amercement (fining) of villeins so as not to deprive them of their livelihood; it protected municipal privileges, and provided that the liberties the king granted to his men should be conferred by them on their men, thus protecting the interests of under-tenants. Indeed, the charter implies the real political power of the knights and the gentry which both king and barons had to take into account in negotiating and drafting.

If these conclusions stress the potential significance of Magna Carta for later generations, in 1215 its immediate occasion was resentment of the king's administration. WEST, looking at the office of justiciar, the king's alter ego, found John's governance to be of the same kind as that of his predecessors. Henry II's and Richard I's justiciars might have been accused of abuses of the type the barons cited: use of the writ *præcipe* which deprived a free man of his court; the exaction of increments above the ancient "farm" of a county; and exaction of heavy amercements and reliefs. In the three reissues of the charter in the minority of Henry III, the clauses that were intrusions into royal administration largely disappeared: the justiciar, Hubert de Burgh, exacted profits above the normal farm of the county; assizes were to be held in the counties once, not four times a year; difficult cases were to come to the court *de banco*, the bench at Westminster, not to an itinerant court. Magna Carta came to be a symbol of good faith, but royal government had to provide the king's necessities. The reissue of 1225, the text which found its way on to the statute book, was "of the king's free will" in exchange for a grant of a 15th on moveables by consent of tenants-in-chief in council. Only in 1237 did Henry III confirm all the liberties granted by earlier reissues "notwithstanding that these charters were completed when we were a minor".

FRANCIS WEST

See also Alexander II; Feudal Law; Henry III; John; Langton; Llywelyn ab Iorwerth; Revenue, Non-Parliamentary; Social Structure: Aristocracy, English

Malaya and Other East Asian Dependencies   20th century

Harper, T.N., *The End of Empire and the Making of Malaya*, Cambridge and New York: Cambridge University Press, 1998

Huff, W.G., *The Economic Growth of Singapore: Trade and Development in the Twentieth Century*, Cambridge and New York: Cambridge University Press, 1994

Miners, Norman, *Hong Kong under Imperial Rule, 1912–1941*, Hong Kong, New York and Oxford: Oxford University Press, 1987

Porritt, Vernon L., *British Colonial Rule in Sarawak, 1946–1963*, Kuala Lumpur, New York, and Oxford: Oxford University Press, 1997

Short, Anthony, *The Communist Insurrection in Malaya, 1948–1960*, London: Mueller, and New York: Crane Russak, 1975

White, Nicholas J., *Business, Government, and the End of Empire: Malaya, 1942–1957*, Kuala Lumpur, New York, and Oxford: Oxford University Press, 1996

Among British dependencies of East Asia, or the "Far East" (a Eurocentric term) – Hong Kong, the Federation of Malaya, Singapore, Sarawak, North Borneo, and Brunei – Malaya has particularly interested scholars, because it was the largest colony, and because there was an unsuccessful communist insurrection in the postwar period. SHORT's account of the latter was based on unprecedented access to the records of the Malayan government and occasioned a legal dispute which held up the book's publication for seven years. He believes that while the Malayan Communist Party (MCP) started its anti-colonial uprising in a conducive political environment, the colonial regime was able to re-establish its authority for a number of reasons: the Chinese community, the main supporters of the MCP, were ideologically divided and numerically weak; Malayans largely supported the colonial regime; military and police forces employed good counterinsurgency tactics; and the colonial authorities, fortunately blessed with good leaders, made the right policy decisions, notably to resettle large numbers of rural dwellers.

HARPER seeks an integration of social and political approaches to a study of the last years of colonial Malaya. He argues that state–society relations were transformed in this period, as the colonial state sought to foster economic development and contain and suppress communist insurrection, and as ethnic Chinese, Malay, and Indian communities had to turn to the state for resources and support. He believes that the insurgency was a societal reaction to state attempts to reimpose control on the use of land and resources in rural areas and that thereafter the colonial state had to employ new strategies which sought to build up loyalty to the colonial and hence to the postcolonial state. He argues this left a legacy of communal- (and thus ethnic-) based politics.

WHITE provides the most up-to-date and comprehensive account of British government and business policymaking towards Malaya in the years before independence. He is particularly strong on the organization of what he argues was a heterogeneous expatriate business community. While he accepts that business and the state shared common liberal values, he argues that there was no close business–state nexus. The state, he notes, often had wider (and thus often divergent) interests at stake, such as the quality of Anglo-American relations, and thus could not support the interests of expatriate capital. He rejects the application of neo-colonial theories to Malaysian history, noting that the wider business community accepted the need for international capital in the post-independence period, while the economic significance of empire to British governments and business interests declined rapidly in the 1950s.

HUFF explores the longer-term relationship between colonialism and economic development in what is the definitive economic history of Singapore. He gives a detailed empirical breakdown of economic growth and structural change in this small city-state, locating his findings in theories of economic development. He concludes that until 1939 trade in staple products such as rubber, tin, and oil – and thus openness to world markets – was the engine of growth because it allowed the colony to exploit its good location and its good access via western and Chinese networks to supplies of capital and labour. After 1959 the growth dynamic changed due to the emergence of a strong (and non-democratic) post-colonial state which regulated savings and wage rates and dealt with market failure.

In a chronologically tighter and thematically wider account, which examines political, social, and economic developments, PORRITT assesses British policies in a small dependency, Sarawak. He argues that significant advances were made in the immediate postwar decades as Sarawak was geared towards independence but that administrators were hamstrung by a reluctance to override traditional attitudes, by the threat of communist rebellions – which drained resources into policing and compromised human rights – and by a reluctance to extend educational opportunities. The authorities also had very little time in which to carry out their programme, a shortage caused in part by a determination to integrate what was perceived as a non-viable political unit into a larger more viable one, Malaysia. He notes that the gains from this period of colonial rule were not distributed evenly: the ethnic Chinese gained most as many were provided with land and commercial opportunities; the non-Muslim indigenous peoples gained least as their customary rights to land and to political autonomy were eroded by the state.

MINERS assesses the relationship between the metropolitan state in London and the colonial state in Hong Kong by exploring policymaking on a range of issues such as the regulation of prostitution, the abolition of *msui tsai* (the traditional Chinese practice of giving up a female child for work as a domestic servant in another family), and the control of opium. These issues shed much light on the social history of this small colonial city-state. He argues London intervened more in colonial affairs in the period, for example by recommending adherence to regulations governing the rights of labour and by insisting that brothels were closed down. But overall power still lay in the territory, where the governor, despite having to take on board the views of members of the legislative and executive councils, could rule "as he saw fit".

DAVID WILLIAM CLAYTON

See also Colonial Wars and Counter-Insurgency; Decolonization; East Asia entries

Malcolm II d. 1034
King of Scotland

Barrow, G.W.S., *Kingship and Unity: Scotland, 1000–1306*, London: Arnold, and Toronto: University of Toronto Press, 1981; reprinted with corrections, Edinburgh: Edinburgh University Press, 1989

Duncan, Archibald A.M., "The Battle of Carham, 1018", *Scottish Historical Review*, 55 (1976): 20–28

Hudson, Benjamin T., "Cnut and the Scottish Kings", *English Historical Review*, 107/423 (1992): 350–60

Hudson, Benjamin T., *Kings of Celtic Scotland*, Westport, Connecticut: Greenwood Press, 1994

Hudson, Benjamin T., *Prophecy of Berchán: Irish and Scottish High-Kings of the Early Middle Ages*, Westport, Connecticut: Greenwood Press, 1996

Kapelle, William E., *The Norman Conquest of the North: The Region and its Transformation, 1000–1135*, Chapel Hill: University of North Carolina Press, and London: Croom Helm, 1979

MacKay, A.E., entry on Malcolm II in *Dictionary of National Biography*, edited by Leslie Stephen and Sidney Lee, 63 vols, London: Smith Elder, 1885–1901

Meehan, D., "The Siege of Durham, the Battle of Carham, and the Cession of Lothian", *Scottish Historical Review*, 55 (1976): 1–19

Stevenson, J.H., "The Law of the Throne: Tanistry and the Introduction of the Law of Primogeniture", *Scottish Historical Review*, 25 (1928): 1–12

If a claim to posthumous fame is based on the success of one's career, then one of the most important early 11th century rulers in Britain was the Scottish king Malcolm II, correctly Máel Choluim mac Cináeda. For historians from the 18th to the 20th century his reign has been used as a chronological marker, with most cursory studies of Scottish history beginning their enquiry with his career. This is partly due to the popular belief that the 11th century saw the transition from "Dark Age" to "Medieval" Scotland during his kingship, and partly to the notice of Malcolm by Irish, Scots, English, and French commentators. Only recently, however, has he begun to receive the recognition for the real accomplishments of his reign. How much he deserved credit was considered by MACKAY. He saw Malcolm as the beneficiary of his ancestors', particularly his father's, gains, but noted that his own actions made those gains permanent.

Information about his early years is provided by the *Prophecy of Berchán* (see HUDSON, 1996), an 11th-century versified history presented as a divinely inspired prophecy, a popular form among Gaelic writers. Malcolm was the son of the late 10th-century king Kenneth II (Cináed mac Máel Choluim) and an Irish princess from Leinster whose name has not survived. During the reign of his cousin and predecessor Kenneth III (Cináed mac Duib) Malcolm was a political exile in the Hebrides, but in 1005 he led a successful rebellion against Kenneth and began his 30-year reign. One of the most important aspects of his kingship was the annexation of southern territories, about which we know more than for any earlier monarch. Malcolm's successes came at the expense of the Britons of Strathclyde and the Anglo-Saxons of Lothian; by 1018 both regions were firmly under his control. Malcolm's interests in Northumbria are the basis for the studies of DUNCAN and MEEHAN. His first foray against the Anglo-Saxons led to his defeat at Durham in 1006, before his success in the battle of Carham in either 1016 or 1018, which extended his realm as far as the Tweed. The former writer argues for the year 1018 as the date of the battle of Carham, while the latter argues for a date of 1016. Central to both arguments is the date of the death of the last known king of Strathclyde, Owen the Bald, as well as the appearance of a comet in 1018. The annexation as far as the Tweed is generally considered contemporary with the Scots annexation of the kingdom of Strathclyde.

In addition to his successful land conquests, Malcolm's other connections with the Anglo-Saxons have received comment. KAPPELLE sees Malcolm as a consummate opportunist, profiting from the confusion in Northumbria during the early 11th century to enlarge his kingdom, both by force of arms and by coercion. The assassination of the Anglo-Saxon ealdorman of Northumbria named Uhtred, as part of the pacification of the region by Cnut, removed a barrier to Scottish ambitions. The marital connections of Malcolm's family with the Northumbrians are seen as part of a process of encroachment. Another problem is the identity of the kings in his entourage for the famous meeting of Malcolm with King Cnut of England and Denmark in 1031, and the reason for that meeting. Accompanied by Macbeth and the king of the Isles named Echmarcach, the English records claim that Malcolm formally submitted to his southern neighbour, an event that is examined by HUDSON (1992). The meeting suggests ties of Malcolm to Scandinavia, while the identification of the kings in his entourage forces a reconsideration of the bounds of his lordship. English materials need to be compared with accounts of Malcolm found in continental records that show the Scots king holding the upper hand in his dealing with Cnut.

A study of many aspects of Malcolm's reign is given by HUDSON (1994), who sees his career intertwined with that of his grandson Duncan I. There it is argued that Malcolm's kingship can be understood only when placed within a general British and Irish context together with a European view. Malcolm is revealed as a powerful monarch whose policy of southern expansion not only brought him into conflict with the powerful successors of St Cuthbert, at Durham since 995, but laid the foundations for the economic expansion that would enrich his successors. His destruction of rivals helped his grandson Duncan I, the son of his daughter Bethoc, to the throne, and also enforced the idea of a single dynasty eligible to put forth candidates to the throne. The implications of these actions within the longer history of Scottish succession is discussed by STEVENSON, who sees Malcolm as an important innovator in the matter of royal succession. Later medieval writers place Malcolm at the heart of administrative change. One such is the 14th-century historian John of Fordun, who claims that the assassination of his father was in part caused by his efforts to have Malcolm succeed him directly, while modern historians see the succession of his grandson Duncan as a momentous shift.

Most modern scholars subscribe to BARROW's estimation of Malcolm as a successful, if mysterious, monarch. He argues that Malcolm generally succeeded in his machinations, within a rapidly changing political situation in northern Britain. The esteem in which he was held by later generations of Scots is testimony to the importance of his time as king. Legal codification, ecclesiastical reorganization, and an early form of state distribution of funds were all credited to Malcolm by Scottish historians in the Middle Ages; while it is almost impossible now to decide how truthful those claims are, they give an indication of the image of this king in the minds of the people. Further study of Malcolm II will add more to our knowledge of a monarch who was influential not only for the Scots kingdom, but for Britain in general.

BENJAMIN HUDSON

See also Æthelred II; Cnut; Duncan I; Macbeth

Malcolm III *c.1031–1093*
King of Scotland

Barrow, G.W.S., *Feudal Britain: The Completion of the Medieval Kingdoms, 1066–1314*, London: Arnold, 1956
Barrow, G.W.S., *Kingship and Unity: Scotland 1000–1306*, London: Arnold, and Toronto: University of Toronto Press, 1981; reprinted with corrections, Edinburgh: Edinburgh University Press, 1989
Cowan, Edward J., "The Historical Macbeth" in *Moray: Province and People*, edited by W.D.H. Sellar, Edinburgh: Scottish Society for Northern Studies, 1993
Duncan, Archibald A.M., *Scotland: The Making of the Kingdom*, Edinburgh: Oliver and Boyd, and New York: Barnes and Noble, 1975
Kapelle, William E., *The Norman Conquest of the North: The Region and Its Transformation, 1000–1135*, London: Croom Helm, and Chapel Hill: University of North Carolina Press, 1979
Lynch, Michael, *Scotland: A New History*, London: Century, 1991; revised edition, London: Pimlico, 1992
McDonald, R. Andrew, "'Treachery in the Remotest Territories of Scotland': Northern Resistance to the Canmore Dynasty, 1130–1230", *Canadian Journal of History*, 34/2 (1999): 161–92
Ritchie, R.L. Graeme, *The Normans in Scotland*, Edinburgh: Edinburgh University Press, 1954
Wall, Valerie, "Malcolm III and the Foundation of Durham Cathedral" in *Anglo-Norman Durham, 1093–1193*, edited by David Rollason, Margaret Harvey, and Michael Prestwich, Woodbridge, Suffolk and Rochester, New York: Boydell Press, 1994

Malcolm III "Canmore" was the longest-reigning and one of the most powerful Scottish kings of the 11th century. The eldest son of King Duncan I (d. 1040), Malcolm spent his adolescence in exile in England during the reign of his rival, Macbeth. Following the defeat of Macbeth in 1054, Malcolm ruled in southern Scotland, and then eliminated Macbeth and his stepson, Lulach, in 1057 and 1058 respectively. Malcolm's path to the throne was bloody, but his 35-year reign, which is generally considered to begin in 1058, was of great importance in Scottish history.

Despite the length of his reign and its generally recognized significance, Malcolm lacks a book-length study, or even comprehensive treatment in a pamphlet or article. He does, however, figure prominently in general histories of the period. A brief but well-rounded and perceptive account of Malcolm's reign will be found in BARROW (1956), while another brief but denser and more technically complex treatment is that of LYNCH. These two works provide good starting-points for an examination of Malcolm's reign.

Malcolm's rise to power is inextricably linked with the dynastic politics of the 11th century. COWAN's account of Macbeth's reign should be considered essential reading for anyone interested in understanding this complex subject, and provides a solid foundation for investigating the rise to power of Malcolm mac Duncan, who figures prominently in the narrative.

One of the key themes of Malcolm's long reign, from its very beginning to its end, is Anglo-Scottish relations; indeed, most historians who have treated Malcolm's reign have done so from this perspective. When Malcolm's father, Duncan, was killed by Macbeth in 1040, Malcolm went into exile in England; some historians, like RITCHIE, have even regarded him as a protégé of King Edward the Confessor. Malcolm's bid for power in 1054 was undertaken with English backing, but, despite this, his reign was dominated by a series of raids and invasions of England.

The most comprehensive treatment of Anglo-Scottish relations in Malcolm's reign is that of KAPELLE, who considers

Malcolm's raids in detail in the broader context of the history of the north of England between 1000 and 1135. He has argued that Malcolm ceased to be an English client almost immediately upon his accession, and became instead the greatest threat from the north. Kapelle pays considerable attention to the motives behind Malcolm's raids, and demonstrates that they were essentially opportunistic; he also shows how they were important in the context of the development of the Anglo-Scottish frontier. DUNCAN has also seen Malcolm's raids and invasions as essentially opportunistic, though he views them as pointless, bringing little profit or territorial gain. BARROW (1981) detects a change of tone in Anglo-Scottish relations around 1066, arguing that up to this point Anglo-Scottish relations were essentially peaceful, while after the Norman conquest they were characterized by "open hostility alternating with sullen suspicion". There are almost as many different opinions on the nature of Malcolm's relations with his southern neighbour as there are commentators upon them.

Foreign relations and domestic affairs during the reign of Malcolm III converge in the issue of matrimonial politics. Malcolm's first wife, whom he married some time around 1065, was Ingibjorg, the widow of the powerful Thorfinn, Earl of Orkney. Barrow (1981) and Lynch relate this marriage to the internal pacification of the kingdom and the need to neutralize the long-standing and traditional threat from the north. But of vastly greater significance was Malcolm's marriage to his second wife, Margaret. An important facet of Anglo-Scottish relations in the aftermath of the Norman Conquest of England in 1066 was the asylum provided to English refugees by Malcolm III. In 1068 Edgar the Ætheling, a representative of the Saxon royal line, arrived in Scotland, accompanied by his sister, Margaret. Her marriage to Malcolm, around 1070 or 1071, had a profound influence on Malcolm himself and on Scottish kingship and society generally, and has been addressed by Barrow (1956, 1981), Duncan, and Lynch, as well as by virtually every commentator on Margaret herself. Barrow (1981) summarizes Margaret's influence in terms of both the immediate, short-term consequences in Anglo-Scottish relations, and the longer-term influences on Scottish society, which was opened to continental and foreign influences of every kind. Duncan has pointed to the fact that Margaret's influence over Malcolm was significant; it is exemplified by the fact that four of their sons were named for Margaret's English ancestors, while names from the house of Alpin are entirely lacking. Ritchie and Duncan are at odds over the degree of English influence in Scotland during this period, but perhaps the greatest significance of the marriage of Malcolm and Margaret lies in the children that it produced: one daughter, Maud, married Henry I of England (providing the link that makes today's British royal family descendants of the royal house of Wessex), while no fewer than three sons, Edgar, Alexander, and David, went on to become kings of Scots and ruled from 1097 to 1153.

In contrast to foreign relations, the domestic affairs of the kingdom under Malcolm remain relatively unexplored. Barrow (1956, 1981) touches briefly on the importance of Malcolm's reign in terms of the political unification of the kingdom. Ritchie has contended that Malcolm ruled relatively untroubled by domestic opposition, but hints of trouble are considered, and their significance for the 12th century explored, by McDONALD. WALL has assessed the role of Malcolm III in the foundation of the new cathedral at Durham in 1093, and her broad-ranging discussion also delves into the Scottish succession and Anglo-Scottish relations after the death of Malcolm.

R. ANDREW McDONALD

See also Alexander I; Duncan I; Edgar the Ætheling; Macbeth; William I, the Conqueror; William II

Malcolm IV *c.*1141–1165
King of Scotland

Anderson, Alan O., *Scottish Annals from English Chroniclers AD 500 to 1286*, London: David Nutt, 1908

Barrow, G.W.S. (compiler and editor), *The Acts of Malcolm IV, King of Scots 1153–1165*, Edinburgh: Edinburgh University Press, 1960

Barrow, G.W.S., *Kingship and Unity: Scotland 1000–1306*, London: Arnold, and Toronto: University of Toronto Press, 1981; reprinted with corrections, Edinburgh: Edinburgh University Press, 1989

Duncan, Archibald A.M., *Scotland: The Making of the Kingdom*, Edinburgh: Oliver and Boyd, and New York: Barnes and Noble, 1975

Lawrie, Archibald Campbell (editor), *Annals of the Reigns of Malcolm and William, Kings of Scotland AD 1153–1214*, Glasgow: MacLeHose, 1910

Lynch, Michael, *Scotland: A New History*, London: Century, 1991; revised edition, London: Pimlico, 1992

McDonald, R. Andrew, "Rebels without a Cause? The Relations of Fergus of Galloway and Somerled of Argyll with the Scottish Kings, 1153–1164" in *Alba: Celtic Scotland in the Middle Ages*, edited by Edward J. Cowan and McDonald, East Linton, East Lothian: Tuckwell Press, 2000

Oram, Richard D., "A Family Business? Colonisation and Settlement in Twelfth- and Thirteenth-Century Galloway", *Scottish Historical Review*, 72/94 (1993): 111–45

Ritchie, R.L. Graeme, *The Normans in Scotland*, Edinburgh: Edinburgh University Press, 1954

Stringer, K.J., *Earl David of Huntingdon, 1152–1219: A Study in Anglo-Scottish History*, Edinburgh: Edinburgh University Press, 1985

Webster, Bruce, *Medieval Scotland: The Making of an Identity*, London: Macmillan, and New York: St Martin's Press, 1997

Malcolm was the eldest son of Henry, Earl of Northumbria, who was the only surviving son of King David I of Scotland (1124–53); his mother was Ada de Warenne. Upon the death of David I, who was predeceased by his own son, Earl Henry, Malcolm succeeded to the Scottish kingship at the age of about 12. He ruled until his premature death in 1165.

Perhaps because his reign was relatively brief, Malcolm lacks a comprehensive, full-scale modern treatment, and his life and reign are best approached through chapters in general studies; even here, however, the reign can sometimes be glossed over. The fullest treatment and essential point of departure for any examination must be BARROW's edition of the royal acts, which includes a detailed introduction that touches upon almost every facet of the reign. It is also worth noting that Malcolm's brothers – William, who followed him as king, and David, Earl of Huntingdon – are the subject of book-length studies that provide many insights on Malcolm's reign.

Although Malcolm's reign, of about 12 years, was relatively short, historians have nevertheless identified several important themes that characterize it.

First and foremost there is the succession, which must be placed in the context of David's reign. From before 1144 David had associated himself in the governance of the kingdom with his own son, Earl Henry, but the premature death of Henry in 1152 dealt a considerable blow to David's plans. The king immediately settled on Henry's eldest son, Malcolm, as his successor, and had him taken about the kingdom by Earl Duncan of Fife. When David died, Malcolm received a traditional inauguration. Some historians, such as BARROW (1981), have regarded the smooth transition between regimes as representing the consolidation of the dynasty, while others, like LYNCH, have preferred to view the fact that Malcolm succeeded young after the premature death of his father, and died childless, as part of ongoing succession problems in the 12th and 13th centuries.

Another important theme marking Malcolm's reign is the maintenance and consolidation of the so-called "Davidian experiment" – the importation of foreign ideas and settlers that gained momentum under David I. Although RITCHIE regarded the process as essentially complete by 1153 and relegated Malcolm's reign to the role of a sequel, most historians, including DUNCAN, Barrow, and STRINGER, now agree that Malcolm's reign was important for the consolidation and expansion of many of David's innovations.

Still on the theme of domestic affairs, it has not escaped the notice of historians that Malcolm's reign was punctuated by several major incidents of domestic disturbance and revolt, including the 1153–57 uprising led by Somerled of Argyll, the "revolt of the earls" at Perth in 1160, and the invasion of Somerled in 1164. The nature of these incidents has been explored by McDONALD, but it is surely significant that each challenge was defeated, and the expansion of royal authority quickened in certain areas such as Galloway, as shown by the work of ORAM.

Relations with England, and especially the personal relations of Malcolm with the formidable Angevin Henry II, constitute another major theme of the reign. Malcolm's cession to Henry of parts of northern England at Chester in 1157, and his submission at Woodstock in 1163, as well as Henry's manipulation of Malcolm's desire to be knighted at his hands, have been seen by Barrow (1981) as serious weaknesses of the reign and as representing major concessions to the English king.

Finally, Malcolm's reign has also been regarded as important for the development of the church in Scotland. Although Malcolm himself has been regarded as personally devout, he was not a founder of monasteries on the same scale as his grandfather, David I. Nevertheless, Malcolm's reign saw the clarification of the important but convoluted issue of the consecration of Scottish bishops in such a manner that the independence of the Scottish church was considerably advanced. This has led Barrow and WEBSTER to regard the reign as instrumental in the development of a distinct Scottish church.

In terms of Malcolm's character and personality, it is well known that he never married and apparently fathered no children (one highly suspect charter notwithstanding), resulting in the development of the epithet "the Maiden" that is sometimes applied to him. Ritchie was among the first to investigate this tradition, while Barrow showed how the earliest sources to use the term did so in a literal sense and not as an epithet. The whole issue is interesting not only for the light that it sheds on Malcolm's career but also for the tradition of chastity surrounding a Scottish king.

Overall assessments of Malcolm's reign are polarized into two camps. On the one hand, it is common among older works to find Malcolm regarded as a weak king who was unable to maintain peace at home or to assert himself against the English king abroad. Typical of this school is the assessment of LAWRIE: "his reign was short; with little success; with greater failure". Increasingly, however, as the historiography of 12th-century Scotland expands, another view is coming to predominate: Ritchie stated that "history places him [Malcolm] among the righteous rulers and victorious captains", while Barrow, whose study of Malcolm's charters has shed important light upon government, also views Malcolm's reign in a favourable light. This view is upheld by Stringer in his study of Malcolm's brother, David of Huntingdon. Some recent studies, however, strike a balance between the two positions: Lynch seems uneasy with the domestic unrest of the reign, and speaks of Malcolm's "mixed legacy" to his successor, William.

The final word on Malcolm has yet to be written, but it is worth noting that, to some contemporaries at least, the verdict was clear cut: William of Newburgh, an English chronicler who described Malcolm's character in some detail, remarked that "in many good qualities he equalled his remarkable grandfather, and in some even surpassed him gloriously; and shone in the midst of a barbarous and perverse race like a heavenly star" (quoted in ANDERSON).

R. ANDREW McDONALD

See also David I; Henry II; William I, "the Lion"

Maldon, Battle of
991

Blake, E.O. (editor), *Liber Eliensis*, London: Royal Historical Society, 1962

Hart, Cyril, *The Danelaw*, London: Hambledon Press, 1990; Rio Grande, Ohio: Hambledon Press, 1992

Keynes, Simon, "The Historical Context of the Battle of Maldon" in *The Battle of Maldon AD 991*, edited by Donald Scragg, Oxford and Cambridge, Massachusetts: Blackwell, 1991

Macray, William Dunn (editor), *Chronicon Abbatiae Rameseiensis*, London: Longman, 1886; Wiesbaden: Kraus Reprint, 1966

Scragg, D.G. (editor), *The Battle of Maldon*, Manchester: Manchester University Press, 1981

Scragg, Donald (editor), *The Battle of Maldon AD 991*, Oxford and Cambridge, Massachusetts: Blackwell, 1991

Swanton, Michael J. (editor and translator), *The Anglo-Saxon Chronicles*, London: Dent, 1996; New York: Routledge, 1998; revised edition, London: Phoenix Press, 2000

The battle of Maldon is recorded in brief prose entries in *The Anglo-Saxon Chronicle* (manuscripts A, F, and E) and in one of the finest short Anglo-Saxon poems. The *Chronicle* entries vary slightly in the amount of detail given, and in the actual date: manuscripts F and E place the event under 991; MS A under 993, but SWANTON shows this to be error. MS F notes simply that in this year Ealdorman Byrhtnoth was killed at Maldon; MS E adds that the ealdorman's death at Maldon followed a raid on Ipswich; and MS A states that the Viking fleet was led by Olafr Tryggvason, that the Maldon attack followed the Ipswich raid, and that Ealdorman Byrhtnoth died in a battle in which the Vikings were victorious. Manuscripts E and F also state that in this year it was first decided to pay tribute to the Danes, on Archbishop Sigeric's advice; MS A, more obliquely, says that after the battle, on Sigeric's advice, the English made peace. It is not appropriate here to discuss the relationship between these *Chronicle* entries, but it should be noted that all three texts associate the battle with the death of Byrhtnoth and with the archbishop's involvement in the subsequent peace negotiations, including the payment of Danegeld. These factors were what were important in contemporary eyes.

The poem, edited by SCRAGG (1981), survives only in Casley's 18th-century transcript of MS Otho A 12, which was lost in the Cotton Library fire of 1731. Casley's transcript shows that his exemplar was incomplete, but the date and extent of the loss are unknown; the beginning and end of the poem are missing but the dramatic unity of the part of the narrative which has survived suggests that the loss may not be that extensive. The date of the poem itself – an important factor in assessing the poem's reliability as evidence of what happened – also remains a bone of critical contention. The poet's seemingly detailed knowledge of events may be genuine but may equally be the traditional poetic device to lend verisimilitude to great actions by an apparently first-hand account. Some indication of the range of critical opinion can be found in the extensive bibliography to SCRAGG's 1991 edition of texts and essays on the battle and in the introduction to his own edition of the poem. Against a fictional reading are the factors that Byrhtnoth's death at Maldon is attested by *The Anglo-Saxon Chronicle* and that, although the extant fragment does not mention Maldon, the poet's topography of the battle site, involving an island in a tidal estuary linked to the mainland by a causeway, points to the banks of the River Blackwater and the causeway to Northey Island (though HART finds an alternative). In favour of an early date of composition are the arguments that a poem celebrating the valour of an army defeated by the Vikings is unlikely to have been composed during the reign of Cnut (1013–35), and the poem's reference to Byrhtnoth's angry refusal to pay Danegeld becomes increasingly a criticism of royal and ecclesiastical policy if the poem is much later than the events it describes. We should trust the poet, but not necessarily the authors of the further extensive accounts of the battle in the 12th-century *Liber Eliensis* (see BLAKE's edition) and the *Ramsey Chronicle* (see MACRAY's edition); the purpose of these accounts is more likely to have been to give a suitable historical context for Byrhtnoth's grants to both houses and to extol the reputation

of their benefactor than to preserve accurate historical record. In this context, the *Liber Eliensis'* detail that the English were greatly outnumbered by the Vikings is dubious, and may simply stress their courage in facing such odds, though the poem also suggests a disparity in numbers by the technique of naming only a representative few of the English and none of the Vikings.

The battle itself, though clearly a great local tragedy – many of the named Englishmen were landowners in East Anglia and Byrhtnoth himself was ealdorman of Essex – was of little lasting significance other than being the occasion of Byrhtnoth's death and of generating a fine poem. The two are related; in its portrayal of Byrhtnoth as a great Germanic warrior the poem is an appropriate lament for the death of a great hero, in which the death of his followers becomes proof of the quality of leadership which could inspire such loyalty. Its overriding theme of loyalty may comment obliquely on the contemporary failures of Æthelred's reign or propose a solution to them in the vanished ethics of a previous age. The poet even dignifies Byrhtnoth's apparent misjudgement in allowing the Vikings access across the causeway by defining it as heroic recklessness (other interpretations are discussed in Scragg's introduction), though it is difficult to see what else Byrhtnoth could have done. To confine the Vikings to the island was a tactical advantage only for as long as the tide was out; once it came back in, their boats could either allow escape or movement up the estuary for an attack on Maldon itself. As the town was the earliest Essex mint, there was every reason for Byrhtnoth to wish to defend it.

KEYNES's account of the significance of the battle shows that it was at the beginning of the series of disastrous raids which culminated in Æthelred's abandoning of England in 1013. Maldon itself seems to have been a comparatively minor skirmish which, had Byrhtnoth not died there, would have received little attention. All three *Chronicle* accounts place it in the context of the raid on Ipswich, and Rochester, London, Sandwich, and Folkestone were also attacked during the 990s, not necessarily by the same fleet. Other attacks occurred in the West Country, presumably from the Irish-based Vikings, and Æthelred clearly saw the dangers of a multiple enemy; his 994 treaty with Olafr Tryggvason was a humiliating compromise which agreed to pay the Vikings £22,000 in return for a guarantee of peace and support against attack from any other Viking force. If, as the poet claimed, Byrhtnoth did refuse to pay Danegeld, it would appear that not all Æthelred's ealdormen suppported the king's policy of paying for peace, despite the archbishop's advice. However, Byrhtnoth's example was not followed; the years following the battle show a steady increase in the price of peace, until in 1007 £30,000 was paid, and the disasters of 1011 were blamed on tax not being paid in time. Even if Byrhtnoth had survived it seems improbable that he could have influenced national policy.

The significance of the battle seems finally to rest upon Byrhtnoth himself. The poem shows that, despite his dissent from Danegeld policy, he was fiercely loyal to the king, unlike a fellow East Anglian, the treacherous Æthelric of Bocking, who was accused of complicity in the plan to receive Swein Forkbeard in Essex. Monastic circles, beyond the houses Byrhtnoth and his family had endowed, also had reason to lament the ealdorman's death. In the anti-monastic reaction after Edgar's death in 975, Byrhtnoth, Æthelwine, and Ælfwold, the sons of Athelstan Half-King, strongly opposed Ælfhere of

Mercia in his efforts to regain some of the lay property which had been handed over to the great abbeys. Resentment against the powerful pro-monastic party was real; Ælfwold is reputed to have executed a certain Leofsige who retook lands round Peterborough; though he subsequently went barefoot to Bishop Æthelwold as a penitent, Ælfwold was absolved of his crime and the estates were handed back to Peterborough. There is no evidence that Byrhtnoth was involved in anything so draconian, though the *Liber Eliensis* speaks of him as taking his place in council against the greed and madness of those who wished to expel the monks, and acting as a wall on their behalf. Byrhtnoth's extensive wealth and landholdings, listed by Hart, would have made him a powerful supporter for the monastic cause, but though the ealdorman's status and reputation seem beyond question, so too does his age. He was appointed ealdorman in 956 by Eadwig, retaining his position under Edgar, and rising, by the time of the battle, to second in the ealdorman hierarchy. His friend Æthelwine died in 992; Ælfwold was dead by 990. Had Byrhtnoth survived the battle it is unlikely that he could have demonstrated his heroic defiance of Vikings, monastic pillagers, or political expediency for much longer.

MARGARET A. LOCHERBIE-CAMERON

See also Æthelred II; Danelaw; Poetry: Old English; Viking Settlement

Malthus, Thomas Robert 1766–1834
Social thinker

Bonar, James, *Malthus and His Work*, London: Macmillan, 1885; 2nd expanded edition, London: Allen and Unwin, and New York: Macmillan, 1924

Dupâquier, J., A. Fauve-Chamoux, and E. Grebenik (editors), *Malthus Past and Present*, London and New York: Academic Press, 1983

James, Patricia, *Population Malthus: His Life and Times*, London and Boston: Routledge and Kegan Paul, 1979

Petersen, William, *Malthus*, Cambridge, Massachusetts: Harvard University Press, and London: Heinemann, 1979

Turner, Michael (editor), *Malthus and His Time*, New York: St Martin's Press, and London: Macmillan, 1986

Winch, Donald, *Malthus*, Oxford and New York: Oxford University Press, 1987

Wood, John Cunningham (editor), *Thomas Robert Malthus: Critical Assessments*, 4 vols, London and Dover, New Hampshire: Croom Helm, 1986

Wrigley, E.A. and David Souden, introduction to vol. 1 of *The Works of Thomas Robert Malthus*, edited by Wrigley and Souden, London: Pickering, 1986

Few thinkers have been the subject of greater debate than Thomas Malthus. His *Essay on the Principle of Population as It Affects the Future Improvement of Society* ... was first published anonymously in 1798 and then, after more reading and observation, in a much expanded, better researched, and re-titled, second edition of 1803. The *Essay* was by far Malthus's most famous work, gaining for him a lasting reputation as a negative thinker who strove to attack the optimistic dreams of William Godwin and the Marquis de Condorcet. Malthus, however, was also the author of many other works, including the important *Observations on the Effects of the Corn Laws* (1815), *Principles of Political Economy* (1820), and *Definitions in Political Economy* (1827). Malthus's contemporaries and near contemporaries were not unanimous when they gave disapproving assessments of his writings, but many considered him an evil man and said so in print. Modern scholarship has tended to be more objective and has increasingly aimed to read Malthus in the context of his times.

BONAR provided the first modern account of Malthus and, although it has now largely been supplanted by better scholarship, his study remains useful. Bonar concentrated his efforts upon an interpretation of Malthus's *Essay on Population* wherein Malthus had laid out his proposition that "population increases in a geometrical, food in an arithmetical ratio". Bonar's book concludes with a short discussion of Malthus's life; this is not always accurate and borrows heavily from the accounts of Malthus's contemporaries, William Otter and William Empson among others. Bonar's account was reprinted twice in the 20th century and has proved influential.

JAMES is the most extensive biography of Malthus published to date. It is a big book and contains much original research. James's text is laced with numerous and lengthy quotations taken from both printed and manuscript sources. Her book reproduces 8 plates and has 38 pages of endnotes. James is strongest on the historical aspects of Malthus's life, giving an accurate and detailed account of the Malthus family background, and setting Malthus's own upbringing, education, career, and writings within the wider English historical context to which they belong.

Published the same year as James, PETERSEN is not as comprehensive as James as a biography. He is, nevertheless, entertaining and effectively portrays Malthus as a man of many faces who lived and wrote within times of great change. However, Petersen's book also occasionally strikes the tone of an ardent apologist in its attempt to rescue Malthus from his detractors. He aims to set the story straight and concludes that Malthus wrote for "the betterment of society and of all the people in it".

The 1980 conference in Paris, "Malthus hier et aujourd'hui", which was sponsored by the Société de Démographie Historique, sprouted two books which are considered here. DUPÂQUIER, FAUVE-CHAMOUX, & GREBENIK provides a collection of 29 essays grouped under six headings: Malthus, Malthus and his Time, Malthus and Religion, Malthusianism, Malthusianism and Socialism, and Malthusianism and Darwinism. TURNER has 15 essays organized around four main themes: Population, Land, Labour, and Capital. In an important essay in Turner, "Malthus's Model of a Pre-Industrial Economy", E.A. Wrigley wrote on a theme that he would take up in his "Introduction" to the *Works of Malthus*.

WOOD, too, is a useful collection of essays on Malthus, in this case reprinting in four volumes works which had originally been published from 1898 to 1984. Wood provides short introductions to each of his book's sections in which each reprinted article is summarized succinctly. Included are classic essays by J. Bonar, J.J. Spengler, R.L. Meek, and J.M. Pullen among many others.

Edited by WRIGLEY & SOUDEN, *The Works of Thomas Robert Malthus* provides in eight volumes a complete edition of

Malthus's writings. This publication will help sustain modern scholarly interest in Malthus's life and thought. Wrigley & Souden's "Introduction" to volume 1 not only outlines the editorial guidelines of the set, but provides an important discussion of Malthus's thought. Here one finds a history of previous editions of Malthus's writings, a brief outline of his life, and a discussion of the "character and setting" of his thought. Malthus is described as a "pragmatic" thinker and Wrigley & Souden argue that the "extent to which his work was informed by his concern to maximize the level of real wages and hence the living standards of the mass of the population has in general received too little emphasis". Their essay effectively puts Malthus's thought within the context of Wrigley's earlier published research into the organic nature of the raw materials of the early Industrial Revolution. Finally, Wrigley & Souden argue that "Malthus's epistemological bent deserves more attention". Their Malthus is less of a deductive thinker than many standard accounts would have it; for them Malthus is an empiricist. It was this empirical Malthus who "bestowed life on population studies as a field of intellectual investigation by showing how strategic to the understanding of the functioning of society a knowledge of its demography might be". Noting that Malthus is separated from the modern world by the intervention of the Industrial Revolution, Wrigley & Souden conclude that "it is peculiarly important to read and to judge Malthus in the context of his times".

WINCH, like so many books in the Past Masters series, offers a concise and reliable account. He provides chapters on Malthus's reputation and life, as well as chapters on Malthus the population theorist of the first and second edition of the *Essay on Population*, Malthus the political economist, and a useful section on "Further reading". Winch aims to put Malthus in his times, asking "what was Malthus attempting to say to his contemporaries?" His answer, in part, is that Malthus was a wide-ranging thinker with much to say about population, morality, politics, and economics. Winch rejects John Maynard Keynes's assessment that "from being a caterpillar of a moral scientist and chrysalis of an historian, [Malthus] could at last spread the wings of his thought and survey the world as an economist". Winch's Malthus was an 18th-century "moral scientist" in the broadest sense of that term.

MARK G. SPENCER

See also Plagues and Famines; Ricardo

Man, Isle of

Belchem, John "The Little Manx Nation: Antiquarianism, Ethnic Identity, and Home Rule Politics in the Isle of Man, 1880–1918", *Journal of British Studies*, 32 (2000): 217–40
Belchem, John (editor), *A New History of the Isle of Man*, vol. 5, *The Modern Period 1830–1999*, Liverpool: Liverpool University Press, 2000
Dickinson, J. Roger, *The Lordship of Man under the Stanleys: Government and Economy in the Isle of Man, 1580–1704*, Manchester: Carnegie, 1996
Duffy, Sean, "Irishmen and Islesmen in the Kingdoms of Dublin and Man, 1052–1171", *Eriu*, 43 (1992)
Hechter, Michael, *Internal Colonialism: The Celtic Fringe in British National Development 1536–1966*, London: Routledge and Kegan Paul, and Berkeley: University of California Press, 1975; as *Internal Colonialism: The Celtic Fringe in British National Development*, with new introduction, New Brunswick, New Jersey: Transaction, 1999
Kinvig, R.H., *A History of the Isle of Man*, Oxford: Oxford University Press, 1944; 3rd edition, as *The Isle of Man: A Social, Cultural, and Political History*, Liverpool: Liverpool University Press, and Rutland, Vermont: Tuttle, 1975
Moore, A.W., *A History of the Isle of Man*, 2 vols, London: Unwin, 1900; reprinted, Douglas: Manx National Heritage, 1992
Train, Joseph, *An Historical and Statistical Account of the Isle of Man, from the Earliest Times to the Present Date; with a View of Its Ancient Laws, Peculiar Customs, and Popular Superstitions*, Douglas: Quiggin, and London: Simpkin Marshall, 1845

The equivocal position of the Isle of Man between Ireland, Scotland, and England had an early impact on historical writing about the island. The first recognizably modern historical account of the Isle of Man was written by Joseph TRAIN and published in 1845. Train was heavily reliant on John Seacome's *Memoirs* of the Stanleys, a work which typified previous explorations of the island's history (*Memoirs, Containing a Genealogical and Historical Account of the Ancient and Honourable House of Stanley*, 1737). Seacome had glorified the Stanleys, papering seamlessly over the evident cracks in their political careers. This was only natural when his major sources, especially for the Isle of Man, were the work known as the *History and Antiquities of the Isle of Man* by James Stanley, seventh Earl of Derby (executed 1651) and the poetical account of the Stanleys by Thomas Stanley, Bishop of Man in the mid-16th century.

Even so, Train was the first to try to locate Man in the complex environment of the Irish Sea. Train was a Scot, born in Ayrshire, and was closely associated with Sir Walter Scott. It was Scott to whom Train supplied details of highland history and myth, and it was Scott who in turn encouraged Train to write a history of Man. Scott's brother Thomas was the receiver-general of the customs in the island. Train's interest in ancient customs and superstitions therefore found ample scope for development in his treatment of the island. Train presented it as an example of continuity in a rapidly changing world – and applied this also to his treatment of the island's constitution, which, he said, adapted "like the willow" across the centuries.

Train's successor, and the author of what remains the most comprehensive account of Manx history, was Deemster (joint chief justice of Man) A.W. Moore. MOORE was educated at Trinity College, Cambridge and became Speaker of the House of Keys. By 1900, when his *History* was published, the island had undergone remarkable changes, including the birth of mass tourism from the north of England and the transformation of the island's constitution. Moore was one of those who responded to these changes by celebrating the island's Celtic identity, especially its connections with Ireland. He therefore expressed that native pride in the island and its history which had been honed in the conflicts of the 19th century over the constitutional position of the island in relation to the United Kingdom and the internal political arrangements of the island. These had seen the defeat of the power of the Atholl lords, who retained considerable influence in the island until 1830, when their remaining manorial rights were bought out by the crown. They had also seen the effective destruction of Manx autonomy through the Revesting Act of 1765 and the associated efforts to end the island's lucrative smuggling trade. Seen initially as an ally against the Atholl lords, then as potential oppressors, the UK government limited its intervention as, for example, the Manx government recovered its hold on harbour administration in 1866. As a consequence the interpretation pursued by Moore turned on two fundamental ideas: the naturalness of the tie to the UK and in particular the British crown, combined with the importance and effectiveness of Manx autonomy under that allegiance. The years between the fall of the independent kingdom of Man and the establishment of settled English lordship through the Stanleys were dismissed as a "dismal period of Manx history, during which the unfortunate island changed its rulers so often that they could have taken but little interest in it". Some ironies emerge from this mixture of Celticism, loyalism, and pride in autonomous institutions, for example the relative failure to celebrate the Scandinavian contribution to the island's history in favour of that from Ireland.

The dominance of Moore's interpretation was such that the next major account of the island, that by KINVIG, did little more than add a stronger emphasis on social, economic, and cultural history, in line with contemporary trends in historiography, and an extended chronological coverage through to the mid-20th century. Kinvig, an historical geographer by profession and another native of the island, was also willing to give greater weight to the Scandinavian influence, as the initial enthusiasm for the rebirth of the Manx language was amended in a more pragmatic direction.

The most recent major contribution to the history of the island discussed here has come from DICKINSON. His thesis "Aspects of the Isle of Man in the Seventeenth Century" (Liverpool University, 1991) and the book which sprang from it present an interpretation of the island's history, especially its economic and social history, which has much in common with the important viewpoint advanced by HECHTER in 1975, known as the internal colonialism thesis. This argues that social, economic, cultural and political difference between the metropolitan core in England and its dependent territories in the rest of England and beyond in Wales, Scotland, Ireland, and the Isle of Man was deliberately maintained by those in power at the centre to enable them to subordinate and exploit these areas more effectively. Dickinson showed that the Manx economy remained primarily agricultural, providing raw materials for the industries of Scotland and especially north-western England. Instead of a celebration of the island's Celtic or Scandinavian influences, therefore, Dickinson provided a more down-to-earth assertion of economic and social domination from England.

Meanwhile, contrasting approaches have been applied to Manx history at two different ends of the chronological spectrum. First, DUFFY has applied the theoretical approaches of the school of historiography known as the "new British History" to the island's experience (see also "The Bruce Brothers

and the Irish Sea World, 1306–29", *Cambridge Medieval Celtic Studies*, 21, 1991). This, along with the perspective of an Irish-based scholar, has allowed him to develop an approach to the period of the kingdom of Man and Isles and the early phases of English intervention in Ireland and the Irish Sea that allows for complexities of connection and allegiance beyond those previously perceived by historians working from rigidly nationalistic perspectives. These, for example, have pointed up the significance of a nobility which might shift in identity as it moved around the Irish Sea and the possibility even in the early 14th century, under the Bruces, of a "pan-Celtic" alliance being formed involving elites in Scotland, Ireland, and Wales, as well as the Isle of Man.

At the other end of the spectrum, BELCHEM's book has argued for the artificiality of the Manx identity forged in the later-Victorian period, seeing it as being a response to the pressures imposed by mass tourism from the north of England (see also his cited article). With an approach influenced by the ideas of Benedict Anderson and his "imagined communities", Belchem describes intellectuals such as Moore and T.E. Brown, with considerable experience of English culture and institutions, looking for Manx identity to save something from what they perceived as the wreck brought in the train of the pleasure-seekers from Lancashire and Yorkshire. Despairing on the whole of using the language as a core for this identity, these men and women turned to a variety of other spheres, such as folklore, dialect, and as we have seen history, to give their land a soul. Recent years have therefore seen contrasting developments – in Dickinson and Belchem the adoption of two models, from Hechter and Andersen respectively, which emphasize the weakness of Manx autonomy in the face of metropolitan English influence, and in Duffy the "New British history" model accentuating the importance of connections and identities which did not necessarily lead inevitably to the English and London or Westminster.

TIM THORNTON

See also Languages: Cornish and Manx; Topography: Coastal

Manchester

Farnie, D.A., *The Manchester Ship Canal and the Rise of the Port of Manchester, 1894–1975*, Manchester: Manchester University Press, 1980

Jones, G.D.B., *Roman Manchester*, Manchester: Manchester Excavation Committee, 1974

Kidd, Alan and K.W. Roberts (editors), *City, Class, and Culture: Studies of Social Policy and Cultural Production in Victorian Manchester*, Manchester and Dover, New Hampshire: Manchester University Press, 1985

Kidd, Alan, *Manchester*, Keele: Ryburn, 1993; 3rd edition, Edinburgh: Edinburgh University Press, 2002

Lloyd-Jones, Roger and M.J. Lewis, *Manchester and the Age of the Factory: The Business Structure of Cottonopolis in the Industrial Revolution*, London and New York: Croom Helm, 1988

Manchester Region History Review (annual), 1987–

Redford, A. with Ina Stafford Russell, *The History of Local Government in Manchester*, 3 vols, London and New York: Longman, 1939–40

Rose, Mary B. (editor), *The Lancashire Cotton Industry: A History since 1700*, Preston: Lancashire County Books, 1996

Timmins, Geoffrey, *Made in Lancashire: A History of Regional Industrialisation*, Manchester: Manchester University Press, 1998

Wadsworth, Alfred P. and Julia de Lacy Mann, *The Cotton Trade and Industrial Lancashire 1600–1780*, Manchester: Manchester University Press, 1931; New York: Kelley, 1968

Willan, T.S., *Elizabethan Manchester*, Manchester: Chetham Society, 1980

Although intermittently inhabited for approaching 2000 years, Manchester acquired its abiding identity during the era of industrialization in the 18th and early-19th centuries. Not surprisingly, the historical literature has concentrated on the "industrial revolution" and the cotton trade. By contrast, studies of Manchester's origins and earlier development are few and the 20th century has been largely neglected. The most recent overview of the city's entire history is Kidd. An extensive bibliography on the 19th century compiled by Terry Wyke can be found in KIDD & ROBERTS and the *Manchester Region History Review* includes an annual list of publications on the history of Manchester and its region.

The historical record reveals little of Manchester's origins in the Roman fort and the civilian settlement (*vicus*) of Mamucium. But archaeology has yielded some information, most recently through the work of the Greater Manchester Archaeological Unit. Earliest Roman levels excavated date from about AD 77–78. Military occupation of the site lasted until the Romans left Britain early in the 5th century. However, the *vicus* did not survive the Romans' departure and the archaeological evidence suggests that there was no urban settlement again for several centuries. JONES is the most accessible entry point into the archaeological literature for the Roman and immediate post-Roman period. Manchester reappears in the historical record in the 10th century as a possible outpost against Viking incursions but the evidence is inconclusive. What is certain is that the medieval town of Manchester which grew up after the Norman Conquest was not of any great significance in Lancashire, let alone England. Unsurprisingly historians have largely ignored it.

Between the 15th and the 18th centuries, Manchester was to develop from the unimportant township of the medieval era into the regional capital of south-east Lancashire and a town of national significance. Its new importance had nothing to do with politics or local government, indeed its manorial administration endured as an anachronism into the industrial era. Manchester's rise had everything to do with its economy. The origins of cloth production in the town remain vague but it is certain that Elizabethan Manchester was already a manufacturing and market centre for woollens and linen, as WILLAN makes clear. However, the crucial 200-year period following the 16th century, during which south-east Lancashire became the cradle of the industrial revolution, has been strangely neglected by modern historians. Part 1 of TIMMINS has done

much to rectify this situation but WADSWORTH & MANN's still invaluable study, now 70 years old, remains essential reading on the economic history of early industrial Manchester.

By the later 18th century the burgeoning status of Manchester, and what was becoming in economic terms the Manchester region, depended upon the wealth generated by the newly mechanized industry of cotton. The broad narrative of Manchester's economic development is difficult to disentangle from that of "Textile Lancashire" as a whole. The history of the cotton industry since 1700 can be best followed in the recent collection edited by ROSE. Yet, as historians are starting to establish, Manchester's economic and social structure marked it out from the necklace of mill towns that grew up around it. In the process some popular myths are being exploded. For instance, in the 19th-century imagination Manchester was "Cottonopolis", the very essence of industrialism, the first factory town. Historical research is undermining this picture. First, an overemphasis upon cotton masks the importance of other industries, notably engineering. But even more important, if the sobriquet "Cottonopolis" involves a focus on the factory, it is doubly misleading. Manchester's commercial importance as the world's entrepôt for cotton outweighed its undoubted industrial significance as a centre of cotton production. Historians have long noted the truth of this for the later 19th century. The work of LLOYD-JONES & LEWIS has produced persuasive evidence that it was as much a feature of the economy of early industrial Manchester.

Historical debate is not confined to the economy of Manchester and its role in the cotton trade. Social historians have become interested in Manchester's broader role in the development of Victorian society and politics. More than any other place in the first half the 19th century, Manchester symbolized to contemporaries the hope and the horrors of the industrial age. Visitors and commentators from Engels to de Tocqueville drew conclusions for the whole of society from the experience of Manchester. The new class-based society Manchester came to represent fascinated the public and figured prominently in the so-called "social problem" or industrial novels of the 1840s and 1850s. For a time the town was the voice of the middle-class "interest" as exemplified in the agitation of the Anti-Corn Law League, the ideology of the "Manchester School", and the political careers of Richard Cobden and John Bright. Equally it symbolized much about the new popular politics of the chartist era and the period leading up to it, and in the Peterloo Massacre of 1819 provided one of the key moments in the development of popular radicalism. Since the collection edited by Kidd & Roberts in the mid-1980s, the town's 19th-century social and cultural history has generated an impressive supply of monographs and articles, too extensive to refer to here. Many of these have reassessed the received picture of industrial Manchester and its identity. However, there have been few attempts at a synthesis and it remains difficult to study Manchester's urban development in the 19th and early-20th century without consulting REDFORD & RUSSELL's three volumes. Much broader in scope than their titles suggest, although now over 60 years old they remain invaluable tools for the historian of Manchester.

In contrast to the 19th century the more recent sinews of Manchester's history are difficult to trace. KIDD's 1993 general history provides the only overview and his conclusions must be considered tentative. The decline of the cotton industry in the face of foreign competition and economic change is the best documented aspect of the era and Rose provides an introduction to the literature. The 20th century in Manchester would have been marked by a more dramatic industrial degeneration had it not been for the Manchester Ship Canal and Trafford Park, the world's first industrial estate. Together they were the last great achievement of Manchester's heyday. Their existence ensured that the town missed the worst of the inter-war depression. FARNIE is essential to an understanding of the development of the 20th-century economy. It was the dramatic collapse of trade on the Ship Canal and at the Manchester docks in the 1960s and 1970s on top of the disappearance of the cotton industry which heralded the shift from a manufacturing to a service-sector economy in late 20th-century Manchester. As yet this latest and crucial stage in the city's evolution awaits its historians.

ALAN J. KIDD

See also Anti-Corn Law League; Bright; Cobden; Industrial Revolution; Peterloo Massacre

Mandated Territories from 1920

Hall, H. Duncan, *Mandates, Dependencies, and Trusteeship*, London: Stevens for the Carnegie Endowment for International Peace, and Washington, DC: Carnegie Endowment for International Peace, 1948

Lugard, Frederick Dealtry, *The Dual Mandate in British Tropical Africa*, London: Blackwood, 1922; reprinted, with a new introduction by Margery Perham, Hamden, Connecticut: Archon Books, and London: Cass, 1965

Perham, Margery, *Lugard*, vol. 1, *The Years of Authority, 1898–1945*, London: Collins, 1960; Hamden, Connecticut: Archon Books, 1968

Temperley, Harold William Vazeille (editor), *A History of the Peace Conference of Paris*, 6 vols, London: Frowde/Hodder and Stoughton, 1920–24

Wright, Quincy, *Mandates under the League of Nations*, Chicago: University of Chicago Press, 1930

The idea that rule of "primitive" people was a trusteeship of civilized powers was not new when the League of Nations was set up after World War I, but clause 22 of its covenant declared territories "inhabited by peoples not yet able to stand by themselves under the strenuous conditions of the modern world" to be "a sacred trust". TEMPERLEY and his contributors, writing shortly after the 1919 Paris peace conference, accepted the victors' view that the defeated Germans had treated their colonies as completely subordinate to German interests, and their native inhabitants as a means to this end, never an end in themselves. Germany must surrender its colonial possessions. The Ottoman empire, a German ally, was also unacceptable as ruler of its former Arab territories. But the Allies had declared during the war that they desired no annexation of enemy territories, only the liberation of peoples subject to misrule. At the peace conference, it was agreed that international administration had never worked – Egypt, Samoa, and the New Hebrides

were cited as unsatisfactory examples – but international control could be exercised through League supervision of nationally held mandates. This mandates system had a Permanent Mandates Commission of nine members, a majority being non-mandatory powers, to which annual reports, on the basis of a detailed questionnaire, must be submitted for comment and criticism, the ultimate sanction being withdrawal of a mandate.

The 15 mandates – six held by Britain, four by British dominions, three by France, one each by Belgium and Japan, the United States having refused suggested mandates and rejected membership of the League – were divided into three categories. Class A consisted of relatively advanced former Turkish territories – Syria, Lebanon, Palestine, Trans-Jordan, and Iraq – for which independence could be foreseen. France held the first two, Britain the last three of these. Class B consisted of the former German colonies in Africa, Britain holding Tanganyika, with the Cameroons and Togoland each being divided between Britain and France, and Belgium holding the mandate for Ruanda-Urundi. These mandates required freedom of conscience, religion, trade, and commerce, with no militarization except for police purposes. Class C consisted of the German Pacific colonies, whose small size, remoteness, and primitiveness made administration as an integral part of the mandatory powers' territory desirable. Japan held the mandate for the north Pacific islands of the Carolines, Marshals, and Marianas, Australia for New Guinea, New Zealand for Western Samoa, and the British empire for Nauru. German South-West Africa became a mandate of the Dominion of South Africa.

If Temperley and his colleagues offered a careful account of origins, a decade later WRIGHT, an American academic, credited President Woodrow Wilson, his advisers being suspicious of the imperial ambitions of Britain and France, with preventing annexation of former enemy colonies and getting the principle of mandates accepted, although Wilson was obliged to recognize the prior claim to a mandate by the power which had actually occupied this particular enemy territory during the war. He also noted a difficulty. Sovereignty was ambiguous: did it belong to the League or to the mandatory power? Was it shared? Juristic opinion divided on national lines and the question remained unresolved. Nevertheless the methods and purposes of mandate administration had been commended by experts, including those experienced individuals who, rather than governments, sat on the Permanent Mandates Commission, although by 1930 there had already been insurrections against the mandatory powers in Syria and Samoa.

When HALL wrote, at the end of World War II, the mandates system had been overtaken by events. Iraq had become independent in 1932, but Syria saw revolts against the French, violently suppressed by General Sarrail in 1925, while Palestine was complicated by British acceptance of a Jewish homeland, with large-scale immigration alongside a large Arab minority. The class B mandates remained untroubled, but, in class C, South-West Africa, with a large German population, saw indigenous riots in 1921 and 1923, as did Western Samoa in 1928, while all the Pacific mandates were disrupted by actual invasion or the logistics of battle after the Pacific war began in 1941. In native welfare, these mandates compared favourably with colonial dependencies, while the international covenants regulating freedom of religion, slavery, labour recruitment, arms and liquor traffic, and "open door" trade policies had generally been observed. But the system had conspicuously failed to deal with Japanese militarization of its mandate, Japan withdrawing from the League in 1935 without relinquishing it. And, although self-government was implied by article 22 of the covenant, it was not a specific objective in the class B and C mandates. Only Iraq in class A became independent. The machinery and procedure of the Permanent Mandates Commission, tied as it was to Geneva, never allowed actual visits of inspection to the mandated territories; its effectiveness rested on governments making truthful reports, upon which there could be no real check whatever suspicions there might be of Japanese and South African policies and practices, and the failure of their official representatives to answer questions at the bi-annual sessions of the Permanent Mandates Commission. Self-government or independence for the mandated territories came only after their transfer to the trusteeship system of the United Nations after the war.

The strength of the Permanent Mandates Commission lay in its expert membership, individuals being nominated by, but neither delegates nor representatives of, governments. The Belgian Orts, the Dutch van Rees, and above all the British Lugard, experienced and knowledgeable in colonial government, together with the Swiss professor Rappard who became its permanent general-secretary, were its core. LUGARD's definition of the dual mandate as a sacred trust to administer people for their own greatest benefit and for the greatest good of the world was a clear enunciation of the principles underlying the League system, and his presence on the Permanent Mandates Commission for 13 years from 1923 to 1936 provided a rare continuity. This, according to PERHAM, tilted the scales away from the cynics, who expected or hoped for little achievement, towards the idealists who expected too much from the mandates system. But even Lugard, noted for his impartiality and lack of prejudice, illustrated a major weakness of the mandates system. Over French actions in Syria in 1925 he remained silent, explaining only much later that the British foreign secretary, Austen Chamberlain, had told him to realize that what he said in criticism as an individual would be attributed to the British government. "Now, where is my duty?"

FRANCIS WEST

See also Colonial Wars and Counter-Insurgency; Decolonization; Palestine, Israel, and the Middle East; World War I: Versailles and Other Treaties

Manorial Economy medieval period

Aston, T.H. and C.H.E. Philpin (editors), *The Brenner Debate: Agrarian Class Structure and Economic Development in Pre-Industrial Europe*, Cambridge and New York: Cambridge University Press, 1985

Bolton, J.L., *The Medieval English Economy, 1150–1500*, London: Dent, and Totowa, New Jersey: Rowman and Littlefield, 1980

Britnell, R.H., *The Commercialisation of English Society, 1000–1500*, Cambridge and New York: Cambridge University Press, 1993

Hallam, H.E., *Rural England, 1066–1348*, Brighton, Sussex: Harvester Press, and Atlantic Highlands, New Jersey: Humanities Press, 1981

Hallam, H.E, (editor), *The Agrarian History of England and Wales*, vol. 2, *1042– 1350*, Cambridge and New York: Cambridge University Press, 1986

Hilton, R.H., *The English Peasantry in the Later Middle Ages: The Ford Lectures for 1973 and Related Studies*, Oxford: Clarendon Press, 1975

Miller, Edward and John Hatcher, *Medieval England: Rural Society and Economic Change, 1086–1348*, London and New York: Longman, 1978; reprinted with corrections, 1980

Miller, Edward (editor), *The Agrarian History of England and Wales*, vol. 3, *1348–1500*, Cambridge and New York: Cambridge University Press, 1991

Postan, M.M., "Medieval Agrarian Society in Its Prime, 7: England" in *The Cambridge Economic History of Europe*, vol. 1, *The Agrarian Life of the Middle Ages*, 2nd edition, edited by Postan, Cambridge and New York: Cambridge University Press, 1966

Postan, M.M., *The Medieval Economy and Society: An Economic History of Britain in the Middle Ages*, London: Weidenfeld and Nicolson, 1972; as *The Medieval Economy and Society: An Economic History of Britain, 1100–1500*, Los Angeles: University of California Press, 1972

Raftis, J.A., *Peasant Economic Development within the English Manorial System*, Montreal and Kingston, Ontario: McGill-Queen's University Press, 1996; Stroud, Gloucestershire: Sutton, 1997

Titow, J.Z., *English Rural Society, 1200–1350*, London: Allen and Unwin, and New York: Barnes and Noble, 1969

In the late 19th century, groundbreaking works by Rogers and Seebohm awakened interest in the manorial economy and society. Other classic works by scholars such as Maitland, Vinogradoff, and Kosminsky intensified study of the origins of the manor and its economic functions. These studies also established a reliance on data drawn from crown sources (e.g. Domesday Book and the Hundred Rolls) and manorial accounts (e.g. wage, price, and rent movements) which would continue until the 1960s. Historians of the manorial economy in the 20th century owe much to these early masters who broke new ground in the study of manors and their sources. The significance of their works for the modern reader, however, is overshadowed by their limited access to documents, relatively unsophisticated analysis of sources, and attempts to promote uniform models of manorialism.

Although evidence extracted from manorial court rolls has since the 1960s increased historians' knowledge of village society, studies of the manorial economy in the 20th century have been coloured by debate over two major theses on its development. The Postan thesis and the Brenner debate have influenced discussion of the manorial economy since the 1960s and 1970s respectively.

POSTAN's chapter (1966), which expands on elements in his earlier works, marks a turning-point in the study of the manorial economy. Here he articulates in a thorough account of the manorial economy and society what was to be henceforth known as the Postan thesis. POSTAN's general text (1972)

further elaborates on elements that underlay the arguments of his earlier essays. His neo-Malthusian, neo-Ricardian model emphasizes population pressure and deteriorating economic conditions preceding the Black Death and improvements realized only after significant population loss in the 14th century.

TITOW, in his volume as part of the "Historical Problems: Studies and Documents" series, presents an overview of sources and problems, landlords and peasants, and debate between Postan and his critics that is generally sympathetic to Postan. Titow also includes transcripts of sources supportive of Postan and Titow's interpretations. MILLER & HATCHER largely follow Postan's lead as well, although with less confidence than Titow, as they survey the themes of population, dependence, inequalities, and forces of change c.1086–1348. BOLTON's work is an attempt to synthesize the findings of historians through the 1970s and set the manorial economy within a wider context of pre-industrial economic development in England. He concludes that the medieval English economy was both highly agrarian and underdeveloped, and that the fundamental economic structures of England altered little in the Middle Ages. Bolton agrees with Postan, Titow, and Miller & Hatcher in his emphasis on the importance of population expansion and contraction and the lack of significant economic or technological innovation. His survey, however, attempts to connect landlords, towns, industrial production, overseas trade, and money and capital with the manorial economy. All in all, the surveys offered by Postan, Titow, Miller & Hatcher, and Bolton are well worth reading, although somewhat dated, and provide background for the more specialized studies of the 1980s and 1990s.

HILTON's work is an excellent example of a survey of the manorial economy c.1300 to c.1500 as seen by one of the best-known English Marxists in this century. Although the peasantry as a socio-economic class is Hilton's primary focus, his conclusions regarding rents, the connection of small towns to peasant institutions, and the role of women set the stage for subsequent investigations and make this volume worth reading.

Robert Brenner's thesis is also essentially Marxist in its notion that social-property systems are a driving force behind economic development. The Brenner debate focused attention on the nature of "feudal" institutions and the manorial economy. Marxist historians such as Brenner, in emphasizing class and class conflict, reject the "demographic determinism" of Postan and his supporters. ASTON & PHILPIN's collection of essays, originally appearing in *Past and Present* between 1976 and 1982, is the best introduction to this debate. It includes Brenner's original essay and a later piece on "The Agrarian Roots of European Capitalism" as well as essays by Postan and Hatcher, J.P. Cooper, Hilton, Guy Bois, and others. The Brenner debate helped focus historians' attention on manorial evidence, interpretations, and a wider context for manorial developments.

The contributions of numerous historians to volumes 2 (1042–1350) and 3 (1348–1500) of *The Agrarian History of England and Wales*, edited by HALLAM and MILLER respectively, with Joan Thirsk as general editor, present significant insights into the manorial economy and society. Like HALLAM's own survey (1981) as part of the "Fontana History of England" series, the contributions to volume 2 collectively represent a critical response to the Postan thesis. The volumes reflect the development of an historical understanding of the manorial economy stemming from the proliferation of case studies from the 1960s through the 1980s based on manorial accounts and court rolls. Great diversity, related to factors such as regional geography, ancient custom, field systems, technology, and landlord-tenant relationships, characterized this manorial economy. The volumes, however, should be read with care. A number of innovative studies in the 1980s and 1990s, which are not reflected in the Agrarian History volumes, have expanded historians' knowledge of such elements as farming practices, technological innovation, productivity, markets, and commercialism as they relate to the manorial economy. The complexity of the manorial economy brought to light by historians in the 1980s and 1990s, however, has been revealed primarily in case studies and specialized investigations rather than in general surveys.

BRITNELL's survey offers insight into the development of the manorial economy, although that is not his only interest. His primary objective is to illustrate the increasing significance of markets, money, and commercial transactions c.1000–c.1500. In doing so, he rejects Postan's population-determinist model and Bolton's dismissal of significant economic change in the medieval period. Britnell's work on commercialization is also valuable as an example of a study that builds a coherent and cohesive survey from disparate strands of localized research and a combination of manorial and extra-manorial sources.

RAFTIS offers another approach to examining the manorial economy. Although the work is essentially an estate study, he argues for the utility of using a limited group of manors to test long-held theories on the manorial economy. In particular, he disputes the belief, shared by historians with such divergent perspectives as Postan, Brenner, Hilton, and their critics, that the essential ingredient in the manorial economy was manipulation of the peasants' economic resources by manorial lords in the era of high farming (the 13th and 14th centuries). In doing so, Raftis opens debate on not only the exploitation of the peasantry but also concepts that have underpinned the historical understanding of the manorial economy in the 20th century.

LORI A. GATES

See also Farming entries; Feudal Law; Feudal Tenures; Feudum; Freedom and Unfreedom; Trade Patterns: Medieval Period; Wages and Rents

Map, Walter d. c.1210
Writer of verse

Aurell, Martin, "La Cour Plantagenêt (1154–1204): entourage, savoir et civilité" in *La Cour Plantagenêt (1154–1204): actes du colloque tenu à Thouars du 30 Avril au 2 Mai 1999*, edited by Martin Aurell, Poitiers: Centre d'Etudes Supérieures de Civilisation Médiévale, 2000

Brooke, Christopher N.L. and R.A.B. Mynors (revising editors and translators), and M.R. James (original editor), *De Nugis Curialium/Courtiers' Trifles*, by Walter Map, Oxford: Clarendon Press, and New York: Oxford University Press, 1983

Cohn, Norman, *Europe's Inner Demons: An Enquiry Inspired by the Great Witch-Hunt*, London: Chatto, and New York:

Basic Books, 1975; revised edition, London: Pimlico, 1993; Chicago: University of Chicago Press, 2000

Harf-Lancner, L., "L'Enfer de la cour: la cour d'Henri II Plantagenêt et la Mesnie Hellequin', *L'Etat et les aristocraties: France, Angleterre, Ecosse, XIIe-XVIIe siècle*, edited by Philippe Contamine, Paris: Presses de l'Ecole Normale Supérieure, 1989

James, Montague Rhodes (editor), *De Nugis Curialium*, by Walter Map, Oxford: Clarendon Press, 1914; reprinted, New York: AMS Press, 1989

Lot, Ferdinand, *Etude sur le "Lancelot" en prose*, Paris: Champion, 1918; expanded edition, 1954

Rigg, A.G., "Golias and Other Pseudonyms", *Studi Medievali*, 3rd series, 18/1 (1977): 65–109

Sharpe, Richard, *A Handlist of the Latin Writers of Great Britain and Ireland before 1540*, Tournai, Belgium: Brepols, 1997

Türk, Egbert, *Nugae Curialium: le règne d'Henri II Plantagenêt (1154–1189) et l'éthique politique*, Geneva: Droz, 1977

Wright, Thomas (editor), *The Latin Poems Commonly Attributed to Walter Mapes*, London: Camden Society, 1841; reprinted, New York: AMS Press, and Hildesheim: Olms, 1968

Wright, Thomas (editor), *Gualteri Mapes De nugis curialium distinctiones quinque*, London: Camden Society, 1850; reprinted, New York: AMS Press, 1968

From at least the 15th century, the name of Walter Map (died *c*.1210) was being bandied around in literary circles as the author of some of the best and bawdiest medieval Latin secular verse, and as the discoverer, perhaps even the author, of the romances underlying the French prose cycle *Lancelot*: the most popular version of the legends of King Arthur and the Holy Grail to have circulated in the Middle Ages. In 1841, WRIGHT filled a hefty volume with Map's Latin poetry, taking it for granted that Map was author of the *Lancelot* cycle in French, although admitting his doubts as to whether one man could have written so diverse and so substantial a collection of Latin verses. More recent scholarship, best approached via the early study by LOT, has entirely stripped Map of any claim to a part in the composition of *Lancelot*, which is now attributed to a northern French milieu and dated to a decade or more after Map's death. At the same time, it has come to be recognized that virtually none of the Latin poetry presented in Map's name was his, but belongs to an anonymous tradition, only later and falsely attributed to specifically named authors. RIGG's valuable study of 1977 credits Map with barely a handful of verses, including none of the so-called "Golias" poems once considered his *chef-d'oeuvre*. Nonetheless, the very fact that Map's name was adopted as a flag of convenience by poets and romancers suggests that the real Walter Map was indeed a familiar figure in 12th-century literary circles, known both as a witty conversationalist and as the author of the one piece of Latin writing with which he can still confidently be credited: the so-called "Courtiers' Trifles" (*De nugis curialium*), a diverse and poorly-organized collection of stories, some of them concerning the court of King Henry II where Map himself served, others addressing such themes as ghosts, fairies, and the fickleness of women. One of these "Trifles", the so-called "Dissuasion of

Valerius", a satire against marriage, circulated fairly widely in the Middle Ages. The remainder of the work seems never to have been published in Map's lifetime, and survived in a single manuscript until its first printing by WRIGHT in 1850. Wright looked upon the work as a literary curiosity, rather than as anything more profound: a judgement that was endorsed by JAMES in his more accurate edition of 1914, which, apart from correcting Wright's Latin, attempted little save the identification of Map's principal classical and patristic sources. Although several English translations were made from James, not until the appearance of the revised edition by BROOKE & MYNORS was an accurate text in both Latin and English supplied with a modern biography of the author, a proper account of his writings, and full historical notes. Brooke & Mynors provide an authoritative source for Map's life and work, and are unlikely to be superseded for many years to come. Meanwhile, TÜRK's study of 1977 had for the first time placed Map's work within its proper literary context, as one of several 12th-century satires written from within the Plantagenet court, to be read not merely as an entertaining selection of anecdotes, but, on a deeper level, as an indication both of the extent of secular learning in the Plantagenet royal circle and of the degree to which the court had come to take on a rich and civilized identity of its own, ripe for satire and parody. HARF-LANCNER's more recent study follows Türk's lead, with particular reference to the image of the diabolic hunt, used by Map and by others of his contemporaries as a metaphor for the volatility and ruthlessness of Plantaganet court life. Much the same basic theme is explored by AURELL, although here drawing attention to the unique richness of the satirical, historical, and administrative literature which flourished in the shadow of the Plantagenet court, unmatched elsewhere in the courts of 12th- and 13th-century Europe. SHARPE's monumental handlist of Latin writers is to be consulted as the chief authority for texts and editions of Map, as of every other medieval English author. Finally, since Map's "Trifles" is one of the earliest texts to refer to the upsurge of heresy in southern France, and in particular to the sect later known as the Cathars, his remarks here have earned him an honourable place amongst the ever burgeoning crop of studies devoted to medieval heresy. COHN's classic study helps to establish Map's story of the heretics and their supposed worship of a monstrous cat within the European-wide context of persecution of religious minorities.

NICHOLAS VINCENT

Marcher Lordships

Davies, R.R., "The Law of the March", *Welsh History Review*, 5 (1970–71): 1–30

Davies, R.R., *Lordship and Society in the March of Wales, 1282–1400*, Oxford: Clarendon Press, 1978

Davies, R.R., "Kings, Lords, and Liberties in the March of Wales, 1066–1272", *Transactions of the Royal Historical Society*, 5th series, 29 (1979): 41–61

Edwards, J.G., "The Normans and the Welsh March", *Proceedings of the British Academy*, 42 (1956): 155–77

Pugh, T.B. (editor), *The Marcher Lordships of South Wales, 1415–1536: Select Documents*, Cardiff: University of Wales Press, 1963

Rees, William, *South Wales and the March, 1284–1415:*
A Social and Agrarian Study, Oxford and New York:
Oxford University Press, 1924
Reeves, A.C., *The Marcher Lords*, Llandybie, Dyfed:
Christopher Davies, 1983

The traditional view of the origins of marcher lordship was that expressed by the 16th-century Pembrokeshire antiquary George Owen of Henllys who maintained that marcher lords enjoyed their particular rights and immunities, which amounted to a virtual independence, because they were originally the Anglo-Norman kingdom's first line of defence against the Welsh. Because of this the king permitted them to retain and rule all the lands they had conquered.

This view was first challenged by Sir Goronwy EDWARDS in his Raleigh Lecture to the British Academy in 1956. He argued that the position of the lords did not stem in any way from the English crown and that marcher lordship, with all its characteristics, was nothing more or less than Welsh kingship in Anglo-Norman hands. What the Norman invaders did as they penetrated Wales was to take over the powers of the Welsh rulers they displaced; this had always been the pattern of Welsh politics. The basic Welsh political and territorial unit, the commote, with its own court, was the basis of Welsh kingship; such evidence as Domesday Book suggested that it was also the unit of Norman penetration and the powers of Welsh kings and Anglo-Norman marcher lords were largely identical, even down to the right of private war. Wherever the Normans went, they tended to take over and adapt the existing political culture and this is what happened in Wales.

DAVIES carried the argument further in his 1979 discussion of marcher lordship, suggesting that Edwards's views had been foreshadowed by some Tudor antiquaries. He saw the Edwards interpretation as something a little too sophisticated for the rough and pragmatic world of the 11th-century Anglo-Welsh border, a world where there was little place for the niceties of constitutional theory; the theoretical justification for marcher powers came later. For many Normans Wales was a land of opportunity, out of the reach of the king of England; here a Norman adventurer could make war and win himself a kingdom in what was a land of war. In their conquests in Wales these lords exercised Welsh political authority because this was the authority they found there. They also came from a feudal and military background and in the frontier zone in which they found themselves everything depended on military power.

Edwards and Davies have made the principal contributions to the debate about the origin and derivation of marcher lordship and have both stressed that the march was an integral part of Wales rather than a kind of no-man's-land between the two countries. There are, however, many other aspects of marcher lordship which have received the attention of historians. Although REES's examination of society and economy in the southern marcher lordships and in the royal lands of south Wales was published three-quarters of a century ago, it has not yet been superseded, nor is it likely to be. This exhaustive archive-based study was a pioneering work in its day and it is still the point of departure for much research on the social and economic history of medieval Wales.

Rees's work has not been superseded by DAVIES's 1978 book on marcher lordship and society as far as social and economic detail is concerned, but the latter is now the definitive study of the march in all its aspects. Rees drew practically all his source material from the Public Record Office, whereas Davies was able to take advantage of the revolution in English and Welsh local archives since World War II and draw on collections now accessible elsewhere. His book examines, among other things, the nature of lordship, with its judicial and military dimensions, the financial and economic aspects of lordship, the relations of lords with the crown, and the two ethnic communities which existed in the march; it is a major contribution to our understanding of that complex world which occupied something like half the total area of Wales in the Middle Ages and it is likewise an indispensable source for anyone studying the contemporary principality.

It was stated more than once in the Middle Ages that the king's writ did not run in the march and DAVIES's 1970 article examines the nature of the law which prevailed there, showing that it was essentially a customary law which varied from place to place and which combined elements of both English and Welsh practice; indeed, the law of the march, outside the sphere of English royal justice, could be described as a mosaic of local law and custom, combining the community's memory and the lord's will.

PUGH edited a number of 15th- and early 16th-century marcher documents, mainly assize rolls and accounts from the lordships of Newport and Brecon, which shed light on the last century of marcher lordship; the editor's introduction discusses the significance of the documents. This collection is important in that it deals with records from a period in the history of the march which has not received as much attention as the thirteenth and fourteenth centuries.

REEVES has written a general book on marcher lords and lordship which is a valuable introduction to the subject; it deals with lordship in its various aspects and concludes with chapters on marcher lords as religious patrons and on their involvement in the politics of the English kingdom at different times. There are numerous other works on the march and marcher lordship, along with several detailed studies of particular lordships (unfortunately some of these remain as unpublished theses submitted for higher degrees; there is an excellent bibliography in Davies's 1978 volume).

ANTONY DAVID CARR

See also Lordships, Palatinates, and Franchises; Wales, Principality of

Margaret of Anjou 1430–1482
Queen and consort of Henry VI

Bagley, J.J., *Margaret of Anjou: Queen of England*, London:
Herbert Jenkins, 1948
Dunn, Diana, "Margaret of Anjou, Queen Consort of Henry
VI: A Reassessment of Her Role, 1445–1453" in *Crown,
Government, and People in the Fifteenth Century*, edited
by Rowena E. Archer, Stroud, Gloucestershire: Alan
Sutton, and New York: St Martin's Press, 1995
Erlanger, Philippe, *Marguerite d'Anjou et la guerre des deux
roses*, Paris: Librairie Académique Perrin, 1961; as

Margaret of Anjou, Queen of England, translated by
Edward Hyams, London: Elek Books, 1970; Coral Gables,
Florida: University of Miami Press, 1971

Griffiths, Ralph A., *The Reign of King Henry VI: The Exercise
of Royal Authority, 1422–1461*, London: Ernest Benn, and
Berkeley: University of California Press, 1981; as *The
Reign of King Henry VI*, Stroud, Gloucestershire: Sutton,
1998

Gross, Anthony, *The Dissolution of the Lancastrian Kingship:
Sir John Fortescue and the Crisis of Monarchy in Fifteenth-
Century England*, Stamford, Lincolnshire: Paul Watkins,
1996

Myers, A.R., "The Household of Queen Margaret of Anjou"
and "The Jewels of Queen Margaret of Anjou" in his
*Crown, Household, and Parliament in Fifteenth Century
England*, edited by Cecil H. Clough, London and
Ronceverte, West Virginia: Hambledon Press, 1985

Watts, John L., *Henry VI and the Politics of Kingship*,
Cambridge and New York: Cambridge University Press,
1996

The queen whom Shakespeare called both "the she-wolf of
France" (in *Henry VI, part 3*) and "thou hateful wither'd hag"
(in *Richard III*) has perhaps not had very fair treatment from
some of her biographers. DUNN makes this point forcefully
basing herself extensively on the accounts printed by Myers as
appendices to his articles on her household and her jewels.
Dunn feels that Margaret's career as the consort of Henry VI can
be divided into two halves, before and after her husband's descent
into severe if intermittent mental illness. Before 1453 she behaved
in the way expected of a medieval queen, showing an interest in
chivalric matters, a love of riding and hunting, and perhaps a
particular interest in gardening. After 1453 she is usually accused
of becoming more involved in politics than was seemly for a
queen and of fighting hard for the rights of her son, Edward,
Prince of Wales against the machinations of the house of York.
For Dunn, even if later events forced her to take a leading political role, before 1453 she is "a dutiful young wife and effective
distributor of patronage rather than an imperious and passionate power-seeker". MYERS draws attention to the lavishness of
her expenditure compared to that of Elizabeth Woodville
[Wydville] as queen to Edward IV, pointing out that this did little
to improve the bad state of Lancastrian finances in general.

ERLANGER's biography, although based on some of the
chronicle evidence, conveys what can only be called a highly
coloured picture of Margaret's life. His imaginative powers are
fully employed in describing her relationship with her husband
and her involvement in some of the more bloody events of the
Wars of the Roses. He also ascribes to her an initiating role in
many of the developments of the later 1450s when the divisions
between the supporters of York and of Lancaster became more
and more clearly defined. His final assessment of her is as a
tragic figure suffering from the anti-French prejudices of the
English and never accorded her due as an "heroic queen" and
a "sublime" mother.

BAGLEY's life, although published as long ago as 1948, is
altogether a more sober account. He makes clear that he is
"unashamed and unrepentant" that his book is "a history
of kings, queens and battles". It does in fact provide a straightforward narrative of her life neither unduly full of romantic

exaggeration nor without a degree of sympathy for his subject,
whom he is also inclined to see as a tragic figure.

A much fuller understanding of the reign of Henry VI and the
place occupied by the queen can be gained from GRIFFITHS's
monumental biography. He looks at the implications for English
policy of the king's marriage with a French princess and the
reports of her support for the cession of Maine at the time of
her marriage. He also accepts the slight evidence of her approval
for a general pardon to those involved in Jack Cade's rebellion
(1450), which is discounted by Dunn. After the birth of the
Prince of Wales in 1453, he sees the king as almost completely
under the queen's domination even if the accusation that the
queen ruled the kingdom as she liked owed more to Yorkist
propaganda than fact. She was involved in the complex developments of the later 1450s, until the victory of Edward IV at
the battle of Towton in 1461 sent her into exile, but to this
point the king had many other supporters. The book does not,
however, cover in detail the period from 1461 until Henry's
murder and the death of the Prince of Wales at the catastrophic
battle of Tewkesbury (1471), which is confined to a brief narrative epilogue. WATTS provides an assessment of her importance
as a source of patronage also during the 1450s but again does
not touch on the period after 1461 and the readeption. GROSS
in his chapter, "Managing Disaster: Margaret of Anjou and the
Formation of Lancastrian Policy, 1453–1471", makes some
attempt to assess the influence of Margaret in her husband's
affairs between these dates but comes to the conclusion that,
despite her energy in the Lancastrian cause, particularly in
France, she had little more grasp of the needs of the situation
than he did.

In many ways, it can be argued that there is no really satisfactory account of the life of Margaret of Anjou in existence
which takes full account of recent work on the complex politics
of the Wars of the Roses. The depiction of her by Shakespeare
as the "she-wolf of France" may be rejected but it is not at all
clear what should be put in its place. Her efforts to secure
support for her husband in the 1460s in France and elsewhere,
culminating in the change of allegiance of Warwick, need further
investigation, as do her earlier activities in England. At the
moment only the earlier years of her marriage have been treated
in a critical and balanced fashion.

SUSAN ROSE

See also Cade Rebellion; Edward IV; Henry VI; Neville

Margaret, "Maid of Norway" 1283–1290

Queen of Scotland

Barrow, G.W.S., "A Kingdom in Crisis: Scotland and the Maid
of Norway", *The Scottish Historical Review*, 69/2 (1990):
120–41

Crawford, Barbara E., "North Sea Kingdoms, North Sea
Bureaucrat: A Royal Official Who Transcended National
Boundaries", *Scottish Historical Review*, 69/2 (1990):
175–84

Dickinson, William Croft, *Scotland from the Earliest Times to 1603*, 3rd edition, revised and edited by Archibald A.M. Duncan, Oxford: Clarendon Press, 1977 (original edition, 1961)

Helle, Knut, "Norwegian Foreign Policy and the Maid of Norway", *Scottish Historical Review*, 69/2 (1990): 142–56

Nicholson, Ranald, *Scotland: The Later Middle Ages*, Edinburgh: Oliver and Boyd, and New York: Barnes and Noble, 1974

Prestwich, Michael, "Edward I and the Maid of Norway", *Scottish Historical Review*, 69/2 (1990): 157–74

Reid, Norman, "The Kingless Kingdom: The Scottish Guardianships of 1286–1306", *Scottish Historical Review*, 61/2 (1982): 105–29

Margaret, Queen of Scotland 1286–90 is more commonly known as the "Maid of Norway". Born in 1283 to King Eric II of Norway and Margaret, the daughter of Alexander III of Scotland, she was the King of Scots' sole surviving heir when he died unexpectedly in 1286. The betrothed wife of Edward of Caernarfon, the heir of Edward I of England, she was the last of the Canmore line. While it is difficult to imagine the historical significance of a girl who did not live past the age of seven and never even set foot on Scottish soil, her death in the islands of Orkney while on the journey to her new kingdom changed the course of Scottish, English, and even Norwegian history. Her demise precipitated a disputed succession known as the "Great Cause" and would result in one of the most famous and extensively studied periods in medieval Scottish history: the first Scottish Wars of Independence.

Her significance in Scotland's history is demonstrated by the fact that *Scottish Historical Review* devoted its entire October 1990 issue to publishing studies commemorating the 700th anniversary of her death. These essays were written by some of the premier Scottish, English, and Scandinavian historians and focus on the political, diplomatic, administrative, and economic connections between these three countries. These four articles should be the focus for any reader interested in this critical time in Scotland's history as they offer the merit of providing her historical significance within the larger context of Scottish, English, and Norwegian viewpoints.

BARROW provides a political and diplomatic analysis of the significance of the Maid from the Scots perspective. He offers a brief analysis of the factions which comprised the six "Guardians" that represented "the community of the realm of Scotland", and was the governing body designed to rule on behalf of the queen. His examination of this period includes an important detailed view of the actions and reactions of the Guardians in response to the enormous crisis in which the country found itself. He also provides insight into the negotiations between Norway and England for the queen's safe passage to her new kingdom as well as for a possible marriage with the king of England's son and heir. Barrow devotes a fair portion of this essay to offering an historical interpretation of the document which was the result of these negotiations, known as the treaty of Birgham (1290). This document has been much debated by historians as much for what it did not say as for what it did. For example, NICHOLSON highlights the ambiguity of the document which he argues worked in Edward's

favour, while Barrow and REID focus on what it did outline: an envisioned union between the Queen of Scotland and the heir to the English throne where the two countries would be ruled separately and independently of one another. Interestingly, Reid furthermore argues that the Scots believed that they had turned Edward from a potential enemy into an ally through the proposed marriage. For his part, PRESTWICH looks at the situation from Edward's perspective and provides a balanced account between the King of England's interactions with the Scots as well as the Norwegians and the motivations behind his dealings with both. Prestwich, more so than the other historians, draws the conclusion that the marriage was never a foregone conclusion and was tenuous at best for many reasons. While these historians do not all agree on Edward's motivations regarding Margaret, they all provide a worthy dialogue and are an important contribution to the historical debate.

HELLE gives an account from the Scandinavian perspective. The article provides a helpful historical overview of foreign relations between Scotland and Norway from the Norwegian point of view. This is becoming increasingly popular as historians realize the importance of placing events in the broader historical context, and this case demonstrates the new understanding that can be gained from such a perspective. Until Helle's contribution, the Maid of Norway's death had never been studied with regard to its repercussions on Scottish-Norwegian as well as Anglo-Norwegian relations. Helle's article goes even further to demonstrate the impact the Maid's death had on Norway's relations with other European countries, including France as well as other Scandinavian countries. This article is a significant contribution towards a clearer understanding of how the death of the Maid of Norway had repercussions for more than simply Scotland and England, which has been the traditional focus of historians.

CRAWFORD wraps up the study of Margaret within a European context by tracing a Scottish royal official who was active in both the Norwegian, Scottish, and English courts during and after the Maid's lifetime. The focus of the article is more on the royal official than on Margaret, and as such it is the least useful of the four. It does, however, provide an interesting example of the diplomatic ties between the three countries during the later 13th century.

There are two general histories that provide an important overview of this critical time period in Scotland's history and enable the reader to more fully understand Margaret's significance within this larger framework. DICKINSON incorporates a short but informative survey while Nicholson contains a much more comprehensive and thorough analysis.

TRACEY L. O'DONNELL

See also Alexander III; Edward I; John Balliol

Markets and Fairs

Britnell, R.H., *The Commercialisation of English Society, 1000–1500*, Cambridge and New York: Cambridge University Press, 1993; 2nd editor, Manchester: Manchester University Press, and New York: St. Martin's Press, 1996

Britnell, R.H., and Bruce M.S. Campbell (editors),
    A Commercialising Economy: England 1086 to c.1300,
    Manchester and New York: Manchester University Press,
    1995
Everitt, Alan, "The Marketing of Agricultural Produce,
    1500–1640" in *The Agrarian History of England and
    Wales*, vol. 4, edited by Joan Thirsk, Cambridge:
    Cambridge University Press, 1967, reprinted, with updated
    bibliography, in *Agricultural Markets and Trade,
    1500–1750*, edited by John Chartres, vol. 4 of *Chapters
    from the Agrarian History of England and Wales*,
    Cambridge and New York: Cambridge University Press,
    1990
Hodges, Richard, *Primitive and Peasant Markets*, Oxford and
    Cambridge, Massachusetts: Blackwell, 1988
Kowaleski, Maryanne, *Local Markets and Regional Trade in
    Medieval Exeter*, Cambridge and New York: Cambridge
    University Press, 1995
Masschaele, James, *Peasants, Merchants, and Markets: Inland
    Trade in Medieval England, 1150–1350*, New York:
    St Martin's Press, and London: Macmillan, 1997
Moore, Ellen Wedemeyer, *The Fairs of Medieval England:
    An Introductory Study*, Toronto: Pontifical Institute of
    Mediaeval Studies, 1985

For much of the 20th century, historians treated markets and fairs as relatively insignificant elements in the social and economic development of England. Traditional wisdom held that the trade occurring in these venues was essentially small-scale and intermittent, and that the real impetus for longer-term commercial growth had to be sought in the economic activities of the mercantile classes in towns and cities. These views have changed considerably over the last generation. Markets and fairs are now seen as major commercial venues in their own right, with a history that, though intimately related to the process of urbanization, merits careful study on its own terms.

The primary impetus for this re-evaluation of the role of markets and fairs in the pre-industrial economy came from EVERITT's seminal article "The Marketing of Agricultural Produce, 1500–1640". Everitt argued that England developed a sophisticated marketing infrastructure under the Tudors and Stuarts, particularly in the decades after 1570. Advances in commercial practices and a realignment of marketing venues allowed goods to flow relatively smoothly between regions, and permitted farmers, or at least some farmers, to transform their operations in two related ways. First, they were able to capitalize on growing population, rising prices, and nascent industrial demand for raw materials to establish farming enterprises that were larger, better managed, and more intensively capitalized. Second, the opportunity to fix eyes on markets further afield allowed farmers in different parts of the country to improve production by specializing in the crops and stock to which their farms were best suited by nature. Changes in marketing practices were thus intimately related to issues of regional diversification, overall economic growth, and fundamental change in the shape of society. Fairs and markets could no longer be seen as economic backwaters; they had to be treated as dynamic institutions that were closely bound up with the other changes that were transforming England from a world of peasant villagers to a world of townspeople and gentry farmers.

Implicit in Everitt's arguments for substantial change in the marketing structures of the early modern world was the assumption that earlier markets had been peripheral features of social and economic life. In the 1980s and 1990s, a significant divergence from this interpretative framework emerged in the work of a number of medieval scholars, who have argued that earlier developments were more substantial than Everitt recognized. BRITNELL, in a series of articles leading up to his 1993 book, initiated this chronological reconfiguration, showing that markets had achieved great prominence already by the middle of the 13th century, although he saw these early markets primarily as localized outlets for the sale of foodstuffs and other basic necessities, and thus not as nodes of regional exchange as described by Everitt. Britnell's work is noteworthy not just for its chronological arguments but also for its attempt to situate markets in a broader medieval context than is evident in most other work in the field. MOORE's work on fairs also argued for an early prominence for these venues, with a heyday reached in the 12th and early 13th centuries. Most historians agree with her contention that fairs were particularly prominent commercial sites in the 12th century, although they find fault with her argument for an undiminished decline after this heyday. Fairs have generally received less attention from historians than markets, though, and a thorough study of their later history is badly needed.

HODGES, working mainly with archaeological data, concurred that sophisticated marketing systems existed well before the early modern period. He sought to push back the origins of routine marketing into the Anglo-Saxon period, but few others have followed his lead. Graeme Snooks, in an article in the volume edited by BRITNELL & CAMPBELL, has argued that Domesday Book reveals a far more commercialized society in the 11th century than is generally recognized, but other contributors to that volume have questioned some of the major assumptions underpinning his interpretation. Certainly, the origins of a number of markets can be traced back before 1066, although the well-documented surge in market foundations and other market activity in the 12th and 13th centuries belies the notion that commercialization had made significant inroads in earlier periods.

A recent study by KOWALESKI implicitly challenges Everitt's model from a somewhat different direction. Through a meticulous prosopographical reconstruction of the merchant community of Exeter and its interactions with producers and consumers in the surrounding Devon countryside, Kowaleski shows that regional commerce was already well advanced by the end of the 14th century. What is not clear from her work is the extent to which Exeter and Devon can serve as models for developments elsewhere. MASSCHAELE's work attempts to generalize for the country as a whole, arguing that medieval markets were closely integrated with each other to form regional networks of exchange. He believes that the dichotomy between a self-sufficient world of medieval peasants and a commercialized world of early modern merchants and gentry capitalists has been overstated by many historians, including Everitt. Structurally, there are many similarities between medieval markets and those of later periods, suggesting that a long-term history of ebbs and flows in the role of markets and fairs might be a better conceptual model for the pre-industrial world than one that emphasizes dramatic change.

Currently, a team of scholars operating under the auspices of the Centre for Metropolitan History at the University of London is engaged in an in-depth examination of sources dealing with medieval markets. Much of this project's work has been published in inaccessible places and tends to lack adequate contextualization for the general reader, but the quality and range of research conducted has been impressive. Details about the centre's publications and works-in-progress, including a gazetteer of markets established before 1516, is available on the centre's website: www.history.ac.uk/cmh/cmh.main.html.

JAMES MASSCHAELE

See also Farming entries; Manorial Economy; Merchant Guilds; Trade Patterns: English (Early Medieval Period); Trade Patterns: Medieval Period

Marlborough, John Churchill, 1st Duke of 1650–1722

Soldier and statesman

Ashley, Maurice, *Marlborough*, London: Duckworth, 1939; New York: Macmillan, 1956

Atkinson, C.T., *Marlborough and the Rise of the British Army*, New York and London: Putnam, 1921

Barnett, Correlli, *Marlborough*, London: Eyre Methuen, 1974; as *The First Churchill: Marlborough, Soldier, and Statesman*, New York: Putnam, 1974

Burton, Ivor F., *The Captain-General: The Career of John Churchill, Duke of Marlborough, from 1702 to 1711*, London: Constable, 1968

Chandler, David, *Marlborough as Military Commander*, London: Batsford, and New York: Scribner, 1973

Churchill, Winston S., *Marlborough: His Life and Times*, 4 vols, London: Harrap, and New York: Scribner, 1933–38; 2nd edition, 2 vols, London: Harrap, 1947

Coxe, William, *Memoirs of John, Duke of Marlborough, with His Original Correspondence*, 3 vols, London: Longman Hurst, Rees, Orme and Brown, 1818–19; revised edition, as *Memoirs of the Duke of Marlborough, with His Original Correspondence*, edited by John Wade, 3 vols, London: Bohn, 1847–48; London and New York: Bell, 1885

Hoff, B. (editor), *The Correspondence, 1701–1711, of John Churchill, First Duke of Marlborough, and Anthonie Heinsius, Grand Pensionary of Holland*, The Hague: Nijhoff, 1951

Horn, Robert D., *Marlborough: A Survey: Panegyrics, Satires, and Biographical Writings, 1688–1788*, Folkestone, Kent: Dawson, and New York: Garland, 1975

Jones, J.R., *Marlborough*, Cambridge and New York: Cambridge University Press, 1993

Lediard, Thomas, *The Life of John, Duke of Marlborough, Prince of the Roman Empire*, 3 vols, London: Wilcox, 1736; revised edition, 2 vols, 1743

Murray, George (editor), *The Letters and Dispatches of John Churchill, First Duke of Marlborough, from 1702 to 1712,* 5 vols, London: John Murray, 1845; New York: Greenwood Press, 1968

Paget, John, "The Duke of Marlborough" in his *The New "Examen"*, London: Blackwood, 1861; 2nd edition, with a critical introduction by Winston Churchill, London: Haworth Press, 1934

Rowse, A.L., *The Early Churchills, an English Family*, London: Macmillan, and New York: Harper, 1956

Snyder, Henry L. (editor), *The Marlborough-Godolphin Correspondence*, 3 vols, Oxford: Clarendon Press, 1975

Taylor, Frank, *The Wars of Marlborough, 1702–1709*, edited by G. Winifred Taylor, 2 vols, Oxford: Blackwell, 1921

Wolseley, Garnet, *The Life of John Churchill, Duke of Marlborough, to the Accession of Queen Anne*, 2 vols, London: Bentley, 1894

Any short list of candidates for the title of the greatest soldier in the history of the British Isles would certainly include Marlborough alongside Henry V and Wellington. In the course of ten successive campaigns from 1702 to 1711 in the War of the Spanish Succession against France, his leadership of the armies of the allies in Flanders and Germany consolidated Britain's emergence as a front-rank European power. He combined the command of armies in the field with the task of maintaining collaborative unity among the countries comprising the Grand Alliance, and this demanded the highest skills of diplomacy. His European prestige as soldier and statesman was achieved through his spectacular victories at Blenheim in 1704 and Ramillies in 1706, and thereafter remained undiminished notwithstanding his difficulties in British domestic politics in the later stages of the war. Blenheim Palace near Woodstock in Oxfordshire, designed by Vanbrugh and completed after Marlborough's death by Hawksmoor, still commemorates his achievements.

Between them, LEDIARD (who had served under Marlborough), COXE, and MURRAY published most of Marlborough's surviving military papers. On the basis of this evidence, modern military historians have arrived at a consensus on Marlborough's distinction as a soldier. ATKINSON and TAYLOR formulated an interpretation which gave equal weight to his capacity as strategist, tactician, and administrator. BARNETT, in a lavishly illustrated study aimed at a wide audience, concluded that Marlborough's success was the product of high competence in a range of different skills. CHANDLER has, perhaps, summarized this consensus most effectively. Chandler remarked upon Marlborough's wide and comprehensive vision at the level of grand strategy, and upon his meticulous planning of individual campaigns. His ability to take advantage of an enemy's weaknesses, to deceive opponents by feints, ruses, and false intelligence, to follow up an initiative by sustained pressure, and to exploit carefully reconnoitred terrain were his principal qualities in terms of battlefield tactics. Marlborough's competence as an administrator was also emphasized by Chandler. He appreciated the importance of keeping his troops fed, paid, and clothed at all times, and he devoted much attention to the detailed organization of the logistics of war. BURTON implied a slightly more critical view by identifying a watershed in Marlborough's career in 1707. Before that year, Marlborough's strategy was limited, and therefore coherent; from 1707 to the end of the war, the new objective of conquering Spain for the Habsburg candidate for the Spanish crown was unrealistic and led, ultimately, to a less decisive Allied victory than had earlier seemed probable. Both Burton and Chandler suggested that possibly Marlborough's victories owed something to the inadequacy of the French generals who opposed him, and that Marlborough's tactics became stereotyped and predictable in his later campaigns. However, all military historians would probably agree that these qualifications do not seriously call into question Marlborough's very high reputation as a general.

HOFF and SNYDER, together with Coxe, published Marlborough's correspondence relating to his activities in international diplomacy and British politics. His problems with his allies, especially the Dutch, are well documented in his letters to Heinsius. The object of his strategy was to invade northern France and to drive towards Paris, and he attributed his failure to achieve this to Dutch over-caution and obstruction. Even more serious were his vicissitudes at home. His original power base in British politics was the favour of Queen Anne, and this proved insecure after his volatile wife Sarah quarrelled with the queen. Thereafter, the ministry of Marlborough's friend Godolphin was sustained by alliances with civilian politicians who could command majorities in the House of Commons. By 1710 the combination of the Sacheverell trial, the transfer of Anne's favour from Godolphin to Robert Harley, and the war-weariness of the electorate produced a new ministry and a parliament eager to bring the war to an end. Marlborough was dismissed from his command and from all his offices in the winter of 1711–12. Britain's armies took no active part in the campaigns of 1712, thus allowing for some last-ditch French successes; and the treaty of Utrecht in 1713 did not fully reflect the scale of Marlborough's earlier victories. Marlborough himself went into self-imposed exile in 1712 and returned to Britain only on the accession of George I in 1714. The bibliography of contemporary writings published by HORN reveals the intensity of the controversy caused by these political difficulties. They clouded Marlborough's fame at home, if not abroad, during the last ten years of his life.

For some earlier historians, Marlborough's career before the outbreak of the War of the Spanish Succession was flawed in a number of quite different respects. Hume, Hallam, and especially Macaulay all criticized aspects of Marlborough's conduct. The youthful John Churchill's rise from obscurity to court favour had been facilitated by his calculating liaison with the Duchess of Cleveland, the ex-mistress of Charles II; by Churchill's sister Arabella's affair with the Duke of York, Charles's brother and heir; and by the friendship between Sarah and Princess Anne. There seemed to the 19th-century mind to be something discreditable about the promotion of a young officer through the influence of the women of the Restoration court. Then, as second-in-command of the army in 1688, Churchill had deserted his friend and patron James II in the course of operations against a foreign invader, the Prince of Orange. Not only did Churchill defect to the enemy in mid-campaign; it was rumoured that he had actually planned to kidnap the king and to convey him as a prisoner to William's camp. After the Glorious Revolution, he had established contact with the Jacobite court in exile, and it was alleged that he had betrayed military secrets to France, notably that of the descent upon Brest in 1694 commanded by his rival Talmash.

The revelation in 1692 of Marlborough's disloyalty to the cause of the Revolution explained, for Macaulay, William's refusal to employ him in the War of the League of Augsburg thereafter. More generally, Marlborough gained a reputation early in life for miserly avarice, which he never succeeded in shaking off. Some of his financial dealings seemed to Macaulay to amount to peculation and even fraud. This alleged personal frailty became a serious political accusation: that Marlborough had wanted to prolong the War of the Spanish Succession for his own advantage against the national interest.

The most serious of these charges, that of betraying military secrets to an enemy, was persuasively dealt with by PAGET. His verdict was that Marlborough (like many others) wished to guard himself against the possibility of a Jacobite restoration by ingratiating himself with the exiled court; however, Marlborough was careful not to give away information to the French unless he was confident that it was already known to them. Paget thus exposed an uncritical use of evidence by Macaulay, but the great Whig historian's influence was so powerful that many biographies of Marlborough have tended to adopt a somewhat defensive tone. This is true of WOLSELEY, ASHLEY, and ROWSE, and also of the exhaustive study of Marlborough's life and career in all its aspects compiled by CHURCHILL. In spite of his natural concern to protect the reputation of his ancestor, Churchill's biography was based on extensive original research in the Marlborough archive, then at Blenheim Palace, and it is scholarly and mostly sound. JONES incorporated the work of more recent historians on the political and diplomatic background of the period, and his description of Marlborough is much the best up-to-date study for the general reader. Jones's sensible conclusion is that it cannot be denied that in some respects Marlborough's conduct might be regarded as discreditable by 20th-century standards, but that his lapses can reasonably be justified by the exigencies of the times through which he lived. They do not diminish his achievements as the manager of a coalition of mutually suspicious allies in a great war and as a soldier who, in Jones's words, "far excelled any other general of his own time".

LIONEL K.J. GLASSEY

See also Anne; Godolphin; Harley; Jacobitism; James VII and II; Marlborough, Duchess of; Spanish Succession, War of; William III and Mary II

Marlborough, Sarah (Jennings), Duchess of 1660–1744

Royal attendant and favourite

Butler, Iris, *Rule of Three: Sarah, Duchess of Marlborough, and Her Companions in Power*, London: Hodder and Stoughton, 1967

Campbell, Kathleen, *Sarah, Duchess of Marlborough*, London: Butterworth, and Boston: Little Brown, 1932

Green, David, *Sarah, Duchess of Marlborough*, London: Collins, and New York: Scribner, 1967

Harris, Frances, *A Passion for Government: The Life of Sarah, Duchess of Marlborough*, Oxford: Clarendon Press, and New York: Oxford University Press, 1991

Hooke, Nathaniel, *An Account of the Conduct of the Dowager Duchess of Marlborough, from Her First Coming to Court, to the Year 1710*, London: James Bettenham for George Hawkins, 1742

Reid, Stuart J., *John and Sarah, Duke and Duchess of Marlborough, 1660–1744: Based on Unpublished Letters and Documents at Blenheim Palace*, London: John Murray, and New York: Scribner, 1914

Thomson, Mrs A.T., *Memoirs of Sarah, Duchess of Marlborough, and of the Court of Queen Anne*, 2 vols, London: Colburn, 1839

At the peak of her career in the first two years of Queen Anne's reign from 1702 to 1704, the Duchess of Marlborough might well have been thought to be one of the most influential women in Europe. Her husband, the first Duke of Marlborough, presided as captain-general of the army over England's military and diplomatic contribution to the allies in the War of the Spanish Succession; the couple were reciprocally devoted. Sarah herself occupied the court offices of groom of the stole, mistress of the robes, keeper of the privy purse, and ranger of Windsor Forest. Their close ally, Lord Godolphin, was lord treasurer, and he supervised the nation's finances. Sarah had for some twenty years – in fact, since 1683 – lived on terms of intimate friendship with the new queen. As is well known, these four powerful individuals at the head of a government conducting a European war discarded formality in their correspondence. They addressed each other as "Mr and Mrs Freeman" (the Marlboroughs), "Mrs Morley" (the queen), and "Mr Montgomery" (Godolphin). Sarah's favour with the queen, who retained and exercised the royal prerogative of choosing and dismissing her own ministers, seemed to make possible Godolphin's adroit financial management and Marlborough's victories on the battlefield. HOOKE, writing in the person of the duchess and with her full approbation and co-operation at the end of her life, implied this view of her services to the nation. THOMSON, REID, and CAMPBELL, successive authors of the best biographies of their respective generations, tended to a greater or lesser extent to take their cue from Hooke, as also did the authors of numerous popular studies not listed here.

The more recent biographers of Sarah and historians of Anne's reign have, however, united in warning against an over-estimation of Sarah's influence. Both BUTLER and GREEN pointed out the paradoxes in her situation. Sarah was a vehement and committed Whig; her mistress the queen distrusted the opportunism and self-interest of party politicians and exhibited an instinctive preference for the Tories. Sarah was largely indifferent to religious issues in politics; the queen was a devout adherent of the Church of England. Sarah was intemperately partisan; Marlborough and Godolphin preferred moderation and conciliation, and were frequently embarrassed by Sarah's violent denunciations of Tories with whom they had to work. Marlborough and Godolphin saw, as Sarah did not, that her importunate advocacy of Whig measures and a Whig ministry first bored, and then offended, the queen. The lack of timing and the erratic judgement which were characteristic of most of Sarah's interventions in affairs tended, more often than not, to undermine rather than to assist the ministry.

Above all, Sarah's relationship with Anne cooled rapidly after Anne became queen. In what is by far the most subtle and

scholarly biography of Sarah, HARRIS charted in detail the development of what had already become an estrangement by the winter of 1704–05 and was a bitter quarrel by 1710. So far from facilitating the careers of her husband and Godolphin, Sarah was for most of the queen's reign a liability to them. Harris made it clear that she was temperamentally unsuited to the role of royal favourite. Highly intelligent and occasionally astute, she was also capricious, impetuous, tactless, and abrasive. She could be volcanically quarrelsome. All her inclinations were in favour of "country" attitudes, as her association late in life with the "patriot" opposition to Sir Robert Walpole suggests; her independence of mind could not be adapted to the skills of governmental politics. Her friendship with Anne had flourished in the 1680s when Anne had been the only adult protestant member of the royal family resident in England during James II's catholic regime, and then in the 1690s when Anne had been the focus of opposition to her brother-in-law William. Their intimate collaboration could not survive Anne's elevation to the throne and the assumption by Anne and Marlborough of patronage and power.

Sarah's real influence on the politics of her time was therefore limited. Harris's biography illuminated another, rather different, aspect of her life: she was a first-rate businesswoman. Her private fortune was maintained separately from that of her husband, and she employed it to great advantage, most notably in selling her South Sea stock at just the right moment in early June 1720 and in investing shrewdly in land. By the time of her death, her fortune, in Harris's words, "must easily have made her the richest woman in her own right in England". Notwithstanding incessant quarrels with her children and grandchildren, perhaps her greatest achievement lay not so much in sustaining her husband through a great war or in her contribution to high politics at Anne's court, but in her consolidation and management of a great aristocratic family and estate.

LIONEL K.J. GLASSEY

See also Anne; Godolphin; Marlborough, 1st Duke of

Marriage

Amussen, Susan Dwyer, *An Ordered Society: Gender and Class in Early Modern England*, Oxford and New York: Blackwell, 1988

Doggett, Maeve E., *Marriage, Wife-Beating, and the Law in Victorian England*, London: Weidenfeld and Nicolson, 1992; Columbia: University of South Carolina Press, 1993

Gillis, John R., *For Better, For Worse: British Marriages 1600 to the Present*, New York and Oxford: Oxford University Press, 1985

Hanawalt, Barbara A., *The Ties That Bound: Peasant Families in Medieval England*, New York and Oxford: Oxford University Press, 1986

Houlbrooke, Ralph A., *The English Family, 1450–1700*, London and New York: Longman, 1984

Ingram, Martin, *Church Courts, Sex, and Marriage in England, 1570–1640*, Cambridge and New York: Cambridge University Press, 1987

Jalland, Patricia, *Women, Marriage, and Politics, 1860–1914*, Oxford: Clarendon Press, 1986; Oxford and New York: Oxford University Press, 1988

Macfarlane, Alan, *Marriage and Love in England: Modes of Reproduction, 1300–1840*, Oxford and New York: Blackwell, 1986

Perkin, Joan, *Women and Marriage in Nineteenth-Century England*, London: Routledge, and Chicago: Lyceum Books, 1989

Stone, Lawrence, *The Family, Sex, and Marriage in England, 1500–1800*, London: Weidenfeld and Nicolson, and New York: Harper and Row, 1977

Stone, Lawrence, *Road to Divorce: England, 1530–1987*, Oxford: Clarendon Press, and Oxford and New York: Oxford University Press, 1990

Stone, Lawrence, *Uncertain Unions: Marriage in England 1660–1753*, Oxford and New York: Oxford University Press, 1992

Stone, Lawrence, *Broken Lives: Separation and Divorce in England 1660–1857*, Oxford and New York: Oxford University Press, 1993

Wrigley, E.A. *et al.*, *English Population History from Family Reconstitution, 1580–1837*, Cambridge and New York: Cambridge University Press, 1997

Emphasizing continuity over change, HOULBROOKE concludes that the nuclear family was the dominant English form of family between 1450 and 1700. His work is a valuable introduction to the sources and concerns of family historians with topics ranging from affective relations to inheritance. The chapters on courtship and marriage, relations between husband and wife, and the end of marriage all emphasize the central place of mutual love, respect, and affection, although Houlbrooke acknowledges that law, theology, and scientific theory all presented women as inferior during the age.

WRIGLEY *et al.* is a companion to Wrigley's monumental *The Population History of England, 1541–1871: A Reconstruction* (1989). This study from the Cambridge Group analyses the results of family reconstitutions for 26 English parishes using Anglican registers. Reconstitution is a technique employing parochial and civil records to reconstruct family histories with focus on births, marriages, and deaths. The results of this study demonstrate a higher average age at first marriage throughout the period than previously thought, explain the reasons why marriages occurred earlier or later at different times, reveal very high levels of "prenuptially conceived" children, and reverse earlier conclusions about a constant rate of marital fertility. The authors' scholarship actually shows an increase in fertility during the 18th century. Readers should approach the work with caution as it is extremely technical demographic history and its conclusions are applied to the whole of England. Despite its limits, this volume, together with the 1989 work, is fundamental reading because of its important methodology and the vast quantity of data it makes available.

GILLIS offers a comprehensive history of lower-class marriage customs and practices, illustrating both regional and class variations. Using a rich blend of primary sources and secondary interpretations, he analyses the fragile nature of marriage among the poorer classes. Gillis concludes that satisfactory companionate marriages were uncommon among the lower orders in both rural and urban environments and that married women especially sought economic and emotional support from family and friends rather than their marriage partners. The study examines courtship and marriage, tracing the shift from public rituals of the earlier period, in which community, family, and friends each played significant roles, to the private, personal ceremonies of modern times. The image of marriage emerging from this study underscores the tensions between the ideal and the actual.

In sharp contrast to Gillis's conclusions, MACFARLANE finds that companionate, egalitarian marriages are the historic norm among lower-class couples. Both scholars are heavily influenced by the methodologies of historical anthropology. Macfarlane emphasizes that the uniqueness of English families is found in their adherence to the Malthusian marriage model since at least the time of Chaucer. Costs and benefits determined when couples married and took precedence over other considerations. Couples delayed the decision until accumulating sufficient financial resources to establish an independent nuclear household. Individuals themselves made the choice of a suitable partner and marriages were based upon love and friendship. Thus, couples did not wed merely to procreate; rather, they accepted children as an inevitable part of a marriage.

While Gillis and Macfarlane address marriage among the lower orders, STONE (1977) focuses his attention primarily on the middle-class, squirearchy, and aristocratic families. He argues that three types characterize English families between 1450 and 1880: open lineage, 1450–1630; restricted patriarchal nuclear, 1550–1700; and closed domesticated nuclear, 1640–1880. The periods are more fluid than rigid and Stone does not see unbridled linear progress over time. The emergence of the modern family is based upon the growth of affective individualism. Families played a far greater role in selecting suitable partners particularly during the first two periods. Freedom of choice in selecting a potential spouse was inversely related to the amount of property at stake. By the latter period, marriages grounded in love rather than in considerations of wealth began to assume greater significance.

Based upon close scrutiny of ecclesiastical court records, particularly the Court of Arches from the province of Canterbury, STONE (1990) surveys the laws, customs, and practices of marriage contracts and the manner in which they could be terminated. He examines the issues connected to proving marital validity and changing parliamentary regulations governing separation and divorce prior to passage of the Divorce Law of 1857. Stone also reviews the law governing separation by private contract and that achieved in ecclesiastical courts. *Road to Divorce* provides the analytical framework for two subsequent collections of case studies (STONE 1992 and 1993). Primary attention in the overview volume focuses on the period between 1660 and 1857, before divorce and separation became commonplace. His extended narrative of the end of marriage is a valuable starting point for this important topic.

Complementing several studies that encompass several historical periods are more focused analyses. HANAWALT presents the richest discussion of family formation and life in 14th- and 15th-century England. Concerned primarily with peasants, her arguments are constructed from coroners' inquests, wills, manorial court rolls, and tax records. She disputes Stone's argument for a sharp cleavage between family life in medieval and early-modern times. Nuclear families were the norm throughout and many were companionate unions built upon affection. Sons did not wait for their inheritance to marry and often acquired their own holdings while parents were still living. The study contains fine descriptions of the communal and personal patterns of married life.

During the 16th and 17th centuries, AMUSSEN argues, popular attitudes regarding patriarchy in the state and family were open to challenge and reinterpretation. Using case studies from Norfolk, rooted in an examination of wills, manorial accounts, deeds, and court records, she explains the elite's obsession with order and sees the family as metaphor for the state. The work raises new questions about the family as both an economic and a political entity. Her conclusions about power and gender relations help explain the changing dynamic of families and the gradual development of a distinction between private and public spheres by the 18th century. In like manner, discussions of sexual honour, wifely obedience, and church seating arrangements add to our understanding of marriage in the three centuries.

INGRAM's analysis of ecclesiastical courts for Wiltshire, Cambridgeshire, Leicestershire, and Sussex in the 16th and 17th centuries illuminates ambiguities between parents and their offspring regarding courtship found in neither Stone nor Macfarlane. It also details the activities of the courts in promoting church marriages and greater sexual morality. There was a marked decline in binding spousals (formal contracts) among villagers and a growing recognition of the need for a church ceremony to legitimize a marriage. The same period witnessed increased condemnation of prenuptial pregnancy and fuller prosecution of bastardy. In these areas, the courts found support within the local communities. Finally, Ingram offers useful analyses of marital breakdown for the lower orders to parallel Stone's findings.

Although ignoring several important studies, PERKIN nonetheless offers a provocative survey of marriage for elite, middle class, and working women. She notes that women at either extreme exercised greater control of personal wealth and more commonly engaged in extramarital affairs than their middle-class sisters. Aristocratic women wed to consolidate property and provide heirs for their class. Male privilege and domination began to subside for these women during the 19th century, according to Perkin; however, most others accepted their roles as wife and mother without question or challenge. Working-class wives, whose income was pivotal to survival, were more commonly acknowledged as full marital partners than wives in any other class. This is a useful introduction to the gradual emancipation of women in marriage in the 20th century.

JALLAND, in a groundbreaking analysis, explores three critical areas: courtship, marriage, and childbirth among approximately 70 prominent Victorian and Edwardian families. She reveals broadly divergent reactions to courtship among this elite. If parents no longer selected suitable partners, particular economic and social assumptions and traditions still governed choices. The author also describes marital intimacy and the difficulties associated with pregnancy and child delivery in rich detail. She provides useful sections on birth control and miscarriages. The work is a superb examination of the private lives of political wives, daughters, and sisters. With its emphasis on the relative freedom in marriage for these women, it serves as a fine complement to Perkin.

DOGGETT adds a fascinating dimension to the study of marriage: wife-beating. She traces the history of the law from Renaissance times through the 19th century and suggests the limited options available to abused wives. Justifications for wife-beating included a husband's legal responsibility for his wife's actions, the custom that wives were subject to their husbands in all things, and the fiction of marital unity. The decision in the Jackson case provided some comfort for abused wives; however, it did not bring equality. Thus, Doggett somewhat moderates some of the positive conclusions found in Perkin and Jalland.

MICHAEL J. GALGANO

See also Birth Control and Abortion; Child Labour; Childbirth, Gynaecology, and Family Planning; Childhood; Divorce Law Reform; Feminism, Second-Wave; Gender and Power; Inheritance, Patterns of; Patriarchy; Sexuality and Sexual Mores; Social Structure entries; Stopes; Women's Legal Status; Women's Movements; Women's Roles and Authority

Marston Moor, Battle of
see Civil Wars entries; Cromwell, Oliver; Fairfax

Martineau, Harriet 1802–1876
Journalist, social campaigner, and novelist

Bosanquet, Theodora, *Harriet Martineau: An Essay in Comprehension*, London: Etchels and Macdonald, 1927
David, Deirdre, *Intellectual Women and Victorian Patriarchy: Harriet Martineau, Elizabeth Barrett Browning, George Eliot*, Ithaca, New York: Cornell University Press, and London: Macmillan, 1987
Fenwick Miller, Florence, *Harriet Martineau*, London: W.H. Allen, 1884; Boston: Roberts, 1885; reprinted, Port Washington, New York: Kennikat Press, 1972
Hoecker-Drysdale, Susan, *Harriet Martineau: First Woman Sociologist*, Oxford and New York: Berg, 1992
Hunter, Shelagh, *Harriet Martineau: The Poetics of Moralism*, Aldershot, Hampshire and Brookfield, Vermont: Scolar Press, 1995
Sanders, Valerie, *Reason over Passion: Martineau and the Victorian Novel*, Brighton, Sussex: Harvester Press, and New York: St Martin's Press, 1986
Walters, Margaret, "The Rights and Wrongs of Women: Mary Wollstonecraft, Harriet Martineau, Simone de Beauvoir" in *The Rights and Wrongs of Women*, edited by Juliet Mitchell and Ann Oakley, Harmondsworth: Penguin, 1976
Webb, Robert K., *Harriet Martineau: A Radical Victorian*, New York: Columbia University Press, and London: Heinemann, 1960

In her lifetime, Harriet Martineau was both influential and controversial. FENWICK MILLER's biographical tribute testifies to Martineau's iconic status, not only through the account of her life itself, but in Martineau's influence upon the author, who became an effective journalist and activist. In the 20th century early interest in Martineau focused on her extraordinary personality. The feminist movement of the 1970s created renewed scholarly interest in her ideas and writings, though, as both Walters and David indicate, Martineau remains a problematic figure for feminist critics.

BOSANQUET's modest aim is "to relate Miss Martineau's life and opinions, and her continual, if sometimes eccentric, progress towards the final phase of her remarkable career, to the personal influences which so clearly and powerfully affected her". Basing her work on Martineau's own *Autobiography* as well as records by her contemporaries, she quotes liberally from these sources, though references are virtually non-existent. Despite this weakness, Bosanquet's range of material makes for a rounded and insightful portrait of her subject, corrects some of the impressions in Mrs Florence Fenwick Miller's 1884 biography, and as Webb notes, her style is "sprightly". James Martineau's lengthy letter to the *Daily News* following the Fenwick Miller biography is included in the appendix.

WEBB offers a scholarly biography, drawing on a most impressive range of manuscript sources, and the journals and newspapers for which Martineau wrote. In particular he was able to use Martineau's own *Daily News* cuttings collection. A historian by background, he approaches his subject in order to discover the forces which formed her opinions. These opinions themselves are characterized as ranging from "penetrating judgements and superb common sense to almost unbelievable dogmatism and just plain silliness". The result is both a fascinating well-documented account of Martineau's extraordinary personality, her work and ideas, and a study of Victorian radicalism. Webb remains essential reading for those interested in Martineau.

WALTERS's essay locates Martineau within a "bourgeois feminist tradition" in which each of the three women discussed "fought alone", working as individuals rather than contributing to a feminist movement. Martineau's widely scattered writings on feminist issues are viewed as a whole. She is seen as a pungent, often audacious, journalist and, if not an original thinker, an exceptionally effective popularizer of ideas. The sympathetic commentary on the *Autobiography* and the remarks on *Deerbrook* highlight the personal conflicts Martineau faced in her approach to the position of women, a theme which Sanders later develops more extensively. This is a brief but very useful starting-point for students interested in this aspect of Martineau's life and work.

HOECKER-DRYSDALE is a sociologist rather than a historian or literary critic, and her subtitle indicates the emphasis of this account of Martineau's life and work. She presents her subject "as a significant figure in the tradition of British social science and of nineteenth century sociological thought". She argues that Martineau's sociological proclivities are evident in virtually all that she wrote from her very earliest work for the *Monthly Repository*, and including her travel writing, fiction, and treatment of such varied subjects as illness and practical advice to intending servants. The slant of the book thus highlights some of those writings that historical and literary-critical approaches may marginalize.

SANDERS's book is valuable in offering a detailed study of Martineau's fiction. Admitting that all her subject's substantial fiction was written between 1827 and 1846, while the decades that followed were filled with her prolific journalistic and polemical writings, Sanders argues that by her contemporary critics Martineau's fiction was highly valued. She points out that her "important and innovatory" work appeared before Elizabeth Gaskell, Charlotte Brontë, and George Eliot embarked on novel-writing, and pre-dated the major works of Charles Dickens and Charles Kingsley on working-class life and social problems. It is within this historical and cultural context that Sanders offers her study of *The Illustrations of Political Economy, Deerbrook,* and the *Autobiography*, as well as many of the short tales, and the travel writings. Martineau is seen as an important precursor of later writers, both in the themes she introduces and in her concern that fiction should reflect all social groups, and that it should reveal the heroism of the struggles of ordinary men. Detailed analyses of particular works support Sanders's theory. Thus *Deerbrook*, in offering "the outwardly-controlled single woman with the powerful 'inner life' . . . pilots the core plots of *Jane Eyre* and other Brontë novels", and her treatment and use of the doctor-hero foreshadow later work by other novelists. Despite its acknowledged weaknesses, that novel is of permanent interest because it poses central questions taken up by Martineau's successors. Sanders's title indicates what she sees as a continuing conflict in Martineau's art as a writer, that between her rationality and her imagination.

DAVID's approach is avowedly feminist. Three remarkable Victorian women – Martineau, Eliot, and Elizabeth Barrett Browning – all of formidable intelligence, all successful and, within their own time, prominent professional writers, are seen as constantly battling against, and yet accommodating themselves to, the patriarchal cultural hegemony: "an insistence that we see these writers as both saboteurs and collaborators is essentially what this book is all about". Martineau is selected not simply because she was so powerful as a political journalist, but because of the variety of genres and modes in which she wrote. Martineau's career is defined by what David calls her "auxiliary usefulness to a male-dominated culture". However convinced and courageous her feminism, the real function of her prodigious literary output was by way of "textual services" to the English middle class and its radical political and economic ideas, which she endorsed. Within this framework David considers Martineau's *Autobiography*, her fiction, history, and political and travel writings. While Martineau's feminism is thus seen as always ambivalent, David treats her subject with sympathy and admires her for her energy, achievements, and tough-mindedness. Within the limits of such an approach the book is stimulating and perceptive.

HUNTER's more recent analysis of Martineau's writing, as its subtitle, "The Poetics of Moralism", suggests, locates it within the tradition of women's didactic literature; a tradition, however, which she extended to include political moral issues such as the abolition of slavery and women's rights.

BARBARA ONSLOW

Marxism

Beckett, Francis, *Enemy within: The Rise and Fall of the British Communist Party*, London: John Murray, 1995
Burns, Emile, *What is the Communist Party?*, London: Communist Party of Great Britain, no date given [1933]

Bruley, Sue, *Leninism, Stalinism, and the Women's Movement in Britain, 1920–1939*, New York: Garland, 1986

Callaghan, John, *The Far Left in British Politics*, Oxford and New York: Blackwell, 1987

Challinor, Raymond, *The Origins of British Bolshevism*, London: Croom Helm, and Totowa, New Jersey: Rowman and Littlefield, 1977

Dworkin, Dennis, *Cultural Marxism in Postwar Britain: History, the New Left, and the Origins of Cultural Studies*, Durham, North Carolina: Duke University Press, 1997

Godden, G.M., *The Communist Attack on Great Britain: International Communism at Work*, London: Burns, Oates and Washbourne, 1935; enlarged edition, 1938

Kaye, Harvey J., *The British Marxist Historians: An Introductory Analysis*, Cambridge and New York: Polity Press, 1984

Kendall, Walter, *The Revolutionary Movement in Britain, 1900–1921: The Origins of British Communism*, London: Weidenfeld and Nicolson, 1969

Laski, Harold J., *Communism*, London: Williams and Norgate, and New York: Holt, 1927

MacIntyre, Stuart, *A Proletarian Science: Marxism in Britain, 1917–1933*, Cambridge and New York: Cambridge University Press, 1980

Martin, Roderick, *Communism and the British Trade Unions 1924–1933: A Study of the National Minority Movement*, Oxford: Clarendon Press, 1969

Pelling, Henry, *The British Communist Party: A Historical Profile*, London: A. and C. Black, and New York: Macmillan, 1958

Pimlott, Ben, *Labour and the Left in the 1930s*, Cambridge and New York: Cambridge University Press, 1977

Shipway, Mark, *Anti-Parliamentary Communism: The Movement for Worker's Councils in Britain, 1917–45*, London: Macmillan, 1988

Whatever the general difficulties associated with writing contemporary history, the "essentially contested" character of Marxism has clearly exacerbated them, both globally and in Britain. Polemical pamphlets such as BURNS and GODDEN must today be treated as "primary sources", rather than independent interpretations of events – and even a more scholarly work such as LASKI did not claim to have presented an "impartial" third description of (international) communism. The most accessible introduction to independent historical discussion of Marxist politics in Britain (PELLING) was not published until 1958, but served an important role in a notable florescence of "labour history" which itself made use of important Marxist concepts – see KAYE. Although individual members of the Labour Party (e.g. supporters of Cripps, Bevan, or Benn) may have described themselves as Marxists, the decline and closure of the Independent Labour Party has directed historians' attention away from "Second International" Marxism and towards "Third" and "Fourth International" versions of the doctrine, despite their limited currency in British society, taken as a whole. The closest approximation to a non-bolshevik Marxist current within the mainstream Labour Party (the Socialist League) only existed for five years (1932–37) and its most significant historian, PIMLOTT, has portrayed its politics as an amalgam of Keynsianism and guild socialism – and not genuinely Marxist at all.

Thus, although the inspiration for revolutionary praxis in 20th-century Britain has not always been Marxism, CALLAGHAN's wide-ranging account has provided the best starting-point for any analysis which assumes the priority of politics over contrary interpretations of Marxism; for example, as a philosophical or sociological perspective. The book was notable for prioritizing the study of both Trotskyist and other Leninist groups to the left of the Communist Party of Great Britain (CPGB), and for its discussion of "the new social movements", which accepted that – in practice – "the proletariat" was by no means the most important recruiting ground for Marxist/communist groups. The text provided a valuable service to historians of the CPGB by arguing that deficiencies of socialist theory among the European Left as a whole were a superior explanation of the party's "bolshevization" and "stalinization". Callaghan was a sceptic who held that the "socialist project is too complex for it to be the monopoly of one organisation" (Callaghan) – which in turn helped to explain the importance of the Labour Party in the history of British socialism.

Previously, historians of the CPGB and its antecedents had emphasized two contrasting explanations of its sectarianism. Pelling and Kendall were both inclined to stress the misjudgements of *individual* Marxists who held leadership positions (e.g. Hyndman, Inkpin, and Pollit) and to argue that, in the case of the CPGB, these were a major factor in its failure to take an independent line from that laid down by the Comintern and (in effect) by the Soviet leadership. In contrast, CHALLINOR's monograph on an earlier British Marxist organization, the Socialist Labour Party, was itself written from a Marxist perspective and argued that "objective conditions" had condemned British Marxists "to play the role of spectators instead of being combatants" (Challinor), which in turn turned revolutionary energies into many inappropriate channels. Subsequently, writing in the 1990s, BECKETT went so far as to blame the sectarian reaction of the British Left to its defeats in the 1980s for the final demise of the CPGB, although he also noted that the British electoral system had always closed off the possibility of a "fourth party" parliamentary strategy.

This factor certainly encouraged the "industrialist" bias of the pro-Soviet wing of the CPGB, and the CPGB's major contribution to 20th-century Britain was perhaps its long-term work within the trade union movement (see MARTIN). The scepticism of the Marxist tradition regarding "bourgeois democracy" was not confined to the Comintern and its successors, however, and ran much deeper in groups to the left of even Trotskyism (e.g. *Workers' Dreadnought*, 1917–24; the Anti-Parliamentary Communist Federation, 1921–45), groups which have enjoyed some influence during periods of proletarian militancy but which have otherwise been completely marginal to British society. Nevertheless, SHIPWAY's polemical (but impeccably researched) study has argued that these groups "kept alive a vision of an authentic alternative to capitalism" and that their decline was largely due to the postwar supersession of a plebian culture of political study, debate, and oratory found in worker's halls and on street corners. Yet the mainstream of this autodidactic, Marxist-oriented subculture was closer to the CPGB than the anti-parliamentary communists (despite the famous split between the party and the Labour Colleges movement) as inspection of MacINTYRE's excellent monograph clearly shows.

Marxism has also been influential in British higher education for, as noted earlier, a significant number of British labour historians have viewed themselves as "Marxists", consciously applying a historiographical approach invented by Marx (and Engels). Alternatively, it could be said that a significant number of heterodox, "intellectual" Marxists have seen themselves as historians – and all five of the writers discussed in Kaye (Dobb, Hilton, Hill, Hobsbawm, and Thompson) were members of the CPGB Historians Group between 1946 and 1956. Kaye's study concluded that one consequence of their work on feudalism, the English Revolution, imperialism, and the 18th-century common people was to create a theoretical space in which both the history of individualism and the possibility of a "truly democratic socialism" could be explored at the end of the 20th century by "post-Marxist" political theorists such as Stephen Lukes.

The connection between organized Marxism and feminism before World War II has been thoroughly examined by BRULEY, while DWORKIN makes numerous references to the feminist, "cultural" Marxists of the History Workshop group of the 1970s and 1980s. Bruley's observations that CPGB "ideology promised that the internal organisation of the party would show no distinction on grounds of sex" but that in reality "the organisation reproduced [unequal] social relations between men and women which mirrored the society which they were seeking to overthrow" could be generalized to cover many other social relations and Leninist groups. This partially explains the movement of many leftist intellectuals into the looser orbits of the *New Left Review* (founded 1959) and *Marxism Today* (which from 1980 to 1992 was in effect an independent magazine, despite its formal connection with the CPGB). Dworkin has recently argued that, despite their small numbers, both the "Marxist historians" and other "cultural intellectuals" (e.g. Anderson and Hall) offered intellectual inspiration to the British Left as a whole from the 1950s to the 1970s, but that during the 1980s a variety of factors subverted this leadership as a variety of Marxist categories were deemed to have become intellectually untenable. Nevertheless, the recent flurry of scholarly interest in the pre-bolshevik "Marxism" of William Morris, for whom E.P. Thompson once acted as biographer, may point to a new style of communist politics for a new century.

CLIVE E. HILL

See also Historiography: Marxist; Industrialization; Socialism

Mary I   1516–1558
Queen of England

Erickson, Carrolly, *Bloody Mary*, London: Dent, and New York: Doubleday, 1978

Loach, Jennifer, *Parliament and the Crown in the Reign of Mary Tudor*, Oxford: Clarendon Press, and New York: Oxford University Press, 1986

Loades, David, *The Reign of Mary Tudor: Politics, Government, and Religion in England, 1553–1558*, London: Benn, and New York: St Martin's Press, 1979; 2nd edition, London and New York: Longman, 1991

Loades, David, *Mary Tudor: A Life*, Oxford and Cambridge, Massachusetts: Blackwell, 1989

Prescott, H.F.M., *Spanish Tudor: The Life of Bloody Mary*, London: Constable, 1940; reprinted, New York: AMS Press, 1970; as *Mary Tudor*, London: Eyre and Spottiswoode, 1952; New York: Macmillan, 1953

Ridley, Jasper, *The Life and Times of Mary Tudor*, London: Weidenfeld and Nicolson, 1973

Tittler, Robert, *The Reign of Mary I*, London and New York: Longman, 1983

The eldest daughter of Henry VIII and Catherine of Aragon, Mary I ruled England for only five years (1553–58). Despite that brief reign she is famous in history as "Bloody Mary", because she ordered the burning of 300 protestants. PRESCOTT's biography was considered the standard for a number of years. This book is solidly documented, though strongly marked by pro-Mary religious sensibilities. Readers today would find its historical analysis rather naive. Though Prescott describes the burning of protestants as a ghastly and mistaken policy, she also tries to justify it as almost inevitable because the protestants posed such danger to Mary's reign. Most historians now agree, however, that it is problematic and suspect to describe those who were burned as a danger to the social order. Prescott portrays Mary as a courageous woman who unfortunately lacked a keen and searching intellect. Prescott believes Mary lacked the qualities necessary to be a successful queen and would have been far better off in private life.

RIDLEY agrees with Prescott that Mary was in no sense fitted for the role of queen. He argues that she had neither worldly wisdom nor political judgement; he is also, however, sympathetic to her as someone who was ill-treated throughout much of her life. His book is beautifully illustrated, but though it lists a bibliography it is without source notes. He includes a useful discussion of not only the protestant martyrs but other aspects of her reign, such as trade with Russia in the 1550s. Ridley argues that because catholicism was central to her life, Mary was often unwilling to face reality. He characterizes her as someone who was kind and considerate, but her religious views earned her the title "Bloody Mary".

This popular nickname is the title for ERICKSON's scholarly but also lively and accessible biography. Erickson argues that while the burning of heretics has to be a major consideration of Mary, there are other important issues as well. Erickson argues that Mary was a survivor, with a full measure of Tudor majesty, who was ruled by her conscience. Erickson's most significant contribution is her discussion of what it meant for a woman to rule in the mid-16th century.

TITTLER's brief but very useful study presents a somewhat more positive view of Mary's reign. Because Mary had so severely broken with the past in terms of foreign and religious policies, her transition had been difficult, though there was considerable continuity in social and economic policy. He argues that there was efficiency in the council and co-operation in parliament once the issue of the Reformation property settlement had been dealt with to members' satisfaction. Members of parliament were not willing to support Mary's restoration of the Roman church in England until current lay ownership of former ecclesiastical land was granted. But the last two years of the reign were dominated by problems and setbacks with the war with France going badly and the persecution of protestants at its height. While the key goals of Mary's reign – alliance with Spain and return to the catholic church – were lost in the reign of her successor, some of her policies, such as searches for new trade routes, reform of the coinage, and revival of the navy, were brought to success in Elizabeth's reign. Tittler suggests that despite Mary's health problems and emotional instability, she and her councillors had not been such failures when the reign came to its end.

LOACH in her study of parliament in the reign of Mary agrees with Tittler and argues that there was much less parliamentary conflict with the crown in Mary's reign than is traditionally believed. She also negates the theory that opposition in parliament worked as an alternative to rebellion. Loach claims success for Mary's parliaments.

LOADES provides the most scholarly and analytical studies of Mary. His biography (1989) is excellent, as is his book about her reign. He argues that though Mary was well educated and as intelligent and strong minded as many of the male nobility, she was also profoundly conventional. She accepted the view that women should be dependent, which made it difficult for her to cope with the stresses imposed by her position. Loades (1979, 1991), like Tittler and Loach, sees Mary's reign as more successful than earlier scholars though Loach disagrees with a number of Loades's conclusions, particularly his view of those in the middle abandoning Mary by 1558. Loades demonstrates that Mary was able to achieve three major goals despite much opposition: the return of the church in England to Rome, her marriage to Philip, and the declaration of war with France. Loades is also, however, less sympathetic personally to Mary than a number of her biographers. He points out that a study of the records does not support the depiction of Mary as the mildest and most merciful of the Tudors. Most of the generous gestures of the reign came at the beginning; her government treated people more harshly as it progressed. She was more ruthless in the execution of traitors than either her father Henry or her sister Elizabeth and also used martial law much more freely. Because of the dictates of her conscience, she zealously and vindictively pursued the burning of heretics. Loades argues that there were a number of achievements of Mary's reign: sound administration, sensible financial policies, and a practical approach to ecclesiastical reconstruction. But the bad harvests and epidemics, as well as the unsuccessful war with France, hurt the end of her brief reign. And even if Mary had had more time, her success with dealing with the problems of her reign was uneven. There is no sign that the English were any more reconciled to the Spanish connection in 1558 than they were in 1554. Philip was even less popular, and Loades contends that if Mary had lived Philip might have dissolved the marriage, something Mary could not have survived. The persecution neither stamped out nor silenced the protestants during the three-and-a-half years in which it was applied. Those politically in the centre who had supported Mary in 1553 were disillusioned by 1558, making Elizabeth's accession much easier than it would have been otherwise.

CAROLE LEVIN

See also Catholic Restoration; Cranmer; Gardiner; Protestant Revolution; Recusancy and Mission

Mary of Guise 1515–1560
Queen and consort of James V of Scotland

Dickinson, William Croft (editor), *John Knox's History of the Reformation in Scotland*, 2 vols, New York: Philosophical Library, 1950; London: Nelson, 1949

Donaldson, Gordon, *Scotland: James V to James VII*, Edinburgh: Oliver and Boyd, 1965; New York: Praeger, 1966

Fleming, Arnold, *Marie de Guise*, Glasgow: McLellan, 1960

Forbes, F.A., *Leaders of a Forlorn Hope: A Study of the Reformation in Scotland*, New York: P.J. Kenedy, 1921; London: Sands, 1922

Fraser, Antonia, *Mary, Queen of Scots*, New York: Delacorte Press, and London: Weidenfeld and Nicolson, 1969

Lee, Maurice, *James Stewart, Earl of Moray: A Political Study of the Reformation in Scotland*, New York: Columbia University Press, 1953

Marshall, Rosalind K., *Mary of Guise*, London: Collins, 1977

M'Kerlie, E. and Marianne H., *Mary of Guise-Lorraine, Queen of Scotland*, London and Edinburgh: Sands, 1931

Thomas, Andrea, "'Dragonis baith and dowis ay in double forme': Women at the Court of James V, 1513–1542" in *Women in Scotland, c.1100–c.1750*, edited by Elizabeth Ewan and Maureen M. Meikle, East Linton, East Lothian: Tuckwell Press, 1999

Mary of Guise has long been ignored, or at least pushed to the periphery, by the vast majority of scholars of 16th-century Scotland in favour of her more exciting and tragic daughter, Mary Queen of Scots (1542–87). As a result, the number of works concerning Mary of Guise is severely limited to a handful of biographies and a few chapters in books about either her husband, James V (1513–42), or her daughter.

Born in November 1515, Mary was the daughter of Claude and Antoinette, the future Duke and Duchess of Guise, and patriarchs of the influential Guise family which rose to power throughout the 16th century. Intelligent and charming, Mary made her public debut in 1531 and by 1534 was married to her first husband the Duke of Longueville. With the duke's death in 1537 she once again became available for marriage, this time catching the eye of the king of Scotland, James V, whom she wed in 1538. James died in December 1542, leaving her to not only raise the six-day-old Mary but somehow hold the kingdom together until Mary was old enough to rule on her own.

Largely due to the protestant reformer John Knox's *History of the Reformation in Scotland*, which has been edited by DICKINSON, scholars interested in Mary of Guise have tended to argue along lines of religion or nationality. Those of protestant persuasion, showing Knox's influence, regardless of nationality, have usually resorted to vilifying Mary of Guise, especially while she served as regent. Catholic and pro-French scholars have gone to the other extreme.

FORBES and M'KERLIE are scholars who challenge Knox's interpretation of Mary and the Reformation, clearly placing themselves in the pro-French/catholic camp. Forbes devotes a significant chapter to Mary of Guise in her account of the

Reformation by placing Mary in the context of several catholic churchmen in Scotland who opposed the protestant Reformation and supported the regent's political policies. The key message of Forbes's work is to show Mary not only as pro-French/catholic and regent but, more importantly, as being morally and legally correct in her dealings with the Scottish nobility and the protestant reformers.

M'Kerlie's approach is biographical and, like later biographies, hers provides an excellent, though romantic, view of Mary's life. In this biography the reader is presented with not only a catholic Mary but also a Mary keenly aware of and in touch with the Scottish people. Furthermore, M'Kerlie argues that Mary of Guise's actions were not only justified but that they should be expected of a mother attempting to protect the life and rights of her daughter.

On the other hand, FLEMING's biography appears as a reluctant criticism of the regent based not on religion so much as on nationality. Ultimately, Fleming dismisses Mary as being ineffective. He sees her problem not as an issue of catholic versus protestant but of being a Frenchwoman unable to understand the ways of the Scots.

The only other full-length work devoted to Mary of Guise was written by MARSHALL, who focuses on the career and personality of Mary. Marshall demonstrates rather well that Mary favoured an independent Scotland until the battle of Pinkie Cleugh (1547), where it was made evident that Scotland could not stand alone and needed France as an ally against England and as a safe haven for her daughter. Furthermore, Marshall provides the reader with an intimate understanding of the relationship of Mary and the Guise family, tying in her political moves with their own, yet being ambitious enough to follow her own path, especially in the beginning years of her regency and the toleration she exhibited toward the reformers.

In fact, after becoming regent, Mary of Guise set out to pursue a conciliatory policy toward the citizens of Scotland as a whole, and especially the nobility. DONALDSON points out her use of patronage to secure the loyalty of certain wayward nobles, and her various appeals to the merchants and burghs of the land. Furthermore, Donaldson contributes insights into Mary's extremely lenient policies toward the reformers, arguing that by allowing reformers to preach in Scotland they might encourage the protestants in England and somehow weaken the Spanish-influenced Mary Tudor's government. This, of course, meant the opposite would be true once the Spanish link to England was severed in 1558 with the accession of Elizabeth I (1558–1603). Therefore, beginning in 1559, under orders from France, Donaldson argues, and in the hope of furthering her daughter's claim to the English throne, Mary ended her policy of toleration toward reformers. LEE concurs with this view, though he adds that it was also no longer necessary to court the protestant nobility since the marriage of Mary of Scotland to the Dauphin had taken place in late 1558.

Like Donaldson and Lee, FRASER's work relegates Mary of Guise to a supporting role and continues the trend towards presenting Mary in a sympathetic light, as a dowager and regent doing the best she can under awful circumstances.

At the end of the 20th century the focus on Mary's intentions or motives has begun to change. Due to the ever-increasing interest in women's history as a whole, scholars such as THOMAS are providing readers with a much broader picture of court life.

More importantly, these types of works go a long way toward presenting women like Mary of Guise as something more than her religion or her nationality.

TIMOTHY G. ELSTON

See also James V; Mary, Queen of Scots; "Rough Wooing"

Mary, Queen of Scots 1542–1587
Queen of Scotland, and France (1559–60)

Cowan, Ian B. (editor), *The Enigma of Mary Stuart*, London: Gollancz, 1971

Cowan, Ian B., *The Scottish Reformation: Church and Society in Sixteenth-Century Scotland*, London: Macmillan, and New York: St Martin's Press, 1982

Dickinson, William Croft (editor and translator), *John Knox's History of the Reformation in Scotland*, 2 vols, London: Nelson, 1949

Donaldson, Gordon, *Mary, Queen of Scots*, London: English Universities Press, 1974

Fraser, Antonia, *Mary, Queen of Scots*, London: Weidenfeld and Nicolson, and New York: Delacorte Press, 1969

Graves, Michael, *Thomas Norton: The Parliament Man*, Oxford and Cambridge, Massachusetts: Blackwell, 1994

Henderson, Thomas F., *Mary, Queen of Scots, Her Environment and Tragedy: A Biography*, 2 vols, London: Hutchinson, and New York: Scribner, 1905; reprinted, New York: Haskell House, 1969

Lee, Maurice Jr, "The Daughter of Debate: Mary, Queen of Scots after 400 Years", *Scottish Historical Review*, 68 (1989): 70–79

Levine, Mortimer, *The Early Elizabethan Succession Question, 1558–1568*, Stanford, California: Stanford University Press, 1966

Lynch, Michael, *Edinburgh and the Reformation*, Edinburgh: John Donald, 1981

Lynch, Michael (editor), *Mary Stewart: Queen in Three Kingdoms*, Oxford and New York: Blackwell, 1988

Marshall, Rosalind K., *Queen of Scots*, Edinburgh: HMSO, 1986

Wormald, Jenny, *Court, Kirk, and Community: Scotland 1470–1625*, London: Arnold, and Toronto: University of Toronto Press, 1981

Wormald, Jenny, *Mary Queen of Scots: A Study in Failure*, London: Philip, 1988; revised edition, London: Tauris Parke, 2001

Although born in Scotland, and succeeding to the throne when only a few weeks old, Mary was the daughter of a French mother, was sent to the French court in 1548, and was married to the Dauphin, Francis, ten years later. She was brought up, and remained, a Francophile catholic, although by the time that she returned to Scotland in 1561 – after the death of her husband and a brief year's reign as Queen of France – the country was under protestant control, and increasingly pro-English in sentiment. Her life, both as queen (1561–68) and during her long captivity in England (1568–87), was lavishly chronicled and commented upon at the time, and has been the subject of complex and sometimes bitter debate ever since.

During her lifetime, Mary's principle enemy and detractor was the protestant preacher and leader John Knox, whose *History*, edited and translated by DICKINSON, should be treated in this respect, as in most others, with extreme caution. She was vigorously defended at the same time by John Leslie, Bishop of Ross, who for a number of years was her faithful agent and representative and whose *Defence of the Honour of . . . Mary, Queen of Scotland* was published in London in 1569. These are worth mention here, because they form the foundation texts for the debate, but they should be approached only through the commentaries of modern writers until the reader has a secure grasp of the context of the queen's life.

Until the 18th century the arguments about Mary tended to run along national and confessional lines. Protestant writers, whether English or Scots, regarded her as a danger to Elizabeth and to the protestant ascendancy in Scotland. During the reign of her son James VI, particularly after his accession to the throne of England in 1603, it was necessary to tread with caution, and the king commissioned William Camden to set the record straight. Consequently his *Annals* (1615) constituted a rare defence of Mary from within the protestant camp. French and catholic writers, on the other hand, always tended to describe her as an innocent victim of political intrigue on both sides of the border, a legitimate queen deprived of her rights by self-seeking heretics, and sometimes as a martyr for her faith. During the 18th century a number of substantial collections of primary material were published, and the numerous 19th-century studies that were based on them broke the confessional mould without in any way diminishing the tendency to pronounce a verdict of innocent or guilty in respect of her alleged complicity in the murder of her second husband, Henry, Lord Darnley. The authenticity of the main incriminating evidence for her involvement, the casket letters, was disputed both at the time and since, and they were edited by HENDERSON, who believed them to be genuine, and whose biography of Mary remains to this day the most closely argued presentation of her guilt.

This judicial imperative in the assessments of Mary had already been abandoned in detailed studies when FRASER's exhaustive biography appeared in 1969. While containing little that was new, this was based on the best available scholarship, and placed unusual emphasis on the queen's emotional and sexual needs in providing explanations for her conduct, a tendency that has been followed in subsequent studies. Fraser is particularly good in explaining how Mary's judgment became distorted by her relationship with James Hepburn, Earl of Bothwell, who became her third husband. This relationship offended her natural supporters as well as her enemies, and led directly to her downfall. In captivity in England, Mary was far more significant for who she was than for anything that she did, and Fraser argues convincingly that she was frequently trapped by intrigues in which she had no direct involvement. However, because Mary had no intention of renouncing her royal status and the claims that went with it, Elizabeth's servants had no option but to treat her with constant hostility and suspicion. Fraser's biography is a romantic tragedy; but it is rigorous in its use of sources and stands up well to critical assessment.

In 1971 COWAN produced a collection of documentary extracts, which are well selected from a large range of sources, some of them original texts, and some historical commentary over four centuries. This has the merit of allowing every point of view to be expressed, without committing the editor. There is a brief and largely historiographical introduction, and an extremely useful bibliography.

DONALDSON accepted that Mary was guilty in respect of some (at least) of the plots against Elizabeth that were alleged against her, but like most modern writers reserves judgment in respect of Darnley. He had already written a more limited study of her trial before the biography appeared, and subjected the evidence to a stricter examination than Fraser attempted, but decided that no conclusion was possible. Donaldson's study is both shorter and more strictly political than Fraser's, and his analysis of the context of Mary's life is sharper and much less personal. MARSHALL's biography, though complete in its coverage, is not particularly original.

Articles and books about Mary have appeared at the rate of about three a year since 1970. The history of the debate about her was usefully summarized in an appendix, "The Continuing Debate", to Donaldson's biography, and LEE's summary brought the controversial history up to date as of 1989. Notable examples among the recent studies of Mary include LYNCH (1988) and WORMALD (1988). Lynch has edited a collection of essays examining every aspect of Mary's life, including her library (by John Durkin) and the Darnley murder (by Julian Goodare). Overwhelmingly concerned with Mary in France and Scotland, only one of the nine papers (by P.J. Holmes) deals with the 19 years of her stay in England. Although in this respect somewhat unbalanced, this is a particularly valuable collection on her personal rule in Scotland. Wormald offers a judicious and up-to-date interpretation by a scholar with no axes to grind. It may be summed up in the key sentence "The central fact of sovereignty, the ability to rule, was the critical area in which Mary failed." As with Lynch, treatment of the period after 1568 is slight.

Because of her political importance, both to England and to Scotland, Mary also features largely in more general studies, both of the reign of Elizabeth, and of the Scottish reformation. Mary's claim to the English succession, derived from her great grandfather, Henry VII, was fiercely debated in the 1560s, and in modern analyses is best handled, and at length, by LEVINE. Anxiety about Mary's presence and intentions pervaded the business of parliament after 1568, and greatly complicated relations between the queen, her council and the House of Commons, a theme indirectly but illuminatingly examined by GRAVES. Conyers Read and, in the 1990s, Wallace MacCaffrey and Penry Williams have also contributed usefully to the Elizabethan and Tudor dimensions, while the Scottish Reformation has been handled by COWAN (1982), WORMALD (1981), and LYNCH (1981). Finally, two editions of primary materials since the 19th century are invaluable resources for the serious researcher – *The Calendar of State Papers Relating to Scotland, 1547–1603* (13 vols, edited by J. Bain *et al.*, 1898–1952), the most comprehensive (though by no means the only) collection of relevant public documents, supplemented, particularly for Mary's French associations, by Alexandre Labanoff's *Lettres, instructions et memoires de Marie Stuart* (1844).

Mary's life, or aspects of it, have also frequently been treated in romantic fiction and drama, and these should be clearly distinguished from serious historical studies.

DAVID LOADES

The Crisis of 1568

Donaldson, Gordon, *All the Queen's Men: Power and Politics in Mary Stewart's Scotland*, London: Batsford, and New York: St Martin's Press, 1983

Fraser, Antonia, *Mary Queen of Scots*, London: Weidenfeld and Nicolson, and New York: Delacort Press, 1969; abridged edition, 1978

Hamilton, Duke of, *Maria R: Mary Queen of Scots, the Crucial Years*, Edinburgh: Mainstream, 1991

MacNalty, Arthur Salusbury, *Mary Queen of Scots: The Daughter of Debate*, London: C. Johnson, 1960

Thomson, George Malcolm, *The Crime of Mary Stuart*, London: Hutchinson, and New York: Dutton, 1967

Wormald, Jenny, *Mary Queen of Scots: A Study in Failure*, London: George Phillip, 1988

Having abdicated her throne at the age of 25, after the civil war caused by her hasty marriage to the Earl of Bothwell, widely believed to be the murderer of her second husband, Lord Darnley, Mary was imprisoned. After escaping, and following another defeat, she made the decision to flee to England and throw herself on the mercy of her cousin Elizabeth. This momentous decision would eventually lead to Mary's execution in 1587. Scholars have had a variety of ways of explaining Mary's fateful decision of 1568.

Mary's escape from prison is presented sympathetically and with great detail in the biography by FRASER. Fraser argues that Mary would have received a strongly supportive reception in France if she had only fled there and that some of her supporters also urged her to stay in Scotland where she could easily have held out for at least another 40 days. Fraser describes Mary's decision to choose England as brave and romantic but hardly wise, and how the ten and a half months of Scottish captivity had sapped her judgement.

MacNALTY takes a medical view of Mary and considers that her imprisonment was actually helpful to her health and mental balance. Also highly favourable to Mary, he attributes her decision to flee to England to a nature that was impulsive, kindly, and romantic. He argues that Mary's character was such that she would not understand the duplicitousness of her cousin Elizabeth. THOMSON has a very different view of Mary's nature. He describes her brilliant escape ending dismally and describes her at the moment of her decision as not only destitute and defeated but defiant and impenitent, a woman who lacked the wisdom of Elizabeth and the patience of Catherine de Medici and was instead blinded by surges of passion.

WORMALD, who is highly critical of Mary's reign in Scotland, argues that Mary had enough support to win back her crown but showed poor judgement in where she gathered her forces, putting herself at risk by going too close to those still loyal to her half-brother, the Earl of Moray. Wormald argues that Mary then panicked. Though her best chance of success meant staying in Scotland since once she fled Scotland her supporters were leaderless, she was too frightened to stay. While France might not have been the safe haven for her described by Fraser, given her former mother-in-law Catherine de Medici's dislike of her, Wormald maintains that Mary had a completely unrealistic, romantic view of Elizabeth, believing that once they met they would become close friends and that Elizabeth would

support her. In Wormald's view, Mary's political judgement was again poor. DONALDSON also suggests that many in Scotland had had time to forget about the scandal of Darnley's murder and Mary's precipitous marriage to Bothwell and were tired of Moray's rule. He argues that had Mary kept her forces intact she might well have won but she was so terrified she fled to England. The Duke of HAMILTON also argues that Mary's side might have vigorously continued if Mary had not fled, but she did so in fear of her life, remembering this was the fate 80 years earlier of her great-grandfather, James III. Hamilton perceives Mary's flight as reasonable, given Scottish history. Though historians have a variety of perspectives on Mary Stuart, they all agree that the decision to flee to England in 1568 was the turning-point of her life.

CAROLE LEVIN

See also Elizabeth I; "Rough Wooing"

Masculinities: To 1800

Bray, Alan, "Homosexuality and the Signs of Male Friendship in Elizabethan England", *History Workshop*, 29 (1990): 1–18

Carter, Philip, *Men and the Emergence of Polite Society, Britain 1660–1800*, London and New York: Pearson, 2001

Cohen, Michèle, *Fashioning Masculinity: National Identity and Language in the Eighteenth Century*, London and New York: Routledge, 1996

Foyster, Elizabeth A., *Manhood in Early Modern England: Honour, Sex, and Marriage*, London and New York: Longman, 1999

Hadley, D.M. (editor), *Masculinity in Medieval Europe*, London and New York: Longman, 1999

Hitchcock, Tim and Michèle Cohen (editors), *English Masculinities 1660–1800*, London and New York: Longman, 1999

The study of masculinity as a gendered history of men and ideals of manliness is a relatively recent development, emerging from feminist historians' insights into the social and historical construction of gender and sexuality. Situating men as gendered beings in their historical contexts has revealed the multiple social meanings of masculinity. In what is claimed to be the first multidisciplinary contribution that aims to theorize and analyse medieval masculinities, the collection of essays edited by HADLEY challenges "the premise, inherent in much scholarly writing on the Middle Ages, that masculinity is universal, unchanging and unquestioned". The concept of hegemonic masculinity, with its associated concept of subordinated masculinities, is a key analytical tool for a number of the essays, highlighting the crucial point that power relations between men were central to the construction of masculinity. Sexuality was also central to notions of appropriate manly behaviour. While this implied the imposition of "compulsory heterosexuality", it created conflicting situations for a clergy who were expected to observe a celibate life-style. Male friendship has been a subject of much interest for historians of masculinity – as has friendship between women for feminist history. The passionate friendship linking pairs of men as "brothers in arms", in the *Chanson de Roland* for example, was one of the most distinctive expressions of male military status, argues Bennett in this volume. This bond, which was often celebrated in deeply emotional terms, has been interpreted to indicate a homosexual relationship between the men. This Bennett rejects, arguing that homosexual behaviour, which was also described in these early sources, was not considered manly.

The fine line that separates the physical and emotional signs of friendship between men from those of sodomy in early modern England is the subject of BRAY's article. Their similarity is only superficial, he argues, for the conventions of friendship in the period required an orderly expression of the relationship, marking its distance from the anarchic and subversive behaviour of sodomites. However, if male friendship and sodomy were incompatible, the dividing line between the two could be ambiguous, and some homosexual relations did occur within social contexts which would have been described as friendship. This ambiguity drew on a tension which is no longer familiar to us because intimacy between men today is protected by the notion of a distinct homosexual minority for whom alone homosexual desire is a possibility. In this essay, then, Bray not only evokes a way of thinking, a symbolic world which has now vanished – a theme he takes up and expands in his chapter in Hitchcock & Cohen – but criticizes those readings which conflate male friendship and homosexuality.

FOYSTER's book explores how men in early modern England experienced their gender in the context of marriage. Her examination of records of marriage breakdown leads her to conclude that masculinity was unstable, shifting, and always being redefined because far from being autonomously determined, it depended on complex networks of relations comprising honour, reputation, and men's relations with other men as well as with women. That sexual reputation was central to the maintenance of masculinity may come as no great surprise. But her important contribution is to show that men's management of their passions and bodies, be it in anger, violence, drunkenness, or love, was also crucial, as failure to control them exposed men's weakness and relative powerlessness. Thus falling in love, which might cause men to lose their reason and self-control, could be effeminating. However, marriage, which restored the balance of power and males' rightful place in the gender order, reinstated their masculinity. Foyster reflects on these issues to address broader questions about continuity and change in the history of early modern manhood.

COHEN discusses the conception of masculinity in the context of politeness, a social ideal for the fashioning of the gentleman in the 18th century. Paradoxically, this ideal also elicited profound anxieties about effeminacy, not only because it was best achieved in the company of women, but also because it was modelled on French practices of sociability. While refinement was necessary to the gentleman, it was also potentially effeminating. She illustrates the paradoxes of politeness for males in relation to manners and language. Though fluent and easy conversational skills, and travel to the Continent on the Grand Tour were requisite components of polite gentlemanliness, they could also compromise masculinity. A loquacious tongue was associated with women and the effeminate French, and the Frenchified manners and language of fops and maca-

ronies testified to their having succumbed to French seduction while abroad, and thus forfeited their claim to sober masculine Englishness. These paradoxes also highlight how "effeminacy" served as a dominant cultural metaphor in the period.

CARTER studies the impact of polite society for 18th-century definitions of the refined gentleman, and its effect on the definition of manliness. Though his book shares common themes with Cohen's, addressing conceptions of manliness in debates over the gentleman's relation to polite society, it differs in some important respects. While she discussed politeness and masculinity in the context of gender, Carter produced a definitive analysis of manliness in relation to politeness and gentlemanliness, culminating in the figure of the fop. Fops highlight the tensions and contradictions associated with aspirations to manly refinement and excessive devotion to the ideals of politeness. One of his important contributions is his discussion of the impact of "sensibility" on the debates surrounding the definition of the ideal gentleman and notions of manliness. The other is his examination of "polite and impolite personalities": based on three diaries, it provides an insight about how real individuals grappled with issues around politeness and refinement. One crucial point that emerges is that these men acknowledged some of the difficulties of attaining manly politeness and refinement when in competition with other men. Ultimately, Carter demonstrates that be it politeness or sensibility, all forms of manliness associated with the 18th-century gentleman could also, potentially, be associated with effeminacy.

The collection edited by HITCHCOCK & COHEN aims to map the diversity of masculinities over the course of the 18th century. In the introduction, the editors discuss main areas of debate and consensus which form the background to the contributions. One area of debate concerns the thesis, put forward by historians of homosexuality, that the 18th century saw the emergence of a specific homosexual identity, and that therefore masculinities were becoming more sharply defined into either a macho heterosexuality or an effeminate homosexuality. One problem with this thesis is that it is largely based on a conflation of effeminacy and homosexuality which fails to address the multiplicity of ways in which "effeminacy" was used and understood in the period. In fact, nearly every essay in the collection refers to effeminacy, none relating to sexual behaviour. Similarly, rather than reducing masculinity to macho heterosexuality, the concerns over manliness explored in the different essays indicate that masculinities were a varied and continually contested set of roles and categories. Thus David Turner shows that men's sexual reputation was vulnerable to gossip and rumour, and that men – not just women – could be both the subjects and spreaders of sexual rumours, while Jeremy Gregory discusses the ideal of Christian manliness promoted in the extensive religious prescriptive literature of the time. The various male identities analysed in the essays, including those practised by a single individual, James Boswell, are taken to suggest that different masculinities emerged over the period, but that the contradictions between them were not resolvable.

MICHÈLE COHEN

See also Gender and Power; Homosexuality

Masculinities: Since 1800

Bourke, Joanna, *Dismembering the Male: Men's Bodies, Britain, and the Great War*, London: Reaktion Books, and Chicago: University of Chicago Press, 1996

Dawson, Graham, *Soldier Heroes: British Adventure, Empire, and the Imagining of Masculinities*, London and New York: Routledge, 1994

Hall, Catherine, *White, Male, and Middle-Class: Explorations in Feminism and History*, Cambridge: Polity, and New York: Routledge, 1992

McLaren, Angus, *The Trials of Masculinity: Policing Sexual Boundaries, 1870–1930*, Chicago: University of Chicago Press, 1997

Mangan, J.A. and James Walvin (editors), *Manliness and Morality: Middle-Class Masculinity in Britain and America, 1800–1940*, Manchester: Manchester University Press, and New York: St Martin's Press, 1987

Mort, Frank, *Cultures of Consumption: Masculinities and Social Space in Late Twentieth-Century Britain*, London and New York: Routledge, 1996

Roper, Michael and John Tosh (editors), *Manful Assertions: Masculinities in Britain since 1800*, London and New York: Routledge, 1991

Sinha, Mrinalini, *Colonial Masculinity: The "Manly Englishman" and the "Effeminate Bengali" in the Late Nineteenth Century*, Manchester and New York: Manchester University Press, 1995

Tosh, John, *A Man's Place: Masculinity and the Middle-Class Home in Victorian England*, New Haven, Connecticut and London: Yale University Press, 1999

The study of the varieties of masculinity is a relatively new subject. It suggests that gender is not simply the product of biology but is actually constructed in various ways at different times. The discussion of masculinities since 1800 has been dominated, for the most part, by considerations of middle-class masculinity and how it has been reshaped and challenged. MANGAN & WALVIN's collection reflects this by focusing on educational practices, sport, and the emphasis on character-building in both Britain and America. It suggests that the channelling of masculine energies was an important question for the elite due to both the rise of industrial society and the expanding burden of administering the empire. Another collection that put masculinity firmly on the historical agenda was that of ROPER & TOSH, which explored changing constructions of manliness over the past two centuries. The issue of masculinity has also been taken up in an array of works on gender although seldom as the central issue.

HALL's exploration builds on her earlier work on empire and race. She argues that attitudes towards race were integral to the constitution of different forms of middle-class masculinity. This essay collection ranges over the development of Victorian masculinities, perhaps most intriguingly in her dissection of the links between attitudes towards race in the context of the Governor Eyre controversy. As Jamaica's governor, Edward Eyre had dealt harshly with the 1865 rebellion, and Hall reveals its ramifications for intellectuals who vigorously debated his actions. While John Stuart Mill characteristically argued that Eyre had overreacted, Thomas Carlyle backed the governor's

actions not only because he believed blacks deserved subjugation, but also because to be a man was to exercise power over the lower orders. Hall shows clearly the links between racism and middle-class masculinity.

This link is also explored by SINHA in the imperial context of India. She examines the way colonial subjects in the subcontinent, particularly Bengalis, were characterized as "effeminate" in order to restrict their advancement towards self-government. Although some groups in India were seen as "martial", and thus worthy of respect, those who focused on educational improvement and advancement through civil service examination were portrayed as "unmanly" and thus ultimately unable to govern themselves. By examining four controversies of the 1880s and 1890s, Sinha uncovers the way ideas about manliness structured attitudes towards colonial subjects and were used to reinforce British rule in India.

Race is not the defining feature of TOSH's study of Victorian middle-class men and domesticity. Instead he recreates the world of the paterfamilias and situates his subject firmly within the family circle rather than the public sphere. The mid-Victorian obsession with male power in the home is illustrated in the discussion of husband–wife and parent–child relations. Rather than the distant figures so beloved of Victorian fiction, Tosh shows these men were fully engaged with family life. This only began to alter in the 1870s as women started to assert their right to a public role, which Tosh argues inevitably led to a re-shaping of domestic relations.

McLAREN investigates the changing roles of men and women through the policing of shifting sexual boundaries. He argues that masculinity was a rather fragile construct which required shoring up by the legal and medical establishments at a time of rapid change. Looking at instances where men over-stepped boundaries, whether by committing a crime or by affronting contemporary sensibilities, McLaren confirms that the policing of masculinity in the late 19th and early 20th centuries was undertaken in order to shore up male power rather than to protect women and children. This phenomenon was part of a trend which characterized most western nations.

Although McLaren's work straddled the period, World War I was one of the events which helped to shape masculinities in the 20th century. Elaine Showalter's chapter on shell shock in *The Female Malady* (1985) had suggested the way attitudes towards masculinity might manifest themselves in the trenches. BOURKE pushes this further in her consideration of the way men's bodies had been physically affected during their military service. For men at the front, their bodies were vulnerable in an obvious way which had seldom been explored by historians before. Fears about the loss of bodily control ranging from incontinence to the loss of a limb to death forced men to constantly re-examine their definition of masculinity. In a war in which the majority of men were not professional soldiers this had great ramifications both in terms of discipline and in the new medical category of shell shock for which doctors strove to find a physiological basis but which was most likely a psychological trauma.

DAWSON's examination of "soldier heroes" is instructive about how military men are employed to construct certain ideals of hegemonic masculinity. He reveals this particularly through his discussion of T.E. Lawrence, who was one of the first heroes created by the new medium of cinema. Newsreel footage established his military prowess and heroism, which was reinforced through popular journalism, and culminated in the 1962 David Lean film *Lawrence of Arabia*. Dawson's exploration of late 20th-century responses to legendary masculinity, not least his own, illustrates the ongoing power of mythic masculinity.

By the end of the 20th century, however, masculinity's evolving construction had moved beyond the battlefield and the family to include the role of the consumer. MORT sees postwar masculinity as dominated not by actions but by the acquisition of possessions. He provides evidence, through his examination of the growth of advertising aimed at men and the expansion of new magazines targeted at men, that masculinity had increasingly become, by the 1980s, a reflection of what men owned or aspired to own. Mort situates this within a consideration of the growth of the gay community, the development of Soho in London as a distinctive gay shopping area, and a series of interviews in which men discuss the intermingling of their masculine identity and their shopping habits. Mort's analysis further demonstrates how masculinity is not unchanging but has been constructed in different ways in the last two centuries.

KELLY BOYD

See also Homosexuality

Matilda 1102–1167
Princess, Empress "Maud" of German territories, later Countess of Anjou

Bradbury, Jim, *Stephen and Matilda: The Civil War of 1139–1153*, Stroud, Gloucestershire: Alan Sutton, 1996

Chibnall, Marjorie, *The Empress Matilda: Queen Consort, Queen Mother, and Lady of the English*, Oxford and Cambridge, Massachusetts: Blackwell, 1993

Davis, R.H.C., *King Stephen 1135–1154*, London: Longman, and Berkeley: University of California Press, 1967; 3rd edition, London and New York: Longman, 1990

Pain, Nesta, *Empress Matilda, Uncrowned Queen of England*, London: Weidenfeld and Nicolson, 1978

Earlier studies of Matilda place her birth at Winchester. However, research indicates that she was born at the Royal Palace in Sutton Courtenay (Berkshire), in 1102. She was the granddaughter of William the Conqueror and Malcolm III of the Scots, and daughter of King Henry I. Her marriage to the 32-year-old German emperor, Henry V, in 1114, produced no children by the time of the emperor's death in 1125. The death of her brother Prince William in the wreck of the *White Ship* (1120) had left her as Henry's only hope for the continuation of his dynasty: the barons swore allegiance to the young princess, and promised to make her queen after her father's death. Matilda remarried, in 1127, Geoffrey Plantagenet, Count of Anjou and Maine. While PAIN recalls that the chroniclers of the time thought the marriage unhappy, it did produce three sons in four years, including the future Henry II. But Matilda's absence from the English court (perhaps because of pregnancy) on her father's death in 1135 provided an opportunity for her cousin Stephen to seize the throne, thus sparking the events that

would lead to civil war in England when Matilda and her husband "invaded" in 1139 to back her claims to the throne.

Matilda's victory at the battle of Lincoln (1141) and capture of Stephen may have seemed to give her complete success, especially when she convinced Stephen's brother, Henry of Blois, the powerful Bishop of Winchester, to support her claim to the throne and declare her queen, and "Lady of the English". However, the victory proved shortlived: BRADBURY argues that it was Matilda's arrogant manner that prevented her from securing allegiance from the citizens of London, who joined with Stephen's queen, Matilda of Boulogne, in a renewed campaign against her. After more fighting, and with Matilda compelled to exchange Stephen for her captured half-brother Robert, the king soon reimposed his authority, and Matilda was to return to the Continent. Eventually, in 1154, her son, Henry, would become succeed to the throne that had eluded her.

In contemporary chronicles, Matilda was described as "always superior to feminine softness and with a mind steeled and unbroken in adversity". In valour and determination Matilda may be compared Elizabeth I, yet much of the serious work on her life and struggle for the throne, and on her historical importance, lies in untranslated German studies of the 19th century. DAVIS discusses the significant social, governmental, and religious developments of the period. His views attracted much scholarly attention from the outset, and the resulting controversies are surveyed in the five new appendices contributed to the 3rd edition. All references have been updated, and particular attention paid to new translations of the sources, especially those references to the German language. (See also the entry on "Stephen" for other works on the period in general and Stephen's contested reign.) CHIBNALL argues that Matilda's fight for the throne was unsuccessful largely because she was a woman: even though there was no actual English law prohibiting a woman from inheriting the throne, this could happen in practice only if the woman in question were considered a "suitable" candidate. Chibnall's view is that in most cases the existence of another male candidate would in itself have been enough to disqualify a woman's candidacy, and so it was difficult for the English court fully to accept Matilda as queen. Chibnall examines the career as a whole of a woman described in her epitaph as "great by birth, greater by marriage and greatest in her offspring" – in her capacities as Henry I's daughter, as the wife and consort of Emperor Henry V, as Countess of Anjou after the emperor's death, and as (vice)regent for her son, Henry II. In her final chapter, Chibnall also examines the various ways in which historians have portrayed Matilda through the ages.

JOSEPH A. DIVANNA

See also David I; Henry I; Henry II; Plantagenet Kingdom; Stephen; Wallingford or Winchester, Treaty of 1153

Medicine: Antibiotics 20th century

Hobby, Gladys L., *Penicillin: Meeting the Challenge*, New Haven, Connecticut and London: Yale University Press, 1985

Macfarlane, Gwyn, *Alexander Fleming: The Man and the Myth*, London: Chatto and Windus, and Cambridge, Massachusetts: Harvard University Press, 1984

Parascandola, John (editor), *The History of Antibiotics: A Symposium*, Madison, Wisconsin: American Institute of the History of Pharmacy, 1980

Rosen, George (editor), "Special Volume: The Antibiotic Era", *Journal of the History of Medicine*, 6/2 (1951): 279–405

Wainwright, Milton, "The History of the Therapeutic Use of Crude Penicillin", *Medical History*, 31/1 (1987): 41–50

Weatherall, Miles, *In Search of a Cure: A History of Pharmaceutical Discovery*, Oxford and New York: Oxford University Press, 1990

Williams, Trevor I., *Howard Florey: Penicillin and After*, Oxford and New York: Oxford University Press, 1984

There are as yet few totally objective accounts of the development of antibiotics. Many of the key texts have been written by participating researchers, anxious to ensure that their contribution is not forgotten. The greatest controversy relates to the development of penicillin, whether the credit should go to the discoverer, Alexander Fleming, or to the Oxford team led by Howard Florey that proved its therapeutic value. Therefore, even those few works which try to offer a history of the drugs have to delve into the personalities involved.

A good example is the chapter on antibiotics in WEATHERALL's highly readable account of pharmaceutical discovery. He discusses the coining of the term antibiosis in 19th-century France, and the development of antibiotic therapy from 1928. He also considers the penicillin discovery controversy, the key question being whether Fleming was aware of the chemotherapeutic possibilities of his discovery before the work of Florey's team. This is generally a balanced account, avoiding much of the vituperation and hagiography which mar some of the literature. Weatherall argues that before 1940 few scientists on either side of the Atlantic had been persuaded of a future for antibiotics despite the 1939 report in America by Dubos and Hotchkiss of their discovery, gramicidin, the first antibiotic whose chemotherapeutic value had been demonstrated. Lack of interest created major financial problems for early research into antibiotics.

The tone of much of the debate was set by Florey himself. In the symposium edited by ROSEN, Florey stressed that penicillin had a two-stage discovery process. The first by Fleming in 1928 with little subsequent research by his team, resulting in penicillin largely being forgotten, and the second and more significant discovery by Florey's team, of its outstanding chemotherapeutic possibilities. At the same symposium Brunel argued that not only should Fleming not be regarded as the discoverer of penicillin but that his failure to allude to earlier work on antibiosis in his inaugural paper on penicillin amounted to scientific fraud.

While little of this impacted on accounts in the 1960s, from the mid-1970s Florey's premise began to be explored. As one of the Oxford team, MACFARLANE set out to explode what he termed the "Fleming myth". He believes that Fleming failed to recognize the full potential of his discovery because of his limitations as a scientist. He does, however, accept that Florey helped to create the "myth". While he initially banned media access to his laboratories in Oxford, journalists received a more sympathetic reception in London. Too late did Florey realize that his failure to court publicity would for evermore link penicillin with Fleming's name.

While WILLIAMS provides much interesting general detail in his biography on Florey, he is unmistakably an apologist on his account. There is a sense of irony, of history repeating itself, in the later research into antibiotics by Florey's team. Abraham developed cephalosporins into viable commercial drugs, when the initial discoverer, Brotzu, could not find a financial sponsor in postwar Italy. Williams is anxious to discount the suggestion that Florey "sold out" a British discovery to the Americans, emphasizing the early work of ICI on penicillin therapy so that by 1943 Britain could meet its own needs.

That the "Fleming myth" became the new orthodoxy can be seen in the symposium edited by PARASCANDOLA. His introduction argues that a "strong" case could be made for dating the antibiotic era before Fleming or a decade after his famous observation. Yet this ignores the content of several papers. Crellin points out that the few papers on antibiosis before 1914, even that of Pasteur, were ignored since they ran counter to the prevailing trend in immunological research, a fate shared by Fleming's work. The symposium was notable for the keynote paper given shortly before his death by Sir Ernst Chain, Florey's partner in 1940, who later made major discoveries in semi-synthetic penicillins. Chain gave Fleming full credit for his part in the penicillin story and argued that the discovery controversy was belittling to all concerned. He believed that Fleming's team was hampered by the technology available to them. Without later advances in techniques and equipment such as partition chromatography and infrared and ultraviolet spectroscopy, Chain argued he could not have taken the research further himself.

WAINWRIGHT's interesting article on the difficulties of using crude penicillin argues that Fleming was unfortunate in choosing his friend Dickson Wright to test penicillin clinically as a topical preparation. Wright's main interest was in the treatment of deep leg ulcers, one of the worst possible tests of the therapeutic effectiveness of crude penicillin. Research a decade later would prove that in ulcers crude penicillin lost its effect within 24 hours and then acted as a medium for bacterial growth, inhibiting the healing process. Wainwright also challenges Brunel, arguing that pre-Fleming accounts of antibiosis are inaccurate in their description of moulds being used since mycology was still an infant science: any green fungus might have been used in these experiments.

By far the most balanced and comprehensive account of the antibiotic story is to be found in HOBBY. While generally highly readable (the author was the microbiologist in the first American team to use penicillin in 1940), sometimes her text can become technical. The synthesis of such a volatile substance would require a large interdisciplinary team: the Oxford team numbered between 10 and 12 at any one time. In this sense, research into penicillin was truly groundbreaking, overcoming the divisions between academic and industrial research, and interesting governments in scientific research. To develop the drug commercially during wartime, corporate co-operation was required. The Therapeutic Research Corporation, which was established in Britain in 1942, included Burroughs Wellcome, Boots, Glaxo, May and Baker, and the British Drug House, with ICI joining later the same year. For all the teams involved it was a story which depended on luck at key moments. Hobby also points out that under modern drug-safety rules, early antibiotics would never have been produced commercially: her team, for instance, were conducting clinical trials on hospital patients within one month of synthesizing the volatile drug. The results of the new treatments were marked: maternal and infant mortality decreased; lifetime expectancy increased. Antibiotics paved the way for further medical breakthroughs: cardiac surgery, organ transplants, and skin graft techniques. With antibiotics the long-awaited chemotherapeutic revolution had arrived.

PATRICIA S. BARTON

See also Fleming

Medicine: Hospital Provision   since 1800

Abel-Smith, Brian, *A History of the Nursing Profession*, London: Heinemann, 1960

Abel-Smith, Brian with Robert Pinker, *The Hospitals, 1800–1948: A Study in Social Administration in England and Wales*, London: Heinemann, and Cambridge, Massachusetts: Harvard University Press, 1964

Ayers, Gwendoline M., *England's First State Hospitals and the Metropolitan Asylums Board, 1867–1930*, London: Wellcome Institute of the History of Medicine, and Berkeley: University of California Press, 1971

Bartlett, Peter and David Wright (editors), *Outside the Walls of the Asylum: The History of Care in the Community, 1750–2000*, London and New Brunswick, New Jersey: Athlone Press, 1999

Digby, Anne, *Madness, Morality, and Medicine: A Study of the York Retreat, 1796–1914*, Cambridge and New York: Cambridge University Press, 1985

Digby, Anne, *Making a Medical Living: Doctors and Patients in the English Market for Medicine, 1720–1911*, Cambridge and New York: Cambridge University Press, 1994

Fissell, Mary, "The Disappearance of the Patient's Narrative and the Invention of Hospital Medicine" in *British Medicine in an Age of Reform*, edited by Roger French and Andrew Wear, London and New York: Routledge, 1991

Foucault, Michel, *Folie et déraison: histoire de la folie à l'âge classique*, Paris: Plon, 1961; as *Madness and Civilization: A History of Insanity in the Age of Reason*, translated from the French by Richard Howard, New York: Pantheon, 1965; London: Tavistock, 1967

Foucault, Michel, *Naissance de la clinique: une archéologie du regard médical*, Paris: Presses Universitaires de France, 1963; revised edition, 1972; as *The Birth of the Clinic: An Archaeology of Medical Perception*, translated by A.M. Sheridan Smith, London: Tavistock, and New York: Pantheon, 1973

Granshaw, Lindsay, *St. Mark's Hospital, London: A Social History of a Specialist Hospital*, London: King Edward's Hospital Fund for London, 1985

Hodgkinson, Ruth G., *The Origins of the National Health Service: The Medical Services of the New Poor Law, 1834–1871*, London: Wellcome Historical Medical Library, and Berkeley: University of California Press, 1967

Jones, Kathleen, *Lunacy, Law, and Conscience, 1744–1845: The Social History of the Care of the Insane*, London: Routledge and Kegan Paul, 1955

Jones, Kathleen, *A History of the Mental Health Services*, London and Boston: Routledge and Kegan Paul, 1972

Jones, Kathleen, *Asylums and After: A Revised History of the Mental Health Services: From the Early-18th Century to the 1990s*, London and Atlantic Highlands, New Jersey: Athlone Press, 1993

Loudon, Irvine, "The Origins and Growth of the Dispensary Movement in England", *Bulletin of the History of Medicine*, 55 (1981): 322–42

Marland, Hilary, *Medicine and Society in Wakefield and Huddersfield, 1780–1870*, Cambridge and New York: Cambridge University Press, 1987

McKeown, Thomas, *The Modern Rise of Population*, London: Arnold, and New York: Academic Press, 1976

Melling, Joseph and Bill Forsythe (editors), *Insanity, Institutions, and Society, 1800–1914: A Social History of Madness in Comparative Perspective*, London and New York: Routledge, 1999

Pickstone, John V., *Medicine and Industrial Society: A History of Hospital Development in Manchester and its Region, 1752–1946*, Manchester and New York: Manchester University Press, 1985

Risse, Guenter B., *Hospital Life in Enlightenment Scotland: Care and Teaching at the Royal Infirmary of Edinburgh*, Cambridge and New York: Cambridge University Press, 1986

Risse, Guenter B., *Mending Bodies, Saving Souls: A History of Hospitals*, New York and Oxford: Oxford University Press, 1999

Rivett, Geoffrey, *The Development of the London Hospital System 1823–1982*, London: King Edward's Hospital Fund for London, 1986

Scull, Andrew, *Museums of Madness: The Social Organization of Insanity in Nineteenth-Century England*, London: Allen Lane, and New York: St Martin's Press, 1979

Scull, Andrew, *The Most Solitary of Afflictions: Madness and Society in Britain, 1700–1900*, New Haven, Connecticut and London: Yale University Press, 1993

Smith, Francis Barrymore, *The People's Health, 1830–1910*, London: Croom Helm, and New York: Holmes and Meier, 1979

Woodward, John, *To Do the Sick No Harm: A Study of the British Voluntary Hospital System to 1875*, London and Boston: Routledge and Kegan Paul, 1974

In recent years, the study of medical history has been transformed. Following the work of Thomas MCKEOWN, historians have adopted a much more sceptical attitude to the claims made by therapeutic medicine in relation to the decline of mortality, and this has led to a much stronger emphasis on the relationship between social and economic factors and the contours of health and disease. At the same time medical historians have also become much more interested in the role played by the medical profession, and by medical institutions, in society at large. One of the most influential single figures in making this reassessment has been the French philosopher Michel FOUCAULT. In *The Birth of the Clinic* Foucault provided a vivid account of the origins of the modern hospital movement, and the birth of modern medicine, at the end of the 18th century. In *Madness and Civilization* he aimed to show how modern ideas about the relationship between reason and madness also originated during this period.

Although Foucault devoted particular attention to the development of modern medical practices at the end of the 18th century, it was in fact during the course of the 19th century that the hospital acquired its present status as the central locus of medical care. This reflected the impact of a number of different developments which took place within the hospitals themselves. In a particularly interesting article Mary FISSELL showed how hospital doctors began to play a much more active role in identifying their patients' symptoms in the late-18th and early-19th centuries, rather than relying on the patients' own accounts to identify the nature of their diseases. This was followed, as RISSE (1999) has pointed out, by the introduction of a range of new techniques, including the use of anaesthesia, and the development of both antiseptic and aseptic operating theatres, which enabled surgeons to offer a much wider range of treatment services.

For many historians ABEL-SMITH's two books on the history of nursing and the history of hospital provision remain the essential starting points, but our knowledge of the terrain which he first mapped out has been greatly enhanced by a large number of more specialized studies which have been published in recent years. Although it is more than a quarter of a century old, WOODWARD's study has continued to provide a valuable overview of the development of voluntary hospitals, and both HODGKINSON and AYERS have provided extremely detailed accounts of the development of Poor Law medical services. LOUDON examines the origins of the dispensary movement at the end of the 18th century, and GRANSHAW shows how one such dispensary, the Benevolent Dispensary for the Relief of the Poor Afflicted with Fistula, Piles and other Diseases of the Rectum and Lower Intestines, grew into St Mark's Hospital at the beginning of the 1850s. RIVETT and PICKSTONE have provided comprehensive accounts of the development of hospital provision in London and Manchester respectively. MARLAND examines the history of medical provision as a whole in the West Riding of Yorkshire and DIGBY (1994) relates the development of hospital services to the rise of the medical profession more generally.

One of the most buoyant areas of historical research in recent years has been the history of mental health and "lunacy". In 1955, when JONES published the first of her series of books (also 1972 and 1993) on the history of mental health service provision, she had little doubt that "lunacy reform ... sprang from a conception of the community's responsibility for the well-being of its members, and revealed a new spirit of humanity in public life", but this confidence has been badly shaken by a number of more recent studies. In 1979 SCULL argued that the rise of the asylum owed less to the "new spirit of humanity", and more to the growing popularity of institutional solutions to social problems, and the success of "medical entrepreneurs" in persuading the English elite that they alone possessed the special expertise needed to deal with the problem of those who were thought to be "mad". In 1993 Scull published a revised edition of his original study, but his basic conclusions remained relatively unchanged.

During the course of the last decade interest in the history of madness has grown considerably, aided at least in part by the munificence of the Wellcome Trust. The current state of play is well reflected in two recent collections. Many of the contributors to MELLING & FORSYTHE's volume have focused their work specifically on Scull. They have tended to take issue with his emphasis on the role of "medical men", and to place a much stronger emphasis on the part played by the asylum inmate's family, and on the relationship between the asylum and the Poor Law. BARTLETT & WRIGHT argue that we need to focus less on institutions and more on the provision of care "outside the asylum". They point out that at any one time fewer than half the people who were registered as "lunatics" were inside asylum walls. However, given that almost half of those who were admitted to public lunatic asylums stayed for 12 months or less, what is perhaps most striking is the number of people who must have passed through the doors of the asylum at some point during the course of the 19th century.

Although there is undoubtedly still much room for more work on the administrative and medical aspects of both hospital and asylum provision, the greatest challenge facing medical historians remains that of reconstructing the patients' experience and, even, their own point of view. In *The People's Health* SMITH made an early attempt to achieve this by making copious use of the writing of hospital doctors and medical journals. However, since Smith's book was first published, historians have begun to make much more progress in reconstructing the careers of different patients by using computers to analyse admission books and other sets of patient records. In her 1985 study DIGBY used the records of patients attending the York Retreat, a psychiatric hospital for members of the Society of Friends, to examine the characteristics and experiences of more than 2000 private psychiatric patients between 1796 and 1910. In the following year, RISSE examined the clinical histories of nearly 4000 hospital patients who attended the Edinburgh Royal Infirmary during the last 30 years of the 18th century. As the use of computers has become more widespread, and as more records come to light, it is reasonable to hope that future researchers will continue to build on these foundations to shed even more light on the history of medical institutions, and the patients who passed through them.

BERNARD J. HARRIS

See also Chadwick; National Health Service; Nightingale; Public Health

Medicine: Medicine, Disease, and Health

Beier, Lucinda McCray, *Sufferers and Healers: The Experience of Illness in Seventeenth-Century England*, London and New York: Routledge and Kegan Paul, 1987

Clark, George N., *A History of the Royal College of Physicians of London*, 2 vols, Oxford: Clarendon Press, 1964–66

Cook, Harold J., *The Decline of the Old Medical Regime in Stuart London*, Ithaca, New York: Cornell University Press, 1986

Kealey, Edward J., *Medieval Medicus: A Social History of Anglo-Norman Medicine*, Baltimore: Johns Hopkins University Press, 1981

Loudon, Irvine, *Medical Care and the General Practitioner, 1750–1850*, Oxford: Clarendon Press, and New York: Oxford University Press, 1986

Orme, Nicholas and Margaret Webster, *The English Hospital, 1070–1570*, New Haven and London: Yale University Press, 1995

Pelling, Margaret, *The Common Lot: Sickness, Medical Occupations, and the Urban Poor in Early Modern England: Essays*, London and New York: Longman, 1998

Porter, Roy and Dorothy Porter, *In Sickness and in Health: The British Experience, 1650–1850*, London: Fourth Estate, and New York: Blackwell, 1988

Rubin, Stanley, *Medieval English Medicine*, New York: Barnes and Noble, and Newton Abbot, Devon: David and Charles, 1974

Webster, Charles, *The National Health Service: A Political History*, Oxford and New York: Oxford University Press, 1998

RUBIN provides a useful introduction to medieval medicine. Constructing a sound argument for its rational foundation, he places special emphasis, the title notwithstanding, on the Anglo-Saxon period. The study makes effective use of archaeological and paleopathological resources and contains fine discussions of leprosy and the development of medicine as a profession. Rubin describes most practitioners as individuals of good sense with solid grounding in classical and contemporary knowledge. The survey includes valuable descriptions of the varieties of extant historical evidence in its appendices and is a good starting point for understanding medieval physicians and disease.

A richer and more thoroughly documented analysis of medieval medicine is offered by KEALEY. His approach, though also centred on practitioners, is more focused and thematic than Rubin. Examining the expansion of healthcare between 1100 and 1154, the work takes into account the contributions of faith healers and others as medical practitioners. The study presents important insights into charitable institutions and emphasizes the prominent role of secular, rather than ecclesiastical, benefactors. Perhaps Kealey's most lasting contribution is his two useful appendices; the first identifies 90 physicians, while the second records 113 hospitals. The study relies extensively on charters and contemporary chronicles. As a consequence, it is less valuable treating medical studies or techniques than Rubin.

ORME & WEBSTER draw particular attention to the hospitals of south-western England, stressing their charitable and religious functions. Though the authors identify many types and properly observe the diversity of these institutions, most hospitals cared for the sick poor and gave sustenance to travellers. The authors caution against accepting earlier arguments regarding the use of hospitals to segregate lepers from the rest of society. The study includes a rich bibliography and is a useful survey of hospitals from Anglo-Norman times through to the Reformation.

Early efforts to professionalize medical practice are detailed in CLARK's survey of the Royal College of Physicians of London from its chartering in 1518 up to passage of the Medical Act of 1858. Drawing extensively on the college's own archives, Clark portrays the group as initially a professional entity serving London; however, it later evolved into a national self-serving elite. The college struggled against the barber-surgeons and apothecaries, and also worked to keep unlicensed practitioners from offering their services to the public. Success was limited because it lacked popular support. It did improve the standards and status of physicians by encouraging dissections, promoting lectures, and insisting upon qualifying examinations for all practitioners. Although Galen's teachings dominated their examinations up to the 16th century and the college was slow to recognize the contributions of William Harvey, Clark nevertheless sees the organization as a positive force up to the next century. Volume 2 covers the period from the late 17th century to 1858. For Clark, the college lost its direction early in the 18th century, yet regained its vigour by the reign of George III, when it laboured conscientiously to improve treatment and conditions for the insane. It also helped to establish national standards in the struggles to address disease and the causes and consequences of poverty. Overall, Clark sees the college providing pivotal leadership in the evolution of English medicine.

COOK focuses his study more narrowly, examining the College of Physicians from its period of dominance in the 1630s to its decline in 1704. His revisionist analysis modifies Clark's interpretation of the 17th century. Cook presents a less attractive portrait of the college, though he does not echo those modern scholars who condemn it as simply seeking to retain its privileged status. Drawing from an impressive array of sources, such as malpractice proceedings, minutes of medical societies and licensing boards, printed treatises, and advertisements, he explains how the college ultimately failed to restrict practice by its rivals. Unlike Clark, he shows how the medical marketplace and developments in the education of physicians led to revisions in philosophy and practice. Competition fuelled publication of medical texts as practitioners sought to trumpet their successes and gain more patients. Finally, Cook interprets the college's political struggles through the late 17th century and illustrates how these problems combined with market realities and changes in medical education to transform the group into a learned society after apothecaries gained the right to prescribe medicines. More balanced than Clark, he provides rich insights into the college's regulatory activities.

BEIER both complements and challenges Cook's conclusions. She rejects the idea of an organized medical profession in the 17th century; instead, she explains in far greater depth how all types of practitioners competed in a consumer-driven open market. Each tried to promote his own skills while discrediting rivals through extensive use of propaganda. Licensed practitioners might attack their antagonists' lack of formal training; however, they seldom criticized their diagnostic skills or success. In the second part of her study, she analyses illness from the perspectives of healers and sufferers. Basing much of her discussion of healers on the casebook of Joseph Binns, a London barber-surgeon, she depicts a cautious healer who treated more than 600 persons during his career. Binns followed traditional practices ranging from purges to blood-letting and each of his patients was treated over long periods with care taken to prevent infection. Beier concludes that barber-surgeons possessed greater manual skills and were more modern in their techniques than the members of the royal college. The concluding section of this important social history of medicine describes common diseases and their victims. Many contemporaries believed that God visited illness on humans because of their sinfulness or to educate them. Others recognized the power of magic and trusted healing to amulets or charms. Beier provides a fascinating window into the world of popular medicine.

Studying the urban environment, age groups and gender, and occupations, PELLING offers a rich blend of essays to interpret the social history of medicine in early modern times. She emphasizes popular preoccupation with disease and disability and underscores Beier's findings about the variety of practitioners who attended the poor and middling sorts. Local authorities retained several kinds of medical practitioner to minister to the health needs of the poor. She also studies nutrition and moderation in medical diagnosis. Among her more significant analyses is a discussion of the 1570 household census for Norwich. From it, she gleans a wealth of information to illuminate public concern for the health needs of the poor and efforts to offer assistance. Her study supplies valuable insights into the omnipresence of disease, as well as treatment for children, the elderly, the disabled, and women.

A survey that continues Pelling's time-frame through the 18th century with a similar focus on the social history of medicine from the perspective of the sick is contributed by PORTER & PORTER. They use traditional literary evidence – diaries, autobiographies, correspondence, fiction, and poetry – creatively to explore health, sickness, and the relationship between suffering and the self. Sickness and death were constant and fears about them consumed most citizens. By the later 17th century individuals became more concerned with prevention and health, though their lives remained dominated by life-threatening illness. The work is filled with detailed first-person descriptions of sickness and reveals the centrality of health concerns among everyday people.

Viewing a portion of the same period, although through a different lens, LOUDON describes the evolution of the general practitioner. In response to rising costs of medical education, new men, trained through practical apprenticeships with hospital experience, presented the types of care sick people wanted. They were accessible, reasonably priced, and their ability to deliver effective care for common ailments and minor injuries made them extremely popular. Loudon successfully uses account books from provincial practitioners to reveal dedicated, hard-working, able professionals. His analysis also adds to an understanding of an important dimension of the professional middle class in the 18th and 19th centuries.

No survey of medical history in Britain would be complete without mention of the National Health Service (NHS), and its pre-eminent historian offers an important interpretation from its origins to the Blair administration. While WEBSTER's primary attention is drawn to the politics and bureaucracy of the NHS, he provides solid analyses of clinical advances and finances. The author credits the special circumstances of World War II and the special vision of Aneurin Bevan for creating the system. If Bevan draws high praise for his commitment and stewardship, few of his successors are similarly singled out. Between 1964 and 1974, the service peaked; yet even then it

suffered from poor leadership, a complicated bureaucracy, and social and geographical inequalities. Webster explains how the Thatcherites worked to discredit the NHS by lengthening waiting lists for services, insisting upon more central control of the system, and increasing the number and power of managers. At the time of writing (1998), he sees little hope for a return to Bevan's vision for the NHS under the (first) Blair government.

MICHAEL JAMES GALGANO

See also DNA and Genetics; Fleming; National Health Service; Nightingale; Public Health

Medicine: 19th-Century Developments

Bynum, W.F., *Science and the Practice of Medicine in the Nineteenth Century*, Cambridge and New York: Cambridge University Press, 1994
Cartwright, Frederick F., *The English Pioneers of Anaesthesia (Beddoes, Davy, and Hickman)*, Bristol: Wright, 1952
Duffy, John, "Anglo-American Reaction to Obstetrical Anesthesia", *Bulletin of the History of Medicine*, 38 (1944): 32–44
Fisher, Richard B., *Joseph Lister, 1827–1912*, London: Macdonald and Jane's, and New York: Stein and Day, 1977
Granshaw, Lindsay, "'Upon This Principle I Have Based a Practice': The Development and Reception of Antisepsis in Britain, 1807–1890" in *Medical Innovations in Historical Perspective*, edited by John V. Pickstone, London: Macmillan, and New York: St Martin's Press, 1992
Hamilton, David, "The Nineteenth-Century Surgical Revolution: Antisepsis or Better Nutrition?", *Bulletin of the History of Medicine*, 56 (1982): 30–40
Youngson, A.J., *The Scientific Revolution in Victorian Medicine*, New York: Holmes and Meier, and London: Croom Helm, 1979

The 19th century was the time of the greatest technological change in human history. Although obscured by the continuing expansion of science and technology, to a place of virtual dominance in historical development in the 20th century, changes over the 19th century were more profound. This is certainly true in the area of medicine. At the end of the 18th century, doctors were only beginning to learn that venesection was not a panacea and had no accurate or systematic understanding of infection. Surgeons, although beginning to combine with apothecaries to become general practitioners and no longer the despised barbers of the past, were not regarded as gentlemen. Unlike physicians (doctors with a university degree), they accepted direct compensation for their service. By the end of the 19th century, the germ theory was fully established thanks to the work of Robert Koch (1843–1910) and the nature of infection clarified by Louis Pasteur (1822–95) and Joseph Lister (1827–1912). Surgery had gone from a bloody, agonizing, life-threatening ordeal in which the practitioner's most important asset was speed to a deliberate science capable of truly amazing benefits to health.

Anesthesia originated in the United States but antiseptic surgery was a largely British innovation.

YOUNGSON provides a thorough introduction to the use of anesthesia and antisepsis in Britain. He surveys the entire century and follows the discoveries and introduction of the new techniques and looks at the opposition to their use as well. Youngson's research is heavily based on medical literature of the period being studied, and he certainly regards the emergence of anesthesia and antisepsis as the keystones to the development of modern scientific medicine. BYNUM, in his more comprehensive examination of the influence of science in medicine, takes greater account of the evolutionary nature of the changes. He also addresses the dispute of how extensively scientific medicine affected the practice of medicine before the 20th century, and he notes that anesthesia and antisepsis were not as widely used as they might have been in the 19th century.

Anesthesia was the first of these two innovations to come into common usage. Although experiments had been going on for some time, the technique became generally known in the 1840s, and the first major, public operation using ether in Britain was done at London's University College Hospital in December 1846. The use of chloroform was introduced to Britain shortly after by Sir James Simpson (1811–70). The background and personalities involved in the growing use of anesthesia in Britain are the theme of CARTWRIGHT. One of the first men to gain fame from the use of anesthesia was John Snow, already the discoverer of the connection of cholera with water supplies, who used it on Queen Victoria during the birth of her eighth child. The queen's acceptance of pain reduction helped ease some of the moral criticism of anesthesia, though the argument continued, especially regarding childbirth because of the biblical imposition of suffering because of the sin of Eve. There were also those who argued that it was too expensive for the poor. Such issues are the theme of DUFFY.

The use of antisepsis is inextricably tied to the name of Joseph Lister, the first medical man advanced to the British peerage (although as Bynum points out, an emphasis on cleanliness and the dangers of infective agents in the environment ("hospitalism") predated and continued during the latter half of the 19th century along with Lister's work). Lister was different from others working on the same ideas in that he tied his work clearly into the emerging scientific understanding of infection that grew from the work of Louis Pasteur. FISHER does an excellent job of covering Lister's life and career. He traces the progress of the experiments and clinical trials that led to Lister's conviction about the absolute necessity of using antiseptic techniques in surgery. He also describes Lister's efforts to teach his techniques, and the opposition to their use, especially in London, to which Lister returned in 1877. It is clear that he admires Lister and has little sympathy for those who rejected his concept. The spread of antiseptic surgery was, in reality, halting and Lister did not move far beyond types of surgery done before antisepsis or to aseptic techniques. GRANSHAW deals with the spread of the method very effectively, taking the evolution beyond the career of Lister. HAMILTON reviews one of the major questions about the impact of antiseptic surgery, suggesting that the decline in deaths in 19th-century surgical cases arose more from improving diets than from better medicine. Thus it is clear that the rise of scientific medicine in the 19th century represented

enormous change and was the foundation for the enormous improvements in healthcare that marked the 20th century, but what that change meant for patients in the 19th century is not as well determined.

FRED R. van HARTESVELDT

See also Chadwick; Nightingale; Public Health

Melbourne, William Lamb, 2nd Viscount 1779–1848
Whig politician, statesman, and prime minister

Brent, Richard, *Liberal Anglican Politics: Whiggery, Religion, and Reform, 1830–1841*, Oxford: Clarendon Press, and New York: Oxford University Press, 1987

Cecil, Lord David, *The Young Melbourne, and the Story of His Marriage with Caroline Lamb*, London: Constable, and New York: Bobbs Merrill, 1939; *Lord M, or, The Later Life of Lord Melbourne*, London: Constable, 1954; both books combined as *Melbourne*, New York: Bobbs Merrill, 1954, and London: Constable, 1965

Mandler, Peter, *Aristocratic Government in the Age of Reform: Whigs and Liberals, 1830–1852*, Oxford: Clarendon Press, and New York: Oxford University Press, 1990

Marshall, Dorothy, *Lord Melbourne*, London: Weidenfeld and Nicolson, 1975

Mitchell, L.G., *Lord Melbourne 1779–1848*, Oxford and New York: Oxford University Press, 1997

Newbould, Ian, *Whiggery and Reform, 1830–1841: The Politics of Government*, London: Macmillan, and Stanford, California: Stanford University Press, 1990

Newman, Bertram, *Lord Melbourne*, London: Macmillan, 1930

Ziegler, Philip, *Melbourne: A Biography of William Lamb, 2nd Viscount Melbourne*, London: Collins, and New York: Knopf, 1976

Lord Melbourne's career has attracted the attention of biographers and historians whose interests range from the scandals of the Regency to the expansion of government in early industrial Britain. While the treatment accorded Melbourne reflects the changing concerns of recent historians, most consider him not as a politician driven by a quest for power, but as an observer who fortuitously achieved high office.

NEWMAN's old-fashioned, leisurely excursion is stylistically ornate, conveys a breezy familiarity with the aristocratic world of high politics, and is dated in its treatment of both political parties and cabinet government. Newman is interested in Melbourne more as the urbane, cosmopolitan man of society than as a formidable politician. Accordingly, Melbourne's relations with Caroline Lamb, Mrs Norton, and Queen Victoria are considered at least as notable as the politics of a decade of reform, when he served as home secretary and prime minister. A cautious conciliator and reluctant reformer, Melbourne presided over concessions he thought marginally better than the conditions they were designed to alleviate.

Politics is almost incidental in CECIL's celebrated first volume, *The Young Melbourne*, as much an elegant evocation of an ostentatious Georgian aristocracy as a study in the character formation of an insouciant nobleman. Cecil depicts an inwardly torn if outwardly detached character, whose centrist politics led him to associate with Canning. Both Newman and Cecil gloss over Melbourne's service as Irish secretary in Canning's and, briefly, Wellington's government. Each justifies, though neither condones, Melbourne's stern treatment of those engaged in agricultural riots and urban distress during his tenure as home secretary in Grey's cabinet. They agree that he neither initiated nor directed the important legislation of the "decade of reform". Rather, Melbourne's principal role as prime minister was to oversee. As Cecil has it, Melbourne's learned scepticism and fundamental tolerance, when combined with a lack of political passion, made him an ideal leader of a fractious Whig government that relied on support from both radicals and Irish repealers as well as on the restraint of moderate Tories in opposition. That Cecil should consider Melbourne's relationship with the young Queen Victoria as the climax of his career is hardly surprising.

MARSHALL agrees that Melbourne had little appetite for power and that good luck propelled him, relatively late in his career, to a leading role in the Whig governments of the 1830s. While not disagreeing in essentials with Cecil's interpretation, Marshall subordinates the private to the public life and provides a far richer and informed discussion of parliamentary reform, Irish questions, rural and urban discontent, and, not least, the constitutional implications of William IV's dismissal of Melbourne's first government in November 1834. Virtually all writers concede that Melbourne's role in the overthrow of Peel's government in 1835 was negligible, notwithstanding his return as prime minister.

While acknowledging Melbourne's equanimity and moderation, Marshall recognizes that his severity as home secretary during the Swing riots and Tolpuddle martyrs episodes reflects a paucity of social conscience, unexceptional for an age of limited government. He lacked familiarity or sympathy with the problems of an emerging industrial society. Nonetheless, while Marshall characterizes Melbourne's as "the ministry of compromise", its various church reforms, remodelling of urban local government, design of a national system of registration for births, marriages and deaths, introduction of the penny post, and founding of London University were indirectly dependent on the prime minister's skill in compromise and conciliation. That Irish grievances defied solution is attributable in part to Melbourne's and the Whigs' neglect of the social and economic roots of many Irish difficulties. Similarly, Melbourne's lack of interest in colonial matters, hardly unusual in the 1830s, may have made him all the more ineffective in dealing with the 1837 Rebellions in Canada and the threat by Jamaican ex-slave-owners to join the United States. Nonetheless, Marshall emphasizes the constitutional importance of Melbourne's government, which functioned at a time when power was shifting from crown to parliament, a matter that made Melbourne's complicated relationship with the young queen all the more significant. ZIEGLER is distinguished by his revisionist interpretation. While cultivating the appearance of the equable amateur, Melbourne is characterized as the calculating professional, "ambitious, cynical and almost wholly without political principle". Indifference becomes a virtue, political vacillation a talent. The interpretation is forced, hardly sustained by the evidence adduced to support it.

Recent reappraisals of Whiggery necessarily require that their authors re-evaluate Melbourne's political significance. BRENT, who tries to associate the Whigs with "liberal Anglicanism", concedes that Melbourne was more inclined towards a learned 18th-century rationalism and that his religious interests were principally intellectual. Opposed to religious enthusiasm of any variety, he considered appointments to the episcopate as seriously on theological as on political grounds. He vigorously pressed for Renn Dickson Hampden's appointment to the Regius chair of divinity at Oxford, despite opposition by both tractarians and evangelicals. MANDLER, on the other hand, considers the "Foxite Whigs" as the leadership group that controlled a more radicalized Whiggery in the 1830s and 1840s. While Mandler argues that the Melbourne–Palmerston circle was not affiliated with this group, Melbourne's government presumably fell under the influence of the Foxite Whigs, who inaugurated an era of sustained social reform that would culminate in the following decade. NEWBOULD's more persuasive, if traditional, interpretation considers Melbourne's government as an amalgam of groups that lacked a unifying philosophy and whose leaders, Melbourne among them, associated the new electoral organizations with radicalism. While Melbourne's government passed some notable legislation, Newbould portrays both the Whigs and their prime minister as reluctant reformers and proponents of limited government.

MITCHELL provides the most astute evaluation of Melbourne as both a public and a private man. He presents a figure whose celebrated and effortless cynicism, however compatible with our image of Whiggery's benevolent condescension, was rooted in the bitter experience of a miserable 22-year marriage. While Mitchell is far too sophisticated a scholar to peddle a simplistic psychological interpretation, he sees in Melbourne's complicated relationships with women an essential source of his character and, along with the Foxite legacy he inherited, of his political conduct. Indeed, his lack of commitment to anything more than a selective Foxite Whiggery and his potential as a figurehead made Melbourne "everyone's second choice" for prime minister. A government beset by disagreements about the corn laws, the ballot, Canada, and foreign affairs welcomed Melbourne's uninspired leadership. His wretchedness in retirement provides material for a painful concluding chapter.

ABRAHAM D. KRIEGEL

See also Anti-Corn Law League; Crimean War; Grey; Peel; Russell; Tolpuddle Martyrs; William IV

Merchant Adventurers

Baumann, Wolf Rüdiger, *The Merchants Adventurers and the Continental Cloth Trade (1560s–1620s)*, Berlin and New York: De Gruyter, 1990

Bisson, Douglas R., *The Merchant Adventurers of England: The Company and the Crown 1474–1564*, Newark: University of Delaware Press, and London and Toronto: Associated University Presses, 1993

Carus-Wilson, E.M., "The Origins and Early Development of the Merchant Adventurers Organisation in London" in *Medieval Merchant Venturers*, London: Methuen, 1954; 2nd edition, 1967

Friis, Astrid, *Alderman Cockayne's Project and the Cloth Trade: The Commercial Policy of England in Its Main Aspects 1603–1625*, Copenhagen: Levin and Munksgaard, and Oxford: H. Milford/Oxford University Press, 1927

Lloyd, T.H., *England and the German Hanse, 1157–1611: A Study of Their Trade and Commercial Diplomacy*, Cambridge and New York: Cambridge University Press, 1991

Palliser, D., *The Company of the Merchant Adventurers of the City of York: A Brief History of the Gild*, York: Company of Merchant Adventurers, 1985

Ramsay, G.D., *The Queen's Merchants and the Revolt of the Netherlands: The End of the Antwerp Mart*, Manchester: Manchester University Press, 1986

As CARUS-WILSON points out, the term "Merchant Adventurer" was often loosely used in the 14th and 15th centuries to mean any merchant engaged in overseas trade who was not a merchant stapler (that is, involved in the wool trade) and whose principal merchandise was cloth. Such merchants could be found in any port in England with a substantial export trade and many ranged widely over the Continent at fairs and markets. A group of Londoners trading with the Netherlands obtained a royal charter in 1407 allowing them to establish a fellowship in the Low Countries. In the course of the century this group became dominant so that the term has often been used subsequently to refer to them under the title of the Merchant Adventurers of England. Carus-Wilson's account of the early years of the company, however, makes clear the way in which this group was subsumed within the Mercers' Company, only meeting regularly as a separate group from 1465. Even so, they never had their own hall or clerks in London. Her article gives a valuable overview of the nature and location of the sources for the Merchant Adventurers in this period, many being among those of the mercers. She also points to the importance of non-metropolitan groups of Merchant Adventurers, particularly in Newcastle and York. PALLISER's brief but cogent history of the York company is very useful in this context. He elucidates their origins and continuing contribution to the city, in later years largely as a social and charitable organization.

The remaining writers all concentrate on the London company and its activities as a monopoly exporter of cloth. LLOYD's book, although mainly concerned with English relations with the German Hanse, has some valuable comments on the Adventurers who were in active competition with the Hanseatic merchants in the cloth trade to Antwerp in the mid-16th century. He sees the Privy Council consulting with the Merchant Adventurers "at every turn" in the 1550s. He also looks at the company in decline when, after the formal loss of its monopoly in 1688, most of the remaining members, who used Hamburg as their staple town, reorganized themselves as the Hamburg Company. This continued till 1809, when they were expelled by Napoleon. From his perspective the Merchant Adventurers were successful in opening much of middle Europe to English trade. BISSON concentrates primarily on the company's trade with Antwerp, seeing their success in estab-

lishing their monopoly as linked intimately with their ability to offer the crown surety for urgently needed loans raised on the Antwerp mart. Their trading practices were in fact the "least adventurous imaginable", but the company provides a striking incidence of "private lucre conducing to the public good". BAUMANN, using mainly material from archives in Germany and the Low Countries and the work of German scholars, is more concerned to evaluate the influence of the Merchant Adventurers on continental markets and economic developments than on English royal policies. He also includes a useful prosopographical appendix of 90 English merchants involved with German trade.

RAMSAY's work is, in fact, the second part of a two-volume consideration of the end of Antwerp as the foremost mart in 16th-century Europe. (The first volume is titled *The City of London in International Politics at the Accession of Elizabeth Tudor*.) It includes a detailed discussion of the political events that led to the Revolt of the Netherlands and ultimately to the blockade of the Scheldt. From the point of view of the Merchant Adventurers, despite their earlier success in achieving a monopoly of the most lucrative aspect of English international trade, the closure of the mart was the beginning of their long decline. The importance of these events in Elizabeth's reign is frequently underestimated, in Ramsay's view. The ending of the regulated but highly profitable connection with Antwerp can be seen as the stimulus that drove London merchants to seek for profits in long-range trade, particularly with the East and West Indies. FRIIS's discussion of Alderman Cockayne's project, though looking at English commercial policy as a whole in James I's reign, has some relevant points to make regarding the Merchant Adventurers. The project itself, to ban the export of unfinished cloth and to grant a monopoly of the finishing and dyeing processes to a company controlled by Cockayne and his associates, was, of course, largely aimed at destroying the privileges of the Merchant Adventurers. Despite being "the most famous company of merchants in Christendom", they were not without enemies. In Friis's view, however, the project had little if any effect in permanently depriving the Merchant Adventurers of what she sees as their "extreme privileges". Much more powerful was the trend away from regulated companies and monopolies visible by the end of the 17th century, though it is hard to see the project itself as having anything much to do with free trade.

SUSAN ROSE

See also Antwerp; Cloth Industry; Guilds and Lay Fraternities; Hanseatic League; Merchant Navy: To 1650; Staple, Company of the; Trade Patterns: English (Early Medieval Period); Trade Patterns: Medieval Period

Merchant Guilds

Bolton, J.L., *The Medieval English Economy, 1150–1500*, London: Dent, and Totowa, New Jersey: Rowman and Littlefield, 1980

Green, Alice Stopford (Mrs J.R.), *Town Life in the Fifteenth Century*, 2 vols, London and New York: Macmillan, 1894

Gross, Charles, *The Gild Merchant: A Contribution to British Municipal History*, 2 vols, Oxford: Clarendon Press, 1890

Miller, Edward and John Hatcher, *Medieval England: Towns, Commerce, and Crafts, 1086–1348*, London and New York: Longman, 1995

Nightingale, Pamela, *A Medieval Mercantile Community: The Grocers' Company and the Politics and Trade of London, 1000–1485*, New Haven, Connecticut and London: Yale University Press, 1995

Reynolds, Susan, *An Introduction to the History of English Medieval Towns*, Oxford: Clarendon Press, 1977; reprinted with corrections, Oxford: Clarendon Press, and New York: Oxford University Press, 1982

In order to understand the significance of merchant guilds in England it is first necessary to define each of the terms. A guild is "a society for mutual aid or the prosecution of a common object"; in the early Middle Ages the term "merchant" could be used to describe small traders or even pedlars but by the later middle ages it had narrowed down and is usually only applied to those whose livelihood largely depended on investment in wholesale trade and commerce. The history of English associations of merchants has been complicated by inappropriate comparisons with guilds in those continental countries that were much more urbanized than England. In England the term "guild" can be applied to trading associations (guilds merchant) found in some English towns after 1066; religious and charitable associations (fraternities) of merchant organizations; specialized organizations of merchants (merchant guilds and companies); and the religious and charitable sections of specialized organizations of merchants.

At the end of the 19th century GROSS set out a neat scheme for the history of merchant guilds in England. As trade expanded after the Norman Conquest and towns grew and prospered traders felt the need of joint action to protect their interests. This action involved the acquisition of privileges that gave the members of the guild merchant a monopoly of trade within the borough. Initially, according to Gross, the guild merchant was a "democratic" organization that included both tradesmen and craftsmen but gradually specialized craft organizations evolved within the guild merchant. Then, in their turn, mercantile interests coalesced within the crafts so that "during the 14th and 15th centuries we find the old Gild Merchant resolved into two general classes of crafts ... those wholly of a mercantile company and those in which the artisan still figured prominently". REYNOLDS puts the diverse forms of association given the name of guild within the context of the history of English towns in the Middle Ages. She establishes that Gross was wrong to claim that merchant guilds were a Norman innovation; originally guilds probably had only "social and convivial purposes" but in the expanding towns of the 12th century these organizations could take on economic and political functions. The membership of guilds merchant would vary according to the size of towns and the nature of the activities carried on in them. In some towns, "Landowners and traders who were not actually resident in the town might join in order to be able to do their business there toll-free, while some guilds were more or less taken over by merchants and wholesalers, as in the cloth towns, where weavers and fullers were excluded". More recently MILLER & HATCHER have shown the importance of guilds merchant in municipal development. "The gild was the 'nucleus of the municipality' ... in that it was a dynamic force in the urban community rather than because later municipal institutions developed from it directly". When towns began to acquire powers of self-government in the 13th century, mayors and governing bodies took over from the guilds merchant the defence of the town's rights and privileges. "Where gilds merchant continued in their twelfth-century role after 1200, the reason was likely to be failure on the part of urban communities to achieve a significant degree of municipal self-government". A few years after Gross had presented his theory of the evolution of the guild merchant GREEN effectively destroyed its final part. There was no "natural process" by which the guild merchant passed painlessly away as industrial conditions changed. The merchant guild did not turn into a "simple social-religious fraternity – a kind of quiet haven of rest for wealthy merchants who had given up the sweets of power and the real government of trade in which their fortunes were concerned, to busy themselves with dirges and masses and chaplains". Instead Green shows how, in the larger provincial towns, the merchant guilds were powerful and wealthy bodies whose membership was very similar to the governing councils of the town, whose policies they controlled in their own interests.

In the matter of merchant guilds London, as in most things, was the exception. There is no trace of an early guild merchant in London; instead there emerged in the 13th century, as BOLTON points out, "groups of traders, not craftsmen or artisans, the mercers, tailors, drapers, grocers, fishmongers, vintners". Specialization was rarely complete as most members of mercantile guilds dealt in cloth but "each gild did seek to regulate one main area of trade and was regarded by the urban authorities as responsible for it". The leading London merchant guilds obtained charters of incorporation from the crown, which transformed them into companies and allowed them to hold landed property and collect rents. Within the general membership of these companies there emerged an exclusive group, the livery, which had its own distinctive uniform and its own fraternity. The members of the livery dominated the company as they dominated city government. NIGHTINGALE's monumental history of the Grocers' Company supersedes older histories of London merchant companies. She starts with the premise that: "Medieval trade guilds were created by a society which had different assumptions from those which underpin the individualistic, secular, and industrialised society of modern Europe". By tracing the history of the guilds of Pepperers and Grocers she establishes that their economic purposes cannot be doubted but that these purposes were not merely protectionist; "rather they set out to expand their trade in foreign markets and were thwarted only by the restrictionist practices of their alien rivals". Nightingale recognizes that each company has a different history because of the specialized nature of their retail and distributive trade but by studying one such company in detail she throws much light on the economic and political history of medieval London and succeeds in relating "the development of the City's guilds, fraternities and livery companies to the changing economic and political circumstances which stimulated their formation and within which they worked".

ANN J. KETTLE

See also Cloth Industry; Guilds and Lay Fraternities; Markets and Fairs; Merchant Adventurers; Staple, Company of the

Merchant Navy: To 1650

Banbury, Philip, *Shipbuilders of the Thames and Medway*, Newton Abbot, Devon: David and Charles, 1971

Burwash, Dorothy, *English Merchant Shipping 1460–1540*, Toronto: University of Toronto Press, 1947; reprinted, Newton Abbot, Devon: David and Charles, 1969

Duffy, Michael *et al.*, *The New Maritime History of Devon*, vol. 1, *From Early Times to the Late Eighteenth Century*, London: Conway Maritime Press / University of Exeter, 1992

Farr, Grahame, *Shipbuilding in the Port of Bristol*, London: National Maritime Museum, 1977

Friel, Ian, *The Good Ship: Ships, Shipbuilding, and Technology in England 1200–1520*, Baltimore: Johns Hopkins University Press, 1995

Hair, P.E.H., "The Experience of the Sixteenth Century English Voyages to Guinea", *Mariners Mirror*, 83 (1997): 3–13

MacGowan, Allan, *Tiller and Whipstaff: The Development of the Sailing Ship 1400–1700*, London: HMSO, 1981

McGrail, Sean (editor), *The Archaeology of Medieval Ships and Harbours of Northern Europe*, Oxford: British Archaeological Reports, 1979

McLaughlin, Roy, *The Sea Was Their Fortune: The Maritime History of the Channel Islands*, Bradford-on-Avon: Seaflower, 1997

Marsden, Peter, *Ships of the Port of London: Twelfth to Seventeenth Centuries AD*, London: English Heritage, 1996

Reddaway, T.F. and Alwyn A. Ruddock (editors), *The Accounts of John Balsall, Purser of the Trinity of Bristol 1480–81*, London: Royal Historical Society, 1969 (*Camden Miscellany*, 23/1)

Salisbury, W. and R.C. Anderson (editors), *A Treatise on Shipbuilding, and a Treatise on Rigging, Written about 1620–1625*, London: Society for Nautical Research, 1958

Scammell, G.V., "English Merchant Shipping at the End of the Middle Ages: Some East Coast Evidence", *Economic History Review*, 2nd series, 13 (1961): 327–41

Scammell, G.V., "Ship Owning in England, c.1440–1550", *Transactions of the Royal Historical Society*, 5th series, 12 (1962): 105–22

Sherbourne, J.W., "English Barges and Balingers of the Late Fourteenth Century", *Mariners Mirror*, 63 (1977): 109–14

Unger, Richard W., *The Ship in the Medieval Economy 600–1600*, London: Croom Helm, 1980

Unlike warships of the same period, the design, building, and use of late medieval and early modern merchant ships is not particularly controversial. The literature therefore is mainly descriptive. A great deal has been written about the trades in particular commodities, from particular ports or to particular destinations within this period; none of that is considered here. Similarly there is a large corpus of work on exploration, cartography, and navigational technology, which is also excluded.

The design and building techniques employed are most fully and generally examined by FRIEL, who also considers fighting ships. His bibliography is extremely useful and relatively (1995) up to date. Guidance to detailed studies of woodworking techniques and other similar crafts should be sought there. Friel's work contains chapters on hulls, measurements, building techniques, rigging and equipment, as well as storage capacity, manpower, and sails. It is also period-specific. Other studies of shipbuilding in particular localities, such as BANBURY and FARR, cover much longer periods, and only parts of them are relevant in this context. MACGOWAN is also period-specific, but is much less general in its coverage, being almost entirely concerned with methods of steering and holding ships upon their predetermined courses. Given the central importance of this quality to a ship's performance, and MacGowan's technical expertise, this is also a very useful study. The other specific study of construction listed is that of SHERBOURNE, which is limited in a different way. Barges and balingers were small trading vessels, largely used for coastal trade; they were technically simple to construct, and were built in large numbers in many small centres all around the coast of Britain. SALISBURY & ANDERSON is a source rather than a study, and is included here as a representative contemporary treatise, which gives considerable insight into the way in which ships were designed, the proportions envisaged, and the technological limitations within which the shipwrights were operating.

BURWASH is the best general study of trading ships in use, covering not only ship design and manning, but also trade routes, volumes of trade, and shipping statistics. The appendices are extremely detailed, being drawn from a wide range of port books; they list not only the number of vessels sailing in given years, but also their ports of destination and the types of vessel. Burwash is based primarily on English sources, but MCGRAIL offers a wider study of a similar nature. He has much less statistical detail, but creates a better impression of the role of English shipping and trade within the European context, at a time when virtually all English commerce was with other ports on the European mainland. SCAMMELL (1961) is again specific, discussing sailings from a number of east-coast ports in the later 15th and early 16th centuries – a period during which the Hanseatic trade, except to London, was in full decline and ports like Boston and Kings Lynn were trying to adjust. SCAMMELL (1962) addresses a different issue: to whom did these ships belong? A few belonged to noblemen or gentlemen (even the king); more were owned by wealthy individual merchants; but by far the largest number were owned by groups or syndicates. The groups might consist of no more than two or three members, but sometimes a dozen or more would co-own a single vessel. Usually these groups were located in the same place, but not always; nor did each individual necessarily hold the same number of shares, or receive a similar return. Large ships (over 150 tons) in particular were like modern companies, in which individuals held one or more shares.

Records of a number of individual trading voyages survive, and several have been published. They are represented here by REDDAWAY & RUDDOCK's edition of the accounts of a Bristol voyage of 1480–81, which give an itinerary of the journey and details of wages and rewards paid, victualling, repairs, and a wide range of incidental expenses. HAIR covers a number of voyages to a specific destination, and is most useful for the light it sheds on the fledgling efforts of English merchants to spread their wings beyond north-west Europe and the Mediterranean. The Guinea voyages, along with those to the Atlantic islands, were the first steps in that diversification of trade that was to characterize the later 16th and early 17th centuries. They had considerable implications both for the way in which longer voyages were organized, and for how the ships were adapted to undertake them.

DUFFY *et al.* offer a wide-ranging regional study, which is included here because the late medieval and early modern periods – particularly the latter – were extremely important for the development of the maritime community in Devon. Not only were fishing and trade major economic activities, but Devon was also in the front line of the long war with Spain from 1585 to 1604. Several of the chief Elizabethan sea captains (such as Francis Drake) hailed from the county, and both piracy and privateering were carried out from there on a large scale. The county elite were deeply involved. MARSDEN is limited more specifically to shipping, but covers the operation of England's premier port for the whole of the period. More than half the customs revenues of England were derived from London in the reign of Henry VIII, and the proportion grew even larger thereafter. London was also the home port of by far the largest number of great merchantmen, which corresponded to the disproportionate wealth of the city's merchant elite. McLAUGHLIN's study is of the very different community of the Channel Islands: well off the beaten track for most purposes, except Elizabeth's campaigns in Brittany, but almost entirely dependent on the sea. Only a small part of the book relates to the period under consideration, but it is included here because of the importance of the seafaring tradition of the islands, and also because (unlike London or Devon) they were largely unaffected by political priorities.

Finally, UNGER offers the most sweeping and relevant way of putting the English merchant marine into the economic context of the period. In the early Middle Ages sea-borne trade was small in scale, and mostly very local. By the 14th century it was central to the economies of the Mediterranean and the Baltic; and by the 15th century equally important to the whole Atlantic and North Sea coasted areas. Apart from short-haul trade to the Low Countries and France, England lagged behind, but by the time that Unger's period ends that situation had been transformed. By 1600 England was one of the two or three major trading economies of western Europe, and her long-distance commerce was second only to that of the Netherlands. Navigational technology and shipbuilding had been forced ahead by commercial priorities. As late as 1650 England was still well behind the Netherlands in merchant tonnage, but over the next 20 years would equal and surpass her rival. It was during the period under consideration here that those foundations were laid.

DAVID LOADES

See also Archaeology: Maritime; Coastal Transport; Hanseatic League; Merchant Adventurers; Staple, Company of the; Trade Patterns: English (Early Medieval Period); Trade Patterns: Medieval Period; Trade Patterns: Scottish

Merchant Navy: 1650–1840

Bosscher, Philip and Robert Gardiner (editors), *The Heyday of Sail: The Merchant Sailing Ship, 1650–1830*, London: Conway Maritime, and Annapolis, Maryland: Naval Institute Press, 1995

Bromley, J.S., *Corsairs and Navies, 1660–1760*, London and Ronceverte, West Virginia: Hambledon Press, 1987

Crowhurst, Patrick, *The Defence of British Trade, 1689–1815*, Folkestone: Dawson, 1977

Davis, Ralph, *The Rise of the English Shipping Industry in the Seventeenth and Eighteenth Centuries*, London: Macmillan, and New York: St Martin's Press, 1962; corrected edition, with new introduction, Newton Abbot, Devon: David and Charles, 1972

Earle, Peter, *Sailors: English Merchant Seamen 1650–1775*, London: Methuen, 1998

Goldenberg, Joseph A., *Shipbuilding in Colonial America*, Charlottesville: University of Virginia Press, 1976

Hope, Ronald, *A New History of British Shipping*, London: Murray, 1990

Howell, Colin and Richard J. Twomey (editors), *Jack Tar in History: Essays in the History of Maritime Life and Labour*, Fredericton, New Brunswick: Acadiensis Press, 1991

Jackson, Gordon, *The British Whaling Trade*, London: Black, and Hamden, Connecticut: Archon Books, 1978

Lloyd, Christopher, *The British Seaman, 1200–1860: A Social Survey*, London: Collins, 1968; Rutherford, New Jersey: Fairleigh Dickinson University Press, 1970

MacGregor, David R., *Merchant Sailing Ships, 1815–1850: Supremacy of Sail*, London: Conway, and Annapolis, Maryland: Naval Institute Press, 1984

MacGregor, David R., *Merchant Sailing Ships, 1775–1815: Sovereignty of Sail*, London: Conway, and Annapolis, Maryland: Naval Institute Press, 1985

Minchinton, Walter E., "Characteristics of British Slaving Vessels", *Journal of Interdisciplinary History*, 20/1 (1989): 53–81

Northcote Parkinson, Cyril (editor), *The Trade Winds: A Study of British Overseas Trade during the French Wars, 1793–1815*, London: Allen and Unwin, 1948

Rediker, Marcus, *Between the Devil and the Deep Blue Sea: Merchant Seamen, Pirates, and the Anglo-American Maritime World, 1700–1750*, Cambridge and New York: Cambridge University Press, 1987

Starkey, David J., *British Privateering Enterprise in the Eighteenth Century*, Exeter: Exeter University Press, 1990

Sutton, Jean, *Lords of the East: The East India Company and Its Ships*, London: Conway Maritime, 1981

Syrett, David, *Shipping and the American War, 1775–1783: A Study of British Transport Organisation*, London: University of London, Athlone Press, 1970

Ville, Simon P., *English Shipowning during the Industrial Revolution: Michael Henley and Son, London Shipowners, 1770–1830*, Manchester and New York: Manchester University Press, 1987

The British merchant navy is so firmly woven into the fabric of British economic and political history that it is difficult to place parameters on its study. Apart from technical studies of the ships themselves, one can fairly claim that the history of the merchant navy is central to all branches of British overseas trade. It played a significant part in the capital accumulation of the 17th and early 18th centuries. Furthermore, it was upon the strength of the merchant marine that the Royal Navy was built.

A good starting-point for a study of the merchant navy under sail is HOPE. While Hope covers a broad sweep of history from 3000 BC to 1988, his chapters from 1649 to 1850 are good narratives of British shipping and its dominance of world trade by the end of the 18th century. He provides a good context for understanding Britain's relationship with the sea. He also provides a good bibliography upon which to build. DAVIS has provided the best study of the shipping industry in the period. He covers many aspects of the merchant marine – shipbuilding, ship-owning, the various overseas trades, the management of the shipping, the conditions of the seamen, and the impact of war upon shipping. As a single-volume study, Davis remains unsurpassed. Nonetheless, the earlier collection of essays, edited by NORTHCOTE PARKINSON, provides a useful addition to Davis in that it extends the themes to cover insurance and ports, demonstrating the breadth of studies that need to be encompassed to understand the merchant navy of this period. Coasting and coastal fishing are not covered in either of these works because the merchant navy has generally been perceived as that segment of maritime activity that deals with deep-sea freight and passenger carriage. Both coasting and fishing were important elements in British maritime enterprise, but they have not yet received the attention they deserve outside specialized articles or general industrial histories. The other important maritime industry, whaling, has been dealt with by JACKSON. By 1774, nearly a third of British-owned merchant ships were built in the American colonies and a good study of this expansion can be found in GOLDENBERG.

Maritime history has been a serious study in Britain since the end of the 19th century. Much of this research has never reached the public in book form, but there is a wealth of information in specialist journals such as the *Mariner's Mirror*, the *Economic History Review*, and more recently founded publications. While much of the research output continues to be published in these journals, there are now many specialized studies that have appeared in books. This is particularly true of work on ship design. MACGREGOR's work has provided detailed studies of the evolution of design as the commercial sailing ship approached the apogee of sophistication. Although the clipper is outside this period it only ever accounted for a small percentage of tonnage, and MACGREGOR shows how the hull form and sail plan of the bulk of merchant ships evolved from the 1770s to the 1830s by reference to the surviving records of British shipbuilders. BOSSCHER has put the matter of British ship design into a European context.

Recent studies continue to improve our understanding of the various branches of seaborne commerce. East India Company shipping is well documented and SUTTON provides a good modern introduction to the study. MINCHINTON is good on slaving vessels. This article is also an example of how important studies on the merchant navy might turn up in journals that are not immediately concerned with the sea. Minchinton has also contributed many other articles on merchant shipping, for which the reader should look out. VILLE has produced a good

study on ship-owning and ship operation in the coal trade at the end of the 18th century. His bibliography is also a good illustration of the range of research that has now been done on the economics and technology of merchant shipping.

When wars broke out, the demand for seamen from the Royal Navy escalated dramatically. The impact of impressment upon seamen and the merchant navy is still a matter of dispute. This and other aspects of the seaman's life are explored in EARLE and in the essays edited by HOWELL & TWOMEY. REDIKER provides an interesting study of different contemporary views of the seaman from honest, plain-dealing, skilled labourer to footloose libertine. For a more traditional view of the British seaman, see LLOYD. The economic impact of impressment on the merchant navy across this period still needs to be extrapolated from the broader statistics of wartime economics. CROWHURST provides a good study of how the merchants adapted their trade in wartime.

One of the merchant navy's other roles in wartime was privateering. This has been studied in important works by STARKEY and BROMLEY. The work of the merchant navy in providing transports for military forces and stores during this period of colonial expansion has been generally neglected, except for the study by SYRETT for the War of American Independence and more recently in articles on the Seven Years War.

While much work remains to be done, studies of the merchant navy are already extensive. They are, however, so diffused in articles and books on related subjects that it is impossible to capture the richness of this history by reference to a few texts. Readers are advised to look out for work in a wide variety of economic, social, and political histories and well as the more obvious journals concerned with ships and seafaring.

RICHARD HARDING

See also Americas, Trade with (to 1870); Archaeology: Maritime; Coastal Transport; East India Company; Exploration entries; Navy: Sailing Navy; Sea Power

Merchant Navy: Since 1840

Davies, Michael, *Belief in the Sea: State Encouragement of British Merchant Shipping and Shipbuilding*, London: Lloyd's of London, 1992

Hope, Ronald, *A New History of British Shipping*, London: Murray, 1990

Kirkaldy, Adam W., *British Shipping: Its History, Organisation, and Importance*, London: Kegan Paul Trench Trubner, and New York: Dutton, 1914

Lane, Tony, *Grey Dawn Breaking: British Merchant Seafarers in the Late Twentieth Century*, Manchester and Dover, New Hampshire: Manchester University Press, 1986

Lane, Tony, *The Merchant Seamen's War*, Manchester and New York: Manchester University Press, 1990

Scholl, Lars U. (editor), *Merchants and Mariners: Selected Maritime Writings of David M. Williams*, St John's, Newfoundland: International Maritime Economic History Association, 2000

Starkey, David J. and Gelina Harlaftis (editors), *Global Markets: The Internationalization of the Sea Transport*

Industries since 1850, St John's, Newfoundland:
International Maritime Economic History Association,
and Seville: Fundación Fomento de la Historia Económica,
1998

Sturmey, Stanley George, *British Shipping and World
Competition*, London: Athlone Press, 1962

Thornton, R.H., *British Shipping*, Cambridge: Cambridge
University Press, 1939

By the mid-19th century, the British mercantile marine was on the verge of establishing a world supremacy that was to last until the outbreak of World War I. A number of significant developments during the 1830s and 1840s provided the launch of the British mercantile marine into a position of unrivalled world power.

However, in 1840 it was not the United Kingdom that held mercantile marine dominance, but American shipowners, whose sailing ships were larger, faster, more cheaply built and subsequently dominated many world shipping routes. HOPE observes that while British sailing vessels maintained a healthy worldwide trade, it was the development of the steam engine and subsequent embrace of new technology by British shipowners that enabled them to break through the dominance of their American counterparts to lead world shipping.

Both Hope and THORNTON acknowledge the vital importance of government involvement in granting mail contracts to the new steamships, thus providing economic stability, and undoubtedly guaranteeing the success of British steam shipping. However, as Thornton observes, it was not until 1868 that the tonnage of steamships exceeded that of sailing ships. There were areas of trade that were dominated by the sailing ship, such as the routes to Australia, and this continued throughout the 19th century, especially given renewed stimulus with the emigration traffic from the 1850s onwards.

In terms of the British mercantile marine's dominance of world shipping, Thornton argues that the repeal of the Navigation Acts under the Whig government of 1848 was the most influential factor that brought this about. Hope notes that, while the repeal of the Navigation Acts was essential in liberating British shipping, the acts themselves had been continually eroded in the quarter of a century before the Whig government came to power. In addition, Hope observes that, despite the rapid post-1848 increase in British tonnage, this was countered by the similarly rapid advancement in both American and Norwegian shipping. Britain's successes in shipping, Hope argues, were its leadership as an industrial nation, its scientific and technical development in shipbuilding, steam power, and communications.

While British shipping enjoyed its ascendancy, there were serious deficiencies in the recruitment and training of officers and crew. A series of legislative measures during the 1840s and 1850s went some way to improve the competence of officers and crew, and the conditions under which they sailed. Government supervision was introduced in the form of the marine department of the Board of Trade. British ships had always been manned by multinational crews, notably the P&O ships. After 1852 with the repeal of a legislative clause, the crew of British ships became increasing international. However, competency remained low, leading to a proliferation of training schools. Despite Thornton's claim that, during the period 1870–1914,

the greatest development was in the advancement of the competency of those manning the ships, the fact remained, and continued to be the case until 1945, that the majority of seafarers received little or no training before going to sea. While conditions for seafarers improved on passenger liners, many others worked and lived in an unhealthy and dangerous environment. Hope provides a useful narrative of the development of seafaring as a career and the conditions under which it evolved. Thornton, in turn, gives a useful insight into the job of the postwar seafarer.

Improvements in conditions that started during World War I, with the building of a significant number of new ships, continued, although even by World War II conditions on older ships remained poor. Advances in recruitment procedures were being made, with the introduction of the National Maritime Board in 1917, finishing off the crimping system once and for all. In 1919 Gravesend Sea School was opened as an attempt to maintain the numbers of new recruits needed to sustain the British merchant fleet.

The evolution of an effective trade union movement and the establishment of sailors' welfare organizations were crucial in achieving improvements in the seafaring career. SCHOLL has selected a number of articles by David M. Williams that, collectively, address a number of issues relating to safety at sea and the welfare of the seafarer throughout the period 1850 to 1914. Several of the articles in this work provide concise accounts of issues surrounding the seafarer: conditions at sea, based on Mayhew's findings, recruitment and training, and reform movements.

By the outbreak of World War I the British mercantile marine carried about half the total of the world's seaborne trade. British shipping was now typified by the steamship, the sailing ship largely unable to meet the demands of an industry in the throes of modernization. It was at this stage in the history of British shipping that KIRKALDY made his contemporary observations about the industry. Kirkaldy's work remains a useful account of British shipping, written by an informed commentator of the time.

The role of the mercantile marine during World War I is usefully narrated in a chapter in Hope, outlining the impact of the war on British merchant ships. STURMEY continues the debate about British shipping during World War I, being critical of an industry that failed to reinvest profits made during the war. Certain sectors of the industry fared very well during the war, but it was the relative success of competitors that damaged British shipping. As Sturmey points out, in the aftermath of World War I, the British shipping industry was faced with the task of winning back its pre-war share of world trade.

Kirkaldy finished his work with the British shipping industry in a very different state to the one described by Sturmey and Thornton when discussing the immediate postwar era. The continuing postwar problem was not one of failing on the part of the British shipping industry – 1919 was a very successful year – but the relative greater success of competitors. Between 1919 and 1931, total British tonnage remained at about the pre-war level. The consequences of postwar economic policies worldwide led to the necessity of intervention on the part of the British government. For example, in 1935 the British Shipping (Assistance) Act was introduced as an emergency measure to shore up the struggling tramp industry.

At the outbreak of World War II, Britain remained a healthy maritime nation, if not the commanding force of the turn of the century. Hope, Sturmey, and Thornton offer insights into the experience of the British merchant navy during World War II, but it is LANE that captures the experience of the seafarer. The British merchant navy provided a vital role during World War II, but what was notable was the struggle among seafarers themselves to gain recognition. Lane's work (1990) explores in detail the discontent of the seafarer, both on a personal and professional level. Although as Hope notes, many measures were introduced during wartime to improve the seafarer's working existence that subsequently extended through to peacetime, Lane's work examines the impact of war on the seafarer as a civilian.

British shipping emerged from World War II to encounter a shipping boom. Also, the postwar years saw rapid improvements in the working conditions of the officers and crew. On an international level, the welfare of the seafarer was acknowledged and addressed. In Britain the Merchant Navy Welfare Board was established in 1948. The education and training of seafarers became more formal, although the problem of training and recruiting sufficient merchant seafarers remained.

Despite postwar prosperity, the disintegration of the British empire affected long-standing shipping companies. In addition the introduction of flag discrimination policies on the part of certain countries affected trade. The postwar years witnessed the globalization of world shipping. It is impossible to speak of British shipping without reference to the complex commercial context in which it now operates. STARKEY & HARLAFTIS present a number of articles that explore aspects of globalization. Lewis Johnman provides an account of the impact of internationalization on postwar British shipping. Frank Broeze examines the impact of containerization and the globalization of worldwide liner shipping over the last 35 years. It is essential to examine the contemporary international shipping scene in order to understand the issues affecting the transformation of the British merchant navy during the postwar period.

The free trade era that reflected the strength of the British empire was supplanted by the need for a more secure economic basis for British shipping during the postwar era. Entry into the European Community was nothing less than an acknowledgement of this by government and industry alike. Sturmey concludes his work with a preview of possible effects of Britain entering the European Community, an argument complemented by the more recent works of Hope and Davies.

British legislative measures were instrumental in the fate of British shipping. DAVIES examines state policy towards shipping, arguing that governments actively supported the growth of merchant shipping and the development of training for seafarers in order to sustain the industry. By the 1990s, the industry was suffering from declining tonnage, declining numbers of seafarers, and a fleet in need of modernization, and eleven years of *laissez-faire* policy on the part of the government. Policies of state intervention in other shipping nations, particularly by other member states of the European Community exacerbated the impact of this arm's-length approach. Concerns over the declining fleet in terms of national defence capabilities were also being voiced.

The plight of the seafarer in the late 20th century is captured in LANE in *Grey Dawn Breaking*. Lane explores the impact of the modernization of the British shipping industry on the seafarer. From the mid-1950s onwards, developments in the shipping industry affected the British seafaring life, enforcing irreversible changes. The 1960s witnessed the advent of container ships, the opening up and diversification of the British shipping industry, the dying years of the passenger liner, and the move from traditional cargo liner to bulk carrier. By the mid-1980s, Lane argues, the only recognizable sector was the coasting trade. International developments also affected British shipping and, consequently, the British seafarer. The 1980s saw British shipping companies increasingly engage in the use of flags of convenience, and the replacement of British by foreign crew. Tony Lane continues to direct contemporary research work into the conditions of seafarers at the Seafarers' International Research Centre at the University of Wales, Cardiff.

RACHEL MULHEARN

See also Coastal Transport; Navy: Modern Navy; Sea Power; Shipbuilding; Trade Patterns: 1800–*c*.1890

Metalwork, Ornamental: Anglo-Saxon and Celtic

Aberg, Nils, *The Anglo-Saxons in England during the Early Centuries after the Invasion*, translated from the Swedish by Sydney Charleston, Uppsala: Almqvist & Wiksell, and Cambridge: Heffer, 1926; reprinted, Hildesheim and New York: Olms, 1975

Backhouse, Janet, D.H. Turner, and Leslie Webster (editors), *The Golden Age of Anglo-Saxon Art 966–1066*, London: British Museum, and Bloomington: Indiana University Press, 1984

Bakka, Egil, *On the Beginning of Salin's Style I in England*, Bergen: Grieg, 1958

Bourke, Cormac (editor), *From the Isles of the North: Early Medieval Art in Ireland and Britain*, Belfast: HMSO, 1995

Brenan, Jane, *Hanging Bowls and their Contexts: An Archaeological Survey of Their Socio-Economic Significance from the Fifth to Seventh Centuries A.D.*, Oxford: Tempus Reparatum, 1991

Bruce-Mitford, Rupert, *The Sutton Hoo Ship-Burial*, 3 vols, London: British Museum, 1975–83

Evison, Vera, *The Fifth-Century Invasions South of the Thames*, London: Athlone Press, 1965

Gogan, L.S., *The Ardagh Chalice: A Description of the Ministral Chalice found at Ardagh in County Limerick in the Year 1868, with a note on its Traditional Conformity to the Holy Grail of Legend*, Dublin: Browne and Nolan, 1932

Haseloff, Gunther, *Die Tassilokelch*, Munich: Beck, 1951

Henry, Françoise, *Irish Art in the Early Christian Period to 800 AD*, revised edition, London: Methuen, and Ithaca, New York: Cornell University Press, 1965

Henry, Françoise, *Irish Art during the Viking Invasions, 800–1020 AD*, London: Methuen, and Ithaca, New York: Cornell University Press, 1967

Henry, Françoise, *Irish Art in the Romanesque Period, 1020–1170 AD*, London: Methuen, and Ithaca, New York: Cornell University Press, 1970

Hines, John, *A New Corpus of Anglo-Saxon Great Square-Headed Brooches*, Woodbridge, Suffolk and Rochester, New York: Boydell, 1997

Hinton, David A., *A Catalogue of the Anglo-Saxon Ornamental Metalwork 700–1100 in the Department of Antiquities, Ashmolean Museum*, Oxford: Clarendon Press, 1974

Kendrick, T.D., *Late Saxon and Viking Art*, London: Methuen, 1949; reprinted, London: Methuen, and New York: Barnes and Noble, 1976

Kilbride-Jones, H.E., *Celtic Craftsmanship in Bronze*, London: Croom Helm, and New York: St Martin's Press, 1980

Kilbride-Jones, H.E., *Zoomorphic Penannular Brooches*, London: Society of Antiquaries, 1980

Laing, Lloyd, *A Catalogue of Celtic Ornamental Metalwork in the British Isles, c.AD 400–1200*, Oxford: Tempus Reparatum, 1993

Leeds, E. Thurlow, *A Corpus of Early Anglo-Saxon Great Square-Headed Brooches*, Oxford: Clarendon Press, 1949

Mahr, Adolf and Joseph Raftery (editors), *Christian Art in Ancient Ireland: Selected Objects Illustrated and Described*, 2 vols, Dublin: Stationery Office of Saorstat Eireann, 1932–41; reprinted, New York: Hacker, 1976

Ryan, Michael (editor), *The Derrynaflan Hoard*, vol. 1, *A Preliminary Account*, Dublin: National Museum of Ireland, 1983

Ryan, Michael (editor) *Ireland and Insular Art, AD 500–1200*, Dublin: Royal Irish Academy, 1987

Salin, Bernhard, *Die Altgermanische Thierornamentik: Selected Objects Illustrated and Described*, Stockholm: Beckman, 1904

Small, Alan, Charles Thomas, and David M. Wilson, *St Ninian's Isle and Its Treasure*, Oxford: Oxford University Press for Aberdeen University, 1973

Speake, George, *Anglo-Saxon Animal Art and Its Germanic Background*, Oxford: Clarendon Press, and New York: Oxford University Press, 1980

Spearman, R. Michael and John Higgitt (editors), *The Age of Migrating Ideas: Early Medieval Art in Northern Britain and Ireland*, Stroud and Dover, New Hampshire: Sutton, and Edinburgh: National Museums of Scotland, 1993

Stokes, Margaret, *Early Christian Art in Ireland*, revised by G.N. Plunket, Dublin: HMSO, 1911; reprinted, Freeport, New York: Books for Libraries Press, 1972

Suzuki, Seiichi, *The Quoit Brooch Style and Anglo-Saxon Settlement: A Casting and Recasting of Cultural Identity Symbols*, Woodbridge, Suffolk and Rochester, New York: Boydell, 2000

Webster, Leslie and Janet Backhouse (editors), *The Making of England: Anglo-Saxon Art and Culture, AD 600–900*, London: British Museum Press, and Toronto: University of Toronto Press, 1991

Wilson, David M., *Anglo-Saxon Ornamental Metalwork, 700–1100, in the British Museum*, London: British Museum, 1964

Youngs, Susan (editor), *The Work of Angels: Masterpieces of Celtic Metalwork, 6th–9th Centuries AD*, London: British Museum, 1989; Austin: University of Texas Press, 1990

There has been no single overview of early-medieval ornamental metalwork in Britain and Ireland, surveys being generally confined to either the Anglo-Saxon or Celtic areas.

Studies of Anglo-Saxon metalwork have in the main concentrated on either the pagan period (*c*.5th–7th centuries) or the Christian period (7th–11th centuries), though an important exhibition catalogue, edited by WEBSTER & BACKHOUSE, discusses a number of major pieces from both periods.

The study of pagan Anglo-Saxon artefacts, particularly metalwork, began in the 19th century, but the definition of the artistic styles of pagan Anglo-Saxon metalwork did not commence until SALIN set Anglo-Saxon material in the wider context of that of contemporary Scandinavia. His seminal work, which defined two major styles (styles I and II) was built upon by a number of scholars, most notably by LEEDS, who developed ideas about typology pioneered by Oscar Montelius. Leeds dominated the study of pagan Anglo-Saxon artefacts in the first half of the 20th century. In 1949 he published a major assemblage of Anglo-Saxon square-headed brooches, which remained the standard work on the subject until HINES's reassessment. Other scholars who built on Salin's work included ABERG, whose key study defined the main types of pagan Anglo-Saxon metalwork and discussed their chronology and stylistic groupings.

Brooch typology dominated the discussions of pagan Anglo-Saxon ornamental metalwork during much of the 20th century. The discovery of the Sutton Hoo ship burial in 1939, however, led to a renewed interest in pagan Saxon ornamental styles, in particular style II. Of the many studies that arose from Sutton Hoo, the definitive report edited by BRUCE-MITFORD not only advanced the study of ornamental style in metalwork but also of technology, which was considered extensively. The development of style II was also considered by SPEAKE, while style I (and by extension, the so-called quoit brooch style that preceded it) received reappraisal by BAKKA. The quoit brooch style was vigorously discussed in a series of studies between 1965 and 2001, debate being focused on whether the style represented a native survival from Roman Britain or a continental import. Most of the discussions were in papers, but the subject was addressed among other topics by EVISON in her study of Frankish settlement in southern England, though her conclusions did not win widespread acceptance. The subject has also been addressed by SUZUKI, with important implications for the study of symbolism in ornament.

A feature of the late 20th-century debates on pagan Saxon metalwork was the growth of interest in the technology of production, and in the symbolic significance of the objects and their decoration. Most of the discussion has appeared in papers rather than in books.

KENDRICK discussed aspects of later Saxon ornamental metalwork, but the first major study was a paper by D.M. Wilson in 1961, in which the Trewhiddle style was defined. This pioneer discussion was developed in WILSON, which not only catalogued major pieces in the national collection but also prefaced the catalogue with a discussion which established a chronology on the basis of historically datable artefacts. To this catalogue was added HINTON's similar survey of material in the Ashmolean Museum in Oxford. An exhibition catalogue edited by BACKHOUSE, TURNER & WEBSTER described and discussed a number of important pieces. Few individual pieces of late Saxon metalwork have received attention in monographs, but mention may be made of HASELOFF's study of the Tassilo chalice, made by an Anglo-Saxon craftsman on the Continent.

Celtic ornamental metalwork attracted the attention of 19th-century scholars, particularly following the discovery of the "Tara" brooch and Ardagh chalice in Ireland. The first major overview of Irish metalwork of the period in volume form appeared in STOKES, which was reprinted several times, most recently 1972. A landmark in the study of Irish metalwork, however, was reached with the publication of MAHR & RAFTERY's two-volume catalogue with its excellent plates and useful descriptive text. Although by no means exhaustive, it illustrated most of the major finds in Ireland to the time of publication. It was left to HENRY to put Irish metalwork in its wider context, which she first did in 1940, and upon which she elaborated in her three books on Irish art (1965, 1967, 1970). Henry's interpretations relied heavily on a belief that Celtic art in Ireland developed from an Iron Age past, with little contribution from Britain. This was particularly apparent in her assumption that hanging bowls of the 5th–7th centuries were Irish products or the work of Irish migrants in Britain, a view now largely discredited. Despite this, her work still remains a major foundation for later study.

Hanging bowls and various forms of dress-fastener, particularly penannular brooches, have long been seen to hold an important key to understanding the development of Celtic ornamental metalwork in the period prior to the Viking raids. Although his chronology has won little acceptance, studies by KILBRIDE-JONES on these subjects have been very influential, while BRENAN has provided a valuable illustrated catalogue of all but the most recent finds of hanging-bowls.

Pictish metalwork became the focus of attention following the discovery of the St Ninian's Isle treasure in Shetland in 1958. The definitive publication by SMALL, THOMAS, & WILSON with its discussion of wider aspects of Pictish metalworking by Wilson, was an important landmark. The discovery of the Derrynaflan hoard in 1980 and its preliminary publication by RYAN et al. (1983) advanced understanding of Irish metalwork of the "golden age" of the 8th–9th centuries. The Ardagh chalice, superior but similar to that from Derrynaflan, was the subject of a major monograph edited by GOGAN.

A catalogue of metalwork by LAING attempted to list all major finds in Britain, with a discussion of penannular brooches and hanging bowls. An exhibition catalogue, edited by YOUNGS, has much useful material on technology as well as art. A series of conference volumes, edited by RYAN (1987), by SPEARMAN & HIGGITT and by BOURKE, have contained much of importance to students of Celtic metalwork.

LLOYD LAING

Metalworking before the Industrial Revolution

Blair, John and Nigel Ramsay (editors), *English Medieval Industries: Craftsmen, Techniques, Products*, London and Rio Grande, Ohio: Hambledon Press, 1991

Cherry, John, *Goldsmiths*, London: British Museum Press, and Toronto and Buffalo: University of Toronto Press, 1992

Crossley, D.W. (editor), *Medieval Industry*, London: Council for British Archaeology, 1981

Hatcher, John, *English Tin Production and Trade before 1550*, Oxford: Clarendon Press, 1973

Haedeke, Hanns-Ulrich, *Metalwork*, translated from German manuscript by Vivienne Menkes, London: Weidenfeld and Nicolson, and New York: Universe Books, 1970

London Museum, *Medieval Catalogue*, compiled by J.B. Ward-Perkins, London: Lancaster House, 1940; corrected edition, London: HMSO, 1954; reprinted, as *London Museum Medieval Catalogue 1940*, Ipswich, Suffolk: Anglia, 1993

Metalworking goes as far back as the invention of time. Historians are forced to accept that some of the survivals from metalworking are often haphazard and sometimes can only be attributed to eras which are often undesignated and untraceable to a particular maker. Once the furnace or fire had been lit with the sole intent of creating or smelting a quantity of metal the craftsman did not know what would be left over or even what he would make with it. Assay marks, hallmarks, and makers' names are therefore relatively modern. Before industrialization and controlled mass production, there were many skilled and practised metalworkers who were mainly anonymous. In seeing and examining such products the LONDON MUSEUM *Medieval Catalogue* is still a cornucopia for those who wish to look at anything from arrowheads, swords, knives, and axes to fine rings, keys, purse frames, and chalices. Although it was originally issued in 1940 it is still a very useful pictorial record of many of the more anonymous results of metalworkers.

One of the best general introductions is HAEDEKE, who simply approaches the subject by considering the metals themselves: copper, bronze and brass, iron, and pewter. He then treats each section chronologically. It is a well produced and illustrated survey by the former curator of the Kunstgewerbe Museum in Cologne and remains a massive contribution to those wishing to understand the pre-industrial metalworking craft.

Most precious of all was gold and in an easily accessible and well-illustrated booklet CHERRY has brought the work of the goldsmith to life. He considers the output of early monastic goldsmiths and then moves towards the regulated days of the London Goldsmiths Company. After considering the goldsmith at work he discusses contracts and distribution. One of the great strengths of his work is the beautiful illustrations.

Britain was known to the ancients as the "Tin Isles" and indeed it was Cornish tin which first brought the Phoenicians here and gave rise to the Stannaries (the tin mines of Devon and Cornwall). Of more use for economic historians is the study by HATCHER. Hatcher remains one of the most recent surveys of the tin industry and trade in pre-industrial England. One of its vital contributions is the statistical data in the two appendices, which have been taken from many surviving records. He considers the organization of the Stannaries and then looks at the patterns of overseas trade between 1300 and 1550. He also analyses the volume of internal trade which fed the pewter industry in many other towns.

A better understanding of the importance of metalworking can be found in CROSSLEY. This is a selection of different works devoted to the archaeology of medieval industry. There are articles on medieval iron smelting, the medieval smith and his products and methods, the medieval bronzesmith, lead mining and smelting, and a survey on the archaeological potential of the Devon tin industry. Crossley examines the development of the bloomery to produce high carbon molten iron and the change which brought the advent of wrought iron. From the 11th century the use of heavier ploughs with iron shares or iron tips meant an increase in metal production. In England it was the Weald which was to produce most of the nails, horseshoes, and arrowheads which were required from the 13th century onwards. Early Saxon and Norman iron-smelting sites are considered from Domesday evidence as well as the accounts of the bloomeries on the Clares, lands near Tonbridge. Consideration is also given to powered bloomeries in the 15th century.

In the same book R.F. Tylecote examines the role of the smith in society and draws the distinction between a blacksmith and a bloom smith. A blacksmith had a high rank and was responsible for the production of horseshoes, stirrups, knives, and other edge tools as well as locks. It was from his particular trade that the lorimer, locksmith, and bladesmith appeared. An archaeological examination is made of various sites as well as the methods and raw materials used. Ian Goodall's paper on the blacksmiths' products reminds us that all tools for iron, wood, stone, textile (tenter hooks and wool combs), and leather working came from the forge. It was important for domestic equipment, personal equipment, and horse equipment. Archaeological evidence for the bronzesmith, whose metal required copper, tin, zinc, and lead, and his methods is less prolific but objects abound. Ian Blanchard uses documentary evidence to review lead mining and smelting and produces a useful picture of the new mines of the 12th century. He then surveys the Durham system which opened up a new epoch in the medieval mines.

As a result of the former work BLAIR & RAMSAY produced a scholarly volume which aimed to update the work of L.F. Salzman (*English Industries of the Middle Ages*, 1913, revised 1923). It does this well and various chapters relate to metalworking. All include ideas for further reading. R.F. Homer writes authoritatively on the non-ferrous metals: tin, lead, and pewter. Claude and John Blair deal with copper alloys (copper and bronze) and concentrate on methods as well as the more specialized bell founding. Gold is dealt with in a large chapter which includes silver and precious stones. Jane Geddes deals with iron, the most common ore, and uses contemporary records to give a real feel of the smith's forge, tools, and products. She considers the formation of the guild, and women as blacksmiths. This is a very helpful, lavishly illustrated, and scholarly volume which builds on the archaeological evidence.

In such a small survey of pre-industrial metalworking it is impossible to give much attention to the crafts associated with monumental brasses and latten or cullen plate which became the vogue for sepulchral monuments. Needless to say they are not

abandoned and societies exist for brasses, pewter, and other metals. Many of the London livery companies associated with metals (Pewterers, Goldsmiths, Lorimers, Cutlers, and Ironmongers) still have a healthy interest in their trade, these long-forgotten skills, and the metals themselves.

ROBIN R. MUNDILL

Methodism

Davies, Owen, "Methodism, the Clergy, and the Popular Belief in Witchcraft and Magic", *History*, 82/266 (1997): 252–65

Davies, Rupert and Gordon Rupp (editors), *A History of the Methodist Church in Great Britain*, vol. 1, London: Epworth Press, 1965

Davies, Rupert A., Raymond George, and Gordon Rupp (editors), *A History of the Methodist Church in Great Britain*, vol. 4, London: Epworth Press, 1988

Gilbert, Alan D., "Religion and Political Instability in Early Industrial England" in *The Industrial Revolution and British Society*, edited by Patrick K. O'Brien and Roland Quinault, Cambridge and New York: Cambridge University Press, 1993

Hempton, David, *Methodism and Politics in British Society, 1750–1850*, London: Hutchinson, and Stanford: Stanford University Press, 1984

Rule, John G., "Methodism and Village Culture in West Cornwall, 1800–1850" in *Popular Culture and Custom in Nineteenth-Century England*, edited by Robert D. Storch, London: Croom Helm, and New York: St Martin's Press, 1982

Semmel, Bernard, *The Methodist Revolution*, New York: Basic Books, 1973; London: Heinemann, 1974

Thompson, E.P., *The Making of the English Working Class*, London: Gollancz, and New York: Vintage, 1963; reprinted, London: Gollancz, 1980

Valenze, Deborah M., *Prophetic Sons and Daughters: Female Preaching and Popular Religion in Industrial England*, Princeton, New Jersey: Princeton University Press, 1985

Walsh, John D., "Origins of the Evangelical Revival" in *Essays in Modern English Church History*, edited by G.V. Bennett and J.D. Walsh, London: A. and C. Black, and New York: Oxford University Press, 1966

Walsh, John D., "Methodism and the Mob in the Eighteenth Century" in *Popular Belief and Practice: Papers Read at the Ninth Summer Meeting and the Tenth Winter Meeting of the Ecclesiastical History Society*, edited by G.J. Cuming and Derek Baker, Cambridge: Cambridge University Press, 1972

Ward, William R., *The Protestant Evangelical Awakening*, Cambridge and New York: Cambridge University Press, 1992

Methodism before the death of John Wesley in 1791 has been less studied in recent years than has its history in the 19th-century, when it had split at last from the Anglican church, became the core of non-conformism in Britain, and itself divided into several separate sections, seven of which were identified in the 1851 religious census. For the 18th century, there have of course been many biographies of John Wesley, of his brother Charles and of their early associate George Whitefield, who so soon after the formative years around 1740 had broken away from the Arminian Wesleys to head a separate Calvinist methodism. The best starting-point, however, is the first volume of the history of the methodist church, edited by DAVIES & RUPP, which appeared in 1965 and serves well as a guide to the historiography up to that point. Useful alongside it is the fourth volume of this official history, edited by DAVIES, GEORGE & RUPP, which is devoted to documents and has an extensive bibliography. Among the contributors to this history is WALSH, whose several essays here and elsewhere make up a major contribution to our knowledge of 18th-century Wesleyanism. Two of these are especially valuable: his definitive explanation of the mob attacks on Wesley and the early methodists and his careful placing of the movement in the context of the Evangelical Revival. Equally distinguished as an historian of the movement is WARD. Although much of his writing is on the 19th century, his book on the evangelical awakening is essential for the wider background.

Following the work of the French historian Elie Halévy early in the 20th century, many historians have seen methodism as a conservative, even reactionary, force in its social and political effects. This view was restated with special force in a startling polemic in THOMPSON's classic study of the early English working class in 1963. For Thompson, methodism was not just counter-revolutionary by the 1790s, but it also gave to the new capitalists of the industrial revolution a means of reinforcing the new discipline needed by labour:

> They weakened the poor from within by adding ... the active ingredient of submission, and they fostered within the Methodist Church those elements most suited to make up the psychic component of the work-discipline, of which the manufacturers stood in most need.

A different view was put forward by SEMMEL in 1973, influenced by the style of social history then known as "modernization theory". He presented the revival as England's particular form of the "democratic revolution". Methodism in spiritual and in social terms, through what he considers to have been essentially a liberal and progressive ideology, helped advance England's transition from a traditional to a modern society, bypassing the need for an overt political revolution. He misleads a little, however, in presenting methodism as an essentially urban phenomenon appealing to the "poor of the nascent proletariat of England's growing factory towns", for the movement had special success in industrial and mining villages. In any case, even by the death of Wesley the factory proletariat was still very much in its infancy, while overall Wesleyan numbers were still too small to carry the full weight of the explanatory role placed on them by Semmel.

The most important contribution to methodist history of recent years has been HEMPTON's examination of the movement's relationship to British society and politics from the mid-18th century beginnings to the mid-19th century, a study which importantly takes in Ireland. Hempton's concern with politics is wider than the specific relationship to radicalism. The issues in which methodist communities took most interest were those involving religious freedom, the promotion of anti-slavery, and an increasingly significant anti-catholicism. Much energy, too, was consumed inside the movement in the management of its own polity. Diversity is emphasized, as is the tension between the undoubted conservatism of the Wesleys, and of later national leaders, and the possible radical tendencies of local chapel members. Hempton does not attempt to offer a clear answer. He leaves instead a picture of the complexities. GILBERT, however, has gone further to suggest that in early industrial England as the 18th century moved into the 19th, it was the moderate radicalism of the grass roots which became politically important, providing an undercurrent of protest and egalitarian sympathy.

Women have been given by Hempton the attention which they merit, for after all in the later 18th-century they exceeded men in methodist membership in the ratio of 3 to 2. Methodism at least spoke the language of spiritual equality and perhaps the movement's older historians were not unaware of women's key role, but if they were not silent, they were at least muted. Hempton suggests that this in part derives from the fact that women's role was less public and official and therefore less featured in the written documentation. Yet, he maintains, they were "the tip of the iceberg of Methodism's oral culture". VALENZE has written on women's role in the early 19th century and in the absence of a dedicated work on 18th-century Wesleyan women it is of much retrospective value. If anything, women are more likely to have played a fuller role in the former period and the lives of many of Valenze's female subjects spanned both centuries. She has stressed the role of cottage religion in enabling women to challenge the institutions and values of industrial society by insisting on the centrality of the home and the local community. Gender and anthropological approaches represent a way towards understanding the local life of methodism. DAVIES, for example, has interestingly discussed the relationship of popular methodism to folk beliefs in witchcraft and magic, as RULE has done for the Wesleyan stronghold of Cornwall. Methodism became a national presence of great influence, but its social history still needs to be sought in the mining villages of Cornwall, Wales, and north-east England, or the manufacturing communities of West Yorkshire and the West Midlands, and those other localities where it came early and grew strongly.

JOHN RULE

See also Identities, Regional: Cornwall; Protestant Dissent; Wesley

Metropolitan Police founded 1829

Emsley, Clive, *The English Police: A Political and Social History*, London: Harvester Wheatsheaf, and New York: St Martin's Press, 1991

Hay, Douglas and Francis Snyder (editors), *Policing and Prosecution in Britain, 1750–1850*, Oxford: Clarendon Press, and New York: Oxford University Press, 1989

Palmer, Stanley H., *Police and Protest in England and Ireland, 1780–1850*, Cambridge and New York: Cambridge University Press, 1988

Philips, David, "'A Just Measure of Crime, Authority, Hunters, and Blue Locusts': The 'Revisionist' Social History of Crime and the Law in Britain, 1750–1850" in *Social Control and the State*, edited by Stanley Cohen and Andrew Scull, Oxford: Martin Robertson, and New York: St Martin's Press, 1983

Radzinowicz, Leon, *A History of English Criminal Law and Its Administration From 1750*, 5 vols, London: Stevens, and New York: Macmillan, 1948–1986

Reith, Charles, *The Police Idea: Its History and Evolution in England in the Eighteenth Century and After*, London and New York: Oxford University Press, 1938

Reynolds, Elaine A., *Before the Bobbies: The Night Watch and Police Reform in Metropolitan London, 1720–1830*, Stanford, California: Stanford University Press, and London: Macmillan, 1998

Taylor, David, *Crime, Policing, and Punishment in England, 1750–1914*, New York: St Martin's Press, and London: Macmillan, 1998

The Metropolitan Police became a subject for serious academic study in the 1930s. Scholars' interests in the founding and development of the force differ in focus and tone, and their conclusions illustrate several points of contention. Central to the historiography of the Metropolitan Police are the questions of who wanted the police, why was the force founded when it was, and what needs central policing met. The orthodox view posits that the police were a state-led product of consensus among the governing elite, a progressive reform. Revisionist historians agree that elites created the force, but they claim that fears of political unrest, not perceived (or real) increases in crime, motivated lawmakers, thus imposing a mission of social control. A third group, striving for synthesis, have integrated the strengths of each view, forwarding theses that look beyond London, and beyond institutional or structuralist loci, to a more complex understanding of the interaction between the police and the policed.

Pioneering works by REITH and RADZINOWICZ established serious study of the origins and goals of the Metropolitan Police. Before their work, police histories were generally anecdotal. Both authors illuminated the chronology of the force's founding using previously neglected archival material, including parliamentary, local, and parish records, copious correspondence, and the enthusiastic pamphlet press. Both describe policing in the metropolis as inept and inefficient before 1829. The Metropolitan Police was the culmination of a progressive, inevitable movement towards change as critics of London's voluntary system of policing argued with complacent traditionalists over how to respond to increasing crime rates. Centralized policing promised a more orderly society by preventing crime; thus the modern preventative police were born. While contributing much to the narrative of the force's development, the consensus view concentrates almost exclusively on history from the view of the governors, not the governed. Little effort is made to examine the depth of support for centralized policing.

In the 1960s, scholars influenced by the revisionist theses of E.P. Thompson and others began to explore the history of modern police from the perspective of its targets, judging the police to be an institution of social control and repression. An excellent example of this conflict view is PHILIPS's contribution to Cohen & Scull, which incorporates many of the themes picked up by the conflict scholars. Arguing for an interdisciplinary approach to analysis of the police, Philips and the other contributors to Cohen & Scull explore the importance of structural innovations designed to manage the poor and to define and control industrial crime and political action. HAY & SNYDER's edited collection of essays continues this wide-ranging treatment of policing, looking at the role of police as prosecutors, thus reinforcing the notion that the police were one part of a new structure of repression, a hallmark of the revisionist or conflict view. Hay's excellent work in this field spans almost three decades. Inherently rooted in an understanding of social and political change as a function of class, the revisionists often assume that lawmakers had more foresight about the effects of the new police than the documents necessarily suggest. The revisionist histories of the police are, however, important contributions for an understanding of the connections between the police and other institutions established during the same era to redefine and manage class relations.

While he follows the conflict school to some degree, PALMER's compelling thesis argues that the Metropolitan Police was not England's first foray into centralized policing: the experiment had begun decades before, in Ireland. Fractious and fragile relations between protestant and catholic Ireland allowed the government a degree of experimentation in state-controlled policing not yet publicly acceptable in England. Results of those experiments influenced the form that England's central policing took from 1829. Palmer owes much to both the consensus and conflict views, and he synthesizes their strengths admirably, adding a new dimension to the history of the police with his explanation of the parallel development of the Irish and English forces. *Police and Protest* is a monumental work that provides perhaps the best bibliography available on the period from 1780 to 1850.

Critics of the consensus and conflict views charge that neither interpretation adequately explains the roots of the police, much less its purposes. Instead, the development of centralized policing can be explained by noting that, at its core, the Metropolitan Police owes its origin to middle-class perceptions that crime was indeed increasing, in numbers and intensity, and to fears of social conflict, amply reinforced by spectacular examples of violent political protest. One aspect of this synthesis view addresses the evolution of public attitudes towards the force. In his brief but thorough overview, TAYLOR deals with the problem of the police's acceptance in society, noting that the force initially faced intense opposition. Beginning in the 1880s, however, Taylor asserts that the police gained acceptance, having adopted more professional and more consistent policies.

EMSLEY has written numerous comparative works on policing, offering detailed analyses of the theoretical and practical considerations that shaped police development in Britain, Europe, and the United States. The most applicable of these works to the development of the Metropolitan Police is also the broadest in scope, chronologically. Modern police evolved in the 19th century partly in response to crime and political disorder, but the form that the force took was based more on considerations such as cost and accountability to local officials.

Elaine REYNOLDS, like Emsley, returns the debate to the issue of by whom, and how, the Metropolitan Police were formed. First, Reynolds places the beginnings of police central-ization and professionalism in the co-operation between London boroughs to better regulate the night watch, a century before the Metropolitan Police Act of 1829. Parliament eventu-ally formalized some of these arrangements. Others remained informal and practical. The Metropolitan Police Act was not, then, innovative, nor was it centred in state action. The gov-ernment centralized and extended many of the practices already in place at the local level. Central to Reynolds's thesis is an understanding that policing was neither inefficient nor ineffec-tive before 1829, and that an increase in crime was the central motivation for the creation of the Metropolitan Police, exacer-bated by complex social and economic changes.

V. SUZANNE BALCH-LINDSAY

MI5 and MI6
see Secret Services and Espionage

Military Logistics: Medicine and Supplies

Cantlie, Neil, *A History of the Army Medical Department*, 2 vols, Edinburgh: Churchill Livingstone, 1974

Creveld, Martin van, *Supplying War: Logistics from Wallenstein to Palton*, Cambridge and New York: Cambridge University Press, 1977

Gabriel, Richard A. and Karen S. Metz, *A History of Military Medicine*, 2 vols, Westport, Connecticut: Greenwood Press, 1992

Macksey, Kenneth, *For Want of a Nail: The Impact on War of Logistics and Communications*, London and Washington: Brassey's, 1989

Tyquin, Michael B., *Gallipoli, the Medical War: The Australian Army Medical Services in the Dardanelles Campaign of 1915*, Kensington: New South Wales University Press, 1993

A cliché in the discussion of military history is that amateurs argue strategy and professionals discuss logistics. It is certainly clear that no military campaign succeeds if the supply and medical services fail to meet their responsibilities. Unfortunately, there is little glory in hauling supplies, and if battlefield doctors sometimes win recognition as they risk life and limb to reach a wounded man, their many hours devoted to the proper mainten-ance of latrines and foot care are more likely to draw derision than the praise they deserve. Soldiers, themselves, often despise logistical duties and look down on those who hold them. Even in Prussia, where the general staff system developed during the 19th century, there was a long struggle over the acceptance of staff officers as the equals of line officers. Military historians have tended to follow the same sort of prejudices, and have devoted relatively little attention to logistical matters.

Although Gustavus Adolphus, King of Sweden and protestant champion in the Thirty Years War, is credited with the first modern effort to provide supplies to an army, most military forces continued to live off the land until the 19th century. General John Burgoyne's surrender at Saratoga during the American Revolution is an example of the problems caused by the inability to provide support to campaigns even at the end of the 18th century. Napoleon's armies were more effectively pro-vided with requirements, but the inability to maintain the lengthy supply line into Russia certainly was a factor in the failure of his invasion in 1812. Technological change, especially in the area of communications, produced much improvement during the course of the 19th century. The importance of rail-roads in the logistics of the American Civil War is clear evidence that supply was becoming one of the key elements in war. Nonetheless, at the very end of the century, the second Anglo-Boer War (South African War) began in October, largely because the Boers had to wait until the grass on the veld was adequately developed to feed their horses. The change in communications and hence logistics became clear with World War I which began as a primarily horse-drawn operation and ended with thousands of trucks carrying supplies and tanks helping to break the stale-mate of the western front.

Both MACKSEY and van CREVELD trace the evolution of logistics and the technology involved. Macksey is restricted to the modern (mid-19th century to the present) aspects of this evolution while van Creveld's canvas is larger. Both of these works are well written and clear, but the latter is significantly more extensively researched. In tracing the evolution of logistical systems over time, each historian emphasizes the tech-nological changes that made possible increased levels of support and discusses the ways that such increased support influenced the nature of combat and strategic decision-making. This pattern led, ultimately, to the global wars of the 20th century because the projection of force was no longer restricted to areas that would supply the needs of the troops and ammuni-tion for increasingly sophisticated weapons could be delivered as well.

The systematic provision of medical services for wounded soldiers is also modern, though it pre-dates the development of medical science to the point that much could be done to help the seriously injured. In the early modern era, the morale of mercenaries and later conscripted or volunteer troops was a growing concern, and a commitment to helping the wounded was a valuable boost. This pattern became increasingly signifi-cant as militaries became citizen armies fighting from national-ist sentiments. Caring for wounded men gave the sense that the sacrifice of the citizen was valued and encouraged others to continue to take the risk of injury. GABRIEL & METZ have surveyed the entire course of military medicine considering both the changing ability of doctors to care for the wounded and the socio-political aspects of providing medical services. Despite a number of unfortunate factual errors, their work is a truly major contribution to the understanding of this important aspect of military campaigning.

As medicine became increasingly sophisticated with the emer-gence of anaesthetics and later antiseptics, weapons, regrettably, far more than kept pace. This became painfully obvious in the American Civil War. Civilians carried aid directly onto battle-fields, and initial official disapproval turned to acceptance out of necessity. Europeans paid little attention to the lessons that were offered by the American conflict, and the British Army Medical Department found itself in great difficulty during the

Anglo-Boer War of 1899–1902. CANTLIE traces the development of the Medical Department as it evolved and changed, ultimately becoming the Royal Army Medical Corps. His volumes make an excellent companion to those of Gabriel and Metz to show the growth and development of military medicine specifically in the British army. TYQUIN's discussion of the medical problems during the Gallipoli invasion of 1915 makes clear that military medicine remained significantly limited during World War I, though it was improving rapidly when compared to even the recent past. Its failure at Gallipoli did, however, clearly add to the Australian and New Zealand disillusionment with Great Britain and the spirit of nationalism that moved those countries toward independence during the postwar era.

The explosion of knowledge in the 20th century has provided military doctors with such marvels as antibiotics (available only to Allied soldiers during World War II) and made military medicine better than even the wildest imaginations of a century earlier might have predicted. GABRIEL & METZ follow this pattern of improvement to the latter part of the century. In the end, modern weapons have been countered by improved tactics (dispersion of forces on the battlefield) and medicine to actually reduce death rates among casualties and eliminate disease as a major element in killing and disabling soldiers.

FRED R. VAN HARTESVELDT

See also Army entries; Army Reforms

Military Technology: Before Gunpowder

Bradbury, Jim, *The Medieval Archer*, Woodbridge, Suffolk: Boydell Press, and New York: St Martin's Press, 1985

Bradbury, Jim, *The Medieval Siege*, Woodbridge, Suffolk and Rochester, New York: Boydell Press, 1992

Brown, R. Allen, *English Medieval Castles*, London: Batsford, 1954; New York: Simmons-Boardman, 1961

DeVries, Kelly, *Medieval Military Technology*, Peterborough, Ontario and Lewiston, New York: Broadview Press, 1992

Hardy, Robert, *Longbow: A Social and Military History*, Cambridge: Stephens, 1976; New York: Arco, 1977; 3rd revised edition, Sparkford, Somerset: Stephens, 1992

Hyland, Ann, *The Medieval Warhorse: From Byzantium to the Crusades*, Stroud, Gloucestershire and Dover, New Hampshire: Sutton, 1994

Lewis, Archibald R. and Timothy J. Runyon, *European Naval and Maritime History 300–1500*, Bloomington: Indiana University Press, 1985

Nicolle, David, *Arms and Armour of the Crusading Era*, 1050–1350, 2 vols, White Plains, New York: Kraus International, 1988; revised edition, London: Greenhill, 1999

The history of pre-gunpowder military technology is contained largely in specialist publications focused on archeology, art history, and history of technology. But more accessible works

of synthesis exist as guides to the intricacies of different fields. And while in many areas there is little to distinguish British from more widely European military technology, the quintessential medieval British weapon, the longbow, has generated its own literature and debates.

DeVRIES is a good general introduction to the field of medieval military technology. Its topical rather than chronological arrangement is useful for investigation of particular types of technology, with sections on arms and armour, artillery (both gunpowder and non-gunpowder), fortifications, and warships. The notes and bibliography are good guides to further reading, and the author intelligently summarizes the state of debates such as the impact of the stirrup on mounted shock combat. Unfortunately for a subject based on the study of actual objects, illustrations are minimal. Every other source listed here, however, is well illustrated.

NICOLLE is basically a guide to the visual sources for arms and armour in the medieval world, both within western Europe and beyond. Hundreds of line drawings reproduce depictions of arms and armour from manuscripts, art, and statuary; the text for each drawing specifies the source and highlights the important details. A valuable glossary of technical terms and an extensive bibliography complete the work, though the list of secondary sources is somewhat dated.

Probably the most important personal weapon in use in the Middle Ages, from a British perspective, was the bow, above all the famous longbow used to such effect by yeoman archers against French chivalry in the Hundred Years War. BRADBURY, in *The Medieval Archer*, sets the longbow within a broader examination of archery in medieval England (and not just England, as Wales often provided substantial contingents of archers to English armies, especially after Edward I's conquest of that country), tracing not only the evolution of various types of bows technologically, but analysing their military uses and effectiveness and the social and administrative arrangements that brought masses of archers into English armies. HARDY focuses even more closely on the longbow itself; in addition to his examination of the social context of archery and its role as a weapon for both war and sport, he provides valuable scientific data on the materials, size, and power of the weapon through analysis of longbows recovered from the wreck of the *Mary Rose* from the reign of Henry VIII. The 16th-century date of the wreck also illustrates the long English adherence to their traditional weapon well into the age of gunpowder.

Outside of personal arms and armour, two military technologies were central to medieval warfare. The first was the castle. BROWN, a classic that is newly available in a reprinted edition, provides an educated tour of castle sites in England, illustrating along the way issues of castle design and construction, placement, and usage. BRADBURY's *The Medieval Siege*, though not detailed about particular castles, is much broader in scope. The author traces the rise of castellation in western Europe and its effect on patterns of warfare, and how those patterns and the use of castles evolved in response to such movements as the Crusades and the rise of centralizing monarchies. All this is explicated through the lens of sieges, one of the most common activities (along with pillaging – battles were relatively rare) in medieval warfare. Bradbury therefore also deals in some detail with the technologies and techniques created to attack castles, including siege engines, or pre-gunpowder artillery, and the laws and conventions of siege warfare. The latter is a good reminder of the culturally bound contexts of technology use.

The other central military "technology" of the pre-gunpowder age was the warhorse. An entire social class who formed the spearhead of medieval armies depended on specially bred, trained, and equipped animals to carry them to and then into battle. HYLAND is an excellent survey of this crucial living technology. Though broadly comparative in scope and method, with chapters on Byzantium, the Muslim world, and the Mongols, the work devotes two chapters to equestrianism in the Anglo-Saxon, Norman, and Plantagenet kingdoms. In the process, Hyland debunks the common image of the western medieval warhorse as a towering giant bred only for size. Rather, medieval warhorses were bred – often on specialized stud farms – to various sizes and capabilities that responded sensitively to such variables as military use (including weight of armour worn by horse and rider as well as style of fighting), climate, and terrain.

Hyland also examines the impact on horses of naval transport. This brings up a final area of military technology, warships. Although there were specialized warships in the Mediterranean – galleys powered by oars – naval warfare in the British world of the North Sea and English Channel was less specialized. Rougher seas prevented the widespread use of galleys, with their shallow drafts, so warships, whether of the Viking longship type or the later roundship, were usually little more than merchant ships filled with soldiers and perhaps fitted with a built-up castle from which archers could fire down at enemy decks. LEWIS & RUNYON is a solid survey of maritime technology and its uses, ranging from late Roman times to "the age of the English and the Hansa in the north" and the fusion of Mediterranean and northern shipbuilding techniques in Iberia which laid the foundation for Atlantic exploration and a new age of maritime connections and conflict. They devote considerable space to military aspects of maritime technology. As in the other books on this list, the presence here of a solid bibliography will guide readers to more specialized literature.

STEPHEN MORILLO

See also Architecture: Medieval Military; Metalworking

Military Technology: Gunpowder, Artillery, and Firearms

Hogg, Ian V., *A History of Artillery*, London and New York: Hamlyn, 1974
Hogg, O.F.G., *Artillery: Its Origin, Heyday, and Decline*, London: Hurst, and Hamden, Connecticut: Archon Books, 1970
Nosworthy, Brent, *The Anatomy of Victory: Battle Tactics, 1689–1763*, New York: Hipppocrene Books, 1990
Parker, Geoffrey, *The Military Revolution: Military Innovation and the Rise of the West, 1500–1800*, Cambridge and New York: Cambridge University Press, 1988
Partington, J.R., *A History of Greek Fire and Gunpowder*, Cambridge: Heffer, and New York: Barnes and Noble, 1960; reprinted, Baltimore: Johns Hopkins University Press, 1999
Rogers, H.C.B., *Artillery through the Ages*, London: Seeley, 1971
Rothenberg, Gunther E., *The Art of Warfare in the Age of Napoleon*, London: Batsford, and Bloomington: Indiana University Press, 1978

The revolution in military technology brought about by the introduction of gunpowder in the late Middle Ages and the subsequent evolution of artillery and infantry firearms, specifically the smooth-bore, muzzle-loading musket equipped with the socket bayonet, can only be understood within the wider context of the "military revolution" of the early-modern European era (roughly 1500 to 1800). Gunpowder radically changed the character of nation-state and dynastic conflict from battlefield tactics to siege warfare. It also increased the "stand-off" distance of weaponry as lethality moved from the direct hand-to-hand combat dictated by the dynamics of the sword, lance, and pike, to distances of thousands of yards by the Napoleonic period.

Building on the concept of a "military revolution" beginning in the early-16th century as championed by Michael Roberts in the 1950s, PARKER asserts that Roberts's concept of a radical change in the art, science, and political, economic, and social nature of European conflict understated the importance of advances in siege and naval warfare made possible by technological innovations in gunpowder weapons. Parker views the implications of those technological advances within the broader context of the rise of Western domination and the establishment of global empires between 1500 and 1750. Clearly, that technology gave the Western imperial powers a commanding advantage against the less-developed, older civilizations of India and Asia as well as the technologically primitive people of the Americas and Africa. In so doing, Parker provides a broad outline of the patterns of European warfare in the 16th and 17th centuries where the evolving gunpowder technology forced significant changes in the operational, tactical, social, political, economic, and technical nature of conflict. Any study of the evolution of gunpowder, artillery, and firearms is enhanced by this contextual background.

Similarly NOSWORTHY addresses the evolution of the battlefield, but at a much lower tactical level than does Parker. In fact, he intentionally defers the study of strategy and the operational art (wherein there is a wealth of existing historiography) to other analysts. In this regard the reader sees the practical result of the revolution in gunpowder, artillery, and firearms at the "sword's point", so to speak. By the late-17th century, the principal technological innovations had already occurred. Other than the profound revolution in military affairs and the conduct of war brought about by the *levée en masse* or citizen army of the French Revolution, and a few improvements in artillery performance and tactical field employment, little changed on the battlefield between 1689 and the early industrial age. Nosworthy provides the specific details as to how the profound technological changes between 1500 and 1700 transformed warfare at the tactical level in the century before industrialization.

ROTHENBERG takes the same tack as Nosworthy in exploring the art and science of war at the tactical level in the last great pre-industrial conflict, the Wars of the French Revolution and Napoleon. Rothenberg goes far beyond a simple analysis of the battlefield dynamics of artillery and firearms, providing a contextual background of the soldierly trade in the age of Napoleon including the organization and doctrine of the various branches of field armies as well as details of the soldiers' daily routine.

The above works set the contextual stage for the gunpowder revolution. Several valuable monographs provide the specific technical details of weaponry from the Renaissance to the Industrial Revolution. Though now dated, PARTINGTON was the first modern survey in English of the history of gunpowder, beginning with a discussion of the "Greek fire" of the Byzantine empire, the first use of mixed chemicals and fire in Western warfare. Partington then explores the early experiments with gunpowder and artillery in the late Middle Ages while questioning some of the myths surrounding the creation of these weapons. Of particular interest is his examination of gunpowder technology in non-Western cultures, especially the Muslim world, China (where gunpowder was first developed), and the Moghul empire of India.

O.F.G. HOGG sets the stage for the importance of artillery in pre-modern nation-state and dynastic conflict by quoting the Prussian King Frederick the Great: "Dont [sic] forget your great guns, which are the most respectable arguments of the rights of kings." Acknowledging that a full history of artillery would encompass numerous volumes, Hogg presents a "brief narrative of the gun and its ancillaries during the last six hundred years". He addresses broad principles of artillery rather than specific technical details. Although the work's scope exceeds the chronological framework by extending to thermonuclear warfare, it does provide a broad-brush survey of the development of artillery from the beginning of the gunpowder age.

ROGERS points out that the first definitive reference to artillery is found in a Ghent manuscript dated 1313. Like O.F.G. Hogg, Rogers examines the evolution of artillery from the medieval beginnings to World War II. Particular attention is paid to the tactical deployment of field and siege artillery and the interplay with other field branches, no doubt owing to the author's broad scope of publications and historiography in many arenas of military history.

Though primarily what might be described as a coffee-table book, I.V. HOGG's history of artillery provides a valuable visual account of the evolution of artillery through photographs, drawings, and diagrams. While it does not provide the depth of technical detail or the broader historical and analytical context of the other works, it is nonetheless a valuable complement to any study of gunpowder, artillery, and firearms.

STANLEY D.M. CARPENTER

See also Army entries; Army Reforms; Defence Capability; Navy entries; Nuclear Power; Royal Air Force

Mill, John Stuart 1806–1873
Utilitarian philosopher, political economist, and politician

Collini, Stefan, *Public Moralists: Political Thought and Intellectual Life in Britain, 1850–1930*, Oxford: Clarendon Press, and New York: Oxford University Press, 1991

Cowling, Maurice, *Mill and Liberalism*, Cambridge: Cambridge University Press, 1963; 2nd edition, Cambridge and New York: Cambridge University Press, 1990

Di Stefano, Christine, *Configurations of Masculinity: A Feminist Perspective on Modern Political Theory*, Ithaca, New York: Cornell University Press, 1991

Gray, John, *Mill on Liberty: A Defence*, London and Boston: Routledge and Kegan Paul, 1983

Haac, Oscar A. (translator and editor), *The Correspondence of John Stuart Mill and Auguste Comte*, New Brunswick, New Jersey: Transaction, 1995

Hamburger, Joseph, *Intellectuals in Politics: John Stuart Mill and the Philosophical Radicals*, New Haven, Connecticut and London: Yale University Press, 1965

Hayek, F.A., *John Stuart Mill and Harriet Taylor: Their Correspondence and Subsequent Marriage*, London: Routledge and Kegan Paul, and Chicago: University of Chicago Press, 1951

Himmelfarb, Gertrude, *On Liberty and Liberalism: The Case of John Stuart Mill*, New York: Knopf, 1974

Mazlish, Bruce, *James and John Stuart Mill: Father and Son in the Nineteenth Century*, London: Hutchinson, and New York: Basic Books, 1975

Mill, John Stuart, *Autobiography*, London and New York: Penguin Books, 1979 (first published, 1873)

Mill, John Stuart, *Collected Works*, general editor, John M. Robson, 33 vols, Toronto: University of Toronto Press, and London: Routledge, 1963–91

Mueller, Iris Wessel, *John Stuart Mill and French Thought*, Urbana: University of Illinois Press, 1956

Okin, Susan Moller, *Women in Western Political Thought*, Princeton, New Jersey: Princeton University Press, 1979

Packe, Michael St John, *The Life of John Stuart Mill*, London: Secker and Warburg, and New York: Macmillan, 1954

Robson, John M., *The Improvement of Mankind: The Social and Political Thought of John Stuart Mill*, Toronto: University of Toronto Press, and London: Routledge and Kegan Paul, 1968

Robson, John M. and Michael Laine (editors), *James and John Stuart Mill: Papers of the Centenary Conference*, Toronto: University of Toronto Press, 1976

Russell, Bertrand, *Portraits from Memory and Other Essays*, London: Allen and Unwin, and New York: Simon and Schuster, 1956

Ryan, Alan, *The Philosophy of John Stuart Mill*, London: Macmillan, and Atlantic Highlands, New Jersey: Humanities Press, 1970

Schumpeter, Joseph A., *History of Economic Analysis*, edited from manuscript by E.S. Schumpeter, New York: Oxford University Press, and London: George Allen and Unwin, 1954

Semmel, Bernard, *John Stuart Mill and the Pursuit of Virtue*, New Haven: Yale University Press, 1984

Skorupski, John, *John Stuart Mill*, London and New York: Routledge, 1989

Skorupski, John (editor), *The Cambridge Companion to Mill*, Cambridge and New York: Cambridge University Press, 1998

Stephen, James Fitzjames, *Liberty, Equality, Fraternity*, London: Smith Elder, and New York: Holt Williams, 1873; new edition, Cambridge: Cambridge University Press, 1967; Chicago: University of Chicago Press, 1991

Thomas, William, *The Philosophic Radicals: Nine Studies in Theory and Practice, 1817–1841*, Oxford: Clarendon Press, and New York: Oxford University Press, 1979

Thomas, William, *Mill*, Oxford and New York: Oxford University Press, 1985

In 1873 Mill died, full of accolades and acclaim. His *Principles of Political Economy* was regarded as the definitive work in most quarters, and his *System of Logic* had been taken up as the standard university text. While his "radical" views on gender and racial equality were widely regarded with disfavour, the man himself had triumphed as a lion of respectable liberalism. *On Liberty* seemed already destined for canonization as a classical text. To be sure, undercurrents of doubt and resentment were circulating, especially among the younger generation. A few months before the philosopher's death, STEPHEN launched the first full-scale attack. He would not question the authority of Mill's early, abstruse theoretical writings, on which he had cut his own intellectual teeth. But now, he felt compelled to take issue with what he perceived as the excessive liberalism and dangerous relativism of the philosopher's later work.

Where Stephen led, others soon followed. The revelations of the posthumously published *Autobiography*, with its paeans to Harriet Taylor and its ringing endorsements of her feminism, did not sit well with Britain's rising cohort of male, imperial intellectuals who were looking for a more manly and red-blooded creed. The Mill / Taylor obsession with individual rights and sentimentalism about the plight of oppressed peoples might be well and good for parlour intellectuals, but something more authoritative (perhaps even authoritarian) was needed by pragmatic potentates who were charged with the difficult task of bringing order to a wayward, recalcitrant world. Of course, the Young Turks of the 1870s became the Old Guard of the 1890s, and were supplanted by a third generation of "new liberals" in their turn. Shorn of his excess individualism, and recognized as a utilitarian precursor of their "new collectivism", Mill was reinducted into the pantheon of liberal patron saints. With the sudden explosion of the women's rights movement at the turn of the century, even his most aberrant crotchet was revealed to be prescient. *On the Subjection of Women* had brilliantly foreshadowed what was to become the liberal, egalitarian agenda for the 20th century.

And yet, at the very moment when Mill the feminist and libertarian was again becoming an inspiration for political activists, Mill the philosopher and economist was being sidelined and dethroned. In economics, the "marginalist" revolution had been at work since the 1870s, undermining the very foundations of the Ricardo / Mill orthodoxy. When the new synthesis was assembled by Alfred Marshall in 1890, Mill's *Principles* were definitively laid to rest (see SCHUMPETER). In philosophy and logic, a parallel trajectory could be traced: the supersession of the old, Aristotelian and inductivist systems by the modern, analytical, mathematical philosophies of Frege and Russell left Mill's *Logic* stranded in the shoals of an antediluvian backwater. According to RUSSELL (Mill's godson), he "was not a great philosopher like Descartes or Hume", and "deserved the eminence which he enjoyed in his own day, not for his intellect, but for his intellectual virtues", for example his ringing defences of progress and liberty.

In 1951, when this assessment was first issued, Mill's reputation had sunk to its lowest ebb. The appearance of PACKE's biography and, later, Robson's massive project of publishing Mill's *Collected Works*, began to lay the foundations for a more dispassionate scholarly reassessment. Nevertheless, the striking renewal of interest in Mill, from the 1960s onwards, is a reflection of the extent to which (more than at any time since his death) his life and work resonate with the perspectives and preoccupations of our day. The most visible source of Mill's new-found relevance has been the rise of the second wave of the women's rights movement. Indeed, for advanced feminists such as OKIN and DI STEFANO, Mill's (admittedly prophetic) formulations do not go nearly far enough today. Grounded in (partly implicit) assumptions of gender essentialism, drawn from Victorian notions of separate gendered spheres, his narrowly formulated demand for women's civic emancipation must remain, in their view, self-defeating and nugatory. By contrast, contemporary conservatives, such as HIMMELFARB and COWLING, have resurrected the charges of Stephen, denouncing what they perceive to be the amoral and even totalitarian implications that are latent in all the "radical" (i.e. Taylor-influenced) productions of the later Mill.

No less remarkable has been the revival of Mill among academic philosophers that has taken place during the last 30 years. This revival began in 1970 with the appearance of RYAN's book, and it has reached its culmination in the work of SKORUPSKI, and *The Cambridge Companion To Mill*, which he edited. During this time the "logical positivism" which displaced Mill during the early 20th century has itself been displaced by a new generation of more pragmatic philosophers who are considerably less detached from the phenomenal world. Uneasy with the "continental", "metaphysical" traditions that have lately been gaining ground, the new analytical philosophers have sought a lucid and logical but "naturalistic" and "empiricist" alternative in the Millite eclecticism which their predecessors had once so contemptuously disdained. For political philosophers, especially those on the Left, the intellectual crisis of Marxism and, in Britain, the impotence of post-Thatcherite social democracy have left a vacancy which Mill is especially well suited to fill. For those, like GRAY, seeking a systematic (but non-dogmatic) foundation for a post-welfare-state liberalism that remains at once steadfastly democratic but also soberly attentive to the degradation of public discourse and the danger of majoritarian tyranny, J.S. Mill is perceived as the best show in town.

The current Mill revival has generated a host of further specialized studies on a wide range of particular topics, whose diversity reflects the breadth and complexity of the man himself. ROBSON & LAINE offer a sampling of recent directions in research. MAZLISH provides a perceptive, albeit speculative, psychobiography which centres on the relationship between the elder and younger Mill. HAMBURGER, THOMAS, and COLLINI have greatly contributed towards placing Mill in his Victorian intellectual context. HAYEK's annotated collection of their correspondence allows the Taylor–Mill relationship to speak for itself. Mill's relationship with French intellectuals is treated by MUELLER, while HAAC has edited and translated his very important correspondence with Comte. Amidst all this flurry of recent specialized literature, one theme remains inadequately developed and imperfectly understood: Mill's innovative empirical vision of an historical social science, and his abortive effort to launch a new bridging social science discipline which he proposed to label "ethology". ROBSON's classic is the indispensable starting-point on these questions, and SEMMEL offers additional useful insights. Much work, however, remains to be done.

THEODORE KODITSCHEK

See also Bentham; Chadwick; Radicalism; Spencer; Utilitarianism

Millenarian and Radical Religious Movements   17th century

Capp, B.S., *The Fifth Monarchy Men: A Study in Seventeenth-Century English Millenarianism*, London: Faber, and Totowa, New Jersey: Rowman and Littlefield, 1972

Davis, J.C., *Fear, Myth, and History: The Ranters and the Historians*, Cambridge and New York: Cambridge University Press, 1986

Hill, Christopher, *The World Turned Upside Down: Radical Ideas during the English Revolution*, New York: Viking Press, and London: Temple Smith, 1972

Hill, Christopher, Barry Reay, and William Lamont, *The World of the Muggletonians*, London: Temple Smith, 1983

McGregor, J.F. and B. Reay (editors), *Radical Religion in the English Revolution*, Oxford and New York: Oxford University Press, 1984

Mack, Phyllis, *Visionary Women: Ecstatic Prophecy in Seventeenth-Century England*, Berkeley: University of California Press, 1992

Marsh, Christopher W., *The Family of Love in English Society, 1550–1630*, Cambridge and New York: Cambridge University Press, 1994

Thompson, E.P., *Witness against the Beast: William Blake and the Moral Law*, New York: New Press, and Cambridge: Cambridge University Press, 1993

HILL is the classic work on radical religion in the 1640s and 1650s and has been inspiring historians since its publication for the simple reason that the author makes 17th-century English history matter on a global scale. However, not all historians have been positively inspired by the author's attempt to explain religious radicalism within a Marxist framework. Revisionists have suggested that Hill's study of those – especially the smoking, drinking, and free-loving ranters – who sought to turn the world upside down during the English Revolution reflects radicalism in the late 1960s as much as revolutionary political and religious ideas in the 1640s and 1650s. DAVIS challenges Hill's interpretation of the Civil War sects by arguing that the ranters were no more than an invention of contemporary propagandists whose anxieties led them to exaggerate ranter numbers and the consistency of ranter thought, which in turn,

Davis argues, has led contemporary historians to do the same. Hill may have used some sources, such as Thomas Edwards's *Gangraena*, too uncritically, but the ranters clearly did not *not* exist even if they would fail the modern definition of a sect. (Hill explicitly writes that "it is extremely doubtful whether there ever was a Ranter organization".) Ultimately, though, Davis and Hill are both polemical in their different ways – if historians should not automatically take contemporaries at face value, readers should treat historians with similar caution.

The place to turn for short but highly informative essays on the major Civil War sects is McGREGOR & REAY. Barry Reay's introduction is helpful historiographically, and his essay on the quakers' socially radical, and anything but pacifist, beginnings is a concise statement of his longer book on the subject; J.F. McGregor in one chapter illumines the transition baptists made in the 1650s from sect to denomination, in another he takes a position on the ranters and seekers which should be read alongside both Hill and Davis; Brian Manning offers an interesting discussion of leveller arguments for religious liberty. Of equal interest are G.E. Aylmer's evenhanded essay on Gerrard Winstanley and Christopher Hill's short, provocative essay on the question of irreligion in histories of radical dissenters.

Bernard Capp's chapter on the Fifth Monarchists in McGregor & Reay is a full-bodied distillation of his book-length study of the ill-fated millenarians, but the reader should also consult CAPP itself, which is still the classic work on the subject. Capp's major argument is that the Fifth Monarchists were driven by their millenarian zeal, which for most of them faded after their political (and religious and economic) failure in Barebone's Parliament. But Capp also provides important information about their socio-economic composition and in so doing sheds light on their economic and political motivations, their geographical dispersal across England and Wales, and the reason why they were primarily an urban phenomenon. He also continues their story past Venner's rising in 1661 in order to explore their diminishing though not insignificant activities during the reign of Charles II. The quantitative side of Capp is excellent. One may wonder if, in light of the ranter controversy, his estimate that the Fifth Monarchists numbered around 10,000 in the 1650s is in fact too high. Capp himself admits this is a probable figure at best; but some contemporaries in that decade thought the riotous millenarians numbered as many as 50,000.

HILL, REAY, & LAMONT is the best work on the 17th-century Muggletonians and the sect's founder, John Reeve, and organizer, Lodowick Muggleton. Like many of the Civil War sects, the Muggletonians were anti-clerical, anti-trinitarian millenarians who believed that the soul died with the body until its resurrection in the Final Judgement; but Reeve and Muggleton were also unique in claiming to have been the two witnesses of Revelation. Reay's first chapter is the strongest in the book and manages to construct a fairly detailed picture of the social composition of the sect despite scarce archival records. At times the interpretations of Hill, Reay, & Lamont are at odds, at other points they overlap, but this apparent weakness is actually one of the book's strengths as the reader gets three angles on a complex subject in a single volume.

E.P. THOMPSON was a planned contributor to this jointly authored work, presumably to take the history of the

Muggletonians up to the 19th century (Muggletonianism technically lasted until the last believer and archivist, Philip Noakes, died in 1979). Thompson's contribution came ten years later in his book on William Blake in which he argues that Blake was profoundly influenced by both the doctrines and songs of the Muggletonians. Thompson spends a large chunk of his study showing the links between Blake and the sectarian and antinomian traditions of the 1640s and 1650s, but the reader gets along the way an impressionistic and inductively ingenious history of the *longue durée* of a religious sect that will be of interest to scholars of radical religion, Blake, and Thompson himself.

Thompson's methods are particularly impressive because of the difficulty involved in historical reconstruction on the basis of scant evidence. A number of authors discussed here have faced similar problems and have turned to new methods to make the elusive more visible. MARSH borrows the social microscope of microhistory, whose lenses were ground by Italian historians but refined by Marsh's mentor Margaret Spufford, in order to uncover the history of the English familists, the followers of the 16th-century Dutch mystic Hendrick Niclaes. Other historians have written on the familists, but Marsh's account is exceptionally sympathetic and reveals a number of surprises. One is that familists could be found at Elizabeth's and James's courts, among the yeomen of the guard, the officers of the Jewel House, the Armoury, and the Wardrobe; the other, related to the first, is that within limitations familists were actually tolerated by their contemporaries. This study is thus of wider importance in showing that by following the "footprint" left by the ostensibly marginal Family of Love, one can come to a better understanding of the larger issues of toleration and the power dynamics of court politics in the 16th and 17th centuries.

In the 1950s Keith Thomas noted the importance of women among the Civil War religious radicals, but the work that has really opened up this subject is MACK. Although on the surface this is a study of early quaker women, it is of broader interest for its treatment of the other sects, its contribution to gender and identity history, and the compelling issues it raises regarding the nature of belief and prophecy. Of more specific interest are the sections on Margaret Fell, Anna Trapnel, Eleanor Davies, George Fox, and James Nayler. The book also contains helpful appendices and a bibliography which should be useful to any student wanting to explore in further detail the various subjects this study raises. Americans received this book more enthusiastically than British reviewers, mainly because it is not entirely clear why, given the book's subtitle, the author decided to jump back and forth across the Atlantic. But this is a minor criticism.

MATTHEW KADANE

See also Baxter; Bunyan; Civil Wars, 1642–1651: Religious Issues; Independency in Religion

Milton, John

see Poetry: Restoration and 18th Century

Mining, Decline of 20th century

Ashworth, William, *The History of the British Coal Industry*, vol. 5, *1946–1982: The Nationalized Industry*, Oxford: Clarendon Press, and New York: Oxford University Press, 1986

Buxton, Neil K., *The Economic Development of the British Coal Industry: From Industrial Revolution to the Present Day*, London: Batsford, 1978

Fine, Ben, *The Coal Question: Political Economy and Industrial Change from the Nineteenth Century to the Present Day*, London and New York: Routledge, 1990

Kirby, M.W., *The British Coalmining Industry, 1870–1946: A Political and Economic History*, London: Macmillan, and Hamden, Connecticut: Archon, 1977

Supple, Barry, *The History of the British Coal Industry*, vol. 4, *1913–1946: The Political Economy of Decline*, Oxford: Clarendon Press, and New York: Oxford University Press, 1987

Without doubt any student of the decline of mining in 20th-century Britain must begin by tackling the large multivolume official history of the British coal industry originally sponsored by the old National Coal Board. Barry SUPPLE, the author of the volume that covers the first half of the 20th century, has eloquently written that the history of coalmining has become symbolic of the complex set of problems, obstacles, and impediments that plagued industrial Britain generally. Indeed, not only does the social and economic history of coalmining share much in common with Britain's other staple industries but the politics of coalmining have frequently reflected and epitomized the political issues facing society at large.

Supple's volume of the official history of British coalmining is at pains to argue that the economic decline of coalmining in the 20th century cannot be attributed to entrepreneurial failure. This complaint, that coalmining suffered from the failure of British entrepreneurs satisfactorily to restructure the industry by increasing the scale of workings, the mechanization of cutting or haulage, and the concentration of ownership, largely dates to the inter-war period itself; but it continues to dominate the historiography of mining. Supple argues that British mining was based on widely scattered units of production that produced for a variety of different markets. This fact alone made modernization a difficult and complicated task. Moreover, there were distinct institutional obstacles to the rationalization of the industry. For example, most colliery companies, even large-scale ones, were family-owned or closely held private companies or partnerships. The resulting fragmented structure of coalmining militated against co-operation with other companies, against large and continuous investments, and against a nation-wide system of industrial relations, all of which presumably would have been necessary for modernization. Other institutional obstacles to modernization included the legal arrangements for mining royalties, relations with the trade unions, and the ambiguous interests of government policymakers. Above all, however, Supple asserts that the most important obstacle to modernization was the nature of the market for coal, which was constantly threatened by overproduction and falling prices, and thus hardly conducive to either large-scale investment or rationalization.

ASHWORTH's concluding volume of the official history necessarily focuses upon the institutional objectives and policy constraints imposed by nationalization. He concludes that the commercial and financial operation of the industry was limited by the statutory prescription to provide a public service. This imposed significant restraints upon both the short-term management and the long-term strategic decision-making within the industry. Overall, Ashworth judges the performance of the industry in terms of output to have been "moderately satisfactory" but its financial results to have been a failure. Ashworth also emphasizes the fact that nationalization was intended in large part to improve industrial relations and in this as well the record is decidedly mixed. While there was no nation-wide strike after nationalization until 1971–72, localized and unofficial strikes continued to plague the industry. And while the nationalized industry was able to keep the industrial peace during the great contraction of the 1960s, from the late 1960s onwards industrial relations in the industry deteriorated decisively.

As noted above, much of the debate among historians has tended to focus on the inter-war period. KIRBY's account of the decline of British coalmining, for example, is presented as "a case study of State intervention within the framework of a free-enterprise economy". He emphasizes the importance of the Coal Mines Act of 1930, the two parts of which are claimed to have been inherently contradictory. Part I introduced a *de facto* cartel system in marketing and pricing while part II attempted to promote the compulsory reorganization of the industry through amalgamation. In Kirby's view, this Act signalled the beginning of a new period of increasing government intervention in the British economy, and not a very auspicious one at that. The Coal Mines Act, he suggests, ultimately functioned to inhibit and not promote amalgamation and rationalization (the goal of part II) because the creation of a statutory marketing cartel (the effect of part I) artificially sustained inefficient producers. BUXTON, on the other hand, attributes a major role in the decline of British mining to the relatively low rate of productivity growth and, consequently, the higher labour costs that existed in Britain than in her European rivals. He has argued that for a variety of technical and structural reasons, British coalowners were relatively slow to mechanize production, especially to introduce mechanical coal-cutters, which was necessary not only to meet foreign competition but also to offset the effects of diminishing returns.

FINE's more recent book adopts a thematic approach to the question and subjects to analysis many of the most prominent theories in the literature on this subject. He not only rejects Kirby's assumption that cartels necessarily inhibited rationalization, but he offers new empirical evidence that seeks to show that the marketing cartel never successfully limited production and that amalgamations were not slowed by government intervention. His detailed analysis of the functioning of the marketing scheme suggests that both the price and quota restrictions of the state-sponsored cartel were unsuccessful. Moreover, Fine also has rejected Buxton's argument that mining suffered from diminishing returns and exhibited few economies of scale. He thus questions the importance Buxton attached to mechanization and posits a potentially significant role for mine size in explaining increases in productivity. Finally, Fine has sought to revive both the theoretical and the empirical evaluation of the role played by royalties and patterns of landownership on the structure, financing, and rationalization of coal production.

In conclusion, while much interesting historical work has been done on the differing factors related to the decline of mining, much work still remains to be done. Many historians have shied away from incorporating the eras of nationalization and privatization into broader accounts, although Fine has perhaps gone furthest in an attempt to counter this tendency. Perhaps now is the time that such a perspective can be brought to bear on this important issue.

JAMES A. JAFFE

See also Electricity; Gas Industry; Nuclear Power; Technology and Employment

Missionary Movements

Berg, J. Van Den, *Constrained by Jesus' Love: An Inquiry into the Motives of the Missionary Awakening in Great Britain in the Period between 1698 and 1815*, Kampen: J.H. Kok, 1956
Porter, Andrew (editor), *Imperial Horizons of British Protestant Missions*, Grand Rapids: Eerdmans, 2002
Stanley, Brian, *The Bible and the Flag: Protestant Missions and British Imperialism in the Nineteenth and Twentieth Centuries*, Leicester: Apollos, 1990
Walls, Andrew F., "The Evangelical Revival, the Missionary Movement, and Africa" and "Missionary Societies and the Fortunate Subversion of the Church" in his *The Missionary Movement in Christian History: Studies in the Transmission of Faith*, Maryknoll, New York: Orbis Books, and Edinburgh: Clark, 1996
Warren, Max, *The Missionary Movement from Britain in Modern History*, London: SCM Press, 1965
Warren, Max, *Social History and Christian Mission*, London: SCM Press, 1967

Although there is a massive number of serious academic publications on the work of British missionaries in the Americas, Oceania, Asia, and Africa during the years 1792 to 1914, and despite the immense impact made by British missionaries on so many parts of the world, writers on the history of the British mainland in the 19th century have tended to ignore the missionary societies. The classic study of 19th century British Christianity, Owen Chadwick's *The Victorian Church*, does not discuss the societies at all.

VAN DEN BERG's study on the origins of the British missionary movements is a revision of his doctoral dissertation and is marked by his particular ecclesiastical background in the Reformed Church of the Netherlands. This is most clearly seen in his attempt to root the 19th century missionary movements in the traditional protestantism of the 17th century ecclesiastical establishments. However, he does work carefully through the founding of the missionary societies that were to dominate the British scene in the 19th century and makes clear that they were shaped both by the evangelical revival of the second half of the 18th century and by the Enlightenment. Despite his particular ecclesiastical perspective he recognizes that the missionary drive found its expression through voluntary societies primarily composed of lay people organized outside the formal ecclesiastical structures of dissent as well as of the establishments of both Scotland and England. He also indicates the close relationship of the early developments of missionary concern with the anti-slavery movement.

That relationship is a theme developed by WARREN in both his volumes of lectures delivered at Cambridge in the 1960s. Warren also reports in his second volume, although only in a preliminary way, on the social mix of those who made up the membership of the many local branches that were the lifeblood of these societies. He found that, at least in the first 70 years of the 19th century, both the people who supported the various societies and the missionaries the societies recruited were drawn from those then designated as "small trades people and skilled artisans". This was also the class that supported the anti-slavery movement and began the first co-operatives, yet little research has been done in this area of 19th century British history. He also shows – but again much more needs to be done in this area – that after 1870 a new evangelical spirit in Oxford and Cambridge led to a significant change in the social classes from which missionaries were drawn, particularly in the Church Missionary Society.

STANLEY focuses on the period from 1870 to 1914. He does take the story of the relationship of the British missionary movements to British imperialism up to the 1960s to some extent, and also looks briefly but perceptively at the pre-1870 period. This work is a uniquely important study for the understanding of the British missionary movements. While it is still a pioneering venture, the author's concentration upon the relationship of the missionary movements to British culture produces a series of important insights into the role of the missionary societies in the history of Britain. The very phrase British culture does raise one question-mark about the work, which is that it does not discuss the way the activities of some elements within the missionary movement challenged the concept of Britishness. A notable example of this is the assertion by Professor Shepperson, late of Edinburgh University, that the Scottish missions in Malawi, as well as being an expression of Christian missionary concern, were also an expression of a nascent Scottish national self-consciousness.

WALLS's lifework has been a radical reappraisal of the entire history of Christian missions. The two essays cited are centred upon the British missionary movements of the 19th century. Walls explores the roles of the British missionary organizations as popular movements that were outside normal ecclesiastical structures and establishments in the United Kingdom and constituted a challenge to them from within the Christian tradition. Again he makes clear how the 19th century missionary movements were an important element from within the Christian tradition challenging the centuries-old concept of Christendom that had survived, in secular as well as in religious thought, the challenges presented to it by the Reformation and Renaissance. The essay also recognizes that this was a difficult struggle that was still not over in 1914.

PORTER's volume of essays, to be published in 2002, is the product of a series of seminars held in the late 1990s. Although three of the essays follow the traditional path of analysing the interaction of missionary activity with African or Asian cultures, the remaining five essays discuss the interaction of the missionary movements with various currents in British politics and culture in the 19th century. Bebbington's essay discusses the relationship of the evangelical faith that underlay the missionary movements with British attitudes to empire. Stanley's and Maugham's essays deal with various patterns of relationship between the missionary movements, imperialism, and governments, including discussions of what, for them, constituted legitimate government. The essays of Ross and Mackenzie reflect upon the interaction of 19th-century science and the missionary movements, including attitudes to the physical environment and the nature and influence of what would now be seen as the pseudo-science of race.

ANDREW C. ROSS

See also Africa: British Interests to 1895; Evangelicalism; Exploration: Since the 18th Century; Livingstone

Modus Tenendi Parliamentum

14th century

Clarke, M.V., *Medieval Representation and Consent: A Study of Early Parliaments in England and Ireland, with Special Reference to the Modus Tenendi Parliamentum*, London and New York: Longmans Green, 1936

Galbraith, Vivian Hunter, "The Modus Tenendi Parliamentum", *Journal of the Warburg and Courtauld Institutes*, 16 (1953): 81–99; reprinted in his *Kings and Chroniclers: Essays in English Medieval History*, London: Hambledon Press, 1982

Prestwich, Michael, "The Modus Tenendi Parliamentum", *Parliamentary History: A Year Book*, 1 (1982): 221–25

Pronay, Nicholas and John Taylor, *Parliamentary Texts of the Later Middle Ages*, Oxford: Clarendon Press, and New York: Oxford University Press, 1980

Sayles, George Osborne, "Modus Tenendi Parliamentum: Irish or English?" in *England and Ireland in the Later Middle Ages: Essays in Honour of Jocelyn Otway-Ruthven*, edited by James Lydon, Blackrock, County Dublin: Irish Academic Press, 1981; also in his *Scripta Diversa*, London: Hambledon Press, 1982

Modus Tenendi Parliamentum is a relatively short medieval treatise on the workings of parliament. The English version of the treatise purports to be a description of how parliament functioned in the reign of Edward the Confessor, produced for William the Conqueror, which had received the Conqueror's formal approval and then constituted a blueprint for the functioning of parliament in the reigns of the Conqueror's successors. The substantially shorter, but clearly related, Irish version purports to be an authoritative instruction from King Henry II to his subjects in Ireland regulating the holding of parliaments in his newly conquered lordship.

The starting point for all modern scholarship on both versions of the treatise is the posthumous work of CLARKE. The earliest surviving manuscripts of the English version of the treatise were written no earlier than the 1380s. This led both Stubbs in his later work and Round to suggest that the treatise itself belonged to that same period. Clarke, however, argued that it was more than half a century older than that and that it belonged to the second half of the reign of Edward II, perhaps more specifically to 1322. She did not suggest a specific author for the work but did suggest that his interest in the petty detail of procedure was "deep enough to characterise him as a zealous and perhaps even a fussy bureaucrat". Stubbs had originally thought quite highly of the treatise but eventually came to judge it virtually worthless. Clarke, however, concluded that the similarities between its description of parliament and parliament as it existed in the second half of the reign of Edward II were sufficiently close to suggest that it had probably been written "as an honest, though tendentious description of Parliament" some time in that period. Clarke knew of the rediscovery in 1931 of an original *inspeximus* of the Irish version of the treatise dated 1419 in the Ellesmere Manuscripts in the Huntington Library in California, which had provided a *terminus ante quem* for that version. She suggested that the Irish version derived from the English version of the treatise, but that it derived from a French translation, not from the original Latin, though it had then been translated back into Latin. She argued that internal evidence suggested that the process of retranslation and adaptation for Ireland was associated with Richard O'Hedigan, Archbishop of Cashel from 1406.

GALBRAITH, while worried by the various statements in the treatise which were provably untrue, on balance accepted Clarke's relatively high valuation of the English version of the treatise. He accepted a date in the second half of the reign of Edward II, but argued that it could be placed no more specifically than between 1316 and 1324. Building on an earlier suggestion by W.A. Morris that the author was a clerical official connected with parliament, Galbraith proposed a specific individual, William Ayreminne, the probable clerk of parliament in this period, as the most likely author. In an appendix Galbraith attempted to refute the, as yet, unsubstantiated suggestion by Richardson and Sayles that the treatise was Irish in origin and that both belonged to the reign of Richard II.

In 1980 PRONAY & TAYLOR provided an accessible modern edition of the English and Irish versions of the treatise and provided a clear restatement of the reasons for assigning the English treatise to the 1320s. They suggested that the treatise belonged to the literature of the legal profession and that its author was most likely an anonymous lawyer. They did not think highly of the author's abilities but also argued that some of the difficulties in matching the treatise with parliamentary practice arose from the fact that the treatise was "probably never intended to be an exact description of a particular parliament" but rather a "statement of how a properly organized parliament ought to be held". In general they accepted Clarke's arguments about the date and provenance of the Irish version.

It was not till 1981 that SAYLES published a paper justifying the earlier views he and his collaborator, H.G. Richardson, had expressed half a century before, insisting on an Irish origin for the treatise. He did not claim that the English version derived directly from either of the two Irish manuscript traditions of the treatise now known. His claim rather was that a lost Irish original lay behind both the English and the Irish versions of the text. It was this alone that explained various features of the English version that appeared to fit the Irish parliament in the reign of Richard II, but not the English parliament in the

reign of Edward II. No particular author or particular purpose was suggested for the work but Sayles proposed that it belonged to a period shortly after 1381. Sayles associated the English version with an attempt to exalt the position of John of Gaunt and his son, the future Henry IV, and he considered the English version likely to have been produced in the later 1380s.

In an extended review of Pronay & Taylor, PRESTWICH also discussed the recently published paper of Sayles. He was not convinced by the arguments of Sayles for a late-14th-century Irish origin for both versions of the treatise, arguing that some of the allegedly Irish late-14th-century features were in fact also paralleled by English phenomena of the first quarter of the 14th-century and that others were simply a reflection of the "imaginative" nature of elements of the treatise. He was equally dismissive of Pronay and Taylor's arguments for seeing it in origin as a legal treatise, even if it later came to be associated with other legal tracts, and argued persuasively for an administrative origin and a bureaucratic author.

PAUL BRAND

Monarchy: England to 1603

Burns, J.H. (editor), *The Cambridge History of Medieval Political Thought, c.350–c.1450*, Cambridge and New York: Cambridge University Press, 1988

Burns, J.H. and Mark Goldie (editors), *The Cambridge History of Political Thought, 1450–1700*, Cambridge and New York: Cambridge University Press, 1991

Burns, J.H., *Lordship, Kingship, and Empire: The Idea of Monarchy, 1400–1525*, Oxford: Clarendon Press, and New York: Oxford University Press, 1992

Chaney, William A., *The Cult of Kingship in Anglo-Saxon England: The Transition from Paganism to Christianity*, Manchester: Manchester University Press, and Berkeley: University of California Press, 1970

Elton, G.R., *The Tudor Constitution: Documents and Commentary*, Cambridge: Cambridge University Press, 1960; 2nd edition, Cambridge and New York: Cambridge University Press, 1982

Fleming, Robin, *Kings and Lords in Conquest England*, Cambridge and New York: Cambridge University Press, 1991

Jolliffe, J.E.A., *Angevin Kingship*, London: A. and C. Black, 1955

Jones, Thomas (editor and translator), *Brut y Tywysogyon, or the Chronicle of the Princes*, Peniarth MS 20 version, Cardiff: University of Wales Press, 1952; Red Book of Hergest version, Cardiff: University of Wales Press, 1955

Kantorowicz, Ernst H., *The King's Two Bodies: A Study in Medieval Political Theology*, Princeton, New Jersey: Princeton University Press, 1957

Kirby, D.P., *The Earliest English Kings*, London and Boston: Unwin Hyman, 1991; revised edition, London and New York: Routledge, 2000

Lander, J.R., *Crown and Nobility, 1450–1509*, London: Arnold, and Montreal: McGill-Queen's University Press, 1976

Sawyer, P.H. and I.N. Woods (editors), *Early Medieval Kingship*, Leeds: privately published, 1977

Wallace-Hadrill, J.M., *Early Germanic Kingship in England and on the Continent*, Oxford: Clarendon Press, 1971

Warren, W.L., *The Governance of Norman and Angevin England, 1086–1272*, London: Arnold, and Stanford, California: Stanford University Press, 1987

Yorke, Barbara, *Kings and Kingdoms of Early Anglo-Saxon England*, London: Seaby, 1990; London and New York: Routledge, 1997

There are numerous biographical studies of individual English kings, and political studies of their reigns; but they are excluded from consideration here, both as being too numerous and not altogether to the point. The study of kingship as a method of government falls broadly into three periods, the early (or emergent), the feudal (or high medieval), and the Renaissance. A number of the works listed here study English kingship in its European context. Neither KANTOROWICZ nor SAWYER & WOODS is specifically concerned with England, although what they say about kingship in general is relevant. The two Cambridge histories edited by BURNS (1988 and 1991) contain essays on the whole range of medieval and early modern monarchy, and although only a minority of them are specifically concerned with England, so many of the characteristics of monarchy in those periods were of general application that a narrow focus is unreasonable. BURNS (1992) contains one chapter on the English crown, but it is an important study. The early Anglo-Saxon kings were semi-sacred figures, and before their conversion to Christianity often claimed kinship with the tribal gods, a theme explored (among many others) by WALLACE-HADRILL. Christian kings lacked that kind of supernatural credit, and instead tended to look to the church for additional legitimation, a search which lay behind the development of the rites of coronation and unction, a theme examined by CHANEY and by KIRBY. The evolution of England from multiple kingdoms into a single realm changed the scale rather than the nature of kingship, but by increasing the uniqueness and authority of the prince, reduced his dependence upon supernatural support. Both YORKE and Kirby explore this phase of development. The evidence for this period is limited and to some extent conjectural, so there are always likely to be disagreements about particular individuals, but there are no major conflicts of interpretation of which the student needs to be aware. There are a few very early charters to provide some record evidence, but most of the sources are literary. The same is true for the even sketchier history of the early Welsh princes, outlined in the *Brut* (edited in two versions by JONES). The tribal nature of their authority survived longer than in the case of the English kingdoms, and remained until the end of the native lines in the 13th century.

The medieval period begins in England somewhat before the Norman Conquest, a point made by FLEMING, who discusses the extent to which the relationship usually called "feudal" between a king and his mesne lords was already established under the Anglo-Danish and old English kings. Nevertheless, Norman kingship was distinct in several ways from its predecessor, and emerged as a blend of English and continental practices. The strength of English law, and the manner in which William and his successors chose to use that, eventually made England quite different from either Normandy or France, a theme explored by both Fleming and WARREN. In this respect the work of JOLLIFFE, although now rather old, is still extremely useful. He explores the consequences of Henry II's decision to exploit the common law for his own purposes, and his expansion of the system of governing by writ, and concludes that the unusual unity and institutional strength of the medieval kingdom arose largely from the success of that policy. It was precisely that strength which was challenged in the 15th century by the collapse of the personal authority of the king. At a time when, as BURNS (1992) makes clear, the theoretical pretensions of kingship were at their height, practical authority in England collapsed, exposing the weaknesses of any system based on personal rule. The authority of the English crown recovered, thanks to the personal competence of Edward IV and Henry VII, and LANDER examines the means by which that was achieved. However, the Tudors learned the lessons of the 15th century, and set out to widen the basis of their support. The monarchy was a national institution, established by God for the benefit of all citizens, and not a superior lord governing in the interest of his peers. Both the sacral nature of kingship, and its unique relationship with the common law (which was a communal law, not made by the king), steered the Tudors in the direction of what would later be known as a "constitutional" monarchy. The title of ELTON'S work on this theme is to some extent anachronistic, in the sense that there was no constitution in the 16th century. There was, however, an awareness that the monarchy was limited, not by powerful individuals, and not even by the church, but by the law, and by the need to obtain widely based consent. The strength of the institutional structure of English royal government eventually came to lie in precisely those forces which inhibited it. The common law and parliament which had been developed originally as instruments of the crown, survived and became stronger because of the political developments of the 16th century, so that the nature of the English crown in 1603 was significantly different from that of its European rivals. There is a very large literature on this subject also, but the essential guide is Elton.

DAVID LOADES

See also entries on individual monarchs; Identities, National: English; Lancaster, Duchy of; Modus Tenendi Parliamentum; Parliament entries; Privy (King's) Council; Purveyance; Revenue, Non-Parliamentary; Royal Supremacy; Union, Act of; Union of the Crowns of England and Scotland

Monarchy: Great Britain since 1603

Brown, Keith M., "The Vanishing Emperor: British Kingship and Its Decline 1603–1707" in *Scots and Britons: Scottish Political Thought and the Union of 1603*, edited by Roger A. Mason, Cambridge and New York: Cambridge University Press, 1994

Cannadine, David, "The Context, Performance, and Meaning of Ritual: The British Monarchy and the 'Invention of Tradition' c.1820–1977" in *The Invention of Tradition*,

edited by Eric Hobsbawm and Terence Ranger, Cambridge
and New York: Cambridge University Press, 1983

Davis, Leith, *Acts of Union: Scotland and the Literary
Negotiation of the British Nation, 1707–1830*, Stanford,
California: Stanford University Press, 1998

Flamini, Roland, *Sovereign: Elizabeth II and the Windsor
Dynasty*, New York: Delacorte Press, and London: Bantam,
1991

Hardie, Frank, *The Political Influence of the British Monarchy
1868–1952*, London: Batsford, and New York: Harper and
Row, 1970

Hill, Jacqueline, "Ireland without Union: Molyneux and
His Legacy" in *A Union for Empire: Political Thought
and the British Union of 1707*, edited by John Robertson,
Cambridge and New York: Cambridge University Press,
1995

Levack, Brian P., *The Formation of the British State:
England, Scotland, and the Union, 1603–1707*, Oxford:
Clarendon Press, and New York: Oxford University Press,
1987

Mason, Roger A. (editor), *Scots and Britons: Scottish Political
Thought and the Union of 1603*, Cambridge and New
York: Cambridge University Press, 1994

Morris, Marilyn, *The British Monarchy and the French
Revolution*, New Haven, Connecticut and London: Yale
University Press, 1998

Poole, Steve, *The Politics of Regicide in England, 1760–1850:
Troublesome Subjects*, Manchester: Manchester University
Press, 2000

Prochaska, Frank, *Royal Bounty: The Making of a Welfare
Monarchy*, New Haven, Connecticut and London: Yale
University Press, 1995

Robertson, John (editor), *A Union for Empire: Political
Thought and the British Union of 1707*, Cambridge and
New York: Cambridge University Press, 1995

The institution of the crown of Great Britain has undergone a tremendous transformation. In an important introduction to the topic, LEVACK explores how the unique British state was formed as England and Scotland moved from the Union of Crowns in 1603 under James VI and I to the Incorporating Union (Union of Parliaments) in 1707. The union of 1603, described as "dynastic, regal, and personal", was problematic from the outset. It did provide for a single sovereign ruler, but the crowns and lines of succession of the two countries remained distinct, and there was no legal, ecclesiastical, or economic unity. Moreover, the union seemed to many contemporaries to be artificial, impermanent, and weak. Throughout the 17th century, Levack contends, rulers beginning with James sought to strengthen the dynastic union economically and politically and thus attain greater political stability through a more effective administration over a more governable territory. The result of the complex negotiations of union was the treaty of 1707, which ended the personal union that had united the two countries, and which established instead one imperial crown, one monarchy, and one parliament of the United Kingdom of Great Britain, while retaining two systems of national law, two national churches, and two national identities.

Two collections of essays, each from a seminar at the Folger Institute, further delve into the origins, perimeters, definitions, limits, and consequences (Scottish, British, and European) of the union. MASON's collection focuses on the implications of the Union of Crowns in 1603 for Scotland in particular, exploring the range of political discourse (especially the positive and negative expectations for union found in pamphlet literature) in Scotland since the mid-16th century, and the problems of identity, self-definition, and status associated with multiple kingship. In particular, BROWN's discussion of the "vanishing emperor" illustrates the problem of maintaining Scottish identity within the regal union. James I had wholeheartedly sought a new dynastic tradition and a new British identity, but in his eagerness to combine the crowns, inadvertently began a tradition of absenteeism from Scotland, so that his descendant Queen Anne would consider herself English, an affront to Scottish nationalism.

Equally significant is ROBERTSON's collection, a companion volume of sorts, which challenges the prevailing conception that the union of 1707 was the result of mercenary and high-handed tactics (limited political and economic concessions, bribery, the suggestion of force), and that any serious debate over the issue was minimal. Instead, the collection focuses on the intellectual (and religious) context of the union. Viewing the union in a far broader context, as an international, not just a Scottish or even a British, event, the authors examine contemporary views and debates concerning the nature of empire, monarchy, sovereignty and union, and consider how those conceptions played out in the British Isles, Europe, and North America. An essay by HILL deals with Ireland's view of the union (a subject that could stand greater scrutiny) and its attempts to strengthen the Irish parliament while under the grip of the English crown. Both of these collections reveal the complexity of the union debate and make an important contribution to the understanding of the British empire.

Taking a more literary approach to the question, DAVIS examines the writings of Scottish and English writers from 1707 to 1830, and the role these authors played in the negotiation of British identity and the imagining of the nation after the union of Great Britain. The nation, Davis claims, was not homogeneous, but rather a space that was simultaneously contested and unitary. By examining the literary dialogue and discursive encounters of certain authors (all male, as it should be pointed out), including Daniel Defoe, Henry Fielding, William Wordsworth, Robert Burns, and Walter Scott, Davis reveals an instability of identity and insecurity over the conception of "nation". In their writings, too, these authors helped invent, and continually renegotiate, the nature, scope, and limits of the union. Although the text is well argued overall, Davis employs a post-colonial theory of national identity that is at times ambiguous and awkward.

In a landmark study, CANNADINE offers great insight into the changing meanings of royal ritual, pageantry and the "secular magic of monarchy" in the modern period. Consciously following a Geertzian model of "thick" description, Cannadine outlines four phases in ceremonial image that developed at the end of the monarchy's real and effective power. Before the 1870s, ritual was inept, private, and of limited appeal due to the monarchy's immense lack of popularity. At the end of Victoria's reign, as the queen became an admired matriarchal figure and London began to regain its national prominence, ceremonies involving the monarchs became elaborate, splendid, and popular. The period before World War I, Cannadine contends, marked the height of "invented tradition" as traditional ceremonies were staged with flair and skill, and new ceremonies outlining the grandeur of the monarchy were self-consciously created. The monarchs appeared to head the nation as their European counterparts did, but of course no longer wielded real power. From the end of World War I to the time of Queen Elizabeth's coronation in 1953, royal ceremonies seemed to embody "consensus, stability, and community" in a time when Great Britain was in its last moments as a leading world power. The media helped convey the grandeur of the monarchy, using awed, hushed tones, refusing to criticize even during such scandalous moments as the abdication crisis. From the 1950s, the media further helped create a fairytale image of monarchy by broadcasting royal ceremonies in which the viewing public could vicariously participate.

MORRIS, loosely following Cannadine's model of invented tradition, suggests that George III's reign, combined with the French Revolution's influence on public discourse, marks the advent of modern kingship and the beginning of monarchy as a cultural icon of British heritage. Since the 17th century, Morris argues, monarchs had refashioned ideas, traditions, and even themselves in order to maintain a semblance of continuity and legitimacy in times of chaos. With the Hanoverian kings, Morris asserts, the monarchy became both demystified and humanized through newspaper press and caricature. By the end of the 18th century, aspects of the modern monarchy had been established. The monarch was working peaceably with the Commons; the political role of the monarchy was diminishing; the public and the press had a new intimacy with the royal family; and royal vice was viewed with amusement. Increasingly, the monarchy was viewed as a tradition-bound institution that underscored the greatness of the nation, even as the crown grew increasingly impotent. This book provides an important overview of the debate over the monarchy, and the contradictions of this subject found in the popular press, in the late-18th century.

In an innovative approach, POOLE examines how the subjects' petitions, in their demands and expectations, helped shape the monarchy. Just as the monarch appeared to retain some semblance of divine right with "the touch" that could cure scrofula, so the petition seemed a magical – albeit secular – document that proved the reciprocal relationship between monarch and subject. In particular, Poole contends that 18th- and 19th-century regicides, while viewed by contemporaries as exemplars of lunacy and "mad politics", actually demonstrate the failure of petitioning and a growing retraction of royal space. By the 18th century, the monarchy had begun to retreat from approachability. Queen Victoria and Prince Albert, often considered the epitome of modern monarchy, were available to the public through their spectacular display, but far less approachable to the individual petitioner.

The monarchy of the last few decades has been the subject of a number of biographies like FLAMINI's popular (but indifferently referenced) sketch of Queen Elizabeth II and her attempts as sovereign to exceed her constitutional limits. Generally speaking, the modern monarchy has received very little scholarly attention by serious researchers, who perhaps have equated the lack of royal power with a lack of royal influence. In 1970, however, HARDIE traced the decline of the monarchy's political influence in domestic affairs and foreign affairs between 1868 and 1952, and noted the crown's gradual move towards political neutrality, in what seems to be an overlooked, but important, insight.

Another notable exception is PROCHASKA's praise-filled discussion of the modern monarchy's philanthropic tradition and public identification with popular causes like healthcare and education. Although its political significance has waned considerably, the royal family still holds an important symbolic presence. Since the 18th century, Prochaska points out, the royal family has been associated with respectability, patriotism, and charitable patronage. The monarchy has long possessed a sense of duty to civil society, but only in recent decades have members of the royal family seemed cognizant of the intangible benefits and public goodwill reaped by their charitable efforts. Although the monarchy steadily lost political clout throughout the 17th and 18th centuries, as an institution, the crown reshaped itself in the 19th and 20th centuries, allowing the tradition of constitutional monarchy to endure and to retain its longstanding social influence.

SUSANNA CALKINS

See also Anglican Establishment; British Republic; Civil Wars entries; entries on individual monarchs; Hanoverian Succession; Jacobite Rebellions; Jacobitism; Parliament entries; Republicanism; Stuart, Charles Edward; Stuart Claimants (1689–1746); Union, Act of; Union of the Crowns of England and Scotland

Monarchy, Attacks on

19th and 20th centuries

Brendon, Piers and Philip Whitehead, *The Windsors: A Dynasty Revealed*, London: Hodder and Stoughton, 1994; revised edition, London: Pimlico, 2000

Cannadine, David, *History in Our Time*, New Haven, Connecticut and London: Yale University Press, 1998

Donaldson, Frances, *Edward VIII*, London: Weidenfeld and Nicolson, 1974; Philadelphia: J.B. Lippincott, 1975

Hibbert, Christopher, *The Royal Victorians: King Edward VII, His Family, and Friends*, Philadelphia: J.B. Lippincott, 1976; as *Edward VII, A Portrait*, London: Allen Lane, 1976

Inglis, Brian, *Abdication*, New York: Macmillan, and London: Hodder and Stoughton, 1966

Lacey, Robert, *Majesty: Elizabeth II and the House of Windsor*, New York: Harcourt Brace Jovanovich, and London: Hutchinson, 1977

Martin, Kingsley, *The Magic of The British Monarchy*, Boston: Little Brown, 1962; as *The Crown and the Establishment*, London: Hutchinson, 1962

Rose, Kenneth, *King George V*, London: Weidenfeld and Nicolson, 1983; New York: Knopf, 1984

Wilson, A.N., *The Rise and Fall of the House of Windsor*, New York: Norton, and London: Sinclair-Stevenson, 1993

Ziegler, Philip, *King Edward VIII*, London: Collins, 1990; New York: Knopf, 1991

Though it might seem that the last decade of the 20th century appeared to manifest the strongest criticisms of the English monarchy, the fact is that agitation against the crown has been frequent since the beginning of the 1800s. Moreover, there were times when the public attack on the monarchy seemed to be significant and effective. Recent scholarship has shed light on this issue both in a historical context and of late.

Kingsley MARTIN, for instance, in a valuable study has pointed out the contempt in which George IV was held thanks to his profligate life-style and the spectacle of attempting to divorce his wife, Queen Caroline. Quoting from *The Times* and other periodicals, he illustrates the lack of respect and the sense of ridicule that was directed toward him. And while his successor, William IV, was married and seemed kinder and gentler, his erratic and crude behaviour also appeared to lower the reverence in which the crown was regarded.

Martin also demonstrates that Queen Victoria encountered a wave of attacks from a number of important political figures, including Bradlaugh and Dilke, as well as other aspects of public opinion, for the way she withdrew from the scene after the death of Prince Albert. Questions were raised about where all of the money was going, if she was not attending to her official duties. Thanks, however, to Disraeli's transformation of the queen into an empress and the veneration in which she was held by the end of the reign, the threat of republicanism had vanished. There was also criticism of Victoria based on her preference for the Conservative Party. As one wag put it, she advised the Tories and warned the Liberals.

In the case of Edward VII, as Martin notes, there was a good deal of scepticism based on his career as Prince of Wales. The fact that, among other things, he was named as a correspondent in a divorce case, raised questions about his suitability for the throne. Christopher HIBBERT also echoes this theme in his study of the king, suggesting that his recovery from a life-threatening illness helped to restore the public's goodwill toward him. In addition, Edward was also criticized for his preoccupation with his mistresses.

Two good monographs on the monarchy in the 20th century are Robert LACEY's *Majesty* and more recently *The Windsors* by BRENDON & WHITEHEAD, which accompanied a recent television series. Both of them acknowledge the major contribution that George V made to establishing the popularity and respectability of the royal family, but at the same time recognize that during World War I, his Germanic ties became such an important issue that he was obliged to change the family name from Saxe-Coburg Gotha to Windsor. Moreover, as Kenneth ROSE noted in his biography, he was prevented from offering asylum to his cousin, the tsar, for fear of public opinion.

The abdication of his son, Edward VIII, does, of course, loom large as an event in the history of the monarchy. Brian INGLIS has written an able study of the abdication itself, while Frances DONALDSON and Philip ZIEGLER have produced very important biographies of Edward himself. These studies reveal that, although the king had some popular support as well as the assistance of figures like Churchill and Beaverbrook, there was also widespread opposition to his decision to marry a twice-divorced American woman. Moreover, the king's neglect of duties, interference with foreign policy on behalf of Germany, and lack of realism were fatal flaws. Thus, although he had

seemed to betoken a new-style modern monarchy, Edward proved unequal to that task.

While George VI and his wife, Queen Elizabeth, get high marks, especially for their wartime service and restoration of the crown after the abdication, the reign of the present Queen Elizabeth II has witnessed a strong wave of agitation against the monarchy. This has been chronicled in such studies as that by A.N. WILSON and also in the essays of David CANNADINE. Some of it is economic criticism of the crown's wealth generated by the social conditions of the Thatcher era, but most has to do with the dysfunctional family which the Windsors have become. The divorces of three of her four children, as well as that of her sister, and the behaviour of the Duchess of York, the Prince of Wales and the late Princess Diana, has led a headline-seeking press to focus on the life-styles of the Windsors. The death of Princess Diana, and the unleashing of pro-Diana anti-Windsor popular feeling, created another sensation. Yet the disappearance of Diana as a focal point of, and catalyst for, popular discontent with the royal family and monarchical institutions also freed the Windsors from a frenzied level of journalistic obsession. In the calmer beginnings of the 21st century, the credibility of the monarchy has risen from mid-1990s slump.

Scholarship has responded to this turn of events in a variety of ways. In the controversial 1990s some argued that Charles might forgo his rights to the throne, and Wilson, writing in 1993, goes so far as to suggest the Duke of Gloucester as an alternative. Cannadine is perhaps more in line with current thinking in suggesting the future lies with a toned-down monarchy with fewer titles, subsidies, and privileges. With the queen now paying taxes, selling the royal yacht, and cutting down on those in her gift, this seems to be the direction the crown will take.

MARC L. SCHWARZ

See also Republicanism

Monasticism: Early

Barlow, Frank, *The English Church, 1000–1066: A Constitutional History*, London: Longman, and Hamden, Connecticut: Archon, 1963

Blair, John and Richard Sharpe (editors), *Pastoral Care before the Parish*, Leicester and New York: Leicester University Press, 1992

Foot, Sarah, *Veiled Women*, 2 vols, Aldershot, Hampshire and Burlington, Vermont: Ashgate, 2000

Gransden, Antonia, "Traditionalism and Continuity during the Last Century of Anglo-Saxon Monasticism", *Journal of Ecclesiastical History*, 40 (1989): 159–207; reprinted in her *Legends, Traditions, and History in Medieval England*, London and Rio Grande, Ohio: Hambledon Press, 1992

Hughes, Kathleen, *The Church in Early Irish Society*, London: Methuen, and Ithaca, New York: Cornell University Press, 1966

Knowles, David, *The Monastic Order in England: A History of its Development from the Times of St Dunstan to the*

Fourth Lateran Council, 943–1216, Cambridge: Cambridge University Press, 1940; reprinted with corrections, 1949; 2nd edition, Cambridge University Press, 1963

Mayr-Harting, Henry, *The Coming of Christianity to Anglo-Saxon England*, London: Batsford, 1972; as *The Coming of Christianity to England*, New York: Schocken Books, 1972; 3rd edition, University Park, Pennsylvania: Pennsylvania State University Press, 1991

Morris, Richard, *Churches in the Landscape*, London: Dent, 1989

Parsons, David (editor), *Tenth-Century Studies: Essays in Commemoration of the Millennium of the Council of Winchester and Regularis Concordia*, London: Phillimore, 1975

Sharpe, Richard, "Some Problems concerning the Organisation of the Church in Early Ireland", *Peritia*, 3 (1984): 230–70

The origins and development of monasticism in pre-Conquest Britain is a subject beset by the difficulties of determining how monasteries themselves should be defined. Prior to the 10th-century monastic reform movement in England, which fostered the standardization of monastic houses and uniform observance of the Benedictine rule, there was no clear definition of the Latin term *monasterium* and its Old English equivalent *mynster*. The nature, function, and role of early Anglo-Saxon monasteries has thus been the subject of a debate which is particularly focused upon the extent of their participation in a pastoral "system". MAYR-HARTING is useful for the overall context of conversion and the influence of Irish, Roman, and Frankish religious models on the foundation of early religious houses. He pays particular attention to Northumbrian monasticism and there are useful summaries of scholarship, prayer, and worship. The debate about the nature of *mynsters* has been a lively feature of several recent specialist articles. A book-length introduction to the subject and other aspects of the pastoral work of the church dealing both with Celtic Britain and Ireland and with Anglo-Saxon England is provided in BLAIR & SHARPE, where all the essays require consultation. Sarah Foot's analysis of the terminology used to define early Anglo-Saxon religious communities concludes that the term *mynster* covered a diverse range of communal institutions, both male and female, including those concerned with the contemplative life and those concerned with ministry to the laity. Such institutions, ruled by abbots and abbesses, were distinguished from those ruled by bishops. The source material is crucial to the debate since it is overwhelmingly composed by monks. The legislation of church synods, noted by Cubitt in the same volume, suggests that priests, and *canonici* (clerks) may well have played a more vital role in pastoral organization than a monastic writer such as Bede implies.

Whereas the early Anglo-Saxon church is marked by a diversity of religious institutions – *monasteria* differing from yet interacting with episcopal sees – the religious history of the Celtic world has tended to be dominated by a view which emphasizes the importance of monasticism and the administrative power of abbots at the expense of episcopally organized communities. HUGHES examined the supposed transition from diocesan to monastic organization said to have taken place in early Ireland and concluded that it "did not happen so rapidly or so uniformly". Her analysis focused around the aims of two opposed parties in the church: the *Romani*, who wished to see greater episcopal control, and a more nativist group who adhered to a system of non-territorial monastic *paruchiae* (confederations of monastic houses), the nativist group emerging as dominant. Recent analysis, most notably by SHARPE, has, however, questioned the existence of any firm organization at all and considers "the assumption that a monastery is a place where monks live the religious life bound by vows . . . under the rule of an abbot, and that an episcopally administered church is different" not to be evident from the sources. To perceive monasticism as the only form of early Irish ecclesiatical organization is, in Sharpe's view, erroneous. Questioning of the overwhelmingly monastic character of the Welsh church is undertaken by Huw Pryce's essay in Blair & Sharpe while the same volume also contains an important survey of the situation in Scotland, where, as houses composed of a group of secular priests serving a large parish became more common, monasticism was to become increasingly eremitic in nature.

Monasteria became more rigidly defined in 10th-century England. Uniformity, regular observance of the Benedictine rule, and the importance of continental practice dominated the 10th-century monastic reform movement undertaken at the behest of three notable clerics: Æthelwold, Oswald, and Dunstan, with the aid of royal support. Monasticism, moreover, became a central element in the organization of cathedral communities as clerks were expelled and replaced by monks. PARSONS is a valuable collection of essays on this subject and the three reformers themselves have all been the subject of essay collections. KNOWLES is the classic account of the "second golden age" of monasticism and is useful for charting the distribution of monastic houses and discussion of their commitment to Benedictinism. BARLOW also provides a valuable survey, dealing with royal patronage of religious houses, the manner in which religious houses came within the aspirations of the aristocracy in an increasingly fragmented political climate, their role as the source for governmental administrators and advisers, and the question of whether late Anglo-Saxon monasticism fell into stagnation after the vibrant efforts of the reform movement. Whereas BARLOW argues for little evidence of cultural activity in monasteries of the late 10th and 11th centuries, GRANSDEN finds cultural vibrancy, in Latin and the vernacular, and considers a lively interest in history, especially the writings of Bede, to have set the cultural agenda for abbeys such as Abingdon, Evesham, and Ramsey on the eve of the Conquest.

Female monastic houses were a key element in the monastic life of this period. Early houses were often double monasteries, mixed communities of men and women such as Whitby, but segregation became more prominent with the 10th-century reform. Royal princesses and powerful aristocratic women, however, remained patrons, founders, and rulers of houses. FOOT shows how the "disappearance" of female communities can be explained by the fact that the later Anglo-Saxon religious woman expressed her devotion outside the cloistered monastery through the medium of the family as a vowed and veiled woman. Such small-scale communities, while ephemeral, nevertheless existed and provided an alternative for the exercise of female spirituality when larger nunneries declined due to the upheaval of war and women's inability to fulfil the full liturgical functions of the church.

Monastic settlement patterns are explored in MORRIS. Pre-Viking sites were often former Iron Age forts or Roman towns. After *c*.850 several important churches were liturgically enlarged but less is known about other aspects of monastic planning. Morris, along with Blair, sees monasticism as a central element in the church's pastoral provision.

SIMON COATES

See also Anglo-Saxon England: Church entries; Bede's *Ecclesiastical History*; Biscop; Columba; Columbanus; Cuthbert; David; Dunstan; Patrick; Wilfrid; Willibrord

Monasticism, Later Periods

see Catholic Church (since 1560); Gilbert of Sempringham; Dissolution of Religious Houses and Chantries; Religious Orders entries

Monck, George, 1st Duke of Albemarle 1608–1670

Military commander

Ashley, Maurice, *General Monck*, London: Jonathan Cape, 1977

Davies, Godfrey, *The Restoration of Charles II, 1658–1660*, San Marino, California: Huntington Library, 1955; London: Oxford University Press, 1969

Dow, F.D., *Cromwellian Scotland, 1651–1660*, Edinburgh: John Donald, 1979

Griffith Davies, J.D., *Honest George Monck*, London: John Lane, 1936

Hutton, Ronald, *The Restoration: A Political and Religious History of England and Wales, 1658–1667*, Oxford: Clarendon Press, and New York: Oxford University Press, 1985

Hutton, Ronald, *The British Republic, 1649–1660*, Basingstoke: Macmillan, 1990; 2nd edition, 2000

Jamison, Ted R., *George Monck and the Restoration: Victor without Bloodshed*, Fort Worth, Texas: Texas Christian University Press, 1975

Warner, Oliver, *Hero of the Restoration: A Life of General George Monck, 1st Duke of Albemarle, KG*, London: Jarrolds, 1936

Not surprisingly, perhaps, his own contemporaries reached no consensus on George Monck and his role as a key instrument of both the English republic and the Restoration. The sermon preached at his funeral compared him with Moses and Gideon: "God was pleased to raise him up to be our Deliverer", the man responsible for the return of the Stuarts in 1660. Contemporary biographies by two of his chaplains sang his praises. Thomas Gumble's *Life of General Monck* (1671) depicted the great general as the father both of the army and of the country. Thomas Skinner's *Life* (published much later in 1723) praised

his political wisdom and principles. Others, however, were hostile. Clarendon and Burnet disliked him; Clarendon called him "an uninspired lout, an opportunist". Pepys, his subordinate in the Admiralty, was unimpressed. John Toland thought that "Monck's dissimulation, treachery, and perjury are like to remain unparalleled in history". Later historians of the 18th and 19th centuries continued to be divided in their assessments. Hume was impressed by his moderation in an age of extremes. Conversely, for Macaulay and Guizot Monck lacked principles.

There continues to be a lively interest in Monck among 20th-century historians. Two books published in 1936 provide the starting-point. WARNER's, without references, bibliography, or even chapter headings, was a chronologically arranged work of popularization. It concentrated on the swashbuckling drama of Monck's life and depicted him chiefly as a soldier. "He was never an imaginative man but he was naturally a brave one". Warner claimed for Monck the main responsibility for the unconditional Restoration that took place in 1660 and underlined how the general's own lack of religious fervour instilled in him an antipathy to fanaticism in others. Monck's greed, in this study as in others, comes across as his most unpleasant characteristic. "Every other passion in time bowed before his avarice. ... He served for money, and the money came". GRIFFITH DAVIES's book, the second offering of 1936, with its 57 pages of documentary appendices, was aimed at a more antiquarian readership. Its chief points were to depict Monck as a professional soldier who broke the power of the army over politics, as a double dealer among double dealers in 1658–60, and ultimately as a tragic figure in that the Restoration settlement "was nothing like the thing he hoped for when he negotiated for the return of the exiled king".

JAMISON aimed to rescue Monck from his contemporary and later critics. Though he was no Marlborough, Monck's role was politically crucial and was underpinned by a deep-rooted consistency. A true patriot, Monck is presented here as "the eternal royalist" who never gave up his determination to serve the Stuarts again between 1644 and 1659, even though circumstances dictated that in this interlude he should do the bidding of parliament and the republic. His merits as a soldier are rehearsed in an account of a long career that spanned more than four decades, and his adroitness celebrated in negotiating the slippery politics in the two years that followed Cromwell's death in 1658. For as long as necessary Monck was expediently all things to all men and covered his tracks. Only when the Restoration was actually announced as about to happen did Monck enter into written, as opposed to oral, communication with the king.

One of the most obvious and remarkable features of George Monck, says ASHLEY in his biography published in 1977, is that he basked in the favour of both Cromwell and Charles II. Both rulers brought order out of anarchy and to both he gave unstintingly loyal service. Pressed by some in 1659–60 to seize power for himself, Monck, this book makes clear, had no such ambition. Better to be a king-maker was clearly the view of this "opportunist awaiting his opportunity". The gamble succeeded, of course, and honours and rewards were heaped on the man of the moment in 1660 – a peerage, lucrative posts and pensions for himself (manna from heaven to a formerly impoverished younger son), and preferments for his circle of dependents.

The most recent studies of Monck have been scholarly and specialized and focused on those dimensions of his career – Scotland and the Restoration – for which he became most famous. DOW deals with the first, and shows Monck in his dual capacity as general and governor. Dow rates Monck highly as a soldier with a "brisk, confident approach to the military problems and his ability to get his requests listened to in Whitehall". He was skilful in playing off factions against each other. As an administrator, however, Monck lacked Broghill's flair and creativity. "Beside him", says Dow, "Monck was a plodder".

What of Monck's role in the Restoration? All the writers deal with it, of course. DAVIES attempted a reassessment of it. More recently HUTTON has returned to the same subject in *The Restoration* and *The British Republic 1649–1660*. As ever this author is penetrating and hard-hitting. Monck's leading role in the complex, fast-moving events of 1658–60 was ultimately made possible by the divisions among those around him. That said, however, "he was the greatest politique of all . . . a master of duplicity [who] managed the army in the interests of Parliament" and who contrived a Restoration without a prior written treaty with Charles. Having done so much to engineer a Restoration, Monck left himself an escape route if, for whatever reason, things went wrong. For Monck himself, as Hutton makes clear, things went marvellously well in 1660 and after. He was generously rewarded by his grateful sovereign, and these rewards, plus the opportunities to do good service in the naval war against the Dutch and during times of domestic crisis like the Great Plague and the Great Fire of London, earned all the public satisfactions that he sought. This old soldier might have been transformed by a title into the Duke of Albemarle but he was by nature not cut out to adorn Charles II's court nor did he exercise real political influence after 1660. Charles II was genuinely grieved by his death and gave him a state funeral but that was only the appropriate recognition for services rendered.

R.C. RICHARDSON

See also British Republic; Charles II; Civil Wars entries; Restoration Settlements

Montgomery, Bernard, Viscount Montgomery 1887–1979
Soldier

Baxter, Colin F., *Field Marshall Bernard Law Montgomery, 1887–1976: A Selected Bibliography*, Westport, Connecticut: Greenwood Press, 1999
Graham, Dominick and Shelford Bidwell, *Coalitions, Politicians, and Generals: Some Aspects of Command in Two World Wars*, London and New York: Brassey's, 1993
Hamilton, Nigel, *Monty*, 3 vols, New York: McGraw Hill, and London: Hamish Hamilton, 1981–86
Ingersoll, Ralph, *Top Secret*, New York: Harcourt Brace, and London: Partridge, 1946
Montgomery, Bernard Law, *The Memoirs of Field-Marshal the Viscount Montgomery of Alamein, K.G.*, London: Collins, and Cleveland, Ohio: World, 1958
Moorehead, Alan, *Montgomery: A Biography*, London: Hamish Hamilton, and New York: Coward-McCann, 1946
Weigley, Russell F., *Eisenhower's Lieutenants: The Campaign of France and Germany, 1944–1945*, Bloomington: Indiana University Press, and London: Sidgwick and Jackson, 1981
Wilmot, Chester, *The Struggle for Europe*, New York: Harper, and London: Collins, 1952

Bernard Law Montgomery was a career soldier. A graduate of the Royal Military College, Sandhurst, he served as a junior officer in World War I. He was a divisional commander at Dunkirk and was subsequently given command of the 8th Army in North Africa, where he won renown for his victory over Erwin Rommel's Afrika Corps at the battle of Alamein in October 1942. He then commanded British troops in Sicily and unsuccessfully raced the American general George Patton for the glory of completing conquest of the island. The situation contributed to his reputation for glory-seeking and egotism. After further service in Italy, Montgomery was made commander of Allied ground forces in Normandy. His conduct in this campaign has produced significant controversy. He has been accused of attempting to use the British 8th Army to break out of the D-Day beachhead via Caen and after failing claiming that his goal had been to draw German forces to that sector to allow an American breakout to the west. He has been criticized for failing to close the Falaise gap and allowing the German army to escape. Most dramatically his Operation Market Garden, which was intended to use paratroops to seize a series of bridges culminating with that in Arnhem, has been portrayed as poorly co-ordinated, beyond his resources, and another egotistical attempt to outshine Patten, whose 3rd Army was driving towards the Rhine. Market Garden ended very badly. Finally, Montgomery's reaction to the German attack that produced the battle of the Bulge in December 1944 has been called too hesitant. In every case Montgomery himself and others have defended his generalship.

The literature concerning World War II in general and discussing, often extensively, Montgomery's role is enormous. BAXTER, despite the limits suggested by his title, has written an extensive historiographical analysis of the writing about Montgomery, and his very good book is the place to start in any investigation of the field marshal. Although Baxter is at pains to give both sides of every controversy, it is clear that he admires his subject.

MONTGOMERY had often been a lightning rod for controversy, but with the publication of his *Memoirs* in 1958, the storm really broke. Relations between Montgomery and American general Dwight Eisenhower, the Supreme Allied Commander in Europe, had during the war and after an icy quality of formal bonhommie punctuated by moments of outrage and bitter criticism. In his *Memoirs*, Montgomery is more openly critical of Eisenhower and seeks to defend his own conduct. Of the criticism that he attempted with inadequate forces to break out of the Normandy beachhead via Caen, Montgomery denies any such intention. He claims that his intention was to threaten the Nazis, drawing attention while the American actually made the breakout on the western flank. INGERSOLL and WEIGLEY reject this claim and argue that the arrogant Montgomery did intend to take the lead. The former goes as far as asserting that the American action at St Lô saved the day in the face of the British failure. WILMOT, however, agrees with Montgomery's version.

Montgomery's official biographer HAMILTON provides a detailed and thorough account of the field marshal's entire life. Not surprisingly, however, the second of his three volumes, *Master of the Battlefield 1942–1944*, covers only the middle three years of World War II, the pinnacle and most controversial time of Montgomery's career. Hamilton is generally positive in his interpretation of Montgomery, though he is willing to criticize. He suggests that Montgomery was rash in Sicily, no doubt to beat Patton to victory, but he does make a case that the hurry was also an attempt to win before the enemy could react. Hamilton argues that Operation Market Garden was a serious blunder that arose not only from Montgomery's desire for glory but also from the effects of stress due to long service and the strain of dealing with Dwight Eisenhower. MOOREHEAD is also a largely sympathetic biographer who tends to take positions quite in line with Montgomery's *Memoirs*.

As the Allied drive towards Germany continued through the latter half of 1944, Montgomery, as he makes clear in his *Memoirs*, disagreed with Eisenhower's use of Allied forces. Montgomery believed that there should be one overall commander, himself or the American Omar Bradley and that such unity of command would have prevented the battle of the Bulge. When the German drive started and the salient (Bulge) was created, Eisenhower gave command of the northern flank to Montgomery, which meant the Englishman was directing two US armies. His handling of the situation has been condemned as hesitant and marked by an overeagerness to withdraw, and unfavourably compared to that of Patton, whose 3rd Army turned and cut off the Bulge. Some criticism of Montgomery, such as Ingersoll's, seems to have its roots in American distaste for a foreigner commanding their forces. GRAHAM & BIDWELL, however, tend to agree with Montgomery and condemn Eisenhower for not concentrating his force. Weigley, though he again comments on Montgomery's arrogance, also argues that he handled this situation well.

Despite the admirable work of Hamilton, Montgomery continues to be a controversial figure. The sources of the criticism are clearly mixed. Some comes from legitimate professional military and historiographical sources while some is tinged with nationalistic jealousy. It is just this sort of mix of interpretation and attitude that gives rise to the saying that every generation can rewrite history, a cliché that seems particularly well applied to the career of Bernard Law Montgomery.

FRED R. VAN HARTESVELDT

See also World War II entries

Montgomery, Treaty of 1267

Carr, A.D., "Anglo-Welsh Relations, 1066–1282" in *England and her Neighbours, 1066–1453: Essays in Honour of Pierre Chaplais*, edited by Michael Jones and Malcolm Vale, London and Ronceverte, West Virginia: Hambledon Press, 1989

Edwards, J. Goronwy (editor), *Littere Wallie Preserved in Liber A in the Public Record Office*, Cardiff: University of Wales Press Board, 1940

Edwards, J. Goronwy, *The Principality of Wales, 1267–1967: A Study in Constitutional History*, Caernarvon: Caernarvonshire Historical Society, 1969

Lloyd, John Edward, *A History of Wales from the Earliest Times to the Edwardian Conquest*, 2 vols, London and New York: Longmans, Green, 1911; 3rd edition, London and New York: Longmans, Green, 1939

Powicke, F.M., *King Henry III and the Lord Edward: The Community of the Realm in the Thirteenth Century*, 2 vols, Oxford: Clarendon Press, 1947; reprinted, Oxford: Clarendon Press, 1966

Smith, J. Beverley, *Llywelyn ap Gruffudd, Prince of Wales*, Cardiff: University of Wales Press, 1998

The treaty of Montgomery, concluded on 29 September 1267, in which Henry III recognized Llywelyn ap Gruffydd of Gwynedd as Prince of Wales and his principality as a constitutional entity, has usually been seen as the crowning achievement of native Welsh rulers in the 13th century. The treaty itself was printed by EDWARDS in *Littere Wallie*, a collection of documents in the Public Record Office dealing with Anglo-Welsh relations in the 13th century; in his introduction he discussed the background and the significance of the treaty and Llywelyn's interpretation of it, an interpretation that was at variance with Edward I's view and therefore contributed to the deterioration of the prince's relations with Edward after 1272. Edwards considered Llywelyn to have overestimated the strength of his own position by failing to realize that the political situation in England had changed completely since the end of the barons' war; the Montgomery settlement had presented the greatest challenge to his statecraft and he proved unequal to it.

CARR examines the course of Anglo-Welsh political relations between the Norman Conquest and the death of Llywelyn ap Gruffydd in 1282 and in doing so he places the treaty in the context of other treaties and agreements between princes of Gwynedd and the English crown, among them the first of such treaties between Llywelyn ap Iorwerth and King John in 1201, the peace of Worcester of 1218, the treaties of Gloucester (1240), Gwern Eigron (1241), Woodstock (1247) and the final treaty of Aberconwy in 1277.

LLOYD was the first historian to examine the sources for the period in detail, although he had to depend on the text of the treaty in Thomas Rymer's *Foedera*. For him Montgomery was the high point of native Welsh political achievement: "since the coming of the Normans no Welsh prince had attained to such a height of authority and landed influence". But he, too, pointed out that the prince's position in 1267 could be described as unreal: "[T]he circumstances of the hour disguised alike the inherent weakness of his own position and the latent strength of that of the English king". Even so, Lloyd saw the treaty as the culmination of the efforts of successive princes in the 13th century to unite Wales under their rule, although it was for later commentators to show the real extent and significance of the changes which occurred in the country, especially during this period.

POWICKE's book is a detailed study of the reign of Henry III and of the first part of that of Edward I. The part played by

Welsh rulers and by Welsh affairs generally in the events of the two reigns received considerable attention and his approach was both sensitive and sympathetic. The treaty was examined in the context of contemporary developments in England; the account of its making formed part of Powicke's discussion of the mission of the papal legate, Cardinal Ottobuono, to aid the process of reconciliation and to bring the civil war to an end. A chapter, appropriately entitled "The Conflict of Laws", was devoted to Anglo-Welsh relations and here both the political background to the treaty and the disputes that arose from its interpretation and that contributed to the succession of crises in Llywelyn ap Gruffydd's relations with Edward I were reviewed. Powicke's treatment of the treaty and, indeed, of Wales generally, is also of interest as a successful attempt by a distinguished English historian to follow the example of T.F. Tout a generation earlier by giving due attention to events in Wales; it may be significant that both Edwards and Powicke had come under Tout's influence, one as a research student and the other as a colleague.

SMITH's substantial study of Llywelyn ap Gruffydd must inevitably give the treaty of Montgomery a central place. As Powicke sets the treaty in its English context, Smith examines the Welsh background in detail, looking at the aims and objectives of the prince and of his grandfather, Llywelyn ap Iorwerth, in quest of a settlement with the English crown that would place the seal of royal approval on the Welsh polity they had both worked so hard to construct. The younger Llywelyn's perception of his position as Prince of Wales and the problems he had to face in creating a new principality based on little more than the uncertain homage of the other Welsh rulers and, as yet, lacking an institutional infrastructure, are studied and analysed in depth, as are the successive disputes with Edward, which may, at least in part, be described as a commentary on the underlying weaknesses of the 1267 settlement. This work is indubitably the most thorough examination of the treaty, its context, and its consequences and must be essential reading for anyone seeking to understand its importance in the history of Wales and, indeed, in the history of that multinational British state, the future of which is the subject of debate in the dawn of the 21st century.

In 1967 EDWARDS gave a public lecture at Caernarfon to mark the seventh centenary of the treaty. This was the swan song of a scholar who, in addition to having made a major contribution to the understanding of the history of medieval Wales, was an outstanding constitutional historian. The treaty, in Edwards's own words, "involved the recognition, on an agreed basis, of the principality of Wales". Llywelyn was killed in 1282 but "while his headless body lay mouldering in the grave in Cwm Hir, his principality went marching on". The principality survived as a constitutional entity, to be granted by Edward I to his son, Edward of Caernarfon, in 1301 and to subsequent princes of Wales. The Acts of Union of 1536 and 1543 did not unite Wales to England; they united Wales within itself, doing away with the distinction between the principality and the march. Wales retained its own courts, the Great Sessions, until 1830. Thus the effects of the treaty of Montgomery were permanent; what had been done in 1267 was not undone.

ANTONY DAVID CARR

See also Edward I; Henry III; Llywelyn ap Gruffydd; Wales before Union with England; Wales, Principality of

More, Sir Thomas 1478–1535
Lord chancellor, scholar, and saint

Ackroyd, Peter, *The Life of Thomas More*, London: Chatto and Windus, and New York: Talese, 1998

Bolt, Robert, *A Man for All Seasons: A Play of Sir Thomas More*, London: French, 1960; New York: Random House, 1962; with notes by E.R. Wood, London: Heinemann, 1963

Bradshaw, Brendan, "More on Utopia", *Historical Journal*, 24 (1981): 1–27

Fox, Alistair, *Thomas More: History and Providence*, Oxford: Blackwell, 1982; New Haven, Connecticut: Yale University Press, 1983

Guy, J.A., *The Public Career of Sir Thomas More*, Brighton, Sussex: Harvester Press, and New Haven, Connecticut: Yale University Press, 1980

Guy, John, *Thomas More*, London: Arnold, and New York: Oxford University Press, 2000

Marius, Richard, *Thomas More: A Biography*, New York: Knopf, 1984; London: Dent, 1985

Martz, Louis L., *Thomas More: The Search for the Inner Man*, New Haven, Connecticut and London: Yale University Press, 1990

Skinner, Quentin, "More's Utopia", *Past & Present*, 38 (1967): 153–68

Sylvester, R.S. and G.P. Marc'hadour (editors), *Essential Articles for the Study of Thomas More*, Hamden, Connecticut: Archon Books, 1977

Sylvester, R.S. *et al.* (editors), *The Complete Works of St Thomas More*, New Haven, Connecticut and London: Yale University Press, 1963–97

The historical and hagiographical literature on Sir or St Thomas More is so vast as to defy comprehension, let alone summary. It commenced even within his lifetime, with a brief epistolary memoir by Erasmus of Rotterdam designed to promote More's scholarly and reformist credentials. The career of this intellectual lawyer turned politician would in any case have left its mark on history, including as it did the composition of a seminal text in political thought, *Utopia*, which baffled its own and succeeding ages even as it gave the world a new word and inaugurated a new literary genre. More's public role as lord chancellor and controversialist, in the refutation and prosecution of protestantism, earned him another (and today largely unsavoury) reputation. And his refusal to support Henry VIII's divorce and break with Rome, which led to his execution for treason in 1535, ensured his eventual canonization as a martyr of the catholic church. His memory was perpetuated, and the cause of his canonization implicitly advanced, by his kindred and their connections in a series of biographies composed from the reign of Mary Tudor onwards. The best known, most widely available, and probably the best, is that by his son-in-law, William Roper, originally written for the Marian edition of More's English works published by William Rastell in 1557, and now often found in editions of *Utopia*.

Serious scholarship on More began in the context of his beatification (1886) and several fine biographies were written in the late 19th and early 20th centuries, mostly by English catholics. However, the monumental labours of the Yale *Complete Works*

(SYLVESTER *et al.*) have set Morean studies on a new basis since the 1960s, not only making almost all his works available in accurate and exhaustively annotated texts, but also adding a wealth of introductory essays and short monographs. The edition of *Utopia* by Edward Surtz and J.H. Hexter was especially influential, for the first time setting that text firmly within the tradition of humanist political thought, and in effect making redundant virtually all previous exegesis by the simple expedient of suggesting that More may, in some sense, have meant what he said. Their work inaugurated a new interpretative tradition, of which the two most significant products are probably SKINNER, who read the text as a paradoxical "humanist critique of humanism" and BRADSHAW, who emphasizes the combination of Platonism and pragmatism in a work which strove to bring together political idealism and realism.

SYLVESTER & MARC'HADOUR amass under one cover a selection of the very best in Morean and Utopian scholarship originally published in a range of academic journals. The most significant new contribution to Morean scholarship in the late 20th century, however, was undoubtedly GUY (1980), closely followed in chronology and importance by FOX. Guy provided a ground-breaking study of More's career as a lawyer, drawing upon court records as well as on state papers, which ended forever any doubts about More's determination and ability to succeed in public life and simultaneously swept away romantic legends about the magical despatch of business in More's three years as lord chancellor. Fox offered the first conspectus of More's intellectual achievement, and made a serious attempt to recapture the synthesis of humanism and Christianity which shaped it. Fox challenges Erasmus's portrait of a "well rounded and humanistically coherent" More with a vision of "contrary impulses" that reflects the tension between the active and contemplative life which certainly vexed early modern humanists. In Fox's view, More's public commitments in the increasingly stressful years of the early Reformation in Europe and England brought that tension to a personally damaging crisis evident in the violence of his controversial writings, and finally resolved only in the enforced enclaustration of the Tower of London. Both Guy and Fox, the latter a little more explicitly than the former, contributed significantly to the "revisionist" re-evaluation of More's career which had been called for and to some extent sketched out by G.R. Elton. The targets of this revisionism were twofold. First, the catholic hagiographical tradition which at times cast the man as a plaster saint, in struggling to cope with the more extreme stretches of More's imagination in his *Utopia*, in his polemics against Luther, Tyndale, and St German, or simply in his "merry jests". And second, the secular parody (in the best sense of the word) of that tradition represented in BOLT, whose brilliant play, subsequently turned into an equally brilliant film, transformed More's martyrdom for the corporate faith of the catholic church into a martyrdom for individual freedom of conscience – just right for the 1960s, but quite possibly the last thing More would ever have contemplated giving his life for.

MARIUS wrote that all More's biographers ended up loving their subject, yet the impression given by his own blockbuster biography is rather the opposite. It marks the high tide of the "revisionist" attack on More's integrity and modern reputation. Notwithstanding its exhaustive and largely reliable factual detail, Marius's work is marred by its methodologically questionable psycho-historical approach, which presents More as a monk *manqué* tormented by sexual guilt which was worked off in verbal and physical cruelty against the protestant heretics who had achieved a fulfilled synthesis of religion and sexuality unavailable to him. It clashes with Paul Scofield's realization of Bolt's 1960s More (*A Man for All Seasons*) in defining a generation's vision of the man, despite the pithy and lucid demolition of the revisionist interpretation offered by MARTZ. A new version of More's life by a major literary biographer, ACKROYD, has deservedly become the standard contemporary account. Significant new information is hardly to be looked for, but the strong sense of the importance of London in More's life and career is a striking interpretative contribution, as is its brief, and almost Plutarchan, contrast between the lives of More and Luther. But despite its narrative flair and its greater sympathy with its subject, it remains a product of the revisionist era in Morean scholarship.

Most recently, GUY's critical investigation (2000) is itself as much historiographical as historical in character, providing a full account of the traditions of Morean scholarship and interpretation. At times the effect of the welter of scholarship is such as to make the quest for the historical More seem, in Guy's eyes, as desperate as the quest for the historical Jesus. However, his closely argued revisions of some "revisionist" theses (More's monastic aspirations and sexual anxieties and his recruitment to Henry VIII's service) in fact justify his original confidence in (rather than his subsequent hesitancy about) the power of sound historical scholarship to resolve or at least to illuminate the controversies surrounding the perennially fascinating Englishman.

Thomas More's career remains a minefield of controversy, as Guy makes clear. Interpretative cruxes include the reading of *Utopia* itself, the contrast between *Utopia* and his later theological polemics, the character of his commitment to catholicism, his political programme, his understanding of conscience, and perhaps above all the perceived contrast between his own martyrdom and his willingness to prosecute others for their religious offences. Twentieth-century scholarship has driven a wedge between the More of faith and the More of history. It remains to be seen whether the scholarship of the next century can do anything to bring them back together.

RICHARD REX

See also Boleyn; Catherine of Aragon; Cranmer; Cromwell, Thomas; Fisher, John; Henry VII; Henry VIII; Henry VIII: Divorce from Catherine; Morton

Morrison, Herbert 1888–1965
Labour politician and statesman

Beckett, Francis, *Clem Attlee*, London: Richard Cohen, 1997

Brivati, Brian, *Hugh Gaitskell*, London: Richard Cohen, 1996

Donoughue, Bernard and G.W. Jones, *Herbert Morrison: Portrait of a Politician*, London: Weidenfeld and Nicolson, 1973

Hollis, Patricia, *Jennie Lee: A Life*, Oxford and New York: Oxford University Press, 1997

Taylor, A.J.P., "The Coalition of 1932–1945" in *Coalitions in British Politics*, edited by David Butler, London: Macmillan, and New York: St Martin's Press, 1978

Morrison has been fortunate in his biographers. DONOUGHUE & JONES is a classic, and it is impossible to envisage it ever being replaced. The authors were lecturers at the London School of Economics, where they researched and wrote the scholarly biography, based on Morrison's *Autobiography* (1960), on over 300 interviews with friends, colleagues, and family, as well as on extensive use of newspapers, national such as the *Daily Herald*, and local such as *Brixton Free Press*.

Part one of the biography is the effort of Jones and deals with the years from 1888 to 1940. Morrison, born on 3 January 1888, was the youngest of seven children of Henry Morrison, a police constable, and his wife Priscilla Caroline Lyon, daughter of an East End carpet-fitter. Within three days of his birth he was totally blind in his right eye, a disability that in later life caused him difficulty. In his early days as a shop assistant he devoured socialist literature; Chiozza Money's *Riches and Poverty* (1906) convinced him that socialism was to be his ideology. He moved from Marxism to ethical socialism, and on the eve of World War I he was the circulation manager of the *Daily Citizen*, a Labour paper.

Morrison saw the potential of local government, and in 1915 became the part-time secretary of the London Labour Party. He took the Independent Labour Party line on the war, opposing it, defending his socialism before the tribunal, and serving his sentence at Letchworth Garden City where he met Margaret Kent, whom he married in 1919. It never became a happy marriage, and in his autobiography he never mentions his wife. Politics was his first concern, his wife and later his daughter were always on the sideline.

His ambition was kindled when he became mayor of Hackney, a member of the London County Council in 1922, and was rewarded by Ramsey MacDonald, who made him minister of transport with a seat in cabinet. It was a busy time for Morrison, for as leader of the Labour group of the London County Council he was responsible for the London Passenger Transport Bill of 1931. He lost the Hackney South seat in 1931 but he had enough to do as a powerful London politician, and when his party gained power in 1934 this enabled him to build the new Waterloo bridge, introduce the green belt, and tackle slum clearances as well as build schools and reform public assistance. In 1935 he was returned for Hackney South but he lost to Clement Attlee in the election for the new party leader. BECKETT shows how that election coloured everything Morrison did for the rest of his life. He resented being passed over. If he had won Hackney South in 1931 he would have been the leader. He and Attlee were the contenders for the Labour leadership. They co-operated against the advice of many of their colleagues in taking effective action against Neville Chamberlain. Churchill rewarded Morrison in the wartime coalition government, appointing him minister of supply, then home secretary, and finally minister of home security.

Part two of the biography written by Donoughue deals with his career from 1940 to 1965. TAYLOR shows how Morrison eventually convinced the Labour Party – against the wishes of Attlee, Bevin, and Dalton – to break up the coalition so as to ensure a victory for the Labour Party, for which he had worked so hard, at the 1945 general election. Returned as MP for Lewisham East, Morrison still hankered for the post of prime minister, but Ernest Bevin, representing the right wing of the party, had complete disdain for him. Members of the left wing of the party also detested Morrison, as we gather from the biography of Aneurin Bevan's wife. HOLLIS, the point of reference, is a superb study of the traditional left. From 1945 to 1951 Morrison was leader of the House of Commons and then for a short spell (March–October 1951) at the Foreign Office as minister. But he was completely out of his depth and a dismal failure.

The last period of his life was very distressing as Donoughue shows. There was the death of his neglected wife in 1951, and then in 1955 the Labour Party refused him again for a younger man as leader in succession to Attlee. It was a bitter disappointment. BRIVATI shows how Morrison refused to continue as deputy leader, a post he had held since 1945. Gaitskell tried his very best to reconcile him, and persuaded Macmillan to create him a peer, with an opportunity in the House of Lords. His second marriage to Edith Meadowcroft of Rochdale in 1955 brought him happiness he had never experienced in his first marriage.

Morrison wrote an important study, *Government and Parliament: A Survey from the Inside* (1954), which brought him some money to enjoy himself. His lasting influence was his impact on British politics in preparing with the help of William Beveridge for the postwar social revolution and as the most powerful politician in the inter-war years, within the London County Council.

D. BEN REES

See also Attlee; Beveridge; Bevin; Churchill, Sir Winston; Dalton; World War II: Home Front

Morton, John c.1420–1500
Lord chancellor, Archbishop of Canterbury, and cardinal

Davies, Clifford S.L., "Bishop John Morton, the Holy See, and the Accession of Henry VII", *English Historical Review*, 102 (1987): 2–30

Davis, J.C., "More, Morton, and the Politics of Accommodation", *Journal of British Studies*, 9(2) (1970): 27–48

Emden, A.B., *A Biographical Register of the University of Oxford to AD 1500*, vol. 2, Oxford: Clarendon Press, 1958

Emden, A.B., *A Biographical Register of the University of Cambridge to 1500*, Cambridge: Cambridge University Press, 1963

Harper-Bill, Christopher, "Archbishop John Morton and the Province of Canterbury, 1486–1500", *Journal of Ecclesiastical History*, 29 (1978): 1–21

Harper-Bill, Christopher, "The *Familia*, Administrators and Patronage of Archbishop John Morton", *Journal of Religious History*, 10 (1979): 236–52

Hook, Walter Farquhar, *Lives of the Archbishops of Canterbury*, vol. 5, London: Bentley, 1867

More, Thomas, *Utopia*, edited by Edward Surtz and J.H. Hexter, vol. 4 of *Complete Works*, New Haven, Connecticut and London: Yale University Press, 1965

Woodhouse, R.I., *The Life of John Morton, Archbishop of Canterbury*, London and New York: Longmans Green, 1895

Initially a firm Lancastrian supporter, Morton eventually gave his support to the Yorkists following the defeat of the Lancastrians at Towton in 1461. A trusted servant of Edward IV, he was appointed an executor of his will and, as a supporter of Edward's sons, was arrested at the usurpation of Richard, Duke of Gloucester. Initially placed in the Duke of Buckingham's custody with whom he conspired against Richard III, he eventually fled to Flanders from where he provided crucial support for Henry Tudor. Following Henry's accession he became a key figure in the king's administration, appointed lord chancellor in 1486. In the same year he became Archbishop of Canterbury and, in 1493, was made a cardinal.

EMDEN's biographical registers of Oxford and Cambridge give a brief history of Morton's life along with a list of his offices, the valuable references providing a useful starting-point for anyone wanting to research his life. HOOK's chapter, although written over 100 years ago, is fully referenced and provides another good starting-point for research into Morton's life. Although a little romantically written in parts, it includes attractive accounts of Morton's residence and famous gardens in Holborn, along with a colourful description of the council meeting at which he was arrested by Richard, Duke of Gloucester in 1483. However, the contextual information should be read with some caution. While WOODHOUSE's dated work provides greater background detail, it is more a collection of sources for Morton's history than a publication of originality. It relies heavily on a number of secondary sources, including Hook, from which large amounts of text are quoted. HARPER-BILL's 1978 article looks at Morton's contribution to the see of Canterbury in light of his dual roles as archbishop and chancellor. Harper-Bill believes that there was actually no conflict between the two roles because Morton was able to maintain a successful balance, something that was unfortunately lost when he died. Comparing him to Wolsey, Harper-Bill claims that, while he was keen to protect the clergy from the criticisms of the laity and to retain a tight control over his province, his motives were not prompted by "personal aggrandizement". He also dismisses Hook's view that an aggressive papal policy, of which Morton was a part, contributed to a reaction under Henry VIII. He sees Morton as a man genuinely concerned for ecclesiastical reform and for "royal solvency", who had the ability to steer a successful course between both interests.

DAVIES focuses on Morton's role in events between 1483 and 1485. Accepting that Morton provided a cohesive element to Buckingham's rebellion and continued to support Henry Tudor from his exile in the Netherlands, Davies proposes that Morton's activities went further. His visit to the pope in 1484–85 was, Davies suggests, crucial as it was instrumental in gaining the valuable papal support that Henry VII enjoyed at the beginning of his reign resulting in the marriage dispensation, swiftly issued, for Henry's union with Elizabeth of York along with measures against sanctuary and provisions for the excommunication of rebels. It is possible that Morton led the papacy to believe that should Henry Tudor become king, England would be more responsive to papal needs and that both Morton and Henry continued to encourage the papacy in these expectations for as long as they could after Henry's accession. HARPER-BILL's 1979 article uses Emden's biographical registers and a study of the archiepiscopal register to try to identify those individuals crucial to ecclesiastical administration who made up Morton's circle. As a result, Harper-Bill is able to give an indication of the nature of Morton's patronage, the support networks he enjoyed, the type of men he wished to attract to his service, and the pattern of advancement for young ecclesiastical lawyers.

Thomas MORE, who served in Morton's household when he was a boy, wrote his *Utopia* in 1515–16. In it he uses Morton to represent the practical and political figure during one of the debates that take place. As a result of More's personal knowledge of Morton, the description of his appearance and manner given by the fictional character, Raphael Hythlodaeus, should not be regarded as mere invention. Consequently, in the absence of accurate contemporary depictions of Morton it provides a brief but useful source of information. While discussing the politics of accommodation in More's *Utopia*, DAVIS looks at More's description of Morton both in *Utopia* and the *History of King Richard III*. His attempts to discern More's attitude to Morton give a useful insight into Morton the man and the character of his household, as well as providing a helpful introduction to More's *Utopia*.

HAZEL PIERCE

See also Bray; Edward IV; Henry VII; More

Mosley, Sir Oswald, 6th Baronet

Mosley 1896–1980

Politician, Labour minister, later leader of the British Union of Fascists

Chesterton, A.K., *Oswald Mosley: Portrait of a Leader*, London: Action Press, no date [1937]

Dalley, Jan, *Diana Mosley: A Life*, London: Faber, 1999; New York: Knopf, 2000

Lewis, D.S., *Illusions of Grandeur: Mosley, Fascism, and British Society, 1931–1981*, Manchester: Manchester University Press, 1987

Mosley, Diana, *Loved Ones: Pen Portraits*, London: Sidgwick and Jackson, 1985

Mosley, Nicholas, *Rules of the Game: Sir Oswald and Lady Cynthia Mosley, 1896–1933*, London: Secker and Warburg, 1982; reprinted in *Rules of the Game / Beyond the Pale*, Elmwood, Illinois: Dalkey Archive Press, 1991; London: Secker and Warburg, 1994; revised edition, London: Pimlico, 1998

Mosley, Nicholas, *Beyond the Pale: Sir Oswald Mosley and Family, 1933–1980*, London: Secker and Warburg, 1983;

reprinted in *Rules of the Game / Beyond the Pale*, Elmwood, Illinois: Dalkey Archive Press, 1991; London: Secker and Warburg, 1994; revised edition, London: Pimlico, 1998

Mosley, Oswald, *My Life*, London: Nelson, 1968; New Rochelle, New York: Arlington House, 1972

Ritschel, Daniel, *The Politics of Planning: The Debate on Economic Planning in Britain in the 1930s*, Oxford: Clarendon Press, and New York: Oxford University Press, 1997

Skidelsky, Robert, *Oswald Mosley*, London: Macmillan, and New York: Holt Rinehart and Winston, 1975; revised edition, London: Papermac, 1981

White, Dan S., *Lost Comrades: Socialists of the Front Generation, 1918–1945*, Cambridge, Massachusetts: Harvard University Press, 1992

It is perhaps appropriate that in the first treatment of his life, a panegyric by CHESTERTON, Sir Oswald Mosley is cast in a heroic mould as fascist "Leader". Although Mosley served successively as a Conservative, an Independent, and then a Labour MP during the 1920s, and as a minister in the 1929–31 Labour government, representations of his life turn on the eight years before his wartime internment in 1940 when he was the leader of Britain's largest fascist movement, the British Union of Fascists (BUF). As the foremost native representative of the 20th century's most reviled politics, even more than 60 years after blackshirts roamed the East End of London, interpretation of Mosley's career remains a matter of controversy, often prompting polemic in place of historical analysis. Nonetheless, while Mosley has been by no means "rehabilitated", he has begun to emerge as more than a one-dimensional fascist monster.

The first step in this process was Oswald MOSLEY's own substantial autobiography which, given that very few of his own papers have survived, is not without value for historians. Nonetheless this is Mosley presented as he wanted to be remembered and his career emerges with a heroic gloss, as driven by high ideals. In seeking to recover his reputation, Mosley conceded error when it was imprudent to do otherwise and dissimulated when practical to do so. Despite the weight of evidence to the contrary, he also sought to wash out the single greatest blot on his record with an expurgatory account of his anti-semitism. Consequently, Mosley's treatment of the most controversial aspects of his career are the most unsatisfactory chapters in the book. Alongside this revisionist project the closing chapter, "Policies for Present and Future", demonstrated that although he had retired from active party politics he had by no means renounced the ambition of a late victory in the war of ideas.

Undoubtedly the decisive step in the re-evaluation of Mosley came with the first full study by SKIDELSKY. Writing with the co-operation of his subject, Skidelsky has been accused of crossing the line from the necessary sympathy of the biographer to uncritically accepting some of Mosley's own arguments. The treatment of the key topic of Mosley's anti-semitism was particularly criticized for seeming to place an over-large share of the responsibility for the policies and actions of the BUF on the Jews themselves. However, it would be going beyond fair comment to suggest this amounted to more than an error of interpretation, and revisions in later editions went some way to address points raised by critics. Despite these caveats and

although not benefiting from the tranche of government files that has since become available, Skidelsky's work remains the authoritative account of Mosley's life, combining detailed research with an open-minded but not uncritical approach.

Skidelsky is particularly strong on the crucial topic of Mosley's economic thought and it is in this area that a chapter in an immaculately researched study by RITSCHEL brings out the role that Mosley played at the outset of the 1930s debate about economic planning. In the first half of his book Skidelsky also provides a full account of Mosley's pre-fascist career, which seemed destined for higher things first in the Conservative Party and then via his apparently meteoric course towards high office in the Labour Party. He also shows the continuity between the different parts of Mosley's career and the significance of his World War I experiences in his thinking. The relationship of Mosley's wartime service to his politics is also central to WHITE's collective political biography of European socialists of the "front generation". This work, while not uncovering any new information, usefully looks at Mosley in comparison with the postwar paths of other socialists. At the same time one might query if the upper-class Mosley, lacking as he did any left-wing political socialization, can be meaningfully spoken of as a socialist "comrade", lost or otherwise.

Given the nature of Mosley's autobiography, it is something of a puzzle that shortly before his death he passed his private papers to Nicholas MOSLEY, his eldest son by his first wife Cynthia (née Curzon) from whom he had long been estranged. By drawing especially on his mother's papers and letters and his own recollections, Nicholas Mosley provides a revealing picture of his father's private life to complement Skidelsky's account of the public career. Although somewhat sketchy on aspects of his political and public activities, a penetrating account emerges which, while not without sympathy, is distinguished by rare candour and intellectual honesty. By travelling into the speculative territory of his father's psychology and personality, Nicholas Mosley also seeks to reconcile the high idealism of the Mosley of *My Life* with the reality of the low politics of fascist anti-semitism and racism.

This "unrecognizable caricature" caused Diana MOSLEY, Mosley's second wife, to break with its author and to pen her own short account of her husband's life. This is of some interest for the insights it gives on its subject's final years, although the account surpasses even Mosley's ability to forget the inconvenient. In writing the life of Diana Mosley herself, DALLEY devotes considerable space to Mosley's political career after breaking with Labour. Lacking ties of either marriage or blood, Dalley is forthright, but generally not polemical, in her evaluations. However, while providing a full picture she offers little new information or novel interpretation, at the same time including a number of factual errors. Although the Mosleys' marriage is at the centre of the story, the reader may turn the final page feeling that they have not been taken beyond the surface of things.

The topic of British fascism has generated numerous books and articles relating to Mosley. Among this literature LEWIS places Mosley in the foreground of what is neither a personal or political biography but – despite the suggestion of its subtitle – effectively a study of the BUF. In a field generally somewhat shy of "theory", Lewis usefully deploys concepts of fascist ideology and the bases of fascist support and is also searching in his treatment of Mosley's anti-semitism. Although nominally covering the period up to Mosley's death, Lewis's treatment of his postwar activities is cursory. A really satisfactory treatment of this part of Mosley's career remains to be written.

PHILIP M. COUPLAND

See also Fascism

Motor Industry

Beaven, Brad, "Shop Floor Culture in the Coventry Motor Industry, c.1896–1920" in *The Motor Car and Popular Culture in the 20th Century*, edited by David Thoms, Len Holden, and Tim Claydon, Aldershot, Hampshire and Brookfield, Vermont: Ashgate, 1998

Church, Roy, *Herbert Austin: The British Motor Car Industry to 1941*, London: Europa, 1979

Church, Roy, *The Rise and Decline of the British Motor Industry*, London: Macmillan, 1994

Dunnett, Peter J.S., *The Decline of the British Motor Industry: The Effects of Government Policy, 1945–1979*, London: Croom Helm, 1980

Lewchuk, Wayne, *American Technology and the British Vehicle Industry*, Cambridge and New York: Cambridge University Press, 1987

Lyddon, D., "Workplace Organization in the British Car Industry", *History Workshop Journal*, 15 (1985): 131–40

Overy, R.J., *William Morris, Viscount Nuffield*, London: Europa, 1976

Rhys, D.G., "Concentration in the Inter-war Motor Industry", *Journal of Transport History*, 3/4 (1976): 241–64

Saul, S.B., "The Motor Industry in Britain to 1914", *Business History*, 5 (1962): 22–44

Thompson, Paul, "Playing at Being Skilled Men: Factory Culture and Pride in Work Skills among Coventry Car Workers", *Social History*, 13/1 (1988): 45–69

Thoms, David and Tom Donnelly, *The Coventry Motor Industry: Birth to Renaissance?*, Aldershot, Hampshire and Brookfield, Vermont: Ashgate, 2000

Tolliday, Steven and Jonathan Zeitlin (editors), *The Automobile Industry and Its Workers: Between Fordism and Flexibility*, Cambridge and Oxford: Polity Press/Blackwell, 1986; New York: St Martin's Press, 1987

Britain entered late into automobile manufacture. Only after experiments with automobiles had taken place in Germany in 1886 and France in 1895 did a motor industry tentatively emerge in Britain in 1896. One explanation for Britain's late entry into motor vehicle production was the success of its light engineering sector. The experimental nature of the motor industry ensured that light engineering firms engaged in the highly successful machine tool and bicycle trades were reluctant to diversify into an untried product. Britain's motor industry began life in Coventry, a city that had been the centre of the bicycle industry until its slump in the late 1890s. The recent book by THOMS & DONNELLY provides a useful analysis of how engineering firms were forced to search for new products after the collapse of the bicycle trade. Firms, which were to become

established marques, in the motor industry such as Rover, Riley, Singer, and Humber all had their origins in the Coventry bicycle industry. Although by 1914 Coventry boasted the lion's share of car manufacturers and component makers, other significant centres included Birmingham and the south-east.

A good insight into the early structures of the motor industry was offered by SAUL, who demonstrated that, prior to 1914, the vast majority of British firms were small in size and were engaged in relatively low production runs. Moreover, there was also a high turnover of firms: almost 200 firms in 1904 claimed to be engaged in car production, a figure which had dropped to approximately 80 in 1910.

The inter-war period witnessed a radical restructuring of the British motor industry. RHYS examined how, during the 1930s, there was a period of increasing concentration in which a handful of firms began to produce cars in volume. In 1929, it was estimated that three manufacturers, Morris, Austin, and Singers, shared some 75 per cent of the British production of cars.

The process of how small firms producing limited production runs transformed themselves into volume producers is explored through the biographical accounts of William Morris and Herbert Austin by OVERY and CHURCH (1979) respectively.

Historical debate surrounding the nature of the British motor industry prior to World War II has focused on the perceived inadequacies of the industry's structure which prohibited the production levels seen in the United States. LEWCHUK has argued that British firms never achieved maximum efficiency due to their failure to adopt Fordist mass-production techniques. The Fordist system not only standardized units to achieve economies of scale, but crucially imposed direct managerial control over the labour force, enforced through a new managerial class and Ford security police. In contrast to the US model, due to the militancy of the British labour, management negotiated a British form of mass production which relied on piece-work, a system that allowed workers to dictate the pace of production since it linked earnings directly to output. Lewchuk's thesis has been vigorously challenged by TOLLIDAY & ZEITLIN who question the validity of Fordist production techniques within the inter-war British domestic market since the company only accounted for 4 per cent of sales in 1929. Moreover, they argue that labour's strength during the inter-war period was much reduced after a failed engineering strike in 1922.

The role of labour in the British motor industry has largely been discussed through the analysis of official trade-union structures. However, with fewer than 25 per cent of car workers unionized at any one time prior to World War II, it is clear that an analysis of institutional structures neglects the vast majority of the workforce. A challenge to this institutional perspective emerged from LYDDON, who argued that workers' attempts at gaining a degree of autonomy in the work process did not stem from unionized "craft" workers but was the semi-skilled workers' response to the structural features of capitalist societies. Recently, THOMPSON and BEAVEN have developed this analysis of work-place informalism and "job control" through an exploration of workplace culture in the Coventry motor industry.

An investigation into the post–World War II reorganization of the industry can be found in DUNNETT's monograph on the decline of the British motor industry. The combined threat of the American producers Ford and Vauxhall, which by 1952 had captured a larger proportion of the market than Britain's leading car makers, persuaded William Morris to agree to a sell-out to Austin. Consequently 40 per cent of Britain's car production was consolidated within one company: the British Motor Corporation. Encouraged by Wilson's Labour government, the mergers continued in the hope of rationalizing the industry. In 1968 the Leyland Motor Company, a buoyant commercial vehicle sector, took over BMC. By the mid-1970s, however, it had become clear that the renamed British Leyland still retained old managerial divisions and rivalries, with volume production such as Austin based in Birmingham, and specialist producers such as Rover and Jaguar based in Coventry.

After an initial period of prosperity, the post–World War II era has largely been characterized as a period of decline. CHURCH's (1994) overview of the British motor industry is perhaps the most accessible analysis of the mergers, government intervention, and the turbulent labour relations that helped erode British firms' dominance of the domestic market in the pre-war era. Church argues that the British motor industry's failure to transform itself into a key international player was due to three interacting factors. First, there were government decisions in which political motives were prioritized over business needs. Second, although the piece-work system had worked effectively when organized labour was weak, the postwar shortage of labour and the growing strength of shop stewards enabled workers to assume a degree of managerial control. Finally, there was an historical weakness in the corporate and managerial structures which had failed to institute systematic planning and organizational change.

The break-up of BL and the sale of firms such as Jaguar and Rover in the 1980s are explored in detail by Thoms & Donnelly. Indeed, this is the most up-to-date monograph on the industry since it includes a commentary on Rover's recent flirtation with the venture capitalists Alchemy, a situation only avoided by the intervention of the Phoenix consortium, which successfully bought the company in May 2000.

BRAD BEAVEN

See also Road Transport

Mount Badon, Battle of later 5th century or
early 6th century

Alcock, Leslie, *Arthur's Britain: History and Archaeology, AD 367–634*, London: Allen Lane, and New York: St Martin's Press, 1971
Burkitt, T. and A. Burkitt, "The Frontier Zone and the Siege of Mount Badon: A Review of the Evidence for their Location", *Proceedings of the Somerset Archaeological and Natural History Society*, 134 (1990): 81–93
Chambers, E.K., *Arthur of Britain*, London: Sidgwick and Jackson, 1927; reprinted with supplementary bibliography, Cambridge: Speculum Historiale, and New York: Barnes and Noble, 1964
Higham, N.J., *The English Conquest: Gildas and Britain in the Fifth Century*, Manchester and New York: Manchester University Press, 1994
Hirst, Susan and Philip Rahtz, "Liddington Castle and the Battle of Badon: Excavations and Research 1976", *Archaeological Journal*, 153 (1996): 1–59
Jackson, Kenneth, "The Site of Mount Badon", *Journal of Celtic Studies*, 2/2 (1958): 152–55
Morris, John, *The Age of Arthur: A History of the British Isles from 350 to 650*, London: Weidenfeld and Nicolson, and New York: Scribner, 1973; revised edition, London: Weidenfeld and Nicolson, 1975

Writing probably some time in the first half of the 6th century, the British cleric Gildas describes an important victory of the Britons over the Saxons at *obsessio Badonici montis*, "the siege of Mount Badon". He claims that the battle was fought the year of his own birth, and that 44 years had passed since then (though here his Latin is a bit obscure). Bede essentially adopts Gildas's account of the battle, adding that it took place about 44 years after the Saxons arrived in Britain (which he dates to AD 449), while the *Anglo-Saxon Chronicle* is completely silent on Badon. The *Annales Cambriae* give the date AD 518 for *bellum Badonis* (a second "battle of Badon" is recorded for the year 667), and both the *Annales* and the *Historia Brittonum* attribute the victory to Arthur, though Gildas had the leader of the Britons as Ambrosius Aurelianus.

Modern scholarship concerning Badon has focused on the date and location of the battle, as well as on the identity of the general who led the Britons to victory. The latter goal, not surprisingly, has often come in the context of investigating an historical King Arthur. This is the case for CHAMBERS, who was the first to present extensive historical and philological reasoning on Badon. Never doubting that the British leader was Arthur, Chambers analysed various candidates for the location of Badon according to tactical military principles, but in the end presented nothing conclusive.

He did, however, leave a clue that was followed by JACKSON, who has tackled the subject of Arthur's battles in several articles. Taking a linguistic approach to the identification of Badon, Jackson argued that the Primitive Welsh name *Badon* would have become in Old English *Badon-byrig*, or Badbury, assuming that it was a hillfort that was besieged. There are several Badburys that fit this description, including Badbury Rings (Dorset), Badbury Hill (Berkshire), and Liddington Castle (Wiltshire), which was once known as Badbury Camp. HIRST & RAHTZ discuss the Roman and sub-Roman evidence from recent excavations at Liddington, and explain the difficulties in using such material evidence to confirm events in early medieval texts.

In the 12th century, Geoffrey of Monmouth had speculated that the battle was fought at the city of Bath. There have been many modern proponents of Bath, including the archaeologist Leslie Alcock. ALCOCK accepted the evidence of the *Annales Cambriae* and the *Historia Brittonum* as confirming the identity of Arthur as leader at Badon, and dated the battle *c.*490 according to Bede's statement that it occurred 44 years after the coming of the Saxons. However, Alcock rejected the Badbury hypothesis on linguistic grounds, arguing that the British name *Badon* was pronounced with a soft *th* rather than a hard *d*, thereby making Bath a better candidate. The battle would not have been fought in the Roman town (Aquae Sulis) itself, but rather on an adjacent hilltop or (less likely for Alcock) at a nearby pre-Roman hillfort. BURKITT & BURKITT have more recently investigated the archaeological evidence for this association of Badon with Bath.

While Alcock himself has since cast doubts on some of his textual conclusions, others have continued to support the candidacy of Bath. MORRIS accepts the philological arguments for Badon = Bath, and suggests that the nearby hill that best fits the description of *mons* is Solsbury Hill by Batheaston. Morris not only identifies Arthur as the leader of British cavalry at Badon (which he dates *c*.495), but suggests that Oesc of Kent was his English opponent. The detailed narrative of Arthur's political and military career as presented by Morris has since come under severe attack by specialists who suggest that Morris was far too accepting of his rather late textual sources.

Several more cautious works on Gildas and sub-Roman Britain appeared in the 1990s, but few have been devoted to discussion of Badon's date and location. An exception is HIGHAM, who has launched an attack on what he calls the "orthodox" view of Badon. Higham does not believe that Badon was a major victory for the Britons, bringing about a period of peace, but rather simply one of the last British victories, followed solely by English successes and eventually a treaty whose terms were unfavorable to the Britons. The main reason for Badon being the sole named battle in the *De excidio*, writes Higham, is that it just happened to occur in the year of Gildas's birth and thus was of purely personal significance to the author. Higham does not identify the location of Badon, but he dates the battle – again against the orthodox view – to *c*.430–40.

The implications of such an interpretation of Badon are immense, for this proposed chronology would date the English conquest of Britain much earlier than has been assumed by both historians and archaeologists. Early critical response to Higham's study highlighted some misunderstanding of the Latin and idiosyncratic interpretations of Gildas's biblical imagery and allegory. It remains to be seen whether Higham's provocative thesis will spark new investigations of the location and character of the battle of Mount Badon.

CHRISTOPHER A. SNYDER

See also Gildas

Mountbatten, Louis, 1st Earl Mountbatten of Burma 1900–1979

Naval commander, Viceroy of India, and chief of defence staff

Dennis, Peter, *Troubled Days of Peace: Mountbatten and South East Asia Command, 1945–1946*, Manchester: Manchester University Press, 1987

Hill, J.R. (editor), *The Oxford Illustrated History of the Royal Navy*, Oxford and New York: Oxford University Press, 1995

Hough, Richard, *Mountbatten: Hero of Our Time*, London: Weidenfeld and Nicolson, 1980

Hough, Richard, *Bless Our Ship: Mountbatten and the Kelly*, London: Hodder and Stoughton, 1991

McGeoch, Ian, *The Princely Sailor: Mountbatten of Burma*, London and Washington, DC: Brassey's, 1996

Mitchell, L.M. *et al.* (editors), *A Summary Catalogue of the Papers of Earl Mountbatten of Burma*, Southampton: University Library, 1991

Murfett, Malcolm H. (editor), *The First Sea Lords: From Fisher to Mountbatten*, Westport, Connecticut: Praeger, 1995

Rasor, Eugene L., *Earl Mountbatten of Burma, 1900–1979: Historiography and Annotated Bibliography*, Westport, Connecticut: Greenwood Press, 1998

Swinson, Arthur, *Mountbatten*, London: Pan, and New York: Ballantine, 1971

Villa, Brian Loring, *Unauthorised Action: Mountbatten and the Dieppe Raid*, Oxford: Oxford University Press, 1989

Whitaker, W. Denis and Shelagh Whitaker, *Dieppe: Tragedy to Triumph*, London: Leo Cooper, 1992

Ziegler, Philip, *Mountbatten: The Official Biography*, London: Collins, and New York: Knopf, 1985

Readers interested in Mountbatten are fortunate in that there is both an excellent and comprehensive biography, and a full and very useful bibliography. ZIEGLER took over the task of writing the authorized biography of Mountbatten from C.S. Forester. He had full access to Mountbatten's very extensive personal archives when they were at the family home of Broadlands and made very good use of them. Despite being very well researched in the Mountbatten archive, the book is easily written, and divides Mountbatten's life story up into five broad chronological sections: up to World War II; through World War II; Mountbatten's time in India; his resumed role in the Royal Navy, concluding with his performance as First Sea Lord and finally Chief of the Defence Staff; and, finally, his retirement and death at the hands of the IRA.

Ziegler shows himself to be sympathetic to his subject, but is by no means sycophantic. He is clearly aware of Mountbatten's vanity, showmanship, and conscious, even ruthless, use of his unparalleled social connections. Such a lordly figure was bound to attract controversy and to spark hostility – sometimes justified, sometimes not. Nonetheless, Mountbatten comes out well from this survey, attentive to the interests and the support of the people who worked for him, an excellent organizer, imaginative and far-seeing (not least over the prospects for India) and not afraid to speak his mind on issues he knew to be unpopular with the government. For instance, Ziegler chronicles Mountbatten's clear opposition to the Suez episode of 1956, his reluctance to support Britain's acquisition of an independent nuclear deterrent, and his continuing scepticism about the utility of nuclear weapons. In short, this model biography should be the starting-point for the study of any aspect of Mountbatten's long and varied career.

RASOR discusses some 450 other treatments of Mountbatten, breaking these down into thematic streams such as Mountbatten's naval career, his role in World War II, his connections with the royal family, and so on. Although the author of this review makes some mistakes of detail, he nonetheless provides a good survey of the works that have appeared up to 1998. His book opens with a short bibliographic review of

Mountbatten's varied career, and ends with an alphabetical and annotated list of all the works Rasor reviews. MITCHELL likewise provides a full list of the Mountbatten archive now held at Southampton University, which comprise about 250,000 papers (many official ones kept illicitly) and about 50,000 photos, tapes, and films. Anyone exploring this archive will be struck by the professionalism with which Mountbatten approached every issue (private, public, and professional), by the extraordinary breadth of his social contacts and his interests, and by his capacity for self-publicity. Nonetheless, his archive is also full of the most admiring comments of many who served with him in all capacities.

MURFETT is useful because it includes not only an essay on Mountbatten's time as first sea lord, but also a review of the benighted career of his father, Lord Battenberg, an earlier first sea lord hounded from office in the early part of World War I because of his German connection. This personal tragedy had a great effect on the young Mountbatten, and perhaps contributed to his acute awareness of the importance of what everyone else thought about him. The background to Mountbatten's naval career is well described in HILL.

During World War II, Mountbatten achieved fame in consequence of his loss of the destroyer HMS Kelly to German air attack during the Battle of Crete in 1941. Although in fact this episode did not reflect particularly well on Mountbatten's tactical or leadership qualities, it was the subject of a eulogistic film, In Which We Serve. This film became something of a trademark for the whole Royal Navy during World War II, and is widely reckoned to have aided Mountbatten's subsequent naval career. Mountbatten was aware of this and is reputed to have written over 800 letters to the men of the Kelly and their survivors. The film was made in close collaboration with Mountbatten's friend, Noel Coward, and the full story of this may be found in HOUGH. SWINSON is a short, popular, and very pictorial introduction to, and account of, Mountbatten's wartime career.

After the Kelly episode Mountbatten became chief of combined operations and, despite his relative youth and inexperience, was treated by Churchill as the equivalent of the three service chiefs. This caused some controversy and is held by the controversial VILLA to have been primarily responsible for the disasters of the 1942 Dieppe raid in which so many Canadians lost their lives. The argument is that Mountbatten relaunched a raid, earlier dismissed as too hazardous, without the consent of the service chiefs and without adequate planning. This thesis is rejected by Ziegler and by WHITAKER & WHITAKER, a Canadian general and veteran of the raid, who argues as well that the Allies learned valuable lessons from this campaign for the invasion of Europe two years later.

After this, Mountbatten went on to the South-East Asia command (and thence to India). The problems for the exhausted British of administering the area in the face of rising local nationalism and the prejudiced interference from the Americans are well told by DENNIS.

HOUGH became something of a chronicler of the family and his second book was one of the first good biographies to appear after Mountbatten's death; it is a good survey, even if written without the benefit of access to the Broadlands archive. It is warmly admiring in tone, although Mountbatten's faults are recognized. McGEOCH is the most recent biography, written

by an ex-sailor who served with Mountbatten. This book makes full use of the Broadlands archive and then existing literature; it comes to Mountbatten's defence over both the Kelly and the Dieppe affairs, lauds him for his conduct of the complex political affairs in South-East Asia and the Indian subcontinent and argues that, through the 1950s and 1960s, Mountbatten did much to modernize the Royal Navy, confirming its place and role within British defence. Mountbatten had his faults, McGeoch acknowledges, but was nonetheless a great man.

GEOFFREY TILL

See also India: Independence Movement to Partition; Navy: Modern Navy; World War II: Far East; World War II: Naval Operations

Murray, Lord George 1694–1760
Jacobite military leader

Burton, John Hill, *The History of Scotland from Agricola's Invasion to the Extinction of the Last Jacobite Insurrection*, vol. 8, Edinburgh: Blackwood, 1873

Lenman, Bruce, *The Jacobite Risings in Britain, 1689–1746*, London: Eyre Methuen, 1980

McLynn, Frank, *The Jacobites*, London and Boston: Routledge and Kegan Paul, 1985

Petrie, Charles, *The Jacobite Movement*, London: Eyre and Spottiswoode, 1932; as *The Stuart Pretenders: A History of the Jacobite Movement, 1688–1807*, Boston: Houghton Mifflin, 1935

Reid, Stuart, *1745: A Military History of the Last Jacobite Rising*, Staplehurst, Kent: Spellmount, and New York: Sarpedon, 1996

Tomasson, Katherine, *The Jacobite General*, Edinburgh: Blackwood, 1958

Until recently, Lord George Murray, the military leader of the Jacobites in the 1745 rebellion, had inspired little historiographical debate. Almost all historians emphasized Murray's military skill and refused to criticize his strategies and decisions. Many histories acknowledged that Murray's arrogance and inflexibility hindered the progress of the rebellion, but most historians attributed the greater share of the responsibility for the strained relationships among the Jacobite leaders to Charles Edward Stuart.

Early histories especially celebrated Murray's leadership and strategic abilities. BURTON called him the "ablest leader in the expedition". He also, however, acknowledged that Murray's arrogance and supreme confidence in his own abilities alienated both his fellow Jacobite leaders and Charles Edward. Their jealousy, and Charles Edward's own arrogance and overconfidence, caused Murray's advice to go often unheard. Burton also believes that Murray was one of the few Jacobite leaders with an accurate picture of their precarious situation and a full realization of the improbability of their success, but that Murray was prepared to continue in the rebellion out of principle. PETRIE concurs with much of Burton's analysis, including the personal conflicts between Murray and the other Jacobite leaders, but adds that Murray was also never able to gain the trust of his fellow Jacobites because he had taken the oath of loyalty and served in the British government until the onset of the '45. Petrie's estimation of Murray's military abilities is even more glowing than Burton's; he asserts that, had Murray not been bound by principle to fight for the Stuarts, he would have gained renown as one of the greatest British generals of all time.

TOMASSON has written the only full-length biography of Murray. Naturally, she is able to consider Murray's character and his impact on the '45 more fully; however, she seems blinded to many of Murray's faults. She emphasizes his virtues: his military skill, his reputation for discipline and organization, his thirst for knowledge, his loyalty to his family as well as to the Stuart cause, his compassion for the poor and for the soldiers under his command, and his abhorrence of corruption. In Tomasson's estimation, Murray was a loyal Briton who saw the Glorious Revolution as an injustice he was anxious to correct. He only swore his loyalty to the Hanoverian monarchs so that he could help his brother be elected to parliament. Murray gained Charles Edward's enmity, not through his arrogance or his refusal to compromise, but simply by being the voice of reason and of the clan chiefs in Charles Edward's Council of War. Charles Edward could not stand to be disagreed with, so grew to hate Murray.

Modern historians of Jacobitism, like LENMAN, tend to provide a much more balanced picture of Murray. Lenman recognizes Murray's intelligence, sophistication, and military ability and gives him credit for most of the Jacobites' early successes. Murray was also smart enough, according to Lenman, to know that a lot of the Jacobites' successes were due to pure luck and to the British army's unpreparedness for the rebellion. However, he also recognizes Murray's arrogance and his overconfidence in his own abilities. Lenman is interested in what motivated Murray to participate in the rebellion. Murray was well-read, intelligent, well-informed about British and European politics and law, and fully aware of the risks and penalties he faced by participating in the rebellion. However, his loyalty to the Stuarts caused him to join the rebellion, despite the apparent unreasonableness of that action.

McLYNN also praises Murray's military abilities, calling him the "military genius of the '45", and adds that he was only able to lead the clans because he was not a clan chief. Thus, the clans could all follow him without worrying about subordinating their pride and reputation to another clan. Despite that advantage, he still faced a great deal of clan factionalism, which he had to resolve in order to organize an effective fighting unit. Although he criticizes Murray's decision to turn back from Derby, arguing that he lost his nerve and that the ease of the Jacobite retreat proved it was unnecessary, McLynn gives less credence to accounts of Murray's flaws than many other recent writers. To McLynn, the conflicts between Murray and Charles Edward were a mixture of personal incompatibility and Charles Edward's unwillingness to take advice from anyone. McLynn asserts that Charles Edward also disliked and distrusted most of the older generation of Jacobites, whom he regarded as too cautious and timid to bring about a Stuart restoration.

The only modern author to write a military history of the '45, REID, is by far Murray's harshest critic. While agreeing that Murray was "unquestionably the most able" of the Jacobites' generals, he harshly criticizes Murray's arrogance and argues that his military knowledge and instincts were not as profound as Murray believed. He believes that Murray was talented and vigilant, but that his virtues as a general were vastly overweighed by his pride and his unwillingness to listen to others' advice. Reid argues that Murray's temper, his impatience, and his unwillingness to work with the other Jacobite officers or to follow orders with which he disagreed seriously handicapped the Jacobites at several key points in the rebellion. Murray's arrogance, his refusal to recognize his own limitations, and his "insubordinate pessimism" may have harmed the Jacobites as much as his skill and knowledge helped them.

Recently, writers such as Reid have attacked Murray's military knowledge and skill, long held in such high esteem by historians of the '45. However, he is still recognized, even by his critics, as the most talented military leader of the rebellion. Flaws in his personality have been recognized all along, especially his impatience, his extreme arrogance, and overconfidence in his own abilities, his pessimistic attitude toward the Jacobite cause, and his strained relationships with the other Jacobite leaders. Appreciation of these flaws, however, has lately led writers to criticize his military strategies during the rebellion.

KRISTEN ROBINSON

See also Jacobite Rebellions; Jacobitism; Stuart, Charles Edward

Music: Instrumental and Operatic after 1660

Burrows, Donald, "London: Commercial Wealth and Cultural Expansion" in *The Late Baroque Era from 1680 to 1740*, edited by George J. Buelow, Basingstoke: Macmillan, 1993; Englewood Cliffs, New Jersey: Prentice Hall, 1994

Caldwell, John, *The Oxford History of English Music*, vol. 2, *c.1715 to the Present Day*, Oxford: Clarendon Press, and New York: Oxford University Press, 1999

Fiske, Roger, *English Theatre Music in the Eighteenth Century*, Oxford and New York: Oxford University Press, 1973; 2nd edition, 1986

Hayes, Deborah, "Some Neglected Women Composers of the 18th Century and Their Music", *Current Musicology*, 39 (1985): 42–65

Johnstone, H. Diack and Roger Fiske (editors), *The Eighteenth Century: Music in Britain*, Oxford and Cambridge, Massachusetts: Blackwell, 1990

Leppert, Richard, *Music and Image: Domesticity, Ideology, and Socio-cultural Formation in Eighteenth-Century England*, Cambridge and New York: Cambridge University Press, 1988

Price, Curtis, Judith Mulhous, and Robert D. Hume, *Italian Opera in Late 18th-Century London*, vol. 1, *The King's Theatre, Haymarket 1778–1791*, Oxford: Clarendon Press, and New York: Oxford University Press, 1995

Purser, John, *Scotland's Music: A History of the Traditional and Classical Music of Scotland from Earliest Times to the Present Day*, Edinburgh: Mainstream/BBC Scotland, 1992

Sadie, Stanley (editor), *The New Grove Dictionary of Music and Musicians*, 20 vols, London: Macmillan, and New York: Grove's Dictionaries, 1980; 2nd edition, edited by Sadie and John Tyrrell, 29 vols and online, 2001

Weber, William, *The Rise of the Musical Classics in Eighteenth-Century England: A Study in Canon, Ritual, and Ideology*, Oxford: Clarendon Press, and New York: Oxford University Press, 1992

White, Eric Walter, *A History of English Opera*, London: Faber, 1983

The late 17th and early 18th century proved to be a time of economic wealth and prosperity for Britain. Yet political unrest and a growing sense of nationalism culminated in uprisings in Ireland and Scotland. These political, social, and economic circumstances, coupled with the increasing influx of European operatic and instrumental practices, greatly influenced and shaped the musical life of this period. While England maintained the largest examples of instrumental and operatic activity, similar examples, though on a smaller scale, were to be found in Scotland and Ireland.

Opera had developed in Italy from the last decade of the 16th century, but England was slow to embrace the developments of the Italian recitative and opera, showing a preference for the masque. With the political and social turmoil caused by the English Civil Wars, it was not until the mid to late 1650s that England saw the rise and development of the practice of semi-opera. WHITE gives a social history of the genre in England, tracing both its precursors and its fully developed form, particularly by Henry Purcell and his contemporaries. In addition, White provides a survey of opera from the death of Purcell in 1695, which saw the abeyance of English opera, until the arrival of Italian operas and George Frederick Handel in England.

By 1720 London could claim to be the Italian opera centre of Europe, boasting the support of the monarch and the nobility. Audiences flocked to see Italian operas but not all in England were enchanted with the practice. Indeed, the great success of the ballad opera *The Beggar's Opera* (1728), written in English by John Gay with music compiled by Christopher Pepusch, which was a satire on the Walpole government, the morals of society, and Italian opera, highlighted the divided opinion in English audiences. It also heralded the rise of the English burlesque opera form. Furthermore, those who followed the Italian opera were divided still further, with two rival Italian opera companies competing for the same audience. As a result, by the 1730s Handel's Italian opera company, which was supported by the king, and the rival Italian "Opera of the nobility" endorsed by the Prince of Wales, were both in financial difficulties and subsequently ruined. Nevertheless, the preference for Italian opera in a large section of British audiences saw the genre flourish in England, Ireland, and to a lesser degree in Scotland.

For opera and its variant forms in England, White remains the authoritative starting-point, giving an overview of Italian and English opera in the early 18th century concentrating on Handel, Thomas Arne, and Charles Dibdin. Following on from this, PRICE, MULHOUS, & HUME provides a most valuable and comprehensive account of the Italian opera, and ballet in London at the King's Theatre, Haymarket in the last part of the

18th century. This text, the first of two proposed volumes covering this period, examines the financial rather than the musical reasons for potential success and inevitable failure during the last half of the century. Alternatively, FISKE gives a broad and authoritative history of theatre music in 18th-century London, including examples of the growing interest in British folk music.

The main musical centres in Ireland, Scotland, and Wales, while still heavily influenced by the art music developments and activities in England, and in Europe, experienced the rise of musical societies, concert series, and festivals, although on a smaller scale. British musical activity of this period displayed an ongoing fascination with Italian vocal and instrumental music, as well as the English operatic forms, and the English oratorio. However, traditional folk and instrumental music still flourished to varying degrees during the late 17th and early 18th century in Ireland, Scotland, and Wales. As a result of political unrest and growing nationalism in Britain, many people turned with an increased interest to their own respective national folk music. The first edition of SADIE provides a brief, but detailed and comprehensive account for Ireland, Wales, and Scotland of musicological debates for both art music and traditional folk music. (For authors of these articles, see entry "Music: Plainsong and Polyphony".) In addition, the revision of Sadie for the second edition (2001), released in print and online formats, provides up-to-date bibliographies, as well as a current summation of musical developments and debates in these areas. For Scotland, PURSER also provides a combined brief history of art and folk music, which has a useful annotated bibliography.

For English art music, the early part of CALDWELL's text, which spans the period from c.1715 to 1815, gives a comprehensive account of 18th-century musical practice focusing on Handel and his English contemporaries. In addition Caldwell includes a bibliography containing the more specialized references for specific musical debates. BURROWS also gives an excellent overview of instrumental and operatic music in London from the 1690s to the 1740s, and includes a useful annotated bibliography.

While the general history of music written by Sir John Hawkins entitled *A General History of the Science and Practice of Music* (1776) included brief biographical accounts of European women composers of the period, the roles of women in recent British music history are not automatically featured. The rise of feminist musicology in the 1980s made some attempt to redress the wholesale omission of women as patrons, composers, performers (both professional and amateur), as well as audience members. As yet the study of women in British music remains a subset of the discipline, and a majority of the general music history texts either omit women or in some instances, as with JOHNSTONE & FISKE, make passing reference to women's musical involvement and musical education. HAYES's brief article attempts to place European (including English) women composers, performers, and instrumentalists in their 18th-century musical context, and shows that European women were among the visiting musical professionals who performed in Britain during this period.

The late 17th and early 18th centuries in Britain saw the rise of musical societies, and concert series and festivals for the performance of "ancient music" and hence the establishment of a canon of musical works. An alternative interpretation to the traditional history of music approach is the research into the ideology of music. From an English perspective, WEBER traces the ideology of this society that established a musical canon, and musical taste. Discussing the rationale of the men and women in British society who subscribed to the establishment of this practice, Weber places this ideology in the political and social context of the period. In addition, Weber analyses the politicized nature of the two 18th-century English general histories of music published by Charles Burney (*A General History of Music*, 1776–1789) and the aforementioned Sir John Hawkins. From a socio-cultural stance, LEPPERT examines the visual representations of private upper-class domestic music-making, and determines not only its social, but also its ideological value and cultural position.

DOLLY MacKINNON

See also Opera and Operetta

Music: Plainsong and Polyphony

Bowers, Roger, "The Performing Ensemble for English Church Polyphony *c.*1320–*c.*1390" in *Studies in the Performance of Late Medieval Music*, edited by Stanley Boorman, Cambridge and New York: Cambridge University Press, 1983

Caldwell, John, *The Oxford History of English Music*, vol. 1, *From the Beginnings to 1715*, Oxford: Clarendon Press, and New York: Oxford University Press, 1991

Crocker, Richard, "Polyphony in England in the Thirteenth Century" in *New Oxford History of Music*, vol. 2, *The Early Middle Ages to 1300*, edited by Richard Crocker and David Hiley, Oxford: Oxford University Press, 1990

Elliott, Kenneth and Frederick Rimmer, *A History of Scottish Music*, London: British Broadcasting Corporation, 1973

Harrison, Frank Ll., *Music in Medieval Britain*, London: Routledge and Kegan Paul, 1958; New York: Praeger, 1959; 4th edition, Buren, Netherlands: F. Knuf, 1980

Higgins, Paula, "Parisian Nobles, a Scottish Princess, and the Woman's Voice in Late Medieval Song", *Early Music History*, 10 (1991): 145–200

Knighton, Tess and David Fallows (editors), *Companion to Medieval and Renaissance Music*, London: Dent, and New York: Schirmer Books, 1992

Lefferts, Peter M., "Medieval England, 950–1450" in *Antiquity and the Middle Ages: From Ancient Greece to the 15th Century*, edited by James McKinnon, London: Macmillan, 1990; Englewood Cliffs, New Jersey: Prentice Hall, 1991

Sadie, Stanley (editor), *The New Grove Dictionary of Music and Musicians*, 20 vols, London: Macmillan, and Washington, DC: Grove's Dictionaries, 1980; 2nd edition, edited by Sadie and John Tyrell, 29 vols and online, 2001

The sporadic and fragmentary survival of manuscripts makes the study of English, Irish, Welsh, and Scottish monophony and polyphony problematic in a number of respects. The number of surviving musical manuscripts identifiable as from the British Isles is small and therefore leaves scant evidence to reconstruct a comprehensive picture of musical life during this period. In addition, from the perspective of sacred music alone, prior to 1066 England had an Anglo-Saxon rite, and Ireland, Scotland, and Wales had a Celtic rite. Furthermore, the Norman Conquest of England in 1066, and its subsequent far-reaching cultural influences, created a highly complex and diverse musical tradition. Wales came under English rule in 1282, and by 1300 Ireland, apart from the north-west and south-west, had been subjected to Anglo-Norman invasion, and partial conquest. Only Scotland remained an independent kingdom, but neither was it unaffected by Norman influence. Hence, to categorize the surviving music from this period by nation state is to place an artificial boundary on a cultural artefact that may represent simultaneously one language (Latin, French, Gaelic) and one religion, but a number of nations, or vice versa.

These issues are compounded by the problem of interpreting accurately early musical notation, tracing the provenance of surviving manuscripts, as well as determining the most appropriate editorial practices for transcribing medieval music for modern publication. All of these issues in musicology have resulted in a significant number of debates, which centre on the interpretation and significance of these findings. Generally, sacred music in Britain has survived in small to moderate quantities from this period; however, the secular music (including traditional vernacular music for Britain) is less represented, and nonexistent in some cases.

For example, in England after the Norman Conquest French was introduced into the court, making it difficult to track "English" music of this period. Indeed the survival of English texts in either monophonic or polyphonic settings is rare. There is also the problem of re-using musical material from a previous source in a new context and new setting, making the actual provenance of a manuscript doubly problematic. While it is clear that there was a tradition of British monophonic music, the earliest surviving examples date from the mid-12th century, with the vast majority of this genre no longer extant. Between the Norman Conquest and the Reformation, a period of 400 years, the history of British music is sparse, and because of this lacuna subject to musicological speculation.

HARRISON charts British medieval music by function, style, and form within the context of French influences, and is still a valuable starting-point and a classic text for this period. A concise account of English music is given by LEFFERTS, who places England in the context of European musical developments from the 10th to the 15th century, and provides a good overview of the major musical developments of the period. However, CALDWELL remains the most comprehensive single account of the development of medieval English monophonic and polyphonic music, tracing the English musical style from its Anglo-Saxon beginnings until the last decade of the 15th century. This text provides a detailed and systematic account of the major musical developments in form and style, such as the "English Sound" or, as it was also known, the *Contenance angloise*.

CROCKER discusses English 13th-century polyphony as not a peripheral to European developments, but rather part of the evolutionary process. English polyphony from this period is then considered an amalgam of cathedral music and the Notre-Dame style. In addition Crocker provides a good bibliography detailing more specific studies in this area.

For Ireland, Scotland, and Wales the articles in SADIE give a brief overview of the nature of the monophonic and polyphonic music of this period, as well as a discussion of surviving examples. Each article in the first edition of Sadie (1980, Ireland: Seóirse Bodley; Scotland: Kenneth Elliott; Wales: Peter Crossley-Holland) includes a detailed bibliography, and these articles and bibliographies have been revised for the second edition (2001, Ireland: Harry White; Scotland: Kenneth Elliott; Wales: Geraint Lewis), bringing them up to date with current musicological debates in these areas. ELLIOTT also provides a brief account of the sparse survival of sacred and secular music of this period for Scotland.

While the medieval manuscripts and works of art contain images that depict women and men in a myriad of activities associated with sacred and secular life, the musical history of that past has simply assumed a male dominance to the exclusion of women. This type of musicological practice is evident in the British music history tradition, and many readers might be forgiven for thinking that women played no role whatsoever in British musical culture. The relatively recent inclusion of women and gender in musicological study has begun to question these assumptions, but has only just started to make any positive inroads into the discipline.

The article by HIGGINS stands somewhat as a lone voice. This article squarely and convincingly questions the validity of the assumption that women composers, writers, and performers were not part of the medieval world, and seeks to rectify the marginalization, or at worst, omission, of women musicians and their voice. Taking an example based on evidence from medieval Scotland, Higgins tackles the early music performance assumption that the male voice was the only performance voice. Rather than opting for the notion that men sang all texts whether the text was from the female or male perspective, Higgins seeks to demonstrate that some female texts were intended to be performed by women. In addition, Higgins makes references to the broader literature on women in western music history, which spans early monastic communities through to the 20th century. Higgins concludes that as research into women in music increases, such lacunae as the absence of women in British medieval music histories will start to be rectified.

BOWERS offers an alternate view that, rather than using the visual and textual aspects of medieval society, has chosen to focus on the musical content as a way of establishing the performance practice. The assumption throughout is that the 14th-century English polyphony under discussion is performed by men. However, an interesting caveat to this debate follows, with a rejoinder to Bowers by Frank Ll. Harrison, regarding the arguments for some female performances. Bower rejects Harrison's findings, but the nature of the discussion is illuminating from the perspective of the need for a more inclusive history of British music.

The collection of essays edited by KNIGHTON & FALLOWS is wide ranging and provides a discussion of recent early music performance debates regarding pitch, instrumentation, voicings, performance practice and authenticity, and audience reception, as well as editorial practice. This text allows the reader to gain an insight into the changing attitudes of performance practice over time in the early music movement.

From a musicological standpoint there has been a tradition of music histories comprising the lives and works of great men, a history of musical forms, or one or both of the above limited to a single country. More recently there has been a greater interest in placing the music of the past in its social and political context, but the literature reflecting the application of these concerns to the history of British music of this period is not yet extensive.

DOLLY MacKINNON

Music: Popular   20th century

Bacon, Tony, *London Live: From the Yardbirds to Pink Floyd to the Sex Pistols: The Inside Story of Live Bands in the Capital's Trail-Blazing Music Clubs*, London: Balafon, and San Francisco: Miller Freeman, 1999

Chilton, John, *Who's Who of British Jazz*, London and New York: Cassell, 1997

Clarke, Donald, *The Rise and Fall of Popular Music*, London: Viking Press, and New York: St Martin's Press, 1995

Cloonan, Martin, "Popular Music and Censorship in Britain: An Overview", *Popular Music and Society*, 19/3 (1995): 75–104

Cloonan, Martin, *Banned! Censorship of Popular Music in Britain, 1967–1992*, Aldershot, Hampshire: Arena, 1996

Davies, Chris, *British and American Hit Singles: 51 Years of Transatlantic Hits, 1946–1997*, London: Batsford, 1998

Frith, Simon, *Sound Effects: Youth, Leisure, and the Politics of Rock 'n' Roll*, New York: Pantheon, 1981; London: Constable, 1983

Gregory, Hugh, *A Century of Pop*, Chicago: Capella, 1998

Hochman, Steve (editor), *Popular Musicians*, 4 vols, Pasadena, California: Salem Press, 1999

Johnstone, Nick, *"Melody Maker": History of 20th-Century Popular Music*, London: Bloomsbury, 1999

Larkin, Colin (compiler and editor), *The Encyclopedia of Popular Music*, 3rd edition, 8 vols, London: Macmillan, 1998; abridged as *The Virgin Encyclopedia of Popular Music*, 4th edition, London: Virgin Books, 2002

MacDonald, Ian, *Revolution in the Head: The Beatles' Records and the Sixties*, London: Fourth Estate, and New York: Holt, 1994; 2nd edition, London: Fourth Estate, 1997

MacKinnon, Niall, *The British Folk Scene: Musical Performance and Social Identity*, Milton Keynes, Buckinghamshire and Philadelphia: Open University Press, 1993

Palmer, Tony, *All You Need is Love: The Story of Popular Music*, edited by Paul Medlicott, London: Weidenfeld and Nicolson / Chappell, and New York: Grossman, 1976

Pickering, David, *Brewer's Twentieth-Century Music*, London, Cassell, 1994; revised edition, as *Cassell Companion to 20th-Century Music*, 1997

Savage, Jon, *England's Dreaming: Sex Pistols and Punk Rock*, London: Faber, 1991; New York: St Martin's Press, 1991; revised edition, as *England's Dreaming: Anarchy, Sex Pistols, Punk Rock, and Beyond*, London: Faber, 2001

Street, John, *Rebel Rock: The Politics of Popular Music*, Oxford and Cambridge, Massachusetts: Blackwell, 1986

Ward, Ed, Geoffrey Stokes, and Ken Tucker, *Rock of Ages: The Rolling Stone History of Rock and Roll*, New York: Rolling Stone Press / Summit Books, and Harmondsworth: Penguin, 1986

Despite the 19th-century German charge that Britain is a land without music, British popular music was the pace-setter for many global trends in the later 20th century. Nevertheless, it must be remembered that the postwar evolution of discrete youth identities, in which music was to play such an important part, owed much to American influence, so that the history of American popular music forms a necessary background and a continuing context. Therefore, the following selection of books is divided between, on the one hand, general popular-music histories or reference works and, on the other, British-orientated studies.

As PALMER explains, with popular music "no one knows a song is good until the public says so". This dependence on commercial success is, in many ways, crippling to the study of popular music because "popularization tends to diminish anything that has pretensions to Art". With this caveat in place, Palmer proceeds to attempt to trace the development of modern popular music from its earliest roots in Africa, and in African-American music from the American South, through ragtime, the birth of jazz in New Orleans, the development of the Blues in the Mississippi delta, the development of "show music" in Tin Pan Alley, burlesque, the development of "hill-billy" music in the Blue Ridge Mountains, to the birth of folk and rock and roll. He takes the story through to the Beatles, and the development of British pop and rock music as a major global influence, but, as his publication date suggests, stops at the point where the grassroots reaction of British Punk music began. Palmer shows that popular music develops as older musical traditions are modified to meld with, or react against, local cultural traditions and pressures.

GREGORY composes the history of the 20th-century's popular music from a very broad background. Arguing that all preceding types of music combined to shape the sounds of the 20th century, Gregory examines over 150 musical genres, some of the technology that drove the music, and the artists who performed it. Using flowcharts, Gregory attempts to trace the influence of early and contemporary styles on each of the genres he examines. Likewise, PICKERING, in a dictionary format, attempts to provide an overview of the 20th century's contribution to popular music. He defines "popular music" as "commercially oriented music" and attempts to provide insight into genres as diverse as punk rock, football songs, and utility music. Although the work lacks in-depth coverage of any one topic, it serves as a useful encyclopedic resource, with many British references. In 1998, LARKIN published the 3rd edition of his immense, alphabetically arranged, eight-volume encyclopedia, which has become the principal library-level reference resource. His single-volume distillation, the *Virgin Encyclopedia of Popular Music*, is now in its 4th edition, and is the most convenient and authoritative reference tool for the individual student and researcher. DAVIES provides a 51-year listing of British and American hit singles, thus encapsulating the trends in popular-music tastes and the rise and fall in the popularity of individual genres and artists.

HOCHMAN's four-volume set may provide the most comprehensive narrative of the history of popular music of the 20th century. Although noticeably skimpy on swing, jazz, and ragtime, the set provides thorough coverage of the development of folk, country, rock, and rap, as well as well-crafted entries covering the major personalities from these genres. The inclusion of a chronology and a discography adds to its value.

The breadth of this subject-matter necessarily means that there are many critical works that focus on just one of the many genres of popular music. Among the most thoroughly covered is rock and roll, and WARD, STOKES, & TUCKER's work, under the auspices of *Rolling Stone* magazine, is one of the most thorough on the subject. Comparing the birth of rock to the American national motto – *e pluribus unum* (out of many, one) – this work argues that rock music evolved as a combination of the best sounds and traditions of all of the varied musical styles that preceded it. A combination of cultural, critical, economic, and narrative evidence makes this a comprehensive and enjoyable analysis of this body of music.

In terms of specifically British-orientated studies, the field is not overpopulated, though there is a proliferation of hagiographical and journalistic material to be found. The Beatles in particular have, however, found their way into serious musicological studies or series mostly devoted to classical music. Out of the many other publications on these most celebrated exponents of British popular music, MACDONALD's much-praised book straddles the line between a general readership level and a student-level cultural study. It balances discussion of the Beatles' songs and their sources, avoiding undue musicological terminology, with an exposition of context, both biographical and cultural.

STREET traces the way that the British popular-music industry functions as an economic entity, and the way in which the industry shapes political values and experiences through its music. He claims his primary goal is to provide "reasons for taking popular music so seriously while trying to understand why it gives me and millions of others so much pleasure". Street posits that while popular music is primarily motivated by commercial ambitions, it also serves as a purveyor of political messages. As Street writes, "here the politics is pleasure". Popular music can give a voice to desires and messages that would otherwise remain unspoken. Street holds that the inherent political messages of popular music force governments to get involved in the popular music industry. It is the history of this relationship, between pop music and politicians, that Street sets forth as the critical history of popular music. However, for the history of political attempts to control and muzzle British popular music – to deny its "voice" – then the publications by CLOONAN, among others, should be consulted. As so often happens with censorship, such accounts say far more about the people, institutions, and sensitivities behind the censoring than they do about the object of the censorship. Attempts by the BBC to ban late-era Beatles records were farcical, in that they so often picked relatively innocent songs while missing more overt drug references in others. In 1977, while a large proportion of the United Kingdom was celebrating the queen's silver jubilee, the Sex Pistols reached number one in the charts with their counter-cultural "God Save the Queen", despite (or perhaps because of) a BBC ban on radio airplay: a particularly vivid expression of establishment and youth cultures seemingly at war with one another. The year

4

38

1977 figures largely in SAVAGE's book, now in an updated edition. A cut above much popular-music journalism in its breadth of comparison and interdisciplinarity, the book combines contemporary history, personal reminiscence and diary extracts (Savage documented the Punk explosion as it happened), and an attempt to situate this most militantly rejectionist of popular-music forms in a context of postwar youth subcultures.

Simon FRITH wrote *Sound Effects* in response to the general lack of serious analysis of British rock. Towards that end, he examines popular music as an industry that produces and consumes meanings. Frith's work details the interrelations among the artists who create popular music, the recording industry, the mass media, and the consumers. Like Street, Frith points out the competing forces that exist in the popular-music industry, the messages of pleasure created by the artists, and the attempts by the industry and government to police those messages. Frith provides a history of the industry and the inherent contradictions involved in this unique relationship. CLARKE also approaches the history of popular music with an understanding that the economic forces within the industry play a vital role in the history of popular music. He argues that popular music must remain commercial in that it must be successful in the open market to survive as a genre. Although the vast majority of the work covers the history of pop before 1960, Clarke does provide minimal coverage of the impact of modern technology on popular music.

JOHNSTONE traces the history of popular music through the articles and columns of *Melody Maker*, the longest-running British popular-music periodical, which existed between 1926 to 2000 before being absorbed into its competitor, the *New Musical Express*. Johnstone uses original *Melody Maker* articles to provide a documentation of popular music as it happened. BACON's history of the London live-music scene provides insight into both the role of the live-music venues as a means of popularizing music genres and the role of live rock performances in London culture.

Finally, although the term "popular music" is so often understood to mean, essentially, pop, rock, and their derivatives, two other popular-music forms that have retained loyal followings are the subject of Chilton and MacKinnon. CHILTON provides over 800 biographies of British jazz musicians, from the dawn of jazz in Britain to contemporary jazz masters. This work provides rare insight into a form of jazz that is often overshadowed by its American counterpart. MACKINNON provides a complete study of the development and history of the British folk-music scene. Including an analysis of the social factors that led to the development of the genre, and which have shaped its forms and themes, MacKinnon offers a unique social-science perspective.

B. KEITH MURPHY
GEORGE WALSH

See also Youth Culture

Music: 16th and 17th Centuries

Bray, Roger (editor), *The Sixteenth Century: Music in Britain*, Oxford and Cambridge, Massachusetts: Blackwell, 1995

Caldwell, John, *The Oxford History of English Music*, vol. 1, *From the Beginnings to 1715*, Oxford: Clarendon Press, and New York: Oxford University Press, 1991

Elliott, Kenneth and Frederick Rimmer, *A History of Scottish Music*, London: British Broadcasting Corporation, 1973

Fellowes, Edmund H., *English Cathedral Music*, 5th edition, revised by J.A. Westrup, London: Methuen, 1969; reprinted, Westport, Connecticut: Greenwood Press, 1981

Flood, William H. Gratton, *A History of Irish Music*, Dublin: Browne and Nolan, 1905; reprinted, 3rd edition, Shannon: Irish Universities Press, and New York: Praeger, 1970

Holman, Peter, "London: Commonwealth and Restoration" in *The Early Baroque Era: From the Late 16th Century to the 1660s*, edited by Curtis Price, Basingstoke: Macmillan, and Englewood Cliffs, New Jersey: Prentice Hall, 1993

Purser, John, *Scotland's Music: A History of the Traditional and Classical Music of Scotland from Earliest Times to the Present Day*, Edinburgh: Mainstream in conjunction with BBC Scotland, 1992

Sadie, Stanley (editor), *The New Grove Dictionary of Music and Musicians*, 20 vols, London: Macmillan, and New York: Grove's Dictionaries, 1980; 2nd edition, edited by Sadie and John Tyrrell, 29 vols and online, 2001

Spink, Ian (editor), *The Seventeenth Century: Music in Britain*, Oxford and Cambridge, Massachusetts: Blackwell, 1992

Spink, Ian, *Restoration Cathedral Music, 1660–1714*, Oxford: Clarendon Press, and New York: Oxford University Press, 1995

Temperley, Nicholas, *The Music of the English Parish Church*, 2 vols, Cambridge and New York: Cambridge University Press, 1979

Walls, Peter, "London, 1603–1649" in *The Early Baroque Era: From the Late 16th Century to the 1660s*, edited by Curtis Price, Basingstoke: Macmillan, and Englewood Cliffs, New Jersey: Prentice Hall, 1993

Among other factors influencing musical development in this period, the staggered experience of religious Reformation in England, Ireland, and Wales between 1536 and 1548, and then Scotland in 1560, coupled with the political upheaval of the Civil Wars, and Scottish and Irish uprisings in the 17th and 18th centuries, are important features. The articles on Ireland, Scotland, and Wales in SADIE (see entry "Music: Plainsong and Polyphony" for authors), give a brief account of the musical circumstances of each nation during this period. Welsh church music tradition basically disappeared with the dissolution of the monasteries, while in the English-dominated centre of Ireland the Gaelic tradition held little or no sway. Elliott & Rimmer provide a concise account of Scottish music prior to and after the Reformation of 1560. Sadie provides detailed bibliographies for the more specialized musical debates, as well as references to the classic music histories of Ireland, Scotland, and Wales.

There are a number of general histories that are still useful starting-points, regardless of their faults and the fact that they do not meet the current musicological standards of scholarship. For Ireland, FLOOD, while problematic for reasons including its patriotism and lack of referencing, still gives a valuable historical overview of the Celtic-Irish and Anglo-Irish music traditions, and can point to possible further avenues of research. The articles for Ireland in Sadie, however, provide current scholarly debates for both "art" music and traditional music, including detailed bibliographies for specialized areas of scholarship.

For Scotland, ELLIOTT & RIMMER, though only a slim volume, provides a valuable starting-point giving a chronological overview of Scottish art music. For a more recent and inclusive general music history, PURSER covers both art music as well as traditional folk music, and includes an annotated bibliography. Again for a brief overview of Scottish music, the article in Sadie is invaluable, and includes specialized bibliographies.

For England, CALDWELL provides the most comprehensive account of the secular and sacred vocal and instrumental music. From the beginnings of the "English sound" (or *Contenance angloise*) that developed in the mid-14th century and influenced the musical practice on the Continent, through to the rise and establishment of English opera in the 17th century (and the arrival of its Italian counterpart in the early 18th century), Caldwell deals with English musical form and style in its social context. Caldwell provides a detailed synthesis of scholarly work, complete with a comprehensive bibliography.

BRAY provides a detailed discussion of the major stylistic developments, and social context for the period predominantly from an English perspective – despite the subtitle of *Music in Britain*. Covering the compositional theory, as well as performance practice, of the period, Bray charts the sacred and secular vocal and instrumental music, focusing on the roles of composer, performer, and audience in the 16th century. In addition he includes a brief reference (several pages) to Scottish and Welsh music.

The loss of the royal court of Scotland in 1603, to the south, placed London as the major musical centre for James VI and I. Concentrating on London during the 17th century, WALLS and HOLMAN provide a detailed overview of the social history of musical patronage, as well as the professional and amateur musicians and audiences of the city. This text discusses musical performances, music education, and musical activities within a social, political, and religious context.

As with Bray, the focus and content of the text edited by SPINK (1992) is predominantly centred on English musical history and practice. However, Spink does provide an excellent starting-point for any musical research of this period not only for England, but also for any study of musical genres. This collection of essays provides a detailed musical overview of the period, drawing on the major social, historical, and musical developments and trends concerning church music, vocal music, and consort music, as well as music for the theatre, and the beginnings of opera in England. This text also contains an extensive bibliography.

FELLOWES provides a concise, but detailed overview of English cathedral music of the period, charting the problematic nature of religious and liturgical upheaval that occurred after the English Reformation, and subsequent rapid alternations between the Latin and the vernacular (English) texts that occurred until the reign of Elizabeth I. His discussion is from the perspective of composers, and musical form and style. Caldwell also offers a discussion of English sacred music from the 15th to the early 18th century, providing a more recent discussion of the period, which includes a detailed bibliography of more specialized material in this area. SPINK (1995) provides a

discussion of choral service, musical sources, and performance practice, as well as individual cathedral and collegiate foundations within the religious context of the period. Spink focuses on the Restoration period, and therefore offers the more detailed account. Both Fellowes and Spink are concerned with the cathedral music (anthems and services) of England, while TEMPERLEY covers the music created for and performed in English parish churches, which was simpler and of a congregational nature. Temperley considers contrasting musical evidence from four regions of England: the West Riding of Yorkshire, Dorset, central London, and the cathedral city of York. This still remains a classic text.

While feminist musicology has been in existence since the 1980s, there has yet to be a major overhaul of the general survey histories of British music from this perspective. At best – and this remains true for the period under discussion here – women remain occasional, but welcome inclusions in some texts, a constant omission in others.

DOLLY MACKINNON

Music Hall
see **Drama and Theatre: 19th Century**

Myths of Origin

Hanning, Robert W., *The Vision of History in Early Britain: From Gildas to Geoffrey of Monmouth*, New York: Columbia University Press, 1966

Kendrick, T.D., *British Antiquity*, London: Methuen, 1950; New York: Barnes and Noble, 1970

Kidd, Colin, *British Identities before Nationalism: Ethnicity and Nationhood in the Atlantic World, 1600–1800*, Cambridge and New York: Cambridge University Press, 1999

MacDougall, Hugh A., *Racial Myth in English History: Trojans, Teutons, and Anglo-Saxons*, Hanover, New Hampshire: University Press of New England, and Montreal: Harvest House, 1982

Piggott, Stuart, *Ancient Britons and the Antiquarian Imagination: Ideas from the Renaissance to the Regency*, London: Thames and Hudson, 1989

Reynolds, Susan, "Medieval *Origines Gentium* and the Community of the Realm", *History*, 68 (1983): 375–90

Simmons, Clare A., *Reversing the Conquest: History and Myth in Nineteenth-Century British Literature*, New Brunswick, New Jersey: Rutgers University Press, 1990

Smiles, Sam, *The Image of Antiquity: Ancient Britain and the Romantic Imagination*, New Haven, Connecticut and London: Yale University Press, 1994

The best introductory work on the history of British origin myths, a seminal study in its time and still an important point of departure, is KENDRICK's study of the development of ideas of origin from the Middle Ages to the Renaissance. Starting with the medieval theories of the Trojan foundation of Britain, especially the enormously influential *Historia Regum Britanniae* written by Geoffrey of Monmouth in the early 12th century, Kendrick goes on to consider the transmission and adaptations of the British myths into the 16th century, where the continuity from archaic origins functioned as a legitimizing basis for the Tudor regime. Later in the 16th century, however, humanist historiography, which had been introduced into England by Polydore Vergil earlier in the century, replaced the myth of Trojan origin with an account of the Teutonic origin of English people, language, and social structures. The transition, in Kendrick's view, is from medieval ignorance and naivety, to modern historical consciousness, arising in the 16th century as historians and antiquarians become increasingly concerned with empirical evidence, as opposed to their forebears' reliance on textual tradition and repetition.

The major medieval texts which produced this tradition of the "matter of Britain" – by Gildas, the author traditionally identified as Nennius, and Geoffrey of Monmouth – are covered by HANNING, who sees these narratives, along with Bede's *Historia ecclesiastica*, as combinations of national and ecclesiastical narratives, a narrative tradition which subsequently, post-Conquest, becomes infused with a number of romance elements in Geoffrey's pseudo-history.

Although REYNOLDS does not consider the origin stories of Nennius and Geoffrey in detail, she does analyse how such origin stories were produced and disseminated throughout Europe in the 8th century and subsequently. This article has considerable bearing on a number of the issues that arise in most considerations of origin myths and their place within national historiography. Reynolds looks at how such narratives of origin – whether Noahic, Trojan, or Teutonic – were credible attempts of various ethnic groups to establish a historical identity. Furthermore, she addresses underlying questions related to the origin myths, in particular how, and to what extent they came into being as part of the development of nations.

Another highly influential view of the medieval–modern transition comes from MACDOUGALL, who argues that the switch in the Renaissance from belief in Trojan origin to the sense of common Saxon descent expresses a sense of history which, while empirically more valid, is similarly driven by contemporaneous political concerns. Whereas the Trojan myth had been instrumental in forging an English national identity in the 12th and 13th centuries, and had been used as support for the dynastic and geographical claims of Plantagenet and later Tudor and Stuart dynasties, the Anglo-Saxon myth postulates a set of racial characteristics for the English, as inherited from their Gothic ancestors, which guarantee a unique, special role for the nation. MacDougall's work is thus one of the seminal texts in the study of "Saxonism": the belief that there is a definable, continuous racial and cultural tradition originating in the Teutonic tribes who settled England in the early Middle Ages.

Nevertheless, the developing interest in Saxon origins did not completely occlude the sense of British origin, and both in

artistic and literary expressions, and in the field of antiquarian discovery and speculation, the ancient British origin myth continued to be the subject of attention throughout the 17th and 18th centuries. PIGGOTT discusses the course of antiquarian discourse on ancient Britons from the end of the 16th to the end of the 18th century. While in Kendrick's study of the Renaissance, the key historical text in the transition from medieval to modern had been Camden's *Britannia* (1586), for Piggott the high point of antiquarianism before the 19th century is the publication in 1695 of Gibson and Tanner's edition of *Britannia*. The late 17th century being the time of the foundation of the Royal Society, Piggott observes that this work is notable particularly in that the study of antiquarian history is shown to depend on inference from material remains. Nevertheless, in Piggott's view, antiquarian investigations continued to be contaminated by myth, particularly the biblical myth of creation and propagation, and the consequent belief in Noahic origin. Crucially, Piggott considers the antiquarian discourse of the 17th and 18th centuries within terms of the *idea* of early Britons; thus, the two images of the early Briton that emerged from the antiquarians' work of the 17th and 18th centuries – the painted naked savage carrying a club, and the druid – went on to have a long-lived and culturally expansive impact.

In the best recent book on British origin myths, KIDD analyses the varying ideologies of ethnicity in the pre-nationalist British world. With regard to current historiographical debates on the question of pre-modern national identity, an area that Reynolds also considers in depth, Kidd views the pre-modern ideology as expressing primordial, or proto-nationalist modes of identity. The three key areas of his analysis of these identities are the theological (including the belief in Noahic migrations and settlements), the constitutional origins and developments of church and state, and the sense of racial lineage and difference. Moreover, in addition to the breadth of analysis and depth of scholarship, Kidd considers the same questions within the various ethnicities of the archipelago, showing how Irish and Scottish ideologies and historiographies expressed the concerns of origin and identity.

SMILES looks at the uses of archaic British myth in art and literature from the beginnings of the Romantic period to the mid-19th century. He regards these uses as examples of a search for national identity, an identity to be constructed through the imagining of mythical origin. Distinguishing between these imaginings and the "scientific" areas of such national constructions as archaeology, he sees artistic and literary images of ancient Britain as "romantic" formations, but argues that such images and formations had, and continue to have, a greater impact on popular notions of the origins of the British than the empirical, specialized historiography of the 19th century and modern archaeologists.

SIMMONS considers the cultural impact of the Anglo-Saxon myth in the 19th century, in the literature of the period, in its influence on such areas as the British monarchy, and on local and national events such as the millennial celebrations for Alfred the Great in 1901 (at the time Alfred was believed to have died in 901; 899 is now the accepted date). These cultural expressions are seen as part of a general and continuing adherence to the Saxonist myth of origin, which had by the 19th century come to occupy the central place in national historiography. Simmons also analyses the development of such concerns with Saxon origins in the work of Saxonist historians, from Sharon Turner at the beginning of the century, to Freeman in the mid-to-late century. However, unlike Kidd and Smiles, Simmons is slightly disappointing in making large claims for the cultural aspects of her analysis, but not fully or consistently developing the links between the various areas of her study: historiography, romance, novel, as well as other cultural forms.

ANTHONY MARTIN

See also Anglo-Saxon Chronicle; Bede's Ecclesiastical History; Chronicles; Gildas; Historia Brittonum; Identities, National entries; Irish Annals

N

Napoleonic Wars: Trafalgar and the War at Sea 1803–1815

Black, Jeremy and Philip Woodfine (editors), *The British Navy and the Use of Naval Power in the Eighteenth Century*, Leicester: Leicester University Press, 1988; Atlantic Highlands, New Jersey: Humanities Press, 1989

Clowes, William Laird, *The Royal Navy: A History from the Earliest Times to the Present*, vols 4 and 5, Boston: Little Brown, and London: Low Marston, 1900

Hill, J.R. (general editor), *The Oxford Illustrated History of the Royal Navy*, Oxford and New York: Oxford University Press, 1995

Howarth, David, *Trafalgar: The Nelson Touch*, New York: Atheneum, and London: Collins, 1969

Marcus, Geoffrey J., *The Age of Nelson: The Royal Navy, 1793–1815*, New York: Viking Press, and London: Allen and Unwin, 1971

Marcus, Geoffrey J., *Heart of Oak: A Survey of British Sea Power in the Georgian Era*, London and New York: Oxford University Press, 1975

O'Brian, Patrick, *Master and Commander*, Philadelphia: J.B. Lippincott, 1969; London: Collins, 1970 (first in a series of 20 historical novels)

Rodger, N.A.M., *The Wooden World: An Anatomy of the Georgian Navy*, Annapolis, Maryland: Naval Institute Press, and London: Collins, 1986

Two excellent histories of the Royal Navy in the French Revolutionary and Napoleonic eras (1789–1815) are available (Clowes and Hill). The choice depends upon the depth and breadth of the reader's interest. Either work stands as an excellent starting point. For a highly detailed history, CLOWES's multi-volume work is preferred. Although a century old, it has stood up well as a purely operational history of British naval affairs to the end of the 19th century. Volumes 4 and 5 cover the period of the French Revolution and Napoleon and focus on what Clowes called the "peculiar circumstances which gave us that victory [Trafalgar]". While acknowledging that the leadership of Vice-Admiral Viscount Horatio Nelson was the seminal ingredient ("great controlling factor") in determining victory over the combined French and Spanish forces under Admiral Villeneuve, other influences such as the superiority of British gunnery both in rate of fire and general effectiveness are cited. In dealing with works of the period immediately prior to World War I, however, the reader is cautioned to remember that naval histories, in particular Clowes and that by Rear Admiral Alfred T. Mahan of the United States, sought both to chronicle operational events and to argue for larger, more capable navies based on the concept of command of the sea ensured by powerful battleships.

By contrast, HILL provides a more concise depiction of the war with France that might be more appropriate as a starting reference point or where the voluminous detail of Clowes is neither necessary nor desired. Articles by the eminent naval historians John Hattendorf on "The Struggle With France, 1690–1815" and Daniel A. Baugh on "The Eighteenth-Century Navy as a National Institution, 1690–1815" provide both a brief operational overview and details of naval finance, shipbuilding, manning, naval architecture, health, discipline, and public perceptions of the naval service. Additionally, articles addressing pre-Georgian naval affairs by J.D. Davies and David Loades establish a baseline for understanding the dominance of British sea power by 1793 from humble Tudor beginnings.

Continuing in this vein of contextual reading, BLACK & WOODFINE provide a series of articles from prominent naval historians on several aspects of the development of British sea power through the 18th century. The rise of British naval, commercial, and imperial maritime dominance by 1789 can only be understood within this context. The central focus of the articles is to "collectively throw light on the extent and limitations of British strength" relative to an increasingly dominant and skilled Royal Navy and the expanding mercantile and political empire spurred on by maritime commerce. Topics include naval finance and the political ramifications of the parliamentary budget process, French naval expansion after the 1730s and the direct challenge to Britain, the impact of economic warfare on national strength, the difficulty in achieving and maintaining naval superiority, the actual use of naval power in relation to its perceived capability, and the laying of the foundations of British power in the post-Napoleonic period through the rise of maritime dominance in the 18th century.

MARCUS (*The Age of Nelson*) provides a keenly focused depiction of naval events of the period. In addition to addressing operational details of the naval war against France, he analyses the period's historical context and "lessons learned". Reacting to the traditional academic prejudice against the study of naval history as well as the 19th-century Admiralty's seeming lack of interest in applying the lessons of the period to the formulation of naval policy for the early 20th century, Marcus analyses the "supremely important lessons for the Navy" including the proper use of intelligence, defence against invasion, joint (military and naval) operations, and commerce protection. The struggle between a land power and a naval power and the resultant issues of formulating policy and strategy play large in his analysis.

MARCUS (*Heart of Oak*) and RODGER both provide a broad view of life in the Georgian navy and the age of Nelson. Reading these in conjunction with the operational histories, one sees a more complete picture of naval affairs from not only the strategic, political, and tactical levels, but also the social, economic, and personal viewpoints as well. Each author analyses manning and personnel issues such as the social background of the various ranks and rates, recruitment patterns, duties, and promotion. Life at sea is featured prominently, especially topics such as health and hygiene, discipline, morale, shore leave, women and children onboard warships, and messing and berthing. The thrust of both Marcus and Rodger is to examine those "important factors which, in the usual narrative treatment of naval history, are likely to be overlooked altogether". Other critical factors include shipbuilding materials and methods, naval strategy and tactics, seamanship and navigation, maritime law and rights, naval administration, and the decisive nature of the war on trade in the ultimate victory over Napoleonic France.

HOWARTH provides a highly readable and thorough chronology of the battle of Trafalgar. He is particularly adept at portraying the personalities and characteristics of the key officers of each side. While not intended as a scholarly research source (as indicated by the lack of foot- or endnotes), it nonetheless is based on significant research into personal archives and letters, as is typical of Howarth's military and naval histories. It should be read in conjunction with and as a capstone to works such as those cited above where a contextual basis has already been established.

The historical novels of O'BRIAN are enjoyed by readers from the casual to highly analytical, scholarly historians. Remarkable for their accurate portrayal of life at sea and the particulars of naval warfare, the 20 novels follow the career of Captain Jack Aubrey and Surgeon Stephen Maturin. Despite their status as historical fiction, the research and scholarship underpinning each novel is extraordinary. O'Brian's novels are a highly recommended companion for any serious study of the Royal Navy, sea power, and maritime affairs in the French Revolutionary and Napoleonic eras.

STANLEY D.M. CARPENTER

See also French Revolutionary Wars; Navy: Sailing; Nelson

Napoleonic Wars: Waterloo and the War on Land 1803–1815

Chandler, David, *Waterloo: The Hundred Days*, London: Osprey, 1980; New York: Macmillan, 1981
Chandler, David and Ian Beckett (editors), *The Oxford Illustrated History of the British Army*, Oxford and New York: Oxford University Press, 1994

Fortescue, John William, *A History of the British Army*, vols 4–10, London and New York: Macmillan, 1899–1930
Gates, David, *The Spanish Ulcer: A History of the Peninsular War*, New York: Norton, and London: Allen and Unwin, 1986
Glover, Michael, *Wellington as Military Commander*, London: Batsford, and Princeton, New Jersey: Van Nostrand, 1968
Howarth, David, *Waterloo: Day of Battle*, New York: Atheneum, 1968; as *A Near Run Thing: The Day of Waterloo*, London: Collins, 1968
Longford, Elizabeth, *Wellington*, vol. 1, *The Years of the Sword*, London: Weidenfeld and Nicolson, 1969; New York: Harper and Row, 1970
Oman, Charles, *A History of the Peninsular War*, 6 vols, Oxford: Clarendon Press, 1902–30; reprinted, New York: AMS Press, 1980
Oman, Charles W.C., *Wellington's Army, 1809–1814*, London: Arnold, and New York: Longmans Green, 1912

In addressing British involvement in land warfare in the French Revolutionary and Napoleonic wars, four major sub-themes make for the best arrangement of reading: the British army's character and general operational history; the Duke of Wellington as a commander; the Peninsular campaign of 1808–13; and the Waterloo campaign of 1815.

No operational and tactical study of the British army is complete without FORTESCUE's multi-volume work, the seminal history of the army from its Elizabethan roots as the Trained Bands (from 1573) through the embodiment of the first standing force, the New Model Army (1645), and into the 19th-century imperial era. It was published over three decades, and all operational histories since flow from its precise and highly detailed accounts of every significant engagement in which British regular and imperial troops participated until 1870. The maps are superior, simple to follow, and attractively presented. For the late Napoleonic wars (1812–15) up to Waterloo, Fortescue supplies two complete volumes of fold-out maps. While Fortescue concentrates most of his efforts on the Napoleonic wars period (1803–15), a brief scan of the earlier volumes gives the reader an appropriate contextual background for the British army of 1793 at the dawn of two decades of conflict with France.

CHANDLER & BECKETT offer the most concise, yet readable and informative (but still scholarly) survey of the history of the army yet produced. Noted historians including Ian Roy, John Childs, David Chandler, Alan Guy, Tony Hayter, and David Gates provide sections detailing the army from the Civil War to Waterloo. As with Fortescue, the work provides a contextual background within which to understand the nature, organization, administration, command structure, personnel, and tactics of the army that fought against France. Reading it in conjunction with selected portions of Fortescue, the reader can adjust his or her level of depth from a general chronological narrative on the character of the army to the highly specific, detailed history of every British military operation in the period.

LONGFORD, a direct descendant by marriage of Arthur Wellesley, the first Duke of Wellington, victor over the French in the Peninsular campaign (Iberia) and Napoleon at Waterloo, strives to "illuminate" the duke's military career using not only official accounts and documents, but also personal letters and journals. In so doing, she humanizes the greatest, and ultimately most successful British personality in the struggle with Napoleonic France. Readers who desire a purely operational history of the war will most likely prefer many of the other, equally respectable biographies of Wellington; however, Longford adds a valuable human quality to the popular image of the cold, distant military genius.

By contrast, GLOVER portrays the purely military aspects of Wellington as a commanding officer. More importantly, he places the duke, his decisions, and the results in the context of the "state of the British army" of the day and the operational environment with which he contended. Glover's analysis of Wellington as a commander is greatly enhanced by an introductory discussion of the character of the British army during the period. One of Wellington's most striking qualities was his ability to extract the maximum military effectiveness from whatever troops he commanded, whether they be regular British, allied Portuguese, or Spanish guerillas (or, as Glover contends, to "make the best use of a situation as he found it").

The single best source for authoritative operational details of the war against the French in the Iberian peninsula, the seat of the most active, direct, and sustained land combat between Britain and France, is OMAN's classic multi-volume history of the Peninsular War. Oman provides the most comprehensive chronological narrative and general history of the campaign to date. The first series of such histories emerged in the 1820s but by 1900 many new primary source materials including memoirs, private correspondence, diaries, and so forth had been located since the first contemporary narratives had been published. Oman incorporated these new sources as well as eliminated the particular biases of earlier writers based on their actual participation in the military and political events of the era.

Oman realized that his historical narrative lacked the contextual quality needed fully to understand the war in the Iberian peninsula and the actions of the major combatants, particularly Wellington. Accordingly, he published in 1912 a study of the duke's Peninsular army (*Wellington's Army*) that addresses the "organization, its day to day life, and its psychology". As a precursor of the modern histories that incorporate the human and organizational aspects of military history into the details of tactics, operations, and strategy, the book broke new ground at the time of its publication. Taken together, the Oman histories represent a truly comprehensive study of the dynamics of the war in Portugal and Spain.

Perhaps as a tribute to Oman's scholarship and authority, no writer published a general history of the Peninsular War for half a century following his last volume. There are, however, several drawbacks to the older works, not least of which is the immense depth of detail, anachronistic writing style, and cost or availability that make them inappropriate for the modern reader. GATES, using traditional as well as newly mined sources, provides a more contemporary and readable analysis of the Peninsular War. While addressing some aspects of the major economic, political, and social factors that influenced the course of the campaign, Gates's work is essentially an operational military history of the Peninsular War and should thus be read in conjunction with other works to obtain the full contextual picture.

A great deal of national mythology surrounds the events of the Waterloo campaign. The French view the episode as a momentary and tragic aberration. The British typically downplay the contribution of the allied Prussian, Dutch, Belgian, and Hanoverian forces; Germans accuse Wellington of failing to support Blücher's Prussians. To clear the air and to place Waterloo in its proper historical context, CHANDLER presents, through a lively text and abundant maps, "a clear visual representation of the whole affair". Additionally, he provides a thorough analysis of events leading up to and resulting from the events of 15–18 June 1815. Embedded in the narrative flow are sections addressing the individual commanders as well as the troops of the opposing sides with an analysis of their strategic concepts, tactical formations, organization, and weaponry.

HOWARTH argues that too much has been written about the controversies surrounding Waterloo and too little about the actual experience of a great cataclysmic battle that shattered the French continental empire and heralded the rise of Great Britain and Germany as the dominant European powers of the 19th century. Howarth thus presents the human experience. Due to the great rise of literacy in the period, it is possible to view Napoleonic war events through the individual soldier's "ground-level, smoke-shrouded point of view". Drawing upon the writings of the troops themselves, Howarth describes the battle of Waterloo as it appeared to the men who actually fought it.

STANLEY D.M. CARPENTER

See also Army: To 1855; Congress System; French Revolutionary Wars; London, Treaty of; Pitt, William, "the Younger"; Wellington

Naseby, Battle of
see Civil Wars entries; Cromwell, Oliver; Fairfax

National Covenant 1638

Cowan, Edward J., "The Making of the National Covenant" in *The Scottish National Covenant in Its British Context*, edited by John Morrill, Edinburgh: Edinburgh University Press, 1990
Donaldson, Gordon, *Scotland: James V to James VII*, Edinburgh: Oliver and Boyd, and New York: Praeger, 1966
Fleming, David Hay, *The Subscribing of the National Covenant in 1638*, Edinburgh: William Green, 1912
Lee, Maurice, Jr, *The Road to Revolution: Scotland under Charles I, 1625–1637*, Urbana: University of Illinois Press, 1985
Macinnes, Allan I., *Charles I and the Making of the Covenanting Movement, 1625–1641*, Edinburgh: John Donald, 1991
Mullan, David George, *Episcopacy in Scotland: The History of an Idea, 1560–1638*, Edinburgh: John Donald, 1986
Mullan, David George, *Scottish Puritanism, 1590–1638*, Oxford and New York: Oxford University Press, 2000

The Scottish National Covenant (1638) is a document of a little more than 4000 words. The first part, following a brief introduction, is the 1581 King's Confession (Negative Confession), committing Scotland to an anti-catholic stance. The second part lists numerous acts of various Scottish parliaments prejudicial to catholic belief and practice, and also those in favour of the kirk's Reformed purity. The third section reaffirms the religious trajectory of an aggressive Reformed theology, and also promises to defend the king against all his enemies. The two commitments were opposed to each other, of course, in that recent changes in religion were the work of King Charles I himself or his continuation of others begun by his father. Those "innovations", whether openly or more covertly attacked, included the restoration of diocesan episcopacy (1610); liturgical changes embodied in the Five Articles of Perth (1618), most contentiously the call for kneeling at communion; *Canons and Constitutions Ecclesiasticall* (1636); and the Scottish *Booke of Common Prayer* (1637).

COWAN has written that "to the making of papers about the making of the National Covenant there is potentially no end." Indeed not even the circumstances of the initial subscription have been left untainted by controversy. FLEMING sifted through the contemporary sources, citing *in extenso*, to ascertain the truth about the time and place of the first signing of this revolutionary document: on Wednesday 28 February 1638 (the day given according to Old Style), inside – and not outside, on a gravestone serving as a table – the Greyfriar's Kirk in Edinburgh. If Charles called it "the damnable Covenant", Archibald Johnston of Wariston, the lawyer, who with the minister Alexander Henderson wrote the document, termed the day of its subscription the "glorious marriage day between God and Scotland". Cowan, hardly less passionately, regards the action as the harbinger "of a new age of social and civil responsibility, of a written constitution, a truly inspirational example which signposted the long road through the American and French revolutions".

If the National Covenant is expressed in legalistic language, its content is profoundly religious, and Cowan emphasizes the religious component due to its collision with Stuart absolutist pretensions, hence provoking a constitutional response. However, religion itself could never have provided the social and political energy to turn the smouldering dissent into a national rebellion. That dynamism came from the political and economic grievances of an aristocracy bereft of a resident monarch since 1603 and now challenged by ill-managed proposals to re-endow the church and also to loosen the ties of lesser landholders to their feudal superiors by enabling them to hold their land directly from the crown. These alterations were embodied in Charles's revocation of 1625 – Sir James Balfour commented that it was "the groundstone of all the mischief that followed after".

DONALDSON emphasized the constitutionalism of the National Covenant in its invocation of statute law, based on the example of England. He wrote that the document did not take direct aim at either the Five Articles or at episcopacy: "It was obviously the intention to revert to the moderate episcopalian regime which had existed during most of the period between the Reformation and King Charles's innovations." He did, however, recognize the ambiguous nature of the covenant itself and the façade of unity it generated.

LEE wrote about the covenant under a rubric generated during the period, namely "the nobility's Covenant". He wrote that "Charles' alienation of his aristocracy was at the root of his troubles", and the combination of religious discontent with fear of a Stuart autocracy flowing now from London spelled disaster. Thus the rebellion was pronouncedly conservative in nature as the nobility sought to re-establish its position. MACINNES also addresses the problems which confronted Scotland during the time of Charles I and concludes that the covenant grew out of years of mounting political disaffection with the king's personal rule.

Mullan has focused on the religious categories incorporated in the National Covenant. MULLAN (1986) argues that while the covenant was couched in moderate terms, the intention of its authors and promoters was always that it entailed a rigidly presbyterian view of the world, hence signalling a return to a golden age without hierarchical, diocesan bishops of any sort, without kneeling at communion, without holy days, etc. Once the covenant was accepted, the ringleaders – Henderson, Wariston, Dickson, Cant, and a number of other dominant figures – were in a position to argue for their own authoritative interpretation. MULLAN (2000) has also attempted to deconstruct the notion of covenanting, and has found two divergent and somewhat incompatible tendencies. One flows from the Hebrew notion of an elect nation; the second is the variant form of Reformed thought known as federal or covenant theology, which has as its focal point the salvation not of nations but of individuals. The National Covenant borrows from the former, and actually flies in the face of the piety preached from many Scottish pulpits since *c.*1590, namely a conversion-based religious experience which had much to do with forsaking the sinful world and journeying as a despised pilgrim to a heavenly city. However, those who preached the covenant attempted to bridge the gap, presenting its acceptance as an act of piety, and publicizing within an atmosphere of revivalistic religious enthusiasm.

The National Covenant is central to any attempt to understand the development of Scottish culture in the early modern period, but its interpretation labours somewhat under a tendency to elevate its moral status without regard to the devastating consequences to which it led. Indeed its influence would reverberate clearly for another two centuries in Scotland and wherever Scots would soon begin to migrate.

DAVID GEORGE MULLAN

National Health Service

founded 1946–1948

Berridge, Virginia, *Health and Society in Britain since 1939*, Cambridge and New York: Cambridge University Press, 1999

Black, Douglas, *Inequalities in Health*, Birmingham: University of Birmingham, 1981; reprinted with Margaret Whitehead's *The Health Divide*, in *Inequalities in Health: The Black Report; The Health Divide*, edited by Peter Townsend and Nick Davidson, Harmondsworth: Penguin, 1990

Klein, Rudolf, *The Politics of the National Health Service*, London and New York: Longman, 1983; 3rd edition as *The New Politics of the National Health Service*, 1995; 4th edition, 2000

Loudon, Irvine, John Horder, and Charles Webster (editors), *General Practice under the National Health Service, 1948–1997*, Oxford and New York: Clarendon Press, 1998

Rivett, Geoffrey, *From Cradle to the Grave: Fifty Years of the NHS*, London: King's Fund, 1998

Titmuss, Richard M., *The Gift Relationship: From Human Blood to Social Policy*, London: Allen and Unwin, 1970; New York: Pantheon Books, 1971; as *The Gift Relationship: From Human Blood to Social Policy, Original Edition with New Chapters*, edited by Ann Oakley and John Ashton, London: LSE Books, 1997

Watkin, Brian, *The National Health Service: The First Phase, 1948–1974 and After*, London and Boston: Allen and Unwin, 1978

Webster, Charles, *The Health Services since the War*, vol. 1, *Problems of Health Care: The National Health Service before 1957*, London: HMSO, 1988

Webster, Charles, *The Health Services since the War*, vol. 2, *Government and Health Care: The British National Health Service 1958–1979*, London: Stationary Office, 1996

Webster, Charles, *The National Health Service: A Political History*, Oxford and New York: Oxford University Press, 1998

The National Health Service was established by the 1946 National Health Service (England and Wales) Act, the 1947 National Health Service (Scotland) Act, and the 1948 Health Service Act (Northern Ireland). The differences between the component parts of the United Kingdom were never negligible; indeed they have been insufficiently acknowledged in historical writing. Nevertheless, since the appointed day of 5 July 1948, over half a century ago, when it came into operation, the NHS has had the same basic shape and essentially the same pattern of development throughout the United Kingdom as a whole.

At its start the NHS had two main characteristics. First, it provided comprehensive care, from basic treatment by a general practitioner, a dentist, or an optician to the most specialized hospital treatment. Second, it provided this for everyone free of charge at the point of delivery. The option of paying for private treatment remained, for those who could afford it, but the scope of private medicine inevitably was severely restricted, and subsequent relations between the public and private sectors are only a minor theme in the NHS's history.

The NHS was, in short, a comprehensive health service, universal in cover, and financed from general taxation. There was a small transfer to it from the new National Insurance Fund created by the 1946 National Insurance Act. As related by Webster (1996) this briefly became an issue in 1956–57, when the Treasury aimed to load a greater proportion of cost on to the Fund. However, no major change in funding in fact occurred at this or at any other time. The NHS has always remained entirely different from insurance-based schemes of health care, which became common in the rest of western Europe after World War II (Webster, 1998).

That its character gave the NHS a moral dimension has always been recognized. In KLEIN's words it was "organized around an ethical imperative . . . to achieve equity in the distribution and use of health care" (preface to first edition). TITMUSS linked this ethical character – equal treatment for all according to need, irrespective of income or any other consideration – to efficiency as well as social justice. He did so particularly in *The Gift Relationship*, a comparison of British voluntary blood donorship and the American commercial system involving the sale and purchase of blood, which showed the former's superiority in terms of lack of contamination and waste as well as of cheapness. Published at a time when the political right was starting to argue that markets were the only effective means of allocating resources, it had a considerable impact as a case study of the superiority of altruism over market forces (see introduction to the 1997 edition).

BERRIDGE is a bibliographical guide to and commentary on recent historical writing, in which the distinctive character of the NHS has become rather lost. Accounts of the origins of the NHS tend to stress its continuity with the past. The first four chapters of WEBSTER (1988) provide the best account of the origins and planning of the service. State intervention in health had been growing since the start of the century with the introduction of national health insurance in 1911, the creation of a Ministry of Health for England and Wales and a Scottish Board of Health at the end of World War I, and the unification of local authority medical services in 1929; and for this reason as well as others private practice and voluntary hospitals were finding themselves in increasing financial difficulty. The outbreak of war in 1939 brought immediacy to a long-standing debate, both on the need to improve public provisions further, and also to co-ordinate them more effectively with the private sector. The Emergency Hospital Scheme brought all hospitals under government control, with a promise made that there would be no return to the pre-war situation, and the NHS emerged from reconstruction planning by the coalition government, as a result of negotiations between civil servants and medical and other interests.

The subsequent story, too, now tends to be written as one of compromise between different interests and objectives, and also of the persistence of problems, especially of reconciling medical improvements with the containment of cost. This is best followed in the various editions of KLEIN, and in Berridge. From the very start, when initial estimates turned out to have been too low, cost has been a source of concern, at some times greater than at others, despite the fact that in the United Kingdom public spending on health as a proportion of gross national product has been below that of most similar countries. The introduction of prescription and other charges, one outcome of the concern over cost, has a complex history. Its main effect, quite recently, has been to curtail severely, if not virtually destroy, the dental and opthalmic parts of the service. For the period before 1979 WEBSTER (1988, 1998) has documented internal government debate and policy in magisterial detail. There is not the same detailed knowledge of the period since then, for which cabinet and departmental papers are closed (see WEBSTER, 1996).

Three related issues attract most attention in surveys of the NHS's first fifty years or so. One is to identify the main phases in its history. Another is to decide whether changes have come essentially through shifts in a predominant consensus or as a result of conflicts of interest and ideology. The last is to evaluate achievements and failures over the long term.

Initially general practice, hospitals, and local authority medical services, though under central supervision, were administered separately at local level. An obvious point of transition, the end of the NHS's "first phase" as WATKIN puts it, came when tripartite administration was abolished in 1973. Medical opinion in particular had argued that unified regional administration was necessary for efficient planning, but its results proved disappointing. The new authorities, responsible for all services in their area, were soon being attacked as cumbersome, and administrative tinkering gradually led to more fundamental bureaucratic change. The quest for better management produced an ideological managerialism, which took business practices as the model for efficiency, and which shifted power away from the medical profession and local representation to a managerial hierarchy, recruited from inside as well as outside the NHS. The paradox was that the high point of its influence coincided with a fragmentation of administration at the start of the 1990s, with the creation of GP fund-holders, hospital trusts, and a purchaser–provider split aimed at creating an internal market. But, however these successive phases of administration are judged, they do not stand out so much when different parts of the service are looked at separately. Webster (1996) provides the best account of the 1962 Hospital Plans for England and Wales, and Scotland, which set out an ambitious building programme. The plans are of major significance, even though their implementation was scaled down. In the mid-1960s a major turning-point for general practice came when a new contract and pay structure replaced the incentive to economize with the opposite incentive to spend on improving the practice. (The essays in LOUDON, HORDER, & WEBSTER are the best account of the history of general practice, in particular David Morrell's "Introduction and Overview".) At the end of the decade a major shift started when the medical officer of health's traditional role in local government began to be questioned and local authority services were fundamentally reorganized. On public health, see especially the writings of Jane Lewis, summarized and commented upon in Berridge.

Behind these changes lay a shifting public debate and substantial divisions of opinion. For the most part, however, disagreements took place as much inside government as between political parties and rival interests. Differences of opinion were limited, practical rather than ideological in character, and contained within a broad measure of agreement. A change came, most commentators agree, only at the end of 1980s, when policies were pushed through in the face of opposition from a great weight of well-informed opinion.

The history of the NHS cannot be written as a linear account, whether of consistent progress or of rise and decline. Its existence has coincided with a therapeutic revolution, and RIVETT, notably in his preface and introduction, emphasizes the clinical advances that have occurred in every decade of its operation. However, the BLACK Report (1980) – reprinted and commented upon in Townsend and Davidson's edition – showed that, despite a general improvement in health, differences in the mortality and morbidity rates of different social classes had not only persisted but had widened slightly between richer and poorer groups. These inequalities in health reflected economic,

social, and environmental factors which the NHS proved powerless to alter. Throughout successive phases of administrative and managerial reorganization it has also been faced with changing needs, demands, and expectations from a society very different at the end of the century from that of 1948. It is the profound change in the context of its operation that makes it so difficult to estimate finally the NHS's failures and achievements.

JOHN BROWN

See also Attlee; Beveridge; Medicine: Hospital Provision; Public Health; Welfare State

Nationalist Politics

Anderson, Benedict, *Imagined Communities: Reflections on the Origin and Spread of Nationalism*, London: Verso, 1983; revised edition, London and New York: Verso, 1991

Boyce, D. George, *Nationalism in Ireland*, London: Croom Helm, and Baltimore: Johns Hopkins University Press, 1982; 2nd edition, London and New York: Routledge, 1991; 3rd edition, 1995

Broun, Dauvit, R.J. Finlay, and Michael Lynch (editors), *Image and Identity: The Making and Remaking of Scotland through the Ages*, Edinburgh: John Donald, 1998

Colley, Linda, *Britons: Forging the Nation, 1707–1837*, New Haven, Connecticut and London: Yale University Press, 1992; new edition, London: Vintage, 1996

Davies, R.R. *et al.* (editors), *Welsh Society and Nationhood: Historical Essays Presented to Glanmor Williams*, Cardiff: University of Wales Press, 1984

Foster, R.F., *Modern Ireland, 1600–1972*, London: Allen Lane, 1988; London and New York: Penguin, 1989

Gellner, Ernest, *Nations and Nationalism*, Oxford: Blackwell, and Ithaca, New York: Cornell University Press, 1983

Grant, Alexander and Keith J. Stringer (editors), *Uniting the Kingdom? The Making of British History*, London and New York: Routledge, 1995

Harvie, Christopher, *Scotland and Nationalism: Scottish Society and Politics 1707–1977*, London: Allen and Unwin, 1977; 2nd edition, as *Scotland and Nationalism: Scottish Society and Politics 1707–1994*, London and New York: Routledge, 1994; 3rd edition, as *Scotland and Nationalism: Scottish Society and Politics 1707 to the Present*, London and New York: Routledge, 1998

Hobsbawm, Eric J., *Nations and Nationalism since 1780: Programme, Myth, Reality*, Cambridge and New York: Cambridge University Press, 1990; 2nd edition, Cambridge: Canto, 1992

Kearney, Hugh, *The British Isles: A History of Four Nations*, Cambridge and New York: Cambridge University Press, 1989

McCrone, David, *The Sociology of Nationalism: Tomorrow's Ancestors*, London and New York: Routledge, 1998

Morgan, Kenneth O., *Rebirth of a Nation: Wales 1880–1980*, Oxford: Clarendon Press, and New York: Oxford University Press, 1981; revised edition, as *Rebirth of a*

Nation: A History of Modern Wales, Oxford: Oxford University Press, and Cardiff: University of Wales Press, 1998

Morton, Graeme, *Unionist-Nationalism: Governing Urban Scotland, 1830–1860*, East Linton, East Lothian: Tuckwell Press, 1999

Robbins, Keith, *Great Britain: Identities, Institutions, and the Ideas of Britishness*, London and New York: Longman, 1997

Smith, Anthony D., *The Ethnic Origins of Nations*, Oxford and New York: Basil Blackwell, 1986

The history of nationalist politics in Britain has been presented in quite contradictory ways: as very recent or very old, as marginal, the actions of extremists, or very central to state formation and monarchical power. These different interpretations do develop into historical debate, but they flow from agenda that fail to overlap. The beginning of nationalist politics has been both an historical and a conceptual problem.

HOBSBAWM states firmly that nationalist politics, meaning nationalism, can be dated no earlier than the late 18th century and the ideas flowing from the French Revolution. Here, then, nationalism is an outcome of the age of the nation state, it is fixed in time and is rooted to a distinct phase in history; other expressions of national identity are, he argues, less complete. Hobsbawm's analysis is based on the work of GELLNER and, to a lesser extent, the influential ideas of ANDERSON, cornerstones of the "modernist school". Of those who argue that nationalism is far from being modern, the leading exponent is SMITH. It is his contention that nationalism is based on very old loyalties and attachments, particularly in non-Western countries, but not exclusively so, and forged on ethnic symbols that are long established and are persistent. The different sides to this debate, and its direct relevance to the British context, are analysed in McCRONE.

While there has been debate between the social theorists on the origins of the very idea of nationalism as political ideology, the narrative historians have searched for the essence of national identity. Here the academic divide has shifted from modern / pre-modern to culture versus state. One of the most influential of historical books of recent times – by COLLEY – locates the creation of Britishness in the formation of the state and the establishment of its monarchy. Prioritizing protestantism, warfare against catholic France and Ireland, and the positive pull of overseas trade with empire and elsewhere, Colley explains how the "British ideal" was forged, superseding older and less progressive identities of Englishness, Scottishness, and Welshness. This new British nationalism, she claims, was in place at the time of Victoria's coronation in 1837. ROBBINS is another whose prolific and influential work focuses upon British nationalism as state-created, although his position has moved further away from Colley recently, re-emphasizing instead persistent cultural and national differences within the United Kingdom. Criticism of Colley pinpoints her failure to deal adequately with the persistence of rival nationalisms to that of Britain; that she underplays the varieties of protestantism within England and between England, Scotland, Wales, and Ireland; and her exclusion of Irish history except in its role as "Other" – the mirror against which protestantism was coalesced in Britain. These criticisms are reviewed in MORTON and stress

that Colley has identified British patriotism rather than British nationalism. Awareness of the propensity of historians to write British history from the standpoint of England – because it is the largest nation and is where the central apparatus of the British state is located – has prompted some historians to attempt to give due weight to all the constituent nations. KEARNEY's history of the British Isles has won many admirers for its even-handed approach. The collection edited by GRANT & STRINGER contains a number of key essays debating how united Britain has become since its medieval foundations, with introductory and concluding essays focusing on the historiographical challenge of writing national history. A similar approach, but for Scotland only, is found in BROUN, FINLAY, & LYNCH. These books do not engage directly with the modern / pre-modern or the culture / state divides in the history of nationalist politics in Britain, but they go a long way to furnishing our interpretation of nationalism in all its forms.

The nationalism of England, as the core nation, is analysed as part of British state formation (as above), or is understood in terms of cultural identity or race. Nationalist political parties are located in the peripheral nations. For political nationalism in Wales, MORGAN is best, primarily because he retains an eye for the British political process. The link between nationalist politics and class in Wales is explored in the essays contained in DAVIES *et al*. To understand the interconnection between Irish nationalism and British nationalism as a symbiosis, not just a one-way fracture, the work of FOSTER is without parallel. It is, however, worth while to complement this with an explicit study of Irish national politics, and here BOYCE is the clearest of many good recent accounts. The modern history of Scottish nationalist politics stems from HARVIE, but this thematic account should be read in conjunction with the historical sociology of McCrone.

GRAEME MORTON

See also Devolution entries; Fascism; Identities, National entries; Identities, Regional entries; Ireland entries; Northern Ireland, Conflict in

Nationalization and Denationalization

from 1945

Ashworth, William, *The State in Business, 1945 to the Mid 1980s*, London: Macmillan, 1991

Chester, Norman, *The Nationalisation of British Industry, 1945–1951*, London: HMSO, 1975

Kelf-Cohen, R., *British Nationalisation, 1945–1973*, London: Macmillan, and New York: St Martin's Press, 1973

Millward, Robert and John Singleton (editors), *The Political Economy of Nationalisation in Britain 1920–1950*, Cambridge and New York: Cambridge University Press, 1995

Pryke, Richard, *The Nationalised Industries: Policies and Performance since 1968*, Oxford: Martin Robertson, 1981

Vickers, John and George Yarrow, *Privatization: An Economic Analysis*, Cambridge, Massachusetts: MIT Press, 1988

The literature on nationalization and privatization has been dominated by economic historians and economists who have asked themselves why industries were taken into and out of public ownership and how this process affected their performance. MILLWARD & SINGLETON argue that economic considerations rather than ideology and politics dominated government discussions in the first half of the century. They believe acts introduced by postwar Labour governments were the culmination of pre-war trends and in part a reaction to perceived failures of earlier state regulation. The issue that concerned ministers, politicians, and civil servants alike was how best to increase efficiency in natural monopolies such as rail, gas, electricity, water, and telecommunications. Consequently infrastructure and extractive industries came under public ownership, while manufacturing and distribution were left in private hands, a pattern for which there was a broad political and intellectual consensus. Nationalization generated economics of scale, cut back the excess profits of private operators, and extended network provision throughout society. Contributors to the volume discuss the different forces influencing the decision to nationalize or not in a range of industries. Coal is the one sector where the issues were very different, as the unions had a more significant role to play and the ability of a nationalized coal industry to reap scale economies was less clear cut.

CHESTER, the official historian of nationalization, focuses on how the Labour Party's electoral programme was introduced. His extremely detailed account is split up into thematic chapters which chronicle the drafting and redrafting of bills, a process of lawmaking which he holds up as an example of how effective the parliamentary system could be. He argues, however, that compensation for private investors, despite being the trickiest aspect of nationalization, was not dealt with in a systematic way, raising some doubts over whether the state got value for its money. He is also critical of the "public corporation", the managerial system for the industries under government control, as it left blurred lines of responsibility between the boards – which ran the industries on a day-to-day basis – and the ministers, who took strategic decisions. Evidence from the records of the industries themselves not having been drawn on, this is not the definitive account, but Chester's stress on the structure of business–state relations is mirrored in other accounts.

A large number of works were written in the postwar period on the performance of the nationalized industries; these have been supplemented more recently by studies of individual industries based on company archives. KELF-COHEN, in one of the better contemporary accounts, surveys the history of various industries and deals with some of the key themes: the relationship between nationalization and macroeconomic management; the financial and political constraints affecting the operation of the boards; and the impact of trade unions on government and management decision-making. He notes that the industries did not perform well against standard financial measures, but argues that this is not surprising, nor necessarily bad, given the broader social criteria set down by trade unions and governments. He sees nationalization as part of a corporate economy where the voices of trade unions and governments were dominant over that of industry.

PRYKE's more damning conclusions have been more influential. He notes that those industries which were subject to national and international competition performed badly after 1973, while even those natural monopolies that did not face direct competition compare unfavourably with their counterparts overseas. He attributes blame in the first instance to the bosses and workers. Most industries were over-manned, riddled with restrictive practices, made bad investment decisions, and distorted the market mechanism by cross-subsidizing non-profit-making activities. However, it was ultimately the structure of ownership, combined with soft-budget constraints used by governments for wider macroeconomic goals, that allowed these practices to continue. Privatization was his solution.

ASHWORTH provides a good historical overview. It is accessible to the non-technical reader and based mainly on secondary and published primary material. He locates nationalization in the debates about monopoly. Consequently he is much less critical of the financial performance of the industries than many accounts by contemporaries. But like others he believes that the problems lay less with the industries themselves than with governments, which set down unrealistic criteria and interfered far too much in day-to-day management.

VICKERS & YARROW, in a sophisticated account based on economic theory and empirical evidence, confirm that privatization in Britain did raise industrial efficiency but caution that what mattered was not ownership *per se* but the unleashing of "the discipline of the market". Introducing competitive forces was easy to achieve for certain sectors such as Cable and Wireless and British Aerospace, who had to operate in international markets, but more difficult for national monopolies, such as gas and telecommunications. The authors are thus critical of a process that failed to establish vigorous regulatory systems to meet the specific requirements of each particular industry.

DAVID WILLIAM CLAYTON

See also Attlee; Consensus in the Postwar Period; Electricity; Gas Industry; Heath; Labour Party; Mining, Decline of; Morrison; National Health Service; Public Transport; Railways; Relative Economic Decline; Steel Industry; Telecommunications; Thatcher

Natural Law

Buckle, Stephen, *Natural Law and the Theory of Property: Grotius to Hume*, Oxford: Clarendon Press, and New York: Oxford University Press, 1991

Gierke, Otto Friedrich von, *Natural Law and the Theory of Society, 1500 to 1800*, translated from the German by Ernest Barker, 2 vols, Cambridge: Cambridge University Press, 1934; 1 vol, Boston: Beacon Press, 1957 (German original, 1913)

Haakonssen, Knud, *Natural Law and Moral Philosophy: From Grotius to the Scottish Enlightenment*, Cambridge and New York: Cambridge University Press, 1996

Skinner, Quentin, *The Foundations of Modern Political Thought*, 2 vols, Cambridge and New York: Cambridge University Press, 1978–79

Tuck, Richard, *Natural Rights Theories: Their Origins and Development*, Cambridge and New York: Cambridge University Press, 1979

Tully, James, *A Discourse on Property: John Locke and His Adversaries*, Cambridge and New York: Cambridge University Press, 1980

Natural law – or natural jurisprudence, as some scholars prefer to describe it – has long been recognized as having made a major contribution to the development of European ideologies and political discourses. Yielding elaborate conjectural histories of human society which serve both to explain and to justify the emergence of particular political arrangements over time, natural law has offered a variety of original and enormously powerful insights into the early origins and legitimate purposes of government. However, recent studies have emphasized that, while modern democratic politics in the English-speaking world received crucial impetus from the philosophy of natural law, particularly during the 17th and 18th centuries, the tradition was in fact as versatile as it was venerable and so was fully capable of promoting authoritarian as well as liberal values.

The indubitable golden age of natural law lay between the late Renaissance and the early Enlightenment. As a result, studies of political thought between the 16th and 18th centuries have inevitably tended to draw attention to its influence. GIERKE, whose work broke new ground in its tracing of key themes in political theory, can be said to have helped initiate the modern appreciation of natural law, drawing particular attention to Hugo Grotius, the most accomplished and influential of early-modern European legal theorists. This outstanding account is in many respects still perfectly satisfactory as an introduction for the general reader, underlying, as it does, many subsequent discussions of the subject.

SKINNER has also proved seminal for the interpretation of natural law among virtually all recent academic historians of British and European political thought. His analysis of the medieval and Renaissance origins of crucial concepts such as rights, resistance, and the state, has come to be regarded as compulsory for all scholars, even where they are inclined to disagree with his interpretation. His account of the 16th-century Thomist engagement with natural jurisprudence has been especially influential, providing a clear explanation of the relationship between the medieval and modern conceptions. His work is also important methodologically because it presents political discourse in terms of successive responses to the problems encountered by statesmen and philosophers, arguing – in a claim which has been widely discussed – that ideas and the language in which they are couched must always be interpreted in historical context. Thus his treatment of natural law has served to emphasize the immediate impact of changing institutional, theological, and ideological circumstances throughout its long and tortuous evolution as a mode of political argument, a view which has given new insights into the origins of modern British political thought in particular.

TUCK, a younger Cambridge colleague of Skinner's and strongly influenced by him, has relied upon a not dissimilar method, tracing the emergence specifically of rights-based discourses from the age of Aquinas, through the Catholic thinkers Vitoria and Molina to the protestant jurist Grotius and his English successors John Selden (whose interest in natural law gave rise to innovative ideas about the conduct of international relations) and Thomas Hobbes. Tuck's account is especially valuable for its conclusive dismissal of the myth, traceable back to the early Enlightenment, that natural rights theories were essentially a modern artefact intrinsic to the emergence of liberal ideologies. Rather, he locates the 17th-century English theorists within a much longer and more complex European tradition, and emphasizes how, in Hobbes as in Grotius, rights became grounded in the universal human desire for self-preservation. Like Skinner's, Tuck's work provides a clear account of the scholastic roots of modern political thought and of the connections of natural law with absolutist theories of government. It also reveals how the controversies of the Reformation and the European turmoil which followed – especially the rebellions or civil wars in France, Germany, and the Low Countries, as well as in England – contributed greatly to the dominance eventually achieved by natural law in the field of political and legal thought.

Scholarly attention has also been diverted towards that significant corollary of natural-jurisprudential thinking, the emergence of the notion of contract as central to the existence and viability of organized political society. Particularly in the interpretation of political philosophers between the mid-17th and late 18th centuries, a group of thinkers in which the English pairing of Hobbes and John Locke are of paramount importance, binding mutual obligation has been seen as underlying the analysis of the legitimacy of the state and the corresponding duties of the subject on the part of Europe's leading theorists. Although originally derived from the sort of primitivist conjectural histories popularized by earlier jurists like Grotius, and achieving its greatest influence in Britain during the early Enlightenment, the possibility that relations between rulers and ruled might be explored in terms of a specific reciprocal agreement has remained important to modern historians of ideas, not least because hypothetical expressions of governmental accountability and popular consent have continued to hold a symbolic importance for many of the liberal political theorists, commentators, and politicians up to our own day.

A related development in recent historiography has been recognition of the extent to which the discussion of property, which had become crucial to British political theory by the 18th century, was similarly indebted to the growing dominance of natural jurisprudence in the 16th and 17th. TULLY in particular has shown how Locke drew his inspiration from Grotius, borrowing from natural-law theory elements of a conceptual vocabulary appropriate to contemporary English society, where substantial land-ownership and dynamic commercial growth were both central facts. Above all, Locke's account of property rights as grounded in labour was to mark a fundamental step in the evolution of modern notions of private ownership. BUCKLE too has supplied a well-regarded study which successfully advances the case for seeing the jurists' fascination with the history of property as contributing to a tradition of political thought to which other British commentators such as the 18th-century theorists Francis Hutcheson and David Hume also belonged.

Another significant and closely related historiographical trend has been the attempt to develop this analysis of 17th-century political thought more broadly into an interpretation of the 18th-century Enlightenment – often in the first instance in technical literature published in specialist periodicals situated at the intersections between law, philosophy, history, and social theory, but also in due course in some seminal and widely respected monographs. HAAKONSSEN above all has shown how British political thinkers can be read as in many other respects the inheritors of the natural-jurisprudential tradition represented by Grotius and his German successor Samuel Pufendorf. His work has suggested that the leading Scottish moralists Hume and Adam Smith were eventually able not only to reformulate politics, but perhaps also to establish the new discipline of economics, on the foundations laid down by the Continental jurists of the previous century. While in no sense a complete explanation of these authors (whose debts to other traditions, such as a possible blending of natural law with stoic discourse in Hutcheson, have also been asserted), an intellectual grounding in jurisprudence makes good sense of the Scots' evident obsession with the material basis of human society from its remotest origins.

The most striking feature of recent historical scholarship has thus been an impressive ability to offer credible and illuminating interpretations of the major texts and thinkers – including the leading English-speaking theorists – in terms of their relationship with a rich, supremely elastic but still recognisably coherent tradition of natural jurisprudence which, though traceable back as far as the 13th century, profoundly shaped political thought in the 17th and early 18th. As a result, it seems likely that the study of natural law, contracts, and rights will remain integral to the evolving historiography of modern British political thought.

DAVID ALLAN

See also Hobbes; Jurisprudence; Locke

Natural Philosophy (in England)

1450–1650

Cohen, I. Bernard (editor), *Puritanism and the Rise of Modern Science: The Merton Thesis*, New Brunswick, New Jersey: Rutgers University Press, 1990

Cormack, Lesley B., *Charting an Empire: Geography at the English Universities, 1580–1620*, Chicago: University of Chicago Press, 1997

Debus, Allen G., *The English Paracelsians*, London: Oldbourne, 1965; New York: F. Watts, 1966

Feingold, Mordechai, *The Mathematicians' Apprenticeship: Science, Universities, and Society in England, 1560–1640*, Cambridge and New York: Cambridge University Press, 1984

Hunter, Lynette and Sarah Hutton (editors), *Women, Science, and Medicine, 1500–1700: Mothers and Sisters of the Royal Society*, Stroud, Gloucestershire: Sutton, 1997

Leary, John E., Jr, *Francis Bacon and the Politics of Science*, Ames: Iowa State University Press, 1994

Merchant, Carolyn, *The Death of Nature: Women, Ecology, and the Scientific Revolution*, San Francisco: Harper and Row, 1980; London: Wildwood House, 1981

Sherman, William H., *John Dee: The Politics of Reading and Writing in the English Renaissance*, Amherst: University of Amherst Press, 1995

Webster, Charles, *The Great Instauration: Science, Medicine, and Reform, 1626–1660*, London: Duckworth, 1975; New York: Holmes and Meier, 1976

Yates, Frances A., *The Occult Philosophy in the Elizabethan Age*, London and Boston, Massachusetts: Routledge and Kegan Paul, 1979

The study of science in early modern England can be characterized as a reaction to post–World War II positivism, and a subsequent search for the origins of the "scientific revolution" of the 17th century. Inquiry into these two main themes has resulted in the transformation of the history of science into an interdisciplinary history of culture that transcends technical considerations and considers revisionist themes of gender and social order.

YATES was one of the first scholars to turn away from the positivistic argument that the development of science involves a tacit classification of magical and hermetic beliefs as "superstitious". Rather, she explained the ultimate source of the "new science" as the reconceptualization of nature that occurred with the introduction of Neoplatonism, hermeticism, and the cabbala in the Renaissance, particularly connecting the acceptance of heliocentrism with Renaissance magic. In an argument known widely as the "Yates thesis", she claimed that magic produced a new conception of man as active controller of natural forces, making more significant knowledge of the natural world and disciplines that could understand nature's hidden forces. Particularly important to the study of English natural philosophy is her argument that the figure of the Renaissance magus was exemplified in the Elizabethan philosopher John Dee (1527–1608).

Yates's work led to further explorations of the role of hermeticism in natural philosophy, of which DEBUS made the most notable contribution in the history of chemistry and medicine. Debus meticulously analysed the influence of the writings of Paracelsus in England, which in the 16th century drew on the experience of craftsmen and divine inspiration to form a new science of alchemy/chemistry and chemical medicine. In the 17th century, Paracelsian medicine would represent a viable alternative among some philosophers and physicians to established institutional medicine, leading to a "Paracelsian compromise" between the Royal College of Physicians and the chemical physicians.

However, the Yates thesis and her portrayal of Dee as a magus have undergone critical reassessment, most recently in the work of SHERMAN. Far from being a secretive and isolated conjurer alienated from the humanistic movement prevalent at Oxford and Cambridge, Dee rather embraced the *vita activa* of the humanists, and utilized his learning and his vast library to establish what Sherman calls England's first "think-tank". Dee also utilized his knowledge as a political commodity, becoming a well-connected producer of studies for influential patrons.

Dee's studies included geographic exploration and establishing the legitimacy of England's imperial claims, a topic covered in CORMACK's excellent analysis of geography at the English universities in the late 16th and early 17th centuries. Cormack demonstrated that not only did the study of chorography and mathematical and descriptive geography help the English develop an imperial ideology, but these disciplines contributed to the development of the new science. The study of geography provided an impetus to the mathematization of the world, placed value on inductive reasoning, and emphasized making that information into a natural philosophy useful for a larger society. Her analysis of the English geographical community further demonstrated the essential role of the relationships between university scholars and artisan craftsmen in the development of new standards for investigating nature.

FEINGOLD also analysed to what extent studies at English universities contributed to the development of science, concentrating upon mathematics. Most important, he challenged previous assumptions (including those made by Yates) that Oxford and Cambridge were inadequate and hostile towards the study and teaching of mathematics, and hence hindered the development of the new science. Instead, his thorough examination of university records illustrated that there were a large number of lectureships established and a high quality of mathematics teaching, an argument that revises previous views that the roots of English natural philosophy were only among puritans at Gresham College and teachers of "practical" mathematics in London.

In 1938 Robert Merton introduced the idea that there was an affinity between English puritanism and the rise of modern natural philosophy in the 17th century, a claim that subsequently caused a good deal of historical debate. A recent anthology edited by COHEN is an excellent overview of the influence of the Merton thesis on the history of 17th-century English science, including essays about recent work that trace the origins of the "new science" in tenets of moderate Anglicanism, opposing views, as well as an article by Merton written especially for this volume.

Charles WEBSTER continued to explore more deeply the connections between puritanism and science, concentrating particularly on the scientific implications of puritan eschatology in the first half of the 17th century. He illustrated that the sciences were utilized to add precision to the "millennial outline" created by theologians and that millennial ideas gave natural philosophers new goals. The puritan revolution became a period of promise when God would allow science to become the means to bring about a new paradise on earth; puritan intellectuals, inspired by the writings of Francis Bacon, became committed to a dedicated attempt via science to remedy the Fall and procure the return of man's dominion over nature.

The shift in religious and social sensibilities about nature, and particularly the primacy of man in nature and in science has been confronted in a variety of feminist scholarship. HUNTER & HUTTON have edited a fine collection of essays about "the scientific lady" in early modern England. Topics include women experimenters in medicine, the role of Renaissance women in the evolution of technical and scientific writing, and an essay concerning the Countess of Pembroke and Elizabethan science. A good deal of feminist works have further revised assumptions about the "father of the scientific method", Sir Francis Bacon. In a sometimes overstated argument, MERCHANT provocatively claimed that Bacon created a new scientific ethic that sanctioned the exploitation of nature and subordination of women. For Merchant, Bacon's programme was exemplified in his "mechanistic utopia", *The New Atlantis*, an agenda that

"transformed the (Renaissance) magus from nature's servant to its exploiter", and "reinforced the tendencies of progress and growth inherent in early capitalism".

LEARY continues to revise our picture of Bacon, exploring the influence his role as a lawyer and a statesman had in shaping his scientific ideology. Just as Bacon's constructive civil policies could be begun only after the populace had been controlled, so Bacon's scheme for his scientific programme presupposed that the "vulgar" must be excluded from the process of inquiry, scientists should be purged of base motivations, and an overarching authority and system of intellectual law should be established to control scientific activity. Rather than portraying Bacon as a progressive, democratic reformer, Leary demonstrated Bacon's scientific agenda reflected more of a "Tudor despotism", illustrating that we have moved a long way from assuming the development of science in early modern England was necessarily beneficent or progressive.

ANNA MARIE E. ROOS

See also Dee; Newton; Physics (and Natural Philosophy); Royal Society of London; Scientific Revolution and the Royal Society

Navy: Modern

Beeler, John F., *British Naval Policy in the Gladstone–Disraeli Era, 1866–1880*, Stanford, California: Stanford University Press, 1997

Bell, Christopher M., *The Royal Navy, Seapower, and Strategy between the Wars*, Stanford, California: Stanford University Press, and London: Macmillan, 2000

Corbett, Julian S., *Some Principles of Maritime Strategy*, London and New York: Longmans Green, 1911; with introduction and notes by Eric J. Grove, London: Brassey's, and Annapolis, Maryland: Naval Institute Press, 1988

Gordon, Andrew, *The Rules of the Game: Jutland and British Naval Command*, London: John Murray, and Annapolis, Maryland: Naval Institute Press, 1996

Grove, Eric J., *Vanguard to Trident: British Naval Policy since World War II*, Annapolis, Maryland: Naval Institute Press, and London: Bodley Head, 1987

Lambert, Andrew, *Battleships in Transition: The Creation of the Steam Battlefleet, 1815–1860*, London: Conway Maritime Press, and Annapolis, Maryland: Naval Institute Press, 1984

Lambert, Nicholas A., *Sir John Fisher's Naval Revolution*, Columbia: University of South Carolina Press, 1999

Mahan, Alfred Thayer, *The Influence of Sea Power upon History, 1660–1805*, London: Hamlyn, and Englewood Cliffs, New Jersey: Prentice Hall, 1980

Marder, Arthur J., *From the Dreadnought to Scapa Flow: The Royal Navy in the Fisher Era, 1904–1919*, 5 vols, London and New York: Oxford University Press, 1961–70; revised and enlarged edition, 1978–

Marder, Arthur J., Mark Jacobsen, and John Horsfield, *Old Friends, New Enemies*, 2 vols, Oxford: Clarendon Press, and New York: Oxford University Press, 1981–90

Roskill, Stephen W., *The War at Sea, 1939–1945*, 3 vols,
   London: HMSO, 1954–61

Roskill, Stephen W., *White Ensign: The British Navy at War,
   1939–1945*, Annapolis, Maryland: Naval Institute Press,
   1960; as *The Navy at War, 1939–1945*, London: Collins,
   1960

Roskill, Stephen W., *Naval Policy between the Wars*, 2 vols,
   London: Collins, and New York: Walker, 1968–76

Sumida, Jon Tetsuro, *In Defence of Naval Supremacy:
   Financial Limitation, Technological Innovation, and British
   Naval Policy, 1889–1914*, London: Allen and Unwin,
   1988; as *In Defence of Naval Supremacy: Finance,
   Technology, and British Naval Policy, 1889–1914*, Boston:
   Unwin Hyman, 1989

Till, Geoffrey, *Air Power and the Royal Navy, 1914–1945:
   A Historical Survey*, London: Macdonald and Jane's,
   1979

Once reigning supreme over the seas, Britain had ceded its maritime dominance to the United States by the mid-20th century. Seeking to understand the Royal Navy's decline, modern scholars examine the impact of financial constraints, inter- and intra-service rivalry, civil–military relations, terminology, and theories of naval warfare. Although they disagree about the primary causes for the decline, they would undoubtedly agree that students of the Royal Navy must first read MAHAN and CORBETT, whose contrasting theories of sea power and its application have influenced modern naval warfare and therefore have formed the basis for, or are the targets of, scholars' contentions.

Addressing transitions in the Royal Navy between 1815 and 1860, Andrew LAMBERT (1984) employs a host of diagrams, photographs, and design schematics to argue that the wooden steam battleship played a key role in developing modern naval warfare. This work also discusses the ideas of the steamship's early proponents, such as Sir Baldwin Walker, creator of the wooden steam battleship, and George Eden (Lord Auckland) and Sir John Graham, who convinced the navy and the government gradually to increase the steam fleet even during periods of financial retrenchment.

Covering the next three decades of British naval history, BEELER argues that Mahan's theories should not be used to evaluate political and naval leaders of the period 1866–80 because they lacked the imperialistic aspirations that fuelled political aims at the end of the century. According to Beeler, the mid-19th-century navy was well prepared for its mission because, despite a pervasive lack of public interest in naval matters, no other nation posed a serious threat to Britain's command of the sea. Beeler also discusses how naval affairs affected national politics, such as when the Gladstone administration's failure to reach an accord on the size-of-the-service estimates contributed to the Tory victory in the 1874 elections.

The first half of the 20th century is perhaps the most provocative period in the Royal Navy's history. Establishing the standard for discussion of the pre-World War I era, MARDER (1961–70) argues that Germany's emergence as a naval power fuelled the nation's defence policy. Despite numerical superiority and an excellent intelligence division, the pre-war Royal Navy had numerous dangerous defects, namely, commanders who, untrained in strategy and tactics, refused to respond to technological changes, regarded gunnery practice as a nuisance,

and grossly underestimated the torpedo's effectiveness. These problems, along with the chaotic state of the Reserve Squadron, caused Britain to enter World War I with a significant disadvantage.

Recent scholarship challenges many of Marder's assumptions. SUMIDA argues that aside from the German navy, economic constraints posed an equally important threat to British naval supremacy in the pre-war period. Financial considerations also shaped the strategic views of First Sea Lord Admiral Sir John Fisher, whom Sumida blames for the navy's failures in World War I. The star of this work is a new system of fire control developed by Allen H. Pollen. According to Sumida, this weapon would have enabled the adoption of the battle cruiser as the navy's new capital ship, which in conjunction with a newly structured fleet that included submarines and used the wireless telegraph, could guarantee Britain's maritime supremacy. Although Fisher originated the new naval force structure and theory of sea power, he undercut his plans by ceding responsibility for adopting new systems to the Admiralty, which subsequently rejected Pollen's fire-control system.

Depicting Fisher in a positive light, Nicholas LAMBERT contends that the admiral's insistence on incorporating new technology revolutionized the Royal Navy. Lambert also excuses Fisher's secretiveness, explaining it as part of an intentional, successful effort to prevent the Liberal Party from slashing the defence budget. Lambert's argument, that financial constraints comprised the dominant force which shaped the Royal Navy in the pre-war period, appears to reject the notion that German naval expansion fuelled naval plans. However, his assertion that these constraints were engendered by the increasingly prohibitive cost of constructing ships superior to those of Britain's European foes, places him, for the most part, in the traditional school of thought.

Containing riveting eyewitness accounts of the battle of Jutland, GORDON's prize-winning book analyses the institutional and personal causes for the Royal Navy's failure to defeat the German fleet during the greatest naval battle of World War I. From this view, Admiral Jellicoe, whose command style was to control his subordinates tightly, bears a significant part of the blame for the losses at Jutland. Gordon also examines the command styles of Admiral David Beatty and Hugh Evan-Thomas, the latter of whom Gordon praises for having a leadership method that encouraged initiative among his subordinates.

Containing numerous maps and appendices for naval strengths, building programmes, and personnel, ROSKILL (1968–76) remains the seminal survey for the Royal Navy between World Wars I and II. The first volume focuses on the Anglo-American naval rivalry, which increased throughout the period until the rise of fascist dictatorships and fear of Japanese intentions caused the United States and Britain to realize that their common interests and enemies outweighed concerns about who would be the strongest naval power. Volume 2 examines the navy's attempt to achieve security and prevent another world conflagration through a series of international conferences and armaments agreements. It also provides extensive coverage of the Royal Navy's rearmament and preparations for World War II.

One recent trend has been to focus on Britain's imperial commitments in the inter-war period as Japan loomed increasingly large in the Royal Navy's calculations. For the fullest treatment of the Royal Navy in the Far East during the 1920s and 1930s, see volume 1, *The Royal Navy and the Imperial Japanese Navy: Strategic Illusions 1936–1941*, of MARDER, JACOBSEN, & HORSFIELD. Examining the navy's war, force structure, and deployment plans, Marder, author of the first volume, attributes Britain's maritime failures in World War II to incompetent navy leaders who doggedly pursued strategies that were defective in conception, despite evidence that they were not working. This work also analyses, though less comprehensively, the interwar activities of the imperial Japanese navy.

Offering a more sympathetic treatment of the preparations for war with Japan, BELL contends that navy commanders understood the ramifications of new technologies and had distinct views about the nature and application of sea power. Synthesizing Mahan's and Corbett's ideas, navy decision-makers argued for a powerful battle fleet, a large network of naval bases and merchant marine, and a healthy shipbuilding industry. A key theme highlighting this thesis is Bell's criticism of traditional interpretations of the "Singapore Strategy". Asserting that the Royal Navy pursued several strategies in Asian waters during the interwar period, Bell maintains that only one generalization can be made about inter-bellum British naval strategy: the bulk of the navy's forces would remain in home waters during peace, whereas during war the maximum available forces would be dispatched to protect the nation's imperial interests.

In the last two decades the shift in scholarly attention from broader surveys of the inter-war Royal Navy to more specific aspects of it has expanded our knowledge of its operations and force structure. Focusing on the development of naval air power in the interwar period, TILL explores a host of reasons that enabled the United States to take the lead over Britain in the race to develop naval air power. These include insufficient finances to fund army, navy, and air forces simultaneously; the loss of personnel and material resources to the Air Ministry in 1918; the lack of an effective political body from which to lobby parliament, for neither the Air Ministry nor the Admiralty considered maritime airpower to be its primary concern; and inter-service rivalries. The latter were particularly obtrusive because the arguments over whether airpower had fundamentally changed the navy's traditional role hindered the incorporation of aircraft and the development of strategies for naval aviation warfare.

ROSKILL's multi-volume official history (1954–61) provides extensive coverage of the Royal Navy's operations in all theatres of World War II. For a more concise version, which presents selected major battles in each theatre of conflict, see ROSKILL (1960).

Writing on the threshold of the Royal Navy's decision whether to become a strategic nuclear naval power, GROVE charts the course the British government has taken to manage its decline as the world's leading maritime power. Insufficient finances continued to plague the navy following World War II as the struggle for resources and a chronic lack of manpower forced the Admiralty to scale down the fleet. The Cold War exacerbated financial problems as both the Attlee and Churchill administrations maintained substantial defence budgets that surpassed those of 1939. Recognizing significant advances in weaponry, especially those in air and nuclear power, naval leaders nevertheless had to scrap, rather than modify, older

battleships when reforming the navy. Consequently, the Revised Restructured Fleet incorporated the carrier as its main surface ship, but restricted the number of airframes under development. The government unsuccessfully attempted to meet the demand for anti-submarine warfare ships by using prefabricated hulls on a second-rate class of frigates, only half of which were delivered, and which required hull reinforcements in any event.

The modern Royal Navy continues to attract widespread popular interest, but is also the subject of an increasingly sophisticated scholarly literature. More than ever, the history of Britain's navy is being linked to its political, economic, social, cultural, and strategic context.

JOYCE E. SAMPSON

See also Churchill, Lord Randolph; Defence Capability; East Asia, Relations with: 1930s to Korean War; Mountbatten; Opium Wars; Shipbuilding; World War I: Naval and Air Operations; World War II: Naval Operations

Navy: Sailing

Andrews, Kenneth R., *Ships, Money, and Politics: Seafaring and Naval Enterprise in the Reign of Charles I*, Cambridge and New York: Cambridge University Press, 1991

Baugh, Daniel A., *British Naval Administration in the Age of Walpole*, Princeton, New Jersey: Princeton University Press, 1965

Capp, Bernard, *Cromwell's Navy: The Fleet and the English Revolution, 1648–1660*, Oxford: Clarendon Press, and New York: Oxford University Press, 1989

Corbett, Julian S., *England in the Seven Years War: A Study in Combined Strategy*, 2 vols, London and New York: Longmans Green, 1907; reprinted, 2 vols, London: Greenhill, and Novato, California: Presidio Press, 1992

Ehrman, John, *The Navy in the War of William III, 1689–1697: Its State and Direction*, Cambridge: Cambridge University Press, 1953

Glete, Jan, *Navies, and Nations: Warships, Navies, and State Building in Europe and America, 1500–1860*, 2 vols, Stockholm: Almqvist & Wiksell International, 1993

Harding, Richard, *The Evolution of the Sailing Navy, 1509–1815*, Basingstoke: Macmillan, and New York: St Martin's Press, 1995

Hattendorf, John B., *England in the War of the Spanish Succession: A Study of the English View and Conduct of Grand Strategy, 1702–1712*, New York: Garland, 1987

Lambert, Andrew, *The Last Sailing Battlefleet: Maintaining Naval Mastery, 1815–1850*, London: Conway Maritime Press, 1991

Lavery, Brian, *Nelson's Navy: The Ships, Men, and Organisation, 1793–1815*, London: Conway Maritime Press, and Annapolis, Maryland: Naval Institute Press, 1989; revised edition, London: Conway Maritime Press, 1990

Loades, David, *The Tudor Navy: An Administrative, Political, and Military History*, Aldershot, Hampshire: Scolar Press, and Brookfield, Vermont: Ashgate, 1992

Richmond, H.W., *The Navy in the War of 1739–1748*, 3 vols, Cambridge: Cambridge University Press, 1920

Rodger, N.A.M., *The Wooden World: An Anatomy of the Georgian Navy*, London: Collins, and Annapolis, Maryland: Naval Institute Press, 1986

Rodger, N.A.M., *The Safeguard of the Sea: A Naval History of Britain, 660–1649*, London: Harper Collins / National Maritime Museum, 1997; New York: Norton, 1998

Syrett, David, *The Royal Navy in American Waters, 1775–1783*, Aldershot, Hampshire: Scolar Press, and Brookfield, Vermont: Gower, 1989

Syrett, David, *The Royal Navy in European Waters during the American Revolutionary War*, Columbia: University of South Carolina Press, 1998

The Royal Navy has been the subject of intense historical scrutiny since the 1880s. The early writings on the navy concentrated on the operations of battlefleets and dominance at sea that characterized the popular image of the navy in this period. In recent decades much more attention has been paid to the navy as one of the largest and most complex organizations of its time. The history of its growth, effectiveness, and its impact on British society are now subjects of a growing historical literature. The result is an enormous range of books on the navy. Most of the operational histories and many of the biographies of famous officers date from the first half of the twentieth century, but remain standard texts, while the newer works seek to place the navy much more into the context of its time. The reader should consult RODGER (1997) to obtain an overview of the period up to 1649 and for an excellent bibliography. There are significant gaps in recent published work after this period. There is also a lack of books that bring together recent scholarship for specific periods. A short synthesis for the period as a whole, with bibliography, can be found in HARDING.

LOADES has summarized the main issues of the establishment of the modern, state navy in the 16th century. His focus is on the creation of an institutional framework to maintain the navy as a permanent organ of the state. The debate about the roles of the Tudor monarchs in this process is well presented. An overview of the operations of the Tudor navy, its fleet action and privateering is presented, but the reader should look to the bibliography for more detailed work on these aspects of the subject.

The early Stuart navy is not well served by modern studies. The period is dominated by questions related to corruption, finance, and the presumed decay of English naval power. Much of the work done on this is to be found in essays and books dealing with the politics of the period rather than explicit works of naval history. Although not considered as thorough as his earlier work on Elizabethan privateering, ANDREWS is the most accessible summary of naval activity during the reign of Charles I. The Civil Wars are in need of re-examination. The older works tend to put a heavy emphasis upon the role of the navy in ensuring parliament's victory. However, it is clear that the naval history of the period has not kept up with the large number of historical studies into other aspects of the conflict that have appeared since 1970. On the other hand, CAPP has produced a very good modern study of the navy under the Commonwealth and Protectorate.

Early histories of the navy following the Restoration in 1660 tended to concentrate on Samuel Pepys and the Anglo-Dutch wars. Recent works have greatly increased current knowledge about ships, naval administration, the officer corps, and the role of the cruising squadrons in the Mediterranean. These have helped produce a much fuller appreciation of development of the operational capability of the navy in this period and have led to some revision of opinion about Pepys. However, all this work has not yet been brought together into a revised overview of the period. The same is true of William III's navy. Although it was engaged in a major war with France, recent examinations of the navy's operational, political, and administrative history during the period have been largely confined to journal articles and unpublished theses. EHRMAN remains the best published work on this period, although it is increasingly difficult to find it in libraries. Queen Anne's navy suffers from the same lack of recent published work. The published operational histories are largely pre-1939. HATTENDORF presents the most recent analysis of British naval power in this period.

The 18th century as a whole has a wealth of published material on the navy. It is the classic period of British naval power under sail, culminating in Trafalgar and the Nelson legend. It is also the period in which significant studies of the administrative and social history of the navy abound. With the exception of the American War of Independence (Revolutionary War), the operational histories tend to be old. RICHMOND and CORBETT remain essential reading and the latter has been reprinted. BAUGH provides an excellent study of naval administration. This type of study has been followed by historians dealing with other periods of the sailing navy, usually in the form of articles, theses, or volumes of the Navy Records Society, although some monographs of naval administration can be found in the bibliographies of the general textbooks noted above. RODGER (1986) is the best study of the internal workings of the navy. The bibliography in this book provides a good list of other works on the social history of the navy, although the works of historians presenting more radical interpretations of seamen's lives are not fully listed.

The American War of Independence has been very well explored in recent years. Administrative, social, political, and operational histories of this war have all been the subject of new published work and current research. SYRETT has provided the most accessible overview of the operational history in American waters. Another, complementary, volume by this scholar concerning European waters has also been published. The French Revolutionary and Napoleonic wars have an even more extensive bibliography. The period has, traditionally, attracted the most attention, and the Nelson bicentenary in 2005 has encouraged the reprinting of old and the production of new works on Nelson and the navy in this period. The bicentenary has led to the production of new work on battles and campaigns, that, for the most part, had not been re-examined in fifty years. Besides these new operational studies there are excellent recent works on privateering, trade protection, the operation of prize law, dockyards, and central administration. The social and political history of the navy of this period is currently being re-examined by scholars, but has not yet reached significant levels of publication to put alongside the older histories. LAVERY provides a good introduction to the navy and the maritime environment of the time. The last years of the sailing navy are explored and assessed in LAMBERT.

A final consideration for students of the navy is its comparative effectiveness in action. The dominance of the Royal Navy after 1793 has often obscured the question of how it achieved this domination and the exact trajectory from the 17th to 19th century. It is a complex subject and the qualitative aspects of this development have been tackled in various monographs. However, the relative size and composition of navies forms the bedrock of this debate and the most complete quantitative study of sailing navies in the period is GLETE.

RICHARD HARDING

See also American Colonies: Loss of; Anglo-Dutch Wars; Anson; Archaeology: Maritime; Blake; Buckingham; Drake; Exploration entries; Frobisher; Hawkins; Howard; Merchant Navy entries; Napoleonic Wars: Trafalgar and the War at Sea; Nelson; Piracy; Ralegh; Seven Years' War; Spanish Armada

Nelson, (Viscount) Horatio, Duke of Brontë 1758–1805

Admiral

Gutteridge, H.G. (editor), *Nelson and the Neapolitan Jacobins: Documents Relating to the Suppression of the Jacobin Revolution at Naples, June, 1799*, London: Navy Records Society, 1903

Mahan, A.T., *The Life of Lord Nelson: The Embodiment of the Sea Power of Great Britain*, 2 vols, Boston: Little Brown, and London: Sampson Low and Marston, 1897; 2nd revised edition, 1 vol., 1899; reprinted, Harmondsworth: Penguin, 1942; New York: Haskell House, 1969

Nicolas, Sir Harris (editor), *The Despatches and Letters of Vice Admiral Lord Viscount Nelson*, 7 vols, London: Henry Colburn, 1844–46; reprinted, London: Chatham Press, 1997

Oman, Carola, *Nelson*, London: Hodder and Stoughton, and New York: Doubleday, 1947; abridged edition, London: Hodder and Stoughton, 1967

Pocock, Tom, *Horatio Nelson*, London: Bodley Head, 1987; New York: Knopf, 1988

White, Colin (editor), *The Nelson Companion*, Stroud, Gloucestershire: Alan Sutton, and Annapolis, Maryland: Naval Institute Press, 1995

Nelson, as Lord Byron observed, was Britannia's "God of War", the only man to match the military genius of Napoleon, and surpass him as a human being. Even in life Nelson achieved mythic status, a fact reflected in one of the largest bibliographies of any British historical figure. Unfortunately the scale of the output has been inversely proportional to its quality. Nelson's naval career is well known. He entered the service under the patronage of his uncle, and made his early reputation and many close connections during the American War of Independence (Revolutionary War). In 1793 he began a six-year tour in the Mediterranean, where he established his credentials as an admiral, showing brilliant initiative at Cape St Vincent, before learning a painful lesson with defeat and the loss of an arm at Tenerife. He returned to annihilate the French fleet at the Nile, and spark enduring controversy with his conduct at Naples. Another masterful performance at Copenhagen in 1801 ensured that he was appointed to command in the Mediterranean when the Napoleonic wars broke out in 1803, and this led to his apotheosis at Trafalgar, where his insight, skill, leadership, and ambition overwhelmed a numerically superior Franco-Spanish fleet. As the first national hero Nelson achieved those heights of popular fame that can only presage a fall. Even before his death the fact that he lived openly with Emma, Lady Hamilton, who had a scandalous past, while still married, closed many doors to him. Despite his Tory politics, unswerving patriotism, and monarchist convictions Nelson did not hide his personal life, and accepted a large degree of ostracism. After his death revelations about his personal life, the execution of Commodore Carracciolo, and his treatment of other Neapolitan Jacobins in 1799 made him profoundly unpopular. His professional merits were outweighed by personal faults.

NICOLAS, an ex-naval officer, began his study convinced that Nelson had not received his due from his country. He recognized that Britain needed an heroic Nelson, and the "talismanic power" of his name, to inspire succeeding generations of naval officers with the highest example of patriotism, duty, skill, and humanity. With the exception of a few pieces relating to Lady Hamilton, which he recognized could only damage his hero, Nicolas printed every item he could find, with considerable editorial skill. This collection remains the basis of any serious study of Nelson's career.

MAHAN, an American naval officer, strategist, and educator, had already secured a global reputation for his work on "Sea Power". He was the first naval professional with the time and the literary skill to assess Nelson's life. Because the book was designed for modern naval education Mahan was obliged to address the most controversial aspects of Nelson's life in detail, and repudiate all those assertions that called into question his honour and integrity. His handling of the Neapolitan Jacobins and Commodore Carracciolo prompted a renewed attack on Nelson, in the popular and the academic press. This forced Mahan to revise his book, the only time he ever did so. The second edition retained the original argument, but doubled the length of the relevant chapters, introducing a wealth of archival evidence to support his case. Despite this magisterial edifice, Mahan did not settle the controversy. This task fell to GUTTERIDGE, a young historian recruited by Mahan's friend Sir John Laughton. His volume established that the major items of evidence used to attack Nelson were forgeries, or dishonest translations.

OMAN, writing during World War II, when the nation needed heroes, particularly one so intimately connected with resistance to continental tyrants, extended the treatment of Nelson's personal life, and enlarged upon his relationship with his wife, and with Lady Hamilton. Like Mahan, Oman found ample material for over 700 densely printed pages, a mark of the sheer scale of the subject, and of the material that is still coming to light. Oman did not consider the old arguments about Naples to be worthy of further note. Sadly they remain controversial. Italian scholars and ministers persist in misunderstanding Nelson's role at Naples, where he was acting with the full authority of the king, and in the Carracciolo case, where his only fault was to insist that the sentence of the Neapolitan court martial be carried out that evening, rather than the following morning. Sadly both issues have become so clouded in fiction, fraud, and misunderstanding, dating back to contemporary gossip, French propaganda, and Italian nationalist writing, that the facts are rarely considered. The product of four decades' research, writing, and travel, POCOCK is now the standard modern life. It widens the perspective on the man, introducing new material, new characters, and fresh insight. It is also a pleasure to read. WHITE takes a different approach, addressing eight aspects of Nelson's impact on the world. It goes a long way towards explaining his enduring celebrity, and takes a critical look at the modern understanding of the man.

Curiously the extant literature, for all its scale, is incomplete. As biography it does not go far enough in assessing Nelson's place in the navy of his day, especially his professional development, relations with older officers in his formative years, and his self-education. The evidence suggest that the basis of his brilliance, as expressed in his simple, direct tactics, and strategic insight, was an uncommon degree of self-education.

ANDREW DAVID LAMBERT

See also French Revolutionary Wars; Navy: Sailing; Napoleonic Wars: Trafalgar and the War at Sea

Neville, Richard 1428–1471
Earl of Warwick

Carpenter, Christine, *Locality and Polity: A Study of Warwickshire Landed Society, 1401–1499*, Cambridge and New York: Cambridge University Press, 1992

Hicks, Michael, *Warwick the Kingmaker*, Oxford and Malden, Massachusetts: Blackwell, 1998

Kendall, Paul Murray, *Warwick the Kingmaker*, London: Allen and Unwin, and New York: Norton, 1957

Lander, J.R., *Government and Community: England, 1450–1509*, London: Arnold, and Cambridge, Massachusetts: Harvard University Press, 1980

Oman, Charles W., *Warwick the Kingmaker*, London and New York: Macmillan, 1891

Pollard, Anthony J., *North-Eastern England during the Wars of the Roses: Lay Society, War, and Politics, 1450–1500*, Oxford: Clarendon Press, and New York: Oxford University Press, 1990

Ross, Charles D., *Edward IV*, London: Eyre Methuen, and Berkeley: University of California Press, 1974; 2nd revised edition, New Haven, Connecticut and London: Yale University Press, 1997

Twentieth-century writings on Richard Neville, Warwick "the Kingmaker", were heir to a long debate stretching back to the earl's own lifetime. Starting with Yorkist propaganda which described him as the "Flower of Manhood" in 1460, he has been admired as the examplar of true nobility. In the 16th-century *Mirror for Magistrates* he was presented as one whose overriding concern was for the common weal, never for his own self-advancement or personal glory. This is a view, sustained through to the 19th century, which has continued to inspire his three

modern biographers. On the other hand Warwick's enemies in the 15th century, especially Edward IV and servants of the Duke of Burgandy, were less enamoured. Edward IV's propaganda in 1470–71 and Burgundian chroniclers writing immediately after his death portrayed him as a double-dealer whose excessive pride and overweening ambition led to his justified fall. This view attracted little atttention in England until the early Victorian era when the combination of a surge of publication of original texts and the emergence of a bourgeois, "Whig" historiography led rapidly to Warwick's demonization in general accounts as the last of the feudal dinosaurs threatening the progress of the English state. Since then views of the Kingmaker have oscillated between the admiring and the condemnatory.

For OMAN Warwick was a great statesman, not only because of his exceptional powers of leadership, but also because of his ability to articulate and represent popular opinion. A man before his time, he was the ideal model for the hard-working, aristocratic leader of a political party at the end of the 19th century: a man such as the prime minister of the day when the book was first published, the Marquis of Salisbury. KENDALL, too, saw Warwick as a man before his time, but in his mind as a self-fashioned Renaissance prince rather than a modern statesman. In Kendall's imaginative treatment Warwick takes on the stature of a superman of almost Wagnerian proportions, "the hero of his own saga"; one acting out his own legend in his lifetime, "who ignored the shackles of his time and reached for what he dared to call his own". HICKS, the last of the three modern biographers, follows the same path, even though his work is founded, unlike his predecessors, on a wealth of scholarship and a detailed command of the sources. Like Oman he stresses the relentless attention to business, and similarly concludes that Warwick was not a power-hungry baron seeking his own advancement, but a man representing public opinion. Like Kendall he admires the man who would attempt anything and who believed that there was no obstacle he could not overcome; a colossus who for 20 years shaped events, his own career, and history itself.

But the Kingmaker's modern biographers have by no means had it all their own way. Indeed the main thrust of 20th-century scholarship was to follow the alternative tradition that he was self-seeking, consumed by ambition, deceitful, and treacherous. ROSS, while he expresses sympathy for the earl as a man pushed aside by Edward IV in the 1460s, stresses his pride, his arrogant refusal to accept any position other than the king's first subject, and his contumacious ambition as the reasons for his rebellion in 1469. This assessment was more forcefully articulated by LANDER, who emphasized his bitter resentment against Edward IV, his inability to tolerate anything less than a dominant position, his inordinate avarice and his rampant acquisitiveness. In this reading the high moral ground occupied by the earl was but a stick with which to beat his enemies rather than a guiding light for his own actions. He deluded himself when he insisted that he had done nothing except what an insulted and disparaged nobleman ought to do. His frequently asserted concern for the common weal reflected his lust for popularity combined with a deep cynicism.

Thus the sides could not be further apart. To his admirers Warwick offered a pointer to the future, to policies and politics that respected and reflected the needs of the common good.

To his critics he summed up the blight of the overmighty subject on 15th-century England, holding back the recovery of effective kingship and the further development of the state. Even the assessment of his generalship divides opinion: his admirers praising his strategic grasp, his detractors noting his tactical incompetence. There does exist, however, a third perspective which holds out the prospect of a more neutral evaluation of the greatest commoner of late-medieval England. CARPENTER and POLLARD have examined the local roots of the earl's power in the west Midlands and the north-east of England. Carpenter concluded that he failed to assert his inherited authority in the region as Earl of Warwick and was unable to build up a powerful following there. Pollard argued, on the contrary, that in the part of England where his family roots lay, Neville secured an authority and sway over the region which made it impossible for his king to ignore him. Examination of the roots of Neville's power, rather than the uses to which he put it, suggests a more structural approach. Warwick, it might be argued, was a prisoner of his vast inheritance and great wealth. He had more to lose than gain; and his career might have been determined more by a desire to preserve his position than by one to enhance it. And as the greatest magnate beyond the ranks of the royal family, thus as an outsider, he had little on which to fall back in a crisis, other than military and popular support. Future writing on the Kingmaker might escape from the shackles of contemporary propaganda, break free of the rival traditions which have dominated ever since, and suggest a more complex if less dramatic figure caught in the tensions and conflicts of his time.

ANTHONY JAMES POLLARD

See also Edward IV; Henry VI; Margaret of Anjou; Towton, Barnet, and Tewkesbury, Battles of

Neville's Cross, Battle of 1346

Campbell, James, "England, Scotland, and the Hundred Years War in the Fourteenth Century" in *Europe in the Late Middle Ages*, edited by J.R. Hale, J.R.L. Highfield, and B. Smalley, London: Faber, and Evanston, Illinois: Northwestern University Press, 1965; reprinted in *The Wars of Edward III: Sources and Interpretations*, edited by Clifford J. Rogers, Woodbridge, Suffolk and Rochester, New York: Boydell Press, 1999

Grant, Alexander, *Independence and Nationhood: Scotland, 1306–1469*, London and Baltimore: Arnold, 1984; reprinted, Edinburgh: Edinburgh University Press, 1991

McKisack, May, *Oxford History of England*, vol. 5, *The Fourteenth Century, 1307–1399*, Oxford: Clarendon Press, 1959

Ormrod, W.M., *The Reign of Edward III: Crown and Political Society in England, 1327–1377*, New Haven, Connecticut and London: Yale University Press, 1990; updated edition, Stroud, Gloucestershire: Tempus, 2000

Perroy, Edouard, *The Hundred Years War*, translated by W.B. Wells, London: Eyre and Spottiswoode, 1951; Bloomington: Indiana University Press, 1959 (French edition, 1945)

Prestwich, Michael, *The Three Edwards: War and State in England, 1272–1377*, London: Weidenfeld and Nicolson, and New York: St Martin's Press, 1980

Rollason, David and Michael Prestwich (editors), *The Battle of Neville's Cross, 1346*, Stamford, Lincolnshire: Shaun Tyas for the North-East England History Institute, 1998

Sumption, Jonathan, *The Hundred Years War*, vol. 1, *Trial by Battle*, London: Faber, 1990; Philadelphia: University of Pennsylvania Press, 1991

The battle of Neville's Cross was fought near Durham on 17 October 1346 between the Scots and English. It resulted in a decisive English victory, heavy Scottish casualties, and the capture of King David II (1329–71), the son of Robert Bruce (King Robert I). Although there are numerous contemporary narratives, conveniently collected in ROLLASON & PRESTWICH, the precise scale, location, and course of the battle remain difficult to establish. Its importance has seldom been fully accepted. It was an occasion when the affairs of England, the Hundred Years War, and of Scotland intersect.

Scotland was allied with France at this stage in the Hundred Years War. The Scots invaded England in response to French appeals for support. Historians of the Hundred Years War, however, have traditionally focused on the continental conflict to the exclusion of that within Britain: thus PERROY in 1951 and SUMPTION in 1990 wrote only the briefest of descriptions of the battle. For English historians also Scotland was essentially a northern problem, hardly central to national affairs. Whereas they recognize that the conquest of Scotland was Edward I's priority and that his son's defeat at Bannockburn in 1314 was a national humiliation, Edward III's not dissimilar efforts in 1333–38 to dominate Scotland, and the north's exposure to Scottish raids thereafter, attracted less attention. MCKISACK in 1959 confined herself to the most basic facts, while noting the active participation of Archbishop Zouche and crediting the English victory largely to Edward's foresight. Even in 1990 ORMROD, Edward III's principal modern biographer, did no more. The battle bulks much larger in Scottish history. For Scots, Neville's Cross was part of the long train of events which commenced with the deaths of Alexander III (1286) and his granddaughter Margaret, the "Maid of Norway" (1290). The brief reign of John Balliol then followed, and Edward I's conquests, Scottish resistance, Robert I's recognition in 1328, and Edward III's attempts to install Edward Balliol as king: in other words, the Scottish wars of conquest and independence.

However, Neville's Cross was not a purely Scottish event nor peripheral in English or European terms. It was first fully contextualized by CAMPBELL in 1965. Commencing in 1333, when Edward Balliol and the disinherited Scottish lords secured Edward III's support and won their victory at Halidon Hill, Campbell traced annual campaigns by the English to conquer Scotland. Like his grandfather, Edward III occupied much of the lowlands; "a wide allegiance", he too found, "could be won by the use of large armies, but were lost when they left . . . He failed and found himself still involved in a war which he could neither win nor abandon". Meantime the young David II fled to France, where Philip VI made a Gascon settlement contingent on David's recognition. Edward combined major expeditions to Scotland with expensive defences against potential French invasions up to 1338, when the French war took priority.

Ill-supplied and unrelieved, English possessions in Scotland were quickly lost, and northern England was exposed to damaging Scottish raids in 1341–42 and again in 1345–46, which were undertaken to force Edward III to recognize David. Neville's Cross is thus both an element in the Scottish Wars of Independence and in the Hundred Years War. It was one of the strongest of Scottish armies that was defeated. Neville's Cross removed the Scottish threat to England and their value to the French. Initially it enabled Edward to take the initiative both in France, where the capture of Calais in 1347 was achieved by one of the largest English armies, and in Scotland, where Balliol overran much of the lowlands, but in the longer term it contributed to Scottish independence. Edward failed to take control. Moreover David II's value as a bargaining chip depended on Scottish recognition of him as king. It was because he was their king that in 1357 the Scots agreed to ransom him for 100,000 marks (£66,666, 13s, 4d.). Despite ten years of negotiation, they had conceded neither overlordship nor territory. Long before then Edward III had abandoned Balliol and now tacitly acknowledged David II as King of Scotland.

Campbell's perceptions entered the mainstream of English history with PRESTWICH's textbook in 1980. Anglo-Scottish warfare is central to his book, which treats the interaction of the two conflicts, and accepts that Neville's Cross enabled Edward to exchange intangible rights for financial advantage. Although no more than a fifth of the ransom was ultimately paid, Edward had found a way to profit from Scotland. International perspectives and evidence are included in GRANT's succinct account of the Wars of Independence. Balliol's successes in the 1330s did not win Scottish co-operation and forced Edward III into conquest, for which he lacked sufficient resources even before French distractions became overwhelming in 1338. By 1341 "the Bruce cause had triumphed again. [Thereafter] David II faced the same task as his father: to make the English crown recognize Scottish independence". With Edward III abroad, the Scots had not expected any opposition. Although ostensibly so similar to Halidon in 1333, Neville's Cross did not lead to the restoration of Balliol, now discredited in Scotland, but to Edward's recognition of David II. Only thus could he exploit David's capture fully. "Paradoxically it was not so much David's triumphant return in 1341 as his disastrous defeat in 1346 that finally ended the Bruce–Balliol civil war. Neville's Cross and David's capture transformed the military and diplomatic relationship between Scotland and England." England accepted David as king, "though not of course Scottish independence".

Rollason & Prestwich published the papers from the conference marking the 650th anniversary of Neville's Cross. Specific items focus on John de Coupland and Thomas Rokeby, captor and custodian of David II, on the Black Rood supposedly captured there and the commemorative monument, on the battlefield site, local landscape, and military archery. The two principal papers by Prestwich and Grant set the battle within its international and Scottish context. Altogether the book sets out the current understanding of the battle in both its local and its widest contexts.

MICHAEL A. HICKS

See also David II; Edward III; Hundred Years' War; Robert II

New Lanark   founded 1784

Blake, George, *"The Gourock"*, Port Glasgow: Gourock Ropework Company, 1963

Butt, John (editor), *Robert Owen, Prince of Cotton Spinners: A Symposium*, Newton Abbot, Devon: David and Charles, 1971

Cullen, Alex, *Adventures in Socialism: New Lanark Establishment and Orbiston Community*, Glasgow: John Smith, 1910; reprinted, Clifton, New Jersey: A.M. Kelley, 1972

Donnachie, Ian and George Hewitt, *Historic New Lanark: The Dale and Owen Industrial Community since 1785*, Edinburgh: Edinburgh University Press, 1993

Harrison, J.F.C., *Robert Owen and the Owenites in Britain and America: The Quest for the New Moral World*, London: Routledge and Kegan Paul; as *The Quest for the New Moral World: Robert Owen and the Owenites in Britain and America*, New York: Scribner, 1969

McLaren, David J., *David Dale of New Lanark: A Bright Luminary to Scotland*, Glasgow: Heatherbank Press, 1983

Podmore, Frank, *Robert Owen: A Biography*, 2 vols, London: Hutchinson, 1906; reprinted, 1 vol., London: Allen and Unwin, 1906; New York: Appleton, 1924

Royle, Edward, *Robert Owen and the Commencement of the Millennium: A Study of the Harmony Community*, Manchester: Manchester University Press, and New York: St Martin's Press, 1998

Taylor, Anne, *Visions of Harmony: A Study in Nineteenth-Century Millenarianism*, Oxford: Clarendon Press, and New York: Oxford University Press, 1987

New Lanark, the factory village on the River Clyde some 40 km (25 m) south of Glasgow, was established by the Scottish entrepreneur and banker, David Dale, in 1785. After Richard Arkwright dropped out of the initial partnership Dale turned New Lanark into an archetype of the philanthropic community, but it was subsequently to become internationally famous as the locus of Dale's son-in-law Robert Owen's social and educational reforms. From the outset New Lanark was much visited, partly because factories employing large numbers of women and children were still unusual, and partly because the mills were located in a spectacular and Romantic setting downstream of the famous (and much painted) Falls of Clyde.

Some early accounts survive from the Dale era (1785–1800), of which the most detailed and interesting is that contributed to Sir John Sinclair's *Statistical Account of Scotland* (1795). This described the generally philanthropic regime prevailing under Dale's managers, a theme developed by McLAREN's important biography of Dale, which emphasizes the nature and extent of the social provision for workers, who included large numbers of child apprentices he recruited from Glasgow and Edinburgh orphanages and parishes. McLaren emphasizes that while Dale, as the founder of a secessionist breakaway from the established Church of Scotland, attached great personal importance to religious observance and morality, education and training nevertheless had a significant role at New Lanark long before Owen's arrival as managing partner.

Owen claims to have made sweeping reforms at New Lanark

and after 1812, when his public career began, it attracted considerable publicity. He initially described his reforms in the series of essays titled *A New View of Society* (1813–16), which attempted to relate character formation to environment. By this time New Lanark was being perceived as a test bed for Owen's ideas on personnel management, factory reform (especially as it affected the employment of children), poor relief, and, more generally, the reform of society. In the uncertain circumstances prevailing in the post-Napoleonic War years, Owen's claim to produce both conforming characters and high profits at New Lanark could hardly fail to appeal to middle- and upper-class audiences.

Descriptions and assessments of the community proliferated, some favourable, others highly critical. Dr Henry Macnab, sent north to investigate by aristocratic Owenites headed by the Duke of Kent, provided a balanced account, but emphasized the strict discipline and policing in the village. This view was also confirmed in a report made by a delegation from the Leeds poor law guardians which also noted the relatively low wages paid. Inevitably, given Owen's views on sectarian religion (aside from marriage and birth control), much of the criticism came from the church, primarily the moral basis of his proposed reforms. But this did not stop Owen using New Lanark as a model for his village scheme, first described in a pamphlet of 1817 and further developed in the *Report to the County of Lanark* (1820). Owen's son, Robert Dale Owen, produced a valuable description (1824) of the schools and institute, with details of the regime and curriculum, which was modelled on the thinking of Joseph Lancaster and J.H. Pestalozzi.

PODMORE's massive biographical study of Owen devoted a great deal of space to New Lanark and examined its place in the early factory system, the reforms Owen carried out, and its role in the further development of Owenism. About the same time another Fabian writer, CULLEN, used the extensive Owen correspondence and the Hamilton of Dalziel papers to produce a comparative study of New Lanark and Orbiston, the first British Owenite community which Owen had planned but abandoned in 1824 after he embarked on another community scheme in the United States at New Harmony, Indiana.

Many of the modern studies of Owen and Owenism devote attention to New Lanark and the reforms Owen carried out, making it a showplace visited by reformers from all over the world. Prominent are the works of HARRISON, ROYLE, and TAYLOR (also noted under the entry on Owen himself). Harrison brilliantly contextualized New Lanark in the history of Owenism, especially its relationship to what he calls the "lost communities", which have left little physical evidence. Taylor takes a much more cynical view of Owen's activities at New Lanark, while Royle's detailed study of the last Owenite community, Queenwood, emphasizes that New Lanark was always the model to which Owen returned and on which he built his theories. DONNACHIE & HEWITT take the view that New Lanark was inappropriate as a building-block for the communities of equality, since it was a capitalist venture, the success of which proved Owen's astuteness as a businessman but did not necessarily provide a model for co-operative ventures.

Not surprisingly the history of New Lanark after Owen's departure has until recently been neglected. BLAKE remedied this to the extent that he devoted some attention to its business history after 1881 under the Birkmyres and later that of the Gourock Ropework Company, which they founded to consolidate their interests in cotton, sailcloth, and rope manufacture. But this was largely superficial and anecdotal and it was left to Donnachie & Hewitt, drawing on the Gourock Ropework papers at Glasgow University Archives, to describe the history of New Lanark under the Walkers, a Quaker family who from 1825 to 1880 seem to have followed the philanthropic tradition set by Dale and Owen. According to their account the Birkmyres were at first less sympathetic to the workers, but subsequently the community was strongly maintained until the mills closed in 1968.

John Hume in BUTT provided a model survey of the industrial archaeology of New Lanark in which he described how the mills and village were built and subsequently extended. This presented further evidence that Owen's contribution to the actual fabric was limited to his institute, the school, and some housing, and that much else that survives dated from the Dale era. The subsequent restoration of the village since the 1970s to UNESCO World Heritage status is also covered by a chapter in Donnachie & Hewitt. However, the best text is the place itself, a monument to those who lived and worked there and the ideas they inspired.

IAN DONNACHIE

See also Factory Reform; Industrial Revolution; Industrialization; Owen; Port Sunlight

New Model Army

see Army: to 1855; Civil Wars entries; Cromwell, Oliver; Fairfax; Lilburne; Putney Debates

New World, Perceptions of

Axtell, James, *The Invasion Within: The Contest of Cultures in Colonial North America*, New York and Oxford: Oxford University Press, 1985

Carroll, Peter N., *Puritanism and the Wilderness: The Intellectual Significance of the New England Frontier, 1629–1700*, New York: Columbia University Press, 1969

Cronon, William, *Changes in the Land: Indians, Colonists, and the Ecology of New England*, New York: Hill and Wang, 1983

Jones, Howard Mumford, *O Strange New World: American Culture, the Formative Years*, New York: Viking Press, 1964; London: Chatto and Windus, 1965

Kupperman, Karen Ordahl (editor), *America in European Consciousness, 1493–1750*, Chapel Hill: University of North Carolina Press, 1995

Pagden, Anthony, *European Encounters with the New World: From Renaissance to Romanticism*, New Haven, Connecticut: Yale University Press, 1993

Turner, Frederick Jackson, "The Significance of the Frontier in American History" in his *The Frontier in American History*, New York: Holt, 1958 (first published in the *Annual Report of the American Historical Association*, 1893)

Since the first publication of Columbus's travel narratives, the idea of the New World has exerted a strong influence upon the European, and later colonial, mind. Following the establishment of the first European settlements, questions arose concerning colonial perceptions of both New World peoples and its terrain. First and foremost, the presence of native inhabitants forced colonists to reinterpret their own positions within a cosmology previously defined by their relationship with God. If there were cultures that had never been exposed to Christianity, it became essential that this "problem" be rectified. Furthermore, to European colonists, American Indian culture seemed backward – they were seen as "savages" who needed to be "civilized". Not only did the inhabitants of the New World confront colonists, but for many transplanted Europeans the very environment itself had a character that shaped, and was shaped by, its interaction with these new settlers. In America, unlike Europe, the presence of a seemingly unlimited frontier had dramatic effects upon the character of the colonists and played a central role in their understanding of the New World.

A number of excellent studies have focused on the colonists' understanding of American Indian culture and customs, highlighting the interactions between the settlers and natives. One of the key factors influencing the colonial position had its roots in European notions of human nature. Howard Mumford JONES provides a perceptive overview of this issue, tracing the evolution of European ideas of the New World from their origins during the late Renaissance through the 19th century. Beginning with the reception of Columbus's reports, Jones explains how early perceptions of the New World as a type of "second Eden" were eventually countered by negative interpretations. As Jones explains, the first reactions to the modern discovery of the Americas were heavily influenced by romantic images of the "noble savage"; Indian culture was portrayed as "virtuous" due to its simplicity and supposedly idyllic character. Jones sketches the process by which these early contacts by travellers and explorers were transformed by settlers to express an increasingly grim view of native Americans. As religiosity among the English colonists rose, the "wildness" and "savagery" of the American Indians came to be seen as stark evidence of their "Satanic" origins. Hoping to "save" them from sin, colonists tried to "civilize" and "Christianize" them.

While Jones does an excellent job explicating the intellectual context within which these early colonial ideas developed, Anthony PAGDEN takes the story forward by focusing more attention upon the theoretical concepts that allowed European colonists to interpret native Americans as "savage". Although much of Pagden's work focuses on the Spanish case, his description of the colonial experiences of administration and acculturation may be easily transported to the situations encountered by French and English settlers. Pagden stresses that the New World was seen as "new" in the most literal sense, that its discovery was almost a "second act of creation". Furthermore, Pagden carefully highlights how the colonial struggle to "civilize" native Americans grew directly out of their perception of the New World as belonging to an earlier age: they were "savage" because their civilization was "younger" than that of the Europeans. As analysed by Pagden the "civilizing process" was also, at a deeper level, a struggle for linguistic supremacy. Faced with the question of which value system was going to dominate the Americas, European colonists sought to prevent the "nativization" of their fellows, while simultaneously trying to convince as many of the "wild" natives as possible to accept their point of view.

Pagden's survey may serve as a good introduction to the broader issues involved with colonial ideas of native civilization, but it is AXTELL's close study of the interactions between the English, French, and native American societies that provides the most detailed analysis of the educational and acculturative influences of these groups upon each other. Axtell provides ample evidence from contemporary sources to support his depiction of the European settlers' strategies of dealing with native Americans. Providing a wealth of detail concerning the interactions between these cultures, Axtell stresses that they English and French primarily sought native American allies through trade and religious conversion. Seeking to first "civilize" and then "Christianize" them, religious missionaries held an unshakable belief in the "essential educability" of the American Indians – while they may have been "backward", they were still "savable" in the sense that they merely needed to be exposed to the "proper" version of the truth. Axtell's study is particularly strong on this point, illustrating the various tactics implemented by the settlers to encourage the complete assimilation of the native population, thus explaining one of the central issues shaping colonial perceptions of the human element of the New World.

Not only did the discovery of the New World introduce settlers to unknown peoples, it also uncovered vast, unexplored territories to their curious eyes. The essays in KUPPERMAN's recent collection are important contributions to understanding the religious, political, economic, and cultural impact of the New World on European consciousness. These pieces help illuminate the wide variety of ways European colonists and explorers sought to reconcile the existence of the Americas with long-held beliefs concerning themselves and their place in the world. For instance, many English settlers were faced with an uncharted frontier, which quickly took on a character of its own. Historiographically, considerations of the American frontier have drawn heavily on the original insights of Frederick Jackson TURNER. Turner's thesis hypothesizes that one of the keys to understanding American thought, from the first stages of colonization until the late 19th century, is the notion of the frontier. Turner suggests that in the social cauldron marking the boundary between settled areas and the wilderness, a constantly changing process of adaptation occurred, moulding the formation of national institutions and acting as a touchstone for colonial understandings of the New World.

Peter CARROLL's study of the New England frontier is an interesting application of Turner's work that seeks to explain the impact of the forest on some of the first American colonists. Carroll claims that the New World wilderness forced an extensive review of puritan theology, testing traditional beliefs and encouraging the application of biblical metaphors to their new situation, thereby transforming their understanding of New World terrain. Grounded more in the actual interactions between colonists and the New World itself, William CRONON's influential study of colonial ecology stresses the fundamental changes wrought upon the daily lives of the settlers by their new surroundings, as well as their effects upon the local environment. Cronon's work provides great insight into the interaction between colonists and the landscape, helping to explicate how settlers understood the New World on a daily basis.

SCOTT C. BREUNINGER

See also American Colonies entries; Americas, Trade with; Australia; Cook; Drake; Exploration entries; New Zealand; Ralegh; Trade Patterns: Early Modern

New Zealand, Settlement of and Relations with

Adams, Peter, *Fatal Necessity: British Intervention in New Zealand 1830–1847*, Auckland: Auckland University Press, 1977

Barratt, Glynn, *Russophobia in New Zealand 1838–1908*, Palmerston North: Dunmore Press, 1981

Belich, James, *Paradise Reforged: A History of New Zealanders from the 1880s to the Year 2000*, Auckland and London: Allen Lane, 2001

McKinnon, Malcolm, *Independence and Foreign Policy: New Zealand in the World since 1935*, Auckland: Auckland University Press, 1993

Orange, Claudia, *The Treaty of Waitangi*, Wellington: Allen and Unwin, and Winchester, Massachusetts: Port Nicolson Press, 1987

Rice, Geoffrey W. (editor), *The Oxford History of New Zealand*, 2nd edition, Auckland, New York and Oxford: Oxford University Press, 1992

Ross, Angus, "Reluctant Dominion or Dutiful Daughter: New Zealand and the Commonwealth in the Inter-war Years", *Journal of Imperial and Commonwealth History*, 10/1 (1972): 28–44

Sinclair, Keith, *A Destiny Apart: New Zealand's Search for National Identity*, Wellington: Allen and Unwin, and Winchester, Massachusetts: Port Nicolson Press, 1986

Wood, F.L.W., *The New Zealand People at War: Political and External Affairs*, Wellington: War History Branch, Department of Internal Affairs, 1958

The relationship between New Zealand and Britain is shaped around two themes: the colonization of New Zealand and the emigration of British people to the country; and the ties of close economic relationship that were dominant for much of the period until British entry into the European Economic Community. The result of these two was visible in a close alignment of New Zealand's social and cultural patterns with those of the homeland, and a close alignment of foreign policy with that of Britain. Although formal attainment of dominion status took place in 1907, shifts in foreign-policy patterns of dependence remained in place for these reasons, and New Zealand was very tardy to adopt the Westminster Convention, providing for independent foreign policy. Since 1970 there has been a radical shift in the economic dependence and migration sources for New Zealand, and the consequence has been reflected in a significant change in social, cultural, and diplomatic alignments.

The historical understanding of these processes began in the years of colonization with classic accounts by both British and New Zealand writers, who gave a very positive gloss to the values of empire and the advantages of a "Britain of the South Seas". Such arguments were quite similar to those used for the Australian experience. The difference lay in the presence of a more powerful indigenous population, the Maori people, in New Zealand. The analysis of colonization therefore focused on the annexation of New Zealand, and its unusual feature: the agreement reached in 1840 at the time of annexation with the Maori through the "treaty of Waitangi". Early accounts emphasized the benevolence of the treaty, but not the motives for the use of a treaty as part of the annexation process. Awareness of the treaty grew sharply after the 1960s. Peter ADAMS analysed its political significance in international affairs, but a notable work by Claudia ORANGE focused on the treaty as a necessity to secure Maori co-operation in the annexation. The discussion on this issue shows no signs of abating.

The annexation was followed in 1854 by the granting of self-government, and thereafter the New Zealand "settler government" succeeded gradually to the full control of the country. In 1907 dominion status was awarded, and during World War II the need to develop diplomatic relations with the United States government led to the creation of the Department of External Affairs. Left-wing New Zealand historians from the 1930s were eager advocates of the fragile seed of New Zealand nationalism. This was a dominating motif in the writings the most prominent of these historians, Keith SINCLAIR, notably in his *A Destiny Apart*. Here and in other works, the argument was that New Zealand's cultural and social distinctiveness and isolation all nurtured the formation of a clear national identity. This view has become an emphatic orthodoxy in recent years.

Yet there was an historical problem, first spelt out by Angus ROSS's seminal article, of a remarkable enthusiasm for the "ties of blood and empire" and a reluctance to take even that measure of independence which Britain offered. For example, virtually the only colonial support for Joseph Chamberlain's idea of an imperial British parliament came from New Zealand politicians, and the Statute of Westminster was not ratified until 1947, well after the other dominions had taken this step. W. David McIntyre in the second edition of the *Oxford History of New Zealand* (RICE), analysed several factors, notably the sense of insecurity induced by distance (sharply accentuated by the Russian scare of the 1880s, as BARRATT has described) and the unusually British character of the immigrants, for while small numbers came from Germany and Scandinavia, the vast majority, in every period of migration, were from the British Isles. Moreover the balance of British settlers fell more towards the Scots, with their enthusiasm for Britishness, and less towards the Irish, who were notorious for their distaste for the empire.

A further factor, which has also very considerable significance was the growing economic dependence on Britain as a market for New Zealand exports. Whereas in the early years of the colony, exports (mostly of flax and timber) largely went to Australia and the United States, the advent of refrigeration tied British consumers and the New Zealand farmers together in a close relationship, which successive governments were forced to defend.

Many of these factors gained huge emotional support during the Anglo-Boer War and in the two world wars of the 20th century. The symbolism of the ANZAC contribution at Gallipoli to the British war effort was in many respects the seminal moment in New Zealand and Australian self-understanding, yet it concerned supporting the empire, as a series of historians have noted. Similarly New Zealand dairy production was in effect set aside for Britain in that period, cementing the close relationship. WOOD in his important book established this point strongly. Thus reformist governments surprisingly did not challenge the closeness of the relationship, as Malcolm McKINNON has showed in his general study. In more recent years there has been a reversion away from interpreting New Zealand history as a process of breaking free from Britain. James BELICH has argued, most recently in this work, that this dependence grew rather than declined from the late 19th century in a process he terms "recolonization". He argues that Britishness was a general commodity and that the ties to the empire were immensely valuable to New Zealand, and that rationality and world-view inclined most people to support it.

PETER LINEHAM

See also Australia; Cook

Newcastle

Bourne, Henry, *The History of Newcastle upon Tyne, or, the Ancient and Present State of that Town*, Newcastle: J. White, 1736; reprinted, Newcastle-Upon-Tyne: Graham, 1980

Brand, John, *The History and Antiquities of the Town and County of Newcastle upon Tyne, Including an Account of the Coal Trade of That Place*, 2 vols, London: B. White, 1789

Gray, William, *Chorographia, or, a Survey of Newcastle upon Tyne in 1649*, Newcastle: S.B., 1649; 6th edition, reprinted, Newcastle: Graham, 1970

Howell, Roger, *Newcastle upon Tyne and the Puritan Revolution: A Study of the Civil War in North England*, Oxford: Clarendon Press, 1967

McCord, Norman and Richard Thompson, *The Northern Counties from AD 1000*, London and New York: Longman, 1998

Mackenzie, Eneas, *A Descriptive and Historical Account of the Town and County of Newcastle upon Tyne, including the Borough of Gateshead*, Newcastle-Upon-Tyne: Mackenzie and Dent, 1827

Middlebrook, S., *Newcastle upon Tyne: Its Growth and Achievement*, Newcastle: Newcastle Chronicle and Journal, 1950

Walker, R.F., *The Institutions and History of the Freemen of Newcastle Upon Tyne*, Newcastle: Stewards' Committee of the Freemen of Newcastle-upon-Tyne, 1997

Welford, Richard (editor), *History of Newcastle and Gateshead*, 3 vols, London: Walter Scott, 1884–87

One of England's most important towns for many centuries, Newcastle, lacking a cathedral, did not become a city until 1882 and remains in the parlance of most of its inhabitants "the town". Its first historian, William GRAY, wrote of it, referring to William Camden's survey of Britain, *Britannia* (1586):

"Camden calls Newcastle Ocellus, the eye of the north, the harth that warmeth the south parts of this kingdom with fire – an Egypt to all the shires of the north, in time of famine, for bread". Here we have three reasons for the town's importance: its military significance because of its strategic position on the lowest convenient crossing of the Tyne and proximity to the Scottish border; the vital nature of its coal trade to the nation; and its role as the granary and financial centre to the northern region. Short but colourful and perceptive, Gray's study was the first real history of the town. Written at a time when the coal trade had become central to the economy of Tyneside, it highlighted "this great trade [which] hath made this town to flourish in all trade", but paid due attention to the town's previous history as a staple town of the wool trade and, naturally, in view of the recent seige by the Scots in 1644, to its strategic importance.

The 18th and 19th centuries were to see a number of histories of Newcastle that were all fuller works than Gray's. None was, however, a history in the conventional sense of an account of the town's development in a consistently chronological format, for they used a topographical and topical approach, essentially surveying the town and exploring the history of each part in turn. Foremost among the studies of the town published in the 18th century were the works of two Newcastle clergymen, the Reverend Henry BOURNE and the Reverend John BRAND. Bourne was the first historian of the town to base his work on the primary documents, which he systematically collected. His book was comparatively short, a folio of 251 pages, but it was a pioneering work and all subsequent histories draw upon it, as did the weightier volumes of John Brand published later in the century. Both these learned men contributed greatly to our knowledge of Newcastle's history, bringing to their work the impulse to retrieve its past and preserve the documentary evidence at a time when the town was changing rapidly. Both placed a considerable emphasis upon ecclesiastical history but what distinguishes them both is their curiosity about all aspects of Newcastle's history. Eneas MACKENZIE, an early 19th-century radical and reformer, whose faith in the progress of the time he lived in provided as tight a framework as Bourne's and Brand's religious faith, synthesized rather than added to the work of the 18th-century historians.

The history of the North-East has found many eminent historians and the fecund period for antiquarianism and history writing of the 18th and early 19th century was continued throughout the latter century. Although there is no *Victoria County History* for Northumberland as there is for Durham, the *Northumberland County History* is an equally excellent and dependable work for those areas it covers. Newcastle is not, however, among them. The most important late 19th-century work on Newcastle was that by Richard WELFORD, who covered the period from the 14th to the 17th centuries in a book rigorously grounded in the primary sources. He employed a year-by-year approach, recording a "diary of the political, municipal, ecclesiastical, commercial and to some extent social life of Newcastle". It was not until the middle of the 20th century, however, that a history of Newcastle that aimed to be "a narrative record of continuous growth" was published. Even then, MIDDLEBROOK's history concentrated upon the modern period with less than a fifth of his book being devoted to the Roman and medieval periods. His book remains, nevertheless, the most complete history of the town.

An important contribution to our understanding of important decades in Newcastle's history was made in 1967 by an American, Roger HOWELL. His work can be said to have transformed interpretations of Newcastle's role during the Civil Wars and Interregnum, explaining developments as much in terms of internal divisions and rivalries as epiphenomena of a national conflict. WALKER's short history of the freemen of the town is wider than the title suggests and is in fact a very useful account of the development of Newcastle's government and merchant companies.

If Newcastle is not as fortunate as many cities of comparable importance in terms of comprehensive histories written in the last two centuries, there is a wealth of detailed work on aspects of its history in *Archaeologia Aeliana*, the annual journal of the Society of Antiquaries of Newcastle, and the excellent recent history of the northern region by McCORD & THOMPSON places Newcastle and its importance in the context of the development of the four northern counties.

A.W. Purdue

Newcastle, Thomas Pelham-Holles, 1st Duke of 1693–1768
Politician and statesman

Browning, Reed, *The Duke of Newcastle*, New Haven, Connecticut and London: Yale University Press, 1975

Henretta, James A., *"Salutary Neglect": Colonial Administration under the Duke of Newcastle*, Princeton, New Jersey: Princeton University Press, 1972

Kelch, Ray A., *Newcastle: A Duke without Money: Thomas Pelham-Holles, 1693–1768*, London: Routledge and Kegan Paul, and Berkeley: University of California Press, 1974

Nulle, Stebelton H., *Thomas Pelham-Holles, Duke of Newcastle: His Early Political Career, 1693–1724*, Philadelphia: University of Pennsylvania Press, and London: Oxford University Press, 1931

Owen, John B., *The Rise of the Pelhams*, London: Methuen, 1957; New York: Barnes and Noble, 1971

Wilkes, John W., *A Whig in Power: The Political Career of Henry Pelham*, Evanston, Illinois: Northwestern University Press, 1964

Williams, Basil, *Carteret and Newcastle: A Contrast in Contemporaries*, Cambridge: Cambridge University Press, 1943; reprinted, Hamden, Connecticut: Archon Books, 1966

Yorke, Philip C., *The Life and Correspondence of Philip Yorke, Earl of Hardwicke: Lord High Chancellor of Great Britain*, 3 vols, Cambridge: Cambridge University Press, 1913; reprinted, New York: Octagon Books, 1977

No 18th-century politician has left behind him such a wealth of detail about his career as the Duke of Newcastle and yet so far he has attracted only one full biography. There are hundreds of volumes of his correspondence in the British Library (among his own papers and those of the Earl of Hardwicke) and this has no doubt daunted some potential biographers, but it is also likely that many historians have been reluctant to spend years of their lives wading through the voluminous correspondence of a man who has become notorious for his fussiness and fretfulness, his petty jealousies, his reluctance to accept responsibility for his actions, and his inability to pursue any political objective to his own satisfaction or to the nation's profit. His personality was lampooned in the memoirs of such contemporaries as Horace Walpole, Lord Hervey, and Earl Waldegrave, and many modern historians have depicted him as the epitome of unredeemed mediocrity and as a veritable buffoon in office.

Such verdicts, however, have unfairly obscured the abilities and merits of a politician at the centre of power for more than 40 years, from the early 1720s to the late 1760s. His reputation is certainly lower than it deserves to be. He was the greatest electoral manager and patronage master of his age, devoting vast amounts of time and money to gaining political support in parliament. As a secretary of state for several decades he played a major role in the conduct of British diplomacy, while, as first lord of the Treasury and prime minister, he found the money to sustain the country's enormous military and naval efforts during the Seven Years War (1756–63) and the supporters to give the administration a majority in parliament.

Newcastle's family background and upbringing, his position in local politics (he was particularly active in Sussex and Nottinghamshire), and his political apprenticeship between 1715 and 1724, when he was appointed a secretary of state, are quite well described in NULLE, though this work clearly betrays its origins as a doctoral thesis. Although one of the richest landowners of his day, Newcastle lived well beyond his means and came close to financial ruin on several occasions. He spent a fortune on election expenses, but even more on maintaining a lavish ducal lifestyle, in part to win over political allies. This aspect of his career has been carefully researched and clearly presented by KELCH, though his study largely ignores Newcastle's wider political career.

Newcastle was particularly interested in distributing crown patronage in order to secure political support. His electioneering activities have not been fully explored, but there are useful articles by S.H. Nulle on his role in the general election of 1727 in the *Journal of Modern History* (1937) and by Basil Williams on his activities in the general election of 1734 in *English Historical Review* (1897). A great deal can be gleaned from a study of the relevant volumes in *The History of Parliament: The House of Commons 1715–1754* (edited by Romney Sedgwick, 2 vols, 1970) and *The House of Commons 1754–1790* (edited by Sir Lewis Namier and John Brooke, 3 vols, 1964). These are now published by Cambridge University Press on a CD-ROM that is searchable. Norman Sykes has examined Newcastle's use of church patronage in an article in *English Historical Review* (1942) and in his book *Church and State in England in the XVIIIth Century* (1934). Philip Haffenden has done the same for Newcastle's use of colonial patronage in an article in the same journal for 1963, while HENRETTA has produced a much more detailed study of Newcastle's general role in colonial administration.

As a secretary of state deeply involved for many years in Britain's diplomatic negotiations with European powers, Newcastle had to face opposition from Earl Carteret. Their decades of political rivalry are described and analysed in a scholarly fashion by WILLIAMS. In an even more impressive work,

OWEN has written much the best account of how Newcastle and his more able younger brother, Henry Pelham, came to dominate government and parliament in the 1740s after the fall of Sir Robert Walpole. Much can be learned about Newcastle by a study of his more able and more illustrious colleagues. The Earl of Hardwicke was Newcastle's closest ally throughout his political career and their long and close relationship has been well explored in the three volumes produced by YORKE. Newcastle's relations with his brother are explored less effectively in the rather disappointing biography of Henry Pelham written by WILKES. Newcastle served almost twenty years under Sir Robert Walpole and was for years a rival or a close colleague of William Pitt the Elder. There are many biographies of both of these more illustrious politicians that contain useful information on Newcastle. The memoirs and histories of his contemporaries – Horace Walpole, Lord Hervey, and Earl Waldegrave – though often highly critical of Newcastle, will repay serious study. Newcastle also looms large in the two seminal works by Sir Lewis Namier: *The Structure of Politics at the Accession of George III* (1929; 2nd edition, 1957) and *England in the Age of the American Revolution* (1930; 2nd edition, 1961).

So far the only full-scale and rounded biography of Newcastle is that written by BROWNING. This is a distinguished work and is essential reading for anyone trying to get to grips with Newcastle's long career. It is based on impressive scholarship, it is clearly structured, and it is well written. It is particularly good on the intricacies of Newcastle's diplomatic activities as secretary of state. It is less valuable on his activities as first lord of the Treasury during the Seven Years War and it needs to be supplemented on some aspects of his career by the works mentioned above. Newcastle's political role in and out of parliament, as distinct from his activities in office, still requires further study.

HARRY T. DICKINSON

See also George I; George II; George III; Pitt, William, "the Elder"; Rockingham; Seven Years' War; Walpole

Newman, John Henry 1801–1890
Founder of the Oxford (Tractarian) movement, writer, later cardinal

Chadwick, Owen, *The Victorian Church*, 2 vols, London: A. and C. Black, and New York: Oxford University Press, 1966–70

Chadwick, Owen, *Newman*, Oxford and New York: Oxford University Press, 1983

Gilley, Sheridan, *Newman and His Age*, London: Darton Longman and Todd, 1990

Hill, Roland, *Lord Acton*, New Haven, Connecticut, and London: Yale University Press, 2000

Ker, Ian, *John Henry Newman: A Biography*, Oxford: Clarendon Press, and New York: Oxford University Press, 1988

Machin, G.I.T., *Politics and the Churches in Great Britain, 1832–1868*, Oxford and New York: Clarendon Press, 1977

Machin, G.I.T., *Politics and the Churches in Great Britain, 1869–1921*, Oxford: Clarendon Press, and New York: Oxford University Press, 1987

Newsome, David, *The Convert Cardinals: John Henry Newman and Henry Edward Manning*, London: Murray, 1993

One of the most celebrated churchmen and writers, Newman is famed for being a founder and leader of the "Oxford" or tractarian movement in the Church of England which commenced in 1833; for being one of the first tractarians to join the Roman catholic church in 1845; for being thereafter a firm defender of British catholics and of his own position against assailants, yet being more moderate and ambivalent towards the papacy and other questions of religion than many converts (such as Henry Edward Manning); and ultimately for receiving a cardinal's hat in 1879 (four years later than Manning, who had joined the Roman church six years later than him). Although Manning rose more quickly in the church of Rome, Newman had attained a much more prominent position in Anglicanism than Manning had done, even if in their Roman catholic lives Newman was more of an outsider and less favoured by church officialdom. Newman was a prolific and felicitous writer of journal articles, pamphlets, and books which are of lasting theological, educational, literary, and autobiographical importance. Devotion, criticism, personal justification, controversy, and poetry are leading ingredients of his large and varied corpus of publications.

KER provides a large, definitive modern biography which gives over 300 pages to Newman's life in the Church of England and over 400 pages to his life in the church of Rome. With the aid of plentiful quotation from Newman's personal and public writings, Ker succeeds in presenting a comprehensive and rounded portrait, in which developing theological opinions and literary felicity share the canvas more than adequately with personal strengths and weaknesses and engagement in controversy. GILLEY's biography, which at over 400 pages is rather less monumental, is similarly accomplished and compelling and forms a lively and perceptive contribution.

The excellent treatments by Ker and Gilley may well be said to tell one almost all there is to know, and almost all that needs to be thought, about Newman. But it is still desirable to read further contextual studies of Newman and his times, such as are given in CHADWICK's two volumes on the Church of England (where the Oxford Movement and its effects are particularly well and intensively covered) and in MACHIN's two on the political relations of the British churches. Those who seek a brief introduction to thought of huge breadth should read the concentrated consideration of Newman given by CHADWICK (1983) in the "Past Masters" series. NEWSOME's dual-biography of Newman and Manning adds splendidly to the high quality of modern work on the two often contesting figures. Fluent and readable, it deals fairly with both cardinals. It implicitly leaves for its readers the fascinating question of whether Manning attained more greatness than Newman on account of his official prominence and social reforming actions, or whether Newman attained more greatness than Manning through the compelling and lasting nature of his literary productions. HILL, in providing a recent large biography of Lord Acton, another leading English catholic who was a contemporary of Newman, deals fully with a field of theological interest (the first Vatican Council and the question of papal infallibility) with which Newman was much involved.

IAN MACHIN

See also Anglican Doctrine and Worship; Catholic Church (since 1560); Oxford Movement; Oxford, University of; Ritualism; Tractarianism

Newton, Sir Isaac 1642–1727
Physicist / natural philosopher and mathematician

Bertoloni Meli, Domenico, *Equivalence and Priority: Newton versus Leibniz*, Oxford: Clarendon Press, and New York: Oxford University Press, 1993

Blay, Michel, *La Conceptualisation newtonienne des phenomenes de la couleur*, Paris: Vrin, 1983

Brackenridge, J. Bruce, *The Key to Newton's Dynamics*, Berkeley: University of California Press, 1996

Brewster, David, *Memoirs of the Life: Writings and Discoveries of Sir Isaac Newton*, 2 vols, Edinburgh: Constable, 1855; reprinted, with an introduction by Richard S. Westfall, 2 vols, New York: Johnson, 1965

Castillejo, David, *The Expanding Force in Newton's Cosmos*, Madrid: Ediciones de Arte y Bibliofilia, 1981

Cohen, I. Bernard, *Introduction to Newton's "Principia"*, Cambridge: Cambridge University Press, and Cambridge, Massachusetts: Harvard University Press, 1971

Cohen, I. Bernard, *The Newtonian Revolution, with Illustrations of the Transformation of Scientific Ideas*, Cambridge and New York: Cambridge University Press, 1980

Dobbs, Betty Jo Teeter, *The Foundations of Newton's Alchemy, or, "The Hunting of the Greene Lyon"*, Cambridge and New York: Cambridge University Press, 1975

Dobbs, Betty Jo Teeter, *The Janus Faces of Genius: The Role of Alchemy in Newton's Thought*, Cambridge and New York: Cambridge University Press, 1991

Dobbs, Betty Jo Teeter and Margaret C. Jacob, *Newton and the Culture of Newtonianism*, Atlantic Highlands, New Jersey: Humanities Press, 1995

Force, James E. and Richard H. Popkin (editors), *The Books of Nature and Scripture*, Dordrecht and Boston: Kluwer, 1994

Gandt, François de, *Force and Geometry in Newton's Principia*, translated from the French by Curtis Wilson, Princeton, New Jersey: Princeton University Press, 1995

Gjertsen, Derek, *The Newton Handbook*, London and New York: Routledge and Kegan Paul, 1986

Hall, A. Rupert and Marie Boas Hall (editors), *Unpublished Scientific Papers of Isaac Newton: A Selection from the Portsmouth Collection*, Cambridge: Cambridge University Press, 1962

Hall, A. Rupert, *Philosophers at War: The Quarrel between Newton and Leibniz*, Cambridge and New York: Cambridge University Press, 1980

Hall, A. Rupert, *Isaac Newton: Adventurer in Thought*, Oxford and Cambridge, Massachusetts: Blackwell, 1992

Hall, A. Rupert, *All Was Light: An Introduction to Newton's Opticks*, Oxford: Clarendon Press, and New York: Oxford University Press, 1995

Herivel, John, *The Background of Newton's "Principia": A Study of Newton's Dynamical Researches in the Years 1664–1684*, Oxford: Clarendon Press, 1965

Jones, Peter (editor), *Sir Isaac Newton: Manuscripts and Papers* (microfilm), Cambridge: Chadwyck-Healey, 1991

Koyré, Alexandre and I. Bernard Cohen (editors), *Isaac Newton's Philosophiae Naturalis Principia Mathematica*, 3rd edition with variant readings, 2 vols, Cambridge: Cambridge University Press, 1972

McGuire, J.E. and Martin Tamny, *Certain Philosophical Questions: Newton's Trinity Notebook*, Cambridge and New York: Cambridge University Press, 1983

Mamiani, Maurizio, *Isaac Newton: filosofo della natura*, Florence: La Nuova Italia, 1976

Mamiani, Maurizio, *Il prisma di Newton: i meccanismi dell'invenzione scientifica*, Rome: Laterza, 1986

Manuel, Frank E., *Isaac Newton: Historian*, Cambridge, Massachusetts: Belknap Press of Harvard University Press, 1963

Manuel, Frank E., *A Portrait of Isaac Newton*, Cambridge, Massachusetts: Harvard University Press, 1968

Manuel, Frank E., *The Religion of Isaac Newton*, Oxford: Clarendon Press, 1974

Shapiro, Alan E., *The Optical Papers of Isaac Newton*, Cambridge and New York: Cambridge University Press, 1984–

Turnbull, H.W. *et al.*, *Correspondence*, 7 vols, Cambridge: Cambridge University Press, 1959–77

Wallis, Peter and Ruth Wallis, *Newton and Newtoniana, 1672–1975: A Bibliography*, Folkestone, Kent: Dawson, 1977

Westfall, Richard S., *Never at Rest: A Biography of Isaac Newton*, Cambridge and New York: Cambridge University Press, 1980

Whiteside, D.T. and M.A. Hoskin (editors), *The Mathematical Papers of Isaac Newton*, 8 vols, Cambridge: Cambridge University Press, 1976–81

The amount of scholarly literature on Isaac Newton is immense. WALLIS & WALLIS offers reliable and exhaustive guidance through the vast maze of literature on Newton to 1975. GJERT-SEN is a bio-bibliographical dictionary of Newton's career, with useful entries on many of his colleagues, rivals, and disciples and chronological lists of his publications and manuscripts. The literature covered here includes publications of primary sources, biographies of Newton, and works focusing on particular aspects of Newton's concerns.

There is no general edition of the collected works and papers of Newton. Rather, there is a series of editions of his correspondence and of his particular fields of study. The editorial apparatus to these editions constitutes much of the best scholarship on Newton, but the compartmentalization of Newton's work is problematic. JONES, which is designed to accompany the microfilm of Newton's manuscripts, simply reproduces the *Catalogue of the Portsmouth Collection* acquired by Cambridge

University Library in 1888 and the *Catalogue of the Newton Papers* sold at Sotheby's in 1936, together with a useful indication of all these papers' current locations. It contains descriptions and summaries of each item: many quite full, some cursory or inaccurate. The *Correspondence* (TURNBULL *et al.*) is the necessary point of departure for anyone concerned with Newton's life as a whole, or with some segment of it. The editors have enhanced this aspect of the work by including a number of manuscripts that had not been published previously. They have also supplied translations of letters and manuscripts not in English, as well as elaborate annotations. The wealth of information in these notes (with a few exceptions) continues to be authoritative.

Newton's career in science began with a lengthy passage in an undergraduate notebook that he entitled, "Quaestiones quaedam philosophicae". Made known by A. Rupert Hall more than 40 years ago, this passage offers insight into the questions in natural philosophy that initially stimulated Newton's interest and continued to hold his attention throughout his career. The "Quaestiones" have remained prominent in Newton scholarship. The McGUIRE & TAMNY edition of the passage prints the original together with a "translation" into 20th-century English with all the abbreviations spelled out, and accompanies the two texts with thorough commentaries that establish the setting and explicate the problems to which Newton first addressed himself.

HALL & HALL is an edition of hitherto unpublished papers that makes available to scholars a number of important, but previously unknown, manuscripts, for the most part on general issues of natural philosophy. These manuscripts have figured prominently in Newtonian scholarship ever since, and anyone interested in the development of Newton's conception of nature will need to become familiar with them. Interpretative commentaries are included with the manuscripts, but inevitably, with the intense scrutiny these papers have received over more than 30 years, alternative interpretations have elsewhere been posited.

Mathematics was an early intellectual passion of Newton's, and his interest continued, with diminished intensity, throughout his life. Surprisingly, in view of the importance of his contribution to mathematics, very few of his papers had been published before the WHITESIDE & HOSKIN edition. This is the pre-eminent edition of Newton's scientific papers, with introductory essays and exhaustive footnote commentaries. Volume 1, which is of special interest, traces Newton's progress from self-taught student to inventor of the calculus.

SHAPIRO is an edition of Newton's optical papers. So far, only one of three projected volumes has appeared, containing the early Cambridge lectures in which Newton worked out the details of his theories of the heterogeneity of light and the phenomena of colours, and established the core of his contribution to the science of optics. The volume also contains Shapiro's explication of Newton's work.

HERIVEL contains the manuscripts on mechanics that preceded the *Principia*, introducing them with an interpretative narrative of Newton's developing grasp of the subject. The manuscripts go back to the same undergraduate years that witnessed the "Quaestiones quaedam philosophicae", when Newton made contact with the new conception of motion and attacked the problems of impact and circular motion. Herivel concludes with

Newton's essay *De Motu* in its three versions, the first composed in 1684, and the manuscripts that accompanied them – in effect, the first drafts of what became the *Principia*. In his *Introduction to the Principia*, COHEN (1971) takes up the story where Herivel leaves off, focusing, as the title promises, on the composition of the book itself. Volume 6 of Whiteside & Hoskin's edition of the *Mathematical Papers* and the KOYRÉ & COHEN edition of the *Principia*, with variant readings from the first two editions and also from the extensive manuscript remains, complete the set of works necessary to the study of this central aspect of Newton's science.

As Cohen proceeded, his attention shifted away from the *Opticks* and toward the *Principia*, of which he was an editor, and a new English translation of that work is imminent. Unlike his earlier work, COHEN (1980) relates Newton (primarily the Newton of the *Principia*) to the ideas and the men who preceded him. Part I defends the concept of a Newtonian revolution, as distinct from the scientific revolution of which it formed the concluding chapter. Central to the Newtonian revolution is what Cohen calls the "Newtonian style", a reciprocal interchange between idealized mathematical theory and empirical measurements, by which the mathematical theory is continually refined in order to embody as fully as possible the complex reality of nature. The second part of the book, entitled "Transformations of Scientific Ideas", treats Newtonian physics as a development and enhancement of the earlier work of Kepler, Galileo, and Descartes.

There is no edition of Newton's extensive papers on alchemy, but some of the most important among them are published as appendices to both DOBBS (1975) and DOBBS (1991).

The first major biography of Newton, by BREWSTER, had access to the great trove of manuscripts then in possession of the Portsmouth family. However, Brewster was a busy scientist who was not prepared to devote a major portion of his career to plumbing the contents of an uncatalogued mountain of papers, and he was a century too early to benefit from the editions of papers mentioned above. He was also afflicted with a serious case of hero-worship, which tinted his perception of his subject. For all that, the *Memoirs* is a remarkable exercise in scientific biography, which held the field as the best source on Newton for more than a century. It can still be read with profit.

WESTFALL accepts that moral excellence does not necessarily accompany intellectual genius. This biography presents a portrait of a neurotic, tortured man, but also gives a detailed account of Newton's scientific achievements. Considering the alchemical papers as part of his scientific career, Westfall draws his account of Newton's religious opinions from manuscripts that were deposited in the Jewish National Library in Jerusalem only after the biography was well in progress. Newton's career as Master of the Mint is also described.

Frank Manuel came to Newton from Renaissance studies, where the split between mysticism and positivism did not exist; he thus had no compunction about studying Newton's various activities from a single perspective. MANUEL (1963) describes the profound methodological and metaphysical relationship between Newton's scientific and other work, including that on the prophetic books of the scriptures (e.g. his derivation of a chronology of ancient kingdoms). The essays in FORCE & POPKIN show that Newton sought to correct the errors he believed had been introduced into the Bible falsely to justify faith in the Trinity.

MANUEL (1974) made use of the Newton manuscripts that had recently been brought to light. The theological manuscripts sold at the Sotheby auction in 1936 had vanished for several decades; Abraham Yahuda, an Alexandrian Jew and friend of Einstein's, had bought them, and bequeathed them to the Jewish National Library in Jerusalem, where they are now known as the Yahuda manuscripts. This event, and Manuel's book, inaugurated serious scholarly study of the content of these papers.

Alchemy is a subject fraught with religious overtones, and Dobbs's work is as much concerned with an examination of the role of religion in Newton's career as a study of alchemy. Until recently, Newton's theological manuscripts were not available for scholarly study, and despite the fact that the manuscripts, which form an immense bulk, are now deposited in libraries, only a tiny fraction of them has been published. DOBBS (1991) is the most recent of the small number of works that rest on these manuscripts. The development in Dobbs's two books reflects the development within the history of science in general: Dobbs (1975) presents Newton's alchemy as a rational, controlled enterprise into fundamental properties of matter, which left major traces in his published work on gravity and light; in Dobbs (1991), emphasis is placed upon the profound relationship between Newton's alchemical work and his religious beliefs, especially his denial of the doctrine of the Trinity.

There are several monographs on special aspects of Newton's career. For his early work on optics, good studies are BLAY on the optical notebooks of the 1660s, MAMIANI (1976) on the Cambridge optical lectures, and MAMIANI (1986) on the development of the prism experiments from the mid-1660s. As part of his editorial work on Newton's correspondence, HALL (1980) produced a book on his notorious dispute with Leibniz on the invention of fluxions and on metaphysics. This chronological survey can now be complemented by a thorough analysis of mathematical and astronomical issues, raised during the dispute studied in BERTOLONI MELI. CASTILLEJO, an early student of the Yahuda manuscripts, eventually summarized some of his own sometimes idiosyncratic work on the relation between Newton's alchemy, theology, and prophetic interpretation. Recent important studies of the dynamics of the *Principia* are BRACKENRIDGE, on the opening sections of the book, and DE GANDT, on the relation between geometry and dynamics. Hall has continued his work on the Newtonian legacy with an accessible biography, HALL (1992), and a well-written introduction to the *Opticks*, HALL (1995).

DOBBS & JACOB is the best introduction to Newton; it is very well written and is popular as a textbook. Building on the work by Manuel and Dobbs, among others, the authors do justice to Newton's theology and alchemy, and, in the latter part of the book, they consider the significance of Newton to the Industrial Revolution.

RICHARD S. WESTFALL
REVIEWED BY SIMON SCHAFFER

See also Coins and Coinage; Natural Philosophy; Physics and Natural Philosophy; Royal Society of London; Scientific Revolution and the Royal Society

Nightingale, Florence 1820–1910
Nurse and nursing reformer

Cook, Sir Edward, *The Life of Florence Nightingale*, 2 vols, London: Macmillan, 1913; abridged by Rosalind Nash, as *A Short Life of Florence Nightingale*, London and New York: Macmillan, 1925

Goldie, Sue M. (editor), *"I Have Done My Duty": Florence Nightingale in the Crimean War, 1854–1856*, Manchester: Manchester University Press, and Iowa City: University of Iowa Press, 1987

Small, Hugh, *Florence Nightingale: Avenging Angel*, London: Constable, 1998; New York: St Martin's Press, 1999

Smith, F.B., *Florence Nightingale: Reputation and Power*, London: Croom Helm, and New York: St Martin's Press, 1982

Reports in *The Times* from the Crimean war and the British hospital at Scutari painted a terrible picture of suffering endured by sick and wounded troops, and urged the despatch of nurses. Through personal connections, notably with Sidney Herbert, secretary of war, Nightingale, who had some experience of hospital administration, secured control of a group of nurses, and supporting funds sent to comfort the British army. Her formidable self-confidence and powers of persuasion enabled her to deal with the opposition of the medical and military authorities who resented her arrival, and rejected her criticism of their work. Her efforts at the Scutari hospital were quickly turned into popular legend by *The Times,* which was seeking an heroic figure as an antithesis to the apparent incompetence of the aristocratic military authorities. At the time she was convinced that her work had saved lives. After the war Nightingale campaigned for improved sanitation in army barracks and in India, and latterly nursing. During the war she made an important contribution to care for the wounded and sick, and if she was never "the Lady of the Lamp" of popular myth, she did raise the national consciousness and establish the role of the nurse in modern military medicine. Her subsequent career was made possible by the celebrity of the war, and much as she disliked her fame, she was prepared to use it to further her ends.

Like all the great Victorians Florence Nightingale received her biography. COOK provided a comforting image of selfless devotion and service to society that met the needs of the day. The two-volume study is a monument to his industry, being based on the vast archive, and achieves a degree of understanding that less thorough efforts have signally failed to match. Until the 1980s it remained the basis of Nightingale studies, supplemented by a steady flow of more limited work, and the widening archival base for fresh research. Although sympathetic and not without insight, the essentially uncritical approach needed revision. A long-term student of the subject and bibliographer, GOLDIE focuses on the Crimean War period, and provides a substantial collection of correspondence.

In the first major revision of the myth SMITH addressed the family background to Nightingale's career, which was full of resentment and rivalry, directed against her mother and her sister, and manipulation of her weak-willed father. In addressing her personal and professional relationships it uncovered more evidence of an obsession with control, often at the expense of the issues for which she fought so hard. Perhaps the most remarkable revelation was that the bulk of all nursing, as understood today, was provided by male orderlies; it was considered highly improper for middle-class women to tend to the mutilated bodies of working-class soldiers. Consequently the "nurses" were restricted to cooking, cleaning, and providing spiritual comfort for the dying, with readings from approved tracts. While at Scutari Nightingale secured control of the funds and the nurses sent out by other groups, often having resort to the most unscrupulous tactics. By mid-1855 she was in control of all the nurses around Istanbul, and went to the Crimea to extend her empire, but her rebuff led to the first of many convenient illnesses. Determined and self-promoting, in Smith's view Nightingale rarely allowed the truth to interfere with her work. Her object was power and reputation; nursing was only the means to that end. Her real contribution to saving life was the result of the superior order, cleanliness, and feeding she imposed. After the war her work was seriously compromised by her refusal to accept the concept that germs spread infection. To the end she remained a "tricky, dogmatic, wheedling manipulator".

SMALL puts forward an altogether different thesis. He argues that Nightingale's postwar career should be viewed in the context of a political struggle for control of the army, waged between the government of Lord Palmerston and the Horse Guards, which had the backing of the queen. To support their case the ministers asked Nightingale to follow up her wartime work with an analysis of the human cost of the war. It was fully expected, based on wartime reporting and Nightingale's own claims, that this would demonstrate the culpability of the medical authorities, and through them the high command, supporting the politicians' demands for increased control over the army. In the event Nightingale's statistical analysis convinced her that the insanitary and unhygienic conditions in her own hospital had been the chief cause of premature death before the arrival of the Sanitary Commission in 1855. By the middle of 1857 she recognized that in her arrogance and ignorance she had organized a hospital that killed 15,000 men. Deeply troubled by these conclusions she wished to publish them, but the government refused her permission, recognizing that they would derail their own agenda. Wracked with suppressed guilt, Nightingale suffered a breakdown in August 1857 and became a psychosomatic invalid for 20 years. After leaking her report, she moved the focus of her work away from nursing and hospitals to public health. This explains her sudden shift towards considering sanitation and hygiene the key to medical success. She saw this work as a way of making some amends for the deaths of so many soldiers. Here her contribution was both profound, and effective. Small argues that her work after the crisis of August 1857 was highly effective, coherent, and essentially correct. Nightingale outlived all her contemporaries, and managed to cover her tracks remarkably well, by keeping a large, but skilfully manipulated archive.

The work of Smith and Small reflects the enduring fascination of Nightingale: her life and work were at once more complex and more important than any of the popular images of her.

ANDREW DAVID LAMBERT

See also Crimean War; Medicine: 19th Century Developments; Public Health

Nine Years' War 1594–1603

Ellis, Steven G., *Tudor Ireland: Crown, Community, and the Conflict of Cultures, 1470–1603*, London and New York: Longman, 1985; revised edition, as *Ireland in the Age of the Tudors, 1447–1603: English Expansion and the End of Gaelic Rule*, London: Longman, and New York: Addison-Wesley Longman, 1998

Falls, Cyril, *Elizabeth's Irish Wars*, London: Methuen, 1950; New York: Barnes and Noble, 1970

Hayes-McCoy, Gerard, "The Completion of the Tudor Conquest and the Advance of the Counter-Reformation, 1571–1603" in *A New History of Ireland*, vol. 3, *Early Modern Ireland 1534–1691*, edited by T.W. Moody, F.X. Martin, and F.J. Byrne, Oxford: Clarendon Press, and New York: Oxford University Press, 1976

Lennon, Colm, *Sixteenth Century Ireland: The Incomplete Conquest*, Dublin: Gill and Macmillan, 1994; New York: St Martin's Press, 1995

Morgan, Hiram, *Tyrone's Rebellion: The Outbreak of the Nine Years War in Tudor Ireland*, Woodbridge, Suffolk and Rochester, New York: Boydell Press, 1993

O'Faoláin, Seán, *The Great O'Neill: A Biography of Hugh O'Neill, Earl of Tyrone, 1550–1616*, London and New York: Longmans Green, 1942

Silke, John J., *Kinsale: The Spanish Intervention in Ireland at the End of the Elizabethan Wars*, Liverpool: Liverpool University Press, 1970

Hugh O'Neill, 2nd Earl of Tyrone, is one of the great romantic heroes of Irish history and is often presented as the leader of the last great attempt to stop the process of anglicization in Tudor Ireland – an early nationalist seeking to preserve the Gaelic Irish nation. This traditional view is best represented by O'FAOLÁIN. The war – traditionally known as Tyrone's rebellion – began with the besieging by Hugh Roe O'Donnell and Hugh Maguire of Enniskillen in June 1594, and the defeat of an English relief force in August. At first Tyrone appeared unwilling to join the rebels. He had supported Sir Henry Bagenal in a campaign against the Maguires ten months earlier; but when he was refused an exclusive commission to govern Ulster, he joined the insurgents. MORGAN's revisionist study is the best examination of the pressures and ambitions that motivated this complex individual.

In the first half of 1595 the English lost control of the Blackwater Fort, Enniskillen, and Sligo, setbacks followed in June by Tyrone's defeat of an English army at Clontibret in County Monaghan. Tyrone was declared "the principal traitor and chief author of this rebellion", having established himself as the leader of the Irish against Elizabeth. In October Tyrone and O'Donnell agreed to a truce and began negotiations which they hoped would gain time to allow military assistance to arrive from Spain. The international implications of the rebellion in connection with England's ongoing war with Spain are examined in some detail by both FALLS and ELLIS. In January 1596, at a meeting near Dundalk, the Irish leaders demanded the dismissal of all English officials in Ulster, liberty of conscience, and the restoration of church lands to catholics. The Ulster roots of the rebellion are best examined by LENNON. Such terms were unacceptable to Elizabeth, who described them as "presumptuous and disloyal petitions"; but as neither side wanted to recommence military operations, it was agreed to extend the truce. In May 1596 Tyrone was pardoned, but by July he was calling upon the Munster leaders to "assist the Catholic religion, and join in confederacy and make war with us". The war settled into a pattern of under-strength English garrisons being besieged by the Irish, and armies sent to relieve them being ambushed. In August 1598 Tyrone obtained his greatest military success in one such action, destroying an English army of 4300 men at the Yellow Ford during an unsuccessful attempt to relieve the Blackwater Fort. The military history of the rebellion has yet to receive a complete study, although the account given by Falls is reasonably full, if now somewhat out-of-date.

By October 1598 Munster was in rebellion and the military situation for England had become desperate. A huge expeditionary force of 17,300 men was assembled under the command of the Earl of Essex. However, arriving in Ireland in April 1599 this distinguished, but in Irish terms inexperienced, noble dispersed half his troops into garrisons and exhausted the remainder during a pointless campaign in Munster. The queen finally ordered her general to move against Tyrone without any further delay. In September he at last did so with 4000 men, only to find the rebel earl waiting for him with an army twice that size. Essex foolishly met with Tyrone alone and agreed yet another truce beneficial to the rebels. The queen disavowed the treaty ten days later, and Essex left for England, contrary to the queen's express command. Both Morgan and Ellis offer important interpretations of this fiasco. These mistakes, coupled with a futile attempt at a court putsch to overthrow his critics, resulted in Essex's execution as a traitor in 1601. Tyrone, in his turn, renounced the truce in early 1600, and undertook what was effectively a royal progress through the midlands and the south, punishing opponents and rallying allies.

Tyrone was then at the peak of his military and political power, but his nemesis was already entering the scene. On 28th February 1600 Charles Blount, Lord Mountjoy was sworn in as lord deputy, and became the leader of an army estimated at between 13,000 and 20,000 men. By May the English were attacking Tyrone's home territory from all directions, and although the rebels could still win battles, they were under increasing pressure. In 1601 the long-awaited Spanish reinforcements, 3500 strong, arrived at Kinsale in Munster. The hard-pressed Ulster leaders had no alternative but to force-march their armies through the worst of winter weather in a desperate effort to join forces with the Spaniards. On Christmas Eve 1601 the Irish forces attacked and were defeated by Mountjoy in an engagement lasting less than three hours in the battle of Kinsale, a campaign which has been thoroughly examined and assessed by SILKE. Tyrone retreated to Ulster while O'Donnell travelled to Spain to request more effective support. The closing stages of the war, most effectively assessed by HAYES-McCOY, were marked by an almost genocidal use of scorched-earth tactics by the English forces; contemporaries noted cannibalism among the Irish population at this time. However, Tyrone and the remnant of his supporters continued a guerilla conflict and Mountjoy informed London early in 1603 that he felt the time had come to offer the remaining rebels pardon if they surrendered. Although initially bitterly opposed to the idea, Elizabeth agreed to the offer being made in February,

as her Treasury could no longer afford the cost of the war. The rebellion ended in April 1603, following negotiations at Mellifort, County Louth. Mountjoy granted generous terms that not only left Tyrone in possession of his lands, but restored much of his pre-war power and independence in Ulster. The reason for the lord deputy's leniency towards the "principal traitor" was that Mountjoy wished to return to London quickly. Elizabeth had died (24 March), and he wanted to greet the new King James, and claim the rewards for ending the Irish war. Resentment against this generous treatment among English officials in Dublin and London led to increasing pressure on Tyrone, which finally resulted in his flight to Spain, and the consequent plantation of protestant settlers in Ulster. The best examination of the political complexities of these events is to be found in Ellis, and the most comprehensive study of the consequences of the rebellion and its failure in Hayes-McCoy.

JOHN M. LYNCH

See also Ireland: Tudor Plantations; O'Neill

Nonjurors late 17th century

Every, George, *The High Church Party, 1688–1718*, London: SPCK for the Church Historical Society, 1956

Hawkins, L.M., *Allegiance in Church and State: The Problem of the Non Jurors in the English Revolution*, London: Routledge, 1928

Mullett, Charles, "Religion, Politics, and Oaths in the Glorious Revolution", *Review of Politics*, 10 (1948): 462–74

Straka, Gerald, *Anglican Reaction to the Revolution of 1688*, Madison: State Historical Society of Wisconsin, 1962

Sykes, Norman, *Church and State in England in the XVIIIth Century: The Birkbeck Lectures in Ecclesiastical History*, Cambridge: Cambridge University Press, 1934; reprinted, New York: Octagon Books, 1975

The nonjurors represent both an interesting and significant movement in the Church of England at the end of the 17th century. By their refusal to take the oath of allegiance to William III after the revolution of 1688, based on their belief that they were still bound by their prior oaths to King James II, this small but influential group of clergy created a schism that helps to illustrate the difficulty some churchmen faced in reconciling themselves to the results of the Glorious Revolution.

Not until recently have the nonjurors received serious and sympathetic attention. This is not difficult to explain given such verdicts as that of Macaulay that their beliefs were outlandish and outdated even by 17th-century standards. Thus, the nonjurors appeared as an anachronism, standing up for a cause already lost, a relic of no real historical importance.

However, in 1926 a scholarly attempt was made to reassess the nonjurors by L.M. HAWKINS. She began by placing them in a respectable tradition which she traced back to King James I and among Caroline divines like William Laud, Robert Sibthorpe, and others whose support for monarchy was exhibited at the time of the forced loan of 1626. In so doing, she suggested that the theories of divine right and passive non-resistance had a long history that continued through the restoration as well. Hawkins saw the views of the nonjurors as both sincere and consistent, thus crediting them with a position that was well thought out. This in itself was significant, since no one had yet embarked on a serious study of them. Thus, she defended their legitimacy and provided a detailed study of their writings. Among other points, for example, she argued that they had an importance for the future in that they challenged the Erastianism of William III's position. She also emphasized the scruples that led to their particular stances on matters of church and state. Moreover, she tended, at times, to consider the non-jurors as synonymous with the High Church party, giving them somewhat greater weight.

Scholars who have followed Hawkins, while recognizing the value of her work, have differed with her over the consistency of the nonjurors and their place in English history. Norman SYKES, for instance, takes issue over their challenge against Erastianism, by noting that the same clergy who refused allegiance to William accepted or did not resist earlier illegal intrusions into church affairs by James II, indicating it was not the theory but the man that was important. Consequently, he sees the nonjurors as caught in this contradiction and not forward-looking, but very much past-oriented.

More recently, George EVERY has added to this historiography with an important book on the high church party at the end of the 17th and beginning of the 18th centuries. Like Hawkins, he searches for roots and finds the genesis of this group in the Tew circle of Lord Falkland in the 1630s and Caroline divines like Laud. Yet Every's High Churchmen are not all nonjurors, although he does treat that party at some length. He does discuss the nonjurors' positions, but he points out their reluctance to give up their offices and the hope of a number of them that they could return to the church at some point. He also emphasizes their opposition to popery and their efforts to convert the Stuart heir, James III, to Anglicanism. In addition, he takes up the question of the willingness of other clergy to occupy positions which the nonjurors were forced to vacate.

Another perspective on the nonjurors is provided by Gerald STRAKA in his study of the reaction of Anglican clergy to the revolution. He makes the point that the nonjurors were not the only ones who stood for divine right, for many other divines found a justification for their conformity in the same theory. Basing their allegiance upon such tenets as divine right by conquest, they were, therefore, able to accept William and Mary without sacrificing their principles. By investigating these churchmen Straka has demonstrated that one did not need to be a nonjuror to still be consistent.

At the same time, Charles MULLETT has taken another tack by indicating the carefulness with which the oaths were written in order to allow scrupulous clerics to swear allegiance to William as *de facto* king, without compromising their oath to James as a *de jure* one. Consequently, as with the argument of Straka, Mullett helps illustrate the availability of alternatives to nonjurism.

MARC L. SCHWARZ

See also Atterbury; Glorious Revolution; Jacobitism; James VII and II; Sancroft; William III and Mary II

Nonsuch, Treaty of 1585

Adams, Simon, "The Outbreak of the Elizabethan Naval War against the Spanish Empire: The Embargo of 1585 and Sir Francis Drake's West Indies Voyage" in *England, Spain, and the Gran Armada 1585–1604: Essays from the Anglo-Spanish Conferences, London and Madrid, 1988*, edited by M.J. Rodríguez-Salgado and Adams, Edinburgh: John Donald, 1991

Adams, Simon, "The Decision to Intervene: England and the United Provinces 1584–1585" in *Felipe II (1527–1598): Europe y la monarquía católica* [Philip II (1527–1598): Europe and the Catholic Monarchy] edited by José Martínez Millán, Madrid: Parteluz, 1998

Bor, Pieter, *Oorsprongk, Begin en Vervolgh der Nederlandsche Oorlogen* [The Origins, Outbreak, and Conduct of the Dutch Wars], Amsterdam: Van Someren, 1679–84

Camden, William, *The History of the Most Renowned and Victorious Princess Elizabeth, Late Queen of England*, edited by Wallace T. MacCaffrey, Chicago: Chicago University Press, 1970

MacCaffrey, Wallace T., *Queen Elizabeth and the Making of Policy, 1572–1588*, Princeton, New Jersey: Princeton University Press, 1981

Motley, John Lothrop, *History of the United Netherlands from the Death of William the Silent to the Twelve Years' Truce, 1609*, London: John Murray, 1860–67; New York: Harper, 1861–68

Oosterhoff, F.G., *Leicester and the Netherlands, 1586–1587*, Utrecht: HES, 1988

"Rapport van de Nederlandsche Gezanten in 1585 naar Engeland gezonden" [Report of the Dutch Envoys sent to England in 1585], *Kronijk van het Historische Genootschap*, 5th series, 2 (1866): 215–77

Read, Conyers, *Mr. Secretary Walsingham and the Policy of Queen Elizabeth*, Oxford: Clarendon Press, 1925; reprinted, Hamden, Connecticut: Archon Books, 1967

Read, Conyers, *Lord Burghley and Queen Elizabeth*, New York: Knopf, and London: Jonathan Cape, 1960

Strong, R.C. and J.A. van Dorsten, *Leicester's Triumph*, Leiden: Sir Thomas Browne Institute at the University Press, 1962; Oxford: Oxford University Press, 1964

Not the least of the complexities of the Anglo-Dutch treaty of Nonsuch of 1585 is the fact that there were three separate treaties: the *traité provisionel* for the relief of Antwerp (2–12 August), the *traité de secours pendant la guerre* (10–20 August), and the English (4–14 September) and Dutch (21–30 September) Acts of Amplification. Although it is probably the central episode in Elizabethan foreign policy, the best sources for the negotiation of the main treaties are Dutch, particularly the "RAPPORT" of the Dutch embassy, which was published in 1866. The modern historiography of the treaty itself has been dominated by MOTLEY, who devoted six out of the eight chapters of volume I of the *History of the United Netherlands* to the diplomacy behind the treaty from the death of William of Orange until the arrival in the Netherlands of the Earl of Leicester at the end of 1585.

Like so many other mid 19th-century historians Motley benefited from the "opening of the archives", specifically the Public

Record Office and the Algemeen Rijksarchief. He made effective use of the older Dutch historians, especially BOR, who prints correspondence from the States of Holland that has since disappeared, but he was also the first historian to employ the report. From it he quotes large sections of Elizabeth's remarkably moving speech to the Dutch envoys at the conclusion of the treaty, a speech completely overlooked in the recent edition of Elizabeth's works. However, like his contemporaries Motley sought to produce a colourful and dramatic narrative and he paid only minimal attention to the details of the negotiations. He was also careless in his handling of the admittedly difficult technical problems created by the simultaneous use of the Julian calendar by the English and the Gregorian by most – though not all – of the Dutch provinces.

Yet despite this, Motley's account of Nonsuch was accepted without much criticism by READ, who, in his biography of Sir Francis Walsingham, judged it to be "in the main excellent" and made no effort to re-examine the Dutch sources himself. *Walsingham* is far from perfect – there are many errors and omissions – but it remains the best-researched study of Elizabethan diplomacy in the period 1572–88, though necessarily circumscribed by the fact that *au fond* it is a biography. In it Read also introduced a factional interpretation of the making of policy that has dominated all subsequent discussion both of Nonsuch and of Elizabethan foreign policy in general in the 1580s. The formulation of a response to the Dutch revolt in the 1570s had provoked a struggle between a puritan interventionist faction largely inspired by Walsingham and a conservative or isolationist faction led by Lord Burghley. The Nonsuch treaties represented the victory of the interventionists.

Read advanced this interpretation on the basis of his discovery of what appeared to be evidence that Burghley and Walsingham had radically different views about foreign policy. This was bolstered by the discovery in CAMDEN, which he believed to have been inspired by Burghley and therefore a "party" history, of a somewhat gnomic passage on a dispute between men of war and men of peace in 1585. Convinced that this was the explanation, he then twisted other evidence to fit the case. Thirty years later, when he came to write his life of Burghley, Read's approach was more nuanced. The discovery of a further passage on a dispute over war in 1585 in another contemporary work associated with Burghley (John Clapham's *Certain Observations*) appeared to justify his confidence in Camden, but he had become less convinced of Burghley's consistent and open opposition to war. Burghley was now the victim of the more aggressive tactics of the interventionist faction.

Subsequent debates over Elizabeth's policy towards the Dutch revolt, such as that between Charles Wilson and R.B. Wernham, have concentrated on the later 1570s and have had little to say on Nonsuch directly. Only MACCAFFREY has gone over the events of 1585 in any detail. Largely because his canvas is broader (in one volume he covers the same period as do the three volumes of *Walsingham*) and his range of research less, he has confirmed rather than challenged Read's overall conclusions. The 1960s saw two new works on the English intervention from the Dutch perspective. STRONG & VAN DORSTEN is an openly descriptive rather than an analytical account and more concerned with the year after Nonsuch, but nevertheless it points to a variety of unused Dutch sources. OOSTERHOFF provided the first full reassessment of the Leicester governor-

generalship based on a command of both the English and the Dutch sources in a thesis written in 1967 though not published until 1988. Her analysis of the way in which many of the problems of the governor-generalship were created by the terms of the treaty is particularly valuable. On the making of the treaty and English policy, however, she has been content to follow Read and MacCaffrey.

The most recent approaches are the two studies by ADAMS, one reappraising the outbreak of the naval war with Spain and the other the making of Nonsuch, an initial sketch from a larger work in progress. He has emphasized particularly the weaknesses of the English evidence on which the factional interpretation is based, and the importance of the Dutch sources to any serious account of the negotiations.

SIMON ADAMS

See also Cecil, William; Dudley; Walsingham

Norfolk, Thomas Howard, 3rd Duke of 1473–1554
Soldier and politician

Grace, F.R., "The Life and Career of Thomas Howard, Third Duke of Norfolk (1473–1554)" (MA dissertation), Nottingham: University of Nottingham, 1961
Head, David M., *The Ebbs and Flows of Fortune: The Life of Thomas Howard, Third Duke of Norfolk*, Athens: University of Georgia Press, 1995
Ives, Eric W., *Anne Boleyn*, Oxford and New York: Blackwell, 1986
MacCulloch, Diarmaid, *Suffolk and the Tudors: Politics and Religion in an English County, 1500–1600*, Oxford: Clarendon Press, and New York: Oxford University Press, 1986
Mattingly, Garrett, *Catherine of Aragon*, Boston: Little Brown, 1941; London: Jonathan Cape, 1942
Robinson, John Martin, *The Dukes of Norfolk: A Quincentennial History*, Oxford and New York: Oxford University Press, 1982; revised as *The Dukes of Norfolk*, Chichester: Phillimore, 1995
Tucker, Melvin J., *The Life of Thomas Howard: Earl of Surrey and Second Duke of Norfolk, 1443–1524*, The Hague: Mouton, 1964
Virgoe, Roger, "The Recovery of the Howards in East Anglia, 1485–1529" in *Wealth and Power in Tudor England: Essays Presented to S.T. Bridoff*, edited by E.W. Ives, R.J. Knecht, and J.J. Scarisbrick, London: University of London/Athlone Press, and Atlantic Highlands, New Jersey: Humanities Press, 1978

Sir Geoffrey Elton said of the second Howard duke (1443–1524) that he left his biographer with scarcely enough to do. Certainly TUCKER's book reflects the modest amount of source material for that life. But surely the third duke, who held the title for 30 years, was twice Henry VIII's chief minister, and whose family history so tumultuously interconnects with that of the royal house, might have filled a few volumes? Until recently the only work wholly devoted to the third duke was GRACE's unpublished MA dissertation. Norfolk is, of course, a familiar figure in all general histories of the period, and in the biographies of his contemporaries. He was almost an old man by non-Howard standards when he succeeded to the dukedom in 1524, and the first 50 years of his life are therefore treated in Tucker's biography of his father. VIRGOE gives the most detailed account of the family background, making good use of such archives as survive. He shows how the Howards were able to recover their landed estate, and the political influence deriving from it, all of which had been lost when the first duke fell with Richard III at Bosworth. Virgoe's chief concern is with the second duke, and the manner in which he rebuilt his local position as a platform for return to national eminence. The third duke, by contrast, had already achieved celebrity through military and naval command before succeeding to the title and the local concerns that went with it.

Norfolk's continuing role as local magnate is best seen in MacCULLOCH's study of the politics of Suffolk. He investigates the uneasy cooperation between Norfolk and Brandon, duke of Suffolk (deliberately given joint authority in East Anglia by Henry VIII, fearful of Howard dominance in the region). The picture is necessarily distorted, because despite his well-organized administration and wide-ranging clientage, Norfolk never managed to control the county of Suffolk as firmly as he did his Norfolk heartland. Even in the acquisition of monastic lands, to which he gave considerable effort, Norfolk's achievements in the southern county were relatively minor.

ROBINSON gives a well-balanced and lively account of Norfolk's career in a book written to celebrate half a millennium of Howard dukes. He does not attempt to clean up the third duke's unlovely image on this family occasion. He acknowledges that his charm was superficial, that he was mean in small things behind a show of liberality, and in general the most oppressive of landlords in a dynasty not noted for its progressive tendencies. He well observes that Holbein's splendid portrait shows Norfolk unfashionably clean-shaven and long-haired, emphasizing his affinity to the previous generation and the remoter past.

Norfolk is invariably condemned as an anachronism, and for seeking political power by hereditary right; and when he actually achieved it, being incapable of the sustained work of government. His periods of dominance are characterized as sterile and purposeless. Norfolk is never likely to appear sympathetic to modern academic writers, who are not often landowners, and whose liberal consciences are dismayed by Norfolk's thuggery and cheerful contempt for learning. His robust attitude to marriage has especially attracted disdain. At best he is an easy target for slighting wit. MATTINGLY wrote of "the ponderous, cold-hearted, chicken-brained Duke, moving sluggishly in the mists of the feudal past like some obsolete armoured saurian [who] would invariably try to talk like a hero out of Malory." Elton considered Norfolk "one of the most unpleasant characters in an age which abounded in them", though this judgement may reflect Norfolk's supposed predominating role in Cromwell's fall, which more recent writers have discounted. IVES's biography of the first of Norfolk's nieces to become queen contains much thoughtful comment on the duke's use of his family for his own political ends. He also judges

Norfolk to have had no principle but self-advantage, and no policy but "spaniel-like sycophancy".

But however disagreeable he was, Norfolk was no comic turn. His sheer tenacity demands serious and extended attention, and this has now been given by HEAD. He does better for his duke than Tucker did for the second, reaching a respectable 350 pages. Even so the first 70 are mostly general history, in which the protagonist only intermittently appears. Head's purpose is political biography. He makes no attempt to disguise his dislike of his subject, and does not labour long in describing his few redeeming features. His account of Norfolk's military and political career is thorough and solidly based. Circumstances no doubt dictated a rather heavy reliance on printed sources; but the author has used more manuscripts than the brief listing in his bibliography suggests. He professes to steer a course between the faction and non-faction interpretations of Henrician politics, though references to the latter are mostly consigned to the notes. He sees Norfolk's two periods of power coming to him almost irrespective of his own efforts to displace Wolsey and then Cromwell. Head's chronicling of these and other central episodes in Norfolk's career is clear and well informed by contemporary comment and modern debate. His closing chapters, in which he attempts to pull together the strands of Norfolk's public and private activities, and then to assess his man, are less well organized. Discussion of court affairs is confused by the apparent belief that chamber, privy chamber, and king's bedchamber are all the same thing. Head is also a little astray with titles of honour, and some of the minor Howards are given wrong names. The details of Norfolk's estate administration and clientage are based largely on data taken secondhand from Virgoe. Here Head's book compares poorly with S.J. Gunn's study of the duke of Suffolk. Head seems almost unwilling to take his leave of the man he has studied for 30 years, wavering between the judgement that his career was a "shallow and futile mockery" and staking claims for its importance. Embedded in this somewhat rambling peroration are two sound reasons for Norfolk's failure: his haughty distaste for the dull work of government did not impress the king; and because of the age difference, Norfolk and Henry had little personal rapport.

C.S. KNIGHTON

See also Cromwell, Thomas; Henry VIII; Wolsey

North, Frederick, 2nd Earl of Guilford 1732–1792

Politician, statesman, and prime minister

Brooke, John, *King George III*, London: Constable, and New York: McGraw-Hill, 1972

Butterfield, Herbert, *George III, Lord North, and the People, 1779–1780*, London: Bell, 1949; reprinted, New York: Russell and Russell, 1968

Cannon, John, *The Fox-North Coalition: Crisis of the Constitution, 1782–1784*, Cambridge: Cambridge University Press, 1969

Cannon, John, *Lord North: The Noble Lord in the Blue Ribbon*, London: Historical Association, 1970

Christie, Ian R., *The End of North's Ministry, 1780–1782*, London: Macmillan, and New York: St Martin's Press, 1958

Lucas, Reginald J., *Lord North: Second Earl of Guilford, K.G. 1732–1792*, 2 vols, London: Arthur L. Humphreys, 1913

Pemberton, W. Baring, *Lord North*, London and New York: Longmans Green, 1938

Smith, Charles Daniel, *The Early Career of Lord North, the Prime Minister*, London: Athlone Press, and Rutherford, New Jersey: Fairleigh Dickinson University Press, 1979

Thomas, Peter D.G., *Lord North*, London: Allen Lane, and New York: St Martin's Press, 1976

Valentine, Alan, *Lord North*, 2 vols, Norman: University of Oklahoma Press, 1967

Whiteley, Peter, *Lord North: The Prime Minister Who Lost America*, London and Rio Grande, Ohio: Hambledon Press, 1996

The reputation of Lord North (who succeeded his father in the earldom of Guilford only two years before death) has recovered progressively over the century from its nadir in the generation after W.E.H. Lecky for whom he was the creature of revived "secret" royal influence after 1760 and the ministerial incompetent who lost the 13 American colonies. A move away from this severe judgement is evident even in LUCAS, who made pioneering use of recently available Royal Commission on Historical Manuscripts (HMC) volumes and some unpublished manuscripts. Lucas accepted that while North was "captive to the king", this had to be set against political ability and an irreproachable private life. For Lucas, North was unlucky in that "in no circumstances could America have remained for ever a group of British colonies." North's further rehabilitation was speeded by the publication of George III's pre-1783 correspondence by Sir John Fortescue in 1927–28 and, above all, by the Namierite revolution in 18th-century British political history. The new thesis was first biographically exhibited in PEMBERTON, who laid down a revisionist line still currently the norm. It pointed to his strengths as a Treasury minister, his skills in the House of Commons, and his defence of the established church. The country gentlemen and independents making up the majority in the lower house, Baring Pemberton argued, respected his competence and character for over a decade as premier and willed North to succeed; so did George III, for whom he was the linchpin of a cabinet whose removal could badly damage Britain in wartime. The author even rescued North from obloquy for his part in the 1783 coalition with Fox, pointing out that North's concern was for strong government, and that his options were limited by Pitt's refusal to serve with him.

Baring Pemberton's ringing apostrophe to "the honest, single-minded Englishman who loved his King, his Church, and his Country" was too much for postwar historians like BUTTERFIELD who had their reservations about the Namierite school. In his seminal 1949 work North is not the villain of the piece, but undoubtedly deficient in crisis management. His indolence encouraged him to shirk responsibility for government policy beyond his own department to neglect the superintending duties essential in wartime. Butterfield came close to pitying North for his over-anxieties and openness to bullying: "In his fidelity to the King, indeed, he endured distress and humiliation under conditions which no other ministry in England ever suffered and survived."

Rather than rush to defend North in principle against Butterfield, younger Namierite scholars in the 1950s and 1960s established a clearer picture of the parliamentary background to his career that permitted more subtle and surer verdicts on his career. CHRISTIE's book is a masterpiece of Namierite technique applied to the 1780 general election results and their aftermath, showing the extent to which North retained parliamentary confidence until very late in the American war. CANNON's Historical Association pamphlet attempted a succinct, measured judgement and it remains the starting-point for anyone looking for a reliable verdict on North in context. Cannon admitted that North's defects "were many and serious", arguing that his "besetting sin" was "irresolution – aggravated for much of his career by gross overwork". In his book on the Fox-North coalition, CANNON (1969) also paid tribute to North's "remarkable character and abilities" as indicated by the survival of personal support after he had resigned as premier in March 1782. For Cannon as the authoritative historian of the Fox-North coalition, Baring Pemberton was correct in blaming Pitt for giving North no alternative but an alliance with Fox. VALENTINE added little to the debate on North. His book did not impress the critics, who castigated the author's numerous factual errors, verbosity, and tendentious judgements. He admitted "I have amplified my text with background interpretation which professional historians may find unnecessary." *Ipse dixit.*

BROOKE's 1972 biography of George III produced some brilliant insights on North that most scholars would still gladly endorse, though they might cavil at "No statesman in our history has been so underrated". Brooke suggested that North's repeated requests to the king for permission to resign in 1778–80 betoken a man who was both afraid of responsibility and ambitious, one who craved reassurance at every turn. Brooke judged that in this wartime crisis "North was irreplaceable. He stood alone. Even those who criticised him most bitterly confessed that they could not find another to take his place." And for all his limitations, North was one of the great parliamentarians of the 18th century, "the Stanley Baldwin or Clement Attlee of his age", a person of charm and social gifts who commanded universal respect even among most of the Rockingham Whigs on the opposition benches. It was, Brooke argued, North's very skills as a House of Commons man that prevented him from being a great wartime leader on the Chatham or Churchill line. THOMAS has fewer rhetorical flourishes but is meticulously accurate and well balanced. It is a short political biography concentrating on the main themes. North's competence is again stressed, as producing solutions to problems of government at home and empire overseas before the American crisis overwhelmed him. Thomas's volume was part of a series in British political biography, so space constraints compelled him to cover ground rapidly. SMITH's approach was more ample. He focused on North's career before 1770, providing less a biography than a look at the factors – many highlighted by earlier scholars – that brought North to power for 12 years from 1770. Finally, the latest biography by WHITELEY, a calm assessment of the prime minister, uses North's private life to explain more satisfactorily his conduct in office.

Whiteley is no more persuaded by North's often-stated disclaim for place than his predecessors and points out that North's respect for authority in the persons of his father and the king did not always do him any favours. He was, Whiteley contends, "by temperament a dove", whom the escalating American crisis turned into "a rather unconvincing hawk".

NIGEL ASTON

See also American Colonies: Loss of; Fox, Charles James; George III; Newcastle, 1st Duke of; Pitt, William, "the Younger"; Rockingham; Seven Years' War; Wilkes

Northern Ireland, Conflict in   from 1960s

Bowyer Bell, J., *The Secret Army: The IRA*, 3rd edition, New Brunswick, New Jersey: Transaction, 1997; Dublin: Poolbeg, 1998 (first edition, 1970)

Bruce, Steve, *God Save Ulster: The Religion and Politics of Paisleyism*, Oxford: Clarendon Press, and New York: Oxford University Press, 1986

Coogan, Tim Pat, *The Troubles: Ireland's Ordeal 1966–1995 and the Search for Peace*, London: Hutchinson, 1995; revised edition, as *The Troubles: Ireland's Ordeal 1986–1996 and the Search for Peace*, London: Arrow, and Boulder, Colorado: Roberts Rinehart, 1996

Gilligan, Chris and Jonathan Tonge (editors), *Peace or War?: Understanding the Peace Process in Northern Ireland*, Aldershot, Hampshire and Brookfield, Vermont: Ashgate, 1997

McGarry, John and Brendan O'Leary, *Explaining Northern Ireland: Broken Images*, Oxford and Cambridge, Massachusetts: Blackwell, 1995

Miller, David (editor), *Rethinking Northern Ireland: Culture, Ideology, and Colonialism*, London and New York: Longman, 1998

O'Leary, Brendan and John McGarry, *The Politics of Antagonism: Understanding Northern Ireland*, London and Atlantic Highlands, New Jersey: Athlone, 1996

Ruane, Joseph and Jennifer Todd, *The Dynamics of Conflict in Northern Ireland: Power, Conflict, and Emancipation*, Cambridge and New York: Cambridge University Press, 1996

Tonge, Jonathan, *Northern Ireland: Conflict and Change*, London and New York: Prentice Hall Europe, 1998; 2nd edition, London: Longman, 2002

MCGARRY & O'LEARY, in *Explaining Northern Ireland*, argue that the conflict erupting since the late 1960s is ethno-national. They see it as a contest between the political organizations of two communities who "want their state to be ruled by their nation". Two ethno-national groups, Ulster unionists and Irish nationalists, both seek self-determination. The rival groups have been formed on the basis of distinctive histories and cultures. These themes are also developed in O'LEARY & MCGARRY, *The Politics of Antagonism*. This concentrates more upon historical issues and provides an excellent analysis of the competing political forces which created partition. Both

accounts indicate how internal conflict exists as Northern Ireland is the site of two competitive national communities. External factors are also crucial, as Northern Ireland is the location of competing British and Irish nationalisms.

Steve BRUCE suggests that a different form of ethnic conflict has taken place. Bruce insists that the conflict is ethno-religious. It is the religious identity of the competing groups that has given the conflict its enduring quality. Unionist politics have been unwilling to transcend, or incapable of transcending, protestant affiliations. Bruce acknowledges that Northern Ireland's is not a "holy war". Clerics are not targeted and religion is often used as a mere ethnic marker. Nonetheless the main unionist parties are linked formally and informally to religious organizations. The protestant Orange Order has voting rights within the Ulster Unionist Party, whose leadership contains numerous members. Free Presbyterians provide a significant number of activists for the Democratic Unionist Party. The founder and leader of this party, the fundamentalist Ian Paisley, insists that his politics stem from his religion.

David MILLER takes issue with both of these interpretations of the conflict. He argues that the conflict is colonial. Ireland was Britain's first colony and, much later via the Act of Union of 1801, Britain attempted to integrate Ireland into the national territory. Rebellion and the creation of the Irish Free State ended the project. Northern Ireland remains Britain's last colony, with Ulster unionists representing settler colonials. Miller is particularly scathing of the "ideological exclusion zone" of academic accounts of the Northern Ireland conflict. He criticizes revisionists for identifying with unionism and others (such as McGarry & O'Leary) for acknowledging the origins of conflict as colonialism, without explaining when this ceased.

RUANE & TODD highlight the complexity of relationships which underpin the conflict. They suggest that it is constituted by the presence of communities with multiple layers of difference. These differences embrace native versus settler quarrels, ethnicity, religion, national identity, and political allegiance. Ruane & Todd suggest that the conflict can only be ended by what they term an "emancipatory" approach. This involves the disentanglement of the complex set of relationships under which the unionist and nationalist communities feel compelled to struggle to advance their interests. Economic, social, and political equality, actively promoted by the British government, will assist in this disentanglement.

BOWYER BELL's account of the conflict is important because he is one of very few authors to gain access to the Irish Republican Army's ruling council. As such, the book's claim to be the "definitive work" on the IRA is perhaps justified, particularly as there are few available written records on the IRA. While clearly sympathetic to republican ideals, the book has nonetheless been praised beyond the confines of its subject group. It offers a well-researched, thorough exposition of the fluctuating fortunes of Irish republicans from the 1916 rising to the "long war" of the 1980s and the peace process of the 1990s. The book is particularly informative on the divisions within the IRA which led to the formation of the Provisionals in 1970 and the revival of "armed struggle" to remove the British presence from Ulster. The split occurred at a time when the IRA, although not dead or even dormant, possessed very few weapons and had come as close as ever in its history to abandoning armed conflict. Bowyer Bell emphasizes the historical continuities and basic beliefs that sustained armed republicanism throughout the 20th century.

While not enjoying the range of IRA contacts offered to Bowyer Bell, COOGAN nonetheless offers a well-sourced account of the conflict. The book is written from a viewpoint unashamedly sympathetic to the nationalist cause, and Coogan's range of contacts and lucid style produce an engaging account. The book is strongest in its analysis of the roles of the republican movement, the SDLP, and the Irish government during the Troubles. Coogan's material on unionism is thinner and he is often critical of what he sees as intransigence within the British government, which has prolonged conflict. Nonetheless, his conclusion is upbeat, arguing that conflict in Ulster need not necessarily be enduring.

The attempts at conflict resolution undertaken in the 1990s are addressed in GILLIGAN & TONGE's edited collection. This includes analysis of the proposals of the main unionist and nationalist parties to address the problem. Other perspectives on the conflict are included, including analysis of education and security policies, and consideration of gender issues. The conclusion is mainly critical, arguing that the British and Irish governments have been torn between competing desires to resolve or merely manage the conflict. The authors suggest that there has been too much ambiguity over what the peace process means. This notwithstanding, the peace process has been important in creating new nationalist allies in attempts to resolve the conflict. "Pan-nationalism" involved a coming together of nationalist parties throughout Ireland, although alliances were often fragile.

A rapid series of events concluded the 20th century – the IRA ceasefire, the loyalist paramilitary ceasefire, the Good Friday Agreement, power-sharing and devolved government, and the emergence of the dissident "Real IRA". TONGE suggests that most of these developments have been facilitated by a moderation of the republican agenda, with Sinn Féin prepared to enter the government of Northern Ireland. Books on the new politics of Northern Ireland are about to emerge.

JONATHAN TONGE

See also Devolution: Northern Ireland; Identities, Regional: Ulster–Northern Irish

Northumberland, John Dudley, 1st Duke of *c.1505–1553*
Soldier and politician

Beer, Barrett L., *Northumberland: The Political Career of John Dudley, Earl of Warwick and Duke of Northumberland*, Kent, Ohio: Kent State University Press, 1973

Hoak, D.E., "Rehabilitating the Duke of Northumberland: Politics and Political Control, 1549–1553" in *The Mid-Tudor Polity, c.1540–1560*, edited by Jennifer Loach and Robert Tittler, London: Macmillan, 1970; Totowa, New Jersey: Rowman and Littlefield, 1980

Hoak, D.E., *The King's Council in the Reign of Edward VI*, Cambridge and New York: Cambridge University Press, 1976

Jordan, W.K., *Edward VI: The Young King; The Protectorship of the Duke of Somerset*, London: Allen and Unwin, and Cambridge, Massachusetts: Belknap Press, 1968

Jordan, W.K., *Edward VI: The Threshold of Power: The Dominance of the Duke of Northumberland*, London: Allen and Unwin, and Cambridge, Massachusetts: Belknap Press, 1970

Loades, David, *John Dudley, Duke of Northumberland 1504–1553*, Oxford: Clarendon Press, and New York: Oxford University Press, 1996

Pollard, A.F., *England under Protector Somerset: An Essay*, London: Kegan Paul, Trench and Trübner, 1900; reprinted, New York: Russell and Russell, 1966

Pollard A.F., *The History of England from the Accession of Edward VI to the Death of Elizabeth, 1547–1603*, London and New York: Longmans Green, 1910

The "Black Legend" of John Dudley, Duke of Northumberland, began shortly after his execution when disappointed protestants, dismayed by his obsequious recantation, blamed him for all the hardships that befell them. It was confirmed by Hayward in the 17th century and reinforced by the Victorians, who admired what they saw as the religious tolerance and generosity to the common man of the Protector Somerset ("the good duke"). In contrast, Northumberland, the "bad duke", was a bigot who was brutal to rebellious peasants and who enriched himself and his family at their expense.

POLLARD continued this interpretation, and his reputation made it the standard view of Northumberland for over 70 years, even though later critics stressed that Pollard worked exclusively with printed sources. Pollard's Northumberland was the embodiment of evil: driven by selfish ambition, his entire life was one of intrigue and deceit culminating in the coup that overthrew the legitimate rule of Protector Somerset and his subsequent scheme to alter the succession, thereby raising Lady Jane Grey and his son to the throne.

JORDAN reinforced Pollard's view with the support of archival scholarship. Although he exonerated Northumberland from the charge of masterminding the plot to subvert the succession, he judged him "psychotic" and "irresponsible" and a Machiavellian schemer whose hysterical attempts to stay in power came close to ruining the country. Jordan added an additional element to the black legend: Northumberland's policies were disastrous for the economy and therefore for England's foreign relations. According to Jordan, under Somerset's guidance England had weathered its economic crisis and recovery was in sight when Northumberland seized power and instituted new policies that plunged the country into hard times once again. And, because of Northumberland's failed economic policies, the monarchy was bankrupt, rendering England impotent in foreign affairs. Consequently Northumberland had to surrender land previously gained in hard-fought campaigns.

BEER was the first to challenge the now-standard Pollard–Jordan interpretation. He argued that there was a dearth of talent within the council when Henry VIII died and that this vacuum allowed Somerset and Northumberland to rise. Rather than constantly intriguing to get to the top, Northumberland was content to serve Henry VIII and then Somerset. Moreover, Beer maintained that Northumberland did not exacerbate the rivalry between the Protector and his brother, Seymour, as the "black legend" had it, but instead attempted to mediate their conflict. Only after Somerset lost his nerve in the face of the Western and Kett's rebellions did Northumberland work to bring him down. Beer replaced Pollard's born intriguer with a Northumberland of above-average talent thrust into a position of power by Somerset's bungling, and concluded that it was the council as a whole that brought Somerset down, not one man. Beer was equally dismissive of other aspects of Northumberland's black legend: he was neither a religious bigot nor a persecutor by nature, but he had learned from Somerset's bungling: hard times called for hard measures. On one key point Beer agreed with Jordan: the "device" in Edward's will that diverted the succession to Lady Jane Grey was the dying king's desperate bid to keep England protestant, not the culmination of the bad duke's quest for power.

HOAK's detailed study (1976) of the Privy Council continued Northumberland's rehabilitation. It convincingly demonstrated that, rather than being the arch-conspirator of the black legend, Northumberland was himself the intended victim of a plot and seized power as a result of outmanœuvering his enemies. This explanation also explains what puzzled earlier biographers: Why should a man with no previous interest in religion suddenly support the reformist cause? Hoak's answer was that he needed the king's and Cranmer's support in the power struggle, and cast his lot in with their religious views.

Hoak's study of the Privy Council coupled with complementary studies of Somerset's rule reveal that so far as the constitution was concerned, the traditional "good duke–bad duke" roles should be reversed. Northumberland restored government by council which had been usurped by the Protector. His genius was in controlling the council as lord president and in controlling royal policy. Jordan had thought that with the fall of Somerset Edward was more and more involved in making policy, but Hoak demonstrated that Northumberland was adept at manipulating him by controlling access and through the force of his personality. For this reason Hoak did not believe that Edward would have been allowed to make the fatal decision to change the succession. He may have agreed with it, but he did not dream it up.

LOADES continued the destruction of Northumberland's black legend with the most complete biography out of the works cited. A member of what Loades calls the "service nobility", Northumberland owed his wealth and his place in society to his ability to do his monarch's bidding. As lord admiral, he proved to be a valiant sailor and a thorough administrator, and it was these qualities rather than his supposed Machiavellian nature that took him to the top. If he was scheming at anything, it was not, as the legend has it, to supplant the legitimate succession; it was to be well placed to benefit when Edward would actually rule. Thus he allied with Cranmer and agreed to religious innovation because this was what the king wanted.

Loades's analysis of Northumberland's rule was the opposite of that of Jordan. Northumberland may have made mistakes in his initial handling of the economy, but then he inherited the effects of Somerset's devaluations and was hit with a succession of particularly bad harvests. In time he developed a strategy that would lead to success. Unfortunately, he and Edward did not live long enough to implement it all, and it was Mary who reaped the benefit of his work. Likewise in foreign policy,

retrenchment made the best of the bad situation created by Somerset's failed policies.

Loades's and Hoak's interpretations of Northumberland solve a contradiction in the traditional view which held that Northumberland was the evil genius responsible for everything that happened, yet he was also grooming the young king to take over and thus let him make important decisions. They show that the view of an active king was an illusion. Northumberland visited Edward secretly bringing "drafts" of papers for him to copy and present to the council as if they were his own, thereby deceiving contemporaries as well as later historians about who was in charge. Northumberland was no longer evil personified, but Edward was still his puppet.

ROBERT C. BRADDOCK

See also Edward VI; Henry VIII; Mary I; Protestant Revolution; Somerset

Northumbria, Anglo-Saxon Dioceses

Aird, William M., *St Cuthbert and the Normans: The Church of Durham, 1071–1153*, Woodbridge, Suffolk and Rochester, New York: Boydell Press, 1998

Bonner, Gerald, David Rollason, and Clare Stancliffe (editors), *St Cuthbert, His Cult and His Community to AD 1200*, Woodbridge, Suffolk and Wolfeboro, New Hampshire: Boydell and Brewer, 1989

Cramp, Rosemary, *Whithorn and the Northumbrian Expansion Westwards*, Whithorn, Galloway: Friends of the Whithorn Trust, 1995

Godfrey, John, *The Church in Anglo-Saxon England*, Cambridge: Cambridge University Press, 1962

Hamilton Thompson, A. (editor), *Bede: His Life, Times, and Writings: Essays in Commemoration of the Twelfth Centenary of His Death*, Oxford: Clarendon Press, 1935; reprinted, New York: Russell and Russell, 1966

Higham, N.J., *The Convert Kings: Power and Religious Affiliation in Early Anglo-Saxon England*, Manchester and New York: Manchester University Press, 1997

Kirby, D.P. (editor), *Saint Wilfrid at Hexham*, Newcastle-upon-Tyne: Oriel Press, 1974

Miles, George, *The Bishops of Lindisfarne, Hexham, Chester-le-Street, and Durham AD 635–1020: Being an Introduction to the Ecclesiastical History of Northumbria*, London: Gardner Darton, 1898

Stancliffe, Clare and Eric Cambridge (editors), *Oswald: Northumbrian King to European Saint*, Stamford, Lincolnshire: Paul Watkins, 1995

The only work which covers the ground almost precisely is MILES. This provides material on three of the bishoprics by detailing each bishop biographically and chronologically. It is not just hagiographic in its treatment but, by discussing each bishop in the context of wider political events of his time, introduces a major theme, namely that the history of the dioceses is not merely, or even predominantly, ecclesiastical but also political and dynastic. This core of factually based material can be supplemented by relevant sections from GODFREY to give background to other volumes in which the dioceses have to be accessed through the works' indexes.

HIGHAM seemingly takes a general theme relating to the whole of Anglo-Saxon England but on closer examination his work makes a very relevant and highly scholarly contribution to the topic under discussion. As the cover to his book indicates, "he looks in great detail at how religious affiliation was interwoven into the political policies and careers of Kings Æthelbert, Edwin, Oswald, Oswiu ... between c.590–670". Edwin, Oswald, and Oswiu form the bulk of the book, thus grounding it very firmly in Northumbrian ecclesiastical politics. Though Chester-le-Street, Hexham, and Whithorn do not appear in the book, it is basic to an understanding of their history, while Lindisfarne forms a significant part of the book's fourth chapter.

Aird, Bonner et al., Cramp, Kirby, and Hamilton Thompson all seemingly cover only parts of our topic but in fact have much to contribute to major themes within it, particularly the most important theme, the intertwined nature of ecclesiastical and secular politics in Northumbria from the 6th to the 11th centuries. Other general themes which the history of the dioceses help to illuminate are: its use to illuminate controversies as to how much of a break with the past the Vikings and the Normans actually were; the interconnected nature of the dioceses and their relative places in a hierarchy of importance; the impact of the central figures of Cuthbert, Oswald, and Wilfrid; the debate about the role of Bede as reliable historical source; and the contest between the Roman and Celtic churches.

The depth of material on each separate bishopric is very variable and often the references to a particular diocese are merely to exemplify the workings of power politics in a certain situation. The exercise of power is usually heptarchic and European rather than just Northumbrian. HAMILTON THOMPSON comments that "the monastery in fact was an ecclesiastical replica of the tribe in whose territory it was founded. Its abbot stood in the position of a tribal chieftain to the community: he himself was in many instances a member of the local ruling family." KIRBY feels that the expulsion of Acca from his see at Hexham in 731–32 was "connected with the attempted deposition of King Ceowulf" and notes that Hexham and Lindisfarne had different loyalties in the dynastic convolutions of the latter half of the 8th century. BONNER, ROLLASON, & STANCLIFFE comment that the "'Northumbrian renaissance' ... may have depended largely on the fruits of conquest" while even the relatively obscure Chester-le-Street diocese was aware of the importance of the patronage of the royal house of Wessex. The biggest example of the close relationship between church and state, and its attendant perils, is Wilfrid (Kirby), while Aird comments that "a large part of the Church of St Cuthbert's success was due to the ability of its leaders to recognise which political entity posed the most serious threat to its liberties", a process to which even the reputedly reclusive Cuthbert was not immune. As Kirby notes, a successful bishop had to forge a modus vivendi with his king. Finally, in the Whithorn bishopric, Cambridge in STANCLIFFE & CAMBRIDGE argues that dedications to St Oswald and St Cuthbert of churches in south-east Scotland, the "farthest outposts of Northumbrian rule" have "political (indeed propagandist) overtones".

The history of the dioceses helps in the fraught calculations of just how intrusive were the Viking and Norman incursions. AIRD, in a book which despite its title devotes half of its pages to a central discussion of the Northumbrian church from 635 to 1065, has important points to make about both incursions, discussing the views of P.H. Sawyer and N. Brooks on the impact of the Vikings, and viewing the Benedictine convent established in Durham in 1083 as "neither a relic of the Northumbrian past nor a provocative innovation of the new Norman ecclesiastical hierarchy ... an amalgamation of both elements; truly Anglo-Norman in constitution". Bonner and Cambridge, in Bonner, Rollason & Stancliffe, have different emphases on the threat posed by the Vikings to the Community of St Cuthbert. John Godfrey in The Church in Anglo-Saxon England, while viewing the settled episcopal line of the Church of St Cuthbert at Chester-le-Street lasting over a century as evidence that the peril was passing, is generally apocalyptic in his view of the Vikings.

The existence of the sees was always subject to the pressures of ecclesiastical politics and invading Northmen. The best example of the sees' history being the results of power manoeuvrings within the church revolve around Cuthbert, Wilfrid, and Oswald. The key political question for both church and state was whether to have a single bishop as head of the Northumbrian church, and which tradition that bishop should represent, the metropolitan Roman or the monastic Celtic. Should the Northumbrian church be one or several sees? The history and fortunes of the Chester-le-Street, Hexham, and Lindisfarne bishoprics revolve around this question. D.H. Farmer in Kirby gives a good, balanced account of Wilfrid's role. Alan Thacker in Stancliffe & Cambridge shows that Cuthbert and Wilfrid exercised influence even in death, arguing that the cult of St Cuthbert was a response by Lindisfarne to the Hexham-inspired cult of St Wilfrid. Cambridge in the same volume concurs and points out that the see of Chester-le-Street owes its existence and extinction to the geographical excursions of the relics of St Cuthbert responding to Viking pressure. CRAMP in an excellent account shows that Whithorn, while linking into Lindisfarne in particular, was really a product of Northumbrian expansionist politics.

Finally, Kirby and Farmer, in separate articles in Kirby, have excellent evaluations of Bede as an historical source.

RAY GRACE

See also Cuthbert; Northumbria; Oswald; Pictland and Dalriada

Northumbria, Kingdom of

Blair, Peter Hunter, Anglo-Saxon Northumbria, edited by Michael Lapidge and Hunter Blair, London: Variorum Reprints, 1984
Bonner, Gerald, Church and Faith in the Patristic Tradition: Augustine, Pelagianism, and Early Christian Northumbria, Aldershot, Hampshire and Brookfield, Vermont: Variorum, 1996
Clemoes, Peter, The Cult of St Oswald on the Continent, Jarrow: St Paul's Church, 1983; reprinted in Bede and

His World: The Jarrow Lectures, 1958–1993, with a preface by Michael Lapidge, vol. 2, Aldershot, Hampshire and Brookfield, Vermont: Variorum, 1994

Higham, N.J., *The Kingdom of Northumbria, AD 350–1100*, Stroud, Gloucestershire and Dover, New Hampshire: Alan Sutton, 1993

Bede and His World: The Jarrow Lectures, 1958–1993, 2 vols, with a preface by Michael Lapidge, Aldershot, Hampshire and Brookfield, Vermont: Variorum, 1994

Marsden, John, *Northanhymbre Saga: The History of the Anglo-Saxon Kings of Northumbria*, London: Kyle Cathie, 1992

Metcalf, D.M. (editor), *Coinage in Ninth-Century Northumbria: The Tenth Oxford Symposium on Coinage and Monetary History*, Oxford: British Archaeological Reports, 1987

Stancliffe, Clare and Eric Cambridge (editors), *Oswald: Northumbrian King to European Saint*, Stamford, Lincolnshire: Paul Watkins, 1995

Story, Joanna Elizabeth, "Charlemagne and Northumbria: The Influence of Francia on Northumbrian Politics in the Late Eighth and Early Ninth Centuries" (dissertation), Durham: University of Durham, 1995

In 1971 in the third edition of his *Anglo-Saxon England*, Sir Frank Stenton referred to Northumbria as lying "almost outside recorded history". In fact the data available on Northumbria are plentiful and complex. Blair in his scholarly and fundamental book records that "No mere mortal can expect to be properly qualified to interpret late Roman, Old Welsh, Old English and medieval Latin records, to say nothing of the archaeological evidence." To this list can be added sculpture (Rosemary Cramp in the Jarrow Lectures), the history of coinage, and the various literary sources well described by Blair. For example, James Booth in Metcalf discusses the intimate link between coinage history and political history and Nicholas Brooks sums up this important symposium as "bringing together experts in various fields – numismatics, metallurgy, philosophy, and history".

A major problem in approaching the history of Northumbria is the amorphous identity of the area covered, in both space and time. BLAIR covers this problem in an etymological and place-name discussion of great depth, allied to factual 7th century political material, of the southern extent of Northumbria (chapter 4). In discussing the boundary between Bernicia and Deira (chapter 5), Blair comments "There is not enough evidence to determine exactly the full extent of Northumbria in Bede's lifetime, and it may be a mistake to suppose that its boundaries were ever clearly defined throughout their whole length." This problem of borders is compounded by the time-scale involved – some eight hundred years. Booth in Metcalf introduces this element when discussing "the new silver coinage introduced in the closing years of the [ninth] century when a Viking state had been established in the smaller southern half of the old Northumbrian kingdom".

There are a number of controversies in discussing Northumbria – notably the discussion of continuity at various times and of the centrality of Bede. In chapter 2 of his book, which is both accessible in style and scholarly in foundation, HIGHAM, under the title "Catastrophe or Continuity?", discusses the issue rather inconclusively in the context of the waxing and waning of Roman, British, and Anglo-Saxon polities around 400. Blair in discussing Coel Hen is quite clearly on the side of continuity. "We seem therefore to have a man bearing a name of Roman formation ... born c.380 ... regarded as head of a family which by the sixth century embraced several native British dynasties ... a successful usurpation by a high military official who remained in the area of his command." Several authors in METCALF discuss the impact of the Vikings on Northumbria around 866–67. D.P. Kirby asserts "under the Viking impact ... the kingdom fractured" but stresses continuities in such key areas as the archiepiscopal succession, though the church in Bernicia, in contrast to the church in Deira, was "totally disrupted". James Booth discusses the debate between Michael Dolley and Peter Sawyer, the latter being more sceptical of the impact of the Viking raids. Booth uses the coin evidence to judge that the raids "disrupted the ailing economy quite radically".

Most scholars accept the central importance of Bede, though many regard him as more reliable on ecclesiastical matters than on other aspects of history. Conversely, however, Blair notes appreciatively that the archaeological excavations at Yeavering support Bede's comment about the *villa regia* found there in Edwin's time, "striking confirmation of his accuracy in such matters of historical detail" but later, discussing the credit claimed by the Welsh church for many Northumbrian baptisms, notes the unreliability of Bede in this discussion, given his strong prejudice against the Celtic church, and the Welsh in particular. One excellent way of assessing the centrality of Bede is to take account of the range and scholarly quality of the JARROW LECTURES under the general title of *Bede and his World*. These volumes, which are beautifully produced and delightful to use, cover architecture, music, archaeology, social class and conditions, visual arts, science, and the wider impact of Northumbria. Many of these compact and scholarly lectures are precursors of later more fully fledged volumes, for example Professor Rosemary Cramp proceeding to a discussion of *Whithorn and Northumbrian Expansion Westwards* (1995).

The Jarrow Lectures foreshadow several important areas later covered by full-length treatments by other authors. For example, Christopher D. Morris in his 1989 lecture gives a taste of archaeological evaluations, which can be followed up in detailed works concerning such sites as Whithorn and Yeavering, while CLEMOES in his 1983 lecture precurses the more detailed work in STANCLIFFE & CAMBRIDGE and the important unpublished thesis by STORY.

Such works are a salutary reminder of Northumbria's widespread external contacts. In his introduction Metcalf notes that "monetary reform (in the ninth century) was no doubt guided by wider considerations of the needs of international and inter-regional trade" which has to be put in a European context. Clemoes in his Jarrow Lecture states he wants to follow "a European trail" which leads him to baroque art in the 1750s and lingering thereafter in folk customs in Bavaria and the Tyrol even later. In his lecture for 1989 Morris notes the links between Northumbria and the north, demonstrating "the crucial role of Northumbria in the development of Christianity there". Blair notes that by 626 the Bernicians and the Welsh had good contacts "and the Deirians for perhaps very much longer".

The last important point to make about the kingdom of Northumbria is that its history is not a matter of the dim and dark past. Blair, aptly enough, discusses the *rapprochement* between Northumbrians and Picts after 711 in terms of personal relationships between leaders, and Metcalf's comments above about the European context of Northumbrian monetary reform in the 9th century all lead to interesting musings about the comparabilities between the kingdom of Northumbria and modern British problems with Europe.

BONNER shows the fundamental importance of religion to Northumbrian politics without being over-ecclesiastical. MARSDEN belittles himself in his dedicatory reference to "a little local history", being with Higham a readable, accessible, and knowledgeable account of learned material. And to end with a novel, C.P.R. Tisdale's *Month of Swallows: Northumbria, England AD 626–633* (1993) is a scholarship-based novel with useful glossaries of phrases, place-names, and maps.

RAY GRACE

See also Aidan; Anglo-Saxon England: Kingdoms; Bede's Ecclesiastical History; Biscop; Cuthbert; Erik Bloodaxe; Hild; Identities, Regional: Border Societies; Identities, Regional: "The North"; Monasticism; Oswald; Wilfrid

Norwich

Atherton, Ian *et al.* (editors), *Norwich Cathedral: Church, City, and Diocese, 1096–1996*, London and Rio Grande, Ohio: Hambledon Press, 1996

Ayers, Brian, *English Heritage Book of Norwich*, London: Batsford for English Heritage, 1994

Evans, John T., *Seventeenth-Century Norwich: Politics, Religion, and Government, 1620–1690*, Oxford: Clarendon Press, and New York: Oxford University Press, 1979

Jewson, C.B., *The Jacobin City: A Portrait of Norwich in its Reaction to the French Revolution 1788–1802*, Glasgow: Blackie, 1975

McClendon, Muriel C., *The Quiet Reformation: Magistrates and the Emergence of Protestantism in Tudor Norwich*, Stanford, California: Stanford University Press, 1999

Pound, John, *Tudor and Stuart Norwich*, Chichester, Sussex: Phillimore, 1988

Tanner, Norman P., *The Church in Late Medieval Norwich 1370–1532*, Toronto: Pontifical Institute of Mediaeval Studies, 1984

AYERS offers a relatively brief but thorough account of the archaeological history of the city of Norwich. While he focuses on the physical and material aspects of Norwich, he nevertheless maintains a sense of the city as a community of citizens, not simply a group of buildings. The book also provides significant historical context for the archaeological evidence presented. The major theme of the book is growth – growth from the earliest palaeolithic settlements into England's second city, based largely on a thriving cloth industry. The majority of the book examines Norwich's medieval heritage, but Ayers also engages with the Reformation period and beyond, bringing the discussion up to the post-1945 era. Effectively illustrated, the book contains ample maps, drawings, and photographs of the city's historic buildings and features. It offers a useful and accessible introduction to Norwich's material past.

The large volume edited by ATHERTON tells the story of one of the major institutions of the city of Norwich, the cathedral. The book chronicles the fabric of the building from its construction beginning in the 11th century to the present, as well as the social, economic, political, and cultural impact of the cathedral and its denizens on the city. Consisting of chapters written by over 30 different authors, it covers a broad variety of topics, from the decorations and monuments to the relations between ecclesiastical authority and civic government. Interactions between cathedral and city were not always pacific; indeed, townsmen attacked the churchmen in 1272. For the most part, however, the town benefited from the presence of the cathedral, which added to the city's significance on the national scale.

TANNER closely examines the religious context of the city in the late medieval period. He focuses not on the institutions of the church, but rather on the practices of religion by the people, as exemplified by the populace of Norwich. Using evidence gleaned largely from wills, Tanner explores the traditional practices of the urban parishes as well as some of the new movements that emerged in the church in Norwich. Tanner concludes that, in Norwich at least, the old church was not in deep decay in the late medieval period. Instead, religious life remained rich and varied, with an actively involved and engaged laity. New movements within the church, represented by individuals like Julian of Norwich, the anchoress and mystic, formed a vital part of religious practice. For Tanner, religion in late medieval Norwich is neither a sharp break with the practices of the earlier Middle Ages nor "fossilized ritualism". Thus for the people, the Reformation came not as a sudden reaction against the church, but as a development from within it.

Norwich has been particularly well served by scholars of its early modern era. McCLENDON's volume on the Reformation in Norwich analyses the impact of religious change on the city in the 16th century. As a significant religious centre in the late medieval period as well as a hotbed of puritan activity during Elizabeth's reign, Norwich might be expected to have suffered from intense religious conflict during the Reformation. Instead, McClendon found that, while conflict existed, it was largely contained by civic magistrates intent on maintaining order. McClendon argues that Norwich's leaders in effect practised religious toleration, compartmentalizing religion as something apart from other political issues. Magistrates certainly embarked on a policy of moral reform to control the inhabitants of the city, but this did not require a specific set of confessional beliefs. Civic identity generally overcame religious division throughout the 16th century. The book may overstate the level of real toleration that existed, but it is an important corrective to some work that assumes division and conflict dominated early modern cities.

POUND directs his focus principally on the economic and social characteristics of Norwich in the Tudor and Stuart periods. Drawing a vivid picture of a bustling early modern industrial town, he provides detailed discussions (including many graphs and charts) of population, wealth, occupational structure, and trade organization in Norwich. He also looks at the social and economic aspects of civic government, examining, for instance, civic finances and the status and occupations of civic leaders. Pound is particularly strong in his treatment of issues of poverty and poor relief, showing that Norwich led the way in finding workable (if harsh) solutions to the problems of poverty.

EVANS published *Seventeenth-Century Norwich* in the first wave of modern scholarship on urban history. In it, he examines the political community of Norwich in the tempestuous Stuart era. His interests lie less with the economic and social stresses of the period than with the response of the city's leading men to political and religious conflicts. In contrast to the relative unity that McClendon saw in the Reformation era, Evans illustrates the sharp conflicts that arose in the 17th century between civic leaders and the crown, town officials and county gentry, and among the townsmen themselves. Contrary to the arguments of other historians, Evans believes that the government of Norwich was becoming less oligarchical rather than more, and that the large and active citizenry continued to play a key role in political and religious issues in the city. Conflicts between royalists and parliamentary puritans in the 1640s and between Whigs and Tories in the 1680s were particularly intense. Evans's book is a good example of how political history can be broadened by the techniques of urban and local history.

JEWSON is one of the few books that specifically focus on the history of Norwich after the 17th century. It offers a systematic treatment of the radical politics that energized the city in the late 18th century. Norwich was one of the cities in which societies, consisting principally of artisans, formed in sympathy with the French revolutionaries, calling for reforms along the lines laid out by Thomas Paine in the *Rights of Man*. The book shows how many of the people of Norwich, especially the substantial dissenting population, responded to the French Revolution and became radicalized by the Jacobins' calls for liberty and equality.

CATHERINE F. PATTERSON

Nottingham, 1st Earl of
see Howard, Charles

Nuclear Power

Eiser, J. Richard, Joop van der Pligt, and Russell Spears, *Nuclear Neighbourhoods: Community Responses to Reactor Siting*, Exeter, Devon: University of Exeter Press, 1995

Gowing, Margaret, *Britain and Atomic Energy 1939–1945*, London: Macmillan, and New York: St Martin's Press, 1964

Gowing, Margaret, with Lorna Arnold, *Independence and Deterrence: Britain and Atomic Energy 1945–1952*, London: Macmillan, and New York: St Martin's Press, 1974

Massey, Andrew, *Technocrats and Nuclear Politics: The Influence of Professional Experts in Policy-Making*,

Aldershot, Hampshire and Brookfield, Vermont: Avebury, 1988

Parker, Mike and John Surrey, "Contrasting British Policies for Coal and Nuclear Power, 1979–1992", *Energy Policy*, 23/9 (1995): 821–50

Peña-Torres, J. and P.J.G. Pearson, "Carbon Abatement and New Investment in Liberalized Electricity Markets: A Nuclear Revival in the UK?", *Energy Policy*, 28/2 (2000): 115–35

Roberts, Jane, David Elliot, and Trevor Houghton, *Privatising Electricity: The Politics of Power*, London and New York: Belhaven Press, 1991

Saward, M., *The Civil Nuclear Network in Britain*, Colchester, Essex: University of Essex, Department of Government, 1989

Williams, Roger, *The Nuclear Power Decisions: British Policies, 1953–1978*, London: Croom Helm, 1980

The United Kingdom produces approximately 13,000 megawatts of nuclear-generated electricity, or 4.1 per cent of the world total, representing some 28 per cent of the country's total domestic electricity generation. Until relatively recently, however, the British public had little to say about the nuclear role in the electricity supply system.

The political history of British civil nuclear power can be divided into four distinct periods: (1) the first several decades of development, the roots of which can be traced to the atomic bomb and the June 1940 establishment of the Committee for the Scientific Survey of Air Warfare; GOWING's two works offer an exhaustive treatment of this phase. During this period the project was the exclusive domain of a technocratic and governmental elite with little, if any, direct accountability to the general public; (2) a period beginning in the mid-1970s when the public became deeply involved and essentially rejected many of the arguments offered by the nuclear elite; (3) a period of official enthusiasm for an expansion in the nuclear role coincident with general policies of privatization and the need to treat nuclear energy as a special case; and (4) contemporary debates about the possibility of a nuclear revival.

The absence of significant public representation in the early phases of nuclear power decision-making is a common theme throughout the literature. WILLIAMS, for instance, asks why civilian nuclear power became "a matter for general political debate only in the seventies – why not in the fifties when civil nuclear power first got underway, or in the sixties when opposition to nuclear weapons prompted major demonstrations?" SAWARD makes a similar point, arguing that until the mid-to-late 1970s the nuclear network was a "closed, insulated, and powerful" policy community. While there were complex and intense struggles over a variety of technical matters, particularly over choice of reactors, "these arguments were essentially 'private' ones between the principal institutional bodies directly involved."

It was not until the 1977 Windscale inquiry regarding the thermal oxide reprocessing plant (abbreviated as THORP) that the public was allowed entrée into the decision-making process. Yet even here "a desire to avoid the politicization of nuclear power was the governing motive of politicians from both political parties ... This technocratic ideology, inherent in the corporatising processes, transmitted itself throughout the public (and private) sectors" (MASSEY). The importance of the Windscale inquiry should not, however, be underestimated, since it was here that the technocratic process, with its insular character and lack of public accountability, first came under challenge. Various public interest groups such as "Town and Country Planning Association and the Friends of the Earth lobbied for an Inquiry not only because they were opposed to the scheme, but because they were also anxious that [British Nuclear Fuels] had made too little information available for a proper review of its future proposals." As noted by Massey, this concern existed despite the fact that the company had made a largely successful "adaptation from a bureaucratic sub-group into a commercially aggressive corporation".

The Windscale inquiry was followed by two other highly charged public investigations, the enormously complex Sizewell B inquiry, which ran from January 1983 to March 1985 and the Hinkley C inquiry, which lasted from October 1988 to November 1989. Both of the inquiries were marked by an exhaustive review of the facts and extensive public participation. In both cases, positive recommendations were made regarding further development, notwithstanding the opposition of the environmental community and other public interest groups (see PARKER & SURREY).

The recommendations of the Sizewell B and Hinkley C inspectors coincided with the third major phase of British civil nuclear politics, which centred on the extraordinary efforts of the Thatcher governments to secure a place for the nuclear industry at Britain's energy table. This technological dedication was rivalled by an equally strong desire to break the power of domestic coal, both politically and as a major force in the supply mix. In addition to breaking the power of the miners' union, Mrs Thatcher's governments had two other key policy objectives, namely, to demonstrate the failure of public ownership and to build a series of large nuclear reactors (see Parker & Surrey).

The first objective was met through a series of policy initiatives, political brinksmanship, and an effort to stigmatize coal through the effective use of public relations and official documents such as the 1981 Flowers report. The second objective was also met and was capped with the privatization of the electric supply industry in July 1989 (ROBERTS, ELLIOT & HOUGHTON). The last objective was never realized: since the commercial start-up in 1995 of Sizewell B and despite the successful conclusion of the Hinkley inquiry, no new plants have been added to the British inventory nor are any under construction. On the day the Berlin Wall fell, "the new Secretary of State for Energy . . . announced one of the most humiliating policy reversals of the Thatcher Governments. British nuclear power stations were not, after all, to be included in the privatization of the electricity supply industry, and the three pressurized water reactors which had been planned as successors to Sizewell B would not now be built" (Roberts). This decision was taken despite ten-years' worth of unflagging government support for the construction of ten new pressurized water reactors initially proposed in 1979.

THORP has also operated in a continuous state of crisis from its very first days. Shipments from abroad routinely result in large-scale public protests and THORP's main domestic customer, British Energy, has recently described reprocessing as "economic nonsense", requesting talks on ending reprocessing. British Nuclear Fuel's international customers have also demanded a renegotiation of long-term contracts and have threatened to stop sending fuel to the facility altogether (*Independent on Sunday*, 13 May 2001).

Despite a 1995 white paper's conclusion that nuclear power should continue to play an important role in meeting the United Kingdom's energy needs, "providing that it is competitive and can maintain rigorous standards of safety and environmental protection", it is doubtful that nuclear technology will experience a revival any time soon (quoted in PEÑA-TORRES & PEARSON). Public enthusiasm for the technology does not seem to have measurably shifted in a more positive direction (see EISER, PLIGT & SPEARS) and while pro-nuclear advocates would like to paint the atom green, it is unlikely that public concerns about climate change and other environmental issues will trump the basic distrust about nuclear energy (see Peña-Torres & Pearson). This bleak prospect for a nuclear revival does not, however, bring an end to civil nuclear politics. The public must now turn its attention to another, even more pressing question: what should it do about the toxic waste that will, for at least the next several thousand years, be the primary legacy of the nuclear experiment?

STEVEN M. HOFFMAN

See also Electricity

Nuns

see **Gilbert of Sempringham; Religious Orders entries**

O

O'Connell, Daniel 1775-1847
Irish nationalist and social reformer

Daunt, William J. O'N., *Personal Recollections of the Late Daniel O'Connell, M.P.*, 2 vols, London: Chapman and Hall, 1848

Gwynn, Denis, *Daniel O'Connell, The Irish Liberator*, London: Hutchinson, 1929; New York: Stokes, 1930; revised edition, Cork: Cork University Press, 1947

Lecky, William E.H., *Leaders of Public Opinion in Ireland*, London: Saunders Ottley, 1861; revised and enlarged edition, London: Longmans Green, 1871; New York: Appleton, 1872

MacDonagh, Michael, *The Life of Daniel O'Connell*, London and New York: Cassell, 1903; revised edition, as *Daniel O'Connell and the Story of Catholic Emancipation*, London: Burns and Oates, and Dublin: Talbot Press, 1929

MacDonagh, Oliver, *The Hereditary Bondsman: Daniel O'Connell, 1775-1829*, London: Weidenfeld and Nicolson, and New York: St Martin's Press, 1988

MacDonagh, Oliver, *The Emancipist: Daniel O'Connell, 1830-1847*, London: Weidenfeld and Nicolson, and New York: St Martin's Press, 1989

Moley, Raymond, *Daniel O'Connell: Nationalism without Violence: An Essay*, New York: Fordham University Press, 1974

Nowlan, Kevin B. and Maurice R. O'Connell (editors), *Daniel O'Connell: Portrait of a Radical*, Belfast: Appletree Press, 1984; New York: Fordham University Press, 1985

O'Faoláin, Séan, *King of the Beggars: A Life of Daniel O'Connell, the Irish Liberator, in a Study of the Rise of the Modern Irish Democracy (1775-1847)*, London and New York: Nelson, 1938; reprinted, Dublin: Figgis, 1970

O'Ferrall, Fergus, *Daniel O'Connell*, Dublin: Gill and MacMillan, 1981

Tierney, Michael (editor), *Daniel O'Connell: Nine Centenary Essays*, Dublin: Browne and Nolan, 1949

During O'Connell's long life he changed the course of both Irish and British politics, his greatest triumph being the granting of catholic emancipation (as a result of which catholics were allowed to sit in the British parliament). Although his rhetoric was often fiery, throughout his life he favoured constitutional methods over physical force. The later years of his life were dominated by his attempts to bring about a repeal of the Act of Union of 1800. However, his conflicts with the radical Young Ireland nationalists, his links with the catholic church, his devotion to the British monarchy, and the catastrophe of the Irish Famine, all served to tarnish his overall political achievements. Consequently, interpretations of his contribution have remained divided and equivocal among historians, biographers, and nationalists. O'Connell left behind a vast amount of correspondence (almost 4000 letters), private papers, speeches, and journals, the great majority of which have been published.

The early account of O'Connell's life by his friend, former political secretary, and political ally, William O'Neill DAUNT, was published only a year after O'Connell's death. Not surprisingly, it is more a hagiography than a biography yet it provides a unique insight based on private conversations, and correspondence no longer extant. Daunt was also concerned to show the private rather than the public side of O'Connell. By referring to O'Connell as the great "Catholic leader", he reinforced the perception of O'Connell's struggle for repeal being linked with catholicism.

The second volume of LECKY's biographies was concerned with O'Connell. It was written in a period when O'Connell's brand of moral force politics was out of favour with Irish nationalists. It also coincided with the publication of memoirs by former members of Young Ireland which were generally critical of O'Connell's adherence to constitutional methods. Lecky's balanced approach to his subject has given the publication an enduring value.

Most biographers of O'Connell believe that his greatest political achievements were made before 1830. GWYNN's sympathetic survey, which was based on a range of primary and secondary sources, was published to coincide with the hundredth anniversary of catholic emancipation in 1829, which was viewed as O'Connell's finest achievement. The book is weighted towards the earlier part of O'Connell's career rather than the post-emancipation years as a member of the British parliament.

Michael MacDONAGH's popular account was also reissued to coincide with the anniversary of emancipation. The author was a political commentator and the style is frequently anecdotal rather than academic yet it remains an early and valuable contribution. O'FAOLÁIN's sympathetic and elegantly written account of O'Connell is generally regarded as a classic, even if at times the praise of O'Connell's achievements is extravagant. Little attention is paid to the failures in O'Connell's career.

A scholarly collection of essays was planned to appear for the centenary of O'Connell's death. The editor, TIERNEY, like many subsequent biographers, was concerned that O'Connell's detractors and enemies had succeeded in discrediting and misrepresenting his many unique achievements. The role played by a number of Young Ireland leaders in damaging O'Connell's reputation, and the enduring legacy of this viewpoint, are assessed. O'Connell is also examined from a variety of more unusual perspectives, including chapters on "English Opinion" and "Continental Opinion". As a consequence, O'Connell's contribution is evaluated in the wider context of 19th-century European politics.

One of the aims of MOLEY's self-styled "essay" was to rescue O'Connell from the political and historiographic wilderness in which he believed he had been languishing since the end of the 19th century. Although based on secondary sources, the perspective is a fresh one as Moley is neither Irish nor an historian, but an American who had worked as a political adviser. Not surprisingly perhaps, he views the American Revolution as having had a major influence on O'Connell's political development. As the title suggests, one of Moley's primary concerns is with O'Connell's commitment to constitutional methods, which he believes offered a model for 20th-century democracies, especially the United States.

Oliver MACDONAGH in *The Hereditary Bondsman* seeks to give a coherence and purpose to O'Connell's prolonged political life which was missing in earlier works. One way in which he does this is by attempting to understand what he refers to as "the curious historical cast of mind" which produced O'Connell. He also shows how O'Connell in his lifetime sought to create an image of his personal and political identity which a number of subsequent histories used uncritically. In *The Emancipist*, published a year later, MACDONAGH focuses on O'Connell's period as an MP, when he changed from being a popular agitator to a professional politician. It is more detailed and scholarly than the earlier publication. The political scene is examined from O'Connell's rather than the wider British perspective. Although MacDonagh includes O'Connell's limitations and failures, he also charts how O'Connell was willing to change his strategies when necessary and developed what the author describes as "a methodology peculiarly appropriate to colonial counter-attack". Throughout, MacDonagh draws on a wide range of primary sources, notably the newly available collection of O'Connell's correspondence, edited by Professor Maurice O'Connell, which had not been available to earlier biographers.

Although part of a series of popular biographies, O'FERRALL'S succinct and incisive publication has utilized a wide range of primary sources. The publication is more than a biography of O'Connell, as it seeks to place him within a broad social and political context. The author also explores the influence of Irish politics on British political developments, which he regards as profound following the Act of Union. O'Connell's political contribution, therefore, is appraised both within the Irish parliamentary party and within the broader sphere of British politics. O'Ferrall is particularly strong on O'Connell's development of a political methodology to deal with the British authorities. Unlike some of the earlier biographies, O'Ferrall also explores the reason for the demise of O'Connell and his movement, and how memories of O'Connell were tarnished by events in his later life.

The collection of essays edited by NOWLAN & O'CONNELL also seeks to place O'Connell not only within a British context, but also within European political development. At the same time, O'Connell is located within a Gaelic and Irish world. Inevitably, a more complex and nuanced view of O'Connell emerges than is evident in many biographies. The editors contend that in order to make an accurate assessment of O'Connell's achievements it is necessary to view him in the context of his own time. However, just as the editors argue that O'Connell has been the victim of shifts in popular attitudes to Irish nationalism, it is worth remembering that this collection was published shortly after the commencement of "the Troubles" in Northern Ireland which reawakened the debate regarding the use of constitutional and physical force.

CHRISTINE KINEALY

See also Catholic Church since 1560; Catholic Emancipation; Ireland entries (19th century); "Irish Question"; Wellington

Oda d. 958
Archbishop of Canterbury

Armitage Robinson, J., *St Oswald and the Church of Worcester*, London: Oxford University Press, 1919

Brooks, Nicholas, *The Early History of the Church of Canterbury: Christ Church from 597 to 1066*, Leicester: Leicester University Press, and Atlantic Highlands, New Jersey: Humanities Press, 1984

Lapidge, Michael, "The Hermeneutic Style in Tenth-Century Anglo-Latin Literature", *Anglo-Saxon England*, 4 (1975): 66–111; reprinted in his *Anglo-Latin Literature 900–1066*, London and Rio Grande, Ohio: Hambledon Press, 1993

Lapidge, Michael, "A Frankish Scholar in Tenth-Century England: Frithegod of Canterbury / Fredegaud of Brioude", *Anglo-Saxon England*, 17 (1988): 45–65; reprinted in his *Anglo-Latin Literature, 900–1066*, London and Rio Grande, Ohio: Hambledon Press, 1993

Schoebe, G., "The Chapters of Archbishop Oda and the Canons of the Legatine Council of 786", *Bulletin of the Institute of Historical Research*, 35 (1962): 75–83

Thacker, A.T., "Cults at Canterbury: Relics and Reform under Dunstan and His Successors" in *St Dunstan: His Life, Times, and Cult*, edited by Nigel Ramsay, Margaret Sparks, and Tim Tatton-Brown, Woodbridge, Suffolk and Rochester, New York: Boydell Press, 1992

Yorke, Barbara, "Æthelwold and the Politics of the Tenth Century" in *Bishop Æthelwold: His Career and Influence*, edited by Yorke, Woodbridge, Suffolk and Wolfeboro, New Hampshire: Boydell Press, 1988

The fullest account of the career of Oda is that in BROOKS. Oda was of Anglo-Danish extraction, the son of a pagan who came to England with the Danish Great Army in the 870s. He was raised in the household of the English thegn, Æthelhelm, with whom, on one occasion, he travelled to Rome. His significance lies in three main areas: as a precursor of the 10th-century monastic reformers (the principal source of his life is the first part of the Life of his nephew, Saint Oswald, now proven by

LAPIDGE (1975), to have been written by Byrthferth of Ramsey); as a lawmaker; and as an example of the integration of Scandinavians into the late Anglo-Saxon state. Elected to the see of Ramsbury by King Athelstan c.927, he fostered the close relationship between kings and bishops which was a characteristic of the reform movement, travelling on the continent to negotiate with Hugh, Duke of the Franks, the safe return of Athelstan's nephew, Louis d'Outremer as King of the Franks in 936. It was most probably during this trip that he was tonsured at Fleury, where he was later to send his nephew, the reformer Saint Oswald, and was appointed Archbishop of Canterbury by Athelstan's successor, Edmund, in 941. Good background to these events is provided by ARMITAGE ROBINSON.

He accompanied Edmund north to resist the invasion of Olafr Gothfrithsson and negotiated a treaty with Archbishop Wulftsan I of York which left the Five Boroughs of the northeast Midlands briefly in Viking hands. In conjunction with Wulfstan, he was the motivating force behind Edmund's first law-code which dealt with many ecclesiastical issues such as the celibacy of the clergy, enforcement of the payment of tithes and the repair of churches. Similar concerns are found in his *Constitutiones* issued between 942 and 946 which was based largely on 10 chapters extracted from the legatine synods of 786 (as described in SCHOEBE) and a synodical letter sent to his suffragans preserved by William of Malmesbury. Since his parental home may well have been in the eastern Danelaw, Oda expressed a strong personal concern to reorganize and renew the church in East Anglia. He re-established the see of Elmham and on 9 May 957 was granted 40 hides of land at Ely by Edmund's son, King Eadwig, perhaps with the intention of re-establishing a monastic regime. In this regard, he may have attempted to recall Oswald from Fleury in order that he should rule there. Such hopes were dashed, however, by the political crisis of 957–58 when Mercia chose Eadwig's brother, Edgar, as king. Late in 957 Oda ceased to attend Eadwig's court and in 958 moved to divorce the king and his queen, Ælfgifu, on the grounds of incest. (YORKE provides a succinct analysis of the politics of the period.)

Oda's concern to promote his lordship of the Canterbury community through building, the acquistion of estates, the promotion of scholarship, and saints' cults is well documented and discussed. He rebuilt the cathedral church by raising the height of the nave 20 feet and accommodated a new altar to house the relics of St Wilfrid acquired in a relic-raid undertaken by King Eadred in 948 when the minster of Ripon was burnt. The relics of St Ouen (Audoenus) were also acquired (see THACKER, which suggests that aside from Oda's activities, Canterbury was little interested in promoting relic cults). Oda commissioned Frithegod, a Frankish scholar whose activities have been thoroughly investigated by LAPIDGE (1988), to compose poems commemorating these acquistions. The work on Audoenus is lost but the *Breviloquium vitae beati Wilfridi* survives and is one of the most difficult Anglo-Latin works of the period prefaced by a flamboyant prose account of the acquisition of Wilfrid's relics purportedly composed by Oda but most likely the work of Frithegod, too. The earliest surviving manuscript of the work provides early evidence of the use of Caroline script at Canterbury (Brooks).

The issue of Oda's acquisition of new estates for Canterbury and his defence of existing church property is fraught by the problems of establishing the authenticity of the diplomas purporting to make the grants (thoroughly discussed by Brooks). A problematic diploma in Eadred's name claims to have granted the monastery of Reculver with 26 hides of land to Canterbury in 949. This survives in two copies on single sheets written in the mid-10th century or soon afterwards, the final attestation claiming that Dunstan wrote it with his own fingers. It is unlikely that Dunstan would have spelt Oda in the continental form Odo. The text is, however, infinitely more skilful than the forgeries produced after the Conquest. Whoever drafted this charter either had access to a witness list or could remember without error the nobles and bishops who would have been present together in 949. The diplomatic (transcription) suggests it could have belonged to a series of diplomas drawn up at Glastonbury and adopted to Canterbury's more flowery linguistic style. Eadred granted £400 in his will to be held at Christ Church; Oda also received a personal bequest of 200 pounds (i.e. 240 mancuses) of gold. Oda's East Anglian connections are again evident in the grant by Ælfgar, ealdorman of Essex, of a Suffolk estate at Eleigh to his daughter, Ælflæd, and her husband, Byrhtnoth, with reversion to his elder daughter if they were childless. This was finally confirmed by Ælflæd after Byrhtnoth had died at Maldon in 991 and the estate became a demesne manor of the monks.

Oda was never the object of a pre-Conquest liturgical cult: his feast was not entered in the calendar, and no hymns, prayers, benedictions, or masses were composed in his honour although he was buried on the south side of the choir in a prominent tomb (Thacker). A post-conquest Life by Eadmer contains many additional statements claiming, for example, that Oda fought alongside Athelstan at Brunanburh in 937. It also provides an account of the acquisition of Audoenus's relics.

SIMON COATES

See also Anglo-Saxon England: Kingdoms; Anglo-Saxon England: Law; Athelstan; Danelaw; Edmund I; Egbert; Erik Bloodaxe; Hagiography; Saint Albans, School of

Offa d. 796
King of Mercia

Fox, Cyril, *Offa's Dyke: A Field Survey of the Western Frontier Works of Mercia in the Seventh and Eighth Centuries AD*, London: Oxford University Press for the British Academy, 1955
Keynes, Simon, "Changing Faces: Offa, King of Mercia", *History Today*, 40, (1990): 14–19
Keynes, Simon, "England 700–900" in *The New Cambridge Medieval History*, vol. 2, edited by Rosamond McKitterick, Cambridge and New York: Cambridge University Press, 1995
Stenton, F.M., "The Ascendancy of the Mercian Kings" in his *Anglo-Saxon England*, Oxford: Clarendon Press, 1943; 3rd edition, Oxford: Clarendon Press, 1971; New York: Oxford University Press, 1990
Stenton, F.M., "The Supremacy of the Mercian Kings" in his *Preparatory to Anglo-Saxon England, Being the Collected Papers of Frank Merry Stenton*, edited by Doris Mary Stenton, Oxford: Clarendon Press, 1970

Wallace-Hadrill, J.M., "Charlemagne and England" in his *Early Medieval History*, Oxford: Blackwell, 1975; New York: Barnes and Noble, 1976

Wood, Michael, "Offa" in his *In Search of the Dark Ages*, London: BBC Books, 1981; New York: Facts on File, 1987

Wormald, Patrick, "The Age of Offa and Alcuin" in *The Anglo-Saxons*, edited by James Campbell, Oxford: Phaidon, and Ithaca, New York: Cornell University Press, 1982

Wormald, Patrick, "In Search of Offa's 'Law-Code'" in *People and Places in Northern Europe, 500–1600: Essays in Honour of Peter Hayes Sawyer*, edited by Ian Wood and Niels Lund, Woodbridge, Suffolk and Rochester, New York: Boydell, 1991

King Offa was the most powerful Anglo-Saxon ruler before Alfred the Great. Claiming descent from a brother of King Penda, he established himself on the throne of Mercia by defeating an obscure rival named Beornred, and gradually built up a Mercian hegemony over southern England that remained more or less intact until his death in 796. Debate still centres on the extent of his power and the nature of his kingship: a ruthless warlord who imposed his will on weaker neighbours, or a skilful statesman who aspired to be king of a united England?

Until fairly recently the modern conception of Offa was defined largely by STENTON in a seminal paper on "The Supremacy of the Mercian Kings", and in greater depth in *Anglo-Saxon England*. Here Offa is rated as one of the greatest rulers of the Anglo-Saxon period. More than just a barbarian potentate with unchallengeable supremacy throughout the south of England, he was a statesman who presided over a sophisticated administrative machine and made an important contribution to the growth of English political unity. He was a force to be reckoned with in international politics, and the only ruler of his time to be treated as an equal by Charlemagne. Stenton's *Anglo-Saxon England* is still invaluable for the sheer depth of coverage and amount of detail provided, but as Keynes points out in "Changing Faces", "the paint on Stenton's magnificent portrait has begun to show its age". Stenton's article on the Mercian supremacy needs to be read with special care. Here he cites the evidence of royal charters that confer on Offa grandiose titles such as "king of the entire nation of the English" to argue that he claimed dominion over the whole of England. However, scholarship moves on and it is now known that these charters are 10th-century forgeries, and that in genuine 8th-century documents Offa is styled simply "king of the Mercians".

In "Changing Faces" KEYNES surveys the development of Offa's formidable reputation, dwelling on the crucial role played by monastic writers at St Albans, who in the 12th and 13th centuries defended and embellished the reputation of Offa, whom they regarded as the founder of their abbey. He then proceeds to a reassessment of Stenton's work and paints a rather different picture. Offa emerges as a brutal warlord: not so much a statesman with a conception of a united England, as a "species of Mercian octopus" with tentacles reaching out to smother the neighbouring peoples who could least resist. KEYNES amplifies this view in *The New Cambridge Medieval History*, and concentrates here especially on Offa's relationship with the kingdom of Wessex. He rejects Stenton's view of Wessex as "a large outlying province of the Mercian kingdom" and uses diplomatic and other evidence to show that West Saxon kings enjoyed a freedom of action that Offa refused to allow to other Anglo-Saxon rulers. Overall, the tide of current scholarly opinion would appear to be with Keynes when he argues that Offa remained fundamentally a king of the Mercians, and that it was left to the West Saxon kings of the 9th and 10th centuries to engender a sense of political unity and national consciousness among the Anglo-Saxons.

Yet to admit this is not to dismiss Offa as a mere brute and bully, and other writers since Stenton have preferred to concentrate on more edifying aspects of Offa's kingship. WALLACE-HADRILL emphasizes some elements of Offa's reign which suggest that he was a king who, like Charlemagne and Alfred, had an understanding of the proper duties of a Christian ruler. Thus Alcuin, the Northumbrian confidant of Charlemagne, sent Offa scholars and praised his commitment to wisdom, and Wallace-Hadrill speculates that he may have intended to establish his own palace school. He also points out parallel developments in English and Frankish ecclesiastical reform and sees Offa's anointing of his son Ecgfrith as a move, inspired by Carolingian practice, to buttress the legitimacy of his dynasty. The general picture is of a ruler whose power Charlemagne would have underestimated at his peril.

WORMALD goes "in search of Offa's law code", a document to which Alfred the Great refers in the preface to his own legislation and which is conventionally thought to have been lost. Wormald believes he has found it embedded in a capitulary that was promulgated in 786 under the auspices of Offa during the course of a legatine visit to England. This ingenious and controversial theory has profound implications, since if correct it reinforces Wallace-Hadrill's perception of Offa as a ruler who knew about the appropriate exercise of Christian kingship, and associates him with legislation that is similar in scope and spirit to Charlemagne's celebrated *Admonitio generalis*.

In one other way Offa emerges as a ruler of great vision and energy. As the architect of Offa's Dyke, he was responsible for the greatest public work of the whole Anglo-Saxon period. It is generally agreed that the dyke stands as evidence of Offa's ability to conscript manpower in very large numbers, which might suggest a high level of administrative efficiency. However, historians and archaeologists still disagree about the dyke's precise function. FOX, in his impressively thorough record of the archaeological fieldwork, regards it as a negotiated frontier between the Mercians and Welsh, a view which is echoed in *Anglo-Saxon England* by Stenton, who believes that Offa's ability to grasp the idea of a negotiated frontier enhances his standing as a ruler and statesman. More recently, the dyke has been interpreted as a more substantial defensive structure than formerly thought, which may imply that it was conceived not as a frontier, but as a continuous military barrier to prevent Welsh raids into Mercia. Recent discussions of the dyke include those by Frank Noble in *Offa's Dyke Reviewed* (edited by Margaret Gelling, 1983), and WORMALD in his chapter on "The Age of Offa and Alcuin".

Wormald's chapter also deserves mention as a very readable general survey. As well as a useful section on economic aspects of Offa's reign, including a consideration of the importance of trade and currency, it contains a large number of illustrations and photographs which help the reader to a better feeling for the material culture of the late 8th century. Finally, the general reader might wish to consult WOOD, whose entertainingly written chapter covers many of the important aspects of the reign, and provides an accessible way into some of the archaeology, though scholars will take issue with some of his more speculative flights of fancy and his tendency at times to push the evidence further than it can reasonably stretch.

ANDREW DENNIS TODD

Old Age

Botelho, Lynn and Pat Thane (editors), *Women and Ageing in British Society since 1500*, Harlow and New York: Pearson, 2001

Minois, George S., *History of Old Age from Antiquity to the Renaissance*, translated by Sarah Hanbury Tenison, Cambridge: Polity Press, and Chicago: University of Chicago Press, 1989 (French edition, 1987)

Pelling, Margaret and Richard M. Smith (editors), *Life, Death, and the Elderly: Historical Perspectives*, London and New York: Routledge, 1991

Quadagno, Jill S., *Aging in Early Industrial Society: Work, Family, and Social Policy in Nineteenth-Century England*, New York: Academic Press, 1982

Rosenthal, Joel T., *Old Age in Late Medieval England*, Philadelphia: University of Pennsylvania Press, 1996

Shahar, Shulamith, *Growing Old in the Middle Ages: "Winter Clothes Us in Shadow and Pain"*, translated by Yael Lotan, London and New York: Routledge, 1997 (Hebrew edition, 1995)

Thane, Pat, *Old Age in English History: Past Experiences, Present Issues*, Oxford and New York: Oxford University Press, 2000

Thomas, Keith, "Age and Authority in Early Modern England", *Proceedings of the British Academy*, 62 (1976): 3–46

It was once believed that the history of old age could not be written, because ageing was essentially a private, undocumented experience. Some questioned whether the aged were even numerous enough to constitute a distinct social group. Over the last 20 years, however, creative use of a variety of primary sources, cultural, legal, personal, and medical, has illuminated the historical construction, status, and experiences of the elderly. Historians who write about old age agree that it is not a fixed category, but rather was culturally constructed (generally negatively), and that the status of the elderly in the past varied considerably. Old age did not begin at a predetermined point in one's life: it depended on status, security, health, and gender.

THOMAS, in an article still frequently cited, debunks the romanticized view of a golden pre-industrial past in which the aged were embraced by community and family, venerated for their wisdom, and held the balance of property and power. Instead, he argues that only those few who maintained fierce control over wealth and property managed to escape the ridicule and victimization of a highly ageist culture. Through a wide reading of cultural texts, Thomas also finds that there were ambiguities in the portrayal of old age, with some writers

emphasizing the experience and authority, and others the wretched degeneration of the aged.

This attention to the social construction of the elderly in literary culture remains popular. SHAHAR focuses on the ambiguous attitudes to the aged in a wide range of printed texts that both reverenced and ridiculed the elderly. She explores the cultural debates about the definitions and duties of the aged, and the symbolic weight their elderly bodies had to bear. Criticized for an insufficiently developed critical approach, and for blurring distinctions between England and the Continent, and over five centuries, Shahar is still successful in presenting the symbolic and religious context of the aged in medieval society. She also addresses the differences between cultural stereotypes and personal reality among the aged in a variety of social positions, including clergy, soldiers, statesmen, townspeople, and peasants.

To answer questions about demography and longevity in the late medieval period, ROSENTHAL examines death records, depositions, wills, and genealogies to devise a "soft demography", tracking age attestations and three-generation families to determine the impact of the aged on their communities. Rosenthal, more concerned with the lived experience than the literary portrayal of the aged, concludes that the elderly were ubiquitous and often able to maintain their status despite cultural representations to the contrary.

Historians of later periods have shifted attention to questions of welfare, family life, and dependency, challenging the "modernization theory" that claims industrialization cost the elderly their place in family units, and charting the development of institutional and state support of pensioners. Writing largely a 19th-century economic history of the elderly, QUADAGNO argues that such changes were in fact the consequence of a new working-class voice in government. She rightly asserts that old age should be studied in its economic and political context, but her insistence on linking the elderly so thoroughly with a discussion of poverty and financial destitution, as passive recipients of state support, limits the range of activities and agency of the aged. Froide's article in Botelho & Thane suggests an alternative view that old age can be a positive time of "autonomy, activity, and authority" for those in the middling ranks.

PELLING & SMITH's collection also focuses mainly on the welfare of the aged, and also grants them considerable agency. Using an impressive array of social history sources, the contributors to this volume find that instead of depending on family alone, the elderly up until the end of the 19th century attempted to maintain their homes and independence through work, charity, and marital relationships, in conjunction with whatever state support was available. In their valuable introduction, Pelling & Smith offer a synthesis of previous work and point the way to new areas, such as the history of medical treatment of the aged.

The most promising new area, however, is the intersection of gender history with studies of old age. Despite the fact that the majority of the elderly have been female, nearly all work to date has focused on representations of male ageing, and the lives of elderly men of import, particularly political leaders and members of the clergy. Women's historians have typically overlooked elderly women, focusing instead on life stages in the reproductive cycle. BOTELHO & THANE redress this gap with a collection of ten articles on such topics as the remarrying widow, old maids, menopause, and female household goods. The contributors to this volume prove that older women's lives are amply illuminated by wills, parish registers, censuses, diaries, inventories, and oral histories. The themes of welfare and poverty, residency patterns, work, and health are examined through a female lens, proving that gender did affect the experience of old age. Kugler's article on the 18th-century diarist Sarah Cowper demonstrates that the elderly engaged actively with cultural stereotypes of old age, both employing and resisting such images as it suited their purpose. Botelho & Thane also provide a bibliographical essay that is a very useful starting-point for any investigation.

Finally, there have been two notable attempts to write comprehensive histories of old age. The work of MINOIS has attracted much attention to the field; he draws on a very wide range of literary sources to show that the status of the elderly cannot be categorized according to a linear progression. He sees a general tendency toward loss of status, especially during periods of historical stability, but his conclusions are necessarily impressionistic and serve more to emphasize the inherent multiplicity and ambiguity of experiences of being old.

THANE also challenges a simplistic view of old age. Based on a survey of secondary literature rather than on extensive primary research, Thane is limited by previous historians' choices of themes, approaches, and time periods. Her premodern chapters deal mostly with cultural representations of the aged, while her chapters on the modern period, which would benefit from similar insights, focus instead on the campaign for old age pensions and the emergence of the pensioner as a new social category. For Thane, increased state support and 20th-century medical advances have allowed the elderly to live contented, independent, socially relevant lives.

AKI CHANDRA LI BEAM

Oldcastle, Sir John c.1378–1417
Leader of the lollards

McFarlane, Kenneth B., *John Wycliffe and the Beginnings of English Nonconformity*, London: English Universities Press, 1952; New York: Macmillan, 1953; as *The Origins of Religious Dissent in England*, New York: Collier Books, 1966; as *Wycliffe and English Nonconformity*, Harmondsworth and New York: Penguin, 1972

Powell, Edward, *Kingship, Law, and Society: Criminal Justice in the Reign of Henry V*, Oxford: Clarendon Press, and New York: Oxford University Press, 1989

Tait, James, entry on "Sir John Oldcastle" in *Dictionary of National Biography*, edited by Leslie Stephen, vol. 42, London: Smith Elder, 1895

Waugh, W.T., "Sir John Oldcastle", *English Historical Review*, 20 (1905): 434–56, 637–58

The Reformation gave birth to two disparate images of the lollard Sir John Oldcastle: to protestant polemicists he was a martyr for the true faith, while in other hands the arch-heretic was transmuted into Prince Hal's roistering boon-companion – Shakespeare's Falstaff. These contradictory constructions of Oldcastle have had some bearing on modern historiography.

TAIT certainly felt the need to dispell the myths both of the "good Lord Cobham" and of the dissolute old knight in his article, which steers a sure course between these rhetorical poles. He notes that John Bale's *Chronicle*, published in 1544 and with John Foxe's *Acts and Monuments* the major source for Oldcastle as "protestant martyr", was informed by Archbishop Arundel's official contemporary account of his career, and so should not be entirely dismissed as a source for Oldcastle's life. However, he takes issue with Bale's and Foxe's attempts to deny the existence of the 1414 lollard rising, or at least Oldcastle's leading role in it, declaring that neither can be "seriously doubted, though the evidence is imperfect, and their treason is perhaps painted blacker than it was".

Ten years after Tait's brief sketch came what is still the standard work on Oldcastle: in his article WAUGH broadly agrees with Tait's depiction of the erstwhile protestant hero "as a commonplace knight whose renown is merely due to his connexion with an unpopular sect". Waugh is able to add much flesh to the bones of Tait's account through his use of a range of records (including some unpublished manuscripts) to supplement the chronicle accounts and Arundel's "official version". These last he treats with circumspection, preferring the parliament roll's account of the 1410 parliament to that of Walsingham's chronicle, but accepting Arundel as broadly trustworthy. The document purporting to be Oldcastle's abjuration, which Bale simply dismissed as a forgery, Waugh believes may have been a draft prepared in case Oldcastle should have relented while in custody. While he doubts the more sensational contemporary accusations made after the 1414 rising – that Oldcastle intended to slaughter the royal family and rule in their place, instigating a general disendowment of the church – he is in no doubt that the rising did take place broadly as described by contemporary sources, and that Oldcastle was its leader. He cannot believe "that a man of Henry V's nature would butcher more than 40 of his subjects merely for the purpose of discrediting a small section of the nation". While some later historians might have been less charitably disposed towards Henry, most agree with Waugh on this point. Opinion has also held with Waugh's characterization of the rising as being only partially motivated by lollardy, since most of those executed suffered as traitors, not heretics, and in his estimation many joined in hope of plunder rather than reform. Waugh's final judgement on Oldcastle is overwhelmingly negative: a man of undoubted courage, he was nevertheless of limited intellectual ability, with little feel for diplomacy, and "by his attempt to restore the waning hopes of his sect he did more to discredit its teaching than any one before or after him".

McFARLANE freely acknowledges his debt to Waugh, with whose interpretation he broadly concurs, although he is more inclined to believe that Oldcastle's plan amounted to a full-scale revolution: "it is difficult to see how they could safely have done less . . . It could hardly have been greater folly than their conqueror's first invasion of France." The major innovation in McFarlane, however, is his use of the presentments made to the commissioners appointed immediately after the collapse of the 1414 rising. From this material he is able to identify the major recruiting grounds for the rebels, and uncover something of their organization, including the crucial role played by unbeneficed clergy, leading him to conclude that there was a reasonably high level of central direction to the revolt.

A substantial body of research on lollardy separates McFarlane's account from POWELL's, and the latter draws upon the work of Aston, Hudson, and others to place the Oldcastle rebellion in a clearer context. For Powell, its origins lay in a reformist movement that grew out of a well-established debate on clerical reform and which was securely grounded in John Wyclif's teachings. Powell follows McFarlane's lead by subjecting the evidence of the presentments to a systematic and detailed analysis, and from this concludes that while only a fraction of the entire lollard community answered the call to arms, those who did were more likely to be unbeneficed clergy, artisans, or small traders – with a stiffening of gentry – than McFarlane's "rustic simpletons". He suggests that Oldcastle's violent challenge to secular authority alienated the greater part of the lollard community, many of whom were pacifist and looked to the king to bring about a "reformation from above". Further, he speculates – a little more tentatively – that the rising was partly motivated by Oldcastle's personal feud with Henry V. Having been a member of the prince's household, and once having looked to him as the potential champion of reform, Oldcastle was disappointed in the new king and shocked when his lord refused to save him from the consequences of his own actions. By 1414, denied the protection of his royal patron, he felt he had no choice but to rebel, and as a faithful vassal unjustly scorned, he felt justified in so doing. Such a "feudal" interpretation, while it has definite echoes of Falstaff and Shakespeare's newly crowned King Henry, does also accord with recent work emphasizing the importance of chivalric culture and ideals to later medieval politics. Powell stresses the importance of the revolt's collapse for the debate on clerical disendowment – not to surface again until the 16th century – and crucially for the growth of royal authority, since the church concluded from this episode (probably mistakenly) that it could not protect itself from the threat of lollardy without the full might of the secular arm: "The real victor of the revolt was the king and his dynasty."

PETER FLEMING

See also Henry IV; Henry V; Lollardy; Wyclif(fe)

O'Neill, Hugh, 3rd Earl of Tyrone

1550–1616
Soldier and Gaelic rebel leader

Canny, Nicholas, "Hugh O'Neill, Earl of Tyrone and the Changing Face of Gaelic Ulster", *Studia Hibernica*, 10/1 (1970): 7–35
Falls, Cyril, *Elizabeth's Irish Wars*, London: Methuen, 1950; reprinted, London: Methuen, and New York: Barnes and Noble, 1970
McGurk, John, *The Elizabethan Conquest of Ireland: The 1590s Crisis*, Manchester and New York: Manchester University Press, 1997
Morgan, Hiram, *Tyrone's Rebellion: The Outbreak of the Nine Years' War in Tudor Ireland*, Woodbridge, Suffolk: Boydell Press for the Royal Historical Society, and Rochester, New York: Boydell, 1993
O'Faoláin, Seán, *The Great O'Neill: A Biography of Hugh O'Neill, Earl of Tyrone, 1550–1616*, London: Longmans Green, and New York: Duell, Sloan and Pearce, 1942; reprinted, Cork: Mercier Press, 1970
Walsh, Micheline Kerney, *Destruction by Peace: Hugh O'Neill after Kinsale, Glaucoucadhaim 1602–Rome 1616*, Dublin: Cumann Seanchais Ard Mhacha, 1986; as *An Exile of Ireland: Hugh O'Neill, Prince of Ulster*, Dublin and Portland, Oregon: Four Courts Press, 1996

With a popular image that ranges from the romantic to the Machiavellian, Hugh O'Neill's historical persona remains nearly as enigmatic and impenetrable today as he was to his contemporaries in the late 16th and early 17th centuries. O'Neill's pivotal role in the Irish transition from Gaelic tradition to English authority has attracted the extra-historical notice of many literary writers. Our fragmented understanding of this historical character, however, is the result of a wide array of Irish, English, and continental sources that defy easy incorporation.

It is this particular limitation that explains the flawed nature of the most prominent attempt at a personal biography of O'Neill, Seán O'FAOLÁIN's popular narrative. Despite his stated intention of "de-mythologizing" this romantic persona, O'Faoláin instead falls into a highly stylized narrative of his own, which differs from the standard 19th-century accounts only through the influence of an early revisionist treatise on the Earl of Tyrone. O'Faoláin's melodramatic style makes for quick reading, but his imagination overwhelms his historical evidence, and readers are presented with long-winded treatments of events that never actually occurred, such as O'Neill's supposed education at the Elizabethan court. Perhaps the truest value of this work comes in providing the reader with an appreciation of the great strides made by Irish and British historiography over the half-century since its composition.

Although Cyril FALLS's account of late 16th-century campaigns in Ireland falls prey to earlier idealized views of Elizabeth's reign, his work still represents a more professional historical treatment than O'Faoláin's literary drama. Writing as a military historian, Falls synthesizes the existing Homeric accounts of individual contests, which historians have previously overlooked as "a series of obscure and savage combats and skirmishes in bog and forest". Falls's incorporation of a number of military sources also reminds his readers of the international significance of the campaigns. His main problem, however, is his acceptance of the traditional conception of the Elizabethan era as some sort of golden age that witnessed the creation of what would become the British empire. This teleology dismisses Irish attempts at resistance with the Whiggish understanding that the ensuing destruction in Ireland stemmed from the natives' ill-considered struggle against English imperial destiny. Free from the budding post-colonial misgivings of his day, Falls's reactionary stance reduces Ireland to little more than a colonial testing-ground where the founding fathers of empire developed their efficient and effective methods of expansion. Nevertheless, although Falls never questions the gilded picture of Elizabethan England, he goes to greater lengths than his predecessors in applying historical methods to his integration of existing primary accounts.

John McGURK's contribution shares Falls's concentration on the Elizabethan expansion of English authority in Ireland, but his less celebratory account of Elizabethan government makes for a more plausible treatment of the Elizabethan campaigns. McGurk's account focuses on the military, financial, and political strains on the crown that resulted from the attempts to subdue Ireland. Furthermore, he effectively links these costs to the fateful policy of confiscation and plantation in former strongholds of Gaelic Ireland. McGurk presents an impressive survey of English state records, utilizing the minutiae of quarter sessions, pay records, and other purely administrative accounts to document the cost of the imposition of English authority in Ireland. In the end, he also clearly points out that this was a price paid by the Irish inhabitants. Although his statistical summary of the Elizabethan campaigns fails to account for less quantifiable motivations behind colonialism, the usefulness of his work extends beyond the realm of the specialist in his account of how and why English colonialism meant the sowing of dragon's teeth in Irish soil.

Nicholas CANNY's article is notable for his analysis of O'Neill's career in Gaelic politics, centralizing Irish traditional authority with an institutional foresight that very nearly succeeds. Canny contests the notion that Gaelic unity could only come under the threat of English military invasion as he describes O'Neill's continued efforts at institutionalized reform following O'Neill's surrender to the Elizabethan commander Mountjoy in 1603. This thorough exploration of similar attempts by earlier O'Neill chieftains, Shane and Turlough Luneach, convey the limited foresight of Hugh's contemporaries, making his innovations all the more remarkable, despite their interruption in 1607. By moving beyond the Whiggish view of a hopelessly moribund Gaelic society in the early 17th century, Canny restores the O'Neills' active role in resisting the encroachment of English authority. Canny's reliance on the distorted pictures offered by the notoriously corrupt English speculators and "undertakers" leads him to overstatement, and he fails to offer a plausible explanation why O'Neill would have abandoned his work to flee Ireland in 1607. Nevertheless, Canny's thorough examination of Gaelic Ulster in the late 16th and early 17th centuries offers a sorely needed account of the courses of action available to the Gaelic Irish.

Micheline Kerney WALSH's work begins with the so-called "Flight of the Earls", although she contests this very name in her attempt to explain O'Neill's departure as a strategic retreat. Walsh's *Destruction by Peace*, and its later edition, *An Exile of Ireland: Hugh O'Neill, Prince of Ulster*, both begin with O'Neill leaving Ireland under duress, faced with imminent arrest and imprisonment by the English. Walsh stresses that O'Neill never intended a permanent departure from his native land, though, and cites numerous letters and documents as evidence of his persistence. His constant appeals to the king of Spain and the pope only brought disappointment, yet Walsh insists that O'Neill's desire to return never waned, and the conventional image of him as a defeated refugee from a lost world stems from propaganda tracts issued by the English court. Although Walsh's continental research represents an unprecedented examination of Spanish and papal archival material, her thesis seems naively to accept at face value O'Neill's words, as well as those of his capricious correspondents. Walsh needs to look beyond Tyrone's correspondence in assessing the sincerity of this often duplicitous figure. In addition, her account should be seen as coinciding with the steady, irreversible encroachment of English authority in O'Neill's former land after 1607.

Finally, Hiram MORGAN's recent work on the Nine Years' War stands in a class of its own for several reasons. Morgan's historiographical treatment of the existing body of work on Hugh O'Neill demonstrates a finely tuned critical ability to assess the respective strengths and weaknesses of the preceeding body of work. This same perspicacious sense governs his use of primary sources, including an impressive range of material from Irish, English, and continental accounts. Morgan's work places O'Neill's rebellion in a new European context by comparing Gaelic resistance to Elizabethan authority in Ireland with the Dutch opposition to Spanish rule in the Low Countries. As do almost all the other works cited here, Morgan's account concentrates on one portion of O'Neill's life: here, the Nine Years' War. Nonetheless, his insight into this historical event offers to us the best chance yet to assess, if not to understand, the motivations of this remarkable historical figure.

MATTHEW J. O'BRIEN

See also Nine Years' War

Opera and Operetta, Rise of

Cannadine, David, "Gilbert and Sullivan: The Making and Un-Making of a British 'Tradition'" in *Myths of the English*, edited by Roy Porter, Cambridge: Polity Press, 1992

Cowgill, Rachel, "'Wise Men from the East': Mozart's Operas and Their Advocates in Early Nineteenth-Century London" in *Music and British Culture, 1785–1914: Essays in Honour of Cyril Ehrlich*, edited by Christina Bashford and Leanne Langley, Oxford and New York: Oxford University Press, 2000

Fiske, Roger, *English Theatre Music in the Eighteenth Century*, Oxford and New York: Oxford University Press, 1973

Hunter, David, "Patronizing Handel, Inventing Audiences: The Intersections of Class, Money, Music, and History", *Early Music*, 28/1 (2000): 32–49

Milhous, Judith, Gabriella Dideriksen, and Robert D. Hume, *Italian Opera in Late Eighteenth-Century London*, vol. 2, *The Pantheon Opera and Its Aftermath 1789–1795*, Oxford: Clarendon Press, and New York: Oxford University Press, 2001

Nalbach, Daniel, *The King's Theatre 1704–1867: London's First Italian Opera House,* London: The Society for Theatre Research, 1972

Price, Curtis, Judith Milhous, and Robert D. Hume, *Italian Opera in Late Eighteenth-Century London*, vol. 1, *The King's Theatre, Haymarket 1778–1791*, Oxford: Clarendon Press, and New York: Oxford University Press, 1995

Sadie, Stanley (editor), *The New Grove Dictionary of Opera*, 4 vols, London: Macmillan Reference, and New York: Grove's Dictionaries of Music, 1992

Weber, William, "L'Institution et son public: l'Opéra à Paris et à Londres au XVIIIe siècle" [The Institution and Its Public: The Opera in Paris and London in the 18th Century], *Annales*, 6 (1993): 1519–39

White, Eric Walter, *A History of English Opera*, London: Faber, 1983

Until recently, much of the work on the history of opera and operetta in Britain was conducted by music and theatre scholars, who were naturally more attentive to the issues important in their fields – illuminating changes in composition and performance practices; charting the architectural and institutional history of the opera houses; and paying close attention to casting, staging, and production patterns – than to the kinds of historiographical debates familiar to historians. In the past few years, however, a small number of scholars have begun to pay closer attention to the social, political, and cultural contexts for the performance of opera and operetta in Britain. The most rigorous and inventive scholarship in recent years has focused on 18th-century opera, with growing attention to the 19th century and much less interest in the 20th century. The literature still favours London over theatres and travelling companies in the provinces or in Wales, Scotland, or Ireland.

The multivolume work edited by SADIE and written by a host of well-known scholars is the best starting-point for novices and specialists alike. Its substantial entry on "London" provides the most up-to-date summary of recent scholarship on the institutional history of the theatres. Although it provides thorough coverage of continental composers, it gives less priority to their English counterparts. It also includes short biographical entries on singers and managers (but almost none on music critics), and its entries on "seating" and the "sociology of opera" provide background on the audience and broader sociopolitical context. Extensive bibliographies following each entry list the most important articles, books, and dissertations on the topic, including published primary sources. A substantial discussion of music critics and the press's coverage of both English and Italian opera from 1785 to 1830 can be found in WHITE.

The available surveys tend to provide narrative chronicles rather than sustained arguments but are nonetheless essential to anyone working in this field. White's history of English opera focuses on the most important composers but also addresses the many failed national opera schemes in the 19th century. His coverage of the 16th- and early-17th-century origins of English opera, and his history of the genre from Sir William Davenant's *The Siege of Rhodes* (1656) to the collaborative operettas of Gilbert and Sullivan, created in 1871–96, is more extensive than his discussion of the 20th century. Unlike White's book, FISKE's more focused treatment of English theatre music in the 18th century furnishes readers with discussions of the plots, tracing the shift from ancient to modern settings, and careful analysis of as much of the music as has survived, whether in published or manuscript form. His book demonstrates the centrality of musical numbers at the dramatic theatres: at Covent Garden in 1747–76, for instance, four of the seven most popular mainpieces were operas, not plays.

While the dramatic theatres, which performed English opera, attracted a broad range of spectators, it was mainly the aristocracy, gentry, and wealthy who patronized the Italian opera in the 18th and early 19th centuries. As the sole book surveying the institutional history of the King's Theatre, which secured an exclusive license to perform Italian opera for much of its history, NALBACH's book provides a useful starting-point: it focuses on the theatre's architecture, management, casts, audience, and production. However, PRICE, MILHOUS & HUME and MILHOUS, DIDERIKSEN & HUME, who have combed the archives for new sources, have uncovered a number of errors and omissions in Nalbach's narrative. These books, a two-volume set on the history of Italian opera in London, 1778–95, provide the best account of the day-to-day workings of an 18th-century theatre yet to be published. An interdisciplinary project, the set closely examines both the operas and ballets produced at the King's Theatre and at a rival company that started out at the Pantheon Theatre, as well as their architectural histories. It also reconstructs in remarkable detail the costumes, lighting, and staffs of these two companies and clearly explains the complex history of their management and finances. More than any previous work, it shows how operas were adapted to suit the audience's tastes and the singers' voices and egos. The fascinating story of how the Pantheon was imagined as a kind of court theatre backed by the lord chamberlain and the Duke of Bedford, with the support of the Prince of Wales, marks an important discovery. In all likelihood, its backers authorized arson to cut their losses after two financially disastrous seasons. Because of the high level of detail and the encyclopedic coverage of the repertoire, specialists will find it more accessible than students, and it is unfortunate that the authors did not do more to fill out the socio-political context for the opera's enormous popularity among the elite in the late 18th century.

Work that has been more attentive to the opera's broader historical context in the 18th century has addressed the persistence of aristocratic patronage. HUNTER criticizes Handel scholars who have maintained that Handel created his oratorios for the middle classes. Hunter relies on the most recent historical writing on the nature of class in British history to demonstrate not only how small the middling order was in Handel's day, but also that the admission prices at the King's Theatre (where many of Handel's operas were performed) and at Handel's oratorio concerts were too high for the middling classes to afford. Hunter also points to the many ways Handel cultivated and relied upon aristocratic and royal patronage for the production of his operas, even though his works were performed in commercial venues. WEBER's article investigates the ways the political culture of London and Paris helped shape the administrative structures of their opera houses in the 18th century. He argues that the resurgence of the British aristocracy in the 18th century, especially with the establishment of the Whig oligarchy, facilitated aristocratic influence at the opera: noblemen helped run the King's Theatre for much of the period from the 1720s through mid-century and revived their interest in the opera house by the 1780s. Although the French nobility also flocked to the opera house, absolutist politics and the relative weakness of the nobility meant that the elite exerted far less influence over operatic affairs than in London: in Paris the opera became a bureaucratic extension of the state largely run by musicians and a few entrepreneurs. While this development opened the way for French intellectuals to play an important role in the operatic *querelles* of the 18th century, the cultural authority of the aristocracy at the King's Theatre effectively impeded any substantial involvement by literary figures.

While Hunter and Weber minimize the influence of the middling sorts on the opera, COWGILL argues that musical taste may have been dividing along class lines by the early 19th century. Her essay addresses the institutional reasons for the belated performance of Mozart's operas in London. She demonstrates that a small group of musicians and bourgeois amateurs from the City used their connections with German merchants in the 1800s to acquire scores of Mozart's operas and perform them in private. On nights when the King's Theatre finally began staging his operas, press coverage in the 1810s and 1820s suggested that businessmen from the City flocked to the opera house while the fashionable classes stayed away.

CANNADINE's essay, which examines the collaborative works of Gilbert and Sullivan as one of many examples of an invented national tradition in the late 19th century, contributes to scholars' understanding of how operetta attracted a middle-class audience. He shows how Gilbert and Sullivan adapted some of the stylistic traditions predominant in earlier working-class theatres to the values of the late Victorian bourgeoisie. In addition to ensuring that their operas were morally respectable, Gilbert and Sullivan drew on some of the main political and economic developments of their day as a means of upholding the traditional order and strengthening national pride. While they omitted references to the social problems so evident to most contemporaries and usually ended their operas with order restored, Cannadine nonetheless argues that their plots tended to suggest the possibility of a world turned upside down, just what many middle-class Britons feared. If these operas were so deeply rooted in the particularities of the late 19th century, Cannadine asks, how did they become such a vital national icon in the 20th century? Part of the answer, he maintains, is that because the D'Oyly Carte family, who held the performance rights into the 1950s, insisted that they be performed as originally written, they took on the aura of an ahistorical tradition, even though that tradition was only decades old. Moreover, events during much of the 20th century continued to resonate with the themes in the Gilbert and Sullivan repertoire; only in the 1980s and 1990s, when Britons began to re-evaluate their relationship with their past, was this invented tradition challenged in any substantial way.

Historians have long shied away from writing about music because it is so much more difficult for laymen to analyse than other artistic forms. However, in the 18th and early 19th centuries many of Britain's aristocrats were arguably more engaged with opera than with most other art forms. And although the history of how the opera was able to accommodate a growing middle-class audience has yet to be written, it promises to shed further light on the complicated subject of class relations in the 19th and 20th centuries.

JENNIFER L. HALL-WITT

See also Music: Instrumental and Operatic

Opium Wars   1839–1842 and 1856–1860

Chang, Hsin-pao, *Commissioner Lin and the Opium War*, Cambridge, Massachusetts: Harvard University Press, 1964

Fairbank, John King, *Trade and Diplomacy on the China Coast: The Opening of the Treaty Ports, 1842–1854*, 2 vols, Cambridge, Massachusetts: Harvard University Press, 1953

Graham, Gerald S., *The China Station: War And Diplomacy, 1830–1860*, Oxford: Clarendon Press, and New York: Oxford University Press, 1978

Gregory, J.S., *Great Britain and the Taipings*, Canberra: Australian National University Press, and New York: Praeger, and London: Routledge and Kegan Paul, 1969

Wong, J.Y., *Deadly Dreams: Opium, Imperialism, and the Arrow War (1856–1860) in China*, Cambridge and New York: Cambridge University Press, 1996

The two Anglo-Chinese wars of the mid 19th-century were outstanding examples of Lord Palmerston's commercial diplomacy, which supported clear objectives with the threat, and actuality, of overwhelming force, to open hitherto closed or tightly restricted markets to British commerce. In both wars major new technologies provided a cutting edge for small, dynamic maritime forces, using sea power to move around the coast and major rivers. Steamships outmanoeuvred existing Chinese coastal forts, while small army units using modern infantry tactics, with or without rifles, easily brushed aside the medieval capabilities of the Chinese troops. It is important to stress that as recently as 1833 a British commercial mission had been rebuffed at Canton, in humiliating circumstances, apparently lacking the power to deal with China.

Changing fashions in scholarship reflect the steady rise of modern China to become a major power, and the relative decline of Britain, together with the increasing use of Chinese language sources. The official Chinese perspective on these conflicts concentrates on the iniquity of the British action, and the heroic response of village communities, in contrast to the supine national leadership.

It is essential to recognize the degree to which both wars in China were concerned with the East India Company, and the economy of the empire. In 1839–42 the bulk of all troops deployed were company soldiers, or British regiments based in India, while the steamships that enabled the fleet to penetrate the great rivers were all company vessels. In 1856–60 the war had to be suspended while the Indian mutiny was suppressed, and the consequent shortage of troops may well account for the failure at the Taku Forts in 1859.

FAIRBANK remains the basis of modern scholarship on the wars, and provides a long-term context for the conflict, stressing Chinese problems with the alarming inflation of the price of silver, due to the drain of coin to pay for opium, and the social concerns over the impact of the drug in society. By focusing on the development of trade this study emphasizes the core issues. Fairbank also assesses the ability of the Chinese to respond to the new challenges, in the light of previous experience, and their assumptions about the Western barbarians.

Although he largely follows Fairbank, CHANG develops the Chinese perspective. He argues that the dramatic increase in opium smuggling forced the Chinese authorities to act, to meet the social chaos caused by widespread addiction, and that the British response was driven by economic need, and greatly influenced by Jardine, Matheson, and other commercial houses. WONG develops this approach in his examination of the origins of the second war, which he attributes to the failure of the first to match up to the hopes of the British, and Chinese duplicity over diplomatic and economic concessions supposedly enshrined in the treaty of Nanking of 1842. His detailed research and challenging conclusions widen historical understanding of the nature of Victorian Imperialism, and stress the free-trade agenda of the Liberal ministry. This approach reflected the cost and strategic problems caused by the expansion of territorial landholdings in India. Wong establishes that Lord Palmerston, as foreign secretary and then as prime minister, was the principal architect of the Opium (or China) wars. In 1839 he was prepared to use force to secure trade concessions from China, to support the economy of India, and with it the imperial financial system. The importance of opium, as the only import the Chinese would buy in sufficient quantities to offset the cost of tea, has lent the war a more sinister character than it had at the time.

In 1856 the Crimean war had just ended, leaving Britain with the specialist naval power for inshore offensive operations, notably steam gunboat flotillas. With the Taiping rebellion raging China was in no position to resist. Palmerston opened discussions with France, the United States, and even Russia to prepare for war, and ensured that a key local official at Canton knew of the need for war. Consequently a crisis was manufactured over the seizure of a local vessel. Censured in the House of Commons, Palmerston called a snap election, and utterly defeated his radical opponents who had completely misjudged the national mood. GRAHAM provides a narrative history from Palmerston's first fumbling effort to open China for trade in the early 1830s through to the ultimate success of the second war. This provides an imperial context, and a degree of continuity that more specific approaches to the wars lack. It does not use Chinese-language material.

GREGORY examines the British response to the pseudo-Christian messianic Taiping rebellion. This provided an opportunity for Britain to further her interests. The Taipings undermined central authority in the coastal cities, while drawing ever more attention to the area through the general rise in lawlessness, and especially piracy. The British seriously considered recognizing the Taiping as the legitimate government, but their interest waned when they realized that the Taiping were no more interested in free trade than the Manchu authorities, and far less capable of organizing the state. After suppressing piracy, and forcing the Chinese to accept a harsh peace in 1860, the British were content to uphold their trading interests, while promoting similar trading patterns in other Asian states, notably Thailand and Japan.

ANDREW DAVID LAMBERT

Oral History: Sources and Uses

Chamberlain, Mary and Paul Thompson (editors), *Narrative and Genre*, London and New York: Routledge, 1998

Evans, George Ewart, *The Crooked Scythe: An Anthology of Oral History*, edited and illustrated by David Gentleman, London: Faber, 1993

Finnegan, Ruth, *Oral Traditions and the Verbal Arts: A Guide to Research Practices*, London and New York: Routledge, 1992

Perks, Robert and Alistair Thomson (editors), *The Oral History Reader*, London and New York: Routledge, 1998

Portelli, Alessandro, *The Death of Luigi Trastulli and Other Stories: Form and Meaning in Oral History*, Albany: State University of New York Press, 1991

Samuel, Raphael and Paul Thompson (editors), *The Myths We Live By*, London and New York: Routledge, 1990

Thompson, Paul, *The Voice of the Past: Oral History*, Oxford and New York: Oxford University Press, 1978; 3rd edition, 2000

Yow, Valerie Raleigh, *Recording Oral History: A Practical Guide for Social Scientists*, London and Thousand Oaks, California: Sage, 1994

Oral history, to quote Ronald Grele, is "the interviewing of eyewitness participants in the events of the past for the purposes of historical reconstruction". Increasingly, electronic media like video or tape recordings capture the interviews. Those historians of modern Britain who use oral history, and many do not for diverse methodological reasons, increasingly recognize that what flows from those interviewed is, in the words of Shaun Nethercott and Neil Leighton, "the tale of events, mediated by memory and shaped by performance". Historians normally utilize oral history to complement, or counter, the evidence found through their study of documentary sources. Linked to the growth of oral history has been a rigorous debate about the value and meaning of historical evidence, partly stemming from a perceived need among historians to continue to justify the use of oral testimony, as the acceptance of its use is not universal.

Oral history has blossomed since the 1960s and there has been a consequent response by various institutions to the archival requirements, and dissemination, of the accumulated material. The oral history section of the British Library's National Sound Archive in London holds the national collection of oral history. This includes the National Life Story Collection (started in 1987), the Millennium Memory Bank, and recordings deposited by many organizations that embrace, among other subjects, BBC sound archive recordings, food, dialect, medicine, politics, various occupational groups, musicians, and artists. Other national collections are connected to the Museum of Welsh Life near Cardiff, the South Wales Coalfield Collection/Miners Library in Swansea, and the School of Scottish Studies, Edinburgh University. There are also significant holdings at the Essex Oral History Archive (University of Essex), the Imperial War Museum's Department of Sound Archives in London, the Modern Records Collection of Warwick University, the Institute of Criminology at the University of Cambridge, and the Mass-Observation Archive at Sussex University. In 1994 the Economic and Social Research Council's

Qualitative Data Archival Resource Centre (Qualidata) was set up within the Department of Sociology at Essex University to support the archiving of qualitative research data, and raise awareness of the existence and possible applications of this data.

Additionally, since the 1970s, the library services of most major British cities and county archives have accumulated their own collections. These have come from community radio sources, the field recordings of local historians, and via oral history projects located within the relevant area. For example, the Centre for Oxfordshire Studies at Oxford's main library holds over 3500 tapes, videos, and transcriptions concerning activities, events, and people in the county. Such archives not only provide a valuable resource for the historian but, critically, provide a vehicle for protecting and conserving recordings.

The (British) Oral History Society first met in December 1969 and its journal has been published since 1970. Oral history was not an unknown entity, having been used in America by Allan Nevins of Columbia University in the 1940s and in British folk-life studies, like the innovative work undertaken by EVANS amid Suffolk farm workers. However, the subsequent application of oral historical study in Britain has been of greatest appeal to those (such as the History Workshop collective) interested in "history from below", and the recovery of the otherwise lost histories of communities, trades, and individuals that would not normally attract the attention of written history. In 1975, three publications appeared that together mark a watershed for the status of oral history within British historiography. These were Paul Thompson's *The Edwardians: The Remaking of British Society*; *Village Life and Labour* edited by Raphael Samuel; and *Fenwomen: A Portrait of Women in an English Village* by Mary Chamberlain. In these illuminating works the authors employ oral history to enhance the evidence gleaned from more traditional historical research methods. The British oral history community has shown a readiness to engage in, and learn and develop from, an energetic discourse carried on with international colleagues. Consequently, publications such as PORTELLI's brilliantly astute work, with its emphasis on deconstructing the memories of a historical event in terms of their symbolic, psychological, and chronological functions, has had a discernable impact on the course of British oral history.

THOMPSON is the standard introductory text, now in its third edition, by one of the leading British pioneers of oral history. Thompson cogently and enthusiastically places the development of British oral historiography within the wider context of Western historiography, discusses devising and undertaking an oral history project, the interpretation and assessment of oral sources, and how to "make history" from them.

Three important anthologies of oral historiography appeared during the 1990s. The essays in SAMUEL & THOMPSON, presented at the International Oral History Conference on "Myth and History" held at Oxford in 1987, represent a critical moment in the discipline's evolution, concentrating on the misunderstandings, substitutions, and exclusions in narrative history that create myths in collective and individual reminiscence. Likewise, CHAMBERLAIN & THOMPSON is an equally important collection of papers that "examine how far the expectations and forms of genre shape different kinds of autobiography and influence what messages they can convey".

(The editors define genre as a "style or category of painting, film, novel etc., characterised by a particular form or purpose".) PERKS & THOMSON is an indispensable volume, gathering together a "carefully selected and edited collection of significant contributions on oral history theory and practice". These cover critical developments, interviewing, advocacy and empowerment (readings from oral history projects with a "very self conscious political purpose"), interpretation, and "making histories".

Much of the methodology of oral history directly borrows from social scientific approaches to fieldwork and there are several works that explore the philosophy and practicalities of the technique. YOW's excellent volume provides a valuable introduction to many issues pertaining to these concerns, including, *inter alia*, legal and ethical questions, and "interpersonal" relations during the interview. Similarly, although FINNEGAN's book was ostensibly written for the Association of Social Anthropologists, it is of great utility to historians wishing to explore the "methods by which oral texts and performances can be observed, collected and analysed".

MARK HATHAWAY

See also Archives entries

Ordainers
see Ordinances of 1311

Ordinances of 1311

Davies, James Conway, *The Baronial Opposition to Edward II, Its Character and Policy: A Study in Administrative History*, Cambridge: Cambridge University Press, 1918; new edition, London: Cass, and New York: Barnes and Noble, 1967

Hamilton, J.S., *Piers Gaveston, Earl of Cornwall, 1307–1312: Politics and Patronage in the Reign of Edward II*, Detroit: Wayne State University Press; London: Harvester–Wheatsheaf, 1988

Hutchison, Harold F., *Edward II: The Pliant King*, London: Eyre and Spottiswoode, 1971

Maddicott, J.R., *Thomas of Lancaster, 1307–1322: A Study in the Reign of Edward II*, London: Oxford University Press, 1970

McKisack, May, *The Fourteenth Century, 1307–1399*, Oxford: Clarendon Press, 1959; Oxford and New York: Oxford University Press, 1991

Phillips, J.R.S., *Aymer de Valence, Earl of Pembroke, 1307–1324: Baronial Politics in the Reign of Edward II*, Oxford: Clarendon Press, 1972

Tout, T.F., *The Place of the Reign of Edward II in English History*, Manchester: Manchester University Press, 1914; 2nd edition, revised by Hilda Johnstone, Manchester: Manchester University Press, 1936; reprinted, Westport, Connecticut: Greenwood Press, 1976

The ordinances of 1311 – propositions for governmental, financial, and legal reform – were imposed on the new king, Edward

II, by the 21 leading aristocrats and churchmen known as the "ordainers". They were also opposed to the king's favourite, Piers Gaveston. The ordinances were repeated in 1322.

Davies and Tout determined the interpretation of Edward II's reign and the crises which dominated it for the better part of a century. They believed that a consistent baronial party challenged the king for control of the government, creating a constitutional struggle to control the departments of state and household agencies. DAVIES sees the ordinances of 1311 as an attempt by the barons to accomplish their aim. Although recent scholarship by Maddicott, Phillips, and Hamilton has broadened our understanding of the ordinances by considering baronial personalities and personal ambitions at the expense of constitutional and administrative questions, Davies's work is still an important scholarly contribution. The author provides extensive notes and bibliography.

HAMILTON's study of Piers Gaveston stresses the importance of personality and personal interests rather than constitutional issues in explaining the ordinances. The author places Gaveston squarely at the centre of the conflict leading to the imposition of the ordinances in 1311. He argues that Gaveston's control of royal patronage and, to a lesser extent, the gifts lavished on the favourite and his haughty behaviour, led to demands for reform. Hamilton sees the constitutional questions raised in the ordinances as a cover for the patronage issue. Edward's inadequacies as a ruler and the personal interests of the barons were minor concerns, according to the author. Hamilton presents an excellent summary of the ordinances as well as annotations and bibliography.

The ordinances of 1311 are also considered in the context of HUTCHISON's biography of Edward II. Hutchison wants to evaluate Edward without taking up the often-discussed constitutional questions but cannot avoid the ordainers and ordinances. He presents an acceptable survey of the issues related to the conflict, and discusses the selection of the ordainers and the key provisions of the ordinances. Hutchison's analysis of the ordinances, however, is inadequate. Gaveston was a major source of contention between the king and his barons; however, Hutchison does not take into account the fact that many barons who believed in a need for reform had individual grievances, and concluded that Edward's leadership was disastrous. This biography provides a readable overview of Edward's reign, but has few footnotes and no bibliography.

MADDICOTT's primary focus is a comprehensive study of Thomas of Lancaster, who was a leading figure in preparing the ordinances and the attempt to enforce them. Maddicott rejects the Davies–Tout thesis that the conflict preceding the ordinances was for control of governmental administrative agencies. He also rejects Davies's claim that the quarrel was a continuation of the conflicts between Edward I and his barons. Maddicott argues that Edward I's magnate opponents were dead, and that most of the earls were young men and companions of the new king who were attached to the king by blood or marriage. He further notes that at an early date in the new reign leading magnates urged the king to initiate reforms and address grievances. Edward's failure to follow baronial advice, Gaveston's growing influence over the king, and the gifts and title granted to Gaveston all galvanized baronial opposition, led to the appointment of the ordainers, and the issuance of the ordinances. Maddicott stresses that the one issue, above all others, which

brought about baronial demands and the ordinances was prices; these had become a heavy burden for many subjects and amounted to taxation without parliamentary approval. The author provides the reader with detailed footnotes and an extensive bibliography.

McKISACK presents a brief but comprehensive overview of the political issues and personalities involved in the appointment of the ordainers and the compilation of the ordinances. She discusses the process of selecting the ordainers and their respective political positions, and summarizes the ordinances. McKisack also reviews some of the scholarly interpretations of the crisis and argues that the ordinances represent baronial interests. McKisack concludes that jealousy of Gaveston's domination of the king, and a determination to reclaim their role as the king's natural advisers, drove the earls to draw up the ordinances in order to dispose of Gaveston and assert control over the departments of state and household.

PHILLIPS's study of Aymer de Valence is important for its discussion of one of the primary figures in the baronial reform movement as well as problems which led to the issuance of the ordinances. He rejects the ideas that the struggle primarily concerned control over the institutions of government and that the barons divided into political parties. He argues that opposition to Edward resulted from political issues, personality differences, and personal interests of the earls. He further asserts that Pembroke and other barons urged Edward to undertake reforms in order to deal with growing unrest throughout the kingdom. Phillips recognizes that Gaveston was an important factor in the controversies which led to the ordinances, but not the only important one. The author provides detailed footnotes and an extensive bibliography. (At the time of writing, Phillips is preparing the volume on Edward II for the "English Monarchs" series.)

The edition of TOUT's work consulted most often by scholars is the 1936 revised edition by Johnstone. Johnstone undertook the modifications based on information which had become available since the original publication and which Tout had contemplated adding to the text. Tout argues that Edward II's reign was uniquely important to the development of medieval English government, for the administration of the kingdom was translated from the king's court to national institutions. In this context Tout views the ordinances as a struggle to control the machinery of government. He further claims that the king's financial situation and Gaveston's influence over the king precipitated the conflict. When Edward refused to accept reforms and to dismiss Gaveston, the barons looked to Henry III's reign as a model of government by magnate council with the purpose of instituting reforms for the household and departments of state. With respect to the ordinances, Tout considers the composition of the committee, the basis of its authority, the role of the Commons, the extent to which the ordinances were implemented, and permanent changes resulting from the ordinances. Although narrowly focused on constitutional and administrative questions, Tout's study still commands attention. The Johnstone text provides footnotes but lacks a bibliography.

BOYD BRESLOW

Orkney and Shetland Islands

Anderson, Peter D., *Robert Stewart, Earl of Orkney, Lord of Shetland, 1533–1593*, Edinburgh: John Donald, and Atlantic Highlands, New Jersey: Distributed by Humanities Press, 1982

Anderson, Peter D., *Black Patie: The Life and Times of Patrick Stewart, Earl of Orkney, Lord of Shetland*, Edinburgh: John Donald, 1992

Ballantyne, John H. and Brian Smith, *Shetland Documents*, 2 vols, Lerwick: Shetland Islands Council and Shetland Times, 1994–99

Clouston, J. Storer (editor), *Records of the Earldom of Orkney, 1299–1614*, Edinburgh: Scottish History Society, 1914

Clouston, J. Storer, *A History of Orkney*, Kirkwall, Orkney: Mackintosh, 1932

Crawford, Barbara E., "The Pawning of Orkney and Shetland: A Reconstruction of the Events of 1460–1611", *Scottish Historical Review*, 48/1 (1969): 35–53

Crawford, Barbara E., *Scandinavian Scotland*, Leicester: Leicester University Press, and Atlantic Highlands, New Jersey: Humanities Press 1987

Fenton, Alexander, *The Northern Isles: Orkney and Shetland*, Edinburgh: John Donald, 1978

Graham-Campbell, James and Colleen E. Batey, *Vikings in Scotland: An Archaeological Survey*, Edinburgh: Edinburgh University Press, 1998

Hewison, W.S., *This Great Harbour Scapa Flow*, Stromness: Orkney Press, 1985

Hossack, B.H., *Kirkwall in the Orkneys*, Kirkwall, Orkney: Peace, 1900

Orkneyinga Saga: The History of the Earls of Orkney, translated by Hermann Pálsson and Paul Edwards, London and New York: Penguin, 1978

Renfrew, Colin (editor), *The Prehistory of Orkney*, Edinburgh: Edinburgh University Press, 1985

Smith, Hance, *Shetland Life and Trade, 1550–1914*, Edinburgh: John Donald, 1984

Thomson, William P.L., *History of Orkney*, Edinburgh: Mercat Press, 1987; revised edition, as *New History of Orkney*, 2001

CLOUSTON (1932) is a general survey of Orkney history written with an infectious enthusiasm and still much admired. The balance reflects a once-common overview of Orkney's past: it tends to hark back to a Norse golden age from which all subsequent history is a decline, attributable to corrupting Scottish influences. The bulk of the book is therefore about saga times and there is a single chapter on the last two centuries. Although it often has perceptive insights into Norse institutions, Clouston's work has at many points been overtaken by more recent research. THOMSON provides a modern general survey; it places more emphasis on recent centuries and on economic history, and includes a large bibliography that is a guide to further reading. There is no general survey of Shetland history. RENFREW is a good account of Orkney's prehistory from the Neolithic period to the Viking Age; it is a useful introduction to Orkney's spectacular monuments such as Skara Brae, Maeshowe, and the brochs.

ORKNEYINGA SAGA is a remarkable source, covering the history of the Orkney earls over a 300-year period. It was written in Iceland *c.*1200 and is most readily available in Pálsson & Edwards's translation. In contrast to Scottish sources, which are often meagre at this date, the saga provides detailed stories with fast-moving action and rich characterization. Orkney is the main location, but the saga contains more information about Shetland than is sometimes realized. Older historians often made uncritical use of saga, accepting it as true unless there was a clear-cut reason to believe otherwise. There is now a greater awareness of its mythical and literary content, and of how political considerations may shape the way the story is told. Historians are increasingly mindful that non-Norse sources fail to corroborate the saga's account at certain important points, with the result that events such as King Harald Fairhair's great voyage of conquest (ostensibly *c.*890 AD) are now regarded as historically doubtful. The *Orkneyinga saga* continues to captivate its readers, and often it is the historian's only source, but it can seldom be taken at face value and it needs to be interpreted with care.

CRAWFORD (1987) and GRAHAM-CAMPBELL & BATEY provide modern authoritative accounts of Viking-age Scotland (*c.*800–*c.*1066). Although they are concerned with Viking activity throughout Scotland, much of the focus is on Orkney and Shetland. There is a particularly full treatment of saga sources in Crawford. Both books adopt an interdisciplinary approach, drawing on place-names and archaeology as well as on saga- and other written sources.

After the *Orkneyinga saga* ends (*c.*1200) the history of Orkney and Shetland is often obscure. The first of BALLANTYNE & SMITH's volumes of documents prints the pitifully few records that have survived from medieval Shetland (1195–1579); it probably contains every document that is ever likely to be discovered. A similar but less complete collection of Orkney documents is printed in CLOUSTON (1914). As the Middle Ages drew to a close Orkney and Shetland were transferred from Danish to Scottish control (1468/9) as a result of the marriage of James III to Margaret, daughter of Christian IV. The political circumstances of the impignoration (pawning) of both groups of islands are discussed in CRAWFORD (1969).

Although the transfer to Scotland was initially fairly painless, the Reformation (1560) and the rule of the notorious Stewart earls brought a period of turbulent change. Ballantyne & Smith's second volume is a rich collection of documents from the comparatively brief period of 1580–1611. Earl Robert Stewart and his son, Earl Patrick, are the subjects of modern scholarly biographies by ANDERSON (1982, 1992).

Fishing, agriculture, and trade in Shetland from 1550 onwards are well covered in SMITH's comprehensive survey. FENTON's large and much-admired ethnological study is an excellent source of information on all the details of traditional folk life in both groups of islands. HOSSACK's large and handsome volume is an account of the former inhabitants of Kirkwall arranged on a house-by-house plan but, since Kirkwall's leading citizens were often merchant lairds with landowning and trading interests, his account is a useful, if somewhat haphazard, source of information about many aspects of Orkney's history. The kelp boom, linen-making, fishing, and whaling are described by Thomson who also provides chapters on the intense period of agricultural change in the mid-19th century which revolutionized Orkney's economy, landscape, and society.

Scapa Flow in two world wars has generated many books, of which HEWISON is the most comprehensive. It deals with the development of Scapa Flow as a naval base, and it describes dramatic incidents such as the scuttling of the German fleet in 1919 and the sinking of the battleship *Royal Oak* by a U-boat in 1939.

WILLIAM P.L. THOMSON

See also Dioceses, Scottish; Identities, Regional: The Highlands and Islands; Viking Seamanship; Viking Settlement

Oswald d. 642
King of Northumbria, and saint

Clemoes, Peter, *The Cult of St Oswald on the Continent*, Jarrow: St Paul's Church, 1983; reprinted in *Bede and His World: The Jarrow Lectures, 1958–1993*, with a preface by Michael Lapidge, vol. 2, Aldershot, Hampshire and Brookfield, Vermont: Variorum, 1994

Dumville, D.N., "The Terminology of Overkingship in Early Anglo-Saxon England" in *The Anglo-Saxons from the Migration Period to the Eighth Century: An Ethnographic Perspective*, edited by John Hines, Woodbridge, Suffolk and Rochester, New York: Boydell Press, 1997

Folz, Robert, "Saint Oswald roi de Northumbrie: étude d'hagiographie royale", *Analecta Bollandiana*, 98 (1980): 49–74

Jansen, Annemiek, "The Development of the St Oswald Legends on the Continent" in *Oswald: Northumbrian King to European Saint*, edited by Clare Stancliffe and Eric Cambridge, Stamford, Lincolnshire: Paul Watkins, 1995

Kirby, D.P., *The Earliest English Kings*, London and Boston: Unwin Hyman, 1991; revised edition, London and New York: Routledge, 2000

Stancliffe, Clare, "Where was Oswald Killed?" in *Oswald: Northumbrian King to European Saint*, edited by Clare Stancliffe and Eric Cambridge, Stamford, Lincolnshire: Paul Watkins, 1995

Stenton, F.M., *Oxford History of England*, vol. 2, *Anglo-Saxon England*, Oxford: Clarendon Press 1943; 3rd edition, Oxford: Clarendon Press, 1971; New York: Oxford University Press, 1990

Thacker, Alan, "Kings, Saints, and Monasteries in Pre-Viking Mercia", *Midland History*, 10 (1985): 1–25

Thacker, Alan, "*Membra Disjecta*: The Division of the Body and the Diffusion of the Cult" in *Oswald: Northumbrian King to European Saint*, edited by Clare Stancliffe and Eric Cambridge, Stamford, Lincolnshire: Paul Watkins, 1995

Wormald, Patrick, "Bede, the *Bretwaldas* and the Origins of the *Gens Anglorum*" in *Ideal and Reality in Frankish and Anglo-Saxon Society: Studies Presented to J.M. Wallace-Hadrill*, edited by Patrick Wormald with Donald Bullough and Roger Collins, Oxford: Blackwell, 1983

Yorke, Barbara, *Kings and Kingdoms of Early Anglo-Saxon England*, London: Seaby, 1990

Oswald succeeded to the kingdom of Bernicia on the death of his brother Eanfrith and reigned from 634 to 642. Having been in exile in Scottish Dalriada during the rule of Edwin, the former Northumbrian king, Oswald was moved to invite the abbot of Iona to send someone to christianize his realm, resulting in the arrival of Aidan. A history of the relations between England, Scotland, and Ireland in the 7th century remains to be written. Such a history would explore the impact that residence among Celtic-speaking peoples had on some of the early Anglo-Saxon kings.

In the year of his accession Oswald conquered Cadwallon, King of Gwynedd (who had been responsible for his brother's death), at the battle of Heavenfield in Northumbria and went on to reunite Bernicia and Deira. He also subjected Lindsey to Northumbrian control. Bede regarded him as the sixth overlord of the peoples south of the River Humber. He was eventually killed at the battle of Maserfelth and his remains were later translated to the monastery of Bardney in Lindsey. The portrait we have of Oswald is essentially that of Bede, which, as YORKE has pointed out, is a century later and accords with 8th-century religious views. Though Oswald was a hero to Bede, Yorke observes that he portrays "an insipid saint-king" with "little of the flavour of the formidable warrior king" that he must have been.

The stages whereby Oswald regained some of the paramount power that King Edwin of Northumbria had held is traced by KIRBY. He points out that there were, however, significant differences from Edwin's period of rule: Oswald never had influence in north Wales; the arrival of Aidan at his behest shifted the focus of the church northwards rather than towards the southern church with its diocesan structure and Roman practices; and the focus of political power in Northumbria shifted away from Deira back to the more northerly kingdom of Bernicia. In his view Bede exaggerated Oswald's power in his claim that those who spoke the Pictish and Irish languages fell under his sway. Yorke's discussion complements that of Kirby in that she examines the development of the Northumbrian kingdom and the relationship through war and marriage of its rulers with other kingdoms in Britain.

When STENTON gave the term *Bretwalda* definition in 1943, Oswald was interpreted as holding such an office even though the term is found only as a dubious reading in one version of the *Anglo-Saxon Chronicle*. Forty years later WORMALD did not repudiate the term completely but suggested that it was "less an objectively realized office than a subjectively perceived status". Thus when Oswald married the daughter of Cynegils, king of Wessex, at the same time sponsoring his baptism and cofounding Dorchester-on-Thames with him, Wormald points out that this could be an instance of overlordship or it might have been a marriage alliance or Oswald may have attested Cynegils's grant simply because he was there. In 1997 DUMVILLE dismissed *Bretwalda* as a ghost-word in a paper where he explored some of the features of an overkingship such as Oswald's, though he cautions that "[t]he sources of early Anglo-Latin political terminology ... still require sustained investigation."

There is as yet no consensus as to where Maserfelth, the place where Oswald died, was located. Most scholars have believed it to be Oswestry and this case has been restated by STAN-CLIFFE. On the other hand, THACKER (1995) argues that it was somewhere on the northern boundary of Lindsey, which would help account for why Oswald's cult was disseminated from the monastery at Bardney.

At this early period translation of a person's remains was a recognized way of proclaiming a saintly cult. In an earlier paper (1985) THACKER had examined the politics of the translation of Oswald's remains, which the Bernician Osthryth, wife of King Æthelred of Mercia, effected sometime between 679 and 697 but which was initially opposed by the monks because of Oswald's conquest of Lindsey. Thacker suggests that the Mercian and Bernician royal families were motivated to make this translation through a common interest in suppressing any support for the memory of the Deiran Edwin, who had brought Christianity to Lindsey.

In the high Middle Ages the cult of Oswald spread widely on the Continent. In recent decades his popular cult has attracted considerable scholarly attention. FOLZ presents a careful survey based primarily on written sources. He first traces the various accounts of the saint's life, beginning with Bede, and then turns to the geographic spread of the cult, which was successful in England because Oswald was the first king to bring about miracles. Folz examines in chronological order the evidence for the cult in martyrologies and calendars. He then traces the migration of relics, following which he explores the distribution of the churches dedicated to him in England and on the Continent. Finally, he also describes the offices, lessons for matins, and the mass of St Oswald preserved in liturgical texts. He observes that the cult was found especially in the north of England, whereas it was rare in the south. Anglo-Saxon missionaries took it to the Continent, where it was ubiquitous in the Holy Roman empire. It was fairly common in Bavaria but more unevenly distributed in Austria. CLEMOES pursues other aspects of Oswald's cult on the Continent, paying particular attention to his visual representation in reliquaries, statues, and painting, which are well illustrated in Clemoes's 1983 Jarrow Lecture. The literary traditions of the cult on the Continent, including the popular poetic epic, *Oswald*, which was edited in 1964, have been explored by JANSEN. The poem probably emanated from Regensburg and may have drawn on the *Life of St Oswald* composed by Reginald of Durham in 1165, though this view is not universally held. Jansen also traces the development in continental sources of the attributes of the raven and the ring with which Oswald has become associated as a saint.

DAVID A.E. PELTERET

See also Aidan; Bede's Ecclesiastical History; Christian Conversion in the British Isles; Hagiography; Northumbria, Kingdom of; Pictland and Dalriada

Owain Gwynedd d. 1170
King of Gwynedd

Davies, James Conway (editor), *Episcopal Acts and Cognate Documents Relating to Welsh Dioceses, 1066–1272*, 2 vols, Cardiff: Historical Society of the Church in Wales, 1946–48
Davies, R.R., *Conquest, Coexistence, and Change: Wales 1063–1415*, Oxford: Clarendon Press and Cardiff: University of Wales Press, 1987; as *The Age of Conquest: Wales 1063–1415*, Oxford: Clarendon Press, and New York: Oxford University Press, 1992
Lloyd, John Edward, *A History of Wales from the Earliest Times to the Edwardian Conquest*, 2 vols, London and New York: Longmans Green, 1911; 3rd edition, London and New York: Longmans Green, 1939
Pryce, Huw, "Owain Gwynedd and Louis VII: The Franco-Welsh Diplomacy of the First Prince of Wales", *Welsh History Review*, 19 (1998): 1–28
Richter, Michael, "The Political and Institutional Background to National Consciousness in Medieval Wales" in *Nationality and the Pursuit of National Independence*, edited by T.W. Moody, Belfast: Appletree Press, 1978
Smith, J. Beverley, "Owain Gwynedd", *Transactions of the Caernarvonshire Historical Society*, 32 (1971): 8–17

Despite his importance in the history of medieval Wales, Owain Gwynedd has not yet been the subject of a detailed study. LLOYD devotes a chapter to him; his *History* is built around the leading rulers and this chapter deals with Owain's life and times, using his career as a basis for the narrative. For Lloyd the 12th century was a period of national revival in native Wales and Owain was one of its most prominent figures. His account, largely based on chronicle evidence, paints an attractive picture of a ruler who laid the foundations for the achievements of the 13th-century princes of Gwynedd, who usually exercised moderation in his dealings with others, and who played the political game with skill; in his words "Welsh history can scarcely show a nobler or a better balanced character". Lloyd's somewhat orotund style is very much a reflection of his age and background, but his account of Owain and of the events of his reign remains the starting-point for any study.

R.R. DAVIES examines the history of medieval Wales from a different and more modern standpoint. Whereas Lloyd tended to construct his narrative around the outstanding rulers, Davies's approach is a thematic one; Owain Gwynedd's importance is not neglected but his career and his significance, along with those of his contemporaries, are mainly woven into two chapters entitled "The Struggle for Supremacy" and "Power, Conflict and Hegemony". Owain is placed firmly in the context of 12th-century Welsh kingship and power politics and Davies considers both the traditional and the innovative aspects of his reign. Like Lloyd, he recognizes the outstanding qualities, above all the prudence on which contemporaries commented and with which this ruler was obviously endowed, and describes him as "a man of breadth of vision unusual among the princes of his day"; while Davies draws attention to the ruthlessness which was an essential concomitant of political power, neither he nor Lloyd mention Owain's mutilation of his nephew

Cunedda ap Cadwallon, the son of his elder brother, a not uncommon method of dealing with dynastic rivals.

Lloyd and Davies both discuss Owain Gwynedd in the context of the general history of medieval Wales. SMITH's article, based on a public lecture, is an assessment delivered to mark the eighth centenary of Owain's death. This is part of a major re-examination and reassessment of 12th- and 13th-century Welsh rulers on which this historian has been engaged for many years and, while questioning some of the assumptions of earlier commentators about the nature of the medieval native Welsh polity, it again perceives Owain to have been "a person of quite exceptional stature". Smith begins by stressing the military dimension of Owain's career; his power, both within his own patrimony of Gwynedd and beyond its borders, rested in the last resort on his ability as a soldier. He goes on to consider the dynastic implications of the reign, particularly the emergence of the concept of the indivisible *regnum* and the nomination of a successor during a ruler's lifetime, a view which provides a convincing challenge to the traditional conception of Welsh kingship as divisible between sons. In conclusion Smith draws attention to the adoption by Owain of a new title, *Princeps Wallensium*, in some of his acts. This study, while lacking the chronological and narrative detail of Lloyd, is a major and original contribution to our understanding of the period.

PRYCE discusses and publishes the texts of three letters from Owain, two of them to Louis VII of France and one to his chancellor, copies of which survive in a manuscript in the Vatican Library. Dates are suggested for the correspondence and its wider significance is considered; Pryce looks at the possible value of a Franco-Welsh alliance to the French king in his struggle with Henry II and at the way in which the letters reflect Owain's own perception of his status. This leads on to a discussion of the styles adopted by Owain in his surviving acts and of the significance of the title of *princeps* (prince), as opposed to that of *rex* (king) in the Welsh world of multiple kingship; there were many kings but only one ruler could be Prince of Wales or of the Welsh. Although Pryce, too, sees the basis of Owain's leadership as essentially military, he also draws attention to his diplomatic activity as illustrated in these letters, and he, like other commentators, emphasizes his stature as one of the greatest of the rulers of Gwynedd.

RICHTER's essay is general rather than specific, dealing mainly with the polarization of political authority in 12th-century Wales around Gwynedd and Deheubarth, but the central figures in this discussion are Owain Gwynedd and Rhys ap Gruffydd and it is essential reading for anyone seeking to understand the political world in which Owain operated. Considerable attention is given to the styles adopted by contemporary rulers and their significance and to the first stirrings of a distinctly Welsh political identity; the study is also valuable as a contribution by a German scholar who is often able to bring a wider perspective to the study of medieval Wales.

Conway DAVIES's examination of the long-drawn-out clash between Owain Gwynedd, Thomas Becket, and the papacy over the appointment of a bishop of Bangor in the 1160s forms part of a massive discussion of the history of the Welsh church which forms the introduction to an uncompleted edition of documents relating to it between 1066 and 1272. Unfortunately the documents relating to the two northern dioceses of Bangor and St Asaph remain unpublished. Davies's account is highly detailed

and remains useful, although it has to be said that conciseness was never among his gifts. He also gives some attention to the accompanying dispute between Owain and Becket over his marriage to his cousin Cristin, a union regarded by Canterbury and Rome as incestuous and one which contributed to the struggle for the succession to Gwynedd after Owain's death.

ANTONY DAVID CARR

See also Becket; Gruffydd ap Cynan; Henry II; Rhys ap Gruffydd; Wales: Medieval Period

Owen, Robert 1771–1858
Entrepreneur and social reformer

Butt, John (editor), *Robert Owen, Prince of Cotton Spinners: A Symposium*, Newton Abbot, Devon: David and Charles, 1971

Claeys, Gregory (editor), *Selected Works of Robert Owen*, 4 vols, London: Pickering, 1993

Cole, G.D.H., *The Life of Robert Owen*, 3rd edition, London: Frank Cass, 1965; Hamden, Connecticut: Archon Books, 1966

Cole, Margaret, *Robert Owen of New Lanark*, London: The Batchworth Press, and New York: Oxford University Press, 1953

Donnachie, Ian and George Hewitt, *Historic New Lanark: The Dale and Owen Industrial Community since 1785*, Edinburgh: Edinburgh University Press, 1993

Donnachie, Ian, *Robert Owen: Owen of New Lanark and New Harmony*, East Linton, East Lothian: Tuckwell Press, 2000

Fraser, W. Hamish, "Owenite Socialism in Scotland", *Scottish Economic and Social History*, 16 (1996): 60–91

Harrison, J.F.C., *Robert Owen and the Owenites in Britain and America: The Quest for the New Moral World*, London: Routledge and Kegan Paul; as *The Quest for the New Moral Order: Robert Owen and the Owenites in Britain and America*, New York: Scribner, 1969

Podmore, Frank, *Robert Owen: A Biography*, 2 vols, London: Hutchison, 1906; reprinted, 1 vol., London: Allen and Unwin, 1906; New York: Appleton, 1924

Pollard, Sidney and John Salt (editors), *Robert Owen, Prophet of the Poor: Essays in Honour of the Two Hundredth Anniversary of His Birth*, London: Macmillan, and Lewisburg, Pennsylvania: Bucknell University Press, 1971

Royle, Edward, *Robert Owen and the Commencement of the Millennium: A Study of the Harmony Community*, Manchester: Manchester University Press, and New York: St Martin's Press, 1998

Taylor, Anne, *Visions of Harmony: A Study in Nineteenth-Century Millenarianism*, Oxford: Clarendon Press, and New York: Oxford University Press, 1987

Robert Owen, entrepreneur and social reformer, was a controversial personality who profited enormously from his enterprise in the era of early industrialization and then set about trying to remedy its excesses. The hero's path from his early life in Newtown, Montgomeryshire, via London, Stamford, Manchester, Glasgow, and New Lanark on to the international stage is well known though still littered with undetected clues to his destiny, all recently and critically reassessed by DONNACHIE (2000). Belying appearances to the contrary, such was Owen's charisma that his ideas on social reform attracted a wide following, though at the same time his propaganda campaigns generated much hostility over his ideas about sectarian religion, the law and lawyers, sexual equality, marriage, divorce, birth control (alluded to, but rarely stated outright), and other social issues.

Robert Owen's autobiography (most recently reprinted in Claeys, vol. 4) was composed of his memories, drew on a lifetime's correspondence (vol. 1A), covered much of his life to 1824, and was published within a year of his death. It had been his intention to write a second volume, but unfortunately he never did so, and while practically all the correspondence he might have used has survived, the bulk of the pre-1820s material was lost. During the last 30 years of his life Owen was involved in many labour, cooperative, and communitarian experiments, generating a flurry of publications (detailed exhaustively in Harrison's bibliography), and creating a movement which for long proved difficult to separate from the man himself.

Owen was thus unfortunate in his early biographers, mainly drawn from the ranks of his followers, who transformed the "Social Father" into the "Father of Socialism", by which sobriquet he is often (wrongly) identified in library catalogues. Biographies by George Jacob Holyoake and William Lucas Sargant are typical of the genre, drawing extensively and uncritically on Owen's autobiography, and it was many years before PODMORE produced a more balanced assessment of Owen's life and role as a reformer.

This monumental study was based on wide-ranging sources, pamphlets, newspapers, parliamentary papers, and the extensive Owen correspondence, and covered the major aspects of Owen's career in Manchester, at New Lanark, his public campaigns for factory reform, poor relief, popular education, the community scheme, his trade union and cooperative phases. Podmore was weakest on Owen's upbringing and early career and, because he had no access to extensive archives there, Owen's period in the United States.

However, Podmore remained the major source for subsequent studies, including those by G.D.H. COLE and Margaret COLE, the former adding important material on Owen's radical phase, the latter producing a concise biography, which brought Owen to a new readership. The modern scholarship is dominated by HARRISON, who draws on extensive research in both Britain and the United States to document Owen's communitarian phase and the history of the Owenite movement from the 1810s to the 1840s. Its extensive bibliography lists practically all surviving publications by Owen and his followers.

The two bicentennial studies of 1971 neatly complemented each other in coverage. The first, edited by BUTT, added important new information on Owen's business successes in Manchester and at New Lanark, his role in the movement for factory reform, as an educational pioneer, his work for the poor, the community scheme, and his relationship with the early

labour movement. The contributions in POLLARD & SALT addressed similar topics but also looked at wider aspects of Owenism in Europe and the United States. DONNACHIE & HEWITT (1993) provided a useful summary of these and later studies in their work on New Lanark.

CLAEYS has edited a critical edition of Owen's major works including *A New View of Society*, the *Report to the County of Lanark*, and all of the most important pamphlets and memorials, and brilliantly annotated the autobiography. This is an invaluable aid to the identities of many notables associated with Owen and his schemes. Owen's American activities have been reassessed in an important comparative study by TAYLOR, who takes a critical view of his ideas and motives both at New Lanark and New Harmony, Indiana, while ROYLE produced a detailed study of Queenwood, the last Owenite community, where Owen evidently displayed customary disregard for the democratic process. FRASER, who produced a useful assessment of Owen and the workers in Butt, later returned to Owen, looking specifically at his activities in Scotland during the 1830s and 1840s. Donnachie, taking account of much of the earlier research and fresh work in all the major archives in Britain and the United States, has subsequently re-examined Owen's life and career to the 1830s. He concludes that early influences, including his boyhood in Wales, were of great significance and that New Lanark was not only a test bed for the collection of ideas Owen picked up in Manchester and Glasgow, but remained the model, however inappropriate, for much of his later thinking.

Apart from the works cited, there is an enormous periodical literature on Owen and Owenism. Moreover Owen was an international figure whose life and thought have also inspired many publications beyond the British Isles, notably in the United States, France, and Japan. The American literature has embraced communitarian and gender issues in Owenism, the French work is mainly concerned with Owenism's contribution to the socialist movement, while Japanese writers looked at Owen's approach to personnel management and philanthropy. The major works are cited in Harrison, Taylor, and Claeys. Much of Owen's philosophy was previously positioned in the history of socialism and Marxism, but this is now generally regarded as mistaken. Taylor reflects on the fact that Owen, having made his fortune and stumbled on his scheme, felt he had been called by some divine being to reform humanity. Whatever his real intentions and no matter how often he was rebuffed, he stuck to his theories with the same determination that had earlier made him rich. While Owen's career is now more fully documented, there are still many unanswered questions and he remains a puzzling figure bridging the eras of Enlightenment and industrialization.

IAN DONNACHIE

See also Factory Reform; Industrial Revolution; Industrialization; New Lanark

Oxford Movement 19th to 20th centuries

Chadwick, Owen, *The Victorian Church*, 2 vols, London:
    A. and C. Black, and New York: Oxford University Press,
    1966–70

Freeman, Peter, "The Response of Welsh Nonconformity to
    the Oxford Movement", *Welsh History Review*, 20/1
    (2001): 435–65

Machin, G.I.T., *Politics and the Churches in Great Britain,
    1832–1868*, Oxford and New York: Clarendon Press,
    1977

Machin, G.I.T., *Politics and the Churches in Great Britain,
    1869–1921*, Oxford: Clarendon Press, and New York:
    Oxford University Press, 1987

Machin, G.I.T., "Reservation under Pressure: Ritualism in the
    Prayer Book Crisis, 1927–1928" in *Continuity and Change
    in Christian Worship*, edited by R.N. Swanson, Woodbridge,
    Suffolk and Rochester, New York: Boydell Press, 1999

Machin, G.I.T., "Parliament, the Church of England, and the
    Prayer Book Crisis, 1927–1928" in *Parliament and the
    Church, 1529–1960*, edited by J.P. Parry and Stephen
    Taylor, Edinburgh: Edinburgh University Press, 2000

Nockles, Peter Benedict, *The Oxford Movement in Context:
    Anglican High Churchmanship, 1760–1857*, Cambridge
    and New York: Cambridge University Press, 1994

Pickering, W.S.F., *Anglo-Catholicism: A Study in Religious
    Ambiguity*, London and New York: Routledge, 1989

Rowell, Geoffrey, *The Vision Glorious: Themes and
    Personalities of the Catholic Revival in Anglicanism*,
    Oxford and New York: Oxford University Press, 1983

Yates, Nigel, *Anglican Ritualism in Victorian Britain,
    1830–1910*, Oxford: Clarendon Press, 1999

The "Oxford Movement" in the Church of England commenced in 1833 and was led by Keble, Newman, Hurrell Froude, and Pusey. It could be said to have had several phases and designations. The mid-19th-century stage was alternatively known as tractarianism (from its published theological series of *Tracts for the Times*), and otherwise as Puseyism. In the later 19th century ritualism became its common if rather loose designation, and thereafter, by the early 20th century, Anglo-catholicism became its usual title. Tractarianism has influenced people of differing religious views and practices in the Church of England, including many of those who prefer the traditional designation of "high churchman" to Anglo-catholic. Originally a reaction against liberal religious thought and concessions, the movement sought to reinforce traditional Anglican identity by emphasizing and extending high church theology. This led to accusations by Anglican evangelicals and broad churchmen, and by nonconformists, that the movement was threatening the protestantism of the Church of England and trying to push it towards reunion with Rome. These accusations were strengthened by a significant number of tractarian adherences to Roman catholicism by the 1850s, including Newman in 1845 and Manning in 1851.

Books about the Oxford Movement began to be published in the 1890s. Some of the early ones were hostile in nature; others put up a restrained and dignified defence of the movement. A number of works, some of lasting importance, appeared at about the time of the movement's centenary in 1933. But modern scholarly and analytical work on the subject is the fullest and most reliable. NOCKLES, in a study which is profound and valuable in both a theological and a historical sense, deals in extensive and masterly fashion with the high church context and the rise of the Oxford Movement from the mid-18th to the mid-19th century. The main focus is on the relationship between "old high church" views and practices and the more intense developments in the Oxford Movement. Nockles sees the latter as a new departure, but one which owed a great deal to previous high churchmanship. CHADWICK's first volume provides a substantial, compelling narrative of the movement and its intensely controversial effects, both at its *alma mater*, Oxford University, and beyond; and the second volume shows how the spread of the movement affected religion and society in various respects in the later 19th century. In a well-introduced work, ROWELL valuably explores the essence of the movement through the religious thought and practice of Keble, Newman, Pusey, John Mason Neale, and Bishop Edward King. His book also includes chapters on tractarian parish clergy and the opposition they encountered; missionary bishops and their controversies; and the interests of many Anglo-catholics in ecumenicalism and social reform.

MACHIN (1977) gives detailed attention to the doctrinal claims of the movement during its first four decades; the conflicts which these claims incurred with rival forms of religious thought; and the effects of the movement on political developments. MACHIN (1987) shows how the religious and political conflicts continued in the later 19th and early 20th centuries – especially in regard to the Public Worship Regulation Act of 1874 and to a decade of particularly fierce dispute over ritualism from 1895 to 1906. MACHIN's two listed articles deal with the antecedents and events of the Prayer Book crisis of 1927–28 (an episode deeply involving ritualism), supplementing previous accounts with the findings of further research.

YATES's work, based on much original research and building on studies which he has published over a long period of time, provides a valuable, comprehensive, and objective examination of the movement and its ramifications. The book sets the movement well in the context of theological and liturgical development in the Church of England since its 16th-century foundation. The extension of tractarian ritualism and the conflicts to which it gave rise are well covered on a national and local basis. A final chapter deals with the varying fortunes of Anglo-catholicism from a crucial report of 1906 on ecclesiastical discipline up to about 1980. Also very illuminating is PICKERING's searching examination and critique of the movement in the 20th century, noting both its successes and failures. The accent on "ambiguity" in his title is illustrated by considerations of the extent of catholicism and the extent of protestantism in the continuing movement; of the matter of how far it can be regarded as a church and how far a sect; and of questions of sexuality among its personnel. Matters regarding decline and division in the movement in recent years are also discussed.

The relations of nonconformity with the Oxford Movement, to which it was a rival and in many ways an opposite trend, were intricate and diverse. Nonconformists who opposed church establishment regarded the tractarian theological developments in the Church of England as additional ammunition for their cause: it seemed all the more important to remove the established status of that church when one of its growing components seemed to be pushing it towards Rome. On the other hand, the discomfort of tractarians within the Church of England because of the hostility they encountered there led some of them to desire disestablishment, and even to join for a time the predominantly nonconformist Liberation Society (originally named the Anti-State Church Association, whose foundation in 1844 was more than a coincidence with the recent appearance of tractarianism). These themes are dealt with in Machin's two volumes, and in the full and original article by FREEMAN which investigates the disputes in heavily nonconformist Wales, not least in connection with tractarian influence in Anglican schools.

IAN MACHIN

See also Anglican Doctrine and Worship; Catholic Church since 1560; Newman; Oxford, University of; Ritualism; Tractarianism

Oxford, Provisions of 1258

Carpenter, David A., *The Minority of Henry III*, Berkeley: University of California Press, and London: Methuen, 1990

Davies R.G. and J.H. Denton (editors), *The English Parliament in the Middle Ages*, Manchester: Manchester University Press, and Philadelphia: University of Pennsylvania Press, 1981

Gillingham, John and J.C. Holt (editors), *War and Government in the Middle Ages: Essays in Honour of J.O. Prestwich*, Cambridge: Boydell Press, and New York: Barnes and Noble, 1984

Holt, J.C., *Magna Carta*, Cambridge: Cambridge University Press, 1965; 2nd edition, Cambridge and New York: Cambridge University Press, 1992

Jacob, E.F., *Studies in the Period of Baronial Reform and Rebellion 1258–1267*, Oxford: Clarendon Press, 1925; reprinted, New York: Octagon Books, 1974

Maddicott, J.R., *Simon de Montfort*, Cambridge and New York: Cambridge University Press, 1994

Powicke, Frederick Maurice, *King Henry III and the Lord Edward*, 2 vols, Oxford: Clarendon Press 1947

Prestwich, Michael, *Edward I*, Berkeley: University of California Press, and London: Methuen, 1988

Richard, Jean, *Saint Louis: Crusader King of France*, edited and abridged by Simon Lloyd, translated by Jean Birrell, Cambridge and New York: Cambridge University Press, 1992 (French edition, 1983)

Richardson, H.G. and G.O. Sayles, *The English Parliament in the Middle Ages*, London: Hambledon Press, 1981

Ridgeway, H., "The Lord Edward and the Provisions of Oxford (1258): A Study in Faction" in *Thirteenth Century England: Proceedings of the Newcastle-upon-Tyne Conference*, edited P.R. Cross and S.D. Lloyd, 4 vols, Woodbridge, Suffolk: Boydell Press, and Wolfeboro, New Hampshire: Boydell and Brewer, 1986–92

Stubbs, William, *The Constitutional History of England in Its Origin and Development*, 3 vols, Oxford: Clarendon Press, 1929 (reprint of volumes from 4th–6th editions; 1st edition, 1874–78); New York: Barnes and Noble, 1967 (reprint of 1897 edition)

Treharne, R.F., *The Baronial Plan of Reform*, Manchester: Manchester University Press, 1932; 2nd edition, as *The Baronial Plan of Reform 1258–1263*, 1971

Warren, W. Lewis, *King John*, London: Methuen, and New York: Norton, 1963; 2nd edition, London: Methuen, 1978; new edition, New Haven, Connecticut: Yale University Press, 1997

The Provisions of Oxford (1258) are a constitutional issue, a milestone in the history of parliament, which can be pursued most thoroughly by reading about four kings, the policies of one of them, and the grievances of the barons, in particular Simon de Montfort, Earl of Leicester. The kings are John, Henry III and his son Edward I, and Louis IX of France. The policies are those of Henry III, in whose reign the Provisions were agreed.

The Provisions were imposed on Henry by disgruntled nobles led by de Montfort. They stipulated the setting up of a baronial council of 15 members, with power over appointments, followed by reforms to the common law. Tensions between, on the one hand, de Montfort and his allies, who regarded the Provisions as a bulwark against royal power, and on the other Henry and his heir Edward, who interpreted the provisions as merely advisory, flared up into the so-called "second baron's war" of 1264–65. Initial success for de Montfort resulted in Henry's and Edward's capture following the battle of Lewes (1264), which left de Montfort effective ruler of England. He famously summoned a parliament, for the first time to include commoners – the knights and burgesses. But in 1265 the military tide turned, and de Montfort was killed at the Battle of Evesham (1265). The Provisions were officially revoked in 1267, leaving the monarch free, again, to choose his advisers.

The literature is excellent, albeit controversial, and the issues and the key players are well served. There are, to begin with, a number of standard, classic texts on the constitutional issues which deserve attention. STUBBS's late 19th-century work has long been a starting-point, and from the Manchester and Oxford schools in the 1920s and 1930s there emerged the work of TREHARNE and JACOB on baronial reform. The views represented here were largely accepted for some time, but have been challenged more recently by the work of RICHARDSON & SAYLES and the volume edited by DAVIES & DENTON. All the above offer important interpretations and should be read.

The path leading to the Provisions begins with King John. WARREN provides a lively study of him and of the intricacies of political life that created Magna Carta. (A transcription of it is included as an appendix.) He is also useful on the French barons and in particular on the Lusignans. It was the dispute between King John and the barons which led to Magna Carta, and during John's reign the basic premise was established that great councils should influence the king's choice of ministers. HOLT focuses on Magna Carta, and he is immensely readable.

John had resented the demands of the barons, and the ensuing civil war put much of England under the control of the King of

France, whose leadership some of the barons sought. For the minority (1216–27) of Henry III turn to CARPENTER. This period saw Magna Carta implanted firmly into constitutional history. William Marshall was regent for Henry, but in the following period the authority of the crown rapidly diminished, and power was dispersed to the communities before being ultimately restored through the work of the justiciar, Hubert de Burgh. Carpenter is particularly helpful in dealing with the constitutional issues and the deteriorating relationship between the barons and the king. He also gives us pointers to further developments – the widespread opposition from the barons to overseas expeditions in Henry's ambitious attempt to reclaim the Angevin empire, the secret marriage of Simon de Montfort to Henry's sister, Eleanor, and the patronage given to Henry's Lusignan half-brothers. In the chapter dealing with the aftermath of the minority, he traces the path from Magna Carta to the Paper Constitution of 1244 – which was essentially an attempt to restore the system existing under the minority – and then to 1258 and the Provisions of Oxford themselves. The later period of Henry III's reign is discussed by POWICKE in another classic volume.

The immediate cause of rebellion in England – and the sequence of events leading to the Provisions – was Henry's Sicilian campaign, which is discussed by MADDICOTT and (for a French view) by RICHARD. In 1254 Henry obtained the grant of the kingdom of Sicily to his second son, Edmund, and, according to the treaty made with Pope Alexander in 1255, Henry had to send troops and a large sum of money to Sicily by the winter of 1256. In April 1258 Henry III called his clergy and barons to explain the papal demands. The immediate effect of this was the demand that parliament be called. It was this parliament that met at Oxford in June 1258, and which produced the Provisions of Oxford. The results were a full surrender by the king, the ridding of the Poitevin favourites, the re-establishment of the great offices of state, and the setting-up of a series of committees with checks and balances. These were issues close to the responsibilities and ambitions of de Montfort, and Maddicott explains them well. In Maddicott's view, the Provisions were inviolable to de Montfort.

The threads of the story after 1258 are picked up by PREST-WICH in his major biography of Henry III's son, the future Edward I. He is not so much concerned with the European issues or the details of the Provisions, but provides us with an account of the changing relationship between Edward and de Montfort. Relations were good in 1258; de Montfort's sons were knighted by Edward. But it was the fluctuating relations among Henry, Edward, and de Montfort after this period that led to the second baronial war. De Montfort's success at Lewes effected a restoration of the Provisions, and ultimately led to the celebrated call for a parliament including knights and burgesses, which opened in January 1265.

For a while after Lewes, Edward was de Montfort's prisoner. Once he was freed, alienated barons flocked to him and began the opposition to de Montfort's self-aggrandisement and his failure to continue the constitutional reforms; this phase, ending with de Montfort's death at Evesham, is dealt with effectively by Maddicott. With Prince Edward as *de facto* ruler from 1265, Magna Carta was confirmed, and although there is general agreement that the Provisions of Oxford were, *per se*, a failure, the principles of the reforms were embodied in the Statute of

Marlborough in 1267. Although Prestwich deals with this in detail, readers should also consult RIDGEWAY's article.

Relations between the monarch and his advisers underwent various changes throughout the period, and Holt, in GILLINGHAM & HOLT, suggests that the impossibility of "imposing an acceptable form of baronial direction on a sane king in his majority" eventually led to a preference for attempting to depose the king, realized in the reigns of Edward II and Richard II.

JUDITH LOADES

Oxford, University of

Brock, M.G. and M.C. Curthoys (editors), *The History of the University of Oxford*, vol. 7, *Nineteenth-Century Oxford, Part 2*, Oxford: Clarendon Press, and New York: Oxford University Press, 2000

Catto, J.I. and Ralph Evans (editors), *The History of the University of Oxford*, vol. 2, *Late Medieval Oxford*, Oxford: Clarendon Press, and New York: Oxford University Press, 1992

Cobban, Alan B., *English University Life in the Middle Ages*, London: UCL Press, and Columbus: Ohio State University Press, 1999

Dowling, Linda, *Hellenism and Homosexuality in Victorian Oxford*, Ithaca, New York: Cornell University Press, 1994

Harrison, Brian (editor), *The History of the University of Oxford*, vol. 8, *The Twentieth Century*, Oxford: Clarendon Press, 1994

Leonardi, Susan J., *Dangerous by Degrees: Women at Oxford and the Somerville College Novelists*, New Brunswick, New Jersey: Rutgers University Press, 1989

McConica, James (editor), *The History of the University of Oxford*, vol. 3, *The Collegiate University*, Oxford: Clarendon Press, 1986

Midgley, Graham, *University Life in Eighteenth-Century Oxford*, New Haven, Connecticut and London: Yale University Press, 1996

Symonds, Richard, *Oxford and Empire: The Last Lost Cause?*, London: Macmillan, 1986; Oxford: Clarendon Press, and New York: Oxford University Press, 1991

Ward, W.R., *Victorian Oxford*, London: Cass, 1965

Since the Middle Ages, the University of Oxford has played a unique role in the cultural and political life of Britain. The university's contribution to religion, to classical studies, to the arts, to life sciences, and to the physical sciences have made it the training ground for future national leaders for hundreds of years. Yet, in addition to educating so many of the kingdom's national leaders, Oxford has inspired and fostered ideas associated with the qualities of England's culture, character, and national temperament. As a result, most 20th-century histories of the university examine its role in particular social and cultural periods, or particular movements and trends.

In the Middle Ages, Oxford acted as a service institution for the bolstering of the existing political, legal, ecclesiastical, and social apparatus, but also provided a considerable degree of social mobility for its graduates of middling to comparatively humble backgrounds. CATTO & EVANS is the definitive study of the medieval university. Its contributors explore the academic pursuits of scholars, the nature of everyday life during the 14th and 15th centuries, and the finances and administration of the colleges. COBBAN also highlights the university-society nexus of medieval Oxford by focusing on the various aspects of English university life, including the undergraduate and postgraduate experiences, the academic periphery, teaching and learning, urban relations and recreations, and university administration.

The 16th and 17th centuries continued to witness vigorous political, ecclesiastical, intellectual, and social power struggles in Oxford: in 1530, Henry VIII forced the university to accept his divorce from Catherine of Aragon; during the Reformation, three Anglican churchmen were tried for heresy and burnt at the stake in Oxford; and Charles I held a counter-parliament in Oxford during the civil wars. The volume edited by MCCONICA provides a history of Tudor and Stuart Oxford which studies the development of the university and its colleges in the context of national history. For example, Henry VIII's dissolution of the monasteries and friaries transferred a large amount of Oxford property to the colleges; yet, during the Reformation, the university's numbers reached an all-time low, its library was dispersed, and there was even a decision to sell the bookshelves. The chapter titled "The Provision of Books" in McConica's volume documents this struggle, noting that there is in the Bodleian Library a 17th-century copy of a letter sent by Christ Church to nobility and gentry as an appeal for funds to found a library. Of course, by the 17th century, Elizabeth I's reign had gone a long way to restoring political and religious stability, and over the next hundred years both city and university were transformed. As contributors to the volume explain, the demand for well-educated professionals, and a recognition among the social elite that academic education was integral to a gentleman's training, led to a sharp increase in university recruitment.

The university played a major role in the civil wars, the Commonwealth period, and the Restoration of Charles; as a result, it expanded both institutionally and intellectually during the 16th and 17th centuries. Yet, by the 18th century, Oxford was characterized less by teaching and learning than by inordinate feasting and drinking, struggles with authority, sports and leisure, political riots, and circuses that delighted both the town and the university. MIDGLEY, both a former student and a don at St Edmund Hall, focuses on this social history in his study of university life in 18th-century. By drawing on a rich array of contemporary sources – student journals, newspaper articles, disciplinary records, satirical pamphlets, poems, reports from foreign visitors, betting books, and recipe books – he presents a series of vignettes and illuminating images that evoke the flavour and spirit of the period.

Nineteenth-century Oxford was an increasingly secular institution. In 1800 it was still bound to the Anglican church, responsible for maintaining the principles of the Church of England. Before the end of the century, the university's transformation to an undenominational, "freethinking" institution was almost complete. After 1871 teachers at Oxford were freed from tests of religious belief. The church was expropriated, and a secular profession of university teaching and scholarship

was created with the resources of the colleges and university. The volume edited by BROCK & CURTHOYS describes the psychological and intellectual climate in which some dons sought a new basis for morality, while many undergraduates turned to the ethic of public service both at home and in the empire. Additionally, the book by WARD outlines the tensions between Anglo-catholicism and rationalism/science in Victorian Oxford, especially in relation to "Oxford's four great humanists" – John Henry Newman, Matthew Arnold, John Ruskin, and Walter Pater. Ward also provides an excellent general overview of the web of art, religion, science, and politics that was Victorian Oxford.

SYMONDS focuses on this influence of the university on the British empire and on the influence of the empire on Oxford between the middle of the 19th century and World War II. The teaching of classics at Oxford had an important place in the university's contribution to the philosophy of, and national attitudes towards, empire. The lessons of the history of the Greek city states were often applied to relations between Britain and the old dominions, while in the government of dependent territories comparisons were frequently made with Rome. Oxford scientists, geographers, and anthropologists supported these motives for empire because they justified expansion in their fields; religious figures supported them because the empire provided a framework within which heirs to the Oxford Movement could advance their work from the slums of Britain to India, Africa, and the Pacific; and Oxford educators saw the empire as a provider of employment to their pupils in posts of responsibility and prestige. Symonds attempts to understand the influence that Oxford exerted in the one direction, on her graduates who went out as administrators, teachers, and missionaries, and on the institutions that they founded; and in the other direction, on those who came both from the dependent colonies and the old dominions to study in the university.

In addition to its role in the building of empire, Greek studies also operated as a "homosexual code" at Oxford during the 19th century – the great age of English university reform. As DOWLING explains, leading university reformers like Benjamin Jowett sought to establish in Hellenism a "ground of transcendent value alternative to Christian theology – the metaphysical underpinning of Oxford from the Middle Ages through the Tractarian movement". Once these reformers had accomplished this goal, Walter Pater, Oscar Wilde, and the Uranian poets could not be denied the means of developing out of this same Hellenism a homosexual counterdiscourse able to justify male love in ideal or transcendental terms: "the 'spiritual procreancy' associated with Plato's *Symposium* and more generally with ancient Greece itself". The single most revolutionary consequence of this hidden or "coded" counter-discourse was conclusively to sweep aside the deep fears of "corruption" and "effeminacy" associated with male love by a classical republican discourse. In fact, Dowling argues that an alternative vision of male love and spiritual procreancy was the direct legacy not simply of Victorian liberal Hellenism but of the revolution in modern historiography lying at the heart of Greek studies at Oxford.

In the 20th century, the debate about degrees for women at Oxford makes clear that an attention to gender roles and gender subversion was still never far from the surface. LEONARDI's study looks at the experience of the women at Somerville

College during the crucial years just before Oxford granted degrees to women. She then looks at six novelists (Dorothy L. Sayers, Muriel Jaeger, Doreen Wallace, Margaret Kennedy, Winifred Holtby, and Vera Brittain), all students at Somerville between 1912 and 1922, and the figure in their fiction of the educated woman. HARRISON's volume also examines Oxford's response to the steady advance of women, as well as a wide range of other issues that helped to shape modern Oxford: the rapid growth in provision for the natural and social sciences; the advance of professionalism in scholarship, sports, and cultural achievement; the diffusion of international influences through Rhodes scholars, two world wars, the university's changing research priorities; and the growing importance of public funding.

CHRISTINE ROTH

See also Newman; Oxford Movement; Tractarianism; Universities entries

P

Paine, Thomas 1737–1809
Political theorist and revolutionary

Aldridge, A. Owen, *Man of Reason: The Life of Thomas Paine*, Philadelphia: J.B. Lippincott, 1959; London: Cresset Press, 1960

Aldridge, A. Owen, *Thomas Paine's American Ideology*, Newark: University of Delaware Press, and London: Associated University Presses, 1984

Ayer, A.J., *Thomas Paine*, London: Secker and Warburg, and New York: Atheneum, 1988

Caron, Nathalie, *Thomas Paine contre l'imposture des prêtres*, Paris: L'Harmattan, 1998

Claeys, Gregory, *Thomas Paine: Social and Political Thought*, Boston and London: Unwin Hyman, 1989

Conway, Moncure Daniel, *The Life of Thomas Paine: With a History of His Literary, Political, and Religious Career in America, France, and England*, with sketch of Paine by William Cobbett, 2 vols, New York: Putnam, 1892

Foner, Eric, *Tom Paine and Revolutionary America*, New York and Oxford: Oxford University Press, 1976

Fruchtman, Jack, Jr, *Thomas Paine and the Religion of Nature*, Baltimore: Johns Hopkins University Press, 1993

Fruchtman, Jack, Jr, *Thomas Paine: Apostle of Freedom*, New York and London: Four Walls Eight Windows Press, 1994

Hawke, David Freeman, *Paine*, New York: Harper and Row, and London: Norton, 1974

Keane, John, *Tom Paine: A Political Life*, Boston: Little Brown, and London: Bloomsbury, 1995

Philp, Mark, *Paine*, Oxford and New York: Oxford University Press, 1989

Despite his lack of much formal education and his very humble origins, Thomas Paine eventually became, through his pen, his intelligence, and his energy, the most widely read political writer in the age of revolution. Soon after emigrating to the American colonies, he began playing a major role in advocating independence from Britain and encouraging the flagging spirits of the rebel troops. His short tract *Common Sense* (1776) urged the colonists to plump for independence, and it was probably the most widely read pamphlet of the age. He went on to write a series of essays, known as the *American Crisis* (1776–83), to stiffen the morale of the rebels after initial reverses. On his return to Britain he wrote several influential radical pamphlets urging political reform, including the celebrated and massively popular *Rights of Man* (1791–92). Fleeing from persecution, he went to France, where he served in the Convention, spent months in prison facing the prospect of execution, and yet still managed to write *Age of Reason* (1794–95), which became another very widely read publication. Returning to the United States, he engaged for a time in polemical debates, before dying virtually alone and neglected.

Paine was much abused by his many critics in Britain and the United States during his lifetime and for many years afterwards. His unorthodox religious views particularly alienated his fellow Americans, while his radical political views made him deeply unpopular with many in Britain. Not until 1892 was there an attempt to do justice to his remarkable achievements in CONWAY's pioneering biography, followed by four volumes of *The Writings of Thomas Paine* edited by Conway (1894–96). It is only more recently, however, with the growing interest in radical ideas, popular politics, and ideological debate and with the general recognition that Paine was a major political propagandist, if not a profound political philosopher, that interest in his writings and his career has mushroomed.

There are now several useful modern biographies of Paine. The earliest of these is probably ALDRIDGE (1959), a generally sound and reliable study of the main outlines of his career, but one lacking depth in both its research and its interpretation of Paine's writings and achievements. Much more substantial is HAWKE, which is extremely detailed on Paine's American career and shows a good understanding of the American context in which he operated for half of his life. It is much less satisfactory in its study of his years in either Britain or France, however, yet an understanding of these aspects of his career is vital to a full appreciation of his many achievements. A.J. AYER's book, though by an eminent philosopher, is disappointing. Ayer is not an historian and he has little understanding of the political context of the three countries in which Paine campaigned for political change. Even in his comments on Paine's thought, Ayer makes few interesting comments and fails to locate these in an intellectual context. There are two recent and very substantial biographies. KEANE has been more assiduous than any previous biographer in tracking down source material about Paine and obscure essays written by him. He tells us much more about Paine's early career, about his personal relations, and about his campaigning journalism than any other biographer. He is very good indeed on Paine's activities during the American War of Independence and during his years in France. He is also very good on the details of the actual publication, distribution, and reception of Paine's works. Unfortunately, he is not an historian and it sometimes shows in the numerous factual errors and in his failure to present the political context effectively. More serious, he makes no real effort to discuss the actual texts of Paine's works. Keane merely gives a précis of the contents of all of Paine's major works and never subjects Paine's ideas or his language to close scrutiny. He is interested in Paine the campaigning journalist, but not in Paine the political thinker, yet Paine's works are what really make him significant. FRUCHTMAN's 1994 biography is also substantial and well researched, but less so than Keane's. His work also suffers from some of the flaws in Keane's biography. He does not fully understand the political context, particularly in Britain, and his work is marred by a number of factual errors. On the other hand, he makes a greater effort than Keane to analyse Paine's writings and to explain their significance. As a political theorist he is prepared to subject Paine's writings to much closer scrutiny.

In many ways the most original studies of Paine are those specialized, deeply researched, and original works which concentrate on specific aspects of his career or his writings. ALDRIDGE's work on his American ideology (1984) offers a very close study of the writing and publication of *Common Sense* and investigates the intellectual influences on it and its reception. On the other hand, it only briefly touches upon his other American writings and spends only a short chapter on the *American Crisis*. FONER also scrutinizes Paine's *Common Sense* and his republicanism, but he devotes even more attention to the radical milieu in Philadelphia and to Paine's ideas on price controls, *laissez-faire*, and moral economy. FRUCHTMAN's study of Paine's religious ideas examines Paine's concept of nature and natural rights, his ideas on civil and economic rights, and his views on political and economic progress. He has some original and important things to say, but he surprisingly fails to give any serious attention to the religious views Paine expressed in the *Age of Reason*. This weakness is redressed, however, in a recent French study by CARON, which subjects Paine's deistical writings to very careful examination and also locates Paine within the wider context of deistical writings. CLAEYS largely ignores Paine's life and career and concentrates on his major writings. His work is based on a very diligent reading of all the available sources on Paine's social and political ideas (and he provides a superb bibliography). He is particularly detailed and valuable in his treatment of *Rights of Man*, and is even deeper and more original in his comments on the neglected *Agrarian Justice* (1797). Throughout his work, he tries to trace the various influences on Paine's thought. While his book is an indispensable study of Paine's ideas, it is less fresh, lucid, and incisive than PHILP's short survey of Paine's major writings. In very short compass, Philp presents a masterly summary of Paine's main ideas and their significance.

HARRY T. DICKINSON

See also American Colonies: Loss of; Burke; Cobbett; London Corresponding Society; Pitt, William, "the Younger"; Radicalism; Republicanism; Wilkes

Pale (Irish)
see Ireland: The Pale

Palestine, Israel, and the Middle East
from 1945

Balfour-Paul, Glen, *The End of Empire in the Middle East: Britain's Relinquishment of Power in Her Last Three Arab Dependencies*, Cambridge and New York: Cambridge University Press, 1991

Brenchley, Frank, *Britain and the Middle East: An Economic History, 1945–1987*, London: Lester Crook, 1989

Cohen, Michael J. and Martin Kolinsky (editors), *Demise of the British Empire in the Middle East: Britain's Responses to Nationalist Movements, 1943–1955*, London and Portland, Oregon: Cass, 1998

Devereux, David R., *The Formulation of British Defence Policy towards the Middle East, 1948–1956*, Basingstoke: Macmillan/King's College, and New York: St Martin's Press, 1990

Kingston, Paul W.T., *Britain and the Politics of Modernization in the Middle East, 1945–1958*, Cambridge and New York: Cambridge University Press, 1996

Louis, William Roger, *The British Empire in the Middle East, 1945–1951: Arab Nationalism, the United States, and Postwar Imperialism*, Oxford: Clarendon Press, and New York: Oxford University Press, 1984

Monroe, Elizabeth, *Britain's Moment in the Middle East, 1914–1956*, London: Chatto and Windus, and Baltimore: Johns Hopkins University Press, 1963; revised edition, as *Britain's Moment in the Middle East, 1914–1971*, London: Chatto and Windus, and Baltimore: Johns Hopkins University Press, 1981

Ovendale, Ritchie, *Britain, the United States, and the End of the Palestine Mandate, 1942–1948*, London and Woodbridge, Suffolk, and Wolfeboro, New Hampshire: Boydell Press/Royal Historical Society, 1989

Ovendale, Ritchie, *Britain, the United States, and the Transfer of Power in the Middle East, 1945–1962*, London: Leicester University Press, 1996

At the end of World War II Britain was still the paramount power in the Middle East. Official British policy reflected the view that other powers were, if possible, to be excluded from the area and that American penetration, even commercial, was to be resisted. British paramountcy in the area was undermined by Zionist terrorism, leading to the surrender of the Palestine mandate in May 1948, and Arab nationalism. Some British officials also thought that Britain's leadership of the Arab world, secure since 1918, had been successfully challenged by the United States and France from 1945, but doubted whether either of those countries was capable of taking Britain's place in the Middle East. The declining British influence in the Middle East matched London's revised defence policy: the Middle East ceased to be one of the three cardinal pillars of British defence. British officials did not always like the growing American involvement in the area, but it was something that Britain had to accept with as good a grace as possible. It was President Dwight Eisenhower's policy during the Suez crisis of 1956 that led to the United States having to take over Britain's burdens in the Middle East. The historical debate has focused on the reasons for British withdrawal from the Palestine mandate, the extent to which British policy in the area was determined by strategic and economic considerations, and whether London was anxious for the United States to take over its role in the area.

MONROE diagnoses a decline of British nerve in the period leading up to and during World War II, followed by a decade of impotence, and offers an epitaph that "Britain in its forty years of dominance in the Middle East earned enough acquiescence, and at times admiration, to save the British skin in two world war". LOUIS has written about British disengagement in the Middle East during the period of the Labour governments of 1945–51. He offers the thesis that Labour's strategy was to refrain from direct intervention and to conciliate the moderate nationalists, hoping to change a relationship of dominance into one of equal partners, and to sustain British influence by economic and social reform. The Palestine issue is viewed as the major disruptive element, one which made it impossible to appease Arab nationalism, and led to divisions with the United States. OVENDALE (1989) examines, against the background of the emergence of the cold war and the birth of the state of Israel, the attempts made by the British foreign secretary, Ernest Bevin, to keep the explosive Palestine situation separate from the deepening needs of the Anglo-American special relationship, while at the same time laying the foundations for Western security.

Looking at the immediately following period, DEVEREUX argues that the Attlee, Churchill, and Eden governments all considered the Middle East as crucial for Britain's security. Using recently released defence documents, OVENDALE (1996) suggests, however, that it was Churchill's peacetime administration that oversaw the dramatic change in British defence policy, the move away from considering the Middle East as one of the three cardinal pillars of British strategy towards the conclusion that it was an area of more limited significance in the age of thermonuclear weapons and at a time when Britain's financial straits meant a limitation of its world role. Churchill personally felt that the Americans should become involved in the area. Eden, when he became prime minister, shifted British policy towards an emphasis on a more direct British role in the Middle East: he thought this necessary to preserve British oil interests, and because of the experience that the British had had of the area London should be willing to pursue a policy without the full agreement of Washington. After the Suez crisis of 1956 Washington began to consult intimately with Britain over policy in the Middle East, and by the time of the crises in Lebanon, Jordan, and Iraq in 1958 the United States had, in effect, acknowledged that it had assumed the leadership of the "Free World" in the Middle East.

COHEN & KOLINSKY have assembled a collection of wide-ranging essays many of which are concerned with Britain's reaction to Arab nationalism in the aftermath of its relinquishing the Palestine mandate, and focus in particular on Britain's relations with Egypt, Jordan, Iraq, and the Arab League, and illustrate what the editors see as the "final eclipse of British imperial power". In an analysis of the British withdrawal from the Sudan, South West Arabia, and the Gulf, BALFOUR-PAUL, who had served as ambassador in various Arabian countries, presents the case that Britain's relinquishment of power followed no uniform pattern in motivation or manner: withdrawal from South West Arabia was forced by public pressure; withdrawal from the Gulf was forced by Treasury calculations and the fading of imperial will.

The economic relationship is examined by KINGSTON who offers an important record of Britain's foreign aid programme in the Middle East in the 1940s and 1950s. Ernest Bevin, the British foreign secretary, had a vision of working with the peasants and not the pashas. But, politically, this policy did not work. A former Foreign Office official and ambassador, BRENCHLEY, suggests that the two supreme influences on the economic relations between Britain and the Middle East have been trade and the oil industry, and he points to the favourable balance of payments and the balance of visible trade that swung in Britain's favour after its withdrawal from direct political involvement in the area.

RITCHIE OVENDALE

See also Bevin; Colonial Wars and Counter-Insurgency; Decolonization; Eden; Mandated Territories; Suez Crisis

Palmerston, Henry John Temple, 3rd Viscount Palmerston 1784–1865

Whig/Liberal politician, statesman, and prime minister

Bell, Herbert C.F. *Lord Palmerston*, 2 vols, London and New York: Longmans Green, 1936

Bourne, Kenneth, *Palmerston, The Early Years, 1784–1841*, London: Allen Lane, and New York: Macmillan, 1982

Brown, David, "Compelling but Not Controlling?: Palmerston and the Press, 1846–1855", *History*, 86 (2001): 41–61

Brown, David, "The Power of Public Opinion: Palmerston and the Crisis of December 1851", *Parliamentary History*, 20/3 (2001): 333–58

Bulwer, Henry Lytton and Evelyn Ashley, *The Life of Henry John Temple, Viscount Palmerston: With Selections from His Diaries and Correspondence*, 5 vols, London: Bentley, 1870–76; vols 1 and 2, Philadelphia: J.B. Lippincott, 1871

Chamberlain, Muriel E., *Lord Palmerston*, Cardiff: University of Wales Press, and Washington: Catholic University of America Press, 1987

Guedalla, Philip, *Palmerston*, London: Benn, 1926; as *Palmerston, 1784–1865*, New York: Putnam, 1927

Henderson, Gavin Burns, *Crimean War Diplomacy, and Other Historical Essays*, Glasgow: Jackson, 1947; reprinted, New York: Russell and Russell, 1975

Krein, David F., *The Last Palmerston Government: Foreign Policy, Domestic Politics, and the Genesis of "Splended Isolation"*, Ames: Iowa State University Press, 1978

Martin, Kingsley, *The Triumph of Lord Palmerston: A Study of Public Opinion in England before the Crimean War*, revised edition, London: Hutchinson, 1963

Partridge, Michael S. and Karen E. Partridge, *Lord Palmerston, 1784–1865: A Bibliography*, Westport, Connecticut: Greenwood Press, 1994

Ridley, Jasper, *Lord Palmerston*, London: Constable, 1970; New York: Dutton, 1971

Southgate, Donald, *"The Most English Minister . . .": The Policies and Politics of Palmerston*, London: Macmillan, 1966

Steele, E.D., *Palmerston and Liberalism, 1855–1865*, Cambridge and New York: Cambridge University Press, 1991

Webster, Charles K., *The Foreign Policy of Palmerston, 1830–1841: Britain, the Liberal Movement, and the Eastern Question*, 2 vols, London: Bell, 1951; New York: Humanities Press, 1969

Palmerston has been lucky in his biographers. His official biography (BULWER & ASHLEY) – a Victorian "five-decker" – was started by a diplomat who had served under him, Henry Lytton Bulwer (vols 1–2, 1870–71), and completed after Bulwer's death by Palmerston's own step-grandson, Evelyn Ashley, who had been his private secretary (vols 3–5, 1874–76). Both men admired him and their work is still an indispensable starting-point for the serious student. Both printed extensive extracts from his papers. The primary material in the biography is less vital now that all the official papers are available to scholars in the Public Record Office and Palmerston's private papers are in Southampton University Library but Bulwer's and Ashley's value as firsthand witnesses remains.

Bulwer was understandably mainly interested in Palmerston's foreign policy and, in any case, by the time he came to write, Palmerston was firmly established in the public mind as the very embodiment of Victorian foreign policy, the patriotic, self-confident John Bull figure. This was the view of the first half of the 20th-century and the popular picture of Palmerston remains the rumbustious figure of GUEDALLA's 1926 biography.

Interwar history was dominated by the study of international relations, perhaps in the hope of averting another catastrophe like World War I. BELL's two-volume biography of 1936 is really a study of Palmerston's foreign policy. MARTIN's very shrewd and pioneering study of public opinion examines Palmerston's role in the public excitement which culminated in the Crimean War. WEBSTER's massive two-volume work, which covers the decade 1830–41, although not published until 1951, belongs essentially to the same genre of interwar fascination with the *minutiae* of foreign policy and is still admiring of Palmerston. Doubts about the accepted interpretations of Palmerston's role had already been raised by HENDERSON but his premature death in an air crash meant that they only survived in a collection of essays. Criticisms such as those of Henderson moved SOUTHGATE to write what was essentially a defence of Palmerston and his policies. This can be regarded as the last of the old-style studies.

Subsequent biographies have tried to look at the whole man and to assess his place in domestic as well as in foreign politics. RIDLEY's 1970 life was a breakthrough, looking at Palmerston through modern eyes and presenting a critical but attractively written survey of his whole career. BOURNE set out to write an exhaustive (and for many readers exhausting) study of every aspect of his life but Bourne died after completing the first volume, which went only to 1841.

Thinking about Palmerston has shifted greatly. This is partly because the modern reader feels less than comfortable with the traditional picture of Palmerston as the symbol of a strong and enlightened England dominating a still backward-looking Europe, and partly because Palmerston himself is now recognized as a complex man. He was the son of an English gentry family, which had acquired Irish lands in the 17th century and, by his time, bore an Irish title. Although a collateral ancestor, Sir William Temple, had been a famous diplomat under William III, Palmerston was by no means predestined to a career in diplomacy. His family had close connections with the City of London and it seemed much more likely that he would become chancellor of the exchequer – a post offered to him at intervals throughout his life. At the University of Edinburgh he had been the pupil of Dugald Stuart, the disciple of the great Adam Smith, and adopted his economic principles. Having entered parliament in 1807 as the MP for the "rotten" borough of Newport in the Isle of Wight, he became in 1809 secretary at war, primarily a financial portfolio, concerned with parliamentary financing of the army. He remained in this comparatively junior office until 1828, through various changes of ministries. He was not a particularly effective speaker and his friends were disappointed in his progress. He seemed an amiable but diffident man – a natural bureaucrat in Bourne's estimation.

No one expected Lord Grey to offer Palmerston the Foreign Office when he became prime minister in 1830 – probably he intended to control foreign affairs himself. But, particularly after Grey was replaced by Melbourne in 1834, Palmerston made the office peculiarly his own. His personality seemed to change gradually to the dominant figure of later years – that portrayed by Guedalla – particularly after 1848. Although Palmerston never liked or trusted the extension of the franchise, he learnt how to control the new expanded electorate. His handling of the great European crisis of 1848–49 was pragmatic and often unsuccessful but he convinced the British public that he was the champion of constitutional causes. Palmerston's growing control of public opinion is interestingly examined in two articles by BROWN (both 2001).

Palmerston is usually regarded as the first Liberal, as distinct from Whig, prime minister and STEELE set out to examine this aspect of his career. Palmerston became prime minister in 1855 in the middle of the Crimean War but the ministry to which the title "Liberal" is first attached is that of 1859, which lasted until Palmerston's death in 1865. Although Palmerston had been an energetic and successful home secretary in 1852–55, pushing through important legislation in penal reform and public health, his premiership was peculiarly devoid of domestic reforms, his interest seeming to revert entirely to foreign affairs. Even here he was less successful. He favoured the South in the American Civil War and his challenge to Bismarck over Denmark finally led to his bluff being called. This ministry is studied by KREIN.

Palmerston has emerged from modern research less as a symbol of the grandeur of Victorian foreign policy and more as a human being. CHAMBERLAIN attempts a survey in a short study but the literature is massive. PARTRIDGE & PARTRIDGE provide a full listing of books and articles about him.

MURIEL E. CHAMBERLAIN

See also Aberdeen; Asia and Africa; Canning; Cardwell; Congress System; Crimean War; "Eastern Question"; Fiscal Politics; Gladstone; Grey; London, Treaty of; Melbourne; Opium Wars; Parliamentary Reform: Acts of 1832–1885; Russell; Trade Patterns: 1800–c.1890; Wellington

Pankhurst, Emmeline 1858–1928
Pankhurst, Christabel 1880–1958
Pankhurst, Sylvia 1882–1960
Women's suffrage and social-political campaigners

Bullock, Ian and Richard Pankhurst (editors), *Sylvia Pankhurst: From Artist to Anti-Fascist,* London: Macmillan, and New York: St Martin's Press, 1992

Castle, Barbara, *Sylvia and Christabel Pankhurst,* London: Penguin, and New York: Viking Press, 1987

Kamm, Josephine, *The Story of Emmeline Pankhurst,* New York: Meredith Press, 1968

Marcus, Jane (editor), *Suffrage and the Pankhursts,* London: Routledge and Kegan Paul, and New York: Macmillan, 1987

Mitchell, David, *The Fighting Pankhursts,* London: Jonathan Cape, and New York: Macmillan, 1967

Mitchell, David, *Queen Christabel: A Biography of Christabel Pankhurst,* London: Macdonald and Jane's, 1977

Romero, Patricia, *E. Sylvia Pankhurst: Portrait of a Radical,* New Haven, Connecticut: Yale University Press, 1987

Winslow, Barbara, *Sylvia Pankhurst: Sexual Politics and Political Activism,* London: UCL Press, and New York: St Martin's Press, 1996

Emmeline, Christabel, and Sylvia Pankhurst are best known for their involvement in the struggle for women's suffrage. Much of the literature on the Pankhurst women concentrates on this part of their lives. Yet, after suffrage, each of them focused on different political activities. For example, Emmeline and Christabel ran for parliament, Christabel became religious and lectured on the apocalypse, and Sylvia supported the Russian Revolution and Ethiopian independence. While the chosen works do consider the Pankhursts' political activities beyond suffrage, more has been written about Sylvia, most likely because her interests were not only more diverse but more successful. Books about them reflect conflicting portraits of these three women, as well as speculation about their sexualities. The main consensus on the Pankhursts is that in terms of their political ideals, they were dedicated and determined women, each demonstrating capable leadership.

MITCHELL's study (1967) of the Pankhurst women demonstrates that their fight for suffrage was based on the issue of equal rights for men and women. All three women needed drama, public recognition, loyalty from their followers, and rapid resolutions to all of their campaigns. Mitchell describes the Women's Social and Political Union (WSPU) as "the largest and most efficient of any political organization in Britain". The author believes the Pankhurst women were neither lesbian nor feminist, but were political activists whose gender was incidental.

Conversely, CASTLE suggests that Christabel and Sylvia Pankhurst exemplify two distinct feminisms. Their differing personalities caused a rift in their relationship, and led them to dichotomous activisms. The only similarity she points to is their determination. She describes Christabel as confident, extroverted, calculated, obsessed with the importance of her leadership, and later in life, morbid and apocalyptic. She shows that Christabel endorsed the movement's militant activities, while securing her own safety by moving to Paris. The author also raises the question of the sisters' sexualities. While she sees Christabel's hatred of men as a political strategy rather than an indication of lesbianism, she presents Sylvia as sensuous and heterosexual. Sylvia was also independent, but in addition nervous, depressive, and torn between art and suffragism, that is, between loyalty to her mother's and her father's causes. The author believes that Sylvia's social vision was much broader than Christabel's because it encompassed wider reform than women's suffrage.

KAMM's biography focuses primarily on Emmeline's suffrage activism, and shows that even as a child she was interested in issues of oppression and revolution. Emmeline demonstrated qualities of leadership that would serve her in her reform work as a poor-law guardian, as well as in the suffrage movement. While Emmeline was an eloquent speaker and a capable leader, the author tells us that she was dictatorial in her running of the WSPU. Yet, she was worshipped as a hero by the union members. The author also describes Emmeline's relationship with the composer Ethel Smyth, who taught the suffrage leader how to aim and throw stones.

MITCHELL's biography of Christabel (1977) presents her as a calculating leader, yet a troubled person. He connects the personal and political by suggesting that she was trapped in her extremist rhetoric, while protected from the violent consequences of suffrage militancy, a contradiction that limited her personal growth. As a suffrage leader, she was encouraged in her personal and political extremism by the suffragists' and her mother's adoration for her. Christabel's possible lesbianism stemmed from her ambivalent feelings for "a neurotic mother". The author's portrait of her is concluded by a comparison between Christabel and Ulrike Meinhof of the West German Baader-Meinhof terrorist group from the 1970s.

BULLOCK & PANKHURST state that the difficulty of writing a good biography of Sylvia lies in the diversity of her activities. Therefore, each essay in this collection focuses on one aspect of her life, including her art, her suffragist activism, her pacifism, her communism, and her anti-fascism. Particularly useful are the two essays on Sylvia's art, where we are given accounts of her artistic education, analyses of her designs for the WSPU, her mural for the Independent Labour Party hall, and her series on working women.

ROMERO interprets Sylvia's life in terms of her personal and political radicalism. She shows that Sylvia's relentless nature, compounded with the ethic of social activism inherited from her father, made her shift her loyalties to different causes many times during her life. The author provides an alternative to Sylvia's autobiography, by trying to balance Sylvia's achievements in suffragism, socialism, and anti-fascism with a picture of a woman who is a political naif, an overly emotional campaigner, an inefficient financial manager, a poor organizer, and a flawed writer. She describes the causes of the split among the three Pankhursts as political differences, Sylvia's jealousy of Emmeline's relationship with Christabel, and Sylvia's illegitimate son.

Instead of interpreting Sylvia's politics as discontinuous, WINSLOW sees Sylvia as the first to connect feminism and socialism. While her political activism began with the woman's suffrage movement, Sylvia became increasingly concerned with the plight of working-class men and women. She saw the issue of women's suffrage in terms of class as well as gender. Sylvia is described as an international feminist whose London organization, the East London Federation of the Suffragettes, later known as the Workers' Suffrage Federation, was both feminist and working class. Sylvia also took stands against racism, imperialism, and colonialism when few people were following suit. While the author believes that it is probable that Emmeline and Christabel were lesbians, she also suggests a lesbian relationship between Sylvia and Zelie Emerson.

MARCUS's introduction to source materials in the Fawcett Library comments on distortions inherent in accounts of the suffragists by both historians of and participants in the suffrage movement. She says that instead of viewing the suffragists as hysterical women, we should read their outspokenness as disruptive of masculine discourse at a time when women were expected to be silent. The hunger strikes, women's refusal to eat and nourish the body, are refusals of motherhood. The author begins and ends with images of force-feeding as rape.

HELEN THOMPSON

See also Women's Movements; Women's Suffrage Movement

Papacy, Relations with medieval period

Cheney, C.R., *From Becket to Langton: English Church Government 1170–1213*, Manchester: Manchester University Press, 1956

Du Boulay, F.R.H., "The Fifteenth Century" in *The English Church and the Papacy in the Middle Ages*, edited by C.H. Lawrence, London: Burns and Oates, and New York: Fordham University Press, 1965

Mollat, G., *The Popes at Avignon 1305–1378*, translated by Janet Love from the 9th French edition (1949), London and New York: Nelson, 1963

Lawrence, C.H. (editor), *The English Church and the Papacy in the Middle Ages*, London: Burns and Oates, and New York: Fordham University Press, 1965

Pantin, W.A., *The English Church in the Fourteenth Century*, Cambridge: Cambridge University Press, 1955; Notre Dame, Indiana: University of Notre Dame Press, 1962

Southern, R.W., *Saint Anselm: A Portrait in a Landscape*, Cambridge and New York: Cambridge University Press, 1990

With the exception of the volume edited by LAWRENCE, which is the only book surveying the complete history of medieval Anglo-papal relations (with essays on the Celtic and Anglo-Saxon churches, as well as those covering the period from the Norman Conquest to the eve of the Reformation), papal relations form but one part of the general history of the English church. This is well illustrated by SOUTHERN's picture of the problems faced by Anselm. The Norman kings of England had not recognized any pope since the death of Gregory VII in 1085, and when William Rufus recognized Urban II rather than Clement III, the papal legate's arrival with the pallium created new problems. In 1097 Anselm's request to visit and consult the pope was refused by the king. When Paschal II succeeded Urban in 1099 and Henry I became king in 1100, the situation changed and Anselm faced what Southern calls "the beginning of a change which became more conspicuous later", a growing bureaucracy, increased regulation, frequent negotiation, and the drawing of power away from the regions towards the central papal government.

The main factor determining the relationship between the English church and the papacy was the plenitude of power and universal jurisdiction belonging to the pope. Innocent III held that he was "judge of all men and judged by none". As CHENEY shows this theological principle was worked out in the Roman canon law ordering the church's life. In order to resolve the numerous conflicts between cited authorities, interested parties appealed to Rome and this practice was greatly increased in the 12th century. The cases were wide ranging and included disputes over the administration of the sacraments, marriage cases, conflicts of jurisdiction, and lawsuits over property. Cheney follows a number of cases and shows how various types of appeals were dealt with by local judges-delegate and by appearance at the Roman curia. The latter involved a hazardous journey – especially when France and England were at war – of seven or more weeks. An exchange of letters took two to four months and the letters might well be meaningless by the time they arrived. It was also possible to deceive curial officers who could not readily confirm testimony. These shortcomings have to be borne in mind when looking at relations with Rome. Long journeys and delay increased costs for appellants but they also needed to pay a large number of officials, up to and including the cardinals, if a case was to be heard.

Cheney lists the other ways in which papal authority was brought to bear on the discipline of the English church: by indulgences, dispensations, especially in marriage cases, exemption of religious houses from diocesan jurisdiction, reserved absolution for certain offences, and the canonization of saints. And petitioners went to Rome seeking benefices, by means of expectatives (an instruction to a patron to provide the next available canonry or living to a given clerk), indulgences, release from the consequences of irregularity, and privileges and indults (a pope's licence for something normally outside canon law). The papal claims to jurisdiction over the English might appear to undermine the authority of the crown, but, as Cheney observes, the popes moved cautiously. When the king objected to papal demands and obstructed them, he generally had the support of the English bishops, who also feared that their authority might be undermined by Rome. Neither king nor bishops were anti-papal, but there was suspicion of foreign intervention in English affairs.

PANTIN continues the story both in his essay in Lawrence and more fully in his own book. He deals first with papal provisions, the system by which men were promoted to offices and benefices by the central authority, the pope, rather than by local methods of appointment. Papal provision was a significant part of the growing centralization of the church in the 12th and 13th centuries to which Cheney also draws attention. In 1265 the pope reserved to himself all the benefices about to become vacant in England. A petitioner seeking a benefice for himself needed to have it presented to the pope by some influential person, a king, cardinal, bishop, or lay magnate. After the petition, there was a process of examination, bull of provision, and execution, with the possibility of an appeal by a rival claimant or local patron. Appeals involved the complex procedures followed by Cheney. Pantin does not think that the evidence supports the usual lurid picture of English benefices filled with aliens, with disastrous results, but acknowledges that much more work must be done on the number of alien and English provisors. Mollat also thinks that the complaint of the "unbridled multitude of apostolic provisions" to strangers was exaggerated and partly unfair. Whatever the facts, Pantin shows that the English laity felt a strong antipathy to aliens and this led to anti-clerical and anti-papal feeling. Papal provision of bishops increased dramatically from the 13th to the mid-14th centuries, perhaps because communication with Avignon was much swifter than with Rome. By this means the king generally got the bishop he wanted and Clement VI (1345) said that if the king of England asked him to make an ass a bishop, he would do so! It was not bishoprics nor parishes that gave rise to conflict but cathedrals, where canonries were sinecures and useful for increasing the income of non-resident clergy employed in the service of church and state. Crown and papacy were usually able to work together in practice, though the king had to steer a course between lay and parliamentary complaint and the advantage gained from cooperation with the pope. The bishops too had to satisfy the claims of both pope and king.

Pantin divides Anglo-papal relations into three periods: 1300–42, 1342–60, and 1360–1400. The first period is one of the fairly smooth relations of Edward I, II, and III with the early Avignon popes, the English subject Clement V, and the two masterful pontiffs John XXII and Benedict XII. The second period, opening the pontificate of the strongly pro-French Clement VI, was one of crisis and struggle, especially because of the Hundred Years' War. Two celebrated statutes were passed during this period: the Statute of Provisors in 1351 and of Praemunire in 1353. Pantin explains that they seem more important to later observers than they did at the time and represented but one aspect of the long struggle between royal courts and church courts. The third period was difficult for both crown and papacy, with the last years of the reign of Edward III and that of Richard II and, on the papal side, the costly reconquest of Italy, the return to Rome, and the Great Schism. It involved protest and conflict on the one hand and constant negotiation on the other. Pantin summarizes 14th-century Anglo-papal relations as a struggle (a) about rival legal claims, and (b) about rival systems of patronage, but not as an attempt at "shaking off the papal yoke".

MOLLAT looks at the same material as Pantin but from a different perspective. He also deals with Ireland and Scotland. He describes the character of each of the Avignon popes and then examines papal relations with Christendom. The section on England is much smaller than those concerned with Italy, the empire, and France. He shows that Edward I needed papal support and "prudently manoeuvred between the malcontents [in parliament] and Clement V". Edward II was less discreet and Pope John XXII took advantage of his difficulties by increasing the number of reserved appointments and papal nominations. The pope resolutely opposed Robert Bruce's invasion of Ulster, but also took an interest in the claim that the king's Irish subjects suffered from acts of oppression. The cardinal legates employed in Ireland were also sent to Scotland. They refused to acknowledge Bruce as king and he refused to accept them; Bruce's excommunication followed, but when summoned to appear at Avignon in May 1320 he justified his actions and sought reconciliation. Mollat largely agrees with Pantin's analysis of the reign of Edward III though he concludes that there was such unrest and rejection of papal demands that a national church was already beginning to form and that "England was gradually becoming ripe for schism".

DU BOULAY begins his account of the last 150 years before the breach with Rome in 1378 and the papal election, of the Italian Urban VI, that led to the Great Schism. It is a period with far fewer significant events in Anglo-papal relations, though the English were committed to ending the schism and to reforming the church. Du Boulay shows how the papacy came to mean less to England and English affairs "seemed neither dangerous nor consequential to Rome".

MARTIN R. DUDLEY

See also Anglo-Saxon England: Church Organization; Christian Conversion in the British Isles

Paris, Matthew *c.*1200–1259
Monk, hagiographer, and chronicler

Galbraith, Vivian H., *Roger Wendover and Matthew Paris*, Glasgow: Jackson, 1944

Knowles, David, *The Religious Orders in England*, 3 vols, Cambridge: Cambridge University Press, 1948–59

Lewis, Suzanne, *The Art of Matthew Paris in the Chronica Majora*, Berkeley: University of California Press, and Aldershot: Scolar Press, 1987

Powicke, Frederick M., "The Compilation of the *Chronica Majora* of Matthew Paris", *Modern Philology*, 38 (1940–41): 305–17; reprinted, with some revisions, in *Proceedings of the British Academy*, 30 (1944): 147–60

Reader, Rebecca, "Matthew Paris and the Norman Conquest" in *The Cloister and the World: Essays in Medieval History in Honour of Barbara Harvey*, edited by John Blair and Brian Golding, Oxford: Clarendon Press, and New York: Oxford University Press, 1996

Stubbs, William (editor), *Memoriale fratris Walteri de Coventria* [The Historical Collections of Walter of Coventry], 2 vols, London: Longman, 1872–73; Wiesbaden: Kraus Reprint, 1965

Tout, Thomas F., *The Political History of England*, vol. 3, *The History of England from the Accession of Henry III to the Death of Edward III, 1216–1377*, edited by William Hunt and Reginald L. Poole, London and New York: Longmans Green, 1905

Vaughan, Richard (editor and translator), *The Chronicles of Matthew Paris: Monastic Life in the Thirteenth Century*, Gloucester: Sutton, and New York: St Martin's Press, 1984

Vaughan, Richard, *Matthew Paris,* Cambridge: Cambridge University Press, 1958

Matthew Paris is best known as a prolific, powerful, and vibrant chronicler of 13th-century affairs who was extremely patriotic in his writing, and quick to condemn clerical vanity, the advancement of non-Anglo-Normans in England's political and ecclesiastical power elite, and abuse of power, as well as an artist who recorded personalities and events with his pen. He spent the majority of his life at the Benedictine abbey of St Albans, Hertfordshire where he benefited from the abbey's emphasis on learning, decorative art, the writing history, and its possession of a well-supplied and busy scriptorium, and sizeable library. His first significant work, *Chronica majora*, is a continuation and revision of the work begun by his fellow monk, Roger Wendover, in which he is primarily responsible for all the material dealing with events that took place between 1236 (when he inherited the position of historian for the abbey upon the death of Wendover) and 1259 (the year of his own death). His contributions to the abbey's chronicle of England was unlike that of any of his predecessors in that he spent a great deal of time and energy gathering information from visitors to the abbey and from a wide variety of sources. He also travelled widely, was a frequent presence at the court and in the king's company, and was a witness to many of the events and ceremonies he related in his works.

His *Historia Anglorum, Flores historiarum,* and *Abbreviatio chronicorum* basically are excerpts from the *Chronica*. In addition to his chronicle accounts, he also wrote four saints' lives in French meant primarily for the use and consumption of the Anglo-Norman population of England. These include *La Estoire de St Aedward le rei, La Vie de St Edmond, La Vie de St Auban,* and *La Vie de St Thomas de Cantorbéry.*

His work as an artist is found spread throughout the above-mentioned works. Sometimes in the form of doodles, fully developed drawings, maps, or diagrams, he supplemented his text with images of participants or visual materials meant to assist the reader in understanding personalities or problems discussed in various sections of his work.

Late 19th- and 20th-century works examining Matthew Paris and his various writings focused on the most basic of issues concerning his authorship of certain works, identification of his handwriting and artwork, and the relationship between copies of his work. Most 19th-century writers who considered Matthew's work became caught up in and admired his patriotism (pro-Norman, anti-Poitevin and Angevin) and his moralistic attacks against clerical corruption and weak kings. STUBBS in his introduction to the works of Walter Coventry and elsewhere was led astray by these sentiments and incorrectly claimed that the greatest condemnations of immorality and political weakness found in the *Flores historiarum* were written by Matthew and not Roger Wendover.

Writing in 1905 TOUT in many ways acted as a bridge between this 19th-century outlook and more critical 20th-century examination of the content of Matthew's writings. Like the Victorians, Tout described Matthew as a patriot with strong anti-clerical biases, but went beyond that to state that he was concise, bold, expressed independent judgement as a historian, and exercised tremendous literary skill. Tout continued by criticizing the author for his preference at times of a good story over fact and indignation at the introduction of non-Normans into England's political and ecclesiastical hierarchy.

By the 1940s work continued to be done on the question of the origins of the surviving manuscripts of Matthew's work as well as his relationship with Roger Wendover and his contributions to the *Flores*. More importantly historians such as POWICKE and GALBRAITH in lectures and in publications turned away from the Victorian tendency to laud Matthew's role as moralist and instead praise three unique characteristics found in his writings: his introduction of personality into chronicle writing, his collection of reliable sources, and the sheer bulk of product. Galbraith found the information Matthew supplied amply offset the extravagance of the prejudices expressed. KNOWLES follows in this pattern and contributes another voice to that group of historians who view Matthew as a man and as a source, but not as a saint.

Contemporary attitudes towards Matthew as a historian have been influenced over the last few decades by the work of VAUGHAN, who continued an unbiased examination of the man, chronicler, and artist. The student of 13th-century chronicle writing, politics, and economic history finds a critical study of the man in his *The Chronicles of Matthew Paris* and in the biography *Matthew Paris*. Vaughan finds Paris often to be mercenary in outlook, constantly mentioning and concerned with the cost of the necessities of life, as well as luxury items. His aristocratic associations and the prejudices of the wealthy Benedictine house to which he belonged are repeatedly demonstrated, as are his narrow parochial loyalties to most things English. As Vaughan points out, Matthew Paris's spirituality is only dimly viewed in his works.

Work continues to be done on Matthew Paris as author and artist, but in much smaller studies that focus on how he reported specific events. Most notable in the current crop of works is READER's article, in which she not only provides a synopsis of Vaughan's work, but specifically examines his handling of the Conquest and compares him with contemporary chroniclers. For those interested in Paris's drawings and artwork, which accompany his texts, LEWIS takes great care to examine them and to relate them to the texts and to the larger artistic tradition of the time.

ILICIA J. SPREY

See also Bede's Ecclesiastical History; Chronicles; Hagiography; Saint Albans, School of

Parishes   medieval period

Cheney, C.R., *From Becket to Langton: English Church Government 1170–1213*, Manchester: Manchester University Press, 1956

Cook, G.H., *The English Mediaeval Parish Church*, London: Phoenix House, 1954

Cutts, Edward L., *Parish Priests and Their People in the Middle Ages in England*, London: SPCK, and New York: Young, 1898

Duffy, Eamon, *The Stripping of the Altars: Traditional Religion in England, c.1400–c.1580*, New Haven, Connecticut and London: Yale University Press, 1992

Gasquet, Francis Aidan, *Parish Life in Mediæval England*, London: Methuen, 1906

Harper-Bill, Christopher, *The Pre-Reformation Church in England, 1400–1530*, revised edition, London and New York: Longman, 1996

Kümin, Beat A., *The Shaping of a Community: The Rise and Reformation of the English Parish, c.1400–1560*, Aldershot, Hampshire and Brookfield, Vermont: Scolar Press, 1996

Moorman, John R.H., *Church Life in England in the Thirteenth Century*, Cambridge: Cambridge University Press, 1945; reprinted with corrections, 1955

The parish was one of the most basic units of English medieval life, placing every dwelling and area of land within a defined area of ecclesiastical jurisdiction. It originated in the Anglo-Saxon period as part of a system of minster parishes, which was gradually converted to a system of local parishes as manorial lords built churches endowed with tithes and claiming the religious observance of local residents. CHENEY shows that the 12th-century parochial system was as unsystematic as the feudal system, with pastoral care being secondary to the benefice and its income. As MOORMAN shows, by the 13th century England was divided into between 8,000 and 12,000 parishes with firm boundaries, rigidly observed and with a requirement, enforced by the parish ban, for a person to seek the sacraments within the parish. Gasquet is clear that the parish was primarily an ecclesiastical unit, answerable to higher authorities within the church but exempt from the control of the local lord. Moorman sees the parish priest as having, at least initially, a dual loyalty, to the bishop and the lord. The parish was also an economic unit in which tithes were paid and which not only supported the clergy but also, and more importantly, alleviated the lot of the poor. The complexities of the tithe system are explained by Gasquet and Moorman, and those of the benefice system by Cheney.

Modern historians remain indebted to the works of 19th-century antiquarians for detailed knowledge of English medieval parish life. The primary sources are visitation reports, churchwardens' accounts, inventories, and wills. Liturgical evidence comes from extant service books and from a wealth of miniatures. Among the antiquaries Cutts and Gasquet remain useful and provide a balance to each other, the former being an Anglican anxious to stress continuity, the latter a Roman catholic anxious to stress discontinuity. CUTTS provides a thorough and well-illustrated account of parishes, parish churches, clergy, services, and customs in rural and urban parishes. The reputation of Cardinal GASQUET as a historian has been reduced by evidence of inaccuracy, polemical intent, and an unwillingness to find anything wrong with medieval Christianity, but his account of medieval parish life provides a helpful and largely accurate picture. Cutts and Gasquet use primary sources but without providing the full notes expected by contemporary historians, and this can be rather frustrating.

As parish churches dot the English countryside and attract many visitors, more attention has been paid to the history of the English parish church than to that of the parish. The majority of books dealing with the former necessarily shed some light on the history of the latter. As COOK says, the social life of medieval England is no less surely written in the stones of parish churches than are the religious beliefs and cults of pre-Reformation days. Cook is concerned with the medieval church building and his careful narrative account, augmented by plans and photographs, provides a clear picture of its changing shape as it was adapted to different patterns of religious devotion and practice, especially by the growth of the chantry cult and the parish guilds. DUFFY shows how the parish was not the only expression of communal religious feeling in late medieval England and charts the activities and evolution of the guilds, which nevertheless used and embellished the parish churches. Moorman sets the 13th-century parish and its church in the broader context of church life, showing the relation to the diocese, to the monasteries, and to the mendicant orders, and also addresses the need for reform of the clergy, the benefice system, and the tithes.

The subject of the religious condition of the parish priests and their people in the Middle Ages takes the historian into a polemical atmosphere, particularly at the point of transition into the history of the Reformation. At one end there are the admirers of medieval religion who see it as "the ages of Faith" and there are others who see it only in terms of false doctrines and manifold superstitions. In current historical writing, the admirers are ascendant. Cook and other historians of the buildings set out to provide the reader with a picture of the parish church and its development. In doing so they provide almost no information about abuses or corruptions, other than in contrasting the splendours of the Middle Ages with the crassness of the late 20th century. Their position is not unlike that of Gasquet in his comparison with the churches before and after what has been called "the great pillage" or, by Duffy in the attack on traditional religion and the "stripping of the altars". By Gasquet's account, there was no need for reform. HARPER-BILL takes the story from 1400 to just short of the Reformation and Duffy takes it from 1400 to the Reformation settlement under Elizabeth I. Harper-Bill gives a very concise account of the English church with chapters on the parish clergy and on religious belief and practice. Duffy gives a long and vivid account of late medieval English religion in the parishes, stressing its richness and vitality, which is, however, open to question at a number of points. He effectively takes up Gasquet's conviction that all was well with English catholicism and traditional religion and the Reformation was unnecessary. There is no consideration of the poverty of the unbeneficed clergy or of the admittedly low level of clerical morality and negligence, noted by Harper-Bill. A somewhat more critical approach to parish life would seem to come closer to the reality, accepting both the vitality of late medieval religion and that the devotional and theological system needed at least some reform. KÜMIN deals in part with this last point.

MARTIN R. DUDLEY

Parker, Matthew 1505–1575
Archbishop of Canterbury

Brook, Victor John Knight, *A Life of Archbishop Parker,* Oxford: Clarendon Press, 1962

Graham, Timothy and Andrew G. Watson, *The Recovery of the Past in Early Elizabethan England: Documents by John Bale and John Joscelyn from the Circle of Matthew Parker,* Cambridge: Cambridge University Library for the Cambridge Bibliographical Society, 1998

Greg, Sir Walter Wilson, "Books and Bookmen in the Correspondence of Archbishop Parker", *The Library,* 4th series, 16/3 (1935): 243–77

James, Montague Rhodes (editor), *A Descriptive Catalogue of the Manuscripts in the Library of Corpus Christi College Cambridge,* 2 vols, Cambridge: Cambridge University Press, 1909–12

McKisack, May, *Medieval History in the Tudor Age,* Oxford: Clarendon Press, 1971

Page, R.I., *Matthew Parker and His Books: Saunders Lectures in Bibliography Delivered on 14, 16, and 18 May 1990 at the University of Cambridge,* Kalamazoo: Medieval Institute Publications, and Cambridge: Research Group on Manuscript Evidence, Corpus Christi College, 1993

Robinson, Benedict Scott, "'Darke Speech': Matthew Parker and the Reforming of History", *Sixteenth Century Journal,* 29/4 (1998): 1061–83

Shirley, F.J., *Elizabeth's First Archbishop: A Reply to Mr J.C. Whitebrook's Consecration of the Most Reverend Matthew Parker,* London: SPCK for the Church Historical Society, 1948

Whitebrook, J.C., *The Consecration of the Most Reverend Matthew Parker, Archbishop of Canterbury,* London and Oxford: Mowbray, and New York: Morehouse-Gerham, 1945

For a man renowned for his moderation and quiet, scholarly temperament, Parker has attracted a great deal of controversy, though much of it not of his own making. BROOK replaced the earlier life by W.P.M. Kennedy (1908) as the standard biography. Such it remains, though necessarily overtaken in points of detail by Norman Jones on the 1559 settlement and William P. Haugaard on the 1563 convocation, and by the work of Patrick Collinson, Christopher Haigh, Felicity Heal, and others on the Elizabethan church generally. Brook's account of Parker's career is solidly based on the printed sources, principally the archbishop's correspondence published by the Parker Society (1853) and the archiepiscopal register edited in several parts for the Canterbury and York Society by W.H. Frere (1928–33). But Brook used no manuscripts; even material in the Parker Library at Corpus Christi College, Cambridge, is cited only by reference to James's catalogue. He has in any case little to say about

Parker's literary work; fairly enough, for this is primarily an account of his central ministry. Brook writes elegantly and with much sympathy for his subject. He well demonstrates how Parker came in some measure to enjoy the exercise of the office which he had so reluctantly accepted. Brook will still be worth reading when, as surely it soon will be, it is replaced by a biography which takes into account the scholarship of the past 40 years, and which incorporates newly printed and still unpublished source material.

There has been much argument about the technicalities of Parker's consecration. To Roman catholics this was the decisive break in the apostolic succession. Anglicans who have wanted their bishops and clergy in orders every bit as holy as those in the pope's church have argued the legitimacy of the Parker ceremony. At the time the main concern was to ensure that the 1550 ordinal was valid in English law (in doubt because the legislation restoring the prayer book in 1559 had not mentioned the separately issued ordinal). Any deficiencies in Parker's consecration were therefore underwritten by royal edict; though this naturally only satisfied those to whom secular control of the church was acceptable in the first place. Catholics and protestants, with different views of what the consecration was supposed to achieve, have consequently had differing reservations about its authenticity. A quite separate issue was raised by WHITEBROOK, who in a heavily documented submission argued that Parker had actually been consecrated some weeks earlier than commonly supposed, at the hands of Kitchen, one of the surviving Marian bishops (and therefore capable of transmitting orders recognized as valid if irregular by the Roman church). Whitebrook short-circuited the debates on the Lambeth consecration service of 17 December 1559 by claiming that this never took place; that records of it were fraudulently concocted, and that documents dated by the year of Parker's episcopate support his case. All this was met with a sweeping rejoinder from SHIRLEY, who had no difficulty in finding flaws in much of Whitebrook's evidence. With his own superior diplomatic and palaeographical skills he showed that Parker indubitably went through a form of consecration at the time and place traditionally supposed (whether or not legitimately in the eyes of the Roman church being not here the question). This was thought by Brook to have settled the matter; yet certain puzzles remain. Whitebrook clearly overstated his case by trying to show that the Lambeth consecration was a fiction. It remains possible that Parker may have hedged his bets by receiving orders according to the old rite before undergoing the newly devised ceremony at Lambeth. Shirley makes much of the fact that the *sede vacante* procedures continued operative after the consecration date alleged by Whitebrook. Surprisingly Shirley makes no allowance for the distinction between *ordo* and *jurisdictio*. If the issue is detached from its polemical context, it may yet yield instructive information about Parker's expectations in 1559 for his own future and that of the church he served.

Debate also continues on Parker's activities as a bibliophile and an editor of historical texts. It was his undoubted achievement to rescue many manuscripts which had been removed from monastic libraries at the dissolution. In 1568 he was specifically authorized by the Privy Council to collect and conserve this material. Much of what he acquired he left to his old college, Corpus Christi, at Cambridge. The catalogue by JAMES is the essential guide. It also lists manuscripts owned by Parker which did not come to the college (as well, of course, as the library's holdings from other sources). GREG usefully collected items of bibliographical interest in Parker's correspondence; he includes some details contributed by James about Cecil's manuscript collection, one from which Parker borrowed. GRAHAM & WATSON document the comprehensive bibliographical survey that Parker superintended. The best summary of Parker's work in collecting and editing manuscripts is given by MCKISACK in a chapter of her general survey. She stresses that this was the work of the team Parker assembled. The extent to which Parker himself wielded the editorial red pencil had been doubted; but to McKisack the issue is of secondary importance. Further discussion is given in PAGE's book, based on his three 1990 Sandars lectures, and illustrated with 75 monochrome photographs by Mildred Budny. Both McKisack and Page are obliged to instance many of Parker's conservation practices which would now be deplored. He would "tidy" books by removing their messier pages, and improve them by cannibalizing others. He cut pictures from a 13th-century psalter to provide frontispieces for an 11th-century book of homilies and a 12th-century Eadmer. He also sent precious volumes to the printing house, whence they returned with inky thumbprints and other marks still painfully visible. But, as Page points out, if Parker destroyed some things we would now preserve, he preserved much more which we would otherwise not have. As editor he is accused of cobbling texts together, and pruning them of "corrupt" passages to suit his vision of the continuity of the English church from Anglo-Saxon times to his own. ROBINSON surveys the recent debate, and reasonably concludes that Parker and his helpers should not be judged by modern standards of textual precision or impartial historiography.

C.S. KNIGHTON

See also Elizabethan Settlement of Religion; Mary I; Protestant Revolution

Parliament: High Court

Beven, T., "The Appellate Jurisdiction of the House of Lords", *Law Quarterly Review*, 17 (1901): 155–70, 357–71

Chrimes, S.B., *English Constitutional Ideas in the Fifteenth Century*, Cambridge: Cambridge University Press, 1936; New York: American Scholar Publications, 1966

Dicey, A.V., *Introduction to the Study of the Law of the Constitution*, 8th edition, London: Macmillan, 1915; reprinted, Indianapolis, Indiana: Liberty, 1982

Edwards, J.G., "Justice in Early English Parliaments", *Bulletin of the Institute of Historical Research*, 27 (1954): 35–53

Elton, G.R., *The Tudor Constitution: Documents and Commentary*, Cambridge: Cambridge University Press, 1960; 2nd edition, Cambridge and New York: Cambridge University Press, 1982

Gough, J.W., *Fundamental Law in English Constitutional History*, Oxford: Clarendon Press, 1955; Littleton, Colorado: Rothman, 1985

Hale, Matthew, *The Jurisdiction of the Lords House, or Parliament, Considered According to Antient Records*, London: Cadell, 1796

Holdsworth, W.S., "Central Courts and Representative Assemblies", *Columbia Law Review*, 12 (1912): 1–31

Kenyon, J.P. (editor), *The Stuart Constitution, 1603–1688: Documents and Commentary*, Cambridge: Cambridge University Press, 1966; 2nd edition, Cambridge and New York: Cambridge University Press, 1986

Maitland, Frederic William (editor), *Records of the Parliament Holden at Westminster, on the Twenty-Eighth Day of February, in the Thirty-Third Year of the Reign of King Edward the First AD 1305*, London: Eyre and Spottiswood, 1893

McIlwain, Charles Howard, *The High Court of Parliament and Its Supremacy: An Historical Essay on the Boundaries between Legislation and Adjudication in England*, New Haven, Connecticut: Yale University Press, and London: Oxford University Press, 1910

Roskell, J.S., *The House of Commons, 1386–1421*, Stroud, Gloucestershire: Sutton, 1993

Selden, John, *Of the Judicature of Parliament*, edited by David Wilkins, London: Walthoe, 1726

Stevens, Robert, *Law and Politics: The House of Lords as a Judicial Body, 1800–1976*, Chapel Hill: University of North Carolina Press, 1978; London: Weidenfeld and Nicolson, 1979

Originally the English parliament was both a consultative assembly and a court of justice, and the latter function was considered to be the more important, which is why the meetings acquired the title of High Court. This was recognized by Sir Edward Coke in the early 17th century, and set out fully by SELDEN a century later. By the time that Selden wrote, the parliament as a whole no longer functioned as a court, its residual judicial function having come to rest in the appellate jurisdiction of the House of Lords. This development was discussed at close quarters by the practising lawyer Sir Matthew HALE in 1796, and in a more academic mode by BEVEN just over a century later. Most of the work on this subject is descriptive rather than controversial. For the early parliaments, there is a good presentation by EDWARDS, while the introduction to the records of the 1305 parliament, published by MAITLAND in 1893, offers an in-depth analysis of the early 14th-century situation by a distinguished legal historian. In the first year of Richard II's reign (1377) the commons actually petitioned the king for the convening of a parliament at least once a year for the hearing of cases where injustice had resulted from the delays of the inferior courts, or disagreements among the judges. This was what would later be called equity jurisdiction, although at this stage it is clear that judgement was to be given in accordance with the common law. Appellate jurisdiction in the proper sense developed during the 15th century, partly as a result of the misuse of the lower courts during the time of misgovernment. It was not until 1585, when the legislative function of parliament was fully developed, that a statute finally confirmed the function of parliament to hear cases on appeal from the court of King's Bench. When Sir Edward Coke defined a void session in the early 17th century, he declared it to be one in which no act had been passed, and no judgement given.

During the 15th century parliament also functioned as a court in a different sense, exercising a process of impeachment to reinforce its various petitions for redress of grievance. In this procedure the House of Lords was properly the court, the Commons acting as prosecutors, and the verdicts had to be confirmed by the crown to have legal effect. This process was revived in the 17th century, and its implications are fully considered by KENYON. The main controversy surrounding the judicial function of parliament has been over when, and how rapidly, it was abandoned. MCILWAIN, who offers the most exhaustive treatment of the whole subject, believed that as late as the reign of Charles I the parliament was still seen primarily as a high court. This position was immediately criticized by Sir William HOLDSWORTH, who pointed out the crucial importance of the Reformation Parliament of 1529–36. McIlwain subsequently acknowledged this correction, and Holdsworth's position was fully explored and developed by ELTON. Elton also pointed out the fact that much of the earlier judicial function of parliament was taken over during the Tudor period by the king's council, particularly in its aspect as the Court of Star Chamber. By the reign of Elizabeth parliament was no longer expected to provide equitable remedies for miscarriages of justice. William Lambarde acknowledged that parliament had a function to provide remedies where the law was defective, but that was rather through legislation than adjudication.

It was as a court of justice rather than as a legislature that parliament first had what would later be called a constitutional function, because it was called upon to make good deficiencies in the royal applications of the law. The early stages of this awareness are examined by ROSKELL in his introduction, but it was during the 15th century that the most important steps were taken, the significance of which were fully appreciated at the time, as is made clear in the thorough (and much wider) study by CHRIMES. The classic, and still useful, study of the relationship between normal judicature and what would later be called constitutional law is that of DICEY. The delicate question of how far a sovereign legislature can be circumscribed by laws which it has the power to make and unmake, and whether any laws are exempt from, or superior to, such treatment, is a subject examined by GOUGH, who comes to the conclusion that the whole notion of fundamental law was undermined by the developments which took place in England between 1529 and 1689. As the sovereignty of parliament became recognized and established, its function as a court became obsolete, because that function was now supplied by legislation and not by judicial decision. The appellate jurisdiction of the House of Lords is an almost accidental survival, or perhaps a typically pragmatic adaptation. Since the end of the 18th century it has a substantial history of its own, which has been set out in detail by STEVENS. There are now arguments for bringing the function of the law lords to an end, and if that were to happen, the final chapter in the history of parliament as a high court would have been written.

DAVID LOADES

See also Law: Structures of Administration entries

Parliament: House of Commons

Cannadine, David *et al.* (editors), *Houses of Parliament: History, Art, and Architecture*, London: Merrell, 2000

Cook, Chris, *A Short History of the Liberal Party 1900–2001*, 6th edition, Basingstoke: Palgrave, 2002

Davies, R.G. and J.H. Denton (editors), *The English Parliament in the Middle Ages: A Tribute to J.S. Roskell*, Manchester: Manchester University Press, and Philadelphia: University of Pennsylvania Press, 1981

Dean, David, *Law-Making and Society in Late Elizabethan England: The Parliament of England, 1584–1601*, Cambridge and New York: Cambridge University Press, 1996

Graves, Michael A.R., *The Tudor Parliaments: Crown, Lords, and Commons, 1485–1603*, London and New York: Longman, 1985

Hanham, H.J., *Elections and Party Management: Politics in the Time of Disraeli and Gladstone*, London: Longman, 1959; Hamden, Connecticut: Archon, 1978

History of Parliament Trust, *The History of Parliament on CD-ROM*, Cambridge: Cambridge University Press / History of Parliament Trust, 1998 (includes 23 volumes); see also the Trust's website: www.ihr.sas.ac.uk/hop

Loach, Jennifer, *Parliament under the Tudors*, Oxford: Clarendon Press, and New York: Oxford University Press, 1991

Neale, J.E., *The Elizabethan House of Commons*, New Haven, Connecticut: Yale University Press and London: Jonathan Cape, 1950

Notestein, Wallace, *The Winning of the Initiative by the House of Commons*, Oxford: Oxford University Press, 1924

O'Gorman, F., *The Emergence of the British Two-Party System, 1760–1832*, London: Edward Arnold, 1982

Parliamentary History (journal), 3 issues yearly, 1982–

Phillips, John A., *Electoral Behavior in Unreformed England: Plumpers, Splitters, and Straights*, Princeton, New Jersey: Princeton University Press, 1982

Ramsden, John, *An Appetite for Power: A History of the Conservative Party since 1830*, London: HarperCollins, 1998

Russell, Conrad, *Parliaments and English Politics, 1621–1629*, Oxford: Clarendon Press, and New York: Oxford University Press, 1979

Russell, Conrad, *Unrevolutionary England, 1603–1642*, London: Hambledon Press, 1990

Sharpe, Kevin (editor), *Faction and Parliament: Essays on Early Stuart History*, Oxford: Clarendon Press, and New York: Oxford University Press, 1978

Smith, David L., *The Stuart Parliaments, 1603–1689*, London and New York: Edward Arnold, 1999

Smith, Robert and John S. Moore, *The House of Commons: Seven Hundred Years of British Tradition*, London: Smith's Peerage, 1996

Thomas, P.D.G., *The House of Commons in the Eighteenth Century*, Oxford: Clarendon Press, 1971

Thorpe, Andrew, *A History of the British Labour Party*, 2nd edition, Basingstoke and New York: Palgrave, 2001

The historiography of the House of Commons reflects its status as a gradually evolving and amorphous institution. Consequently, any survey acts as a "snapshot" rather than a thoroughly comprehensive overview. Nevertheless, much can be found in general works covering parliamentary history. The journal *Parliamentary History*, which began as a yearbook and is now a thrice-yearly publication, is a key source for up-to-date articles, and regularly publishes specialist issues on specific areas.

It is also possible to recommend certain texts which serve either as fundamental points for reference or, alternatively, as key guides to debates. The fullest overall reference work is the series of volumes, some published and others still ongoing, by the HISTORY OF PARLIAMENT TRUST. While the published works run to 23 volumes, these have been conveniently brought together onto a single CD-ROM. The scale of this project is vast. It is multilayered, serving both as a history and as a work of reference, and consists of 15,559 biographies of MPs, over 1600 constituency reports, six lengthy introductory surveys, and a series of statistical tables covering election results alongside material covering the details of individual constituencies. The CD-ROM provides a valuable research tool, though there are, however, inconsistencies between the various sections. Also, while it may appear feasible to pursue searches across entire periods and, for example, it takes little time to investigate, say, all MPs returned for a particular constituency, the availability of evidence may sometimes limit the results obtained. Biographical information on MPs is naturally much more prevalent for the 18th century onwards than for the medieval and Tudor periods. Overall, it is perhaps the biographical sections that present particular problems, since they sometimes interlock rather insufficiently across the volumes. Despite such drawbacks, however, the work of the History of Parliament Trust continues, and the intention is to publish volumes covering parliamentary history from the earliest assemblies until the Reform Act of 1832, with the possibility of expanding the work on the history of the Commons until the present day.

Both the advantages and shortcomings of the History of Parliament Trust's work are reflective of wider, underlying issues in the historiography of parliament, particularly the impact of a Namierite, Whiggish approach with its teleological emphasis on the development of parliamentary democracy. Whereas early works such as NOTESTEIN tended to emphasize the inevitable rise to power of the Commons, there is now a much more marked concern to stress the limits of government and the manner in which the maintenance of a delicate balance between crown, Lords, and Commons remains a dominant theme. Emphasis on the collective biographies of political elites and parliamentary procedure, which dominates the Trust's work, has been countered by a concern to consider political ideology and the manner in which the Commons found a political "voice".

Of the books purporting to offer short surveys of the Commons' history, the essays collected in SMITH & MOORE – a companion volume to that which appeared on the Lords under the same editorship – offer the most concise and up-to-date introduction. The overall tone of the work is to emphasize how, because of the previously limited nature of the franchise, the present dominance of the Commons in parliamentary history is a recent phenomenon: the Lords, overall, remained the dominant body before 1911, while the crown was the ulti-

mate ruling body before 1800. The volume's main emphasis, given its title, is thus upon continuity rather than change. It stresses the manner in which dialogue and political balance remained at the heart of government. Before the 19th century, it contends, there was little in the way of a demand for "parliamentary government", still less a genuinely "popular politics". Instead, this view is dismissed as part of an over-optimistic Whiggish historiography.

Those seeking the origins of parliament have primarily concentrated on the 13th century and, above all, on the issue of state finance. Carpenter's essay in Smith & Moore provides a succinct overview showing how, during the course of the early 13th century, the frequency with which knights and burgesses were summoned to attend meetings began to increase. The granting of taxation, or rather the constant refusal to grant it, placed parliament on the political map in this period. This point is made particularly forcefully in the series of essays collected in DAVIES & DENTON. As changes in the structure of local magnate society occurred and knights and burgesses began increasingly to demand a role in local affairs, so this led them to develop a political voice through the exercise of local office. Davies & Denton contains a valuable assessment of the need to identify the relationship between clerical and parliamentary assemblies, showing how, during the 14th century, the clergy came to sit in a separate house: convocation. Moreover, their work also points to the persistent significance of war in the calling of parliaments and the creation of a common identity. The involvement of the Commons in assenting to taxes and helping to provide answers to petitions led to the eventual development of legislation proper, so that by 1489 all valid legislation required the consent of the Commons.

The early modern Commons has been the subject of a plethora of studies. Whereas NEALE and Notestein held the view that the 16th and 17th centuries saw the Commons' power come to eclipse that of the Lords, a perspective broadly defined as "revisionism" has come to question such assumptions. Graves, Loach, Russell, Smith, and Sharpe serve as useful means of investigating key early modern developments; but, it should be emphasized, these studies are merely the tip of an extremely large early modern iceberg.

The most striking element in the historiography of Tudor parliaments concerns the manner in which consensus has come to replace conflict as a dominant theme underlying relations between crown and parliament. Neale's approach, emphasizing conflict, has been challenged by GRAVES and LOACH, both of whom concentrate on the manner in which the crown-in-parliament acted as the supreme legislative authority. When it acted in collaboration with parliament, rather than in conflict with it, the crown was strengthened, as the experience of Henry VIII's successors showed. Nevertheless, there remains substantial evidence of ideological disagreement in Elizabethan parliaments as DEAN has shown through a concentration on parliamentary "lobbying". While the Elizabethan parliaments saw a rise in the number of members returned, what was represented was property rather than people. Seats were often taken for social prestige rather than to advance particular causes.

Given the collapse and reconstruction of monarchical government, the 17th century is, crucially, seen as pivotal to the entire history of the Commons. SMITH provides a guide both to the historiography and to detailed factual information on the parliamentary machine. The succinct overviews of historiographical debates, such as discussion of the work on committees and elections, are valuable, but the Interregnum is rather less well covered. Nevertheless, the attempt to contextualize 17th-century parliamentary history and to relate developments to the ongoing evolution of the Commons itself is ambitious, and Smith shows how, by the end of the century, and the events of 1688–89, the provision of public finance by parliament was no longer a matter of the crown's financial necessity but a means of underpinning the entire tax base of the state. Of more specific studies, RUSSELL (1979 and 1990) has been concerned to overturn the inevitability of teleology and Notestein's notion of a strong Commons by investigating the Commons' history from the "centre" yet "on the ground" through the minutiae of Commons debates. Rather than moving inevitably towards the climax of the civil wars, MPs were hampered by their inability to understand the true costs of government, especially in times of war. Russell's concentration on parliaments has been criticized for its "court-centred" approach. It can usefully be balanced alongside the essays collected in SHARPE, which emphasize how the quarrels between crown and Commons were often produced by divisions among royal councillors, how the peerage was important to the political process, and how "court' and "country" were not opposed groupings but overlapping spheres.

The historiography of the post-1688 period is dominated by a number of themes: the strengthened position of the Commons in relation to the crown; the emergence and consolidation of political parties; the gradual extension of the franchise in an atmosphere of increasing industrialization; and the eventual dismantling of the power of the Lords from 1911 onwards. O'GORMAN and THOMAS both provide comprehensive overviews of 18th-century developments and the emergence of party politics. While the traditional view of the Hanoverian Commons was that it was unrepresentative, not merely of the people at large but of the actual electorate too, there is now an emphasis on how electors expected MPs to reflect their own localized interests. PHILLIPS offers a valuable reassessment of 18th-century elections by illustrating how electoral behaviour was less constrained by influence and corruption than previously assumed. HANHAM is a useful guide to party politics and management in the Victorian Commons and can be supplemented by the numerous published biographies of key figures. Parliamentary reform and party politics in the 20th century is best covered by works dealing with the history of individual parties, such as RAMSDEN, COOK, and THORPE, while general historical works on the 20th century provide useful narratives on election results and major legislation.

Finally, the character of the Commons has been greatly shaped by the buildings in which it has operated. In 1547 St Stephen's chapel formed the meeting place of the Commons and was only superseded by the rebuilding of the Palace of Westminster after the great fire of 1834. CANNADINE et al. provides an up-to-date and well-illustrated guide.

SIMON COATES

See also "Politics" in Thematic List for relevant entries; Magna Carta; Oxford, Provisions of; Parliamentary Reform entries; Women's Suffrage Movement

Parliament: House of Lords

Cannadine, David et al. (editors), The Houses of Parliament: History, Art, and Architecture, London: Merrell, 2000

Cannon, John, Aristocratic Century: The Peerage of Eighteenth-Century England, Cambridge and New York: Cambridge University Press, 1984

Cokayne, George E. and Peter W. Hammond, The Complete Peerage; or, A History of the House of Lords and All Its Members from the Earliest Times, vol. 14: Addenda and Corrigenda, Stroud, Gloucestershire: Sutton, 1998

Foster, Elizabeth R., The House of Lords, 1603–1649: Structure, Procedure, and the Nature of Its Business, Chapel Hill: University of North Carolina Press, 1983

History of Parliament Trust: www.ihr.sas.ac.uk/hop/lords

Jenkins, Roy, Mr Balfour's Poodle: An Account of the Struggle between the House of Lords and the Government of Mr Asquith, London: Heinemann, 1954; new edition London: Collins, and New York: Chilmark Press, 1968

Jones, Clyve and David Lewis Jones (editors), Peers, Politics, and Power: The House of Lords, 1603–1911, London: Hambledon Press, 1986

Longford, Frank Pakenham, Earl of, A History of the House of Lords, updated edition, London: Sutton, 1999

McCahill, Michael W., Order and Equipoise: The Peerage and the House of Lords, 1783–1806, London: Royal Historical Society, 1978

Pike, Luke Owen, A Constitutional History of the House of Lords, from the Original Sources, London and New York: Macmillan, 1894; reprinted, New York: Burt Franklin, 1964

Powell, Enoch J. and Keith Wallis, The House of Lords in the Middle Ages: A History of the English House of Lords to 1540, London: Weidenfeld and Nicolson, 1968

Smith, E.A., The House of Lords in British Politics and Society, 1815–1911, London and New York: Longman, 1992

Smith, Robert and John S. Moore (editors), The House of Lords: A Thousand Years of British Tradition, London: Smith's Peerage, 1994

Stevens, Robert, Law and Politics: The House of Lords as a Judicial Body, 1800–1976, Chapel Hill: University of North Carolina Press, 1978; London: Weidenfeld and Nicolson, 1979

Swatland, Andrew, The House of Lords in the Reign of Charles II, Cambridge and New York: Cambridge University Press, 1996

Turbeville, A.S., The House of Lords in the Reign of William III, Oxford: Clarendon Press, 1913; Westport, Connecticut: Greenwood Press, 1970

Turbeville, A.S., The House of Lords in the Age of Reform, 1784–1837: With an Epilogue on Aristocracy and the Advent of Democracy, 1837–1867, London: Faber, 1958

Among the plethora of works on parliamentary history and the structure of government, the Upper Chamber – the House of Lords – has, on the whole, taken a historiographical second place to the Commons. The work of the HISTORY OF PARLIAMENT TRUST will provide the key reference tools, but its work on the Commons at present far outstrips that on the Lords. But a forthcoming volume edited by Ruth Paley for the project, which will cover the Lords between 1660 and 1832, will be a fundamental reference work for the Lords in the long 18th century, with key insights into composition and biographical information. In the 19th century historians were more concerned with the history of the peerage than with the House of Lords as an institution, as the publication of *The Complete Peerage* showed (COKAYNE & HAMMOND should be consulted for guidance here). The only full survey of the Lords before 1900 was PIKE, which is largely concerned with legal matters. The controversy over the Parliament Bill in 1911 led to an upsurge of interest in the Lords. Responding to this debate, a series of books on the House from the Restoration to the early 19th century were published, of which TURBEVILLE (1913) remains one of the most important for its establishment of a historiographical precedent. TURBEVILLE (1958) was the culmination of this pioneering work.

As the Namierite and Whig dominance of historiography has receded so interest in the House of Lords has grown. It is now recognized that the history of the House of Lords should deal not merely with the institution or the peerage alone but with the families that formed the ruling elite, at national and county level, whose power was based on a number of key elements: possession of land, military functions, jurisdictional control over the localities, and access to the sovereign and the levers of government.

Few volumes have attempted to deal with the history of the House of Lords in its entirety. But of these the fundamental starting place is SMITH & MOORE, while LONGFORD is a readable and informed insider guide written by a peer of great longevity. Given the nature of its agenda, all of the essays in Smith & Moore are of relevance. Moreover, this agenda, as the very title of the work suggests, illustrates two key elements: first, that the Lords' origins as an institution should be traced back beyond the 13th century to the Anglo-Saxon *witan*, the assembly of the king and his great men; secondly, the great ability of the ruling class to absorb change and adopt to particular sets of historical circumstances. On the whole, the volume fulfils its goal of showing how the history of the House of Lords is, largely, the history of the nobility itself and, as a consequence, the survival of a changing elite. A large number of the contributors, such as David Cannadine, John Cannon, David Carpenter, and John Miller, have written about the aristocracy in the round.

The medieval House of Lords is magisterially covered in POWELL & WALLIS, which has yet to be superseded. This, too, lays a great emphasis on the Lords as an embodiment of tradition, illustrating how much its survival, as well as the calls for its destruction, depends on its maintenance of habitual modes of behaviour. The book defends a strict chronological approach to its subject matter on the grounds that this reflects the gradual evolution of a long-term institutional body. Its conclusion – that the early 16th century saw the decline of a nobility characterized by service in war, personal favour, and the dominance of churchmen in the administration and the rise of a nobility composed of civilian, lay administrators – remains fundamental to discussions of the transformation of the nobility which took place in the early modern period.

This process, which saw the dismantling and reconstruction not only of the aristocratic elite's ethos and function but also of

the institution of the Lords itself, with the execution of the king and the foundation of the Republic, has dominated discussion of the House's history in the period 1603–1911. The best starting place here is the excellent collection of essays contained in JONES & JONES, which contains an annotated bibliography as well as a historiographical introduction, and which brings together a series of seminal pieces conveying the major arguments and approaches. The Tudor and early Stuart period is dominated by the history of certain key aristocratic families. Gunn's chapter in Smith & Moore is a valuable survey, while FOSTER's study opened up the historiography of the Lords in the well-covered early 17th century. Until recently the Restoration remained largely uncovered. SWATLAND's work is now fundamental here, and emphasizes how fear of abolition made the Lords conscious of their need to assert their privileges and judicial powers. The work does, however, tend to concentrate on the legislative and political roles of the Lords and lacks a broader contextualization of its place in the overall politics of government and the court. Nevertheless, the book fills an important gap in the somewhat cursory coverage of the period 1660–89, which can largely be explained by the continuing focus on the long 18th century as the "golden age" of the House of Lords.

When 20th-century work on the history of the Lords began to grow, the 18th century, and particularly the "first age of party", proved to be fertile ground. Division lists and diaries have been valuable sources here. CANNON's work sets the century in context and summarizes much of the tone of the historiography (for a summary see his chapter in Smith & Moore). In the 15th century the nobility exercised a rough and ready regional power; in the 18th century it ran the government. Great houses replaced castles, control over parliamentary seats and patronage replaced war and local dominance, and, while land and its ownership remained central, the nobility's power remained largely unchallenged. The "golden age of the aristocracy" was, however, for a time buried under the weight of 19th-century historiography, emphasizing the history of the Commons. The 18th century was thus eulogized as a parliamentary and liberal age, a golden age of party rather than one of shared aristocratic interests, while the 19th century's emphasis on party rhetoric disguised the dominance of an oligarchical elite. Cannon's work brings out these points forcefully, illustrating how 18th-century parliaments served as focal points for local and specialist interests where the values of a shared community promoted private aims by legislative means. Such points apply, in particular, to the first half of the 18th century. The latter half has been less well covered, although MCCAHILL provides an important overview showing how, once again, the Lords was able to adapt to changing circumstances: the decline of rural society and the expansion of domestic industry, trade, and colonization. McCahill emphasizes how a large proportion of new peers created in the period c.1780–1810 were professional men who served as servants of the state in the armed and diplomatic services. The 19th and 20th centuries, however, saw the extension of the franchise and ever more increasing industrialization. The Lords' adaptability remains a dominant historiographical theme and the prevailing mood is one where, while there was aristocratic decline, the upholding of tradition prevented a complete fall.

Despite a series of measures that chipped away at the Lords' power – the Reform Acts of 1832, 1867, and 1884–85; the abandonment of voting by proxy in 1869; and, most importantly, the Parliament Act of 1911, "the single most symbolic event in the decline and fall of the British aristocracy", which ensured that Money Bills eventually became law and other Public Bills became law if passed by three successive sessions of the Commons – the Lords has, nevertheless, taken a long time to decline. The most up-to-date guide to these developments is provided by SMITH, who emphasizes how, despite the triumph of the middling orders, the inherent conservatism of Victorian society allowed the House of Lords to survive and reinvent itself as an important restraining influence on policy and legislation, while the standard account of the struggle leading up to the events of 1911 is JENKINS.

Despite two world wars and the further dismantling of long-held hereditary benefits, accounts of the post-1918 Lords tend to emphasize how it has managed to survive, largely by providing a check on the growing power of the Commons, serving as an embodiment of tradition, ritual, and ceremony and by increasing its judicial function. Continuing interest in the aristocracy as a social body, exemplified in the works of David Cannadine (see his chapter in Smith & Moore for further bibliography) will ensure ongoing interest, while advances in computerized records will assist with detailed research into individual noble families. On criticism, most standard works on 20th-century British politics include accounts of attempts at reform, while STEVENS is the best book on the Lords as a judicial body. Finally, CANNADINE et al. provide an up-to-date and marvellously illustrated guide to the buildings of parliament, where the sections on the House of Lords cement its status as a visual expression of ceremonial order and hierarchy.

SIMON COATES

See also "Politics" in Thematic List for relevant entries; Magna Carta; Oxford, Provisions of; Parliamentary Reform entries; Privy (King's) Council

Parliament: Representation and Suffrage to 1918

Biagini, Eugenio F., Liberty, Retrenchment, and Reform: Popular Liberalism in the Age of Gladstone, 1860–1880, Cambridge and New York: Cambridge University Press, 1992

Colley, Linda, Britons: Forging the Nation, 1707–1837, London: BCA, and New Haven, Connecticut: Yale University Press, 1992

Cowling, Maurice, 1867: Disraeli, Gladstone, and Revolution: The Passing of the Second Reform Bill, Cambridge: Cambridge University Press, 1967

Gash, Norman, Pillars of Government and Other Essays on State and Society, c.1770–1880, London and Baltimore, Maryland: Arnold, 1986

Hempton, David, Methodism and Politics in British Society, 1750–1850, London: Hutchinson, and Stanford, California: Stanford University Press, 1984

Kitson Clark, G., The Making of Victorian England, London: Methuen, and Cambridge, Massachusetts: Harvard University Press, 1962

Marwick, Arthur, The Deluge: British Society and the First World War, London: Bodley Head, 1965; Boston: Little Brown, 1966

O'Gorman, Frank, The Long Eighteenth Century: British Political and Social History, 1688–1832, London and New York: Arnold, 1997

Parry, Jonathan, The Rise and Fall of Liberal Government in Victorian Britain, New Haven, Connecticut and London: Yale University Press, 1993

Thompson, E.P., The Making of the English Working Class, London: Gollancz, 1963; New York: Pantheon, 1964

The history of the reform of representation and suffrage – or parliamentary reform – in Britain is linked to challenges to the constitution from two principal sources: from domestic pressure, usually reacting to real or perceived abuses of power by those with the vote, and from external factors, such as the impact of the American and French revolutions. When examined over a period of 300 years, both sources of pressure change character but, by the end of the 18th century at least, become inextricably interlinked. The wealth of books and journal articles reflects the fundamental importance of this subject to understanding the evolution of the modern political state and the increasingly industrialized society that that state reflects. It is for this reason also that there is no standard text on the subject, although the main points and sequence of events are covered in most general surveys of the history of British politics and society from the 18th century onwards. KITSON CLARK's work on the 19th century provides a superior example of this genre.

Although old and, some would argue, profoundly intellectually out of date, THOMPSON's neo-Marxist study of the relationship between politics and society in the late 18th and early 19th centuries remains of great importance. It enables the reader to see how a model can be developed that can be applied to all historical periods from 1215 to the early 19th century to explain the ways in which challenges to political authority manifested themselves and how the ruling elite responded to them. Thompson therefore enables us to draw comparisons, for example, between the baronial challenge to King John that led to the signing of Magna Carta, the deposition of Charles I, and the passage of the Great Reform Act in 1832. He places great emphasis on the Whig constitution that emerged as a result of the Glorious Revolution, which Thompson argues resulted in a form of institutionalized protestant tyranny that was bound to lead to disenchantment among the masses. This dissatisfaction was inflamed by a desire for greater involvement in the political process brought about by the increased wealth that many outside the ruling elite experienced as a result of the Industrial Revolution. Also implicit in Thompson's study is the Rousseau-esque right of the working class to rise up and demand greater political representation. Thus it is possible to extend Thompson's work and view the three reform acts of the later 19th century as three stages in a class struggle. Historians of the early

20th century, such as MARWICK, would argue that that conflict was only reconciled through the cataclysmic consequences of World War I, which resulted in women being given the vote and a move towards discrediting the class system.

The idea of "forging the nation" is the subject of COLLEY's most well-known work on the 18th and early 19th century. A high-profile study that is reputed to be a favoured text within the circles of New Labour, Colley identifies the common forces and experiences that characterize British society during this period and which have led to the development of the idea of "Britishness". She argues that the framework created by these experiences is so strong that it can withstand challenges to it and evolve to meet those challenges. Thus she sees the calls for and responses to parliamentary reform in the 18th century and 19th century in an essentially Whiggish way, that is, one that sees no need for revolutionary change similar to that experienced in France after 1789. Colley's work is also relevant to those seeking to explore the theme of parliamentary reform beyond the chronological bounds of this article because she sees regional devolution as the next stage in the process of democratizing the people. Within her historical context, she highlights the strength of regionalism in Britain in the 18th and 19th centuries, and the nature of those differences – a concept that is of fundamental importance to debunking the long-held view that the process of industrialization occurred evenly across the country, or, indeed, that there was an "industrial revolution" at all.

An important aspect of the regionalism that Colley identifies is diversity of religious traditions, with the development of nonconformity being most notable in Scotland and Wales as well as in areas of rapid industrialization such as the Midlands and the north of England and often associated with calls for parliamentary reform. HEMPTON's work provides a useful synthesis of a growing body of material on religious nonconformity in the 18th and early 19th centuries and the connection between debating societies and other organizations that agitated for the extension of the franchise. He criticizes previous historians for devoting too much attention to debunking the Halévy thesis on the connection between the growth of nonconformity in Britain and the absence of a cataclysmic political revolution similar to that in France. Rather than having a calming influence on British society in the late 18th and early 19th centuries, Hempton sees methodism in particular as providing a moral and spiritual legitimacy to the radical cause. One cannot, he argues, understand the rise of the former without understanding the passion of the latter.

The work of Hempton and others did much to encourage a reappraisal of the way in which political agitation for the extension of the franchise has been viewed. This point has been taken up by O'GORMAN in his important political and social study of the 18th century. His work provides the first comprehensive coverage of the whole of the century and does much to update and extend many of the points made 30 years earlier by Thompson. O'Gorman, who is an expert on the Whig party in the 1770s, suggests that to view the movement for parliamentary reform in the 18th century in black-and-white terms of oppressed and oppressors is to so oversimplify the situation as to make any analysis meaningless. There were, O'Gorman argues, those within parliament who were sympathetic to the cries of Thomas Paine and John Wilkes and who

would have been prepared to have extended the franchise much earlier than 1832. Likewise, there were members of the unenfranchised classes who had little desire to participate in politics and so were unconcerned that they did not possess the vote. The historical "truth", he claims, lies somewhere between the two poles.

There is a massive literature on British parliamentary reform in the 19th century. One of the most accessible studies is the collection of 15 essays by GASH on the development of the role of parliament in this period. Gash, who is the biographer of Lord Liverpool and Sir Robert Peel – two politicians who had contrasting views on the rights of the masses to a say in the political operation of the country – includes an essay on the three reform acts of the 19th century. Gash argues that, although often discussed, historians have failed to acknowledge that all three acts were passed by governments that had little interest in parliamentary reform. What is more, it is dangerous to assume that the passage of the first act in 1832 started an evolutionary process that was smooth and consistent. Gash points out that the first three reform acts were passed for different reasons, by very different governments and in different manners.

This interpretation challenges the widely accepted view expressed by COWLING and others who have declared that liberalism was a coherent ideology in the 19th century. Cowling argues that too much emphasis has been placed on the role of the radical societies in bringing about parliamentary reform and that to assume that the governments that oversaw the passage of the acts did so because they had been forced to take a defensive stance by circumstances presents an incomplete picture. He discusses two points: the extent to which class consciousness prompted governmental resistance to parliamentary reform and whether the radical agenda succeeded later in the century because it had the "respectability" of coming from the chamber of the House of Commons rather than from extraparliamentary agitation. This argument has been developed by a subsequent generation of historians wishing to explain that more modern manifestation of Gladstonian liberalism – Thatcherism – after 1979. PARRY, for example, argues that Gladstone and Hartington were in favour of further extensions of the franchise only if they presented the opportunity to "convert" the newly enfranchised to the merits of liberalism. If the new voters were not persuaded, Parry argues that Gladstone favoured a return to the 18th-century Whig view that the constitution was perfect and thus not in need of reform. Thus parliamentary reform, Parry argues, was a means of ensuring the dominance of the Liberal Party from the 1860s until the outbreak of World War I, which destroyed this approach to mass politics for good. This theme has been extended by BIAGINI, who views Gladstonian liberalism as part of the movement of mass politics by the end of the 19th century and thus in a position politically and ideologically to promote the extension of the franchise. It was thus a Conservative-dominated coalition, fuelled by the legacy of traditional liberal ideas that gave the vote to women for the first time in 1918.

GAYNOR JOHNSON

See also Chartism; Lilburne; Parliamentary Reform entries; Proportional Representation; Putney Debates; Women's Suffrage Movement

Parliament of Ireland

Bolton, G.C., *The Passing of the Irish Act of Union: A Study in Parliamentary Politics*, London: Oxford University Press, 1966

Falkiner, C. Litton, "The Parliament of Ireland under the Tudors", *Proceedings of the Royal Irish Academy*, 25 / section C (1904–05): 508–41; 553–66

Farrell, Brian (editor), *The Irish Parliamentary Tradition*, Dublin: Gill and Macmillan, London: Macmillan, and New York: Barnes and Noble, 1973

Hayton, D.W. (editor), *The Irish Parliament in the Eighteenth Century: The Long Apprenticeship*, Edinburgh: Edinburgh University Press, 2001

Johnston, Edith Mary, *Great Britain and Ireland, 1760–1800: A Study in Political Administration*, Edinburgh: Oliver and Boyd, 1963; reprinted, Westport, Connecticut: Greenwood Press, 1978

Johnston-Liik, Edith Mary, *History of the Irish Parliament 1692–1800*, 6 vols, Belfast: Ulster Historical Foundation, 2002

Moody, T.W., "The Irish Parliament under Elizabeth and James I", *Proceedings of the Royal Irish Academy*, 45 / section C (1939–40): 41–81

Richardson, H.G. and G.O. Sayles, *The Irish Parliament in the Middle Ages*, Philadelphia: University of Pennsylvania Press, 1952; 2nd edition, 1964

The legislature of the modern Irish state (the Oireachtas) was created by the Irish Free State Constitution of 1922. Ireland had last possessed its own separate legislature, then known as the Irish parliament, at the end of the 18th century. That parliament had first come into existence during the first half of the 13th century as the parliament of the English colonial lordship of Ireland. It had then enjoyed a continuous existence, but gone through a series of major transformations, down to 1800 when the passing of the Act of Union created a single parliament of the United Kingdom of Great Britain and Ireland and abolished the separate Irish parliament. Only the volume of papers edited by FARRELL attempts to deal with the whole stretch of that history, but the papers, which were originally delivered as part of a series of radio lectures, are brief and relatively lightly footnoted. They are also written by a variety of authors who adopt a variety of approaches to the chronological periods allotted to them.

Other works on the Irish parliament cover only specific periods. The fullest and most satisfactory of these more detailed studies is that of RICHARDSON & SAYLES. This discusses the history of the Irish parliament from the beginnings to the late 15th century, when the operation of parliament was radically transformed by Poynings' Law (1494). Richardson & Sayles draw on their unrivalled knowledge of the relevant surviving material to describe what can be known of the composition of the Irish medieval parliament; its functions in regard to legislation, taxation, and the remedying of grievances; and its place within the wider framework of the governmental machinery of the medieval lordship.

For the succeeding Tudor period, the only general survey available is that of FALKINER. This provides a general survey of some of the significant developments in the history of parliament which took place during this period, such as the ending of the practice of holding parliamentary sessions away from Dublin and of the participation of clerical proctors in the work of the Irish parliament. It also surveys and edits some of the Elizabethan evidence for what took place at parliamentary sessions. Much of Falkiner's work has been modified by subsequent, more detailed scholarship on such topics as the Reformation parliament and the application of Poynings' Law. MOODY also covers the history of the Irish parliament during the reign of Elizabeth and looks in detail at James I's parliament of 1613–15. This was the first parliament to take place after the general "pacification" of Ireland and the first to contain representatives from the various newly created counties and a large number of newly created boroughs. It was also a parliament which saw a major conflict between the old English and native Irish catholic representatives on the one hand and the new Irish protestants and the king's government in Ireland on the other.

JOHNSTON is a fascinating attempt to apply some of Namier's methodology to the Irish parliament as it existed in the second half of the 18th century. Part II of her book focuses on "The Irish Electoral System" and surveys the different kinds of constituency that returned members to the Irish House of Commons and the extent of government influence over parliamentary elections. Part III looks at the composition of the Irish parliament as a whole: the different kinds of members who sat in the Irish House of Commons and the members of the Irish House of Lords. What is lacking, however, is any kind of detailed consideration of what the Irish parliament actually did: the kind of legislation it passed, the financial measures it approved, and the appeal cases it heard after 1782.

Two recent publications, billed as marking the bicentenary of the Acts of Union, have contributed to the study of the 18th-century parliament. Edith Mary Johnston (now as JOHNSTON-LIIK) has followed up her earlier publications with a six-volume resource of statute information (categorized by constitution, education, law and order, and local government), constituency histories, and biographical studies of the MPs who sat between 1692 and 1800. HAYTON's collection looks at various aspects of the workings, legislation, and make-up of parliament from the 1690s to 1800. Topics include taxation, criminal legislation, public expenditure, "Poynings' Law in the 1760s", "Electors, Patrons and Irish Elections", and Sir Henry Cavendish.

The ending of a separate Irish parliament in 1800 through the enactment of Acts of Union enacted by the parliaments of Ireland and Great Britain and the creation of a single parliament of the United Kingdom of Great Britain and Ireland at Westminster was politically contentious in Ireland from the beginning and the story of how this was brought about soon acquired a legendary element. BOLTON provides a detailed and convincing account of the political context and mechanisms that actually brought about the Act of Union and the end of the separate Irish parliament.

PAUL BRAND

See also Dublin; Grattan; Ireland entries; Kilkenny, Statutes of; *Modus Tenendi Parliamentum*; Poynings

Parliament of Scotland

Duncan, Archibald A.M., "The Early Parliaments of Scotland", *Scottish Historical Review*, 65 (1966): 36–58

Ferguson, William, introduction to "The Scots and Parliament", special edition of *Parliamentary History*, edited by Clyve Jones (1996): 1–10

Goodare, Julian "Parliamentary Taxation in Scotland, 1560–1603", *Scottish Historical Review*, 68 (1989): 23–52

Goodare, Julian, "The Scottish Parliament of 1621", *Historical Journal*, 38 (1995): 29–51

Goodare, Julian, "The Estates in the Scottish Parliament, 1286–1707" in "The Scots and Parliament", special edition of *Parliamentary History*, edited by Clyve Jones (1996): 11–32

Goodare, Julian, "The Scottish Parliamentary Records, 1560–1603", *Historical Research*, 72 (1999): 244–67

Goodare, Julian, "Scotland's Parliament in Its British Context, 1603–1707" in *The Challenge to Westminster: Sovereignty, Devolution, and Independence*, edited by H.T. Dickinson and Michael Lynch, East Linton, East Lothian: Tuckwell Press, 2000

Goodare, Julian and Norman Macdougall, entry on parliament in *The Oxford Companion to Scottish History*, edited by Michael Lynch, Oxford and New York: Oxford University Press, 2001

Goodare, Julian, "The Admission of Lairds to the Scottish Parliament", *English Historical Review*, 116 (2001): 1103–33

Jones, Clyve (editor), *The Scots and Parliament*, Edinburgh: Edinburgh University Press, 1996; also as special issue of *Parliamentary History* (1996)

Lee, Ronnie, "Retreat from Revolution: The Scottish Parliament and the Restored Monarchy, 1663" in *Celtic Dimensions of the British Civil Wars*, edited by John R. Young, Edinburgh: John Donald, 1997

MacDonald, Alan R., "'Tedious to Rehers'? Parliament and Locality in Scotland c.1560–1651: The Burghs of North-East Fife", *Parliaments, Estates, and Representation*, 20 (2000): 31–58

Mackie, John D. and George S. Pryde, *The Estate of the Burgesses in the Scots Parliament and Its Relation to the Convention of Royal Burghs*, St Andrews: Henderson, 1923

Rait, Robert S., *The Scottish Parliament before the Union of the Crowns*, London: Blackie, 1901

Rait, Robert S., *The Parliaments of Scotland*, Glasgow: MacLehose Jackson, 1924

Scally, John, "Constitutional Revolution, Party and Faction in the Scottish Parliaments of Charles I" in "The Scots and Parliament", special edition of *Parliamentary History*, edited by Clyve Jones (1996): 54–73

Tanner, Roland, *The Late Medieval Scottish Parliament: Politics and the Three Estates, 1424–1488*, East Linton, East Lothian: Tuckwell Press, 2001

Terry, Charles Sanford, *The Scottish Parliament: Its Constitution and Procedure, 1603–1707*, Glasgow: MacLehose, 1905

Thomson, Edith E.B., *The Parliament of Scotland, 1690–1702*, London: Oxford University Press, 1929

Walker, David M., *A Legal History of Scotland*, vol. 2, Edinburgh: W. Green, 1990; vols 3–4, Edinburgh: T. and T. Clark, 1995–96

Young, John R., *The Scottish Parliament, 1639–1661: A Political and Constitutional Analysis*, Edinburgh: John Donald, 1996

Young, John R., "The Scottish Parliament and the Covenanting Revolution: The Emergence of a Scottish Commons" in *Celtic Dimensions of the British Civil Wars*, edited by Young, Edinburgh: John Donald, 1997

Young, John R., "Seventeenth-Century Scottish Parliamentary Rolls and Political Factionalism: The Experience of the Covenanting Movement", *Parliamentary History*, 16 (1997): 148–70

Young, John R., "The Scottish Parliament and National Identity from the Union of the Crowns to the Union of the Parliaments, 1603–1707" in *Image and Identity: the Making and Re-making of Scotland through the Ages*, edited by Dauvit Broun, Richard J. Finlay, and Michael Lynch, Edinburgh: John Donald, 1998

Young, John R. "The Scottish Parliament and the War for the Three Kingdoms, 1639–1651", *Parliaments, Estates, and Representation*, 21 (2001): 103–23

Young, Margaret D. (editor), *The Parliaments of Scotland: Burgh and Shire Commissioners*, 2 vols, Edinburgh: Scottish Academic Press, 1992–93

The standard work on the history of the Scottish parliament is that of RAIT (1924). Strongly constitutional in tone, it provides a detailed overview of the origins of parliament to the end of its existence in 1707. Impressive as it is, it is permeated with overtones of political Darwinism, with the Scottish parliament being compared unfavourably with its English counterpart. Westminster, as the "mother of parliaments", was viewed as the ideal constitutional model for parliaments and thus the Act of Union of 1707, followed by the creation of a British parliament, was regarded by Rait as a further step in the march of "progress". His earlier book (RAIT, 1901) looked at parliament in the pre-1603 period. Scholars now accept that Rait's work is in need of substantial revision and that the parliamentary history of Scotland pre-1707 needs a re-examination, based on scholarly archive research. Easier to read but less in-depth is TERRY's book of 1905, which covers the period following the Union of the Crowns, 1603–1707. Terry concludes, however, that the Scottish parliament was playing a greater role in national life than hitherto, and had developed its political and constitutional powers, at the time when it voted itself out of existence in 1707. This book also contains an appendix of some documents relating to parliamentary history, which may be useful to students and teachers. THOMSON's study of the Williamite parliament of 1690–1702 also belongs to this early 20th-century genre, and it is also in need of substantial revision and archive research. In terms of the study of specific estates which made up the Scottish parliament, the estate of the burgesses received particular attention from MACKIE & PRYDE in 1923.

The historiography of the Scottish parliament remained static for much of the 20th century, and it is only in recent years that it has found a new lease of life in scholarly books and articles. The best introductory overview is the section on parliament (GOODARE & MACDOUGALL) in the *Oxford Companion to Scottish History*. The most recent monographs have been those of John YOUNG (1996) and TANNER. Young provides a detailed analysis of parliamentary activities in the 1640s, when parliament was a vibrant institution during the British civil wars. Particular emphasis is put by Young on the role of parliamentary committees, which were of an innovative nature during this period, and analysis of original manuscript committee registers is an important theme in this book. Tanner provides an original and long-overdue study of the medieval Scottish parliament between 1424 and 1488. This should be of considerable importance for a greater understanding of late medieval Scottish political life. The seminal article on the early parliamentary history of Scotland remains that of DUNCAN.

In terms of a broad coverage and overview, the parliamentary sections in WALKER provide a sound commentary and are written by one of the leading Scottish legal historians, bringing a refreshing legal perspective. These sections should be of particular importance for academics and advanced students. The essay collection edited by JONES includes some important articles on the pre-1707 Scottish parliament. FERGUSON's introduction is useful from a historiographical perspective, especially in terms of an intellectual assault on the blinkered perspective of Rait in the early 20th century. A modern overview of the concept and role of estates in the Scottish parliament is provided by GOODARE (1996). The parliamentary politics of the Covenanting parliaments of the 1640s are discussed in the article by SCALLY. John YOUNG's 1998 article in the collection edited by Broun *et al.* provides an overview of Scottish parliamentary developments, 1603–1707, within the context of the collection's theme of Scottish national identity. An overview of the same period has recently been offered by GOODARE (2000), in his article in *The Challenge to Westminster*: it looks at Scottish parliamentary developments within a British context.

Specific themes of Scottish parliamentary history have also been the subjects of books and articles in recent years. The nature of the Scottish parliamentary records for the period 1560–1603 period has been discussed by GOODARE (1999). In terms of recent articles on individual parliaments, GOODARE's 1995 article provides a detailed reassessment of the controversial parliament of 1621. Voting lists and analysis are also provided here. The Restoration parliament of 1661–63 has received particular attention in John Young's monograph (1996) and LEE's article. Chapter 12 of Young's book provides a detailed analysis of the 1661 parliamentary session with the reassertion of the royal prerogative and the rescinding of the Covenanting constitutional revolution. Lee's article provides a broader context to this, 1661–63, with further consideration of the parliamentary sessions of 1662 and 1663. GOODARE's article (1989) in the *Scottish Historical Review* has analysed the complex nature of parliamentary taxation in Scotland between the Reformation and the Union of the Crowns. MACDONALD's article is one of the few examples of a local case-study. The activities of the seven parliamentary burghs of northeast Fife are discussed and analysed for the period 1560–1651. This represents the most recent work on parliamentary burghs. The foreign policy of the Scottish parliament

in the 1640s has been explored by John YOUNG (2001) in his article in *Parliaments, Estates, and Representation*. This looks at Scottish parliamentary attitudes, structures, and actions towards the Palatinate and the United Provinces of the Dutch Republic, *c.*1641–47. It considers the attitude of the Scottish parliament to the Thirty Years' War (1618–48) during the 1640s and it examines the role of a Scottish diplomatic mission to the United Provinces and the reception of a Swedish diplomatic mission to Edinburgh in 1644, showing that the Scottish parliament had a European political vision and was not limited to a British or Scottish perspective.

The admission of the lairds to the Scottish parliament has been discussed in a recent important article by GOODARE (2001) in the *English Historical Review*. The political dynamics of the relationship between the different parliamentary estates of a single-chamber institution have been looked at by John YOUNG (1997) for the 1640s in his article in *Celtic Dimensions*. This argues for the development of a Scottish commons in the 1640s. It argues that the estate of the barons/shire commissioners and the estate of the burgesses became relatively more powerful than hitherto in relation to the estate of the nobility. This has aroused debate within the broader schema of Scottish history, but in terms of recent writings on specific Scottish parliamentary history, Scally's article challenges this view and asserts that magnate/noble influence remained the dominant force. John YOUNG's article (1997) in *Parliamentary History* analyses the nature of political factionalism in the Covenanting movement of the 1640s, based on an examination of parliamentary rolls and attendance data. In terms of useful research tools for studying Scottish parliamentary history, Margaret YOUNG's edited volumes provide useful bibliographical data on the burgh and shire commissioners as estates of the unicameral Scottish parliament. Appendix 1 of volume 2 provides a list of parliaments from 1290 to 1707, including dates and locations. Appendix 2 of volume 2 consists of constituency lists, arranged alphabetically under their constituencies. Burgh constituencies are listed first, followed by shire constituencies. Thus, readers can identify the personnel of particular constituencies and then quickly proceed to the appropriate member or members for that area at any given time. Appendix 3 of volume 2 provides a useful historical assessment of the period.

Important additions to the historiography of the Scottish parliament will come with a three-volume publication on various aspects of Scottish parliamentary history, edited by members of the History of the Scottish Parliament project based at the University of St Andrews. These volumes are planned for publication by Edinburgh University Press in 2002–03.

JOHN R. YOUNG

Parliamentary Reform I: Reform Acts of 1832–1885

Brock, Michael, *The Great Reform Act*, London: Hutchinson, 1973
Cannon, John, *Parliamentary Reform, 1640–1832*, Cambridge: Cambridge University Press, 1973

Gwyn, William B., *Democracy and the Cost of Politics in Britain*, London: Athlone Press, 1962

Hart, Jenifer, *Proportional Representation: Critics of the British Electoral System, 1820–1945*, Oxford: Clarendon Press, and New York: Oxford University Press, 1992

Jones, Andrew, *The Politics of Reform, 1884*, Cambridge: Cambridge University Press, 1972

Kinzer, Bruce L., *The Ballot Question in Nineteenth-Century English Politics*, New York: Garland, 1982

Machin, Ian, *The Rise of Democracy in Britain, 1830–1918*, London: Macmillan, and New York: St Martin's Press, 2001

Moore, David Cresap, *The Politics of Deference: A Study of the Mid-Nineteenth Century English Political System*, Brighton, Sussex: Harvester Press, and New York: Barnes and Noble, 1976

O'Leary, Cornelius, *The Elimination of Corrupt Practices in British Elections, 1868–1911*, Oxford: Clarendon Press, 1962

Seymour, Charles, *Electoral Reform in England and Wales: The Development and Operation of the Parliamentary Franchise, 1832–1885*, London: Oxford University Press, and New Haven, Connecticut: Yale University Press, 1915

Smith, F.B., *The Making of the Second Reform Bill*, Cambridge: Cambridge University Press, 1966

Witmer, Helen Elizabeth, *The Property Qualifications of Members of Parliament*, New York: Columbia University Press, and London: King and Staples, 1943

1832 saw the first broad parliamentary reform in the modern period. A Whig government passed three acts (for England and Wales, Scotland, and Ireland respectively) to make the franchise more uniform on the basis of property qualifications (though the county and borough franchises remained clearly separated), and to provide for the transfer of seats from small boroughs which now lost all or some of their representation. The surplus seats were divided between counties and large towns. After 1832 a good deal of generally fruitless agitation, and many failed efforts in parliament to carry further electoral reform, took place before a second trio of important reform acts was carried, by a minority Conservative ministry with radical support, in 1867–68 (the Scottish and Irish measures were passed in 1868). These measures doubled the borough electorate but did not much extend the county franchise, and included only a restricted redistribution of seats from small boroughs to counties and large towns (about a third of the number redistributed in 1832). A Liberal government carried the third Reform Act (the first to apply to the whole United Kingdom) in 1884, equalizing the borough and county franchises and giving the vote to all adult males who could meet a residence qualification. In consequence about two-thirds of adult males could vote in parliamentary elections until the next franchise enlargement occurred in 1918. The 1884 Act was allowed through by the Lords (which had a Conservative majority) in return for Gladstone's ministry agreeing to a fundamental redistribution, on the basis of dividing most constituencies into single-member ones and making them congruent (by no means entirely, but to a much greater degree than before) with local social class weighting and with relative population size.

CANNON gives a detailed and enlightening introduction to this subject which should be read in order to understand its lengthy antecedents. SEYMOUR remains an extemely useful, if somewhat austere, work. It has an impressively wide factual range, and considers the minor measures of electoral reform as well as the major acts and their effects. MACHIN is a general study of the development of parliamentary democracy from 1830 to 1918, including substantial examination of the various measures. BROCK is a masterly, highly detailed, and analytical study of the passage of the first reform bills and the intentions behind them. This intelligent and perceptive work continues to provide a scholarly basis for examination of the 1832 bills and their context. MOORE advances controversial propositions about the maintenance and extension of deference in politics by the acts of 1832. These views have attracted wide criticism, especially on their first appearance in article form. But, although seeming excessive in his detailed contentions, he has left a well-justified impression that political deference continued to be important, especially in certain types of constituency where there was effective patronage and control for many years after 1832. SMITH provides an extensive study of the antecedents and passage of the 1867–68 reform bills, paying much useful attention to parliamentary reform in the period from 1848 to 1865 as well as to the critical years of 1866–68. JONES, though having a less straightforward style, is a similarly useful investigation of the 1884–85 bills in their political context, and displays a subtle and impressive mastery of detail.

A number of monographs have given, both collectively and within the chosen limits of each work, authoritative coverage to important aspects of democratic demand and development apart from the major reform acts. GWYN and O'LEARY focus, in regard to this period, on the question of illegal electoral bribery and the difficulty of suppressing this until a strong and determined act was passed in 1883 and small borough constituencies (where bribery mainly flourished) ended in 1885. WITMER concentrates on the issue of property qualifications which from 1711 were officially (though not always in practice) demanded of MPs returned in England and Wales; and on the abolition of this requirement by an act of 1858 – the first enactment of one of the democratic six points of the "People's Charter" of 1838. KINZER covers in much detail a question represented by another point in the charter – that of a secret ballot in parliamentary elections. He investigates the strong call for this reform in the 1830s and the chequered history of the question until 1872, when it was finally enacted (with significant securities). HART studies the still unrealized demand for proportional representation of parties in the House of Commons, beginning mainly with a small campaign launched by published works of Thomas Hare in the later 1850s and continued by pressure groups and individual MPs.

IAN MACHIN

See also Chartism; Derby; Disraeli; Gladstone; Grey; Parliament: Representation and Suffrage; Russell; William IV

Parliamentary Reform II: Act of 1911

Asquith, H.H., *Fifty Years of British Parliament*, 2 vols, London: Cassell, and Boston: Little Brown, 1926

Blackburn, Robert, "The Duration of Parliament: Historical Perspectives on the 1911 Amendment to the Septennial Act", *Journal of Legal History*, 9/1 (1988): 98–106

Blewett, Neal, *The Peers, the Parties, and the People: The General Elections of 1910*, London: Macmillan, and Toronto: University of Toronto Press, 1972

Dangerfield, George, *The Strange Death of Liberal England, 1910–1914*, New York: Smith and Haas, 1935; London: Constable, 1936

Hanham, H.J. (editor), *Nineteenth-Century Constitution, 1815–1914: Documents and Commentary*, London: Cambridge University Press, 1969

Jenkins, Roy, *Mr Balfour's Poodle: An Account of the Struggle between the House of Lords and the Government of Mr. Asquith*, London: Heinemann, 1954; as *Mr Balfour's Poodle: Peers v. People*, New York: Chilmark Press, 1968

Newton, Thomas Wodehouse Legh, *Lord Lansdowne: A Biography*, London: Macmillan, 1929

Nicolson, Harold, *King George the Fifth: His Life and Reign*, London: Constable, 1952; New York: Doubleday, 1953

Phillips, Gregory D., *The Diehards: Aristocratic Society and Politics in Edwardian England*, Cambridge, Massachusetts: Harvard University Press, 1979

The constitutional reform of 1911 joins the reforms of 1832, 1867, 1884–85, and 1918 as milestones on Britain's road to political democracy. It affirmed in law what long had been practice, namely the pre-eminence of the popularly elected House of Commons over the hereditary House of Lords. The 1911 reform embodied four important measures: (1) it limited the ability of the House of Lords to delay money bills (including budgets) to at most one month; (2) it limited the ability of the Lords to delay other bills to approximately two years, by stipulating that legislation would become law without the approval of the Lords if passed by Commons in three successive sessions; (3) it amended the Septennial Act of 1716 by requiring a general election for Commons at least every five years; and (4) it provided for the first time compensation to members of Commons for their services, initially £400 per annum. The text of the Parliament Act of August 1911, which incorporated the first three of these measures, is included in HANHAM along with commentary by the editor.

The story of the 1911 constitutional reform lies not only in its provisions, but also in the circumstances of its passage amid constitutional crisis. The crisis began to develop with the introduction in April 1909 of the budget by David Lloyd George, chancellor of the exchequer in Prime Minister H.H. Asquith's Liberal government. Challenged to find additional revenues to pay for warships, old-age pensions, and other social services, Lloyd George proposed increased taxes on higher incomes, inheritances (death duties), land, and luxuries, all designed to extract more revenue from those with greater wealth, especially landed wealth. The Conservatives mounted a determined opposition to the budget in Commons, but did not have the votes to block it. The Conservative leadership, A.J. Balfour in Commons and Lord Lansdowne in Lords, then decided to veto the budget in the House of Lords where they had an overwhelming majority. This created a constitutional crisis since the Lords traditionally did not tamper with revenue measures. The Liberals declared the peers' action "a breach of the Constitution and a usurpation of the rights of Commons". The Conservatives defended their actions in terms of the revolutionary nature of the budget and the addition of non-revenue tack-ons to the bill. The budget bill crisis led to a general election in January 1910 to resolve the conflict of "the Peers against the People", as the Liberals cast it. Although the key election issue was the budget, the question of the future role of the House of Lords loomed large. The results were disappointing for both major parties. The Conservatives made substantial gains, but fell short of a majority. The Liberals lost over one hundred seats and their outright majority, but still had a plurality and, with their Labour and Irish allies, a majority. The Liberals remained in office and proceeded to pass Lloyd George's budget, which the Lords did not challenge. However, the Liberals were determined to enact constitutional reform that would limit the power of the Lords. But would the Lords agree to such legislation or would they fight?

Surprisingly, not a single monograph has been published on the constitutional reform or Parliament Act of 1911. However, there are three valuable studies of the constitutional crisis and circumstances that produced reform. JENKINS tells the story of the parliamentary struggle from the introduction of the "People's Budget" in April 1909 until the passage of the Parliament Act in August 1911. Taking his catchy title from Lloyd George's 1908 comment that the Lords "is not the watchdog of the Constitution, it is Mr Balfour's poodle", Jenkins believes the Conservative leadership erred in rejecting the budget. He also observes that the dog eventually bit its master as over 100 Conservative "diehards" or "last ditchers" repudiated their leaders, Balfour and Lansdowne, who advocated acceptance of the inevitable – after a second election in December 1910, fought on the issue of constitutional reform, left Asquith and his allies in power, and following King George V's pledge to create enough new peers to assure passage of the Parliament Act. The "diehards" were determined to reject the bill and damn the consequences. Jenkins does not see the consequences of the bill to have been as dire as some of its opponents predicted. It did not lead to the destruction of the House of Lords, and only three pieces of legislation were passed without the Lords' approval between 1911 and 1954 when Jenkins published his book.

BLEWETT's study, based on extensive research in contemporary sources, focuses on the two general elections of 1910, which were necessary for the passage of the 1911 constitutional reform. Opening with a lengthy discussion of the politics of the preceding quarter-century, he examines in detail the political contexts, parties, press, pressure groups, campaigns, and results of the January and December elections. He sees these contests as decisive, confirming the class and regional polarities that were present but less clearly apparent in earlier elections dating to 1886. He views the Parliament Act of 1911 as remarkably tame and its Liberal sponsors as having muffed an opportunity to identify with the nation's democratic sentiments.

Complementing Blewett's analysis of the 1910 elections for Commons is PHILLIPS's study of the actions of the Lords in the constitutional crisis. His focus is on the 112 "diehards" who rejected the advice of Balfour and Lansdowne in voting against the Parliament Act of 1911. Defying conventional wisdom, Phillips shows that most of the "diehards" were not "backwoodsmen" – those peers who usually stayed on their country estates, cared little about politics, and attended Lords only to veto Liberal legislation – but rather were politically active locally and nationally. He sees them as "radical conservatives rather than simple reactionaries". One of the historians Phillips challenges is DANGERFIELD, whose brilliant, if somewhat eccentric, book on the pre–World War I years includes some 50 pages on the 1909–11 constitutional crisis. He portrays the "diehards" as reactionary "backwoodsmen" and the Parliament Act itself as important more as a symbol for a passing older order than for what it did to alter the constitution.

In the absence of major book-length studies of the 1911 reform, a useful source of information is journal literature. BLACKBURN contributes to our understanding of an often neglected feature of the Parliament Act, the reduction in the maximum life of an elected Commons from seven to five years. After contextualizing the issue by recounting its history, he shows that the 1911 reduction, which is still in effect, was a bargaining device in a measure that increased the power of Commons in relation to that of Lords.

Another useful approach in exploring the constitutional reform of 1911, in particular the crisis that produced it, is through autobiographical and biographical accounts of major players: Asquith and Lloyd George, Balfour and Lansdowne, and the kings, Edward VII and George V. Three of the fuller accounts are those of Asquith, Newton, and Nicolson. In ASQUITH's memoirs of his public life, he devotes five chapters to the crisis, beginning with the budget and concluding with the Parliament Act. He reveals his own thoughts and actions and shows, from his perspective, the roles of various players. NEWTON, himself a peer in 1911, and Lansdowne's authorized biographer, includes chapters on "The People's Budget" and "The Parliament Bill". He believes Balfour and Lansdowne made a major tactical error in opposing the 1909 budget, thus precipitating the constitutional crisis. He has empathy for Lansdowne in the midst of the 1911 crisis, and thinks his acceptance of the inevitability of the bill's passage after the December election and the king's pledge (which he became aware of in July) was responsible and statesman-like. However, he believes Lansdowne could have been more vigorous in using his leadership position and personal influence to try to persuade the "diehards" of the folly of resistance. NICOLSON also devotes two chapters to George V's role in the crisis following his accession to the throne in May 1910. In Nicolson's view the new king genuinely tried to be non-partisan, but desperately wanted to avoid having to create the necessary new peers, perhaps up to 500, to override the large Conservative majority in Lords. He had high hopes for the constitutional conference of government and opposition leaders in the summer and fall of 1910. When the conference failed to reach agreement, the king reluctantly gave Asquith his pledge to create sufficient peers to overcome the opposition to constitutional reform in the Lords if the Liberals prevailed after a second election in which the focal issue would be reform. Nicolson reveals that the king gave his pledge mistakenly believing Balfour was unwilling to form a government if Asquith resigned. He also accepted, to his later regret, Asquith's insistence that the November pledge remain secret.

It was not made known to the Conservative leaders until 19 July. George was greatly relieved when 37 Conservative peers joined the Liberals and bishops to defeat the "diehards" by 17 votes (Lansdowne and the majority of his fellow Conservatives abstained), thus allowing the Parliament Act to become law without the necessity of invoking his creation pledge.

JOHN L. GORDON, JR

See also Asquith; Balfour; George V; Lloyd George; Parliamentary Reform: House of Lords

Parliamentary Reform III: House of Lords 20th century

Baldwin, Nicholas, "The Composition of the House of Lords: Reform Options and Consequences", *Representation*, 36/1 (1999): 53–66

Butt, Ronald, "The Case for a Stronger Second Chamber" in *People and Parliament*, edited by John P. Mackintosh, Farnborough, Hampshire: Saxon House for the Hansard Society, 1978

Crick, Bernard, *The Reform of Parliament*, London: Weidenfeld and Nicolson, 1964; New York: Anchor Books, 1965; revised edition, 1968; further revised edition, 1970

Dorey, Peter, "The Labour Party and the Problems of Creating a 'Representative' House of Lords", *Representation*, 37/2 (2000): 117–23

Morgan, Janet P., *The House of Lords and the Labour Government 1964–1970*, Oxford: Clarendon Press, 1975

Richard, Ivor and Damien Welfare, *Unfinished Business: Reforming the House of Lords*, London: Vintage, 1999

Shell, Donald, "The House of Lords" in *The Politics of Parliamentary Reform*, edited by David Judge, London: Heinemann, 1983; Rutherford, New Jersey: Fairleigh Dickinson University Press, 1984

Shell, Donald, "Labour and the House of Lords: A Case Study in Constitutional Reform", *Parliamentary Affairs*, 53/2 (2000): 290–310

Although the 1911 and 1949 Parliament Acts reduced the House of Lords's power of delay, with the former legislation also preventing their lordships from obstructing "money bills", it was only from the 1960s onwards that more serious and systematic attention was focused on reform of the House of Lords, invariably in the context of more general constitutional reform and modernization of Britain's political institutions.

While MORGAN's analysis is clearly of the Wilson governments' general relationship with the House of Lords during the latter half of the 1960s, it necessarily includes *inter alia* one of the few detailed accounts of Labour's failed attempt at reforming the House of Lords in 1968–69. Having been elected in 1964, and then re-elected with a comfortable parliamentary majority in 1966, the Labour Party had no specific proposals for House of Lords reform, but was urged to "do something" by Richard Crossman after he had been appointed lord president of the Council, and assumed responsibility for parliamentary reform. Yet it soon became apparent that there was a marked lack of unanimity within the cabinet and among Labour backbenchers as to how precisely the House of Lords should be reformed, for once it was decreed that hereditary peers should no longer be permitted to vote, a host of vexatious questions were raised about the composition of the House of Lords, the means by which peers should subsequently be appointed, and the extent to which a reformed – and thus revitalized – second chamber might actually be imbued with increased powers or enhanced legitimacy (and thus be more inclined to prove obstructive to governments). Unable to answer such questions satisfactorily, Wilson abandoned the proposals for Lords reform that had been enshrined in the 1969 Parliament (No. 2) Bill.

BALDWIN shows that after Labour's failed attempt during the late 1960s, there were numerous proposals for reforming the composition of the House of Lords during the remainder of the 20th century, with recommendations and blueprints emanating not just from the Labour and Liberal parties, but from the Conservatives too. The various proposals invariably sought to tackle the anomaly of hereditary peerages, proposing either an appointed House of Lords or one elected via some form of proportional representation. Baldwin explains, however, that the eclectic character of these proposals militated against wider or bipartisan agreement on any one particular programme, while also raising a host of further troublesome questions about the relationship of a reformed House of Lords *vis-à-vis* the House of Commons. Indeed, Baldwin rightly concludes that any proposals for reforming the Lords must also delineate the subsequent functions and powers that the reformed second chamber will exercise, a constitutional conundrum which then remained unresolved.

Some of these issues are examined by SHELL (1983) in an essay that is generally supportive of the House of Lords, but which does acknowledge that the hereditary element is "eccentric, even offensive" and should therefore "be removed". What Shell proposes instead is some form of election to the House of Lords, preferably providing for proportional or regional representation. Yet Shell presciently recognizes that even if a government could agree on a suitable method of election or mode of representation, it might still decline to proceed, because of recognition that an elected House of Lords would probably become a more effective House of Lords, thereby at least slightly tilting the balance of power away from the executive towards parliament. Few governments genuinely wish to strengthen parliament, and so proposals to reform the House of Lords (beyond reducing the power of delay and permitting the creation of life peerages) have invariably come to naught.

CRICK also observes that repeated criticism of "the comedy and scandal of the House of Lords" has consistently failed to yield widely agreed solutions because of lack of agreement over the precise purpose of Lords reform: to strengthen or weaken, to "improve or to impair" it? In Crick's view, the problem that reformers ultimately need to resolve concerns the actual *function* of the House of Lords, rather than its powers and composition.

A singularly robust defence of the House of Lords is presented by BUTT, who is dismissive of the Labour Party's traditional "ridicule" of the second house and its perennial criticisms of the hereditary principle, and even suggests that the quality and calibre of debate in the Lords has usually been somewhat superior to debates heard in the House of Commons. Butt nonetheless feels obliged to acknowledge that the pressure for an elected component cannot be resisted indefinitely, and thus proposes that elected peers serve 12-year terms, with elections for one-third of them being held every four years, thereby providing at least some continuity. Crucially, however, Butt hopes that such a reform will enhance the legitimacy of the House of Lords, thereby permitting a significant increase in its powers of scrutiny and delay.

The Blair government's apparent commitment to reform of the House of Lords provides the impetus for RICHARD & WELFARE's study. They delineate the general case for reform before suggesting specific proposals to render the House of Lords more accountable and effective. In particular, Richard (Labour's leader in the House of Lords 1992–98) and Welfare recommend that two-thirds of the upper chamber's members be directly elected, with the remainder being nominated as non-political "experts". However, they also insist that while a more accountable, expert, and legitimate House of Lords could and should revitalize parliament, and contribute towards a more effective system of checks and balances, the House of Commons should remain pre-eminent. Of course, this really means that the will of the government should prevail. As such, Richard & Welfare are unable to overcome the dilemma that has undermined virtually all previous attempts at Lords reform, namely that a more representative or accountable membership will imbue it with greater legitimacy and authority, and thus increase its scope and willingness to challenge the government. Richard & Welfare attempt to square the circle by claiming that greater scrutiny by the Lords will improve the quality of a government's policies and legislation; but the argument is convenient rather than convincing.

The Labour Party's difficulties in seeking to agree on House of Lords reform throughout the postwar era are delineated in DOREY's short article, while SHELL (2000) examines how the first Blair government sought to succeed where previous Labour governments had failed. While Blair had succeeded in removing most of the hereditary peers, presenting this is as "phase one" of New Labour's programme of reform, Shell remained sceptical about the extent to which "phase two" will ever be realized in the form of a more democratic and accountable House of Lords. Indeed, at the beginning of 2002, the Blair government published a White Paper for the "second phase" of Lords reform, which proposed a 600-member chamber, in which only 20 per cent of members would be directly elected, a further 20 per cent would be appointed by a new Appointments Commission, and the remaining 60 per cent would be nominated by the parties themselves, in proportion to their share of the vote in the most recent general election. To date, Shell's scepticism seems to have been entirely justified.

PETER DOREY

See also Blair; Parliamentary Reform: Act of 1911

Parnell, Charles Stewart 1846–1891
Politician and Irish nationalist leader

Bew, Paul, *C.S. Parnell*, Dublin: Gill and Macmillan, 1980; reissued as *Charles Stewart Parnell*, 1991

Boyce, D. George and Alan O'Day (editors), *Parnell in Perspective*, London and New York: Routledge, 1991

Callanan, Frank, *The Parnell Split, 1890–1891*, Cork: Cork University Press, and Syracuse, New York: Syracuse University Press, 1992

Claydon, Tony, "The Political Thought of Charles Stewart Parnell" in *Parnell in Perspective*, edited by D. George Boyce and Alan O'Day, London and New York: Routledge, 1991

Ervine, St John, *Parnell*, London: Benn, 1925; Harmondsworth and New York: Penguin, 1944

Foster, R.F., *Charles Stewart Parnell: The Man and His Family*, Hassocks, Sussex: Harvester Press, and Atlantic Highlands, New Jersey: Humanities Press, 1976

Healy, T.M., *Letters and Leaders of My Day*, 2 vols, London: Butterworth, 1928; New York: Frederick A. Stokes, 1929

Johnston, R., *Parnell and the Parnells: A Historical Sketch*, London and Dublin: no publisher given, 1888

Kee, Robert, *The Laurel and the Ivy: The Story of Charles Stewart Parnell and Irish Nationalism*, London: Hamish Hamilton, and New York: Penguin, 1993

Loughlin, James, *Gladstone, Home Rule & the Ulster Question 1882–1893*, Dublin: Gill and Macmillan, and Atlantic Highlands, New Jersey: Humanities Press, 1987

Lyons, F.S.L., *The Fall of Parnell, 1890–1891*, London: Routledge and Kegan Paul, and Toronto: University of Toronto Press, 1961

Lyons, F.S.L., *Charles Stewart Parnell*, London: Collins, and New York: Oxford University Press, 1977

MacNeill, J.G. Swift, *What I Have Seen and Heard*, London: Arrowsmith, 1925

O'Brien, Conor Cruise, *Parnell and His Party 1880–1890*, Oxford: Clarendon Press, 1957; corrected reprint, Oxford: Clarendon Press, 1964

O'Brien, R. Barry, *The Life of Charles Stewart Parnell, 1846–1891*, 2 vols, London: Smith and Elder, and New York: Harper and Row, 1898

O'Brien, William, *The Parnell of Real Life*, London: Unwin, 1926

O'Connor, T.P., *The Parnell Movement, with a Sketch of Irish Parties since 1843*, London: Kegan Paul Trench, and New York: Benziger, 1886

O'Connor, T.P., *Charles Stewart Parnell: A Memory*, London and New York: Ward Lock, 1891

O'Connor, T.P., *Memoirs of an Old Parliamentarian*, London: Benn, 1929

O'Day, Alan, *Parnell and the First Home Rule Episode 1884–1887*, Dublin: Gill and Macmillan, 1986

O'Day, Alan, *Charles Stewart Parnell*, Dundalk: Historical Association of Ireland, 1998

O'Day, Alan, *Irish Home Rule 1867–1921*, Manchester: Manchester University Press, 1998

O'Hara, M.M., *Chief and Tribune: Parnell and Davitt*, Dublin and London: Maunsell, 1919

O'Shea, Katharine, *Charles Stewart Parnell: His Love Story and Political Life*, 2 vols, London: Cassell, 1914; reprinted, 1 vol., London: Cassell, 1973

Robbins, Sir Alfred, *Parnell: The Last Five Years*, London: Butterworth, 1926

Sherlock, Thomas, *The Life of Charles Stewart Parnell: With An Account of His Ancestors*, Boston: Murphy and McCarthy, 1881

Charles Stewart Parnell is celebrated by poets, writers, and historians, and he has been the protagonist of a Broadway stage production, a Hollywood film, and a BBC costume drama. The "Chief" or "uncrowned king of Ireland" was the first recognized champion of the Irish "race" throughout the world. Parnell's fame owed much to political accomplishments. During the general election campaign in 1918 Sinn Fein speakers vied with one another to claim his mantle. A protestant landlord, scion of an Ascendancy vilified in national demonology as the West Briton backbone of the English garrison, he was an unlikely object of popular veneration. Parnell possessed few of the gifts usually found in those who inspire mass adoration. He was a dull, precise speaker, had an aloof manner, and his political energy was concentrated in the "alien" parliament at Westminster. No doubt he is remembered today mainly because of his liaison with Katharine O'Shea, wife of Captain William Henry O'Shea, which exposed him to the fury of the catholic church and the multitudes who set store by traditional morality.

There are four phases in the transmission of Parnell's identity; contemporaries who treated Parnell as the coming man; the publication of formative lives; reminiscences by contemporaries, and modern scholarship arising from the revolution in Irish historiography beginning in the 1930s. Certain of the standard features of the portrait make an early appearance. SHERLOCK in 1881 focused on Parnell's ancestral inheritance, his rise to power, moderating influence, and ability to make rational political choices. In 1886 T.P. O'CONNOR, a political colleague, claimed that Parnell's outlook was shaped by the 1798 and 1867 rebellions, though he balanced these revolutionary influences with the message that throughout the land war Parnell urged the Irish people to eschew violence and to seek their aims by constitutional means. Two years later JOHNSTON pointed to the importance of the Parnell family's traditional liberal attitude towards catholics as a key ingredient in his make-up.

The divorce crisis in 1890–91 marked a transition. Emphasis upon Parnell's exemplary character disappeared and his political acumen received less attention, while biographers dwelled on the mysterious, romantic, and dramatic aspects of his life along with the Greek-like tragedy of the fall. Establishing the tone, O'CONNOR's hurried biography (1891) foreshadowed the main element in subsequent interpretations – the enigma. Concluding his portrait, O'Connor proclaimed "there is no doubt about Parnell's greatness. He was a portent, a great and tragic exception to Nature's ordinary laws, like an eclipse or an earthquake". Lyons's modern scholarly estimate is similar.

In 1898 R. Barry O'BRIEN, a London journalist, published the *Life*, which became the yardstick for measuring future biographies. O'Brien's purpose was to contrast the sad state of national politics in the 1890s with the unified movement directed by Parnell. O'Brien laid down three of the chief ingredients in the story – Parnell the instinctual prescient leader who comprehended the emotive force of Fenianism and saw membership in the House of Commons in terms of its tactical utility; Parnell who welded together the disparate strands of the nation; and Parnell the man who would have secured home rule but for the divorce crisis.

Parnell's affair with Katharine O'Shea cast a spell over subsequent writers and this effect can be traced in a bevy of memories and recollections by contemporaries published in the three decades after Barry O'Brien's biography. Among these are accounts by Katharine O'SHEA herself, O'HARA, ERVINE, MacNEILL, William O'BRIEN, ROBBINS, HEALY, and O'CONNOR.

It was not until Conor Cruise O'BRIEN's *Parnell and His Party*, published in 1957, in which Parnell was repositioned firmly within his movement, that the romantic legend began to be displaced by the astute rather than the mystic figure. Cruise O'Brien argued that Parnell was imbued in constitutionalism. Nevertheless, much of Barry O'Brien's interpretation is retained. Parnell, in Cruise O'Brien's hands, skilfully equivocated about violence, walking the tightrope between extremists and moderates. Also, Cruise O'Brien endorses Barry O'Brien's picture of Parnell as the man of iron determination who bent the national movement to his will. LYONS (1961) portrayed the fallen leader not as the giant felled by pygmies but as the maker, too often the duplicitous manufacturer, of his own fate. Parnell appeared as an increasingly desperate and undisciplined shadow of a former self. Despite an absence of empathy for Parnell, Lyons still saw him as an incomparable figure.

Subsequent academic studies expand upon Cruise O'Brien's contextual analysis, examining Parnell's family, caste, and political environment. FOSTER explores his outlook through family heritage, not the alleged anti-English views of Parnell's mother, reinforced by a progressive gentry tradition flourishing in east Wicklow. Tony CLAYDON's perceptive study, from the collection by BOYCE & O'DAY, integrates an inherited political ideology, emphasizing the virtue of local responsible institutions, developed and extended by Parnell to fit Irish circumstances in his own time. LYONS (1977) underlines Parnell's preoccupation with 1782. Four Parnells emerge: the country gentleman; an instinctive political genius; engaging companion; and a man of passion driven by demonic pride and self-will. In two studies from the 1980s O'DAY and LOUGHLIN reassessed the parameters of the home rule incident. Instead of Parnell holding British politicians to ransom, O'Day sees him as at their mercy. Placing Parnell in context receives a significant twist from BEW, who develops two themes – Parnell's weak perception of Ulster before 1891 and his southern protestant landlord-inspired concerns on the self-government and land questions. Bew turns Barry O'Brien on his head. Among studies of the 1990s, the rapid drift toward viewing Parnell as intent upon mediating between Ireland's communities, as someone trying to ease the excesses of ethnic Catholic nationalism, is advocated by CALLANAN. For Lyons the principle at stake during the divorce episode was the "independence" of the Irish party from British combinations. O'DAY in *Irish Home Rule* pictures Parnell as part of a protestant tradition, holding that self-government was a formula to reconcile the interests of Ireland's peoples, and in *Charles Stewart Parnell* he portrays him as a sincere champion of House of Commons traditions and as someone who tried even in 1891 to make parliament the focus of Irish political attention. Interspersed with academic studies are a number of popular biographies of which KEE's is a worthy example suited to a general readership.

ALAN O'DAY

See also Butt; Fenian Movement; Gladstone; Ireland entries (19th century); "Irish Question"; Kilmainham "Treaty"

Patriarchy

Clark, Alice, *Working Life of Women in the Seventeenth Century*, London: Routledge and Kegan Paul, and New York: Dutton, 1919; reprinted, London: Routledge and Kegan Paul, 1982

Fell, Christine, Cecily Clark, and Elizabeth Williams, *Women in Anglo-Saxon England; and The Impact of 1066*, London: British Museum, and Bloomington: Indiana University Press, 1984

Hamilton, Roberta, *The Liberation of Women: A Study of Patriarchy and Capitalism*, London and Boston: Allen and Unwin, 1978

Murray, Mary, *The Law of the Father? Patriarchy in the Transition from Feudalism to Capitalism*, London and New York: Routledge, 1995

Pinchbeck, Ivy, *Women Workers and the Industrial Revolution 1750–1850*, London: Routledge, 1930; New York: Kelley, 1969

Stone, Lawrence, *The Family, Sex, and Marriage in England 1500–1800*, London: Weidenfeld and Nicolson, and New York: Harper and Row, 1977

The view that patriarchal authority is inherent in human nature, arising either naturally and spontaneously or as a direct result of divine intention, has been challenged by historical and feminist research and writing. Roberta Hamilton and Mary Murray in their studies consider the nature of and shifts and changes in patriarchal authority during the transition from feudalism to capitalism in England. HAMILTON's view is that an understanding of patriarchal authority requires that we consider material, ideological, and biological factors. She combines an explicitly feminist analysis of patriarchal ideology, which locates the source of male domination of women in biological differences between the sexes, with a Marxist analysis of the economic impact of the development of capitalism. The thrust of her argument is that the emergence of capitalism undermined the family as the basic economic unit and in so doing undermined women's role in production, thereby increasing female dependency within all classes of society. Meanwhile changes occurred in patriarchal ideology. While protestantism saw women as godly companions of their husbands rather than, as in medieval catholicism, natural allies of the devil, protestantism also defined women's role more closely as that of housewife and asserted the spiritual authority of husbands and the inferiority of wives.

In MURRAY's book patriarchy is seen as indivisible from other aspects of social structure such as class. Her general argument is that patriarchy and class relations are particular expressions of the fundamental social relation of property which together they constitute. Her particular focus is on rights in and to property, political power and office, kinship structures, and the idea that women themselves were property. In Murray's view, Anglo-Saxon, feudal, and capitalist society in England were constructed through and articulated specific kinds of patriarchal relations. At the heart of the transition from feudalism to capitalism was a fundamental shift in property relations which were patriarchally structured: rather than seeing patriarchal authority as part of natural law and divine intention, patriarchal authority is seen as a product of the structure of social relationships.

Whereas Hamilton and Murray construct their arguments at a fairly high level of theoretical abstraction and draw largely on secondary rather than primary sources, Fell, Stone, Clark, and Pinchbeck make more use of primary sources to construct more detailed empirical accounts of patriarchal relationships between men and women. Drawing on wills, charters, letters, chronicles, archaeological discoveries, place-names, and poetry, in *Women in Anglo-Saxon England* Christine FELL provides plenty of evidence to suggest that relationships between women and men were socially rather than naturally or divinely produced. (Her study was published in the same volume with Clark and Williams's *The Impact of 1066*.) Chapters focus on myth and legend, daily life, sex and marriage, family and kinship, manor and court, the religious life, and Viking women in Britain. Attention is also given to the impact of Norman feudalism on the position of women. The scholarly and erudite compilation of evidence discussed by Fell suggests that women in Anglo-Saxon society were neither submissive nor subordinate. Women's rights were recognized within kinship structures as well as within marriage and upper-class women exercised a considerable degree of political power and influence.

Fell does not attempt to engage with metatheoretical debates about the nature of and shifts and changes in patriarchy as do Hamilton and Murray, concentrating instead on a richly textured historical and empirical approach. Lawrence STONE however does attempt to combine detailed historical data with a theoretical approach. His focus on patriarchal and natural law authority comprises part of his study of *The Family, Sex, and Marriage in England 1500–1800*. He identifies and analyses three kinds of family structures: the open lineage family of 1450–1630; the restricted patriarchal nuclear family of 1550–1700; and the closed domesticated nuclear family of 1640–1800. In his analyses of these family structures he signals shifts and changes in patriarchal relations. He discusses the reinforcement of patriarchy in the 17th century by the state. He argues that:

> What seems to have happened is that a diffuse concept of patriarchy inherited from the middle ages that took the form of "good lordship" – meaning dominance over kin and clientage – was vigorously attacked by the state as a threat to its own authority. Patriarchy was now reinforced by the state, however in the much modified form of authoritarian dominance by the husband and father over the woman and children within the nuclear family. What

had previously been a real threat to political order was thus neatly transformed into a formidable buttress to it.

He also sees as significant the protestant view that husbands and fathers should be the spiritual and secular heads of households. However, by the late 17th century patriarchal authority was being explicitly challenged. John Locke's contract theory challenged political theories of state power and consequently challenged ideas about patriarchal power within families and the rights of individuals. Stone (165) quotes Mary Astell: "If absolute sovereignty be not necessary in a state, how comes it be so in a family? . . . If all men are born free, how is it that all women are born slaves?" Stone contends that as the power of absolute monarchy declined in the state so too did patriarchal authoritarianism within the family decline.

While Stone provides us with some understanding of the dynamics of patriarchy with family and state, a fuller understanding needs to include the relationship of women and men within the workplace – both inside and outside the home. Two books which do this are Clark's and Pinchbeck's. Moreover, while the work of Stone and Fell provides us with more of an understanding of the relationship between women and men within the upper echelons of society, Clark and Pinchbeck are more focused on women within the lower and middling ranks of society. CLARK sees the 17th century as the critical period in which productive and familial relations were transformed. The capitalist mode of production is identified as "the means by which the revolution in women's economic position was effected". She discusses the way in which the emergence of a family wage system (as opposed to individual wages) benefited men; how the employment of wage-earners within the master's premises prevented the employment of the wage-earner's wife in her husband's occupation; and how a rapid increase in wealth led to the withdrawal of upper-class women from activity within the sphere of business. Overall, the emergence of capitalism during the 17th century undermined the productive role and contribution of women. Even so, Clark points out that before the emergence of capitalism "women's relation to the 'home' was regarded as an immutable law of Nature, inviolable by any upheaval in external relations". Consequently she argues that:

> the idea that the revolution in women's economic position was due to deliberate policy may be dismissed . . . the subjection of women to their husbands was the foundation stone of the structure of the community in which Capitalism first made its appearance. Regarded as being equally the law of Nature and the Law of God, no one questioned the necessity of the wife's obedience, lip service being rendered to the doctrine of subjection, even in households where it was least enforced.

Writing about developments a century later in the employment of women in agriculture as well as trade and industry, Ivy PINCHBECK argues that in the long run the Industrial Revolution was beneficial to women's social and economic position. Pinchbeck is acutely aware that being paid inadequate wages, without the vote, and with little protection from the law, women suffered the consequences of being second-class citizens. She is also clearly aware that paid employment was for many women a forced "choice" to enable them to supplement family incomes. Even so, Pinchbeck considers that being an independent wage-earner provided women with the first step towards social and economic emancipation. Writing well before feminists and historians engaged explicitly in theoretical debate about the relationship between patriarchy and capitalism, Pinchbeck provides a wealth of historical data which brings to life the struggles of working-class women against both patriarchy and capitalism.

MARY MURRAY

See also Gender and Power; Inheritance, Patterns of; Marriage; Masculinities entries; Social Structure entries; Women's Movements

Patrick c.400–c.493
Missionary and patron saint of Ireland

Bieler, Ludwig (translator and editor), *The Works of St. Patrick; Hymn on St. Patrick by St. Secundinus*, London: Longmans Green, and Westminster, Maryland: Newman Press, 1953

Binchy, D.A., "Patrick and His Biographers: Ancient and Modern", *Studia Hibernica*, 2 (1962): 7–173

Carney, James, *The Problem of St. Patrick*, Dublin: Dublin Institute for Advanced Studies, 1973

De Paor, Liam (editor and translator), *Saint Patrick's World: The Christian Culture of Ireland's Apostolic Age*, Dublin: Four Courts Press, and Notre Dame, Indiana: University of Notre Dame Press, 1993

Dumville, David N. (editor), *Saint Patrick, AD 493–1993*, Woodbridge, Suffolk and Rochester, New York: Boydell and Brewer, 1993

Hood, A.B.E. (editor and translator), *St Patrick: His Writings and Muirchu's Life*, London: Phillimore, and Totowa, New Jersey: Rowman and Littlefield, 1978

Howlett, D.R. (editor and translator), *Liber epistolarum Sancti Patricii episcopi / The Book of Letters of Saint Patrick the Bishop*, Dublin and Portland, Oregon: Four Courts Press, 1994

O'Loughlin, Thomas, *St Patrick: The Man and His Works*, London: Triangle, 1999

Patrick is the patron saint of Ireland and was one of the first Christian missionaries to the country. He has been the subject of many academic debates over the years. In some respects, we know more about Patrick than any other figure in Irish history in the 5th century, yet we still cannot create a traditional biography.

To begin a study on Patrick, one should start with two of his writings that have survived. In his translation of Patrick's *Epistola* and *Confessio*, BIELER puts the original Latin into clear English. He does not include the Latin text, so a novice to Patrick's work will find it easy to read. His introduction follows the arguments of early 20th-century writers on Patrick, however, and therefore should be read with caution as many of his conclusions are no longer accepted. Bieler's translation forms the foundation on which many other translations are based.

HOOD's work includes the *Vita Sancti Patricii* by Muirchú, written in the 7th century, as well as Patrick's *Epistola* and *Confessio*. Hood provides a short introduction, which again must be read with caution as it supports older ideas within Patrician historiography. However, Hood includes the Latin text of the writings and follows each with the English translation. Thus, the English translation can be confirmed by a reader who can translate the Latin.

A slightly different approach has been used for HOWLETT's version of Patrick's writings. Howlett is concerned with examining the style of Latin that Patrick used. Many scholars have summed up Patrick's Latin as either inarticulate or at least uneducated. Disputing this, Howlett examines in minute detail how Patrick used Latin, and the excellent literary style that he produced. This volume has the Latin version of the text on one page and the English translation on the facing page. It is done line by line and includes analysis and commentary after each section. Howlett's work is for a reader interested in medieval Latin as well as the history of the saint. The general reader may find this more technical than they might want.

For the reader interested in Patrick's writings and other sources for early Christianity, DE PAOR's effort will be extremely valuable. De Paor has gathered numerous ancient and medieval writings covering the history, culture, and religion of early medieval Ireland. He provides these sources in English translation. Each source has an introduction and commentary to keep it in context. Some of the sources include texts of church councils, early chronicles and annals, papal letters, and various saints' lives. As a resource for the study of the original sources for both Patrick and early medieval Ireland, De Paor's work is essential.

Once familiar with Patrick's writings, the reader can delve into the historical debate that has raged during the last century. Writing on Patrician studies has been prolific due to the numerous problems that revolve around how little we actually know about the saint. Although we have his writings, Patrick did not leave any solid information such as dates. The specific places he mentions have not yet been positively identified either. One of the foremost of these controversies in Patrician studies has been the dates of both his life and his mission to Ireland. This particular controversy is important because of the rancour that surrounded it in the 1950s and 1960s.

CARNEY was involved heavily in the debate about dates. At one time, it was generally accepted that Patrick's mission began c.432 and his death occurred c.493. However, in order for these dates to make sense, Patrick would have been around 120 years old at the time of his death, which seemed unlikely. A re-evaluation was done, and the conclusion was that his mission began c.432, and his death occurred c.461. Carney, however, following on Thomas F. O'Rahilly's work, suggested that Patrick's mission actually began in the later half of the 5th century, c.456, and his death c.493. Carney's book is a collection of articles, some of which had been published previously, covering his interpretations about this dating problem. Carney's work is pivotal because most scholars now accept that Patrick's mission started in the second half of the 5th century and that he died in the last decade of that century, which alters Patrick's dates to c.400–c.493.

However, Carney faced severe opposition from those who supported the earlier view. BINCHY's article discusses in length the controversy over this issue. He provides a thorough summary of the major arguments and their proponents, while also commenting on their merits or lack thereof. However, Binchy is not limited to the dating problem; other controversies are also examined in this article. Binchy's work is important in order to understand the controversies that have begun to be settled since the 1970s.

In more recent times scholars have continued to discuss these controversies, but without the rancour that characterized the earlier period. DUMVILLE has brought together an excellent group of commentators to examine these issues. The purpose of this volume was to see where the controversies had been left and attempt to move them forward. This collection covers a variety of topics including dates, Patrick's missing years, later hagiographers, missionary activity in Britain, and the spread of Christianity in Ireland. This provides an excellent and thorough discussion of where Patrician studies stand today.

O'LOUGHLIN's fairly slim volume provides a summary of some of the major issues in Patrician studies as well. However, it is designed for the general reader, providing an introduction that places the study of Patrick into context in terms of what Patrick's worldview may have been. Above all, O'Loughlin makes it clear that while we can gain much from the study of Patrick, we will never be able to produce a conventional biography of the man or his times. This work contains a translation of Patrick's writings as well. The main benefit of his translation is the extensive index of Patrick's use of scripture. O'Loughlin has made copious notes on each reference in Patrick's writings that originate in scripture, and it is probably the most exhaustive index available.

KAREN E. MILLER

See also Anglo-Saxon England: Church Organization; Christian Conversion in the British Isles; Ireland: Before the Normans; Irish Annals

Patronage and Politics, Early Modern

Dickinson, H.T., *The Politics of the People in Eighteenth-Century Britain*, London: Macmillan, and New York: St Martin's Press, 1994

Elton, G.R., "The Points of Contact" in his *Studies in Tudor and Stuart Politics and Government*, vol. 3, *Papers and Reviews 1973–1981*, London and New York: Cambridge University Press, 1983

Hay, Douglas and Nicholas Rogers, *Eighteenth-Century English Society: Shuttles and Swords*, Oxford and New York: Oxford University Press, 1997

Hill, Brian, *The Early Parties and Politics in Britain, 1688–1832*, London: Macmillan, and New York: St Martin's Press, 1996

Holmes, Clive, *Seventeenth-Century Lincolnshire*, Lincoln: History of Lincolnshire, Commission for the Society for Lincolnshire History and Archaeology, 1980

Holmes, Geoffrey, *Augustan England: Professions, State, and Society, 1680–1730*, London and Boston: Allen and Unwin, 1982

Holmes, Geoffrey, *The Making of a Great Power: Late Stuart and Early Georgian Britain, 1660–1722*, London and New York: Longman, 1993

Hughes, Ann, *Politics, Society, and Civil War in Warwickshire 1620–1660*, Cambridge and New York: Cambridge University Press, 1987

MacCaffrey, Wallace C., "Place and Patronage in Elizabethan Politics" in *Elizabethan Government and Society: Essays Presented to Sir John Neale*, edited by S.T. Bindoff, J. Hurstfield, and C.H. Williams, London: Athlone Press, 1961

Morgan, Victor, "Some Types of Patronage, Mainly in Sixteenth and Seventeenth Century England" in *Klientelsysteme im Europa der frühen Neuzeit*, edited by Antoni Mazak with Elisabeth Muller-Luckner, Munich: Oldenbourg, 1988

Namier, Lewis B., *The Structure of Politics at the Accession of George III*, 2 vols, London: Macmillan, 1929; 2nd edition, London: Macmillan, and New York: St Martin's Press, 1957

Neale, John E., "The Elizabethan Political Scene" in his *Essays in Elizabethan History*, London: Jonathan Cape, 1958

O'Gorman, Frank, *Voters, Patrons, and Parties: The Unreformed Electoral System of Hanoverian England, 1734–1832*, Oxford: Clarendon Press, and New York: Oxford University Press, 1989

O'Gorman, Frank, *The Long Eighteenth Century: British Political and Social History, 1688–1832*, London: Arnold, and New York: St Martin's Press, 1997

Patterson, Catherine F., *Urban Patronage in Early Modern England: Corporate Boroughs, the Landed Elite, and the Crown, 1580–1640*, Stanford, California: Stanford University Press, 1999

Peck, Linda Levy, *Court Patronage and Corruption in Early Stuart England*, Boston and London: Unwin Hyman, 1990

Perkin, Harold, *The Origins of Modern English Society, 1780–1880*, London and New York: Routledge and Kegan Paul, and Toronto: University of Toronto Press, 1969

Sharpe, Kevin, "Crown, Parliament, and Locality: Government and Communication in Early Stuart England" and "The Image of Virtue: The Court and Household of Charles I, 1625–1642" in his *Politics and Ideas in Early Stuart England: Essays and Studies*, London and New York: Pinter, 1989

Smith, Robert A., *Eighteenth-Century English Politics: Patrons and Place-Hunters*, New York: Holt Rinehart and Winston, 1972

Stone, Lawrence, *The Crisis of the Aristocracy, 1558–1641*, Oxford: Clarendon Press, 1965

Williams, Penry, *The Tudor Regime*, Oxford: Clarendon Press, and New York: Oxford University Press, 1979

Political patronage is the right of control over appointment to an office or privilege, especially court and government offices, titles, sinecures, pensions, contracts and commissions, and some church livings. As the art of governance consisted largely in its most effective distribution, patronage was a powerful means by which early modern rulers ensured stability. With the consolidation of royal power under the Tudors, monarchs became adept at securing the loyalty and service of the political elite through royal favour, which, in the absence of a professional bureaucracy, allowed them to rule from the centre to the localities. Local leaders, in turn, dispensed patronage to clients and maintained channels of access and communication between the court and the localities. Sweeping political change in the 16th and 17th centuries altered the contours and dimensions of royal patronage, which by the 18th century had greatly increased through the expansion of the Treasury, the customs and excise, and the army and navy.

Recent work on early modern politics has examined the functions and distribution of patronage as a means of promoting stability as interest has turned from the structures of formal power to the informal ties that bound government and society, court and elite, and patron and client. NEALE sparked interest in Elizabethan patronage with the range of bounty in the queen's gift, much of which was contested by petitioners either at court through intermediaries linked with the Privy Chamber or from the localities; the scale of fees and gratuities in patron-client relationships; and the symbiotic nature of patronage and faction. Faction was pivotal in the competition for royal favour and thus control of patronage. Patronage, in turn, was the glue that held faction together.

MACCAFFREY takes patronage to the localities and shows how the crown secured the service and loyalty of the peers and gentry through a wide distribution of bounty. Favour and office were the tools of patronage in the crown's quest for loyalty aimed at securing the "good will" and "confidence" of the political elite. In binding the material interests of the polity to the fate of the regime, Elizabeth I sought to strengthen government and minimize conflict. Political elites, in turn, were responsible for local recruitment and the system cohered through patronage and connection. For the ambitious the court acted as a "magnet".

ELTON accents "points of contact" in his study of the nature of court patronage. The royal household as the largest employer lured place-seekers, and positions especially within the Privy Chamber were fiercely contested. As intermediaries were arbiters of patronage, issues of access to the monarch, exclusion, and brokerage were critical to aspirants. Elton demonstrates that the court cannot be identified exclusively with the person of the monarch, and high politics between 1509 and 1558 was dominated by the unsuccessful attempts of court factions to gain "exclusive control". Unlike Henry VII and Elizabeth, Henry VIII appeared to foster division; nevertheless both father and daughter used faction as a counterbalance to monopoly and corruption. By the 1590s, however, the queen had ceased to dispense patronage skilfully, which led to rebellion and the dangerous isolation of her court. WILLIAMS adds insights into the Tudor art of "winning compliance" through patronage.

The focus on court, place, and favour has encouraged scholars of state-building to examine the interplay of aristocratic and government patronage. Lawrence STONE suggests a decline in the importance of aristocratic authority and thus of patronage with the growth of the centralized state under the early Tudors. Alternatively, MORGAN posits that the centralized state provided new channels for patronage which he calls "patrimonial".

Historians including Clive HOLMES and Ann HUGHES have explored political patronage from the point of view of the gentry elite and their reactions to the lure of royal bounty.

PATTERSON takes patronage to provincial towns to examine its role in establishing reciprocal relations between civic leaders and elites. A strengthened state with increased demands on civic officials caused them to seek patronage in high places using the traditional tools at their disposal: honour and deference, gifts and hospitality, local office and parliamentary seats. She argues that connection as much as conflict explains the development of early modern government.

Current opinion on political patronage in 17th-century politics has been shaped by challenges to Whig interpretations of the causes of the civil wars from around the mid-1970s as revisionists have shifted the focus from constitutional issues to political clientage. SHARPE's work on the "processes of communication" at court, both to and from the king, places Elton's "points of contact" in a broader context. A monopoly of court patronage under the early Stuarts weakened the aristocracy and the effectiveness of the council; it deprived court rivals and jeopardized local patronage networks. Local leaders excluded from favour turned to the House of Commons to exercise their influence and early Stuart parliaments railed at the inaccessibility of the court. Charles I's rule without parliament exacerbated tensions. Parliament came to govern "only reluctantly" and largely because "of the breakdown of patronage and communications". PECK, however, questions the recent focus on faction as a major cause of political discord in her study of early Stuart patronage and corruption in the context of contemporary politics and ideology. Corruption, she argues, was a major concern for contemporaries evident "in statute, proclamation, language and behavior".

The nature of political patronage altered after the settlement of 1688–89 which created parliament as a central feature of constitutional monarchy. The system enabled royal ministers to manage parliament and to secure the majority necessary in the Commons "to do the King's business". The opposition argued that it enabled the crown to buy parliament, though current opinion mostly refutes the monolithic power once attributed to first ministers. Nonetheless, as a minister could influence selection for public office, positions in the army, navy, and the church and promote candidates for titles, pensions, and contracts, an MP's support was often bought by patronage. Political patrons among the landowners who influenced the election of MPs were, in turn, courted by crown ministers to return men who would support the administration.

Scholarly debate on late 17th- and 18th-century political patronage was largely dominated by Whig historians until NAMIER's influential repudiation of their work in the 1920s. Namier focused on patron-client relationships using prosopography which enabled him to collect detail on the personal life, career, and connections of every MP during the early years of George III's reign to establish the factors which determined the political actions of an individual or group. He stressed patronage, corruption, and self-interest to the exclusion of ideas and principles, which inspired criticism and revision from the 1950s, according to different orthodoxies. Modern research, nevertheless, remains indebted to the Namierite view on the uses of political patronage.

Historians less interested in high politics than social history have explored political patronage in terms of class or culture. PERKIN argues that before the Industrial Revolution England was a classless society organized around vertically linked relationships based on property and patronage. It was these vertical ties which, more than the horizontal ties of class, bound society. Political patronage was a system of personal recruitment from one's own family or contacts. It provided the means by which property could affect selection for those positions which were not decided exclusively by property. The patronage system was dominated by landowners and clients from court to county politics.

SMITH is instructive on the relationships of patronage which enabled the king's ministers to manage parliament. Outlining patterns of allegiance in the Commons and the Lords, the court and Treasury group was composed of administrators and courtiers loyal to office rather than connection, and the "professional place-hunters" whose patronage depended on the government of the day. The distribution of patronage was the means by which ministries gained parliamentary support, and its administration required great skill and the backing of the monarch. The work of Geoffrey HOLMES (1993) on the reigns of William III and Anne and Frank O'GORMAN (1997) are useful here.

HOLMES (1982) discusses "state" professionals in both civil and military service whose presence was felt at least by the end of Anne's reign. A more centralized political culture and the expectation of favour and place in an expanding and increasingly professional bureaucracy attracted individuals to London. The plum positions were the ministerial posts, whose occupants were political placemen rather than bureaucrats, Smith's place-hunters; but rich opportunities existed at every level for the well connected.

For DICKINSON too much attention has been accorded the "propertied elite" and their exploitation of patronage in parliamentary constituencies, to the detriment of the voters themselves. While not disputing their influence, he contends that evidence for MPs' election through aristocratic patrons is often inflated. He argues that the electorate exercised their informed judgement in casting their vote. O'GORMAN (1989) and HILL are instructive on 18th-century electoral protest and patronage, respectively.

HAY & ROGERS illuminate the friction between the private and exclusive world of patronage politics and the extraparliamentary politics of the first half of the 18th century. To some extent it was contained by the ideological allure of Whiggery in the face of Jacobite and catholic concern. Once the concern waned, however, the patronage system was threatened by a vigorous political culture whose opposition the government was increasingly forced to address. After 1760 the old system lost ground and the formal system of parliamentary politics seemed increasingly anachronistic, as the politicization of the people transformed the arena of national politics.

LOUISE GILL

See also Prime Minister; Tories entries; Whigs entries

Peacekeeping Operations   since 1945

Harbottle, Michael, *The Blue Berets*, London: Leo Cooper, 1971; Harrisburg, Pennsylvania: Stackpole Books, 1972; revised edition, 1975

Her Majesty's Government Foreign Affairs Committee, *The Expanding Role of the United Nations and its Implications for United Kingdom Policy*, vol. 2, London: HMSO, 1993

Jensen, Erik and Thomas Fisher (editors), *The United Kingdom: The United Nations*, London: Macmillan, 1990

Murray, Rupert Wolfe (editor), with photographs by Steven Gordon, *IFOR on IFOR: NATO Peacekeepers in Bosnia-Herzegovina*, Edinburgh: Connect, 1996

Rose, Michael, *Fighting for Peace: Bosnia 1994*, London: Harvill, 1998

The United Nations, *The Blue Helmets: A Review of United Nations Peace-Keeping*, New York: United Nations, 1985; 3rd edition, 1996

Whittaker, David J., *United Nations in Action*, London: UCL Press, and Armonk, New York: Sharpe, 1995

Whittaker, David J., *United Nations in the Contemporary World*, London and New York: Routledge, 1997

Peacekeeping involving the United Kingdom since 1945 has taken place as part of either United Nations or NATO operations; there is thus a dearth of literature confined purely to Britain's peacekeeping role. However, Britain's contribution is, naturally, included in studies of the UN's peacekeeping activities, and significant information can be derived from these works. One of the studies that does focus on the United Kingdom's contribution is the edited volume by JENSEN & FISHER, which assembles a unique collection of insights into the evolving relationship between the United Kingdom and the UN. Among the contributors are three former British ambassadors to the UN, including Sir Brian Urquhart, whose contribution focuses particularly on the question of peacekeeping. Urquhart's first sentence highlights one of the most widespread misunderstandings of the role of the UN, pointing out that:

> [t]he phrase "peace-keeping" does not occur in the United Nations Charter, nor is there any description of the concept of peace-keeping as we now understand it. The term came into general use in the early 1960s to describe the use of military personnel and forces in a non-violent international capacity as the observers of cease-fires or the controllers of conflict.

It is, thus, immediately obvious why the UN's ability to *enforce* peace usually fails to meet public expectations, because, as Urquhart demonstrates, the UN's charter does not actually cover the role which people have come to expect it to play.

The implications of Britain's contribution to the UN's peacekeeping effort are also covered in the FOREIGN AFFAIRS COMMITTEE publication listed, where the emphasis is placed on the level of troops required for such operations as Somalia and Bosnia in relation to Britain's overall military strength. It is pointed out that it does not follow "that because demand is increasing, every demand will be met". The balance of nuclear versus conventional troops is also discussed, the implication being that the ending of the cold war altered the perceived need for a powerful nuclear arsenal, and that "it seems hardly likely that Trident is going to be very useful in Somalia or Bosnia or Angola, but indeed the actual on-the-ground presence of a cohesive, well-disciplined ... British force would enhance Britain's role in foreign policy decision-making within the international community."

Brigadier HARBOTTLE, former chief of staff of the UN peacekeeping force in Cyprus in 1966–68, looks at the major incidents in which UN forces have been involved during the organization's first 30 years. He refers to his study as a "guide book" to the more prominent of the peacekeeping efforts that the UN has mounted, and as such provides a comprehensive bibliography to help guide the reader towards further detailed studies. Harbottle underlines the "rules of the game" by which the Security Council must abide in carrying out its authority to "take such action by air, sea or land forces as may be necessary to maintain or restore international peace", including the important criterion that all UN peacekeeping operations must have the consent of one or more of the parties concerned. He examines in detail the UN actions in Cyprus, in which Britain played a large part, and which literally did involve keeping the peace – a fragile and tenuous affair – for many years.

General Sir Michael ROSE also looks at peacekeeping from the soldier's perspective, this time in Bosnia as commander of the United Nations Protection Force in 1994. His account includes contemporary documents and photographs as well as diary entries, and describes the difficult task of attempting to sustain the peace process in the face of opposition both from within the former Yugoslavia and from the outside world. The UN's role in Bosnia is a prime example of the restrictions placed upon the organization; initially its role was nominally to provide humanitarian aid, but it was then expected to assume a peacekeeping role without, however, the invitation or cooperation of the parties involved. When the year-long struggle to stabilize the military conflict was over, and aid convoys were reaching their destinations, the UN's place was taken by the NATO Ifor contingent (see below).

The UNITED NATIONS' own review of its peacekeeping activities, *The Blue Helmets*, gives an extremely detailed account of its worldwide involvement, including facts and figures, covering the nature and extent of financial, military, and civilian contributions by individual countries. The sheer scale of the international dimension of UN operations is very clearly demonstrated, underlining, perhaps, the difficulty of extracting purely national statistics.

WHITTAKER's 1995 volume devotes a chapter to "Peacekeeping and Collective Security", again looking in detail at areas in which British forces have been involved. His 1999 volume also contains a chapter on peacekeeping, this time in terms of the confusion and criticism with which the world views the UN's efforts. "Contemporary opinion, as the media mirrors it, seems to regard peacekeeping in three lights: horror, confusion and criticism." The three basic types of peacekeeping which Whittaker analyses are preventive diplomacy, preventive deployment, and peace-building. The question of *enforcement* of peace "must be the last resort of the peacekeeper".

This question of enforcement leads away from the diplomacy and peace-building of the UN to the more military intervention of NATO. British forces have been involved in recent years in the NATO contingents in the former Yugoslavia, notably the Implementation Force (Ifor) in Bosnia and the more recent involvement in Kosovo. Much of the published work to date on Kosovo has involved debate on the role of NATO as a whole, and little has yet been written specifically on the British involvement. However, MURRAY & GORDON have produced a fascinating account of Ifor's role in Bosnia. Less academic and more personal in character than the studies referred to so far, this book contains more than 200 photographs of the troops, the people, and the beautiful, but difficult, terrain with which the earlier UN forces had to contend. The volume examines the participating forces by donor country, and thus covers the British division in some detail.

CAROLYN J. KITCHING

See also Defence Capability

Peasants' Revolt 1381

Dobson, R.B. (editor), *The Peasants' Revolt of 1381*, London: Macmillan, and New York: St Martin's Press, 1970; 2nd edition, 1983

Eiden, Herbert, "Joint Action against 'Bad' Lordship: The Peasants' Revolt in Essex and Norfolk", *History*, 83 (1998): 5–30

Fryde, E.B., *Peasants and Landlords in Later Medieval England, c.1380–c.1525*, Stroud, Gloucestershire: Alan Sutton, and New York: St Martin's Press, 1996

Hilton, Rodney, *Bond Men Made Free: Medieval Peasant Movements and the English Rising of 1381*, London: Temple Smith, and New York: Viking Press, 1973

Hilton, R.H. and T.H. Aston (editors), *The English Rising of 1381*, Cambridge and New York: Cambridge University Press, 1984

Justice, Steven, *Writing and Rebellion: England in 1381*, Berkeley: University of California Press, 1994

Oman, Charles, *The Great Revolt of 1381*, Oxford: Clarendon Press, 1906; new edition, with new introduction and notes, Oxford: Clarendon Press, and New York: Greenwood Press, 1969

OMAN's comprehensive narrative of the course of events in the revolt of 1381, although labouring beneath certain 19th-century aphorisms (it was first published in 1906), is still a good, concise introduction that helps to establish the chronology of the rebellion. All the counties involved in the revolt are covered and the narrative description of events in and around London is particularly useful for untangling the somewhat confusing sequence of the movement here.

HILTON (1973) attempts to place the revolt in its European context by describing medieval peasant communities as consolidated social entities where socio-economic tensions created the need for social movements. Peasant rebellions are seen as becoming more complex over time; continental European examples from the earlier Middle Ages are described in terms of simple movements for peasant emancipation from the pressures of oppressive lordship, whereas the widened scope of peasant rebellion in the later Middle Ages is epitomized by the rising of

1381. It is convincingly argued that although it was initially a reaction to the fiscal demands of the new poll tax the rebellion had a deeper ideological base (religious as well as socio-economic), exemplified by the confident demands of the peasant leaders for the imposition of an egalitarian social order free of serfdom. The rebels' demands are considered as a true expression of peasant expectations in the aftermath of changed socio-economic conditions caused by the Black Death, and the failure of the revolt not as proof of the ephemeral nature of this ideology but as a result of the strength of feudal lordship in 14th-century England.

The strength of feudal lordship is also a feature in DOBSON. Seventy-nine original documents (translated), each with a short introduction, provide a valuable insight into the reaction and opinions of contemporaries of the rebellion. The hostility towards the rebels reflected in the class bias of these sources is emphasized, and seen as "a touchstone of the emotional prejudices of the medieval chronicler". But this hierarchical social attitude also helps to explain the failure of the revolt in the face of a feudal lordship that held a monopoly on literary propaganda and, as the trials of the insurgents in the months following the revolt proved, a firm grip on judicial authority. The general introduction highlights the social and political failure of the rebellion and suggests that a crude sociology of the revolt should be avoided; the ideology behind the movement is seen as fragile and ephemeral. The revolt is adjudged a short-term reaction to socio-economic conditions lacking a coherent purpose and was thus ultimately doomed to failure.

The collection of papers in HILTON & ASTON is especially useful for comparative analyses of the revolt. Cazelles's and Cohn's essays both use European precedents and antecedents (the French Jacquerie and Florentine movements) to contextualize the 1381 English rising. Both emphasize the importance of the involvement of the gentry and town patricians in the various examples of social unrest usually described as peasant movements, which can be seen either as correlative with gentry and clerical involvement in 1381 or in contrast to the English revolt which was *predominantly* made up of the peasantry and hinged on their grievances. Also useful are the comparisons between the urban and rural dimensions of the revolt. Dyer sees the rebels' demands as reflecting rural concerns over oppressive lordship articulated by members of village elites who genuinely believed in the possibility of self-governing village communities. Butcher and Dobson focus on the urban dimension to the revolt, using Canterbury, York, Scarborough, and Beverley as examples. Although important centres of rebellion, towns are seen as intrinsic parts of their regions and their occupants as still concerned with the issues of lordship and serfdom.

A regional approach to the revolt is taken in a stimulating article by EIDEN, where the rebellion in Norfolk and Essex is examined. The names, and many of the occupations, of the rebels are recovered from government indictment records, demonstrating the essentially rural character of the revolt. Also highlighted are the many examples of the burning of manor court rolls, interpreted as a direct statement of defiance against oppressive lordship: destroying the prime evidence for the customary service at the very places – the manor courts – where the justice of this lordship was administered. Using this evidence it is clear that the main intention of the rebels was to eliminate certain key members of the regional jurisdictional administra-

tion, but more importantly to eradicate the court rolls that symbolized their villeinage.

A good introduction to the agrarian background to the movement is FRYDE. The revolt is seen as the culmination of the socio-economic conditions caused by the Black Death and the attempts by landlords to maintain their custumal rights (i.e. rights over services and land). Especially useful are the sections describing agrarian conditions in the West Midlands as evidenced by the estate records of the bishop of Worcester. Although the West Midlands were not directly affected by the revolt, the chronology of the changeover from direct exploitation of demesne on the bishops' manors to farming out leaseholds agrees with the situation that prevailed in eastern England. The inability of landlords to adapt their concepts of serfdom to the new conditions created by the leasing of demesnes is seen as exacerbating social tensions among the peasantry. It is suggested that the bishop of Worcester's estates escaped peasant rebellion because of the better treatment of its demesne workers, and that some servile renders were abated as an effect of the revolt, so quelling potential social unrest.

A very different approach is used by JUSTICE. The techniques of new historicism are utilized to analyse six texts from the chronicles of Henry Knighton and Thomas Walsingham that purportedly record the spoken words and written letters of various rebels. The assumption that the socio-cultural values of the rebels can be recovered even from within the official doctrine of chronicles is based on close textual analysis and the theory that the leaders of the rural peasantry were articulating a genuine class-driven ideology in words and actions. The arguments are not consistently convincing but they introduce a stimulating new dimension to the study of the 1381 revolt.

NEIL S. RUSHTON

See also John of Gaunt; Richard II; Social Conflict: Medieval (English); Taxation: Parliamentary

Peel, Sir Robert 1788–1850
Politician, prime minister, and founder of the Metropolitan Police

Clark, G. Kitson, *Peel and the Conservative Party: A Study in Party Politics, 1832–1841*, London: Bell, 1929; reprinted, London: Frank Cass, and Hamden, Connecticut: Archon Books, 1964

Crosby, Travis L., *Sir Robert Peel's Administration, 1841–1846*, Newton Abbot, Devon: David and Charles, and Hamden, Connecticut: Archon Books, 1976

Gash, Norman, *Mr Secretary Peel: The Life of Sir Robert Peel to 1830*, London: Longman, and Cambridge, Massachusetts: Harvard University Press, 1961; revised edition, London and New York: Longman, 1985

Gash, Norman, *Sir Robert Peel: The Life of Sir Robert Peel after 1830*, London: Longman, and Totowa, New Jersey: Rowman and Littlefield, 1972; second edition, London and New York: Longman, 1986

Kerr, Donal A., *Peel, Priests, and Politics: Sir Robert Peel's Administration and the Roman Catholic Church in Ireland,*

1841–1846, Oxford: Clarendon Press, and New York: Oxford University Press, 1982

Machin, G.I.T., *The Catholic Question in English Politics, 1820 to 1830*, Oxford: Clarendon Press, 1964

Machin, G.I.T., *Politics and the Churches in Great Britain, 1832 to 1868*, Oxford: Clarendon Press and New York: Oxford University Press, 1977

Mahon, Lord and Edward Cardwell (editors), *Memoirs by the Rt Hon. Sir Robert Peel*, 2 vols, London: John Murray, 1856–57

Parker, C.S. (editor), *Sir Robert Peel, from his Private Papers*, 3 vols, London: John Murray, 1891–99; reprinted, Kraus Reprint, 1970

Ramsay, A.A.W., *Sir Robert Peel*, London: Constable, and New York: Dodd Mead, 1928

Peel has bequeathed less of a personal impression to history than Palmerston, Gladstone, Disraeli, Lloyd George, or Churchill. But his contribution to British history was arguably as great as that of any of these statesmen. Like his disciple Gladstone, he was famous for moving with the times. He executed a notable shift from ultra-Toryism to liberal conservatism. The major milestones in this progress were his acceptance (despite his nickname of Orange Peel) of catholic emancipation in 1829; his acquiescence in parliamentary reform after it had passed in 1832; his initiation in 1835 of an ecclesiastical commission to reform the temporal affairs of the Church of England; his agreement with a certain amount of reform to promote the civil equality of dissenters; his Maynooth grant (benefiting the Irish catholics) in 1845; and his liberal commercial policy of the 1840s. His main political concerns were the Irish situation, finance and commerce, ecclesiastical policy, and law and order. He led one generally unsuccessful minority government (1834–35) and a much more successful majority one (1841–46). But he was unable to escape political disaster in this government's later stages. In the last four years of his life he was politically weakened, retaining some influence but leading an uncertain and divided group of "Peelites" against the Liberal Party and the majority of Conservatives. His religious beliefs and attitudes were usually kept in reserve, but were decisively held. His legislative achievements in the 1840s were impressive, and included important religious and social reforms as well as the act repealing the Corn Laws for which he is chiefly known. Although he did not question *laissez-faire* in general, his achievements (especially legislation for labour in factories and mines) exemplified the gradual growth of state intervention.

Peel's politics and policies have been extensively explored and analysed, but his personality has remained comparatively hard to fathom, and he appears almost a model of the stiff and uniform Victorian monolith. He was a loyal and supportive paterfamilias, apparently a stranger to adultery. Those who look very hard in the vast historical literature on 19th-century Britain will be able to find glimpses of a sense of humour which a naturally reserved surface ("the smile of Peel is like the gleam of brass on a coffin", claimed Daniel O'Connell) could not invariably conceal. Almost entirely, however, the known characteristics of Peel are efficiency, responsibility, courage, and determination, combined with shyness and sensitivity and a touch of self-righteous impatience (the latter being directed in exasperation at his firmly protectionist back-benchers in the 1840s).

About a dozen biographies of Peel, including ones by Guizot and Rosebery, appeared in the 19th century. There were also two published collections of his letters and memoirs, edited respectively by MAHON & CARDWELL and by PARKER, before the end of that century. A smaller collection in one volume, edited by his grandson George Peel, appeared in 1920. Following this, two academic scholars produced studies of Peel, RAMSAY in 1928 and Kitson CLARK in 1929. But although these two works, supplemented by a brief biography by Kitson Clark in 1936, used the Peel papers and helped to place the study of Peel on a more modern academic footing, they were little more than foretastes of the greater riches opened up by GASH. His two volumes of detailed biography, making full use of the Peel papers and other original records, appeared in 1961 and 1972 respectively. This fluently written, solid, and reliable monument to historical scholarship continues to form the centrepiece of Peel studies. Peel's conscientiousness and zeal find a full and worthy reflection in these highly informative and well considered volumes, whether they are dealing with his policies as chief secretary for Ireland, as home secretary, or as prime minister. Their author is clearly disposed in favour of Peel, without allowing objectivity to suffer, and his study of a single important figure is set widely in social and political context.

Peel awaits a further full-scale treatment. Apart from some brief accounts in the form of booklets and articles, the more recent literature on Peel comprises studies of some of his policies and of his encounters with Benjamin Disraeli, his noted Conservative antagonist who helped to bring him down in 1846. MACHIN (1964) examines the details of Peel's conversion to the support of Wellington's policy of catholic emancipation in 1829, and MACHIN (1977) contains much information about Peel's ecclesiastical policies of the 1830s and 1840s, including (unusually) those concerned with the Church of Scotland, which experienced disruption in 1843. CROSBY presents a concise and useful account of Peel's great ministry of 1841–46, and KERR provides a thorough and objective examination of that ministry's constructive policies towards the Irish catholics. Peel's public face and policies have thus been very thoroughly treated, but more might be done to rescue his personality from its comparatively shadowy position.

IAN MACHIN

See also Anti-Corn Law League; Canning; Cardwell; Catholic Emancipation; Chartism; Dalhousie; Derby; Disraeli; Factory Reform; Fiscal Politics; George IV; Gladstone; Ireland entries (19th century); Metropolitan Police; Wellington; William IV

Penal Reform

Block, Brian P. and John Hostettler, *Hanging in the Balance: A History of the Abolition of Capital Punishment in Britain*, Winchester, Hampshire: Waterside Press, 1997

Blom-Cooper, Louis (editor), *Progress in Penal Reform*, Oxford: Clarendon Press, 1974

Cross, Rupert, *Punishment, Prison, and the Public: An Assessment of Penal Reform in Twentieth Century England* by an Armchair Penologist, London: Stevens and Sons, 1971

Forsythe, W.J., The Reform of Prisoners 1830–1900, London: Croom Helm, and New York: St Martin's Press, 1987

Forsythe, W.J., Penal Discipline, Reformatory Projects, and the English Prison Commission, 1895–1939, Exeter, Devon: Exeter University Press, 1990

Garland David, Punishment and Welfare: A History of Penal Strategies, Aldershot, Hampshire and Brookfield, Vermont: Gower, 1985

Harding, Christopher et al., Imprisonment in England and Wales: A Concise History, London and Dover, New Hampshire: Croom Helm, 1985

Howe, Adrian, Punish and Critique: Towards a Feminist Analysis of Penality, London and New York: Routledge, 1994

Ignatieff, Michael, A Just Measure of Pain: The Penitentiary in the Industrial Revolution, London: Macmillan, and New York: Pantheon Books, 1978

McConville, Seán, A History of English Prison Administration, vol. 1, 1750–1877, London and Boston: Routledge and Kegan Paul, 1981

Morris, Norval and David J. Rothman (editors), The Oxford History of the Prison: The Practice of Punishment in Western Society, Oxford and New York: Oxford University Press, 1995

Pugh, Ralph B., Imprisonment in Medieval England, Cambridge: Cambridge University Press, 1968

Radzinowicz, Leon and Roger Hood, A History of English Criminal Law and its Administration from 1750, vol. 5, The Emergence of Penal Policy, London: Stevens, 1986; Oxford and New York: Oxford University Press, 1990

Thomas, J.E., The English Prison Officer since 1850: A Study in Conflict, London and Boston: Routledge and Kegan Paul, 1972

Ian McLachlan in BLOM-COOPER points out that the three European founding fathers of modern British criminology – Max Grunhut, Hermann Mannheim, and Sir Leon Radzinowicz – all had a fundamental interest in penal history that "has given a valuable historical dimension to criminological study in Britain less evident elsewhere". Despite the reference to Britain, the overwhelming quantity of this study is of England and of male imprisonment. Books such as Ron Ramdin's The Making of the Black Working Class in Britain (1987) discuss the police rather than the prison service. The best book to discuss capital punishment is BLOCK & HOSTETTLER, which is described as recording "the stance taken by key organizations and countless individuals in a dubious phase of British legal history when humanity, morality and decency came face-to-face with deterrence, retribution and expediency". This example shows the basic debate between rehabilitation on the one hand, and deterrence and retribution on the other, in its most extreme form. It also shows the major problem with the discussion of penal reform, that the history almost always gets mixed up with the author's view on the morality of the situation.

Blom-Cooper declares that a complementary aim of his book is to move opinion away from imprisonment while CROSS deliberately acknowleges the problem when discussing "What is penal reform?" He regards this as "a surprisingly difficult

[task]" and his resulting definition is consciously value-laden. After querying whether the phrase would cover the reintroduction of the death penalty, his conclusion is that "any change aimed at the rehabilitation of the offender can properly be described as penal reform". McLachlan in Blom-Cooper is not so sure: "not all penal reform is enlightened, nor penal reformers invariably wise". He thus posthumously restores the reputation of mid-Victorian judges and politicians who spoke against the abolition of transportation by noting (in considering the views of A.G.L. Shaw in Convicts and Colonies, 1966) that "it was probably more humane and progressive than the penitentiary system which eventually replaced it". McLachlan in Blom-Cooper discusses, as does Blom-Cooper, the "naive Whiggish view" of much penal reform history, preferring to view the century before 1974 as "very largely (though not entirely) a mistake, a blind alley into which the British Government wandered as much through short-sighted financial and political expediency as from any considered penal policy".

The main discussion of penal reform centres on the period after 1750. Morris & Rothman has a useful introduction on the medieval use of imprisonment, as has HARDING. Thomas commends PUGH. Writers such as IGNATIEFF view the prison as one of several institutions – workhouse, schools, hospitals, asylums – invented in the 18th century as social control mechanisms by the middle and upper classes of industrializing England. The use of the Mental Health Act of 1913 to incarcerate single mothers and thus attempt to contain a social problem is a prime example of this approach. Interestingly, however, Harding, in a chapter heading, talks about the rediscovery of the prison.

Ignatieff feels that this is a legitimate starting-point for a discussion of the motivation of penal reform, as it was at this time that "John Howard, Jeremy Bentham and Cesare Beccaria first placed prisons on the agenda of social concern of their class". He ends his book in 1850 with industrialization well established and Marx in writing mode. FORSYTHE in his excellently detailed book (1987) – which is well constructed in compact chapters covering important themes in a disciplined chronology, with precise conclusions – discusses as his starting point Ignatieff and Michel Foucault (Surveiller et punir, 1975; translated as Discipline and Punish: The Birth of the Prison, which falls outside the scope of this essay dealing as it does largely with France), noting their scepticism about claims to progressive policies, which they saw as "camouflage". Forsythe's introduction is a valuable bibliographical note on the main debate in this field, whether the motive behind penal policy was (and is) retribution and deterrence or rehabilitation. Discussing Margaret DeLacy's Prison Reform in Lancashire (1981), he argues that Foucault and Ignatieff assumed that the policies laid down by national administrators were actually carried out in the localities. He also criticizes the choice of 1850 for Ignatieff's end-date as distorting the debate, echoing Radzinowicz in noting that the debate should also encompass the late 19th and early 20th centuries, in order to take account of factors such as the diminution of the size and impact of the prison system in this period. Thus FORSYTHE (1990) takes 1939 as his end date. For his opening date he agrees with Cross and Harding about the fundamental importance of the Gladstone Report of 1895, which Cross considered to be the most fundamental statement of penal policy until the 1959 white paper, largely because of the paucity of such statements in the interim. It spoke positively of the reformatory aim of imprisonment. However, Forsythe judges that the work of Foucault and the revisionists in the 1970s "has deeply compromised or even discredited the reformatory endeavours in prisons". In the political world of the 1980s this became the stock-in-trade of many leading politicians, though for widely differing reasons. In fact Ignatieff, as his introduction makes clear, is reacting to the same stimuli as these politicians, the prison disturbances of the late 1960s and the early 1970s in the United States, Spain, France, Canada, Britain, and Italy, though his conclusions tended in a left-wing direction while the politicians made off in the opposite direction.

Ignatieff in his preface claims that "reform-minded administrators have liberalized the security and custody of many institutions . . . [and this] . . . has broken the fragile order inside the prison". One of Forsythe's conclusions is that between 1895 and 1939 the course of prison development depended not just on philosophy and policy but also on "the spirit, enthusiasm and courage of personnel". Both these approaches are illuminated by THOMAS, who takes as his starting-point a *Times* leading article of 27 November 1969: "There should be no conflict in an ideal prison system between security and rehabilitation." Thomas says these do conflict, agreeing with Lord Denman in the 1840s when he declared that "the combination of reform and deterrence as aims of imprisonment to be a contradiction in terms" (cited in Cross). According to Thomas the problem of coping is undertaken by the basic-grade uniformed officer, who is excluded from the debate which leads to the attempted implementation of reformative aims. Thus Thomas condemns sociologists and historians alike for assuming that "the primary conflict in prison is between reformation and deterrence". His book is important because it places the prison officer at the centre of a succinct and detailed historical account of the English system with change and evolution as a central theme, well cataloguing official enquiries, reports, and legislation. In contrast Forsythe aims to test the claims of officials in his period – chaplains, borstal housemasters, governors, and prison commissioners – that they were forwarding a very important reformatory ideal.

Forsythe records the power of what he calls the classical view, that punishment is publicly measured and defined, to which institutions and officials returned like homing pigeons when they needed security and certainty in assessing their role. GARLAND views the period from 1895 to 1914 as the one in which this classical view came under the greatest scrutiny, in a book which Seán McConville in Morris & Rothman refers to as "a much acclaimed attempt to place penal history into a broader context of social policy and control". Forsythe thus seconds Garland in his criticism of the end point adopted by Ignatieff.

What then is the balance between theory and practice in discussing the motivation for penal reform? Harding cites McLachlan in Blom-Cooper approvingly to state that "penal reform has never been wholly empirical, not least because the causes of delinquency and rule breaking have been imperfectly understood". The whole cellular, silent period was strictly ideologically based, testing some prisoners to complete destruction. Benthamism, humanitarianism, and classical political economy all affected penal reform.

Thomas notes that women "deserve separate study . . . [but] . . . they are usually excluded". Harding mentions them in passing but only to show how their experience of penal reform differed from his main interest, male imprisonment. Ann D. Smith in Blom-Cooper is a useful short discussion. HOWE firstly deals with the relevant theory and models, for example the "new" histories of punishment regimes, propounded by such writers as Rusche and Kirchheimer, Melossi, Jankowicz, Ignatieff, and Cohen. She then discusses feminist approaches to the analysis of women's penality, in a thorough, in-depth review of the relevant literature (Carleton, O'Brien, Perrot).

Three books too large for a general read are MORRIS & ROTHMAN, RADZINOWICZ & HOOD, and MCCONVILLE. McConville in Morris & Rothman describes Radzinowicz & Hood as a work of "great virtuosity, unraveling numerous strands of penal policy and skillfully placing imprisonment in its broader setting". It is a shrewd mixture of discussion on debates and historical narrative; unusually, the table of contents is a stimulating and thought-provoking read in its own right – the socialist interpretations of crime and Marxist connections, the inevitable imperfections of the measuring rod, draining the reservoir of crime, cutting the supply of recidivism. McConville is a mine of information and interpretation. Both have huge bibliographies. Morris & Rothman is slightly coffee-tableish, being unreferenced, but well written by experts in their field, with useful bibliographical notes, and puts English experience well in context with European and American discussions. The bibliography in Blom-Cooper is also worthy of attention.

And after all this? As Forsythe (1987) sums up, we are as confused now as 200 years ago. Evangelical reform to 1860, followed by a general view that no hope of reform of prisoners could be entertained, a view reversed from 1900 to 1975, and since 1975 "an erosion in the belief in the reformation of the offender". Preventative detention may well have died "unmourned" in 1967 (Forsythe), but currently spirited attempts are being made to exhume it.

RAY GRACE

See also Law Enforcement: Since 1840; Poverty: Poverty and Deprivation

Peninsular War

see French Revolutionary Wars; Napoleonic Wars

Periodical Press and Critical Reviews

18th and 19th centuries

Couper, W.J., *The Edinburgh Periodical Press: Being a Bibliographical Account of the Newspapers, Journals, and Magazines Issued in Edinburgh from the Earliest Times to 1800*, 2 vols, Stirling: MacKay, 1908

Graham, Walter, *English Literary Periodicals*, New York: Nelson, 1930; reprinted, London: Cass, and New York: Octagon Books, 1966

Myers, Robin and Michael Harris (editors), *Serials and Their Readers: 1620–1914*, Winchester: St Paul's Bibliographies, and New Castle, Delaware: Oak Knoll Press, 1993

Pottinger, George, *Heirs of the Enlightenment: Edinburgh Reviewers and Writers, 1800–1830*, Edinburgh: Scottish Academic Press, 1992

Shattock, Joanne and Michael Wolff (editors), *The Victorian Periodical Press: Samplings and Soundings*, Leicester: Leicester University Press, and Toronto: University of Toronto Press, 1982

Shattock, Joanne, *Politics and Reviewers: The Edinburgh and The Quarterly in the Early Victorian Age*, London, and New York: Leicester University Press, 1989

Srebrnik, Patricia Thomas, *Alexander Strahan: Victorian Publisher*, Ann Arbor: University of Michigan Press, 1986

Vann, J. Don and Rosemary T. VanArsdel (editors), *Victorian Periodicals and Victorian Society*, Toronto: University of Toronto Press, and Aldershot, Hampshire: Scolar Press, 1994

Early 20th-century scholarship on the periodical press and critical reviews of the 18th and 19th centuries was most concerned to recover the bibliographic details of this press and the biographical particulars of the men and women who produced it. COUPER is representative of this literature. His pioneering work on early Scottish periodicals with Edinburgh imprints remains authoritative to this day. GRAHAM, one of the first to discuss English periodicals at book length, similarly prevails as a useful, single-volume introduction to serials from the 17th to the early 20th centuries. These works chronicle the titles (with changes), days of publication, length of runs, and prices of the major Scottish and English periodicals and hundreds of their lesser-known kin. They also sought to describe the physical layout of those periodicals' pages, the nature of the discussions contained therein, and the identity and character of their many contributors, editors, and publishers. Graham differentiated single-essay periodicals, critical reviews, miscellanies, and other quarterly, monthly, and weekly serial publications from the more widely studied daily newspapers. On his pages one might discern the early glimmerings of a choate scholarly appreciation of the periodical as a window on questions of wider historical significance.

More recently a proliferation of published directories, indexes, and microfilm collections have identified and made more accessible tens of thousands of English and Scottish periodicals and critical reviews for the period under survey. The British periodical press had clearly come into its own by the late 18th century and in the early 19th century and later it expanded exponentially. Not surprisingly, secondary literature related to these periodicals has also multiplied in recent years – so much so that there are now a number of published bibliographies of relevant secondary sources as well as modern journals devoted to the history of journals.

This historiography has largely been dominated by essays and monographs that take as their subjects the most prominent periodicals and their personalities – an approach that continues to have much to offer the history of periodicals, as evidenced by POTTINGER. His far-ranging study throws new light on the well-known *Edinburgh Review* and *Blackwood's Edinburgh Magazine* by situating them more completely in appropriate intellectual and cultural contexts. Pottinger argues, in part, that the *Review*'s early 19th-century founding (by the "Happy Warriors" Sidney Smith, Francis Jeffrey, Francis Horner, and Henry Brougham) and quick success owed considerable debts to the Scottish Enlightenment to which it was an unaffected heir.

But the study of individual periodicals and reviews has also broadened in recent years as lesser-known serials and publishers find their historians. A good example is SREBRNIK. Her study of Alexander Strahan (1834?–1918) is fascinating for the light it casts on the life of a late 19th-century British (a Scot transplanted to London) periodical publisher and the book world within which he lived. Srebrnik convincingly argues that Strahan, although largely overlooked by modern historians, had an extensive reputation in his own day as the latitudinarian publisher of the *Contemporary Review*. Strahan's "nonpartisan and nonsectarian" disposition was even more widely known through his *Good Works*, "a sixpenny monthly that in the late 1860s was the best-selling magazine in the English-speaking world".

Scholarly appreciation of the periodical's potential role in attempted reconstructions of the cultural past has been augmented in recent years and in no small way by the growing prominence of the history of the book. MYERS & HARRIS, in a volume devoted to serials in their Publishing Pathways series, illustrate this affiliation and show where it might lead. The eight papers that make up the collection are somewhat disparate, spanning the 17th to the 20th centuries, but taken together are united in that they illustrate an historiographic shift in recent scholarship on periodicals. Focus has moved away from strict bibliographic and biographical matters and has gravitated towards heightened concerns over periodicals' circulations, readership, and cultural influence or reflection. Some of the most promising new work in these emerging fields is encountered in recent books that take as their subject the periodicals of Victorian Britain.

The 14 essays in SHATTOCK & WOLFF are a case in point. Subdivided into three main fields – the influence of the periodical form on authors, economic aspects of periodical publication, and the readership of periodicals – the essays in this volume are collectively more rewarding than the title's modest "Samplings and Soundings" suggests and go a significant way towards advancing the periodical press's potential as a key to unlocking the minds and society which produced and consumed it. So too does SHATTOCK's more recent monograph. Her specialized study of the *Edinburgh* and *Quarterly* reviews in the decades of the 1820s and 1830s is not, she says, "directly concerned with what the quarterlies actually said on particular issues or events", but rather "with the impact of the quarterlies" and "their role in the literary and cultural world in general". She finds that, while the quarterly reviews remained influential well into the 19th century, the expansion of the newspaper press in the 1840s weakened their political backbone, leading to their eventual demise.

VANN & VANARSDEL bring together 18 essays concerned with specialized periodicals from the Victorian era. The essays in this volume offer concise introductions and an accompanying range of bibliographic aids for topically specific periodicals from a range of fields (law, medicine, architecture, military, science, music, illustration, theatre, transport, financial and trade press, advertising, agriculture, temperance, comic periodicals, sport, workers' journals, and student journals). Collectively the volume illustrates nicely the "pervasiveness of periodical literature in nineteenth-century British society".

Significant steps forward have been made in the recovery of the basic factual details of 18th- and 19th-century British periodicals and critical reviews. These primary sources have been successfully roused from their once sleepy obscurity and are slowly working their rightful way into general histories of the period. As more of their multitudinous bibliographic and biographical records are uncovered, and as our understanding of their dissemination, readership, and impact deepens, we might hope to integrate the periodical press even more fully into the social history of ideas in Britain.

MARK G. SPENCER

See also Ephemera

Perpetual Chantries late medieval period

Binski, Paul, *Medieval Death: Ritual and Representation*, Ithaca, New York: Cornell University Press, and London: British Museum Press, 1996

Boase, T.S.R., *Death in the Middle Ages: Mortality, Judgment, and Remembrance*, New York: McGraw Hill, and London: Thames and Hudson, 1972

Burgess, Clive, "Strategies for Eternity: Perpetual Chantry Foundation in Late Medieval Bristol" in *Religious Belief and Ecclesiastical Careers in Late Medieval England*, edited by Christopher Harper-Bill, Woodbridge, Suffolk and Rochester, New York: Boydell, 1991

Cook, George H., *Mediaeval Chantries and Chantry Chapels*, London: Phoenix House, 1947; 2nd edition, 1963

Dobson, R.B., *Church and Society in the Medieval North of England*, London and Rio Grande, Ohio: Hambledon Press, 1996

Duffy, Eamon, *The Stripping of the Altars: Traditional Religion in England c.1400–c.1580*, New Haven, Connecticut and London: Yale University Press, 1992

Horrox, Rosemary, "Purgatory, Prayer, and Plague: 1150–1380" in *Death in England: An Illustrated History*, edited by Peter C. Jupp and Clare Gittings, Manchester and New York: Manchester University Press, 1999; New Brunswick, New Jersey: Rutgers University Press, 2000

Kreider, Alan, *English Chantries: The Road to Dissolution*, Cambridge, Massachusetts: Harvard University Press, 1979

Le Goff, Jacques, *The Birth of Purgatory*, translated from the French by Arthur Goldhammer, Chicago: University of Chicago Press, and London: Scolar Press, 1984 (French edition, 1981)

McGuire, Brian Patrick, "Purgatory, the Communion of Saints, and Medieval Change", *Viator*, 20 (1989): 61–84

Raban, Sandra, *Mortmain Legislation and the English Church, 1279–1500*, Cambridge and New York: Cambridge University Press, 1982

Ward, Rachel E., "The Foundation and Functions of Perpetual Chantries in the Diocese of Norwich *c.*1250–1547" (dissertation), Cambridge: Jesus College, University of Cambridge, 1998

Wood-Legh, K.L., *Perpetual Chantries in Britain*, Cambridge: Cambridge University Press, 1965

Perpetual chantries were late medieval intercessory institutions established in hopes of guaranteeing their beneficiaries continuous chains of masses aimed at lessening the pains of Purgatory for those who were neither saints nor unrepentant sinners. Five excellent commentators explore the concept's antecedents as a divine halfway house from different perspectives. LE GOFF, the groundbreaking scholar, examines the theological evidence, tracing the conviction that the dead could amend their lives to the Christian Neoplatonists Clement of Alexandria and Origen, who saw God's fire as purifying, not punishing. McGUIRE assesses donors' mindsets and motives, claiming that what mattered most was their feeling of closeness to the dead and confidence that their prayers would help them gain salvation. BOASE pinpoints additional stimuli in the iconography of the period, demonstrating the gruesome portrayals of death, decay, hellfire, and damnation which reminded parishioners graphically of life's tenuousness. HORROX studies the interpersonal aspects of the late 12th-century church's formalization of Purgatory, as it influenced the concept of penitence, family, community, parish obligations, and the dead's dependence on the living. BINSKI concentrates primarily on the ritual aspects of the era's fixation on death and the iconography of remembrance.

Funded by gifts of property, rents, and other valuables donated by individuals, families, fraternities, or guilds who could not afford pricier beneficia, English perpetual chantries ranged from great collegiate foundations like St William's College at York Minster, with many beneficed clergy resident within a major cathedral, to hospitals for the indigent elderly, to chapels of ease, to specially designated altars in parish churches served by single chaplains and their successors chosen by the donors and installed by the local bishop. Less secure but serving the same intercessory function for poorer patrons were unbeneficed stipendiary priests or "vicars choral" hired for specific occasions to conduct anniversary masses or "obits".

Scholarly interest in English chantries and chantry chapels founded between their advent in 1170 and their suppression under the Henrician and Edwardian Chantries Acts (1545 and 1547) as "superstitious uses" has increased greatly since 1947 when COOK published the first architectural and functional study of these foundations. This was followed by WOOD-LEGH's comprehensive study of English and Scottish perpetual chantries based on her 1954–55 Birkbeck Lectures. Considered to be the definitive work in this neglected area when it appeared in 1965, it provides an excellent overview of the various chantry forms and foundation processes, the chaplains' daily lives and religious duties, their relationships with other clergy, and the provisions made for illness, disability, old age, and retirement. Working primarily with Essex, Warwickshire, Wiltshire, and Yorkshire data, KREIDER thoroughly documents the Henrician and Edwardian commissioners' zealous but frequently uneven efforts to confiscate chantry endowments, property, and movables, allegedly for "the relief of the poor" but actually for more dubious government priorities. Nothing, however, better contextualizes perpetual chantries than DUFFY's superb study, which succeeds admirably at the two tasks he sets for himself: to capture the "richness and complexity of the religious system by which [late medieval English catholics] structured their world" and "to tell the story of the dismantling and destruction of that symbolic world".

RABAN's carefully researched analysis of the causes and effects of Edward I's 1279 legislation restricting alienation of real property to the "dead hand of the church" has sparked particular interest in testators' and their executors' handling of perpetuities funded by such conveyances. Three regional historians interested in this area are especially noteworthy. The first, BURGESS, looks at 15th-century Bristol merchants wealthy enough to afford perpetual chantries after satisfying their family obligations and astute enough to ensure their survival. Using the same strategies that enriched them, they hand-picked trustees from the same hard-headed business elite and founded their chantries in parish churches whose wardens had vested interests in the same values. Drawing on a "somewhat remarkable collection of forty-one original deeds and other documents [in the City of York archives] which relate to ... chantries founded in the city ... between 1321 and 1528", DOBSON reaches similar conclusions about the strong religious convictions of the canny elite who founded perpetual chantries in medieval York. All but four of them established chantries in their parish churches, frequently choosing chaplains who were friends and advisers. Cathedral officers and clergy, conversely, found the minster more congenial, preferring to trust their spiritual well-being to colleagues. WARD, in an unpublished PhD dissertation, ends this progression by analysing the broader functions of perpetual chantries in the diocese of Norwich to illuminate ongoing discussions about contemporary religion. Chantry chaplains were not engaged simply in securing their founders' happy exit from Purgatory, she concludes, but functioned instead as integral members of the regional community who enjoyed immense trust and high regard.

JEAN COAKLEY

Persons, Robert

see Jesuits in the British Isles

Peterloo Massacre 1819

Bamford, Samuel, *Passages in the Life of a Radical*, 2 vols, Heywood: J. Heywood, 1841–43; with preface by Tim Hilton, London: MacGibbon and Kee, 1967, and reprinted, Oxford and New York: Oxford University Press, 1984; as vol. 2 of *The Autobiography of Samuel Bamford*, London: Cass, and New York: Kelley, 1967

Belchem, John, *"Orator" Hunt: Henry Hunt and English Working-Class Radicalism*, Oxford: Clarendon Press, and New York: Oxford University Press, 1985

Epstein, James, "Understanding the Cap of Liberty: Symbolic Practice and Social Conflict in Early Nineteenth-Century England", *Past & Present*, 122 (1989): 75–118

Read, D., *Peterloo: The "Massacre" and Its Background*, Manchester: Manchester University Press, 1958; reprinted with additional notes, Manchester: Manchester University Press, and Clifton, New Jersey: Kelley, 1973

Thompson, E.P., *The Making of the English Working-Class*, London: Gollancz, and New York: Vintage, 1963; reprinted London: Gollancz, 1980

Walmsley, Robert, *Peterloo: The Case Re-opened*, Manchester: Manchester University Press, and New York: Kelley, 1969

The Peterloo massacre of 16 August 1819 is regarded as one of the milestone events of English working-class history and, as such, has attracted controversy, both from participants and contemporaries and later from historians. The main debate then as now surrounds the question of responsibility for the killing of 11 people and the injuring of hundreds. There is no shortage of eye-witness accounts which historians have drawn upon but the best and most compelling has been provided by BAMFORD, the Lancashire radical. Although biased – he was after all in the crowd on the day of the massacre – his account provides good detail to the build-up to the meeting and convincingly argues that the drill practice and marching on the moors beforehand by working men was to instil order and discipline in their ranks. Such quasi-military behaviour was not, he maintained, revolutionary or aggressive in intent. The actual massacre is described in detail but the popular reaction of Lancastrian radicals has probably been toned down. It must be remembered that this book was written over twenty years after the event and its author was keen to portray himself as a sober and law-abiding individual.

THOMPSON, in what has become the classic left-wing interpretation, is critical of Bamford's account, in that the latter overstates the novelty of the discipline and pageantry displayed by the participants. In taking a much wider perspective Thompson has been able to place the meeting in the context of both early trade unionism and constitutional radical traditions. He also gives it a prominent place in the development of class consciousness. However, he agrees that the presence of a large and orderly crowd was something that evoked alarm and fear in the local authorities. The factors of the size of the Peterloo crowd and its orderly behaviour are two elements which Thompson believes have been lost in accounts of the meeting. The event was also, in his opinion, quite literally a massacre since there was a large number of women and children present in the peaceful and unarmed crowd. In terms of responsibility he argues that the Manchester magistrates intended to break up the meeting forcibly and that the home secretary, Lord Sidmouth, knew and agreed with the local authority's plan to arrest Henry Hunt on the hustings and disperse the crowd. The fact that no documents within the Home Office papers exist which provide evidence of Sidmouth's involvement does not, in his opinion, invalidate this view.

READ, author of one of the best accounts, had earlier taken a different stance when he argued, from the evidence provided by Home Office papers, that Sidmouth had strongly advised the Manchester magistrates to act with great caution and not interfere with the meeting unless violence broke out. He therefore places responsibility for the massacre very much with William Hulton, the chairman of the Manchester magistrates, and his colleagues. By placing Peterloo in the local context Read has been able to show the extreme hatred and contempt which the local loyalists had for working-class political reformers. This interpretation offers a middle way between Thompson and the right-wing revisionist case put forward by WALMSLEY, a Manchester antiquarian bookseller and local historian. In a lengthy and detailed study of the actual day of the massacre the latter author puts up a spirited defence of William Hulton and the other magistrates. In doing so he fails to place Peterloo in the context of either national or local politics. His main purpose in clearing the magistracy of responsibility is to argue that the events of 16 August have been distorted and exaggerated by radicals and newspapers antagonistic towards political loyalists. His main conclusion, which most other historians have found unconvincing, was that no one was to blame for the massacre. All the different parties, from the radicals to the yeomanry and, most especially, the magistrates, were victims of a tragedy. However, his argument that Hulton ordered the yeomanry into the crowd to arrest Hunt and that this action sparked off an attack by a militant minority in the crowd suggests that he, by implication, blames radical militants. Their attack on the yeomanry, he argued, led the latter to retaliate in self-defence. All other historians have rejected this interpretation of events, especially his defence of Hulton who, it has to be said, displayed little common sense on the day of the meeting.

In the broader history of political radicalism Peterloo has been regarded as a moral victory for working-class radicals but, as BELCHEM has argued, it represented a failure of Hunt's tactics of the "mass platform" and forcible intimidation in which the massed ranks of disciplined workers were meant to advance the cause of political constitutionalism. When this approach of popular pressure politics was met with repression Hunt was unwilling to employ physical force or call for full-scale mass confrontation. The government's repressive "Six Acts" restricted the radical press and mass meetings and effectively halted any advances political radicalism had gained from the massacre.

One other interesting and relatively new approach has provided new insights on Peterloo. EPSTEIN has examined the meanings and importance of symbols such as the "cap of liberty" – the most prominent symbol of popular radicalism – which figured prominently in contemporary prints of the massacre and was described by Bamford in his account. The cap was not simply a cultural trimming providing colour to the meeting but possessed the same significance and importance as military colours did to a regiment, and as a consequence the yeomanry did their utmost to capture these heavily defended icons on the actual day of the massacre. In furthering our understanding of cultural symbols such as the "cap of liberty", Epstein claims to have provided historians with an entry point for a more general exploration of radical ideology, language, and mobilization.

JOHN E. ARCHER

See also Chartism; Manchester; Radicalism; Social Conflict: Modern Period

Petition of Right 1628

Burgess, Glenn, *The Politics of the Ancient Constitution: An Introduction to English Political Thought, 1603–1642*, London: Macmillan, 1992; University Park, Pennsylvania: Pennsylvania State University Press, 1993

Flemion, Jess, "The Struggle for the Petition of Right in the House of Lords: The Study of an Opposition Party Victory", *Journal of Modern History*, 45 (1973): 193–210

Flemion, Jess, "A Savings to Satisfy All: The House of Lords and the Meaning of the Petition of Right", *Parliamentary History*, 10/1 (1991): 27–44

Foster, Elizabeth Read, "Petitions and the Petition of Right", *Journal of British Studies*, 14 (1974): 21–45

Guy, J.A., "The Origins of the Petition of Right Reconsidered", *Historical Journal*, 25 (1982): 289–312

Reeve, L.J., "The Legal Status of the Petition of Right", *Historical Journal*, 29 (1986): 257–77

Relf, Frances Helen, *The Petition of Right*, Minneapolis: University of Minnesota, 1917

Russell, Conrad, *Parliaments and English Politics 1621–1629*, Oxford: Clarendon Press, and New York: Oxford University Press, 1979

Sommerville, J.P., *Politics and Ideology in England, 1603–1640*, London and New York: Longman, 1986; revised edition, as *Royalists and Patriots: Politics and Ideology in England, 1603–1640*, 1999

RELF is the classic investigation of the Petition of Right and how it came to be. Relf examines the derivation of the petition, starting with the events of the "Five Knights" case, the unsatisfactory outcome of which and fears of the abuse of royal powers impelled the House of Commons to curb the king's prerogative. The petition and the king's answer to it were not considered to be a public statute, and the judges would later interpret it in the narrowest way. But Relf suggests that, while the principles enunciated in the petition could not really be enforced, the general statement of English rights made it a milestone in the development of constitutional government.

FOSTER places the Petition of Right in the context of procedure by petition in parliament in general. Petitions were a "middle way", a non-statutory means of getting a point across in a form acceptable to the king. The process of petitioning in the Tudor and Stuart eras developed out of parliament's attempts to gain redress of grievances. By 1628, when the procedures for petitioning had become solidified, a petition of right presented a particular grievance which was shown to be illegal. Enumerating specific wrongs, it presumed that there would be an item-by-item response. The Petition of Right was in some ways unique, but it also demonstrated the persistence of the idea that petitioning was the proper way to express the grievances of the realm.

While covering a much broader subject, RUSSELL includes a significant discussion of the Petition of Right and the parliament of 1628. This book, which was an early major statement of the revisionist view of Stuart politics, plays down the role of ideology in these parliaments. The petition is placed in the context of the crisis of war and the financial difficulties of the crown. Yet Russell stresses the uniqueness of the parliament of 1628, which met with a clear intention of asserting English liberties.

Russell emphasizes that the petition was intended to confirm existing liberties and that the procedure by petition was a traditional form used intentionally to defuse conflict with the king. Still, he argues that the Petition of Right crisis was critical in creating distrust between king and parliament.

GUY's interests lie not so much in the Petition of Right itself, but in the events that precipitated it. He wishes to explain parliament's adamance about making these particular statements of right, especially their questioning of the king's authority to imprison without cause shown. Guy firmly concludes that it was Charles and his officers who precipitated the crisis, rather than a power-hungry House of Commons. In the manuscripts of King's Bench, Guy uncovered the records of the "Five Knights" case which attorney general Sir Robert Heath was alleged to have falsified. Guy argues that it was this "felonious" perversion of the official record that made the Commons fear that the king was willing to manipulate the law in order to achieve his own ends. (This argument for the illegal behaviour of Heath in purposely falsifying public records on the king's behalf has been strongly questioned by Mark Kishlansky, "Tyranny Denied: Charles I, Attorney General Heath, and the Five Knights' Case", *Historical Journal*, 42 (1999): 53–83.) The petition was thus a direct response to the subversion of due process laws by the crown, and it explains why the parliament pursued its ends so tenaciously. The Commons' forced retreat from procedure by bill to procedure by petition is seen as a major blow to their desires.

REEVE takes issue with Relf's earlier characterization of the Petition of Right as merely a judicial measure that did not attain the Commons' legislative goals. Attacking Relf on the grounds of both fact and argument, Reeve asserts that the petition was fundamentally legislative in nature because it allowed for interpretation. He argues that Sir Edward Coke saw the petition as a means to bind the king as far as the law could do so. While the Lords feared inhibiting the prerogative of the king, the Commons fully intended to constrain the prerogative. It was a strong response to perceived innovations in the constitution and it posed a challenge to King Charles to govern in a traditional manner. Reeve characterizes the Petition of Right crisis as a true precursor to the civil wars, an argument that may overstate the connection between one period of political antagonism and the other. FLEMION (1991) disagrees with both Reeve and Russell in their characterizations of the Lords' role in the petition. She suggests that the Lords were not persuaded to the Commons' view, but rather that they understood the petition differently. For them, the petition did not affect the king's legitimate exercise of the discretionary power of imprisonment; the prerogative was not touched. Flemion's views thus revise the interpretation expressed in her earlier article (1973).

Unlike Reeve, BURGESS does not see the Petition of Right as an outright attack on the royal prerogative. Looking at the debates over the petition in the context of the larger discussion of political ideology in early Stuart England, he sees consensus as the model for the period. With the petition, the parliament did not wish to limit the royal prerogative, but to state clearly what the law actually was and to get the king to agree with this interpretation of law. The problem behind the debates was the confusion of prerogative and law; the failure to resolve this confusion led to the breakdown of the language of common law as the dominant language of political consensus. SOMMERVILLE, on the other hand, would argue that consensus did not exist, that common law language was not the dominant discourse, but one of several. Hence the Petition of Right demonstrates an ideological clash between absolutist theory that upheld the strict prerogative rights of the crown and common law theory that defended English liberties. Two fundamentally different interpretations existed. Even after signing the petition, the king believed it did not infringe upon his sovereign prerogative; in contrast, anti-absolutists would argue that this statement of old law did indeed bind royal power.

CATHERINE F. PATTERSON

See also Charles I; Civil Wars, 1642–1651: Constitutional Issues; Taxation: Parliamentary

Physics (and Natural Philosophy)

Berman, Morris, *Social Change and Scientific Organization: The Royal Institution, 1799–1844*, London: Heinemann Educational, and Ithaca, New York: Cornell University Press, 1978

Brown, Laurie M., Abraham Pais, and Brian Pippard (editors), *Twentieth Century Physics*, 3 vols, Bristol: Institute of Physics Publishing, and New York: American Institute of Physics Press, 1995

Cantor, Geoffrey, David Gooding, and Frank A.J.L. James, *Faraday*, London: Macmillan, 1991; revised edition, as *Michael Faraday*, Atlantic Highlands, New Jersey: Humanities Press, 1996

Caroe, G.M., *William Henry Bragg, 1862–1942: Man and Scientist*, Cambridge and New York: Cambridge University Press, 1978

Crombie, A.C., *Augustine to Galileo: The History of Science, A.D. 400–1650*, 1 vol., London: Falcon Press, 1952; Cambridge, Massachusetts: Harvard University Press, 1953; 2nd edition, London: Falcon Press, and Cambridge, Massachusetts: Harvard University Press, 1961

Goldman, Martin, *The Demon in the Aether: The Story of James Clerk Maxwell*, Edinburgh: Harris, and Bristol: Hilger, 1983

Gowing, Margaret, *Britain and Atomic Energy, 1939–1945*, London: Macmillan, and New York: St Martin's Press, 1964

Hall, A. Rupert, *Isaac Newton, Adventurer in Thought*, Oxford and Cambridge, Massachusetts: Blackwell, 1992

Hermann, Armin *et al.*, *History of CERN*, 3 vols, Amsterdam, Oxford, and New York: North-Holland, 1987–96

Hunt, Bruce J., *The Maxwellians*, Ithaca, New York: Cornell University Press, 1991

Hunter, Michael (editor), *Robert Boyle Reconsidered*, Cambridge and New York: Cambridge University Press, 1994

Hunter, Michael and Simon Schaffer (editors), *Robert Hooke: New Studies*, Woodbridge, Suffolk and Wolfeboro, New Hampshire: Boydell Press, 1989

Jungnickel, Christa and Russell McCormmach, *Cavendish*, Philadelphia: American Philosophical Society, 1996; revised edition, as *Cavendish: The Experimental Life*, Lewisburg, Pennsylvania: Bucknell University Press, 1999

Keller, Alex, *The Infancy of Atomic Physics: Hercules in His Cradle*, Oxford: Clarendon Press, and New York: Oxford University Press, 1983

Knight, David, *Humphry Davy: Science and Power*, Oxford and Cambridge, Massachusetts: Blackwell, 1992

Olby, Robert, *The Path to the Double Helix*, Seattle: University of Washington Press, and London: Macmillan, 1974; enlarged edition, New York: Dover, and London: Constable, 1994

Olson, Richard, *Scottish Philosophy and British Physics, 1750–1880: A Study in the Foundations of the Victorian Scientific Style*, Princeton, New Jersey: Princeton University Press, 1975

Smith, Crosbie, *The Science of Energy: A Cultural History of Energy Physics in Victorian Britain*, London: Athlone, and Chicago: University of Chicago Press, 1998

Smith, Crosbie and M. Norton Wise, *Energy and Empire: A Biographical Study of Lord Kelvin*, Cambridge and New York: Cambridge University Press, 1989

Wilson, David B., *Kelvin and Stokes: A Comparative Study in Victorian Physics*, Bristol: Hilger, 1987

Physics, or more properly until the end of the 19th century natural philosophy, in Britain has a long history. There is, however, no adequate single text devoted either to the subject generally, or even to physics within specific periods. Most, though not all of the books here, are accessible biographical studies of some of the key figures in the development of physics.

CROMBIE deals with medieval science in Europe generally. But there is a significant component dealing with natural philosophy in England, particularly optics and dynamics and especially those scholars connected with Merton College, Oxford. Crombie argued that there was a continuity in scientific knowledge between the medieval period and the Renaissance. This thesis was criticized severely at the time, and to some extent he did not later adhere to it so strongly.

The so-called "scientific revolution" which occurred in the Renaissance was initially centred elsewhere in Europe. Copernicus in Poland, Galileo in Italy, Kepler in Germany, and Descartes in France, over a period of a century or so, transformed human understanding of the universe and laid the foundations for the development of physical theory. In England there was little scientific activity of note until the 17th century. At the beginning of that century, William Gilbert produced some original work on magnetism, while Francis Bacon developed a philosophy of empirical and collaborative science which, if it was not exactly followed by his successors, formed the template in which they framed their arguments.

The second half of the 17th century was when English natural philosophers such as Robert Boyle, Robert Hooke, and above all Isaac Newton made major contributions to the subject. Although perhaps most widely known for physical laws which every student of physics learns, Boyle and Hooke were major figures in natural philosophy and in society and HUNTER and HUNTER & SCHAFFER place them respectively in their contemporary contexts, and, especially with Boyle, his religious context. But it was Newton (HALL) who was most influential through two books. First was the *Principia* (1687), which dealt

with dynamics and developed the notion of force which he used to produce his theory of gravity including the inverse square law. The second book was the *Opticks* (1704) which provided a geometrical theory of optics, an explanation for the colours of the spectrum, and a theory that light was particulate in nature, although there was room for interpreting what Newton really thought. Newton undertook this work against a background of holding unorthodox (and thus, in post-Restoration England, dangerous) unitarian religious beliefs and an extensive study of alchemy from which he may well have derived the concept of force. Newton had a number of opponents, including Hooke, who criticized Newton's ideas of colour and also of dynamics. Despite such opposition, Newton's view of the world became the scientific orthodoxy during the 18th century.

Much natural philosophical work undertaken in England during the 18th century was directed towards understanding phenomena such as electricity and heat that Newton had only speculated about. The work of Henry Cavendish (JUNGNICKEL & McCORMMACH) illustrates this. He made some of the most precise measurements of physical phenomena that had been made up to this time and then applied Newtonian theory to them. This book, however, provides more than its title suggests since it deals with the place of science in 18th-century aristocratic society. The 18th century, as OLSON shows, also saw the start of Scotland's contribution to natural philosophy during the Scottish Enlightenment. Henceforth Scottish natural philosophers would play a major role in the development of the subject in Britain.

In 1799 the Italian natural philosopher Alessandro Volta announced the invention of the electric battery, and also the Royal Institution was founded in London. BERMAN provides an account of the first 40 years or so of the Institution, concentrating on its public role rather than the scientific research that was undertaken in its laboratories. Both these events in 1799 exerted a profound influence on natural philosophy during the 19th century. The Royal Institution possessed in the 19th century one of the few research-capable laboratories in Europe. It was here, using the electric battery, that Humphry Davy (KNIGHT) and Michael Faraday (CANTOR, GOODING, & JAMES), and later John Tyndall, James Dewar, and Lord Rayleigh carried out much of their major work. Elsewhere George Stokes (WILSON) in Cambridge developed the formidable mathematical theory of fluid mechanics, while William Thomson (later Lord Kelvin: SMITH & WISE) in Glasgow enunciated the laws of the new science of thermodynamics and worked out the cosmological implications of them in the heat death of the universe (SMITH). Thomson also worked on electrical phenomena and together with his younger contemporary James Clerk Maxwell (GOLDMAN) mathematized Faraday's theory of the electromagnetic field, thus, as HUNT shows, making it into one of the cornerstones of modern physics.

In the second half of the 19th century the universities started establishing laboratories of their own with the Cavendish at Cambridge and the Clarendon at Oxford. At the former J.J. Thomson in 1897 detected the subatomic particle that would later be called the electron, although its existence was announced at a lecture at the Royal Institution.

The opening of the 20th century not only saw the beginning of the Nobel Prize for Physics (first awarded 1901) but also the start of an enormous change in the approach to physics with the invention of quantum mechanics and relativity theory mostly in the German-speaking countries (BROWN, PAIS, & PIPPARD). British physicists not only took advantage of these new theoretical insights, but also developed them, for example in the work of P.A.M. Dirac. British physics in the 20th century benefited greatly from the base that had been established in the 19th century and this was added to from the mid-1930s onwards when the rise of fascism in Europe drove many top physicists, for example Max Born and Dennis Gabor, into exile in Britain, where they made enormously important contributions.

The first British winner of the Nobel Prize for Physics, in 1904, was Rayleigh for his discovery of the inert gas argon. In 1915 the prize was awarded jointly to the father-and-son team William and Lawrence Bragg (CAROE) for their method of analysing crystal structures by the means of X-rays. Lawrence Bragg, at the age of 25, remains the youngest ever winner of the Nobel prize. In 1923 William Bragg moved to become head of the Royal Institution, where he established a major crystallographic research team, members of which included his son, W.T. Astbury (who was arguably the first molecular biologist), J.D. Bernal (who later established a laboratory at Birkbeck College), and Kathleen Lonsdale (who did likewise at University College London).

Britain, as KELLER discusses, was also well placed in the field of atomic physics with C.T.R. Wilson and J.D. Cockcroft at the University of Cambridge, James Chadwick, also at the Cavendish, who discovered the neutron, and P.M.S. Blackett at the University of Manchester, who worked especially on cosmic rays. With such a wealth of talent in this and other fields of physics, Britain was well placed to meet the scientific needs of the 1939–45 war in such diverse areas as the degaussing of ships, the invention of radar at various wavelengths, and, of course, to start work to build an atomic weapon (GOWING), although with the entry of the United States into the war against Germany in December 1941, the British contribution was moved to America.

The end of the war left Britain a victor but by the 1950s it had become clear that it no longer possessed the resources for large-scale scientific research. Thus it joined CERN in Geneva (HERMANN *et al.*) following the realization that it could not build its own world-class particle accelerator. The history of Britain's collaborations in physics closely parallels the overall problems that it has experienced with European integration. However, where resources required were not as demanding as for particle physics, Britain was and is able to produce world-class research. Thus Francis Crick and James Watson working at the Cavendish, then directed by Lawrence Bragg, determined the double helical structure of DNA in 1953 (OLBY). That year Bragg moved to the Royal Institution where, like his father, he established a major crystallographic research group. There Max Perutz and John Kendrew in part did their work on the structure of proteins for which they won the Nobel Prize for Chemistry in 1962 and David Phillips worked out the structure of lysozyme, the first enzyme to be so analysed.

Although it may appear that physics is in decline in Britain, especially with the closure during the 1990s of a number of university physics departments, it seems as if physics has expanded into other areas of science, most notably electrical engineering and molecular biology. However, British physics as such continues to flourish but to a large extent within the international collaborative efforts that modern big science now requires.

FRANK A.J.L. JAMES

See also Boyle; Natural Philosophy; Newton; Royal Institution

Pictland and Dalriada

Anderson, Marjorie O., *Kings and Kingship in Early Scotland*, Edinburgh: Scottish Academic Press, 1973; revised, 1980; Totowa, New Jersey: Rowman and Littlefield, 1974

Anderson, Marjorie O., "Dalriada and the Creation of the Kingdom of the Scots" in *Ireland in Early Mediaeval Europe: Studies in Memory of Kathleen Hughes*, edited by Dorothy Whitelock *et al.*, Cambridge and New York: Cambridge University Press, 1982

Bannerman, John, *Studies in the History of Dalriada*, Edinburgh: Scottish Academic Press, 1974

Chadwick, H. Munro, *Early Scotland: The Picts, the Scots, and the Welsh of Southern Scotland*, Cambridge: Cambridge University Press, 1949

Cummins, W.A., *The Age of the Picts*, Stroud, Gloucestershire: Alan Sutton, 1995

Foster, Sally M., *Picts, Gaels, and Scots: Early Historic Scotland*, London: Batsford, 1996

Fraser, John, "The Question of the Picts", *Scottish Gaelic Studies*, 2 (1927): 172–201

Friell, J.G.P. and W.G. Watson (editors), *Pictish Studies: Settlement, Burial, and Art in Dark Age Northern Britain*, Oxford: British Archaeological Reports, British Series 125, 1984

Henderson, Isabel, *The Picts*, London: Thames and Hudson, and New York: Praeger, 1967

Wainwright, F.T. (editor), *The Problem of the Picts*, Edinburgh: Nelson, 1955; New York: Philosophical Library, 1956; reprinted, Perth: Melvin Press, 1980

Pictland and Dalriada (or Dál Riata) have attracted the attentions of scholars for centuries, beginning with Bede in the 8th century and continuing to the present. Part of the reason is the uncertainty about much of their history and another part is their contribution to what became the kingdom of Scotland. About the Picts there have been two other mysteries: the question of whether they practised matrilineal succession to the kingship; and the problem of the meaning of the numerous carved stones, with their symbols. Dalriada has its own curiosity for historians, as an outpost of, and avenue for, Irish culture in Britain.

CHADWICK saw the history of the two areas as complementing one another. He stressed the elasticity of dominion and the unknown factor contributed by intermarriage (aggravated by the matrilineal question) and shared religious institutions. This led to his suggestion that the relations between the two regions were not marked by constant warfare, but rather by peaceful contacts interrupted by occasional hostilities. Their merger was the result of the energetic Scots subsuming the reactionary Picts, a conclusion he drew from his study of the king lists. ANDERSON (1973) used the same existing sources to identify specific rulers and their dynasties. She sees those materials as presenting an essentially accurate picture of the royal lines among both the Picts and the Scots, with competition among the dynasties visible in the succession to the various kingships. FOSTER uses aspects of the studies of Chadwick and Anderson as she sees both peoples developing along similar paths and the union of the two as a logical progression. The continued domination of the aristocratic lineages of Dalriada after their movement eastwards into Pictavia was only one aspect of constancy. The union of the Picts with the Scots is studied by ANDERSON (1982). She sees the ending of Pictish culture as a deliberate action on the part of the Scots, who installed their own institutions in the aftermath of Kenneth I's triumph.

The two regions have more often been studied in isolation, with the greater share of attention given to the Picts. This led FRASER to complain that "for a people who played no very great part in the history of Europe, the Picts might very well be thought to have already received their due share of attention". His ground-breaking study employed the witness of linguistics to attempt to answer questions of ethnography, using a comparative European methodology. He successfully set out a rational scholarly basis for further speculations. While much of his discussion deals with language, the witness of historical records is called into service. Other scholars see an interdisciplinary approach to be a sensible method of study, and this has produced a number of important collected studies. Modern work on the Picts has been shaped by the very influential essays edited by WAINWRIGHT. Each is important and covers a different area, such as history, art history, archaeology, language. Wainwright's own essay places the Picts within the general development of British history and finally rescues them from the tender mercies of those who had transported them to the realm of fantasy. Integrating pictorial sources with the contemporary annals and king lists, HENDERSON complements her historical survey with a detailed consideration of art in Pictish society. She sees the stylistic developments of the symbol stones together with the aptitude in their execution as revealing a culturally sophisticated society. From this she suggests that both Pictish identity and their cultural contacts with their neighbours are visible, literally, in their artistic productions. The meagre materials provided by the written or sculpted records have been usefully expanded by other disciplines. The essays edited by FRIELL & WATSON study farming and settlement patterns in addition to the remains of habitations in an attempt to reconstruct the social and economic foundations of Pictish society. In common with other European peoples, this society exhibits signs of social stratification in the material remains, limitation of agriculture imposed by physical geography, and adaptation of settlement to climate. CUMMINS takes a completely political reading of the period and argues that the eventual merger of the Picts and Scots and the early years of the united kingdom are evidence of peaceful relations among them, in contrast with the violent unions found elsewhere in Europe. He sees the location of the Picts and the ambitions of their neighbours as being as much determining factors in their history as their embrace of Christianity.

Dalriada has had less specific study devoted to it, mainly because it is more often examined in the general context of the later Scottish kingdom. BANNERMAN argues that the tract "The History of the Men of Britain" is an important document for understanding the settlement of the kingdom and the relative power of the dominant kindreds. The purpose of this document he sees as tied to the military reverses of the kingdom at the hands of the Anglo-Saxons of Northumbria, and is connected with the collection of tribute. His investigation of the entries on northern British affairs in the Irish annals led him to propose a chronicle maintained on Iona. Although administratively sophisticated by the standards of the day, the eventual success of the Dalriadan princely line could not have been predicted from the kingdom's precarious existence. As other scholars have also noted, the complex intermarriages with neighbouring dynasties add an element of uncertainty to any attempt to judge the success of the kingdom.

There are a number of more specialized works dealing with the symbol stones, arguing for or against the practice of matrilineal succession among the Picts, and the place of the church in Pictish or Dalriadan societies. While individual historians need to judge for themselves the usefulness of such studies, it is clear that the scarce written records are usefully supplemented by the evidence from other disciplines.

BENJAMIN HUDSON

See also Picts and Scots

Picts and Scots

Anderson, Alan Orr (editor and translator), *Early Sources of Scottish History AD 500–1286*, 2 vols, Edinburgh: Oliver and Boyd, 1922; reprinted with author's corrections and a bibliographical supplement edited by Marjorie O. Anderson, Stamford, Lincolnshire: Paul Watkins, 1990

Anderson, Marjorie O., *Kings and Kingship in Early Scotland*, Edinburgh: Scottish Academic Press, 1973; revised, 1980; Totowa, New Jersey: Rowman and Littlefield, 1974

Chadwick, H. Munro, *Early Scotland: The Picts, the Scots, and the Welsh of Southern Scotland*, Cambridge: Cambridge University Press, 1949

Crawford, Barbara E., *Scandinavian Scotland*, Leicester: Leicester University Press, and Atlantic Highlands, New Jersey: Humanities Press, 1987

Dickinson, William Croft, *Scotland from the Earliest Times to 1603*, London and New York: Nelson, 1961; 3rd edition, Oxford: Clarendon Press, 1977

Duncan, Archibald A.M., *Scotland: The Making of the Kingdom*, Edinburgh: Oliver and Boyd, and New York: Barnes and Noble, 1975

Innes, Thomas, *Critical Essay on the Ancient Inhabitants of the Northern Parts of Britain or Scotland*, 2 vols, London: W. Innys, 1729; reissued, 1 vol., Edinburgh: W. Paterson, 1879

Robertson, Eben William, *Scotland under Her Early Kings: A History of the Kingdom to the Close of the Thirteenth Century*, 2 vols, London: Edmonston and Douglas, 1862

Skene, William Forbes, *Celtic Scotland, A History of Ancient Alban*, 3 vols, Edinburgh: Edmonston and Douglas, 1876–80; Freeport, New York: Books for Libraries, 1971

Watson, William J., *The History of the Celtic Place-Names of Scotland*, Edinburgh: William Blackwood, 1926; reprinted, Shannon: Irish University Press, 1973

The early history of the peoples who would make up the medieval Scottish kingdom is obscure and complex. The later medieval state was an amalgam of five distinct cultural and linguistic groups, assembled under one lordship over the course of several centuries, beginning with the merger of the *Picti* of northern Britain with the *Scoti* of Dalriada (or Dál Riata) in the 9th century. The physical shape of the kingdom changed over a longer period and the process continued until the very end of the medieval period. This has presented scholars with the difficult task of explaining the process of assimilation and its consequences at a very early date; to add to the problem the historical sources are few, brief, and in most instances preserved in manuscripts copied centuries after the events they describe. Beginning in the 18th century, the basic source-collecting and criticism was begun, leading to the important, and enduring, work from the mid-19th century to the third quarter of the 20th, which more recent studies largely follow.

The methodology to be used in studying the early period has occupied the attention of historians from an early date. Still important today, although composed early in the 18th century, INNES's essay became the model for later interpretations, even though much of his work is an attack on the work of George Buchanan, the tutor of James VI and I. Innes's reliance on original source materials together with his employment of basic comparative historiography ensure that his observations are relevant today, especially his arguments for strong monarchs working together with a single church. That methodology was used in the 19th century by ROBERTSON, who made his own contribution by employing the technique of the legal argument (he was a solicitor from Leicestershire) to show how revealing a close reading and comparison of all source materials could be for an understanding of this period, especially of the nature of Anglo-Scottish relations. His arguments, particularly for caution when using English sources for Scottish history, are still compelling and were much admired by SKENE. Skene's pioneering work on early Scottish history incorporated Gaelic-language materials into his researches, and he opened a new era in the field as he used Irish annals, hagiography, and other written works to reveal the Celtic aspect to Scottish history that had largely been ignored. His views on various topics now need to be modified, but his volumes are still a useful survey for a well-rounded overview. All more recent works are indebted to those pioneers whose sound scholarship has stood the test of time.

The search for source materials leads through many languages and texts, making A.O. ANDERSON's monumental source collection all the more valuable. While not a narrative history as such, the scholarly apparatus for those texts contains a wealth of historical information. More than previous scholars, he demonstrated the helpful nature of interaction among the various peoples. Yet the very disparate nature of the communities that formed the early Scots kingdom ensures that cultural history is particularly difficult to discern, a topic that is addressed, in part, by WATSON. His analysis of place-names provides an immense amount of information on ecclesiastical houses, habitation sites, and the relationship of literature to geography. He argues for layers of habitation, as newcomers take over the good land or easily defensible sites from earlier dwellers. Traditional historical writing is provided by DICKINSON, who sees the developing Scots kingdom of the early Middle Ages in terms of a typically European formation. The growth of the monarchy was part of the general tendency towards a strong central government. A more elaborate study, DUNCAN's classic work on the Scottish kingdom is an important survey of political, ecclesiastical, and material history. His examination of developments in the course of more than a thousand years argues for the longevity and continuity of institutions within a changing political context, especially the influence from Gaelic society.

More specialized studies have been as important as general surveys. CHADWICK's study of king lists and notices of kings in the chronicles led him to propose that the division of Picts and Scots was less definite than the written records would suggest. Using political records as a source for ethnography, he argued that the societies of the Picts and Scots were less distinct than believed and that their merger had been occurring since the late 8th century, made obscure for modern students by the annals' conservatism in the use of population terms. Using much the same materials, a political investigation is found in M.O. ANDERSON's analysis of king lists, genealogies, and annalistic materials. The wealth of interpretative material is supplemented by editions of the source material. While this is largely a textual history, there is much of importance for political history. Her argument that these king lists and annals are valid contemporary record even though they survive in manuscripts from centuries later than their original composition leads to the extrapolation of a political situation that is uniquely complicated. More wide ranging is a history of Viking Scotland by CRAWFORD, whose synthesis of history, archaeology, geography, and art history illuminates an area whose contribution is often not recognized. She demonstrates that the material wealth of the Vikings and their political importance throughout the North Atlantic allowed them to influence the development of the Scots and Picts economically, culturally, and politically.

In the future, uncovering the historical landscape will be assisted by the work of archaeologists and art historians. As more of the material remains are uncovered and interpreted, this will supplement the brief surviving records.

BENJAMIN HUDSON

See also Kenneth I; Pictland and Dalriada; Strathclyde, Gododdin, Rheged, "Kingdoms" of

Pilgrimage of Grace   1536–1537

Bush, Michael, *The Pilgrimage of Grace: A Study of the Rebel Armies of October 1536*, Manchester and New York: Manchester University Press, 1996

Davies, C.S.L., "Popular Religion and the Pilgrimage of Grace" in *Order and Disorder in Early Modern England*, edited by Anthony Fletcher and John Stevenson, Cambridge and New York: Cambridge University Press, 1985

Dickens, Arthur Geoffrey, "Secular and Religious Motivation in the Pilgrimage of Grace" in *The Province of York: Papers Read at the Fifth Summer Meeting of the Ecclesiastical History Society*, edited by G.J. Cuming, Leiden: E.J. Brill, 1967

Dodds, Madeleine Hope and Ruth Dodds, *The Pilgrimage of Grace 1536–1537 and the Exeter Conspiracy, 1538*, 2 vols, Cambridge: Cambridge University Press, 1915

Elton, G.R., "Politics and the Pilgrimage of Grace" in *After the Reformation: Essays in Honour of J.H. Hexter*, edited by Barbara C. Malament, Manchester: Manchester University Press, 1980

Haigh, Christopher, *Reformation and Resistance in Tudor Lancashire*, London and New York: Cambridge University Press, 1975

Hoyle, R.W., *The Pilgrimage of Grace and the Politics of the 1530s*, Oxford and New York: Oxford University Press, 2001

James, Mervyn Evans, "Obedience and Dissent in Henrician England: The Lincolnshire Rebellion, 1536", *Past and Present*, 48 (1970): 3–78

Reid, R.R., *The King's Council in the North*, London: Longmans Green, 1921; reprinted, Wakefield: EP Publishing, and Totowa, New Jersey: Rowman and Littlefield, 1975

Historians have long debated the nature and causes of the Pilgrimage of Grace. This great rebellion, which erupted across the northern counties of England in October 1536, provided the Tudor regime with what was, perhaps, the greatest challenge to its authority. The most detailed account of the rebellion was that written more than 80 years ago by the Misses DODDS. Their two-volume study, based upon a detailed examination of the Henrician state papers, has remained the definitive narrative account of the pilgrimage. As such, it presents what is now regarded as the traditional view of the revolt, that of a spontaneous mass protest of the conservative north against the upheavals caused by the policies of the Henrician regime during the early 1530s. In this interpretation, straightforward political concerns are closely interlinked with overt religious grievances.

Over the years, however, historians have sought to venture beyond the scope of the Dodds' analysis. Their study, although still regarded as impressive in its detailed narrative approach, has been criticized in recent times for being idealistic and too readily accepting of the evidence put forward by the rebel leaders. A few years after the Dodds' interpretation, REID addressed the subject of the pilgrimage in her study of the Council in the North. While acknowledging the religious and political dimensions of the revolt, Reid went on to suggest that economic and social grievances played an equally important part. In her view, tenurial anxieties over increased rents, enclosures, and rising entry fines, set against a background of rising prices and poor harvests, lay at the root of the problem for the mass of the pilgrims. DICKENS, writing some fifty years later, agreed with Reid's view. In his influential essay, written in the late 1960s, he saw the inspiration for the pilgrimage emanating, largely, from the reactions of a "disgruntled peasantry and yeomanry" to a multiplicity of localized, primarily secular, concerns and grievances.

Nevertheless, discussion surrounding the importance of religious issues has continued to loom large, perhaps not surprisingly, given that the pilgrims' leader Robert Aske presented the revolt, from its earliest stages, as a religious crusade. HAIGH has stressed the religious nature of the revolt in his study of the Reformation in Lancashire, suggesting that resistance to the religious reforms of the Henrician government provided the major impetus for rebellion within that county. While it concedes that some of the concerns regarding the suppression of the monasteries may have had economic overtones, Haigh's study seeks to emphasize the strong attachment of that locality to the pre-Reformation church. DAVIES, returning to a theme explored by him in an earlier article, similarly underlines the importance of religion in the rebellion, not least for its unifying capacities. As he points out, the whole concept of the pilgrimage was enshrined in religious imagery. Moreover, the religious dimension gave the rebellion the necessary justification, by virtue of its appeal to the ultimate power of the Almighty, for the challenge to royal authority.

The Henrician regime of the early 1530s, which, under the direction of Thomas Cromwell, sought a more effective enforcement of royal authority in the north, aroused considerable upper-class resentment. The role played by political grievances in the pilgrimage, therefore, remains a subject of much debate. Several historians, sensing elements of upper-class manipulation in evidence behind the scenes, have questioned the traditional notion of a commons-inspired revolt. JAMES has written widely on the issues surrounding the pilgrimage and on the role of the crown and upper orders in the revolt. His study of the earlier Lincolnshire phase of the rebellion, which preceded the Pilgrimage proper, discusses the extent to which the intrusions of central authority engendered the resentment which led to members of the upper orders assuming the leadership of and providing momentum for the rebellion. Another assessment of the political issues surrounding the rebellion is that in the influential and controversial article by ELTON, which suggests that the leadership and inspiration behind the revolt lay with members of the defeated pro-Aragonese court faction. The aim of this group, in Elton's view, was to discredit the dominant court clique, headed by Cromwell, by exploiting the grievances of the men of the north.

Modern research, however, is moving once more towards the view of the Pilgrimage of Grace as a popular revolt. BUSH argues that it was indeed a rebellion of the lower orders inspired primarily by agrarian concerns. However, he also goes some way towards reconciling the differing points of view by suggesting the existence of a second "strand of revolt", based upon the political grievances of the northern gentry, which became enmeshed with the first. The initial rising by the commons was thus translated into more "formidable" proportions, because of the sympathetic support of the upper orders, which, although tacit in the beginning, became more committed as the revolt gathered momentum. The recent major study, that by HOYLE, also stresses the "popular and spontaneous" nature of the revolt, "with the commons in the driving seat". Hoyle highlights the diversity of regional characteristics, in terms of the rebels' aims and motivations, illustrating how the religious concerns of some areas came to be merged with the agrarian and socio-economic grievances of other localities.

The pilgrim host, which had succeeded in securing various

concessions from the king in December 1536, had dispersed in disarray by the following March. Nevertheless, Bush's study, which focuses on the recruitment and mobilization of the pilgrim host, serves usefully to re-emphasize the extent of the potential threat to the Henrician regime posed by the rebels, in terms of numbers and military preparedness, during the course of their revolt in the winter months of 1536–37.

CHRISTINE M. NEWMAN

See also Cromwell, Thomas; Dissolution of Religious Houses and Chantries; Henry VIII; Social Conflict: Early Modern Period

Piracy

Anderson, J.L., "Piracy and World History: An Economic Perspective on Maritime Predation", *Journal of World History*, 6/1 (1995): 25–50

Barbour, Violet, "Privateers and Pirates of the West Indies", *American Historical Review*, 16/3 (1911): 529–66

Bromley, John, "Outlaws at Sea: Liberty, Equality, and Fraternity among Caribbean Freebooters" in his *Corsairs and Navies, 1660–1760*, London and Ronceverte, West Virginia: Hambledon Press, 1987

Cordingly, David, *Life among the Pirates: The Romance and the Reality*, London: Little Brown, 1995; as *Under the Black Flag: The Romance and Reality of Life among the Pirates*, New York: Random House, 1996

Exquemelin, Alexandre, *The Buccaneers of America*, Harmondsworth: Penguin, 1969; London: The Folio Society, 1972; Glorieta, New Mexico: Rio Grande Press, 1990 (1st editions, 1678, 1684, 1686)

Hill, Christopher, "Radical Pirates" in *The Collected Essays of Christopher Hill*, vol. 3, *People and Ideas in Seventeenth-Century England*, Brighton, Sussex: Harvester Press, and Amherst, Massachusetts: University of Massachusetts Press, 1986

Hughson, Shirley Carter, "The Carolina Pirates and Colonial Commerce, 1670–1740", *Johns Hopkins University Studies in Historical and Political Science*, 12th series, 5–7 (1894): 1–134

Johnson, Charles, *A General History of the Pyrates*, edited by Manuel Schonhorn, London: Dent, and Columbia: University of South Carolina Press, 1972; as *A General History of the Robberies and Murders of the Most Notorious Pirates*, edited by David Cordingly, London: Conway Maritime Press, 1998 (1st editions, 1724, 1728)

Karraker, Cyrus Harreld, *Piracy Was a Business*, Rindge, New Hampshire: R.R. Smith, 1953

Lane, Frederic C., "Economic Consequences of Organised Violence", *Journal of Economic History*, 18/4 (1958): 401–17

Pares, Richard, *War and Trade in the West Indies, 1739–1763*, Oxford: Clarendon Press, 1936

Peterson, "An Historical Perspective on the Incidence of Piracy" in *Piracy at Sea*, edited by Eric Ellen, Paris: International Maritime Bureau, 1989

Rediker, Marcus, *Between the Devil and the Deep Blue Sea: Merchant Seamen, Pirates, and the Anglo-American Maritime World, 1700–1750*, Cambridge and New York: Cambridge University Press, 1987

Rediker, Marcus, "Hydrarchy and Libertalia: The Utopian Dimensions of Atlantic Piracy in the Early Eighteenth Century" in *Pirates and Privateers: New Perspectives on the War on Trade in the Eighteenth and Nineteenth Centuries*, edited by David J. Starkey *et al.*, Exeter, Devon: University of Exeter Press, 1997

Ritchie, Robert C., *Captain Kidd and the War Against the Pirates*, Cambridge, Massachusetts: Harvard University Press, 1986

Ritchie, Robert C., "Government Measures Against Piracy and Privateering in the Atlantic Area, 1750–1850" in *Pirates and Privateers: New Perspectives on the War on Trade in the Eighteenth and Nineteenth Centuries*, edited by David J. Starkey *et al.*, Exeter, Devon: University of Exeter Press, 1997

Stanley, Jo (editor), *Bold in her Breeches: Women Pirates Across the Ages*, London and San Francisco: Pandora, 1995

Starkey, David. J., *British Privateering Enterprise in the Eighteenth Century*, Exeter, Devon: University of Exeter Press, 1990

Wickens, P.L., "The Economics of Privateering: Capital Dispersal in the American War for Independence", *Journal of European Economic History*, 13/2 (1984): 375–96

Zahedieh, Nuala, "Trade, Plunder, and Economic Development in Early English Jamaica, 1655–1689", *Economic History Review*, 39/2 (1986): 205–22

Zahedieh, Nuala, "'A Frugal, Prudential, and Hopeful Trade': Privateering in Jamaica, 1655–1689", *Journal of Imperial and Commonwealth History*, 18/2 (1990): 145–62

The first port of call for any serious student of colonial piracy must be the contemporary narratives of EXQUEMELIN and JOHNSON, both of which are available in modern editions. Exquemelin's detailed description of the 17th-century buccaneers is the earlier and more bloodthirsty of the two. The graphic accounts of banditry Exquemelin gives have influenced all historical studies of this subject, and his book retains its position as the standard work more than three centuries after its first publication in Dutch in 1678. It is admirably complemented by Johnson's later portrayal of the "golden age" of piracy during the War of the Spanish Succession (1701–14) and the decade following the treaty of Utrecht. Primarily concerned with heists at sea rather than organized raids on land, this work forms the basis of many literary and historical treatments of piracy. For many years a debate has raged over whether the book should be attributed to Daniel Defoe. Modern scholarship has failed to provide convincing evidence of Defoe's authorship; it has also, however, failed to illuminate the personality of the shadowy Captain Johnson.

Caribbean piracy is but one example of the phenomenon of violence and brigandage at sea that is many centuries old. Two articles which provide a valuable context in which to locate the American manifestation of piracy are ANDERSON and PETERSON. Both relate historical inquiry to current concerns, proving a reminder that piracy is a living subject. Similar in intent, but written from a quite different perspective, is the work of CORDINGLY, who concerns himself with the image of the pirate band and its evolution over time. The metamorphosis of the seafaring bandit from marauding psychopath to the civilized urbanity of Errol Flynn forms the basis of a compelling counterpoint as Cordingly contrasts romance with reality.

The immense literature that has been generated on the West Indies and North America may be conveniently if loosely grouped under three headings: political or diplomatic history, social history, and economic history. An outstanding example of the first approach is provided by PARES, who takes as his subject the war against trade during the 18th century and the use of trade as a continuation of European conflict during peacetime. The close associations between legitimized raiding, manifested in the form of the privateers, is also the subject of a more recent work by STARKEY, which is the authoritative text in the field. Recent developments in this area are set out by RITCHIE (1997), who relates the decline of piracy during the second half of the 18th century to the rise of fiscal-military bureaucracies and attempts by the early modern state to establish a monopoly in the exercise of violence. Though this approach has recently become popular, a number of ideas may be traced to an earlier article by LANE, who derived his conclusions from the study of Mediterranean piracy. Mention must also be made here of RITCHIE (1986): a deeply researched and skilfully written work, which makes a valuable contribution under all three headings and which succeeds in locating the experiences of Kidd's company within the context of the developing Atlantic world of the late 17th century.

Piracy is one field of historical study where radical approaches to social history are alive and well. REDIKER (1987 and 1997) is the leading torch-bearer and interprets piratical communities as alternative societies of masterless men (and a few masterless women) who rejected the brutal working conditions and hierarchical authority characteristic of both the merchant marine and the royal navy. The potential for treating piracy in this way is also recognized by HILL and BROMLEY, who attempt to integrate it into a developing tradition of protest. STANLEY and her collaborators introduce gender as an instrument of social analysis and focus on female-specific experiences of piracy. Their gender (and gender-bending) treatment of the subject shares some similarities with Cordingly in that it also analyses the visual representation of female pirates. Common to all these contributions is the assumption that the Atlantic economy was capitalistic in nature: Rediker going furthest in this respect by viewing the ship in Marxist terms as the means of production and sailors as a nascent proletariat. One distinctive feature of his work is the examination of the relationship between piracy and slavery.

An appreciation that pirates, though formally outlaws, interacted with colonial communities and formed an important element in the process of market exchange is a feature common to most of the works reviewed above. Older but valuable contributions in the general area of economic history are the studies of BARBOUR, HUGHSON, and KARRAKER. Collectively, these authors demonstrate that if pirates brought violence and disruption to some colonial regions they brought goods, services, and employment to others. More recent investigations of the economic role of piracy in the process of colonial settlement have been undertaken by WICKENS and ZAHEDIEH (1986 and 1990). The difference between these and earlier studies lies in the greater emphasis placed by Wickens and Zahedieh on capital accumulation and the economics of crime and predation. They suggest that piracy shared the characteristics of other rent-seeking activities and the problems of common resource industries. Zahedieh concludes from studying Jamaica that though important at an early stage of colony formation, over the longer term the high level of piratical activity during the later 17th and the 18th centuries was unsustainable. A similar conclusion is reached by Ritchie in his examination of Kidd's relationship with the merchants of the continental colonies. Piracy's rise and fall may thus be viewed like a barometer, measuring the development of colonial port towns from primitive frontier settlements to sophisticated commercial centres.

S.D. SMITH

See also Americas, Trade with; Drake; Hawkins; Merchant Navy entries; Navy entries; Ralegh

Pitt, William, "the Elder", Earl of Chatham 1708–1778
Politician, statesman, and prime minister

Ayling, Stanley, *The Elder Pitt, Earl of Chatham*, London: Collins, and New York: McKay, 1976

Black, Jeremy, *Pitt the Elder*, Cambridge and New York: Cambridge University Press, 1992

Brooke, John, *The Chatham Administration, 1766–1768*, London: Macmillan, 1956

Green, Walford Davis, *William Pitt, Earl of Chatham, and the Growth and Division of the British Empire, 1708–1778*, New York: Putnam, 1900

Middleton, Richard, *The Bells of Victory: The Pitt-Newcastle Ministry and the Conduct of the Seven Years' War, 1757–1762*, Cambridge and New York: Cambridge University Press, 1985

Peters, Marie, *Pitt and Popularity: The Patriot Minister and London Opinion during the Seven Years' War*, Oxford: Clarendon Press, and New York: Oxford University Press, 1980

Peters, Marie, *The Elder Pitt*, London and New York: Longman, 1998

Ruville, Albert von, *William Pitt, Earl of Chatham*, translated by H.J. Chaytor assisted by Mary Morison, London: Heinemann, and New York: Putnam, 1907 (German edition, 1905)

Williams, Basil, *The Life of William Pitt, Earl of Chatham*, 2 vols, London and New York: Longmans Green, 1914

Scholarly interest in the "Great Commoner" was appreciable in the early 20th century, fuelled by the availability of new materials and widespread interest in the challenges of empire. GREEN, first off the mark, had access to materials in the Bowood manuscripts as well as utilizing recent Historic Manuscripts Commission (HMC) volumes and Sir William Anson's edition of Grafton's journal. Though it appeared in a series called "Heroes of the Nations", Green's account is not entirely uncritical of its subject. Though leaving its readers in no doubt of "the unquestionable greatness of his [Pitt's] public action" and his capacity "to rule, to lead a nation, to mould a people, to act in great crises as the instrument of fate", Green was not ashamed to note what he called the "pose and charlatanism" of Pitt's private life. Even so, this was essentially a Carlylean exercise in heroics with Pitt pushed into the disparate company of Caesar and Napoleon, Alexander, and Attila. It was left to the German scholar, Albert von RUVILLE, to produce the first of two detailed biographies of Pitt to appear before 1914. Ruville used the huge Newcastle archive in the British Museum as well as diplomatic sources in London and Berlin in what the introduction (by Hugh E. Egerton) with some justice called a "new and solid contribution to world history". In his three volumes, Ruville worked so hard to be impartial that he appeared lacking in sympathy at times. His Pitt is an able egoist, playing a part in 18th-century politics with consummate ability, yet with many contradictions and signs of political insincerity. For all the scholarship, Ruville cannot resist the prophetic touch as "with his whole soul he aspired after the new age, yet without the power to become part of it". Ruville concentrated on Pitt the minister of 1757–61, while not neglecting his later career. He was the first scholar to demonstrate that Pitt's resignation in 1761 involved no breach with the young George III, and his judicious comments on Pitt's taking a peerage in 1766 are still worth consideration. This flurry of interest in Chatham culminated in 1913 with WILLIAMS, which has remained the standard authority. His work confirmed the picture of Pitt as the indispensable and omnipresent directing minister of the 1757–61 government, a strategic master who ensured that, in "vast portions of the world the Protestant Anglo-Saxon – not the French Roman Catholic – civilisation should hereafter prevail". Williams was, however, sufficiently cautious not to claim that there was either consistency or originality in Pitt's colonial policy overall.

Williams held the field in the interwar period, with just one biography (Brian Tunstall's of 1938) appearing. A combination of reduced popular interest in British imperialism and the apparently definitive nature of Williams's text best explains this. Postwar Namierite scholarship had essentially parliamentary preoccupations and found a traditionally heroic figure like Pitt rather awkward to discuss. Work in the 1950s and 1960s anyway concentrated less on the Seven Years' War than on the first 20 years of George III's reign in which Pitt (Earl of Chatham after 1766) figured as a gouty maverick who first contributed to the ministerial instability of 1760–70 and then, in the 1770s, had a last patriotic incarnation as an opponent of British policy in the American War of Independence. BROOKE's 1956 text on the Chatham administration of 1766–68 highlighted the importance of Pitt's career *after* leaving office in 1761 and sensitively incorporated him into a refined Namierite framework; even so, this accomplished text did not wholly relinquish a sense of its subject's imperial vision. AYLING in 1976 was the next to attempt a sophisticated popular biography, one that was coolly post-imperial in tone and perspective. It was well-written and accurate, but neither introduced new source material nor seriously departed from an heroic portrayal.

That was left to MIDDLETON who, in 1985, in a scholarly scrutiny of the wartime administration, insisted that his book was necessarily influenced by the non-heroic values of contemporary society. Middleton insisted that any close reading of departmental correspondence and other contemporary material compelled the abandonment of any superhuman view of Pitt the prime minister singlehandedly dominating the government and imposing policy on cabinet colleagues. Middleton's Pitt was a more hesitant figure, so lacking in confidence in 1757 that he was anxious to enlist Spain as a British ally, and far more dependent on the energies of fellow ministers like Newcastle and Anson than writers like Williams had appreciated. He also questioned the extent of Pitt's popularity with the public and noted "the fortunate timing of Pitt's admission to office" in 1757 when French attention began to shift from the maritime war to events in Europe.

The most recent approaches are less self-consciously iconoclastic than Middleton, or ready to subscribe to his reading of the *Zeitgeist*. BLACK's of 1992 is probably better based in archival sources than any previous biography, taking full advantage of the deposit of the Dropmore Papers (Series II) in the British Library; he is particularly useful on Pitt's life before the Seven Years' War. He gives us Chatham as outsider, a gifted but selfish politician dogged by mental instability and poor health. It was, Black sensitively argues, Chatham's very absence from the world of courts and the "old Whig" phalanx, that helped him embody the national interest during the Seven Years' War, and Middleton, Black argues, goes too far in denying him credit for the success of the wartime coalition. He concludes that "Chatham was a Hanoverian hero, tarnished no doubt by the exigencies, complexities and compromises of politics, but a hero for a country that gave that description to no other politician". Black also suggests that Pitt, despite his hunger for office, was temperamentally most at home in opposition.

The leading modern authority on Chatham is Marie PETERS, who established her reputation on him with her monograph of 1980, and subsequent articles. She returned to the subject with a thematic biography in 1998. Like Middleton and Black, Peters regards his combination of physical and mental ill-health (probably clinical depression) as the key to his entire career, and the book's closer examination of his later political life can only diagnose failure. She does not deny the heroic aspect of his role in wartime, but raises doubts about the real substance of his achievements. And Peters confirms Middleton's view that his conduct of the war was an *ad hoc* affair. And he was not, by contemporary standards, a minister for peacetime, showing himself unable in 1766–68 to end British international isolation or introduce new policies in either India or North America. He had none of his son's ability to familiarize himself with a subject and then bring on policy initiatives. It was, in the end, "the vision thing" that inspired Chatham and the British parliament and people rather than any administrative competence he possessed. "He was a great man, perhaps", Peters concludes, "but one of flawed greatness who only briefly was able to rise to the challenge of his age. By his last decade, time had passed him by."

NIGEL ASTON

See also George II; George III; Newcastle, 1st Duke of; Rockingham; Seven Years' War; Walpole

Pitt, William, "the Younger" 1759-1806
Politician, statesman, and prime minister

Barnes, Donald Grove, *George III and William Pitt, 1783-1806: A New Interpretation Based upon a Study of Their Unpublished Correspondence*, Stanford, California: Stanford University Press, and London: Humphrey Milford / Oxford University Press, 1939; reprinted, New York: Octagon Books, and London: Cass, 1965

Black, Jeremy, *British Foreign Policy in an Age of Revolutions, 1783-1793*, Cambridge and New York: Cambridge University Press, 1994

Breihan, John, "William Pitt and the Commission-on-Fees, 1785-1801", *Historical Journal*, 27 (1984): 59-81

Derry, John, "Governing Temperament under Pitt and Liverpool" in *The Whig Ascendancy: Colloquies on Hanoverian England*, edited by John Cannon, London: Arnold, and New York: St Martin's Press, 1981

Ehrman, John, *The Younger Pitt: The Years of Acclaim*, London: Constable, and New York: Dutton, 1969; reprinted with corrections, London: Constable, 1984

Ehrman, John, *The Younger Pitt: The Reluctant Transition*, London: Constable, and Stanford, California: Stanford University Press, 1983

Ehrman, John, *The Younger Pitt: The Consuming Struggle*, London: Constable, and Stanford, California: Stanford University Press, 1996

Emsley, Clive, "Repression, Terror, and the Rule of Law in England during the Decade of the French Revolution", *English Historical Review*, 100 (1985): 801-25

Harling, Philip, *The Waning of "Old Corruption": The Politics of Economical Reform in Britain, 1779-1846*, Oxford: Clarendon Press, and New York: Oxford University Press, 1996

Holland Rose, J., *William Pitt and National Revival*, London: Bell, 1911; reprint, included in *Life of William Pitt*, London: Bell, and New York: Harcourt Brace, 1924

Holland Rose, J., *William Pitt and the Great War*, London: Bell, 1911; reprint, included in *Life of William Pitt*, London: Bell, and New York: Harcourt Brace, 1924

Mori, Jennifer, *William Pitt and the French Revolution, 1785-1795*, Edinburgh: Keele University Press, and New York: St Martin's Press, 1997

Sack, J.J., "The Memory of Burke and the Memory of Pitt: English Conservatism Confronts Its Past, 1806-1829", *Historical Journal*, 30 (1987): 623-40

Wells, Roger, *Wretched Faces: Famine in Wartime England 1793-1801*, Stroud, Gloucestershire: Alan Sutton, and New York: St Martin's Press, 1988

Despite two centuries of speculation about the ideas and policies of the younger Pitt, it remains difficult for modern historians to separate the man from the myth. Pitt, canonized in his own time as the "Pilot who weathered the Storm" of the French Revolutionary wars, was an aloof and enigmatic leader whose motives for action were never easy for any but his intimates to ascertain. Modern scholars find it no easier to explain the true Pitt. HOLLAND ROSE, long the standard academic life of Pitt, remains an entertaining and informative read though it has been superseded by Ehrman.

The Ehrman biography, in total 2172 pages of text, functions at two levels: as a detailed account of Pitt's life and times for the general reader and an unbiased research resource for the student or scholar. Readers may find Ehrman frustratingly inconclusive about many of Pitt's motives for the adoption of controversial policies, and this ambivalence is intentional on the author's part. Few scholars have challenged Ehrman's meticulous research though a few dissenting voices have been heard. BREIHAN's work on the Public Accounts Commissions of the 1780s has demonstrated that Pitt's commitment to economical reform – the quest for greater efficiency and accountability in Whitehall – was not strong on account of his conventional court Whig views respecting the maintenance of a state bureaucracy free from parliamentary scrutiny. HARLING has recently suggested that Pitt's entire reform career during his first decade in office was a public relations exercise intended to rehabilitate the image of aristocratic government in the eyes of a public demoralized by Britain's recent defeat at the hands of revolutionary America. Harling's work, though impressionistic, characterizes a current shift in research interest from Pitt's policies to his public image. BLACK's study of foreign policy during the 1780s, based upon extensive primary source research in British and foreign archives, finds Pitt a subordinate figure in the diplomacy of the decade, giving the credit instead for the pursuit of an active and aggressive foreign policy to his first foreign secretary, the Marquis of Carmarthen.

Volume 1 (1969) of EHRMAN dealt with Pitt's youth and establishment in office. Volume 2 (1983), which addresses the French Revolutionary wars, is much less satisfactory than volume 1, in part because the documentation for this period of Pitt's life is patchy. The academic profession is still digesting the contents of volume 3 (1996), which covers Pitt's life from the end of 1796 to his death. The strengths of volumes 2 and 3 lie in their detailed coverage of foreign and military policy. While Pitt's personal thoughts on these subjects can get lost in the details of the narrative, volume 2 remains an exhaustive account of British warfare and diplomacy during the 1790s. It is far less satisfactory on domestic and intellectual issues, particularly Pitt's thoughts on sedition, treason, and the French Revolution. The government response to popular radicalism during the 1790s has received much coverage from many angles, many hostile to Pitt, but a balanced account of his public order policies, both in terms of conception and law enforcement, can be found in EMSLEY. WELLS, despite a Marxist slant, provides the best account of Pitt's socio-economic policies during the later 1790s.

MORI's book was written to elucidate Pitt's little-known thoughts on war, radicalism, and the French Revolution. It also contributes to a long-running debate about the intellectual orientation of Pitt's political principles. While a liberal identity was suggested, both to contemporaries and historians, by the policies of the 1780s, Pitt's foreign and domestic policies during the following decade seemingly marked a change of heart identified by Holland Rose or revealed a latent conservatism endorsed by Ehrman. Pitt's 19th-century reputation as a founding father of the British Conservative Party has, moreover, led authors all too readily to identify him as some kind of Tory despite the fact that Pitt always called himself an "independent Whig".

Few people called themselves Tories, much less conservatives or liberals, at the end of the 18th century. Though many scholars have seen Pitt as the leader of a "new" Tory party based upon support for a strong crown and Church of England, his resignation over catholic emancipation in 1801 suggests that, whatever his followers thought, Pitt was no Tory. Many of Pitt's followers nevertheless, argues SACK, ignored Pitt's indifference to religion in life to construct a posthumous identity for him as a devout member, whatever his views on emancipation, of the established church. Pitt, as Sack demonstrates, was more useful in death than in life, for his memory could be appealed to by future "liberal" and "ultra" Tories to unite a British right bitterly divided over the emancipation issue. BARNES's claims that Pitt deferred to the wishes of George III from 1785 onwards have not stood the test of time. The king loathed the prospect of peace with revolutionary France but Pitt, as Ehrman notes, urged this on both the crown and his cabinet colleagues throughout the later 1790s. While Pitt was willing to encourage the cult of monarchy during the 1780s and 1790s, there is little evidence that he subscribed to it himself, and Edmund Burke, the supposed doyen of 19th-century British conservatism, was as Sack and Mori note, little admired either by Pitt or the vast majority of MPs during the 1790s or 1800s. DERRY has suggested in a speculative article that Pitt was a conservative independent Whig rather than a Tory and this remains a plausible explanation for a lifetime of policies whose contradictions remain otherwise difficult to explain.

JENNIFER MORI

See also American Colonies: Loss of; Burke; Catholic Emancipation; Fox, Charles James; French Revolutionary Wars; George III; George IV; Paine; Napoleonic Wars entries; North; Rockingham; Tories: 1714–1830; Whigs: c.1760 to c.1860; Wellington

Plagues and Famines: Effects on Demography

Appleby, Andrew B., *Famine in Tudor and Stuart England*, Liverpool: Liverpool University Press, and Stanford, California: Stanford University Press, 1978

Crawford, E. Margaret (editor), *Famine: The Irish Experience 900–1900, Subsistence Crises and Famines in Ireland*, Edinburgh: John Donald, 1989

Devine, T.M., *The Great Highland Famine: Hunger, Emigration, and the Scottish Highlands in the Nineteenth Century*, Edinburgh: John Donald, 1988

Finlay, Roger, *Population and the Metropolis: The Demography of London 1580–1650*, Cambridge and New York: Cambridge University Press, 1981

Gottfried, Robert S., *Epidemic Disease in Fifteenth Century England: The Medical Response and the Demographic Consequences*, New Brunswick, New Jersey: Rutgers University Press, and Leicester: Leicester University Press, 1978

Hatcher, John, "Plague, Population, and the English Economy, 1348–1530", The Economic History Society, 1977; in book form, *British Population History: From the Black Death to the Present Day*, edited by Michael Anderson, Cambridge and New York: Cambridge University Press, 1996

Jordan, William Chester, *The Great Famine: Northern Europe in the Early Fourteenth Century*, Princeton: Princeton University Press, 1996

Kershaw, Ian, "The Great Famine and Agrarian Crisis in England, 1315–1322", *Past and Present*, 59 (1973): 3–50; in book form, in *Peasants, Knights, and Heretics: Studies in Medieval English Social History*, edited by R.H. Hilton, Cambridge and New York: Cambridge University Press, 1976

Razi, Zvi, *Life, Marriage, and Death in a Medieval Parish: Economy, Society, and Demography in Halesowen, 1270–1400*, Cambridge and New York: Cambridge University Press, 1980

Slack, Paul, *The Impact of Plague in Tudor and Stuart England*, London and Boston: Routledge and Kegan Paul, 1985; reprinted with corrections, Oxford: Clarendon Press, and New York: Oxford University Press, 1990

Smith, Richard M., "Demographic Developments in Rural England, 1300–1348: A Survey" in *Before the Black Death: Studies in the "Crisis" of the Early Fourteenth Century*, edited by Bruce M.S. Campbell, Manchester: Manchester University Press, 1991

Walter, John and Roger Schofield (editors), *Famine, Disease, and the Social Order in Early Modern Society*, Cambridge and New York: Cambridge University Press, 1989

Wrigley, E.A. and R.S. Schofield, *The Population of England, 1541–1871: A Reconstruction*, London: Arnold for the Cambridge Group for the History of Population and Social Structure, and Cambridge, Massachusetts: Harvard University Press, 1981

Historical publications on the demographic effects of plague and famine tend to focus on specific eras and episodes. Medieval studies have largely relied on manorial documents to debate the extent of demographic expansion before the 14th century and the timing and extent of decline within that century. A combination of factors has also made the early-modern period especially attractive for study of particular events as well as developments over the course of the pre-modern era. However, recent studies of long-term demographic trends have also incorporated impacts of mortality crises. In addition, studies of famines in Ireland and Scotland can also provide useful contrasts to English studies regarding sources, methodology, and findings.

KERSHAW's classic examination of the impact of the Great Famine c.1315–22 fits within larger debate regarding medieval population trends and their significance. He sets his examination within the context of debate between historians led by M.M. Postan who identify the Great Famine with a 14th-century subsistence crisis, and those led by J.C. Russell who hold that famine and epidemic disease had no significant impact before the Black Death. Kershaw argues convincingly on the basis of manorial and other evidence that the Great Famine did have a significant economic and demographic impact on England. JORDAN sets the English experience within the context of northern European developments. Although his work is not limited to Britain or demographic impact in particular, it is the first full-length study of the Great Famine. Jordan's work relies extensively on secondary and chronicle sources to review debate over demographic and other consequences. This work reflects the widespread acceptance of the view that the Great Famine was a significant demographic catastrophe, whether interpreted as Malthusian check or as tragic fluke.

SMITH's essay is an excellent introduction to previous studies, sources of evidence, methodology, and theoretical debates concerning population trends and potential "Malthusian" checks in the pre-plague era. He judiciously reviews the work of Postan, Russell, Razi, Hatcher, and others. Smith concludes that although medieval sources offer greater challenges for systematic analysis than those used by early-modern demographers, there is a need to proceed with a combination of practices that have borne fruit in manorial case studies. RAZI's manorial case study is explicitly and extensively concerned with demographic patterns. Razi uses manorial court rolls to track population trends, particularly the demographic effects of the Black Death. However, his methodology, discussed in Smith's essay, is the subject of intense debate.

HATCHER presents an introduction to controversy over population patterns after the initial shock of the Black Death, particularly debate over the chronological and quantitative extent of population decline after c.1350, the impact of successive epidemics, and the onset of demographic recovery. Hatcher's thorough examination of direct (demographic) and indirect (economic) evidence leads him to conclude that mortality remained high and population low into the 16th century due to the impact of epidemic and infectious diseases. GOTTFRIED offers a more focused demographic study of epidemic disease in the 15th century. He sets his findings within the context of Malthusian (fertility-driven) and biological (mortality-driven) population models and between J.A. Saltmarsh's portrait of frequent and devastating plagues c.1348–1480 and J.M.W. Bean's assertions of the minimal effects of plague in the 15th century. Gottfried's testamentary evidence from East Anglia supports his argument that epidemic disease delayed population recovery until at least the 1470s.

Peter Laslett's query "Did the peasants really starve?" (in *The World We Have Lost*, 1965) inspired discussion on early modern as well as medieval mortality crises. APPLEBY's pioneering work on famine and its demographic impacts in north-western England details three local mortality crises c.1587–1623 and sets them within a national context. Appleby's groundbreaking and articulate study provides an affirmative answer to Laslett's question. FINLAY examines London in the first full-length study of the demography of an early modern metropolis. He uses London parish records to argue that "background" mortality in normal years was perhaps more significant than occasional epidemics, including plague itself. SLACK uses death records from two counties, three provincial towns, and London to investigate patterns of demographic impact by plague c.1485–1670. Slack's work offers an alternative approach to Appleby's and Finlay's in methodology and his emphasis is on the impact of plague and its disappearance. WALTER & SCHOFIELD's collection, dedicated to Andrew Appleby, showcases work in historical demography by members of the Cambridge Group for the History of Population and Social Structure and others. The collection includes essays by Slack, Keith Wrightson and David Levine, Wrigley, and others. An excellent introductory chapter by the editors on famine, disease, and crisis mortality in the early

modern era offers a thorough review of basic concepts, sources, and methodological issues.

No discussion of British demography would be complete without reference to WRIGLEY & SCHOFIELD's monumental work based on aggregative data from 404 parishes. Here demographic effects of plague and famine are placed within the context of short-term variations and long-term patterns of fertility, nuptiality, and mortality. An appendix masterfully identifies, charts, and discusses local mortality crises in terms of their distribution over time, causes, spread, and structure. Although the analysis of family reconstitution data from 26 parishes by Wrigley, Schofield, R.S. Davies, and J.E. Oeppen (*English Population History from Family Reconstituion 1580–1837*, 1997) provides refinement of findings, Wrigley & Schofield's earlier study remains one of the most significant historical works since the 1980s.

Studies of other parts of the British Isles have also been produced utilizing a variety of sources. The volume edited by CRAWFORD contains nine essays that explore the effects of famine and plague before 1500 based on literary rather than manorial data, new aspects of the Irish potato famine, and other crises. DEVINE examines the Highland famine c.1846–55 and its demographic consequences, including effects on birth, marriage, emigration, and migration patterns. The work is important for its discussion of 19th-century Scottish sources and examination of contrasts between Highland regions and between the Highland and Irish experiences.

LORI A. GATES

See also Farming entries; Great Irish Famine; Highland Clearances; Malthus

Plantagenet Kingdom

Barlow, Frank, *The Feudal Kingdom of England, 1042–1216*, London and New York: Longmans Green, 1954; 5th edition, London and New York: Longman, 1999

Carpenter, Christine, *The Wars of the Roses: Politics and the Constitution in England, c.1437–1509*, Cambridge and New York: Cambridge University Press, 1997

Harding, Alan, *England in the Thirteenth Century*, Cambridge and New York: Cambridge University Press, 1993

Holmes, George, *The Later Middle Ages, 1272–1485*, Edinburgh: Nelson, 1962; New York: Norton, 1966

Jacob, E.F., *The Fifteenth Century, 1399–1485*, vol. 6 of *Oxford History of England*, Oxford: Clarendon Press 1961; Oxford and New York: Oxford University Press, 1993

Lander, J.R., *Government and Community: England 1450–1509*, London: Arnold, and Cambridge, Massachusetts: Harvard University Press, 1980

McKisack, May, *The Fourteenth Century, 1307–1399*, vol. 5 of *Oxford History of England*, Oxford: Clarendon Press 1959

Poole, Austin Lane, *Oxford History of England*, vol. 3, *From Domesday Book to Magna Carta, 1087–1216*, Oxford: Clarendon Press, 1951; 2nd edition, 1955

Powicke, Frederick Maurice, *The Thirteenth Century, 1216–1307*, vol. 4 of *Oxford History of England*, Oxford: Clarendon Press, 1953; 2nd edition, 1962

Prestwich, Michael, *The Three Edwards: War and State in England, 1272–1377*, London: Weidenfeld and Nicolson, and New York: St Martin's Press, 1980

Warren, W. Lewis, *The Governance of Norman and Angevin England 1086–1272*, London: Arnold, and Stanford, California: Stanford University Press, 1987

The term Plantagenets refers to those monarchs who ruled England for 331 years, beginning with the reign of Henry II in 1154 and ending with the defeat and death of Richard III at the battle of Bosworth in 1485. The name derives from Geoffrey Plantagenet, Count of Anjou (hence the adjective "Angevin"), father of Henry II.

The *Oxford History of England* is an essential reference work, each volume providing a detailed narrative account of the period it covers. The reign of each monarch is encompassed along with topics such as society, towns, culture, and the church. England is put into its European context while Wales, Scotland, and Ireland are also given attention. Although not an easy read, the volumes by POOLE, POWICKE, McKISACK, and JACOB are useful for swiftly obtaining an overview of various aspects of this period, with the contents page of each helpfully listing each subject within a chapter.

BARLOW's volume provides an effective introduction to the reigns of the first Plantagenets. Explaining the ancestry of the first Plantagenet king, Henry II, his accession and establishment of authority is set against the background of not only his predecessor Stephen's problems, but those of his parents. His legal reforms, dispute with Thomas Becket, and problems with his family are dealt with while the social changes which took place in England at this time, along with the so-called "12th-century Renaissance", are also discussed. Richard I's arrangements for England during his absences are contemplated while the king's manoeuvrings abroad are not ignored. A measured look at John's reign notes the difficulties he faced on his accession along with his achievements. However, John's character does emerge as a crucial contributory factor towards the problems that occurred during his reign leading to the events of 1215, and the book draws to a close with John's death from dysentery in 1216. Robbed by his own household and abandoned, his was, in Barlow's words, "a squalid end to an ignoble life". A clear style of writing together with the inclusion of comprehensive genealogical trees, a list of recommended reading, and occasional anecdotes and quotes from contemporaries, such as the monk who could not cope with the strict discipline of his life, combine to make this an accessible read. WARREN's book provides an invaluable insight into the workings and development of Angevin government. In covering the first four Plantagenet monarchs, the significance of their reigns is clearly revealed, an appreciation of which is necessary for any scholar of this period. Although it is an often tortuous topic, the use of contemporary material combined with Warren's methodical approach and descriptive style of writing make this a surprisingly interesting, as well as an approachable work.

Chapter 1 of HARDING's volume is an example of historiography at its best and is helpful both to the academic and the reader coming to the subject for the first time. Succeeding chapters demonstrate how royal lordship was transformed during this period into "state power" and that this was facilitated by "the growth of the towns and of a class of professional administrators based within them". Elements of society, along with administrative changes both locally and nationally, are tracked throughout this period and chapters encompass peasants, knights, magnates, the manor and parish, towns and townsmen, with a particularly fascinating section on professional people. Chapter 7 looks at the politics of the period covering the reigns of John, Henry III, and Edward I, and a guide to further reading is included at the end of the book. Although not an easy read, and generally not the most suitable introduction for the absolute beginner because of an expectation of previous knowledge in this area, it is an important addition to the scholarship on the 13th century. HOLMES's work "takes the reader by the hand" to provide an overview of the period 1272–1485. In addition to topics including the organization of society, church, and government, individual monarchs and their period of rule are also looked at. Divided into two sections, 1272–1361 and 1361–1485, some events are briskly covered without a full discussion of the facts, perhaps inevitable considering that this is a general introduction to a period of 213 years. With a useful chronological table and comprehensive genealogical trees, PRESTWICH's book is an excellent introduction to, and reference for, the period 1272–1377. Well written, lively, and clearly explained, Prestwich has found the right balance by meeting the needs of both beginner and academic. Not only are the crucial events and developments of this period thoroughly addressed, but the book is made more fascinating by Prestwich's assessment of the characters of the first three Edwards. Thus the kings emerge from behind the conventional medieval images associated with them as three-dimensional human beings, as men rather than monarchs.

LANDER's volume provides a first-rate opening into the 15th century despite its start date of 1450. Part 1 gives a fluid, breezy account of aspects of government and society including education, the arts, economic and religious life, royal finance, and government. Part 2 deals with politics, comprising chapters on Richard of York and the reigns of Edward IV, Richard III, and Henry VII. Throughout the book Lander's pacy style is complemented by contemporary accounts, for instance, of Henry VI's pathetic procession on foot through London in 1471 with his sword of state borne before him by a peer who, in Lander's words, "had one foot in the grave", to an extract from one of Richard III's personal prayers possibly indicating that, towards the end, "he had become in the highest degree schizophrenic". Demolishing many of the myths and misconceptions surrounding the 15th century, Lander has produced an excellent piece of factual history which is also thoroughly readable.

Although not a general narrative of the period, CARPENTER's refreshing look at the Wars of the Roses is an essential addition to any study of the 15th century. Sources and historiography for the period, including the latest research, are discussed and the backdrop to events successfully recreated. An analysis of kingship as it had developed by the 15th century is conducted along with a re-evaluation of bastard feudalism (services provided to lords for fees rather than land), while the organization of local government and the role of the nobility and gentry are also considered. As a result, Carpenter believes that the magnates of the 15th century were not all ambitious opportunists simply taking advantage of an unfortunate situation and sees the much maligned royal councillor William de la Pole, Duke of Suffolk, more as a prisoner of events. Containing an annotated bibliography, this book is a well-written, clearly explained account of an often controversial episode in English history.

HAZEL PIERCE

See also Angevin Empire; Edward I; Edward II; Edward III; Edward IV; Henry II; Henry III; Henry IV; Henry V; Henry VI; Hundred Years' War; John; Matilda; Richard I; Richard II; Richard III

Poetry I: Old English

Aertsen, Henk and Rolf H. Bremmer, Jr (editors), *Companion to Old English Poetry*, Amsterdam: VU University Press, 1994

Bradley, S.A.J. (editor and translator), *Anglo-Saxon Poetry: An Anthology of Old English Poems in Prose Translation*, London: Dent, 1982

Calder, Daniel G. and Michael J.B. Allen (translators), *Sources and Analogues of Old English Poetry: The Major Latin Texts in Translation*, Cambridge: Brewer, and Totowa, New Jersey: Rowman and Littlefield, 1976

Krapp, George Philip and Elliott Van Kirk Dobbie (editors), *The Anglo-Saxon Poetic Records: A Collective Edition*, vols 1–6, New York: Columbia University Press, and London: Routledge and Kegan Paul, 1931–53

Liuzza, R.M. (editor and translator), *Beowulf: A New Verse Translation*, New York: Broadview Press, 2000

Nicholson, Lewis E. and Dolores Warwick Frese (editors), *Anglo-Saxon Poetry: Essays in Appreciation for John C. McGalliard*, Notre Dame, Indiana: University of Notre Dame Press, 1975

O'Brien O'Keeffe, Katherine, *Visible Song: Transitional Literacy in Old English Verse*, Cambridge and New York: Cambridge University Press, 1990

Owen-Crocker, Gale R., *The Four Funerals in Beowulf and the Structure of the Poem*, Manchester and New York: Manchester University Press, 2000

The Old English poetry that survives from the 7th to the 12th centuries runs to some 30,000 lines, which is 10 per cent of the entire literary corpus for the period. It is diverse and complex and encompasses many different genres, each bringing with it interpretative difficulties that have resulted in a large body of critical analysis.

A standard introduction to the body of poetry extant from the Anglo-Saxon period (all of which is edited in the six major, and still standard, volumes by KRAPP & DOBBIE) is BRADLEY's superb volume presenting the majority of Old English poems in translation. Although the translations are written as prose, they are exactingly accurate, often highly evocative, and Bradley arranges the material by manuscript, giving a good sense of the positioning of texts within their physical context. Each poem is preceded by an excellent introduction that succinctly appraises the themes and central subjects of the text. This is an indispensable volume which allows any reader easy access to the earliest sustained body of poetry in any vernacular.

NICHOLSON & FRESE's collection of essays on Old English poetry ranges widely through heroic verse, biblical verse, the elegies, hagiographic texts, and wisdom poems, each contribution providing detailed readings, and eloquent criticism. It is still one of the more coherent and important volumes published on poetic texts, and certain essays are of particular note, including David Chamberlain's contribution on "*Judith*: A Fragmentary and Political Poem", Thomas D. Hill's "The Fall of Angels and Man in the Old English *Genesis B*", and Alain Renoir's "A Reading Context for *The Wife's Lament*".

Another similarly comprehensive and valuable collection of essays analysing poetic texts is that edited by AERTSEN & BREMMER. Each of the contributions offers an original insight into its subject text(s), David F. Johnson, for example (in "Old English Religious Poetry: *Christ and Satan* and *The Dream of the Rood*"), demonstrating the originality of the eschatological allusions present in *The Dream of the Rood*. Mildred Budny offers an exemplary essay on "Old English Poetry in its Material Context", examining the manuscripts that contain poetic texts, and the manner in which they were produced.

Work on Old English poetry has encompassed many different scholarly approaches in recent decades. One of the major models for analysis has been that of source studies: evaluating the poetic texts in the light of possible and probable Latin or vernacular predecessors. Assisting considerably in this method is CALDER & ALLEN's volume that seeks to provide Latin analogues for Old English texts, explicating the cultural context of the specific work, and highlighting the means by which the vernacular poet adopted and adapted his or her source materials. Much of the corpus is included in this volume, from biblical and hagiographic poetry, to the Riddles, the Elegies, and *The Battle of Maldon*. Rather than insisting on the dependency of vernacular poets on works that preceded them, this volume illustrates most effectively how composition in this period was influenced and pervaded by all manner of texts: liturgical, scriptural, historical, and patristic.

A volume that also seeks to contextualize, but within a different framework, is O'BRIEN O'KEEFFE's. This important contribution to the growing debate concerning orality-literacy and manuscript studies has had a major impact on scholarship in the last decade. O'Brien O'Keeffe focuses on Caedmon's *Hymn*, *Solomon and Saturn I*, Alfred's *Metrical Preface* to the *Pastoral Care*, and the *Anglo-Saxon Chronicle* poems to describe the particular characteristics of evolving literacy in Anglo-Saxon England, and the ways in which levels of literacy can be tracked through manuscript layout and visual cues.

The most famous Old English poem, *Beowulf*, has always received the greater concentration of scholarship in Anglo-Saxon literary studies. In recent years, students and teachers alike have benefited from the numerous editions and translations of the text, each considerably different from the other. Of particular note here is LIUZZA's excellent contribution. Published hot on the heels of Seamus Heaney's *Beowulf* (1999), Liuzza's translation is the work of a scholar whose own poetic sensibilities are brought to bear in the sensitive reading of the text. In addition to a fine translation, Liuzza also includes a thorough and erudite introduction that illuminates the current status of *Beowulf* criticism; and then, helpfully, in a series of appendices, a substantial amount of relevant material (such as West Saxon royal genealogies, Old Norse and Old English homiletic analogues, and texts illustrating the Anglo-Saxons' concerns with pagan practices) is incorporated to permit a more informed understanding of the poem.

OWEN-CROCKER's volume is a model of clarity in the frenzy that is *Beowulf* criticism. She offers a holistic, multidisciplinary approach to the poem in which she utilizes archaeological and literary evidence to provide a revisionary reading of the text. The funerals give structure to and establish the tone of the poem; the fourth funeral, that referred to in "The Lament of the Last Survivor", assists in resolving the interlinking complexity of the whole. This reading leads to a conclusion that "The recognition that there are four funerals in the poem establishes four fixed points from which thematic patterns radiate", patterns that are fully investigated in the course of this important book.

ELAINE M. TREHARNE

Poetry II: Medieval Vernacular (English and Scots)

Bennett, J.A.W. and G.V. Smithers (editors), *Early Middle English Verse and Prose*, Oxford: Clarendon Press, 1966

Burrow, J.A., *A Reading of Sir Gawain and the Green Knight*, London: Routledge and Kegan Paul, 1965; New York: Barnes and Noble, 1966

Dinshaw, Carolyn, *Chaucer's Sexual Poetics*, Madison: University of Wisconsin Press, 1989

Gray, Douglas, *Robert Henryson*, Leiden: E.J. Brill, 1979

Patterson, Lee, *Chaucer and the Subject of History*, London: Routledge, and Madison: University of Wisconsin Press, 1991

Pearsall, Derek, *Old English and Middle English Poetry*, London and Boston: Routledge and Kegan Paul, 1977

Robertson, D.W., *A Preface to Chaucer: Studies in Medieval Perspectives*, Princeton, New Jersey: Princeton University Press, 1962

Woodward, Daniel and Martin Stevens (editors), *The Ellesmere Chaucer: Essays in Interpretation*, San Marino, California: Huntington Library, and Tokyo: Yushodo, 1995

After the Norman Conquest the development of vernacular poetry in England was heavily influenced by French genres (e.g. lyric, romance) and conventions such as rhyme that eventually predominated over the native alliteration; early poems such as *The Owl and the Nightingale* (*c.*1200) show the mixture of influences. In the 14th century the alliterative form was revived by regional poets such as Langland (*Piers Plowman*) and the anonymous writer of *Sir Gawain and the Green Knight* and *Pearl*, but continental influences dominate the works of the London-based Chaucer (principally *Troilus and Criseyde* and *The Canterbury Tales*). Fifteenth-century poets such as Lydgate in England, and Henryson in Scotland, sought to imitate Chaucer's mastery. Little vernacular poetry survives in Scotland prior to this point; the earliest datable work is Barbour's

patriotic poem *The Bruce* (1375). PEARSALL gives a comprehensive and very readable survey of the history of verse in the Middle English period, including its development from Old English; his discussion of 15th-century poetry, which is too often dismissed as derivative or dull, and his comments on Scots poetry, all too easily viewed as a mere adjunct to poetic activity south of the border, are particularly useful.

Much of the energy of late 19th- and early 20th-century scholars of Middle English was expended upon the recovery of texts so that the poems might simply be read. Such is the complexity of the manuscript tradition of many major medieval poems (*Piers Plowman* and *The Canterbury Tales* in particular), that textual criticism remains a key area of scholarly interest, as witnessed by the continuing editorial endeavours of the Early English Text Society and the Scottish Text Society, founded in 1864 and 1882 respectively. The study of Middle English poetry was also linked to the establishment of English as a university discipline, since it was believed that the reading of texts written in early forms of the language would add much needed rigour to the otherwise frivolous pastime of reading English literature. The view that Middle English poetry was primarily a vehicle for the study of the development of the English language persisted in the early part of the 20th century, and the residue of this approach may be seen in an anthology such as that of BENNETT & SMITHERS where the extracts are supported by commentaries whose focus is principally linguistic and where the introduction summarizes key developments in the history of Middle English language rather than literature.

As the 20th century progressed, the pendulum swung very much the other way as developments in modern literary criticism had an impact upon the study of medieval poetry. The influence of the so-called New Criticism, a movement that focused upon the text to the exclusion of all else, encouraged the reading of Middle English poetry as poetry, and approaches that privilege literature above language have held sway ever since. BURROW is an excellent example of a sustained attempt to extract meaning from the text by close reading. Indeed, since nothing whatsoever is known about the author of *Sir Gawain and the Green Knight* (not even his name), a focus on the text itself is well-nigh inescapable. Much medieval poetry has survived anonymously, and even in the case of known authors biographical details may be sparse. Despite this disadvantage, detailed critical evaluations of individual poets and their works have been achieved; one typical example is GRAY, who summarizes what is known of Henryson's life, analyses his poetry, and assesses his contribution to the development of Middle Scots as a literary language.

A different type of close reading lies at the heart of feminist criticism, an increasingly influential force in the study of medieval poetry during the final two decades of the 20th century. DINSHAW's book was one of the first full-length studies of medieval poetry to pay attention to matters of gender. Focusing on Chaucer's women characters, she underlines the masculine aspects of his work (what she terms "reading like a man"), developing an analogy between the text and the female body. Her book is not an easy read, but it offers perhaps the most thorough feminist reading of Chaucer's poetry.

The view that all medieval literature was designed to teach Christian doctrine, whether directly or through allegory, was deeply influential between the 1960s and 1980s. The foremost proponent of this school of exegetical criticism was ROBERT-SON. His insistence on the importance of medieval literary exegesis and focus on patristic-allegorical interpretation also served to foster the belief that there was no such thing as personal identity in the Middle Ages. In fact the relation of self to society is an important element in many medieval poems, and the notion that the idea of the individual only arose in the Renaissance is one that various critics since the 1980s, in particular Patterson, have sought to debunk.

By the early 1980s any approach which ignored context was increasingly felt to be inadequate. One response to this was the critical practice of New Historicism with which PATTERSON is also closely associated. Another strand of critical activity that has attempted to recover the historical context of Middle English poetry has focused on the manuscripts in which that poetry survives. These are no longer regarded as mere sources of textual reference, but instead are examined for the extra information that their physical composition, layout, and ordering of material may yield. A good example of the added insights about readership and textual production that can be gained by paying attention to manuscript evidence may be gleaned from the volume of essays produced by WOODWARD & STEVENS to accompany the publication of the facsimile of perhaps the most famous manuscript of Middle English poetry, the Ellesmere manuscript of Chaucer's *Canterbury Tales*.

Chaucer has been and continues to be the dominant figure in studies of medieval poetry, and many of the more recent critical and theoretical approaches have been developed most fully in relation to Chaucer's works, and are yet to be extended to other areas of Middle English and Middle Scots poetry.

MARGARET CONNOLLY

Poetry III: Renaissance to 1660

Bush, Douglas, *English Literature in the Earlier Seventeenth Century, 1600–1660*, Oxford: Clarendon Press, 1945; revised edition, 1962

Corns, Thomas N. (editor), *The Cambridge Companion to English Poetry: Donne to Marvell*, Cambridge: Cambridge University Press, 1993

Hester, M. Thomas (editor), *Seventeenth-Century British Nondramatic Poets*, series 1–3, Detroit: Gale Research, 1992–93

Kinney, Arthur F. (editor), *The Cambridge Companion to English Literature, 1500–1600*, Cambridge: Cambridge University Press, 2000

Lewis, C.S., *English Literature in the Sixteenth Century, Excluding Drama*, Oxford: Clarendon Press, 1954

Loewenstein, David and Janel Mueller (editors), *The Cambridge History of Early Modern English Literature*, Cambridge: Cambridge University Press, 2002

Malcolmson, Christina (editor), *Renaissance Poetry*, London and New York: Longman, 1998

Parfitt, George, *English Poetry of the Seventeenth Century*, London and New York: Longman, 1985; 2nd edition, 1992

Patrides, C.A. and Raymond B. Waddington (editors), *The Age of Milton: Backgrounds to Seventeenth-Century Literature*, Manchester: Manchester University Press, 1980

Richardson, David A. (editor), *Sixteenth-Century British Nondramatic Writers*, series 1–4, Detroit: Gale Research, 1993–96

Waller, Gary F., *English Poetry of the Sixteenth Century*, London and New York: Longman, 1986; 2nd edition, 1993

Ward, A.W. and A.R. Waller (editors), *The Cambridge History of English Literature*, vol. 4, *Prose and Poetry: Sir Thomas North to Michael Drayton*, Cambridge: Cambridge University Press, 1909

Woudhuysen, H.R. (editor), *The Penguin Book of Renaissance Verse: 1509–1659*, introduced by David Norbrook, London: Allen Lane/Penguin Press, 1992; revised edition, London and New York: Penguin, 1993

So many fine and diverse historical studies of English Renaissance (or "early modern") poetry have been produced in the last century, and particularly in the last several decades, that any brief guide to such scholarship is bound to ignore much valuable work. This is especially true because recent study of Renaissance literature in general has become increasingly, and quite self-consciously, historical in emphasis: a much higher proportion of scholarship is explicitly historical than would have been the case, say, even 30 years ago. Moreover, fundamental debates about the very nature of historical writing and about the possibilities of achieving historical "truth", along with wholesale transformations in the very practices and subjects of historical scholarship, have made the field an ever exciting but sometimes bewildering arena of contention and discovery. Many of these transformations are helpfully reviewed in the introduction to the important volume edited by LOEWENSTEIN & MUELLER. They, while acknowledging the real value of the earlier work of WARD & WALLER (and also of the venerable studies prepared for Oxford University Press by Douglas BUSH and C.S. LEWIS), also explain why they have chosen to do many things differently. In both content and format, the Loewenstein & Mueller volume best exemplifies the current state of the art, and its very full bibliography also makes it especially valuable. Similarly rich in coverage and in bibliographical depth is the volume edited by PATRIDES & WADDINGTON.

Meanwhile, the collection edited by WOUDHUYSEN shows how recent scholarly trends have affected the compilation of literary anthologies; the lengthy introduction to this volume relates many of these developments to numerous specific poetic texts.

Several principal trends in recent historical approaches to Renaissance verse seem worth noting. In the first place, most commentators now agree that the relations between early modern poetry and historical events are crucial, rich, and complex topics of study. Second, the range of historical topics now considered relevant to poetry is ever expanding. No longer are "historical approaches" to poetry mostly confined to histories of prominent persons or "key" ideas or obviously "significant" events. Now, almost any and every topic can be seen as bearing, in some way, on an understanding of the larger culture from which poetry emerged and to which it in turn contributed. In particular, there has been a huge upsurge of interest in topics or groups or persons once considered "marginal". Many of these trends are outlined in the extremely clear and judicious introduction to the volume edited by MALCOLMSON, which also offers a good selection of representative essays as well as detailed bibliographies. The new interest in previously under-studied groups has especially benefited women authors, but it has also led to increasing concern with such other groups as religious, ethnic, national, and sexual minorities. Meanwhile, "politics" – however broadly or narrowly that term is conceived – has become a central concern of many scholars, as has "theory" (especially of the feminist, Marxist, "new historicist", "poststructuralist", and "multicultural" varieties). Although some scholars have expressed unease over any attempt to make our understanding of the past reflect current notions of political or social correctness, some of the most heated debates of recent decades have, in fact, involved questions of whether historical scholarship can ever (or should ever) claim to be "objective" or "disinterested". Many of the changes that have taken place in the field in the last 30 years are reflected in the contrasts between PARFITT's more traditional, genre-based narrative and Gary WALLER's more self-consciously theoretical approach. The importance of recent interest in gender issues can also be seen in the changes made in the second editions of these two books: Parfitt added a chapter specifically devoted to women writers, whereas Waller added a chapter dealing not only with women's poetry but also with "gay voices". For all the reasons just mentioned, multi-author essay collections (such as those listed above), along with series of books that include the work of diverse writers (such as numerous volumes in the "Cambridge Companion" series), are likely to give readers the best sense of the range of recent debates. Claude J. Summers and Ted-Larry Pebworth, for instance, have co-edited a highly useful series of proceedings from the biennial Renaissance conferences at the University of Michigan-Dearborn, beginning in 1976. This series, like the field itself, has become increasingly historical in emphasis; figures and topics covered have included (in chronological order) Robert Herrick; George Herbert; Ben Jonson; John Donne; religious lyrics; poetry and politics; Andrew Marvell; discourses of desire; matters of wit; women writers; the Civil Wars; literary circles; and "faultlines in the field". The Summers and Pebworth volumes have the advantage of being unusually broad, both in their openness to different perspectives and in their coverage of "major" and "minor" authors. The volumes edited by KINNEY and by CORNS provide less specialized essays and are therefore likely to be of particular value to general readers or to students.

Similarly useful, and perhaps even more explicitly biographical and historical in emphasis, are a number of volumes in the "Dictionary of Literary Biography" series, which can be found in most academic (and many good public) libraries. RICHARDSON, for instance, has edited four large volumes devoted to *Sixteenth-Century British Nondramatic Writers*, and HESTER edited three equally impressive volumes focusing on *Seventeenth-Century British Nondramatic Poets*. The scope, detail, and format of these volumes, and the guidance they provide to both primary and secondary sources, make them essential sources of information, particularly to beginning students. Many other volumes in the DLB series, as well as other volumes published in additional series issued by the Gale Research group, are highly relevant to historical study of early modern poetry in English. Similarly useful are the individual volumes included in the venerable "Twayne's English Authors Series". Many of these volumes are now in second editions, and they are specifically designed to place their subjects in detailed

historical contexts and to offer broad, accessible coverage of the most important secondary scholarship. This series of books, like many others, has recently been moving more and more toward inclusion of "topic" volumes (rather than volumes simply devoted to individual canonical authors). All the volumes mentioned in this paragraph, along with the earlier volume edited by Ward & Waller, now have the added advantage of being easily accessible on-line.

ROBERT C. EVANS

Poetry IV: Restoration and 18th Century

Bate, Walter Jackson, *The Burden of the Past and the English Poet*, Cambridge, Massachusetts: Belknap Press of Harvard University Press, 1970; London: Chatto and Windus, 1971

Doody, Margaret Anne, *The Daring Muse: Augustan Poetry Reconsidered*, Cambridge and New York: Cambridge University Press, 1985

Rothstein, Eric, *Restoration and Eighteenth-Century Poetry 1660–1780*, London and Boston: Routledge and Kegan Paul, 1981

Terry, Richard, *Poetry and the Making of the English Literary Past 1660–1781*, Oxford: Oxford University Press, 2001

Trickett, Rachel, *The Honest Muse: A Study in Augustan Verse*, Oxford: Clarendon Press, 1967

Weinbrot, Howard D., *The Formal Strain: Studies in Augustan Imitation and Satire*, Chicago: University of Chicago Press, 1969

Weinbrot, Howard D., *Britannia's Issue: The Rise of British Literature from Dryden to Ossian*, Cambridge and New York: Cambridge University Press, 1993

The poetry of this period – especially that of the 18th century – suffered long and seriously from Matthew Arnold's condescending late 19th-century label for the period as an "age of prose and reason". Some of the power and complexity of the poetry has since been rediscovered, yet it is still too common to view it as characteristically decorous, polite, safe, and unsubtle. This is why several of the studies listed below stress opposite qualities, such as its verve, generic instability, and overall diversity. Newer labels for the period also need questioning: terms such as "neoclassical", "Augustan", "Augustan humanism", and "age of sensibility" have provided all-too-handy formulae with which to simplify a complex continuum.

TRICKETT's respected book is a study of "attitudes" in 18th- and some 17th-century poetry. She focuses on the "Augustan ideal of honesty" – honesty both in the sense of truth to fact, and in the sense of "integrity", hence applying both to the subjects of poetry and to the poet's stance. She has most to say on the satires of John Dryden, Jonathan Swift, John Oldham, the Earl of Rochester, Alexander Pope, and Samuel Johnson, and the book is most useful in conveying a sense of the broad development of some poetic genres over time. Johnson, who for Trickett "seems to epitomize the principles, the experience, and the genius of the Honest Muse", is the poet with whom she is most in tune.

WEINBROT's 1969 book explores the background and conventions of Augustan imitation and formal verse satire, thence developing readings of the most important later examples. More specifically, work in these genres by major 18th-century poets – Pope, Johnson, and Edward Young – is viewed in the context of earlier work by Abraham Cowley, Rochester, Oldham, and others. Though not an introductory book, it is still a standard treatment of several major 18th-century poems – Young's *Love of Fame*, Pope's *Imitations of Horace*, and Johnson's *London* and *The Vanity of Human Wishes*.

BATE's readable and provocative book has been very influential, but its thesis has been increasingly called into question in recent years. For Bate, the 18th century is crucial in making the transition from Renaissance to modern ways of writing poetry and thinking about poetry, in that this period shows in acute forms "the remorseless deepening of self-consciousness, before the rich and intimidating legacy of the past". Dryden, Pope, and others, Bate contends, felt themselves to be "latecomers", unable to compete with the achievement of the "Ancients" and of English classics such as Milton. One problem is that this thesis is based almost entirely on the discursive remarks of the writers discussed, together with those of contemporary aestheticians such as David Hume. There is much evidence in the poetry of the 18th century itself that, for major writers at least, knowledge of the literary past was not a burden but an inspiration.

ROTHSTEIN's study is well conceived if not eminently readable. Though a work of literary history, it aims to go beyond the mere "survey": Rothstein hopes to assist in dispelling old myths (as he sees them) about the period's poetry – the "fissure" between classicism and Romanticism, the "age of prose and reason". The book consists of four long chapters, on the use of the genres before and after 1720, on poetic style, and on the adaptations of classical, national, biblical, and Ossianic poetic traditions. Here he anticipates Weinbrot (1993, see below). Rothstein's reading of 18th-century poetry is conspicuously thoughtful and often persuasive, but probably requires to be approched *en bloc*, and by experienced students. A very extensive appendix consists of a useful listing of the major poems and poetry collections published over the whole period.

DOODY's book is an overtly revisionist account of English poetry from the Civil War to George Crabbe. Its emphasis is on "the excitement of the works, and on their strangeness"; the image of "dull correctness" for the period is exploded. This is an enjoyable and provocative survey, not least provocative in its questioning of the assumptions often implied in the use of the term "Augustan" for the period. For Doody, 18th-century poetry is most notable for such features as its innovative mingling of genres, modes, and styles, and its self-consciousness. Her strengths as a critic lie in catholicity of taste, an engaging enthusiasm, and an ability to say interesting things about individual works without wishing to have the last word on them. The volume also includes a batch of well-chosen illustrations from early printings of the poetry, useful for acquiring a sense of the way it was presented and read.

WEINBROT's 1993 volume is a bulky and demanding study of the creation of a British literary consciousness through a complex set of negotiations with classical norms, especially in poetry. It has polemical aims: Weinbrot questions the usefulness of concepts such as Augustanism, neoclassicism, and Harold Bloom's "anxiety of influence". He delves into several of the less well-charted waters of the period's verse, such as responses to Hebrew literature (especially in Christopher Smart), Scottish writing, and the phenomenon of Ossian, the Gaelic bard "translated" by James Macpherson. But he also surveys the development of better-known territory, such as the ode and Homeric imitation. Weinbrot shows the emergent canon of British poetry mixing native and foreign elements, and the 18th century appropriating the power and prestige of the traditional literary models in the service of a modern commercial empire.

TERRY engages with current concerns about the historical development of the English poetic canon in suggestive new ways. His study of how the literary past was understood in the years 1660–1780, and of how antiquarians, scholars, and critics unearthed, invented, and mythologized it, begins by examining the shifting limits of the concept of poetry itself, as well as of "literature" and "criticism", in the period. Later chapters include discussions of the status of pre-Chaucerian poetry, Samuel Johnson's *Lives of the Poets*, women poets, and classical *vs* Gothic models. The opening-up and ordering of the English literary past, Terry argues, occurs before 1750, earlier than has previously been assumed.

STUART GILLESPIE

Poetry V: Romantic Era

Abrams, M.H., *The Mirror and the Lamp: Romantic Theory and the Critical Tradition*, New York: Oxford University Press, 1953

Abrams, M.H. (editor), *English Romantic Poets: Modern Essays in Criticism*, New York and London: Oxford University Press, 1960

Bloom, Harold, *The Visionary Company: A Reading of English Romantic Poetry*, New York: Doubleday, 1961; London: Faber, 1962; revised and enlarged edition, Ithaca, New York: Cornell University Press, 1971

Bowra, C.M., *The Romantic Imagination*, Cambridge, Massachusetts: Harvard University Press, 1949; London: Oxford University Press, 1950

Frye, Northrop, *A Study of English Romanticism*, New York: Random House, 1968; reprinted, Brighton, Sussex: Harvester Press, 1983

Furst, Lilian R., *Romanticism*, London: Methuen, and New York: Barnes and Noble, 1969; 2nd edition, London: Methuen, 1976

Gaull, Marilyn, *English Romanticism: The Human Context*, New York: Norton, 1988

Mellor, Anne K. (editor), *Romanticism and Feminism*, Bloomington: Indiana University Press, 1988

Watson, J.R., *English Poetry of the Romantic Period, 1789–1830*, London and New York: Longman, 1985; 2nd edition, 1992

The critical discussion of Romantic poetry depends, as far as the scope of individual research is concerned, largely on whether the term is understood as an historical period or a particular mode of literary expression; both categories create difficulties. On the one hand, the Romantic era also saw the publication of non-

Romantic poetry; on the other hand, the philosophical, formal, and thematic characteristics of Romantic poetry remain under debate. Some of the major concepts of Romantic poetry are: a turn towards individual perception, an imagination based on the author's self, and an increased interest in the supposedly "true" reality of nature.

The importance of the imagination as understood by Romantic poets is the central focus of BOWRA. Contrasting the new idea of the author as creator of an imaginative product with the predominantly mechanistic 18th-century world-view in the tradition of Locke and Newton – which allocated only a minor role to sense-perception – Bowra outlines the epistemological and poetological concepts of both the theoretical and the poetic works of William Blake, Samuel Taylor Coleridge, and Percy Bysshe Shelley. Their belief in the existence of free will is shown to contrast sharply with the stern rationalism of their age. The study then analyses individual texts concentrating on the theme of the imagination. The final chapters explore the influence of Romantic poetry in the works of Christina and Dante Gabriel Rossetti, and in Swinburne's poetry. In the final chapter Bowra outlines the inherent limitations and the lasting contributions of Romantic poetry.

The status of the term Romanticism in criticism is the topic of a seminal essay by A.O. Lovejoy, included in the 1960 collection edited by ABRAMS. One of three general, introductory pieces, Lovejoy's analysis sets out by tracing the numerous historical and philosophical roots of the term, as well as the wealth of differing meanings associated with it, only to reach a by now famous conclusion: "The word 'romantic' has come to mean so many things that, by itself, it means nothing." While the author immediately rejects the option of completely avoiding the term, he instead proposes the usage of the plural of Romanticism. Exemplary realizations of such "Romanticisms" in all their contradictory elements are supplied by the remaining contributions in Abrams's authoritative volume. ABRAMS's *The Mirror and the Lamp* also remains an excellent interpretation of theoretical aspects of Romantic poetry.

Written within the framework of one theoretical approach, BLOOM reads Romantic poetry from a position he later outlined in *The Anxiety of Influence: A Theory of Poetry* (1973). His earlier voluminous text on Romantic poetry delineates the various literary influences of the poems under discussion, offering convincing interpretations of the Romantic canon. In addition to analyses of the six great poets (Blake, Coleridge, William Wordsworth, Shelley, John Keats, and Lord Byron), Bloom also offers a brief chapter on those lesser known and epigonic authors who bridged the gap between Romantic and Victorian poetry. However, none of these poets appears to deserve, in Bloom's opinion, more prolonged attention.

A different reading of the Romantic movement and its poetic mythology is offered by FRYE. Proceeding from his approach of archetypal criticism, Frye focuses on Thomas Lovell Beddoe, Shelley, and Keats, outlining the archetypal images present in their works. Frye insists on treating Romanticism as a purely literary phenomenon separated from social or historical actualities, seeing as its starting-point a myth based on man's relationship with nature, which is centred around a sense of loss. Frye sets Romantic experience apart from reality as studied by science, and thus further supports the importance accorded the poet's imagination and artistic insight. A critical reader might occasionally have misgivings about Frye's rather lax use of citations.

GAULL offers in many respects a view that complements the strictly literary focus in both Frye and Bloom. Maintaining Romantic poetry as her central theme, Gaull offers the "historical, social, cultural, political, economic, intellectual, philosophical, artistic, and scientific background" to the field. The obviously very broad approach is convincingly realized. This appraisal is particularly true for the discussion of the literary marketplace, and for the section of the book entitled "The Illusion of History". Both parts provide comprehensive overviews of the subject matter in question. However, Gaull's encyclopedic scope brings with it an inescapable brevity in the treatment of individual themes.

A major aspect of Romantic poetry neglected in many other works is discussed by MELLOR. Her volume sets out to investigate the often neglected role of women in Romantic poetry. Mostly written within the tradition of Anglo-American feminist criticism (though in parts also influenced by French feminist theory), the individual contributions all subscribe to the notion that the female voice has been silenced by the canonical poets of the era, as well as by the academic discourse at large. The articles in Mellor, in turn, claim recognition for women writers' tremendous contribution to the period. Some essays deal with the roles women played in the lives of particular authors (Wordsworth and Byron); others look at the positioning of femininity within the poetic works of the predominantly male authors of the time.

A more traditional introduction to Romanticism as a general phenomenon is the slim volume by FURST. This book offers a very general but nevertheless perceptive discussion of basic terminology in the field, as well as its major critical and aesthetic concepts. Similar to Furst, though both more narrowly focused on Romantic poetry and more comprehensive in scope, is WATSON. Published as a volume within the Longman "Literature in English" series, Watson's book arguably presents one of the most valuable single-volume studies on Romantic poetry. Chapters on the poet and his or her imaginative framework, on the philosophical background to Romanticism in European philosophy and history, on the central themes of nature, dreams, and the human condition, and finally on the six major authors of the period, combine to make Watson an excellent point of reference for a preliminary, yet extensive orientation. A chapter on minor poets rounds off the volume, followed by a chronology, an annotated bibliography, and by biographical sketches of individual authors, which list further critical sources.

GERD BAYER

Poetry VI: Victorian and Edwardian

Armstrong, Isobel, *Victorian Poetry: Poetry, Poetics, and Politics*, London and New York: Routledge, 1993
Campbell, Matthew, *Rhythm and Will in Victorian Poetry*, Cambridge and New York: Cambridge University Press, 1999
Christ, Carol T., *Victorian and Modern Poetics*, Chicago: University of Chicago Press, 1984

Leighton, Angela, *Victorian Women Poets: Writing Against the Heart*, London and New York: Harvester Wheatsheaf, 1992

Richards, Bernard, *English Poetry of the Victorian Period: 1830–1890*, London and New York: Longman, 1988

Rose, Jonathan, *The Edwardian Temperament: 1895–1919*, Athens: Ohio University Press, 1986

Shaw, W. David, *The Lucid Veil: Poetic Truth in the Victorian Age*, London: Athlone Press, and Madison: University of Wisconsin Press, 1987

Major publications on Victorian and Edwardian poetry reflect a diversity of approaches to literary analysis and literary history. RICHARDS's comprehensive study of the formal, generic and thematic features of Victorian poetry provides readers with a useful introduction to this area of study. In 15 focused chapters, Richards examines the work of major authors and provides readers with a general history of Victorian poetry. Attention is paid throughout to historical context and to related tensions characterizing this body of work, tensions which Richards outlines in terms of "escapism and realism, frivolity and utility, activity and lethargy, religiosity and secularity, solidarity and alienation, elitism and populism". Of particular note are Richards's arguments concerning the influence of utilitarian thought on poetry produced in this period. The volume also contains helpful and instructive appendices. These include a detailed biographical and bibliographical discussion of poets and a chronology which pairs the publication of poetic works with major historical and cultural developments.

In a study aimed at more advanced readers, SHAW explores connections between Victorian poetry and changing conceptions of both language and knowledge. In this sophisticated and provocative book, he discusses and outlines the predominant poetic theories of the period and links developments in science, theology, and philosophy to developments in poetry. Taking his title from Alfred Tennyson's *In Memoriam*, Shaw evokes the metaphor of a lucid veil to point to the limited transparency of representation and to emphasize the importance of representational and expressive theories of language and knowledge. In three sections focusing on the relation of poetry to science, to agnosticism, and to prophecy, Shaw examines Victorian conceptions of knowledge and discusses 19th-century attitudes towards the mimetic and representational capabilities of poetry. The resulting study relies heavily on the analysis of prose writings by influential figures. Indeed, as Shaw himself notes in his preface, this book is not focused on poetic examples, but seeks instead to develop a framework for analysis.

CAMPBELL's study takes as its focus the prosodic handling of questions of human agency in the work of four 19th-century poets: Tennyson, Browning, Hopkins, and Hardy. The book is shaped by an interest in "poetic form and its relation to the concern that the poets considered here show with decision, action and event". Drawing evidence from a generically diverse selection of poems, among them elegies, dramatic monologues, and lyrics, Campbell argues for the interconnectedness of poetics and ethics. In the process, he undertakes a detailed consideration of prosody, offering readers thorough and perceptive discussions of rhythm and metre. Indeed, it is Campbell's call for a reconsideration of prosody that marks this book as a significant contribution to recent scholarship on Victorian poetry and poetics.

ARMSTRONG's critical history of Victorian poetry identifies two major traditions: "one exploring various strategies for democratic, radical writing, the other developing, in different forms, a conservative poetry". In chronologically arranged sections, Armstrong maps the relation of Victorian poetry to philosophical and historical developments, among them Benthamism and revolution in Europe. Stressing the importance of Victorian conceptions of modernity and of culture, Armstrong distinguishes between "aestheticized politics" and "politicized aesthetics", terms she applies to the poetry of Browning and Tennyson respectively. Armstrong also makes interesting links between politics and the grotesque, most notably in relation to Browning's later poetry. Also of note are her readings of the poetics and politics of Swinburne, Hopkins, Meredith, and Thompson.

Like Armstrong, LEIGHTON also addresses poetry from a political perspective. She, however, takes as her subject the work of Victorian women poets, a group of writers who have received significant critical attention in the last two decades. Influenced by a commitment to the rediscovery and rereading of non-canonical texts, Leighton looks at the writings of both major and minor women poets. Throughout she argues for a self-conscious female tradition and characterizes women's poetry of this period as a "distinct genre". Her more narrow focus lies with women's sensibility. She contends that Victorian women's poetry "grows out of struggle with and against a highly moralized celebration of women's sensibility". Pairing biographical material with textual readings, she also investigates the professionalization of poetry and the sexual politics of literary production and reception. Close attention is paid to the imaginative impact of Sappho and Corinne, two figures Leighton identifies as active models for female creativity in this period.

CHRIST's compact and thought-provoking book focuses on connections between Victorian and modernist poetry. Responding to what she perceives as a failure fully to acknowledge the influence of the Victorians on the moderns, Christ rewrites literary history with a new emphasis on continuities existing between the work of two Victorians, Tennyson and Browning, and three modernists, Yeats, Eliot, and Pound. Emphasis is placed on their shared interest in the dramatic monologue and their common rejection of romantic conceptions of the poet's subjectivity. While acknowledging the anti-Victorianism of many modernists, Christ manages to identify and analyse traditionally overlooked continuities between these two eras of poetry. In the process, she provides readers with an insightful and thorough discussion of both traditions.

ROSE's is one of relatively few books devoted to the study of Edwardian culture. As Rose himself notes in his introduction: "Intellectual historians do not know quite what to make of Edwardian Britain. They generalize easily about 'Victorianism' and 'modernism,' but it has proved far more difficult to define a peculiarly 'Edwardian turn of mind'". Rose attempts to uncover the character and history of Edwardian literature. He achieves this, in large part, by reading the literature produced in this period in relation to contemporary economic, political, and cultural developments. Characterizing the period as one of social and cultural revolution, Rose discusses the legacy left by Victorian thinkers and writers and maps changes in the understanding of, and societal attitudes towards, religion, sexuality, childhood, and community. Rose also includes a census of books published in Britain between 1870 and 1924.

VANESSA WARNE

Poetry VII: Since 1914

Acheson, James and Romana Huk (editors), Contemporary British Poetry: Essays in Theory and Criticism, Albany, New York: State University of New York Press, 1996

Howe, Irving (editor), *The Idea of the Modern in Literature and the Arts*, New York: Horizon, 1967

Jones, Peter and Michael Schmidt (editors), *British Poetry since 1970: A Critical Survey*, New York: Persea, and Manchester: Carcanet Press, 1980

Kenner, Hugh, *The Pound Era*, Berkeley: University of California Press, 1971; London: Faber, 1972

Kenner, Hugh, *A Sinking Island: The Modern English Writers*, New York: Knopf, and London: Barrie and Jenkins, 1988

Martin, Bruce K., *British Poetry since 1939*, Boston: Twayne, 1985

Rosenthal, M.L. and Sally M. Gall, *The Modern Poetic Sequence: The Genius of Modern Poetry*, New York and Oxford: Oxford University Press, 1983

Spender, Stephen, *The Struggle of the Modern*, Berkeley: University of California Press, and London: Hamish Hamilton, 1963

"Make it new" was the modernist battle cry, and ever since the early years of the century, poets and critics have, in World War I's aftermath, fought over the ruins of the Tradition. The primary works of the century extol the new or ignore it; they claim a new generation supplants it, or has created the new anew. Many critics agree that the early 20th-century "movement" was, in the main, discontinuous with the past, but others have viewed it as a continuation of the tradition.

For SPENDER, the modernists, unlike their successors today, treated the world as a unity. They almost wholly rejected the past, although he finds "connections with the nostalgic aestheticism of the end of the nineteenth century". Arguing for a balance between old and new, he claims "Language . . . is neither new nor completely traditional. It is always evolving and accumulative".

In *The Pound Era*, KENNER suggests that Ezra Pound, an American, was the centre of the vortex that was international modernism, in which two British writers (Irish James Joyce and American-turned-Briton T.S. Eliot) played important roles. It was Pound the modernist for whom the modern world could not exist, since "nothing exists which does not understand its past or future". An American expatriate could be the most important figure in Anglo-American poetry only perhaps through the first several decades of the century, until the British championed their native voices again. The anxiety over Pound's and Eliot's influence, however, has lasted.

Aware that those who don't study the past are condemned to repeat it, ROSENTHAL & GALL place emphasis squarely on William Butler Yeats as well as Pound as co-founders of modernist poetry. Yeats's final poetic sequence of physical and spiritual renewal, Pound's *Cantos*, and Ted Hughes's *Crow* continue a tradition of poetic sequences stretching back through Tennyson to Shakespeare, each sequence being composed of poems and fragments conceived under the same psychological pressure.

To assert that nihilism is the centre of modernist literature, HOWE assembles many of the seminal documents of the century from European and Anglo-American sources. The modern's wish for nothingness struggles against its passion for psychic renewal and ends, with the lone exception of Samuel Beckett, in self-parody.

MARTIN focuses not on the modernists but on those who wrote a socially concerned, political poetry before the mid-century. This thoroughly British group centred on Auden and its own dilemma, which for all British poets since that period has been to decide between a personal poetry such as Yeats often indulged in and writing on the public level as Seamus Heaney fully achieves in *The Bog People*. Martin ignores modernism as the dominant movement of the century, although he stresses one of its elements, internationalism, as playing a vital role in the Spender–Auden line as well as in the contemporary Charles Tomlinson, Ted Hughes, Thom Gunn, and others.

Few critics still wish entirely to ignore the international, particularly the Anglo-American quality of 20th-century verse, but those who do study the English movement in isolation from the American and even from the Irish include KENNER. Continuing as chief advocate for modernism into the 1980s, in *A Sinking Island* he deprecates the current fashion with unique insight. Although there is no longer an English literature, for each poet has a separate following, there is no dearth of talent. Youth reads as a penance, dismissing the canon as "nothing but a list of Great Names".

Looking at British poetry after 1970, JONES & SCHMIDT identify nostalgia for and rejection of past dominating illusions with a new inner-directed poetry, as modernists are relegated to the shadows. Narratives strongly based in history once again have their day, and the independent lyric poem is shunned. The demands of the university and the market now determine the course of poetry in Britain and America, which have separated again into distinct traditions after some decades of a joint modernist thrust. As these poets of disillusion have begun to make money as performers (after the discovery of the public poetry reading to great acclaim in the 1960s), and through foundations and Arts Council grants, they are no longer in opposition to society; they have become its servants.

Contrariwise, ACHESON & HUK find many divergent streams branching out from the well of British poetry since World War II. A central thrust and the desire for seeing the most important voices as one movement (as in the 1960s and 1970s) is no longer desirable. The postmodern "rules", meaning that writers exhibit post-feminist, post-patriarchal, and post-colonial rejections of tradition, including the tradition of modernism. Breakdown of any received order (conformity) is again the catchword, as at the inception of modernism when Wyndham Lewis's *Blast* appeared on the scene to shock the enfranchised. New directives and directions are celebrated, and excitement is praised and exclusiveness condemned.

At the same time that the editors express concern for marginalization of new poets, they themselves, in an unintentional parody of recent American "politically correct" scholarship, establish categories as rigid as any known in the past. They relegate black poets to a group identity based on their skin colour, and they weed out women from the general culture of poets considered as a whole of imagination's disciples, so that the women are forced into a pre-fab room of their own.

Acheson & Huk champion this new anarchy with its new rigid categories, naming it diversity. Although attempts are made in the essays herein collected to detect modernist roots, such attempts fail from the vagueness and indecisiveness of new critical theories. This book is under the American spell (even to the extent of championing the now-defunct L=A=N=G=U=A=G=E movement), the least desirable internationalist trend.

Pleading lack of space, the editors, irresponsibly given their title, omit all Irish contemporary poets, the best of whom, Seamus Heaney, is very likely the best poet in English today.

CARL JAY BUCHANAN

Poitiers, Battle of
see Edward III; Hundred Years' War

Police
see Law Enforcement entries; Metropolitan Police

Politeness and Gentility

Andrew, Donna, "The Code of Honour and Its Critics: The Opposition to Duelling in England, 1700–1850", *Social History*, 5 (1980): 409–34

Barker, Hannah and Elaine Chalus (editors), *Gender in Eighteenth-Century England: Roles, Representations, and Responsibilities*, London and New York: Addison Wesley Longman, 1997

Barker-Benfield, G.J., *The Culture of Sensibility: Sex and Society in Eighteenth-Century Britain*, Chicago: University of Chicago Press, 1992

Brewer, John, "This, That, and the Other: Public, Social, and Private in the Seventeenth and Eighteenth Centuries" in *Shifting the Boundaries: Transformation of the Languages of Public and Private in the Eighteenth Century*, edited by Dario Castiglione and Lesley Sharpe, Exeter, Devon: Exeter University Press, 1995

Brewer, John, *The Pleasures of the Imagination: English Culture in the Eighteenth Century*, London: HarperCollins, and New York: Farrar Straus Giroux, 1997

Bryson, Anna, *From Courtesy to Civility: Changing Codes of Conduct in Early Modern England*, Oxford: Clarendon Press, 1998

Carré, Jacques (editor), *The Crisis of Courtesy: Studies in the Conduct-Book in Britain, 1600–1900*, Leiden and New York: E.J. Brill, 1994

Colley, Linda, "Womanpower" and "Manpower" in her *Britons: Forging the Nation, 1707–1837*, New Haven, Connecticut: Yale University Press, 1992

Davidoff, Leonore and Catherine Hall, *Family Fortunes: Men and Women of the English Middle Class, 1780–1850*, Chicago: University of Chicago Press, and London: Hutchinson, 1987

Dwyer, John, *Virtuous Discourse: Sensibility and Community in Late Eighteenth-Century Scotland*, Edinburgh: John Donald, 1987

Elias, Norbert, *The Civilizing Process*, translated by Edmund Jephcott, 2 vols, Oxford: Blackwell, and New York: Urizen, 1978–82; revised edition, Oxford and Cambridge, Massachusetts: Blackwell, 2000 (German edition, 1939)

Goldsmith, M.M., *Private Vices, Public Benefits: Bernard Mandeville's Social and Political Thought*, Cambridge and New York: Cambridge University Press, 1985

Habermas, Jürgen, *The Structural Transformation of the Public Sphere: An Inquiry into a Category of Bourgeois Society*, translated by Thomas Burger with the assistance of Frederick Lawrence, Cambridge, Massachusetts: MIT Press, and Cambridge: Polity Press, 1989 (German edition, 1962)

Herrup, Cynthia, Felicity Heal, Nigel Llewellyn, Faramerz Dabhoiwalla, Elizabeth Foyster, and Laura Gowing, symposium on "Honour and Reputation in Early Modern England", *Transactions of the Royal Historical Society*, 6/6 (1996): 137–248

Hitchcock, Tim and Michele Cohen (editors), *English Masculinities, 1660–1800*, London and New York: Longman, 1999

Hundert, E.J., *The Enlightenment's Fable: Bernard Mandeville and the Discovery of Society*, Cambridge and New York: Cambridge University Press, 1994

James, Mervyn, "English Politics and the Concept of Honour, 1485–1642" in his *Society, Politics, and Culture: Studies in Early Modern England*, Cambridge and New York: Cambridge University Press, 1986

Klein, Lawrence, "Property and Politeness in the Early Eighteenth Century Moralists: The Case of *The Spectator*" in *Early Modern Conceptions of Property*, edited by John Brewer and Susan Staves, London and New York: Routledge, 1995

Klein, Lawrence E., *Shaftesbury and the Culture of Politeness: Moral Discourse and Cultural Politics in Early Eighteenth-Century England*, Cambridge and New York: Cambridge University Press, 1994

Klein, Lawrence, "Politeness for Plebes: Consumption and Social Identity in Early 18th-Century England" in *The Consumption of Culture, 1600–1800: Image, Object, Text*, edited by Ann Bermingham and John Brewer, London and New York: Routledge, 1995

Langford, Paul, *"A Polite and Commercial People": England, 1727–1783*, Oxford and New York: Oxford University Press, 1989

Langford, Paul, *Englishness Identified: Manners and Character, 1650–1850*, illustrated by Martin Rowson, Oxford and New York: Oxford University Press, 2000

Mason, John E., *Gentlefolk in the Making: Studies in the History of English Courtesy Literature and Related Topics from 1531 to 1774*, Philadelphia: University of Pennsylvania Press, 1935

Mullan, John, *Sentiment and Sociability: The Language of Feeling in the Eighteenth Century*, Oxford: Clarendon Press, and New York: Oxford University Press, 1988

Vickery, Amanda, *The Gentleman's Daughter: Women's Lives in Georgian England*, New Haven, Connecticut and London: Yale University Press, 1998

Wahrman, Dror, *Imagining the Middle Class: The Political Representation of Class in Britain, c.1780–1840*, Cambridge and New York: Cambridge University Press, 1995

Wahrman, Dror, "Percy's Prologue: From Gender Play to Gender Panic in Eighteenth-Century England", *Past and Present*, 159 (1998): 113–59

The best places to begin are with the balanced account in LANG-FORD (1989) of the integral relationship between the social, cultural, and political history of the 18th century and with the panorama in BREWER (1997) of English politeness as national self-imagining. While 18th-century summary is thus well served, its predecessor is less well supplied, though Langford's newest work (2000) now looks in both directions to cover the entire period between 1650 and 1850.

In itself, the history of manners has a long pedigree. MASON's survey of courtesy literature (see now also CARRÉ) dates originally from the second quarter of the 20th century; ELIAS on the relationship between manners, court society, and the absolutist state dates from 1939. Yet these had to wait some 40 years before their full import began to be recognized, particularly for the task of actually pinning down the perennially rising "middle class". Even then, the features of this most nebulous of all historical phenomena, especially the close inter-twining of commerce, consumption, and gender in its cultural forms, have continued to be partially masked by anachronistic backward extrapolation from a period which did describe itself in the languages of class to one in which such entities had yet to be imagined, let alone named as such in social description. The clearest example is the long-reigning paradigm of "class struggle without class", which reduces post-Restoration and Hanoverian cultural history to the dialectic interplay of a patrician proto-capitalist elite and proto-proletarian plebs. This saves the appearances by the *nonsequitur* of denying the middling orders any cultural expression beyond the servile aping of their hierarchical superiors, even though it was they who for the most part drove the process as a whole. Similar extrapolation from the seeming institutionalization of proto-Victorian gender division in English middle-class culture between 1780 and 1850 (DAVIDOFF & HALL) generated an almost equally misleading and long-lasting paradigm of "separate spheres" for the whole of the preceding century. This was reinforced by the initial English-language reception of HABERMAS on the evolution from the late 17th century onwards of a presumptively masculine "bourgeois public sphere" of open discussion, intermediate between the authority of the absolutist state and the privacy of the family.

In effect the complement of Elias, Habermas's concept has been the other major influence on current writing, but its initial implications have been extensively revised. The more recent work of WAHRMAN on the pre-Victorian middle class delays the institutionalization of its gender divisions until the 1830s. As for the 18th century, BREWER's examination (1995) of

usage and VICKERY's outstanding example of what happens to preconceived categories when close attention is paid to real people both show that while the age may have known two "spheres", they were not "separate". On the contrary, they overlapped and were intimately connected: to the extent that an 18th-century "public sphere" without the active participation of women in some of its most characteristic manifestations could hardly have existed, let alone functioned. The overriding feature of this revision has in fact been the recognition that while social relationships in the age of the American and French revolutions certainly moved towards a clearer demarcation of roles, which has been likened by some to "gender panic", this did not of itself produce female domestic segregation. The lesson of COLLEY is quite the opposite.

Reinterpretation of the "long century" stretching from the Restoration to the 1820s also means that Hanoverian and Georgian England is no longer seen as simply "leading to" a meeting with "Victorian values" in the "Age of Reform". This has moved the focus back to the late Stuart and early Hanoverian decades. Here, the task is to recover the ways in which the codes of a hieratic and corporate yet also potentially anarchic post-feudal culture of honour and reputation formally overseen by monarchy, church, and court were changed into 18th-century conventions of urban politeness: in which they had to be domesticated and privately remoralized because whatever public rhetoric might proclaim, political stability now depended in reality on commerce, credit, and the orderly behaviour of individuals in pursuit of their passions and their interests. On the former state, the key works are JAMES, the volume of *Transactions of the Royal Historical Society* (HERRUP et al.), and now BRYSON. The central features of the transformation, which reflected the fundamental philosophical changes associated with Hobbes and Locke, are the reciprocal connection made by the third Earl of Shaftesbury between politeness and liberty and therefore the revaluing of religion, which are discussed by KLEIN; and *per contra*, the controversy surrounding Bernard Mandeville's disconcerting *Fable of the Bees* and its eventual assimilation, which is the subject of GOLD-SMITH and HUNDERT. Of two other works which consider the literary and philosophical implications, MULLAN's treatment of Richardson, Sterne, and Hume is the more systematic; and BARKER-BENFIELD's account of sensibility as not just a literary vogue but a comprehensive culture derived from a Lockeian "nerve paradigm" comes close to Shandeian chaos in its zeal to get everything in, but suggests much. Its account of the reformation of male manners on the one hand, and on the other of the corresponding dangers of effeminacy and false politeness, opens the way towards the progression from sensibility to sentiment, and thence to sincerity and proto-Victorian "character" towards the end of the century. The final discussion of Hannah More and Mary Wollstonecraft is equally valuable. The practical outcomes of the theoretical centrality of manners in the Scottish Enlightenment are well handled by DWYER. Indeed, the prominence of Scots among the public moralists and philosophers of manners in the century's later years substantially discounts any peculiarly English claim to politeness. HITCHCOCK & COHEN and BARKER & CHALUS are useful collections of current essays, a number of them stressing particularly the continuous importance of religious influences throughout the century. Meanwhile ANDREW on the duel serves as a reminder of the time that it took for the fit between honour, reputation, and politeness – between the *virtù* of the gentleman and the "virtue" of the genteel – to become perfect: if it ever did.

JOHN MONEY

Poor Laws

see Medicine: Hospital Provision; Poverty entries; Public Health; Speenhamland Poor Relief System

Popular Religion

Brigden, Susan, *London and the Reformation*, Oxford: Clarendon Press, and New York: Oxford University Press, 1989

Cuming, G.J. and Derek Baker (editors), *Popular Belief and Practice: Papers Read at the Ninth Summer Meeting and the Tenth Winter Meeting of the Ecclesiastical History Society*, Cambridge: Cambridge University Press, 1972

Duffy, Eamon, *The Stripping of the Altars: Traditional Religion in England, c.1400–c.1580*, New Haven, Connecticut and London: Yale University Press, 1992

Gilley, Sheridan and W.J. Sheils (editors), *A History of Religion in Britain: Practice and Belief from Pre-Roman Times to the Present*, Oxford and Cambridge, Massachusetts: Blackwell, 1994

Larkin, Emmet, *The Historical Dimensions of Irish Catholicism*, New York: Arno Press, 1976; reprinted with new introduction, Washington, D.C.: Catholic University of America Press, and Dublin: Four Courts Press, 1984

McLeod, Hugh, *Religion and Society in England, 1850–1914*, Basingstoke: Macmillan, and New York: St Martin's Press, 1996

Pantin, W.A., *The English Church in the Fourteenth Century*, Cambridge: Cambridge University Press, 1955; Notre Dame, Indiana: University of Notre Dame Press, 1962

Stephens, W.R.W. and William Hunt (editors), *A History of the English Church*, 8 vols, London and New York: Macmillan, 1899–1924

The eight volumes under the general editorship of STEPHENS & HUNT – the fullest account of Christianity in England until the beginning of the 20th century – provided a good insight into the *status questionis*. The writers of the individual volumes, mostly Anglican clergymen, produced primarily an institutional history of the church but the work contains a great deal about what may be described as popular religion. Chapter 16 of volume 2, on the medieval church, turned explicitly to popular religion, rather unfavourably: "The practical religion of the illiterate was in many respects merely a survival of the old paganism thinly disguised". It drew a distinction between "the religion of the common people" and the "philosophy of the learned". On the whole, however, the history moves quite easily, without obvious tension or consciousness, between institutional history and popular religion and is quite appreciative of the latter.

PANTIN's publication of a revised version of his Birkbeck Lectures at Cambridge University in 1948, seven years after they had taken place, shows the best of the developments that had taken place in the next half century with respect to the late Middle Ages. He, too, managed a balance and interchange between the institutional, intellectual, and popular sides of religion. He did not address the issue of popular religion directly, perhaps feeling that to treat the issue separately led to false and artificial problems. He was, nevertheless, very appreciative of the religious practices of the laity, taking them seriously in their own right and not simply as superstitious or as derivative of clerical religion. The "rise of the devout layman" he saw as "one of the most important phenomena of the religious history of the later Middle Ages".

The papers edited by CUMING & BAKER show, as the title of the volume indicates, that popular religion had obtained an official place in British academia by the early 1970s. The 26 scholars in question, who covered the full chronological sweep of Christian history, were mostly prominent academics from England and Scotland and in about half the cases wrote about British topics. The approach is eclectic and there is no introduction nor does any single paper discuss explicitly the nature of popular religion. The sociological interests of continental historians lie in the background but their more theoretical approaches and the resulting dichotomies and oppositions between popular and official religion, between the lay majority and clerical elites, are largely lacking.

Twenty-two years later, in 1994, GILLEY & SHEILS collected the work of 24 British scholars, this time to produce a continuous history of religion – largely though by no means exclusively of Christianity – in England, Scotland, and Wales from Roman times to the present day. In this case, too, there is no open discussion of the nature of popular religion and the phrase appears nowhere in the titles of the chapters. The omission may have been deliberate, a desire once again to avoid treating popular religion as a separate category. The emphasis, however, is very much upon the religion of the people, a "from below" approach, and there are useful bibliographical surveys.

At about the same time DUFFY was causing a sensation with his treatment of popular religion just before and in the early years of the Reformation. Bringing together the recent insights of other scholars, and producing much additional material of his own, especially from East Anglia, he argued that popular religion – or "traditional religion" as he usually preferred to call it – on the eve of the Reformation was very much alive and flourishing, against the earlier orthodoxy of decline and decadence. He also argued that the Reformation in its early years was not readily welcomed by the majority of people, rather it was largely imposed on them against their wishes. His book has been very influential and the ensuing debate has extended well beyond academic circles.

For the 19th century, McLEOD has provided the best summary of the debate. The introduction gives his position: "This book will argue that in England during the period 1850 to 1914 a relatively high degree of religious consensus existed . . . [which] included acceptance by most of the population of Protestant Christianity".

Much of the study of popular religion has been local history and BRIGDEN's brilliant study of London is among the finest. The city, itself untypical as the capital and much the largest city in the country, reveals the variety of individual responses and warns against generalizations.

For Ireland, LARKIN brought together three articles published previously in *The American Historical Review*. Particularly seminal is the second article, "The Devotional Revolution in Ireland, 1850–75", in which he argues that in this quarter-century, under the vigorous leadership of Cardinal Cullen, the devotional life of Irish catholics was transformed from an unorganized, superstitious, and home-centred religion into a church-based, Romanized and clerically dominated one, with huge and lasting consequences for both Ireland and the wider Church influenced by Irish catholicism. His thesis has become a new orthodoxy in Irish history.

NORMAN P. TANNER

See also Anglican Doctrine and Worship; Catholic Church since 1560; Evangelicalism; Fundamentalism (Christian); Independency in Religion; Kett's and Western Rebellions; Lilburne; Lollardy; Methodism; Millenarian and Radical Religious Movements; Protestant Dissent; Salvation Army

Port Sunlight   founded 1888

Bradley, Ian Campbell, *Enlightened Entrepreneurs*, London: Weidenfeld and Nicolson, 1987
George, W.L., *Labour and Housing at Port Sunlight*, London: Alston Rivers, 1909
Hubbard, Edward and Michael Shippobottom, *A Guide to Port Sunlight Village: Including Two Tours of the Village*, Liverpool: Liverpool University Press, 1988
Jolly, W.P., *Lord Leverhulme: A Biography*, London: Constable, 1976
Lever, William Hulme, *Viscount Leverhulme: By his Son*, London: Allen and Unwin, 1927
Musson, A.E., *Enterprise in Soap and Chemicals: Joseph Crosfield & Sons Limited, 1815–1965*, Manchester: Manchester University Press, 1965; New York: A.M. Kelley, 1967
Sellers, Sue, *Sunlighters: The Story of a Village*, London: Unilever External Affairs Department, 1988
Tigwell, Rosalind E., *Cheshire in the Twentieth Century*, vol. 12, *A History of Cheshire*, Chester: Cheshire Community Council Publications, 1985

When William Hesketh Lever in 1888 founded the village of Port Sunlight adjacent to the village of Lower Bebbington on the Cheshire side of the River Mersey, he was combining two typical aims of the period, the creation of a model village and enlightened self-interest.

When selecting a bibliography for Port Sunlight it is therefore important to remember that references to the village can be found in works relating to enlightened entrepreneurs of the late-19th century, which usually include Lever, as well as in histories of the county of Cheshire and of Port Sunlight itself.

Port Sunlight was by no means the first model industrial village. It was preceded by Styal in Cheshire and New Lanark in Scotland (both founded 1784), Saltaire in Bradford (1850), and Bromborough Pool in Wirral (1853) and was built at roughly the same time as Bourneville (founded 1879). Yet, with perhaps the exception of Bourneville, Port Sunlight village

has been, and to some extent still is, regarded as the classic example of a planned industrial village, providing model housing and facilities for the founder's labour force. William Hesketh Lever's aims and ambitions for Port Sunlight are well documented in his biography written by his son, William Hulme LEVER. Published in 1927, this detailed work has provided the foundation for many further studies of the village. The work emphasizes the fact that Lever was as anxious to avoid the mistakes of some of the early industrial towns, where uncontrolled building had resulted in the creation of slums – some examples of which he had witnessed as a child growing up in Bolton – as he was to attract loyal and healthy workers to his soap factory.

A less dated account of the planning of Port Sunlight can be found in JOLLY's biography of Lever, who later became Lord Leverhulme. This work provides a readable account of the life and career of Lever, setting the creation of Port Sunlight in the context of an ambitious, energetic man who had business interests at home and abroad. This must indeed be the classic account of Lever's ideas and ideals in founding the village. BRADLEY's more scholarly volume is useful but it is an analytical study of enlightened entrepreneurship rather than a specific work about Port Sunlight.

It does not seem possible to study thoroughly the development and character of Port Sunlight without a consideration of the career of Lever. Of works that specifically relate to the village itself, GEORGE's book, published in 1909, is an early example. Indeed, George was the first historian of the village and although the book is very dated in style he gives detailed descriptions of the village and its buildings, which he describes as "a new Arcadia, ventilated and drained on the most scientific principles". Indeed, it is remarkable how little the village has changed since its foundation, a fact that those who are acquainted with the village will appreciate on reading George's book, which dates back to before World War I.

Other volumes consider Port Sunlight village in the context of the history of the county of Cheshire in which the village was located until the boundary reorganization of 1974. Such volumes tend to be fairly general in approach – out of necessity – an example being TIGWELL's section on Port Sunlight. Another approach is that of MUSSON. Although his work is a history of the soap and chemicals business of Joseph Crosfield, he cannot avoid some comparisons between Crosfield's business in Warrington and Lever's Port Sunlight. Always a fierce competitor of Crosfield, Lever's soap works were adjacent to Crosfield's until a lack of space to expand his business persuaded Lever to look for another site. The outcome was the founding of Port Sunlight. The wisdom of Lever's decision becomes very clear when reading Musson's work.

The publication by Unilever in 1988 of SELLER's study of the "Sunlighters" coincided with the village's centenary. Tracing the developments and changes through its hundred years, this is an interesting and informative work even though it is written very much from a "pro-Lever" stance. It is the most thorough of recent publications and is particularly well illustrated with photographs of the village and villagers from throughout the century. In particular, the accounts of the impact of the two world wars makes a new addition to the historical account of Port Sunlight and provides evidence that the villagers were not as insular as some of the literature might suggest. Indeed, Sellers demonstrates how villagers, fully involved in village life and work, nevertheless saw events beyond the world of the factory and responded to the outbreak of both wars with patriotic enthusiasm. Also published during Port Sunlight's centenary year was HUBBARD & SHIPPOBOTTOM's work which describes the architecture of the village. It demonstrates the many different architectural styles and the variety of building materials used to create what George describes as "the charms of irregularity", a village in which the workers were proud to live.

Literature of substance that focuses on Port Sunlight tends to fall into one of two categories: those works published before World War I and those published around the time of the centenary of the village. In both categories there is a tendency for the author to eulogize the work of Lever. Perhaps the handing over in April 1999 of Port Sunlight – now a Grade II listed village – by Unilever Merseyside Ltd (UML), the subsidiary entrusted with the estate's management, to an independent conservation trust will prompt further research into the history of this unique community.

ROSALIND ELIZABETH TIGWELL

See also New Lanark

Poverty I: Poverty and Charity to the 16th Century

Clay, Rotha Mary, *The Mediaeval Hospitals of England*, London: Methuen, 1909; New York: Barnes and Noble, 1966

Dyer, Christopher, *Standards of Living in the Later Middle Ages: Social Change in England c.1200–1520*, Cambridge and New York: Cambridge University Press, 1989

Gilchrist, Roberta, *Contemplation and Action: The Other Monasticism*, London and New York: Leicester University Press, 1995

Harvey, Barbara, *Living and Dying in England 1100–1540: The Monastic Experience*, Oxford: Clarendon Press, and New York: Oxford University Press, 1993

Heal, Felicity, *Hospitality in Early Modern England*, Oxford: Clarendon Press, and New York: Oxford University Press, 1990

Jordan, W.K., *The Charities of Rural England, 1480–1660*, London: Allen and Unwin, 1961; New York: Russell Sage Foundation, 1962

Leonard, E.M., *The Early History of English Poor Relief*, Cambridge: Cambridge University Press, and New York: Barnes and Noble, 1900

Moore, Ellen Wedemeyer, "Aspects of Poverty in a Small Medieval Town" in *The Salt of Common Life: Individuality and Choice in the Medieval Town, Countryside, and Church*, edited by Edwin Brezette DeWindt, Kalamazoo: Medieval Institute of Western Michigan University, 1995

Nicholls, George and Thomas MacKay, *A History of the English Poor Law, in Connection with the Legislation and Other Circumstances Affecting the Condition of the People*, 3 vols, London: John Murray, 1854–99; revised edition, London: King, 1904; reprinted, New York: Kelley, 1967

Rubin, Miri, *Charity and Community in Medieval Cambridge*, Cambridge and New York: Cambridge University Press, 1987

Slack, Paul, *The English Poor Law, 1531–1782*, London: Macmillan, 1990; Cambridge and New York: Cambridge University Press, 1995

Tierney, Brian, *Medieval Poor Law: A Sketch of Canonical Theory and Its Application in England*, Berkeley: University of California Press, 1959

The sometimes fierce debates that have characterized evaluations of the so-called Speenhamland system and the Victorian poor law are largely absent from the rich but discursive studies of medieval poverty and charity. Local studies abound, based on manuscript and printed documents of specific institutions, but from the welter of evidence generalizations must be tentative, if attempted at all. "The poor always ye have with you" (John 12.8) is the oft-quoted biblical text for the medieval perception of poverty, as a condition to be alleviated, not a problem to be solved. However, the dislocations occasioned by the Black Death led to changing attitudes, reflected by a desire to make distinctions between the deserving and undeserving poor, both in law and in the practice of alms-giving. It is not until the 16th century that the first formulations of a comprehensive poor law occur, with the writings and preachings of Christian humanists and "Commonwealth" men in the immediate background. Before the Tudor era poverty and charity were treated piecemeal in a few statutes, in charities of or within municipalities, in various agencies of the church, and as an inseparable thread in the fabric of medieval society.

It is a measure of the diffidence recent historians have in attempting a synthesis of the early history of poverty and charity in England that the best book may be by LEONARD, writing in 1900. SLACK considers her work "still the most thorough account of the period before 1640", but he questions some of her arguments. Leonard begins in the Anglo-Saxon period and her first five chapters deal with pre-1530 England, at least in part. She emphasizes the role of the medieval church, traditions of alms-giving, and the increasing importance of municipalities in relieving distress. Building on the municipal records of London and Norwich, the statutes and state papers, the story she tells smoothly unfolds to what she sees as the key work of the Privy Council under Charles I (during 1629–40) in inducing the justices of the peace to enforce existing laws.

Slack, whose principal focus is the post-1531 poor law, agrees with Leonard that the belief that the community, not just the family, ought to support the needy was not new in the 16th century but was rooted in the late medieval period. Slack looks primarily to innovations in poor relief that were germinating throughout western Europe in the early 16th century, partly under the influence of Christian humanism. The Protestant Reformation was not the cause, he believes, but the facilitator in England because it made it easier for government to intervene, and it destroyed much of the institutional structure for providing relief through church institutions, guilds, and fraternities.

But if one digs back further than the 16th century the picture is murkier. It is indicative that the magisterial *Agrarian History of England and Wales* edited by Joan Thirsk (1991) has no indexed references to poverty before volume IV, covering

1500–1640. In exploring the earlier history NICHOLLS (who wrote the first two volumes) builds chiefly on laws, beginning in late Anglo-Saxon times. He, like Leonard, has a synthetic view, but goes beyond the early history of the poor law to examine the law as it evolved to the late Victorian era. Of course, statutes are at an altitude distant from the plains where poverty was, or was not, relieved. The same holds true for canon law, brilliantly analysed by TIERNEY. Canonical theory held that the impotent poor should be supported by public authority and that parishes had a responsibility to support their own poor, even to the point of sanctioning specific laws to enforce giving. However, these medieval communities fell foul of the perennial problem of how to help the able-bodied unemployed. Tierney argues that the really important innovation of Tudor poor law was, from 1536 onwards, attempting to deal constructively with this segment of the poor rather than lumping all such people under the category of vagabonds.

DYER attempts to probe the realities but, on his own admission, comes up short. He writes: "The survival of the medieval poor still remains something of a mystery". Dyer provides an excellent point of departure for exploring both the realities and the historical literature. He stresses that the unpredictability of life required an abundance of private charity, which was underpinned by the theological emphasis on the value of alms-giving for the professed Christian. However, his analysis of extant records suggests little was actually done for the poor that can be measured. Monastic alms, for example, may have averaged a scant 2 per cent of monastic income, while only 0.5 per cent of the population was served by the various hospitals and alms-houses designed to aid the deserving poor. The undeserving poor could expect nothing from such sources. Dyer examines bishops' alms, fraternities, guilds, the parish, lay aristocratic charity, bequests, and parliamentary initiatives, the latter being generally restrictive and punitive except in relieving some tax burdens. He then concludes that the overall quantity of charity was low. He, as Leonard and Slack, sees Tudor concerns and initiatives prefigured in late medieval attitudes and actions affecting the poor, and suggests that the solution to the mystery may have been the aid of relatives and neighbours in the country and informal charity in the towns – in short, the unmeasurables. The towns also had whatever institutional charity that was on offer.

The criticism JORDAN's work generated, chiefly in the pages of the *Economic History Review*, has served as a caution to those who would measure charitable giving. Providing a wealth of specific detail, in three major books (only one of which is cited here), Jordan's overall conclusion that the degree and pace of charitable giving increased significantly between 1480 and 1660 is now suspect, according to Slack and Dyer. When variables are so many and the sources so few, historians take refuge in examinations of specific localities or institutions where conclusions can be supported with sufficient illustrative detail to gain credence. One of the best in this genre is RUBIN, whose study of medieval Cambridge is frequently cited by other historians of medieval poverty. While focused on Cambridge, she attempts to locate this community within a wider context, including research in France and Belgium, especially the work inspired by Michel Mollat at the Sorbonne in the 1960s. Her study is of the period 1200–1500, and she sees Cambridge as "a pregnant example" of a community contending with poverty,

in which there was a shift "from communal and cooperative forms of charitable organization towards a more personal and individual search for religious and social benefits".

Caution pervades Rubin's work and other more recent studies of medieval poverty rather than the clear syntheses of the early 20th century. Focusing on institutions, for example, the earlier study by CLAY provides much useful information on medieval hospitals, concluding that the some 750 such institutions served a population no larger than that of early 20th-century London. In contrast Dyer emphasizes how uncharitable most of these institutions were in actually meeting need. HARVEY provides more detail, surveying monastic charity from the late 11th century to the early 16th century, stressing its scale and discrimination. But one of the most fascinating books on medieval charitable institutions is by GILCHRIST. In a chapter entitled "Houses of Mercy: The Archeology of Medieval Hospitals" she provides, through text, sketches, and photographs, the material dimension to indoor relief before the poor laws.

One of the problems for the student of medieval poverty and charity is that of definitions. The social engineering of modern times connects poorly with a time when giving bed and shelter to a pilgrim or merchant was of a piece with providing the same service to the indigent. HEAL explores the separation of hospitality, as we define it today, from the relief of true need through private charity.

No brief essay could do justice to all the scholarly studies, chiefly in article form, having to do with medieval English poverty and charity, and focused on specific communities. There are too many gaps in the evidence to cherish the positivist hope that a sure and certain synthesis will ever emerge from the materials available for study. But perhaps one essay may serve as representative, and as at least a partial answer to Dyer's mystery of how the poor survived. MOORE's study of a small medieval town, St Ives in the East Midlands, reveals "a community attitude towards financial distress which tried to minimize the isolation and helplessness of poverty". Basing her studies on court records, especially of fines levied and remitted, she concludes that the poor "were enveloped by a social network of support". This was no doubt true of some medieval communities and perhaps more often the ones whose records have survived to modern times. By whatever means the poor survived, it was the views and practices of late medieval England that provided the seed ground for the first welfare state in the Tudor era.

JAMES STEPHEN TAYLOR

Poverty II: Poverty and Social Control, 17th and 18th Centuries

Blaug, Mark, "The Myth of the Old Poor Law and the Making of the New", *Journal of Economic History*, 23/2 (1963): 151–84

Cage, R.A., "The Making of the Old Scottish Poor Law", *Past and Present*, 69 (1975): 113–18

Innes, Joanna, "The 'Mixed Economy of Welfare' in Early Modern England: Assessments of the Options from Hale to Malthus (c.1683–1803)" in *Charity, Self-Interest, and*

Welfare in the English Past, edited by Martin Daunton, London: UCL Press, and New York: St Martin's Press, 1996

King, Steve, "Reconstructing Lives: The Poor, the Poor Law, and Welfare in Calverley, 1650–1820", *Social History*, 22/3 (1997): 318–38

Landau, Norma, "The Laws of Settlement and the Surveillance of Immigration in Eighteenth-Century Kent", *Continuity and Change*, 3/3 (1988): 391–420

Marshall, Dorothy, *The English Poor in the Eighteenth Century: A Study in Social and Administrative History*, London: Routledge, 1926; reprinted, London: Routledge, and New York: A.M. Kelley, 1969

Mitchison, Rosalind, "The Making of the Old Scottish Poor Law", *Past and Present*, 63 (1974): 58–93

Slack, Paul, *Poverty and Policy in Tudor and Stuart England*, London and New York: Longman, 1988

Snell, K.D.M., *Annals of the Labouring Poor: Social Change and Agrarian England 1660–1900*, Cambridge and New York: Cambridge University Press, 1985

Solar, Peter M., "Poor Relief and English Economic Development before the Industrial Revolution", *Economic History Review*, 48/1 (1995): 1–22

Thompson, E.P., *Customs in Common*, London: Merlin Press, and New York: New Press, 1991

Webb, Sidney and Beatrice Webb, *English Poor Law History*, vol. 1, *The Old Poor Law*, London and New York: Longmans Green, 1927

Wrightson, Keith and David Levine, *Poverty and Piety in an English Village: Terling, 1525–1700*, New York: Academic Press, 1979; revised edition, Oxford: Clarendon Press, and New York: Oxford University Press, 1995

The majority of works relating to poverty and social control in Britain in the 17th and 18th centuries concern practices and developments in England. This entry will deal first with England and Wales; Wales was technically governed by the same laws as England, although in practice the authors quoted here tend to mention Wales only in passing. It will then touch briefly on debates about Scotland; scarcity of relevant records has stifled work on Ireland.

Modern scholarship of the statutory management and control of poverty in England and Wales begins with the vast researches of the Webbs and of Marshall. These early 20th-century writers undertook the monumental task of compiling comprehensive histories of the laws relating to poverty and vagrancy. The WEBBS outlined the legislative framework governing parish responses to poverty and gave details of different experiences of administration. They stressed both the origins of the old poor law in the 16th-century desire forcibly to suppress vagrancy and the punitive aspects of subsequent local enforcement of the law, particularly the use of institutions like workhouses and houses of correction. MARSHALL concentrated on contemporary attitudes to poverty and consequential variations in the workings of the poor law in the 18th century, with some emphasis on its impact on the lives of the poor. Both the Webbs and Marshall identified common elements of welfare policy and (less often) variations in the outcome of local experiments. They characterized the efforts of parishes to deal with poverty as harsh, relief taking place in what the Webbs called a "frame-work of repression". Local policy was insufficiently financed or too poorly managed to ensure an acceptable minimum standard of material resources for paupers but paradoxically (particularly towards the end of the period) the same measures were judged likely to inflame the very problems they sought to alleviate, by tending to increase the proportion of the population necessarily dependent on a measure of parochial relief.

Challenges to these orthodoxies began to emerge in the 1960s. BLAUG analysed the claim that certain practices of the old poor law had had an adverse effect on the incidence of poverty and the need for relief. In particular he overturned the assumption that the format of relief actively encouraged early marriage (and consequent population growth), fostered low wages, and exacerbated underemployment; instead, he found that relief measures were formulated to counter these problems after they had started to impinge on local awareness. Blaug's work cleared the way for a much more positive assessment of the old poor law.

Subsequently, some historians have continued to exonerate the old poor law from the accusations of the Webbs and Marshall by observing the medieval precedents for local relief of the poor, contextualizing the criticisms levelled at the system by contemporaries and stressing the successes among parish efforts, particularly before the late 18th century. SNELL has written about the quality of life in southern England in the 18th and 19th centuries, particularly for agricultural workers. He concentrates on the damaging impact of enclosure, the seasonality of rural unemployment, consequential population mobility, and experiences of poverty. He stresses the importance of ready access to poor relief since his pessimistic view of standards of living for the southern labouring poor casts an advantageous light over established welfare procedures. The poor law in the 18th century is posited as both a miniature welfare state, offering generous, humane relief, and a lynchpin in social relations, supplying the opportunity for mutual respect between different groups in local society.

SLACK provides a good, modern account, particularly for the 17th century. He charts the evolution of thought and practice from the social-order problems which exercised the minds and consciences of 16th-century legislators through to an acceptance of and desire to quantify the "deserving" poor which prompted the formulation of the old poor law. He also identifies some typical experiences of recipient paupers, with an emphasis on residents of urban parishes. He argues that while legislation aimed at social control, the latitude granted to local managers and their personal knowledge of applicants led to a system characterized by the generosity of its distributions and an expanding range of items typically provided.

Nevertheless, not all research has been keen to present the ameliorative face of the English poor laws. LANDAU has taken issue with Snell; she questions his apparent assumption that the laws of settlement were employed solely to remove people who were nearly or actually destitute and concludes that, before 1795, they were used to monitor the in-migration of individuals and families who were not poverty-stricken. Snell rightly observes that the settlement laws were designed specifically to modify the workings of the poor laws but did not entertain the possibility that permissive laws might be turned to unintended uses. Settlement legislation may have been implemented in such a way as to permit surveillance of in-migration, but if this was the case then widespread acknowledgement by contemporaries was lacking (which is not proof but is at least suggestive). Landau's case is not yet proven conclusively but at the least her research provides a useful check to automatic assumptions about the manner of law enforcement and, if proven, will require a radical revision of the perceived extent of past control over population mobility.

An explanation for motives underlying an apparently increasing desire to control the poor in the early 17th century has been advanced by WRIGHTSON & LEVINE. They argue that in the Essex parish of Terling tightening social discipline originated in a religious, mainly puritan, impulse. The middling sorts were spurred by their consciences, as well as by a long-standing desire to manage poverty, to control and discipline the poor and their culture. Wrightson & Levine claim that the rate of regulatory prosecutions in the early 17th century, initiated by local officials in extra-parochial courts, is explicable in terms of the spread of Reformation discourses of godly ideals and social order. This has been a controversial thesis, generating challenges on the basis of the character of English puritanism, the nature of social-control structures which predated the 17th century, and the extent to which the Terling example typified developments elsewhere.

In contrast, and for the 18th century, THOMPSON points to the vibrancy of customary culture for the plebian population and its resistance to external control by law or local authority. Custom was defined flexibly and might have originated from legal provision, traditional practice, or from favoured innovations which required some additional weight to be deemed justified. The identification of a practice as customary legitimized it in the eyes of participants and secured the caution, if not the approval, of observers or opponents. In the 18th century, the labouring poor used custom to preserve preferred practices, such as skimmingtons or wife sales (ritualized secular divorces), and to delay and contest change, particularly where change epitomized the advance of industrial capitalism.

In the 1990s two, often contrasting, strands of research have dominated work on the management and experience of poverty in the 17th and 18th centuries. One holds that parish relief was the dominant source of welfare assistance for the very poor in most places and at most times; it did a relatively good job at supporting the poor in the context of inflexible, local taxation and the average standard of living experienced by the labouring poor. SOLAR has taken this furthest by arguing that parishes manipulated poor-law provisions to suit local perceptions of labour supply and demand. The net effect of these adaptations, he claims, provided a near-universal welfare system, conciliatory rather than coercive, which minimized subsistence migration and promoted a mobile, responsive national workforce. The second approach increasingly doubts the comprehensive, universal character of parish relief and points to both the regionally varied nature of the poor-relief safety net and also to the patchwork economies which shored up poor households. KING has demonstrated the extent to which a positive view of the poor law misrepresents the situation for the poor in the north of England. The poor rate in Calverley, in the West Riding of Yorkshire, supported a smaller proportion of the poor, with lower-value payments and over shorter periods than was apparently the case in southern parishes. Survival strategies employed by the poor involved parish relief as merely one of a range of props including borrowing and lending, exploitation of kin, and management of varying employment opportunities. Assessments of the national picture have also emphasized the diversity of structures available to relieve and manage poverty. INNES has argued that in the "mixed economy of welfare" of the late 17th and 18th centuries voluntary charities persisted and often flourished alongside statutory relief because the technical and practical limits of parish relief prompted voluntary action to extend the range of benefits available to the poor. An examination of contemporary debates about the supply of voluntary charity shows that opinion tended to favour charity over relief, for its supposedly beneficial effect on the poor and its attractions for donors, and some commentators advocated a drastic reduction of parish poor relief; in practice it was accepted that both brands of support should represent parts of a wide range of welfare measures including self-help strategies.

Treatment of the poor in Scotland in the 17th and 18th centuries was fundamentally different from that in England, since the poor laws offered a less comprehensive support system. Controversy has arisen over the tenor of Scottish attitudes to the poor and the extent to which relief was offered to the able-bodied poor. MITCHISON argued that no relief was given to the able-bodied poor and that insufficient help was given to the impotent poor to provide them with the necessaries for life. Policy was oriented primarily to avoid the levy of a compulsory tax; any other considerations relating to the relief or control of the poor were secondary. CAGE challenges these conclusions by qualifying their applicability. He identifies opportunities for relief of the able-bodied which were available within the poor law provisions, questions whether scanty support for the impotent poor can be proven, and points out the limited geographical spread from which Mitchison drew evidence, particularly her omission of urban parishes.

ALANNAH TOMKINS

See also Social Conflict: Early Modern Period

Poverty III: Poverty and Deprivation, 19th and 20th Centuries

Barnett, Correlli, *The Audit of War: The Illusion and Reality of Britain as a Great Nation*, London: Macmillan, 1986; as *The Pride and the Fall: The Dream and Illusion of Britain as a Great Nation*, New York: Free Press, 1987

Blaug, Mark, "The Myth of the Old Poor Law and the Making of the New", *Journal of Economic History*, 23 (1963): 151–84

Burnett, John (editor), *Destiny Obscure: Autobiographies of Childhood, Education, and Family from the 1820s to the 1920s*, London: Allen Lane, 1982; reprinted, London and New York: Routledge, 1994

Checkland, S.G. and E.O.A. Checkland (editors), *The Poor Law Report of 1834*, Harmondsworth and Baltimore: Penguin, 1974

Collini, Stefan, *Public Moralists: Political Thought and Intellectual Life in Britain 1850–1930*, Oxford: Clarendon Press, and New York: Oxford University Press, 1991

Dean, Mitchell, *The Constitution of Poverty: Toward a Genealogy of Liberal Governance*, London and New York: Routledge, 1991

Fraser, Derek, *The Evolution of the British Welfare State: A History of Social Policy since the Industrial Revolution*, London: Macmillan, 1973; revised edition, 1984

Fraser, Derek (editor), *The New Poor Law in the Nineteenth Century*, London: Macmillan, and New York: St Martin's Press, 1976

Harris, José, "Enterprise and the Welfare State: A Comparative Perspective" in *Britain since 1945*, edited by Terry Gourvish and Alan O'Day, London: Macmillan, 1991

Himmelfarb, Gertrude, *The Idea of Poverty: England in the Early Industrial Age*, New York: Knopf, 1984; London: Faber, 1985

Himmelfarb, Gertrude, *Poverty and Compassion: The Moral Imagination of the Late Victorians*, New York: Knopf, 1991

Johnson, Paul, *Saving and Spending: The Working-Class Economy in Britain, 1870–1939*, Oxford: Clarendon Press, and New York: Oxford University Press, 1985

Lees, Lynn Hollen, *The Solidarities of Strangers: The English Poor Laws and the People, 1700–1948*, Cambridge and New York: Cambridge University Press, 1998

Prochaska, Frank, "Philanthropy" in *The Cambridge Social History of Britain 1750–1950*, vol. 3, *Social Agencies and Institutions*, edited by F.M.L. Thompson, Cambridge and New York: Cambridge University Press, 1990

Rowntree, Benjamin Seebohm, *Poverty: A Study of Town Life*, London and New York: Macmillan, 1901

Townsend, Peter, "The Meaning of Poverty", *British Journal of Sociology*, 18 (1962): 210–27

Vincent, David, *Bread, Knowledge, and Freedom: A Study of Nineteenth-Century Working-Class Autobiography*, London: Europa, 1981; London and New York: Methuen, 1982

Vincent, David, *Poor Citizens: The State and the Poor in Twentieth-Century Britain*, London and New York: Longman, 1991

Webster, Charles, "Healthy or Hungry 'Thirties?", *History Workshop Journal*, 13 (1982): 110–29

Williams, Karel, *From Pauperism to Poverty*, London and Boston: Routledge and Kegan Paul, 1981

Winter, Jay, "Infant Mortality, Maternal Mortality, and Public Health in Britain in the 1930s", *Journal of European Economic History*, 8 (1979): 439–62

Before embarking on a survey of the historiography of poverty, it is important to recognize the different ways in which the terms "poverty" and "the poor" have been understood during the period under review. During the first half of the 19th century many writers were keen to distinguish between *poverty* – "the state of one who, in order to obtain a mere subsistence, is forced to have recourse to labour" – and *indigence* – "the state of a person unable to labour, or unable to obtain, in return for their labour, the means of subsistence" – and it was only during the second half of the century, following the work of such authors as Henry Mayhew, that the term poverty itself became clearly associated with lack of means (Checkland & Checkland;

Thompson & Yeo, *The Unknown Mayhew*, 1971). It is in this sense that the term will be used during the remainder of this essay.

One of the greatest difficulties facing the historian of poverty is the difficulty of giving a voice to those who were themselves poor. However, as both BURNETT and VINCENT (1981) have demonstrated, it is possible to address this difficulty at least in part by drawing on the evidence provided by working-class autobiographies and, for more recent periods, by oral history. In recent years, a number of historians have also attempted to address this issue by conducting detailed investigations into the ways in which working-class people made their own attempts to protect themselves against the economic hazards of daily life by cooperating with friends and neighbours, by pawning valuable items, by joining friendly societies, and by engaging in other forms of what JOHNSON calls "saving and spending".

For the historian of the poor, as for the 19th-century poor themselves, it can be difficult to escape from the shadow of the Poor Law. For those interested in the history of public policy towards the poor, the *Poor Law Report* of 1834 remains an essential starting-point. As CHECKLAND & CHECKLAND observed, "the English Poor Law Report . . . is one of the classic documents of western social history . . . the record of the attempt by Parliament, within the first industrialising society, to comprehend the condition of the labouring poor, and to formulate a policy". However, as the Checklands themselves recognized, the report was also a deeply flawed document, which provided a highly jaundiced view of the operation of the old Poor Law. In 1963, the economist Mark BLAUG concluded that "hardly any of the dire effects ascribed to the Old Poor Law stand up in the light of available empirical evidence".

One of the most controversial questions in the historiography of the new Poor Law concerns the extent to which the Poor Law Amendment Act of 1834 actually made much difference to the conduct of Poor Law policy. Several of the contributors to FRASER's edited collection, including both Anne Digby and Michael Rose, argued that even though the new Poor Law was specifically designed to abolish the practice of outdoor relief, the vast majority of paupers continued to receive relief outside the workhouse, and so the characteristic feature of Poor Law policy after 1834 was one of continuity rather than change. However, this interpretation was sharply challenged by WILLIAMS in 1981. This writer claimed that the main aim of the new Poor Law was not to abolish outdoor relief *per se*, but rather to abolish the distribution of outdoor relief to able-bodied males, and he was able to present statistical evidence which suggested that the pursuit of this aim was largely successful. However, other writers have counselled against placing too much emphasis on national statistics. LEES argues that "a high proportion of the unemployed married men with families simply did not make it into national records". She concludes that "the Poor Law Commission may not have succeeded in cutting off aid to the unemployed, but it did manage to force support for this group outside the normal administrative procedures for the poor law".

During the 20th century, the historiography of poverty has continued to be influenced by debates over the meaning of poverty. In 1901 ROWNTREE tried to measure the incidence of poverty by observing the living conditions of the working-class population of York. He drew a famous distinction between *primary poverty* – the state of those "whose total earnings were insufficient to obtain the minimum necessaries for the maintenance of merely physical efficiency" – and *secondary poverty* – the state of those "whose total earnings would have been sufficient for the maintenance of merely physical efficiency were it not that some portion of them was absorbed by other expenditure". In 1962 TOWNSEND criticized Rowntree's approach on the grounds that it failed to take account of the relative nature of poverty – in other words, the extent to which the definition of poverty should take account of the normal standards and expectations of the society in which they lived. Even though some writers have criticized Townsend's interpretation of Rowntree, it is difficult to deny the fact that the formulation of the concept of *relative poverty* had a major impact, not only on the public policy debates of the 1960s, but also on subsequent attempts to measure the incidence of poverty in Britain and elsewhere.

In view of the highly political nature of debates over the subject of poverty, it is not surprising that it should be difficult to separate the historiography of poverty from attitudes to the role of the state in providing welfare services more generally. This is true of both the 19th and the 20th centuries. For writers and historians working in a social-democratic or Marxist tradition, such as FRASER and DEAN, the new Poor Law represented at best an abdication of society's collective responsibility to care for its disadvantaged members, and at worst a deliberate attempt to use the institutions of social policy to coerce the poor into participation in the labour market. However, for more conservatively inclined historians, such as HIMMELFARB, the most important legacy of the new Poor Law was not so much its direct impact on the poor themselves, as the incentive which it provided to middle-class Victorians to use their "moral imagination" to develop alternative means of reducing the burden of poverty. This very different view of Victorian attitudes to poverty was also reflected in PROCHASKA's work on the importance of philanthropy in 19th-century society, and, in a rather different way, in COLLINI's study of the role played by altruism in the thought of the Victorian "public moralists".

The interaction between politics and history also played an important part in debates about the impact of poverty and unemployment on health and living conditions during the interwar period. In 1982, WEBSTER examined a series of small-scale local studies, and concluded that

> in view of the impressive body of evidence suggesting that the health problems experienced during the 1930s were rooted in economic disadvantage . . . the Depression must be regarded as a significant exacerbating factor, tending to worsen still further prevailing low levels of health, and so contributing towards a crisis of subsistence and health different in kind but similar in gravity to the crises known to students of pre-industrial societies.

However, even though it is clear that unemployment did have a significant effect on the health of some sections of the population, the aggregate statistics show that the standard of living for the population as a whole continued to improve. In 1979 WINTER concluded that "the most important feature of the aggregate data . . . is the persistence of the trend towards better . . . health . . . despite the economic crisis of the early [1930s]".

The historiography of poverty has also been closely bound up with attitudes to the welfare state during the postwar period. In *Poor Citizens*, VINCENT (1991) cast doubt on some popular assumptions about the role of welfare services when he suggested that economic policy was at least as important as social policy in ensuring that levels of poverty continued to decline. However, other writers have suggested that the Attlee government's determination to focus on the improvement of welfare provision was achieved at the cost of economic regeneration. In 1986, BARNETT alleged that the foundation of the welfare state had resulted in the "dank reality of a segregated, subliterate, unskilled, unhealthy and institutionalised proletariat hanging on the nipple of state maternalism". However, even though Barnett expressed his views with particular pungency, they did not rest on the most solid empirical foundations. In a paper first published in the *Transactions of the Royal Historical Society* in 1990, José HARRIS put his hypothesis to the test by comparing levels of welfare expenditure and economic growth in a range of other countries. If anything, the statistical evidence suggested that public expenditure on social welfare was associated with higher rates of economic growth, and not the reverse.

BERNARD J. HARRIS

See also Chadwick; Medicine: Hospital Provision; Rowntree; Welfare State

Powys, Kingdom of
see Wales before Union with England

Poynings, Sir Edward 1459–1521
Statesman and lord deputy of Ireland

Brady, Ciaran, "'Constructive and Instrumental': The Dilemma of Ireland's First 'New Historians'" in *Interpreting Irish History: The Debate on Historical Revisionism 1938–1994*, edited by Brady, Blackrock, County Dublin, and Portland, Oregon: Irish Academic Press, 1994

Bradshaw, Brendan, "The Beginnings of Modern Ireland" in *The Irish Parliamentary Tradition*, edited by Brian Farrell, Dublin: Gill and Macmillan, and New York: Barnes and Noble, 1973

Chrimes, Stanley B., *Henry VII*, London: Eyre Methuen, and Berkeley: University of California Press, 1972

Conway, Agnes, *Henry VII's Relations with Scotland and Ireland, 1485–1498*, Cambridge: Cambridge University Press, 1932; reprinted, New York: Octagon Books, 1972

Curtis, Edmund, "The Acts of the Drogheda Parliament, 1494–1495, or 'Poynings' Laws" in *Henry VII's Relations with Scotland and Ireland, 1485–1498*, by Agnes Conway, Cambridge: Cambridge University Press, 1932; reprinted, New York: Octagon Books, 1972

Edwards, R.D. and D.B. Moody, "The History of Poynings' Law: Part I, 1494–1615", *Irish Historical Studies*, 2 (1940–41): 415–24

Ellis, Steven G., *Tudor Ireland: Crown, Community, and the Conflict of Cultures, 1470–1603*, London and New York: Longman, 1985; as *Ireland in the Age of the Tudors, 1447–1603: English Expansion and the End of Gaelic Rule*, 1998

Palmer, William, *The Problem of Ireland in Tudor Foreign Policy, 1485–1603*, Woodbridge, Suffolk and Rochester, New York: Boydell Press, 1994

Quinn, D.B., "The Early Interpretation of Poynings' Law, 1494–1534", *Irish Historical Studies*, 2 (1940–41): 241–54

Quinn, D.B., "Aristocratic Autonomy, 1460–1494", "'Irish Ireland' and 'English' Ireland", and "The Hegemony of the Earls of Kildare, 1494–1520" in *A New History of Ireland*, vol. 2, *Medieval Ireland 1169–1534*, edited by Art Cosgrove, Oxford: Clarendon Press, and New York: Oxford University Press, 1987; revised edition, Oxford: Clarendon Press, 1993

Richardson, H.G. and G.O. Sayles, *The Irish Parliament in the Middle Ages*, Philadelphia: University of Pennsylvania Press, 1952; new edition, 1964

Although Sir Edward Poynings was celebrated under the early Tudors as a captain, councillor, and statesman, he is chiefly remembered as Henry VII's lord deputy of Ireland (1494–96), an English dependency ruled from Dublin. One of "Buckingham's rebels" of 1483, Poynings joined Henry Tudor in exile in Brittany and returned with him to defeat Richard III at Bosworth in 1485. A knight of the Garter, he saw active service abroad and became deputy lieutenant of Calais in 1493. As ELLIS makes clear, Sir Edward's tasks in 1494 were threefold: to pacify both Gaelic chiefs and old English nobles and eliminate support for the Yorkist pretender, Perkin Warbeck; to oversee financial reform aimed at administrative self-sufficiency; and to undertake administrative reform designed to strengthen royal control.

While the crown's experiment in direct rule under Poynings features largely as a chapter or two in more general studies of Ireland under the Tudors, or as the basis for a seminal article, it has been well served by 20th-century scholarship. Ellis offers a balanced study, although for sheer detail drawn from manuscript sources CONWAY and QUINN (1987) remain influential. Driven by military and financial goals, for Conway, Poynings's success against the "Yorkist faction" was complete though he failed to make Ireland "pay its way". Quinn illuminates the crown's concerns both within and beyond the Pale, and Sir Edward's ability as a soldier and a politician. More circumspect than Conway in his military appraisal, none the less Poynings eliminated the dynastic threat. Importantly, the period created a framework for effective rule for the crown until 1534.

Central to historical debate on the significance of the Poynings era is the reform legislation of the Drogheda parliament summoned by Sir Edward in 1494, of which CURTIS provides the most detailed analysis and CHRIMES a judicious potted version. Chrimes categorizes the reforms thus: financial and legal, law and order, defence, constitutional, governmental or parliamentary. Curtis views the legislation as the crown's immediate response to its dynastic enemies, and in the long term as a means of extending royal authority in Ireland. Of importance is the ninth of a series of 49 acts which became known as Poynings's Law and resonated in the political arena until its

virtual repeal in 1782. As QUINN (1940–41) states in the first full account of its operation to 1534, the act required the king's formal consent under the Great Seal before the Irish parliament could be convened, and approval of its intended legislation by the English council. Traditionally scholars have viewed it as a convenient line of demarcation in Irish history between medieval and modern, and while modern historians remain divided over its intention and effect all acknowledge its profound role in the history of the Irish parliament.

A number of 18th- and 19th-century interpretations of Poynings's Law reflect the influence of Irish politics on the historiography of the late medieval period. EDWARDS & MOODY confidently assert, however, that the "old view" of the law as an effective means of silencing the Irish parliament, promoted by 18th-century patriots and read in the 19th-century histories of Plowden (1812) and Gilbert (1865) among others, has no place in the 20th-century works of "standard" historians such as H.A.L. Fisher's *History of Ireland* (1913). The influence of Quinn, Edwards, and Moody in Irish historiography is evident in the volume and quality of revision articles published in the academic periodical *Irish Historical Studies (IHS)* founded by Moody in the 1930s. Edwards & Moody adopted and encouraged a critical approach towards received orthodoxy and set in train what might almost be described as revisionist orthodoxy in Irish historical scholarship.

Their analysis of the constitutional and political significance of Poynings's Law, together with Quinn's work, embodies this approach. Quinn's study of the law to 1534 based on manuscript sources argues that it fulfilled its intended function, which altered only with the end of the Kildare ascendancy and the establishment of an English administration in Dublin. Edwards & Moody explore in two stages the workings of the act to 1615 and the attempts of both the Irish executive and the legislature to alter the law at critical times. The periods 1613–15 and 1634–35 mark a watershed in its history: formerly it had curbed the Irish executive and was supported by the Irish parliament; henceforth it was used by the government to control parliament. Subsequently it was vilified by the "national" party, composed in 1641 and 1688 of Irish and catholic interests, and in the 18th century of protestant and planter interests, until Yelverton's Act in 1782 made it redundant. Aidan Clarke (*IHS*, 1972) augments their research with his study of Lord Deputy Wentworth's manipulation of the function of Poynings's Law in 1634–35, and the failure of a section of the Irish parliament to have the traditional interpretation of its provisions restored in 1640–41.

The Edwards-Moody school has had its critics. Indeed conflicting views of the law reflect the force of the debate between revisionism and nationalism in recent Irish scholarship, on which BRADY sheds much light. It gained momentum in the 1970s when BRADSHAW, responding to RICHARDSON & SAYLES for whom Poynings's Law was not intended as part of a fundamental programme of parliamentary reform, argued its profound significance: the Irish council, now a partner in the legislature, had usurped parliament's role of formally initiating legislation and left it only with the function of veto and a power of amendment which it exercised "with dubious legality". Ellis, on the other hand, supports the earlier view. The law was not an attempt to curb the functions of the legislature, nor had it farsighted constitutional implications. It was aimed at preventing the use of parliament for private gain or for ratifying the claims of would-be kings, and as a means of extending royal control.

PALMER's sharp summary of Poynings's Law in the context of England's foreign policy and France's role in shaping the crown's Irish policy updates earlier work. Henry VII's dynastic insecurity, Yorkist enemies with European allies, and the uncertainty of France created a potent mix. Thus when the political crisis deepened in 1494 Poynings was sent to counter the dynastic threat and to ensure that henceforth pretenders would be unable to gain parliamentary approval.

LOUISE GILL

See also Henry VII; Ireland entries

Priestley, Joseph 1733–1804
Chemist and clergyman

Anderson, R.G.W. and Christopher Lawrence (editors), *Science, Medicine, and Dissent: Joseph Priestley (1733–1804)*, London: Wellcome Trust / Science Museum, 1987

Bolton, Henry Carrington (editor), *Scientific Correspondence of Joseph Priestley*, New York: privately printed, 1892; reprinted, New York: Kraus Reprint, 1969

Crook, Ronald E., *A Bibliography of Joseph Priestley, 1733–1804*, London: Library Association, 1966

Gibbs, F.W., *Joseph Priestley: Adventurer in Science and Champion of Truth*, London: Nelson, 1965

Golinski, Jan, *Science as Public Culture: Chemistry and Enlightenment in Britain, 1760–1820*, Cambridge: Cambridge University Press, 1992

Lindsay, Jack (editor), *Autobiography of Joseph Priestley*, Bath: Adams and Dart, 1970

McEvoy, John G. and J.E. McGuire, "God and Nature: Priestley's Way of Rational Dissent", *Historical Studies in the Physical Sciences*, 6 (1975): 325–404

McEvoy, John G., "Joseph Priestley, 'Aerial Philosopher': Metaphysics and Methodology in Priestley's Thought 1772–1781", *Ambix*, 25 (1978): 1–55, 93–116; 26 (1979): 16–38

Priestley, Joseph, *Memoirs of Dr. Joseph Priestley to the Year 1795, Written by Himself*, London: Johnson, 1806

Rutt, John Towill (editor), *The Theological and Miscellaneous Works of Joseph Priestley, LL.D., F.R.S.*, 25 vols in 26, London: George Smallfield, 1817–31

Schaffer, Simon, "Priestley's Questions: An Historiographical Survey", *History of Science*, 22 (1984): 151–83

Schofield, Robert E., *The Lunar Society of Birmingham: A Social History of Provincial Science and Industry in Eighteenth-Century England*, Oxford: Clarendon Press, 1963

Schofield, Robert E. (editor), *A Scientific Autobiography of Joseph Priestley (1733–1804)*, Cambridge, Massachusetts: MIT Press, 1966

Schofield, Robert E., *The Enlightenment of Joseph Priestley: A Study of His Life and Work from 1733 to 1773*, University Park: Pennsylvania State University Press, 1997

Joseph Priestley was a clergyman, political theorist, and physical scientist whose work contributed to advances in liberal, political, and religious thought as well as in experimental science. In the history of science, he has most commonly been depicted as a foil for Antoine Lavoisier in the chemical revolution of late 18th-century chemistry. Thus, Priestley's discovery of what Lavoisier was subsequently to call oxygen, while continuing to adhere to the old phlogiston theory, has been employed to emphasize the revolutionary nature of Lavoisier's thinking. More recently, Priestley's emphasis on democratic values in science has been used to highlight Lavoisier's elitist form of science. Priestley's open support for the French Revolution resulted in a mob burning down his house, library, and laboratory, and he was driven from his home. Eventually, Priestley emigrated to the United States. Priestley has been of interest not only to historians of science; there is also a tradition of scholarship on Priestley by dissenters. Priestley wrote on theological matters too, such as his six-volume history of the Christian church.

BOLTON provides access to the part of Priestley's correspondence that was recognizable as science at the time of editing in 1892. RUTT, a co-dissenter and personal friend, republished a great deal of Priestley's work. The focus of these massive 25 volumes, as the title implies, is on theology, but much of Priestley's work, which ostensibly is more of a chemical nature, is included too. The Thoemmes Press is planning to reissue Rutt's edition, in two volumes, in late 2002 or early 2003.

PRIESTLEY's autobiography has been republished by LINDSAY, who provides a short introduction covering Priestley's career, his relations with David Hartley and Boscovich, and his doctrines of materialism and phlogiston.

There are two useful biographies of Priestley. GIBBS is reliable and fairly comprehensive: Priestley's science and its application to the arts is covered and there is a good account of his post-Revolutionary life, including a detailed description of the mobbing which led to his house being burnt down. Unfortunately the book is incompletely documented: there are few footnotes and only a short bibliographical essay.

SCHOFIELD's long-awaited volume (1997) covers only the first half of Priestley's life, although a second volume is planned. SCHOFIELD (1966) does not actually contain Priestley's autobiography. Rather, it depicts his life through a selection of slightly edited correspondence. It contains a very useful (but not comprehensive) index of Priestley's correspondents.

Much literature which is not of a biographical nature bears on Priestley: institutional history, works on specific aspects of Priestley's activites, and contextualizations of Priestley's written work within the society of his day.

CROOK is the standard bibliography, containing a listing of Priestley's own publications, including his many pamphlets. The physical details of each are described meticulously, and locations are listed of where each item can be found. Most of these locations are in the British Isles, but many are also deposited in Canada, Germany, Switzerland, and the United States. Priestley's non-periodical publications are listed by category: theological and religious, political and social, educational and psychological, philosophical and metaphysical, historical, and scientific. The book also contains a section on secondary literature which, more than three decades later, is now out of date.

SCHOFIELD (1963) is an indispensable account of Priestley's principal philosophical network. The Lunar Society was a group of natural philosophers and industrialists in Birmingham with whom Priestley was involved for the central part of his career. The book describes the industrial context of the application of chemistry to the useful arts.

McEVOY & McGUIRE is a useful introduction for historians of science to Priestley's philosophical and theological thought. The authors argue that Priestley's constructive empiricism represents a major philosophical reform in 18th-century attitudes to science, and that Priestley sets out a way to link rationalism and empiricism: things are as they are because a wise God has made them so. McEVOY interprets Priestley's pneumatic chemistry in the light of his philosophical and theological convictions. For example, Priestley saw the qualities of different kinds of of air as a part of divine design. McEvoy argues, not always convincingly, that all parts of Priestley's chemistry can be linked to such convictions.

SCHAFFER surveys the strange contradiction in Priestley's scientific reputation – that he was too empirical, and guided too much by the mere appearances of chemical phenomena; and that he was too theoretically prejudiced, and thus too driven by an overarching commitment to the phlogiston theory. In order to resolve this apparent contradiction, it is argued that we need a developmental account of Priestley's natural philosophical work instead of assuming that he held one single set of methodological or chemical beliefs. Schaffer also points out that Priestley's scientific and political careers have been used to teach morals about the fate of the scientist, and this may help explain why he has been seen as both conservative and radical, empiricist and theoretician.

GOLINSKI is a history of chemistry in Britain in relation to the forms of civic life characteristic of the Enlightenment, a period when scientific practice and discourse became an established part of the public domain. The book contains two chapters on Priestley, who is interpreted as a communicator whose aspiration was to spread the knowledge of science.

ANDERSON & LAWRENCE is the first collection to bring together in one volume papers covering the various aspects of Priestley's work, such as science, applied science, philosophy, and theology. There is a paper on the relation between Priestley and Whewell, and there are several good papers on Priestley's politics and millenarianism (Priestley was a millenarian in the sense that he believed that prophecies of the scripture would be fulfilled and had a relevance to his time).

ARNE HESSENBRUCH

See also Electricity; Radicalism; Utilitarianism

Prime Minister: Emergence and Development of Office 18th century

Black, Jeremy, *British Foreign Policy in the Age of Walpole*, Edinburgh: John Donald, and Atlantic Highlands, New Jersey: Humanities Press, 1985
Cannon, John, *The Fox-North Coalition: Crisis of the Constitution, 1782–1784*, Cambridge: Cambridge University Press, 1969
Clark, J.C.D., *The Dynamics of Change: The Crisis of the 1750s and English Party Systems*, Cambridge and New York: Cambridge University Press, 1982
Dickinson, William Calvin, *Sidney Godolphin, Lord Treasurer, 1702–1710*, Lewiston, New York and Lampeter, Dyfed: Edwin Mellen, 1990
Eccleshall, Robert and Graham Walker (editors), *Biographical Dictionary of British Prime Ministers*, London and New York: Routledge, 1998
Feiling, Keith Grahame, *The Second Tory Party, 1714–1832*, London: Macmillan, 1938; reprinted, London: Macmillan, and New York: St Martin's Press, 1959
Hill, Brian W., *Robert Harley, Speaker, Secretary of State, and Premier Minister*, London and New Haven, Connecticut: Yale University Press, 1988
Hill, Brian W., *Sir Robert Walpole: "Sole and Prime Minister"*, London: Hamish Hamilton, and New York: Penguin, 1989
Namier, Lewis, *The Structure of Politics at the Accession of George III*, 2 vols, London: Macmillan, 1929; 1 vol., London: Macmillan, and New York: St Martin's Press, 1957
Namier, Lewis and John Brooke (editors), *The House of Commons, 1754–1790: Introductory Survey*, London: HMSO for the History of Parliament Trust, 1964
Owen, John B., *The Rise of the Pelhams*, London: Methuen, 1957; reprinted, London: Methuen, and New York: Barnes and Noble, 1971
Owen, John Beresford, "George II Reconsidered" in *Statesmen, Scholars, and Merchants: Essays in Eighteenth-Century History Presented to Dame Lucy Sutherland*, edited by Anne Whiteman, J.S. Bromley, and P.G.M. Dickson, Oxford: Clarendon Press, 1973
Plumb, J.H., *Sir Robert Walpole*, 2 vols, London: Cresset Press, and Boston: Houghton Mifflin, 1956–61
Pares, Richard, *King George III and the Politicians*, Oxford: Clarendon Press, 1953; corrected edition, 1954; London and New York: Oxford University Press, 1967
Roberts, Clayton, *The Growth of Responsible Government in Stuart England*, Cambridge: Cambridge University Press, 1966
Sedgwick, Romney (editor), *The House of Commons, 1715–1754, Introductory Survey*, 2 vols, London: HMSO for the History of Parliament Trust, and New York: Oxford University Press, 1970
Thomas, Peter D.G., *Lord North*, London: Allen Lane, and New York: St Martin's Press, 1976

The emergence and development of the office of the prime minister during the 18th century is discussed in two types of publications: political biographies and high politics texts. ROBERTS, whose definition of the post acts as a benchmark for all scholars of the 18th century, identified as prime, chief, or first minister the man who "monopolized the counsels of the King ... closely superintended the administration, ... controlled patronage and ... led the predominant party in parliament". The union of all these duties in one individual distinguished a "prime" minister from other leading ministers of later Stuart England; but several candidates have been presented as the first holder of the office.

Majority academic opinion still nominates Robert Walpole as Britain's first prime minister although Robert Harley and Sidney Godolphin have been presented as alternative candidates by HILL (1988) and DICKINSON. Both men, or so their defenders claim, exercised all the powers identified by Roberts and add to this list the general direction of British foreign policy. Neither, however, did so under the conditions of political stability and undisputed party leadership enjoyed by Walpole and partially covered in PLUMB's magisterial biography, which has never been completed. Walpole, interestingly enough, rejected the title of prime minister on the grounds that it smacked of French absolutism but, as HILL has demonstrated in a concise short biography, Walpole exercised sole leadership over all branches of executive government in a manner hitherto unseen in British politics.

As the post of chief or prime minister had emerged from the crucible of party conflict with no legal or constitutional status, its powers and duties were never clearly defined. A premier's authority depended on the strength of his personality, the closeness of his relations with the crown and the degree of reliable support he could command from colleagues and followers. As PARES put it, "The history of the Prime Minister before 1832 – and perhaps after it – is . . . like that of the Cheshire Cat: sometimes there is almost a whole cat, sometimes no more than a grin, and it is not always the same end that appears first". This state of affairs can only be traced through detailed studies of party politics and ministerial relationships with the crown: here Pares surveys the reign of George III with balance, wit, and detachment while ECCLESHALL & WALKER give short and up-to-date biographical entries on each premier complete with suggestions for further reading.

The powers of the crown, much like the powers of the premier, were what incumbents made of them. OWEN's work (1973) reassesses the reputation and statesmanship of George II in a positive light and, though his book on the Pelhams (1971) is now looking dated, it is still highly informative on the politics of court Whiggery during the 1740s. Readers are warned that Hill changes his perspective half way through his work to reflect changes in academic perceptions of the 18th-century party system. The Tory party, once thought to have died shortly after 1715, has now been rediscovered as an active political force up to at least 1760 and CLARK, who has helped resurrect its ideas, influence, and identity, gives the most detailed and nuanced account of court and party politics during the 1750s. The 1760s, a decade of extreme instability, has been the subject of numerous books and articles, none devoted to the office of prime minister though much has been written on individual politicians and office-holders.

NAMIER (1929) is crucial to any understanding of an 18th-century parliament comprised of court, country, and independent MPs to whom modern notions of party discipline and ideology were unknown. The political world described here and in SEDGWICK, OWEN, and NAMIER & BROOKE is dominated by factions and family interest: a place where "men no more dreamt of a seat in the House in order to benefit humanity than a child dreams of a birthday cake so that others may eat it." What, if any, intellectual leadership a premier exercised over his followers in this political environment is difficult to ascertain, as is the extent to which a two-party system survived into the later 18th century. Although ideas and principles have returned to the high politics of mid-Hanoverian Britain, Namier & Brooke remains essential reading for its lucid and scholarly portrait of an unreformed House of Commons where self-interest reigned supreme, while the introductory surveys in the "History of Parliament" series (Namier & Brooke, Sedgwick) provide a wealth of detail on constituencies, elections, and individual MPs.

Premiers from Walpole to the younger Pitt constructed working majorities from two sets of politicians: the independents and the court. By 1780 the latter group had turned into the King's Friends, those MPs who would support any government possessing the confidence of the king. FEILING identified the King's Friends under Lord North's leadership as the core of an embryonic second Tory party loyal to a strong crown, but the presence of the 185-odd king's friends at Westminster did not necessarily strengthen the hands of a chief minister because they saw the king, not the premier, as their leader. North's relations with George III lie at the heart of a THOMAS biography that sees no Toryism in the king, the premier, or their Commons followers, who after North's fall transferred their loyalty to William Pitt the Younger. CANNON's monograph on the causes and effects of the 1783 constitutional crisis illustrates that the choice of a chief minister, in this case Pitt, remained a prerogative of the crown rather than the choice of parliament and that the powers of the prime minister had changed little since 1721. The determination of George III to uphold his royal rights, notes Pares, ensured that no premier would gain further authority at the expense of the crown until madness overcame the king in 1810.

JENNIFER MORI

See also Anne; Godolphin; Tories entries; Whigs entries; Fox, Charles James; George I; George II; George III; Harley; Newcastle, 1st Duke of; North; Pitt, William, "the Elder"; Pitt, William, "the Younger"; Rockingham; Walpole

Privy (King's) Council of England

Baldwin, James Fosdick, *The King's Council in England During the Middle Ages*, Oxford: Clarendon Press, 1913; Gloucester, Massachusetts: Smith, 1965

Bayne, C.G. and William Huse Dunham (editors), *Select Cases in the Council of Henry VII*, London: Quaritch, 1958

Cust, Richard, "Charles I, the Privy Council and the Parliament of 1628", *Transactions of the Royal Historical Society*, 6th series, 2 (1992): 25–50

Elton, G.R., "Tudor Government: Points of Contact, II: The Council", *Transactions of the Royal Historical Society*, 5th series, 25 (1975): 195–211

Elton, G.R. (editor), *The Tudor Constitution: Documents and Commentary*, Cambridge: Cambridge University Press, 1960; 2nd edition, Cambridge and New York: Cambridge University Press, 1982

Fitzroy, Almeric, *The History of the Privy Council*, London: John Murray, 1928

Goodman, Anthony, "Richard II's Councils" in *Richard II: The Art of Kingship*, edited by Goodman and James Gillespie, Oxford: Clarendon Press, and New York: Oxford University Press, 1999

Guy, J.A., *The Cardinal's Court: The Impact of Thomas Wolsey in Star Chamber*, Brighton, Sussex: Harvester Press, and Totowa, New Jersey: Rowman and Littlefield, 1977

Guy, J.A., "The Privy Council: Revolution or Evolution" in *Revolution Reassessed: Revisions in the History of Tudor Government and Administration*, edited by David Starkey and Christopher Coleman, Oxford: Clarendon Press, and New York: Oxford University Press, 1986

Hoak, D.E., *The King's Council in the Reign of Edward VI*, Cambridge and New York: Cambridge University Press, 1976

Jensen, J.V., "The Staff of the Jacobean Privy Council", *Huntington Library Quarterly*, 40 (1976): 11–44

Kenyon, J.P. (editor), *The Stuart Constitution, 1603–1688: Documents and Commentary*, Cambridge: Cambridge University Press, 1966; 2nd edition, Cambridge and New York: Cambridge University Press, 1986

Lander, J.R., "The Yorkist Council and Administration, 1461–1485", *English Historical Review*, 73 (1958): 27–46

Lander, J.R., "Council, Administration, and Councillors", *Bulletin of the Institute of Historical Research*, 32 (1959): 138–80

Pulman, Michael Barraclough, *The Elizabethan Privy Council in the Fifteen-Seventies*, Berkeley: University of California Press, 1971

Sharpe, K., "Crown, Parliament, and Locality: Government and Communication in Early Stuart England", *English Historical Review*, 101 (1986): 321–50

Swatland, A., "The Role of the Privy Councillors in the House of Lords, 1660–1681" in *A Pillar of the Constitution: The House of Lords in British Politics, 1640–1784*, edited by Clyve Jones, London and Ronceverte, West Virginia: Hambledon Press, 1989

Turner, Edward Raymond, *The Privy Council of England in the Seventeenth and Eighteenth Centuries, 1603–1784*, 2 vols, Baltimore: Johns Hopkins University Press, 1927–28

Virgoe, R., "The Composition of the King's Council, 1437–1461", *Bulletin of the Institute of Historical Research*, 43 (1970): 134–60

Weikel, A., "The Marian Council Revisited" in *The Mid-Tudor Polity, c.1540–1560*, edited by Jennifer Loach and Robert Tittler, London: Macmillan, and Totowa, New Jersey: Rowman and Littlefield, 1980

Because it was the principal vehicle for advice, administration, and the enforcement of the royal will, the king's council – or Privy Council – plays a major part in the political study of every English reign from the Anglo-Saxon period until the 18th century. Such a vast literature is far beyond the scope of this essay, which will merely select from secondary works devoted specifically to its composition and function. For much of this period, the records of the council have been printed: *Proceedings and Ordinances . . . 1386–1542*, by N.H. Nicolas (1834–37); *Acts . . . 1542–1603*, by J.R. Dasent (1890–1907); and *Acts . . . 1613–1631* (1921–64). Other relevant series are the domestic, colonial, Irish, and Scottish state papers, published by the Public Record Office over the last 150 years, none of which will be considered here.

The standard general history of the medieval council is still that of BALDWIN, which has never been replaced because interest in its working has shifted to more specific studies with a much narrower focus. The council was also very much a reflection of the monarch's personal style, a point made with particular clarity by GOODMAN. Even the minority councils of Henry VI have been discussed mostly in the context of the whole reign. FITZROY has an even wider focus, covering the whole history of the council, but is a comparatively slight popular work, as well as being out of date in most particulars. TURNER is the equivalent of Baldwin, covering the last two centuries of the Privy Council's meaningful existence, and is again included because of its scope, rather than because its scholarship is now highly regarded. Over the last half-century, interest in the history of the council has focused mainly on the period from 1450 to 1650, during which it not only changed its nature, but also developed a number of differentiated functions. The provincial councils which developed after 1485 in the north and the Marches of Wales will not be considered here, because although they discharged many of the functions of the Privy Council in those regions, they were separate and subordinate institutions. The judicial function of the council, however, was an aspect of the main body, and that is considered in this context by BAYNE & DUNHAM, who look at the early development of that specialization, and by GUY (1977), whose study of Wolsey's responsibility for the emergence of a fully fledged Court of Star Chamber is now the standard treatment of that controversial subject.

VIRGOE, looking at the personal council of Henry VI, is concerned more with its composition than its function, because at that time, more than any other, membership of the council was an expression of the political forces which were operating on the king, and the way in which he was responding to them. By contrast, LANDER's two articles on the Yorkist council discuss mainly the way in which Edward IV and Richard III used their advisers to manipulate and control the great aristocratic affinities which were such a feature of the political life of the late 15th century. Interest in the Tudor council has focused mainly on two periods: the 1530s, when the old royal council is alleged to have changed its nature, and the reign of Edward VI (1547–53), when the minority councils embarked upon a number of controversial policies. ELTON's article "Points of Contact" (1975) is somewhat wider in scope, looking at the way in which the Tudors used their councils to keep in touch with the local political elites, and to manage them in the interests of the crown. His view of the changes of the 1530s was first set out in *The Tudor Revolution in Government* (1953), and somewhat modified in the second edition of *The Tudor Constitution* (1982). Elton's main thesis was that the council was reduced at this time from a large and rather amorphous body to a tightly organized group of office holders, through the influence of the king's chief minister, Thomas Cromwell. In his contribution to *Revolution Reassessed* (a general attack on Elton's 1953 thesis) GUY (1986) argued that although some such change took place, it was neither sudden nor the result of Cromwell's influence. The council in the reign of Edward VI was discussed in 1975 by M.L. Bush in *The Government Policy of Protector Somerset*, and in 1996 by D.M. Loades in *John Dudley, Duke of Northumberland*, but the most satisfactory study is that of HOAK, who covers the whole reign, and discusses policy as well as composition and effectiveness. Queen Mary's council has also been a focus of some interest, and has been examined by Hoak, and by Loades in *The Reign of Mary Tudor* (1991). The useful work of WEIKEL should be read in conjunction with the latter.

The records of the Privy Council are missing for much of the 1560s, and the only work devoted specifically to the Elizabethan council is that of PULMAN, which, although it covers only the 1570s, is instructive on the reign as a whole. The scholarly and substantial works of Conyers Read, *Mr Secretary Cecil and Queen Elizabeth* (1955) and *Lord Burghley and Queen Elizabeth* (1960) also consider the working of the council in some detail throughout the reign. James I continued to use his council in the Tudor manner, and SHARPE in particular picks up some of the themes on communication and management explored for the earlier period in Elton's "Points of Contact". JENSEN is a more detailed study of the mechanics of conciliar administration, but is useful for this period, when such mechanics were becoming more controversial. Charles I's council, by contrast, became more detached from local politics, and more court based, which was a serious disadvantage in dealing with the "country" opposition which began to develop in the 1620s. The origins of these problems can be clearly seen in the parliament of 1628, a situation examined effectively by CUST. During the period of personal government and the Civil War, the functioning of the council is usually subsumed under studies of the king himself, or of specific ministers, particularly Strafford.

After the Civil War, the council reverted to its early 17th-century function, but being increasingly dominated by peers, played its communicating role in the House of Lords, rather than in the House of Commons or the counties, a situation explained by SWATLAND in the context of the history of that house. The best general account of the council in the later 17th century is probably still that contained in KENYON, although it inevitably features in every political analysis of the period. The Privy Council declined in power and importance along with the person of the monarch, and by the early 19th century most of its advisory and executive functions had been taken over by the cabinet. The Privy Council still exists, but membership is an honour rather than a job, and it works mainly as a judicial review body. Unlike the cabinet, the Privy Council is not even indirectly responsible to the electorate, and consequently has no political role.

DAVID LOADES

See also Parliament: House of Lords; Tudor "Revolution in Government"; Wolsey

Proportional Representation

19th and 20th centuries

Bogdanor, Vernon, *Proportional Representation: Which System?*, London: Electoral Reform Society, 1992
Commons, John Rogers, *Proportional Representation*, Philadelphia: American Academy of Political and Social Science, 1892; 2nd edition, New York: Macmillan, 1907
Fear, G.H.L., *The "Pros" and "Cons" of Proportional Representation*, published privately, 1983
Hart, Jenifer, *Proportional Representation: Critics of the British Electoral System, 1820–1945*, Oxford: Clarendon Press, and New York: Oxford University Press, 1992
Humphreys, John H., *Proportional Representation: A Study in Methods of Election*, with an introduction by Lord Courtney of Penwith, London: Methuen, 1911
Machin, Ian, *The Rise of Democracy in Britain, 1830–1918*, London: Macmillan, and New York: St Martin's Press, 2001

Proportional representation means the return of representatives in proportion to the number of votes cast for their parties. The conventional, and still mainly practised, British electoral system of "first past the post" frequently enables a party which gains most seats, but fewer votes than the main opposing party, to form the government. But this would be far less likely under proportional representation. "First past the post" favours the larger parties at the expense of the smaller, and encourages the formation of comparatively long-lasting single-party administrations. Proportional representation would strengthen the smaller parties by giving them the prospect of obtaining more seats, but would weaken single-party government and encourage the formation of brittle coalitions. Proportional representation is clearly more democratic than "first past the post", but it could produce more instability of government. Not surprisingly, the strength of major party interest has meant that proportional representation has been usually opposed by majorities in parliament. It has been advocated since the 1850s, however, by some notable individuals (such as Thomas Hare, John Stuart Mill, Leonard Courtney, and Sir John Lubbock) and by some notable pressure groups (such as the Proportional Representation Society and the Electoral Reform Society). In 1867 parliament adopted a "limited vote" in certain British constituencies, which aimed to give more hope of representation to the minority party in those areas. But the "limited vote" was abolished in 1885. The cause of proportional representation later made more obvious headway, if only periodically until the later 20th century. It was employed in the elections to the Northern Ireland parliament from 1921 to 1929, and to the Northern Ireland Assembly from 1973. It was partly used in the elections to the Scottish parliament and the Welsh Assembly in 1999. But there are as yet no government plans to adopt proportional representation in the British parliament.

MACHIN deals with proportional representation in the context of general democratic advance, up to the hopeful but unsuccessful parliamentary moves in 1917–18. HART provides the only full, modern, and scholarly history of the question in Britain. Beginning with early critics of the electoral system, particularly with the appearance of published claims for proportional representation from 1853, Hart proceeds to examine the schemes of the tireless campaigner Thomas Hare in the later 1850s. Thence she covers the activities of the Representative Reform Association (1868–74) and the Proportional Representation Society (this was founded in 1884, but soon languished, and was revived in 1905 with J.H. Humphreys as secretary). The Proportional Representation Society failed to gain its end in the electoral reforms of 1884–85. Thereafter there was a lull in advocacy of the cause until there was a renewal of strength in the years from 1905 to 1918, which were pregnant with electoral change. Proportional representation, unlike manhood suffrage and limited women's suffrage, did not eventually succeed at this time, although in 1917–18 it rivalled the other two causes in the amount of parliamentary time given to debating it. The Lords favoured the reform, but the Commons were opposed, and the cause failed again in parliament. A royal commission was appointed to consider the matter, and it proposed a partial system of proportional representation. But no legislative reform emerged, although (as noted above) the cause obtained its first success in being adopted in the Northern Ireland elections in 1921.

COMMONS, an American professor, presented a detailed advocacy of proportional representation in congressional and state elections in the United States, making ample comparative reference to the electoral system in the United Kingdom and elsewhere. HUMPHREYS, who served as secretary of the Proportional Representation Society, wrote at a time when several countries had adopted a proportional system and there was the prospect of more doing so. Basing his case on the under-representation of minorities in the British electoral system, he argued (with constant reference to foreign practices) for a method of transferring votes from one candidate to another in the same party (the "transferable vote"), in order to obtain a more proportionate allocation of party allegiance in the final result. The transferable vote has remained the preferred method of British supporters of proportional representation. After considering objections to proportional methods which arose from the interests of single-party government, Humphreys declared that the latter would be far less damaged by a proportional system than was often argued.

Proportional representation has remained a matter of considerable debate in Britain without ever being adopted as the means of electing the House of Commons. Nevertheless, in spite of the failure of hope in this respect after 1918, proportional representation made advances in being adopted in Northern Ireland elections and in the party list system adopted for the return of a minority of members of the Scottish parliament and Welsh Assembly in 1999. As a matter of continuing interest and argument, proportional representation has been the subject of numerous brief publications which oppose or advocate it: FEAR is an example of the sceptical treatment and BOGDANOR (recommending the single transferable vote) of the vindicatory argument.

IAN MACHIN

See also Devolution entries; Parliamentary Reform entries; Women's Suffrage Movement

Prostitution

Bartley, Paula, *Prostitution: Prevention and Reform in England, 1860–1914*, London and New York: Routledge, 2000

Finnegan, Frances, *Poverty and Prostitution: A Study of Victorian Prostitutes in York*, Cambridge and New York: Cambridge University Press, 1979

Henderson, Tony, *Disorderly Women in Eighteenth-Century London: Prostitution and Control in the Metropolis, 1730–1830*, London and New York: Longman, 1999

Karras, Ruth Mazo, *Common Women: Prostitution and Sexuality in Medieval England*, New York and Oxford: Oxford University Press, 1996

Mahood, Linda, *The Magdalenes: Prostitution in the Nineteenth Century*, London and New York: Routledge, 1990

McHugh, Paul, *Prostitution and Victorian Social Reform*, New York: St Martin's Press, and London: Croom Helm, 1980

Spongberg, Mary, *Feminizing Venereal Disease: The Body of the Prostitute in Nineteenth-Century Medical Discourse*, London: Macmillan, and New York: New York University Press, 1997

Walkowitz, Judith R., *Prostitution and Victorian Society: Women, Class, and the State*, Cambridge and New York: Cambridge University Press, 1980

Today, as in earlier times, women are most often the focus when the subject of prostitution is addressed. Whether the observer assumes a moral stance or an interest in social control, prostitution is generally considered a female problem, despite the infrequent acknowledgment of the male prostitute. Women traditionally bear the scrutiny, the blame, and the rigours of attempted regulation. In the 19th century, policing and community activity remained firmly focused on the "common" prostitute, the very adjective denoting class condescension in addition to vague fears of numbers too large for comfort. Although historians have charted centuries of concern with females who trade sexual congress for money, the voices of the prostitutes themselves are often muted, manipulated, or even ignored.

KARRAS begins her investigation of prostitution in the late Middle Ages by noting that the term itself was unknown and the very definition was significantly different than in later centuries. The "common woman" or whore was recognized not through "the exchange of money, nor even multiple sexual partners, but the public and indiscriminate availability of a woman's body". Public shaming or labelling of women as whores threatened any woman not under the control of a man.

Medieval prostitution was unlike that on the Continent, Karras explains, because most English towns did not have official brothels nor were there any serious attempts to reform prostitutes or to provide havens. The regulations that did exist tended to focus on maintaining social order through the grouping of common women on the margins of society; there was no thought of protecting the women physically or medically.

Central to Karras's interpretation is the dramatic change in attitudes toward prostitutes that occurred in the 16th century. This can be attributed in part to syphilis, the Reformations, and an increasingly repressive moral view, but mainly, she notes that as the population rose, "and with it unemployment and the fear of disorder . . . the elites felt sufficiently threatened to suppress prostitution, at least at the level that catered to the lower classes". It was the desire to control male sexuality that caused the end of the toleration of prostitution.

HENDERSON also views prostitution from the angle of public control although his study focuses on London in the century before Victoria's ascension to the throne. Henderson concentrates on the chronic problem of public order and, like Karras, he charts a changing attitude toward prostitutes and their trade. This shift led from the vicious harlot of late medievalism to the penitent magdalen familiar to the later Victorians. Henderson finds that prostitutes were drawn from the most impoverished sections of London and while the average prostitute was in her late teens or early twenties, she worked the streets only intermittently or for a brief time. These young women were not geographically or socially separated from others of their social level, for the most part, although by 1830, Henderson argues that they were increasingly seen as distinct from other women, willing but unable to reform themselves.

Far from being faint-hearted and too prudish to address the issue of prostitution, Victorians centred a long public debate on this issue, and modern historians have followed suit. The plethora of studies has taken different approaches that often mirror current historical concerns. One of the first texts to undertake a serious critical approach to the subject was FINNEGAN. Before hers, many books relied upon contemporary writings, such as that of Sir William Acton, and pornographic works, in an uncritical manner and unthinkingly reflected the biases of the sources. Central to Finnegan's approach is a rejection of these assumptions that depicted prostitutes as having "iron bodies", as choosing this life because of an innate love of fun and profit. She focuses on prostitutes in the second half of the 19th century in York, and asserts that these women were, in general, a poor, ill-nourished, drunken, and diseased lot. This is largely an empirical history; Finnegan wishes to contradict the breezy conclusions of those before her and ventures no further in her investigations.

McHUGH aims to redress what he sees as a bias in the examination of the Contagious Disease Acts of 1864, 1866, and 1869. This legislation gave local police powers to arrest suspected prostitutes on the streets of garrison towns and naval ports, force them to undergo an internal examination, and detain the women at will. These CD Acts, as they were known, were repealed in 1886 after much opposition among public groups. Instead of interpreting the repeal movement only in terms of women's social and political emancipation, with Josephine Butler as the sainted heroine, McHugh places the repeal movement within a wider social and political scene. He concludes that the feminists would not have succeeded in the repeal of the acts without help from other quarters and that the CD Acts themselves may actually have improved the health of women and did much to diminish prostitution.

WALKOWITZ also uses the CD Acts to illuminate the social reality of prostitution and she has produced one of the major creative works in the field. Hers is primarily a study of the machinations of the state in controlling prostitutes and in dealing with the opposition of the Contagious Disease Acts. In addition, she presents a clear picture of the women who became prostitutes in places under the jurisdiction of the CD Acts, as well as a full account of the lives they led before and after their lives on the street. Walkowitz moves past McHugh's concerns with the centrality of feminist opposition; she argues such broad discretionary powers were handed to the police that the focus passed from concern with disease to a control of the urban poor. The results of the acts were that prostitutes were isolated from the community into which they had been integrated and that working-class culture was destroyed. Where McHugh denied the centrality of feminist groups, Walkowitz finds that

the feminists were still couched within the ideology of separate spheres and that they assumed women were essentially moral, spiritual creatures who needed protection. These early defenders of women had yet to discover that state protection of young women led inevitably to repressive and coercive measures against those same women. Unlike Finnegan, who views prostitutes as silent and oppressed, Walkowitz paints a scene roiling with the struggle for control over the policing of working-class sexuality.

MAHOOD also views prostitutes as a potentially threatening social problem although, despite the title of this study, she concentrates on Scotland, particularly Glasgow. The repressive Glasgow Magdalene homes became more interventionist and targeted more of the female working class as potential objects of moral reform. They began to use the police to enforce entry into what had previously been voluntary reform asylums.

Mahood's conceptual framework is underpinned by Foucauldian discourse, social control theories, and a feminist historiography. She maintains that reformers in conjunction with the medical world and the local state enabled those in power to socialize working-class women into the social and sexual mores of the middle class. Unlike Henderson or Walkowitz, prostitutes themselves are marginalized in this study of power and control.

Another work that draws on recent theoretical constructs is that of SPONGBERG, who investigates prostitution by drawing on medical and legal documents. She offers a textual analysis of the medical literature of period and sets it within a wider cultural analysis. Spongberg examines medical literature on syphilis and gonorrhea and demonstrates how these views influenced the construction of the prostitute as pathological female and contaminated Other. Much of the Victorian medical discourse regarding prostitution and venereal disease grappled with the contradictions between pure women and male sexual freedom; by scientifically "proving" that prostitutes were inherently diseased, irreconcilable ideologies were made consistent.

In the most recently published study, BARTLEY too seeks to place prostitutes within the context of the reform and prevention movements which gathered influence in the later 19th century. Bartley builds upon the work of Walkowitz and McHugh by providing an expanded framework of class, gender, race, and religion. The most significant contribution of this study is a detailed discussion of the influence of the eugenics movement and the linking of prostitution and feeble-mindedness. The social purity movement aimed at the suppression and elimination of prostitution rather than upon the reformation of prostitutes. Individuals themselves are lost in Bartley's careful delineation of organizations determined to eradicate the female sexual trade.

CYNTHIA CURRAN

See also Poverty: Poverty and Deprivation; Poverty: Poverty and Social Control; Public Health; Sexuality and Sexual Mores; Women and Employment to 1914; Women's Roles and Authority

Protectorate of Cromwell 1653–1659

Aylmer, G.E. (editor), *The Interregnum: The Quest for Settlement, 1646–1660*, London: Macmillan, and Hamden, Connecticut: Archon, 1972; revised edition, London: Macmillan, 1974

Barnard, T.C., *Cromwellian Ireland: English Government and Reform in Ireland 1649–1660*, London: Oxford University Press, 1975

Durston, Christopher, *Cromwell's Major Generals: Godly Government during the English Revolution*, Manchester: Manchester University Press, 2001

Firth, C.H., *The Last Years of the Protectorate, 1656–1658*, London and New York: Longmans Green, 1909

Gardiner, Samuel Rawson, *History of the Commonwealth and Protectorate, 1649–1656*, revised edition, 4 vols, London and New York: Longman, 1894–1903 (see vols 2 and 3)

Sherwood, Roy, *Oliver Cromwell: King in All But Name, 1653–1658*, Stroud, Gloucestershire: Sutton, and New York: St Martin's Press, 1997

Woolrych, Austin, *Commonwealth to Protectorate*, Oxford: Clarendon Press, and New York: Oxford University Press, 1982

Given the fact that literally thousands of books have been written about the period of the "English Revolution" of 1640–60, it is an astonishing fact that there has been no single book devoted to the Protectorate, the period from December 1653 to May 1659 during which Oliver Cromwell and then (briefly) his son Richard served as "Lord Protector of the Commonwealth of England, Scotland, and Ireland and the dominions thereunto belonging". There is not even a study devoted to Cromwell's time as lord protector, every biography telling the story of his whole life and devoting less than 40 per cent of its space to the Protectorate. No systematic account has been published of the precise nature of Cromwell's power as lord protector: how far was he *primus inter pares* in his council, how far all the major decisions were made in his presence or in his absence. Almost all the biographies assume that he ran the government as monarchs had. Maybe so; maybe not. There is no systematic study of the role of the army during the Protectorate. How was policy made (or policy made elsewhere subverted) at the unminuted meetings Cromwell had weekly with the officers currently in London? There has been no systematic study of the legislation (and the failed legislation) of the three Protectorate parliaments; of the exercise of protectoral patronage in the residual state church – indeed the whole parliamentary history remains patchily rather than systematically studied.

As a result, gaining a real understanding of this crucial period is a matter of a piecemeal approach, and it has to be said that much of the best work is to be found in scattered articles and essays. The best – indeed the only – really thorough narrative remains that of Gardiner and Firth. GARDINER had completed a 12-volume narrative history of British history from 1603 to 1642 and a four-volume history of the Civil War (1642–49), when he set out, in his seventies, to write his *History of the Commonwealth and Protectorate*. He had got down to the parliamentary elections of the summer of 1656 when he died in

1902. Gardiner's method was to sit in the Public Record Office and the British Museum and to read everything they had on the period and subject in hand. He wrote it as he researched it, chapter by chapter. Gardiner was a brilliant historian, who tested the veracity, accuracy, and biases of every source and picked his way through the evidence with a care and clarity of exposition which brooks no equal for this or any other period. In these final volumes, foreign affairs – and foreign military and naval adventures – take an especially prominent place. Following his death, his project was taken over by FIRTH, and he added two volumes to take the story down not to the end of the Protectorate, but to the end of Oliver's life. Firth was Gardiner's intellectual disciple, and he had spent much of the previous 20 years editing the work of many of the principal actors in the drama of the 1650s – of the republicans Edmund Ludlow and Lucy Hutchinson, of William Clarke (secretary to the army), as well as of diplomats and soldiers. His knowledge was even broader than Gardiner's, but his ability to discriminate between the sources was less refined, and his writing lacked the exceptional fluency of Gardiner. Firth, too, dealt especially well with foreign and military matters. A century on they remain the fundamental narrative with commentary on the course of events, which is why both have stayed more or less continuously in print.

Beyond these volumes, one has to turn to accounts of particular episodes. WOOLRYCH offers an exceptionally careful and detailed account of the establishment of the Protectorate, and offers the best available commentary on the "Instrument of Government", the paper constitution imposed on the country in December 1653 by the Army Council until it was replaced by a parliamentary written constitution ("The Humble Petition and Advice") in June 1657. DURSTON has taken one of the most contended and contentious devices of the Protectorate, the rule of the major generals (1655–56), and located it within the broader history of the period. The major generals created a select militia of demobbed New Model veterans paid for by a discriminatory tax on all former cavaliers (which allowed Cromwell to run down the standing army in England and to reduce direct taxation) and he added to their duties responsibility for a "reformation of manners", a puritan programme of moral rearmament. Durston has produced a far more nuanced account of their work than was available hitherto. SHERWOOD examines the vexed question of how far Cromwell became "a king in all but name" by examining the public ritual (installations, opening of parliaments, accreditation of ambassadors, funerary rites, etc.) and public symbols (seals, coins, medals, liveries, etc.) of the Protectorate before and after Cromwell (with great hesitation) declined to be crowned as king in 1657. Sherwood overstates a good case; but it is a good case. BARNARD examines the relatively benign aspects of English policy towards Ireland after the brutal conquest and the ethnic cleansing of the early 1650s: the development of economic, educational, and legal reforms alongside the hopeless quest for protestant evangelism. First published in 1975, the book appeared refurbished in 2000.

And that is essentially all there is. There are innumerable biographies of key players in the Interregnum, but none is outstanding; and many of the county and borough studies that proliferated in the 1960s and 1970s contain excellent chapters on the impact of the protectoral regime on the ground. The way forward beyond the above is essentially through reading the many articles on key aspects of the period. A representative sample can be found in the volume edited by AYLMER, which contains important essays on the parochial system, the early legislation of the Protectorate, settlement in the counties, and "the last quests for settlement". This remains a period that needs taking by the scruff of the neck.

JOHN MORRILL

See also Anglo-Dutch Wars; Baxter; Blake; British Republic; Cromwell, Oliver; Long Parliament; Millenarian and Radical Religious Movements; Monck

Protestant Dissent 16th to 20th centuries

Bebbington, D.W., *The Nonconformist Conscience: Chapel and Politics 1870–1914*, London and Boston: Allen and Unwin, 1982

Binfield, Clyde, *So Down to Prayers: Studies in English Nonconformity 1780–1920*, London: Dent, and Totowa, New Jersey: Rowman and Littlefield, 1977

Bradley, James E., *Religion, Revolution, and English Radicalism: Nonconformity in Eighteenth-Century Politics and Society*, Cambridge and New York: Cambridge University Press, 1990

Collinson, Patrick, *The Elizabethan Puritan Movement*, London: Jonathan Cape, and Berkeley: University of California Press, 1967

Koss, Stephen, *Nonconformity in Modern British Politics*, London: Batsford, and Hamden, Connecticut: Archon Books, 1975

McGregor, J.F. and B. Reay (editors), *Radical Religion in the English Revolution*, Oxford and New York: Oxford University Press, 1984

Spufford, Margaret (editor), *The World of Rural Dissenters, 1520–1725*, Cambridge and New York: Cambridge University Press, 1995

Watts, Michael R., *The Dissenters*, vol. 1, *From the Reformation to the French Revolution*, Oxford: Clarendon Press, 1978

Watts, Michael R., *The Dissenters*, vol. 2, *The Expansion of Evangelical Nonconformity*, Oxford: Clarendon Press, 1995

Much of the history of protestant dissent has been written by those who belong to it. Some of it is redolent of idealistic loyalty and a desire to perpetuate (or even invent) a continuous tradition. This is evident in two of the most important aspects of the debate as to the nature of English dissent. One concerns the relative contribution of Continental European movements and of the earlier English heretics, notably the lollards, to its development. A second concerns the extent to which nonconformity separated itself from society as a whole, with a purity of principle and a reforming zeal, relatively untainted by worldly corruptions.

WATTS supersedes all previous general histories of dissent. Based upon meticulous research, which draws upon many local and denominational studies, Watts emphasizes the English rather more than the Continental influences upon dissent. He sees dissent in a continuous, if sometimes wandering, line, from the Tudor puritan movement, to the radical outpouring of the 1640s and 1650s, to the age of persecution under the Restoration (1660–88) and the relative decline during the period of toleration thereafter, followed by the invigorating effects of the evangelical revival. Watts's work is hampered neither by excessive sympathy with dissent, nor by a secularist bias against it.

Subsequent generations of dissenters looked to the puritans as their spiritual ancestors. For the 16th-century origins of dissent, the best study is that of COLLINSON. He identifies puritanism primarily as an expression of discontent with the religious settlement of 1559 and with an urge to carry the Church of England in a more protestant direction than Queen Elizabeth or the ecclesiastical hierarchy would accept. His detailed examination of opinion and practice at parish level demonstrates that support for puritanism within the Elizabethan church was considerable, but that in the main it did not take a separatist or revolutionary form; it sought to reform the church from within. Its failure was largely due to Archbishop Whitgift's enforcement of uniformity, and Collinson concludes with the tantalizing possibility that, given rather more flexible statesmanship under James I, much puritan opinion could have been accommodated within the church.

That this did not happen probably owed more to the vehement hostility of Charles I and Archbishop Laud towards puritanism than to any inherent tendency towards separatism on the part of the ancestors of dissent. A rather different view, however, is presented by the essays edited by McGREGOR & REAY. They focus upon the Civil Wars and Interregnum and, with chapters by distinguished authors on several of its principal strands, they depict dissent as a strongly radical force with social protest, as well as theological grievance, at its heart. There are excellent chapters on the levellers, ranters, quakers and Fifth Monarchists, but by giving less attention to the more moderate dissenting groups, notably the presbyterians, the authors perhaps give undue prominence to the revolutionary, at the expense of the more accommodating, elements of dissent.

Because of its association with commerce, there has been an understandable tendency to perceive dissent in primarily urban terms. The essays edited by SPUFFORD form a valuable corrective to such a view. Patient reconstruction of a series of rural communities shows the persistence of dissent, particularly in areas where parochial and gentry control was relatively weak and where there was a mixed local economy. Two essays by Bill Stevenson reveal the extent to which late 17th-century rural dissenters achieved a substantial measure of social integration, while retaining their theological and organizational distinctiveness.

BRADLEY's study is the most thorough analysis of 18th-century dissent. He shows that many local dissenters, despite the Test Acts, took an active part in local government and formed an important electoral force. He argues that, faced with a more authoritarian regime under George III and Lord North, much of dissent came to identify with the grievances of the American colonists and, in alliance with low-church Anglicans, rediscovered a Whig and sometimes a radical identity. Bradley associates dissent increasingly with lower-middle class, artisan elements in society and sees in its campaigns the beginnings of "modern" class and party conflict. Although perhaps overstating the case, and underestimating the theological factors behind the developments which he examines, Bradley offers a convincing thesis as to the mentality of late-18th-century dissent.

During the 19th century, growing wealth and social respectability led to the gradual supersession of the term "dissent" by "nonconformity". That transition is best encapsulated by BINFIELD's highly original work. Binfield brings to light a series of nonconformist family connections, support groups, and educational opportunities, which help to explain nonconformist expansion and consolidation, together with studies of leading campaigners for nonconformist causes. His chapter on Edward Baines and the *Leeds Mercury* is particularly impressive. Binfield's book is all the more valuable for its discussion of the cultural, as well as the political and social, dimensions of nonconformity.

A more explicitly political study is that of BEBBINGTON, which examines the nonconformist contribution to public life and social issues, notably temperance. While confirming the traditional identification of nonconformity with the Liberal Party, Bebbington shows that some of the more conservative nonconformists, notably the Wesleyan Methodists, were turning towards the Conservative Party, especially during the Home Rule crisis of the 1880s. Bebbington renders an important service by exposing the variety of party political opinions within nonconformity.

KOSS's first-rate volume is the best study of 20th-century nonconformity. Both Bebbington and Koss have important points to make about the rising importance of class and economic questions on the determination of political allegiance. Koss interprets politics in the widest sense and emphasizes the connection between the numerical losses of nonconformity, the marginalization of religious issues in politics, and the decline of the Liberal Party. Nonconformity, faced by a haemorrhage of support and wholly dependent upon the voluntary principle in an increasingly secular age, began to seek ecumenical solutions as a means of survival. Such an irenical approach towards other protestants would have been recognizable to many of its 16th- and 17th-century predecessors.

G.M. DITCHFIELD

See also Anglican Doctrine and Worship; Anti-Catholicism and the Test Acts; Arminianism; Askew; Bale; Baxter; Bunyan; Cartwright; Civil Wars, 1642–165: Religious Issues; Elizabethan Settlement of Religion; Emigration: From England and Wales; Evangelicalism; Fundamentalism (Christian); Hampton Court Conference; Independency in Religion; Knox; Laud; Lilburne; Methodism; Millenarian and Radical Religious Movements; Popular Religion; Putney Debates; Salvation Army; Test and Corporation Acts, Repeal of; Toleration and Comprehension; Wesley

Protestant Revolution 1548–1553

Brigden, Susan, *London and the Reformation*, Oxford: Clarendon Press, and New York: Oxford University Press, 1989

Dickens, A.G, *The English Reformation*, 1st edition, New York: Schocken Books, and London: Batsford, 1964; revised edition, London: Collins, 1967; 2nd edition, University Park: Pennsylvania State University Press, 1989

Duffy, Eamon, *The Stripping of the Altars: Traditional Religion in England, c.1400–c.1580*, New Haven, Connecticut: Yale University Press, 1992

Haigh, Christopher, *English Reformations: Religion, Politics, and Society under the Tudors*, Oxford: Clarendon Press, and New York: Oxford University Press, 1993

Hughes, Philip, *The Reformation in England*, vol. 2, *Religio Depopulata*, London: Hollis and Carter, and New York: Macmillan, 1953; revised edition, London: Burns and Oates, 1963

Kümin, Beat A., *The Shaping of a Community: The Rise and Reformation of the English Parish, c.1400–1560*, Aldershot, Hampshire and Brookfield, Vermont: Scolar Press, 1996

Loades, David, *Revolution in Religion: The English Reformation, 1530–1570*, Cardiff: University of Wales Press, 1992

MacCulloch, Diarmaid, *Thomas Cranmer: A Life*, New Haven, Connecticut and London: Yale University Press, 1996

MacCulloch, Diarmaid, *Tudor Church Militant: Edward VI and the Protestant Reformation*, London and New York: Allen Lane, 1999

Pettegree, Andrew, *Foreign Protestant Communities in Sixteenth-Century London*, Oxford: Clarendon Press, and New York: Oxford University Press, 1986

Whiting, Robert, *The Blind Devotion of the People: Popular Religion and the English Reformation*, Cambridge and New York: Cambridge University Press, 1989

It was during the years 1548–53 that the English church became for the first time protestant, and the historiography of the experience has been dominated for centuries by historians' opinions as to whether or not this was a good thing. Traditional Anglican historiography, represented here by DICKENS, has always claimed that the pre-Reformation English church was ripe for change, having lost its spiritual drive and sense of direction. The Reformation was consequently supported by a large number of people at all levels of society, to whom the thrust of royal policy from 1533 to 1553 was welcome. The new church polity was also able to build on the foundations left in the soil by the Wyclifite or lollard movement of the previous century. Traditional catholic historiography, on the other hand, represented here by HUGHES, has always emphasized the negative and destructive effects of the Reformation. From their point of view, although the catholic church needed shaking up, it was doing a perfectly good job, and the vast majority of the population was entirely satisfied with it. It was the egotism of Henry VIII and greed of the lay aristocracy that destroyed a perfectly viable church, and replaced it with a department of state that had no claim to spiritual authority.

Until the 1980s the Anglican tradition was the accepted orthodoxy. Since then, however, this interpretation has been vigorously attacked, both by historians unconnected with the traditional catholic school, such as Haigh, and by a new generation of catholics, such as Duffy. HAIGH, in a number of works now summarized in *English Reformations*, has argued that the Henrician and Edwardian changes were almost entirely political in their inspiration, and were imposed from above, without regard to the wishes of the population. DUFFY, approaching from a different angle, has drawn attention to the elaborate and well-supported nature of pre-Reformation piety, and has argued that the protestant leadership had nothing adequate to offer in its place. As a result of these disagreements, the basis of discussion has now shifted away from general interpretation to more specific studies, of which the most important and influential is BRIGDEN. London, although it contained many parishes of determined conservatism, did largely welcome the Reformation, and particularly the protestantism brought in by Edward VI. It cannot be pretended that London was dragged along reluctantly by the king; indeed some parishes were problems for the opposite reason, that they wanted reforms more radical than the council was willing to tolerate. London was also influenced by the willingness of both the government and the city authorities to welcome the establishment of protestant refugee communities, a subject examined in detail by PETTEGREE. Other historians, looking at different evidence, have tended to agree with the general thesis advanced by Haigh, but have also argued that the issues were less clearcut than he claimed. WHITING, looking at the conservative diocese of Exeter, was impressed by the willingness of people to obey the king and council, however much they might grumble about what was being done. KUMIN, with a wider brief, also found much grassroots discontent, but a significant minority who welcomed the changes, and were usually more vocal and assertive than their opponents. Many parishes became deeply and bitterly divided, and to that extent the immediate impact was negative. Some sceptics, represented here by LOADES, have also pointed out that 16th-century England was not a democratic polity, and that what people wanted was much less important than what they could be persuaded or forced to accept. Given that the coercive powers of the crown were limited, and that the introduction of protestantism was never effectively resisted, either under Edward VI or under Elizabeth, it must follow that catholic convictions (as distinct from mere conservatism) were less strong than has been claimed.

In this somewhat negative historiographic climate, the work of MacCULLOCH has been refreshingly positive. Without making any extravagant claims for the strength of protestant support, he has pointed out the positive nature of the spiritual message that the "new religion" could bring. It appealed particularly to the literate, who were a small but growing minority, and to those of a pragmatic turn of mind who could not understand how a physical body could be in two (or more) places at once. The quality of the intellectual and spiritual leadership offered by Cranmer and his circle was much higher than his opponents claimed, both at the time and since. They also managed to domesticate protestantism through the English bible and liturgy, so that it no longer appeared German, and consequently the disadvantage of "foreignness" could be shifted entirely onto the pope. Important as this "revolution" is,

however, it cannot be understood in isolation. Had Mary lived longer, or Elizabeth been a different sort of person, it might have been an episode of little lasting significance.

Finally, it should be noted that since the literature on this subject is very large, each of the works discussed above contains a bibliography that should be consulted for further guidance.

DAVID LOADES

See also Bale; Cranmer; Edward VI; Henry VIII; Northumberland; Royal Supremacy; Somerset

Public Health 19th century

Berridge, Virginia, "Health and Medicine" in *The Cambridge Social History of Britain, 1750–1950*, vol. 3, *Social Agencies and Institutions*, edited by F.M.L. Thompson, Cambridge and New York: Cambridge University Press, 1990

Cullen, M.J., *The Statistical Movement in Early Victorian Britain: The Foundations of Empirical Social Research*, New York: Barnes and Noble, and Brighton, Sussex: Harvester, 1975

Finer, S.E., *The Life and Times of Sir Edwin Chadwick*, London: Methuen, 1952; New York: Barnes and Noble, 1970

Floud, Roderick, Kenneth Wachter, and Annabel Gregory, *Height, Health, and History: Nutritional Status in the United Kingdom, 1750–1980*, Cambridge and New York: Cambridge University Press, 1990

Hamlin, Christopher, *Public Health and Social Justice in the Age of Chadwick: Britain, 1800–1854*, Cambridge and New York: Cambridge University Press, 1998

Hardy, Anne, *The Epidemic Streets: Infectious Disease and the Rise of Preventive Medicine 1856–1900*, Oxford: Clarendon Press, and New York: Oxford University Press, 1993

Lambert, Royston, *Sir John Simon, 1816–1904, and English Social Administration*, London: McGibbon and Kee, 1963

MacDonagh, Oliver, *Early Victorian Government, 1830–1870*, London: Weidenfeld and Nicolson, and New York: Holmes and Meier, 1977

McKeown, Thomas, *The Modern Rise of Population*, London: Arnold, and New York: Academic Press, 1976

Smith, F.B., *The People's Health, 1830–1910*, New York: Holmes and Meier, London: Croom Helm, and Canberra: Australian National University Press, 1979

Szreter, Simon, "The Importance of Social Intervention in Britain's Mortality Decline c.1850–1914: A Reinterpretation of the Role of Public Health", *Social History of Medicine*, 1/1 (1988): 1–37

Wohl, Anthony S., *Endangered Lives: Public Health in Victorian Britain*, London: Dent, and Cambridge, Massachusetts: Harvard University Press, 1983

The survey by BERRIDGE provides a very good and recent overview of the subject. There are also two excellent comprehensive works by SMITH and by WOHL. The latter in particular is impressive in its combination of a strong line of analytical narrative with telling quantitative and qualitative detail.

The history of public health tended until recent decades to be dominated by approaches which treated it more from the perspective of the growth of government than from that of the history of medicine. Examples are the lives of the two most important early figures: that of Sir Edwin Chadwick by FINER and of Sir John Simon by LAMBERT. Historians such as MacDONAGH have tended to treat the movement along with factory reform and the Poor Law as important dimensions of a "19th-century revolution in government": a concept which in itself produced much controversy among historians. The visitations of cholera, the "plague" of the new urban society, acted as a powerful driver of the concern with public health which emerged in the 1830s and 1840s, but as important was the rise of new forms of data gathering and presentation being pioneered by statisticians such as William Farr. Public health in the 1840s was constructively about sewers, but it was intellectually dependent on epidemiology, as CULLEN has demonstrated. More recently a new and very different account of the politics of the public health movement has been offered by HAMLIN. He sees the Chadwick of public health reform as very much of a piece with the Chadwick who implemented the harsh new Poor Law and who was eager to establish an expanded police force. The disinclination of working-class radicals and chartists to associate themselves with the movement becomes explicable.

The perception that early industrial progress was not being accompanied by improving mortality was what drove Chadwick and his associates. Indeed mortality was increasing in urbanizing Britain. That adverse trend was reversed from the late 1860s onwards, so that by the beginning of the 20th century expectation of life at birth had reached 45 years for males and 49 for females, never having before exceeded 40. At the same time infant mortality rates also began to fall significantly. The first era of public health reform had faced many difficulties. Resistance to Chadwick's determined centralization had driven him out by 1854. Effective sewage disposal, his "big idea", dominated the discourse of health reform for two decades before it was put into effective place in most large towns. Early problems apart though, there seemed no reason for historians to doubt that the eventual, if delayed, outcome of public health reform was the great mortality decline of the late 19th century.

That certainty was seriously challenged in 1976 by a scholar whose background was not in political history. Thomas McKEOWN was a professor of social medicine, who had an established reputation as an historical epidemiologist and demographer. The "McKeown thesis" inverted the traditional framework of explanation. Not only public health reform, but also developments in medicine itself, were dismissed as insignificant factors in the decline in mortality. By default the answer had to lie in improvements in standards of living, especially in nutrition. In the case of medical advances, the thesis seems to have stood the test of time. The simple argument that most of the fatal diseases that had taken a severe toll in early 19th-century Britain had in fact begun to decline significantly before the arrival of effective counteracting medicines, antibiotics, or immunization generally carried conviction. Since he believed that the greatest contribution to mortality had been made by diseases transmitted through the air, such as tuberculosis and smallpox, and the childhood diseases such as diphtheria,

whooping cough, and scarlet fever, rather than via contaminated water or food causing diseases such as cholera or typhoid, McKeown also argued that the impact of the early public-health movement, which was essentially about sanitation and hygiene, had been seriously overstressed by historians.

After a ten-year period of near orthodoxy, the "McKeown thesis" came under serious challenge. Historians, among whom SZRETER can be considered representative, began to re-establish public health reform as a significant player in the mortality decline. McKeown had given nutrition a primary role by default. There was no established correlation between indices of dietary improvement and periods of measured mortality decline. When in the 1980s historians began to measure data on children's stature, this key indicator strongly indicated a period between the 1820s and 1860s in industrial Britain when childhood height was falling, despite a general upward trend in real wages. There are obviously health benefits from improved nutrition, but clearly, as FLOUD, WACHTER, & GREGORY have shown, they could be lost in otherwise deteriorating environments. Szreter has indicated other problems with McKeown's approach. Public health's contribution was not simply in the area of sanitation and thereby irrelevant to airborne diseases; immunization, first for smallpox and then for diphtheria, must be accounted public-health measures. Tuberculosis was stressed by McKeown as a killer, but although it did decline by 50 per cent from its mid-century level by 1901, this trend had only set in at the end of the 1860s. By then smallpox reduction, the outcome of a public-health measure, was already leading the overall mortality improvement. This, if added to cholera and typhoid, strongly suggests that it was among those diseases which could be reduced by public-health measures that the 19th-century fall in mortality began.

Recently historians have begun to take a more positive view of the 19th-century public-health reforms. Pivotal to this revision is a stress on a significant second phase beginning in the mid-1860s and therefore coinciding with the point from which the anthropometric evidence indicates that improved nutrition was beginning at last to have a stature-raising effect. It was over the last third of the century that properly effective sewage systems were built, especially after greater powers were conferred on local authorities by the Public Health Act of 1875. The important work of HARDY on London displays the increasing effectiveness of public health in this later period, which was due at least in part to the improving quality of its own professional agents, its increasing educational role, and not least the greater willingness of the population to accept its message.

JOHN RULE

See also Chadwick; Medicine entries; Poverty: Poverty and Deprivation; Prostitution

Public Transport

Armstrong, John, "From Shillibeer to Buchanan: The Impact of Transport on the Urban Environment" in *The Cambridge Urban History of Britain*, vol. 3, *1840–1950*, edited by Martin J. Daunton, Cambridge: Cambridge University Press, 2000

Barker, Theo C. and Michael Robbins, *A History of London Transport: Passenger Travel and the Development of the Metropolis*, 2 vols, London: Allen and Unwin, 1963–74; revised edition, 1975

Barker, Theo C., "Urban Transport" in *Transport in Victorian Britain*, edited by Michael J. Freeman and Derek H. Aldcroft, Manchester: Manchester University Press, 1988

Buckley, R.J., *A History of Tramways: From Horse to Rapid Transit*, Newton Abbot, Devon: David and Charles, 1975

Hart, Harold W., "The Sedan Chair as a Means of Public Conveyance", *Journal of Transport History*, 5/4 (1962): 205–18

Hibbs, John, *The History of British Bus Services*, Newton Abbot, Devon: David and Charles, 1968

Public transport today has become identified almost by a negative: it is anything that is *not* the motor car. This view arose in the second half of the 20th century because of the dominance of the motor car in moving people, rather than freight. There are several possible definitions of public transport, each of which has had more relevance in some periods than others. Public transport could be defined economically as "publicly owned". This might apply to several forms of transport from the 1940s to the 1980s when nationalization was instituted for the railways, airlines, buses, and coaches. Even earlier, some trams and buses were owned by municipalities. It ceased to have this meaning from the 1980s when British Airways, National Bus, and British Rail were all privatized in one way or another, and bus routes were deregulated and made open to competition. An extension of equating public transport with public ownership might be that it attracted an element of subsidy. Certainly some railway services were paid a public service obligation for routes which were uneconomic but socially necessary. Also some tram and bus services were subsidized by local authorities. However, subsidies in the form of using surpluses from popular routes or busy times of day, to support those less popular, are a commonplace of all forms of transport and hardly a defining characteristic. A much more comprehensive and useful definition is that public transport is that which is available to anyone willing to pay the fare. Hence it excludes private carriages and cars but includes railways, airlines, trams, buses, coaches, and (in theory) canals. Several of these forms of transport are treated separately in this volume; it makes more sense here to regard public transport as essentially urban passenger traffic, with only passing reference to other aspects.

In the pre-industrial British city there were forms of public transport, namely the man-borne sedan chair and the horse-drawn hackney carriage. Both appeared in London in the early 17th century as HART has shown, and by the 1650s were common in the capital and beginning to appear in a number of provincial cities, such as Exeter, York, and Chester, as well as outside England in Dublin and Edinburgh. The use of these forms of conveyance, he argues, was restricted to the upper classes because the fares were very high. There was no benefit of speed as congestion ensured neither chair nor carriage proceeded at more than walking pace, and hence their advantages over walking were in effort saved and in ensuring one's garments were not spoiled by rain or mud.

In the early 19th century these forms of public transport were joined by the hansom cab, which was two-wheeled and there-fore lighter and more manoeuvrable. It was patented in 1834 and the number of them registered grew steadily until about 1890. They too were expensive, and hence the preserve of the middle and upper classes. The workers continued to walk, as they had done for centuries, as BARKER (1988) points out. One breakthrough in urban public transport was the advent of the horse-drawn omnibus, as shown by BARKER & ROBBINS. Its introduction to London is usually attributed to George Shillibeer in 1829, when he ran one from Paddington to the Bank. It carried about a dozen passengers inside plus a handful on the roof and was drawn by three horses. Like hansoms and hackneys, Barker & Robbins argue, it was little faster than walking and decidedly expensive. Hence its use was confined to the middle classes, perhaps clerks and other white-collar workers. To a large extent, that the fares were too expensive for use by workers did not matter since they could no more afford the time to travel than the money, and in the early 19th century tended to live near to their workplaces. For the middle classes, however, the horse bus provided the possibility of moving out to more distant suburbs where the conditions were cleaner, quieter, and less threatening.

The horse tram, as BUCKLEY has shown, was an improvement over the horse bus as it could carry double the number of passengers with less horse power. Since horses were expensive to run, this reduced the fares and made it available to artisans. This was abetted by introducing cheap workmen's fares for early morning trams, as Barker demonstrates, and comfort was much greater. Buckley explains that the construction of tramways began in England in the 1860s but became widespread in the 1870s when the step rail was replaced by the much more convenient flush rail, which did not interfere with other traffic. The horse tram had a great impact on artisan life styles, allowing them to move away from living near their work place and hence continuing the outward spread of large cities, and the improvement of living conditions.

The end of the 19th century saw yet another great breakthrough in intra-urban transport with the advent of the electric tram, as ARMSTRONG has shown. Producing electricity was much cheaper than maintaining the 11 horses an average tramcar needed, the tram's capacity was greater, and the speed of travel could be doubled. From 1891, when the first electric service operated in Leeds, it took a while to catch on, but in the first decade of the 20th century, as Buckley shows, most large towns developed electric tramways often coincident with municipalization. The growth of electric tram networks had a great effect on suburbanization, with many people choosing to live in cleaner conditions with gardens and trading off the cost of fares against the lower rents available in the new suburbs. Equally important for London was the growth from the 1860s of the underground railways, as explained by Barker & Robbins, which avoided surface congestion and provided workmen's tickets. The arrival of electric traction and the deep-level underground railways by the early 20th century, and their overground extensions in the interwar period, aided commuting from the suburbs to the centre, just as the main-line railways became more orientated to suburban services.

Motor buses began to appear in the early years of the 20th century, as HIBBS has shown. It was a hesitant start until a reliable, tough vehicle was developed which could tolerate continued stop-start conditions. Initially motor buses often built upon existing rail routes or tramways, extending public transport into areas which had not been served by those means. As the motor bus became more reliable, and as pneumatic tyres reduced running costs and improved comfort, bus services spread, and by the inter-war period began to compete against tramways, as Hibbs elaborates. Because they needed no dedicated tracks or overhead wiring their capital costs were much lower and their flexibility of deployment much greater. Over time they were seen as cheaper alternatives to trams, and by the early years after World War II tram mileage was shrinking. The heyday of public transport, Hibbs argues, was the 1950s and early 1960s, for later in the 1960s car ownership became so ubiquitous as to cause a decline in demand for bus services. After the oil price rises of the 1970s there was some pressure to encourage people out of their cars and onto public transport, but declining petrol prices, in real terms, in the 1980s plus renewed construction of motorways and bypasses worked in the opposite direction. The 1990s saw a "green" movement, keen to stress the role of public transport, combined with much greater freedom of operation for bus proprietors, and growing congestion. The balance seemed to be shifting against private transport and towards public, but only time will tell if this is a long-term trend or short-term fad.

JOHN ARMSTRONG

See also Aviation; Engineering entries; Railways; River and Canal Transport; Road Transport; Sea Travel in the 20th Century

Puritanism
see **Protestant Dissent**

Purveyance

Aylmer, G.E., "The Last Years of Purveyance, 1610–1660", *Economic History Review*, 2nd series, 10 (1957–58): 81–93
Given-Wilson, C.J., "Purveyance for the Royal Household, 1362–1413", *Bulletin of the Institute of Historical Research*, 56 (1983): 145–63
Given-Wilson, C.J., *The Royal Household and the King's Affinity: Service, Politics, and Finance in England 1360–1413*, New Haven, Connecticut and London: Yale University Press, 1986
Maddicott, J.R., *The English Peasantry and the Demands of the Crown 1294–1341*, Oxford: Past and Present Society, 1975 (*Past and Present* supplement, 1)
Prestwich, Michael, *War, Politics, and Finance under Edward I*, London: Faber, and Totowa, New Jersey: Rowman and Littlefield, 1972
Smith, A. Hassell, *County and Court: Government and Politics in Norfolk, 1558–1603*, Oxford: Clarendon Press, 1974
Stewart, Richard Winship, *The English Ordnance Office 1585–1625: A Case-Study in Bureaucracy*, Woodbridge, Suffolk and Rochester, New York: Boydell for the Royal Historical Society, 1996
Woodworth, A., *Purveyance for the Royal Household in the Reign of Queen Elizabeth*, Philadelphia: American Philosophical Society, 1945

Purveyance was a means by which, up to the mid-17th century, the English crown gained access to material resources, both for war and for the household. Goods were taken either at the market or at an agreed price, and there was clearly scope for unfairness and corruption in the activities of the crown's purveyors. It was in origin a duty of service to the monarch but in the early-modern period it was, increasingly, commuted into a cash payment. To an extent, therefore, purveyance was a means by which the crown gained access to the moveable wealth of its subjects, in the absence of effective indirect taxation. Serious questions about the propriety of purveyance were raised in the Elizabethan and Jacobean parliaments and the crown lost the right to impose the obligation in 1640. Thereafter the crown paid for its supplies at the market rate, a significant part of the income necessary to do this coming from indirect taxation. In a sense, therefore, purveyance was superseded by effective taxation systems, which also allowed government to tax the moveable wealth of its subjects.

By the 1290s some people claimed that the right of the crown to take timber, meat and drink, to requisition carts, and to raise military supplies was a grievance. Purveyance for the household, although a regular irritant, was not the main grievance. It was the demands of the crown during periods of warfare that caused most friction during the medieval period. The burdens of purveyance figure prominently in the accounts of PRESTWICH and MADDICOTT, the latter taking the story through to the mid-14th century. The best examination of the use of purveyance to provide for the household and of the impact of purveyance during the 14th century is that of GIVEN-WILSON's important article in the *Bulletin of the Institute of Historical Research*. The raising of purveyance for the household has to be placed in the context of the household finances as a whole, of course. For a full account of household finances the book by GIVEN-WILSON (1986) is indispensable.

WOODWORTH provides an excellent guide to purveyance in the later-16th century, examining aspects of local administration and parliamentary debate about the propriety of the duty. It draws on the papers of influential politicians and of parliamentary debate, as well as the records of the Greencloth. For the early-17th century, the standard work is AYLMER. In this very important article he traces the transformation of purveyance from a duty of service into, effectively, a tax. This transformation occurred in two stages. The inequities resulting from the visits of purveyors into the counties, taking goods as they found them, were manifold. As an alternative, it was suggested that counties could arrange for the transport of the goods themselves, covering the difference between the market price and the crown's price, by raising a local rate. The second stage in the transformation of the service was simply to raise the rate which was sent to the court to subsidize whatever purchases were felt necessary there. In this form purveyance came increasingly to resemble a tax, one for which consent had not been sought. Under Elizabeth and the early Stuarts, therefore, purveyance was a grievance both in the localities and in parliament. Administrative and constitutional concerns were raised, although historians differ as to how much weight to give to each as the real cause of concern.

SMITH provides a detailed account of the local hostilities that were aroused by these transactions, the pressures at work in the making of composition agreements, and the resentments that attended the purveyors' activities. His study clearly demonstrates how the issue could intersect with other concerns to produce an escalating political problem. These issues entered national political debate on a number of occasions, and so the issue of purveyance can also be followed in political histories of the early Stuart parliaments. Military activity spawned other kinds of imposition too, for example the activities of saltpetre men and cart-taking, as well as the more familiar evolution of the militia. STEWART offers a full discussion of the problems of military supply in the early Stuart period, including detailed discussion of these questions, without, perhaps, making the political implications of these activities clear to the non-specialist.

MICHAEL J. BRADDICK

See also Revenue, Non-Parliamentary; Taxation: Parliamentary

Putney Debates 1647

Aylmer, G.E. (editor), *The Levellers in the English Revolution*, London: Thames and Hudson, and Ithaca, New York: Cornell University Press, 1975

Cleissner, R., "The Levellers and Natural Law: The Putney Debates of 1647", *Journal of British Studies*, 20/1 (1980): 74–89

Glover, Samuel Dennis, "The Putney Debates: Popular vs Elitist Republicanism", *Past and Present*, 164 (1999): 47–80

Kishlansky, Mark A., "Consensus Politics and the Structure of Debate at Putney", *Journal of British Studies*, 20/2 (1981): 50–69

Macpherson, C.B., *The Political Theory of Possessive Individualism: Hobbes to Locke*, Oxford: Clarendon Press, 1962; Oxford and New York: Oxford University Press, 1964

Morrill, John and Philip Baker, "The Case of the Armie Truly Re-Stated" in *The Putney Debates of 1647: The Army, the Levellers, and the English State*, edited by Michael Mendle, Cambridge and New York: Cambridge University Press, 2001

Woodhouse, A.S.P. (editor), *Puritanism and Liberty: Being the Army Debates (1647–49) from the Clarke Manuscripts, with Supplementary Documents*, London: Dent, 1938; Chicago: University of Chicago Press, 1951

Woolrych, Austin, *Soldiers and Statesmen: The General Council of the Army and Its Debates, 1647–1648*, Oxford: Clarendon Press, and New York: Oxford University Press, 1987

Just one phase in a long series of debates within the army which took place between May 1647 and January 1649, the arguments about freedom, the franchise, and the rights of men rehearsed in the parish church at Putney in October and November 1647 have been elevated to the status of a watershed in the evolution of the western political tradition, a position securely occupied until relatively recently.

Wishing primarily to make available the texts of the various army debates of 1647–49, as well as an array of pamphlet material, WOODHOUSE presented what happened at Putney as "a spontaneous and unconscious revelation of the Puritan mind" which he characterized as spiritually dogmatic and politically authoritarian, yet simultaneously libertarian and democratic. The debates illustrated these inward contradictions, offering a commentary on the divisions among the puritan victors of the war, and in particular the cleavage between the Independents, or "the party of the centre", and "the parties of the Left" (levellers, sectarians, and others), their erstwhile allies in the struggle against the presbyterian "party of the right". His, then, was an interpretation which foregrounded the conflict between radical and conservative voices at Putney, emphasizing the question of the franchise and the coercive power of the magistrate over the conscience of the individual.

AYLMER belongs well within this particular tradition of leveller scholarship, which sees Putney as the high-water mark of radical influence within the ranks of the New Model Army. The tradition thus asserts that Putney was the moment when the levellers wrestled for control of the army as the equals of the military "grandees". With the levellers threatening to win, the grandees threatened and cajoled their antagonists, used delaying tactics, and ultimately dissolved the General Council to forestall an embarrassing defeat. The levellers had come close to capturing the initiative within the army, and their advance had to be brutally crushed, first at the rendezvous at Ware, Hertfordshire in November 1647, and ultimately at Burford, Oxfordshire in May 1649.

Although contentious and widely disputed, MACPHERSON gives an account of the importance of the debates in the transformation of English political theory with which all others needs must engage. For him, the ideas on display at Putney marked a key stage in the development of a narrow ideology of "liberty", in which property ownership and economic independence were the basis of political "interest", itself the only qualification for political right or participation.

More recently, historians have down-played the ideological significance of the confrontation at Putney, concentrating instead on its significance for the politics of the parliamentary alliance in the aftermath of the king's defeat. Although not the first to point out the incoherence and divisions among the diverse group of men who came to be tarred with the same levelling brush, KISHLANSKY has done more than most to puncture the myth of the New Model Army as a body of "saints in arms" thirsting to put into practice leveller schemes for the reformation of society. Discussing Putney, he has pointed out differences of opinion among the supporters of the *Agreement of the People*, as well as the common ground shared by both grandees and "levellers". As a further extension of his arguments elsewhere for the importance of establishing and maintaining consensus in 17th-century political culture, he has also asserted that efforts were made by all parties to the debate to ensure agreement. Unfortunately in this respect they were a failure, revealing "the erosion of consensus politics" and the emergence of a more adversarial model of political decision-making, in particular during the famous debates on the franchise, on which so much of the great liberal tradition of leveller historiography has dwelt.

WOOLRYCH offered a reassessment of the significance of the Putney debates by means of close examination of the General Council of the army within which they took place, as well as the widespread misgiving among soldiers concerned by their commanders' attempts to negotiate with the king. Woolrych challenged Kishlansky, arguing that Cromwell and Ireton did not seek consensus, but rather to cut the ground from under the levellers by asserting that their *Agreement of the People* ran contrary to the army's prior commitment to restore government by king, Lords, and Commons. The appointment of subcommittees to thrash out thorny points of disagreement, and prayer meetings to solicit divine assistance in their resolution, were not so much the methods of consensualism, as Kishlansky had claimed, but rather the tactics of the ideological battle-front. The silence which followed the order that William Clarke stop reporting the debates on 9 November was, then, eloquent testimony to the depths of genuine disagreement. Perhaps fittingly, the two authors have more in common than this comparison might suggest. Kishlansky was always at pains to acknowledge the degree of conflict at Putney, while Woolrych emphasizes the loyalist consensus with which the debates ended as testimony to how shallow the roots of leveller support in the army really were.

The most important recent reappraisal of the debates has been offered by MORRILL & BAKER, who have cast doubt on the presence at Putney of anyone who could be labelled at that time, or indeed ever, as a "leveller", thus destabilizing the entire tradition of a stand-off between radicalism and conservatism. They have also found serious divisions among the "new agents" observable in the "running skirmish" between the authors of *The Case of the Armie*, which the General Council had met to discuss, and the *Agreement of the People*, on which so much of its time was spent. Most importantly, they have disputed the primacy of the franchise as the primary topic under discussion, its true significance having been vastly overinflated by 19th- and 20th-century historians engaged in the real struggle to broaden parliamentary representation. Morrill & Baker emphasize instead the significance of the debates about the monarchy and its future settlement. In so doing, they probably exaggerate slightly, for as they note it was the far more specific question of negotiation with Charles I which caused the greatest division among the officers.

Alongside political historiography, there still thrives a tradition of intellectual history in which the debates are analysed for their ideological content. Such interpretations, as those of CLEISSNER and GLOVER, tend to uphold the older, increasingly untenable idea of a leveller "party", with a coherent set of ideas on display throughout the debates at Putney. The latter is at least interesting in providing instances in which the highbrow, literary neoclassicism of mainstream republicanism was articulated in a populist, more accessible fashion during the debates.

SEAN KELSEY

See also Civil Wars, 1642–1651: Constitutional Issues; Independency in Religion; Lilburne

Pym, John 1584–1643
Politician

Brett, S. Reed, *John Pym, 1583–1643: The Statesman of the Puritan Revolution*, London: John Murray, 1940

Glow, Lotte, "Pym and Parliament: The Methods of Moderation", *Journal of Modern History*, 36/4 (1964): 373–97

Hexter, J.H., *The Reign of King Pym*, Cambridge, Massachusetts: Harvard University Press, and London: Oxford University Press, 1941

Lambert, Sheila, "The Opening of the Long Parliament", *Historical Journal*, 27/2 (1984): 265–87

Morrill, John, "The Unweariableness of Mr Pym: Influence and Eloquence in the Long Parliament" in *Political Culture and Cultural Politics in Early Modern England: Essays Presented to David Underdown*, edited by Susan D. Amussen and Mark A. Kishlansky, Manchester: Manchester University Press, 1995

Roberts, Clayton, "The Earl of Bedford and the Coming of the English Revolution", *Journal of Modern History*, 49 (1977): 600–16

Russell, Conrad, "Parliament and the King's Finances" in *The Origins of the English Civil War*, edited by Russell, London: Macmillan, and New York: Barnes and Noble, 1973

Russell, Conrad, "The Parliamentary Career of John Pym, 1621–1629" in *The English Commonwealth, 1547–1640: Essays in Politics and Society Presented to Joel Hurstfield*, edited by Peter Clark, Alan G.R. Smith, and Nicholas Tyacke, Leicester: Leicester University Press, and New York: Barnes and Noble, 1979

The only scholars to pay much heed to Pym's family background and formative years have been Reed Brett and Conrad Russell. During his wardship he was brought up in the Cornish household of his stepfather Sir Anthony Rous, friend of Francis Drake, helping foster Pym's distinctly godly protestantism, and perhaps too his taste for colonial adventuring. The Cornish connection also brought Pym to the attention of his most important political patron, Francis Lord Russell, the Earl of Bedford, and thence the wider circles of puritan political activism in which he would later move.

That activism has been the subject of intense debate. Writing in a tradition which saw the Civil War in England as resistance to tyranny, HEXTER credited Pym as the master strategist of the Long Parliament, the man who laid the foundations of its Civil War fiscal and military administration, architect of the Scottish alliance which made possible the defeat of the king, and hence the triumph of liberty. "Like an industrious hen, Pym, when he was not busy hatching one batch of schemes, set about laying another". Hexter's achievement was to question the convention that Pym was the leader of the war party, describing him instead as the spiritual father of the "middle group", the political "trimmers" who swapped repeatedly between war and peace parties for reasons of both private ambition and public principle, depending on how their ideals of protestantism and good royal governance might best be served at any given time. This was a group and a cause whose unity Pym "carried with him to the grave" in December 1643 – the Solemn League and Covenant, "Pym's last legislative masterpiece ... saved the parliamentary cause for a time [but] ultimately destroyed it".

GLOW endorsed this view of Pym, identifying his "skilful manipulation" of the Commons, and his "adroit exploitation" of circumstances. To these ends, Pym successfully "used" all parties within the Commons as the occasion demanded. His favoured managerial tool was the parliamentary committee, more easily "controlled" than the whole House. The death of the great architect was a pivotal moment in the politics of the parliamentarian coalition, shattering the volatile middle group and prompting wholesale realignment of party adherences.

The reputation of Pym the great liberator has suffered the same fate as the "Whig" historiography on which it had been predicated. Although unwaveringly adulatory in his account of "King Pym", BRETT presented with reasonable impartiality the evidence, none of which Hexter considered, for Pym's tremendous loyalism and "almost excessive moderation" in the early days of his parliamentary career, a time when he was rarely to be found challenging directly the rights of the crown, and far more commonly concerned with the sound health of royal finances. RUSSELL went even further in demoting Pym from the leadership of the 1620s "opposition", asserting that he was a political nonentity until securing the electoral patronage of the Earl of Bedford in the mid-1620s, the importance of which connection is also laid out by ROBERTS. Pym consistently displayed a strong devotion to the crown, was immensely defensive of its powers and its rights, and if anything his loyalty was probably "excessive" (Russell), at least until 1625, and probably down to the collapse of the "bridging appointments" scheme by which Bedford's clique had sought to grasp power in 1641. Pym's views on the nature and function of a parliament were "inoffensive to the monarchy, even if offensive to [Sir Edward] Coke". However, he was a devout puritan, and it was the rise of Arminianism which first sent him scurrying for the cover of law and liberty, though it was probably the death of his patron, Bedford, which more than anything else compelled him to champion their cause.

Reed Brett portrayed Pym's colonial adventure as treasurer to the Providence Island Company and Saybrook patentee in the 1630s as the beginnings of his political militancy. It was also, of course, the confirmation of his place at the hub of the political faction which would rise to pre-eminence in the parliaments of 1640. *A propos* of his career after 1640, LAMBERT argued that the extent of Pym's influence was deliberately exaggerated in order to protect many others among the parliamentarian leadership from having to take their own share of the responsibility. Above all, the mythology surrounding Pym consciously suppressed the primacy of the parties within the House of Lords in the first months of war. It also bears little relation to the rather second-rank nature of Pym's performance as a committeeman, nor is his claim to primacy much advanced by the fact that he never once acted as a teller during a division in the Commons. MORRILL does much to advance and strengthen the case against Hexter's interpretation of Pym the political puppet-master, disputing his credentials as the reputed engineer of the Long Parliament's administrative machinery and the tactician controlling its political alignment. In particular, Morrill questions Pym's influence over the development of the parliamentarian programme for financial reform prior to the outbreak of war, and points out that Pym was certainly no legislator, neither introducing nor speaking to a single measure of his own nor anyone else's devising. He also shows Pym's complete absence from recorded debates on almost all of the more contentious issues confronting the House of Commons in 1641, although he was obsessively involved in manufacturing the impeachment cases against Strafford and Laud. Morrill concludes that Pym was "neither ubiquitous nor omnicompetent". The reputation of King Pym has been more or less shattered. The challenge remains, nonetheless, to work through the full implications of Hexter's reinterpretation of the party allegiances and ideological alignments which criss-crossed the Long Parliament, in the midst of which Pym and his colleagues were entangled.

SEAN KELSEY

See also Arminianism; Charles I; Civil Wars entries; Laud; Long Parliament; Strafford

Q

Quo Warranto, Writ of

Bolland, William Craddock (editor), *The Eyre of Kent, 6 and 7 Edward II, A.D. 1313–1314*, vol. 3, London: Quaritch, 1913

Brand, Paul, "'Quo Warranto' Law in the Reign of Edward I: A Hitherto Undiscovered Opinion of Chief Justice Hengham" in his *The Making of the Common Law*, London and Rio Grande, Ohio: Hambledon Press, 1992

Cantle, A., *The Pleas of Quo Warranto for the County of Lancaster*, Manchester: Chetham Society, 1937

Plucknett, Theodore F.T., *A Concise History of the Common Law*, Rochester, New York: Lawyers Co-operative, 1929; 5th edition, Boston: Little Brown, and London: Butterworth, 1956

Sutherland, Donald W., *Quo Warranto Proceedings in the Reign of Edward I, 1278–1294*, Oxford: Clarendon Press, 1963

Quo warranto writs required persons to demonstrate "by which warrant" they exercised franchises, exemptions, or privileges that belonged to the crown. Despite their controversial use under the Tudors and Stuarts, their medieval origin and use have received but little attention, especially since the publication of Sutherland's definitive study in 1963. BOLLAND, for example, in the introduction to volume 3 of his edition of the *Eyre of Kent, 6 and 7*, described the procedure for defending a franchise under a writ of *quo warranto*, but made no effort to describe the origins of the procedure, nor its sudden decline and near eclipse in the early 14th century.

CANTLE, in his introduction to the pleas of *quo warranto* for Lancashire, was the first historian in modern times to deal with this issue – the origins of the medieval process and its relatively sudden demise. His study dealt with both the particulars of the Lancashire eyre of 1292, and *quo warranto* pleas in general. He noted that the writ itself went back to the time of Richard I as an enquiry for holding land, but that Henry III's government was the first to use it against franchises. Like Bolland, he also discussed – but in greater detail – the procedures used in the *quo warranto* enquiries, based on the evidence of their use at the 1292 eyre. He noted that a variety of persons were subjected to summons under the writ – 15 monasteries and sundry other ecclesiastical persons and corporations, the three boroughs of Lancaster, Liverpool, and Preston, and a number of laymen, including the king's own brother – and most of those summoned were forced to appear in person before the justices to defend their claims of franchise. Of these claims, inquiries into administrative practices far outnumbered those into tenurial arrangements, and mostly concerned feudatory courts and the justice administered there. Other franchise claims involved the assizes of bread and ale, grants of various fiscal privileges, and various executive liberties. Inquiries into grants of free warren and chase in the forests also formed a sizeable part of the eyre's *quo warranto* work.

Some years later, PLUCKNETT provided a good general introduction to the early history of the *quo warranto* writ in the few pages (35–50) that he devoted to the matter in his general history of the common law. He noted that the question of the legal title to a franchise came to the fore only slowly, first in the 1254 eyre, then in the Hundred Rolls inquests of 1274–75. The medieval *quo warranto* writ itself, when used at all, was normally employed between and against private persons, but only rarely by the king. Nonetheless, this pattern of usage was the method chosen by the king, as seen in the 1278 statute *De libertate clamanda*, as the best way to attack the "broad social and political problems of the liberties". This statute engendered a stream of heavy *quo warranto* litigation, worries over the growth of royal power, and public resentment over what seemed yet another effort by the king to wring money out of his subjects without their consent. In the end, all this, along with endless delays and costs in hearing *quo warranto* inquiries, led to the 1290 Statute of *Quo Warranto*, which effectively ended the crown's use of the writ to enhance its revenue.

SUTHERLAND's study, which remains definitive, concentrated on the development of *quo warranto* law in the reign of Edward I, appropriately since Edward's *quo warranto* campaign of 1278–94 determined the shape of the law of franchises through to the various Stuart regimes from 1603. This campaign stemmed, as with many other Edwardian administrative and legislative efforts, from the information gathered through the Hundred Roll inquests, and its purpose was to expeditiously claim and maintain crown rights in franchises through renewed use of the general eyres. The problem, however, was that these revived eyres moved excessively slowly, especially when it came to the *quo warranto* inquiries, which arose from the lack of a set body of franchise law. Thus, when confronted by a question involving a franchise, the eyre justices were reluctant to make an authoritative decision. These questions were then forwarded for decision to king and council which, however, due to the press of other business, meant that only a few of these cases were ever decided. One such question that was decided was that franchises could not be claimed by long tenure. However, the immediate outcry from the community of the realm led to the promulgation of the 1290 Statute of *Quo Warranto*, which explicitly reversed this decision, and also provided that thenceforth *quo warranto* writs could only be heard and determined in a general eyre. In essence, political expediency, in the conflict for power between the king and his baronage and clergy, was more important in the development of *quo warranto* and franchise law than any legal theory. Thus, by the end of the *quo warranto* campaign in 1294, the law was a compromise: the king could force any subject to answer for his liberty without cause by a writ of *quo warranto*, while a subject could claim good warrant by a claim of holding since 1189, or "from time out of mind". The end result was that *quo warranto* had little effect for the rest of the medieval era, both because of this compromise, and because very few of the important issues raised by usage of the *quo warranto* writ were ever settled.

The only work done on medieval *quo warranto* since that of Sutherland is that provided by BRAND, whose study discusses a set of questions and answers relating to *quo warranto* law found in three medieval manuscripts, and contributes to our understanding of the failure of the Edwardian *quo warranto* campaign. The questions were those put by the justices on the Northamptonshire eyre of 1285 to the chief justice of the King's Bench, Ralph de Hengham, who responded with definitive answers. The reason for the questions and answers were simply that there was no settled consensus as to what the law relating to *quo warranto* entailed, which, of course, led to the general failure of the *quo warranto* campaign as Sutherland discussed. A first memorandum had been drawn up by the judges on the Yorkshire eyre of 1279–81, and a series of *ad hoc* decisions had been rendered by the king or his council by 1285, but no detailed nor authoritative exposition of the law existed. These were provided by Hengham. The questions concerned (1) the use of *quo warranto* writs for recovering free tenement; (2 and 3) various procedural delays available to defendants; (4) whether the franchises of return of writs, warren and market could be alienated without royal confirmation; (5) whether a failure to claim a franchise at the proper time was a tacit renunciation of the franchise; and (6) whether seisin (possession) since "time out of mind" was sufficient warrant for holding a franchise. To all these questions, the king's chief justice took a moderate to non-royalist line, which, Brand contends, had more to do with Hengham's disgrace and removal from the bench in 1290 than alleged judicial corruption. In turn, the reaction to Hengham's answers, a highly aggressive royalist position provided by the new chief justice, Gilbert de Thornton, contributed immeasurably to the opposition of the community of the realm which ended in the compromise embodied in the 1290 *quo warranto* statute, which effectively ended the usefulness of the *quo warranto* writs for the rest of the medieval period.

JEROME S. ARKENBERG

See also Edward I

R

Race Relations and Immigration

20th century

Chadwick, Owen, *Michael Ramsey: A Life*, Oxford:
    Clarendon Press, and New York: Oxford University Press,
    1990
Goulbourne, Harry, *Race Relations in Britain since 1945*,
    London: Macmillan, and New York: St Martin's Press,
    1998
Green, Jeffrey, *Black Edwardians: Black People in Britain,
    1901–1914*, London and Portland, Oregon: Cass, 1998
Hansen, Randall, *Citizenship and Immigration in Post-War
    Britain: The Institutional Origins of a Multicultural
    Nation*, Oxford and New York: Oxford University Press,
    2000
Hill, Clifford, *Immigration and Integration: A Study of the
    Settlement of Coloured Minorities in Britain*, Oxford:
    Pergamon, 1970
Hiro, Dilip, *Black British, White British: A History of Race
    Relations in Britain*, London: Eyre and Spottiswoode,
    1971; 2nd edition, Harmondsworth: Penguin, and New
    York: Monthly Review Press, 1973; 3rd edition, London:
    Grafton, 1991
Holmes, Colin, *John Bull's Island: Immigration and British
    Society, 1871–1971*, London: Macmillan, 1988
Layton-Henry, Zig, *The Politics of Immigration: Immigration,
    "Race" and "Race Relations" in Post-War Britain*, Oxford
    and Cambridge, Massachusetts: Blackwell, 1992
Morgan, Kenneth O., *The People's Peace: British History
    since 1945*, Oxford and New York: Oxford University
    Press, 1990; 2nd edition, 1999
Patterson, Sheila, *Immigration and Race Relations in Britain,
    1960–1967*, London and New York: Oxford University
    Press, 1969
Scarman, L.G., *The Brixton Disorders, 10–12 April 1981:
    Report of an Inquiry*, London: HMSO, 1981; with a new
    preface by Lord Scarman, as *The Scarman Report: The
    Brixton Disorders 10–12 April 1981: Report of an Inquiry*,
    Harmondsworth and New York: Penguin, 1982
Walvin, James, *Passage to Britain: Immigration in British
    History and Politics*, Harmondsworth: Penguin/Belitha
    Press, 1984

The settlement and impact of ethnic minorities in Britain provided one of the main social issues of the second half of the 20th century, and the issue remains powerful at the beginning of the 21st. The subject has attracted, and continues to attract, the publication of numerous books in the form of histories and contemporary analyses of non-white settlement, statutory and institutional changes, and race relations in society. Rioting between rival white bodies of native British and immigrant Irish was commonplace in the 19th century. But the first riots of a black/white racial kind in Britain appear to have taken place, on a small scale, over the question of employment at the end of World War I. Thereafter, disturbances occurred between black and white American troops resident in Britain during World War II; and serious rioting took place in 1958 – ten years after the beginning of a wave of black immigrants who entered the country to take up jobs in the expanding British economy. The first half of the 1980s and the year 2001 saw further violent outbreaks produced by the continuing social tensions that have arisen from the settlement and treatment of the non-white minorities.

WALVIN gives a broad and concise introduction to the subject, the first half of his book being a historical treatment up to 1962, and the second a more detailed investigation of conditions from the Commonwealth Immigrants Act of 1962 to the early 1980s. GREEN provides a fascinating examination of black people in Edwardian Britain, illustrating their social diversity and the reactions to them, and showing that even at that time they were more than a scarcely noticed marginal presence. HOLMES deals with the subject during a century of (mainly white European) immigration to Britain up to 1971, beginning in mid-Victorian times and ending with the controversial 1960s, when non-white influx had become much more frequent than in earlier times.

Coloured immigration began to be a major issue, causing much tension, in the 1950s. The problems which arose and the legislative attempts to cure them are given a comprehensive and critical survey, in quite a small compass, by GOULBOURNE. Also critical, but fuller and distinctly more pungent, is HIRO's lively and challenging account of the whole postwar question of ethnic minorities in Britain, set in its imperial and post-imperial context. Immigration and race relations are well placed in the general context of British postwar history by MORGAN. The more formal questions of citizenship and nationality in connection with immigrants, rather than the social frictions which are abundantly treated elsewhere, are fruitfully if somewhat technically examined by HANSEN. The attitudes of politicians and political parties to immigration are presented, very clearly and informatively, by LAYTON-HENRY, with the help of many statistics and a chapter on comparisons with continental European countries.

After race riots in London and Nottingham in 1958, issues regarding the control of immigrant numbers and the treatment of those allowed into Britain came to a head in the 1960s. Several major acts of legislation were passed in that decade, aiming both to reduce the influx of immigrants and to lessen and preferably eliminate social discrimination against them. PATTERSON, dealing with crucial years from 1960 to 1967, gives the fullest available account of the issue during this time, in the form of a very detailed study (undergoing criticism for some of its assumptions), which makes abundant use of statistics and displays general scholarly effectiveness. Most of the relevant acts of the 1960s are thoroughly covered in this study – as are social questions in connection with immigrants, such as employment, housing, education, health, and crime, and the attitudes of the churches, the Campaign against Racial Discrimination, and other organizations (including anti-immigrant groups, notably the National Front). CHADWICK deals with the activities and collisions of Michael Ramsey, Archbishop of Canterbury in this decade, in his search to repel intolerance of immigrants and establish more harmonious race relations. HILL's very useful study also concentrates on the legislation and racial problems of the 1960s, and provides a great deal of statistical and other information.

After a famous inflammatory verbal contribution by Enoch Powell in 1968, the issue did subside somewhat in the 1970s, though the period did witness the rise of the pro-repatriation right-wing National Front. But there were widespread outbreaks of urban interracial rioting in the first half of the 1980s, for which a sharp growth in unemployment was at least partially responsible. SCARMAN's influential report, based on a thorough investigation of some of these riots, taking place in south London in April 1981, made many recommendations on desirable improvements in black-white relations. The report illustrates many of the still-continuing racial problems and the need to eliminate them. Riots on a similarly widespread scale did not recur until another 20 years had passed, when there were serious, largely racial, disturbances in Bradford, Oldham, Burnley, and Glasgow in the summer of 2001. These occurred at a time when unemployment was much lower than at the previous time of widespread disturbance. The riots had a variety of contributory causes, one of which (affecting Glasgow, where the racial element was less marked than in the other places mentioned) was the settling of asylum-seekers in Britain. It remains unclear how far tensions in these areas were manipulated by fringe political groups, such as the British National Party. Soon after these riots came some attacks on Muslims in Britain, brought about by the enormous terrorist atrocities perpetrated in the United States on 11 September 2001. These recent examples of a recurring problem will doubtless receive the attention of chroniclers and analysts in due course.

IAN MACHIN

See also African-Caribbean Community in Britain; Decolonization; Immigration since 1945

Radcliffe, Thomas

see **Sussex, Thomas Radcliffe, 3rd Earl of**

Radicalism in Politics

later 18th and 19th centuries

Biagini, Eugenio F. and Alastair J. Reid (editors), *Currents of Radicalism: Popular Radicalism, Organised Labour, and Party Politics in Britain, 1850–1914*, Cambridge and New York: Cambridge University Press, 1991

Brewer, John, *Party Ideology and Popular Politics at the Accession of George III*, Cambridge and New York: Cambridge University Press, 1976

Briggs, Asa (editor), *Chartist Studies*, London: Macmillan, and New York: St Martin's Press, 1959

Clark, J.C.D., *English Society, 1688–1832: Ideology, Social Structure, and Political Practice during the Ancien Regime*, Cambridge and New York: Cambridge University Press, 1985; revised edition, as *English Society, 1660–1832: Religion, Ideology, and Politics During the Ancien Regime*, Cambridge and New York: Cambridge University Press, 2000

Clarke, P.F., *Lancashire and the New Liberalism*, Cambridge: Cambridge University Press, 1971

Cole, G.D.H. and Raymond Postgate, *The Common People, 1746–1938*, London: Methuen, 1938; 2nd, enlarged edition, 1946; as *The British People, 1746–1946*, New York: Knopf, 1947

Kirk, Neville, *Change, Continuity, and Class: Labour in British Society, 1850–1920*, Manchester and New York: Manchester University Press, 1998

Pocock, J.G.A., *The Machiavellian Moment: Florentine Political Thought and the Atlantic Republican Tradition*, Princeton, New Jersey: Princeton University Press, 1975

Prothero, I.J., *Artisans and Politics in Early Nineteenth-Century London: John Gast and His Times*, Folkestone, Kent: Dawson, 1979

Stedman Jones, Gareth, *Languages of Class: Studies in English Working-Class History, 1832–1982*, Cambridge and New York: Cambridge University Press, 1983

Tanner, Duncan, *Political Change and the Labour Party, 1900–1918*, Cambridge and New York: Cambridge University Press, 1990

Thompson, E.P., *The Making of the English Working Class*, London: Gollancz, and New York: Vintage, 1963; reprinted, London: Gollancz, 1980

During Britain's "long 19th century", political radicalism was a multifaceted and eclectic phenomenon. It not only encompassed parliamentary reform, as the term is most commonly understood, but it also included an extraordinary variety of social and political movements including Owenite socialism, trade unionism, and insurrectionary politics. The heritage and impact of political radicalism has recently become the subject of renewed debate among historians, particularly under the influence of both the adoption of new political perspectives and the postmodern interest in language and discursive analysis. Nevertheless, throughout this century the history of political radicalism has continued to be a lively, contentious, and especially fruitful subject of research.

COLE & POSTGATE, like many writers of their generation, suggested that modern radicalism began with John Wilkes's attack on the King's Speech in 1763. They produced detailed and politically committed narrative histories that traced 18th-century radicalism from Wilkes's campaign through Major John Cartwright's programme for parliamentary reform to the Reverend Christopher Wyvill's association movement. More recent work, however, has tended to view "popular politics" within a much broader framework. BREWER, along with many others, has shifted the emphasis of much recent research away from "high politics" and towards a more subtle and variegated appreciation of the popular symbolism and rituals of 18th-century political culture that acted as both a source of populist pressure for reform and a reserve of traditional support. It is perhaps this new sense of politics as cultural practice that has most marked recent research into this period.

Still, it would not be too far wrong to say that most historians, especially before the 1980s, assumed that 18th-century radicalism was generally progressive and emancipatory. J.C.D. CLARK has gained a great deal of not necessarily favourable attention for attempting to reject this notion. In a contentious and highly revisionist work, Clark attacks what he labelled the "economic-reductionist" nature of earlier political histories and particularly faults their use of the term "radical". Clark envisions 18th- and early-19th-century Britain in very much the same way that historians have traditionally described contemporary European *anciens régimes*. That is, rather than seeing Britain as an emerging industrializing nation with its attendant consequences of a growing bourgeoisie and democratization, as was implicit in earlier works, the Britain that appears in Clark's book is patriarchal, aristocratic, and dominated by an established church. For Clark the ideological dominance of the church was so thorough that it is impossible to understand radicalism outside this theological framework. In fact Clark unequivocally states that "all forms of radicalism in early-modern England had a religious origin. This was true both doctrinally and practically." Doctrinally, radicalism was rooted in the rejection of trinitarianism while practically radicals fought against the Anglican church's established status. This definition, however, has yet to gain any significant number of adherents.

The last two decades have also witnessed the development of important new perspectives among intellectual historians seeking to explain radicalism's ideological origins. It was once common to insist that radicalism drew largely upon the language and legacy of John Locke. Thus, it was argued, radicalism was founded largely upon premises of political or civil rights. However, such notions have been brought into question principally by POCOCK's work, which has been instrumental in directing attention toward the classical republican or "civic humanist" tradition that underlay much radical sentiment. For Pocock, demands for reform based upon Lockean rights were much less important than those derived from classical republican theory that privileged the duty of landowners to fight corruption by participating in public affairs. The social foundation of such radicalism was necessarily much narrower and largely restricted to the nation's elites.

By all accounts, however, the 1790s marked a turning-point in the history of political radicalism. The influence of the French Revolution generally and the publication of Thomas Paine's *Rights of Man* in particular appeared to presage a transformation of the political scene. A new understanding of political rights as both immanent and inalienable was introduced into the language of radicalism. As E.P. THOMPSON's important and lengthy work made well known, the impact of Paine was not limited to his contributions to political theory. Under Paine's influence and with his help, local corresponding societies were soon established and these societies are now considered by historians to be the first popular, or working-class, radical organizations of the modern period. Indeed Thompson's book, first published in 1963, was arguably the most important work in the field for at least two decades after its publication. Thompson asserted that the period 1789–1832 witnessed the "making of the English working class", by which he meant the creation of an autonomous working-class culture forged in the experience of repression and exploitation of both the French and Industrial revolutions of the period. The breadth of Thompson's book was quite remarkable and spawned an entire generation of later research, for within this general thesis lay a new understanding not only of political radicalism, which was now accorded a more pronounced socio-economic inflection, but also of the role of urban and rural artisans who were brought to the forefront of the movement, and later examined in even more detail by PROTHERO. For Thompson these radical artisans were the real heroes of England during these years. They were responsible, he argued, both for nourishing liberty in the face of government repression and for articulating a distinct moral economy that placed production for use before profit. In an oft-quoted extract from the book's introduction, Thompson admitted that one of his goals was to rescue such people and their ideas from the "enormous condescension of posterity". While historians continue to argue over many aspects of Thompson's book, this magisterial work certainly did accomplish that goal.

Interestingly, Thompson's influence has been most notably questioned not for the period of his study but for the later periods of the 19th century. In particular, historians' debates over the nature of chartism have precipitated the most significant disagreements among those who specialize in the history of radicalism as well as within the much broader field of social history. As far back as Friedrich Engels observers have been divided over whether chartism was fundamentally a proletarian class movement against exploitation and oppression or a "respectable" political movement for reform of the constitution. BRIGGS's important collection of essays published in 1959 had the great advantage of emphasizing the wide variety of local chartist experiences but its influence among subsequent historians may have had the unintended effect of obscuring the importance of the national movement as a whole. However, STEDMAN JONES's more recent contribution to the debate has not only brought renewed attention to the movement as a whole but was also the first major contribution to the literature that adopted an avowedly postmodernist stance.

Stedman Jones ultimately rejected class as a fundamental element of chartist agitation on the basis of his lengthy discursive analysis of its language of protest. Unlike Thompson, who posited an important role for "experience" in the making of the English working class, Stedman Jones assigned an "autonomous weight" to language that both mediated and structured the efficacy and aspirations of radicalism. Viewed in this light, Stedman Jones recognized chartist language as distinctly political in character. He argued that the language of chartism was not the property of a specific class nor did it express a fundamentally class-based view of society. Instead it drew upon the inheritance of earlier radical analyses that posited the aristocratic monopoly of state power as the source of social and economic evils. Even after 1832, when the middle classes effectively became integrated into the political system and the language of radicalism became the *de facto* property of the working classes, this did not vitiate the fundamentally political analysis of chartism's "totalizing critique" of society's problems. In fact, Stedman Jones concluded, the seeds of the ultimate failure of chartism lay in the language's inability to respond to the changing role of the state as parliament increasingly adopted measures of reform and withdrew from the arena of class interests. Under such circumstances, as increasingly proved to be the case during the administrations of Russell, Peel, and Gladstone, chartism lost not only its power to make sense of society but also its credibility.

Subsequent writers have eagerly taken up Stedman Jones's argument and extended it in one form or another well into the second half of the 19th century. Most notable among these historians have been BIAGINI & REID, who have argued that working-class radicalism and middle-class liberalism shared the same political heritage and expressed themselves in much the same political idioms. They have recently labelled this shared radical heritage "popular radicalism" and have claimed that it was characterized by a faith in pragmatic reforms, open government, and individualism. There was, they emphasize, a pronounced continuity in 19th-century radicalism that stretched not only back to the 18th century but also across fundamental class divisions.

Indeed the influence of this new "continuity thesis" does not stop at the mid-Victorian period for, as other historians have argued, the purchase of popular radicalism was an essential ingredient in the founding and initial growth of the Labour Party. Several historians have drawn on and elaborated P.F. CLARKE's early work that had posited the importance of a progressive "new liberalism" in Lancashire in the period before World War I. TANNER, for example, has emphasized a profound continuity and coherence to pre-war radicalism that linked together a variety of liberal and labour radicals into a broad progressive alliance. In his detailed work based on local constituency data, Tanner generally devalues the importance of class-based politics for the rise of labour and asserts the importance of particular local developments and political configurations.

The "continuity thesis", it should be noted in conclusion, has still not been universally accepted. Many earlier historians had attributed the rise of labour to the rise of a self-conscious and organized working class, especially as symbolized by the "new unionism" of the 1880s and the growing appeal of socialism. This view has recently been forcefully reiterated by KIRK and, until relatively recently, much of the historical research on radicalism undertaken since the mid-20th century had been in some way influenced by this view. At this time, however, the problem of radicalism's history and future is still very much a contested issue.

JAMES A. JAFFE

See also Chartism; Cobbett; Locke; London Corresponding Society; Paine; Priestley; Republicanism; Wilkes

Radio

see **Broadcasting; Reith, John**

Railways

Chandler, Alfred D. Jr, *The Visible Hand: The Managerial Revolution in American Business*, Cambridge, Massachusetts: Belknap of Harvard University Press, 1977

Channon, Geoffrey, "A.D. Chandler's 'Visible Hand' in Transport History: A Review Article", *Journal of Transport History*, 2/1 (1981): 53–64

Donaghy, Thomas L, *Liverpool and Manchester Railway Operations 1831–1845*, Newton Abbot, Devon: David and Charles, 1972

Gourvish, T.R., *Railways and the British Economy 1830–1914*, London: Macmillan, 1980

Hawke, G.R., *Railways and Economic Growth in England and Wales 1840–1870*, Oxford: Clarendon Press, 1970

Kirby, Maurice W., *The Origins of Railway Enterprise: The Stockton and Darlington Railway, 1821–1863*, Cambridge and New York: Cambridge University Press, 1993

Lewis, M.J.T., *Early Wooden Railways*, London: Routledge, and Kegan Paul, 1970

Mitchell, Brian R., "The Coming of the Railway and United Kingdom Economic Growth", *Journal of Economic History*, 24/3 (1964): 315–36

O'Brien, Patrick (editor), *Railways and the Economic Development of Western Europe, 1830–1914*, London: Macmillan, and New York: St Martin's Press, 1983

There has been an enormous amount of research on the history of Britain's railway system and, although much of it has been undertaken by enthusiasts, there is also a solid body of academic work. It continues to be a controversial topic. It is impossible to cover all aspects; this essay can only skim the surface of a vast literature.

There are two contestants for the title of Britain's first railway: the Stockton and Darlington, which opened in 1825, and the Liverpool and Manchester, which commenced operations in 1830. This is not to ignore the huge number of wagonways and other forms of mainly coal transport drawn by horses or gravity from mine to waterside, which are so ably charted and explained by LEWIS. These did not carry passengers for gain and neither were they steam propelled. They usually used wooden rails, or later wrought iron plates attached to the wooden rail. KIRBY has written the early history of the Stockton and Darlington line, showing that locomotives were not the only form of propulsion – horses and stationary steam engines were also employed – and that initially track usage was open to all carriers rather than being the monopoly of the railway company. It was these characteristics that, in the view of some commentators, disqualify the Stockton and Darlington from the title of first modern railway. By contrast, as DONAGHY has shown, the Liverpool to Manchester Railway (LMR) from its commencement used only locomotive power and, for safety reasons, ran all of the trains itself. Hence the LMR, with its Stephenson-designed locomotives, is seen by some as the first fully modern railway system in the world, defined in organizational as well as engineering terms.

There were several railway booms in the early 19th century which saw the basic network of main railway lines built by the middle of the century. The impact of railways on politics, economy, and society has been the subject of much disagreement. Contemporaries saw their significance as quite startling – a large increase in speed and potential mobility for both goods and people. This continued to be the view into the 1960s, most cogently and analytically propounded by MITCHELL, who divided the impact of the railway into three categories: as an idea, in construction, and as an operating entity. The building of railways, he argued, had a great impact on iron, brick, and coal production as well as in engineering practices. Their operation revolutionized transport in terms of speed, volume, comfort, and price, and most importantly they had a radical impact on ideas in terms of mobilizing capital and hence in attitudes to: saving and investment; the need for standard time; ideas on space, time, and mobility; and even ideas of evolution and creationism.

This radical interpretation was questioned initially by scholars in the United States, in the context of their railroads, and the doubts were taken up subsequently in the UK. The leading proponent of an alternative view of British railways was HAWKE, who used statistical techniques to try and estimate the "social saving" of the railway. That is, how much greater costs the economy would have incurred if the railways had never been built. This was dubbed the "counterfactual" proposition. In America the role of the railways had been much downplayed, and Hawke too took this line. He calculated that between 7 and 11 per cent of the British national income in 1865 would have been saved by the railways, depending on the cost of comfort on other forms of transport. There has been much controversy over this finding. GOURVISH has criticized both the methods and the results. Hawke omitted many features of railway transport, Gourvish claims, and some of his figures for freight rates are dubious or poorly based. Gourvish made his own calculations of the possible social saving from railway operation and arrived at a minimum of 2.7 per cent and a maximum of nearly 23 per cent. This enormous range casts doubt on the value of the exercise because small variations in the assumptions make a large impact. Hence there is a degree of disillusionment with the social-savings approach, despite attempts to extend the technique to other European countries, best evinced in the work edited by O'BRIEN.

Another debate about the impact of railways has centred on their role in business history. In the United States CHANDLER stressed that railway companies were among the biggest businesses of the 19th century, and indeed the first large-scale firms ever. They far exceeded other corporations in their geographic scope, scale of employment, the revenue they generated, and the amount of capital invested in them. Their sheer size meant they had problems organizing and controlling such large operations. Chandler claimed that the way in which the railway solved these organizational problems acted as a model for other large-scale firms later on. So railways in America were claimed to be pioneers of big-business methods. There was controversy over the degree to which transfer of techniques took place, and the extent of the novelty of the railways' solutions, with the army proposed

as one obvious model. More importantly there was an attempt to see if these ideas applied in Britain. CHANNON was an early proponent of this approach, demonstrating that British railway companies were the largest business enterprises in the country, a situation paralleling that of America, but that they were concentrated at an even earlier date than in the United States. Channon also stressed that the government played a much larger role in Britain than in the United States in relation to railways. The British government prevented further mergers beyond a certain point as it feared oligopoly, thus encouraging railways to find less formal forms of co-operation, such as pools and conferences. Also, government concern over monopoly, and public protest, led to legislation freezing freight charges in the 1890s, so in another way the government affected British railways to a greater extent than in the United States. The profitability of British railways after 1870 was far from robust and hence there is doubt as to whether high-order decisions made by the railway directors were as optimal as Chandler suggested.

Of late, with radical changes in the structure of British railways, more interest has been shown in the rationale of nationalization and hence in government–railway relationships. Controversy is likely to heighten rather than diminish.

JOHN ARMSTRONG

See also Brunel; Engineering entries; Freight Transport; Industrial Revolution; Public Transport; River and Canal Transport; Stephenson; Telford; Transport Development

Ralegh, Sir Walter c.1554–1618
Courtier, seaman, and writer

Fussner, F. Smith, *The Historical Revolution: English Historical Writing and Thought, 1580–1640*, London: Routledge and Kegan Paul, and New York: Columbia University Press, 1962

Greenblatt, Stephen J., *Sir Walter Ralegh: The Renaissance Man and His Roles*, New Haven, Connecticut and London: Yale University Press, 1973

Hill, Christopher, *Intellectual Origins of the English Revolution*, Oxford: Clarendon Press, 1965; reprinted with corrections, Oxford: Clarendon Press, and New York: Oxford University Press, 1980; revised and enlarged edition, as *Intellectual Origins of the English Revolution – Revisited*, Oxford: Clarendon Press, and Oxford and New York: Oxford University Press, 1997

Lawson-Peebles, Robert, "The Many Faces of Sir Walter Ralegh", *History Today*, 48/3 (1998): 17–24

Quinn, David B., *Raleigh and the British Empire*, London: Hodder and Stoughton for the English Universities Press, 1947; New York: Macmillan, 1949

Strathmann, Ernest A., *Sir Walter Raleigh: A Study in Elizabethan Skepticism*, New York: Columbia University Press, 1951

Trevor-Roper, H.R., "The Last Elizabethan: Sir Walter Raleigh" in his *Historical Essays*, London: Macmillan, and New York: St Martin's Press, 1957; as *Men and Events: Historical Essays*, New York: Harper, 1957

Sir Walter Ralegh is certainly one of the most fascinating figures to emerge from the Renaissance period. As one writer puts it, there are as many sides to his personality and reputation as there are ways of spelling his name. Few have as many dimensions as the man termed by Hugh TREVOR-ROPER, "The Last Elizabethan".

For example, David QUINN has focused attention on Ralegh's role as a supporter and propagandist of British colonization. While England had been slow to take part in the creation of an empire, Ralegh became the leading spokesman for this view. Along with his half-brother Humphrey Gilbert, who sought to establish a colony in Newfoundland, Sir Walter wrote of the benefits of such endeavours not only for socio-economic reasons, but also as an aspect of his strong anti-Spanish stance. In addition, as Quinn notes, Ralegh was associated with the Hakluyts, whose publications gave voice to Sir Walter's arguments and included some of his own works such as *The Discovery of Guiana*. Finally, Quinn discusses the experience that Ralegh had in Ireland, in common with other English seamen, and his role in the establishment of the abortive Roanoke colony in North Carolina.

Sir Walter has also been seen by scholars such as Strathmann and Christopher HILL as a key figure in the history of science. Among his associates or clients were such significant figures as Thomas Hariot and John Dee, and Ralegh was aware of the newer scientific trends. He also occupied himself in the Tower with various experiments and medical cures. But STRATHMANN argues against the view of some contemporaries that his ideas, conversations, and friendships could support a charge of atheism.

In this connection, scholars like Hill, Strathmann, and FUSSNER have dwelt in depth on Ralegh's *History of the World* written while the author was a prisoner in the Tower during the reign of James I. This work has become the focus of great interest, despite the fact that it ends around 130BC. Now considered a landmark in English historical writing in terms of its efforts at analysis and causation, the *History* also interests scholars because it had a remarkable popularity among puritans, Oliver Cromwell, for example, recommending it to his son as required reading. Scholars have emphasized the importance of the preface and its development of the idea of the working of God's providence in history. Within the scope of the *History* itself, moreover, God remains the first cause.

At the same time, historians have also noted the political impact of the *History*, for Ralegh makes a number of judgements about rulers and ruling. These, it is pointed out, are not limited to the ancients for, in the preface, Ralegh has a number of things to say about English history. Thus Ralegh supported the notion that monarchs might be criticized, a fact that led James I to regard the *History* as too inflammatory. Finally, as Hill notes, Ralegh's other political writings lent support to the pretensions of the commons.

Another feature that scholars like Hill and LAWSON-PEEBLES, especially, have noted is the strong strain of anti-Spanish feeling which flowed from Ralegh and his circle. Behind the colonization efforts lay the desire to use such settlements as bases from which to attack the Spanish. Moreover, Ralegh was also prepared to raid Spanish possessions himself. Hence, the irony in his conviction for the treason of aiding Spain.

The same authors note the significance of Ralegh's execution as a symbol of England's appeasement of Spain and the posthumous role Sir Walter was to play as a recurrent reminder of English patriotism. Larger than life, he became both a source of strength and a lightning-rod of opposition to the early Stuarts.

In this connection, scholars have also noted the careful way in which Ralegh went about a fashioning a self-image. GREENBLATT, for instance, has discussed this in relationship to his role as a courtier and during his trial for treason. In addition, as he and Lawson-Peebles have pointed out, Ralegh handled his own execution as a set piece, carrying it off in such a way that he could create the kind of death scene that he wanted. Certainly, he was successful in this effort.

It should be noted that, thanks to the work of Greenblatt and others, Ralegh has acquired a more significant literary reputation, not only in terms of his prose work, but also regarding his poetry. Such scholars now regard him as a leading author of the period.

It is safe to assume that Ralegh will continue to demand scholars' attention. That he has become a critically important figure is evidenced by the fact that Hill saw him as one of three men, along with Francis Bacon and Edward Coke, who laid the foundations for the English Revolution.

MARC L. SCHWARZ

See also American Colonies: Carolinas and Georgia; Dee; Drake; Exploration: To the 18th Century; Frobisher; New World, Perceptions of the; Piracy

Rawdon-Hastings, Francis, 1st Marquis Hastings, 2nd Earl of Moira 1754–1826

Soldier and imperial administrator

Bayly, C.A., *Imperial Meridian: The British Empire and the World, 1780–1830*, Harlow and New York: Longman, 1989

Dodwell, H.H. (editor), *The Cambridge History of the British Empire*, vol. 4, *British India, 1497–1858*, Cambridge: Cambridge University Press, and New York: Macmillan, 1929

Dodwell, H.H., "The Development of Sovereignty in British India" in *The Cambridge History of the British Empire*, vol. 4, *British India, 1497–1858*, edited by Dodwell, Cambridge: Cambridge University Press, and New York: Macmillan, 1929

Edwardes, S.M., "The Final Struggle with the Marathas, 1784–1818" in *The Cambridge History of the British Empire*, vol. 4, *British India, 1497–1858*, edited by H.H. Dodwell, Cambridge: Cambridge University Press, and New York: Macmillan, 1929

Ehrman, John, *The Younger Pitt*, vol. 2, *The Reluctant Transition*, London: Constable, and Stanford, California: Stanford University Press, 1983

Hibbert, Christopher, *George IV*, vol. 1, *Prince of Wales 1762–1811*, London: Longman, and New York: Harper and Row, 1972; vol. 2, *Regent and King 1811–1830*, London, Allen Lane: 1973; one-volume edition, Harmondsworth: Penguin, 1976

Kavanaugh, Ann C., *John Fitzgibbon, Earl of Clare: Protestant Reaction and English Authority in Late Eighteenth Century Ireland*, Dublin and Portland, Oregon: Irish Academic Press, 1997

Luard, C.E., "The Indian States, 1818–1857" in *The Cambridge History of the British Empire*, vol. 4, *British India, 1497–1858*, edited by H.H. Dodwell, Cambridge: Cambridge University Press, and New York: Macmillan, 1929

MacDonagh, Oliver, *The Inspector General: Sir Jeremiah Fitzpatrick and the Politics of Social Reform, 1783–1802*, London: Croom Hill, 1981

Mehta, Mohan Sinha, *Lord Hastings and the Indian States: Being a Study of the Relations of the British Government in India with the Indian States, 1813–1823*, Bombay: D.B. Taraporevala, 1930

Pancake, John S., *This Destructive War: The British Campaign in the Carolinas, 1780–1782*, Alabama: University of Alabama Press, 1985

Pearson, Lilian M., "The Bengal Administrative System, 1786–1818" in *The Cambridge History of the British Empire*, vol. 4, *British India, 1497–1858*, edited by H.H. Dodwell, Cambridge: Cambridge University Press, and New York: Macmillan, 1929

Despite the abundance of materials for a biography in the Huntington Library and elsewhere, historians have shied away from offering a comprehensive assessment of Hastings's varied career. He was an imperial official second only in stature to Lord Cornwallis, in personal appearance every inch the part, the "Timon of the present age", as Wraxall dubbed him, but the activities of this public servant can still only be examined episodically, with his time in the American war and as Governor-General of Bengal attracting most attention.

Where he is mentioned at all, Lord Rawdon (as he was styled before 1793) emerges creditably from both British and American scholars charting his career in the American War of Independence from Bunker Hill in 1775 (where he was wounded) to Camden in 1780 and beyond. The consensus is that Rawdon was a fine combat officer. PANCAKE's study of the war in the south judges Rawdon's victory over Nathanial Greene at Hobkirk's Hill (near Camden) on 25 April 1781 a British strategic failure, but attaches no personal blame to Rawdon who, having retreated to Charleston, left for Britain (he was captured at sea by the French), his health broken by 15 months of hard campaigning under Cornwallis.

Rawdon's role in Irish politics (admittedly subordinate to his army career) has attracted no single study. He was a major landlord in Ulster after succeeding his father as 2nd Earl of Moira in 1793 and, as a moderate Whig, sympathetic to catholic emancipation. Attention focuses on Moira as the butt of Lord Chancellor Clare's three-hour, hardline speech (the "rope speech" as it was known to the Whigs) in the Irish House of Lords in February 1798, replying to Moira's motion denouncing the "coercion and severity ... by which this kingdom is ruled", and requesting that a committee of peers consider independently the causes of discontent. The latest student of the exchange, KAVANAUGH, observes that "Moira himself could scarcely be dismissed merely as a hypocrite and opportunist with a short memory". Moira's importance as one of the strongest

advocates of patriotic union between Britain and Ireland, a union that included catholic emancipation, has been persuasively noted by MACDONAGH.

EHRMAN's magisterial biography of Pitt shows what little use government made of his proven qualities in the French revolutionary wars. Ehrman exonerates Moira for the failure of his expedition to make landfall in the Vendée late in 1793 and shows how the following year he pressured Pitt and Dundas into abandoning a descent on the Breton coast; Ehrman considers Moira's brief period as master-general of the Ordnance to have been insignificant, though he sympathizes with his frustration over the conduct of the expedition to the Ile d'Yeu in late 1795. Moira's British political career in England between c.1790 and 1813 has also not been put under the spotlight, a surprising omission in view of his role as George, Prince of Wales's trusted adviser and confidant. HIBBERT's biography of George IV offers no extended treatment of Moira's actions as intermediary between the prince and the Foxite and Grenville Whigs beyond noting the earl's generosity in lending money to the prince and mentioning his importance during George III's illnesses in 1801 and 1804. Hibbert is content to restate Creevy's verdict, that Moira was "the greatest political coward in the world" in connection with the earl's failure to negotiate a new government based around himself and Wellesley Robert, Earl of Mornington, in February 1812 following Perceval's assassination and the prince becoming regent. There is a sense from general works that Moira was temperamentally unsuited to the rough-and-tumble of Westminster and was more than content to go to Bengal after the regent had confirmed Lord Liverpool's administration in power.

The starting-point for 20th-century study of Hastings in India is the DODWELL volume (1929) in the *Cambridge History of the British Empire*, from which Hastings emerges with the utmost credit in all aspects of policymaking. His eventual decision to continue Wellesley's forward policy towards the Indian states is thoroughly vindicated here. As EDWARDES puts it:

> Lord Hastings fully realised that, if India was ever to prosper, orderly government must be substituted for the lawless and predatory rule of chief antagonists, and he brought to the achievement of his complex task a singular combination of firmness and moderation.

In the same spirit, in their contributions PEARSON lauds Hastings's constant attention to the Bengal administrative system, where he improved the working of Cornwallis's code; DODWELL considers the "definite and full" assertion of sovereignty over the Moghul empire self-evidently desirable; while LUARD vindicates his consolidation of empire despite the misgivings of the East India Company directors. British rule was under threat when he arrived, not so when he left. Several contributors, among them Edwardes and Luard, make the point that the marquess (advanced a step in the peerage in 1817) was well served by able subordinates such as Sir David Ochterlony, the victor at Makwanpur over the the Gurkha state of Nepal, Sir John Malcolm in central India, Mountstuart Elphinstone in the Deccan, Sir Thomas Munro in Madras, and Sir Charles Metcalfe in Delhi and Hyderabad.

MEHTA's volume is in much the same vein. He concluded that Hastings stood only at a short remove from Wellesley in his impact on British rule in India. According to Mehta, "He was essentially a militarist, but at the same time there was in him a conciliatory spirit, which did not make him a ruthless conqueror", who proceeded on the basis that all Indian states would have subordinate status within the Raj, a strategy made possible by the defeat of the strong independent powers in 1816–18 after the Maratha leaders had mounted their final challenge to British rule. Mehta makes the same point as Dodwell over Hastings's good fortune in having capable subordinates in place.

The most recent treatment of Hastings's rule in India occurs in BAYLY. He argues that the marquess was continuing the Wellesley policy of providing stability for the subcontinent through achieving British paramountcy. For Bayly, Hastings is one of the key players in "the second British Empire" of c.1780–1830 when, following the disasters of the American War of Independence, British imperial power expanded on an unprecedented scale. This period of empire was characterized by an emphasis on benevolent authority rather than any rights of subjects, and Hastings played the archetypal proconsular figure to perfection.

NIGEL ASTON

See also East India Company; George IV; India: Conquest

Rebecca Riots 1838–1844

Davis, Natalie Z., "Women on Top" in The Reversible World: Symbolic Inversion in Art and Society, edited by Barbara A. Babcock, Ithaca, New York: Cornell University Press, 1978

Evans, Henry Tobit, Rebecca and Her Daughters, Being a History of the Agranian Disturbances in Wales Known as "the Rebecca Riots", Cardiff: no publisher given, 1910

Howell, David, "The Rebecca Riots" in People and Protest: Wales 1815–1880, edited by Trevor Herbert and Gareth Elwyn Jones, Cardiff: University of Wales Press, 1988

Howkins, Alun and Linda Merricks, "'Wee Be Black as Hell': Ritual, Disguise, and Rebellion", Rural History, 4/1 (1993): 41–53

Jones, David J.V., Rebecca's Children: A Study of Rural Society, Crime, and Protest, Oxford: Clarendon Press, and New York: Oxford University Press, 1989

Thompson, E.P., Customs in Common, London: Merlin Press, and New York: New Press, 1991

Williams, David, The Rebecca Riots: A Study in Agrarian Discontent, Cardiff: University of Wales Press, 1955

The so-called Rebecca riots – their name stemming from a biblical allusion – took place in Wales, and began as a series of night attacks by local people (sometimes men in women's clothes) in protest against tolls and turnpikes. The first monograph on the riots was by Henry Tobit EVANS whose Rebecca and Her Daughters appeared posthumously in 1910, edited by his daughter. Less than 10 per cent of the volume, however, was in the author's own words, the bulk of the text comprising unattributed extracts, mainly from the Welshman newspaper. There is a narrative of the main events thrown together in some sort of chronological order but hardly any analysis was attempted.

In complete contrast was The Rebecca Riots by David WILLIAMS, an immaculate "study in agrarian discontent", meticulously researched – not least through a trawling of the Home Office papers (HO.45) – and rigorously examined both with regard to causation and to forms of protest. Anxious to establish that the causes of the riots were far more deep-seated than the oppressive toll gates, Williams was at pains to examine the various other hardships afflicting the peasantry, such as low prices for the food they produced, high farm rents, burdensome poor rates, and exacting tithes and church rates, and also to emphasize the growing poverty arising from the remarkable growth of population. Wholly aware of the harsh lives of the peasantry exacerbated by gentry indifference, and acknowledging their "recklessness born of despair", Williams nevertheless stood back as it were from the nocturnal outrages. For him,

> . . . the inevitable consequences of this defiance of the rule of law was that the forces which engendered it were perverted to other purposes for, in a social upheaval, the scum may rise to the surface as well as the cream. The more law-abiding members of the community were kept in constant fear of a summons to attend at the destruction of a gate, and of the lurid threat of retaliation which accompanied it.

Particular condemnation was reserved for the "gang of miscreants" led by Shoni Sgubor Fawr in late summer 1843, who, as "the lunatic fringe of the Rebecca movement", lurched it into new levels of violence.

It is in his contrast to his old tutor's detachment that David JONES's Rebecca's Children makes a new departure. For Jones, "Rebeccaism grew naturally out of a fertile soil" given that "private, social and political life in West Wales had always been impregnated with violence". In his view, the chemistry of the Rebecca movement did not change in the late summer of 1843 as both Tobit Evans and David Williams contended, moving away from the toll gates into more violent, more distasteful forms of direct action like arson, vandalism, animal maiming, and brutality. Such activities, insisted Jones, had been there from the start and Shoni Sgubor Fawr and Dai'r Cantwr simply "brought them to a fine art". Jones accepted this violence as a natural response of the west-Wales peasantry. Altogether, states Kenneth O. Morgan, Jones "was more emotionally and politically committed by far" (Crime, Protest, and Police in Modern British Society, co-edited with David Howell, 1999) than David Williams and he "invested them [the rioters] all with humanity and a kind of heroisim". Building on the observation made by Tobit Evans's daughter in her introduction to her father's book, David Jones was, moreover, keen to point to the continuation of Rebeccaism "in a variety of guises" during the 1850s and 1860s in the south-western counties. Again, he was to lay greater stress than Williams upon the political "feelings of independence" among the west-Wales peasantry, feelings of independence that he detected before the riots but that were significantly catalysed by them.

Other scholars have made helpful contributions. The custom of carrying the ceffyl pren (wooden horse), so intimately associated with Rebecca's mission of doing good to the poor and distressed, has been placed within the wider context of early modern British and European popular culture by writers like Natalie Z. Davis, Alun Howkins and Linda Merricks, and Edward Thompson. DAVIS, in demonstrating how a carnival right of criticism and mocking sometimes spilled over into real social protest, drew attention to the case of the Rebecca riots among others. Just as important as the disguise afforded by the black face and female attire, she argued, were the various ways in which the female persona sanctioned resistance, as males drawing upon "the sexual power and energy of the unruly woman and on her license (long assumed at carnivals and games) to promote fertility, to defend the community interests and standards, and to tell the truth about unjust rule". For their part, HOWKINS & MERRICKS contended that participation in the ritual of blacking up and wearing female clothes transformed those involved, for the real element of concealment was against the self, the ritual of mask, female garb, and acting the "pantomime" of resistance allowing respectable farmers (in Rebecca's case) to become transformed into the community's conscience and to carry out acts of protest totally out of character with their respectable selves. Edward THOMPSON similarly extends our grasp by placing the *ceffyl pren* alongside similar rituals in the rest of Britain, notably riding the stang, skimmington, and rough music.

Thompson also amplifies our understanding of the way in which Rebecca was perceived by the "poorest and most despised" of the community as the dispenser of popular justice by citing the correspondence of Edward Lloyd Hall to the Home Office concerning his turning away "a poor idiot girl" begging at his door, who quietly replied that she would "tell Becca". Furthermore, Thompson, like David Jones concerned to emphasize the continuing spiritual authority of Rebecca, cited the presence of a "Rebecca" gang at Llanbister in Radnorshire as late as 1898 punishing an adulterous couple.

David HOWELL's essay on the riots cautioned against downplaying the importance of the toll gates in causing the riots while, at the same time, suggesting that if high farm rents had been lowered sooner the riots would not have occurred.

DAVID W. HOWELL

See also Road Transport; Social Conflict: Modern Period

Recusancy and Mission

Aveling, J.C.H., *The Handle and the Axe: The Catholic Recusants in England from Reformation to Emancipation*, London: Blond and Briggs, 1976
Bossy, John, *The English Catholic Community 1570–1850*, London: Darton, Longman and Todd, 1975; New York: Oxford University Press, 1976
Duffy, Eamon, *The Stripping of the Altars: Traditional Religion in England c.1400–c.1580*, New Haven, Connecticut and London: Yale University Press, 1992
Haigh, Christopher, *Reformation and Resistance in Tudor Lancashire*, Cambridge and New York: Cambridge University Press, 1975
Haigh, Christopher, *English Reformations: Religion, Politics, and Society under the Tudors*, Oxford: Clarendon Press, and New York: Oxford University Press, 1993
Hughes, Philip, *The Reformation in England*, vol. 3, London: Hollis and Carter, and New York: Macmillan, 1954
McCoog, Thomas M., *The Society of Jesus in Ireland, Scotland, and England 1541–1588: "Our Way of Proceeding?"*, Leiden and New York: E.J. Brill, 1996
Trimble, William Raleigh, *The Catholic Laity in Elizabethan England 1558–1603*, Cambridge, Massachusetts: Belknap Press of Harvard University Press, 1964
Walsham, Alexandra, *Church Papists: Catholicism, Conformity, and Confessional Polemic in Early Modern England*, Woodbridge, Suffolk and Rochester, New York: Boydell Press for the Royal Historical Society, 1993

Traditionally historians such as BOSSY, AVELING, HUGHES, and TRIMBLE have seen the English catholic community in 1558 as small and needing the presence of the Douai priests and the Jesuits to rally them to loyalty to pope and Roman church, even though this meant loss of property (especially after the 1581 and 1587 recusancy statues imposed a fine of £20 per lunar month or forfeiture of all moveable goods and two-thirds of one's property), liberty, and, possibly, life. Attention has focused on those who refused "to go to church, chapel, or usual place of common prayer". DUFFY and especially HAIGH look at the presence of Marian clergy in England and how they ministered to those who preferred the traditional religion. Rome did not forbid attendance at Anglican services until Pius V did so in 1566, resulting in the mission in England of William Allen and Laurence Vaux. Haigh notes that recusancy (refusal to attend church) increased in Lancashire after that mission, while some lay catholics questioned Vaux's authority and continued to conform on occasion.

Once the priests from the Douai seminary arrived in 1574 and the Jesuits in 1580, they condemned occasional conformity and demanded that all catholics should be recusants. Haigh believes that the placement of the priests in London and the south, areas not traditionally attached to the old religion, led to the loss of traditional catholic areas to Anglicanism.

WALSHAM widens the concept of catholic by looking at the church papists, that group of men and women who saw themselves as catholic yet periodically attended the established church. They were condemned by the seminary priests and Jesuits and also by Anglicans. Walsham holds that recusancy was a clerical construct and that a significant number of those attached to the old religion conformed occasionally, which forced the clergy to produce literature to convince recusants to be firm in their refusal to attend Anglican services. While the clergy publicly condemned occasional conformity, casuistry allowed the clergy to permit occasional conformity in certain situations. They would never, however, publicly admit that.

Haigh and Bossy both see Elizabethan recusancy as a seigneurial sect. Haigh sees the persecution of 1581–92 and the arrival of seminary priests and Jesuits as changing the nature of Elizabethan catholicism, which became more and more dependent upon the gentry. The priests were recruited from university graduates and the sons of the gentry, so that when they returned to England they lived and worked with family, friends, and their social equals.

Haigh claims that the government's claim that catholics were disloyal subjects was misleading because the clergy, especially the Jesuits, were charged to minister to catholics and to avoid contact with heretics. That explanation underestimates the political and international context of recusancy and the English mission. The papacy still claimed the right to excommunicate and depose monarchs as Pius V had Elizabeth in the bull *Regnans in excelsis* after the 1569 rising of the northern earls. McCOOG places the Jesuit mission in an international context. The presence of Jesuits in England must be seen in the light of what Jesuits were doing in Ireland and Scotland. A Jesuit chaplain to the Spanish troops in Ireland might have given Cecil and the council some cause to wonder about the loyalty of catholics.

The queen and council certainly worried about recusant loyalty in the years prior to the Armada when some of the nobility and gentry were confined and when all recusants were deprived of their weapons. Loyalty was again in the fore during the archpriest controversy (basically an in-house disagreement between some seculars and the Jesuits over governance of the mission, control of the secular seminaries on the Continent, and ecclesiastical governance of the mission), when some of the seculars attempted to devise an oath of loyalty to the queen that would please both monarch and pope. Bossy sees the importance of loyalty in the 1585 declaration of loyalty offered to the queen by Sir Thomas Tresham in his own name and in the names of Lord Vaux and Sir John Arundell. In it the recusant gentry offered their loyalty to the queen while claiming the right to use their own priests.

Bossy notes that Sir Thomas Tresham again wrote a petition to James I upon his accession asking for toleration for catholicism. In return the gentry would employ priests who would take an oath of loyalty to the monarch and all other priests would be sent to the Continent. After the Gunpowder Plot the question of loyalty again arose in the 1610 Oath of Allegiance, which was an attempt to test the loyalty of recusants by having them swear that the Bishop of Rome had no authority to depose kings. The oath did not mention the spiritual authority of the pope.

For documentary material on recusancy and mission see the publications of the Catholic Record Society and its journal *Recusant History*.

JOHN J. LaRocca

See also Allen; Anti-Catholicism and the Test Acts; Catholic Church since 1560; Catholic Emancipation; Jesuits; Mary I; *Regnans in excelsis*; Royal Supremacy; Sander(s)

Reform Acts
see Parliament and Parliamentary Reform entries; Women's Suffrage Movement

Reformation in the British Isles
see "Religion" in Thematic List for relevant topics

Regnans in excelsis 1570

Cecil, William, *The Execution of Justice in England*, edited by Robert M. Kingdon, Ithaca, New York: Cornell University Press, 1965

Dures, Alan, *English Catholicism, 1558–1642: Continuity and Change*, London: Longman, 1983

Holmes, Peter, *Resistance and Compromise: The Political Thought of the Elizabethan Catholics*, Cambridge and New York: Cambridge University Press, 1982

Hughes, Philip, *The Reformation in England*, vol. 3, "*True Religion now Established*", London: Hollis and Carter, and New York: Macmillan, 1954; revised edition, New York: Macmillan, and London: Burns and Oates, 1963 (3 vols in 1)

LaRocca, John J., "'Popery and Pounds': The Effect of the Jesuit Mission on Penal Legislation" in *The Reckoned Expense: Edmund Campion and the Early English Jesuits*, edited by Thomas M. McCoog, Woodbridge, Suffolk and Rochester, New York: Boydell Press, 1996

Law, T.G., "Cuthbert Mayne and the Bull of Pius V", *English Historical Review*, I (1886): 141–44

Loades, D., "Relations between the Anglican and Roman Catholic Churches in the Sixteenth and Seventeenth Centuries" in *Rome and the Anglicans: Historical and Doctrinal Aspects of Anglican-Roman Catholic Relations*, edited by Wolfgang Haase, Berlin and New York: de Gruyter, 1982

McGrath, Patrick, *Papists and Puritans under Elizabeth I*, London: Blandford, and New York: Walker, 1967

McGrath, Patrick, "The Bloody Questions Reconsidered", *Recusant History*, 20/2 (1991): 305–19

Meyer, Arnold Oskar, *England and the Catholic Church under Queen Elizabeth*, translated from the German by J.R. McKee, London: Kegan Paul, Trench, Trübner, 1916; reissued with new introduction by John Bossy, London: Routledge and Kegan Paul, and New York: Barnes and Noble, 1967 (original German edition, 1911)

Pollen, John Hungerford, *The English Catholics in the Reign of Queen Elizabeth, A Study of their Politics, Civil Life, and Government*, London and New York: Longmans Green, 1920

Tierney, M.A. (editor), *Dodd's Church History of England from the Commencement of the Sixteenth Century to the Revolution in 1688*, with notes, additions and a continuation, 5 vols, London: Dolman, 1839–43; reprinted, New York: AMS Press, 1971

Walsham, Alexandra, *Church Papists: Catholicism, Conformity, and Confessional Polemic in Early Modern England*, Woodbridge, Suffolk and Rochester, New York: Boydell Press, 1993

In February 1570 Pope Pius V sealed a bull declaring Queen Elizabeth to be a heretic, and deprived her of her pretended claim to the crown of England. TIERNEY printed the full Latin text of this bull as an appendix to *Dodd's Church History*, and Hughes reprinted an English translation by David Lewis from his edition of Nicholas Sander's *Rise and Growth of the Anglican Schism* (1877). It was promulgated (unofficially) in London in May by being nailed to the Bishop of London's front door. Protestants at the time, and protestant-minded historians since, have described this bull as a "declaration of war", but that was not exactly the original intention. Pius was responding, far too late for his intervention to have the desired effect, to a plea from one faction of those who had risen in rebellion in the north of England in 1569. Those among the rebels whose agenda included the immediate overthrow of Elizabeth believed that many catholics were holding back from joining them because they were uncertain of their allegiance. Pius's bull was designed to remove that obstacle by declaring all allegiance to Elizabeth to be null and void. As both POLLEN and HUGHES have pointed out, it stopped at that, and did not issue any call to English catholics to rise against the pretender. The bull was never officially published, and no briefs were issued to catholic princes to put it into effect. Consequently catholic (and catholic-minded) historians, such as Pollen, Hughes, McGrath, and LaRocca have tended to argue that it was a non-event, which made practically no difference to the attitude of English catholics towards the queen. Christopher Haigh, in his recent *English Reformations* (1993), dismisses it in a single sentence on the grounds that recusancy was already an established phenomenon.

From this point of view it is argued that, far from stirring up catholics against Elizabeth, the main consequence of the bull was to stir up protestants against catholics, resulting in that penal legislation which subsequently forced many catholics unwillingly into treason. That is the main thrust of LAROCCA'S argument, and the underlying assumption in McGRATH's examination of the proceedings against arrested priests. However, as William CECIL pointed out a few years after the event, in his work of 1583, the logic of the situation created by the bull was irrefutable, whatever the intention may have been. If an English catholic could owe no allegiance to the queen, he had to be regarded as a potential traitor, whether he did anything or not. The penal laws did not, in fact, punish opinion; but harbouring a priest or attending clandestine masses were overt declarations that the individual would obey the church rather than the state. Traditional English historiography, represented here by MEYER and LOADES, has accepted the validity of this argument, drawing attention to the numerous plots laid against the queen's life, and the actual fate of William of Orange in 1584. Loades also draws attention to the "private but unequivocal" sanctioning of Elizabeth's murder by the cardinal secretary of state in December 1580.

Whatever action it may or may not have provoked, *Regnans in excelsis* set the agenda for the political debate concerning conscience and obedience which followed for more than a century. This debate is surveyed by DURES in a brief but extremely useful study, which examines the catholic position as a whole. WALSHAM focuses specifically upon the theoretical debate, but covers many aspects over an extended period, while HOLMES is concerned exclusively with the issue of resistance during Elizabeth's lifetime. There is a large, but not directly relevant, literature concerned with the search for an acceptable oath of allegiance for catholics which took place in the early part of James I's reign. Despite pressure from some quarters in the curia, Elizabeth's excommunication was not renewed, and a declaration to that effect at the time of the Armada in 1588 was issued by Cardinal William Allen, and not the pope. The significance of this was hardly noticed in England, where Allen's

action was taken as confirmation of the malevolent intent of the catholic church, and its determination to support the queen's enemies.

As both Pollen and Hughes have pointed out, the circumstances which prompted Pius to issue the bull in the context of the curial politics of 1569–70 have been little studied. That remains as true now as it was in 1954 (or 1920). Philip II was not consulted, and did not welcome the pope's action, which is the main reason why no action was taken upon it. Pius probably knew that the northern rebellion in England had failed, and acted mainly to re-establish his credibility as a decisive leader, after having had that called in question, not least by the English catholics themselves. Partly because the text of the bull has been familiar for a long time, and partly because what it was thought to mean has always been more important than what it actually said, *Regnans in excelsis* has not been subjected to much close critical examination, although its significance for one early missionary priest was examined by T.G. LAW over a century ago. However justified (and indeed overdue) it may have seemed in the eyes of the catholic church at the time, it has always been remembered in England as the decisive move which transformed catholics from being troublesome old believers into the adherents of a foreign and hostile power.

DAVID LOADES

See also Catholic Church since 1560; Elizabeth II; Jesuits; Recusancy and Mission

Reith, John, 1st Baron Reith 1889–1971
Director of the BBC, later government minister, and administrator

Boyle, Andrew, *Only the Wind Will Listen: Reith of the BBC*, London: Hutchinson, 1972
Briggs, Asa, *The History of Broadcasting in the United Kingdom*, vol. 2, *The Golden Age of Wireless*, London and New York: Oxford University Press, 1965; revised edition, 1995
McIntyre, Ian, *The Expense of Glory: A Life of John Reith*, London: HarperCollins, 1993
Reith, John, *Into the Wind*, London: Hodder and Stoughton, 1949
Stuart, Charles (editor), *The Reith Diaries*, London: Collins, 1975
Whitehouse, Mary, *Cleaning Up TV: From Protest to Participation*, London: Blandford Press, 1967

An engineer by training and a soldier and business manager by early experience, Reith filled many important positions during his life. But he owes his national prominence and a place in history chiefly to his period as director of the British Broadcasting Company (1922–27) and director-general of the British Broadcasting Corporation (1927–38). During these years public radio and public television were inaugurated and supervised by Reith. A man of strong religious views, set in a Victorian mould with a marked touch of dogmatism in his make-up, Reith saw his broadcasting role as a mission to strengthen and elevate the cultural appreciation and the Christian proclivities of the nation.

To this end, Reith's management of the then monopoly position of the BBC did give room to comedy programmes and dance music, but only alongside considerable allocations to religious services, classical music and plays, instructive talks and serious discussions. Some elements of his distribution of programme time have remained even to the present, but only amid greater time given to pure (or impure) entertainment, especially on television. Even in the 1930s, listeners who wanted to hear only dance music and comedy all day tuned in to the more accommodating off-shore English-language stations of Radio Luxemburg and Radio Normandy.

Reith later bitterly regretted leaving the BBC in 1938. Among his later posts were ministerial ones in the wartime coalition government in the early 1940s, but he had poor relations with Churchill and was dismissed in 1942. Thereafter he did so well in offensive operations at the Admiralty that he received a decoration from Churchill. After holding further important posts he retired in 1959. Though "autocrat" and "paternalist" were terms readily applied to his character and style, Reith did not always appear to have personal traits to match the roles of super-efficient administrator and far-sighted planner. He made rapid instinctive judgements which sometimes damaged him (though in regard to the interests of others his judgement was much surer). He saw himself as a failure, but this view was belied by the considerable successes he attained in the high positions he held.

STUART's introduction to his selection from Reith's diaries provides a perceptive biography in microcosm, and is an excellent summary of the life and personality of Reith. The diary extracts – samples from a large archive now kept by the BBC – should also be read as illustrating Reith's clear-cut attitudes and trenchant responses to situations that confronted him. REITH's own memoirs, dealing with his life up to the end of World War II (with a "postscriptum" to 1947, "nearly ten years since leaving the BBC", as he feelingly noted), contain much of interest and importance on personal and public matters. Like the diaries, the memoirs can be taken as displaying the man. BOYLE, though handicapped by not being allowed access to the diaries (which were only opened to scholars after Reith's death), provides from other sources an interesting and detailed biography up to 1945. This book gives much information about Reith's difficulties and successes as director of the BBC, in relation (where appropriate) to national events such as the general strike of 1926 and the abdication ten years later. The same ground is covered, in rather shorter compass, in the life by McINTYRE, who had the advantage of being able to study the diaries. McIntyre also goes further than Boyle in time, terminating a lively, rounded, and informative study at Reith's death in 1971.

The second of the five volumes of BRIGGS's history of the BBC covers Reith's directorship of early radio and early television in appreciative but objective detail. Other volumes in this work should be read in order to place Reith's directorship in context by observing how far his policies persisted in the following decades. Reith apparently did not become a member of the National Viewers' and Listeners' Association which was founded by Mrs Mary Whitehouse in 1964 to protest against the new permissiveness in broadcasting. But WHITEHOUSE clearly shows (if mainly by implication) how far broadcasting, especially television, departed in the 1960s from the assump-

tions and policy of Reith, and in fact takes his approach as a talisman and model of broadcasting policy.

IAN MACHIN

See also Broadcasting

Relative Economic Decline

20th century

Barnett, Correlli, *The Audit of War: The Illusion and Reality of Britain as a Great Nation*, London: Macmillan, 1986
Coates, David, *The Question of UK Decline: State, Society, and Economy*, London and New York: Harvester Wheatsheaf, 1994
Coates, David and John Hillard (editors), *The Economic Decline of Modern Britain: The Debate between Left and Right*, Brighton, Sussex: Harvester Wheatsheaf, 1994
Crafts, Nicholas, *Britain's Relative Economic Decline, 1870–1995: A Quantitative Perspective*, London: Social Market Foundation, 1997
Edgerton, David, *England and the Aeroplane: An Essay on a Militant and Technological Nation*, Basingstoke: Macmillan, 1992
Elbaum, Bernard and William Lazonick (editors), *The Decline of the British Economy*, Oxford: Clarendon Press, and New York: Oxford University Press, 1986
English, Richard and Michael Kenny (editors), *Rethinking British Decline*, London: Macmillan, and New York: St Martin's Press, 2000
Hutton, Will, *The State We're In*, London: Jonathan Cape, 1995
Lee, Simon, "Explaining Britain's Relative Economic Performance" in *The Political Economy of Modern Britain*, edited by Andrew Cox, Simon Lee, and Joe Sanderson, Cheltenham, Gloucestershire: Elgar, 1997
Lewis, Mark, Robert Fitzgerald, and Charles Harvey, *The Growth of Nations: Culture, Competitiveness, and the Problem of Globalization*, Bristol: Bristol Academic Press, 1996
Newton, Scott and Dilwyn Porter, *Modernization Frustrated: The Politics of Industrial Decline in Britain since 1990*, London and Boston: Unwin Hyman, 1988
Pollard, Sidney, *Britain's Prime and Britain's Decline: The British Economy, 1870–1914*, London and New York: Arnold, 1989
Weiner, Martin J., *English Culture and the Decline of the Industrial Spirit, 1850–1980*, Cambridge and New York: Cambridge University Press, 1981

COATES has furnished a welcome overview of the vast literature on decline and attempted to organize the literature in terms of the evidence presented about labour, capital, and the state. In identifying four "packages" or explanations of decline, namely conservative nationalist, liberal, social democratic, and Marxist, Coates has contended that Marxist explanations are the strongest, but only where they are complex and nuanced. As an alternative introduction to the literature, LEE's detailed analysis of decline explores the relationship between culture and

British economic performance, the role of the state in industrial modernization, the politics of de-industrialization, and the role played by the City of London.

Those seeking a comprehensive introduction to the debate about national decline are also well served by COATES & HILLARD. A valuable analysis of de-industrialization in Britain is followed by a series of essays on decline, in turn, from the Right, the centre, and the Left. The book concludes with a number of contrasting overviews of the debate.

CRAFTS has provided a very concise analysis of the trajectory of relative economic decline, from the second highest level of real GDP per person in 1870 to eleventh in 1979 and seventeenth in 1994. He has identified the period from the 1950s through to the 1970s as the most damaging for the United Kingdom's relative economic performance, and weak productivity and innovation rather than merely low investment as the principal causes of national decline.

POLLARD's highly detailed analysis of the question of decline in the period from 1870 to 1914 has highlighted the extent to which the idea of relative decline and the accusation of economic failure are dependent upon the benchmark for comparison chosen and the nature of the prior expectation of economic performance. In any event, Pollard's conclusions are that national decline was limited to certain sectors of the economy only, and could not be attributed to a failure in entrepreneurship.

ELBAUM & LAZONICK's wide-ranging collection of essays provides a prime example of an institutionalist perspective on decline. Relative economic success elsewhere is accounted for in terms of the presence of the institutions of corporate capitalism, which enabled mass production and scientific managerial organization to be diffused among the new industries of the second Industrial Revolution in Germany, Japan, and the United States. By comparison, cultural conservatism, reflected in a matrix of rigid institutional structures, locked the United Kingdom into the archaic and less-efficient institutions of the competitive capitalism characteristic of the first Industrial Revolution.

NEWTON & PORTER's account of the politics of industrial decline during the 20th century furnishes one of the best examples in which the responsibility for national decline is laid squarely at the door of the City of London, the Bank of England, and the Treasury. Their liberal economic orthodoxy is held to have prevented the construction of a dominant ideology of state-led industrial modernization at Westminster and in Whitehall.

WEINER's attribution of relative national decline to a "century of psychological and intellectual de-industrialization", led and propagated by education institutions among the governing and business elites, remains one of the most widely cited contributions to the decline literature. BARNETT's more recent assault upon what he depicts as a liberal, Christian, anti-industrial, and anti-militaristic middle-class governing elite has enjoyed a similar resonance among politicians of both the Left and the New Right.

Despite the popularity of the monocausal simplicity of the cultural perspective on British decline, LEWIS, FITZGERALD & HARVEY have delivered an extensive critique of the work of Weiner and Barnett which has exposed the limitations of this approach to understanding economic performance, not only in the United Kingdom but also in rival national economies. In a similar vein, EDGERTON's essay on the history of the aircraft industry has also vividly demonstrated the extent to which the United Kingdom's governing elites, rather than being the perpetrators of an anti-industrial culture, have actively embraced science and technology in successive industrial modernization strategies.

HUTTON's polemic on the impact of Thatcherite prescriptions for national decline on both economic performance and the cohesion of society is one of the most important critiques of the political economy of the New Right. His conclusion is that Thatcherism failed to stem relative economic decline and therefore nothing less than a comprehensive programme of economic and constitutional reform must be implemented to remedy long-standing and recent constraints on economic growth.

ENGLISH & KENNY's edited collection is a new and refreshing attempt to rethink decline. A series of interviews with leading contributors to the debate, including Martin Weiner, Correlli Barnett, and Will Hutton is followed by a number of thematic analyses exploring the role played by party ideology, institutional approaches, European integration, globalization, and the end of empire. The editors conclude their collection by pointing to the importance of directing attention away from decline itself and towards "declinism", the proclivity for leading politicians, economists, and historians to couch their arguments and agenda within the discourse of national decline, irrespective of the necessity for or the validity of such an approach.

SIMON DAVID LEE

See also Consensus in the Postwar Period; Cripps; Dalton; Industry, Heavy: Decline; Mining, Decline of; Technology and Employment; Welfare State

Religious Orders: Canons Regular

Colvin, Howard Montagu, *The White Canons in England*, Oxford: Clarendon Press, 1951

Dickinson, J.C., *The Origins of the Austin Canons and Their Introduction into England*, London: SPCK, 1950

Dickinson, J.C., "Canons Regular of St Augustine" in *New Catholic Encyclopedia*, vol. 3, New York: McGraw Hill, 1967

Knowles, David, *The Religious Orders in England*, 3 vols, Cambridge: Cambridge University Press, 1948–53

Graham, Rose, *S. Gilbert of Sempringham and the Gilbertines: A History of the Only English Monastic Order*, London: Stock, 1901

Salter, H.E. (editor), *Chapters of the Augustinian Canons*, London: Canterbury and York Society, 1922

Wills, Garry, *Saint Augustine*, London: Weidenfeld and Nicolson, and New York: Viking Press, 1999

The ideal of the canons regular appeared in the early time of the church with various efforts to establish common ways of life for groups of clergy, but their real origin dates from the 11th century in close connection with the reform movement of Pope Gregory VII. During the next century they largely adopted the so-called rule of St Augustine of Hippo and became known as the Augustinian (or Austin) canons. There were also other independent congregations, the most notable being the Premonstratensians (or Norbertines) and the Gilbertines in England.

The most recent life of St Augustine is by WILLS, who has frequent useful quotations. For three years before his ordination to the priesthood, Augustine lived a sort of monastic life with a few friends near his birthplace, Tagaste, in North Africa. During his time as Bishop of Hippo from 395 until his death in 430, though he devoted himself to defending Christian faith and morals and refuting heresy and schism, he also took a prominent part in the various attempts then being made to establish a full common life for clerical houses. He had the clergy of his cathedral live under a common rule and possess no private property.

Until the middle decades of the 11th century, almost the only order in the Western church was the Benedictine; but by then some clerical communities in northern Italy and southern France sought to lead a common way of life. Discipline, nevertheless, became much relaxed among the clergy of several of the cathedrals in the Frankish empire. Accordingly a council was held at Aix-la-Chapelle in 816 which drew up a rule for such a life, but as it did not absolutely forbid the acquisition or enjoyment of private property, abuses again appeared. Accordingly councils were held at Rome in 1059 and 1063 which amended the rule of Aix-la-Chapelle and in particular bound the clergy to a community life and to the renunciation of private property.

By the early 12th century such communities had spread widely in western Europe, but there were clergy in churches who lived in much the same way as before, and those who obeyed the prescribed rule sought to distinguish themselves from these recalcitrants by being known as "canons regular".

Most of them were Augustinian canons who adopted the rule of St Augustine, which they claimed was based upon his writings. It cannot be shown, however, that St Augustine ever composed a rule, properly so-called. He did, indeed, write a treatise, *De moribus clericorum*, and a letter laying down a rule of life for the religious women under his direction, not compelling them to strict enclosure, but requiring them to renounce all individual property. It is not known how the injunctions contained in this letter came to be adapted to communities of men, and, indeed, the Augustinians had to supplement them by reference to the Benedictine rule.

The observance of a rule facilitated the formation of independent bodies of regular canons, neither connected with cathedrals nor with collegiate churches as they had been previously. DICKINSON (1950) summarizes the controversy about their rule as well as describing their establishment and their arrival in England in 1105; and in DICKINSON's article in the *New Catholic Encyclopedia* (1967) he takes their story up to the 1960s.

The Augustinian canons, however, did not observe the rule completely, and attempts were made to get their houses to adopt greater uniformity. In the late 13th century this was done (as SALTER has shown) by the general chapters of the English Augustinian canons.

A congregation of the Augustinian canons was commonly known as the Lateran canons. This name was derived from the fact that during several centuries until 1391 they formed the chapter of the great Lateran basilica in Rome. Their office for the feast of St Gelasius I, pope from 492 to 496, states that it was this pontiff who established them at the Lateran.

The Premonstratensian canons were founded by St Norbert at Prémontré, near Laon in France, in 1120. They adopted the so-called rule of St Augustine but with stricter discipline and additional austerities, including the entire abstinence from meat, and, like the Cistercians, they frequently chose to settle in remote places. In England they were known as the "White Canons" from the colour of their woollen habit, while the Augustinian canons were called the "Black Canons" for a similar reason. COLVIN gives a valuable account of origins of the Premonstratensian order and the circumstances of the foundation of each of their abbeys in England, but does not go beyond the early 15th century.

This deficiency is remedied by KNOWLES, who gives considerable attention to the 14th and 15th centuries, a period which he declares has been neglected by historians. He contrasts the activities of the two main orders of the canons regular during this time. The Premonstratensians were monastic rather than apostolic and were engaged in parochial duties more often than missionary activity, while the Augustinians had never recognized the cure of souls as part of their vocation, but by the end of the 14th century papal privileges accorded to them enabled them to hold benefices, often as purely nominal incumbents, with the result that they "were by the fifteenth century the least fervent, the worst disciplined and the most decayed of all the religious houses".

A unique English order is described by GRAHAM. When parish priest of Sempringham in Lincolnshire, St Gilbert established a company of lay brothers and lay sisters, which became the Gilbertine order in 1139. When the Cistercians refused his request to incorporate them into their order, he arranged (with additional statutes of his own) for the women to follow the rule of Benedictine nuns and for the men to follow that of Augustinian canons, and henceforward his communities became largely a double order, which received papal approbation in 1148. In the double monasteries, only the church was common to the nuns and the canons, and here neither could see nor hear the other; the other buildings were erected a considerable distance apart. Its houses numbered 13 when dissolved in the 16th century, nine being double and four for men.

LEONARD COWIE

See also Gilbert of Sempringham

Religious Orders: Catholic after 1560

Basset, Bernard, *The English Jesuits from Campion to Martindale*, London: Burns and Oates, 1967; New York: Herder and Herder, 1968

Edwards, Francis, *The Jesuits in England from 1580 to the Present Day*, Tunbridge Wells, Kent: Burns and Oates, 1985

Flynn, Thomas S., *The Irish Dominicans, 1536–1641*, Dublin: Four Courts Press, 1993

Guilday, Peter, *The English Catholic Refugees on the Continent, 1558–1795*, vol. 1, *The English Colleges and Convents in the Catholic Low Countries, 1558–1795*, London and New York: Longmans Green, 1914

Lunn, David, *The English Benedictines, 1540–1688: From Reformation to Revolution*, London: Burns and Oates, and New York: Barnes and Noble, 1980

McCoog, Thomas M., *The Society of Jesus in Ireland, Scotland, and England, 1541–1588: "Our Way of Proceeding?"*, Leiden and New York: E.J. Brill, 1996

McNamara, Jo Ann Kay, *Sisters in Arms: Catholic Nuns through Two Millennia*, Cambridge, Massachusetts: Harvard University Press, 1996

Peters, Henriette, *Mary Ward: Ihre Persönlichkeit und ihr Institut*, Innsbrück: Tyrolia, 1991; as *Mary Ward: A World in Contemplation*, translated by Helen Butterworth, Leominster, Herefordshire: Gracewing, 1994

GUILDAY provides a sound starting-point for studying the English catholic colleges and convents established in the Low Countries from the Reformation through the 18th century. He focuses on the Benedictines, the Carthusians, and Jesuits and also describes the foundations for women. For him, government persecutions compelled catholics to seek exile in order freely to practice their faith. Though its conclusions are somewhat dated, the study remains valuable for its breadth of coverage and valuable bibliography.

BASSET attempted the first full survey of the English Jesuits. As his title suggests, his approach is largely biographical and he contributes valuable insights into the personalities of prominent English Jesuits from 1580, when the Jesuits first came to England, until the eve of World War II. The study begins with a fruitful examination of Jesuit sources which Basset contends must be used instead of their critics' writings to correct myths about the society. His less than critical history emphasizes Jesuit triumph over persecution, ignorance, and isolation. Despite its limitations, Basset's work remains a useful introduction.

Complementing and extending Basset is the more scholarly analysis offered by EDWARDS. Like his predecessor, he does not explain why the English legitimately saw the 1580 Jesuit mission as a threat to church and state. While he presents the contradictions inherent in the instructions given to Parsons and Campion, he fails to analyse their implications. The early Jesuits were charged to keep the faith alive in England and not engage in political discourse; yet, they were also to encourage the overthrow of Elizabeth by negotiating with Mary and plotting with Philip's Spain. Edwards also denies Jesuit involvement in the Gunpowder or the Oates plots; however, despite these significant shortcomings, his work is overall balanced and rich. He carefully describes individual Jesuits with emphasis on their spirituality, without neglecting their political and polemical activities, and presents a thorough chronological account of the English province.

The most scholarly treatment of the early Jesuit mission to the British Isles is found in McCOOG. Firmly rooted in a mastery of the appropriate archival evidence, this study skilfully interprets the complex relationship between the order, its supporters in Rome and Madrid, and its English adversaries, both protestant and catholic. Its focus is narrowed to the period between the first arrival of Jesuits in Ireland in 1541 and the defeat of the Armada. Although McCoog is sympathetic to the Jesuits, he does address their mistakes and misdeeds critically and offers a thorough, realistic analysis of English attitudes and the policies that resulted. His work details the active efforts of the Jesuits to overthrow Elizabeth's government and restore catholicism to the islands.

The fullest analysis of the Dominicans during the period of catholic revival is FLYNN's scholarly study on Ireland. This impressively researched volume explains how they endured after being nearly destroyed by the monastic dissolution in 1536 to become an essential element of the catholic Counter-Reformation in Ireland by the early 17th century. Flynn attributes their survival to the fortitude of old friars and the persistence of the Observant movement, which antedated the Reformation. The Dominican revival was characterized by the founding of vibrant Irish Dominican houses in Lisbon and Louvain, and a house for nuns in Portugal. Its successes were capped in 1632 when the Irish province was established. The work examines the tensions between the Irish Dominicans and the Franciscans, the largest religious order in Ireland.

Though it embraces a somewhat broader chronological period, LUNN's volume on the English Benedictines parallels Flynn by tracing that order's revival following the Reformation. He examines that transformation against the backdrop of the Appellant controversy, which stalled the re-establishment of a Benedictine mission to England from 1594 until 1602. According to Flynn, one factor motivating the effort to return was the assumption that their former properties and monastic holdings would be lost to the Jesuits should catholicism be restored to England without their presence. Throughout, Lunn carefully describes how the Benedictines reconstructed the order from its medieval monastic foundations to create a new form emphasizing tight central organization and regimented piety. Like Flynn, he examines the tensions and conflicts among the religious orders as well as the issues separating catholics from protestants.

PETERS has written perhaps the most scholarly volume detailing catholic religious orders for women after the Reformation. Her study of Mary Ward depicts the establishment of a new form of religious community for women: the institute. In keeping with the spirit of the catholic revival of the 16th century, Ward founded an academy in Flanders to instruct women, some of whom would return to England to teach and counsel their catholic families. Thus, her foundation was designed to appeal to women who wished to serve but who were not interested in a cloistered, contemplative life. The account is distinguished by its careful documentation of the institute's first two decades and its influence across Europe in the 17th century. Based upon careful archival research, Peters addresses Ward's personal spirituality, as well as her trials and achievements in establishing and sustaining the institute. After its suppression in 1631, owing to opposition from the Jesuits and Benedictines, Ward persevered and ultimately founded a new house in Rome before returning to her native Yorkshire, where she died in 1645. This painstakingly thorough analysis offers valuable insights into the spiritual lives of Mary Ward and catholic women in the period.

Surveying the history of Christian women in religious orders across nearly two millennia, McNAMARA offers essential insights into the lives and struggles of catholic nuns globally.

Her scope is monumental as she focuses on independent nuns who forged new opportunities for women in a hostile environment. The chapters describing the Counter-Reformation and the roles of monastic teaching orders in Europe are especially relevant. McNamara provides an enormous body of evidence illustrating monastic life and argues throughout that control over women has characterized ecclesiastical policy and practice to the present day. She emphasizes a catholic sisterhood and offers a full array of evidence to support her conclusions. Her central thesis is, of course, controversial; however, the work will remain essential reading for any serious student of women in religion.

MICHAEL JAMES GALGANO

See also Jesuits

Religious Orders: Conventual (Benedictines, Cluniacs, Cistercians)

Berman, Constance Hoffman, *The Cistercian Evolution: The Invention of a Religious Order in Twelfth-Century Europe*, Philadelphia: University of Pennsylvania Press, 2000

Burton, Janet, *Monastic and Religious Orders in Britain 1000–1300*, Cambridge and New York: Cambridge University Press, 1994

Constable, Giles, *Cluny from the Tenth to the Twelfth Centuries: Further Studies*, Aldershot, Hampshire and Brookfield, Vermont: Ashgate, 2000

Coppack, Glyn, *The White Monks: The Cistercians in Britain 1128–1540*, Stroud, Gloucestershire: Tempus, 2000

Coulton, G.G., *Five Centuries of Religion*, 4 vols, Cambridge: Cambridge University Press, 1923–50

Cowdrey, H.E.J., *The Cluniacs and the Gregorian Reform*, Oxford: Clarendon Press, 1970

Cox, Giles, *Cluniac Studies*, London: Variorum Reprints, 1980 (articles first published 1956–77)

France, James, *The Cistercians in Medieval Art*, Stroud, Gloucestershire: Sutton, and Kalamazoo, Michigan: Cistercian Publications, 1998

Knowles, David, *The Religious Orders in England*, 3 vols, Cambridge: Cambridge University Press, 1948–59

Knowles, David, *Cistercians and Cluniacs: The Controversy between St Bernard and Peter the Venerable*, London and New York: Oxford University Press, 1955

Lackner, Bede K., *The Eleventh-Century Background of Early Cîteaux*, Washington, D.C.: Cistercian Publications, 1971

Lawrence, C.H., *Medieval Monasticism: Forms of Religious Life in Western Europe in the Middle Ages*, London and New York: Longman, 1984; 3rd edition, 2001

Leclercq, Jean, *Love of Learning and the Desire for God: A Study of Monastic Culture*, translated by Catharine Misrahi, New York: Fordham University Press, 1961; 3rd edition, 1982

Lekai, L.J., *The White Monks: A History of the Cistercian Order*, Okauchee, Wisconsin: Cistercian Fathers, 1953

Norton, Christopher and David Park, *Cistercian Art and Architecture in the British Isles*, Cambridge and New York: Cambridge University Press, 1986

O'Conbhuidhe, Colmcille, *Studies in Irish Cistercian History*, edited by Finbarr Donovan, Dublin and Portland, Oregon: Four Courts Press, 1998

Platt, Colin, *The Abbeys and Priories of Medieval England*, London: Secker and Warburg, and New York: Fordham University Press, 1984

Robinson, David (editor), *The Cistercian Abbeys of Britain: Far from the Concourse of Men*, London: Batsford / English Heritage, and Kalamazoo, Michigan: Cistercian Publications, 1998

Stalley, Roger, *The Cistercian Monasteries of Ireland: An Account of the History, Art, and Architecture of the White Monks 1142–1540*, New Haven, Connecticut and London: Yale University Press, 1987

Turner, D.H. *et al.*, *The Benedictines in Britain*, London: British Library, and New York: Braziller, 1980

Williams, David H., *The Welsh Cistercians: Aspects of Their Economic History*, Pontypool, Monmouthshire: Griffin Press, 1969; revised edition, as *The Welsh Cistercians*, 2 vols, Tenby: Cyhoeddiadau Sistersiaidd, 1984

Wood, Susan, *English Monasteries and Their Patrons in the Thirteenth Century*, London: Oxford University Press, 1955

The religious fervour that persuaded men to reject the world and pursue a life of devotion to God in the isolation of a monastery had its roots in the arrival in England of St Augustine (d. *c*.604) and in the intellectual spirit of St Benedict of Nursia (*c*.480–*c*.550). The Benedictine movement was then reformed and influenced at the monastery of Cluny, in Burgundy, during the Anglo-Saxon period, but both the Benedictine and Cluniac orders failed to offer the life that many sought, and this led to the foundations of the Carthusians, who arrived in England in the late 12th century, and the Cistercian order, founded in France (with an Englishman, Stephen Harding, as third Abbot, and whose first English foundation was at Waverley in 1128). The great Cistercian houses included Fountains and Rievaulx, which became places of great learning.

The literature for this whole subject is enormous. Included in the selection here are, to begin with, some books that give an overview of the movement that began with St Benedict and that spread across Europe to flourish in England, Ireland, and Wales, and to a lesser degree in Scotland. For many years the standard work on the history of monasticism in England was COULTON's four-volume history. While it remains of interest, it was superseded by KNOWLES's magisterial *The Religious Orders in England*. Although Knowles's work remains a recommended starting-point, it has been criticized, notably by Brian Golding, for failing to recognize the work of the lesser orders and in particular of the contribution of Gilbert of Sempringham. A brief introduction to the early history of monasticism can be found in TURNER *et al.*. It is a slender volume, divided into sections, each written by an expert in the field. The illustrations are numerous and well chosen, some from the British Library's collection, but many from farther afield. The text is comprehensive, simply set out and can be readily understood. It is particularly good on the Benedictine rule and the liturgy, and there is an excellent section on libraries and writers. The notes, too, are informative. The volume by LAWRENCE is more detailed. It is a conventional textbook, by a historian who is well-versed in the subject, and the narrative is organized under useful headings. Those new to the subject would find this an excellent starting-point. BURTON is widely recognized as one of the leading scholars of monastic history. Her book is the culmination of her wide research and it demonstrates her detailed knowledge as well as her mastery of the literature. Her references, too, are invaluable, in particular those to her own work on the great Yorkshire houses, such as Rievaulx and Fountains, on which she is the acknowledged expert.

The Cluniacs did not become a dynamic force in England as they had in France. Founded in 909, the order pursued a life of reformed observance of liturgy and freedom from the restrictions of the secular church. Cluny became increasingly liturgical with its elaborate ceremonial, which attracted some, but which led others to seek a more austere life. The young Anselm, full of a desire for learning, felt that Cluny was so obsessed with the liturgy that it left no time for study. The first Cluniac priory in England was founded at Lewes in 1077, and eventually there were some 30 priories. But their subjection to the central control from Burgundy meant they were identified as having a French connection, and support for them faded. They were easily "nationalized" in times of war against France. CONSTABLE's book is an invaluable collection of studies from one of the leading scholars on Cluny, and can usefully be read in conjunction with COX.

Cluny was at its height when the first exodus of monks went from Benedictine Molesme in 1098 and founded the monastery of Cîteaux, and thus the Cistercian order. LACKNER provides a useful assessment of the early period of Cîteaux, though it is marred chiefly by the author's uncritical dependence on limited sources and unfamiliarity with recent literature. Cluniacs were closely associated with the papal reform movement and, in the 12th century, had a reputation for the beauty of their liturgical music and the ornate grandeur of their abbeys. And for these qualities they were heavily criticized by the Cistercians, and in particular by St Bernard of Clairvaux. The clearest history of the Cistercians is LEKAI's book, which runs from the foundations to modern times, and which makes accessible copies of the original documents of the order. This is a straightforward work, and has been long used as an introduction to the order. A more recent study is that of BERMAN. Her work is scholarly and detailed, and demonstrates her years of research on the subject. To understand the dispute between the Cistercians and the Cluniacs, the study by KNOWLES (1955) – actually the text of his inaugural lecture at Cambridge – is important. He shows the contrasts between fanaticism and moderation demonstrated in the views of two men: the Cistercian, Bernard of Clairvaux, who was a zealous, impulsive reformer, and the Cluniac, Peter the Venerable, who personified the reasonable and charitable defender of custom and tradition. While the disagreement took place in continental Europe, it was the focus of differences between the two interpretations of the Benedictine order throughout Western Christendom. The impact of the reform movement and Cluny can be found in the impressive work of COWDREY.

For a study of monastic spirituality LECLERCQ is invaluable. In the introduction to his book the author suggests that it has long been established that the 12th century is the key period in the history of religious orders. Leclercq has written extensively, and this book is essential reading for a proper understanding of monastic learning and the spiritual context in which it was nurtured. The author writes with rare lucidity, and inevitably his life as a monk permeates his writing. He explains the study of the Bible and patristics, but he also takes us through the practical side of the monastic culture – the organization of the scriptorium where copyist-rubricators, painter-illuminators, and binders were employed. He shows the need for accuracy and how the "inter-library loan system" functioned, which ensured that the best copies were available for copying. This book is the monastic mind at work.

To understand more of the circumstances under which these orders lived PLATT's work is one of the most important to be published. The author has a comprehensive knowledge of his subject. ROBINSON's edited volume focuses on the Cistercian houses. A more detailed study of Cistercian art and architecture can be found in NORTON & PARK and in FRANCE, while COPPACK's immensely readable book contributes significantly to our knowledge of Cistercian sites and the history behind them. It is also important to know how the monks acquired their land, and WOOD writes with authority on this aspect in the 13th century.

The distinctive nature of monasticism in Wales has been very well served by WILLIAMS, generally regarded as the greatest historian of Welsh monasticism; his extensive references and illustrations make his work particularly valuable. STALLEY has researched Irish monasticism deeply, making his work a significant contribution to the subject. It complements O'CONBHUIDHE's book, which is an academic collection of writings dealing with a wide range of Cistercian developments in Ireland.

JUDITH LOADES

See also Aelfric; Christian Conversion in the British Isles; David; Dunstan; Edgar I; Gilbert of Sempringham; Hild; Monasticism; Saint Albans, School of; Wilfrid

Religious Orders: Female

Burton, Janet, *Monastic and Religious Orders in Britain, 1000–1300*, Cambridge and New York: Cambridge University Press, 1994
Elkins, Sharon K., *Holy Women of Twelfth-Century England*, Chapel Hill and London: University of North Carolina Press, 1988
Gilchrist, Roberta, *Gender and Material Culture: The Archaeology of Religious Women*, London and New York: Routledge, 1994
Oliva, Marilyn, *The Convent and the Community in Later Medieval England: Female Monasteries in the Diocese of Norwich, 1350–1540*, Woodbridge, Suffolk and Rochester, New York: Boydell, 1998
Power, Eileen, *Medieval English Nunneries: c.1275 to 1535*, Cambridge: Cambridge University Press, and New York: Macmillan, 1922
Thompson, Sally, *Women Religious: The Founding of English Nunneries after the Norman Conquest*, Oxford and New York: Oxford University Press, 1991

When Henry VIII dissolved the monasteries of England and Wales in the late 1530s there were almost 150 nunneries, of which half were Benedictine houses and a quarter Cistercian. Until recently the histories of these female houses have been largely omitted from accounts of monastic life in England in the Middle Ages and the contribution of women religious marginalized. The trivializing tone was set by POWER's pioneering work on English nuns and nunneries. Based on a very wide selection of documentary sources it aimed to "give a general picture of English nunnery life during a definite period, the three centuries before the Dissolution". Power has been criticized for her assumption that nuns came almost entirely from the upper classes in society and that nunneries were full of superfluous daughters and elderly widows. "A career, a vocation, a prison, a refuge; to its different inmates the medieval nunnery was all these things". She has also been criticized for undue concentration on the financial difficulties faced by all but the largest nunneries and for her assumption that the nuns ran their houses incompetently. The most entertaining parts of Power's work are those based on an insufficiently critical use of visitation records. She used these inspection reports by bishops to show how for the majority of nuns any religious vocation had been compromised by worldliness. Many of them were immoral and bored; they kept pets, wore rich clothes, and entertained their friends both inside and outside their convents.

In spite of the recent growth of interest in women's history and, in particular, in women's spirituality in the Middle Ages, historians have been slow to challenge the stereotypes established by Power. THOMPSON's study of the 139 nunneries founded after the Norman Conquest aimed to fill the gap left by Power and cover the era of monastic expansion in the 12th and early 13th centuries. Thompson believes that the shortage of sources for the study of women leading the religious life during this period is "an indication of the problems of the women themselves, reflecting poverty, lack of learning and the vagaries of their intrinsic dependence on men". Communities of women developed slowly and often lacked any real stability. Women religious were vulnerable because they were dependent on men "to act for them as priests and to help with their temporal affairs"; yet any "association of the sexes depended on an uneasy foundation, one undermined by distrust of sexuality and fear of scandal". Although acknowledging the atmosphere of suspicion faced by women who wished to lead holy lives, ELKINS paints a more optimistic picture of female monasticism in the 12th century. She shows how women made "numerous accommodations" in order to lead religious lives and how they were especially "adaptive" in their relations with celibate men. Thanks to these "flexible, practical and pragmatic" women, by the end of the century "religious women lived in a vast network of monasteries, so widespread that women of all social strata, in every part of England, could easily enter religious life". BURTON, in the most recent survey of the monastic and religious orders in the period from 1000 to 1300, devotes only a short chapter to women on the grounds that no modern synthesis yet exists "which places the contribution of women within the context of both male and female religious life". Although there is no evidence for Britain comparable to that found on the Continent, Burton suspects that women may have turned in the 13th century to forms of "organised and religious life outside the nunnery".

GILCHRIST, an archaeologist by training, offers a fresh perspective on medieval English nuns by using gender as a category of analysis in order to explore the "archaeology of religious women". Nunneries were distinguished from male houses by a paradox of isolation and dependence; they were founded in isolated or marginal places but were dependent on their local communities for "labour, religious services, market commodities and cash gifts". Gilchrist also shows how monastic architecture was central to the "social construction of difference" between monks and nuns. Nunnery buildings tended to be smaller and more domestic and they differed from male houses in the arrangement and use of space within the monastic enclosure; in particular the orientation of churches in nunneries may reflect the same feminine religious symbolism which can be found in the iconography of nunnery seals.

In her study of eleven female monasteries in the diocese of Norwich from 1350 until the Dissolution OLIVA effectively questions Power's three basic assumptions that nuns came predominantly from the upper ranks of society, that their religious vocations were tarnished by increasing worldliness, and that small convents were always on the brink of collapse because they were poorly endowed and badly managed. By reconstructing the social composition of the nunneries Oliva demonstrates that the vast majority of the nuns came not from the aristocracy but from the middling social ranks of society. In addition, the patterns of patronage revealed by wills shows that nunneries were not the "frivolous and moribund institutions" described by Power. The fact that their local communities were prepared to support the nuns reveals both the nuns' commitment to those communities and also local perceptions of the high quality of the nuns' religious vocation. Oliva also traces a pattern of office-holding in the convents which included a career ladder based more on merit than, as Power believed, on social status. "A hierarchy of household offices appears to have existed ... whereby nuns could acquire and hone administrative talents which were recognised and rewarded by assignments to higher status positions with more responsibilities and greater prestige". Like Gilchrist, Oliva argues that "gender made a difference between female and male monastic life in the later middle ages". Generally women were accorded a lower status in society and so nuns may have been more esteemed because "they had greater obstacles to overcome in their pursuit of a religious life". This esteem and feelings of self-worth nourished by their successful management of their meagre resources must have given the nuns "positive and lasting self-images" which in many cases seem to have survived the dissolution of their communities.

ANN J. KETTLE

Religious Orders: Mendicant

Egan, Keith, "Medieval Carmelite Houses: England and Wales" and "An Essay Towards a Historiography of the Origin of the Carmelite Province in England" in *Carmel in Britain: Essays on the Medieval English Carmelite Province*, edited by Patrick Fitzgerald-Lombard, Rome: Institutum Carmelitanum, 1992

Fitzgerald-Lombard, Patrick (editor), *Carmel in Britain: Essays on the Medieval English Carmelite Province*, Rome: Institutum Carmelitanum, 1992

Gwynn, Aubrey, *The English Austin Friars in the Time of Wyclif*, London: Oxford University Press, 1940

Hinnebusch, William, *The Early English Friar Preachers*, Rome: Sabinae, 1951

Knowles, David, *The Religious Orders in England*, vol. 1, Cambridge: Cambridge University Press, 1948

Knowles, David and R. Neville Hadcock, *Medieval Religious Houses*, London and New York: Longmans Green, 1953; 2nd edition, London: Longman, 1971

Shannon, A.C., entry on "Augustinians" in *The New Catholic Encyclopedia*, vol. 1, New York: McGraw-Hill, 1967

The mendicant orders are those forbidden to own property in common. KNOWLES & HADCOCK list all the known houses in England and Wales of the four main mendicant orders, the Dominican (Black) Friars or Friars Preachers, Franciscan (Grey) Friars or Minors, Carmelite (White) Friars and the Austin or Augustinian Hermits, also known as Friars, together with other friar-like groups, including the Friars of the Sack and the Pied Friars. The Crutched Friars or Friars of the Cross, were also to be found in England. They followed the Rule of St Augustine, with constitutions borrowed from the Dominicans, and showed many characteristics of the mendicant orders but evolved into an order of canons regular and were recognized as non-mendicant.

KNOWLES's history, though over 50 years old, still provides the best summary history of the appearance of the mendicants in England. He shows that each of the four orders made rapid progress during the first 40 or 50 years after arriving in England, and that a settled way of life was consolidated thereafter, with fewer new foundations made after this time.

The Dominicans arrived first, in 1217, under the protection of the Bishop of Winchester, and immediately gained the support of Archbishop Stephen Langton. HINNEBUSCH gives a very detailed history of the early English Friars Preachers, their foundations at Oxford and London, and the spread of their houses across the country, together with an account of Dominican architecture, spirituality, and preaching. There were 36 houses by 1260 and 47 by 1272. In England, as Knowles shows, the Black took second place to the Grey Friars in the intellectual sphere, but the Dominicans excelled in diplomacy and were counsellors of the great.

The Franciscans arrived next, in 1224, only 14 years after Pope Innocent III gave verbal approval to Francis's first rule. Nine carefully chosen friars arrived at Dover and made three settlements within six weeks, at the ecclesiastical, civil, and intellectual centres of English life, namely Canterbury, London, and Oxford. Initially they lodged with the Dominicans but soon established their own houses. By 1240 there were 34 friaries. Knowles, using the writings of the contemporary historian Thomas of Eccleston, gives an excellent account of the way in which the Franciscans established their houses among the people in towns and how, aided by Bishop Robert Grosseteste's patronage, and by attracting young scholars, they made a growing intellectual contribution at Oxford. In the years after 1240 the English province of the Dominican order reached its zenith and was held up as an example to others, and though

there were those who were prepared to abandon the requirement of pronounced poverty, England kept to a strict observance of the rule.

The Carmelites were rather different from the Dominicans and Franciscans. They appear to have begun as a band of hermits on Mount Carmel in the Holy Land under a rule granted by the Patriarch of Jerusalem early in the 13th century. Under pressure from Muslim incursions, the started to leave for Cyprus, Sicily, Provence, and England from 1238. EGAN remarks that there is no adequate history of the English Carmelites; but he notes that they arrived, according to Eccleston, when Richard of Cornwall returned from his crusade in January 1242. Egan believes that the Carmelites, who had originally been hermits and had became mendicants in 1229 by decree of Gregory IX, and who had only just begun academic and intellectual development, would have faced great difficulties in establishing an identity in England given the evident popularity of the well-established Dominicans and Franciscans. Their first four foundations were all rural and reflected the order's eremitical origins; they were at Hulne near Alnwick in Northumberland (by 1242), Aylesford in Kent (1242), Losenham, Newenden, Kent (1242–47), and Bradmer, Norfolk (1242–47). Following a revision of the statutes in 1247 the Carmelites were allowed to establish urban houses as well. Egan holds to the idea that Simon Stock seems to have been responsible for guiding the changes in England, though Knowles says that we know almost nothing of his life and character "save that they were endowed with talents of the highest order". But Knowles & Hadcock conclude that he and "his reputed achievements must be relegated to the realm of myth". FITZGERALD-LOMBARD includes Egan's list of the 39 English Carmelite houses (repeated in Knowles & Hadcock), an account of the 15th-century English province, and an annotated bibliography.

The Augustinian hermits, who became known as Friars, originated in Tuscany and spread to Spain, Germany, and southern France before 1243 when the papacy put them under the rule of St Augustine and consolidated the various houses in the Little Union of 1244 and the Great Union of 1256 into an order of hermits. Like the Carmelites they moved from rural hermitages into the more active life of towns. The earliest English house was founded at Clare, Cambridgeshire, in 1248. According to SHANNON, the province of England and Ireland had 27 foundations with 500 religious but Knowles & Hadcock give 40 houses. GWYNN gives an account of their arrival in England, showing that the most important house was that in London, founded in 1253, while a centre of study was established in Oxford in 1268. The Austin Friars enjoyed high patronage and they made foundations in the English midlands and on the east coast.

All the mendicant orders enjoyed a new period of growth at the end of the reign of Edward I and the beginning of that of Edward II, but they suffered great losses during the Black Death in the mid-14th century, and though new houses were founded thereafter they were generally rather small. Friars of all kinds started to leave England between 1534 and 1538 when the suppression of their houses began. There was, however, a house of Dominicans at St Bartholomew's, Smithfield, during the reign of Queen Mary, and another of Franciscans at Greenwich.

MARTIN R. DUDLEY

Religious Orders: Observants (Franciscans)

Hutton, Edward, *The Franciscans in England 1224–1538*,
    London: Constable, and Boston: Houghton Mifflin, 1926
Little, A.G., *Introduction of the Observant Friars into
    England*, London: Oxford University Press, 1923
Moorman, John, *A History of the Franciscan Order from Its
    Origins to the Year 1517*, Oxford: Clarendon Press, 1968;
    reprinted, Chicago, Illinois: Franciscan Herald Press, 1988

Observants may be described as those within a religious order who seek to observe the rule in its original form and regardless of relaxations, changes, and dispensations subsequently introduced, even by lawful authority. Although observants existed in a number of monastic and religious orders, the term is specifically applied to the Franciscans. MOORMAN, who touches on the English Franciscans only in passing, nonetheless provides the broader context for the other studies. The history of the order, he writes, during the century from 1417 to 1517, is the story of how attempts were made first to carry out extensive reforms, and then to keep the friars together as two groups, more or less independent of each other, but both under the jurisdiction of the minister general. So difficult was this that papal intervention was required. Martin V encouraged the observants and Eugenius IV gave constitutional form to their existence by establishing, in 1443, two vicars general for them, Giovanni Capistrano for the cismontane "family" in the Italian provinces and Jean Perioche Maubert for the ultramontane "family", those north of the Alps. This arrangement, providing for the parallel existence of conventual and observant branches of Franciscans, was consolidated by the bull *Ut sacra ordinis minorum religio* of 1446.

HUTTON traces the origin of the observants back to the disputes over poverty in the time of the Avignon Pope John XXII. For those friars who wanted to observe strictly the rule of St Francis, poverty – individual and corporate – was essential. Hutton sees the bull that restored ownership of property to the order in 1322 as the beginning of the Franciscan revolution. The danger of strict observance was always that of drifting into what Hutton calls the "absurdities and abuses" of the Fraticelli. The Italian friar Pauluccio Trinci of Foligno (d. 1390) avoided the extremes and opposed the Fraticelli. His friars, though traditionally barefoot, wore wooden sandals (*zoccoli*) for protection against snakes, and the Italian observants became known as *Zoccolanti*. With Pauluccio as commissary general, the observants grew and by 1414 had 34 houses in Italy. The most notable individual among them was to be St Bernardino of Siena (1380–1444), described by Hutton as the St Bernard of the observants. The observant movement appeared independently in every country and pursued an independent career in each.

Little and Hutton both tell the story of the introduction of the observants into England. Hutton also notes that it was from the province of Cologne, where the observants appeared in 1420, that they came to Scotland in 1447, at the request of that country's king, James I. Little reports that papal permission for houses in Ireland was granted in 1449. It cannot be firmly asserted that the observants had a convent in England until the one in Greenwich was founded in 1484, but Little says that the earliest reference to the observant friars in connection with England comes in a letter of Giovanni Capistrano to King Henry VI, dated October 24, 1454. This letter refers to a request for Giovanni to come and assist in the founding of some new observant houses, a request he refuses because of his going to Hungary. He sent the incapacitated Henry relics of St Bernardino of Siena "in the hope that with faith they may help to restore you to health". Henry recovered suddenly at Christmas 1454, but the outbreak of the troubles of the Wars of the Roses meant that he did not found any observant houses.

Little believes that one of the reasons for the slowness in introducing the observants was the very high standard of observance in the English province. In England the vow of poverty was widely observed and there is no evidence of widespread immorality or popular discontent with the friars. Sometime before January 1481, however, Edward IV "acting under suggestion from abroad and moved", says Little, "by a well-founded anxiety for the safety of his soul" invited the ultramontane vicar general to establish the house at Greenwich. The vicar general would not accept the offer without papal permission, and this was obtained in January 1481. Little, who gives a full account of the foundation based on documents at Corpus Christi College, Cambridge, believes that the influence from abroad came from the king's sister, Margaret of Burgundy. The only other observant house established in the 15th century was at Richmond and, like that at Greenwich, was a royal foundation and attached to a royal palace.

Little shows that when the Franciscans arrived in 1224 they spread rapidly and 36 houses were founded by 1240. From 1482 until 1498 Greenwich stood alone as the only observant house in England. The houses in Canterbury, Newcastle, and Southampton were transferred, at the request of Henry VII, from the conventuals to the observants who seemed to have a special devotion to the latter. Little observes that at the Dissolution there were two houses in Southampton, one conventual, one observant, which suggests a division in an original single house. A house was founded in Newark in 1507. Little concludes that in England "the Strict Observance was a plant of foreign origin; it required much artificial stimulation, and took long to strike its roots in the soil".

"When Henry VIII came to the throne of England in 1509", writes Hutton, "he was no less an admirer of the observants than his father had been". The house at Greenwich vigorously supported the claim of Catharine of Aragon and was suppressed in 1534, the house being given to the Austin friars. The wardens of the observant houses at Canterbury and Richmond were involved with Elizabeth Barton, the "Holy Maid of Kent", and executed at Tyburn in April 1534. Hutton narrates the fate of the Friars. In 1534 the Imperial ambassador Chupuys wrote: "All the Observers of this kingdom have been driven out of their monasteries for refusing the oath against the Holy See, and have been distributed in several monasteries, where they are locked up in chains and worse treated than they could be in prison." Some were smuggled abroad; 50 died in prison. In May 1538 one of their leaders, Friar Forrest of Greenwich, a doctor of divinity, was burned at Smithfield.

MARTIN R. DUDLEY

Religious Orders: 10th Century to 1540

Burton, Janet E., *Monastic and Religious Orders in Britain, 1000–1300*, Cambridge and New York: Cambridge University Press, 1994

Donkin, R.A., *The Cistercians: Studies in the Geography of Medieval England and Wales*, Toronto: Pontifical Institute of Mediaeval Studies, 1978

Harvey, Barbara, *Living and Dying in England, 1100–1540: The Monastic Experience*, Oxford: Clarendon Press, and New York: Oxford University Press, 1993

Knowles, David, *The Monastic Order in England: A History of Its Development from the Times of St Dunstan to the Fourth Lateran Council, 943–1216*, Cambridge: Cambridge University Press, 1940; reprinted with corrections, 1949; 2nd edition, 1963

Knowles, David, *The Religious Orders in England*, 3 vols, Cambridge: Cambridge University Press, 1948–59

Oliva, Marilyn, *The Convent and the Community in Late Medieval England: Female Monasteries in the Diocese of Norwich, 1350–1540*, Woodbridge, Suffolk, and Rochester, New York: Boydell, 1998

Platt, Colin, *The Abbeys and Priories of Medieval England*, London: Secker and Warburg, and New York: Fordham University Press, 1984

Robinson, David. M., *The Geography of Augustinian Settlement in Medieval England and Wales*, 2 vols, Oxford: British Archaeological Reports, 1980

Youings, Joyce, *The Dissolution of the Monasteries*, London: Allen and Unwin, and New York: Barnes and Noble, 1971

Essential to modern historical scholarship on British monasticism is KNOWLES. *The Monastic Order* is a comprehensive discussion of the development of cloistered religion from the time St Dunstan became Abbot of Glastonbury in 943 until the fourth Lateran Council in 1215–16. A lucid narrative follows the 10th-century monastic revival under Dunstan, the development of post-Conquest Benedictine monasticism, and the arrival of the new orders of Cistercians and Carthusians in the 12th century. But the work is far more than a historical narrative; the socio-economic, spiritual, intellectual, and administrative aspects of monastic life are all explored in depth with great sensitivity and understanding. The three-volume *Religious Orders* takes the narrative from 1216 to the Dissolution, but again, monasticism is treated in its social and religious context. Particularly useful are the chapters in the first two volumes on episcopal visitations, where the evidence from bishops' registers are interpreted in terms of both what they tell us about the moral condition of the religious orders in the Middle Ages, and of relations between bishops and monasteries over a period of three centuries. The final volume is a comprehensive survey of the condition of monasticism in all its aspects in the early 16th century, picking out for detailed scrutiny personalities such as Prior More of Worcester, and themes such as humanism at Evesham Abbey. The various stages of suppression are then described in a dextrous narrative that is indispensable for its reconstruction of the events and characters involved.

BURTON's treatment of the period 1000–1300 involves a series of themes which deal with the internal organization of religious houses and the social context of monasticism. Particularly important is the section dealing with the socio-political reasons for the patronage of monasteries by lay patrons in the earlier period, and how the expansion of new foundations had all but dried up by 1300. The mutual benefits of foundations and donations for both patron and monastery are seen as exemplifying certain medieval attitudes to religion where the benefits of spiritual and economic reciprocity were articulated in the lay-monastic relationship.

A seminal approach to the development of a single order is DONKIN. The techniques of historical geography are deployed to full effect in order to assess the economic success of the Cistercian order after their arrival in the 12th century. The strategies used by the white monks to manage their estates are described in concise language, explaining how sheep- and cattle-farming played such a major role in the order's economic expansion, and how this was consolidated by the assarting (clearing) of marsh and woodland. The time-scale is limited to before the Black Death but it is still an essential study for any reconstruction of Cistercian settlement and economic consolidation. A geographic methodology is also used by ROBINSON to interpret the development of the Augustinian order in Britain. Most especially the national taxation assessments, the *Taxatio Ecclesiastica* (1291), and the *Valor Ecclesiasticus* (1535) are utilized to demonstrate the relative economic wealth of the order and how the spiritual and temporal endowments of houses were administered. Particular use is made of maps and tables to explain how Augustinian houses, most of which were only middle-ranking in wealth, consolidated their estates and carried out effective land management.

PLATT's emphasis is on the architecture of the religious orders and what the structural remains of monasteries can tell us about the changing priorities of monasticism from the Conquest to the Dissolution. The text skilfully fuses archaeological and historical evidence to provide a unique and wide-ranging assessment of the socio-cultural aspects of monastic life. A notable feature is the range of illustrations used to great effect to clarify the text and strengthen the textual arguments.

HARVEY analyses the internal social structure of religious houses, drawing most of the evidence from the large surviving archive of Westminster Abbey. The three central sections elucidate the daily routine of this wealthy Benedictine abbey in terms of diet, sickness, and mortality. The skilful manipulation of data from the abbey's account rolls allows for a window to be opened on a cloistered social group in the later Middle Ages, which shows in great detail their material requirements and expectations. These expectations are generally seen as mirroring the upper-class lifestyles of the outside world, and thus demonstrate some general social trends. Despite the slackened observance of the Benedictine rule by the later Middle Ages, the monks of Westminster are still portrayed in a sympathetic light, carrying out their spiritual and material (especially almsgiving) tasks to the best of their ability while attempting to adapt to the social expectations of their upper-class rank.

Female monasticism in the later Middle Ages is dealt with by OLIVA by reference to nunneries in the diocese of Norwich. These nunneries were poorly endowed in comparison to their male counterparts. But it is shown, by reference to a wide range of documentary sources, that they maintained their religious and economic integrity throughout the period by the retention of local patronage and the efficient management of their estates. A prosopographical approach is taken which demonstrates that, as opposed to the long-established view, the vast majority of nuns were local women from the middling social ranks rather than from the aristocracy. There is also an excellent bibliography on the female religious orders.

The best approach to the Dissolution of the monasteries is through YOUINGS. A series of primary documents illustrating the course of the Dissolution is preceded by an extensive analysis of the mechanisms behind the suppression, largely from a central government perspective. A clear narrative of events supports the interpretation that once the suppression of the smaller houses was set in motion a total dissolution became inevitable. Extensive use is made of the voluminous, and largely unpublished, material from the Court of Augmentations and also the state papers of Henry VIII's reign to demonstrate how the government was able to undertake such an enforced requisitioning of monastic lands. The Dissolution is thus interpreted as a legal ploy by central government, under the direction of Thomas Cromwell, to acquire land for redistribution, and not necessarily as an intrinsic part of the religious Reformation in Britain.

NEIL S. RUSHTON

See also Monasticism

Republic, British (1649–1660)
see British Republic

Republicanism in the 19th Century

Cannadine, David, "The Context, Performance, and Meaning of Ritual: The British Monarchy and the 'Invention' of Tradition *c.*1820–1977" in *The Invention of Tradition*, edited by Eric Hobsbawm and Terence Ranger, Cambridge and New York: Cambridge University Press, 1983

Harrison, Royden, *Before the Socialists: Studies in Labour and Politics 1861–1881*, London: Routledge and Kegan Paul, and Toronto: Toronto University Press, 1965

Kuduk, S., "'A Sword of a Song': Swinburne's Republican Aesthetics in *Songs before Sunrise*", *Victorian Studies*, 43/2 (2001): 253–78

Poole, Steve, *The Politics of Regicide in England, 1760–1850: Troublesome Subjects*, Manchester: Manchester University Press, 2000

Royle, Edward, *Radicals, Secularists, and Republicans: Popular Freethought in Britain, 1866–1915*, Manchester: Manchester University Press, and Totowa, New Jersey: Rowman and Littlefield, 1980

Rumsey, Christopher, *The Rise and Fall of British Republican Clubs 1871–1874*, Oswestry, Shropshire: Quinta Press, 2000

Taylor, Antony, *"Down with the Crown": British Anti-Monarchism and Debates about Royalty since 1790*, London: Reaktion Books, 1999

Williams, Richard, *The Contentious Crown: Public Discussion of the British Monarchy in the Reign of Queen Victoria*, Aldershot, Hampshire and Brookfield, Vermont: Ashgate, 1997

At the end of the 18th century Tom Paine prophesied the end of monarchy in Europe. His book, *The Rights of Man*, took the British monarchy as the epitome of the high monarchical style, and openly criticized the excesses of the court, "Old Corruption", and venal office-holding surrounding the throne. For Paine monarchy was an abuse, rooted in the accident of birth, unearned privilege, and the dubious or counterfeit pedigrees of royal bloodlines. Most studies of British republicanism begin with Paine. He provided it with its cardinal text, and created a link to the world of the Atlantic revolution at the end of the 18th century.

In truth, however, British republicanism was seen by contemporaries as weak and imported French Jacobinism. Beyond Paine it generated no further major texts, and attracted nationwide public attention only once during the seclusion of Queen Victoria following the death of Prince Albert in 1861. This short-lived phase of republican activity, reaching a peak in 1870–71, highlighted the detrimental effect on the British throne when the incumbent was, in effect, an absentee head of state, whose invisibility led to the suspension of the public ceremonial of the royal state.

Most early studies of Victorian republicanism depict the agitation as weak and impotent. In CANNADINE the weakness of republicanism is seen as a measure of the strength and virility of 19th-century monarchism. For this author the republicans are easily dismissed, providing an impetus for the revitalization of royal ceremonial and splendour in the period 1872–87, but having little real substance in their own right. Indeed he challenges the very integrity of the term "republicanism" in a British context, depicting radicals as fundamentally loyalist in nature, and the British royal state as Bagehot's "veiled republic" in which even reformers realized that the rights of the freeborn Englishman flourished under the protection and largesse of a benevolent monarch, safeguarding, rather than challenging, the traditional liberties of the ancient constitution. For WILLIAMS the monarchy under Queen Victoria was perfectly suited to the new representational politics of the post-1867 reform period. At a time when notions of democracy, civic participation, and political accountability were expanding through reform of parliament itself, a public monarchy came to symbolize the compact between governors and governed in a renewed public sphere.

Historians of a Marxist turn have also diminished the notion of British republicanism. Dismissive of constitutional agendas, and reliant on notions of "movements" in history, they have traditionally viewed republicanism as an aberration that distracted the masses from their true interests in social welfare reform. In HARRISON the republican trappings of the Land and Labour League in the 1870s are scorned. Here the organization is described less as a republican sect, and more as an early focus for radical collectivist and redistributionist energies after the collapse of the Reform League in 1869. Some historians, following the lead of contemporaries, have portrayed British republicanism as a derivative political style, rooted in French precedents, but providing little more than an anaemic imitation of the French republican tradition that flourished in Europe at the time of the Paris Commune.

Historians who have taken British republicanism seriously have tended to pay undue homage to the Paine legacy in popular politics. ROYLE sees British republicanism as part of the British freethought tradition, motivated in particular by the desire to strip away the superstitions of priestcraft and a rapacious state church. He argues that for secularists like Charles Bradlaugh the mystifications of priests and the religious sanctification given to royal ceremonial by the Anglican church were quite simply inseparable.

More recently, however, attempts have been made to locate the republican campaign of 1870–71 in the broader tradition of popular politics and to escape from notions of British republicanism as a flawed and ephemeral movement. TAYLOR has portrayed republicanism in Britain as a submerged and often ignored component of radicalism, rooted in a reverential Cromwellianism and an abhorrence of the corruption of the executive that was very evident during the 1830s, and in the later stages of the chartist movement. Here he has tried to reclaim the murmurings against the excessive and unjust financial exactions apparently extorted from the British public for the upkeep of royalty as an agitation that deserves consideration on its own terms, rather than simply as a traditional style of anti-tax discourse. For some reformers, a movement dedicated to an overhaul of the royal state formed part of a broader populist critique of craven politicians, corrupt courtiers, and royal interference in politics, as well as a way of maintaining a platform for agitation separate from the blandishments of a reformist liberalism in the 1870s and 1880s.

Much of the history of British republicanism remains unresearched. Nevertheless, some recent publications indicate possible areas for future inquiry. POOLE opens up the field of attempted royal assassinations by an analysis of the tensions between the increasingly approachable public face of monarchy, and the frustrations of disaffected petitioners, loyalists, and the fantasists of royalty. The lyrical and poetical inheritance of British republicanism is also beginning to receive attention. KUDUK explores its influence on Swinburne in her work on the republican engagement with the poetic mainstream. Finally there is a much needed examination of the local dimension to British republicanism in RUMSEY that scrutinizes the dynamics of republican club-life in areas where the movement was both strong and weak. Contemporary work on anti-monarchism is informed by the recent travails of the British monarchy and emphasizes that British republicanism should be seen, not as a passive barometer of a successful monarchism, but rather as a movement grounded in the British radical tradition, and offering an apparent antidote to the excesses of kingship.

ANTONY TAYLOR

See also London Corresponding Society; Monarchy, Attacks on; Paine; Radicalism; Wilkes

Restoration Settlements 1660–1662

Bosher, Robert S., *The Making of the Restoration Settlement: The Influence of the Laudians, 1649–1662*, London: Dacre Press, and New York: Oxford University Press, 1951; revised edition, London: Dacre Press, 1957

Green, I.M., *The Re-establishment of the Church of England, 1660–1663*, Oxford and New York: Oxford University Press, 1978

Habakkuk, John, "The Land Settlement and the Restoration of Charles II", *Transactions of the Royal Historical Society*, 5th series, 28 (1978): 201–22

Hutton, Ronald, *The Restoration: A Political and Religious History of England and Wales, 1658–1667*, Oxford: Clarendon Press, and New York: Oxford University Press, 1985

Seaward, Paul, *The Cavalier Parliament and the Reconstruction of the Old Regime, 1661–1667*, Cambridge and New York: Cambridge University Press, 1989

Spurr, John, *The Restoration Church of England, 1646–1689*, New Haven, Connecticut and London: Yale University Press, 1991

Thirsk, Joan, "The Restoration Land Settlement", *Journal of Modern History*, 26 (1954): 315–28

Whiteman, E.A.O., "The Restoration of the Church of England" in *From Uniformity to Unity*, edited by Geoffrey F. Nuttall and Owen Chadwick, London: SPCK, 1962

Set to remain for some time the best general account of the period, the study by HUTTON has comprehensively routed the notion of a single "Restoration settlement" denoting the legislation of 1660–62 which reversed the revolutions of the previous two decades. In fact there were two settlements, "of differing character and produced by different groups of men working in different circumstances". The first took place in 1660. Its statutory portion comprised indemnity and oblivion, the crown's financial settlement, and payment of the army and navy, and was the somewhat flawed achievement of the Convention; while its more *ad hoc* elements included the restoration of church and crown lands. Whereas the first was at least begun in a spirit of reconciliation, the second Restoration settlement was the far more partisan undertaking of the Cavalier Parliament of 1661–62 (described in great detail by SEAWARD). It reversed parts of the constitutional and ecclesiastical revolutions of 1641–48, replaced key elements of the first Restoration settlement, and the essence of national reunification was dissipated utterly by measures such as the Corporation Act, the Act of Uniformity, and the burning of the Covenant, though again much of the reconstruction of episcopacy and persecution of dissent arose in an *ad hoc* manner. Hutton qualifies considerably the conventional judgement that the Restoration was a victory for Charles II, pointing out the limited extent to which the king was able to get his way, and arguing that the second Restoration settlement was "a defeat [for Charles] to be avenged".

Key features of the Restoration settlements have been treated individually to great effect. Although recognizing that there would be no return to the heyday of clerical wealth and political power in England, BOSHER sees the ecclesiastical legislation of 1662 as the final triumph of high church Laudianism, whose essence had been distilled by persecution during the Interregnum, and whose devotees had laid their plans for episcopal restoration in advance of the king's return. The explanation for the miraculously swift recovery of episcopacy lay, however, in the complexities of court and parliamentary factional politics, not least the machinations of Edward Hyde (the Earl of Clarendon), who manipulated the unfurling settlement, inasmuch as he was able, in order to trump factional rivals.

GREEN has criticized Bosher's use of the "Laudian" label, which he describes, reasonably enough, as anachronistic (WHITEMAN, recording her own misgivings on the same score, nevertheless does Bosher the courtesy of acknowledging his own awareness of the label's shortcomings). Green also questions the extent to which any party, "orthodox" or otherwise, was truly able to corner the control of church patronage, which remained throughout firmly in the hands of a king who could not by any stretch of the imagination be described as "Laudian". The popular impetus for the restoration of episcopal government has been exaggerated, and it took much longer than Bosher estimated, too. The two authors have a great deal more in common, however, than Green allows, particularly in their respective accounts of the unpredictability of the Restoration ecclesiastical settlement and the contingencies from which it emerged.

Lacking some of the penetration of the other two authors, Whiteman's nevertheless remains a lucid account of the nuts and bolts of the ecclesiastical restoration. It amplifies Bosher's analysis of the role of those devotees of the Church of England who had done the most to avoid collaborating with the Interregnum regimes, men such as Gilbert Sheldon, George Morley, and John Cosin. It also anticipates some of the criticisms made by Green, particularly the assumption that the ecclesiastical restoration was patterned to a blueprint drawn up before 1660. SPURR painstakingly reconstructs the conformist Anglicanism of the 1650s, and does more than most to reinstate the "moderates" and their theology to their rightful place in the orthodoxy and ecclesiastical establishment created after 1660, as for example in their shaping of a Book of Common Prayer which at least left a door open to puritans prepared to accept episcopal ordination.

The settlement of the church also points up the importance of the land settlement as a feature of Restoration politics. The sale of property belonging to the crown, the church, and to royalist "delinquents" since 1646 had created important interest groups whose influence was felt in shaping the stratagems and tactics of Restoration. THIRSK first demonstrated the skill with which the issue was handled by the king and his advisors, who simultaneously managed to persuade the purchasers of the prospect of confirmation of land sales, or at least compensation for any losses, while assuring churchmen and dispossessed royalists that they might expect to come back into their own. Restitution of crown and church lands was ultimately achieved through a combination of statute and the accommodation of purchasers' interests by the granting of leases to the properties they had acquired outright. Private lands had already begun making their way back into the hands of their original owners before the royal Restoration. Although Charles and Hyde remained reluctant to add any formal impetus to the process for fear of upsetting the policy of "oblivion", Thirsk demonstrates emphatically that "royalists regained their land in all but

exceptional circumstances", contrary to the assertions of other historians that the Interregnum land sales achieved a permanent shift in the balance of English landownership. HABAKKUK points out some of the characteristics of the original sales which made it easier for the new regime to avoid confirmation of land sales. For the most part, purchasers had not settled on their new estates, merely collecting rents from sitting tenants, and therefore had no attachment other than financial to their purchases. More importantly, most purchasers had made good on their investments by 1660, especially if they had bought land as creditors of the state. The tactics of Charles II and his lord chancellor were thus vindicated by circumstances. Wishing to avoid confirming sales, they found the pressure for them to do so relatively short-lived and easy to resist, not least due to lack of unity among an extremely diverse group of purchasers.

SEAN KELSEY

See also British Republic; Charles II; Clarendon; Protectorate of Cromwell

Retail Revolution   20th century

Birchall, Johnston, *Co-Op: The People's Business*, Manchester and New York: Manchester University Press, 1994

Jefferys, James B., *Retail Trading in Britain, 1850–1950: A Study of Trends in Retailing with Special Reference to the Development of Co-Operative, Multiple Shop, and Department Store Methods of Trading*, Cambridge: Cambridge University Press, 1954

Lancaster, Bill, *The Department Store: A Social History*, London and New York: Leicester University Press, 1995

MacKeith, Margaret, *Shopping Arcades: A Gazetteer of Extant British Arcades, 1817–1939*, London and New York: Mansell, 1985

MacKeith, Margaret, *The History and Conservation of Shopping Arcades*, London and New York: Mansell, 1986

Mathias, Peter, *Retailing Revolution: A History of Multiple Retailing in the Food Trades Based upon the Allied Suppliers Group of Companies*, London: Longman, 1967

Redfern, Percy, *The Story of the C.W.S.: The Jubilee History of the Co-Operative Wholesale Society Limited, 1863–1913*, Manchester and New York: CWS, 1913

Redfern, Percy, *The New History of the C.W.S.*, London: Dent, 1938

Schmiechen, James and Kenneth Carls, *The British Market Hall: A Social and Architectural History*, New Haven, Connecticut and London: Yale University Press, 1999

Seth, Andrew and Geoffrey Randall, *The Grocers: The Rise and Rise of the Supermarket Chains*, London: Kogan Page, 1999

Williams, Bridget, *The Best Butter in the World: A History of Sainsbury's*, London: Ebury Press, 1994

Winstanley, Michael J., *The Shopkeeper's World, 1830–1914*, Manchester and New York: Manchester University Press, 1983

While the 19th century is associated with the Industrial Revolution, the history of the 20th century is increasingly being written as the age of the retail revolution. Consumer spending has increased dramatically, especially since the 1950s. Since the 1980s the pace of change has accelerated remarkably, so much so that a relatively small number of businesses now account for the majority of consumer spending in most sectors. Four firms enjoy two-thirds of the grocery market. The total number of shops has declined dramatically, but their average size has increased. Investment in retailing is now global rather than national. Supermarkets, "out-of-town" shopping malls, and e-commerce seem poised to challenge the traditional high street and the style of shopping associated with it.

There are, as yet, few readable general surveys of these dramatic changes, but the emergence of the supermarket giants of the grocery world – Tesco, Sainsbury, Asda, Safeway, and Marks & Spencer – is the subject of SETH & RANDALL's lively and informative book. They attribute much of these firms' expansion to astute entrepreneurship and their ability to forecast, or even mould, consumer spending, but they acknowledge that the pace of change is so rapid that their continued success cannot be guaranteed. Individual histories of successful firms are also common, but the problem with such histories is that they are often written with the overt or tacit support of the businesses and tend to adopt an uncritical, even laudatory approach. Nevertheless, the best of them, such as Bridget WILLIAMS's profusely illustrated history of how Sainsbury's transformed itself from a high-class family grocer in the London area into a chain of supermarkets, are well worth reading and highlight many of the broader trends in retail history over the course of the century, particularly the growth of national companies. These are also the subject of JEFFERYS's seminal survey of the development of multiple retailing from the 1870s. Although it was published as long ago as 1954 and has long been out of print it remains, and is likely to remain, essential reading for anyone who wishes to understand how and why chains of shops emerged at different times and with different levels of success in the food, clothing, and household goods sectors. His statistical tables are still widely quoted and are unlikely to be bettered, while his analysis of the specific nature of retail developments affecting each trade is both measured and clear. Equally impressive is MATHIAS's history of the various grocery firms which had come together by the 1960s as the Allied Suppliers Group including Liptons, Home and Colonial, and Maypole. Like Jefferys, he sets their emergence in the context of a revolution in international trade and rising living standards from the 1870s but he is primarily concerned with providing a detailed business history of the individual firms. Yet another aspect of the retail revolution is charted by LANCASTER, who explores the department store with its emphasis on fashion and style from its origins in the mid-19th century, through the "Golden Age" prior to World War I to the rather more chequered fortunes of the postwar years.

But concentration on the emergence of new forms of retailing can impart a false impression of the speed and extent of change earlier in the century. This was neither as dramatic nor as linear as such histories imply, and it was characterized by significant regional variations. The independent shopkeeper proved remarkably resilient until comparatively recently, as did market trading and the cooperative movement. Insights into the way in which "traditional" independent shopkeepers functioned can be gleaned from the oral histories collected by

WINSTANLEY, who focuses on the patterns of trade which characterized the 1890s to 1910s. During the 19th century huge market halls were erected across much of England, particularly in Lancashire and Yorkshire. These were the working class's retail cathedrals, the municipal authorities who sponsored and ran them viewing them not just as retail centres, but as architectural statements of their town's commercial importance and civic dignity. SCHMIECHEN & CARLS have written the first comprehensive survey of them in a beautifully illustrated volume which traces both their rise and decline. They have also compiled a fairly complete gazetteer. Their book deserves a wide readership; the surviving halls deserve visiting. Equally distinctive and worth exploring are the covered shopping arcades which characterized late 19th-century urban redevelopment schemes in many cities. These have been rescued from oblivion by MacKEITH, whose two volumes are well worth searching out. She traces their origins, changing architectural styles, and ultimate decline, while her gazetteer provides a guide to those which survived further redevelopment schemes in the 1960s and 1970s, particularly in Leeds and Cardiff.

The biggest casualty of recent retail change, however, has been the cooperative store, which has now all but disappeared from many towns. The cooperative movement was once the largest voluntary association in the country, if not the world, boasting over 8 million members in the late 1930s. As BIRCHALL shows in his affectionate study, written to mark the movement's 150th year, it was always much more than a retail business; for many members it was a way of life with a mission to transform the world on non-profit-making cooperative lines. Its vision was international, as were its trading activities. REDFERN's two histories of the Cooperative Wholesale Society's ventures are breathtaking in their coverage. It was a vertically integrated concern capable of growing, manufacturing, or importing virtually everything that the retail societies sold. It was the first universal provider capable of supplying virtually every household need. The depressing collapse of the movement since the 1950s and its subsequent low profile belies its earlier significance as a pioneer of an alternative to the capitalist consumer society which is now so pervasive.

MICHAEL J. WINSTANLEY

See also Consumerism

Revenue, Non-Parliamentary

medieval and early modern periods

Alsop, J.D., "The Revenue Commission of 1552", *Historical Journal*, 22 (1979): 511–33

Barratt, N., "The Revenue of King John", *English Historical Review*, 111 (1996): 835–55

Bernard, G.W., *War, Taxation, and Rebellion in Early Tudor England: Henry VIII, Wolsey, and the Amicable Grant of 1525*, Brighton, Sussex: Harvester Press, and New York: St Martin's Press, 1986

Challis, C.E., *The Tudor Coinage*, Manchester: Manchester University Press, and New York: Barnes and Noble, 1978

Dietz, F.C., *English Government Finance 1485–1558*, Urbana: University of Illinois, 1921; reprinted, in *English Public Finance 1485–1641*, 2 vols, New York: Barnes and Noble, 1964

Dietz, F.C., *English Public Finance, 1558–1641*, New York and London: Century, 1932; reprinted, in *English Public Finance 1485–1641*, 2 vols, New York: Barnes and Noble, 1964

Fryde, E.B., *William de la Pole: Merchant and King's Banker (1366)*, London and Ronceverte, West Virginia: Hambledon Press, 1988

Gras, Norman Scott Brien, *The Early English Customs Service: A Documentary Study of the Institution and Economic History of the Customs from the Thirteenth to the Sixteenth Century*, Cambridge, Massachusetts: Harvard University Press, 1918

Hallam, Elizabeth and David Bates (editors), *The Domesday Book*, Stroud, Gloucestershire: Tempus, 2001

Harriss, G.L., *King, Parliament, and Public Finance in Medieval England to 1369*, Oxford: Clarendon Press, 1975

Hoyle, R.W. (editor), *The Estates of the English Crown 1558–1640*, Cambridge and New York: Cambridge University Press, 1992

Jones, N.G., "Long Leases and the Feudal Revenue in the Court of Wards, 1540–1645", *Journal of Legal History*, 19 (1998): 1–22

Mayhew, N.J. (editor), *Edwardian Monetary Affairs (1279–1344): A Symposium*, Oxford: British Archaeological Reports, 1977

Ramsey, James H., *A History of the Revenues of the Kings of England 1066–1399*, Oxford: Clarendon Press, 1925

Richardson, Walter C., *A History of the Court of Augmentations, 1536–1554*, Baton Rouge: Louisiana State University Press, 1971

Steel, Anthony, *The Receipt of the Exchequer 1377–1485*, Cambridge: Cambridge University Press, 1954

Woolfe, B.P., *The Crown Lands 1461–1536: An Aspect of Yorkist and Early Tudor Government*, London: Allen and Unwin, and New York: Barnes and Noble, 1970

Woolfe, B.P., *The Royal Demesne in English History: The Crown Estate in the Governance of the Realm from the Conquest to 1509*, Athens: Ohio University Press, 1971

Before the 13th century, the crown had three main sources of revenue: rents and fines from the royal demesne; related feudal revenues, such as wardship and escheat; and the profits of justice from the shires, the "sheriffs' tourn". All these continued throughout the period with which we are concerned, although the third was of minimal importance by the 16th century, and the second came to an end with the end of military tenure in 1645. These were known as the ordinary revenues of the crown, and when there were claims that the king should "live of his own", this was what was meant. They were distinct from the extraordinary revenues, granted by parliament, which are considered separately. The first and greatest survey of the royal demesne was incorporated in Domesday Book (1087). This has been the subject of much scrutiny, and much scholarly writing, represented here by one of the latest contributions, a useful collection of essays edited by HALLAM & BATES. The best general study of the demesne is WOOLFE (1971), although it

is sketchy on the early period. Both the studies of the late medieval and early modern demesne are useful, although they are very different. WOOLFE (1970) is a lucid but fairly brief introduction, intended for students, and supported by selected documents. HOYLE is a collection of specialized learned articles, which are extremely informative, particularly on estate management in the early 17th century, but definitely not for beginners. When the monasteries were dissolved between 1536 and 1540, and the chantries in 1547, there was a very large, albeit temporary, expansion of the royal demesne. These acquired lands were managed separately from the ancient demesne, through the Court of Augmentations. This court existed as a separate institution only from 1536 to 1554, and RICHARDSON is the definitive study of its workings. After 1554 what was left of the acquired land was managed by an augmentations office within the exchequer.

In the later Middle Ages, apart from parliamentary taxes, such as tenths and fifteenths, and later Subsidies, two other sources of revenue were added: customs and the profits of the mint. It was the king's prerogative to coin money (or to license others to do so), and the mints were always expected to show a working profit. However, for a few years, between 1540 and 1551, the crown pursued a deliberate policy of debasement for gain. This had an extremely adverse effect on the economy, and was not repeated thereafter in spite of extreme pressure. There are several studies of this debasement, but the most useful and comprehensive is CHALLIS. There are many studies of English trade, and of specific aspects of it, but the old work on the customs by GRAS has never been replaced. These revenues are treated here as ordinary, because they were based on the king's prerogative right to control movement in and out of the realm, but in fact they occupied a grey area, because they were traditionally voted by parliament at the beginning of each king's reign. The crown also borrowed money, both at home and abroad. Both FRYDE and HARRISS are studies devoted largely to this process in the 15th century, although approaching the subject from different angles. The Lancastrians and Yorkists tended to borrow from their own subjects, a process which carried a political price, but which was easier to control. Before that, borrowing had mainly been from Italian (particularly Florentine) bankers, a matter covered, among others, in the collection of essays edited by MAYHEW. When Henry VIII was struggling to finance his second war with France, in 1525, he also attempted to resort to a forced loan, a process which parliament had declared illegal in 1484. The failure of this so-called "Amicable Grant" is the subject of the work by BERNARD.

There is no modern study of medieval revenue in general, and the work of RAMSEY from 1925 has not been superseded. Most recent work has been specific, either to reign or to type of revenue, and that genre of scholarship is represented here by BARRATT, although there is much more. The early modern period has been no better served, and although the two works by DIETZ (1921 and 1932) have been frequently criticized and corrected in detail, neither has been replaced. (The two-volume edition of 1964 was a reprint.) Here too the best modern scholarship is highly specific. JONES offers an excellent insight into the operations of one of the old feudal revenues, managed by a separate court since the 1530s, in the last days of military tenure; and he suggests some reasons why that system ended a generation after the failure of the Great Contract. A scholar who has done a great deal of work on mid-Tudor finance is ALSOP, and his significant output is represented here by his study of the revenue commission of 1552, which effectively addressed the legacy of debt left by the foreign wars of Henry VIII and Protector Somerset. It was the Tudors who finally demonstrated that the increasing costs of government had, by the 16th century, made it impossible for the crown to survive on its ordinary revenue, however flexibly that was interpreted. It was essential for the monarch to resort to direct taxation, not only for war, but also to survive. Elizabeth knew that, but never admitted it, and the Stuarts were finally forced to learn it the hard way.

Discussions of the central machinery of financial administration are included in all the general surveys listed, and in most textbook studies of the different chronological periods. Richardson on augmentations and STEEL on the "receipt of exchequer" are the most immediately relevant in this connection, although works on the Duchy of Lancaster and the Court of First Fruits and Tenths should also be consulted.

DAVID LOADES

See also Feudum; Lancaster, Duchy of; Purveyance; Taxation: Parliamentary

Rheged
see **Strathclyde, Gododdin, Rheged, "Kingdoms" of**

Rhodes, Cecil 1853–1902
Imperialist and entrepreneur

Flint, John, *Cecil Rhodes*, Boston and Toronto: Little Brown, 1974; London: Hutchinson, 1976
Lockhart, J.G. and C.M. Woodhouse, *Rhodes*, London: Hodder and Stoughton, 1963; as *Cecil Rhodes: The Colossus of Southern Africa*, New York: Macmillan, 1963
Marlowe, John, *Cecil Rhodes: The Anatomy of Empire*, London: Elek, 1972
Roberts, Brian, *Cecil Rhodes: Flawed Colossus*, London: Hamish Hamilton, 1987; New York: Norton, 1988
Rotberg, Robert I. with Miles F. Shore, *The Founder: Cecil Rhodes and the Pursuit of Power*, New York and Oxford: Oxford University Press, 1988
Thomas, Antony, *Rhodes*, London: BBC Books, and Johannesburg: J. Ball, 1996; as *Rhodes: The Race for Africa*, London: Penguin/BBC Books, 1997
Williams, Basil, *Cecil Rhodes*, London: Constable, and New York: Holt, 1921; new edition, London: Constable, 1938

Eulogized by white Rhodesians as the founder of their country and for laying down the principle of "equal rights for all civilized men", often regarded as the father of English-speaking South Africans, seen as the promoter of cooperation between Boer and Briton – a role which led to his sacrificing the political rights of blacks in the interests of appeasing the Afrikaner

Bond in the Cape to achieve that end – Rhodes has also been vilified as the founder of apartheid, for leaving a legacy of antagonism between Afrikaners and English speakers in South Africa, and for displaying a ruthless entrepreneurship in his exploitation of gold and the amalgamation of the diamond mines. There is general agreement that he sought to promote the British imperial vision.

Of the many eulogistic early biographies of Rhodes that by WILLIAMS has endured, partly because of its careful scholarship. Williams sees at the heart of Rhodes's imperialism qualities that have done service to mankind: at the pinnacle of his success in 1895 Rhodes had painted "the map of Africa red" to a greater extent than had ever been achieved before; it was due to Rhodes more than any other man that English speakers and Afrikaners saw that a union of South Africa would serve the ends they both wanted. In the 1960s, the account by LOCKHART & WOODHOUSE, which makes extensive use of the Rhodes papers in Oxford, was widely anticipated as being definitive, but was criticized for overlooking many Colonial Office documents which contained material critical of Rhodes. Lockhart & Woodhouse postulate the verdict that Rhodes's memory at the time they were writing was embodied in two symbols: the name of a country which could prove to be the model of a multiracial partnership; and the Rhodes scholarships established to enable Commonwealth, American, and German students to benefit from an Oxford education.

In the early 1970s MARLOWE analysed the development of Rhodes's thought and career as a mirror of the development of imperialist thought and activity, and saw Rhodes as both inspiring and being inspired by British imperialism. Two years later, J.H. Plumb, in his introduction to FLINT's volume, offered the diagnosis of Rhodes as someone who spent his life pursuing one objective – the amassing of the largest fortune ever controlled by one man – to enable him to realize his dream of a secret elite of white Anglo-Saxons, dedicated like Plato's philosopher kings to the bringing of authority and order to the world, in effect to the ruling of other peoples for their own good. Flint's actual text is more circumspect.

The late 1980s saw the publication of two major reassessments of Rhodes's career and personality. ROBERTS concentrates on the man as a product of his time, and depicts Rhodes as a ruthless, energetic, and idealistic man, whose fortune, amassed through diamond mining, enabled him to pursue his political ambition, the crazy dream of painting red as much of the map of the world as he could. In his detailed and extensive biography, Rotberg not only considers Rhodes in terms of his subject's own era, but has also collaborated with the psychologist, Shore, to offer a "psychodynamic interpretation". ROTBERG & SHORE try to answer the question of why Rhodes proved so creative and effective in his multifarious pursuits. Their conclusion is that Rhodes exuded power and smelled of success: he appealed to the idealism of men. A belief in Rhodes became a substitute for religion; it was Rhodes's skills with people and his capacity for visions that enabled him to consolidate the diamond mines – he was a superb strategist and skilled manager. They see Rhodes as viewing blacks as standing in the way of imperial progress, and argue that Rhodes's need for cheap labour and legislative power necessitated an alliance with the Afrikaner Bond and the imposition of limitations on the Cape's colour-blind franchise, the Glen Grey legislation of

1894, which laid the basis for 20th-century rural segregation in South Africa. These authors also attribute the great gulf between English and Afrikaans speakers in South Africa to Rhodes's plans for, and complicity in, the Jameson raid of 1895–96, aimed at overthrowing Paul Kruger's Transvaal, and the subsequent distrust that cancerously grew into a "fatal antagonism" between the two elements of the white population. They conclude that there is an irony that in implementing Rhodes's positive gift to the world, the Rhodes scholarships, committees have selected men and women according to criteria in defiance of the design of their founder.

In the late 1990s, a lavish BBC television production revived an interest in Rhodes. The work on which this was based was by an English-speaking South African, THOMAS. It betrays a hostility both to Rhodes and to the author's own people. Thomas attributes the foundations of apartheid to Rhodes and the actions he took in 1894 to solve the labour problems. Rhodes's blueprint for a new South Africa promised to solve the country's labour problems at a stroke by ending black self-sufficiency through the confining of rural Africans to tribal reserves and the imposition of a tax on every hut. This meant that to survive blacks would have to enter the cash economy and sell their labour to whites. Alongside these territorial changes, Thomas argues, Rhodes and his ministers imposed apartheid in the towns. Thomas suggests that Rhodes only embraced the imperial idea when it served his own purpose. He saw profiteering as a "patriotic duty": after Rhodes's mercenaries had destroyed the Matabele nation and thereby added another 70,000 square miles to Rhodesia, Rhodes told his British shareholders that the value of their investment had increased by 2000 per cent. In Thomas's view, the progress of Rhodes "from cotton farmer and diamond digger to 'African Colossus' had the shape and scale of classical tragedy – the massive tragedy of a young man's corruption in pursuit of power".

RITCHIE OVENDALE

See also Africa entries; Anglo-Boer Wars; South Africa, Relations with

Rhodri "the Great" d. 878
Hywel "the Good" d. c. 949

Dumville, David , "The 'Six' sons of Rhodri Mawr: A Problem in Asser's *Life of King Alfred*", *Cambridge Medieval Celtic Studies*, 4 (1982): 5–18

Kirby, David, "Hywel Dda: Anglophile?", *Welsh History Review*, 8 (1976–77): 1–13

Lloyd, John Edward, *A History of Wales from the Earliest Times to the Edwardian Conquest*, 2 vols, London and New York: Longmans Green, 1911

Loyn, H., "Wales and England in the Tenth Century: The Context of the Athelstan Charters", *Welsh History Review*, 10 (1980–81): 283–301

Maund, Kari, *The Welsh Kings*, Stroud, Gloucestershire, and Charleston, South Carolina: Tempus, 2000

Rhodri the Great, or Rhodri Mawr, was the son of Merfyn Frych, or Merfyn "the Freckled", the progenitor of the second dynasty of Gwynedd. He succeeded his father as King of Gwynedd in 844, and by the time of his death in 878, at the hands of Anglo-Saxons, he had gained control of the kingdoms of Powys, Ceredigion, and Ystrad Tywi.

LLOYD was in no doubt that Rhodri deserved the title "Great", both for his "strenuous and gallant resistance to the northern marauders" (the emotive language is typical), and for uniting most of Wales into a single realm: henceforth, to be of the blood of Rhodri Mawr was the first qualification for rule in Gwynedd, and Deheubarth. MAUND – the only historian to have written a comprehensive account of the medieval Welsh kings since Lloyd – has seen Rhodri as an effective military leader, whose defence of the prime agricultural terrain of his Anglesey heartland probably turned potential Viking settlers towards other targets in Ireland, England, and the Western Isles. Rhodri's death in 878, following his restoration after a brief, Viking-induced exile in 877, is put down either to Scandinavian-controlled Mercian forces expanding their hegemony and defending their border against potential Welsh hostility, or to Anglo-Saxon forces seeking refuge from Viking rule. A lull in Anglo-Saxon interest in Wales in the middle years of the 9th century gave Rhodri the time to consolidate his position in Gwynedd and to expand his power outside. After the death of Cyngen of Powys in 856, Rhodri may have taken control of that kingdom – Cyngen was the last of the independent kings of Powys. After the death of Gwgan of Ceredigion in 872, Rhodri appears to have annexed that kingdom too: Ceredigion became the property of the descendants of Merfyn Frych, and its historical traditions were grafted onto the foundation legend of Gwynedd.

DUMVILLE, in a study of the textual history of part of Asser's *Life of King Alfred*, has shown that the traditional attribution of six sons to Rhodri Mawr is the result of a copying error, where *ui* (Latin, "by the might") was mistaken for a Roman numeral, vi. The loose deductions made by Lloyd concerning the nature of the succession to and development of Rhodri's political power are undermined by Dumville's article, which shows how our appreciation of the development of the overlordship of the second dynasty of Gwynedd must be restricted.

Rhodri Mawr's grandson, Hywel Dda ("the Good"), began his career in the south, gradually expanding his dominion until, by 942, he was in control of most of Wales (only Glywysing and Gwent remained independent of his rule). Hywel was a regular visitor at the English court, and in 928–929 he made a pilgrimage to Rome. Lloyd thought that these facts, taken with the conventional linking of his name to legal reform, were evidence that Hywel maintained a pro-English policy, and even that he may have modelled himself on Alfred the Great. This is a view with which LOYN has expressed sympathy. Whereas Hywel is not to be seen as an anglophile in any anachronistic sense, nevertheless, he was prepared to learn from his experience in England and further afield in Europe at large. Hywel, the most powerful ruler in a fragmented Welsh polity, was probably interested in the precepts of Alfred's grandsons, which had unified the kingdom of England.

KIRBY, on the other hand, has taken a more cynical view, seeing Hywel's compliance with the English kings as more apparent than real: his attitude may have been tempered not with admiration, but with a pragmatic acceptance of Athelstan's superior power, leading him to avoid confrontation or provocation. Kirby has also argued that the surviving medieval Welsh material relating to Hywel may be interpreted as an indication that after his death, Hywel became at least temporarily the centre of a cult, focusing upon ideas of him as an ideal of kingship – just, pious, and militarily effective.

For Maund, Hywel Dda's submission to the Anglo-Saxon kings was probably a more reliable alternative for the Welsh ruler than an alliance with Vikings. She has contrasted Hywel's cordial relations with the English with those of his cousin Idwal Foel, King of Gwynedd, whose hostility to Anglo-Saxon domination led to his humiliation, and eventual defeat, by Athelstan. The later part of Hywel's reign, apparently a period of relative peace, largely free from Viking raids and problems on the borders, is put down to the strength of Hywel and his ability to maintain peace and order. While this may be the case for internal Welsh affairs, we should note that the English and Scandinavians were otherwise occupied at this time, wrestling for power in Northumbria. Maund has, furthermore, seen the traditional attribution of the codification of native Welsh law to Hywel Dda as a possible reflection of 12th- and 13th-century south Welsh attempts to re-establish the importance and influence of their line in an age dominated by the princes of Gwynedd.

Hywel's death – the date of which is variously attested in annalistic sources as 948, 949, or 950 – did not lead to the smooth succession of a new pan-Welsh king but, in line with both previous and subsequent Welsh experience, to warfare and conflict between the next generation of the line of Merfyn.

JOHN REUBEN DAVIES

See also Alfred the Great; Athelstan; Edmund I; Wales before Union with England: Early Kingdoms; Welsh Law

Rhuddlan (Wales), Statute of 1284

Carr, A.D., *Medieval Anglesey*, Llangefni: Anglesey Antiquarian Society, 1982

Davies, R.R., *Conquest, Coexistence, and Change: Wales 1063–1415*, Oxford: Clarendon Press, and Cardiff: University of Wales Press, 1987; as *The Age of Conquest: Wales 1063–1415*, Oxford: Clarendon Press, and New York: Oxford University Press, 1992

Griffiths, Ralph A., *The Principality of Wales in the Later Middle Ages: The Structure and Personnel of Government*, vol. 1, *South Wales 1277–1536*, Cardiff: University of Wales Press, 1972

Jenkins, Dafydd, "Law and Government in Wales before the Act of Union" in *Celtic Law Papers: Introductory to Welsh Medieval Law and Government*, edited by Dafydd Jenkins, Brussels: Librairie Encyclopédique, 1973

Smith, J. Beverley, "The Legal Position of Wales in the Middle Ages" in *Law-Making and Law-Makers in British History: Papers Presented to the Edinburgh Legal History Conference, 1977*, edited by Alan Harding, London: Royal Historical Society, 1980

Smith, L.B., "The Statute of Wales, 1284", *Welsh History Review*, 10/2 (1980): 127–54

Waters, W.H., *The Edwardian Settlement of North Wales in its Administrative and Legal Aspects (1284–1343)*, Cardiff: University of Wales Press, 1935; Westport, Connecticut: Greenwood Press, 1981

The statute of Rhuddlan (or Wales) of 1284 contained the legal, judicial, and administrative components of Edward I's settlement of his newly acquired lands in North Wales following the conquest of 1282–83. In his discussion of the Edwardian settlement DAVIES examines the statute in its historical context, dealing with its administrative and legal provisions in turn, and pointing out the conservative and radical elements in Edward's arrangements, especially in the field of law. He discusses the extent to which native Welsh law was retained in some fields and English criminal law introduced in others and he considers Welsh reactions to the new order. This account, included as it is in the most comprehensive work on the history of medieval Wales, is the best introduction to the subject.

WATERS's book, based on his thesis, was a pioneering work when it first appeared more than six decades ago and it has not been superseded. This is an archive-based study in depth of the working of the administrative and legal changes introduced by the statute in the principality of North Wales; the first part deals with the central and local administration of the principality under Edward I, his son, and his grandson, while the second part is a detailed examination of the working of the various courts set up by the statute, from the justice's sessions to the hundred court, followed by a discussion of the administration of criminal and civil justice. Waters remains the standard work on law and administration during the first 60 years of the new regime and is still the essential point of departure for anyone working in this field. There is a need for a further study, looking at the period between the grant of the principality to the Black Prince and the outbreak of the revolt of Owain Glyn Dŵr (although Wales under the Black Prince was the subject of an Oxford thesis in the 1920s), but administrative history is no longer a popular field of study. Waters's closely argued study does not always make easy reading, but it does indicate how much source material survives in the public records.

Waters looked at the statute and its operation from the point of view of a historian; L. (Llinos) B. SMITH, on the other hand, concentrates on the legal dimension. As she says, it has been "more remarked upon than studied", and she discusses it as a statute in the general context of Edward I's legislation. She goes on to show how some of the processes provided in the statute differed from English practice, while others did not previously exist in England. Use is made of the rich corpus of Flintshire judicial records among the archives of the palatinate of Chester to illustrate the working of the statute and its interpretation in the courts; these records are particularly valuable because of the loss of practically all the medieval judicial records of the principality of North Wales. Considerable attention is given to the new writs provided for Welsh litigants in the statute and they are compared with what was available in England. This is an important study; most discussion of the statute has been of its significance as part of the Edwardian settlement of North Wales and commentators on Edward's legislation (T.F.T. Plucknett, for example) have tended to ignore it. Smith shows here that it should stand alongside the great Edwardian statutes, while at the same time recognizing the separate identity of the new royal lands in Wales. And, like other scholars, she reminds us that, although it is sometimes known as the Statute of Wales, it only applied to the four new counties of Anglesey, Caernarfon, Merioneth, and Flint.

CARR devotes a chapter of a detailed local study to the operation of the legal and administrative provisions of the statute in one of the new counties which it established; this chapter actually goes beyond the working of the statute on the ground to consider the personnel of local government and the financial dimension. GRIFFITHS's book is the first part of a prosopography of the two principalities of South and North Wales and it includes an important introduction which examines local government at all levels in the former, along with judicial and financial administration. Although the statute does refer to the counties of Carmarthen and Cardigan, most of the administrative machinery there was already in place in 1284; nevertheless, most discussion of the statute is of it as part of the Edwardian settlement and as Waters is the starting-point for any study of the administration of the northern principality, so is Griffiths for its southern counterpart. The northern volume is in preparation.

JENKINS's article provides an overview of the interrelation of law and government in medieval Wales, both in the royal lands and in the march; he goes beyond the 1284 statute to discuss the penal legislation rushed through parliament at the start of the Glyn Dŵr revolt and the Acts of Union. Considerable attention is given to questions of law and procedure in the march and also to the impact of the statute itself on the practice and survival of Welsh law, a subject on which this author is the acknowledged authority, in the later middle ages.

J.B. SMITH's essay on the legal position of Wales in the middle ages is above all a discussion of the position of the courts at Westminster (King's Bench and Common Pleas) in relation to Wales both before and after 1284. This brings with it a discussion of the place of the common law in medieval Wales; the central courts had no jurisdiction in the principality because the judicial system established by the statute of Rhuddlan was self-contained and because the royal lands in Wales were not part of the kingdom of England. The argument here is mainly concerned with the marcher lordships; although the king's writ did not run in the march, actions from there did come to Westminster from time to time and Smith considers the issues arising from this.

ANTONY DAVID CARR

See also Edward I; Glyn Dŵr Revolt; Welsh Law

Rhys ap Gruffydd c.1132–1197
King of Deheubarth

Davies, R.R., *Conquest, Coexistence, and Change: Wales 1063–1415*, Oxford: Clarendon Press, and Cardiff: University of Wales Press, 1987; as *The Age of Conquest: Wales 1063–1415*, Oxford: Clarendon Press, and New York: Oxford University Press, 1992

Lloyd, John Edward, *A History of Wales from the Earliest Times to the Edwardian Conquest*, 2 vols, London and New York: Longmans Green, 1911; 3rd edition, London and New York: Longmans Green, 1939

Jones, Nerys Ann and Huw Pryce (editors), *Yr Arglwydd Rhys*, Cardiff: University of Wales Press, 1996

Richter, Michael, "The Political and Institutional Background to National Consciousness in Medieval Wales" in *Nationality and the Pursuit of National Independence*, edited by T.W. Moody, Belfast: Appletree Press, 1978

Turvey, Roger, "The Defences of Twelfth-Century Deheubarth and the Castle Strategy of the Lord Rhys", *Archaeologia Cambrensis*, 144 (1995): 103–32

Turvey, Roger, *The Lord Rhys: Prince of Deheubarth*, Llandysul: Gomer, 1997

Warren, W. Lewis, *Henry II*, London: Eyre Methuen, and Berkeley: University of California Press, 1973

Rhys ap Gruffydd, also known as the Lord Rhys, the ruler of the South Wales kingdom of Deheubarth from 1155 to 1197, was the dominant figure in late 12th-century Wales. LLOYD's discussion of this period is largely built around Rhys and his achievements. One chapter bears his name and he is also a leading figure in the preceding and following chapters. It is significant of Lloyd's approach that the first sub-heading of his chapter on Rhys is "The Greatness of the Lord Rhys"; in his treatment of the history of Wales between the coming of the Normans and the Edwardian conquest Lloyd tended to use the leading native rulers as the cornerstones of his narrative. This was the first major work of historical scholarship to be written from a Welsh perspective, although it has to be stressed that its author never allowed his sympathies to distort his scholarly integrity or rigour.

Lloyd's portrait of Rhys, based on the evidence of chronicles and on the writings of the prince's kinsman Gerald of Wales, is an attractive one and he has appeared in a similar light to subsequent commentators; the picture is of a shrewd and intelligent ruler who extended the borders of his territory, who read the signs of the times and was open to new ideas, and who was able to build up a fruitful and effective working relationship with Henry II. DAVIES refers to Rhys's "genial self-assurance and easy confidence" and his pragmatic approach; "he knew when and how to bend, with good grace and without grovelling". He examines his career in relation to other contemporary Welsh rulers, but he also points out the underlying weakness of the position Rhys had built up; however great his power and his influence during his lifetime, it depended entirely on his own personality and when he died the Deheubarth he had built up fell apart. Personality was not enough; no polity could survive its creator without a secure institutional framework to sustain it. Even the good relations with the English crown depended on the friendship of Rhys and Henry II; they did not survive Henry's death in 1189.

WARREN's treatment of Rhys ap Gruffydd is included in the chapter on "The Lordship of the British Isles" in his biography of Henry II. If Lloyd and Davies examine the Welsh dimension, Warren is concerned with Rhys's career in the context of Henry's political position within the British Isles and he therefore concentrates on the period of *détente* in Anglo-Welsh relations after 1171, which he sees as the consequence of a rethinking of his policy towards the Welsh on the part of the king and a simultaneous reappraisal of their position by the Welsh rulers. He also emphasizes the importance of Rhys to the king in the wake of the Norman invasion of Ireland, an invasion mounted from south-west Wales. The Council of Oxford in 1177 is seen as particularly significant, marking a polarization of political authority in Wales around Rhys in South Wales and Dafydd ab Owain Gwynedd in the north. Rhys's relationship with Henry II is described as one of "good sense and goodwill".

The volume edited by JONES & PRYCE (in Welsh) appeared in 1997 to commemorate the eighth centenary of Rhys's death. It is a collection of studies of various aspects of his reign rather than a biography and these aspects are examined by a number of scholars. The topics range from the nature of the Deheubarth patrimony to which Rhys succeeded in 1155 to the works of the court poets who sang in his praise, along with the poetry itself. This is an important and useful collection, the more so in the absence of a detailed monograph, but it demands from its readers some preliminary knowledge of the history of 12th-century Wales as well as a knowledge of the Welsh language.

RICHTER's discussion of politics and national consciousness in pre-conquest Wales devotes considerable attention to Rhys, especially in connection with the styles and titles used in his *acta* which reflect his perception of his position and with the polarization of political power and authority in late 12th-century Wales also discussed by Warren; it is also valuable as a contribution by a German scholar who is able to look at Wales from a different perspective.

TURVEY's 1995 article discusses the castles built and rebuilt by Rhys and their significance, not only for his defensive policy but also for the definition of the borders of Deheubarth. This is an important exercise in the study of the military geography of medieval Wales, which sees three phases of castle construction and adaptation during Rhys's reign; it is also a reminder that he was probably the first native Welsh ruler to use castles as residences and court centres.

In 1997 TURVEY published a short study of Rhys intended, like the Jones & Pryce volume, to mark the anniversary of his death; he describes it as "a short, popular study intended for scholars, students and the general reader" and as an introduction to a detailed forthcoming study. This must be regarded as the standard work on the life and reign of the Lord Rhys, at least until the appearance of the promised monograph; the evidence, both historical and literary, is re-examined and Rhys emerges with his reputation intact. He could act ruthlessly on occasion and his private life was less than blameless, but as every commentator has agreed, there can be little doubt that he was the outstanding Welsh ruler of the 12th century. As Turvey points out, the only person to express dislike of him was Walter Map, a contemporary at the court of Henry II, although Map added that he would not wish his personal hatred to blind him to Rhys's undoubted personal qualities. This man to all intents and purposes created a kingdom; had it survived him and had his heirs been able to carry on his work, the history of 13th-century Wales might have been different, a conclusion which the reader may draw from most of what has been written about him.

ANTONY DAVID CARR

See also Henry II; Owain Gwynedd; Richard I; Wales before Union with England: Early Kingdoms

Ricardo, David 1772–1823

Political economist

Blaug, Mark, *Ricardian Economics: A Historical Study*, New Haven, Connecticut: Yale University Press, 1958

Cannan, Edwin, "Ricardo in Parliament", *Economic Journal*, 4 (1894): 249–61; 409–23

Carlson, Mattieu J., "The Epistemological Status of Ricardo's Labour Theory", *History of Political Economy*, 26/4 (1994): 629–48

Checkland, S.G., "The Propagation of Ricardian Economics in England", *Economica*, 16 (1949): 40–52

Eatwell, John, "The Interpretation of Ricardo's Essay on Profits", *Economica*, 42 (1975): 182–87

Fetter, F.W., "The Rise and Decline of Ricardian Economics in England", *History of Political Economy*, 1 (1969): 370–87

Findlay, Ronald, *Trade and Specialization*, Harmondsworth: Penguin, 1970

Gordon, Barry, *Political Economy in Parliament, 1819–1823*, London: Macmillan, 1976; New York: Barnes and Noble, 1977

Hollander, Jacob H., *David Ricardo: A Centenary Estimate*, Baltimore: Johns Hopkins Press, 1910

Hollander, Samuel, "The Reception of Ricardian Economics", *Oxford Economic Papers*, 29 (1977): 221–57

Hollander, Samuel, *The Economics of David Ricardo*, Toronto: University of Toronto Press, and London: Heinemann, 1979

Meek, R.L., "The Decline of Ricardian Economics in England", *Economica*, 17 (1950): 43–62

Paglin, Morton, *Malthus and Lauderdale: the Anti-Ricardian Tradition*, New York: Kelley, 1961

Ricardo, David, *The Works and Correspondence of David Ricardo*, edited by Piero Sraffa with the collaboration of M.H. Dobb, 11 volumes, Cambridge: Cambridge University Press, 1951–73; paperback edition, Cambridge and New York: Cambridge University Press, 1981–

Sraffa, Piero, *Production of Commodities by Means of Commodities: Prelude to a Critique of Economic Theory*, Cambridge: Cambridge University Press, 1960

St Clair, Oswald, *A Key to Ricardo*, London: Routledge and Kegan Paul 1957; New York: Kelley, 1965

Stigler, George, "Ricardo and the 93% Labour Theory of Value", *American Economic Review*, 48 (1958): 357–67

Viner, Jacob, *Studies in the Theory of International Trade*, London: Allen and Unwin, and New York: Harper, 1937

The starting point for all serious students of David Ricardo must be RICARDO's published works. Familiarization with his extensive literary output has been made easier by Sraffa's fine edition of the complete works and correspondence. Sraffa's high standard of editorial method has been universally hailed and one of the many strengths of his edition is the masterly treatment of the problems posed by the multiple editions of Ricardo's key text *On the Principles of Political Economy, and Taxation*. The introduction to the first volume of this series is a major contribution in its own right and provides an excellent summary of Ricardo's contribution to economic theory. Many students have also benefited from ST CLAIR's guide to the *Principles*, which is more than just a simple crib and presents Ricardo's opinions on a variety of key issues.

The best single-volume study of Ricardo remains that of BLAUG, which provides a clear and balanced exposition of Ricardo's economic theories and places them in their historical context. Blaug is particularly valuable for the light he sheds on Sraffa's reinterpretation of Ricardo's approach to value and income distribution and on Marxian readings of Ricardo. The older study by Jacob HOLLANDER remains a useful supplementary guide and the first half of the volume consists of a valuable biographical sketch.

Several authors have attempted to chart the contemporary reception of Ricardo's theories. The articles by CHECKLAND, Samuel HOLLANDER (1977), MEEK, and FETTER all deal with the impact of Ricardo on economic theorists and policy makers during the 19th century. One of the earliest and most important critical responses to Ricardo was that of Thomas Robert Malthus. The intellectual relations between the two men may be studied using Sraffa's edition of Ricardo's works which includes correspondence with Malthus and Ricardo's notes on Malthus's *Principles of Political Economy*. This subject is examined in depth by PAGLIN, who also supplies valuable information about the connections between Ricardo, Malthus, and James Maitland, the eighth Earl of Lauderdale. A complementary field of study is Ricardo's political career after his election as member for Portarlington in 1819. This field is surveyed in an article by CANNAN and in a longer study by GORDON. Cannan's eloquent account is based on the Hansard debates and concentrates on Ricardo's proposals for currency reform and his position on the question of the Corn Laws. Gordon's more prosaic study presents a chronological narrative of the issues preoccupying Ricardo in parliament and attempts to link these episodes with the rise of classical political economy to a position of economic orthodoxy.

The most debated aspects of Ricardo's economic system are his theory of value (or the lack of it) and his theory of profits. STIGLER's article has inspired a great deal of research on the role of the labour theory of value in Ricardo's thought and his search for an invariable measure of value. A useful summary of the twists and turns of the debate on this question is provided by CARLSON. The controversy on profits is closely related to SRAFFA's work on the mechanism of income distribution. EATWELL and Samuel HOLLANDER (1979) both address the issue of how profits are related to high or low wages in the Ricardian system; Eatwell endorses much of Sraffa's analysis while Hollander dissents from it. The aspect of Ricardo's economics best known to the general reader is his theory of comparative advantage. VINER's commentary remains the best introduction to Ricardo's theory of trade, while FINDLAY provides a clear exposition of the principle of comparative advantage and specialization.

S.D. SMITH

See also Malthus

Richard I, "the Lionheart" 1157–1199
King of England, and Duke of Normandy and Aquitaine

Appleby, John T., *England Without Richard, 1189–1199*, London: Bell, and Ithaca, New York: Cornell University Press, 1965

Brundage, James A., *Richard Lion Heart*, New York: Scribner, 1974

Flori, Jean, *Richard Coeur de Lion: le roi-chevalier*, Paris: Payot, 1999

Gillingham, John, *Richard Coeur de Lion: Kingship, Chivalry, and War in the Twelfth Century*, London and Rio Grande: Hambledon Press, 1994

Gillingham, John, *Richard I*, New Haven, Connecticut and London: Yale University Press, 1999

Henderson, Philip, *Richard Coeur de Lion: A Biography*, London: Robert Hale, 1958; New York: Norton, 1959

Nelson, Janet L. (editor), *Richard Coeur de Lion in History and Myth*, London: King's College Centre for Late Antique and Medieval Studies, 1992

Norgate, Kate, *Richard the Lion Heart*, London: Macmillan, 1924; reprinted, New York: Russell and Russell, 1969

Turner, Ralph V. and Richard R. Heiser, *The Reign of Richard Lionheart: Ruler of the Angevin Empire, 1189–1199*, London and New York: Longman, 2000

Richard I was idolized in his own lifetime, and legends accrued around him in the later Middle Ages, including the setting of the story of Robin Hood during his reign (witness his cameo appearance in Hollywood versions). But later historians, from Gibbon to Stubbs and beyond, vilified him as a bad son, a bad husband, and a bad ruler. In the second half of the 20th century debate was often dominated by speculation about his sexual orientation. The eighth centenary of his ten-year reign occasioned reassessments of this and more weighty questions.

NORGATE's biography of Richard appeared in 1924 and deservedly held the field for the following half-century. It is a scholarly treatment, demonstrating the author's complete familiarity with the available sources. It is, however, little concerned with Richard as King of England; as Norgate admitted in her preface: "that sovereign's island realm figures scarcely more than in the background, and the life of its people not at all." Richard's visit to England as its new king in 1189 is described in a chapter entitled "The Year of Preparation", and the book is dominated by the story of the Third Crusade. Consequently Norgate portrays Richard as the romantic hero, but casts no light – flattering or otherwise – on his rule in England.

An altogether less heroic depiction is to be found in HENDERSON's biography of 1958. The author claimed to present Richard as a "relatively complicated character", but the text is intensely subjective and adduces "evidence" that is no more than a debased Freudianism. Henderson's explanation of the king's treatment of Glanville reads: "To Richard he was probably a father-figure, and therefore someone to be done to death." The epilogue makes a quite outrageous and anachronistic reference to the Inquisition and to the Dominicans as "the forerunners of the modern political police", in a paragraph that is no more than an unfounded guilt-by-association condemnation of

Richard, culminating in the view that "while his whole life is mainly a record of cruelty and lust in its various forms, our own age, with its overwhelming addiction to violence, should find Richard a sympathetic figure". The book devotes little space to English affairs. It would not warrant discussion at all, were it not that it represents a view of Richard and his reign as English king that has gained popular currency.

This view, though not the emotive approach, was perpetuated by APPLEBY in his account of England during Richard's reign as absentee king. The book is simply structured with a chapter for each year of the reign, beginning with "1189" when, during Richard's visit to England, "he had done almost everything possible to break up the firm and orderly government that his father had imposed on the country". Appleby went on to indict Richard for replacing efficient administrators with new men; persuading the more capable barons to accompany him on crusade; antagonizing the church; exacting unprecedented sums of money; and finally, failing to designate an heir and thus leaving England prey to John. In the final chapter, "1199", Appleby conceded Richard's glorious reputation in his overseas enterprises, but he concluded that "it is almost meaningless to say that Richard was a bad king; for all practical purposes he was king in name only". Paradoxically, though, "Richard's neglect was England's good fortune", for – Appleby claimed – in his absence the barons of England developed a political consciousness that led them directly to confront King John at Runnymede in 1215. In Appleby the Whig interpretation of history lives on.

BRUNDAGE avoided this trap by writing a biography that dealt with the government of England or political history only where these impinged on Richard personally. He also wrote for the general reader, so although he based his account on the primary sources, reference has to be made to Norgate to trace the evidence at any point. This biography is a much more balanced interpretation than Henderson's, but Brundage's view of Richard is still a negative one, except in his role as a crusader – the role that is central to the book. It is convenient to mention at this point two other biographies written for the general reader, by Régine Pernoud (*Richard Coeur de Lion*, 1988 [in French]) and Antony Bridge (*Richard the Lionheart*, 1989). Both are sound narrative accounts but, like Brundage, the authors do not challenge the orthodox view.

This is regrettable, for GILLINGHAM had started his long campaign to restore Richard's reputation as early as 1973, with *The Life and Times of Richard I*, a book that is still valuable for its many well-chosen illustrations. A more developed interpretation was offered in *Richard the Lionheart* (1978, 2nd edition 1989). But both these books, plus much, but not all, of the essays in *Richard Coeur de Lion* (1994), were superseded in 1999 by the publication of *Richard I*. Gillingham has argued cogently that it is a nationalistic anachronism to condemn Richard as a "bad king", because England was only a small part of his Angevin empire, the whole of which he was defending vigorously even at the time of his death, and which was lost by his brother John.

Gillingham also took account of the collection of essays edited by NELSON in 1992. This included an excellent brief account of Richard's reign by J.O. Prestwich and several examinations of the Lionheart legend in European literature. The legendary Richard was also given due, if not disproportionate, weight by

FLORI in another study (in French) published for the 800th anniversary of Richard's death. Flori's account was exhaustively researched and discursively presented and, in accordance with the preoccupation of Flori's own long career, he devoted the second part of the book to Richard as a chivalric figure. Like Gillingham, Flori discussed Richard's sexuality, but he arrived at a different conclusion. His major originality probably lay in the claim that Richard nurtured his own legend, revelling like his predecessors in the diabolical reputation of his family. TURNER & HEISER completed the rehabilitation of Richard as ruler: disregarding his reputation as a soldier, and even as a person, they demonstrated the administrative competence that enabled him to rule his lands even *in absentia*. The first and last chapters of their study are excellent reviews of Richard's reputation and his achievements.

SUSAN B. EDGINGTON

See also Angevin Empire; Crusades; Eleanor of Aquitaine; Henry II; John; Walter Hubert; William I, "the Lion"

Richard II 1367–1400
King of England

Bennett, Michael, *Richard II and the Revolution of 1399*, Stroud, Gloucestershire: Sutton, 1999

Gillespie, James L. (editor), *The Age of Richard II*, Stroud, Gloucestershire: Sutton, and New York: St Martin's Press, 1997

Given-Wilson, Chris, *The Royal Household and the King's Affinity: Service, Politics, and Finance in England, 1360–1413*, New Haven, Connecticut: Yale University Press, 1986

Given-Wilson, Chris (translator and editor), *Chronicles of the Revolution, 1397–1400: The Reign of Richard II*, Manchester: Manchester University Press, 1993

Goodman, Anthony, *The Loyal Conspiracy: The Lords Appellant under Richard II*, London: Routledge and Kegan Paul, and Coral Gables, Florida: University of Miami Press, 1971

Goodman, Anthony and James Gillespie (editors), *Richard II: The Art of Kingship*, Oxford: Clarendon Press, and New York: Oxford University Press, 1998

Hector, L.C. and Barbara F. Harvey (editors), *The Westminster Chronicle, 1381–1394*, Oxford: Clarendon Press, and New York: Oxford University Press, 1982

O'Leary, De Lacey Evans, *England under Richard II*, London: Simpkin Marshall, 1908

Oman, Charles, *The History of England: From the Accession of Richard II to the Death of Richard III, 1377–1485*, London and New York: Longmans Green, 1906

Saul, Nigel, *Richard II*, New Haven, Connecticut: Yale University Press, 1997

Steel, Anthony B., *Richard II*, Cambridge: Cambridge University Press, 1941

Tuck, Anthony, *Richard II and the English Nobility*, London: Arnold, 1973; New York: St Martin's Press, 1974

Richard was born in 1367, the son of Edward the Black Prince and Joan, known as the Fair Maid of Kent. His father having predeceased him, he succeeded his grandfather Edward III on the throne at the age of nine in 1377. During a lengthy minority, which is best remembered for the dramatic events of the Peasants' Revolt (1381), the country was governed by the Council, under the leadership of John of Gaunt. In 1382, at the age of 15, Richard married Anne of Bohemia, the eldest daughter of Emperor Charles IV. The period was one of economic and political stress, caused partly by the radical after-effects of the Black Death, and partly by the collapse of the English war effort against France towards the end of Edward III's reign. The facts of Richard's eventful, and eventually disastrous, career are not in dispute. A scholarly outline was established by OMAN and O'LEARY nearly a century ago, and the standard account of the reign, until recently, was that provided by STEEL in 1941. For reasons which are still in dispute, Richard developed a view of his office and its powers that brought him into head-on conflict with many of his most powerful nobles. In 1386 his chancellor, Michael de la Pole, was impeached in parliament. Richard's attempt to reassert his authority was defeated, and in 1388 de la Pole and several others were "appealed", a crisis reflected vividly in the *Westminster Chronicle* (edited by HECTOR & HARVEY), and examined in depth by both GOODMAN (1971) and GILLESPIE. Having recovered his position in 1397, somewhat ironically with the assistance of his uncle John of Gaunt, the king gained his revenge against his opponents, appealing them in turn, a success which led directly to his overthrow two years later at the hands of Gaunt's son and heir, Henry Bolingbroke (Henry IV).

The traditional view that this situation was created simply by Richard's wilful disregard for the traditional limitations of his office is challenged in some measure by both Goodman and Gillespie. Although the latter's focus is mostly on political and legal events, including Haxey's petition of 1397 and the Oxford trial of 1400, the essays which he has assembled cover many other aspects of the reign. Subjects such as public health and religious foundations do not much advance an understanding of the king's actions, but both foreign trade and courtly art are relevant, because the reign must be seen in its European context, and images of authority were among the king's chief weapons. Goodman is more exclusively concerned with Richard, particularly his relations with the church and the higher nobility, and his controversial uses of literature and the visual arts for his own purposes. Like Goodman, GIVEN-WILSON in his works and BENNETT concentrate particularly on the two crises provoked by the Lords Appellant, the former drawing particularly upon contemporary chronicles, which he edited (GIVEN-WILSON, 1993)

Richard was an idealist who may perhaps have been unduly influenced by his tutor, Simon Burley. As is made clear by SAUL in the recent (and to date by far the best) biography of the king, it was not so much that Richard did not understand the forces arrayed against him but rather that he considered it his duty to overcome them. Like Charles I 250 years later, he was unable either to make concessions honestly or to accept defeat, failings which proved fatal to him as they would become to Charles. As both Saul and Bennett demonstrate, Richard's overthrow by Bolingbroke was due to the collapse of his own support rather than to the great power of his enemies. Richard was disposed

to settle his problems by force rather than law, and although this worked in 1387, and ten years later (at least to begin with), it was a mistaken strategy. His choice of Isabella, the seven-year-old daughter of Charles VI of France, as his second wife in 1396, was probably also a mistake. Improved relations with France were not desired by the English nobles, and, as both Saul and TUCK have argued, the key to any monarch's success in this period lay in his ability to handle relations with his magnates. Richard may, or may not, have been a "Renaissance Prince" ahead of his time, but his fall in 1399 and somewhat mysterious death, probably in the following year, laid up a store of trouble for the following century.

GOODMAN & GILLESPIE (1998) represents a sampling of the most recent views on the nature of Richard's kingship.

JOSEPH A. DiVANNA

See also Henry IV; John of Gaunt; Peasants' Revolt

Richard III 1452–1485
King of England

Armstrong, C.A.J. (editor and translator), *The Usurpation of Richard III: Dominicus Mancinus ad Angelum Catonem de occupatione regni Anglie per Riccardum Tercium Libellus*, London: Oxford University Press/Humphrey Milford, 1936; 2nd edition, Oxford: Clarendon Press, 1969; Gloucester and Wolfeboro, New Hampshire: Alan Sutton, 1984

Dockray, Keith (editor), *Richard III: A Reader in History*, Gloucester: Alan Sutton, 1988; as *Richard III: A Sourcebook*, Stroud, Gloucestershire: Sutton, 1997

Hanham, Alison, *Richard III and His Early Historians 1483–1535*, Oxford: Clarendon Press, 1975

Horrox, Rosemary, *Richard III: A Study of Service*, Cambridge and New York: Cambridge University Press, 1989

Hughes, Jonathan, *The Religious Life of Richard III: Piety and Prayer in the North of England*, Stroud, Gloucestershire: Sutton, 1997

Pollard, A.J., *Richard III and the Princes in the Tower*, Stroud, Gloucestershire: Alan Sutton, and New York: St Martin's Press, 1991

Potter, Jeremy, *Good King Richard? An Account of Richard III and His Reputation, 1483–1983*, London: Constable, 1983

Ross, Charles, *Richard III*, London: Eyre Methuen, and Berkeley: University of California Press, 1981

Richard III has never ceased to attract attention, and in most interpretations the mystery that bulks large is the fate of the princes in the Tower. First and second in line of succession when Richard's brother Edward IV died on 9 April 1483, the boys were taken into their uncle's protection, were declared bastards, and disappeared from view; Richard assumed the throne on 26 June. After a reign of only 26 months Richard was faced with Henry Tudor's invasion, and died defeated at the battle of Bosworth on 22 August 1485. Little reliable contemporary material has survived, and that from the next generation is tainted, since the Tudor monarchy had every reason to proclaim its own legitimacy in terms of Richard's unfitness to rule. With so short a reign, unnaturally begun and ended, incapable of engendering impartial observation or matured reflection in contemporaries, it was inevitable that the study of Richard III would become much more the study of the growth of legends and traditions about this king, and the twists and turns of historiographical writings about him, than is the case with any other medieval English monarch.

ARMSTRONG's publication forms a watershed in studies of Richard III. The bilingual Latin/English edition of the report on Richard's coup compiled, before 1 December 1483, by an Italian visitor with no personal interest in English internal politics, divides the historiography of Richard into commentaries written before Mancini was known to historians, and those written with knowledge of his text. Mancini may not be as objective as was initially thought, having little understanding of the English language and access to only comparatively restricted social circles in London, but he reveals the circulation of some rumours and interpretations earlier than had previously been supposed.

HANHAM focuses attention on the writings of Mancini, the Crowland chronicle second continuator, other native chroniclers, Polydore Vergil, and Sir Thomas More, giving some consideration to documentary evidence. She covers the key period for the development of any Tudor spin on Richard; if his reputation is to be deemed the victim of Tudor propaganda it is here we should expect to find its deliberate application. But Hanham, writing with the benefit of Mancini's text, believes there is very little evidence of Henry VII and his supporters deliberately blackening Richard's already dark reputation. She also suggests that More's history of the king was a joke against historians. Hanham's focus on a short period of historiography is pitched at a more academic readership than POTTER, who covers the whole period from Richard's reign to the present, interweaving two approaches: tracing the evolution of the well-known images of Richard as deformed and monstrous, a serial killer, and child murderer; and explaining the ebb and flow of Richard's reputation over the centuries. Early writings to please Tudor patrons established the outlines of the tale, and these were popularized by mid-Tudor chroniclers, where Shakespeare picked up the details for his play. Three widely separated attempts to rehabilitate Richard, by Sir George Buck in 1619, Horace Walpole in 1768, and Sir Clements Markham in 1892 and 1906, have had little lasting success in obliterating the traditional picture.

Both Hanham and Potter take essentially the same approach, looking at Richard through the development of writings about him. ROSS, however, attempts something different. Taking Richard's slot in a series of studies of English monarchs, Ross offers a good historiographical introduction, more condensed than Potter, but highlighting the salient trends, then proceeds to investigate the life and times of the king, and the actual achievements of his reign. The work was quickly accepted as the definitive 20th-century biography of Richard, and it reflects the non-judgemental ethos of its decade, making Richard out to be a man of his time, which happened to be a violent era. As a well-balanced and well-informed, judiciously written study, this cannot be bettered, and it does much to open up the daily activities of Richard's government, which have often been lost

sight of in works taking a more sensational approach to the king.

Recently writers have chosen to give specifically angled perspectives on the subject. HORROX looks at the retinue which helped to elevate Richard to the throne, and provided the manpower to keep him there, until it eventually failed him. This is interesting on two levels, because it accounts for Richard's actual power base and the personal politics of the reign, and it offers a case study of the mechanics of lordship and retinues, with the focus on a following rooted in the north of England but eventually used to shore up a regime nationally. Richard's northern connections have been most forcefully interpreted by POLLARD. In simplest terms this perspective offers to account for the polarization of opinions about, and support for, Richard in terms of a north-south divide, northern followers looking to Richard as their good lord, opening prospects of upward mobility for them all over the country, southerners, especially after Buckingham's rebellion, resenting being pushed out of office in their ancestral shires by northern newcomers preferred by the king. The northern perspective is also developed in HUGHES, who sets out boldly to correct what he sees as previous failure to appreciate the role of religion in Richard's actions and self-perception.

The questionability of the source material permits wide-ranging interpretation, and it is appropriate therefore, finally, to stress the fact that even those who try to be objective about Richard cannot ignore the colourful writings of earlier times. DOCKRAY offers extracts from the various contemporary or near-contemporary writings about Richard which are so major a factor in all later historiographical works. The selected passages often stop short of what anyone familiar with the cited source would like to see included, but accepting that non-specialists cannot read everything, and cannot be expected to want to, Dockray offers juicy nuggets which give a good flavour of the sources and commentaries and have been purposefully selected and arranged in relation to particular events and issues; note that the revised version should be preferred.

HELEN M. JEWELL

See also Bosworth, Battle of; Edward IV; Henry VI; Henry VII; Neville; Thomas, Cardinal Bourchier; Towton, Barnet, and Tewkesbury, Battles of

Ritualism   later 19th century

Chadwick, Owen, *The Spirit of the Oxford Movement: Tractarian Essays*, Cambridge and New York: Cambridge University Press, 1990

Church, R.W., *The Oxford Movement: Twelve Years, 1833–1845*, London and New York: Macmillan, 1891; new edition, edited by Geofrey Best, Chicago: University of Chicago Press, 1970

Faber, Geoffrey C., *Oxford Apostles: A Character Study of the Oxford Movement*, London: Faber, 1933; New York: Scribner, 1934

Franklin, R.W., *Nineteenth-Century Churches: The History of a New Catholicism in Württemberg, England, and France*, New York: Garland, 1987

Pickering, W.S.F., *Anglo-Catholicism: A Study in Religious Ambiguity*, London and New York: Routledge, 1989

Reed, John Shelton, *Glorious Battle: The Cultural Politics of Victorian Anglo-Catholicism*, Nashville, Tennessee: Vanderbilt University Press, 1996; London: Tufton, 1998

Rowell, Geoffrey, *The Vision Glorious: Themes and Personalities of the Catholic Revival in Anglicanism*, Oxford and New York: Oxford University Press, 1983

Yates, Nigel, *Anglican Ritualism in Victorian Britain, 1830–1910*, Oxford: Oxford University Press, 1999

Two prominent movements within Victorian Anglicanism were tractarianism (and the Oxford Movement) in the early 19th century and ritualism in the later 19th century. Hence, the fundamental historical question has been the relationship, if any, between the two movements. CHURCH's influential "insider" history (he had known all the participants) sees little connection between the two. For him, tractarianism was strictly Oxford-centred, primarily a matter of academic theology, and effectively came to an end with John Henry Newman's conversion in 1845. What happened later had to do with another generation of men, with another agenda of issues. So powerfully did Church set the terms of discussion that 20th-century historians have had difficulty breaking free of his paradigm. Anglo-catholics, as adherents of ritualism were called, wanted to claim the tractarians as their spritual fathers, and argued that the development of ornate, catholic ceremonial in the High Anglican church later in the 19th century followed logically from tractarian theology. Writing to celebrate the centenary of tractarianism in 1933, FABER depends largely upon Church for his account of the movement's origins and leaders. However, he extends his study's chronological reach beyond 1845 to encompass the second half of the 19th century, thereby implying that ritualism later in the century had connections with tractarianism. But his work is a collection of sparkling character sketches, informed by a deep knowledge of the personalities involved, not a sustained and analytical narrative. Hence later historians judged his hints at continuity between the two movements to be little more than a pious wish.

The following decades saw biographies of ritualist leaders, histories of ritualist parishes, and accounts of the foundation of religious orders for women and men. Yet no synthesis was forthcoming. CHADWICK's collection of essays written during the quarter century after 1960 was the product of deep knowledge and sympathy for his subject. He argues that indeed there was something in tractarian thought that "cohered" with the advance of ritual in public worship, but he failed to spell out just what that something was. He hints that the something had to do with the movement's Romantic, poetic, and aesthetic spirit. But Chadwick devotes more space to explaining how ritualism really had its origins in the Cambridge Camden Society, how it was much wider and more influential a movement than that of the tractarians, and how the tractarian leadership thought the introduction of elaborate vestments, decorations, and ceremonial to be "undesirable and improper, and advised their disciples against them". He attributes the spread of such practices to "the less guarded desires" of a younger generation of unrestrained parochial clergy. Chadwick's interpretation was received wisdom for the following 30 years.

Tractarianism's sesquicentenary in 1983 saw little change in interpretation, at least from the pens of Anglo-catholic historians. ROWELL's work is a collection of sketches rather than a coherent history. Its structure, with chapters on movement leaders, ritualist parishes in the slums of East London and the southern seaside resorts, Anglican sisterhoods, missionary bishops, and liberal Anglo-catholics, is similar to those of Chadwick, and of Faber 50 years earlier. This structure fits Rowell's belief that ritualism was about sacramental spirituality, the pursuit of a holy life, and the church as a part of the mystery of the incarnation. He contends that Anglo-catholicism arose from fear of the changing industrial social order and from Romantic medievalism, but his book's structure prevents him from investigating ritualism's cultural and social history and from demonstrating continuity with tractarianism.

Within a matter of years, however, the interpretative landscape changed. FRANKLIN's major comparative study argues that tractarian doctrine and ritualist worship had analogies elsewhere in Europe. Further, he moves the Oxford theologian E.B. Pusey to centre stage. Social reform, Franklin argues, was a major component of Pusey's tractarian theology, for tractarianism was an attempt to grapple with the problems of modern, industrial society, not an escape from those problems into Romantic medievalism. When Pusey put his social theology into action, he chose the industrial north as his sphere of action and he expressed his theology by means of ritualism. PICKERING is concerned to explain ritualism's decline in the second half of the 20th century, but along the way he provides much history. He calls ritualism the "second stage" of tractarianism, "a movement within a movement" that shared a common theological thread with the more extreme tractarians. He stresses that the ritualists were divided among themselves, some using the 3rd- and 4th-century church as their model, others calling for a return to medieval practices, and a few imitating the practice of the 19th-century catholic church.

Two important analytical and comprehensive narratives of ritualism appeared at the end of the 20th century. REED studies ritualism's roots in tractarianism, the movement's spread into the parishes, the theological and social ideologies that ceremonial revival symbolized, the movement's evolution and internal conflict from generation to generation, and the reasons why the movement survived strenuous attempts to suppress it. Ritualism was a countercultural movement that challenged middle-class values as much by creating an alternative lifestyle as by its writing and preaching, and which appealed to people disaffected from those values. Finally, Reed argues that ritualism survived parliament's attempt to outlaw it in 1874 because it was entrenched, because persecution both created martyrs and gained support from traditional High churchmen, and because ritualists themselves changed over the years, abandoning the argument for ceremonial in the name of doctrinal uniformity in favour of the argument for ceremonial in the name of freedom of conscience.

YATES, the author of numerous local studies of ritualism throughout England, shows that ritualism appeared as early as the late 1830s and flourished in places other than London slums and seaside resorts. He minimizes ritualism's tractarian roots. He asserts that ritualists, lay and clerical, used the movement to escape the rapid social changes of the 19th century. The movement's long-term consequences were to bring disunity to worldwide Anglicanism and to help undermine the consensus about the relationship between church and state. Both Yates and Reed are agreed on their final conclusion: ritualism, beginning as a movement to transform and (for Reed) scandalize the Church of England, ended as a church party, thereby enjoying respectability, acknowledging the right of other church parties to exist, and sowing the seeds of its own decline in the late 20th century.

DENIS PAZ

See also Anglican Doctrine and Worship; Newman; Oxford Movement; Tractarianism

River and Canal Transport

Duckham, Baron F., "Canals and River Navigations" in *Transport in the Industrial Revolution*, edited by Derek H. Aldcroft and Michael J. Freeman, Manchester and Dover, New Hampshire: Manchester University Press, 1983

Dyos, H.J. and D.H. Aldcroft, *British Transport: An Economic Survey from the Seventeenth Century to the Twentieth*, Leicester: Leicester University Press, 1969

Hadfield, Charles, *British Canals: An Illustrated History*, London: Phoenix House, 1950; 7th edition, Newton Abbot, Devon and North Pomfret, Vermont: David and Charles, 1984

Jackman, W.T., *The Development of Transportation in Modern England*, Cambridge: Cambridge University Press, 1916; revised edition, London: Cass, 1962; New York: Kelley, 1965

Prior, Mary, *Fisher Row: Fishermen, Bargemen, and Canal Boatmen in Oxford, 1500–1900*, Oxford: Clarendon Press, and New York: Oxford University Press, 1982

Szostak, Rick, *The Role of Transportation in the Industrial Revolution: A Comparison of England and France*, Montreal and Kingston, Ontario: McGill-Queen's University Press, 1991

Ward, J.R., *The Finance of Canal Building in Eighteenth-Century England*, London: Oxford University Press, 1974

Willan, T.S., *River Navigation in England 1600–1750*, Oxford: Oxford University Press, 1936; reprinted, New York: Kelley, 1965

Willan, T.S., *The English Coasting Trade 1600–1750*, Manchester: Manchester University Press, 1938; reprinted, New York: Kelley, 1967

Willard, J.F., "Inland Transportation in England during the Fourteenth Century", *Speculum*, 1 (1926): 361–74

JACKMAN's study, though originally published as long ago as 1916, still provides an authoritative guide to water transport in England from the Middle Ages until the Victorian period. Based on substantial research, and with an excellent bibliography of primary sources consulted, this book outlines the main contours of the subject. It shows that substantial impediments to river navigation existed in the late medieval period as a result of obstructions by private persons and the high charges that watermen made for providing barges, boats, and ferries. For these reasons, and lack of improvements, rivers were not used as much in the transport of goods as they might have been. Few advances occurred in the 16th century, when only eight acts of Parliament dealt with river navigation. The Stuart era witnessed more attempts to make rivers navigable in order to reduce carriage costs on heavy commodities such as coal. This was in train after 1650. Jackman traces the complementary growth of improved river navigations and canals after 1750, showing how they developed significantly at a time of industrial expansion. His account covers the opposition to canal building from vested interests such as road trustees and participants in the coasting trade as well as the beneficial effects of canals on manufacturing enterprise, domestic and foreign trade, agricultural produce, the carriage of bulk commodities across regions, and the reduction in carriage costs. The book concludes by discussing the methods deployed by railway companies to establish their ascendancy over waterways by the 1840s.

Modern research on medieval English waterways is very sparse; indeed, the most detailed treatment is still WILLARD's article of 1926. The early modern period is better served by WILLAN's two classic studies, based on an Oxford doctorate of 1934 and still not superseded. Willan demonstrates the complementarity between river navigations and the coasting trade and their significance for the development of internal commerce in England. In the period 1600–1750, industry and agriculture depended on the coasting trade for raw materials and for the sale of products in urban markets. The coasting trade remained important while land communication was defective; only with the coming of the railways, which opened up the hinterlands of ports, did the coasting traffic decline. Rivers were considerably improved by parliamentary statute in the late Stuart and early Hanoverian eras, increasing significantly the mileage of navigable rivers in England. Rising provincial wealth coupled with the operation of joint-stock companies lay behind the improvements. Industrial expansion necessitated the carriage of heavy goods by water transport. River improvements also expanded the market for agricultural produce. Willan concludes that improved water communication was a legacy of the 17th and 18th centuries that was essential for the commercial and industrial revolutions.

HADFIELD's book is the starting-point for understanding the basic narrative history of British canals. He covers regional developments, the role of engineers, and the legislative battles over the promotion of individual waterways. The popularity of the book is reflected by its having appeared in numerous editions since 1950, when it was first published. The author has published several other specialized books on regional waterways in Britain.

Hadfield's publications are those of a well-informed amateur enthusiast; they make no pretence at economic history. DYOS & ALDCROFT have more to offer on the economic history of waterways. They place river navigation and canal development within the overall context of transport's contribution to the economy, with particular emphasis on the cheapness of water transport compared with road transport.

PRIOR's study of Fisher Row, a Thameside community in Oxford, is the best discussion of the people who worked on waterways. She examines the local significance of bargemen, canal boatmen, and their family history and social relations over four centuries between the Tudor and Edwardian periods. Her book includes a good section on the links between the River

Thames and the various canals surrounding Oxford in the early Industrial Revolution.

WARD dissects the finance of canal and river improvement in the 18th century. He finds that most improvers of waterways were local commercial and agricultural men, but an important minority came from London, especially from the legal community. Ward covers the geographical background of investors, their social and economic status, and their motives for investing in waterways. He analyses the problems of raising capital, especially the supplementary finance needed to cover an increase in the cost of works over the original estimate. He shows that the canal investments of the main occupational classes in England were roughly proportional to their shares of the nation's larger incomes. Thus landowners did not play a disproportionately large part in waterway investment.

DUCKHAM's essay is the best single recent overview of the contribution of waterways to the Industrial Revolution in Britain. He covers the promotion and chronology of waterways, financial investment, and operational aspects succinctly. His conclusion looks at the impact of waterways on the economy. The statistical significance of canals is difficult to determine, given the patchy survival of data confined to particular localities. But canals were crucial for the distribution of coal from inland coalfields and for thereby stimulating the growth of the iron industry; they also served urban centres and the agricultural economy, helping to accelerate "the trend towards a more national market and a closer integration of the regions".

SZOSTAK's study is one of the few detailed attempts to set English transport developments in a comparative international context. He compares the rapid progress made in promoting English waterways in the 18th century with France's slow development of waterways in the same century; and he also includes material on roads. His main argument is that transport improvements were necessary for English industrialization because they aided regional specialization, the emergence of new industries, and an increase in the scale of production. Whereas French reliance on a centralized institutional structure proved inefficient in promoting waterways, English use of local initiatives, private bills in parliament, and arbitration of land prices proved to be a much better institutional framework for the development of waterways.

KENNETH MORGAN

See also Brunel; Coastal Transport; Engineering entries; Freight Transport; Industrial Revolution; Public Health; Railways; Telford; Transport Development

Road Transport

Albert, Bill, *The Turnpike Road System in England 1663–1840*, Cambridge: Cambridge University Press, 1972

Barker, Theo and Dorian Gerhold, *The Rise and Rise of Road Transport, 1700–1990*, Basingstoke: Macmillan, 1993; Cambridge and New York: Cambridge University Press, 1995

Chartres, J.A., *Internal Trade in England, 1500–1700*, London: Macmillan 1973

Chartres, J.A., "Road Carrying in England in the Seventeeth Century: Myth and Reality", *Economic History Review*, 30/1 (1977): 73–94

Freeman, Michael J., "Road Transport in the English Industrial Revolution: An Interim Reassessment", *Journal of Historical Geography*, 6/1 (1980): 17–28

Gerhold, Dorian, "The Growth of the London Carrying Trade, 1681–1838", *Economic History Review*, 41/3 (1988): 392–410

Gerhold, Dorian (editor), *Road Transport in the Horse-Drawn Era*, Aldershot, Hampshire: Ashgate, and Brookfield, Vermont: Scolar Press, 1996

Pawson, Eric, *Transport and Economy: The Turnpike Roads of Eighteenth-Century Britain*, London and New York: Academic Press, 1977

Thompson, F.M.L., "Nineteenth-Century Horse Sense", *Economic History Review*, 29/1 (1976): 60–81

Turnbull, Gerard L., "Provincial Road Carrying in England in the Eighteenth Century", *Journal of Transport History*, 4/1 (1977): 17–39

Walsh, Margaret (editor), *Motor Transport*, Aldershot, Hampshire and Brookfield, Vermont: Ashgate, 1997

Webb, Sidney and Beatrice Webb, *English Local Government: The Story of the King's Highway*, London and New York: Longmans Green, 1913

No one doubted the importance of roads to the Romans; the physical manifestations were there for all to see. The "dark ages", which are traditionally viewed as closing over Britain with the departure of the legions, seemed for road transport to extend to the 20th century, when motor vehicles burst on the scene and soon dominated all forms of transport, whether of goods or people. In these dark ages one or two lights appeared – Macadam's road surfacing, turnpike trusts, and the stagecoach – but faintly. Of course it was more complicated than this. For short-distance traffic road transport was always essential – from port to workshop, from canal wharf to factory, or, in the 19th century, from railway goods yard to mill. In the last couple of decades there has been a radical rethink of the role of road transport.

Based on travellers' complaints of the poor quality of roads in the early modern period, it was largely believed that few people used them. CHARTRES (1973 and 1977) and TURNBULL turned this idea on its head, suggesting the roads were churned up by the growth in the traffic using them. They looked at the number of carriers calling at various inns to show that there was indeed rapid growth in goods carriage by road wagon from the 17th to the 19th centuries, and that much of it was long distance. They arrived at an annual rate of growth of about 11 per cent over 100 years, demonstrating how dynamic this sector was. Research followed to trace the networks of carriers in various parts of the country, and FREEMAN was among these scholars, demonstrating that carriers were crucial to market towns as well as to the long-distance inter-city trade.

The role of turnpike trusts in transport history also underwent drastic revision. These stretches of road were brought to a high level of efficiency by local worthies banding together to finance the work and then recouping their expenditure by charging tolls to traffic using the improved roads. The tolls were collected at a barrier – the turnpike – hence the name. Until the

1970s, following the lead of the WEBBs, it was thought that turnpikes had little impact on transport or economic growth because they were local initiatives with no logic or systematization and scattered across the country haphazardly. Thus, long-distance trunk traffic faced a patchwork of improved and unimproved roads and delays at numerous toll collection points. ALBERT refuted this view, showing that although arising through local initiative the separate trusts, by the late 18th century, did form a system of trunk roads radiating from London. Also, he demonstrated that locals often banded together to create a turnpike to carry through traffic. Since road maintenance was a local duty, through traffic contributed nothing to its upkeep. The introduction of a turnpike allowed locals to charge long-distance carriers for some of the wear and tear they caused. This view of the national role of the turnpikes and their essential economic rationality was reinforced by PAWSON who looked at them from a historical geographer's viewpoint and emphasized their contribution to economic expansion.

Albert's and Pawson's views remain the current orthodoxy, but the views of Chartres and Turnbull have come under attack from GERHOLD (1988 and 1996). He used similar methods and sources but calculated that the rate of growth was much lower than previously estimated, mainly because Chartres and Turnbull had significantly underestimated the extent of carriers in the early 18th century and earlier. Thus while there appeared to be very rapid growth this was much reduced when the much larger network of the early period was taken into account. Thus, while Chartres and Turnbull estimated for the period 1715 to 1796 that the number of ton miles worked rose tenfold, or roughly 11 per cent per annum, on services to the capital, Gerhold reduced this to threefold for the period 1681 to 1838, a drastic revision.

Gerhold has shown that road transport in the industrial revolution was crucial to trade and economic growth, and that its special strengths compared to canals and coasters were reliability, frequency, and a small consignment size. The drawback was the cost, it being much dearer than water-borne goods carriage. This was less important for high-value commodities such as draperies and cloth, high-quality steel files, bullion, and perishables, as Gerhold has shown. The carriage of low-value bulky goods over any substantial distance was not the forté of horse-drawn road transport.

It should not be assumed that the advent of the railway caused a decline in road transport. Long-distance services died when rails paralleled their routes, but there was such a growth in trade and commerce that there was a steady increase in the number of horses in the United Kingdom during the 19th century, as THOMPSON has shown. Horses were needed for the short but crucial journeys from railway station or port to factory or warehouse. The traffic was particularly concentrated in the cities and industrial towns where traffic jams of horse-drawn and pedestrian traffic became common, Thompson argues. The horse population and congestion problems on the roads were added to by the need for intra-urban passenger transport such as horse buses and then trams. After a struggle among steam, electricity, and petrol for dominance as the motive power, well brought out in BARKER & GERHOLD'S succinct book, petrol won the day in the early 20th century. Since then the rise of road transport has been dramatic and largely unchallenged, though

bemoaned, as Barker and Gerhold explain ebulliently. Despite the massive growth of road transport in the 20th century there has been little historical debate about its rise or the causes of this. As both Barker & Gerhold and WALSH explain there has been more interest in the technical and business history of car manufacture, much less on commercial vehicles, and little interest in the effect of motor vehicles on society and the economy. We still need to know who bought and used road vehicles and the precise impact they had.

JOHN ARMSTRONG

See also Bicycles and Bicycling; Freight Transport; Motor Industry; Public Transport; Rebecca Riots

Robert I, the Bruce 1274–1329
King of Scotland

Barrow, G.W.S., *Robert Bruce and the Community of the Realm of Scotland*, London: Eyre and Spottiswoode, and Berkeley: University of California Press, 1965; 3rd edition, Edinburgh: Edinburgh University Press, 1988

Brown, J.T.T., *The Wallace and The Bruce Restudied*, Bonn: Hanstein, 1900 (*Bonner Beiträge zur Anglistik*, vol. 6)

Duncan, A.A.M., "The Community of the Realm in Scotland and Robert Bruce: A Review", *Scottish Historical Review*, 2nd series, 45/140 (1966): 184–201

McDiarmid, Matthew P. and James A.C. Stevenson (editors), *Barbour's Bruce: A Fredome is a Noble Thing!*, 3 vols, Edinburgh: Scottish Text Society, 1980–85

McNamee, Colm, *The War of the Bruces: Scotland, England, and Ireland, 1306–1328*, East Linton, East Lothian: Tuckwell Press, 1997

Prestwich, Michael, *War, Politics, and Finance under Edward I*, London: Faber, and Totowa, New Jersey: Rowman and Littlefield, 1972

Reid, Norman H., "Crown and Community under Robert I" in *Medieval Scotland: Crown, Lordship, and Community: Essays Presented to G.W.S. Barrow*, edited by Alexander Grant and Keith J. Stringer, Edinburgh: Edinburgh University Press, 1993

Watson, Fiona J., *Under the Hammer: Edward I and Scotland, 1286–1306*, East Linton, East Lothian: Tuckwell Press, 1998

Watson, Fiona J., "The Enigmatic Lion: Scotland, Kingship, and National Identity in the Wars of Independence" in *Image and Identity: The Making and Re-making of Scotland through the Ages*, edited by Dauvit Broun, R.J. Finlay, and Michael Lynch, Edinburgh: John Donald, 1998

Young, Alan, *Robert the Bruce's Rivals: The Comyns, 1212–1314*, East Linton, East Lothian: Tuckwell Press, 1997

Robert Bruce is one of the two great patriotic heroes in Scotland's national history; the other is William Wallace. Their victories in battle against superior English forces, at Bannockburn in 1314 and at Stirling Bridge in 1297 respectively, have remained potent nationalist rallying cries. Pointing out that the historical record may be less than unequivocal in the legacy of these battles and of these leaders has done little to dampen enthusiasm. Inevitably, Bruce has received ample attention from authors peppering the popular market with "lives of", producing many duplicate and – although often beautifully illustrated – somewhat shallow biographies. The source of the popular and the academic account comes from John Barbour's *The Bruce*, dating from 1375. Selected extracts are used to stir patriotic blood, and while one must be aware that patriotic heroes often attract unwarranted attention, we should be suitably grateful that one classic account that has stood the test of time exists to guide us. BARROW can rightly claim to have written the definitive history, and this is the starting-place for any scholar. Duncan, who along with Barrow did so much to shape the modern teaching of Scottish history in Glasgow and Edinburgh universities, described this work in a long and critical review essay as "one of the landmarks of historical writing set up by this generation".

The main debate is Barrow's confidence in the establishment of the "community of the realm" and its importance to Bruce's capture of the throne. The community of the realm is especially contentious for the importance attached to the concept by later generations, with emphasis on "freedom" and the creation of a bond between the people and their government, forging nation and national identity before the age of nationalism. This concept has also served to support the construction of a popular Scottish ethos, a collective spirit, a greater (than in England) sense of community. The concept, of course, has its main historical relevance in the time of Bruce. Barrow has placed the community of the realm at the heart of 13th- and 14th-century political theory, stressing the centrality of the relationship between the people and the feudal elites to a Scottish nationhood which encompassed "the totality of the King's free subjects". The prominence of this concept was its use by Bruce to justify his capture and consolidation of the throne after 1306, despite his claim being less than clear-cut. The balance of power between the community of the realm and Bruce is often presented as reaching its most critical juncture in the Declaration of Arbroath (1320), a document readily identified as the first and one of the finest pieces of nationalist rhetoric in the medieval period. A valuable discussion on whether the declaration signalled the power of Bruce over the realm, cementing his position as king, by presenting himself as the choice of the community, is laid out in the work of REID. He argues that if one examines the legislation produced, the events of 1320 were a continuation of trends rather than a high-point of change, but still they marked an important period in the interdependence of the community and Bruce. DUNCAN, however, has remained sceptical over just how consistently representative of the people the community of the realm was throughout this period, or how consistent was its independence of action. His work offers an invaluable counterpoint to the over- positive and coherent interpretation of these themes presented in much of this literature.

Analysis of Barbour's *The Bruce* can be usefully found in the work of BROWN, whose comparison with Blind Harry's epic verse upon the life and deeds of Sir William Wallace is highly instructive. It should be read along with the Scottish Text Society's reproduction of *The Bruce*, edited by McDIARMID & STEVENSON, which is the standard point of entry to the source. Other works are notable for placing the life and actions

of Bruce in the wider context of his times. The intricacies of England's attempts to conquer Scotland during the age of Edward I are best found in WATSON (*Under the Hammer*). This monograph does much to unearth the political and military state of Scotland, and its larger neighbour, in the years immediately prior to Bruce's seizure of the throne. It builds on the work of PRESTWICH, who provides an interesting viewpoint from the English sources, too often ignored when dealing with such patriotic biographies. Based on government records detailing the cost of Edward I's military endeavours, Prestwich and Watson provide in their work balance to our understanding of Bruce. Wider histories of the patriotic king in this period include the interesting contribution by McNAMEE, who takes Robert Bruce, and his brother Edward, as his focus on warfare during the period 1306 to 1328. Further context is offered by YOUNG, who presents a powerful corrective account of the Comyn family, the rivals to Bruce. The work is also notable for tracing the construction of the Bruce myth in the chronicles of John of Fordun, Walter Bower, and Andrew of Wyntoun. These chronicles, by contrast, also show the rhetorical means by which John Comyn was undermined, being subsumed within the over-patriotic chronicles which accuse him of siding with Edward I against Robert I. WATSON's contribution to a book of essays entitled *Image and Identity* shows the attractiveness to Bruce of promoting national identity to enable him to maintain his power and, equally, the attractiveness of Bruce to the concomitant creation of a national identity around him, backing up the patriotic prejudices identified by Young. There are many sides to the history of Bruce and these themes have all benefited from scholarly yet accessible accounts, despite the proliferation of potboilers which exist. All are, it must be said, reflections of Barrow's masterly exposition.

GRAEME MORTON

See also Arbroath, Declaration of; Bannockburn, Battle of; Bruce; Edward I; Edward II; John Balliol; Wallace

Robert II 1316–1390
King of Scotland

Barrell, A.D.M., *Medieval Scotland,* Cambridge and New York: Cambridge University Press, 2000

Boardman, Stephen I., *The Early Stewart Kings: Robert II and Robert III, 1371–1406,* East Linton, East Lothian: Tuckwell Press, 1996

Donaldson, Gordon, *Scottish Kings,* London: Batsford, and New York: Wiley, 1967; revised edition, London: Batsford, 1977

Grant, Alexander, *Independence and Nationhood: Scotland, 1306–1469,* London and Baltimore: Arnold, 1984; reprinted, Edinburgh: Edinburgh University Press, 1991

Lynch, Michael, *Scotland: A New History,* London: Century, 1991; revised edition, London: Pimlico, 1992

Nicholson, Ranald, *Scotland: The Later Middle Ages,* Edinburgh: Oliver and Boyd, and New York: Barnes and Noble, 1974

First of the Stuart (or Stewart) dynasty of Scotland, Robert (ruled 1371–90) was the grandson of Robert Bruce. Lynch argues that, because of the lack of evidence, many previous historians have rushed to a critical judgement of the first Stewart king. DONALDSON provides a bleak picture of these 19 years. He points out that Robert II's right to the crown rested on the basis of statute: this legal enactment supposedly settled the question concerning the legitimacy of Robert's first three sons, whose mother, Elizabeth, was related within prohibited degrees to her husband. He emphasizes the dissent against Stewart rule, which was manifested in a demonstration, described by Boardman as a display of "political disaffection", by William, first Earl of Douglas. Donaldson castigates Robert for an undistinguished life, and thinks very little of his reign: he argues that powerful magnates ignored a king increasingly prone to physical and mental collapse; ambitious subjects, as he writes, concealed, from an unadventurous king, their intentions to renew Anglo-Scottish warfare. Donaldson finishes his appraisal of the reign by analysing the association in government of Robert's eldest son, the Earl of Carrick, due to the inadequacies of the monarch.

NICHOLSON also sees the first Stewart king as a failure: he considers that Robert II lacked the masterful political touch, and this absence of determination led to bad government and subsequent internal problems. He stresses how Robert bought off the opposition of the Douglas family after the "royd harsk begynnyng" of the staged protest mounted by the Douglases at Linlithgow. Nicholson links this to the question of the legitimacy of Robert II's eldest sons; indeed, he argues that the French court expected future troubles concerning the succession.

The financial difficulties of the 1380s are studied by Nicholson; he emphasizes, as did Donaldson, the lawless state of the kingdom. Nicholson considers that this drift was also evident in royal conduct of Anglo-Scottish relations. He diminishes the importance of the king; the peace-loving Robert could in no measure control the warlike propensities of the nobility. In this view the king made no contribution to the Scottish victory, in 1388, over the English at Otterburn in Redesdale – the first substantial military success at the expense of the English since the late 1320s.

Grant, Lynch, and to a lesser extent Barrell, give more considered and balanced assessments of the reign of Robert II. GRANT, in his analysis, can discern a reign "not so unsuccessful"; political tension had decreased, and he argues that the demonstration by the Douglas family was aimed at winning patronage, rather than the crown, and the majority of the nobility continued to support Robert. Moreover, as he narrates, after this fracas all sides were rewarded and satisfied, a considerable political trick. As Grant maintains, Robert used his sons to dominate the nobility: 8 out of 15 earldoms were in their hands, and no crown lands were used to endow his sons; Lynch describes this process as creating a "family consortium". Overall, as analysed by Grant, Robert II's patronage was handled in a more tactful fashion, when compared to the deeds of David II (ruled 1329–71). And unlike Nicholson, Grant considers that Robert was financially secure, although not rich when compared to his English and French counterparts.

Grant suggests a *coup d'état* in 1384 on Carrick's part, and downplays the supposed senility of the king. He sees a faction fight within the royal family as the reason for the events of that year; Grant goes further and suggests that the king, in moving against an injured Carrick in 1388 (the earl had been incapacitated by a kick from his horse), and in personally arranging Scotland's participation in the Anglo-French truce of 1389, was no mere "spectator" of events. LYNCH stresses little break, in the years 1371–84, with the continuity established by the previous reign. Like Grant, he thinks there was no dislocation in government or finance. Moreover, Lynch sees Robert's policy of allowing the consolidation of the territorial power base of the Black Douglases, the origin of political troubles in the 1450s, not as a weakness, but an example of the *laissez-faire* policy followed by David II, to the applause of historians. Finally, Lynch agrees with Grant in seeing 1384 as a coup. BARRELL does not go so far in rescuing this reign: he thinks Robert's personality lacked consistency of purpose, and argues that he ruined his inheritance from David II. He admits, however, that the position of David was better than Robert's, because he had no brothers or children to cause dissent, and the Stewart dynasty was new and needed to establish itself.

BOARDMAN has recently completely reassessed the reign of Robert II, and in so doing he goes beyond the position of Lynch and Grant. He sees that Robert's pre-royal career was one of ruthlessness in the consolidation of his own and family's interests, often in the teeth of opposition from the court favourites of David II. As king, he argues, his propaganda was adept: the 14th-century history of the family was rewritten; and an attempt was made to trace the family's descent from legendary Scottish figures. Boardman argues for the importance placed on the figure of Robert I (ruled 1306–29): he collects evidence from books of arms which suggest the linkage in the period of 1378 of the Stewart/Bruce arms; John Barbour's epic *The Bruce,* although not necessarily the product of Robert's patronage, certainly reflected a state of affairs, including baronial unity, desired by the crown. Like Grant, Boardman argues for the successful outcome of Robert's handling of the nobility; a non-interventionist policy was the best-suited strategy to adopt.

Boardman explodes many of the myths surrounding Anglo-Scottish relations in the 1370s and 1380s. Many of the contemporary writings of the Scottish literary tradition, in his analysis, describe Robert as a successful inheritor of Robert I's anti-English stance; rather than a king who desired peace, Robert was in agreement in committing the Scots to an English invasion in the early 1380s. Boardman also argues it was Carrick who, on gaining power in 1384, spread the picture of Robert as a king unwilling to face the English. Like Grant, Boardman sees Carrick's ascent in that year as a coup; historians like Donaldson, in his view, believe Carrick's propaganda, which was actually designed to discredit his father. Boardman does think, however, that Robert should have been more menacing.

M.J. PEARSON

See also David II; Edward III; Richard II; Robert III

Robert III c.1337–1406
King of Scotland

Barrell, A.D.M., *Medieval Scotland*, Cambridge and New York: Cambridge University Press, 2000

Boardman, Stephen I., *The Early Stewart Kings: Robert II and Robert III, 1371–1406*, East Linton, East Lothian: Tuckwell Press, 1996

Brown, Michael, *James I*, Edinburgh: Canongate Academic, 1994; revised edition, East Linton, East Lothian: Tuckwell Press, 2000

Donaldson, Gordon, *Scottish Kings*, London: Batsford, and New York: Wiley, 1967; revised edition, London: Batsford, 1977

Grant, Alexander, *Independence and Nationhood: Scotland, 1306–1469*, London and Baltimore: Arnold, 1984; reprinted, Edinburgh: Edinburgh University Press, 1991

Lynch, Michael, *Scotland: A New History*, London: Century, 1991; revised edition, London: Pimlico, 1992

Nicholson, Ranald, *Scotland: The Later Middle Ages*, Edinburgh: Oliver and Boyd, and New York: Barnes and Noble, 1974

John, Earl of Carrick, eldest son of Robert II (ruled 1371–90), on his accession in 1390 took the name of Robert, to become the third Scottish king to bear that name, and the second Stuart (or Stewart) king. Like that of Robert II, the reign of Robert III is treated harshly by DONALDSON – it is well to recall his scathing opening comment that "after nineteen years of the increasingly senile Robert II, Scotland was to have sixteen years of the infirm Robert III". Thereafter, he presents an unflattering account of those years: the king was dominated by his brother, the Duke of Albany, apart from a period in the 1390s when the king regained his power, and according to Donaldson, plunged the kingdom into anarchy. He presents a picture of a king unable to control his brothers: apart from Albany, Alexander Stewart, "the Wolf of Badenoch", burnt Elgin cathedral. Donaldson finishes his account by relating the death of Robert's elder son, the Duke of Rothesay, while a prisoner of Albany (and perhaps at his hands), and the capture of Robert's younger son, James, who on being sent to France was captured by English pirates.

NICHOLSON argues that Robert III was a failure because, like his father, he was not masterful. As the dominant power in Scotland in the 1380s, Carrick, he contends, presided over a breakdown in law and order, as evidenced by the number of legal cases. Moreover, Nicholson considers Carrick's inglorious military career did not help his position. He contends that Carrick's lameness, subsequent to a kick from a horse, was the excuse needed to remove him from power. "Nothing much was to be hoped for in the heir apparent" are his damning words; indeed, he links the destruction of Elgin by "wyld wykkyd Heland-men" to the perceived view of the failure of the king to control the kingdom and punish wrongdoers.

Nicholson stresses the growing hostility between the king's brother, Robert Stewart, and the heir apparent, David, Earl of Carrick. By the late 1390s, as he argues, Carrick was growing in political importance; the king's reaction to their friction, in creating his brother Duke of Albany and his son Duke of Rothesay, was in Nicholson's view a placatory measure that did no good – the king would help anyone, he writes, as long as they were called Stewart. He then narrates how Rothesay, with the help of Robert's queen, Annabella, became in 1399 the king's lieutenant for three years.

The political trouble this caused is analysed by Nicholson: Rothesay jilted the daughter of the Earl of March, and the latter invited Henry IV of England (1399–1413) to invade Scotland and settle the breach of promise. The deaths of Rothesay's major supporters, including, in 1401, the queen, left him exposed and, as Nicholson writes, the king in his desperation at being unable to control his son's actions asked Albany to arrest him; Rothesay died in prison in March 1402, shortly after observing a comet, "brycht stern and clere". The capture of James, in his estimation, broke the king. Indeed, using the chronicles, Nicholson states that Robert possessed an intense feeling of personal failure, evidenced by his instruction to Annabella to bury him in a midden with the epitaph "Here lies the worst of kings and the most wretched of men in the whole realm" – although this did not, in the end, happen.

BARRELL argues that Robert III cannot be seen as a forceful ruler; his period of personal rule, which commenced in 1393 after Robert Stewart's five-year guardianship had ended, was in his view disastrous. He considers the instability created by the feuds of the royal family caused trouble on the border, culminating in the Scottish defeat at Humbleton (or Homildon) Hill in September 1402. In Barrell's analysis, Robert was physically and psychologically unable or unwilling to be a king, and he used his sons to counteract Albany; even in that he failed. He argues that Robert's statement to his queen, even if real, and uttered out of humility, is still a fitting epitaph on the reign.

Grant and Lynch are more positive in their assessments of Robert III. GRANT considers Robert a poor king, but unlike Donaldson and Nicholson he thinks that it might have been worse: there was no civil war between Albany and the king; Rothesay's fall was probably his own fault; and in general, the power struggle was confined to the royal family, and did not involve the wider political community. LYNCH stresses that the early years of the reign witnessed no real collapse in government; and the king's infirmity, in his estimation, did not stop him besieging Dumbarton in 1400. Moreover, he questions the extent of Robert's injury, in the light of the one illegitimate and six legitimate children the king fathered after 1388. Indeed, Lynch thinks the king's adoption of the name "Robert" was a sign of future potential. He views many of the problems of lawlessness in the 1390s against the background of disorder in the far north – typified by the deeds of the Stewarts of Badenoch, and the lack of respect to the crown the Lord of the Isles started to display. Lynch argues that the problems of the far north defeated even a vigorous king like James I (ruled 1406–37). He adds that overall the arguments within the Stewart family were not conducive to good governance. Finally, Lynch sees the financial difficulties of Robert III as the ultimate cause of his problems.

In BOARDMAN's examination of the reign, he sees many of the problems as originating in the death of his major supporter, James, second Earl of Douglas, at Otterburn in 1388. He details how Robert's regional supremacy, built up south of the Forth, fell to pieces because of the squabble by the Douglas family over James's inheritance. Boardman argues that Carrick's subsequent loss of his guardianship was a blow to his prestige that was never corrected, and as he consequently states, Robert started his reign on the defensive. BROWN agrees with this interpretation, and describes Robert as being in "political eclipse"; according to Boardman this was never reversed. As his analysis displays, Robert III's troubles stemmed from his father's creation of his sons as major territorial lords – rival power bases to challenge the king's; these, he argues, formed the deeper roots to the troubles of Robert III's reign.

M.J. PEARSON

See also Henry IV; Robert II

Rockingham, Charles Watson-Wentworth, 2nd Marquis of

1730–1782
Politician, statesman, and prime minister

Elofson, W.M., *The Rockingham Connection and the Second Founding of the Whig Party, 1768–1773*, Montreal and Kingston, Ontario: McGill-Queen's University Press, 1996

Hoffman, Ross John Swartz, *The Marquis: A Study of Lord Rockingham, 1730–1782*, New York: Fordham University Press, 1973

Langford, Paul, *The First Rockingham Administration, 1765–1766*, London: Oxford University Press, 1973

Namier, Lewis and John Brooke, *The House of Commons, 1754–1790*, 3 vols, London: HMSO, and New York: Oxford University Press, 1964; reprinted with corrections, London and New York: Secker and Warburg, 1985

O'Gorman, Frank, *The Rise of Party in England: The Rockingham Whigs, 1760–1782*, London: Allen and Unwin, 1975

Rigg, James McMullen, entry on Rockingham in *Dictionary of National Biography*, 66 vols, edited by Leslie Stephen and Sidney Lee, London: Smith Elder, and New York: Macmillan, 1885–1906

Charles Watson-Wentworth, second Marquis of Rockingham (1730–82), was the only surviving son of Thomas Watson-Wentworth and his wife Mary, daughter of Daniel Finch, second Earl of Nottingham and sixth Earl of Winchelsea. During his father's lifetime, Charles was styled Viscount Higham and Earl of Malton. Rockingham was educated at Westminster School and Cambridge University. Upon his father's death in December 1750, he succeeded to all his honours, assuming his seat in the House of Lords the following spring. Rockingham was raised in a strongly Whig family, and inherited that loyalty. Rockingham is noted for being the leader of a group of aristocratic Whig politicians, more out of office than in, from the 1760s until his death. However, he was pre-eminently a local politician. His birth and landed wealth contributed to his being much more engaged in the social and political affairs of his native Yorkshire than he was, for most of his career, with the intricacies of power at the court of St James. Rockingham served Yorkshire

as lord lieutenant of, at various times, the North, East, and West Ridings, and as vice-admiral for the county.

Rockingham briefly led two administrations, from July 1765 to July 1766 and then again from March to July 1782. In the intervening years the Rockingham connection, which included among others, Edmund Burke, William Dowdeswell, the Duke of Portland, Lord John Cavendish, and Sir George Savile, organized a strong parliamentary opposition and helped remake the Whig agenda. In his recent study of Rockingham's political connection, ELOFSON argues that this outsider position came to suit the group's objectives and temperaments perfectly, and helped Rockingham craft the image of himself as the upholder of patrician virtue and Whig principles that he wished to hand down to posterity.

Rockingham was lauded in his own time for his unquestioned character and sturdy political principles. Historians have maintained this very high opinion of the marquis and his closest political allies. However, compared to other statesmen of his time, especially flashy orators, Rockingham has subsequently received little notice. While his administrations have been the subject of excellent monographs by O'GORMAN and LANGFORD, focusing mainly on the long-term importance of policies and party development, the marquis himself has been given little attention as an individual. His biographer, HOFFMAN, laments this, calling Rockingham one of the "foremost men of politics in the age" and attributes the lack of attention to the marquis's quiet persistence, lack of speaking skills, and extended self-imposed political exile. Likewise, the biographical entry by RIGG in the *Dictionary of National Biography* refers to Rockingham's "sterling honesty" and commends him for having "contended manfully against a corrupt system of government". Rigg, however, condemns him to an earned obscurity by dismissing Rockingham as "by no means a great statesman". Elofson argues that Rockingham and his friends have been misunderstood, and that this has led them to seem both less interesting and more virtuous than they actually were. He maintains that a careful examination of their writings and actions reveals that Rockingham and his followers were indeed principled politicians, but that maintaining their exile from office was no great burden. Elofson maintains that with the exception of Edmund Burke, the marquis and his connection did not hunger for office, instead deriving satisfaction from pursuing their goals outside of government. They were not, as NAMIER & BROOKE suggest, chafing for the opportunity to storm back into power. Rather, they were instrumental in shaping what Elofson identifies as the Whiggish branch of a nascent country party in the 1760s and 1770s. From that vantage, Rockingham was able to help reconfigure what it meant to be "Whig", moving from the staunch defenders of the constitutional *status quo,* to being identified with moderate reform and critical of the court. At the same time the Rockinghams maintained ideological continuity between early and late 18th-century politicians who wore the Whig label.

During his first tenure in office, Rockingham favoured a moderate treatment of the restive American colonies. He successfully carried the repeal of the Stamp Act against a strong opposition, which included the Bedford-Grenville faction and the king's friends. This was balanced by the passage of a new Mutiny Act, which required the colonial assemblies to provide for the quartering and maintenance of British troops. His administration also carried resolutions condemning the use of general warrants in the Wilkes case, hardly a move calculated to ingratiate him with the king.

Although Rockingham was dismissed in July 1766, he did not ask his followers to leave office for more than a year, as he was indecisive about moving into opposition. When he finally did, that opposition lasted for 16 years. During that time Rockingham opposed war with the American colonies, and worked to limit extensions of royal prerogative and patronage. He also censured the government for neglect of affairs in Ireland.

The second Rockingham administration was briefer than the first, lasting only from March to July 1782, when it ended with Rockingham's death. During that time, Rockingham won legislative independence for Ireland, cut the size of the royal household, thus eliminating a rich source of royal patronage, and barred government contractors from the House of Commons. Rockingham was buried in York minster in July 1782. His marriage having produced no children, his honours became extinct.

SUSAN MITCHELL SOMMERS

See also American Colonies: Loss of; Burke; Fox, Charles James; George III; North; Pitt, William, "the Elder"; Pitt, William, "the Younger"; Whigs: *c.*1760 to *c.*1860

Roman Britain: British Tribes

Cunliffe, Barry, *Iron Age Communities in Britain: An Account of England, Scotland, and Wales from the Seventh Century* BC *until the Roman Conquest*, London and Boston: Routledge and Kegan Paul, 1974; 2nd expanded edition, London and Boston: Routledge and Kegan Paul, 1978; 3rd expanded edition, London and New York: Routledge, 1991

Handford, S.A. (translator), *The Conquest of Gaul*, by Julius Caesar, Harmondsworth and New York: Penguin, 1951; revised and with a new introduction by Jane F. Gardner, Harmondsworth and New York: Penguin, 1982

Hartley, Brian R. and R. Leon Fitts, *The Brigantes*, Gloucester and Wolfeboro, New Hampshire: Sutton, 1988

Salway, Peter, *Roman Britain*, Oxford: Clarendon Press, and New York: Oxford University Press, 1981; reprinted with corrections, London: Book Club Associates, 1982

Wacher, John, *Roman Britain*, London: Dent, 1978; revised edition, Stroud, Gloucestershire: Sutton, 1998

Webster, Graham, *Boudica: The British Revolt against Rome* AD 60, Totowa, New Jersey: Rowman and Littlefield, and London: Batsford, 1978

Webster, Graham, *The Roman Invasion of Britain*, New York: Barnes and Noble, and London: Batsford, 1980; revised edition, London: Batsford, 1993; reprinted, London and New York: Routledge, 1999

Webster, Graham, *Rome against Caratacus: The Roman Campaigns in Britain* AD 48–58, London: Batsford, 1981; Totowa, New Jersey: Barnes and Noble, 1982; revised edition, London: Batsford, 1993

Although all written evidence of British tribes derives from the Roman perspective of their conquerors, literary sources augmented by archaeological evidence provide extensive information on the island's native peoples. CUNLIFFE synthesizes a judicious mixture of literary and archaeological data to illuminate the formation of communities from the Bronze and Iron Ages, and to trace the destabilizing influence of continental trade contacts starting in the 2nd century BC. His rejection of invasion theory as a monocausal factor of change in pre-Roman society does not neglect the role of war and migration in Celtic tribal society. Moreover his study of settlement patterns, social stratification, and the economy provides a nuanced portrait of native society. The nature of the disputes over historical interpretation of tribal origins opens SALWAY's essential text, which provides throughout a detailed chronological narrative augmented by notes and appendices guiding readers through historiographical controversies and the latest archaeological discoveries. WACHER's survey offers less historical detail, but interprets more clearly for the general reader the meaning and mysteries of the material evidence. Both of these texts give clear accounts of the Roman experience in Britain, Wacher being graced with drawings, plans, and photographs.

Caesar's own writings on the Gallic campaigns, translated by HANDFORD, provide the first views of the native tribes of Iron Age Britain. Although previously contacted by continental traders, the peoples of south-east England earned Rome's hostility when they offered aid to Caesar's Gallic enemies, thus precipitating invasion in 55 and 54 BC by his unprepared but ultimately victorious forces. Internal problems within the tribal kingdoms gave even those brief reconnaissance missions a lasting influence and provided warring clans with a new ally in Rome. WEBSTER's *Roman Invasion of Britain* describes the tribal divisions that emerged between the Caesarian and Claudian invasions. Using evidence of coin distribution and wine imports, he tracks the rewards given to Rome's native allies such as the Trinovantes and Atrebates, and the hostility expressed by the Catuvellauni against both the Roman invaders and weaker neighbouring tribes. The Catuvellauni suffered defeat in AD 43 when Claudius's need for military victory and increased sources of wealth prompted a new invasion force of four legions. The natives' hillforts and chariots were no match for the disciplined Roman troops. Roman victory relieved the tribes oppressed by the Catuvellauni, but the victors then had to protect the new province by establishing the road and fortress network needed to hold territory. Client relationships and diplomacy were also offered to the tribal kingdoms. Intentionally degrading to the natives, however, was the seizure of the Catuvellauni centre Camulodunum (Colchester) and the establishment there of Roman urbanization and later a legionary veterans' retirement enclave.

Although both the emperor and the governor knew that the natives' most effective assimilation of Roman culture could best occur over a generation of peaceful trade and contact, several tribes refused to allow the process to take hold. The Catuvellauni leader Caratacus had escaped the victorious Roman forces even as one of the legions pursued rebels into the west. WEBSTER continues the story in *Rome Against Caratacus*, synthesizing literary sources such as Tacitus' *Annals* with archaeological evidence of the tribal leader's last stand in the Welsh hills. Webster carefully analyses the weaknesses of

Roman policy towards native allies, noting the long-term hostilities that developed from forcibly disarming even friendly tribes, lending them money on ambiguous terms, and brutally settling discharged soldiers at Colchester. With two legions and *auxilia* troops, Governor Scapula followed Caratacus into the upland regions of Wales, where the native leader and his confederation of rebellious tribes hoped to decimate the Romans with guerrilla tactics. Superior Roman training again won the day, although Caratacus escaped to the Brigantes of northern England. Unable to convince the tribe's queen to abandon her alliance with Rome, Caratacus was turned over to the enemy and paraded through Rome, later to be awarded by Tacitus a renowned speech contrasting the rebel's integrity with imperial excesses.

WEBSTER completes his historical trilogy with *Boudicca*, examining the Iceni tribe of eastern England and the brutal ways in which Rome treated its client king. Prasutagus had named the emperor co-heir with his two daughters, but upon his death in AD 60, the procurator seized all royal assets. The royal family's resistance was treated as rebellion, the widowed queen being flogged and her daughters raped, the latest in a series of short-sighted Roman actions against the tribes. Queen Boudicca and the Iceni found several other tribes eager to rise in revolt, beginning first with the destruction of Colchester and the slaughter of an ambushed Ninth Legion, then moving on to the destruction of London itself. Superior Roman tactics again overcame British ardour, but the imperial government was shaken enough by tribal insurrection to send reinforcements from Germany and to curb the worst of the governor's vengeance.

Tribal power was essentially broken by the end of the 1st century AD. The building of Hadrian's Wall in the 120s and the Antonine Wall two decades later established a frontier line and troops in the Brigantian tribal area. These actions annoyed the Brigantes sufficiently for serious attacks to occur in the 150s, resulting in Rome's withdrawal from the more northerly wall. HARTLEY & FITTS focus solely on the Brigantes because of their important early alliance with Rome, their proximity to major frontiers, and their role as Rome's defenders against tribes to their north. A pastoral people largely uninterested in the civilizing elements Rome could bring, the Brigantes contributed mining, metalwork, and stone in small amounts, returning quietly to Iron Age traditions by the early 5th century as post-Roman kingdoms developed. By then Rome had far less to fear from remaining British tribes than from Germanic invaders and the Picts and Scots of the far north.

LORRAINE ATTREED

See also Boudicca

Roman Britain: Crafts, Trade, and Agriculture

De la Bédoyère, Guy, *English Heritage Book of Roman Villas and the Countryside*, London: Batsford, 1993
Hartley, Brian R., *Notes on the Roman Pottery Industry in the Nene Valley*, Peterborough: Peterborough Museum, 1960

Hingley, Richard, *Rural Settlement in Roman Britain*, London: Seaby, 1989
Merrifield, Ralph, *London: City of the Romans*, Berkeley: University of California Press, and London: Batsford, 1983
Rivet, A.L.F. (editor), *The Roman Villa in Britain*, London: Routledge and Kegan Paul, and New York: Praeger, 1969
Strickland, Tim, *The Romans at Wilderspool: The Story of the First Industrial Development on the Mersey*, illustrated by Graham Sumner, Clive Constable and Gordon Lawrence, Warrington: Greenalls, 1995
Wacher, John, *Roman Britain*, London: Dent, 1978; revised edition, Stroud, Gloucestershire: Sutton, 1998
Wild, J.P., *Textile Manufacture in the Northern Roman Provinces*, Cambridge: Cambridge University Press, 1970

Our understanding of Roman Britain's economy is helped considerably by WACHER's emphases on material culture and the interpretation of archaeological evidence even within a general survey. Trade brought Britain to Rome's attention long before thoughts of invasion and conquest. Celtic Iron Age inhabitants had pursued lively commercial contacts with the Continent since the 7th century BC, but the exchanges noted by the Greek geographer Strabo writing at the end of the 1st century BC were more humble. The natives traded cattle, grain, hides, hunting dogs, metal, and slaves for the luxury goods of the Roman world, chiefly pottery, glassware, wine, and olive oil. Already possessed of coins and a stratified society using luxury goods to demarcate social levels, natives of south-east Britain embraced long-distance trade, urbanism, and industry with more enthusiasm than their northern neighbours, but no corner of Britain was entirely free of Roman influences.

Discussion of trade is incomplete without study of the physical and commercial nature of London. MERRIFIELD offers a clear and detailed account of what archaeology has revealed of the administrative and economic capital of Roman Britain. Neither *colonia* nor *civitas* nor *municipium*, Londinium possessed unique status but its origins remain a mystery. Merrifield provides generous discussion of the variety of theories seeking to explain the origins of London, examining whether military needs alone in the years following the Claudian invasion could account for the site's selection and development, or whether the credit for London's origins ought to go solely to traders. Less doubtful is London's growth in prosperity after recovery following the Boudiccan raids of AD 60, evidenced by the building of substantial wharves, warehouses, and ships, in addition to the administrative and military buildings that crowded the site. Merrifield traces decline in trade from the 3rd century, blamed mostly on political upheavals in the empire, although government functions continued and inhabitants remained into the early years of the 5th century. Merrifield's lively sense of the challenges of archaeology and his ability to re-create the commerce and industry of the British capital make this an invaluable guide to economic history.

Although London and other cities sheltered industry as well as trade and markets, recent research emphasizes the widespread and rural nature of manufacture. Certain industries, such as iron production, were directly linked to government requirements, but access to the transport network could transform local production beyond modest levels. HARTLEY studies the pottery industry in the Nene valley near Peterborough, an area graced with access to Fenland waterways and river connections to transport the wares to both military and civilian clients. WILD takes a broader view, examining clothing manufacture techniques in Britain, Belgium, and Germany, to reveal the existence of small civilian markets as well as the greater needs of the army. STRICKLAND offers the most detailed and colourful study of industrial development as revealed by archaeology. Wilderspool (its Roman name is unknown) caught Roman attention when troops easily crossed the Mersey there to reinforce Brigantian loyalty in the wake of Caratacus's revolt. The Twentieth Legion settled in the area during the 70s, and the new legionary fortress of Chester was less than 20 miles away. These factors sparked Wilderspool's growth as a frontier boom town, taking advantage of Mersey navigation and the convergence of Roman roads to develop wharves, warehouses, and the production and transport of pottery, iron tools, and woollen cloth. Manufacture slowed late in the 2nd century, discouraged less by imperial political turmoil than the rise of mass-production centres elsewhere. Strickland traces the site's reversion to farming, and concludes with a helpful discussion of modern archaeological methods.

Native Celtic influence and the persistence of small farmsteads dominate discussion of British agriculture, in the wake of decades of concentration on villa sites and the elites who inhabited large estates. DE LA BÉDOYÈRE provides the best overview of the issues at stake, beginning with the prehistoric landscape and tracking those Roman influences that terminated in "a devastating cultural change in the way that the population of Britain organized and expressed themselves, recorded their affairs and stored their wealth". His judicious mixture of history, archaeology, geography, and environmental factors takes note of the late Iron Age expansion of agriculture, population, and trade links with the Continent, an expansion magnified by Roman contacts and coercion after the Caesarian invasions. Military and commercial markets, as well as tax and tribute demands, gave Celtic farming the impetus to expand beyond subsistence levels of cereal production and livestock raising. Moreover the development of urban centres and a transport network assisted distribution of goods.

Since the late 1960s historians have tried to expand their view of agriculture and rural society from villa sites and urban consumption to include the single farmstead and local village markets. HINGLEY argues for the value of studying the poor and lowly in Roman British society, discussing the unit system theory of villa development that asserts the continued existence of Celtic extended family organization within the Romanized villa structure. He is particularly interested in why villas were scarce in the north and west, adding to the usual factors of poor climate and distance from markets the lasting cultural influence of Celtic values, which did not display wealth and power by building in the Romanized format. Hingley forces readers to acknowledge the lasting strength of native forms and values when history and archaeology have so far concentrated heavily on Roman culture and its material survivals. RIVET has written extensively on the villa in Roman Britain, and this collection of essays showcases the best of his own work as well as the writings of scholars with newer approaches, many of which have been acted upon since the book was published. Contributions by Smith on mosaics and Liversidge on interior decoration

emphasize the wealthiest estates of the 1st and 2nd centuries, as well as the optimum period for villa building in the early 4th century, but their heavily illustrated chapters provide valuable insights into Romanized British life. Knowledge of villa owners, tenant relations, land use, and the ultimate fate of villa organization upon Saxon incursion may remain beyond reach, but study of the economic history of Roman Britain has an increasingly broad perspective.

LORRAINE ATTREED

Roman Britain: Defence

Blagg, T.F.C. and A.C. King (editors), *Military and Civilian in Roman Britain: Cultural Relationships in a Frontier Province*, Oxford: British Archaeological Reports, 1984
Breeze, David J. and Brian Dobson, *Hadrian's Wall*, London: Allen Lane, 1976, revised 3rd edition, Harmondsworth: Penguin, 1987
Holder, P.A., *The Roman Army in Britain*, London: Batsford, 1982
Johnson, Stephen, *The Roman Forts of the Saxon Shore*, London: Elek, and New York: St Martin's Press, 1976
Jones, Michael E., *The End of Roman Britain*, Ithaca, New York: Cornell University Press, 1996
Salway, Peter, *Roman Britain*, Oxford: Clarendon Press, and New York: Oxford University Press, 1981; reprinted with corrections, London: Book Club Associates, 1982
Webster, Graham, *The Roman Imperial Army of the First and Second Centuries AD*, London: Black, 1969; New York: Funk and Wagnalls, 1970; 3rd edition, with new introduction by Hugh Elton, Norman: University of Oklahoma Press, 1998

The Roman world was guided by the belief that the best defence is an effective offence. Such a philosophy inspired the growth of empire, secured by both wartime and peacetime activities of the army. WEBSTER provides a concise survey of the development of the Roman army throughout the empire, with special attention paid to Britain. Drawing on the work of ancient historians such as Livy, Plutarch, and Tacitus, Webster offers a sound guide to army composition, camps and forts, tactics in the field, and civilizing influences during peacetime, in an account graced with helpful notes and an extensive bibliography. Complementary to his imperial focus is the more narrow purview of HOLDER. Utilizing literary and archaeological evidence, he examines what was expected of the army in war and peace, and an appendix provides short histories of all the units known to have served in Britain. Holder is especially clear on the changes in legionary and auxiliary structure over the centuries, analysing recruitment patterns, the command structure, and peacetime activities such as construction.

The role of the army in British society is addressed in the BLAGG & KING collection of essays focusing on urbanism, the economy, and trade. The defence of the province involved the army in the formation of towns and the spread of mints and markets. Other essays trace the differences in military and civilian diet, religious practices, and attitudes towards monumental building in towns. The papers make excellent use of archaeological discoveries while seeking the humanity behind military policy.

Roman Britain's concern for defence began in 55 BC, when Julius Caesar perceived the need to invade the island to secure his pacification of Gaul. Native tribes defended their homeland with hillforts and chariots, but were no match for the drilled and disciplined Roman legionary and auxiliary forces. A more concerted effort at invasion and conquest occurred under Claudius in AD 43, after which consolidation of Roman defence took the form of constructing the roads, fortresses, garrison posts, and settlements essential to establishing a frontier. SALWAY studies these developments but details of defence must be extracted from the political context of his chronological narrative. For the army in Britain, there existed a fine line between active conquest and defensive entrenchment, as native tribes continued to resist the invaders into the 4th century, by which time Picts, Scots, and eventually Germanic peoples had begun their raids.

The 2nd-century frontier demarcations of Hadrian's Wall and the Antonine barrier find full analysis in BREEZE & DOBSON. Hadrianic imperial policy to cease expansion made particular sense for Britain, where civilizing attempts to inculcate Roman values in the natives knew increasing success in the south but met with bitter opposition from northern tribes. From AD 122, Hadrian's Wall began to be built in stone at the eastern end, and in turf in the far west (later replaced in stone), and reinforced with milecastles and small forts for the patrolling garrison. A ditch in front and an earthwork (the *vallum*) to the rear marked out a protected military zone, the total structure acting as a means to control but not prevent movement and communication. Far from serving as the settled boundary of the civil province, the wall sought to maintain order by dividing native groups and encouraging the development of a settled agricultural and commercial area on the Cumbrian plain to supply the army as it defended the Roman way of life. Breeze & Dobson study the society of army life on the wall as well, examining recruitment, health and religion, and relations with civilians.

With such a frontier, Hadrian effected a radical change within the army, decreeing its role to be that of keeping order rather than winning new territory. More conventional ways of thinking returned, however, upon the accession of Antoninus Pius, whose ambition for military victory coincided with renewed threats from Scotland. The army successfully reoccupied the Lowlands for the first time since the mid-80s, building from AD 143 a new turf wall across the Forth-Clyde isthmus. Although more heavily garrisoned than its southern counterpart, the northern frontier fell back to Hadrian's Wall during the 150s upon attack by the Brigantian tribe, and was only briefly reoccupied early in the following decade.

The closing years of the 2nd century saw Romano-British townspeople taking defence in their own hands by building first earthworks and then masonry walls around their cities, when civil war in the empire involved the army in political plots, often to the neglect of their military duties. Although division of Britain into two provinces followed shortly thereafter, and Britain briefly joined the breakaway empire of the Gallic provinces, such administrative changes had little effect on basic defences. Innovative steps began to be taken early in the

3rd century with the construction of new forts on the south coast. Originally intended to protect merchant shipping into London, these forts formed the origins of the Saxon Shore defence lines built in greater numbers between 276 and 284. JOHNSON argues the case for the early and mercantile origins of the forts, asserting their linkage to similar structures in Gaul to protect against piracy. Designed for use with artillery, the bases acted as heavily fortified guard posts defending ports and river estuaries rather than strategic military positions. Later raids by Germanic invaders gave the system its name, but Johnson insists upon its earlier origins and mercantile role.

The last century of Roman control in Britain had serious consequences for defence. Division of the province into four parts included a radical restructuring of the command system and of the army itself into field and frontier forces. Breeze & Dobson remain helpful on this confusing period as command of frontier troops passed to the *dux Britanniarum* while a detachment of the field army obeyed the *comes Britanniarum*, with help on the south coast from the count of the Saxon Shore. JONES examines the final decades of Roman Britain, arguing strongly against blaming solely the Germanic tribes for the deterioration of imperial rule. He insists that the role of the natural environment be taken seriously, with such factors as climatic deterioration occurring in the 5th century associated with harvest failure, famine, and changes in migration patterns. Moreover, Jones notes that civil wars, usurpations, northern invasions, and heavy taxes had left the British with negative views of Roman society. With an elite never fully integrated into imperial society, Britain was not fully Romanized. After 410, Roman Britain decided it could defend itself no worse than had the imperial government, little realizing the ferocious nature of the Germanic invaders already on its shores.

LORRAINE ATTREED

Roman Britain: General Surveys

Collingwood, R.G. and J.N.L. Myres, *Roman Britain and the English Settlements*, Oxford: Clarendon Press, 1936; reprinted 2nd edition with corrections, Oxford: Clarendon Press, 1949

Frere, Sheppard, *Britannia: A History of Roman Britain*, London: Routledge and Kegan Paul, and Cambridge, Massachusetts: Harvard University Press, 1967; 3rd revised edition, London and New York: Routledge and Kegan Paul, 1987; 3rd edition, further revised, London: Folio Society, 1999

Haverfield, F., *The Romanization of Roman Britain*, London: H. Froude for the British Academy, 1905; 2nd edition, enlarged, Oxford: Clarendon Press, 1912; 4th edition, Oxford: Clarendon Press, 1923; reprinted, Westport, Connecticut: Greenwood Press, 1979

Liversidge, Joan, *Britain in the Roman Empire*, London: Routledge and Kegan Paul, and New York: Praeger, 1968

Millett, Martin, *The Romanization of Britain: An Essay in Archaeological Interpretation*, Cambridge and New York: Cambridge University Press, 1990

Reece, Richard, *My Roman Britain*, Cirencester: Cotswold Studies, 1988

Richmond, I.A., *Roman Britain*, Harmondsworth and
    Baltimore: Penguin, 1955; 3rd revised edition,
    Harmondsworth: Penguin, 1995
Salway, Peter, *Roman Britain*, Oxford: Clarendon Press, and
    New York: Oxford University Press, 1981; reprinted with
    corrections, London: Book Club Associates, 1982
Todd, Malcolm (editor), *Research on Roman Britain,
    1960–1989*, London: Society for the Promotion of Roman
    Studies, 1989

Britain must rank among the most carefully surveyed regions of
the Roman empire. Although literary evidence for the province
is scarce, archaeological study has been intense during the last
one hundred years or so. This process has been aided by a
growing body of scholarly opinion that work needs to be done
on topics and regions well beyond the traditional foci of classical studies. Ancient Britain, for example, is no longer thought
of as a topic inferior to ancient Italy or ancient Greece. This has
resulted in a steady stream of volumes focused upon Roman
Britain. Those works selected in this survey, therefore, are only
those which have made a particular contribution in their own
right. HAVERFIELD is, perhaps, the most influential early 20th
century work. Its pioneering contribution was to bring to the
fore the notion of Romanization, that is the adoption of Roman
culture by the native population. The reasons for this process
were understood to lie in the superiority and desirability of the
classical culture which was promoted by the imperial authorities. This view of the civilizing of barbarians can be seen in the
light of contemporary attitudes to the peoples of the colonial
empires.

COLLINGWOOD & MYRES was the most important work
on the topic in the immediate pre-war years. It is really two
books bound together, the former treating Roman Britain and
the latter the arrival of the English. The book examines the geography of Britain and the background to the Roman invasions.
It is careful to stress the partial nature of Romanization and the
prevalence of native cultural traditions, as well as to bring out
the high level of regional variation in Britain. The outline given
in Collingwood & Myres remained the main text through to the
1950s, by which time, however, a flood of new information from
aerial photography and from rescue digs on areas of bomb
damage and sites of new high-rise blocks began to pour out in
specialist publications. This new material was employed in a
number of influential textbooks of which FRERE was
one of the more prominent. His layout is similar to Collingwood
& Myres, but the focus was more strongly archaeological. Of
other textbooks from the same period LIVERSIDGE is interesting because it eschewed the traditional political outline to concentrate on topics in social and economic life, above all the
towns and villas.

One of the greatest experts of this period, Ian RICHMOND,
only produced a short summary of the subject. With his death
in 1965, Oxford University Press turned to Peter Salway to
revise the Roman portion of Collingwood & Myres (the English
portion was revised by Myres himself and published separately
in 1986). The pace of archaeological discoveries had been so
dramatic that it was decided that it would be best to write an
entirely new book, which duly appeared in 1981. SALWAY drew
upon archaeological discoveries but did not focus upon them.
The text is striking and seems, perhaps, a little old-fashioned
because of its paucity of maps, diagrams, and illustrations. It
first presents a detailed narrative of events in so far as that may
be recovered from the expeditions of Caesar through to the
arrival of the Anglo-Saxons. Then, in a final section, Romanization, geography, town and country, economy, religion, and
society are treated. Salway covers much the same ground as
Collingwood although, tellingly, his organization is different.
In the earlier work the rise of Roman Britain led into a discussion of the Romanized province, which then led to the "End
of Roman Britain" which began, apparently, in the early 3rd
century. This arrangement is rooted in the then prevalent
view of late antiquity as an inferior period, whereas it is now
known that Britain was at its most prosperous in the early 4th
century and that clear economic "decline" only becomes evident
after 350.

TODD, through a series of essays on a wide range of topics,
provides summaries of the major new archaeological discoveries from 1960 to 1989. It also gives occasional hints of the theoretical shifts taking place in archaeology during this period
which are obscured in Salway. A very interesting corrective is
provided by REECE, which is an informal counterblast against
a range of assumptions made by mainstream scholarship. His
ideas are rooted in a perception of Roman Britain as representing a break in a longer Celtic continuity in north-west Europe.
In other words, the Roman occupation did not represent a rise
in cultural achievement and did not last, but was rather something of an aberration. Britain was far more British than Roman
and its cities were not like the bustling centres of the
Mediterranean but were little more than villages or, as he calls
them, TCTs (things called towns).

MILLETT presents another modern archaeological view, but
this time in a formal monograph, extensively illustrated and
with full apparatus. His analysis refers back to Haverfield's
examination of Romanization, but sees this in terms of the
meeting of two evolving cultural streams and their intercom-
munication. The emphasis is not simply in describing the history
of towns or villas, but in trying to understand their economic,
and to a lesser extent social, functioning. Millett and Reece represent a trend in recent studies which aims to avoid seeing one
cultural tradition as necessarily superior and tries to understand
people working within the cultural choices that are available to
them. No longer is it reasonable to concentrate on towns and
villas, as Liversidge had done, when the vast majority of the
population lived in neither. Archaeological work, through
analysis of wooden remains and techniques such as surface
survey, is producing great quantities of new information on
everyday life in Roman Britain, while the recovery of the
Vindolanda tablets shows that exciting new written evidence
may still await discovery. This bounty of source material has
meant that many of the above monographs have appeared in
several revised editions and new general surveys will be needed
in the future.

DOMINIC JANES

See also Settlement: Early Distribution

Roman Britain: Government and Social Structure

Alcock, Joan P., *English Heritage Book of Life in Roman Britain*, London: Batsford for English Heritage, 1996

Allason-Jones, Lindsay, *Women in Roman Britain*, London: British Museum Publications, 1989

De la Bédoyère, Guy, *English Heritage Book of Roman Villas and the Countryside*, London: Batsford, 1993

Frere, Sheppard, *Britannia: A History of Roman Britain*, Cambridge, Massachusetts: Harvard University Press, and London: Routledge and Kegan Paul, 1967; revised edition, London and Boston: Routledge and Kegan Paul, 1978; 3rd revised edition, London and New York: Routledge and Kegan Paul, 1987; 3rd edition, further revised, London: Folio Society, 1999

Hingley, Richard, *Rural Settlement in Roman Britain*, London: Seaby, 1989

Jones, Michael E., *The End of Roman Britain*, Ithaca, New York: Cornell University Press, 1996

Salway, Peter, *Roman Britain*, Oxford: Clarendon Press, and New York: Oxford University Press, 1981; reprinted with corrections, London: Book Club Associates, 1982

Wacher, John, *The Towns of Roman Britain*, London: Batsford, 1974; Berkeley: University of California Press, 1975; 2nd revised edition, London: Batsford, 1995

Provincial government, at least at its highest levels, has not attracted the same attention as those aspects of Roman Britain able to be illuminated by the fruitful partnership of history and archaeology. The survey accounts of SALWAY and FRERE provide the basic outline of government, describing the chain of command from governor to local council, and tracking the changes in structure consequent upon division of the province in the late 2nd and early 4th centuries. Britain was a consular province with two arms of government, each directly responsible to the emperor. The governor of the province, an ex-consul of senatorial rank, served as the *legatus Augusti* with a staff headed by a centurion of senior status. Governors commanded the army, personally leading troops for the most important campaigns of the period, and so peripatetic that their administration did not settle permanently in London until the end of the 1st century AD. The governor also served as chief justice, hearing petitions and presiding at trials, although legal duties were usually left to the *legatus iuridicus* able to apply Roman law and Celtic codes appropriately to different members of society. Directly responsible to the emperor and not the governor was the financial secretary (*procurator Augusti*) of equestrian status. The *procurator* and governor followed different policies during the early years of invasion and conquest, when the most important task was the establishment of peaceful relations with the client kingdoms and native settlers. The procurator's harsh financial policy incited the Iceni to revolt in AD 60, and the damage they inflicted on both legions and administrators prompted a more diplomatic policy thereafter.

JONES discusses the changes in government structure under Diocletian and Constantine, who divided Britain into four (and later five) separate provinces as a complete diocese within the prefecture of Gaul, headquartered at Trier. Responsible directly to the prefect's *vicarius* in London, provincial governors thereafter exercised only civil powers and headed a growing and increasingly specialized civil service. Throughout the empire Constantine reorganized the command structure of the army by removing it from its provincial basis. For Britain this meant forces led by a *dux Britanniarum* and a *comes litoris Saxonici*, able to draw troops from more than one province. For both civil and military servants, these changes denied the Romano-British active participation in imperial government and by the start of the 5th century encouraged their deliberate rejection of an overbearing government that did little for them.

Local government knew greater stability. During the 1st century large areas of Britain remained under direct military rule or else were administered with the co-operation of client kingdoms. These arrangements were replaced by the establishment of urban centres from which to spread Roman law and culture, while collecting the taxes and supplies necessary for government maintenance. WACHER provides the essential discussion of urban development in an illuminating mixture of historical and archaeological evidence. Chartered cities, beginning with Colchester in AD 49, combined defensive, administrative, and civilizing purposes to effect the Romanization of the province. The *coloniae* (Colchester was soon joined by Lincoln, Gloucester, and York) formed self-governing units housing Roman citizens, usually retired veterans and their families. The *municipium* at Verulamium (St Albans), founded at the same time as Colchester, gained the status given normally to pre-existing towns with non-veteran Roman citizens. The ruling body in these units was the *ordo*, a council composed of 100 oligarchic members (*decuriones*) responsible for the maintenance of the imperial cult, the law courts, the construction and upkeep of public buildings and amenities, and the administration of surrounding territory. Beneath these units in rank were the *civitates*, whose controversial relationship with the ancient tribal units Wacher fully discusses. Common to both *coloniae* and *civitates*, however, were the Roman cultural amenities of the baths, forum, imperial cult, and entertainment facilities, all administered by local councils and intended to inculcate Roman values to civilize the natives.

Analysis of British social structure begins with the late Iron Age tribes, divided into a military aristocracy and a farming peasantry, with the presence of slaves used both for their labour and as trade goods for Roman merchants. For the period after the Claudian invasion the process of Romanization dominates discussion of social structure, not least because the amenities of Roman culture left considerable physical remains. Literary and archaeological evidence for the poorest classes, and for rural life in general, is slender. Although no modern author portrays the invaders as pure Romans bringing the light of civilization to the backward British, Salway, Frere, and Wacher generally discuss social structure in terms of urban living, spread of Latin, participation in local government, and adoption of continental art forms. Native elites adopted Roman building styles, dress, and language, and began to acquire citizenship and the responsibilities of government. ALCOCK provides a more general view of everyday life, focusing on material culture and reconstructing lifestyles in the province. She pays some attention to the influence of Celtic values on Romano-British life in a work whose glossary, bibliography, and list of places to visit serve readers well. Celtic influences are of vital importance to

HINGLEY, who asserts their influence on extended family groupings in villas and in strong communal organization that influenced how wealth was displayed and social status conveyed. DE LA BÉDOYÈRE combines the traditional archaeological focus on elite villa sites with new interest in villages and farmsteads, to analyse how much we can know about rural society. Tenants, workers, and slaves find equal treatment with villa owners in this lushly illustrated volume. ALLASON-JONES studies the social, biological, and intellectual experiences of women in Roman Britain, concluding that Romanization gave British women a cosmopolitan experience that the Germanic invaders on the horizon would not match. There is general agreement among all the authors that invaders and natives created a hybrid form of Roman culture in Britain, the impermanence of which finds fullest explanation in Jones's theory of increasing alienation and separation. Through his study of changes in land use during the 4th and 5th centuries, he reveals the increased hardship known by the lower classes, punished by high taxes, colder and wetter weather, absentee landlords, and a governmental structure unable to provide basic protection for residents of any social position.

LORRAINE ATTREED

Roman Britain: Invasion and Conquest

Handford, S.A. (translator), *The Conquest of Gaul*, by Julius Caesar, Harmondsworth and New York: Penguin, 1951; revised and with a new introduction by Jane F. Gardner, Harmondsworth and New York: Penguin, 1982

Hawkes, Christopher, "Britain and Julius Caesar", *Proceedings of the British Academy*, 63 (1977): 125–92

Holder, P.A., *The Roman Army in Britain*, London: Batsford, 1982

Mattingly, H. (translator), *Tacitus on Britain and Germany: A New Translation of* The Agricola *and* The Germania, Harmondsworth: Penguin, 1948; Baltimore: Penguin, 1962; as *The Agricola and The Germania*, revised by S.A. Handford, Harmondsworth: Penguin, 1970

Peddie, John, *Invasion: The Roman Invasion of Britain in the Year AD 43 and the Events Leading to Their Occupation of the West Country*, New York: St Martin's Press, 1987; as *Invasion: The Roman Conquest of Britain*, Gloucester: Alan Sutton, 1987

Salway, Peter, *Roman Britain*, Oxford: Clarendon Press, and New York: Oxford University Press, 1981; reprinted with corrections, London: Book Club Associates, 1982

Wacher, John, *Roman Britain*, London: Dent, 1978

Webster, Graham, *The Roman Invasion of Britain*, New York: Barnes and Noble, and London: Batsford, 1980; revised edition, London: Batsford, 1993; reprinted, London and New York: Routledge, 1999

Our knowledge of Rome's invasion and conquest of Britain depends upon the written sources of its military leaders and historians, and also upon the archaeological and cultural anthropological methods of the modern age. WEBSTER opens his study of the Caesarian and Claudian invasions with a review of the written and material evidence, their strengths and omissions. He dedicates his early chapters as well to a study of Britain's native tribes, their Celtic roots, and the Iron Age society the Romans found first through trade contacts in the 2nd century BC and later during military invasions. Julius Caesar himself provided the first full description of Britain and the Britons in his history of the Gallic campaigns, translated with a useful introduction by HANDFORD. Caesar's motivations for his two invasions of 55 and 54 BC are best understood through the full historical context provided by SALWAY's chronological narrative. The Britons' assistance to their Gallic neighbours during Caesar's campaigns, combined with the military leader's political ambitions, decided him even late in a campaign season to invade the island with five legions. Traders had not given Caesar the geographical information he needed, so the strikes took the form of useful reconnaissance missions, providing insights on harbours, native fighting techniques, and potential alliances with tribal leaders. HAWKES makes a useful addition to the political context and military movements by his personal knowledge of the Kentish terrain and of pertinent archaeological finds there. Battered by bad weather and drawn back to Rome during political crisis, Caesar never returned to Britain and Roman policy in general neglected the island for several decades.

Renewed trade and offers of clientage further destabilized internally warring tribes, so that rescue of native allies became one of the reasons Claudius launched a second invasion in AD 43. WACHER rejects the idea that the invasion was a conscious effort at empire building, discussing in detail the personal political benefits that Claudius understood would accrue from a military victory, as well as the wealth from Britain's mines and food supplies. Salway emphasizes the Roman belief in their absolute moral right to conquer native kingdoms, citing the writers of the age who expressed this. Under the command of Aulus Plautius, four legions and auxiliaries totalling 40,000 men landed at Richborough and two other sites. Native tribes at first refused to give battle but the Catuvallauni finally engaged, only to be defeated; the tribes they themselves had conquered surrendered to Rome. The native leader Caratacus retreated to the Welsh hills to continue resistance. While Claudius made a brief visit to glory in the victory, the Second Legion led by the future emperor Vespasian pursued the rebels into the west country, and the remainder of the forces established the fort and road networks needed to hold a new province.

PEDDIE provides an unusual perspective on the invasion and western campaigns by focusing on the capabilities of the Roman military machine. He transfers modern experiences of military engineering, troop movement, and even the activities of contemporary re-enactment groups such as the Ermine Street Guard to illuminate battle conditions of the 1st century. Some of his conclusions may be suspect, but his sections on logistics, weaponry, construction, food supplies, and medical treatment contribute valuable insights to the Roman experience. HOLDER provides a more traditional examination of the units, officers, and men of the Roman army in war and peace, and he carefully incorporates archaeological discoveries in his studies of forts and supply bases.

Further campaigns were needed to complete the conquest. Caratacus had established himself in Wales, finding new allies among tribes there such as the Silures. Hoping to use the hilly terrain and native guerrilla tactics to their advantage, the natives were nonetheless overcome by the superior training and discipline of two Roman legions in a total force of 25,000 men. Unable to persuade the queen of the neighbouring Brigantes to abandon her alliance with Rome and join him, Caratacus was captured in AD 51 and exhibited in Rome as a defeated rebel; his dignity and courage impressed writers such as Tacitus. Continued resistance by the Silures, internal turmoil among the Brigantes, and the revolt of the Iceni AD 60–61 occupied the following decade of the conquest. Of them all, the initial successes of widowed queen Boudica, fighting to defend her late husband's client kingdom, her daughters' honour, and the integrity of the Iceni and other tribes, instilled the most fear in Roman leaders. Governors such as Scapula and Paulinus had pursued a vengeful policy towards native tribes, the consequences of which resulted in the slaughter of the Ninth Legion, the destruction of Colchester and London, and the adoption of a more sensitive policy by the new governor. MATTINGLY's translation of and introduction to *Agricola* by Tacitus provide useful insights into the policies of a governor and military leader intent upon bringing the benefits of Roman civilization to the natives, although the author's family ties to Agricola (Tacitus was his son-in-law) colour the account.

The last three decades of the 1st century witnessed the occupation of Wales and the advancement of the frontier into Scotland with garrisons north of the Forth. Legionary fortresses were now rebuilt in permanent masonry and citizen colonies (*coloniae*) such as Lincoln and Gloucester housing discharged legionary soldiers helped to hold territory and inculcate Roman values. Early in the 2nd century southern Scotland had to be abandoned as problems with the Brigantes and northern tribes escalated. In keeping with policy effected elsewhere in the empire, Hadrian decided to establish a linear fortified frontier, starting in 122 and proceeding westwards from Newcastle. Its mixture of masonry and turf, its 15 garrison forts, and its military zone marked by a forward ditch and an earthwork to the rear were meant more to impress and control the native population than to stop any concerted effort at rebellion. By the end of the first quarter of the 2nd century, Rome's period of British invasion and conquest was over, and the task of holding and influencing a foreign land had begun in earnest.

LORRAINE ATTREED

Rosebery, Archibald Primrose, 5th Earl of 1847–1929

Liberal politician, statesman, and prime minister

Brooks, David (editor), *The Destruction of Lord Rosebery: From the Diary of Sir Edward Hamilton, 1894–1895*, London: Historian's Press, and Atlantic Highlands, New Jersey: Humanities Press, 1986

Crewe, Robert Offley Ashburton Crewe-Milnes, Marquis of, *Lord Rosebery*, 2 vols, London: John Murray, 1931; New York and London: Harper and Brothers, 1931 single volume

James, Robert Rhodes, *Rosebery: A Biography of Archibald Philip, Fifth Earl of Rosebery*, London: Weidenfeld and Nicolson, 1963

Raymond, E.T., *The Man of Promise, Lord Rosebery: A Critical Study*, London: Fisher Unwin, 1923

Stansky, Peter, *Ambitions and Strategies: The Struggle for the Leadership of the Liberal Party in the 1890s*, Oxford: Clarendon Press, 1964

The Earl of Rosebery's active political career spanned just fifteen years, from 1881 until his retirement from the leadership of the Liberal party in 1896. For the next decade until the Liberals again came to power in 1906, he was a tempting alternative leader whose presence hovered over the party. Thereafter he faded quickly as a political force, especially once his latent conservatism came to the fore.

A gifted speaker and writer, Rosebery made a profound impact on his age. Those who admired him read like a *Who's Who* of late Victorian England. Gladstone, Disraeli, Herbert Asquith, Sir Edward Grey, the young Winston Churchill found Rosebery alternately attractive, fascinating, and frustrating. Despite admirable personal qualities such as great charm, wit, and an indefinable charisma, there was something lacking in Rosebery. Words like "baffling", "mysterious", and "enigmatic" have been used to describe this wealthy Scottish peer who married a Rothschild heiress and twice won the Derby while prime minister. Despite his positive qualities, Rosebery's political career was largely a failure. This is the paradox that those who have written about him seek to resolve.

Rosebery inspired an enormous number of newspaper and magazine articles in his lifetime, most of them ephemeral. RAYMOND was the first attempt to assess his career with any degree of objectivity. A talented journalist, Raymond based his book on Rosebery's public speeches and writings. He traced Rosebery's problems to his youth, especially his inability to form close relationships and a degree of hypersensitivity that made him avoid responsibility. After his wife's death in October 1890 Rosebery was isolated and without firm attachments. Raymond argues that the presence of health problems, especially insomnia, helps explain Rosebery's difficulties with his colleagues. While painting a sympathetic personal portrait, Raymond provides little that is new about Rosebery and the state of the Liberal Party in the 1880s and 1890s.

Raymond's study devotes considerable attention to Rosebery's historical writings, which included highly praised lives of the younger Pitt and Rosebery's friend, Lord Randolph Churchill. He finds great charm if not depth in them, treating Rosebery as "more the literary nobleman than the nobleman of letters".

After Rosebery's death his son-in-law, the Marquis of Crewe, undertook a formal biography. CREWE's work is an example of the two-volume life favoured by the Victorians, being in effect a massive mausoleum rather than a true biography. It's strongest point is Crewe's access to Rosebery's private papers, which are quoted extensively. The coverage of Rosebery's political career is best when dealing with his two terms as foreign secretary. Crewe gives Rosebery high marks for his handling of British foreign policy in the 1880s and early 1890s, especially the thorny question of Anglo-German relations. He also devotes considerable attention to Rosebery's conception of Liberal imperialism. Rosebery personified this concept, seeking to portray the British empire as a force for good in the world and not just as a lucrative business concern for Great Britain.

Crewe is frank in his analysis of Rosebery's faults in his dealings with Gladstone and others in the Liberal Party. Rosebery was a difficult colleague. He constantly had to be courted to take an active role in the party at times of crisis in 1886 over Irish Home Rule and again when Gladstone formed his last government in 1892. The need to court Rosebery and literally beg him to aid the party *in extremis* created animosity that later hurt him during his brief 15-month tenure as prime minister. Crewe is circumspect in his dealings with Rosebery's private life, although he does convey the intensity of his love for his wife Hannah.

JAMES's definitive biography of Rosebery appeared in 1963. James amassed an enormous amount of new material, including papers put at his disposal by Rosebery's heirs. His biography supersedes all else written about Rosebery. It is thorough, well written, and astute in its analysis of Liberal difficulties in the 1880s and 1890s over issues such as imperialism and social reform as well as the personal difficulties associated with finding a successor to Gladstone.

James is excellent on foreign policy issues including those involving imperial difficulties. He shows how on complex questions, such as relations with Japan during the first Sino-Japanese War or the possible annexation of Uganda, Rosebery could use his prestige within the Liberal Party and the nation to get his way against the judgement of his colleagues. Rosebery, he notes, was proud of his claim to have instituted the concept of the continuity of foreign policy whereby a change of government did not mean a change of the nation's external policies. His actions as foreign secretary in 1886 and again between 1892 and 1894 reveal a similarity in his views to those of his predecessor, Lord Salisbury.

James's account of Rosebery's brief premiership in 1894–95 is the story of a failure. Sir William Harcourt – arguably Gladstone's logical successor, and also Liberal leader in the House of Commons – was a difficult colleague but Rosebery was largely to blame for his administration's flaws. As a young man it was said that Rosebery sought the palm without the dust. As prime minister he found the day-to-day dealings of politics repulsive and gradually withdrew into isolation.

James's study also traces Rosebery's drift to the right. Rosebery was out of touch with Liberal views in the last decade of the 19th century. He disagreed with the party on issues such as imperialism, Irish Home Rule, and even social questions such as higher death duties. As Rosebery himself recognized towards the end of his life, he had joined the wrong party.

Rosebery's growing isolation is revealed in STANSKY, who makes it clear that the troubles of British liberalism from the 1880s were personal as well as ideological. Gladstone had so dominated liberalism for 30 years that no successor was able to flourish. When he left office the ensuing struggle to control the Liberal Party was ugly and eventually isolated British liberalism for a decade. Rosebery won the struggle for power with the equally difficult and cranky Harcourt, but he had nothing to offer the Liberal Party in the way of ideas. Despite his position as the first chairman of the London County Council, Rosebery did not foreshadow the new liberalism taking hold among younger Liberals. His appeal – aside from his imperialism – to young Liberals like Asquith, Grey, and R.B. Haldane was personal not ideological. By the time he became prime minister he was already out of touch with the party on most domestic and even foreign policy issues, as Stansky makes clear.

Just how bad the years of Rosebery's premiership were is made clear in BROOKS. His long introduction to the diary for 1894–95 of Sir Edward Hamilton, a close friend of Rosebery, is a portrait of disaster. From the opening days of his ministry when Rosebery cast doubt on the viability of Irish Home Rule as a Liberal measure, Brooks shows that he was unqualified to lead. Hamilton was a great admirer of Rosebery, but it was Harcourt who led the party to its only great success in the 1894–95 government, the budget act that introduced high death duties. He did this without Rosebery's support. Rosebery's personal reaction to the death duties act revealed him, in Harcourt's words, as extreme a Tory as Lord Eldon.

Brooks's portrait of Rosebery as prime minister is a sad one, of a man who finally achieved an office he had long yearned for, only to find it deeply unsatisfying. Brooks, through Hamilton's diary, shows Rosebery to be the architect of his own problems. When he left office in 1895 he was only 48, apparently with a great future ahead of him, yet he never again held power of any kind. Rosebery's career is summed up by the subtitle of Raymond's biography, "Man of Promise". It might better be put, "Promise Unfulfilled".

JOHN P. ROSSI

See also Anglo-Boer Wars; Asquith; Campbell-Bannerman; Gladstone

Roses, Wars of the

see Bosworth, Battle of; Edward IV; Henry VI; Henry VII; Margaret of Anjou; Neville, Richard; Richard III, Towton, Barnet, and Tewkesbury, Battles of

Rothschild, Lionel de   1808–1879
Merchant banker, philanthropist, and advocate of Jewish emancipation

Bermant, Chaim, *The Cousinhood: The Anglo-Jewish Gentry*, London: Eyre and Spottiswoode, 1971; as *The Cousinhood*, New York: Macmillan, 1972

Davis, Richard, *The English Rothschilds*, London: Collins, and Chapel Hill: University of North Carolina Press, 1983

Ferguson, Niall, *The World's Banker: The History of the House of Rothschild*, London: Weidenfeld and Nicolson, 1998; as *The House of Rothschild*, 2 vols, New York: Viking Press, 1998–99

Gilam, Abraham, *The Emancipation of the Jews in England, 1830–1860*, New York: Garland, 1982

Roth, Cecil, *The Magnificent Rothschilds*, London: Robert Hale, 1939

Salbstein, M.C.N., *The Emancipation of the Jews in Britain: The Question of the Admission of the Jews to Parliament, 1828–1860*, Rutherford, New Jersey: Fairleigh Dickinson University Press, and London: Associated University Presses, 1982

Wilson, Derek, *Rothschild: A Story of Wealth and Power*, London: André Deutsch, 1988; revised edition, London: André Deutsch, 1994; original edition as *Rothschild: The Wealth and Power of a Dynasty*, New York: Scribner, 1988

Baron Lionel de Rothschild was the eldest son of Nathan Mayer Rothschild (1777–1836), founder of the British branch of the celebrated banking family, who was regarded as the wealthiest businessman in England. Like his father, Lionel was a baron of the Hapsburg empire, but unlike his father he generally employed this title in British public life. Entering the family merchant bank, he was responsible for raising a number of important loans to foreign governments, and was chiefly responsible for British government borrowing to finance the Crimean War. He floated a loan of £16 million for that purpose in 1854.

A man of philanthropic outlook who helped to raise huge sums for Irish famine relief, in 1861 he severed financial connections with the Tsarist regime in protest at Russia's brutal suppression of the Polish revolt. His most notable deal occurred in 1875 when he enabled the government of his friend Benjamin Disraeli to purchase the Suez Canal shares from the Khedive of Egypt with a loan of £4 million. On his death he left a personal fortune of £2,700,000. He was dedicated to the welfare of Jews at home and abroad. He was among those members of the Anglo-Jewish elite who, chafing under the notion that they were, despite their wealth and standing, second-class citizens until Jews won the right to sit in parliament, pursued "Jewish emancipation" as a matter of principle. In 1847 he was elected to parliament for the City of London in the Liberal interest, but was prevented from taking his seat because he could not swear the Christian oath necessary to do so. Over the next decade he was re-elected for the same constituency several times, and following his election in 1857 a compromise was effected between Lords and Commons that permitted each House to insist on the form of oath that it chose. Thus freed from the necessity to swear "on the true faith of a Christian", Rothschild was in 1858 able to take his seat as Britain's first Jewish serving member of parliament. Ironically, although he sat for 15 years he never addressed the Commons. Gladstone failed to persuade Queen Victoria to raise Rothschild to the British peerage; she explained that the elevation of a Jew would raise antagonism and that it would be untoward to reward one whose wealth was based on "a species of gambling" rather than "the legitimate trading which she delights to honour". In 1885, however, his eldest son, Sir Nathan Mayer Rothschild also a Liberal MP, was thus elevated, becoming Britain's first Jewish peer. Lionel de Rothschild was the model for "Sidonia" in Disraeli's novel *Coningsby, or, The New Generation* (1844).

In a pioneering work on the British branch of the Rothschild family, ROTH surveys the baron's life and career in lively style, but the account reads anecdotally. While useful as an introduction it has been all but superseded by the highly recommended works of DAVIS and of WILSON. The former, the first book based on archival material from N.M. Rothschild and Sons, is a study not of the bank but of the men who ran it. As such it provides, over several chapters, a sensitive and scholarly account of Rothschild in his domestic and socio-political setting. The latter, which also treats the baron over several chapters, is likewise a serious and well-researched account that concentrates more on the human side than on the minutiae of banking and

on economic detail. Between them these three books contain much illustrative material pertaining to the baron, including several portraits; all include genealogical tables. BERMANT sets the baron in the context of the close coterie of Anglo-Jewish elite families to whom he was connected.

The massive, magisterial work by FERGUSON, drawing on hitherto unaccessed primary sources, is the definitive work on the Rothschild banking empire Europe-wide. As such, it is indispensable for information regarding Lionel's financial career.

In the course of academic accounts of Jewish and non-Jewish attitudes to Jewish emancipation GILAM and SALBSTEIN discuss the baron's ultimately successful campaign to take his seat in the House of Commons.

HILARY L. RUBINSTEIN

See also Disraeli; Jewish Emancipation; Suez Canal Purchase

"Rough Wooing" 1544–1548

Bonner, Elizabeth, "The Genesis of Henry VIII's 'Rough Wooing' of the Scots", *Northern History*, 33 (1997): 36–53

Bush, M.L., *The Government Policy of Protector Somerset*, Montreal: McGill-Queen's University Press, and London: Arnold, 1975

Crowson, P.S., *Tudor Foreign Policy*, London: A. and C. Black, and New York: St Martin's Press, 1973

Donaldson, Gordon, *Scotland: James V to James VII*, Edinburgh: Oliver and Boyd, 1965; New York: Praeger, 1966

Guy, John, *Tudor England*, Oxford and New York: Oxford University Press, 1988

Jordan, W.K., *Edward VI: The Young King: The Protectorship of the Duke of Somerset*, Cambridge, Massachusetts: Belknap Press of Harvard University Press, and London: Allen and Unwin, 1968

Nicholls, Mark, *A History of the Modern British Isles, 1529–1603: The Two Kingdoms*, Oxford and Malden, Massachusetts: Blackwell, 1999

Paterson, Raymond Campbell, *My Wound is Deep: A History of the Later Anglo-Scots Wars, 1380–1560*, Edinburgh: John Donald, 1997

Phillips, Gervase, *The Anglo-Scots Wars, 1513–1550: A Military History*, Woodbridge, Suffolk and Rochester, New York: Boydell Press, 1999

The "rough wooing" was an attempt by the English government to force the Scots to fulfil the terms of the treaty of Greenwich (1543) wherein the future Edward VI would marry the Scottish princess, Mary Stuart, and thus accomplish a union of the two kingdoms under English rule. The political and military efforts to force this agreement began with the conclusion of the treaty under Henry VIII, and ended unsuccessfully with the abandonment of the Scottish garrisons and the fall of Protector Somerset six years later. Historiographical debate has centred largely on the effectiveness of English policy, especially on the strategic considerations, the development of an "English party" among the Scottish earls, the use of propaganda, and the establishment of garrisons to intimidate the Scots into submission.

Until 1975, the conventional view was that the "rough wooing" was initiated by Henry VIII to put an end to the "auld alliance" between Scotland and France, which had hindered – by leaving the nation exposed to the possibility of foreign invasion from the north – English attempts to force their territorial and dynastic claims in France. The invasion of Scotland in 1542 and the devastating defeat of the Scots at Solway Moss, soon followed by the death of James V, enabled the English to develop a largely protestant, English party of Scottish nobles who would assist in Henry's goal of union. DONALDSON reflected this view, which has not been completely overtaken by more recent scholarship. Henry's ambassadors used both the carrot and the stick, the former coming mostly in the offer of the Princess Elizabeth as a bride for the Earl of Arran's son. These traditional interpretations stress the primacy of the French war, for which the Scottish campaign was largely a screening effort, and of the English king's belief that once the negotiations broke down (after the release of his arch-opponent, Cardinal Beaton, from prison) a scorched-earth policy would be the most effective way, ultimately, of forcing the Scots to submit. Such appeal to "force and fear", however, only served to diminish England's Scottish supporters in 1544–45. CROWSON went even further, blaming Henry VIII for underestimating Scottish patriotism by thinking the nobility would side with Henry against the queen and her party. Crowson seemed to think that negotiation was not given enough of a chance to effect the desired recasting of alliances.

The watershed reinterpretation of the "rough wooing" looked at it from the vantage point of Protector Somerset's government policy. BUSH's controversial, but largely accepted, view is that Somerset's preoccupation with Scotland led him to sacrifice effective government overall. The protector had some reason to be optimistic that he would be successful ultimately, considering his earlier string of decisive victories in the previous king's reign. But Bush believed that his reliance on costly and ineffective garrisons demonstrated the regent's opportunism, recklessness, and lack of judgement. This view flies in the face of many other scholars who hold that Somerset could have been successful had luck been more on his side. Crowson thought the propaganda of the time (including a treatise by the protector) demonstrated his sincere conviction that the Anglo-Scottish alliance was best for both nations. JORDAN was most trusting of Somerset's motives, insisting that he was outraged at violations of the Greenwich treaty. This is part of an overall pre-Bush acceptance of a humanitarian and just "good duke". Bush also cast the war in Scotland as rife with important war aims in its own right, and not just as a stepping stone toward a larger objective in France.

Recent surveys of Tudor England, such as that by GUY, tend to accept Bush's analysis, and the conviction that the "rough wooing" ended unsuccessfully when the French King Henry II sent troops to Scotland in April 1548 and Mary Stuart was taken to France, thereby leading to the abandonment of the garrisons by the end of 1549. From that point the reason for the war no longer existed and the policy became defensive.

More recent interpretations of the "rough wooing" have attempted to place the event more within a long-standing Anglo-Scottish conflict which led to particular responses by the Scots that minimize the French affinities.

BONNER traced the origins of the "rough wooing" to Francis I's convincing James V to forego his scheduled meeting with Henry VIII in York in 1541, so that the latter could not provoke a pretext for war with France. She held that Henry was resurrecting Thomas Cromwell's policy of using Scotland to achieve aims in France, but that the king unwisely insisted on the use of force when initial diplomatic overtures proved unsuccessful.

Most other scholars also blame Henry for many of the failures connected with the "rough wooing", especially the lost opportunities with the English party in Scotland, the "assured Scots". PATERSON concluded that the king expected too much of his Scottish allies. Instead of providing them with adequate support all along, he rather launched large punitive raids that drove Scotland, and eventually many English sympathizers, toward an active French alliance. PHILLIPS called this a "strategy of destruction" and stressed that the assured Scots were a vacillating group who needed much coddling, being most concerned about protecting their lives and property.

NICHOLLS, however, has found this approach too Anglocentric. In his view, Henry extracted promises of support and made important gestures, such as returning the prisoners taken at Solway Moss. He only turned to violence after becoming impatient with the impotence of the assured Scots while the pro-French party of Cardinal Beaton displayed greater skill and determination in working to achieve a strong pro-French alliance. Nicholls held also that the rejection of the treaty of Greenwich by the Scottish parliament did not guarantee a French alliance, while after the victory at Pinky (1547) the English lost the initiative by not following it up effectively. This led to Arran's treaty with France, even though he did not trust the French king.

BEN LOWE

See also Edward VI; James IV; James V; Mary of Guise; Mary, Queen of Scots; Somerset; Union, Act of; Union of the Crowns of England and Scotland

Rowntree, Benjamin Seebohm

1871–1954

Social reformer, industrialist, and analyst of poverty

Briggs, Asa, *Social Thought and Social Action: A Study of the Work of Seebohm Rowntree 1871–1954*, London: Longman, 1961

Fitzgerald, Robert, *Rowntree and the Marketing Revolution, 1862–1969*, Cambridge and New York: Cambridge University Press, 1995

Rowntree, B. Seebohm, *Poverty: A Study of Town Life*, London and New York: Macmillan, 1901

Rowntree, B. Seebohm, *The Human Needs of Labour*, revised edition, London and New York: Longman, 1937

Simey, Lord, entry on Rowntree in *Dictionary of National Biography*, supplementary volume, 1951–1960, edited by E.T. Williams and Helen M. Palmer, London and New York: Oxford University Press, 1971

Stitt, Sean and Diane Grant, *Poverty: Rowntree Revisited*, Aldershot, Hampshire and Brookfield, Vermont: Avebury, 1993

Townsend, Peter, *Poverty in the United Kingdom: A Survey of Household Resources and Standards of Living*, London: Allen Lane, and Berkeley: University of California Press, 1979

Veit Wilson, John, "Seebohm Rowntree" in *Founders of the Welfare State: A Series from New Society,* edited by Paul Barker, London and Portsmouth, New Hampshire: Heinemann, 1984

It would be mistaken to view Seebohm Rowntree as a philanthropist or paternalist. His view of life was formed by his experience as Quaker, liberal, scientist, and businessman in a manner that consistently bonded all four elements. SIMEY, a long-time colleague and friend, writing in the *Dictionary of National Biography*, showed how Rowntree's work went logically from "the needs of the individual . . . [to] the kind of industrial conditions which promote efficiency". Thus his work on poverty led directly to his work in the study and practice of management. Asa Briggs pointed out that as an employer in York ROWNTREE's work on his survey *Poverty: A Study of Town Life* was much facilitated, for example in being able to obtain wage statistics from the North Eastern Railway. Also "As an employer, he was naturally drawn to the criteria of 'physical efficiency'", while his training as a chemist led him to speculate whether scientific methods could be used to help resolve disputes as to the level of poverty in society.

It was these criteria and his use of them in dividing poverty into primary and secondary categories that became the most controversial elements in Rowntree's work. Simey in 1971 notes this cause of conflict and denotes it "unintentional". TOWNSEND in his monumental study regarded Rowntree's criteria as narrow and absolute compared with his own relativistic views on poverty. He saw Rowntree's category of secondary poverty as equating to the right-wing view of poverty as mismanagement. This led him to relegate Rowntree to the backwater of history, irrelevant to the discussion of poverty in the last quarter of the 20th century. Briggs in 1961 foreshadowed the subsequent debate in discussing Rowntree's *Poverty and Progress* (1941), by stating that "his emphasis was on the inadequacy of the changes, even when taken together, to provide what he regarded as an acceptable society".

As STITT & GRANT point out, the first to spring to Rowntree's defence was VEIT WILSON, who in 1984 attacked the label "absolute" attached to Rowntree's analysis of poverty by Townsend. Veit Wilson's *New Society* article, reproduced in Barker, is based on an earlier, more theoretical article in the *Journal of Social Policy* (15/1), "Paradigms of Poverty: a Rehabilitation of B.S. Rowntree". Veit Wilson feels that Townsend's judgement is faulty because the whole of his academic career "has been marked by his desire to overturn this paradigm of minimum subsistence poverty which he implies Rowntree established", thus ignoring Rowntree's own explanation of the distinction as a device "to convince individualists that the life style of the poor was at least in part caused by low income and not by improvidence". To Veit Wilson it was the state which unthinkingly converted Rowntree's minima into maximum incomes. Ironically, as a Liberal, Rowntree believed that the state should lay down a minimum standard of living below which no one should fall. Townsend's strictures do appear harsh in light of a half-page description of secondary poverty in *Poverty: A Study of Town Life* in which laudable expenditure such as a halfpenny newspaper or a tram ride to a healthy seaside beach would detract from "mere physical efficiency". Concerning the plight of old people, Rowntree wrote in 1941: "Of course, they *do* get an occasional ounce of tobacco, or a glass of beer, but only by suffering a little more from cold or undernourishment" (*Poverty and Progress*).

Veit Wilson is concerned with protecting Rowntree's place in history. Stitt goes further, his intention being "to step into Seebohm Rowntree's shoes and establish a primary poverty line for Britain in 1992". In so doing he raises the question of how relevant Rowntree is to current debate on poverty. BRIGGS cites three areas of interest. In 1914 in the *Financial Review of Reviews* ROWNTREE wrote an article supporting the idea of a minimum wage, following this in 1918 in *The Human Needs of Labour* with a discussion of the size of a "minimum efficiency wage" to be secured by Trades Boards, as distinct from the "desirable" wage to be secured by collective bargaining. This latter element is a change of view from 1905, when he wrote advocating individual pay levels for each employee rather than wage rates settled by collective bargaining, allowing *inter alia* for performance-related pay. In fact Rowntree's attitude to trade unions was ambivalent. He believed that his social workers could represent both management and labour. In 1924, after starting a profit-sharing scheme in 1922, his reorganization of his business led to redundancies. In a step foreshadowing others in the coal and steel closures in the 1980s and 1990s, 100 people were assisted by Rowntree to set up their own businesses.

There is less controversy about Rowntree's significance in the world of industrial management, perhaps because this part of his life is less remembered. Colonel Lyndall Urwick – a former Rowntree employee – writing in *The Golden Book of Management* (1956) called him "the British management movement's greatest pioneer" (cited in Briggs). Simey indicates that under Rowntree, first as labour director from 1897 and then chairman from 1923 to 1941, the company stood out in the practice of scientific management, which Briggs typified as lacking any philanthropic paternalism. His supplementary unemployment benefit scheme of 1921 anticipated much boosted schemes in 1955 in the American car industry.

In the end the basic question is whether Rowntree was primarily an employer, as Townsend would see him, or a humanitarian. His concerns with efficiency are basic, for without them he could see no way that industry could afford reasonable wages and good employment conditions. However, the timing of many Rowntree reforms suggests an intelligent swimming with the liberal tide. The works medical and dental provision of 1904 only just precede state provision in schools. The 1906 joint contribution pension scheme comes just before the state scheme of 1908, while New Earswick came three years before the Town Planning Act of 1909. Does this justify Simey's favourable use of Beatrice Webb's description of Rowntree as "more a philanthropist than a capitalist"? FITZGERALD is clear that it is quite wrong to label the company after 1897 as paternalist. Moreover, despite the high profile of the Rowntree Company in York, Briggs notes that in the York of the 1890s "there was precious little social security". In fact the local council did not appoint a full-time medical officer of health until 1900.

RAY GRACE

See also Poverty: Poverty and Deprivation

Royal Academy   founded 1768

Baile de Laperriere, Charles (editor), *Royal Academy Exhibitors, 1971–1989: A Dictionary of Artists and Their Work in the Summer Exhibitions of the Royal Academy of Arts*, Calne, Wiltshire: Hilmarton Manor Press, 1989

Graves, Algernon, *The Royal Academy of Arts: A Complete Dictionary of Contributors and their Work from its Foundation in 1769 to 1904*, 8 vols, London: Henry Graves and George Bell, 1905–06; reprinted, New York: Franklin, 1972

Hutchison, Sidney C., *The History of the Royal Academy 1768–1968*, London: Chapman and Hall, and New York: Taplinger, 1968; 2nd edition as *The History of the Royal Academy 1768–1986*, London: Robert Royce, 1986

Pye, John, *Patronage of British Art, an Historical Sketch: Comprising an Account of the Rise and Progress of Art and Artists in London, from the Beginning of the Reign of George the Second*, London: Longman, Brown, Green and Longmans, 1845

Royal Academy of Arts, *Royal Academy Exhibitors 1905–1970: A Dictionary of Artists and their Work in the Summer Exhibitions of the Royal Academy of Arts*, 6 vols, Wakefield, West Yorkshire: EP Publishing, 1973–82

Sandby, William, *The History of the Royal Academy of Arts from Its Foundation in 1768 to the Present Time: With Biographical Notices of All the Members*, 2 vols, London: Longman, Green, Longman, Roberts and Green, 1862

Solkin, David H., *Painting for Money: The Visual Arts and the Public Sphere in Eighteenth-Century England*, New Haven, Connecticut and London: Yale University Press, 1992

Stevens, Mary Anne (editor), *The Edwardians and After: The Royal Academy 1900–1950*, London: Royal Academy of Arts in association with Weidenfeld and Nicolson, and New York: I.B.M./Gallery of Arts and Sciences, 1988

Taylor, Brandon, *Art for the Nation: Exhibitions and the London Public, 1747–2001*, Manchester: Manchester University Press, and New Brunswick, New Jersey: Rutgers University Press, 1999

Valentine, Helen, *From Reynolds to Lawrence: The First Sixty Years of the Royal Academy of Arts and Its Collections*, edited by Mary Anne Stevens, London: Royal Academy of Arts, 1991

The Royal Academy of Arts was founded on 10 December 1768, when its instrument of foundation was signed by George III. Its inaugural exhibition was held the following year. Most discussions of the history of the Royal Academy have been concerned with the circumstances surrounding its foundation, particularly with regard to its often controversial character as an institution sponsored by royalty on the model of the French Academy, to which many artists in Britain, most notably Hogarth up to his death in 1764, were opposed in principle. PYE's account is one of the most detailed and informative, giving exhaustive documentary evidence in his history of the rise of art exhibitions and societies in 18th-century England, particularly artists' donation of works to the Foundling Hospital from 1746, and the exhibitions of the Society of Artists from 1760, out of which

the organization of the Royal Academy evolved, and with illuminating insights into the personal antagonisms and rivalries between the principal artists. Pye, however, as an engraver by profession, has his own axe to grind, in presenting his book as an argument for the admission of engravers as full members of the Royal Academy. Despite this, he provides a still valuable reference source, to which later scholars such as Hutchison and Solkin have had considerable recourse. Other essential documentary material for exhibitors and their works are the meticulous dictionaries of exhibitors from 1768–1989 compiled by BAILE DE LAPERRIERE, ROYAL ACADEMY OF ARTS (a multi-contributor work), and most notably GRAVES.

SANDBY also offers a very detailed account of almost the first century of the Academy's history, with highly valuable biographical accounts of the members, making it another important documentary source, a series of appendices providing useful information about members, officers, works and the Academy's laws and constitution. However, it is unreliable in places, and is imbued with a mid-Victorian evangelicalism over the morally elevating function of art, on the premise that the "history of art ... is in reality little less than the history of the taste and moral refinement of the people, their advancement in civilisation". Yet, this Arnoldian sensibility makes Sandby's account an illuminating sidelight on mid-Victorian academic aesthetics, which needs to be considered against the backdrop of the contemporary challenges being posed to the pedagogic principles of the Academy by Pre-Raphaelitism and the rise of realism in art.

The most important and wide-ranging survey of the Academy's history remains that by HUTCHISON who, in his second edition, provides a very clear, well-organized, though hardly critical, account of the Royal Academy over the whole of its existence up to 1986, chronicling its history by period and venue, from the first exhibition in Pall Mall to its current address at Burlington House. Hutchison's celebratory tone (the book was originally published in 1968 to celebrate the Academy's bicentenary) and its breadth of coverage detract from its academic value, entailing a somewhat superficial analysis. Nonetheless, the admirable capacity to account for such a complex history within a single volume make this the most significant introduction to the history of the Royal Academy available.

By contrast, the most sophisticated and nuanced discussions of the significance of the establishment of the Royal Academy within the contexts, respectively, of 18th-century British aesthetics and commercial ideology on the one hand, and of the history of national, public art institutions in London on the other, are those by Solkin and Taylor. Although similar to Hutchison in the breadth of period covered, TAYLOR places his account of the Royal Academy within an overall history of museums and galleries, much influenced by recent scholarly developments in museology and museum studies. His account of the Academy, though brief and generally confined to its foundation, for which he is clearly indebted to Solkin, is illuminatingly placed in a comparative chronological analysis with other public institutions such as the National Gallery or the Tate, and considered within the modern discourse on art as it relates to the construction and interpretation of national identity, and to the formation and enactment of state policy on art. From this approach, the crucial characteristic of the Academy that emerges for Taylor is its royal sponsorship, which rendered it at the outset an institution "in the image of the king".

SOLKIN's account of the foundation of the Royal Academy forms the culmination of his book, which may be seen as a multifaceted analysis of the social, political, and ideological aspects of art and the public sphere in 18th-century England (more precisely, London) leading to the formation of the Royal Academy. Like Taylor, he is very concerned with the Academy's royal association, but within a more plural and precisely focused analysis. Starting with the conflicting discourses on art and aesthetics at the beginning of the century, typified by the writings of Anthony Ashley Cooper, 3rd Earl of Shaftesbury, and Bernard Mandeville, which are held to represent the opposite poles of civic humanism versus commercial ideology, the developing discourse on art and the public sphere is analysed within the wider dialectic of commercial versus public interests, taking in art's relation to morality, to dominant concepts of sympathy and charity, urbanization, and the rise of an empowered, industrial middle-class interest. The circumstances surrounding the foundation of the Academy, therefore, are firmly set against the contemporary urban politics of Wilkite protest and anti-royal sentiment, whereby the discourse on the Academy becomes a site of ideological contest over the very nature of the 18th-century urban public. This is a demanding, specialized, but rewarding and important book.

Other studies deal with specific periods in the Academy's history: VALENTINE's exhibition catalogue considers the first 60 years of the Academy, through an interesting examination of the Academy's own collection of diploma works. Though perceptive, it is only a brief survey of the works. STEVENS is also an exhibition catalogue, drawing attention to a little-considered period in the Academy's history, and containing an illuminating and thoughtful account of the Academy in relation to the rise of modernism in the first half of the 20th century.

GEOFF QUILLEY

See also Art: *c.*1750–1914; Scientific Revolution and the Royal Society

Royal Air Force 20th century

Deighton, Len, *Fighter: The True Story of the Battle of Britain*, London: Jonathan Cape, 1977; New York: Knopf, 1978

Goulter, Christina J.M., *A Forgotten Offensive: Royal Air Force Coastal Command's Anti-Shipping Campaign 1940–1945*, London and Portland, Oregon: Cass, 1995

Hoffman, Bruce, *British Air Power in Peripheral Conflict 1919–1976*, Santa Monica, California: RAND Corporation, 1989

Hough, Richard and Denis Richards, *The Battle of Britain: The Jubilee History*, London: Hodder and Stoughton, 1989; as *The Battle of Britain: The Greatest Air Battle of World War II*, New York: Norton, 1989

Mason, Francis K., *The British Fighter since 1912*, London: Putnam Aeronautical, and Annapolis, Maryland: Naval Institute Press, 1992

Mason, Francis K., *The British Bomber since 1914*, London: Putnam Aeronautical, and Annapolis, Maryland: Naval Institute Press, 1994

Robertson, Scot, *The Development of RAF Strategic Bombing Doctrine 1919–1939*, Westport, Connecticut: Praeger, 1995

Perhaps because it is a relatively new and highly technological phenomenon, the strategic, operational, and tactical history of the Royal Air Force (RAF) has elicited little of the controversy and historiographical debate relative to that of the army and Royal Navy. Rather, the bulk of historical works are of a technical or biographical nature. The exception is the strategic bombing campaign of 1942–45, particularly over its morality and effectiveness in winning the war. Operational histories, particularly of World War II, are plentiful; however, postwar events and technological trends are typically treated as subsets of more general operational histories (e.g. Desert Shield / Desert Storm).

Any RAF historical analysis should start with MASON's two volumes on fighters and bombers. Every aircraft fielded by the RAF from its inception just prior to World War I as the Royal Flying Corps is addressed with both technical specifications and operational history. Mason literally provides a highly detailed encyclopedia of British air power. Despite its strictly technical nature, one can discern a great deal about the operational history of the RAF, particularly in the two world wars.

Despite his prominence as a novelist rather than historian, DEIGHTON provides a highly competent history of the Battle of Britain with a particularly good analysis of the strategic assumptions of both German and British air commanders. Both sides assumed that the future of warfare lay in strategic bombing as advocated by interwar air theorists such as the Italian General Giulio Douhet and the American Brigadier General Billy Mitchell. Accordingly, both the RAF and the Luftwaffe emphasized strategic bombing and the employment of fighters primarily for bomber and homeland defence throughout most of the war. Typically, air/ground operations were regarded as secondary missions by both the American and British air staffs in the European theatre of operations. The Germans, following the defeat in the Battle of Britain, lost interest in strategic bombing and concentrated on homeland defence on the western front with its shrinking fighter force. Deighton credits Air Chief Marshal Sir Hugh Dowding with rescuing the British fighter from its subordinate role and with winning the Battle of Britain through the superb employment of Britain's limited air defence assets. Deighton's analysis of fighter tactics and weapons, though not as technical and comprehensive as Mason, nonetheless provides a compelling analysis of the events of the battle, no doubt aided by his literary skills as an action-adventure novelist.

HOUGH & RICHARDS offer a more scholarly approach to the Battle of Britain based on official documents and personal memoirs (although their work is intended for the general reader). The authors provide an operational narrative as well as analysing the key building-blocks of the British victory put in place during the interwar years. Hough & Richards address: interservice rivalries and budget battles of the 1920s that threatened the junior service's survival; creation of an effective, technologically advanced air defence system; fielding of modern fighters despite the ascendancy of the strategic bombing doctrine among many senior officers; and the rise of Fighter Command despite "competing claims" for resources.

The strategic context within which nations derive their foreign and defence policies has largely been ignored in the historiography of international relations until the last two decades. In terms of the development and implementation of the strategic bombing policy, ROBERTSON addresses that weakness through a case study analysis of the interrelationship between foreign policy and national strategy in terms of Britain's interwar air defence doctrine. The services, Treasury, Foreign Office, and other governmental departments debated not only the financial and technological aspects of fielding evolving aeronautical technology and weapons systems, but how air power supported national and imperial interests and how the RAF could support diplomatic initiatives. Robertson demonstrates how the strategic bombing doctrine fitted the interwar development of British national strategy.

GOULTER provides the first in-depth analysis of the vital, yet oft-overlooked RAF Coastal Command anti-shipping campaign against German merchant interests. Though usually associated with anti-submarine warfare, Coastal Command's economic offensive struck directly at Germany's ability to provide the raw materials for war such as Swedish iron ore imported through Norway. Goulter examines the development of anti-shipping operational techniques as well as the value of intelligence, using primary sources previously overlooked by World War II historians.

While most works on the RAF deal with World War II, the air service was heavily engaged in imperial operations in the interwar years as well as in cold war and post–cold war peripheral operations, most recently the Gulf War (1991) and Balkans operations of the late 1990s. HOFFMAN found several constants in various RAF peripheral operations including: the lack of a technologically advanced opponent; a minimal air defence threat wherein modern aircraft were not necessarily better; a need for close air-ground coordination; the ineffectiveness and inappropriateness of air power in rural or urban contexts against a loosely organized and dispersed insurgent force; and, finally, the economic efficiency that air power often provides over ground operations, assuming that the operational context is appropriate to air warfare. Though the study ends in 1976, the lessons learned are clearly applicable to current peripheral conflicts, particularly where political authorities view air power as a relatively inexpensive (in blood and treasure) alternative to extended ground operations.

STANLEY D.M. CARPENTER

See also Aeronautics and the Aerospace Industry; Aviation; Defence Capability; Harris; Hoare; World War II: Air Operations

Royal Institution   founded 1799

Bence Jones, Henry, *The Royal Institution: Its Founder and Its First Professors*, London: Longmans Green, 1871; reprinted, New York: Arno Press, 1975

Berman, Morris, "The Early Years of the Royal Institution, 1799–1810: A Re-evaluation", *Science Studies*, 2 (1972): 205–40

Berman, Morris, *Social Change and Scientific Organization: The Royal Institution, 1799–1844*, London: Heinemann, and Ithaca, New York: Cornell University Press, 1978

Caroe, A.D.R., *The House of the Royal Institution*, London: Royal Institution, 1963

Caroe, Gwendy, *The Royal Institution: An Informal History*, London: John Murray, 1985

Chilton, Donovan and Noel G. Coley, "The Laboratories of the Royal Institution in the Nineteenth Century", *Ambix*, 27 (1980): 173–203

Forgan, Sophie, "The Royal Institution of Great Britain, 1840–1873" (dissertation), London: Westfield College, University of London, 1977

McCabe, Irena M. and Frank A.J.L. James, "Collections X: History of Science and Technology Resources at the Royal Institution of Great Britain", *British Journal for the History of Science*, 17 (1984): 205–59

Martin, Thomas, *The Royal Institution*, London: Longmans Green, 1942; revised edition, 1949

Royal Institution, *Minutes of the Managers' Meetings 1799–1900*, 15 vols in 7, Ilkley, Yorkshire: Scolar Press, 1971–76

Throughout the 19th century, the Royal Institution possessed one of the finest scientific laboratories in Europe. For much of that time it was the only laboratory in Britain where experimental science could be pursued effectively. It was in this laboratory that Humphry Davy and Michael Faraday conducted their fundamental chemical and physical researches, particularly into electricity. Later, John Tyndall, James Dewar, William Henry Bragg, his son William Lawrence Bragg, George Porter, and others held professorial appointments at the Royal Institution. Much concerning the history of the Royal Institution can therefore be learned from reading accounts of their lives. With such a distinguished record of research, it was thus natural that, when the history of the Royal Institution came to be written, there was a tendency to concentrate on this at the expense of the many other activities that also take place there.

This approach skewed accounts of the founding of the Royal Institution and its early history, since scientific research was never envisaged by the founders as one of the aims of the Royal Institution; rather, the dissemination of scientific knowledge was its initial primary aim. BENCE JONES, who wrote the first history of the Royal Institution, gave Benjamin Thompson, Count Rumford, the leading role in its foundation. This perspective allowed Bence Jones to stress the importance of research, and hence Davy's significance as a scientific discoverer; indeed, this account ends with Davy's departure from the Royal Institution. Moreover, as the first account to be published, Jones formed the agenda for much subsequent writing on the Royal Institution; for example, both MARTIN and G. CAROE follow his lead in their accounts of the early years of the Institution, by concentrating on research.

The archives of the Royal Institution contain a remarkably large and comprehensive collection of institutional records, which more recent historians have used to provide a different account of the early Royal Institution. Some of the ROYAL INSTITUTION's records were published in the *Minutes of the Managers' Meetings*, which photographically reproduced and indexed the minute books. They provide a good picture of the management of the Royal Institution during its first century, though the informative quality of the minutes is variable depending on who the assistant secretary was at a given time. McCABE & JAMES provide a brief overview of the archival holdings of the Royal Institution, both as administrative records and as personal papers of the professors.

Using such archival sources, BERMAN draws attention to the importance of agricultural and imperial interests, as well as those of social reform, in the formation and early years of the Royal Institution. Berman rightly pointed out the importance of Joseph Banks, Lord Spencer, and Thomas Bernard, among others, to the Royal Institution and thus reduced the significance of the crucial role assigned previously to Rumford. Berman, however, swung too far in the opposite direction from other historians of the subject, by neglecting almost completely the role of research. He somewhat overstated the case, by portraying Faraday as an instrument of government policy (for example, in the inquiry of 1844 into the Haswell Colliery disaster) which, he argued, did violence to Faraday's supposed commitment to "pure science".

FORGAN, in an unpublished dissertation, takes a more balanced view of the development of the Royal Institution in the middle third of the 19th century. She examines the role of the managers who ran the Institution and its two secretaries during this period, John Barlow and Bence Jones, showing that they had more influence than the professors, including Faraday and Tyndall. One of the major concerns of the secretaries, Forgan shows, was the success or failure of the lecture courses from which the Royal Institution earned much of its income. It was only towards the end of this period, under the influence of Bence Jones, that research was seen to be an integral part of the activities of the Royal Institution, rather than just of its professors.

For the remainder of the 19th century, and indeed for the 20th century, knowledge of the history of the Royal Institution is sketchier than for the years before 1873. CHILTON & COLEY contains useful information for the whole of the 19th century, including floor plans showing the development of the laboratory, while A. CAROE looks at the development of the building as a whole up to c.1940. Chilton & Coley also provide some detail of laboratory finance and, very rare in any kind of historical literature, a list of technicians working in the Royal Institution up to 1925.

Bence Jones's aspirations to make research central to the activities of the Royal Institution were further reinforced in 1896, when the new Davy-Faraday Research Laboratory was opened following an endowment by Ludwig Mond. It was in this laboratory that Dewar, the Braggs, Porter, and more recent directors have conducted their scientific research. These developments are covered in Martin and G. Caroe (a daughter of William Henry Bragg). Apart from brief mentions in the latter, however, many of the recent major developments in the Royal Institution, such as the schools lectures, the televising of the Christmas lectures, and the Institution's expanding role in the promotion of the public understanding of science, have received little or no attention.

FRANK A.J.L. JAMES

See also Davy; Faraday; Physics and Natural Philosophy; Royal Society of London

Royal Mint
see Coins and Coinage

Royal Society of London   founded 1660

Atkinson, Dwight, *Scientific Discourse in Sociohistorical Context: The Philosophical Transactions of the Royal Society of London, 1675–1975*, Mahwah, New Jersey: Erlbaum, 1999

Barton, Ruth, "'An Influential Set of Chaps': The X-Club and Royal Society Politics, 1864–1885", *British Journal for the History of Science*, 23 (1990): 53–81

Feingold, Mordechai, "Of Records and Grandeur: The Archive of the Royal Society" in *Archives of the Scientific Revolution: The Formation and Exchange of Ideas in Seventeenth-Century Europe*, edited by Michael Hunter, Woodbridge, Suffolk: Boydell Press, 1998

Gascoigne, John, *Science in the Service of Empire: Joseph Banks, the British State, and the Uses of Science in the Age of Revolution*, Cambridge and New York: Cambridge University Press, 1998

Hall, Marie Boas, *All Scientists Now: The Royal Society in the Nineteenth Century*, Cambridge and New York: Cambridge University Press, 1984

Hall, Marie Boas, *Promoting Experimental Learning: Experiment and the Royal Society, 1660–1727*, Cambridge: Cambridge University Press, 1991

Hunter, Michael, *Establishing the New Science: The Experience of the Early Royal Society*, Woodbridge, Suffolk: Boydell Press, 1989

Lyons, Henry, *The Royal Society, 1660–1940: A History of Its Administration under Its Charters*, Cambridge: Cambridge University Press, 1944; reprinted, New York: Greenwood Press, 1968

McClellan, James E. III, *Science Reorganized: Scientific Societies in the Eighteenth Century*, New York: Columbia University Press, 1985

Shapin, Stephen, *A Social History of Truth: Civility and Science in Seventeenth-Century England*, Chicago: University of Chicago Press, 1994

Sorrenson, Richard, "Towards a History of the Royal Society in the 18th century", *Notes and Records of the Royal Society of London*, 50 (1996): 29–46

Sprat, Thomas, *History of the Royal-Society of London for the Improving of Natural Knowledge*, London: Martyn and Allestry, 1667; edited by Jackson I. Cope and Harold Whitmore Jones, St Louis, Missouri: Washington University, and London: Routledge and Kegan Paul, 1959

Weld, Charles Richard, *A History of the Royal Society, with Memoirs of the Presidents*, 2 vols, London: Parker, 1848

As the oldest still active scientific institution, the Royal Society of London has naturally attracted much scholarship. Nearly all important English and most Scottish, Welsh, and Irish scientific figures, as well as those from beyond the British Isles, have been members. It has been a significant venue that has organized the pursuit of science for more than three centuries, both within its walls and over the entire globe. It was widely copied throughout the British empire and the United States, and its history can usefully be split into three eras: from its founding to the 1830s, from the 1840s to World War I, and from World War I to the present. The beginnings of the first era have attracted a huge amount of modern scholarship, the rest of this era comparatively little; the beginnings of the second era quite large amounts, the rest of it less so; the third era none. The most significant and representative literature on the society is discussed here; there is very much more available, which can be traced by following the footnotes in these works.

The history of the society has not been easy to interpret. It was supposedly founded to support the new experimental philosophy, but, as HALL (1991) points out, experimentation was not the dominant mode of investigation, even in the society's early years. The Royal Society was meant to be useful, but, as HUNTER argues, its members had virtually no interest in practical matters. It was not even particularly royal at its founding. Charles II gave it a charter and a mace in 1662, and little else. This was quite in contrast to the Royal Greenwich Observatory, the only other significant Stuart scientific institution, which the king in parliament funded fairly consistently. Subsequent Stuarts and Hanoverians continued this policy of zero funding for the Royal Society with very few specific exceptions. Therefore, according to Hunter, fellows had to look to their own resources; it was they who paid the society, not the society them. They were members of a London club that turned out to be rather important; they were not pensioned academicians. These simple facts had profound consequences. To survive the society had to recruit many members – often numbering into the hundreds, but never female – to pay the bills for the rooms, the secretary, the demonstrator of experiments, the instruments themselves, and the publication of the society's journal, *Philosophical Transactions*. It also had to provide enough intriguing or important scientific material to keep the general membership interested. Thus a fellow might be an obscure country parson with only a passing interest in botany or he could be Isaac Newton. This huge range in the abilities and interests of the membership made the society, as MCCLELLAN demonstrates, very different from the more exclusive European academies.

While the society may not have been particularly empiricist, utilitarian, royal, or academic, it has, however, as FEINGOLD's account shows, taken a deep interest in its past, and its fellows have produced several histories. But when a fellow wrote one, did he speak for himself, or the society? This question has bedevilled Sprat, Weld, and Lyons whose interests as fellows and their position in the society must be carefully considered when reading their accounts. SPRAT has been particularly problematic in this regards. Written only seven years after the society's founding, it was a programmatic announcement of the society's ideals as held by a certain number of the fellows, not a dispassionate account of the actual activities of the entire membership. WELD, though an apologetic text, is still surprisingly good in its treatment of the society's transition from a place where experimental effects were shown to a place where they were instead talked about. It is also important for its material on the presidents of the society in the 18th and early 19th centuries. LYONS contains some useful details on the adminis-

trative structure of the society, but is unusually Whiggish in its attempts to decide which fellows were "scientific" and which were not.

The modern scholarship surrounding the founding of the society, which is substantial and interesting, can only be touched upon. Hunter provides an excellent introduction to that literature, which concerns, among other things: the founding rhetoric of the society; the relations between science and religion; and the social status of the fellows and the science they advocated. The society's early attempts to establish an appropriate scientific discourse – both spoken and written – and to maintain a regularly published journal have attracted rhetorical analysis, most recently and extensively in ATKINSON, which gives a detailed analysis of the *Philosophical Transactions*. The fellows' early attempts to make experiments and instruments work, and to create norms for assigning credit for discoveries, have been the subject of much sociological work, including the always interesting SHAPIN, which, however, tends rather too easily to take one fellow, Robert Boyle, as representative of all the fellows.

If the society underwent no dramatic changes in the 18th century, it was not therefore unimportant. SORRENSON notes that it continued to follow its founding principles in respecting the plain fact, and those who could produce it, and to be suspicious of generalizations and generalizers. While it revered its greatest fellow, Sir Isaac Newton, its fellows mostly ignored his mathematizing methodology and concentrated on the production of novel experimental effects, accurate measurement, and meticulous natural history. The society remained a club, but one that used shared correspondence networks, economic interests, observations, instruments, and readings of papers to maintain sociability. GASCOIGNE studies Sir Joseph Banks's very long presidency (1778–1820), which coincided with the almost continuous conflict of the American and French Revolutions and the Napoleonic wars. The society made vigorous attempts to be useful to its nation, while the social make-up of the fellowship and the self-funded nature of the society remained relatively unchanged.

BARTON describes the substantial, but none the less rather slow, changes which the society underwent after Banks's presidency, and these constitute the beginning of the second era. The Royal Society had to adjust to the fact that it was no longer the only substantial scientific society in London once a host of single-discipline societies, such as the Geological, sprung up. It also chose to stop electing members who were more patrons than practitioners of science and sought and received more state support. The political struggles that accompanied these changes have attracted much scholarly attention. HALL (1984) gives a broad but scholarly overview of the entire 19th century with especial emphasis on just when the society became "scientific". Thereafter, quite remarkably, the scholarship dries up. The society changed greatly in its third era from World War I onwards – as the British state took a much greater interest in all aspects of science, and as university dons came almost completely to dominate the fellowship – but there are no works as yet devoted to the society's 20th-century history.

RICHARD SORRENSON

See also Natural Philosophy; Newton; Physics and Natural Philosophy; Scientific Revolution and the Royal Society

Royal Supremacy from 1534

Elton, G.R., *England under the Tudors*, London and New York: Methuen, 1955; 2nd edition, 1974; 3rd edition, London and New York: Routledge, 1991

Elton, G.R. (editor), *The Tudor Constitution: Documents and Commentary*, Cambridge: Cambridge University Press, 1960; 2nd edition, Cambridge and New York: Cambridge University Press, 1982

Haigh, Christopher, *English Reformations: Religion, Politics, and Society under the Tudors*, Oxford: Clarendon Press, and New York: Oxford University Press, 1993

Jones, Norman L., *Faith by Statute: Parliament and the Settlement of Religion, 1559*, London: Royal Historical Society, and Atlantic Highlands, New Jersey: Humanities Press, 1982

Lehmberg, Stanford, *The Reformation Parliament, 1529–1536*, Cambridge: Cambridge University Press, 1970

Neale, J.E., *Elizabeth I and Her Parliaments*, vol. 1, *1559–1581*, London: Jonathan Cape, 1953; New York: St Martin's Press, 1958

Ogg, David, *England in the Reigns of James II and William III*, Oxford: Clarendon Press, 1955; reprinted, Oxford and New York: Oxford University Press, 1984

Spurr, John, *The Restoration Church of England, 1646–1689*, New Haven, Connecticut and London: Yale University Press, 1991

In 1534, a year after it had extinguished papal jurisdiction in England by passing the Act in Restraint of Appeals, parliament enacted the Act of Supremacy. Earlier, in 1531, the Convocation of the Clergy had acknowledged Henry VIII to be the Supreme Head of the church, "so far as the law of Christ allows". This saving phrase was deleted from the statute, which instead referred to the king as the Supreme Head "in earth". The circumstances under which convocation and parliament acted can be studied in LEHMBERG's history of the Reformation parliament. As Lehmberg points out, the statute was more clearly directed against Rome than the earlier statement of the clergy: it allows God, or Christ, to hold some variety of supremacy, but not the pope.

Mary Tudor's second Act of Repeal (1554) repealed the Act of Supremacy along with the other religious legislation of her father's reign. At the time of her succession Mary actually held the title Supreme Head but masked it by using "etc." as part of her royal style. Queen Elizabeth's first parliament enacted a new supremacy statute as part of the Elizabethan religious settlement of 1559. In his older account of this parliament NEALE said that the original supremacy bill restored the title Supreme Head but that a second version, introduced after Easter, gave her the title Supreme Governor instead, probably because of doubts that a woman could be head of the church. Neale's evidence was slight and his account of the settlement has been substantially revised by JONES. In any case the act reaffirmed royal control of the English church and once again denied the jurisdiction of the pope. These events can also be traced in HAIGH's volume, which includes an account of the way in which the government used the oath of supremacy as a means of ejecting catholic clergy who were unwilling to swear allegiance to the queen as governor.

While most writers have viewed Elizabeth's position as Supreme Governor as being basically the same as Henry VIII's role as Supreme Head, ELTON argued that there was an essential difference between head and governor. He saw Henry as the highest ecclesiastical dignitary in the realm, taking precedence over the Archbishop of Canterbury and ruling the church from within. Elizabeth, in contrast, ruled it from outside, acting through her archbishops and the groups of royal commissioners which she appointed from time to time. "No . . . quasi-ecclesiastical character appertained to the supreme governorship. While the queen lived it made little practical difference, but the change profoundly affected the position of her successors" (*England under the Tudors*). Elton concluded that "the Elizabethan supremacy was essentially parliamentary, while Henry VIII's had been essentially personal" (*The Tudor Constitution*).

Royal supremacy was of course extinguished during the interregnum of the 17th century, following the execution of Charles I, but like the monarchy it returned at the time of the Restoration. Charles II's Cavalier Parliament reasserted the validity of the supremacy statute. SPURR's book includes a substantial discussion of the king's use of supremacy as a justification for his appointment of bishops and his visitations of the church. He suggests that royal supremacy was a guarantee of the unity of the national church and quotes Richard Hooker's famous phrase, "there is not any man of the church of England but the same man is a member of the commonwealth, nor a member of the commonwealth which is not also a member of the Church of England". The royal supremacy left bishops and cathedral chapters in day-to-day control of the church but did not allow them to gather in synods or issue canons without royal leave. OGG discusses the continuing significance of supremacy through the Glorious Revolution and considers whether the catholic sovereign James VII and II was justified in some of his actions, including the appointment of the controversial Ecclesiastical Commission, because he retained the royal supremacy. The title "Supreme Governor", together with the designation "Defender of the Faith" granted to Henry VIII by Pope Leo X in 1521, remains part of the royal style.

In the 20th century there were those who argued that a divorced man, such as the Duke of Windsor or Prince Charles, could not exercise royal supremacy, and Charles, acknowledging the existence of other denominations outside the Church of England, spoke of his desire to be head of the churches, "defender of the faiths", not a unitary state church. These issues have not yet been resolved.

STANFORD LEHMBERG

See also Anglican Establishment; Henry VIII

Russell, John, 1st Earl Russell

1792–1878

Whig politician, statesman, and prime minister

Brent, Richard, *Liberal Anglican Politics: Whiggery, Religion, and Reform 1830–1841*, Oxford: Clarendon Press, and New York: Oxford University Press, 1987

Brock, Michael, *The Great Reform Act*, London: Hutchinson, 1973

Conacher, J.B., *The Aberdeen Coalition 1852–1855: A Study in Mid Nineteenth-Century Party Politics*, London: Cambridge University Press, 1968

Kriegel, Abraham D., "Liberty and Whiggery in Early Nineteenth-Century England", *Journal of Modern History*, 52/2 (1980): 253–78

Mandler, Peter, *Aristocratic Government in the Age of Reform: Whigs and Liberals, 1830–1852*, Oxford: Clarendon Press, and New York: Oxford University Press, 1990

Mitchell, Austin, *The Whigs in Opposition, 1815–1830*, Oxford: Clarendon Press, 1967

Newbould, Ian, *Whiggery and Reform, 1830–41: The Politics of Government*, London: Macmillan, and Stanford, California: Stanford University Press, 1990

Parry, Jonathan, *The Rise and Fall of Liberal Government in Victorian Britain*, New Haven, Connecticut and London: Yale University Press, 1993

Prest, John, *Lord John Russell*, London: Macmillan, and Columbia: University of South Carolina Press, 1972

Southgate, Donald, *The Passing of the Whigs, 1832–1886*, London: Macmillan, and New York: St Martin's Press, 1962

Given his long and distinguished career in British politics, it is remarkable that Lord John Russell has not attracted a greater number of modern biographers. While Russell is well represented in the traditional 19th-century "life and times" genre, the paucity of modern biographical studies may be a consequence of his prominence at a time when party politics were exceedingly complicated. Indeed, Russell's intimate connection with the cause of parliamentary reform cast him in the role of transforming the political world in which he became a central character.

MITCHELL discusses Lord Russell's abortive efforts for modest parliamentary reform bills in the 1820s, and his promotion of civil and religious liberty when he successfully advocated parliament's repeal of the Test and Corporation Acts in 1828. Prest considers Russell's greatest achievement to be his preparation of the Reform Bill of 1832 and his steady direction of parliamentary reform through the House of Commons. BROCK provides a comprehensive treatment of Russell's indispensable role during the Reform Bill struggle, particularly among the committee of four who drafted the legislation for the cabinet's consideration. Once Russell was awarded a place in Lord Grey's cabinet, he became the Whigs' most determined advocate of equitable treatment for Ireland. The generally accepted notion that he "upset the coach" in pressing for the appropriation of surplus Irish church revenues to secular purposes in 1834 is challenged by NEWBOULD, who holds Edward Stanley, later the 14th Earl of Derby, rather than Russell responsible for splitting the Whigs on that divisive issue. Parry differs, as he suggests that Russell's insistence on the appropriations clause in the Irish Church Temporalities Bill "was probably the most important single step in the formation of the Liberal party", perhaps a strained interpretation given the government's ultimate abandonment of the clause later in the decade. Both

Newbould and PREST argue that, notwithstanding opposition from radicals as well as conservatives, Russell impressively managed the House of Commons from 1835 to 1841, when he served first as Melbourne's home secretary and, subsequently, secretary for war and colonies. Indeed, Prest suggests that Russell's achievement in the 1830s augured greater distinction in the future. Nonetheless, despite Russell's advanced liberal views, Prest claims that a singular combination of pride and reticence made him a difficult colleague, and a prime minister from 1846 to 1852 who achieved no more than an equivocal success. His inability to deal with the enormity of the Irish famine was all the more ironic for a politician who had been so vigorous a spokesman for the redress of Irish grievances.

While Prest attempts to rescue Russell from the neglect he has incurred, it is inadvertently reinforced by the author's acknowledgment that he should have retired from politics in 1852 when his government was turned out. CONACHER sees in Russell the personification of Whiggery fighting to retain its old ascendancy during the fractious Aberdeen coalition, in which Russell served as foreign secretary, minister without portfolio, and lord president of the council. Prest accepts Conacher's characterization of Russell's difficulties, but attributes his loss of stature in part to his prolonged and increasingly bitter feud with Palmerston, who was indisposed to assist Russell's various efforts to immortalize himself by a second parliamentary reform bill. That Russell was denied that distinction has its analogue in his acceptance of free trade before Peel embraced it, only to witness the latter secure the credit for repealing the Corn Laws. Having accepted a peerage in 1861, he failed in his last effort at parliamentary reform during his brief ministry of 1865–66, to which Prest devotes little space.

Russell's prominence has made him a central figure in conflicting interpretations of mid-19th-century liberalism. KRIEGEL discusses the political culture of aristocratic Whiggery that Russell inherited and sought to apply in his early career. SOUTHGATE treats him as "the arch Whig of the nineteenth century", devoted to the idea of an enlightened aristocracy promoting civil and constitutional liberty, but disinclined towards enacting social reforms. Russell also subscribed to a broad-church Anglicanism that BRENT considers essential to an understanding of politics in the 1830s and 1840s. Indeed, Brent treats Russell as the key figure among the "liberal Anglicans", a group that allegedly rescued the Whig party from political disintegration. They supplanted an antiquated preoccupation with constitutional questions with a passionate concern for the moral improvement of the people. Brent attributes this intellectual and moral transformation primarily to Russell, "who saw a liberal Anglicanism as ensuring the preservation of the state". He characterizes Russell's frequently uncertain policies as "deliberately ambiguous", and his sometimes vacillating behaviour as "prudent inactivity". By contrast, MANDLER portrays Russell as the leader of the "Foxite Whigs", who presumably helped to inaugurate and sustain social reform in the 1830s and 1840s, favouring not only an activist but a centralized state. These "Foxite" activist and centralist tendencies, Mandler claims, culminated in the reforms of Russell's government, notably the legislation for a ten-hour day (1847) and a sweeping measure of centralization, the Public Health Act of 1848. Accordingly, Mandler refers to the disintegration of Russell's ministry in 1852 as marking the fall of the "last Whig government", heralding the end of the age of reform, the emergence of the mid-Victorian age of equipoise, and the triumph of *laissez-faire* liberalism in place of Foxite Whig interventionism.

PARRY also restores the Whigs as the guiding force of 19th-century liberalism, with Russell conspicuous among their leaders. Just as Parry's interpretation of Whiggery and liberalism is more intricate than those of other scholars, so his appraisal of Russell is all the more nuanced. Parry contends that 19th-century liberalism "owed most to the whig tradition". He argues "that the *parliamentary* whig-Liberal tradition was central to British politics", far more so "than undisciplined radicalism". Indeed, rather than finding the beginnings of the Liberal Party in the alliance between Palmerston and Gladstone

in 1859, he considers aristocratic Whiggery of the 1820s and 1830s as the Liberal Party's true inspiration. In such a major revisionist interpretation, Lord John Russell emerges as a seminal figure, "the most effective interpreter of the Liberal frame of mind". Given Parry's findings, one can hardly be surprised at his conclusion that "a powerful discussion of Russell's central role in Liberal history is long overdue".

ABRAHAM D. KRIEGEL

See also Aberdeen; Catholic Emancipation; Derby; Factory Reform; Great Irish Famine; Grey; Melbourne; Palmerston; Parliamentary Reform: Acts of 1832–1885; Public Health; Test and Corporation Acts, Repeal of

S

Saint Albans, School of

Galbraith, Vivian H. (editor), *The St Albans Chronicle, 1406–1420*, Oxford: Clarendon Press, 1937

Galbraith, Vivian H., *Roger Wendover and Matthew Paris*, Glasgow: Jackson, 1944

Gransden, Antonia, *Historical Writing in England*, 2 vols, London: Routledge and Kegan Paul, and Ithaca, New York: Cornell University Press, 1974–82

Jenkins, Claude, *The Monastic Chronicler and the Early School of St Albans*, London: SPCK, and New York: Macmillan, 1922

Rerum Britannicarum Medii Aevi scriptures; or, Chronicles and Memorials of Great Britain and Ireland during the Middle Ages ("Rolls Series"), London: HMSO, 1858–1911; reprinted, New York and Vaduz, Liechtenstein: Kraus Reprint, 1964–81

Taylor, John, *English Historical Literature in the Fourteenth Century*, Oxford: Clarendon Press, and New York: Oxford University Press, 1987

Vaughan, Richard, *Matthew Paris*, Cambridge: Cambridge University Press, 1958

The Benedictine abbey of St Albans enjoyed an unrivalled reputation for learning throughout the Middle Ages and was renowned especially for its tradition of historical writing. Between the 12th and 15th centuries it produced a succession of chroniclers – Roger Wendover (*c*.1180–1235), Matthew Paris (*c*.1200–59), William Rishanger (*c*.1260–1312), and Thomas Walsingham (*c*.1340–1422) – whose works are acknowledged to be among the most valuable sources for English history. The St Albans chronicles are remarkable not only for their longevity but also for their thematic and stylistic coherence: each chronicler consciously built upon the work of his predecessor, creating a continuous, even seamless narrative which extends for more than 250 years.

The value of the St Albans chronicles was recognized by the very first generation of modern historians, and the texts of almost all of them were included in the *Rerum Britannicarum*. It was in these editions that the works of Wendover, Paris, and their successors were first described as representing a distinct "school" of historical writing. It was believed that – like the French royal abbey of St Denis – St Albans served some kind of public role, providing an official historical record for the use of the English crown. It was even suggested that there had been a post of "historiographer" established at the abbey which each of the chroniclers had held in turn.

An early challenge to these views came from JENKINS, who focused on the origins of the St Albans "school" in the 12th century. He argued that the abbey had never been formally constituted as an official centre for historical writing, and dismissed the idea of an office of "historiographer" as the "pure invention" of the Rolls Series editors. In fact he claimed that there was no clear evidence to show that any monk of St Albans had begun to write chronicles much before the second quarter of the 13th century.

Where Jenkins concentrated on the early chroniclers, in his first book on the subject, GALBRAITH (1937) was concerned with the last of them, Thomas Walsingham. Like Jenkins, Galbraith was critical of the conclusions of the Rolls Series and offered an alternative view of the "school" based on his own analysis of the manuscripts. His most important discovery was of a section of the chronicle (to 1422) by Walsingham that had been omitted from the Rolls Series. He also challenged the concept of the "school", claiming that the writing of chronicles at St Albans had never been "a continuous activity" but that the tradition was revived at regular intervals at the initiative of individual monks, of whom Walsingham himself was the last. Indeed Galbraith depicted Walsingham as the dominant figure in a community where learning was already in decline. He believed that all of the chronicle manuscripts dating from this period were the work of his hands and also identified for the first time a number of other texts, including commentaries on classical literature, which could be attributed to him. In his next contribution GALBRAITH (1944) returned to the work of the early chroniclers. Here he agreed with Jenkins that the tradition of historical writing had begun with Roger Wendover. He again rejected the notion of an official "historiographer", although he did believe that the compiling of chronicles was "a task laid upon an individual monk and . . . there was only ever a single author working at one time". In fact it was "these successive continuators who constitute the St Albans school of history and not a number of competing contemporaries writing at one time". Galbraith also re-examined the relationship between Wendover and Matthew Paris and suggested that Paris had been far more dependent on the work of his predecessor than had been recognized. The two were also closely bound together by a common political outlook, which he characterized as a "constitutional perspective", supportive towards the barons, suspicious of the crown.

VAUGHAN was the first to make a complete study of Matthew Paris's contribution to the St Albans tradition. Drawing on a detailed analysis of all the surviving manuscripts associated with Matthew, Vaughan was able to demonstrate for the first time the full extent of his historical writing. Not only did Matthew compile a *Chronica majora (Greater Chronicle)* covering the years 1235–59; he was also the author of shorter histories, the *Flores historiarum*, the *Historia Anglorum*, and a documentary collection, the *Abbreviatio chronicorum*. His scholarly interests also extended into other disciplines – especially hagiography, but also cartography, heraldry, and science. Vaughan confirmed Galbraith's suggestion that Paris had borrowed extensively from Wendover's chronicle, and it was Wendover who was the first "original St Albans historian". In Vaughan's opinion, Matthew's outlook was more populist than political, presenting "the point of view . . . the foibles and prejudices of the ordinary man in the street . . . a crusty old gossip . . . but stolid, earthy and kind".

GRANSDEN drew together the researches of Galbraith and Vaughan to offer a summary account of the St Albans "school" from its beginnings to its fading in the 15th century. She considered Matthew Paris to be among the most important of all chroniclers in the whole tradition of medieval historiography: "he did not possess the wisdom of Bede or the mental acumen of William of Malmesbury, but he deserves to rank with them". His real significance was in his development of a critical method. He was "the first historian in England who had a sustained and consistent attitude to authority".

Focusing on the final century of the St Albans chroniclers, TAYLOR bases much of his discussion on the work of Galbraith. Like Galbraith, he sees Walsingham as the spearhead of the very last revival of chronicle writing at the abbey. He demonstrates that Walsingham not only became a dominant figure at St Albans but that the influence of his writing – and of the St Albans "school" as a whole – could be found wherever history was read or written for much of the period.

JAMES G. CLARK

See also Oda; Paris, Matthew; Religious Orders: Conventual

Salisbury, 1st Earl of

see Cecil, Robert

Salisbury, Oaths of 1086

Barlow, Frank, *William I and the Norman Conquest*, London: English Universities Press, 1965
Cronne, Henry Alfred, "The Salisbury Oath", *History*, 19 (1934–35): 248–52
de Bouard, Michel, *Guillaume le Conquérant*, Paris: Presses Universitaires de France, 1958; expanded edition, Paris: Fayard, 1984
Harvey, Sally P.J., "Domesday Book and Anglo-Norman Governance", *Transactions of the Royal Historical Society*, 5th series, 25 (1975): 175–93
Holt, Sir James Clarke, "1086" in *Domesday Studies*, edited by J.C. Holt, Woodbridge, Suffolk; and Wolfeboro, New Hampshire: Boydell Press, 1987
Stenton, F.M., *The First Century of English Feudalism, 1066–1166*, Oxford: Clarendon Press, 1932; corrected edition, 1954; reprinted, Westport, Connecticut: Greenwood Press, 1979
Stenton, F.M., *Anglo-Saxon England*, Oxford: Clarendon Press, 1943; 2nd edition, 1947; 3rd edition, 1971, reprinted Oxford and New York: Oxford University Press, 1990 (*Oxford History of England*, vol. 2)

What oath was sworn to William the Conqueror at Salisbury at Lammastide (1 August) in 1086, and who swore it? These questions of definition arise because the incident was described by two important contemporary primary sources: John of Worcester (formerly "Florence") in Latin and the Peterborough version of the *Anglo-Saxon Chronicle* in English. According to John, the king summoned his archbishops, bishops, abbots, earls, barons, and sheriffs with their knights to meet him at Salisbury on 1 August; when they came there he made their knights swear fealty (*fidelitatem*) to him against all men. The entry in the Peterborough *Chronicle* runs, in Bishop Stubbs's translation:

> . . . the king's wise men [*witan*] came to him at Salisbury at Lammastide, and all the land-holding men of any account over all England, whosoever men they were, and they all bowed down to him, and became his men, and swore him hold-oaths, that they would be faithful to him against all other men.

The *Chronicle*, according to some, described an act of homage (Latin *homagium, hominium*), an acknowledgement of dependence which was sworn by a knight on his knees to his lord in respect of land which he held directly of that lord and in respect of that land only; John, however, uses the word "fealty" (Latin *fidelitas*), which means an oath of allegiance sworn to the king by a subject not in respect of any particular piece of land but because the subject believed that the lord could and would protect him and was ready to serve the lord in that expectation. Before 1066 kings had sometimes demanded such oaths. The difficulty is that the *Chronicle* appears to be describing not one transaction but two, if we suppose that bowing to the king and becoming his man was one transaction and swearing an oath of allegiance was another. But in fact becoming the king's man and swearing allegiance to him were one transaction with two aspects, which today we describe as doing fealty. Those who think that one transaction only was involved may describe him who bowed and swore either as doing homage or as swearing fealty. The key Old English words "landsittende" and "hold a[eth]as" occur seldom in Anglo-Saxon usage outside this particular passage, and the account in John of Worcester reflects much better than that of the Peterborough chronicler and the vocabulary used by ecclesiastics who describe these matters.

Accordingly, some have deduced that those who came to Salisbury swore homage to the king, others that those present swore fealty to him. The argument here is that fealty, not homage, was sworn. If the king could enforce loyalty, one oath was as useful as the other. In either case the link was the swearer's land, of which the king could, if powerful enough, find means to deprive him. Homage was done only to the man (normally a tenant-in-chief) of whom a knight held, immediately, the land which created the bond of homage; it was done kneeling, and the inferior put his hands between those of his superior.

To E.A. Freeman, one of the first modern historians to touch on what he chose to call the Conqueror's "great Gemot at Salisbury", the assembly symbolized the obliteration of the English ruling class (*Norman Conquest*, 1876). Later writers saw the need to say what actually happened.

F.M. Stenton, as early as 1908 in his *William the Conqueror and the Rule of the Normans*, set his readers on the right track by treating the oath as one of fealty; but later, STENTON (1943) began a weighty paragraph of *Anglo-Saxon England* with a blunt statement that those present, i.e. "all the land-holding men of any account in England, whosoever men they were ... did him [i.e. the king] homage, became his men, and swore him fealty, that they would be faithful to him against all other men"; Stenton defined those present as mostly the "honorial barons" (a term already invented by him in *The First Century of English Feudalism*), i.e. mainly "the better-endowed and responsible tenants" of the king's tenants-in-chief, who would have taken only "a few days" to swear their oaths and thus create "a personal relationship" between under-tenants and king which was paramount for the stability of the English state. The leading French biographer of William I, DE BOUARD, gives space to the problems posed by the oaths, i.e. the legal situation of mesne-tenants, and the need for medieval states to ensure loyalty from subjects of varying levels in the feudal hierarchy. BARLOW has described the oath as one of fealty (1965, also in the multi-author collection *The Norman Conquest: Its Setting and Impact*, 1966).

It is not difficult to name individual "honorial barons" who would surely have come to Salisbury in 1086, such as Alvred the Breton (a leading tenant of the king's half-brother Robert of Mortain), Reinaud de Bailleul (a prominent vassal of Roger de Montgomery in Shropshire where he was Roger's sheriff, and a minor tenant-in-chief in Staffordshire), and Wadard (a tenant of Odo of Bayeux in Oxfordshire and elsewhere, who appears in the Bayeux Tapestry). These and other tenants enjoyed financial resources which in material terms put them on a level with many tenants-in-chief.

The first article of major significance on the oath during the 20th century came in 1934–35 when CRONNE stressed the practical rather than the constitutional importance of the oath and after a good survey of earlier views, from Blackstone to Stenton, commended H.W.C. Davis for seeing the seriousness of the emergency facing the Conqueror in 1086. In 1975 HARVEY argued that the oath was a consequence of Domesday Book, which had reached the king and his ministers and confirmed the existence of men whose loyalty must be assured.

Appropriately, it was in 1986 that a magisterial lecture by HOLT changed the nature of the argument. Holt argued that the *breves* which contained the findings of the Domesday commissioners were available by 1 August 1086, and that admittedly later evidence (in this case Richard fitzNeal in 1179) showed that a skilled minister could interpret them. Holt shifted the emphasis more than any previous writer had done: to him the oath was a complement to Domesday, and the search for the Conqueror's motivation in arranging the Domesday enquiry was over. The book and the oath had both been the subject of the "deep speech" between the Conqueror and his great men at Gloucester during the Christmas feast of 1085. (Holt had earlier argued in another context – "Politics and Property in Early Medieval England", *Past & Present*, 57 [1972] – that in consequence of the oath under-tenants could expect security of tenure from the Crown in return for loyalty, and got it.)

It has not been difficult to find reasons why in seven months and more from Christmas 1085 to Lammas 1086 William I should have worried about loyalty and wanted information quickly about those with territorial power. One possible factor, indeed, may on any interpretation diminish in importance: the threat of a descent on England meditated by the Danish king, who was murdered at Odense in July 1086, had in fact receded. But disquiet at the attitude of the king of Scotland and above all of France (however weak they were, each had opportunities for damaging William) was recurrent for much of the reign, and soon after the oath William set sail for France for the campaign during which he died. Like Anglo-Saxon rulers before him, William had reminded everyone who mattered where his duty lay, as Henry I was to do on behalf of his son, William the Ætheling, at a similar juncture in 1116.

JOHN F.A. MASON

Salisbury, Robert Gascoyne-Cecil, 3rd Marquis of 1830–1903

Conservative politician, statesman, and prime minister

Bentley, Michael, *Lord Salisbury's World: Conservative Environments in Late-Victorian Britain*, Cambridge: Cambridge University Press, 2001

Blake, (Lord) Robert and Hugh Cecil (editors), *Salisbury: The Man and His Policies*, Basingstoke: Macmillan, and New York: St Martin's Press, 1987

Cecil, Gwendolen, *Life of Robert Marquis of Salisbury*, 4 vols, London: Hodder and Stoughton, 1921–32; reprinted, 2 vols, New York: Kraus Reprint, 1971

Grenville, J.A.S., *Lord Salisbury and Foreign Policy: The Close of the Nineteenth Century*, London: Athlone Press, 1964; corrected edition, 1970

Hughes, Judith M., *Emotion and High Politics: Personal Relations at the Summit in Late Nineteenth-Century Britain and Germany*, Berkeley: University of California Press, 1983

Marsh, Peter, *The Discipline of Popular Government: Lord Salisbury's Domestic Statecraft, 1881–1902*, Brighton, Sussex: Harvester Press, and Atlantic Highlands, New Jersey: Humanities Press, 1978

Pinto-Duchinsky, Michael, *The Political Thought of Lord Salisbury, 1854–1868*, London: Constable, and New York: Archon, 1967

Roberts, Andrew, *Salisbury: Victorian Titan*, London: Weidenfeld and Nicolson, 1999

Robinson, Ronald and John Gallagher, with Alice Denny, *Africa and the Victorians: The Official Mind of Imperialism*, London: Macmillan, and New York: St Martin's Press, 1961; 2nd edition, Basingstoke: Macmillan, 1981

Shannon, Richard, *The Age of Salisbury, 1881–1902: Unionism and Empire*, London and New York: Longman, 1996

Smith, Paul (editor), *Lord Salisbury on Politics: A Selection from His Articles in the Quarterly Review, 1860–1883*, Cambridge: Cambridge University Press, 1972

Steele, David, *Lord Salisbury: A Political Biography*, London: University College London Press, 1999

Until very recently, the best account of the life of Robert Gascoyne-Cecil, the 3rd Marquis of Salisbury – three-time prime minister and four-time foreign secretary – continued to be the excellent corpus written by his daughter Gwendolen CECIL between 1921 and 1932. This work remains valuable for its inclusion of correspondence, lively narrative of office-holding, and "insider" descriptions of Salisbury's personality, attitudes, and characteristic behaviour. Cecil never completed the volume covering the last decade of her father's career, however, and she was unable to incorporate in her work much material outside his own papers. (An excerpt from Cecil's unpublished reminiscences of her father's private life is contained in BLAKE & CECIL's collection of essays.)

The most ambitious short appraisal of Salisbury's personality and cast of mind came in the brief introduction SMITH appended to his edition of Salisbury's political essays. Smith presents a man whose ideas and actions must be understood as originating in a deeply neurotic personality, a man who was depressive, agitated, introverted, fearful of change and loss of control, and self-effacing but capable of extraordinary combativeness. Smith follows Cecil in noting how Salisbury managed to lessen the most extreme manifestations of these traits through courage, intense religious devotion, and a wonderfully happy domestic life. And HUGHES argues that Salisbury's need to keep conflict at a distance actually contributed to the steady, consensual functioning of his cabinets by allowing for ministerial autonomy and a low emotional temperature in interactions. But Smith's vivid portrait (which, it should be noted, both Roberts and Steele do much to refute) helps to dramatize the paradox always noted about Salisbury – that this aloof and suspicious patrician found himself presiding over the rowdy forces of democracy in Britain and the accommodation of the Conservative Party to the expanded electorate.

Smith follows PINTO-DUCHINSKY in arguing that Salisbury's major contribution to the transformation of Conservatism into a modern, electorally viable movement was intellectual. Deeply out of sympathy with the emotional or reverential appeals of Conservatism, Salisbury argued for resistance to legislative change using the objective tone, logical structures, and evidentiary methods that characterized the scientific fields he so admired. This "most formidable Conservative Party intellectual ever" (Smith) grounded British Conservatism in utilitarian, empiricist methods of discourse, thus weakening the drift towards romantic and irrational allegiances that would transform the European right in the decades after his death.

The works just discussed are especially good at analysing Salisbury's political outlook before he assumed increasingly heavy official responsibilities from the Disraeli ministry of 1874 until his own retirement in 1902.

Two important studies, by Marsh and by Shannon, frame a recent debate over Salisbury's role as leader of the Conservatives in an era of extraordinary change for the party and the nation. MARSH began a revival of scholarly interest in late-Victorian Conservatism in a work that presents Salisbury's greatest achievement as control of the democratic process through recognition that "effective Conservatism" was a matter not of public policy but of "political craft". This is Salisbury as a reluctant but eventually effective manipulator: of the electorate through the development of local organization and imperial rhetoric, of the Commons through judicious submission to the views of the Unionist majority, and of colleagues through "prosaic adjustments" to the varied interests and personalities that constituted the Conservative-Unionist alliance. In this construction, Salisbury would be neither surprised by nor responsible for the disasters that overtook the party as more "radical" forces gained prominence after his retirement.

SHANNON challenges this assessment in two important ways. First, he stresses continuity, rather than adaptation, in Salisbury's ideas and methods of operating between the early and late stages of his career, believing that Salisbury was always looking backwards in his understanding of political forces. Second, the period of Conservative success that Salisbury enjoyed appears as the lucky result of "internal laws of transformation" that were creating a modern party based on urban and suburban forces which Salisbury not only disliked but had little responsibility for mobilizing. Instead, the success of party operatives like Middleton and Akers-Douglas allowed Salisbury, and subsequently Arthur Balfour, to continue aristocratic methods of cabinet management and parliamentary leadership long after these had become detrimental to the party as a whole. Shannon's work embodies a new approach to political narrative that stresses the chaotic multitude of forces, institutions, and characters that constituted the late-Victorian Conservative movement, rather than the masterly control of key individuals.

Masterly control has been the general assessment of Salisbury's performance in the assignment he most preferred, that of foreign secretary. A number of important scholarly studies of Salisbury's foreign and imperial policy appeared in the 1960s (see the bibliography and footnotes in BLAKE & CECIL), of which GRENVILLE and ROBINSON & GALLAGHER may be taken as representing a consensus. Salisbury, in this school, "towered above his contemporaries" in the knowledge and practice of foreign affairs (Grenville). He was never the "splendid isolationist" of popular myth, but rather a patient, pragmatic practitioner, with a keen understanding of Britain's historic interests that was widely appreciated by his countrymen. As such, he oversaw the partitioning of Africa, the emergence of Germany and the United States as imperial powers, and the transfer of British attention from the Dardanelles to Suez without provoking a serious confrontation of the great powers, much less a European war. In an essay in Blake & Cecil, A.N. Porter makes a laudable attempt to link the "official mind" of the foreign secretary, objectively assessing Britain's interests and capacities in a rapidly changing international situation, to the aristocratic statesman's broader understanding of how taxation demands for imperial defence would affect the landed interest's class, party, and social agendas.

Two new biographies of Salisbury are indispensable. Both use the private archives at Hatfield House, the Cecil family seat, extensively, as well as scores of other collections. ROBERTS has written the more vivid and readable book. His study provides a clear chronological narrative, and he excels at using Salisbury's own words to capture the flavour of the man's mind and personality. Its approach is hagiographic, however, praising

Salisbury as a man whose caustic attitudes and "patient obstructionism" were justified by the sorry developments of modernity. It does not deeply engage controversies over Salisbury's roles in domestic and foreign policy. STEELE remedies this with a study whose chapters on topics like the "Eastern Question" or the "New Conservatism in Practice" are sustained analytical essays. His Salisbury emerges less clearly as a personality, but much more nuanced as a statesman and a politician. Steele's new and unusual position is that Salisbury, grounded in a deep sense of religious duty, was in fact always forward-looking, more in sympathy with "underdogs" at home and in the empire than has been supposed, and as ready as Gladstone himself to adopt constructive platforms.

BENTLEY provides another interesting collection of essays attempting to situate Salisbury's preoccupation with various topics (the church, empire, property, the party) in the context of the collective mind-set of his "chosen circle" of late Victorian Tories.

NANCY W. ELLENBERGER

See also Carnarvon; Chamberlain, Joseph; Churchill, Lord Randolph; Conservative Party; Devonshire, 8th Duke of; Disraeli; "Eastern Question": The Dardanelles

Salvation Army from 1865

Booth-Tucker, F. de L., *The Life of Catherine Booth: The Mother of the Salvation Army*, 2 vols, New York: Ewell, 1892; London: Salvation Army, 1893

Ervine, St John, *God's Soldier: General William Booth*, 2 vols, London: Heinemann, 1934

Horridge, Glenn K., *The Salvation Army: Origins and Early Days, 1865–1900*, Godalming, Surrey: Ammonite Books, 1993

Murdoch, Norman H., *Origins of the Salvation Army*, Knoxville: University of Tennessee Press, 1994

Sandall, Robert (vols 1–3), Arch R. Wiggins (vols 4–5), and Frederick Coutts (vols 6–7), *The History of the Salvation Army*, 7 vols, London and New York: Nelson, 1947–86

Walker, Pamela J. *Pulling the Devil's Kingdom Down: The Salvation Army in Victorian Britain*, Berkeley: University of California Press, 2001

Three recent books are of considerable value in researching the early history of the Salvation Army. WALKER (2001) is probably the best single volume currently available. It is the only full-length study which emphasizes the gender aspect of the Army, and it is a pioneer in treating the Army as a "neighbourhood religion". Walker also provides a fine discussion of the significance of the Army's theology.

Another excellent study is MURDOCH (1994), which emphasizes the North American antecedents of the Army's revivalism. Murdoch agrees with HORRIDGE (1993) that the Salvation Army failed to make significant inroads in the London slums, despite its popular reputation as being uniquely successful with the urban underclass. It did not succeed in gaining large numbers of adherents until it spread into provincial towns, which already had a long tradition of being friendly to dissent.

Murdoch emphasizes the rigid sectarian discipline within the Salvation Army, which had adopted an imperial, non-democratic structure by the 1880s. This is a fine but critical history of the Salvation Army with accurate and full biographical information on its founders, William Booth and his often overlooked wife, Catherine.

Horridge traces the Salvation Army from its origins, placing it firmly in the context of its Victorian religious and social environment. East London, Manchester, Honiton, Guildford, and Wales are used as case studies. The book is well illustrated, with useful tables, and useful if ugly maps, which probably survive from its origin as a doctoral thesis. The substantial appendices bring together rare and hard-to-find material from a wide range of primary sources. Horridge subjects two basic and often-repeated assumptions about Salvation Army growth to close empirical scrutiny – that it enjoyed unprecedentedly fast growth from 1878 and that it had considerable impact on the urban working class (whereas membership data suggest that the Army floundered until it moved into the provinces). He also studies the backgrounds and careers of officers and converts more generally. The detailed narrative is not always arresting but is reliable and useful as an adjunct to Murdoch. Horridge presents a well-rounded picture of early salvationist history, discussing periods of decline, resignations, low recruitment, and loss of membership as well as periods of rapid growth. This account emphasizes numerical growth and decline as an explanation for policy and theological changes. Horridge's main contribution is his careful analysis of which occupational and social groups were most likely to join, and of the socio-economic backgrounds of officers – who he argues were not converts from the submerged tenth (the destitute urban poor), as the Army liked to suggest, but often former methodist industrial workers. Despite his criticism of the Army's methods and governance, he points out that by 1900 it had attracted a British membership of 100,000, making it second only to the Primitive methodists (200,000) as an organized working-class denomination – an enormous achievement for a 35-year-old organization.

The reader is left with little to choose from in the way of general histories, aside from these works and a few slight popularizations, ordinarily published under the auspices of the Army. The popularizations may be entertaining reading, but their active allegiance to the Army's cause makes them useless for serious study. The one exception is the official Army history, currently in seven volumes by SANDALL, WIGGINS, & COUTTS. This has its uses, if the reader is seeking a general overview of the Salvation Army's activities, especially as an international organization. It does give considerable detail, which may not be available elsewhere, particularly with regard to the Army's international expansion, but the approach is solidly confessional and the work as a whole is essentially uncritical of the Army in all its aspects. It also perpetuates a number of myths, most notably by playing down of the role of Smith in the development of the "Darkest England" campaign. It makes considerably less use of primary sources than the big biographies of William Booth and Catherine Booth.

For those interested in the early years of the Army, the best biographies of William and Catherine Booth give far more detail and are much more revealing in their use of primary sources than the official history of the movement. While ERVINE's biography of William Booth is uncritical and defensive regarding its subject, it is reasonably full and accurate. The large biography of Catherine Booth by her son-in-law F. de L. BOOTH-TUCKER is also, effectively, a history of the Army to 1890, the year of her death. While Booth-Tucker is adoring, he also quotes voluminously from a wide range of sources bearing on the early years of the Army, including some that are no longer available to the researcher. The book is far wider than a simple biography, and it is a useful resource despite its age; a later abridgement is of much less value.

SUSAN MUMM

See also Evangelicalism; Popular Religion; Protestant Dissent

Sancroft, William 1617–1693

Archbishop of Canterbury and nonjuror

D'Oyley, George, *The Life of William Sancroft, Archbishop of Canterbury*, 2 vols, London: John Murray, 1821

Every, George, *The High Church Party, 1688–1718*, London: Society for Promoting Christian Knowledge, 1956

Hawkins, L.M., *Allegiance in Church and State: The Problem of the Nonjurors in the English Revolution*, London: Routledge, 1928

Hutton, W.H., entry on Sancroft in *A Dictionary of English Church History*, edited by S.L. Ollard and Gordon Crosse, London: Mowbray, and Milwaukee: Young Churchman, 1912; 2nd revised edition, London: Mowbray, 1912; 3rd revised edition, edited by S.L. Ollard, Gordon Crosse, and Maurice F. Bond, London: Mowbray, and New York: Morehouse-Gorham, 1948

Straka, Gerald, *Anglican Reaction to the Revolution of 1688*, Madison: State Historical Society of Wisconsin, 1962

Sykes, Norman, *Church and State in England in the XVIIIth Century: The Birkbeck Lectures in Ecclesiastical History*, Cambridge: Cambridge University Press, 1934; Hamden, Connecticut: Archon Books, 1962

Sykes, Norman, *From Sheldon to Secker: Aspects of English Church History, 1660–1768*, Cambridge: Cambridge University Press, 1959

Few archbishops of Canterbury seem to have achieved great historical fame. Thomas Becket and Thomas Cranmer achieved immortality by dying for their beliefs in opposition to the crown, and William Laud will be remembered for creating a vision of the church which captured the support of King Charles I but cost Laud his life at the hands of the puritans and Scots during the Civil Wars. One would think that William Sancroft might also have received considerable scholarly attention by virtue of his leadership in the "seven bishops" case that helped provoke the revolution of 1688–89, and his conscientious refusal to take the oath of allegiance to King William III. Yet despite these impressive gestures, Sancroft seems to have been cast into oblivion. In part, this is because of Sancroft's association with the nonjurors, a group of clergy generally regarded, despite HAWKINS's attempt at rehabilitation, as clinging to a nostalgic and anachronistic lost cause. Nonetheless, Sancroft was a most important figure who deserves more modern treatment than the biography by D'OYLEY of 1821.

For example, HUTTON, in his article on Sancroft in the *Dictionary of English Church History*, published at the beginning of the 20th century, speaks of the archbishop in quite laudatory terms, emphasizing his courage, charity, and integrity. In addition, Hutton provides important information on Sancroft's life before he became a leading churchman after the Restoration.

Some recent historians have also noted Sancroft's significance, especially as it affected the religious aspect of the revolutionary settlement. SYKES, for instance, points out that the archbishop, despite his Tory political inclinations, was a supporter of and a friend to foreign protestants and an advocate of comprehension, having been involved in the unsuccessful attempt to achieve this end in the parliament of Charles II. Later, under James II, Sancroft continued this effort; and, as Sykes notes, the aim of comprehension was referred to in the petition of the seven bishops. Moreover, after the deposition of James II, and after his own refusal to recognize William of Orange, Sancroft continued to pursue a comprehensive solution. The result was the establishment of a commission to present the matter to convocation. In light of the failure of this effort, Sykes deplores the nonjuring schism because it deprived those who attempted comprehension of their leadership at this decisive moment. He saw this as a situation that had a disastrous effect on the Church of England. At the same time Sykes pointed out the important work that Sancroft was involved in concerning the reform of the canon law. Dealing with issues like excommunication, pluralism, and the problem of scandalous clergy, Sancroft formulated a series of changes that would have improved the quality and character of churchmen. This, of course, also failed to happen because of the actions of the nonjurors.

Additional information on Sancroft can also be found in an earlier, but important, study by George EVERY, who goes into great detail about the attempt to achieve comprehension in the wake of the Glorious Revolution, indicating the important role that the archbishop played. At the same time, however, Every indicates the various factors, both internal and external, which prevented that goal from being obtained. He also provides a helpful guide to the archbishop's odyssey as Sancroft sought unsuccessfully to find a way out of an ideological dilemma. This involved supporting a regency and possible efforts at a conditional restoration of the Stuarts. However, as Every notes, Sancroft was not optimistic about the chance of such a resolution and preferred to exhort William of Orange to adhere to the terms of the declaration he had issued on arriving in England. But in the final analysis, Sancroft could not remain as archbishop, because of his failure to recognize William III as king. Thus he entered the ranks of the nonjurors, where he remained until his death in 1693.

Historians have continued to discuss the nonjurors since Hawkins's favourable account. Every pointed out the number of high churchmen who were able to accommodate themselves to the new regime; Sykes criticized their consistency and logic. More recently, STRAKA noted the readiness of many clergy to find a divine sanction for William's accession.

There is, then, much in Sancroft's character and career that should attract the attention of scholars. Certainly, there is a need for an up-to-date study that will do justice to his contribution and significance.

MARC L. SCHWARTZ

See also Charles II; Glorious Revolution; James VII and II

Sander(s), Nicholas *c.1530–1581*

Scholar and catholic polemicist

Clancy, Thomas H., *Papist Pamphleteers: The Allen-Persons Party and the Political Thought of the Counter-Reformation in England, 1572–1615*, Chicago: Loyola University Press, 1964

Holmes, Peter, *Resistance and Compromise: The Political Thought of the Elizabethan Catholics*, Cambridge and New York: Cambridge University Press, 1982

Milward, Peter, *Religious Controversies of the Elizabethan Age: A Survey of Printed Sources*, Lincoln: University of Nebraska Press, and London: Scolar Press, 1977

Pollen, John Hungerford, *The English Catholics in the Reign of Queen Elizabeth: A Study of Their Politics, Civil Life, and Government*, London and New York: Longmans Green, 1920

Sander, Nicholas, *De origine et progressu schismatis Anglicani liber*, Cologne, 1585; translated, as *The Rise and Growth of the Anglican Schism*, with introduction and notes, by David Lewis, London: Burns and Oates, 1877; reprinted, Rockford, Illinois: Tan, 1988

Southern, A.C., *Elizabethan Recusant Prose, 1559–1582: A Historical and Critical Account of the Books of the Catholic Refugees Printed and Published Abroad and at Secret Presses in England Together with an Annotated Bibliography of the Same*, London: Sands, 1950

Veech, Thomas McNevin, *Dr. Nicholas Sanders and the English Reformation 1530–1581*, Louvain: Bureaux du Recueil, Bibliothèque de l'Université, 1935

Warnicke, Retha M., *The Rise and Fall of Anne Boleyn: Family Politics at the Court of Henry VIII*, Cambridge and New York: Cambridge University Press, 1989

Dr Sander, an important English defender of catholicism who was educated at Oxford University, left England in 1559, shortly after the accession of Elizabeth I, whom he subsequently plotted to overthrow. He lived in Rome, Louvain, and Madrid, attended the council of Trent, was proposed for a cardinal's hat, and participated in a catholic expedition to Ireland, where he died in 1581. His most famous work is *De origine et progressu schismatis Anglicani* (*The Rise and Growth of the Anglican Schism*), published posthumously in 1585 by Edward Rishton (who completed it) and perhaps best known for its unflattering portrayal of Anne Boleyn as a lustful, deformed witch who was the child of an illicit union between her eventual husband Henry VIII and her mother Lady Elizabeth Boleyn, and whose own daughter Elizabeth I was the product of Anne's incestuous relationship with her brother. Sander also produced many theological works.

Sander drew sharp criticism from early modern English protestant historians such as William Camden, Peter Heylyn, John Strype, and George Wyatt; and Bishop Gilbert Burnet wrote his famous *History of the Reformation of the Church of England* (1679–1715) specifically to refute Sander's *De origine*. Sander drew fire in the 19th century from J.A. Froude among others and continued to polarize opinion along catholic-protestant lines well into the 20th century, though recent accounts are more dispassionate.

Lewis's introduction to his copiously annotated translation of SANDER recounts the historiographical controversy surrounding the work from a decidedly pro-catholic stance. Both text and commentary must be used with caution, for the editor takes the author's account essentially at face value; however, recent scholarship has shown that Sander got many facts right, and even his more outrageous errors (e.g., regarding Anne) were based upon popular belief, to which they are thus a useful key.

POLLEN, a Jesuit, devotes substantial attention to Sander, drawing partly on his biographical sketch in *English Historical Review*, 6 (1891). Pollen is sympathetic but describes Sander as both a "really great Churchman" and "an extremist", the latter opinion being shared by anti-Jesuit appellants during the archpriest controversy of Elizabeth's last decade.

VEECH, like Lewis and Pollen, carries the catholic imprimatur, so it is no surprise that this is a largely favourable biography. However, Veech does blame Sander for failures of papal diplomacy, allowing family and friends to fall into enemy hands, and other shortcomings. While Veech devotes considerable attention to *De origine*, he argues that Sander's theological works, especially *De visibili monarchia ecclesiae* (1571), are more significant.

SOUTHERN is primarily concerned with Elizabethan recusant prose, which he finds equal in quality to that of contemporary English protestants. Because his work terminates in 1582, he does not discuss *De origine*, focusing instead on Sander's theological works. Crediting Sander with founding the Louvain school of apologetics, he examines several works that Sander produced there. Southern does not really address Sander's theological arguments in *The Supper of Our Lord* (1565), *The Rocke of the Church* (1567), and *A Treatise of the Images of Christ* (1567); rather, he emphasizes the clarity and economy of expression they manifest. Discussing *A Briefe Treatise of Vsurie* (1568), he notes that Anglicans and English recusants shared an antipathy to usury, in contrast to the Calvinists, and suggests that Sander's target was the latter.

CLANCY, another Jesuit, distinguishes Louvainists, including Sander, from the appellants and the party led by William Allen and Robert Persons, concentrating on the last. Nevertheless, in discussing political thought, he links Sander and the Allen-Persons party in desiring "a revolution . . . in the name of ancient rights and conservative values" and particularly in criticizing Elizabeth's regime for fostering heresy, economic distress, clerical marriage, and so on. However, he stresses that Sander was alone in defending the papal bull excommunicating Elizabeth (*Regnans in excelsis*) and that Allen distanced himself from Sander's Irish expedition. Southern credits Sander as one of the earliest defenders of the papal deposing power.

HOLMES emphasizes Sander's role in developing resistance theory with *De visibili monarchia ecclesiae*, though he also briefly discusses *De origine* as an actual act of resistance. Examining the former alongside works by John Leslie and Richard Bristow, he demonstrates that Sander was the first to develop a theoretical justification for catholic resistance to Elizabeth during its initial phase 1569–73 (thereafter catholics for a time drew back from resistance). This work antagonized the Elizabethan regime by defending papal supremacy, chronicling catholic opposition (which helped inspire the "bloody questions" used against priests in the 1580s), and justifying the papal bull of excommunication against the queen. Holmes shows that Sander developed an innovative approach to the limits of royal power, arguing that a monarch acknowledged subordination to the church in both baptism and the coronation.

Naturally, biographers of Anne Boleyn, from Wyatt in the 16th century to Eric Ives in the 20th, have addressed Sander's account. WARNICKE, the most recent scholarly biography, not only discusses Sander in the main body of the text but also includes an appendix, "The Legacy of Nicholas Sander". Warnicke rejects Sander's description of Anne's physical deformities, which some previous scholars have regarded merely as exaggeration (whereby, for example, a mole becomes a wen and a tiny nail on the side of a finger becomes a sixth finger). Warnicke says that it is pure invention and that, in order to prove Anne a witch, Sander drew on the Neoplatonic tradition that inner evil manifests itself in outer deformity.

MILWARD briefly comments on each of Sander's works and places them in the context of ongoing political and theological debate in and about England.

Although the religious controversies in which Sander participated have died down, he himself remains controversial, and the degree to which historians can rely upon *De origine* as a source continues to be debated. However, there is more agreement across denominational lines now about Sander's importance as a polemicist and a theologian and about the caution with which his work must be approached.

WILLIAM B. ROBISON

See also Boleyn; Recusancy and Mission

Schooling: Before Compulsory Education 1300–1870

Aldrich, Richard, *An Introduction to the History of Education*, London: Hodder and Stoughton, 1982

Bagworth, Hazel, "The Changing and Developing Roles of British and Foreign School Society Agents and Inspectors 1826–1870, with particular reference to Lieut. J. Fabian, Reverend J.H. Dobney, and Dr. W. Davis", *History of Education Society Bulletin*, 61 (1998): 15–28

Barnard, Howard Clive, *A History of English Education from 1760*, London: University of London Press, 1961; revised edition, 1969

Bartle, G.F., "The Role of the British and Foreign School Society in the Country Towns of South-East England during the Nineteenth Century", *History of Education Society Bulletin*, 56 (1995): 7–16

Charlton, Kenneth, *Education in Renaissance England*, London: Routledge and Kegan Paul, 1965

Cook, T.G. (editor), *Local Studies and the History of Education*, London: Methuen, 1972

Ferguson, John (editor), *Christianity, Society, and Education: Robert Raikes, Past, Present, and Future*, London: Society for Promoting Christian Knowlede, 1981

Gosden, P.H.J.H. (editor), *How They Were Taught: An Anthology of Contemporary Accounts of Learning and Teaching in England 1800–1950*, Oxford: Blackwell, 1969

Horn, Pamela, *Children's Work and Welfare 1780–1880s*, Basingstoke: Macmillan, 1994; as *Children's Work and Welfare, 1780–1890*, Cambridge and New York: Cambridge University Press, 1955

Hyndman, Michael, *Schools and Schooling in England and Wales: A Documentary History*, London and New York: Harper and Row, 1978

Jewell, Helen M., *Education in Early Modern England*, Basingstoke: Macmillan, and New York: St Martin's Press, 1998

Jones, Gareth Elwyn, *The Education of a Nation*, Cardiff: University of Wales Press, 1997

Lawson, John and Harold Silver, *A Social History of Education in England*, London: Methuen, 1973

Lowe, Roy (editor), *History of Education: Major Themes*, vol. 4, London and New York: Routledge / Falmer, 1992

McClelland, Vincent Alan (editor), *The Churches and Education*, Leicester: History of Education Society, 1984

Maclure, J. Stuart, *Educational Documents: England and Wales 1816–1963*, London: Chapman and Hall, 1965; 5th edition, as *Educational Documents: 1816 to the Present Day*, London and New York: Methuen, 1986

Orme, Nicholas, *Medieval Children*, New Haven, Connecticut: Yale University Press, 2001

Scotland, James, *The History of Scottish Education*, 2 vols, London: University of London Press, 1969

Sylvester, D.W., *Educational Documents, 800–1816*, London: Methuen, 1970

Willis, Richard, "William Ballantyne Hodgson and Educational Interest Groups in Victorian Britain", *History of Education Society Bulletin*, 67 (2001): 41–51

A parent conferred no considerable benefit on his child by bringing him into the world, if he afterwards entirely neglected his culture and education and suffered him to grow up like a mere beast to lead a life useless to others and shameful to himself.

Thus Sir William Blackstone argued, in the 18th century, that the education of the masses was vital to safeguard freedom. The issues raised about the purpose of education and the responsibility for its provision have been discussed since the Middle Ages.

There are several works which have a broad chronological sweep. ALDRICH, in the first three chapters of his book, analyses the role of family, gender, rank, order, and class set against population, investment and consumption, and occupation, maintaining that these issues have not merely influenced the history of education but largely constituted it. (LOWE includes an essay by Marsden examining these issues in the context of the 19th century and challenging the view that schooling reflected a polarization between the upper and lower classes resulting from the lengthy education of the elite and the short elementary education of the lower orders. He analyses views on the appropriateness of different kinds of education for differing levels of society.) LAWSON & SILVER, in their survey of schooling from 1300 to 1870, explore population structure and distribution, particularly changes brought about by the industrial revolution and urbanization after 1850. They argue that throughout the period religious issues, attitudes towards educational philanthropy, and concern for the extent and function of literacy are related to educational developments. The reader can trace the response to the need for education from 1350 to 1870 in Aldrich, who surveys primary education, and stresses the role of the parish priest and the song schools in the medieval period; the development of reading schools, petty schools, and private schools (some free in the 16th century); and the expansion of elementary education through the provision of charity schools in the 17th and 18th centuries. Lawson & Silver provide a more detailed study of the period, with many local examples illustrating dame schools – private-enterprise schools that were often small and badly organized, held in teachers' houses, their existence depending on local demand. SYLVESTER provides a study of the period 1340 to 1816 based on contemporary documents and commentary. The documents on the petty school include illustrations of an ABC primer of 1538 intended to teach children about religion and church services.

Most of the studies under consideration here concentrate on shorter periods. ORME considers the medieval period. He challenges the view that childhood in medieval times was a brutal, unpleasant experience. His research has provided evidence of children's learning to read and complaining about school, and of informal education resulting from games that children played with each other and with adults. CHARLTON writes in detail of education in the 16th century, discussing humanism and its exemplar in Castiglione's *Book of the Courtier* (1528). He considers the value of books, copybooks, and letter-writing material in English. JEWELL examines who is being taught in early modern England, what is being taught, and to what purpose, asking what was achieved in terms of basic literacy and individual attainment. The book includes a useful outline of the development of education in the period. With the introduction of printing into London by William Caxton in 1476, the mass production of books, reasonably cheaply, particularly in English, gave a great incentive to literacy and informal self-education from the 16th century on.

The civil wars led to a re-examination of all aspects of education to ensure that all would make the maximum use of their capacities. Part of this radical thinking stressed the need for formal education for agricultural labourers. The scientific tradition of the 17th century also influenced opinions. FERGUSON's collection examines the response in the 17th century to the need for more formal education. The essays consider the work of Robert Raikes and the Sunday school movement. They not only cover a history of the movement but include an essay on the 18th-century background, a local study of Sunday schools in Stockport as an example of education in an urban area, and a consideration of the Sunday school in 19th-century literature.

McCLELLAND's collection includes two essays which complement Ferguson's studies, considering the factors that promoted mass schooling in the period 1780–1840. The early history of the Society for Promoting Christian Knowledge (SPCK) and its role in promoting charity schools is discussed critically. In the essay "Religion and the Origins of Mass Schooling: The English Sunday School 1780–1840", Dick discusses the existing studies of the Sunday school movement in an attempt to explain the provision of such schools and concludes that "Sunday Schools enabled mass schooling to secure acceptance within the traditionally-minded upper and middle

classes". BARNARD describes the various types of schools that provided some kind of elementary education in the early years of the 19th century. The institutions included dame schools, common day schools, charity schools, schools of industry, and Sunday schools.

The need to increase the provision of popular education in the 19th century led to the work of Andrew Bell (an Anglican) and Joseph Lancaster (a Quaker) in developing the monitorial system, a system of mass production in education. The monitorial schools gave rise to a "religious difficulty" in education and led to the formation of two societies – the National Society for promoting the education of the poor in the principles of the Established Church in England and Wales and the Royal Lancastrian Society (later renamed the British and Foreign School Society). The latter had schools open to pupils of any denomination, although attendance at a place of worship on Sunday was required. BARTLE examines the problems faced by the schools of the British and Foreign School Society. He discusses fees, funding, attendance, and enrolment of teachers and considers their successes and failures. BAGWORTH discusses the changing roles of agents and inspectors of the British and Foreign School Society from 1826 to 1870, arguing that "the importance of this portion of the society's labours can scarcely be overestimated".

COOK includes an essay by Sanderson – "The National and British School Societies in Lancashire, 1803–1830: The Roots of Anglican Supremacy in English Education" – which stresses the role of religion and the conflicts of church and dissent but emphasizes the hostility of both to a state system of education. In his conclusion, Sanderson urges the reader to be aware of the fundamental problem that arises with topographical studies in history: these often reveal developments in the provision of local education which contrast with information given in national reports. Sanderson considers the national policies of the National and British Schools Societies and their modification and interpretation by the local communities of Lancashire.

HYNDMAN has an interesting introduction, examining attitudes about education in the 18th and 19th centuries, followed by a chapter illustrated by extracts from contemporary documents on the societies and their schools between 1800 and 1861. He includes an assessment of the work of individual pioneers, including Robert Owen. GOSDEN, using contemporary documents, describes the condition of elementary schools and the teaching methods used in the classroom before 1862. He then examines the increasing involvement of the state in the provision of elementary education through the Revised Code of 1862. By imposing standards nationally, the government hoped to avoid a breakdown of society under the strain of developing urbanization. HORN examines changes in the employment of children as they affected education from 1780 to 1890. Legislation controlling the mining and textile industries demonstrated the government's claim to authority over children, which often conflicted with that of the parents.

While the state exerted influence on educational developments, other pressure groups also brought about changes. WILLIS looks at the work of four groups in Victorian Britain: (1) the Lancashire Public School Association, (2) the College of Preceptors, (3) the Scholastic Registration Association and the National Union of Elementary Teachers, and (4) the Association for the Promotion of Social Science. He examines William

Hodgson's support for these societies, describing Hodgson's desire to provide education for needy children and his interest in the "ragged school" movement and the education of workhouse and factory children. Hodgson advocated better education for women and girls, and he encouraged the "spiritual enlightenment, union, [and] cohesion" of the teaching profession.

MACLURE illustrates the increasing involvement of the government in providing education following the creation of the Committee of Council for Education in 1839. The appointment of commissioners to inquire into the state of popular education in 1858 led to recommendations to improve education. Presented through documents on the Newcastle Commission are the arguments for and against state aid, payment by results, attendance and compulsion, and the religious control of schools.

In 1870 W.E. Forster posed the question, "How can we cover the country with good schools?" His speech, included in Maclure, summarizes the factors that he had to consider in shaping the Education Act of 1870. Lawson & Silver discuss the problems faced by Forster in 1870, particularly the shift in support from voluntarist approaches to the programme of the National Education League for compulsory, free, and unsectarian schools maintained from local rates and inspected by government, following the Reform Act of 1867 which enfranchised working men in towns. The Education Act of 1870 incurred opposition and criticism, but the creation of school boards did eventually "fill the gaps" and increase the number of school places. Lord Sandon's Act of 1876 set up school attendance committees in districts where there were no school boards. The act placed on parents the responsibility for ensuring that their children received "efficient elementary instruction in reading, writing, and arithmetic".

Many of the surveys of educational history in the long period between the Middle Ages and 1870 concentrate on England and Wales. SCOTLAND's two-volume study discusses Scottish education; JONES considers the essential role of Welsh education in upholding Welsh culture and society. (Jones also considers the significance of the Report of the Commissioners of Inquiry into the State of Education in Wales in 1847, and its influence on Kay Shuttleworth and English education.)

EVELYN E. COWIE

Schooling: Compulsory 19th and 20th centuries

Mangan, J.A. (editor), *A Significant Social Revolution: Cross-Cultural Aspects of the Evolution of Compulsory Education*, London and Portland, Oregon: Woburn Press, 1994

Rubinstein, David, *School Attendance in London, 1870–1904: A Social History*, Hull, Tyne, and Wear: University of Hull, and New York: Kelley, 1969

Silver, Harold, *Education as History: Interpreting Nineteenth- and Twentieth-Century Education*, London and New York: Methuen, 1983

Simon, Brian, *Education and the Labour Movement, 1870–1920*, London: Lawrence and Wishart, 1965

Simon, Brian, *Education and the Social Order, 1940–1990*, London: Lawrence and Wishart, and New York: St Martin's Press, 1991

Stephens, W.B., *Education in Britain, 1750–1914*, London; Macmillan, and New York: St Martin's Press, 1998

Sutherland, Gillian, *Policy-Making in Elementary Education, 1870–1895*, London: Oxford University Press, 1973

Writing in 1857, Horace Mann referred to "the social wretchedness which blights all educational promise". His analysis of the failure of working-class parents to send their children to the growing number of elementary schools highlights the problems faced by the advocates of compulsory education. The conflict between school attendance and child labour and the need for children's wages, however small, remained a dominant issue in the provision of education throughout the 19th century. SUTHERLAND, in her study of policymaking in 1870–95, demonstrates the dependence and progress of educational legislation on the regulation and control of child labour.

Throughout the 19th century compulsory schooling was a controversial issue. Joseph Lancaster considered it unacceptable to an Englishman, with his "spirit breathing the language of independence". Andrew Bell argued that the practice of universal compulsion "does not admit of being universally adopted, and if it did, would not be productive of general benefit".

SILVER traces the attempts to limit child labour and the principle of education for factory children from the Health and Morals of Apprentices Act of 1802. In his chapter "Ideology and the Factory Child" he examines attitudes towards half-time education as a solution to the problem of losing children's earnings. For many parents the question was "education on the half-time plan or no education at all".

STEPHENS examines the effect from the 1830s of legislation designed to restrict excessive hours of work for the very young, women, and children, and the impact it had on the provision of education. Compulsory education is distinct from compulsory schooling, since it can be obtained outside the school. Stephens considers the education available to working-class children in England: dame schools, common schools, voluntary schools promoted by the denominations, Sunday schools, and ragged schools (free schools for poor children). SIMON in *Education and the Labour Movement, 1870–1920* discusses popular education and working-class attitudes towards its provision and use. The preoccupation of trade union leaders with the right to education and the need for free compulsory education are discussed in detail together with the reactions of members of the labour movement towards the emergence of class-based systems of education.

In 1861 the Newcastle Commission examined the state of popular education. Silver analyses the change in the strongly held views on compulsory school attendance expressed by the commission that Englishmen would never permit state compulsion such as existed in Germany because it would be too "great a shock to our educational system", and the "metamorphosis of opinion between 1870 and 1880". Sutherland examines the role of politicians in changing public opinion and explores the confused ideas of the Liberal Party on the need for universal direct compulsion if elementary education was provided nationally.

The Education Act of 1870 provided the administrative machinery to increase the provision of school places in England and Wales. Popularly elected school boards could be set up to remedy deficiencies. The act failed to provide for compulsory attendance at school, free school places, or a revised elementary school curriculum, although employers in an increasingly technological and industrial society needed a literate and skilled workforce. The act of 1870 gave school boards the right to demand attendance in their schools, and in 1876 this right was extended to school attendance committees in areas where no school board existed. RUBINSTEIN examines the creation of the London School Board and the tasks its members faced in providing some 100,000 school places and enforcing school attendance. Rubinstein argues that the London School Board has received too little attention from historians, and his detailed study appraises the educational needs of children in London and the social and political problems of Londoners, particularly the poorer groups of the working class.

The permissive powers of compulsion of the school boards and attendance committees were ended by the Education Act of 1880. Children were required to attend school until the age of 10 years, when they could receive an education certificate allowing them to leave. Sutherland, in his section "The Learning Process 1880–1888", considers the problem faced after 1880 by local authorities trying to enforce the act, the supportive role of the Department of Education, and the gradual increase in the numbers of children attending school.

Following the act, the Department of Education established a Code Committee; as a result, the curriculum of the elementary schools was broadened. For the parents of pupils at both voluntary and board schools, the payment of school fees was a burden. The Education Act of 1891 resolved the problem by allowing voluntary and board schools to admit pupils free and receive a grant from the government. Sutherland discusses the opposition of the department to free education, and the political calculations which brought a change of policy. Compulsory, free education to the age of 10 led to improvements in literary skills, and the issue of raising the age of leaving school and the future of part-time education, at a time when the demand for child labour was declining, became significant.

SIMON, in *Education and the Social Order, 1940–1990*, discusses the issue of raising the age of leaving school, from 1870 on, analysing it against a background of social and political change and examining pressure groups such as the Trades Union Congress. The age was raised to 12 in 1899. The Education Act of 1918 ended the half-time system and raised the age to 14. The age was raised to 15 in 1947 and to 16 in 1972.

MANGAN provides a valuable international perspective on the evolution of compulsory education, considering educational, economic, cultural, and political issues.

EVELYN E. COWIE

See also Fisher, H.A.L.

Schooling: Medieval

Leach, Arthur F., *English Schools at the Reformation, 1546–1548*, London: Constable, 1896
Leach, Arthur F., *The Schools of Mediaeval England*, New York: Macmillan, and London: Methuen, 1915
McMahon, Clara P., *Education in Fifteenth-Century England*, Baltimore, Maryland: Johns Hopkins University Press, 1947
Miner, John N., *The Grammar Schools of Medieval England: A.F. Leach in Historiographical Perspective*, Montreal and Kingston, Ontario: McGill-Queen's University Press, 1990
Moran, Jo Ann Hoeppner, *The Growth of English Schooling, 1340–1548: Learning, Literacy, and Laicization in a Pre-Reformation York Diocese*, Princeton, New Jersey: Princeton University Press, 1985
Orme, Nicholas, *English Schools in the Middle Ages*, London: Methuen, 1973
Orme, Nicholas, *Education in the West of England, 1066–1548: Cornwall, Devon, Dorset, Gloucestershire, Somerset, Wiltshire*, Exeter: University of Exeter, 1976
Orme, Nicholas, *Education and Society in Medieval and Renaissance England*, London and Ronceverte, West Virginia: Hambledon Press, 1989
Parry, A.W., *Education in England in the Middle Ages*, London: Clive, 1920; reprinted, New York: AMS Press, 1975
Simon, Joan, *Education and Society in Tudor England*, Cambridge: Cambridge University Press, 1966

Just before the turn of the 20th century, many details related to the history of medieval schooling remained shrouded in uncertainty. Since that time, scholars have tried to discern the details of this important aspect of medieval society. This scholarly endeavour developed in stages. First, a framework needed to be established. Then, the research turned to establishing details, focusing on specific eras and various historical techniques. Finally, these approaches were integrated to give an increasingly clearer picture.

LEACH pioneered the modern study of medieval English education. In *The Schools of Mediaeval England* (1915), he analysed educational trends, dismissed long-held assumptions, and attempted to place ecclesiastical and secular influences over education in their proper perspective. Unlike most of the scholars following him, Leach examined the whole of medieval English educational history from its Anglo-Saxon beginnings to the reign of Edward VI. Despite his own over-broad assumptions and missteps, his work – both in this book and in his earlier study *English Schools at the Reformation* (1896) – spurred on this area of scholarship.

Just five years after *The Schools of Mediaeval England*, PARRY began to scrutinize Leach's findings, adding more detail to this area of scholarship. In *Education in England in the Middle Ages* (1920) he too covered the entire period, describing a three-step or three-stage process: Anglo-Saxon, church control, and secular control. In the second stage, he studied monastic education, curriculum, and cathedral schools in addition to the more recent grammar and song schools. His analysis of education in the later medieval period considered the social factors behind the growing laicization of schools: the necessity of literacy for the nobility, the Black Death, lollardy, and the Reformation. In this work, Parry took a broad view and began to theorize about how social factors affected schooling.

A generation later, McMAHON focused on a particular period of educational activity rather than offering an overall survey. She analysed the importance of the traditional elements of education, such as the philosophers and scholasticism, stressing the growing need for education in English society. She also analysed educational trends in different social subgroups, such as chivalric education for boys and girls, and practical education. She gave greater attention to distinct types of schools as well as types of lay foundations. (She discussed the chantry schools in depth, for example.) McMahon's study gave credence to studying specific centuries and the increasing emphasis of social factors in educational development.

SIMON opposed earlier scholarship. In the middle to late 1960s, various scholars began to take apart Leach's original findings and sought to focus on specific trends rather than sweeping processes. Thus Simon, in her preface, takes exception to Leach's point concerning the "sweeping away of schools" during the Reformation, asserting that the 16th century was a time of renewal for the English educational system, not, as her predecessor had asserted, its ending. Like McMahon, Simon produced a concentrated study of one period, but Simon relegated 15th-century educational processes, including the struggle over secular versus ecclesiastical control of education, to the background. Instead, Simon's work focused on the Reformation as the second starting-point for English education, pondering the effect of the relationship between the state and education both before and after 1547. Simon also illuminated the respective policies and legacies of the later Tudor monarchs, culminating in the "triumph of the vernacular".

Starting in the early 1970s, ORME re-examined the history of medieval English education and contributed several elements of his own. In *English Schools in the Middle Ages* (1973) he assessed the strengths and weaknesses of earlier scholarship. Like Leach's *Mediaeval Schools*, Orme's work surveyed the entire evolution of medieval English education. However, Orme focused on how people were educated and on forces affecting the educational process. In his analysis he divided the subject into several parts: education between 1100 and 1400; education between 1400 and 1530; religious orders and education; and learning during the reigns of Henry VIII, Edward VI, and Elizabeth I. With regard to grammar schools, Orme looked at the founding institutions, curricula, schoolmasters, and students. He inserted local history into his study by including lesser-known schools. His next book, *Education in the West of England, 1066–1548: Cornwall, Devon, Dorset, Gloucestershire, Somerset, Wiltshire*, also emphasized local history as an element of educational history. Orme charted two intertwined courses, detailing both education and the role of the educational process in these counties. He looked at the development, evolution, and increasing specialization of the educational process, whether in the old "general school", which later became the grammar school, or in the relationship between individual masters and pupils – a relationship that attracted others to the learning process, forming the first classes. In addition, Orme followed Simon in stressing the importance of humanism to educational procedures. Finally, in *Education and Society in Medieval and Renaissance England*, Orme applied this technique to still other schools. More importantly, however, he offered his readers viewpoints from the people of that period, such as Langland and Shakespeare, as well as greater detail on aspects of individual schools. In his works, Orme took the rough processes of his earliest counterparts, added the periodization and the exact trends of Simon and McMahon, and started to humanize all this by a liberal application of the local-history model.

MORAN, like her predecessors, provided a periodized analysis of education. First, she adopted Leach's and Orme's emphasis on medieval rather than Renaissance education. Then, after a comprehensive discussion of earlier studies and trends, she looked at local records for mention of grammar schools before the 16th century. She emphasized interconnectivity in the educational process. As she noted, the expanding educational resources in later medieval England provided the groundwork for the later Reformation. She asserted that the Reformation had been spurred by a need for more literacy among clerics as well as laypeople's increasing need to be literate – not the other way around. Finally, her look at people's secular reading added another dimension to this study.

MINER contributed to this field in three ways. First, he charted Leach's research and developing ideas between 1890 and 1915. Then, he reprised the reviews of Leach's work that were written after Leach's death. Finally, in his historiographical essay, he added Moran's and Orme's works to this perspective. In short, Miner developed the historiographical tradition and provided a good starting-point and signature for future endeavours.

DAVID J. DUNCAN

See also Literacy: Before Printing

Scientific Revolution and the Royal Society from 17th century

Butterfield, Herbert, *The Origins of Modern Science, 1300–1800*, London: Bell, 1949; New York: Macmillan, 1951; revised edition, London: Bell, and New York: Macmillan, 1957

Cohen, H. Floris, *The Scientific Revolution: A Historiographical Inquiry*, Chicago: University of Chicago Press, 1994

Gascoigne, John, *Science in the Service of Empire: Joseph Banks, the British State, and the Uses of Science in the Age of Revolution*, Cambridge and New York: Cambridge University Press, 1998

Golinski, Jan, *Science as Public Culture: Chemistry and Enlightenment in Britain, 1760–1820*, Cambridge and New York: Cambridge University Press, 1992

Hall, A. Rupert, *From Galileo to Newton, 1630–1720*, London: Collins, and New York: Harper and Row, 1963

Hall, A. Rupert, *The Scientific Revolution, 1500–1800: The Formation of the Modern Scientific Attitude*, London and New York: Longmans Green, 1954; 3rd revised edition, as *The Revolution in Science, 1500–1750*, London and New York: Longman, 1983

Hall, Marie Boas, *Promoting Experimental Learning: Experiment and the Royal Society, 1660–1727*, Cambridge and New York: Cambridge University Press, 1991

Hunter, Michael, *Science and Society in Restoration England*, Cambridge and New York: Cambridge University Press, 1981

Hunter, Michael, *The Royal Society and Its Fellows, 1660–1700: The Morphology of an Early Scientific Institution*, Chalfont St Giles, Buckinghamshire: British Society for the History of Science, 1982; reprinted with corrections, 1985

Hunter, Michael, *Establishing the New Science: The Experience of the Early Royal Society*, Woodbridge, Suffolk; and Wolfeboro, New Hampshire: Boydell, 1989

Hunter, Michael, *Science and the Shape of Orthodoxy: Intellectual Change in Late Seventeenth-Century Britain*, Woodbridge, Suffolk; and Rochester, New York: Boydell, 1995

Isis Current Bibliography of the History of Science and Its Cultural Influences (annual), Chicago: Chicago University Press for History of Science Society, yearly

Merton, Robert, *Science, Technology, and Society in Seventeenth-Century England*, New York: Harper and Row, 1970; reprinted with new introduction by the author, Brighton, Sussex: Harvester Press, and Atlantic Highlands, New Jersey: Humanities Press, 1978

Miller, David P., " 'Into the Valley of Darkness': Reflections on the Royal Society in the Eighteenth Century", *History of Science*, 27/76 (1989): 155–66

Osler, Margaret (editor), *Rethinking the Scientific Revolution*, Cambridge and New York: Cambridge University Press, 2000

Rousseau, George and David Haycock, "Voices Calling for Reform: The Royal Society in the Mid-18th Century, Martin Folkes, John Hill, and William Stukeley", *History of Science*, 37 (1999): 377–406

Sargent, Rose-Mary, *The Diffident Naturalist: Robert Boyle and the Philosophy of Experiment*, Chicago: University of Chicago Press, 1995

Schaffer, Simon, "Natural Philosophy and Public Spectacle in the Eighteenth Century", *History of Science*, 21 (1983): 1–43

Schaffer, Simon, "Priestley and the Politics of Spirit" in *Science, Medicine, and Dissent: Joseph Priestley (1733–1804)*, edited by Robert Anderson and Christopher Lawrence, London: Wellcome Trust and the Science Museum, 1987

Schaffer, Simon, "Glass Works: Newton's Prisms and the Uses of Experiment" in *The Uses of Experiment: Studies in the Natural Sciences*, edited by David Gooding, Trevor Pinch, and Simon Schaffer, Cambridge and New York: Cambridge University Press, 1989

Schaffer, Simon, "The Consuming Flame: Electrical Showmen and Tory Mystics in the World of Goods" in *Consumption and the World of Goods*, edited by John Brewer and Roy Porter, London and New York: Routledge, 1993

Shapin, Steven, *A Social History of Truth: Civility and Science in Seventeenth-Century England*, Chicago: University of Chicago Press, 1994

Shapin, Steven and Simon Schaffer, *Leviathan and the Air Pump: Hobbes, Boyle, and the Experimental Life, Including a Translation of Thomas Hobbes, Dialogus physicus de natura aeris, by Simon Schaffer*, Princeton, New Jersey: Princeton University Press, 1985

Sorrenson, Richard (editor), "Did the Royal Society Matter in the Eighteenth Century?" special issue, *British Journal for the History of Science*, 32/2 (1999); includes: Larry Stewart, "Other Centres of Calculation, or, Where the Royal Society Didn't Count: Commerce, Coffee Houses, and Natural Philosophy in Early Modern London"; Andrea Rusnock, "Correspondence Networks and the Royal Society, 1700–1750"; John Gascoigne, "The Royal Society and the Emergence of Science as an Instrument of State Policy"; David Miller, "The Usefulness of Natural Philosophy: The Royal Society and the Culture of Practical Utility in the Later 18th Century"

Stewart, Larry, *The Rise of Public Science: Rhetoric, Technology, and Natural Philosophy in Newtonian Britain, 1660–1750*, Cambridge and New York: Cambridge University Press, 1992

Webster, Charles, *The Great Instauration: Science, Medicine, and Reform, 1626–1660*, London: Duckworth, 1975; New York: Holmes and Meier, 1976

Westfall, Richard S., *Never at Rest: A Biography of Isaac Newton*, Cambridge and New York: Cambridge University Press, 1980; abridged as *The Life of Isaac Newton*, Cambridge and New York: Cambridge University Press, 1993

The title of this entry requires an opening disclaimer of what one commentator has called "the sceptred-isle version of the scientific revolution". The issues raised by the concept in its entirety obviously dwarf any such particular appropriation. Nevertheless there are more valid reasons than specious patriotism for narrowing the focus. From whatever standpoint the scientific revolution is viewed in the "great tradition" of debate about defining philosophical issues which opens COHEN's comprehensive investigation of the history of science as a discipline – plural continuity or radical break marked by the mechanization and mathematization of nature; idealization and paradigmatic achievement of precision, but *per contra* the differing roles of experiment in the Baconian and classical sciences; therefore whether the revolution comprehensively overthrew all previous thought about nature or was specific to cosmology and mechanics however much it affected other fields incidentally – the circumstances of natural philosophy in Restoration England constituted a crucial conjuncture in the history of early modern natural knowledge.

Three points of entry lead from Cohen's "great tradition" to the English situation. BUTTERFIELD gave the initial concept of the scientific revolution its currency among English-speaking historians at large. In the sequence of more detailed works by A. Rupert HALL and Marie Boas HALL on its internal characteristics, the transformation was spread out into something with many origins and no single chain of causes which nevertheless cohered in the cumulative uniqueness of emerging rationalism. In a different mode, the Weberian connection made by MERTON between science and puritanism has been taken up particularly by Marxist general historians to support an "English revolution" in which radical protestantism, though itself defeated in the reactionary aftermath, acted as the vehicle for the capitalist overthrow of feudalism. A good deal of ink has been spilled on the controversy over the "Merton thesis", much of it on what exactly was meant by puritanism and therefore – this being a protean appellation – who was or was not a puritan and in either case when. The uninitiated reader may be forgiven for finding not a little of this redolent of Mark Twain on what the future will know about subjects on which research continues to cast much darkness. Nevertheless, the connections between religious and scientific developments cannot be simply set anachronistically aside, any more than they can be reduced to a single formula. Both the enquiry itself and its results are therefore central.

For the first phases of how the scientific revolution was received in England, the most conspicuous result, although its profuse detail undermines Merton's specifically puritan hypothesis, is WEBSTER's recovery of the links between the original Baconian ideal, inspired by millenial protestantism, of a restored knowledge of the natural world, and the broader impulse towards comprehensive material and social reform during the interregnum, inspired particularly by the influence and associates of Samuel Hartlib.

HUNTER's initial study (1982) of the early Royal Society and of Restoration science more generally seeks to balance the intensive work of Webster and others on the interregnum by accounting for the "equal success" of science "before and after 1660". In arriving at a true picture of the Royal Society and its context, Hunter directs his attention against exaggerations and easy generalizations, especially regarding (1) the impact of Baconianism; (2) the effect of projected scientific utility on state policy, mercantile initiative, and the economy at large; and (3) the apparently rapid transition to latitudinarian and Newtonian stability in church and state, based on the synthesis of natural and revealed knowledge expressed from 1692 onwards in the Boyle lectures. As a formal institution, the Royal Society which emerges from these corrections is a good deal less obviously imposing, less cohesive, and more heterogeneous in its membership and outlook than either its title or its earliest aspirations may seem to suggest. It was also less than universally accepted or respected, not only among the learned, but also among the gentlemen virtuosi who, rather than mercantile interests, made up most of the late 17th-century scientific community. In the effective absence of any similar previous organization, the Royal Society had to learn by doing what its effective role could be and how to go about fulfilling it; and that took time. There is, in other words, a considerable element of historical illusion by back-projection from the society's Newtonian and post-Newtonian prestige about the usual depiction of its early prominence.

This is carried further in Hunter's edited collections as well as in his own later writing: not only on the Royal Society, but even more so on its most prominent early Fellow, Robert Boyle. The particular concern in this case is the account of the social origins of modern science put forward by SHAPIN & SCHAFFER. According to these authors, the potentially disruptive side-effects of the rapid supersession of Aristotelian natural philosophy by differing varieties of corpuscularian mechanism in the middle decades of the century were brought quickly within the figurative confines of the "House of Experiment". There, they could be controlled and productively harnessed by a new breed of experimentalist, of which Boyle was the prototype and chief instigator, operating according to rules of procedure and decorum which constituted a social technology for the witnessed making and communication of probabilistic facts. On the providentially undergirded authority of such evidence, religious, political, and social order could be securely rebuilt after the turmoil of the civil wars. This argument, whose social constructionism strikes not only at the core of present debate about the scientific revolution but, implicitly, at the claims of scientific objectivity itself, is criticized in general terms in Cohen's third chapter, and more particularly by SARGENT for

its foreshortening of Boyle's own epistemological and ontological concerns. It also postpones, or only obliquely addresses, the relationship between Boyle's experimentalism and the "mathematical way" of Newton, best treated in WESTFALL, and thus the unresolved (and unresolvable) metaphysical and theological issues which continued to dog the new science long after its appearance.

These issues are now the subject of an important collection of essays edited by OSLER. Nevertheless, Shapin & Schaeffer offer a powerful heuristic means of explaining the relationship between the continued momentum of the revolution and the wider contingencies which affected its course. By showing how a conflation of truth and gentility in the 17th century provided the cultural matrix necessary for the development of social trust in experimental knowledge, SHAPIN ties the revolution's form in far-reaching ways to the history of manners and the transition to civil politeness. On the other hand, SCHAFFER's many articles, of which only the more general are listed here (see further in *Isis*), elucidate and contextualize the actual development of experimental practice and instrumentation. They also establish public demonstration as not just a sideline left to popularizers, but a vital condition of the reception of experimental natural knowledge in society at large during the following century, and as therefore central to its pursuit.

If Schaffer shows both the conservative and the potentially subversive aspects of this process, STEWART shows fully how "public science" established itself as an essential constituent of an entrepreneurial but still traditional-minded society in which politeness and utility were joined in improvement, during the 50 years after the convergence of the classical and Baconian traditions in Newton's *Opticks* of 1704. GOLINSKI carries the same general themes forward to the absorption, during the early 19th century, of what Butterfield had called the "delayed" scientific revolution in chemistry. In the course of this, the focus moves beyond the confines of the original "House of Experiment" to the relationship between the scientific revolution and the history of technological invention and development. This, however, should not be taken to imply that the Royal Society retreated from "cutting-edge" discovery into complacent fashionability – a notion which used to be invoked to explain the apparent loss of forward momentum in basic science after Newton and the hundred-year lag between the scientific revolution and the delayed arrival of science-based industrial innovation. The account of 18th-century society now being mapped out in MILLER, ROUSSEAU & HAYCOCK, and SORRENSON suggests rather that once again it was learning new roles by doing. As it did so, it continued to be strategically important, not only, as GASCOIGNE shows, in the evolution of state and empire, but also in legitimizing, and therefore shaping, the developing culture of invention which began to transform the country from the 1760s onwards.

JOHN MONEY

See also Boyle; Natural Philosophy; Newton; Royal Academy; Royal Society of London

Scotland, Early Medieval

see **Pictland and Dalriada; Picts and Scots**

Scotland, Early Modern: General Surveys

Allan, David, *Virtue, Learning, and the Scottish Enlightenment: Ideas of Scholarship in Early Modern History*, Edinburgh: Edinburgh University Press, 1993

Brown, Keith M., *Kingdom or Province? Scotland and the Regal Union, 1603–1715*, New York: St Martin's Press, and London: Macmillan, 1992

Daiches, David, Peter Jones, and Jean Jones (editors), *A Hotbed of Genius: The Scottish Enlightenment, 1730–1790*, Edinburgh: Edinburgh University Press, 1986

Gibson, A.J.S. and T.C. Smout, *Prices, Food, and Wages in Scotland, 1550–1780*, Cambridge and New York: Cambridge University Press, 1995

Goodare, Julian, *State and Society in Early Modern Scotland*, Oxford and New York: Oxford University Press, 1999

Houston, R.A., *Social Change in the Age of Enlightenment: Edinburgh, 1660–1760*, Oxford: Clarendon Press, and New York: Oxford University Press, 1994

Houston, R.A. and I.D. Whyte (editors), *Scottish Society: 1500–1800*, Cambridge and New York: Cambridge University Press, 1989

Macinnes, Allan I., *Clanship, Commerce, and the House of Stuart, 1603–1788*, East Linton, East Lothian: Tuckwell Press, 1996

Maclean, Fitzroy, *Highlanders: A History of the Clans of Scotland*, London: Adelphi, 1995; as *Highlanders: A History of the Scottish Clans*, New York: Viking Penguin, 1995

Mason, Roger A., *Kingship and the Commonweal: Political Thought in Renaissance and Reformation Scotland*, East Linton, East Lothian: Tuckwell Press, 1998

Mitchison, Rosalind, *Lordship to Patronage: Scotland 1603–1745*, London and Baltimore, Maryland: Arnold, 1983; Edinburgh: Edinburgh University Press, 1990

Mitchison, Rosalind and Leah Leneman, *Sexuality and Social Control: Scotland, 1660–1780*, Oxford and Cambridge, Massachusetts: Blackwell, 1989; revised edition, as *Girls in Trouble: Sexuality and Social Control in Rural Scotland, 1660–1780*, Edinburgh: Scottish Cultural Press, 1998

Sher, Richard B., *Church and University in the Scottish Enlightenment: The Moderate Literati of Edinburgh*, Princeton, New Jersey: Princeton University Press, and Edinburgh: Edinburgh University Press, 1985

Symonds, Deborah A., *Weep Not for Me: Women, Ballads, and Infanticide in Early Modern Scotland*, University Park: Pennsylvania State University Press, 1997

Early modern Scotland has given rise to a particularly rich body of historical study, ranging from very broad and inclusive works to narrowly focused and detailed analyses of specific topics. As with English history, Scottish historians of the early modern period focus their research on society, the economy, and politics, but they have the additional challenge of examining the impact of Scotland's relationship with England during a period that saw the growth of the nation-state, its incorporation into the English state, and its subsequent dissolution as an independent political entity. The ramifications of these events echo throughout early modern Scottish history, regardless of any intent to address – or ignore – them. They are fundamental not only to Scotland's history but also to the emerging "British" history that followed in their wake.

The best place to start is usually at the beginning, and for modern scholarship on the period, MITCHISON's concise history (1983) of Scotland, from the union of the crowns under James VI to the union of parliaments, is a very good if necessarily superficial beginning. Arguing that the union of Scotland and England has typically distorted Scottish history by prompting continual comparisons between the two countries, Mitchison tries instead to place Scotland in a European context, emphasizing links and similarities with other European countries. Drawing on political, constitutional, religious, economic, and social studies, Mitchison describes the growing bonds between England and Scotland, beginning with the succession of James VI and culminating in the Act of Union in 1707. Although the analysis suffers from space constraints, this text is a readable introduction to broad themes of early modern Scottish historiography.

Although political history is both a relevant and a popular topic for historians of early modern Scotland, the people receive their due in a variety of social and cultural studies. One relatively early, but still important, series of essays is HOUSTON & WHYTE's edited volume. Admitting that the collection represents preliminary research, they seek to present topics that go beyond the three interpretive models of Scottish history – peripheral, romantic, and contextual – and instead view the country in comparison with other European nations. The essays cover a wide range of subjects, from diet to population mobility to the role of women in Scottish society, and while not all are equally profound, they are informative and extensively researched, providing an excellent starting-point for further research and debate. The concluding essay by Keith Wrightson notes the need for additional research and suggests that there is some benefit in thinking of Scottish history with an awareness of its "shared identity of the British past".

Following his own lead, HOUSTON (1994) offers a painstakingly researched urban history that he hopes will serve as a model for further study of other urban areas, with an eventual goal of a collection that could serve as the basis for a synthesized history of Scottish urban society. His comprehensive study of Edinburgh between 1660 and 1760 provides intricate details on the transformation of urban life. More broadly, he explores the relationship between changes in social attitudes and values and the development of Enlightenment philosophies. The chapters are more thematic than progressive, although Houston does attempt to find common elements between them. The first chapter deals with Edinburgh's social structure, and the factors that played a role in the changes it underwent in the late 17th and early 18th centuries. The following chapters look at the impact of those changes on the city's physical space; its value systems; its attitudes towards the poor; and the function of public protest, politics, and economics. Throughout, he shows that the most important change was a breakdown of the community egalitarianism of earlier centuries. Social status became associated with authority, lifestyle, wealth, and belief, and class increasingly divided society. Mobility and authority were the prerogative of the wealthy, and led to the institutionalization of charity and the breakdown of consensus in public protest.

Moving from the city to the country, MITCHISON & LENEMAN's work (1989, revised 1998) seeks to measure and evaluate social responses to sexuality in non-urban areas of Scotland over the 120-year period from 1660 to 1780. Through extensive investigation into parish records, Mitchison & Leneman discovered that the primary engine of social control was the Church of Scotland, which had more than a little success in its efforts to regulate moral and social behaviour. Acting as the conscience of the people, the church worked to ferret out irregular marriages that promoted fornication, expose and punish parents of illegitimate children, and impose rigid standards on an often resisting populace.

In a similar vein, but using entirely different methods, SYMONDS looks at the issue of infanticide in Scotland from the late 17th century on. Examining a fascinating combination of source material – ballads, court records, personal memoirs, and a novel by Sir Walter Scott – Symonds suggests that infanticide, a transgression of social mores that had always existed, was made visible by the passage in 1690 of a draconian act regarding child murder. Over the course of the century, shifting attitudes towards women created the perception that, as a sex, they were incapable of child murder, rendering the existing law essentially academic. Symond argues that although the male-dominated court system rejected the idea of infanticide, Scottish women continued to accept and acknowledge its reality. Though this book suffers from an overuse of broad generalizations unsupported by fact, it offers many avenues for further research.

Another aspect of social control is economic, as GIBSON & SMOUT show in their study of prices. Offered largely as a source document for historians, this text nonetheless provides a view into the economic experiences of the average Scot in the early modern period. In addition to collections of prices presented and arranged in tables and graphs, the authors provide a chapter on the regulation of prices in the burghs, a survey of food consumption, and an analysis of the fiar system, which determined prevailing prices for grains, meal, and animal products. Although they respect the significance of long-term price changes, they are more interested in the impact of short-term price fluctuations on the welfare of the Scottish people. Overall, this text is a complex but extremely useful collection that offers a wealth of data for continuing research into the lives of the people in 16th- and 17th-century Scotland.

Moving from society to politics, GOODARE's monograph is intended to provide an overview of the nature of Scottish state building in the 16th and 17th centuries. Goodare begins with an explanation of sovereignty and absolutism, arguing that absolutism is a process, not a product – a position that many contest, particularly in regard to Scotland. Regardless, he continues to find absolutist tendencies in the Scottish court in its relationship to the kirk, the borders and Highlands, and its nobles and clients, at least until the middle of the 17th century as Scotland and England grew more closely together. While many points of Goodare's thesis are debatable, his work still provides a welcome summary of the recent scholarship in this area.

BROWN analyses Scottish political history from 1603 to 1707. Eager to offer a readable and accessible text, he dispenses with references in favour of an extensive bibliography and reading list. The central theme of the book is that there was little interest in union in Scotland before 1707. The political and economic instability of absentee governance by the Stuart kings created a succession of crises that eventually forced the country to accede to union with England. Brown illustrates his thesis with chapters on economics, the growth of the covenanting movement, the exclusion crisis of 1679–81, and the decline in trade with Europe and England. The narrative is readable, and the text provides a good introduction to 17th-century Scottish history from a Scottish perspective.

MASON's collection of essays represents more than a decade of research into the political thought and culture of Renaissance and Reformation Scotland. An important survey of the history of the period, the essays include detailed studies of the writings of John Mair, John Knox, George Buchanan, and James VI and I, along with broader analytical studies of the Scottish political community during an era of great change. Though the subject is very different, Mason's essays, like Houston & Whyte's collection, are intended to raise more questions than they answer and provide suggestions for future research.

Perhaps one of the most widely studied areas of early modern Scottish history is the Enlightenment, for reasons that DAICHES, JONES, & JONES make clear in their survey of the topic. Some histories of the Enlightenment skirt intellectualism altogether while others fall victim to excessive intellectualism; this book happily avoids both traps and offers an accessible introduction to the subject. Daiches's introductory essay provides an overview of the Enlightenment, and subsequent chapters present more detailed studies of the men who contributed to fields from philosophy to science, among them David Hume, Adam Smith, Joseph Black, and James Hutton. The final chapter explores the relationship between Scotland and America and shows how Enlightenment ideology was transplanted to American institutions of government and higher education.

In contrast to this broad overview, SHER's work focuses on the relationship between philosophers and the Church of Scotland, which he says was a good one, despite seeming differences. The rise of the Moderate Party in the 1750s had helped to create a more liberal climate in the church. Sher looks at five of the churchmen who supported the party – William Robertson, Hugh Blair, Alexander Carlyle, Adam Ferguson, and John Home – and traces their rise to prominence. He examines their emphasis on the importance of polite learning and economic and social progress, their advocacy of the existing political system, and their tolerance for doctrinal differences within and outside the church. Defining moderatism as a blend of presbyterianism, Christian stoicism, and civic humanism, he argues that it kept religious thought at the centre of Enlightenment ideas and public education.

In a similar vein, ALLAN seeks to trace the historiography of the Scottish Enlightenment back to Renaissance humanism and Calvinism, traditions which he also believes shared an emphasis on the virtue of scholarship. Unlike Sher, however, he separates the two lines of moral discourse – Calvinism and moderatism – and sees them as progressing on slightly different though compatible trajectories. Allan is more interested in the wider role of Enlightenment thought, and he relates the moral principles of the literati to the greater social and political context of 18th-century Scotland. He examines the Scots' belief that moral and commercial virtue was a necessary qualifier for social leadership, and he suggests that the idea was deliberately fostered by the intellectuals to replace the sense of political autonomy which was lost after the union of 1707.

of operational commitments by the inner German frontier. With hindsight these arguments can be seen as products of their time. They demonstrate that theoretical and historical studies of sea power are not immune to the passage of time and the changing climates of the age.

GRAY has inherited Mahan's mantle. As a political scientist he was concerned "to demonstrate how sea power has worked strategically to confer advantage or to avert or offset disadvantage". Unlike his famous predecessor, Gray is not a polemicist for sea power or a partisan of any particular navy or naval strategy, and he carefully examines the options available to land powers. He recognizes that all major wars require a mixed strategy and shows how such strategies vary over time, reflecting the nature of the nations involved, the level of technology, the geostrategic character of the combatants, and the full panoply of political factors. Gray's work is not a history of sea power but a study of how sea power works. Significantly, he opens the concluding chapter with a quote from Richmond: "Sea power did not win the [Second World] War itself: it enabled the war to be won".

GLETE provided a fresh starting-point for naval historical studies, by analysing the naval construction of all significant powers over a period of 360 years. He considered the nature of naval power and the role played in the creation of modern states by the bureaucratic, industrial, economic, and fiscal policies necessary to support the navies which exerted that power. He demonstrated that naval policy and strategy can be assessed from a close study of procurement. Sea power was a costly tool, one that only the richest and most determined polities could use.

HARDING offers a fresh historical perspective on the extant literature of the era of the sailing navy, suggesting that it has now lost the utility in naval education and thinking that it had in Mahan's time but that many of agendas it embodies still reflect the concerns of the early 20th century. Consequently, core assumptions – from the utility of battle fleets in sea power to the inevitability of naval development through this period – should now be re-examined. Perhaps it is time to assess the history of writing on sea power, to demonstrate the division between naval history and strategic analysis.

ANDREW LAMBERT

See also Engineering: General Surveys; Merchant Navy: 1650–1840; Merchant Navy: Since 1840

Sea Travel in the 20th Century

Armstrong, John, "Transport and Communications" in *Western Europe: Economic and Social Change since 1945*, edited by Max-Stephan Schulze, London and New York: Longman, 1999
Broeze, Frank, "Containerisation and the Globalisation of Liner Shipping" in *Global Markets: The Internationalization of the Sea Transport Industries since 1850*, edited by David J. Starkey and Gelina Harlaftis, St John's, Newfoundland: IMEHA, 1998
Craig, Robin, *Steam Tramps and Cargo Liners 1850–1950*, London: HMSO, 1980
Hope, Ronald, *A New History of British Shipping*, London: John Murray, 1990
Maber, John M., *Channel Packets and Ocean Liners 1850–1970*, London: HMSO, 1980
Miller, William H., *Transatlantic Liners, 1945–1980*, Newton Abbot, Devon: David and Charles, and New York: Arco, 1981

HOPE shows that in 1914 the ship was the most important method of moving goods and passengers in intercontinental trade. By 1999 it had a negligible role in passenger transport but retained the lion's share of cargo traffic, though patterns and methods had changed drastically. In 1914, he argues, Britain was by far the leading maritime nation, with about 40 per cent of the world fleet. By the 1990s it owned less than 5 per cent. The 20th century saw huge changes in Britain's position as a maritime nation. The interwar period was the heyday of the large, luxurious passenger liner, carrying middle- and upper-class travellers in comfort across the Atlantic, as MILLER has shown, and between the mother country and its colonies and dominions. In addition there were many ferries for short sea crossings to Ireland and the Continent of Europe, and a network of coastal liners around the shores of the UK, as MABER explains. Air travel was inefficient, using small-capacity aircraft of limited range. Although a little faster than travel by sea, it was expensive and tedious, encountering turbulent conditions and requiring frequent halts to refuel. By comparison the liners were romantic, elegant, and relaxed, Miller suggests. The health benefits of a sea cruise were an added bonus, and coastal ships offered mini-cruises in the summer in Scotland and even around Great Britain. Of course, conditions for third-class or steerage passengers were much less pleasant.

There was a marked decrease in the number of economic migrants from Britain in the interwar period, compared with the period before World War I, as Maber shows – from nearly 600,000 a year just before the Great War to fewer than 400,000 a year in the 1920s and 250,000 in the 1930s. This is largely explained by the closing down in 1921 and 1924 of virtually free emigration for Britons to the United States. Quotas were established which, though relatively favourable to Britain compared with eastern European countries, imposed tight controls. This situation was compounded in the 1930s, Hope argues, when the world price of many agricultural and mineral products plunged, so that countries relying on exploiting such raw materials became less attractive destinations for migrants. Indeed in this decade slightly more people came back to Britain by sea than left it, so unattractive were economic conditions in those countries relying on extractive economies. Throughout the interwar period Britain owned the largest merchant fleet in the world, although, as Hope has shown, its share of merchant shipping dropped from about one-third in 1921 to a quarter in 1939.

The main technological breakthrough was the growing dominance of the motor ship over the steamer, as CRAIG has explained. A diesel engine running on oil fuel reduced manning costs for stoking boilers and taking coal on board, used less space for engine and bunkers, and was a better economic proposition, though Britain has been accused of being slow to adopt the motor ship.

After World War II liners continued to dominate intercontinental traffic, but eventually the advent of the jet aeroplane with higher speeds and capacities and greater range spelled the end for the liner. Whereas in 1951, as ARMSTRONG has shown, about 750,000 people crossed the Atlantic by sea and 300,000 by air, in 1957 the two modes reached parity with one million each, and a decade later 5.5 million went by air but only 500,000 by sea. The huge increase in the price of fuel oil in 1973, as a result of the Arab-Israeli war and an oil embargo by the Organization of Petroleum Exporting Countries (OPEC), raised operational costs and doomed the liner trade, he suggests. By 1975 regular passenger liners ceased to cross the Atlantic. Those liners which remained in service were often altered to become cruise liners, little more than mobile luxury hotels, which were accessed by air and so became more part of the leisure industry than utilitarian transport.

For short sea crossings a number of new types of vessel were introduced. One of the most unusual was the hovercraft, a British invention, which began a passenger service across the English Channel in 1968 and carried cars as well in 1978. Hovercraft were fast, travelling at speeds up to 40 knots and halving journey times. Hydrofoils were also introduced on various short sea journeys, as were catamarans. All were fast movers and much reduced journey times compared with conventional craft.

Since World War II there has been a revolution in cargo shipping. As BROEZE has argued, large ships are expensive pieces of capital equipment which need to be kept moving to make a good return. Slow loading and unloading were the bane of the ship owners, so ways around using port labour were sought. Containerization was one very successful solution to the problem. Broeze argues that it speeded up loading, giving much better turnaround times, and reduced pilferage. Containerization began in the mid-1960s, and by 1995 95 per cent of all liner trade was containerized. Ship design was aimed at maximizing the number of containers, and even larger ships were built. In 1971, Broeze says, Great Britain had the second largest container fleet in the world, but by the 1990s it was well down the list. Despite the high capital cost, many new players entered the industry, often from less developed countries where ship operating costs were lower.

Containers were ideally suited to long-distance intercontinental routes. The equivalent for short sea crossings was roll-on-roll-off or "ro-ro", as HOPE has shown. This allowed "seamless" journeys from factory to final destination across water, with no need to discharge lorries into the ship's hold or the ship's load into lorries at the other end. It became particularly important, as ARMSTRONG argues, when Britain's trade became less oriented to its empire and more to the European Continent. Like containerization, it speeded up journey times and dramatically reduced dock labour. As a result of the need for deep water and large acreages on which to park containers, many conventional docks were found wanting and the centre of activity moved downstream – as occurred in London, where Tilbury became the container terminal and the docks in the city centre were developed into offices, shops, and apartments.

Just as container ships grew in size to take advantage of the economies of scale, so too did other specialized forms of cargo ships, such as bulk carriers and tankers, as Hope reminds us. These grew to such an extent that terms like "supertanker" and "very large crude carrier" were coined for them. The *Seawise Giant* weighed more than 500,000 dead-weight tonnes and was more than 1,500 feet long. These ships sailed slowly to conserve fuel but carried very large quantities at low unit cost. The use of larger ships was boosted after the closure of the Suez Canal in 1967; and despite some concern over their safety and economy after the rise in oil prices in 1973, size did reduce costs. Britain remained the largest European ship-owning nation until 1976 but thereafter was overtaken by Greece and Norway.

JOHN ARMSTRONG

See also Public Transport

Secret Services and Espionage

Aldrich, Richard J., *Intelligence and the War against Japan: Britain, America, and the Politics of Secret Service*, Cambridge, 2000

Andrew, Christopher, *Secret Service: The Making of the British Intelligence Community*, London: Heinemann, 1985

Balfour, Michael, *Propaganda in War: Organisations, Policies, and Politics in Britain and Germany*, London and Boston: Routledge and Kegan Paul, 1979

Bennett, Ralph, *Behind the Battle: Intelligence in the War with Germany, 1939–1945*, London: Sinclair-Stevenson, 1994; enlarged edition, London: Pimlico, 1999

Brook-Shepherd, Gordon, *Iron Maze: The Western Secret Services and the Bolsheviks*, London: Macmillan, 1998

Curry, John, *The Security Service 1908–1945: The Official History*, Kew, Surrey: Public Record Office, 1999

Erskine, Ralph and Michael Smith, *Action This Day*, London, 2001

Fergusson, Thomas G., *British Military Intelligence, 1870–1914: The Development of a Modern Intelligence Organization*, London: Arms and Armour Press, and Frederick, Maryland: University Publications of America, 1984

Foot, M.R.D. and J.M. Langley, *MI 9, the British Secret Service That Fostered Escape and Evasion, 1939–1945, and Its American Counterpart*, London: Bodley Head, 1979; 2nd edition, as *MI 9: Escape and Evasion, 1939–1945*, Boston: Little Brown, 1980

Garnett, David, *The Secret History of PWE: The Political Warfare Executive, 1939–1945*, London, 2002.

Hesketh, Roger, *Fortitude: The D-Day Deception Campaign*, London: St Ermin's Press, 1999; Woodstock, New York: Overlook Press, 2000

Hinsley, F.H. *et al.*, *British Intelligence in the Second World War: Its Influence on Strategy and Operations*, 5 vols, London: HMSO, and New York: Cambridge University Press, 1979–90

Howard, Michael, *British Intelligence in the Second World War*, vol. 5, *Strategic Deception*, London: HMSO, 1990

Jones, R.V., *Most Secret War*, London: Hamish Hamilton, 1978; as *The Wizard War: British Scientific Intelligence 1939–1945*, New York: Coward McCann Geoghegan, 1978

Jones, R.V., *Reflections on Intelligence*, London: Heinemann, 1989

Judd, Alan, *The Quest for C: Sir Mansfield Cumming and the Founding of the British Secret Service*, London: HarperCollins, 1999

Kahn, David, *The Codebreakers: The Story of Secret Writing*, New York: Macmillan, and London: Weidenfeld and Nicolson, 1967, revised edition, New York: Scribner, 1996

Lampe, David, *The Last Ditch*, London: Cassell, and New York: Putnam, 1968

Mackenzie, W.J.M., *The Secret History of SOE: The Special Operations Executive 1940–1945*, London: St Ermin's Press, 2000

Sparrow, Elizabeth, *Secret Service: British Agents in France, 1792–1815*, Woodbridge, Suffolk; and Rochester, New York: Boydell Press, 1999

Stafford, David, *Churchill and Secret Service*, London: John Murray, 1997; Woodstock, New York: Overlook Press, 1998

All these subjects have ancient roots, but early evidence is extremely slight. Secret services were handled at the highest levels by the monarch and a few closely trusted courtiers; and within living memory it was still held a grave offence against good manners to refer to them in public at all. In Anglo-Saxon England and in the Middle Ages the only evidence for the existence of any such bodies is indirect: it would not have been possible for Alfred or any other of the great warrior kings to win their campaigns without reasonably sound intelligence about enemies and terrain.

In early modern times the mists part a little. KAHN quotes some evidence to show that Mary, queen of Scots, was framed by Walsingham's deciphering expert, Thomas Phelipes, who broke the code she was using in messages smuggled out of Fotheringay in her laundry and, by adding forgery to his deciphering, discovered the names of some young men who sought to rescue her; they went, as she did, to the scaffold. The early death of the dramatist Christopher Marlowe was supposedly due to some entanglement with the secret service, but what it was remains obscure. Oliver Cromwell was regarded as the best-informed ruler in Europe; his lord chancellor, John Thurloe, took care of the details for him. William Blathwayt (1649?–1717), an accomplished linguist, may have handled intelligence matters for William III as his secretary at war, but this is mere conjecture.

At the time of the Jacobite risings, the government set up an extra secret body called by the few in the know the "foreign letter office" to investigate potential Jacobite traitors. Of its work hardly anything is known, though the failure of the risings is clear enough.

Late in the 18th century, a mob controlled London for a week during the Gordon Riots of 1780 and had to be put down by the army. In 1793 an Alien Office was established, ostensibly to control immigration, and the foreign letter office was subsumed under it. In fact it provided cover for espionage, mainly into revolutionary France. Elizabeth SPARROW has rediscovered its papers and recounts its activities. At the time of the Nore mutinies of 1797 those in authority were edgy about even the mildest revolutionary doctrines – hence the prosecutions of various correspondence societies and the radical antagonism to authority of such figures as Francis Place.

After Waterloo (1815) there seems to have been a hiatus in organized, government-inspired secret activity. Such activity was revived with the creation in 1883 of the Special Irish Branch of Scotland Yard, intended specifically to protect government installations against Irish dynamiters (one of whom set off a

bomb outside Scotland Yard itself). For years, one of the home and Irish secretaries' worst headaches had been the presence in Ireland every hunting season, *incognita*, of Empress Elizabeth of Austria, until 1882 when she stopped riding (she fell victim to an anarchist assassin's dagger in Switzerland in 1898). In 1887, as ANDREW established, the Special Irish Branch was absorbed into a nationwide Special Branch, which still survives.

Simultaneously, as FERGUSSON has shown, the army began to pull together its hitherto quite informal arrangements for collecting intelligence. Wellington had been well served in the Peninsula by spies, organized for him by Colquhoun Grant, but thereafter it had been left to officers' private initiative to collect information while ostensibly on holiday abroad and pass that information back to the authorities.

Threats from abroad – revolutionary socialism, anarchism, and the new German navy – made clear the need for systematized intelligence. In 1909 the cabinet was persuaded by the committee of imperial defence to put at least the intelligence and security services on a permanent, though unavowed, footing. A secret service bureau was set up under two officers: Lieutenant-Commander Cumming, RN, to handle intelligence; and Captain Vernon Kell, South Staffordshire Regiment, to deal with security. From these two men derived the two departments now commonly known as MI6 and MI5.

During World War I, the staffs of both services multiplied many times over; each had several hundred employees by 1918, and each had some successes to report. The spy networks the Germans had established in the United Kingdom before the war began were all tidied up, and there were no further serious incursions during the war. Cumming provided much vital intelligence from spy networks, most of them train watchers, from close behind the German lines.

More spectacular work, if of less operational weight, was done in the Levant by T.E. Lawrence and his friends, working with dissident Arabs against the Turkish empire, which they helped to overturn. Such guidance as they got from higher authority they received from a staff branch in Cairo called MO4. London played no part. Cumming, according to JUDD, provided a few sabotage stores, though Judd does not say to whom.

At the start of the war, the navy began a systematic study of German wireless codes; from Room 40, O[ld]B[uilding], at the Admiralty both the main naval and the main diplomatic codes of Germany were mastered, with an important political result: the conversion of the United States from neutrality to belligerency through the deciphered Zimmermann telegram.

After World War I secret service staffs, like so many others, were cut back severely. BROOK-SHEPHERD, who (like Judd) was given privileged access to some MI6 files, has illustrated the service's obsession with revolutionary Russia and recounts both the successes of Lieutenant Agar, VC, in sinking Bolshevik shipping in the Baltic and the eventual failure of the man who called himself Sidney Reilly.

Andrew and STAFFORD have deftly presented, from different angles of sight, how the secret services were weaned away from a concentration on Russia and persuaded to focus on the more immediate danger from Nazi Germany. Andrew considers the institutional dimension and Stafford the personal. After Churchill became prime minister in May 1940 the forging of a proper secret intelligence community could begin.

By the middle of World War II there were as many as nine British secret services: (1) the auxiliary units, small teams of devotees whose task it would have been to hamper the rear areas of the German invasion that never happened; (2 and 3) MI5 and MI6, both much expanded; (4) the radio security service; (5) the escape service; (6) the special operations executive, to promote sabotage and subversion in enemy-occupied countries; (7) the political warfare executive, which grew out of it; (8) the deciphering service, vital to all the rest; and (9) the deception service, the smallest and most senior of the lot.

Of the radio security service practically nothing has been published in print. On the auxiliary units the best book remains LAMPE's, a good outsider's book. On escape, FOOT & LANGLEY cover the headquarters ground; there is a large, less formal literature on escape adventures. For MI5 there is the official history by CURRY; its presentation is anonymous, as good secret manners dictate, but it contains a frontispiece inserted by Andrew, who edited it. There is also one volume, the fourth in HINSLEY's series, *Security and Counter-Intelligence*, written jointly by Hinsley and by C.A.G. Simkins, which overlaps it.

For MI6 there is nothing officially published (Hinsley apart), but R.V. JONES's two magnificent books explain with force how scientific intelligence could be applied to the problems of modern warfare (Jones's cover was that he was a scientific adviser to the air ministry). Hinsley's first three volumes (in four parts) ostensibly cover the work of MI6 but in fact cover the work of the deciphering service (in which Hinsley himself worked). The head of MI6, who had been a Life Guards officer, took political responsibility for this, though its methods were far too complex for him to master. The decipherers' work gave a tiny group of strategists an insight of unexampled quality into the enemy's mind, and 10,000 discreet staff members stayed silent about it for 30 years. On deciphering method, we find at least a few useful pages in ERSKINE & SMITH.

The Special Operations Executive (SOE), the subversion service, was never a popular department. Its in-house history, written just after the war (and after its own disappearance) by MACKENZIE, was recently published. Mackenzie had been close to the centre of policymaking in the air ministry during the war, and after it he had full access to SOE's archives and council. He explains lucidly how it fitted into the rest of the war machine and considers that its strategic weight was high. ALDRICH's book gives a clear example of how it had to struggle with allies as well as enemies.

The work of the political warfare executive, never quantifiable, was also discussed in an in-house history by the Bloomsbury novelist David GARNETT, who had served in it. Michael BALFOUR's book, which overlaps Garnett's, also covers Germany.

On deception, HOWARD's fifth volume in the Hinsley series, *Strategic Deception* (1990), is decisive; however, it often contradicts what lesser authors assert. HESKETH's book provides a colourful supplement, spelling out how the largest and most important deception to cover the Normandy invasion worked; and BENNETT's magisterial survey puts both the deciphering service and the deception service into the strategic context.

M.R.D. FOOT

See also Cold War

Secularization

Berman, David, *A History of Atheism in Britain: From Hobbes to Russell*, London and New York: Croom Helm, 1988

Bruce, Steve (editor), *Religion and Modernization: Sociologists and Historians Debate the Secularization Thesis*, Oxford: Clarendon Press, and New York: Oxford University Press, 1992

Budd, Susan, *Varieties of Unbelief: Atheists and Agnostics in English Society, 1850–1960*, London: Heinemann Educational, 1977

Chadwick, Owen, *The Secularization of the European Mind in the Nineteenth Century: The Gifford Lectures in the University of Edinburgh for 1973–1974*, Cambridge and New York: Cambridge University, 1975

Gilbert, Alan D., *The Making of Post-Christian Britain: A History of the Secularization of Modern Society*, London and New York: Longman, 1980

MacIntyre, Alasdair, *Secularization and Moral Change: The Riddell Memorial Lectures, 36th Series, Delivered at the University of Newcastle-Upon-Tyne on 11, 12, and 13 November 1964*, London: Oxford University Press, 1967

Martin, David, *A General Theory of Secularization*, Oxford: Blackwell, and New York: Harper and Row, 1978

Sommerville, C. John, *The Secularization of Early Modern England: From Religious Culture to Religious Faith*, New York and Oxford: Oxford University Press, 1992

Wilson, Bryan, *Religion in Sociological Perspective*, Oxford and New York: Oxford University Press, 1982

Secularization is mentioned in most recent studies of modern British religious history and in many general social histories as well. Numerous works offer evidence for or against a decline in religion, giving figures for, e.g., church attendance or expressions of belief. However, there is no agreement on the definition of "secularization"; it has been taken to mean, among other things, declining church attendance; anticlericalism; a wish to disestablish the Church of England; expression of religious doubts or disrespect; the rise of heresies, occultism, or freethinking societies; and the institutionalization of science. In general, historians use the term to mean a decline in the respect or attention given to Christian institutions or thinking, rather than to religion in a more general sense. While it is impossible here to cover the vast literature offering facts relevant to these developments, we can note the works of most help in conceptualizing secularization.

Academic interest in secularization began early in the 20th century when German sociological theory, under the influence of Karl Marx and Max Weber, directed attention to rationalization and bureaucratization, which were thought to be uncongenial to religious thought and practice. Industrialization and urbanization were presented as primary factors in secularization. WILSON's historical-sociological works are the most current expression of this tradition, though Wilson, like others, rejects a "secularization thesis" or paradigm that would seem too deterministic.

Historians then began to trace secularization backwards to the Renaissance or scientific revolution in an effort to find its philosophical roots, assuming that the process was primarily intellectual. Whereas sociologists had argued that thinking and ideology reflected more basic processes, works like CHADWICK's suggested that changes at the level of philosophy and science initiated doubts which then seeped downwards through the population. Chadwick's account places English developments within a European context.

SOMMERVILLE took issue with both these viewpoints. He asked a basically sociological question: when had a host of disparate activities lost their religious associations? He found that urbanization, industrialization, and science came late in this process. Secularizing tendencies seemed rather to reflect political and even religious movements, including protestantism – for religious movements can have a secularizing effect, if they desire to prune away religious expressions which are rejected as "superstitious" (a point made by Weber). This is an instance of the fact that a population can become more religious in mentality at the same time that the society is becoming more secular in its structures, which may have been the case around 1800 in Britain.

From some perspectives superstition has as much right to be considered religion as what the dominant culture has approved as such. But historians normally assume that in the British context religion means, or should mean, Christianity, and deviant beliefs may be counted as irreligious. This leads to confusion, since what some recognize as a decline of religious culture may seem to others to be an increase in spirituality. British historians have been slow to adopt the French practice of discussing "de-Christianization".

Sommerville saw intellectual developments as being more the result than the cause of the four different processes which we tacitly define as secularization: (1) social differentiation, (2) institutional autonomy, (3) the transfer of religious activities to secular institutions, and (4) mental distraction from or denial of religion. But the 18th century did bring the development of a consistently secular rationalism, which had previously lacked a conceptual language. This amounted to a "cultural grammar" of atheism which Lucian Febvre had searched for in vain among Renaissance writers. BERMAN went further, to show how difficult consistent atheism would have been psychologically, as well as intellectually, in the early modern period.

There have been numerous studies of the development of a secular consciousness in the 19th century. The most comprehensive is BUDD's *Varieties of Unbelief*, which draws on the works of many others. This development can be traced, partly, in the rise of organized free thought, which may never have become a widespread or respectable force but whose unconscious effects may have been considerable. Some have noted that efforts to refute such attacks on religion may themselves have raised doubts in the general population, since one can loosen the hold of religious assumptions simply by bringing them into full consciousness.

Whether religious doubts were raised more by the sciences, historical scholarship, or cultural relativism is an unresolved question. The fact that doubts often centred on moral questions suggests deeper psychological and social factors at work than are normally dealt with in intellectual history. MACINTYRE's treatment of this question could be followed further.

MARTIN has shown how the larger social process takes a different course in different countries, and he is able to relate this to political circumstances. The complexity of his account shows

how inadequate the earliest social-scientific generalizations were. His comparative approach helps to put Britain's case into a wider perspective.

Though it is becoming dated, the most comprehensive view of the whole subject is GILBERT's. Gilbert suggests some of the factors working against secularization; these have become a common theme among scholars who find reason to doubt the cruder formulations of the secularization thesis, in which changes were thought of as uniform, linear, and inevitable. BRUCE's contributors bring the debate up to date, but they exhibit some of the confusion that persists. Progress on the subject will depend upon using the mass of social, political, and cultural data already gathered within a more consistent scheme.

C. JOHN SOMMERVILLE

See also Anglican Doctrine and Worship

Service Industries   20th century

Aldcroft, Derek H., *British Transport since 1914: An Economic History*, Newton Abbot, Devon; and North Pomfret, Vermont: David and Charles, 1975

Channon, Derek F., *The Service Industries: Strategy, Structure, and Financial Performance*, London: Macmillan, 1978

Clayton, G., *British Insurance*, London: Elek, 1971

Holloway, J. Christopher, *The Business of Tourism*, Plymouth, Devon: Macdonald and Evans, 1983; 5th edition, London and New York: Longman, 1998

Jefferys, James B., *Retail Trading in Britain 1850 to 1950: A Study in Trends in Retailing with Special Reference to the Development of Cooperative, Multiple Shop, and Department Store Methods of Trading*, Cambridge: Cambridge University Press, 1954

Lee, Clive, "The Service Industries" in *The Economic History of Britain since 1700*, vol. 2, *1860 to 1939*, edited by Roderick Floud and Donald McCloskey, second edition, Cambridge and New York: Cambridge University Press, 1994

Michie, Ranald C., *The City of London: Continuity and Change, 1850–1990*, Basingstoke: Macmillan, 1992

Millward, Robert, "Productivity in the UK Services Sector: Historical Trends 1865–1985 and Comparisons with the USA 1950–1985", *Oxford Bulletin of Economics and Statistics*, 52/4 (1990): 423–36

By 1900 services already accounted for a much larger proportion of total output in Britain than in most other countries. Throughout the 20th century, the service sector's share of the British economy continued to grow. Despite this, services have received far less attention than manufacturing industries from historians. The main theme addressed in the work that has been published is whether a large service sector imposes a burden on the growth of an economy. Some particular service industries and individual firms have also been subjects of historical study.

LEE gives a useful introduction to the historical analysis of the service sector, covering the late 19th century and the first half of the 20th century. He provides a clear and succinct account of the tricky matter of defining the service sector, and an overview of theories alleging the growth-inhibiting effect of services on the economy. Lee also includes a range of statistical information on service output and the growth of the labour force in services. Disaggregated statistics reveal a decline of domestic service in the interwar years but show that most other services saw continual expansion in numbers over the period reviewed.

CHANNON offers a pioneering and ambitious analysis of the 100 largest service industry corporations over the period 1950 to 1975. Comparative analysis shows that services followed a broadly similar pattern of development to manufacturing, becoming more diversified and more internationally oriented, and adopting multidivisional structures. However, the service businesses tended to adopt these changes at a later date and rather more slowly than firms in manufacturing. Channon discusses the extent to which firms in particular service industries – including banking, insurance, retailing, and the public sector – adopted new strategies and new forms of organization.

MILLWARD provides a revisionist analysis of trends in the growth of productivity in the UK service sector from the mid-19th century to the 1980s. Official statistics suggest that the growth of productivity in services was consistently well below the average for the UK economy. Millward's alternative estimates show services in a much more favourable light, consistently close to the average growth rate for productivity in the UK, except duirng major recessions, when the service sector may have absorbed some of the surplus employment from other sectors, depressing its productivity.

ALDCROFT gives an overview of the transport sector in the first three-quarters of the 20th century. By 1900 the railway companies were among the largest service businesses and dominated inland transport provision. Aldcroft documents the decline of railways and the remarkable growth of road transport during the 20th century. Also, by mid-century, a large proportion of the transport sector was in public hands; but, Aldcroft argues, transport policy often tended to exacerbate problems in the sector by imposing frequent organizational changes on the industries. Other themes tackled in his wide-ranging book include the demand for infrastructure expenditure, notably road building, the growth of civilian air traffic since 1945, and the decline of the UK shipping industry.

JEFFERYS gives an economic analysis of the development of retailing. Before 1850 this sector consisted of small, independent traders. Jefferys focuses on the growth of large-scale retailing since then, including multi-shop firms, department stores, and cooperative retailing. After a brief summary of the main trends, the bulk of the book is devoted to a series of in-depth studies of the development of particular trades within retailing, such as the grocery trade, the milk trade, clothing, footwear, chemists, and newsagents. Jefferys documents the use of standardized techniques by large firms, their exploitation of economies of scale, and their pricing policies and advertising strategies.

MICHIE seeks to provide a long-term perspective on the development of the City of London as a commercial and financial centre, and to assess its contribution to the British economy. He demonstrates that the City has changed significantly over time, in response to wars, government intervention, and shifting patterns of international trade. In the 19th century firms in the City of London were actively involved in the actual buying and selling of commodities, but over the course of the 20th century the role of the City moved increasingly to the provision of financial services. Michie is eager to refute the widespread idea that the City of London had harmful effects on the British economy, stressing both its dynamism and the value of its contribution to industry and trade. He also argues that governmental restrictions on the City's activities between 1914 and the 1970s were damaging and tended only to direct business to other financial centres. Since the 1970s, however, governmental restrictions have lessened and competitive pressures have increased.

CLAYTON describes and analyses the growth of the insurance industry in Britain. The main strength of his book is a discussion of the general economic background and its influence on the insurance business. In the 19th century, a growing population and rising living standards encouraged the formation and expansion of many insurance companies. Clayton documents the development of insurance for weekly wage-earners in the later 19th century; the growing intervention by the state, which also began at that time; and the wave of amalgamations which occurred in the insurance industry in the first quarter of the 20th century. After World War II, the industry experienced further growth; but Clayton argues that this growth was at the expense of profits, so that by the late 1960s the industry was ailing.

Leisure industries, such as tourism, have been among the fastest-growing parts of the service sector in recent years. There is no fully satisfactory general history of tourism in Britain, but HOLLOWAY includes some historical chapters and gives an extensive discussion of the development of the industry since 1945. The growth of tourism is traced back to the proliferation of railways and the rising standard of living of the mass of the population during the 19th century. The British seaside holiday became popular in this period, and it was augmented by the rise of holiday camps in the interwar years. From the 1960s on, cheaper air travel enabled many to take holidays abroad. Against this historical background, Holloway addresses a number of analytical themes, including the role of tourism in the economy, the evolving structure of the industry, the role of government in promoting tourism, and growing concerns about the social and environmental consequences of tourism.

ANDREW JENKINS

See also Leisure and Recreation

Settlement: Border Societies

Donnan, Hastings and Thomas M. Wilson, *Borders: Frontiers of Identity, Nation, and State,* Oxford and New York: Berg, 1999

Green, Stanton W. and Stephen M. Perlman (editors), *The Archaeology of Frontiers and Boundaries,* Orlando: Academic Press, 1985

Hooke, Della, *The Landscape of Anglo-Saxon England,* London and Washington: Leicester University Press, 1998

Millward, Roy and Adrian Robinson, *The Welsh Borders,* London: Eyre Methuen, 1978

Parry, M.L. and T.R. Slater (editors), *The Making of the Scottish Countryside,* London: Croom Helm, and Montreal: McGill-Queen's University Press, 1980

Salway, Peter, *The Frontier People of Roman Britain*, Cambridge: Cambridge University Press, 1965

Sawyer, P.H. (editor), *English Medieval Settlement*, London: Arnold, 1979

Witney, K.P. *The Jutish Forest: A Study of the Weald of Kent from 450 to 1380 A.D.*, London: Athlone Press, 1976

The material on this theme is rather a "thing of shreds and patches". We do not find books concentrating on settlement and land use in border regions; rather, it is necessary to isolate material on land use and settlement in general books on the border, or material on the border in books on land use and settlement.

Modern writers on borders tend to be highly theoretical and international in approach. This is true of DONNAN & WILSON; nevertheless, their book is an important way of locating concepts which enrich the study and understanding of such areas in British history. For example, J.R.V. Prescott in Donnan & Wilson discusses the distinction between the "border", the area adjacent to a boundary; and "borderlands", "the transition zone within which the boundary lies". This underlines the importance of the approach of MILLWARD & ROBINSON, who base their book on:

> . . . a strip of country on either side of the boundary dividing England and Wales and in this political sense it can rightly claim distinctiveness over the past thousand years. To think of it solely in these historical terms would be misleading, however, for the area also possesses a unity based on its transitional character, lying as it does between the English lowlands to the east and the Welsh uplands to the west.

G.R.J. Jones in SAWYER also sees political changes as misleading, in that "in the late seventh century, and possibly also the early eighth century, settlements bearing Old English names could nevertheless still house Britons". Millward & Robinson highlight this tension between the transitional nature of the borderland and the political nature of the border in discussing the impact of Offa's Dyke. Despite the entry of non-Celtic Mercians, "Opinion leans to the view that this was a piecemeal and mainly peaceful settlement of tracts that had been cleared and farmed since prehistoric centuries". Thus the combination of the theory in Donnan & Wilson and the detailed example in Millward & Robinson points to a possible generalization for borders which are not precisely discussed, as in PARRY & SLATER, whose work contains a scholarly discussion of land use and settlement in Scotland but no real reference to border societies.

Added to this tension between border and borderland are changes of emphasis in the same geographical area, which take place over the 2,000-year history of a theme. Again, Millward & Robinson are useful in giving a detailed example, because they are dealing consciously with a border area. In the chapter "Communications of a Corridor" they discuss periods of relative strength and weakness of the Anglo-Welsh border, from the Bronze Age to the present. "Bronze Age man was anxious to carve out east–west routes . . . across the borderland region", while the Romans imposed a north–south emphasis on communications, which was reinforced by the Mercians. The

Norman Marcher lords and Welsh princes created important, if subsidiary, east–west roads, by encouraging Cistercian monasteries, "raising the commercial potential of the borderland through the organisation of the wool trade". From 1750 onwards turnpike trusts and industrial needs predominated over a north–south political focus. This east–west focus was strengthened in the railway age, as "many companies . . . were anxious to provide a link between the industrial towns of England and south Wales and the coast of Cardigan Bay", the Cambrian railways adopting an east–west policy in an unsuccessful bid to access the lucrative London–Dublin trade. This extended analysis of the focus of transport of the Welsh borderland is highly suggestive of points to look for elsewhere. It is probable that land use is of subsidiary importance in forming the character of border regions and that settlement also has a fairly low-key role. Such matters as underlying political trends and military, industrial, and trade requirements are of much greater immediacy. SALWAY notes similar issues on the frontiers of Roman Britain.

Nevertheless, certain important issues connected with land use and settlement can be discerned. Examples include forest regions, commons, and the general area of internal colonization. WITNEY, in a well-researched and clearly written book, gives a sustained account of the manner in which the change from oak commons to cultivation changed the nature and borders of local societies. "It was for the ubiquitous acorn yield that [the Jutes] valued the forest, and this led them in time into every corner of it". HOOKE gives a picture in which borders were non-conflictual phenomena quite unlike Hadrian's Wall or Offa's Dyke. In this situation crucial parts of the argument are land use and settlement – or often their lack. Reiterating the point that political borders may have fluctuated but land use would remain constant in the local community, Hooke notes "how frequently the boundaries of kingdoms seem to have been drawn through relatively empty regions. In some cases, woodland may have been allowed to regenerate in such locations". The same picture can be seen in the Welsh Marches in the years after the arrival of the Normans.

The history of the woodland is often also the history of local colonization. In GREEN & PERLMAN, Stanton Green gives a useful introductory review of the literature, noting that some settlers were attracted to the nearest edge of the frontier to maximize the economic advantages of this land. In Sawyer, P.H. Sawyer, discussing new interpretations of medieval English settlements, indicates that recent research had led to a fundamental change in viewpoint: "The period between the English and Norman conquests was therefore not marked by a great movement of colonization". There are thus important debates about the continuity of land use and settlements on the Anglo-Welsh and Anglo-Scottish borders, and on the boundaries of Roman, Anglo-Saxon, and Norman societies. Hooke, for example, indicates the complexity of the concept of border societies: "In Anglo-Saxon England a hierarchy of boundaries can be recognized, some of them probably ancient, some evolving as the period progressed". J.R.V. Prescott in Donnan & Wilson comments that "as a discipline, history has increasingly looked at borderlands as social or cultural systems which often transcend the state boundary", while Sawyer sees the theme as one in which historians work cooperatively with archaeologists, geographers, and scholars of place names.

RAY GRACE

Settlement: Early Distribution

Dark, Petra, *The Environment of Britain in the First Millennium* A.D., London: Duckworth, 2000

Fox, Cyril, *The Personality of Britain: Its Influence on Inhabitant and Invader in Prehistoric and Early Historic Times*, Cardiff: National Museum of Wales, 1932; revised edition, with additional maps by Lily F. Chitty, 1938; reprinted, New York: AMS Press, 1979

Higham, Nicholas, *Rome, Britain, and the Anglo-Saxons*, London: Seaby, 1992

Jones, Barri and David Mattingly, *An Atlas of Roman Britain*, Oxford and Cambridge, Massachusetts: Blackwell, 1990

Myres, J.N.L., *The English Settlements*, Oxford: Clarendon Press, and New York: Oxford University Press, 1986

Rahtz, Philip *et al.*, *Cadbury Congresbury 1968–1973: A Late/Post-Roman Hilltop Settlement in Somerset*, Oxford: Tempus Repartum, 1992

Welch, Martin, *English Heritage Book of Anglo-Saxon England*, London: Batsford / English Heritage, 1992

West, Stanley, *West Stow: The Anglo-Saxon Village*, East Anglican Archaeology 24, Ipswich: Suffolk County Planning Department, 1985

The cessation of Roman authority in Britain in the early 5th century marks the start of the conventional medieval period. The subsequent c.650 years, until the Norman Conquest in 1066, have variously been called the "Saxon" period and the "dark ages", the latter term reflecting a relative dearth of archaeological and historical sources. The history of this period has largely been written from early narrative accounts such as Bede and Gildas, which themselves focus upon political and ecclesiastical history; on the day-to-day life of ordinary folk our documents are largely silent, and one of the major contributions that archaeology has made for the medieval period is in uncovering evidence of early settlement.

The early writers such as Bede famously described the invasion and conquest of England by the Angles, Saxons, and Jutes during the 5th century, and the early work of archaeologists appeared to confirm the historical record. FOX, for example, attempted to show how marked regional variations in the distribution of different classes of artefact, notably the weapons and jewellery deposited as grave goods in cemeteries, reflected the areas colonized by the different Germanic immigrants. MYRES similarly used archaeological evidence, particularly different styles of pottery, to write a history of Anglo-Saxon invasion, conquest, and colonization.

This early scholarship had a number of common elements: archaeology was used to support an essentially historical narrative; that narrative was largely one of political events, written in terms of the progress of Anglo-Saxon migration and kingdom-formation; and the archaeological data were dominated by assemblages of material from cemeteries. It was also assumed that the Anglo-Saxons arrived in the context of a mass folk migration, and that they arrived in a largely deserted and even heavily forested landscape. In recent years, however, archaeological surveys and excavations, alongside the examination of palaeoenvironmental remains, have transformed our understanding of this period.

From the 1960s, there was a growing awareness that the landscape of Roman Britain was more heavily populated than had previously been thought. Field-walking (the systematic collection of artefacts from the surface of ploughed fields) and aerial photography (which can reveal buried sites through differential crop growth) indicate a density of settlement suggestive of a population of c.4 million (as opposed to earlier estimates of c.1 million). The intensity with which the landscape of Roman Britain was used is reflected in JONES & MATTINGLY's *Atlas of Roman Britain*, which also reflects the marked regional variation in the patterns of settlement, rural industry, and military disposition.

DARK has recently drawn together the palaeoenvironmental evidence (notably pollen) for this period, which suggests that while there was a decrease in the intensity of landscape exploitation, se well as a shift from arable to pastoral farming, there was no widespread woodland regeneration. It would appear, therefore, that the Anglo-Saxons arrived in a landscape which was both well-populated and still used for farming.

Another area of recent revisionism has been the scale and nature of the Anglo-Saxon settlement. Some scholars, such as WELCH, argue that there was indeed a mass folk migration of peoples from the Continent. Indeed, the title of his review of this period, "Anglo-Saxon England", is itself telling: this traditional view is that early medieval England was dominated by a wholly new population and its culture. In contrast, other scholars, such as HIGHAM, see much greater continuity with the Romano-British period and argue that the arrival of the Anglo-Saxons was in the context of an elite takeover rather than mass migration. These revisionist scholars even argue that many of those buried in "Anglo-Saxon" cemeteries may have been natives who simply adopted new styles of dress (jewellery, etc.). Even the title of Higham's book – *Rome, Britain, and the Anglo-Saxons* – reflects the modern view that this was a period with highly complex social interactions between different ethnic groups.

The settlement of early medieval England can be thought of not just in terms of the landscape-scale processes of migration and continuity, but at the local scale of individual sites. From the 1960s, archaeology has also made remarkable progress in this area. The advent of large-scale excavations, usually in advance of developments such as gravel extraction and road building, have for the first time revealed the settlements in which both natives and immigrants were living during this period. One of the largest excavations was at West Stow in Suffolk; WEST has shown how during the course of several hundred years this settlement shifted its location as buildings decayed and were rebuilt on a slightly different site. Each farm consisted of a main timber-framed hall and several ancillary buildings with distinctive sunken floors. Plant and animal remains suggest a mixed economy with both arable farming and the raising of livestock.

West Stow is typical of early "Anglo-Saxon" settlements in that it was located on relatively poor soil, well away from areas that had been occupied during the Roman period. Unfortunately, very little is known about the surviving native sites in much of Britain, as the collapse of the Romano-British economy meant that there was very little durable and datable material culture; presumably ceramic vessels were replaced by baskets and wooden bowls which do not survive in most archaeological sites. Only in the west of Britain have a number of native settlements been excavated, such as the hilltop site at Cadbury Congresbury in Somerset. Although RAHTZ et al. were able to investigate only a small part of the interior of this reoccupied Iron Age hill-fort, the range of material culture showed clear contact with the Mediterranean world, for example in the form of imported pottery. It would appear, therefore, that towards the end of the 5th century there was some migration of Germanic peoples into the east of the former province of Britannia where there was what is still an ill-understood relationship with the surviving native population, while in the west the "Romano-British" peoples were attempting to maintain links with their "Roman" past.

STEPHEN RIPPON

See also Archaeology: Prehistoric; Roman Britain: General Surveys

Seven Years' War 1756–1763

Brewer, John, *The Sinews of Power: War, Money, and the English State, 1688–1783*, London: Unwin Hyman, and New York: Knopf, 1989

Doran, Patrick Francis, *Andrew Mitchell and Anglo-Prussian Diplomatic Relations during the Seven Years War*, New York: Garland, 1986

Eldon, Carl William, *England's Subsidy Policy towards the Continent during the Seven Years War*, Philadelphia: University of Pennsylvania Press, 1938

Frégault, Guy, *Canada: The War of the Conquest*, translated by Margaret M. Cameron, Toronto: Oxford University Press, 1969

Furneaux, Rupert, *The Seven Years War*, St Albans, Hertfordshire: Hart Davis MacGibbon, 1973

Gipson, Lawrence Henry, *The British Empire before the American Revolution*, vols 6–7: *The Years of Defeat, 1754–1757* and *The Victorious Years, 1758–1760*, New York: Knopf, 1946–49

Guy, Alan J., *Oeconomy and Discipline: Officership and Administration in the British Army 1714–1763*, Manchester: Manchester University Press, 1985

Houlding, J.A., *Fit for Service: The Training of the British Army 1715–1795*, Oxford: Clarendon Press, and New York: Oxford University Press, 1981

Jennings, Francis, *Empire of Fortune: Crowns, Colonies, and Tribes in the Seven Years' War in America*, New York: Norton, 1988

Leach, Douglas Edward, *Roots of Conflict: British Armed Forces and Colonial Americans, 1677–1763*, Chapel Hill: University of North Carolina Press, 1986

Middleton, Richard, *The Bells of Victory: The Pitt-Newcastle Ministry and the Conduct of the Seven Years' War 1757–1762*, Cambridge and New York: Cambridge University Press, 1985

Nash, Gary B., *The Urban Crucible: Social Change, Political Consciousness, and the Origins of the American Revolution*, Cambridge, Massachusetts: Harvard University Press, 1979

Parkman, Francis, *Montcalm and Wolfe*, Boston: Little Brown, 1884; numerous subsequent editions, including *Montcalm and Wolfe: The French and Indian War*, New York: Da Capo Press, 1995

Rogers, Alan, *Empire and Liberty: American Resistance to British Authority, 1753–1763*, Berkeley: University of California Press, 1974

The tendency of most English-language works, such as the single-volume survey by FURNEAUX, is to treat the war in Continental Europe as an adjunct to events in North America, where the war was to become better known by its 19th-century designation as the French and Indian War (with an earlier starting date of 1764). And many historians, such as NASH, have focused on the war as a cause of the American Revolution. However, some more recent studies have tended to use the term Seven Years' War for North America too, and have placed the conflict in its broader context, utilizing changes in both ethnohistory and new military history.

British policy has been reappraised in a number of important studies. ELDON analyses the controversy surrounding British subsidies to Continental rulers, including the Convention of Westminster, which helped trigger a reversal of alliances, as well as the wartime assistance given to Prussia, Hessen-Kassel, Hanover, and other north German territories. These findings are extended considerably by DORAN's published dissertation, which analyses Anglo-Prussian relations and the activities of Andrew Mitchell, the remarkable British ambassador to Frederick II. As Doran demonstrates, Britain did not leave Frederick in the lurch after 1760, seeking instead a way to extract itself from the war without unduly harming its ally; but a series of mutual misunderstandings prevented effective coordination and soured relations for many years to come. MIDDLETON offers the most recent interpretation of British war management and the role of William Pitt the Elder, which tones down the Victorian glorification of Pitt as the sole architect of victory and gives greater credit to both the Duke of Newcastle and George II in the formulation of policy.

Britain's armed forces have also been the subject of a number of important works which, while not dealing with the war directly, nonetheless are essential for understanding how it was conducted. GUY investigates the transformation of command and officership along increasingly professional lines before the war; HOULDING discusses preparation in both peace and war, indicating how domestic duties as a police force, together with financial and political constraints, proved a greater hindrance to effective training than the purchase system behind officers' appointments. Advanced training often had to be carried out in encampments after a conflict had already broken out, and it benefited only a small proportion of the total force. Nonetheless, British officers retained a lively interest in tactical and technical innovation, leading to the growth of an extensive contemporary specialist literature. Like Guy, Houlding presents a picture of a relatively professionalized army that was not inferior to its Continental contemporaries. BREWER extends these findings by analysing British war finance in a path-breaking study which coined the term "fiscal-military state" to encapsulate the accumulation of the means to project military power as a policy instrument. Brewer dispels the myth that British policy was made and enacted by gentlemen amateurs, arguing that Britain was better able than the absolute monarchies on the Continent to mobilize the resources needed for waging war effectively. Parliamentary institutions provided a forum for political consensus and a mechanism for legitimizing high levels of taxation, while a flexible fiscal structure enabled the government to tap the resources of a growing economy. Combined with Eldon's study of subsidy politics, and the recent reappraisal of policy formulation, these findings go a long way towards explaining Britain's victories during the war.

PARKMAN's book, written in a grand literary style, is a classic study of the North American war. Parkman was one of the first historians to examine the war in detail and explore its relationship to the American Revolution. However, this work is important not because of its content but because of the influence it has had upon later historians. It must be read with great care, as it is almost as much story as history. Parkman is extremely selective in his use of sources, and all but caricatures Frenchmen as evil and scheming adversaries and Native Americans as brutal savages.

JENNINGS's *Empire of Fortune* is an example of a work heavily influenced by and written partly as a corrective to Parkman. Examining the course of relations between Native Americans and Europeans from the late 1740s to the Treaty of Paris in 1763, Jennings stresses the importance of pressure from both local and imperial sources on the native inhabitants of North America. He concludes that the origins of the war lay almost exclusively in the greed of colonial and British officials. The work is a good study of the involvement of the Native American peoples in the conflict and provides an expert analysis of diplomacy between Europeans and Native Americans and among the Native American peoples themselves. Unfortunately, the book is weaker in its analysis of the acts of imperial officials and tends to reduce them to a series of conspiracies and plots.

FRÉGAULT provides a French Canadian perspective on the war, paying particular attention to military affairs. He sees the origins of the conflict in the underlying tension between the British and French empires, claiming that the British were determined to destroy French Canada. He thus portrays the war as a struggle for the survival of French Canada and depicts French Canadians as struggling desperately to retain control of their future against the overwhelming might of the British colonies. However, Canada was conquered not because of the might of the British – Frégault stresses the inability of British and Anglo-American forces to win a decisive victory – but rather because of the unwillingness of France to provide adequate support for its North American colony.

GIPSON provides an extremely detailed account of the military and naval aspects of the war from a global and imperial perspective – a perspective reflected in his name for the conflict, the "Great War for the Empire". He argues that the war was a turning-point in the history of North America, for it removed the possibility that the French would block western expansion and gained the security which Americans required as a precondition of a bid for independence. He pays particular attention to the many logistical and tactical problems faced by the British, and he stresses the extent of the military failures before 1757. The work emphasizes how greatly the colonies depended upon Great Britain for military and financial support and refutes the notion that the colonists were capable of defending themselves. Victory in North America was won by British blood, according to Gipson, blood spilled because of concern for the North American colonies rather than for the British empire as a whole.

LEACH analyses the many problems faced by the British in waging war in North America. Although his work examines warfare throughout the colonial period, more than half of it is devoted to the Seven Years' War. Leach argues that the colonists' innate dislike of a standing army created tension with the British army, heightened by a basic rivalry between colonists and Englishmen. Conflicts multiplied in the mid-18th century, as the need for colonies to participate in warfare increased. The colonists increasingly viewed the British as tyrannical despots, while the British viewed colonists as cowardly profiteers. Such tension naturally served to undermine the foundations of the empire, and it contributed to the revolutionary movement.

ROGERS also examines how the war generated tension between colonists and British army officers and how it laid the groudwork for the American Revolution. He takes a less sympathetic view of the British, arguing that the oppressive methods used by British officers to recruit men and obtain supplies and transport led many colonists to see the government as arbitrary. He argues that this created a fertile ground for the development of Whig ideology. Colonial assemblies quickly found themselves cast in the role of defenders of traditional liberties against the tyranny of the British military machine. Once the assemblies had taken this stance, they continued to make these claims after the war, with disastrous consequences for the British empire.

MATTHEW C. WARD (ON NORTH AMERICA)
PETER H. WILSON (ON EUROPE)

See also Navy: Sailing; Newcastle, 1st Duke of; North

Sexuality and Sexual Mores

Ariès, Philippe and André Béjin (editors), *Sexualités occidentales*, Paris: Seuil, 1982; as *Western Sexuality: Practice and Precept in Past and Present Times*, translated by Anthony Forster, Oxford and New York: Blackwell, 1985

Donoghue, Emma, *Passions between Women: British Lesbian Culture 1668–1801*, London: Scarlet Press, 1993; New York: HarperCollins, 1995

Epstein, Julia and Kristina Straub (editors), *Body Guards: The Cultural Politics of Gender Ambiguity*, London and New York: Routledge, 1991

Foucault, Michel, *Histoire de la sexualité I: La volonté de savoir*, Paris: Gallimard, 1976; as *The History of Sexuality*, vol. 1, *An Introduction*, translated by Robert Hurley, New York: Pantheon, 1978; London: Allen Lane, 1979

Fout, John C. (editor), *Forbidden History: The State, Society, and the Regulation of Sexuality in Modern Europe: Essays from the Journal of the History of Sexuality*, Chicago and London: University of Chicago Press, 1992

Nye, Robert A., *Sexuality*, Oxford and New York: Oxford University Press, 1999

Porter, Roy and Mikulá, Teich (editors), *Sexual Knowledge, Sexual Science: The History of Attitudes to Sexuality*, Cambridge and New York: Cambridge University Press, 1994

Rowse, A.L., *Homosexuals in History: A Study of Ambivalence in Society, Literature, and the Arts*, London: Weidenfeld and Nicolson, and New York: Macmillan, 1977

Spencer, Colin, *Homosexuality: A History*, London, Fourth Estate, 1995; as *Homosexuality in History*, New York: Harcourt Brace, 1995

Tannahill, Reay, *Sex in History*, London: Hamish Hamilton, and New York: Stein and Day, 1980; revised edition, London: Cardinal, 1989; Chelsea, Michigan: Scarborough House, 1989

Young, Wayland, *Eros Denied*, London: Weidenfeld and Nicolson, 1965

After having been marginalized as a branch of gender history, the history of sexuality is quickly gaining recognition as a field in its own right. Just as early gender history was motivated by an interest in grounding feminist thought historically, the history of sexuality has been politicized so that, for many historians, the history of sexuality equates with the history of sexual repression, especially of same-sex relations. This is evident in the work of YOUNG in the 1960s. Young charts the history of sexual repression in both England and America, examining the presentation of sex and sexuality in art and literature as well as in political and religious writings. Viewing sex as marginalized in western society, he produces a history that concentrates on images, actions, and words excluded from "normal" social interactions. His extensive use of literary and artistic images makes this work a good introduction to the history of pornography and erotica, but his historical survey of the subject matter is less satisfying, consisting of a series of thematic essays rather than a synthesized assessment of repression across time. At times the work appears disjointed, and it is not helped by a paucity of notes.

This emphasis on repression was noted, and rejected, by FOUCAULT in his important volume on the history of sex. Foucault envisaged this as the first in a comprehensive six-part history of sex, though the chronological range of the project was subsequently curtailed. Beginning with a challenge to the commonly held notion of Victorian sexual repression, Foucault poses a series of questions relating to what he sees as a "discursive explosion" regarding sex from the 17th century to the present. He argues that as modern societies emerged there were fundamental changes in the ways sexuality was regulated and talked about. Expertly dissecting pre-modern attitudes towards sex, Foucault demonstrates how the regulation of sexuality became increasingly complex, with the state drawing on science, social science, and medical knowledge to underpin its changing regulatory systems. He is predominantly interested, however, in why sex commands such a high status in western consciousness; and it is notable that as early as the 1970s he had detected a theme which was to continue to dominate subsequent histories of sexuality – an obsession with repression and censorship.

Foucault's assertion of a universal interest in the subject of sex is partially proved by the prevalence of histories of sex that appeal to the popular as well as the scholarly market. Of these, TANNAHILL's *Sex in History* is probably the most useful, covering a wide range of material both chronologically and geographically. Because of its scope, this book lacks some detail, and the text does suffer as a result; but it is still a useful introduction to changing sexual practices and attitudes over time.

SPENCER's volume on the history of homosexuality suffers from similar problems. Spencer consciously adheres to the model of repression highlighted by Foucault. Admitting that he is preoccupied with homophobia, he sets out to explain its origins in a study of the oppression of homosexuality from pre-history to the present. Geographically diverse, the work is descriptive rather than interpretive.

Some excellent work has emerged, however, in the form of essay collections containing detailed studies on themes of sexuality. The most useful example is provided by ARIÈS & BÉJIN's collection on European sexuality. Concentrating on the history of the Christian ideal of marriage from ancient Rome to the present, the essays variously assess attitudes towards sexual relations – such as same-sex relationships, divorce, premarital sex, and prostitution – that support or challenge this ideal. This is a fascinating study of the varying impact of Christianity on sexual behaviour throughout the ages and across cultural boundaries, and also of the resilience of the pattern of marriage as a "binding tie, monogamous and indissoluble" alongside the increasingly open acceptance by western cultures of other types of sexual union. This is an accessible but learned contribution, and because of the eminence of its contributors it avoids the prurience which can plague less scholarly collections.

PORTER & TEICH's volume of wide-ranging essays encompasses a rigorous attempt to chart changing sexual attitudes in the world of science. It concentrates on the intellectual ownership of knowledge concerning sex, challenging the assumption that increased sexual knowledge is correlated with sexual freedom. Rejecting the model of sexual history as a story of repression, Porter & Teich have chosen essays that explore the extent to which the view of sexual knowledge as liberating has been adopted and modified throughout history. Though it includes work from across Europe, the collection contains a considerable amount of work on Britain. Concentrating predominantly on the writing and thinking of the medical profession, it is a fascinating history of scientific interpretations of sexuality.

EPSTEIN & STRAUB's collection of essays explores the theme of gender ambiguity through the history of hermaphrodism, lesbianism, transsexuality, and sodomy. Examining those individuals who threaten set definitions and divisions of sexuality, each essay attempts to place these ambiguous representations of gender in historical context and to examine their function in relation to the dominant system of sexuality and gender. Beginning with an essay that expertly delineates the notion of gender ambiguity, Epstein & Straub present a body of complementary essays that demonstrate the extent to which behaviour and identities blurring the boundaries of gender and sexuality have been perceived as a problem in societies divided both geographically and chronologically.

Another useful essay collection is provided by FOUT, addressing the history of the regulation of sexuality by the state and society. The essays have all been collected from the *Journal of the History of Sexuality*. The work has a strongly modern bias – only three of its 15 contributors work on material earlier than 1700 – but in terms of subject matter and approach it is a well-balanced collection. The essays catalogue a history of attempts to regulate sexual expression, reproduction, motherhood, and masculinity and demonstrate the social, legal, and intellectual changes that have produced the culture of sexuality in which we now live. The essays are neatly sandwiched between two considerations of the history of sexual disease: one on syphilis in the 15th century and the other on AIDS in the 1980s. The collection manages to demonstrate expertly the permanence of moral, political, and medical influences in the regulation of sexuality, and also the changing emphasis of each of these within the specific cultural context of differing time periods.

An invaluable introduction to source writings on sexuality is NYE's multidisciplinary resource book, containing 150 selections from the works of historians, philosophers, psychotherapists, and sociologists throughout the ages on the question of sexuality. An excellent essay on the usefulness of a historical viewpoint in understanding human sexuality leads into a chronologically arranged set of sources, both primary and secondary, from the Greeks to the present day. The book charts the history of attitudes towards sexuality, gender, the body, and the family, and provide an overview of the development of philosophical thought concerning sexuality throughout history.

The human impact of sexual regulation is often best seen in autobiographical writings by people whose behaviour such regulation curtailed. ROWSE provides a series of case studies of famous artistic men throughout history and their experiences of homosexuality (either as homosexuals themselves or as accused homosexuals). Examining how his subjects expressed themselves, often covertly, through art, poetry, and plays, Rowse demonstrates that the ambivalence such men felt about their sexuality was mirrored in the duality of their lives and their art. This is a book less about societal attitudes towards homosexuality than about the ways individuals have managed to express their sexuality. As a study of the tension between masculinity and homosexuality it is both interesting and enlightening.

Lesbianism has raised noticeably less historical interest than homosexuality, an imbalance that DONOGHUE attempts to redress. She wants to break down what she views as "rigid divisions between friendship and sex" that have hampered historical discussions of lesbianism. Examining a range of representations of lesbian culture in British elite and popular print media from 1668 to 1801, she is concerned with how female relations were depicted. Donoghue offers a fascinating exploration of the cultural variety of closeness between women from pseudo-romantic friendships to sexual relations. Though her work is concerned mainly with the texts of early modern Britain, it serves as an interesting and useful text for scholars of all periods interested in the cultural history of same-sex relationships.

SARAH A. TODD

See also Feminism, Second-Wave; Gender and Power; Homosexuality; Marriage

Shaftesbury, Anthony Ashley Cooper, 1st Earl of 1621–1683

Politician

Brown, Louise Fargo, *The First Earl of Shaftesbury*, New York and London: Appleton-Century, 1933

Christie, W.D., *A Life of Anthony Ashley Cooper, First Earl of Shaftesbury 1621–1683*, 2 vols, London and New York: Macmillan, 1871

Haley, K.H.D., *The First Earl of Shaftesbury*, Oxford: Clarendon Press, 1968

Martyn, Benjamin and Andrew Kippis, *The Life of the First Earl of Shaftesbury*, edited by G. Wingrove Cooke, 2 vols, London: Richard Bentley, 1836

Traill, H.D., *Shaftesbury (The First Earl)*, London: Longmans Green, and New York: Appleton, 1886

Anthony Ashley Cooper, first Earl of Shaftesbury, is one of the most fascinating figures of 17th-century England, yet relatively little has been written about him. Although he does appear in nearly every major examination of politics during the interregnum and the Restoration, he has been the subject of only two biographies in the 20th century. Shaftesbury's life intersected with the most significant upheavals of his era, including the mid-century civil wars and the exclusion crisis – indeed, he was largely responsible for the latter. Whether Shaftesbury is viewed as an ambitious iconoclast motivated solely by a quest for power or as a champion of progressive political and religious views, scholars concur that he had a genius for organizing political support.

MARTYN & KIPPIS establish the tone that characterizes most 19th-century examinations of Shaftesbury when they unabashedly compare him to the great Roman senator Marcus Tullius Cicero. Arguing that Shaftesbury's political actions were motivated by concern for his country's best interests, these authors ignore Cooper's changing loyalties during the civil wars, explaining instead that he was involved in several elaborate schemes throughout 1643 to end the conflict. Cooper, a consummate Whig patriot, took every opportunity to expose Oliver Cromwell's "design of enslaving his country" during the short-lived Barebones Parliament and engineered opposition to the Protectorate in 1654 so effectively that the new government began to be called into question. Although such lavish praise creates a rather unbelievable portrait of the earl, the inclusion of several complete reprints of letters by Shaftesbury and some of his contemporaries makes this biography worthwhile. Especially useful for students and advanced scholars are the discussions of John Locke's treatment of Shaftesbury's manuscripts and the earl's published supporters and detractors such as Roger L'Estrange, Sir William Temple, and Gilbert Burnet.

Nearly four decades passed before another serious study of Shaftesbury appeared. Paying only slightly less homage to the earl than Martyn & Kippis, CHRISTIE contends that Shaftesbury was incorrupt in an age of political corruption. Christie addresses Cooper's service in the king's forces but explains that he was not a vehement royalist. His independence and strength of character arose from his having been orphaned during childhood, and events in the reign of James II proved that Shaftesbury was justified in supporting the Exclusion Bill. Another interesting point not mentioned in most biographies of Cooper is his lifelong belief in astrology, an interest imparted to him by his boyhood mentor, one Dr Olivian, a German astrologer. Christie is an excellent starting-point for students or advanced scholars, especially because it includes numerous primary sources such as Shaftesbury's autobiography, correspondence, and personal and official papers regarding the exclusion crisis, and suppressed passages of Edmund Ludlow's *Memoirs*.

Arguing that Shaftesbury's "master passion" was ambition, TRAILL was the first biographer to examine his subject's less admirable characteristics. Cooper overstated his role at Oxford University in abolishing "tucking", a 17th-century form of hazing, and he married to improve his social status and political connections. Sceptical of the explanation that he abandoned the king's cause for religious reasons, Traill contends that Cooper left the king's service because he was angry over having lost the governorship of Weymouth and Portland to Colonel William Ashburnham. Yet Traill recognizes Shaftesbury's significant contribution to the development of modern political behaviour, portraying him as having one foot in the 17th century and one in the late 19th. A master rhetorician with great technical knowledge, the earl intentionally weakened each party that came to power until the Restoration and subsequently rose to the zenith of his career as a member of Charles II's cabal. In swaying parliament and manipulationg the passions of the London mob, Shaftesbury's method of debating presaged modern political debate.

Whereas 19th-century biographers view Shaftesbury as a consummate republican who created modern politics, 20th-century scholars present more balanced portraits, accounting for the influences that shaped his thought and actions. Portraying Shaftesbury as the bridge between middle and late 17th-century parliamentary leaders, BROWN argues that the earl taught John Pym's political methods to the generation of men who ousted James II. Shaftesbury was an unscrupulous politician who extended the exclusion crisis by capitalizing on the Popish Plot of 1678. He was also responsible for the Revolution of 1688 in the sense that it was based on his political principles – the insistence that England should have a parliamentary government, without standing armies or ecclesiastical domination. Although Shaftesbury created the Whig party and influenced its characteristics for the next 100 years, he did not control it during his political career. Brown was also the first biographer to examine Shaftesbury's other great bequest to posterity, the Carolina settlements. As in politics, he was expert in adopting policies that had withstood the test of time, but he was also judicious in allowing the colonies to experiment and develop on their own.

The most recent contribution to scholarship on Shaftesbury is HALEY's thorough analysis of primary sources and 19th-century historiography, which creates the most balanced portrait of the earl to date. Accepting several of Christie's arguments, Haley contends that Shaftesbury was progressive in politics and religion but conservative in upholding many of the aristocracy's traditional rights and beliefs. Although he favoured religious toleration, he believed in an established church based on tithes and thus supported the Test Act of 1673. He also supported monarchy, and he did not advocate universal male suffrage. The "no popery" issue dominated Shaftesbury's political life, but he did not oppose catholicism unless it posed a political danger, as it did in James II's reign. Haley also casts doubt on the argument that Locke's *Two Treatises of Government* was an exclusionist tract written in support of Shaftesbury.

JOYCE SAMPSON

See also Anti-Catholicism and the Test Acts; Burnet; Charles II; Exclusion Crisis; Locke

Shaftesbury, Anthony Ashley Cooper, 7th Earl of 1801–1885
Social reformer, philanthropist, and politician

Battiscombe, Georgina, *Shaftesbury: A Biography of the Seventh Earl, 1801–1885*, London: Constable, 1974; as *Shaftesbury: The Great Reformer, 1801–1885*, Boston: Houghton Mifflin, 1975

Best, Geoffrey F.A., *Shaftesbury*, London: Batsford, 1964

Chadwick, Owen, *The Victorian Church*, 2 vols, London: A. and C. Black, 1967–70; New York: Oxford University Press, 1966–70

Finlayson, Geoffrey B.A.M., *The Seventh Earl of Shaftesbury, 1801–1885*, London: Eyre Methuen, 1981

Hammond, J.L. and Barbara Hammond, *Lord Shaftesbury*, London: Constable, 1923; New York: Harcourt Brace, 1924

Hodder, Edwin, *The Life and Work of the Seventh Earl of Shaftesbury, K.G.*, 3 vols, London and New York: Cassell, 1886

Hollis, Patricia (editor), *Pressure from Without in Early Victorian England*, London: Arnold, and New York: St Martin's Press, 1974

A conventional future on the Tory benches might have been predicted for the young Lord Ashley when he entered parliament in 1826. Yet although he remained a member for most of his life, first of the Commons and after 1851 of the Lords, his career took a different direction. As a Tory paternalist he agreed to take over the parliamentary leadership of the Ten Hours movement in 1833; and he then went on, inspired by his evangelicalism, to embrace a host of social and moral causes in and out of parliament. Although he dominated the age as reformer, philanthropist, and churchman he preferred to do so largely as an outsider who held no major office and was often at odds with the leaders of his own party. Biographers and historians have not found it easy to do justice to the range and scale of Shaftesbury's activities or to the competing elements within them: private and public, philanthropic and political, urban and rural, *laissez-faire* and interventionist, conservative and radical. It has also proved difficult to establish the criteria by which his achievements over a career of nearly six decades can be judged.

Shaftesbury chose a friend as official biographer, fed him material and anecdotes, and instructed him to "tell my life in its entirety". But although HODDER's *Life* was respectful and admiring, it was also unexpectedly revealing, since Hodder, who wished his subject to tell his own life, quoted copiously from the private diary that Shaftesbury had finally allowed the author to use. The intense sense of strain and self-doubt that Shaftesbury had hidden from view was now visible, and he emerged as a complex and vulnerable individual rather than a plaster saint. The biography portrays Shaftesbury as he had wished, as "an Evangelical of Evangelicals" who never led an evangelical party and held some unpopular religious views, his millenarianism in particular. Hodder also defines him as the "Working Man's Friend", a tireless activist labouring on behalf of some two hundred moral and social reform societies, which sent representatives to his funeral. Historians have treated some of the reminiscences in Hodder's biography with caution, but they have generally respected its comprehensiveness and used it as a starting-point.

HAMMOND & HAMMOND reworked Hodder's material to their own ends in their selective study. As progressive Liberal social historians with a special interest in the impact of the Industrial Revolution on labour, they were more interested in the times than the man and more interested in the political campaigns than the moral and religious campaigns. In the edition of 1936 they defended themselves against critics who had accused them of being fundamentally out of sympathy with Shaftesbury, and particularly with his religious outlook, but they clearly disliked some aspects of evangelicalism and were much more critical than Hodder. They argued that Shaftesbury lacked the necessary qualities for political success, failed to press home his victory over the Ten Hours Bill, and then turned away into philanthropy and arid quarrels with the ritualists. They exaggerate the extent to which Shaftesbury changed direction after 1847, and they are certainly guilty of wishful thinking when they complain that he should have allied himself with the Christian socialists; but their judgements are penetrating, and they found much to admire as well as criticize.

Like Hammond & Hammond, BEST produced a thematic review rather than a biography, but he gives a more rounded picture. His lively and stimulating study remains the best brief historical account of Shaftesbury, whom he depicts sympathetically, yet as flawed and difficult: at once representative and unique, Shaftesbury personified the conscience of his age. Best sees Shaftesbury's lifelong efforts on behalf of the mentally ill as his noblest achievement but argues that in general Shaftesbury did his best work as a member of the House of Commons.

BATTISCOMBE's was the first conventional biography since Hodder's. Written for the general reader and with a light touch, it is thoroughly researched and perceptive in its understanding of Shaftesbury's family and public life, although it adds nothing that is strikingly new.

FINLAYSON was the first to provide an exhaustive and scholarly modern biography, which puts Shaftesbury in historical context and relates him to other individuals and to contemporary events. As well as giving particularly full attention to the causes that Shaftesbury himself thought important and to the legislation and charities that absorbed his time, Finlayson includes neglected subjects such as Shaftesbury's interest in foreign and imperial policy. He sees Shaftesbury as someone who defies political or religious stereotyping and was never imprisoned in the social order that he wished to maintain. Finlayson is careful to describe change over time and Shaftesbury's responses to shifts of opinion in society, particularly in religion, where the earl's reactions were by no means exclusively conservative. He views the diary as a treacherous source but uses it circumspectly to describe Shaftesbury's complex personality, his inner torments, and his hypersensitivity. These Finlayson sees as important in explaining Shaftebury's motives and actions and the opposition that he provoked. Finlayson is fair both to Shaftesbury and to his critics. In assessing Shaftesbury's achievements he points out the dangers for the biographer, even of an individual with such stature, of exaggerating the importance of the subject.

In this respect HOLLIS's collection of essays on pressure groups between the first and second Reform Acts can offer a useful corrective. The essays demonstrate how varied these crusades were in their composition, nature, and objectives, although they shared a desire to exert pressure on parliament from within and without. Shaftesbury is compared with other campaigners and located within the overlapping and highly populated worlds of the moral and social reformers.

A broad context for Shaftesbury as Anglican evangelical is provided by CHADWICK's classic study of the Victorian church. Although this tends to play down the importance of evangelicalism in general, it makes an exception for Shaftesbury, who is described as the noblest philanthropist of the century, although also as the man who later helped to lead the evangelicals along a harsher, more political path.

FRANCES WALSH

See also Evangelicalism; Factory Reform

Shipbuilding, Rise and Decline of

19th and 20th centuries

Arnold, A.J., *Iron Shipbuilding on the Thames, 1832–1915: An Economic and Business History*, Aldershot, Hampshire; and Burlington, Vermont: Ashgate, 2000

Gordon, G.A.H., *British Seapower and Procurement between the Wars: A Reappraisal of Rearmament*, Annapolis, Maryland: Naval Institute Press, and London: Macmillan, 1988

Grove, Eric J., *Vanguard to Trident: British Naval Policy since World War II*, Annapolis, Maryland: Naval Institute Press, and London: Bodley Head, 1987

Jones, Leslie, *Shipbuilding in Britain: Mainly between the Two World Wars*, Cardiff: University of Wales Press, 1957

Lorenz, Edward H., *Economic Decline in Britain: The Shipbuilding Industry, 1890–1970*, Oxford: Clarendon Press, and New York: Oxford University Press, 1991

Peebles, Hugh B., *Warshipbuilding on the Clyde: Naval Orders and the Prosperity of the Clyde Shipbuilding Industry, 1889–1939*, Edinburgh: John Donald, 1987

Pollard, Sidney and Paul Robertson, *The British Shipbuilding Industry, 1870–1914*, Cambridge, Massachusetts: Harvard University Press, 1979

Ritchie, L.A. (editor), *The Shipbuilding Industry: A Guide to Historical Records*, Manchester and New York: Manchester University Press, 1992

Slaven A.J., "Self Liquidation: The National Shipbuilders Security Ltd, and British Shipbuilders in the 1930s" in *Charted and Uncharted Waters: Proceedings of a Conference on the Study of British Maritime History*, edited by Sarah Palmer and Glyndwr Williams, London: Trustees of the National Maritime Museum/Department of History, Queen Mary College, 1981

Slaven, A.J., "Management and Shipbuilding, 1890–1938: Structure and Strategy in the Shipbuilding Firm on the Clyde" in *Business, Banking, and Urban History: Essays in Honour of S.G. Checkland*, edited by Anthony Slaven and Derek H. Aldcroft, Edinburgh: John Donald, 1982

Slaven, A.J., "Marketing Opportunities and Marketing Practices: The Eclipse of British Shipbuilding, 1957–1976" in *From Wheel House to Counting House: Essays in Maritime Business History in Honour of Professor Peter Neville Davies*, edited by Lewis R. Fischer, St John's, Newfoundland: International Maritime Economic History Association, 1992

Sumida, John Tetsuro, *In Defence of Naval Supremacy: Financial Limitation, Technological Innovation, and British Naval Policy, 1889–1914*, London: Allen and Unwin, 1988; as *In Defence of Naval Supremacy: Finance, Technology, and British Naval Policy, 1889–1914*, Boston: Unwin Hyman, 1989

A major problem in modern British economic history lies in explaining why an industry, shipbuilding, in which Britain had long dominated the world had by the end of the 20th century shrunk to statistical insignificance in international terms. In 1920, Britain launched almost 60 per cent of world output, and as late as 1948 it still held over 50 per cent. By the 1990s registering just over 1 per cent could be hailed as an achievement.

POLLARD & ROBERTSON explain how and why it was that a shipbuilding industry based on wooden construction and sail propulsion, under severe competitive and technological pressure from the United States and France in particular, was able to transform itself and achieve world dominance in the 1860s. Ultimately, a combination of a rise of building in iron, and later steel, and the development of steam technology bestowed world leadership on the British shipbuilding industry. This, however, was not a simple case of one technology replacing another: wood and sail reached their apogee at the same time as metal and steam technology came into their own.

The new technology was based on a series of inventions and innovations centred on the west coast of Scotland and the north-east coast of England. At the microeconomic level, the geographical shifts which these changes caused are analysed by ARNOLD. He examines why the United Kingdom's major shipbuilding centre, the Thames, was able to transform itself in the era of wood and sail and again in the era of iron and steam but still experienced a precipitous decline. The British shipbuilding industry had undergone two industrial revolutions in the span of a few years. The whole configuration of these revolutions – industrial relations, management attitudes, and an air of technological supremacy – may have suited the pre-1914 period, but they would not *per se* suit a world economy ravaged by World War I.

Before 1914, however, almost all major inventions and innovations in shipbuilding technology were pioneered in Britain. Iron construction was quickly supplanted by steel. With regard to propulsion, the compound, triple, and quadruple expansion engines linked to Scotch and water tube boilers were all pioneered on the Clyde and the north-east coast of England. The last major innovation was the direct-acting steam turbine as a means of propelling ships, pioneered on the Tyne by Charles Parsons, although its major application to ships was marked on the Clyde. Turbine propulsion made rapid advances before 1914, and the only technological breakthrough not to be made in Britain was the motor ship, better known as the diesel (after its inventor's name). Although it made little progress before World War I, the diesel was a portent of the future. Before 1914

British shipbuilding, sustained by technical expertise, a vast empire, growing world trade, and overseas demand, dominated the world market.

The impact and aftermath of World War I was to damage the British shipbuilding industry beyond repair, although this was not realized at the time. A combination of trade dislocation, economic slump, and economic nationalism all contributed to a situation where there was a vast over-supply of ships available for the volume of world trade. JONES (1957) and SLAVEN ("Management and Shipbuilding", 1982) track the course and impact of the recession, and then the depression, on British shipbuilding. Although it was published in the 1950s, Jones's *Shipbuilding in Britain* remains the best study of the interwar years. The contraction of naval demand, which had been an important element in the growth of the industry before 1914, was underlined by the signing of the Washington Conference treaty of 1921, which severely curtailed the building of warships. The impact of naval policy on shipbuilding is well captured in SUMIDA (1989), and the policies which underpinned disarmament are outlined in GORDON (1988). The best study that takes the viewpoint of the industry rather than naval policy is PEEBLES (1987).

As naval orders evaporated, so too did overseas and domestic mercantile orders. With British mercantile growth stagnant and foreign orders at around two-thirds of their pre-1914 levels, at least in theoretical terms, Britain could have supplied the whole of world demand between 1921 and 1938. As a result Britain's share of world output fell from 60 per cent in 1913 to 42 per cent in the late 1930s. The interwar years also marked significant changes in the composition of the world's carrying trade and in the way it was carried. Oil gradually began to replace coal – a major staple of the British tramp trade – as one of the world's main carrying trades, and this spawned new types of ships, the tanker and the bulk carrier, which once again were portents of things to come.

The impact of the recession was to induce brutal competition, prices below cost, yard closures, bankruptcies, wage cuts, unemployment, and embittered industrial relations. The response of the industry is encapsulated in SLAVEN ("Self Liquidation", 1981). The builders set up a trade association, the Shipbuilding Conference, designed to limit competition; this body settled, as policy, upon the need to reduce capacity more in line with anticipated demand. In 1930 it established, with support from the Bank of England, a rationalization agency, National Shipbuilders Security Ltd (NSS), to buy up and remove from production redundant shipyards and berths. Between 1930 and 1938 this organization removed some 1.4 million gross registered tons of berth capacity – some 35 per cent of the total available in 1930. The cuts fell disproportionately hard on the Clyde and the north-east coast of England, where the closure of the giant Palmer's yard at Jarrow led to unemployment of more than 70 per cent and ultimately provoked the Jarrow Hunger March, perhaps the most potent symbol of the situation in shipbuilding in particular and of the depression in Britain in general. The straitened circumstances of British shipbuilding in this period were exacerbated by the subsidies and schemes of credit support established by many other countries to aid their industries. This competition was heightened by new forms of technical competition as the motor ship and the transport of oil came into their own. Despite the fact that Britain did move into these areas, there was a strong residual commitment to carrying trades and their vessel types and propulsion systems, which had allowed Britain to achieve world domination in the maritime trades. In effect, it was naval rearmament that pulled the industry out of the depression, although as late as 1939 mercantile demand remained flat.

World War II eventually propelled the industry into full production and seemed to restore Britain's position as the premier shipbuilding country in the world. The growth of world trade from 1948, sustained by the Korean war and the absence of serious competition in world shipbuilding markets, ensured British dominance, and Britain held more than 50 per cent of the world market. The market situation, however, was an entirely false one, with Britain enjoying a sellers' market, dominated by cost-plus contracts and little competition. Despite these propitious conditions for British shipbuilding there was an intensification of competition in the period after World War II, with West Germany, Japan, and Italy all re-entering world markets and countries such as Sweden, Norway, the Netherlands, Belgium, France, and Spain all providing stiff competition. After 1950 the world shipbuilding market expanded unprecedentedly as world trade boomed in hitherto unknown ways. The world mercantile fleet expanded by 33 million tons between 1950 and 1958, but British builders adopted a steady-state approach to the market. In all probability this attitude of mind was a reaction to the horrendous conditions of the interwar years, but it doomed British shipbuilding to failure. Even in the easy market conditions of 1945 to 1955, a range of criticisms were advanced against British shipbuilders: lack of reasonable credit facilities, late delivery dates, high prices, and a general unwillingness to consider new types of ships and new shipping markets. Such criticisms were intensified in the wake of the Suez crisis of 1956, which fundamentally altered the nature of the shipbuilding and shipping markets. The sellers' market turned to a buyers' market, and Britain rapidly lost market share, being overtaken in quick succession by Japan and then West Germany. In addition to new ship types and propulsive methods, there were new construction techniques based on welding and prefabrication methods, developed in the United States during the war and taken up with gusto on the Continent and in Japan, but not with any degree of enthusiasm in Britain.

The mild recession of 1958–61 merely interrupted the astonishing growth of demand for shipping, but it was enough to convince the industry that its stubborn refusal to expand after 1945 had been correct. As world demand boomed, British shipowners began increasingly to order abroad, and British builders' share of world output fell from 15 per cent to under 4 per cent between 1960 and 1974. The expansion of competition was based heavily on the emergence of a market for very large and ultralarge crude carriers, one which benefited those builders who had embraced the new technology of prefabrication and flow-line production methods. The British retained their traditional approach to the market, despite the obvious evidence that the airliner had replaced the ocean liner as the favoured method of crossing the Atlantic, and that worse was probably to come. Thus, as SLAVEN ("Marketing Opportunities", 1992) has demonstrated, British shipbuilders operated in what was a marketing and information vacuum.

The failure in the market marked the beginning of the end of British shipbuilding as a volume producer. Some 17 yards closed

between 1958 and 1963, mostly voluntary liquidations, until in the mid-1960s high-profile bankruptcies began to occur. The state now weighed in with lavish support, beginning with the Shipbuilding Credit Scheme of 1963, to be followed by the Shipbuilding Inquiry Committee of 1966, which established further measures of support and reorganization of the industry through the Shipbuilding Industry Board. Despite all the effort and money – £220 million between 1967 and 1972 – that went into restructuring the industry, it was increasingly being spent on sustenance rather than competition. The world economy was then hit by OPEC's increased oil prices of 1974, which destroyed the demand and supply schedules that had pertained for almost 30 years; inflation rocketed, world trade slumped, and the tanker market, which represented half of all new building, collapsed. Orders were reduced by 50 per cent between 1975 and 1976. In the wake of this crisis the Labour government nationalized the industry as British Shipbuilders in 1977, a step which saved the industry from total extinction. By the later 1980s, with a radically free-market-oriented Conservative government in power, the industry was privatized, in an episode of almost unprecedented industrial vandalism, designed to reduce British capacity to next to nothing. It worked. By the late 1990s only the major naval yards and a very few mercantile yards were left. GROVE's analysis (1987) of naval policy since 1945 explains why the vicarious nature of this policy meant that there could be little support for the industry. There is no commensurate study for the period after 1945 with regard to shipbuilding to match Peebles.

The academic debate on the decline of British shipbuilding has been intense and vociferous. Slaven has consistently asserted a managerial-failure thesis, while LORENZ has maintained that decline can be explained only through the medium of institutional economics. This is a complex and difficult explanatory mechanism, but it basically holds that the way in which the industry developed, its attitudes to markets, and its industrial relations had bred a system wherein trust could not be achieved or had broken down. The lack of trust between management and labour, in this view, largely explains the inability of the British shipbuilding industry to reform itself. Whatever the explanatory mechanisms, it had been a remarkable dénouement, with the dominance of British shipbuilders wiped from the face of the market in less than 40 years.

Those wishing to pursue research on British shipbuilding should follow RITCHIE (1992) as the definitive guide to the primary sources available for the study of the industry in Britain. These are rich sources for what is, ultimately, a sorry tale.

LEWIS JOHNMAN

See also Engineering: General Surveys; Industry, Heavy: Decline; Merchant Navy: Since 1840; Navy: Modern

Simnel, Lambert, Rebellion of 1487

Bennett, Michael, *Lambert Simnel and the Battle of Stoke*, Stroud, Gloucestershire: Sutton, and New York: St Martin's Press, 1987

Chrimes, S.B., *Henry VII*, London: Eyre Methuen, and Berkeley: University of California Press, 1972

that undermined customary ideas about human bondage and servitude. The emergence of evangelicalism, which at once stressed personal responsibility and emphasized the dangers of moral complacency, was also a factor: this movement identified slave trading and slavery – as John Wesley put it – as great sins of the world which would soon be judged. The success of abolition, then, came not from economics but largely from intellectual and religious developments.

Between the debate over the nature of the slave trade and its abolition is a significant body of scholarship about the plantations of the West Indies. DUNN has argued that the slave trade to the West Indies came about because neither European nor indigenous labourers were able to adapt to the Caribbean. PATTERSON paints a picture of Jamaica as a slave society which disregarded most traditional mores. GOVEIA's analysis of the Leeward Islands offers a less exotic picture: the combination of the slave trade and the practice of plantation slavery produced a society which was highly stratified and exploitative.

Finally, scholars have also explored the attempts by the Royal Navy to suppress the trade in slaves. LLOYD examined the relationship between the 19th-century slave trade, British domestic politics, and naval operations; for this reason, his account remains useful after more than half a century. HOWELL added to this literature by not only examining naval policies in detail but also showing that at many stages the suppression of the slave trade was brought about as much by determined individuals as by government policy.

STEPHEN L. KECK

See also Africa I: British Interests to 1895; Bristol; Exploration: To the 18th Century

Slave Trade: Anti-Slavery Movement

Anstey, Roger, *The Atlantic Slave Trade and British Abolition, 1760–1810*, London: Macmillan, and Atlantic Highlands, New Jersey: Humanities Press, 1975

Coupland, Reginald, *The British Anti-Slavery Movement*, London: Thornton Butterworth, 1933

Davis, David Brion, *The Problem of Slavery in the Age of Revolution, 1770–1823*, Ithaca, New York: Cornell University Press, 1975; Oxford and New York: Oxford University Press, 1999

Drescher, Seymour, *Econocide: British Slavery in the Era of Abolition*, Pittsburgh: University of Pittsburgh Press, and London: Feffer and Simons, 1977

Oldfield, J.R., *Popular Politics and British Anti-Slavery: The Mobilisation of Public Opinion against the Slave Trade, 1787–1807*, Manchester and New York: Manchester University Press, 1995

Temperley, Howard, *British Antislavery, 1833–1870*, London: Longman, 1972

Turley, David, *The Culture of English Antislavery*, London and New York: Routledge, 1991

Walvin, James, *Black Ivory: A History of British Slavery*, London: HarperCollins, 1992; Washington, D.C.: Howard University Press, 1994

Williams, Eric, *Capitalism and Slavery*, Chapel Hill: University of North Carolina Press, 1944; London: André Deutsch, 1964

The first major achievement of British anti-slavery was the campaign to end the transatlantic slave trade in the British empire. Analysis of this topic has emphasized either the moral arguments and effective propaganda of the abolitionists as the key to success or economic considerations relating to the slave trade and the British Caribbean as a more compelling reason for the demise of British transatlantic slaving. Before World War II, the chief explanation offered for the abolition of the British slave trade was the humanitarian work of anti-slavery campaigners. COUPLAND, the leading advocate of this point of view, argued that the statutory ban on the British slave trade was a moral triumph for saintly Christian evangelicals and quakers, clustered around the Clapham Sect and the leadership of William Wilberforce in the House of Commons. According to this interpretation, philanthropic individuals achieved a striking success as humanitarianism triumphed in 1807.

A challenge to these arguments came from WILLIAMS, a Trinidadian, who presented a strong case for economic reasons why Britain abolished its slave trade. In direct opposition to Coupland's ideas, Williams adapted data from Lowell Joseph Ragatz's *The Fall of the Planter Class in the British Caribbean, 1763–1833* (1928) to argue that the British West Indian plantation economy was in serious decline after the Seven Years' War. The causes of the decline were soil exhaustion on sugar estates, interruptions to the marketing of sugar during the American War of Independence, and planters' indebtedness in the period 1793–1807. Williams also argued that during the late 18th century the British economy was undergoing a shift from mercantilism to industrial capitalism, with an accompanying change from an emphasis on slavery to free wage labour in the empire: thus Britain abolished its slave trade primarily for economic reasons.

ANSTEY argued that Williams had not provided systematic statistics to support his case and that little evidence on economic matters was produced in the parliamentary debates over abolishing the slave trade. Anstey traced the origins and progress of abolitionist thought, especially its emphasis on Christian benevolence and a belief in God's providence. These beliefs led anti-slavery campaigners to single out the slave trade as an act of national wickedness. The difficulties of war with revolutionary and Napoleonic France delayed the progress of the campaign in parliament against the slave trade. But a turnaround occurred in 1806–07 when the newly formed coalition ministry (the "Ministry of All the Talents") campaigned first to restrict the supply of slaves to foreign territories in wartime and then to abolish the British slave trade altogether. According to Anstey, a particular and fortuitous set of politico-economic circumstances impelled the British to abolish their slave trade in the national economic interest.

The most direct attack on Williams's views can be found in DRESCHER's book. Marshalling an impressive array of statistics, Drescher argued that the British slave trade was abolished at a time of propitious economic circumstances for the British Caribbean. Soil exhaustion and the planters' indebtedness were temporary phenomena. According to the evidence, sugar plantations were still making profits, on average, even during difficult wartime years. At the turn of the 19th century, Britain was expanding its Caribbean plantation system in newly acquired territories such as Trinidad and British Guiana. British West Indian trade comprised as significant a share of total British foreign commerce in the 1820s as it had in the 1770s. For these reasons, Drescher argued, the abolition of the British slave trade was as an act of economic suicide: the economic decline of British Caribbean slavery, *pace* Ragatz and Williams, came after 1815.

The implication of this conclusion was to return the arguments over philanthropy and economics full circle to a position favourable to Coupland. Recent work on the battle against the British slave trade has pointed to the sheer effectiveness of the philanthropic campaign and to the popularity of this crusade, as evidenced by the number of signatures on petitions presented to parliament. The mobilization of abolitionist activities in London and the provinces is discussed thoroughly by OLDFIELD, who provides much material on the diffusion of visual and written anti-slavery propaganda. DAVIS explores how the growth of anti-slavery formed part of the ruling classes' ideological hegemony over the lower classes. Drawing on ideas of the Italian thinker Gramsci, Davis suggests that the British acted from self-interest in abolishing the slave trade. Whigs, Tories, evangelicals, and quakers came together in a campaign that emphasized subjection to the law. Parliament demonstrated its liberal progress to the nation by ameliorating and abolishing the slave trade and, later, slavery itself.

Numerous books follow the progress of the anti-slavery cause in Britain through to the mid-19th century. WALVIN, in *Black Ivory*, provides a readable narrative of black peoples' resistance to plantation slavery in the British Caribbean and the crusade to abolish slavery in the British empire – themes that he has also explored in several other books. TEMPERLEY concentrates on the ways in which British abolitionists pursued an international attack on slavery after 1834. Taking the stance (contrary to Williams's) that industrial capitalism did not destroy slavery, Temperley shows that the international work of British abolitionists was beset by internal factional struggles, ideological differences, and the problem of achieving results in foreign territories such as Cuba and Brazil. TURLEY analyses the culture of English anti-slavery; he perceives abolitionist campaigners as a series of coalition groups embracing different religious traditions that were active in other 19th-century reform movements. He detects a distinctive "reform mentality" that influenced public opinion and politicians, but he also shows that abolitionists were only one group, and certainly not the major group, in the process of significant social and constitutional change that occurred in Britain during the 1820s and 1830s.

KENNETH MORGAN

Sluys, Battle of 1340

Allmand, Christopher T., *The Hundred Years War: England and France at War, c.1300–c.1450*, Cambridge and New York: Cambridge University Press, 1988

Friel, Ian, *The Good Ship: Ships, Shipbuilding, and Technology in England 1200–1520*, London: British Museum Press, and Baltimore, Maryland: Johns Hopkins University Press, 1995

Hewitt, H.J., *The Organization of War under Edward III, 1338–1362*, Manchester: Manchester University Press, and New York: Barnes and Noble, 1966

Hutchinson, Gillian, *Medieval Ships and Shipping*, London: Leicester University Press, and Rutherford, New Jersey: Fairleigh Dickinson Press, 1994

Richmond, Colin, "The War at Sea" in *The Hundred Years War*, edited by Kenneth Fowler, London: Macmillan, and New York: St Martin's Press, 1971

Rodger, N.A.M., *The Safeguard of the Sea: A Naval History of Great Britain*, vol. 1, 660–1649, London: Harper Collins and the National Maritime Museum, 1997; New York: Norton, 1998

Rose, Susan, "Edward III: Sluys 1340" in *Great Battles of the Royal Navy: As Commemorated in the Gunroom, Britannia Royal Naval College, Dartmouth*, edited by Eric Grove, London: Arms and Armour Press, 1994

Rose, Susan, *Medieval Naval Warfare, 1000–1500*, London and New York: Routledge, 2002

Sumption, Jonathan, *The Hundred Years War*, vol. 1, *Trial by Battle*, London, Faber, 1990; Philadelphia: University of Pennsylvania Press, 1991

The battle of Sluys, fought in the estuary of the River Scheldt on 24 June 1340 between the English and the French, was the first significant encounter of the Hundred Years' War. It has achieved greater renown than other medieval sea battles between these two adversaries, perhaps because the victor, Edward III, celebrated his achievement by striking a gold noble with an obverse showing himself on board a cog ship.

The background to the battle and a rousing narrative of the sea-fight itself can be found in SUMPTION (1991). This meticulously researched and elegantly written narrative of the opening years of the Hundred Years' War, providing a detailed account of the events leading to the outbreak of war and of events before and after the battle itself, has no equal among recent writings. Sumption explains the diplomatic manoeuvring and the deployment of forces by both sides before the engagement. He describes the collapse in the morale of the French after their defeat, and the joy with which the news of the victory was received in London. Significantly, a copy of Edward III's own account of the battle in a letter to his son is preserved in the City of London archives.

RODGER, in his overview of British naval history, provides more analysis of the action itself, placing it firmly in the context of developments in naval warfare in the 14th century. He is concerned to point out the benefits to the French of being allied with both Genoa and Castile and also to draw attention to the lack of strategic thinking on naval matters in England at this date. What had the greatest success against an enemy was not an encounter between royal fleets but coastal raids that created panic onshore, destroyed valuable property, and interrupted trade. Rodger vigorously denies that the victory at Sluys gave the English command of the seas, pointing out that by August the French were able to launch further raids all along the south coast of England. ROSE (1994) also presents a detailed account of the battle itself, drawing attention to the divergent chronicle accounts of events, including the French method of chaining galleys together to form a kind of fighting platform.

A valuable discussion of the objectives of naval warfare throughout the Hundred Years' War is provided by ALLMAND, who also sets out the nature of the naval forces available to each side. RICHMOND also sees the concept of "command of the sea" as inappropriate at this period; instead, he uses the idea of "zones of control" that could be established in the immediate vicinity of a fleet at sea. The importance of Sluys was that it restored the confidence of the English in their forces and allowed them to take the initiative, leading eventually to the successful siege of Calais in 1347 and the conversion of Calais into an English base on the border of France. Richmond extends his discussion to the end of the war in 1453, concluding that war at sea, whether successful or unsuccessful, had "none of the far-reaching consequences" so noticeable in later centuries. The whole question of the strategic use of naval forces in this period is also discussed, in relation to the Mediterranean and northern European powers, in ROSE (2002).

FRIEL and HUTCHINSON are both primarily concerned with shipping in general throughout the medieval period, concentrating on the technical aspects of shipbuilding and types and uses of ships, but they also include chapters on warships. Hutchinson looks particularly at the use of galleys by the English crown in the 14th century; Friel includes a discussion of the weaponry used at sea. Both provide many informative illustrations from contemporary sources as well as plans and drawings, some based on the results of underwater archaeology. HEWITT's book is concerned with the organization and logistics of warfare in general; its material on the use of ships helps the reader appreciate the difficulties facing any medieval monarch who wished to keep a fleet in being. Hewitt devotes space to the methods applied in raising a fleet and to the accumulation of the necessary supplies.

War at sea in the later Middle Ages could result in dramatic conflicts, of which Sluys is probably the best-known example. Its overall strategic importance, however, can be exaggerated. Although this battle ended in a famous victory, it had few if any long-term consequences for either side. From that point of view, the relief of Harfleur by a naval force under the command of the Duke of Bedford in August 1416 was of greater importance, since it ensured the continued success of Henry V's invasion of France. These conclusions emerge strongly from the works discussed above.

SUSAN ROSE

See also Edward III; Hundred Years' War

Smillie, Robert 1857–1940
Miners' leader

Aitken, Keith, *The Bairns O'Adam: The Story of the STUC*, Edinburgh: Polygon, 1997

Arnot, R. Page, *The Miners: A History of the Miners' Federation of Great Britain*, vol. 2, *Years of Struggle from 1910 Onwards*, London: Allen and Unwin, 1953

Arnot, R. Page, *A History of the Scottish Miners from the Earliest Times*, London: Allen and Unwin, 1955

Bellamy, Joyce and John Saville, *Dictionary of Labour Biography*, vol. 3, London: Macmillan, and Clifton, New Jersey: A.M. Kelley, 1976

Clegg, Hugh Armstrong, *A History of British Trade Unions since 1889*, vol. 2, *1911–1933*, Oxford: Clarendon Press, and London and New York: Oxford University Press, 1964

Gregory, Roy, *The Miners and British Politics, 1906–1914*, Oxford: Oxford University Press, 1968

Howell, David, *British Workers and the Independent Labour Party, 1888–1906*, Manchester: Manchester University Press, and New York: St Martin's Press, 1983; reprinted with corrections, 1984

Howell, David, "'All or Nowt': The Politics of the MFGB" in *Miners, Unions, and Politics, 1910–1947*, edited by Alan Campbell, Nina Fishman, and David Howell, Aldershot, Hampshire; and Brookfield, Vermont: Scolar Press, 1996

Smillie, Robert, *My Life for Labour*, London: Mills and Boon, 1924

Perhaps the most remarkable thing about Robert Smillie is how little he is now remembered. Although BELLAMY & SAVILLE have no doubt that "Smillie takes his place among the greatest of the miners' leaders" and as the "first prominent personality to bring a socialist outlook into the whole of his trade-union work", he barely rates a mention in most of the more recent general histories of trade unionism other than as one member of the Sankey Commission on the mining industry in 1919. Yet Smillie was president of the Scottish Miners' Federation (which he had been largely responsible for bringing into existence) from 1894 until 1918 and again from 1921 until 1928, and president of the Miners' Federation of Great Britain in the turbulent years from 1912 until 1921. Part of the reason why so little attention has been given to him is that few of his personal papers survive; there is only a rather poor volume of rambling reminiscences: SMILLIE (1924), published when he had just been elected to parliament after seven earlier unsuccessful attempts.

Smillie (the family name was in fact Smellie) was born in Belfast and moved to Scotland in 1871 at the age of 15. Becoming a miner in Lanarkshire, he came under the influence of an emerging movement for independent labour representation. He became the president of the Larkhall Miners' Association in 1885 and president of the Scottish Miners' Federation in 1894. He was already associated with Keir Hardie's Scottish Labour Party, and in 1893 he joined the new Independent Labour Party (ILP). In this he was out of line with the English miners' leaders who retained their traditional loyalty to Liberalism. Smillie never wavered in his belief that the political and industrial organization of labour had to go on side by side, and he was the key figure in winning the miners away from the Liberal Party to support Labour.

Bellamy & Saville present Smillie as warm-hearted, utterly sincere, and not particularly theoretical. CLEGG, quoting a contemporary, describes him as "well-read . . . the mildest and most humorous of men . . . quietly spoken, but ruthlessly logical and always cautious and far-sighted". HOWELL (1983) notes the significance of Smillie's presiding, in January 1900, over the inaugural meeting of the Scottish Workers' Parliamentary Election Committee, a body which anticipated the Labour Representation Committee; he concludes that "perhaps more than anyone else, Smillie epitomised the possibility of a rapport between the ILP and trade unionism". It was at Smillie's prompting that the Miners' Federation agreed to affiliate with the Labour Party in 1908, and GREGORY shows how Smillie severed the miners' connection with Liberalism in the following decade.

Smillie's firm commitment to socialism had given him a reputation for militancy by the time he took over as president of the Miners' Federation in 1912, an appointment which ARNOT (1953) sees as a victory of the new generation over the old. Lloyd George criticized Smillie for "fanatical obstinacy", but as Clegg points out, in industrial affairs Smillie was generally a moderate. His concern was with maintaining miners' unity, and in the national coal strike of 1912 he came down firmly on the side of settlement. He had little time for syndicalism. According to AITKEN, Smillie told the Scottish Trades Union Congress, of which he had been the founding chairman, that much of the militancy within unions in the years before 1914 was due to "a few discontented members who are not in a position to rise with sufficient rapidity into official positions because of the leaders not dying off quickly enough".

Smillie parted company with most miners in his opposition to World War I. However, he continued to lead the Miners' Federation at the same time as he campaigned against the introduction of military conscription, which he believed would be followed by industrial conscription. His socialism was unswerving, and Howell sees him as leading a shift within the Miners' Federation towards support for nationalization of the industry and towards fitting mining priorities "into a wider political agenda". Smillie's commitment to nationalization was strengthened by his experience as a member of the Sankey Commission; Clegg believes that in 1919–20 getting the government to continue with control of the industry was Smillie's overriding objective. Smillie pleaded with the miners – though in vain – to accept arbitration in 1920 rather than antagonize the public with a strike which might also break the Federation. Clegg concludes that Smillie's time in these years might "have been better spent negotiating with the owners over a permanent pay settlement and with the government over their proposals for the future of the industry than in scheming for nationalisation".

A divided and demoralized group of county miners' unions in Scotland brought Smillie back as chair of the Scottish Federation in 1921; but, as ARNOT (1955) shows, he had little of his former vigour. Smillie's hope of creating a single union was shattered by communist-led splits and bitter infighting to which he could contribute little. He resigned in 1928 and stood down as MP for Morpeth in 1929.

W. HAMISH FRASER

See also Independent Labour Party

Smith, Adam 1723–1790
Economist and philosopher

Campbell, R.H. and A.S. Skinner, *Adam Smith*, New York: St Martin's Press, and London: Croom Helm, 1982
Griswold, Charles L., *Adam Smith and the Virtues of Enlightenment*, Cambridge and New York: Cambridge University Press, 1999
Muller, Jerry Z. *Adam Smith in His Time and Ours: Designing the Decent Society*, New York: Free Press, and Toronto and New York: Maxwell Macmillan, 1993
Rashid, Salim, *The Myth of Adam Smith*, Cheltenham, Gloucestershire; and Northampton, Massachusetts: Elgar, 1998
Ross, Ian Simpson, *The Life of Adam Smith*, Oxford: Clarendon Press, and New York: Oxford University Press, 1995

As the Industrial Revolution began, astute observers noted the limits of mercantilism and argued for policies encouraging freer trade. Adam Smith is generally considered the herald of this new economic theory, capitalism. Smith is one of the few 18th-century British philosophers whose names are familiar today, and his continued appeal for scholars, as well as the educated public, is astonishing. Indeed, a complete bibliography of works in English about, or relating to, Smith would run into thousands of items. Perhaps not surprisingly, many of his devotees appear to have read more about him than by him.

The most reliable and readable recent biographies are by CAMPBELL & SKINNER and ROSS. Campbell & Skinner's slim volume is intended as a guide for those who are intrigued by Smith's work but know little of his life. The authors have created an immensely useful handbook, based on their broad working knowledge of Smith's writings, that integrates Smith's life with his works. For a more exhaustive treatment of Smith's life the reader should turn to Ross, who drew on his experience as co-editor of the Glasgow Edition of Smith's works (1976–83) to write the definitive biography of Smith in his time.

Smith was well regarded by his contemporaries for his prescient critique of mercantilism, his recognition of the potential productivity of the free market, and his elucidation of the new field of political economy, which he is credited with founding. It is his long-term impact, however, that is most important. Particularly in the 20th century, Smith was considered the patron saint of the free market, and by extension, of economic libertarianism, which is distinguished by a fiercely optimistic adherence to unrestrained free trade as the chief producer of wealth. Many scholars point out that, ironically, Smith would probably be dismayed by recent one-sided interpretations of his chief works, *The Theory of Moral Sentiments* (1759) and *An Inquiry into the Nature and Causes of the Wealth of Nations* (1776). Nonetheless, much of the popular literature on Smith consists of arguments invoking his endorsement of either liberal or conservative political and economic agendas, or claiming his authority on behalf of a particular cause, ranging from reforming child labour to financing religious education.

Smith's early work was in ethics, and much of it was influenced by his participation in the Scottish Enlightenment. *The Theory of Moral Sentiments* was the first volume of what Smith envisioned as a series which included *The Wealth of Nations* as the second volume; a third volume, *Essays on Philosophical Subjects*, dealing with the arts and sciences and published posthumously; and a fourth volume, on the history of law and justice, that was never begun. Seen in this context, *The Wealth of Nations* appears to be not only the first comprehensive system of political economy but also part of a much larger work describing the historical development of modern society.

The Theory of Moral Sentiments lays the psychological foundation for Smith's philosophy. In it Smith describes universal and unchanging human nature, which is the basis for social institutions and social behaviour. Smith is interested in the ability to form moral judgements, including judgements of one's own behaviour, especially in the face of what would appear to be an imperative for self-preservation and self-interest. He also, and more importantly, observes that humans are regulated by reason and sympathy as well as by passions and instincts. This aspect of Smith's work is gaining greater recognition, as scholars seeking a more balanced view emphasize his insistence on the necessity of individual virtue for a stable society. GRISWOLD's book is indicative of this new line of inquiry, which is by no means limited to historical analysis of Smith's work but finds its way into a variety of critiques of modern society and governments. Griswold examines Smith's systematic philosophy of morality, which is based on individuals' making decisions as though they were "impartial spectators" rather than from pure self-interest.

In *The Wealth of Nations*, Smith continues his examination of how the inner struggle between passions and reason works itself out in society. MULLER points out that Smith's interest in creating a "decent society" was influenced by his study of Stoicism. Smith was interested in how this basic conflict affected both historical and current societies. Muller describes Smith as being interested, in high Enlightenment style, in laying out a coherent system for civilization. Smith saw the development of private property as the catalyst for society and described a mythic evolution of society in which each stage is dominated by the relationship between individuals and private property. He described the new era, dominated by what has come to be known as laissez-faire capitalism, as the culmination of history.

Smith's most famous work, however, is in economics, and it was influenced by his contact with the French physiocrats. Most of *The Wealth of Nations* consists of Smith's detailed description of how the "invisible hand" operates in the commercial stage of society, which Smith sees as the most perfect phase of human development. Smith argues that conflict within and between individuals leads to competition, as each seeks to better himself. To protect themselves and their property men create order. Smith carefully examines, as part of this process, the conflicting claims and desires of the three great classes – labourers, landlords, and manufacturers – and the underlying laws that govern their interactions and regulate the division of the wealth of the nation.

Thus Smith describes a reliable "machine" for growth, depending only on the predictable complexity of human nature for its perpetuation. Smith's optimism and his progressive tone provide the foundation for his enduring popularity. And Smith remains an iconic figure, claimed by people adhering to widely disparate political and economic ideologies. Like the Bible, his works are routinely mined for evidence in debate. It is not remarkable that his works lend themselves to this, running as they do into thousands of pages. What should be noted is that Smith remains an almost unquestioned authority on many topics ranging from politics and ethics to foreign relations and education. Even attempts to demonstrate Smith's lack of originality, such as that by RASHID, leave his image intact. Rashid demonstrates rather persuasively that Smith, like other men, was motivated by passion as well as reason, and that much of his work was derivative. Ultimately, however, it is the image rather than the man that is crucial.

SUSAN MITCHELL SOMMERS

See also Capitalism; Economic Theory entries; Locke

Snowden, Philip 1864–1937
Independent Labour, then Labour, politician and statesman

Andreades, A., *Philip Snowden: The Man and His Financial Policy*, translated by Dorothy Bolton, London: King, 1930 (French edition, 1930)
Cross, Colin, *Philip Snowden*, London: Barrie and Rockliff, 1966
"Ephesian" [C.E. Bechhofer Roberts], *Philip Snowden: An Impartial Portrait*, London and Toronto: Cassell, 1929
Laybourn, K., *Philip Snowden: A Biography 1864–1937*, Aldershot, Hampshire: Temple Smith, 1988
McKibbin, Ross, "The Economic Policy of the Second Labour Government, 1929–1931", *Past & Present*, 68 (1975): 95–123
Skidelsky, Robert, *Politicians and the Slump: The Labour Government of 1929–1931*, London: Macmillan, 1967
Snowden, Philip, *An Autobiography*, 2 vols, London: Nicholson and Watson, 1934
Thompson, Noel, *Political Economy and the Labour Party: The Economics of Democratic Socialism, 1884–1995*, London: UCL Press, 1996

Few Labour politicians apart from Ramsay MacDonald have been the butt of such unrelenting execration as Philip Snowden. His name has entered Labour folklore as the epitome of political betrayal, and his period as chancellor of the exchequer in the second minority Labour government is seen as a major cause of its demise. This may account for the fact that, aside from two essentially hagiographical biographies of Snowden by ANDREADES and "EPHESIAN" (Roberts) which appeared before 1931, the only substantial studies of Snowden's life and political career are those of CROSS and LAYBOURN. Few on the left seem desirous of disinterring the memory of one who was so clearly buried outside the hallowed ground of the labour movement. That said, there is another important reason why Snowden's life and work have suffered neglect from historians: Snowden himself took pains to ensure that his personal papers would be destroyed after his death. This is sad for a number of reasons, but particularly because the excellent studies by Cross and Laybourn remind us that there was much more to Snowden than the figure presented in popular Labour mythology – the parsimonious Labour chancellor who was prepared to sacrifice the unemployed to the Treasury's obsession with balancing the nation's books.

Cross, in particular, makes it clear that there is much to be admired in Snowden's political career. Specifically, there was his courageous and principled opposition to many aspects of the conduct of World War I, as well as his energetic and consistent support for the cause of women's suffrage. Cross is particularly good on Snowden's apprenticeship as a Labour politician, drawing out the capabilities it instilled but also the limitations it imposed on his intellectual horizons. While Snowden's period as an itinerant propagandist gave him an intimate understanding of the constituency he addressed, it also prevented any systematic or profound development of the ideas he sought to purvey. As Cross intimates, what Snowden's audiences responded to was an ethical denunciation of capitalism and an evocation of a socialist utopia, even though that utopia was ill-defined and left a prescriptive lacuna which Snowden was never able to fill adequately.

Cross displays a particular empathy with his subject. This is no bad thing. Biographies driven by a desire to denigrate serve little purpose other than as therapy for their authors. Yet Cross's empathy does not and cannot obscure the fact that when push came to shove Snowden could be as vindictive a piece of work as British politics can boast. This comes across with particular force in his own two-volume autobiography, SNOWDEN (1934), published shortly after the traumatic events surrounding the collapse of the second minority Labour government. The work is self-serving – few such works are anything else – but it provides, nonetheless, both an insight into Snowden's mind and a detailed account of the events of 1931 which historians may wish to discount but cannot neglect. Running through the work is a determination to eviscerate those who had challenged Snowden's credo or crossed political swords with him. This is particularly evident in his treatment of MacDonald. Like Captain Ahab, Snowden seemed driven to stab at the great white whale of MacDonald's reputation even as the political waters closed over the heads of both. What his autobiography also conveys is an image of intransigence, compounded equally of obsession and conscience and making for a personality who rarely if ever bethought himself in the bowels of Christ that he might be wrong.

LAYBOURN's study is less sympathetic. To a greater extent than Cross, Laybourn reads the subject's life with an eye to the "betrayal of 1931", perceptively explaining Snowden's actions in that decisive year in terms of his values and attitudes of mind. Those values came out of nonconformist and essentially liberal views which Snowden brought with him from his upbringing and early political activism in the textile districts of Yorkshire. For Laybourn, what happened in 1931 was a consequence of the fact that "Snowden's generation of ILP members, influenced by [such] Liberal Radical and non-Conformist views had grown out of touch with the new more trade union-oriented policies of the Labour Party". At some juncture they were therefore "bound to come into conflict in their approach to matters such as unemployment benefit". In this reading, 1931 was a tragedy waiting to happen. Laybourn also argues, though less persuasively, that Snowden was able to dominate economic policy-making because Labour was a party bereft of ideas. In some measure, therefore, the party brought the tragedy on itself. Yet Laybourn does not miss his man; such arguments are not used to exonerate Snowden. The fact remains that "on the one major charge levelled against him – that he betrayed the Labour Party in 1931 – there is no doubt".

While there are few substantial studies of Snowden's life, his period as chancellor has been an object of intense scrutiny, more often than not highly critical. In this regard one of the most acerbic studies has been that of SKIDELSKY. Written at a time when Keynesianism was the received wisdom for economic policymakers on both sides of the political divide, Skidelsky's work is part of an historiographical traditon that saw the economic policy of the interwar period as underpinned by an understanding of the economic world which rendered policymakers impotent when confronted by mass unemployment. Shackled to an economic philosophy of balanced budgets, sound money, the gold standard, and free trade, a chancellor like Snowden was driven to act in ways which both exacerbated the nation's economic problems and disadvantaged Labour's traditional social constituency.

However, with the demise of Keynesian social democracy, the efficacy of Keynesian remedies as applied to the problem of unemployment is now no longer taken for granted, and this has altered our perspective on what governments could and should have been doing in the interwar period. This has laid the basis for a more sympathetic treatment of policymakers, as reflected in McKIBBIN's article. McKibbin argues that the Labour government did not have unlimited freedom to manoeuvre, and in 1929–31 it did about as well as could be expected – and better than many other administrations of the period. Skidelsky responded vigorously to this view in the second edition of his work, but subsequent econometric research on the interwar period has in part substantiated the argument, and it deserves serious consideration. Whether, of course, this will be sufficient to rescue Snowden's reputation for posterity is another matter.

None of the works cited discusses the totality of Snowden's thought in any detail. Cross and Laybourn do touch on some of the important elements of his political economy, but these are not considered at any length or in relation to the thinking of Snowden's contemporaries in the labour movement. This omission is partly repaired in THOMPSON's volume. Thompson looks at Snowden's writing on economic and social questions during his period of prominence and power within the Labour Party and throws light on Snowden's economic and social philosophy and also on the ideological currents that ebbed and flowed through the Labour Party in the first three decades after its formation. However, none of these works is likely to rescue Snowden from execration or from the historical oblivion to which he was relegated by the British left.

NOEL THOMPSON

See also Depression; Independent Labour Party; Labour Party; MacDonald

Social Conflict: Early Modern Period

Amussen, Susan Dwyer, *An Ordered Society: Gender and Class in Early Modern England*, Oxford and New York: Blackwell, 1988

Cressy, David, *Travesties and Transgressions in Tudor and Stuart England: Tales of Discord and Dissension*, Oxford and New York: Oxford University Press, 2000

Erickson, Amy Louise, *Women and Property in Early Modern England*, London and New York: Routledge, 1993

Fletcher, Anthony, *Gender, Sex, and Subordination in England 1500–1800*, New Haven, Connecticut, and London: Yale University Press, 1995

Roberts, Michael and Simone Clarke (editors), *Women and Gender in Early Modern Wales*, Cardiff: University of Wales Press, 2000

Sharpe, J.A., *Crime in Early Modern England 1550–1750*, London and New York: Longman, 1984

Sharpe, J.A., *Early Modern England: A Social History 1550–1760*, London and Baltimore, Maryland: Arnold, 1987; reprinted with corrections, 1988

Stone, Lawrence, *Broken Lives: Separation and Divorce in England, 1660–1857*, Oxford and New York: Oxford University Press, 1993

Wood, Andy, *The Politics of Social Conflict: The Peak Country, 1520–1770*, Cambridge and New York: Cambridge University Press, 1999

Wrightson, Keith, *Earthly Necessities: Economic Lives in Early Modern Britain*, New Haven, Connecticut, and London: Yale University Press, 2000

Social conflict in the early modern period took many forms. Tudor, Stuart, and 18th-century commentators frequently spoke of the need to maintain order, especially social order, community order, and gender order. While perhaps there was no "general crisis" at the heart of this period as assumed by previous historians, early modern society was concerned with threats to social stability and did have to grapple with an upheaval of most political, social, and religious traditions following the Reformation. While much has been written on social conflict in England, far less scholarship has centred on the other parts of Great Britain.

SHARPE's masterful overview (1987) of the social history of early modern England provides an important synthesis of the roots and dimensions of social crises and conflicts. Between 1550 and 1760 the population of England doubled, social stratification among the different orders increased (although Sharpe hesitates to use the more loaded term "class"), and there was a consistently high mortality rate (attributed principally to poverty, disease, bad harvests, famine, and childbirth). A developing court and government system balanced rising crime rates, increased taxation, and increased vagrancy. In this period, too, a distinct household ideology emerged, placing the pious protestant father at the head of a dutiful household. The subordination of females and the obedience of children became fundamental to maintaining the tenuous order of society. In the Tudor and early Stuart eras, ad hoc decisions of crown and parliament, rather than carefully constructed long-term strategies, dominated the response to pervasive social and economic problems. By the mid-17th century, chaos and instability within society and government had brought England to its maximum pressure point, resulting in the profound rupture of the civil wars. Sharpe – unlike many earlier Marxist and economic historians – is unwilling to ascribe the mid-17th century rupture to a rising middle class caught in the transition from feudalism to capitalism. Nevertheless, he contends that the process of modernization caused a profound transformation within English society. After the intense political and social shake-up of the mid-17th century, England became more stable and better able to deal with the agents of social conflict in a sustained and systematic way.

Sharpe's text is complemented, at least in part, by WRIGHTSON's study of the social and economic history of early modern Britain, in which Wales and Scotland (regions deliberately avoided by Sharpe) are also discussed. Wrightson examines the transition in economic life and the process of commercialization, particularly the uneven economic and social developments. He argues that as the old medieval conception of a society of estates was shifting, a new economically stratified social order with different goals and ambitions was emerging in England and Wales.

In an illuminating regional study, WOOD examines the politics of social conflict through the contentious relations between miners (plebians) and local elites (lords and entrepreneurs) in the Peak District in north-west Derbyshire (1520–1770). Elites, holding onto a fictional social hierarchy, in which the gentry and nobility were born to command and plebians were born to obey, did not know what to make of the rapid social and economic flux caused by the beginnings of industrialization. A fear of the "lawless" mining villages that lacked an elite developed into a prominent social concern. Subsequent localized disputes over free mining customs demonstrate how social conflict became politicized (both in local custom and in material resources) as miners responded to a loss of their rights with protests, riots, and litigation.

AMUSSEN takes up the theme of gender and class in early modern England, focusing on the family as an economic unit and the foundation for political and social order in a highly complex patriarchal society. She argues that throughout the early modern era in England there was a prevailing idea of the disciplined family as being at the heart of the social order. Wives were expected to obey their husbands, servants their masters, and children their parents. In return for this obedience and fidelity, the head of the household, more a "benevolent patriarch" than a tyrant, was expected to perform his duties as husband, father, or master properly. This relationship of responsibility and obedience operated outside the family as well: those with higher status governed and took care of those with lower status. Those who were being governed were expected to be obedient and to cooperate with the local government. In a generally convincing discussion, Amussen points out how the social hierarchy, ever fluctuating and nuanced, was a source of much heated conflict in the early modern period. For example, seating arrangements at church – with all the symbolic and visual representations of the social hierarchy and status conveyed by the location of the pew – led to both fistfights and lawsuits. In time, by the early 18th century, challenges to the class order were even more direct. Families were still expected to be orderly, but with less intervention from outsiders; ultimately, control of gender disorder (especially disorderly women) continued to affirm the proper social order. Since Amussen focuses on the records of three Norfolk villages, it is hard to say how well her study reflects patterns in other regions of England. With the exception of ROBERTS & CLARKE's more localized collection of essays on women and gender in early modern Wales, gender as a source of social conflict in other parts of Great Britain remains vastly uncharted territory.

The breakup of the family through divorce thus caused fears of a breakdown in social and communal harmony. In his third and last volume on marriage, STONE discusses the history of divorce during the highly litigious age of the early modern era. Using 12 case studies drawn from marital life among the elite, Stone suggests a highly controversial theory: that the early modern family was disaffected and uncaring but gradually evolved into the modern loving family. Since the 1970s Stone's theories on marriage and divorce have prompted a wave of scholarship presenting alternative interpretations that maintained, challenged, or even rejected his notion of the family.

The transfer of property was another aspect of contested gender and family relations that helped shape the structure of English society. Focusing on the stages of "ordinary" women's lives (maids, wives, widows), ERICKSON discusses women's participation in the transmission and creation of wealth, the nature of women's property rights, and how these rights were often controlled by the courts. There was often more parity among the sexes in the distribution of an inheritance than is commonly assumed; but widows still often had to resort to probate court to claim their wealth or property, even when it came from an earlier inheritance or they had earned it with their own labour.

FLETCHER provides an important synthesis of the scholarship of sex and gender in England, offering a thoughtful overview of the construction of gender and the changing interpretations of masculinity and femininity between 1500 and 1800. Focusing on the upper levels of English society, and using literature about, though not by, women, Fletcher probes the social anxiety towards patriarchy experienced by men and women. Arguing against a general crisis in gender relations, Fletcher agrees that gender gradually began to provide a foundation (albeit an insufficient one) for early modern patriarchy. In the Tudor period gender shaped sex and was constructed only as a balance of body humours. Later, gender became hierarchical and grounded in the physical body, based on dress and demeanour and enforced by honour codes, sexual virtue (for women), and male control of expressions of friendship and erotic attraction; and it would be a means of maintaining order and making sense of society. Visible sexual differences helped maintain the masculine sense of privilege and control over various sources of power. Rather than simply being misogynistic, as some feminist scholarship has asserted, men instead had to mask their fear of female assertiveness and their own potential inadequacy. To Fletcher, the early modern period was characterized by men's struggle to maintain their tenuous hold on patriarchy and by women's struggle to decide between accepting and rejecting patriarchal notions of femininity.

SHARPE (1984) looks at a different source of social conflict in his careful study of crime. He argues that in the highly litigious early modern age, the control of crime was dependent on private initiative as wronged individuals sought to prosecute a felony. To Sharpe, an intense fear of disorder, compounded after the Reformation by distrust of religious consensus, resulted in the growing control by the state over the individual. At the same time, however, aberrant behaviour within the community was not always a source of conflict. CRESSY's collection of 15 essays provides a useful, if not provocative, glimpse into the lives of ordinary people and how they dealt with agents of social conflict. At heart the essays reflect scandalous and often divisive local issues, but Cressy places them within a larger national context. They show how people may have tolerated some odd occurrences and bizarre behaviour on the part of the neighbors to preserve the larger, and more important, communal order and harmony in their lives.

SUSANNA CALKINS

See also Pilgrimage of Grace; Poverty: Poverty and Social Control, 17th and 18th Centuries

Social Conflict: Medieval (English)

Barnie, John. *War in Medieval Society: Social Values in the Hundred Years War 1337-1399*, London: Weidenfeld and Nicolson, 1974; as *War in Medieval English Society*, Ithaca, New York: Cornell University Press, 1974

Bean, J.M.W., *The Decline of English Feudalism, 1215-1540*, Manchester: Manchester University Press, and New York: Barnes and Noble, 1968

Bellamy, John, *Crime and Public Order in England in the Later Middle Ages*, London: Routledge and Kegan Paul, 1973

Carpenter, Christine, *The Wars of the Roses: Politics and the Constitution in England, c.1437-1509*, Cambridge and New York: Cambridge University Press, 1997

Carpenter, D.A., *The Minority of Henry III*, London: Methuen, and Berkeley: University of California Press, 1990

Davies, J.C., *The Baronial Opposition to Edward II: Its Character and Policy – A Study in Administrative History*, Cambridge: Cambridge University Press, 1918; reprinted, London: Cass, and New York: Barnes and Noble, 1967

Dyer, Christopher, *Lords and Peasants in a Changing Society: The Estates of the Bishopric of Worcester, 680-1540*, Cambridge and New York: Cambridge University Press, 1980

Fryde, E.B., *Peasants and Landlords in Later Medieval England*, London: Sutton, and New York: St Martin's Press, 1996

Fryde, Natalie, *The Tyranny and Fall of Edward II, 1321-1326*, Cambridge and New York: Cambridge University Press, 1979

Harvey, Barbara, *Westminster Abbey and Its Estates in the Middle Ages*, Oxford: Clarendon Press, 1977

Hilton, Rodney, *The Decline of Serfdom in Medieval England*, London: Macmillan, and New York: St Martin's Press, 1969

Hilton, Rodney, *The English Peasantry in the Later Middle Ages: The Ford Lectures for 1973 and Related Studies*, Oxford: Clarendon Press, 1975

Hilton, Rodney, *Class Conflict and the Crisis of Feudalism: Essays in Medieval Social History*, London: Hambledon Press, 1985; revised edition, London: Verso, 1990

Holmes, G.A., *The Estates of the Higher Nobility in Fourteenth-Century England*, Cambridge: Cambridge University Press, 1957

Holt, J.C., *The Northerners: A Study in the Reign of King John*, Oxford: Clarendon Press, 1961

Holt, J.C., *Magna Carta*, Cambridge: Cambridge University Press, 1965; 2nd edition, 1992

Homans, George Caspar, *English Villagers of the Thirteenth Century*, Cambridge, Massachusetts: Harvard University Press, 1941

Hyams, Paul R., *Kings, Lords, and Peasants in Medieval England: The Common Law of Villeinage in the Twelfth and Thirteenth Centuries*, Oxford: Clarendon Press, 1980

Jacob, E.F., *Oxford History of England*, vol. 6, *The Fifteenth Century, 1399-1485*, Oxford: Oxford University Press, 1961

Kaeuper, Richard W., *War, Justice, and Public Order: England and France in the Later Middle Ages*, Oxford: Clarendon Press, and New York: Oxford University Press, 1988

Keen, M.H., *England in the Later Middle Ages: A Political History*, London: Methuen, 1973

Levett, A. Elizabeth, "Studies in the Manorial Organization of St Albans Abbey" in A. Elizabeth Levett, *Studies in Manorial History*, edited by H. M. Cam, M. Coute, and L. Sutherland, Oxford: Clarendon Press, 1938; New York: Barnes and Noble, 1963

Levett, A. Elizabeth and A. Ballard, *The Black Death*, Oxford: Clarendon Press, 1916 (Oxford Studies in Social and Legal History, vol. 5)

Lipson, E., *The Economic History of England*, vol. 1, *The Middle Ages*, London: A and C Black, 1915; reprinted, 1971

Maitland, F.W., *Domesday Book and Beyond: Three Essays in the Early History of England*, Cambridge: Cambridge University Press, and Boston: Little Brown, 1897; reprinted, 1987

McFarlane, K.B., *Lancastrian Kings and Lollard Knights*, Oxford: Clarendon Press, 1972

McFarlane, K.B., *The Nobility of Later Medieval England: The Ford Lectures for 1953 and Related Studies*, Oxford: Clarendon Press, 1973

Pike, L.O., *A History of Crime in England*, 2 vols, London: Smith Elder, 1873–76

Powell, Edward, *Kingship, Law, and Society: Criminal Justice in the Reign of Henry V*, Oxford: Clarendon Press, and New York: Oxford University Press, 1989

Powicke, F.M., *King Henry III and the Lord Edward: The Community of the Realm in the Thirteenth Century*, 2 vols, Oxford: Clarendon Press, 1947

Powicke, F.M., *Oxford History of England*, vol. 4, *The Thirteenth Century, 1216–1307*, Oxford: Clarendon Press, 1953; 2nd edition, 1962

Prestwich, Michael, *The Three Edwards: War and State in England, 1272–1377*, London: Weidenfeld and Nicolson, and New York: St Martin's Press, 1980

Ramsey, J.H., *Lancaster and York: A Century of British History*, A.D. 1399–1485, 2 vols, Oxford, 1892

Saul, Nigel, *Knights and Esquires: The Gloucestershire Gentry in the Fourteenth Century*, Oxford: Clarendon Press, and New York: Oxford University Press, 1981

Stacey, Robert C., *Politics, Policy, and Finance under Henry III, 1216–1245*, Oxford: Clarendon Press, and New York: Oxford University Press, 1987

Storey, R.L., *The End of the House of Lancaster*, London: Barrie and Rockliffe, 1966; revised, Gloucester, England: Sutton, 1999

Tout, T.F., *The History of England from the Accession of Henry III to the Death of Edward III, 1216–1377*, London: Longman, 1905; reprinted, New York: Haskell House, 1969

Tout, T.F., *The Place of the Reign of Edward II in English History, Based upon the Ford Lectures Delivered in the University of Oxford in 1913*, Manchester: Manchester University Press, 1914

Vinogradoff, Paul, *Villainage in England: Essays in Mediaeval History*, Oxford: Clarendon Press, 1892; reprinted, 1968

From Hastings to Bosworth, violence, conflict, and strife shaped relations between the English social classes. In writing about these interactions, scholars have focused on two connections in particular. Kings and nobles maintained uneasy relations as each side sought to expand its own interests at the cost of the other. Often, this interaction exploded into armed conflict, rebellion, and lawlessness. Likewise, the relationship between lord and peasant deteriorated from the 13th century onwards, leading to armed rebellion and another tug of war for control.

Several historians have examined the effects of crime and lawlessness on society as a whole. For example, BELLAMY (1973) followed PIKE's earlier analysis (1873–76) in considering this issue from all angles. In the reign of Edward II, for example, revolts resulted from constant bickering and failures on the battlefield. Likewise, McFARLANE (1972 and 1973) was instrumental in tracking violence across social lines. While the majority of his works focused on the 15th century, *The Nobility of Later Medieval England* contained essays spanning the entire period. BARNIE (1974) concurred with these assessments and added the element of popular anti-papal sentiment. KAEUPER (1988) investigated pressures from above and below: first how the expansion of royal authority and the formation of the wartime state in the later Middle Ages met with resistance from the nobles, and then how the presence of a *vox populi* shaped many policies. Following in McFarlane's and Bellamy's footsteps, POWELL (1989) offered short-term and long-term summations of lawlessness in the countryside, royal efforts to combat it, and the results of those efforts. In *Kingship, Law, and Society* he summarized these trends for the long term and the reign of Henry V.

The struggle between monarch and nobles has received attention in several accounts, particularly over the past 50 years. POWICKE (1947 and 1953) gave expansive accounts of the civil wars during the reigns of John and Henry III, as did HOLT (1961, 1965), STACEY (1987), and D.A. CARPENTER (1990). DAVIES (1918), TOUT (1914), and FRYDE (1979), writing about the reign of Edward II, provided still more coverage of issues in the mid-14th century. KEEN (1973) illustrated how the continual warfare between 1290 and 1485 led to social unrest. Like Keen, RAMSEY (1892), STOREY (1966), and JACOB (1961) provided a comprehensive view of the 15th century as well. BEAN (1968) examined how royal legislation in the 14th century, such as the Ordinance of 1356 and the statutes of *Quia emptores* and *Mortmain*, punctuated a period of efforts by royalty in the 13th and 14th centuries to cut into the vassals' local landholdings and the abuses of their customary rights. While not nearly as specific, D.A. Carpenter's survey of the minority of Henry III did provide some detail. PRESTWICH (1980) related the events of the late 13th and 14th centuries in great detail; and SAUL (1981) provided an excellent example of how "bastard feudalism" led to lawlessness in one county, Gloucestershire.

The brewing conflict between lord and peasant has also received coverage in scholarly accounts over the past century. VINOGRADOFF (1892), MAITLAND (1897), and – a century later – HYAMS (1980) emphasized the beginnings of this process, showing how the Normans pushed the formerly free landholders into villeinage between the Conquest and the 12th century, utilizing the Domesday Book as a checkpoint. These authors, especially Maitland, expertly conveyed the distinctions between the various peasant classes.

Other scholars have tracked the general process over the entire period, detailing the explosion of the peasants' resentment against their lords' demands. LIPSON (1915) sketched the developing strife leading to conflicts and uprisings, separated out the views of the Roman and Germanic schools towards the question of how the manor developed as it did, and showed how the villeins' independence disappeared as their lords gained the upper hand. To his credit, Lipson did not try to impose uniformity on the peasant population but rather differentiated between various free and unfree tenants. In his work, the Black Death and the commutation of services are stressed as turning-points in the villeins' voicing of their demands. LEVETT & BALLARD (1916), minimized the role of the Black Death relative to other disasters befalling England in the 14th century; however, they too mention tenants' restlessness as demands for increased work were imposed after that point. HOMANS (1941) echoed this sentiment, and HOLMES (1957) detailed how the lords pressed their rights while the tenants strove to maintain their own position. HILTON's three studies (1969, 1975, 1990) provide further detail on this struggle. Hilton notes that the Peasants' Revolt should not be considered an isolated event.

Following suggestions in the earlier scholarly accounts concerning local differences in these relationships, other scholars focused on distinct regions. LEVETT (1938) depicted how tension built up between lords and tenants because of the lords' method of exacting rents and obligations, causing the tenants to rebel in the later 14th century. Likewise, Hilton (1975) detailed conflicts between villagers, as well as tension between lord and tenant, in his fourth essay ("Conflict and Collaboration"); in another essay he detailed the friction between these parties in Staffordshire. HARVEY (1977), like Lipson, surveyed the entire period, but she looked at only one specific abbey in detail; in this work she illustrated both the loss of the freeholders' rights to the abbey in the 11th and 12th centuries and the struggle between lords and tenants for control over the lands. She also detailed disputes over labour services on these estates. DYER (1980) examined these issues in the bishopric of Worcester. Although he did not find the kind of organized revolts that took place in other parts of England, he did discern tension between the parties, breeding resistance in the peasantry, particularly with the enclosing of land in the 13th century and the increasing reluctance of tenants and, later, rentiers to perform their duties after the Black Death.

Two works combining general and localized analyses must also be considered. Hilton (1985) reprints essays on various issues such as the 13th-century dispute between the Abbot of Leicester and the inhabitants of Stoughton over labour services, the struggles of peasants with other social classes, the effect of the 14th-century popular movements, the social ideology behind the Great Rising (Peasants' Revolt) of 1381 and other peasant revolts, and how the upward movement of the lowest classes affected English society as a whole. FRYDE (1996) has provided an excellent summary of this scholarship in two ways. First, he traces the general history of the rise and fall of the relationship

between peasants and landlords; then he analyses its regional derivations. He looks at the oppression of the peasantry by the lords between 1066 and the late 14th century, and then at the way the relationship continued after commutation transformed the economy from barter to monetary transactions. The turning-points in this process are identified as the Black Death and the Peasants' Revolt. In chapter 2 Fryde looks at the socio-economic and legal background of the Peasant's Revolt; in chapter 3 he discusses the revolts of 1349–81 as tenants attempted to gain a new social position while the lords attempted to retain theirs; in chapter 5 he analyses the tension related to the early leasing of demesnes; in chapter 8 he talks about the continued conflicts between lords and peasants. He views the enclosure issue (chapter 12), continued oppression (chapter 13), and the depression of the mid-15th century (chapter 11) as contributing to social tension. Finally, in chapter 15 he discusses the legal changes in tenurial status.

DAVID J. DUNCAN

See also Peasants' Revolt

Social Conflict: Modern Period

Best, Geoffrey, *Mid-Victorian Britain, 1851–1875*, London: Weidenfeld and Nicolson, 1971; New York: Schocken Books, 1972; revised edition, St Albans: Panther, 1973

Bohstedt, John, *Riots and Community Politics in England 1790–1810*, Cambridge, Massachusetts: Harvard University Press, 1983

Calhoun, Craig, *The Question of Class Struggle: Social Foundations of Popular Radicalism during the Industrial Revolution*, Chicago: University of Chicago Press, and Oxford: Blackwell, 1982

Clark, J.C.D, *Revolution and Rebellion: State and Society in England in the Seventeenth and Eighteenth Centuries*, Cambridge and New York: Cambridge University Press, 1986

Harrison, Brian, *Peacable Kingdom: Stability and Change in Modern Britain*, Oxford: Clarendon Press, and New York: Oxford University Press, 1982

Hobsbawm, E.J., *Labouring Men: Studies in the History of Labour*, London: Weidenfeld and Nicolson, 1964; New York: Basic Books, 1965

Hobsbawm, E.J. and George Rudé, *Captain Swing*, New York: Pantheon, 1968; London: Lawrence and Wishart, 1969

Hollis, Patricia, *The Pauper Press: A Study in Working-Class Radicalism of the 1830s*, London: Oxford University Press, 1970

Jones, Gareth Stedman, *Languages of Class: Studies in English Working Class History, 1832–1982*, Cambridge and New York: Cambridge University Press, 1983

Joyce, Patrick, *Work, Society, and Politics: The Culture of the Factory in Later Victorian England*, New Brunswick, New Jersey: Rutgers University Press, and Brighton, East Sussex: Harvester Press, 1980

Joyce, Patrick, *Visions of the People: Industrial England and the Question of Class, 1840–1914*, Cambridge and New York: Cambridge University Press, 1991

Kirk, Neville, *The Growth of Working Class Reformism in Mid-Victorian England*, Urbana: University of Illinois Press, and London: Croom Helm, 1985

Linebaugh, Peter, *The London Hanged: Crime and Civil Society in the Eighteenth Century*, London: Allen Lane, 1991; Cambridge and New York: Cambridge University Press, 1992

Palmer, Stanley H., *Police and Protest in England and Ireland, 1780–1850*, Cambridge and New York: Cambridge University Press, 1988

Perkin, Harold, *The Origins of Modern English Society 1780–1880*, London: Routledge and Kegan Paul, 1969; Toronto: University of Toronto Press, 1971; as *The Origins of Modern English Society*, London and New York: Routledge, 1991

Price, Richard, *Labour in British Society: An Interpretive History*, London and Dover, New Hampshire: Croom Helm, 1986

Prothero, I.J., *Artisans and Politics in Early Nineteenth-Century London: John Gast and His Times*, Folkestone, Kent: Dawson, 1979

Randall, Adrian, *Before the Luddites: Custom, Community, and Machinery in the English Woollen Industry, 1776–1809*, Cambridge and New York: Cambridge University Press, 1991

Rudé, George, *The Crowd in History: A Study of Popular Disturbances in France and England, 1730–1848*, New York: Wiley, 1964; revised edition, London: Lawrence and Wishart, 1981

Thompson, Dorothy, *The Chartists*, London: Temple Smith, 1984; as *The Chartists: Popular Politics in the Industrial Revolution*, New York: Pantheon, 1984

Thompson, E.P., *The Making of the English Working Class*, London: Gollancz, and New York: Vintage, 1963; reprinted, London: Gollancz, 1980

Thompson, E.P., *Customs in Common*, London: Merlin Press, and New York: New Press, 1991

Thompson, F.M.L., *The Rise of Respectable Society: A Social History of Victorian Britain, 1830–1900*, London: Fontana, and Cambridge, Massachusetts: Harvard University Press, 1988

Wells, Roger, *Insurrection: The British Experience, 1795–1803*, Stroud, Gloucestershire: Alan Sutton, 1983

Wells, Roger, *Wretched Faces: Famine in Wartime England, 1793–1801*, Stroud, Gloucestershire: Alan Sutton, and New York: St Martins Press, 1988

The recent historiographical debate on social conflict in modern Britain has played itself out in the shadow of E.P. THOMPSON's classic works. In his "Moral Economy of the English Crowd" (reprinted in *Customs in Common*, 1991; originally 1971) he hypothesized that an implicit code was involved in much 18th-century social conflict. This was a calculated trade-off, which authorized the plebs to engage in limited protest but only in ways that obliquely buttressed the ability of the patriciate to rule. Thompson posits a pervasive normative belief that the protection of the community should take precedence over the maximization of individual profit. As this belief was abandoned by Britain's aristocracy, enforcement of the moral economy became the province of the plebeian crowd.

So long as such riots remained essentially "pre-political", directed against aliens or middlemen in the tumultuous cities, and towards moderating the price of grain in the increasingly commercialized countryside, they could, as RUDÉ demonstrated, be safely tolerated. During the 1790s, however, in the aftermath of the French Revolution, traditional protest took on a newfound potency and militancy, becoming connected with political radicalism and the rise of an increasingly industrial working class.

The classic account of this double transformation remains THOMPSON (1963). In this path-breaking work Thompson showed how the combined impact of capitalistic exploitation and governmental repression reshaped traditional genres of plebeian expression and remoulded them into increasingly self-conscious, politically organized forms. For incipient trade unionists, deprived of the right to organize legally, notions of "moral economy" and the "freeborn Englishman" were transmuted into what Hobsbawm aptly termed "collective bargaining by riot". In the Luddite movement of 1812 both the strengths and the limitations of this approach became clear. After the war, especially in the increasingly urbanized manufacturing districts, popular protest became public and open. Secret conspiracies gave way to political associations and trade unions. The village crowd expanded into a national mass movement. The riot was replaced by the monster meeting, where hundreds of thousands gathered to express their solidarity. Baptized in blood on the field of Peterloo (1819), these new forms were reinforced during the 1820s by the intellectual cross-currents of Owenite socialism and a vigorous radical press. With the parliamentary reform agitation of the early 1830s, Thompson thought, his working class had come of age.

For the next two or three decades after Thompson's *magnum opus*, much scholarly energy was devoted simply to extending his argument and fleshing out its details. WELLS catalogued the hunger and insurrectionary violence of the 1790s, LINEBAUGH traced the contours of the plebeian cultures of transgression, and PROTHERO examined the transformation and politicization of London's artisan trades. The textile outworkers were surveyed by RANDALL, among many others; and HOLLIS produced a valuable study of the radical press. HOBSBAWM & RUDÉ reconsidered the rural "Swing" movement; in the countryside, open organization remained impossible and the secret tradition assumed increasingly incendiary forms, which ran parallel to the urban campaign for parliamentary reform. The history of the police, and its relation to social protest, both in England and in Ireland, is painstakingly reconstructed by PALMER. Since Thompson (1963) ended his account at the year 1832, the field was left open to his followers to re-examine the great mass movements – factory reform, industrial trades unionism, chartism, and agitation against the poor laws – that took place during the 1830s and 1840s, when the genre of protest whose origins he had delineated reached its peak. Specific works here are too numerous even to mention, but it is fitting that the best single synthesis of the material written after Thompson's can be found in the book on chartism by his wife, Dorothy THOMPSON (1984).

The most critical problem generated by the Thompsonian paradigm of social conflict is to explain the subsequent social stabilization during the midddle and late Victorian period, when the mass mobilizations of the 1819–48 period precipitously

stranglehold on the land and the sagacity of its members in encouraging economic development, financing the state, and winning foreign conflicts. As THOMPSON points out, in a work that was one of the first to use private estate collections for the modern period, most peers also proved able to reform their manners, education, and work habits to make themselves the "natural leaders" of the nation long after land ceased to be the most profitable investment and sons of the middle class acquired the attributes of gentlemen. Cannadine provides an exhaustive study, compiling much recent research, of the accumulating challenges to the entitlements of the nobles that faced this group after about 1880, as well as the not always graceful responses of individual peers as corporate identity collapsed.

The question how a system of aristocratic power and privilege was able to survive so long in the earliest "modern" nation was traditionally answered by noting the relative fluidity at the top of British society: younger children, barred from inheriting land, moved easily into professional and service occupations; enterprising businessmen bought estates and gradually gained access to political power. Stone & Stone argued forcefully, however, that this was a national myth. Studying the histories of houses, rather than of families, they found very low rates of acquisition by people who were not already members of the extended elite. Although that argument was widely accepted in the 1980s, SPRING & SPRING mounted vigorous rebuttals, using Stone & Stone's own data on the ownership of country houses to demonstrate that at any one time up to one-third of country estates were owned by "new men" rather than by relatives of the existing elite. In an important prosopographic study of membership in the House of Commons from the medieval period to 1914, WASSON discovered a similar percentage of men new in the national elite who established a continuing family presence in either the Commons or the Lords.

Another broad debate has concerned the contribution of the aristocracy to the economic modernization of Britain. WIENER argued that the prestige given to politics, amateurism, and an impractical education by the aristocracy corrupted the entrepreneurial spirit of the business classes and undermined Britain's economic adaptability once other national competitors emerged. CAIN & HOPKINS, however, countered that Wiener's concentration on the fortunes of British industry missed the point, since the aristocracy had, since the 17th century, demonstrated plenty of concern for the sector of economic activity that mattered most to Britain in any case: investment capitalism and global trade and finance.

NANCY W. ELLENBERGER

See also Aristocratic Affinity; Magna Carta

Social Structure: Aristocracy, Scottish

Barrow, G.W.S., *The Anglo-Norman Era in Scottish History*, Oxford: Clarendon Press, and New York: Oxford University Press, 1980

Brown, Keith M., *Bloodfeud in Scotland, 1573–1625: Violence, Justice, and Politics in an Early Modern Society*, Edinburgh: John Donald, and Atlantic Highlands, New Jersey: Humanities Press, 1986

Brown, Keith M., "Aristocratic Finances and the Origins of the Scottish Revolution", *English Historical Review*, 104 (1989): 46–87

Brown, Michael, *The Black Douglases: War and Lordship in Late Medieval Scotland, 1300–1455*, East Linton, East Lothian: Tuckwell Press, 1998

Colley, Linda, *Britons: Forging the Nation, 1707–1837*, New Haven, Connecticut, and London: Yale University Press, 1992

Macinnes, Allan I., *Clanship, Commerce, and the House of Stuart, 1603–1788*, East Linton, East Lothian: Tuckwell Press, 1996

Paul, Sir James Balfour (editor), *The Scots Peerage Founded on Wood's Edition of Sir Robert Douglas's Peerage of Scotland; Containing a Historical and Genealogical Account of the Nobility of That Kingdom*, Edinburgh: David Douglas, 1904–14

Stringer, K.J. (editor), *Essays on the Nobility of Medieval Scotland*, Edinburgh: John Donald, and Atlantic Highlands, New Jersey: Humanities Press, 1985

Wormald, Jenny, *Lords and Men in Scotland: Bonds of Manrent, 1442–1603*, Edinburgh: John Donald, and Atlantic Highlands, New Jersey: Humanities Press, 1985

Modern scholarship on the Scottish nobility has been influenced by two problems. On the one hand, within Scottish social history there has been an emphasis on the working lives and daily experiences of the rest of the population – usually being at the expense of the privileged elite, whose activities were traditionally regarded as the exclusive province of the political historian. On the other hand, the nobility, in Scotland perhaps more than in most other countries, have been the focus of genealogists and amateur researchers. Their exactness has not always matched their enthusiasm; and it is clear that their primary concern has invariably been to establish lineages rather than to explore the rich fabric of elite social existence.

The result is that our present understanding of Scotland's historical nobility remains deficient in crucial respects. There is as yet no equivalent, for example, of Lawrence Stone's studies of the modern English elite in the early modern period, work which has offered a thought-provoking interpretative synthesis built on impressive foundations of comprehensive prosopographic research. Instead there exists an accumulated body of essentially descriptive and factual work on Scotland's nobility which might easily inform more analytical or interpretative studies but which has yet to be fully exploited.

The indispensible reference source in any consideration of the Scottish nobility as a social class remains PAUL's encyclopedic work, a multivolume Edwardian compilation which mirrors, though it does not straightforwardly recapitulate, the familiar works cataloguing the descent of the British peerage as a whole. Numerous individual family histories by the late Victorian scholar Sir William Fraser – a doyen of students of the Scots nobility – also continue to provide definitive narratives on the careers of many famous names: the Scotts, the Leslies, the Montgomeries, the Carnegies, the Grants, and so forth. Whatever the intellectual limitations of these often massive compendiums (Fraser, for example, was a meticulous and indefatigable recorder of dynastic *minutiae* rather than a man inclined to pursue a larger vision of the nobles' social history), they nevertheless offer the Scottish historian an incomparable resource on kinship, education, marriage, office, longevity, mortality, and inheritance, from which it is at least possible to imagine much more insightful studies of the elite's changing nature ultimately flowing.

More interpretatively sophisticated studies, of much greater value for an understanding of the nobles' social experience in the round, have begun to emerge in recent years, though they have often focused primarily on the thorny problem of magnates' unruly and acquisitive behaviour and its ostensible relationship to the conduct of national politics. BARROW's major study of the Anglo-Norman period and a valuable edited collection by STRINGER remain important here as a marker for what might eventually be possible in the context of the medieval Scottish nobility. The recent study by Michael BROWN, examining part of the complex Douglas kinship grouping, also offers a cerebral analysis of the most important noble dynasty of late medieval Scotland as it battled its way to the forefront amid the nation's bitter conflict with England.

For the 15th and 16th centuries there is also the groundbreaking work of WORMALD, who gives many intriguing glimpses into the true nature of Scotland's elite during the troubled Renaissance and Reformation eras. The cultivated character of the nobility, and the complexity of its relations with a politically sophisticated monarchy, are highlighted in this study. Perhaps Wormald's most influential contribution, however, has been to challenge (though not, in the view of many current scholars, fully to dispatch) the conventional understanding of the late medieval scene: that Scotland's unfortunate and feeble crown had simply laboured beneath the excessive burdens imposed by an "overmighty nobility".

A different but no less innovative perspective on a slightly later period has been offered by Keith M. BROWN. He has shown how until at least the end of the 16th century feuding and private violence were recognized as legitimate institutions among the Scottish elite, even as religious and political pressures increasingly bore down disapprovingly upon such disruptive and morally questionable practices. He has also published a number of original scholarly articles which explore the growing fiscal problems and distinctive political concerns of the 17th-century nobility, seeing these as a significant cause of the troubles of the Stuart crown in Scotland during the age of the Covenant.

Coherent studies of the Scottish nobility in more recent times are unfortunately even less numerous, though interest in the phenomenon of clanship and the social transformation of the Scottish Highlands during and after the Jacobite period has produced some useful insights not only into political behaviour but also into the economic and cultural context in which this important part of the national elite operated. In particular, MACINNES has provided a pioneering account of the social structures and practices which connected political dissidence, religious affiliation, and material change in the Highland nobility between the age of the Covenant and the onset of the clearances, showing how the mighty Campbell name – ultimately borne by dukes of Argyll, marquises of Breadalbane, earls of Loudoun, and lords Cawdor – prospered at the expense of many distinguished older families.

For the Lowland nobility of the 18th and 19th centuries the present state of substantial social history – as opposed to passing comment by political historians – is unimpressive. COLLEY's controversial study of the 18th-century British elite contains provocative thoughts on the assimilation of Scotland's landed classes into the wider mainstream after the Union; Colley argues that this was a vital precondition for the creation of a new national and imperial identity. But convincing studies of the Hanoverian or Victorian Scottish nobility as such have not been forthcoming, making it difficult to subject this part of Colley's work to the sceptical scrutiny that many suspect it deserves. It is therefore hardly surprising that the nobility of 20th-century Scotland have also gone virtually unstudied by recent historians (except in so far as they might again be considered simply a subset of an embattled British aristocracy – a perspective which begs rather than tackles the most interesting questions).

Scottish historiography as a whole has thus been slow to adapt to the recent fashion in British and European scholarship which has recognized the nobility as a compulsory subject for the social historian. The result is a patchy understanding of the historical evolution of the elite as a social class, notwithstanding the generally robust quality of the factual information available for the Scottish nobility, and notwithstanding some important individual efforts to reconstruct certain aspects of their unquestionably profound historical influence and experience. Future work can be expected to shed much-needed light on this important but neglected field.

DAVID ALLAN

See also Aristocratic Affinity; James II ; James III

Social Structure: Aristocratic Families

Gathorne-Hardy, Jonathan, *The Rise and Fall of the British Nanny*, London: Hodder and Stoughton, 1972

Gerard, Jessica, *Country House Life: Family and Servants, 1815–1914*, Oxford and Cambridge, Massachusetts: Blackwell, 1994

Girouard, Mark, *Life in the English Country House: A Social and Architectural History*, New Haven, Connecticut, and London: Yale University Press, 1978

Habakkuk, John, *Marriage, Debt, and the Estates System: English Landownership, 1650–1950*, Oxford: Clarendon Press, and New York: Oxford University Press, 1994

Hollingsworth, T.H., "The Demography of the British Peerage", *Supplement to Population Studies*, 18 (1964): 1–168

Lewis, Judith Schneid, *In the Family Way: Childbearing in the British Aristocracy, 1760–1860*, New Brunswick, New Jersey: Rutgers University Press, 1986

Macfarlane, Alan, *Marriage and Love in England: Modes of Reproduction, 1300–1840*, Oxford and New York: Blackwell, 1986

Mertes, Kate, *The English Noble Household, 1250–1600: Good Governance and Politic Rule*, Oxford and New York: Blackwell, 1988

Rutherford, Jonathan, *Forever England: Reflections on Race, Masculinity, and Empire*, London: Lawrence and Wishart, 1997

Spring, Eileen, *Law, Land, and Family: Aristocratic Inheritance in England, 1300 to 1800*, Chapel Hill: University of North Carolina Press, 1993

Staves, Susan, *Married Women's Separate Property in England, 1660–1833*, Cambridge, Massachusetts: Harvard University Press, 1990

Stenton, Doris Mary, *The English Woman in History*, London: Allen and Unwin, and New York: Macmillan, 1957

Stone, Lawrence, *The Family, Sex, and Marriage in England 1500–1800*, New York: Harper and Row, and London: Weidenfeld and Nicolson, 1977

Trumbach, Randolph, *The Rise of the Egalitarian Family: Aristocratic Kinship and Domestic Relations in Eighteenth-Century England*, New York and London: Academic Press, 1978

Serious study in the history of families at different levels in the social hierarchies of western Europe is barely one generation old. Already, however, the portion of the field that deals with the British aristocracy has produced an important, overarching paradigm of family development, as well as recent, furious, rebuttal.

Before the 1970s discussions of the family that were more than anecdotal tended to elucidate the situation at law. STENTON can still be profitably read for her survey of women's property rights and legal standing, based on court actions, wills, charters, and statutes. Much can also be gleaned from HOLLINGSWORTH's demographic statistics on marriage ages and partners, fertility rates, morbidity, life expectancy, and more for the extended peerage (including grandchildren of titleholders) throughout the centuries. GIROUARD provides another window through which to observe changes in elite family life since the Conquest. In describing the evolution of country mansions, he describes the transformation from the encastellated warrior households of the Middle Ages, with their great halls, to the formal, ordered, but still public spaces of the Tudor–Stuart magnates to the private, intimate plans of the Victorians, whose servants were no longer flaunted but discreetly relegated to separate wings, floors, or blocks.

Work on the aristocratic family is less extensive for medieval times than for later periods, and MERTES makes it clear that observations regarding the continental nobility should not be simply grafted onto the British Isles. The establishment of feudal law after the Conquest made a very significant change, for it promoted "patrilineality, primogeniture and a dynastic sense of kinship" that was at odds with the earlier horizontal, cognatic structure of elite identity. The notion that younger children did not share the inheritance – that they were, indeed, commoners – lessened extended kinship ties and produced households in which kin provided a much smaller portion of servants, escorts, and retainers than was characteristic, for example, in southern Europe. Mertes shows that the nobility, even if their households were much larger, shared in the nuclear family structure that MACFARLANE found dominant in lower levels of English society quite early in the nation's history. What distinguished the aristocracy was a drive to keep real property intact and in the hands of a male member of the patriarchal bloodline, as this provided the basis for both local and national power.

What then of relations within family units? STONE devised a striking hypothesis based largely upon records left by, or relating to, the aristocracy. Using legal, demographic, and literary evidence, he argued that families had progressed in stages from an open-lineage structure in the late Middle Ages to rigid patriarchy in the early modern period and finally to an affectionate, companionate domestic relationship in the Enlightenment. Stone presented a harsh image of pre-modern families focused on property and lineage rather than the happiness of individual members, and characterized by arranged marriages, aloofness, limited emotional expression, and pervasive abuse or neglect of children. Central to the changes he detected were questions of the treatment of aristocratic wives, widows, and younger children at law in an estates system that conferred all benefits on the single male heir. Stone argued that generous provisions for widows and unborn children written into marriage settlements from the early 18th century onwards demonstrated a new concern on the part of fathers for immediate family members, and he posited a revolution in affective relations as the century progressed.

TRUMBACH surveyed the private papers of a substantial portion of the 18th-century peerage, and his findings paralleled those of Stone. Both historians argued that increasing informality of address and names, greater choice in selecting marriage partners, more generous provisions for younger offspring, and greater concern for the nurturing of children originated with the aristocracy decades before developing in the rest of educated society. The rise of the "egalitarian" family of the modern era was thus intimately linked to acceptance of domesticity by the English aristocracy. LEWIS provided striking evidence of improvement in the domestic lives of women, including more regular contact with the birth family, in her study of marriage and childbirth among three generations of peeresses in the 18th and 19th centuries.

Stone and Trumbach's thesis came under attack, however. Macfarlane, as noted earlier, found that nuclear households, with their distinct emotional patterns and their encouragement of personal autonomy, had characterized middle and lower levels of English society much earlier than was originally thought and probably could not be said to have originated with the aristocracy. HABAKKUK, who had been one of the first to speculate about what property settlements suggested regarding family relations, later became sceptical that legal instruments implied anything meaningful about affection within families. He did conclude, though, that financial provisions for widows and younger children probably improved from the 18th century onwards and that this, combined with greater life expectancy, helped to build up substantial debt on 19th-century landed estates. Habakkuk provides an enormous compendium of information and examples regarding aristocrats' property arrangements, inheritances, marriage strategies, and family fortunes, although his discussions do not directly engage those of other historians and definitive conclusions are hard to find. His work can be usefully supplemented by STAVES, who provides a grimmer view of how legal devices that appeared to improve the position of women worked in practice to reduce their economic independence.

SPRING launched the fullest attack on Stone's and Trumbach's theses. She argued that the most important story contained within the refinement of legal devices to protect aristocratic estates and provide for family members was not that benefits to women improved but rather that women should have held substantial estates under the common law were dispossessed. Given the lack of real property inherited by women from at least the 14th century onwards, she noted that arranged marriages or the heartless pursuit of heiresses would have been pointless within the aristocracy; she also questioned whether a limited capacity for affection was a common pattern in their families. Spring's work, based on restricted evidence but compelling in its sustained argumentation, reinserted the realities of patriarchal power, if not emotional tyranny, into a story that had threatened to obscure the disabilities under which aristocratic women continued to function long after the 18th century.

Other implicit critiques of Stone and Trumbach come from historians of family life in the Victorian aristocracy. Though Stone had noted in passing an evangelically inspired resurgence of aloof and patriarchal family relations after the permissive 18th century, GATHORNE-HARDY and others presented a notably dismal picture of child-rearing practices among Victorian aristocratics. Boys, especially, were raised mostly by servants – as their parents preoccupied themselves with the great world – and were ejected from the family circle into all-male boarding schools from about the age of seven. RUTHERFORD, among others, used this distinctive pattern, which middle-class families embraced as the century progressed, to construct a paradigm of an emotionally crippled, secretly narcissistic, but outwardly conformist and dutiful imperial ruling class. GERARD, however, noted that landed fathers busy around the estate might be more present than professional men in their sons' lives; she discovered close and affectionate family ties in the country households she investigated. Gerard cited David Roberts's finding that the memoirs of aristocratic offspring indicate unusual personal autonomy, as well as affection and respect for parents. In this assessment, there would be little to distinguish 19th-century aristocratic families from either their 18th-century forebears or the families of the professional middle classes in the same era. At this point, scholars have yet to resolve the question whether, how, and when aristocratic families differed from families in other sections of the educated classes in Britain.

NANCY W. ELLENBERGER

Social Structure: English Gentry

Heal, Felicity and Clive Holmes, *The Gentry in England and Wales, 1500–1700*, Stanford, California: Stanford University Press, and London: Macmillan, 1994

Jenkins, Philip, *The Making of a Ruling Class: The Glamorgan Gentry, 1640–1790*, Cambridge and New York: Cambridge University Press, 1983

Mingay, G.E., *The Gentry: The Rise and Fall of a Ruling Class*, London and New York: Longman, 1976

Rosenheim, James M., *The Townshends of Raynham: Nobility in Transition in Restoration and Early Hanoverian England*, Middletown, Connecticut: Wesleyan University Press, 1989

Spring, Eileen, *Law, Land, and Family: Aristocratic Inheritance in England, 1300 to 1800*, Chapel Hill: University of North Carolina Press, 1993

Stone, Lawrence and Jeanne C. Fawtier Stone, *An Open Elite? England, 1540–1880*, Oxford: Clarendon Press, and New York: Oxford University Press, 1984

Tawney, R.H., "The Rise of the Gentry, 1558–1640", *Economic History Review*, 11/1 (1941): 1–38

Trevelyan, G.M., *English Social History: A Survey of Six Centuries, Chaucer to Queen Victoria*, London and New York: Longmans Green, 1942

Trevor-Roper, H.R., "The Gentry, 1540–1640", *Economic History Review Supplement*, 1 (1953) [Supplement is free-standing]

G.M. TREVELYAN first introduced "the gentry" as a category of analysis in his pathbreaking study (1942). He described Elizabethan gentlemen not as isolated, rural squires but as economic opportunists who kept in personal touch with the modern world. Since then, historical debate has focused on the issue of modernity. Were the gentry forward-thinking leaders of the English Revolution (and, later, the Industrial Revolution)? Or were they fundamentally conservative in their attitudes towards political and social change?

In the 1950s and the 1960s historians divided over the question whether a "rising," new class of gentry could be held responsible for the English civil wars. R.H. TAWNEY argued that changes in the distribution of property, in favour of the gentry and away from the church and the crown, led to a corresponding political adjustment in the 1640s. H.R. TREVOR-ROPER disagreed. He argued that power did not necessarily follow property and that the gentry did not rise as a class. The resulting debate, known as the "storm over the gentry", captured the attention of a national audience and led to a great deal of statistical work on the relative wealth of the landed classes. During the decade 1955–65 a flurry of doctoral theses focused on the finances of individual families such as the Percys or Hastingses, on groups of families in areas such as Northamptonshire or East Anglia, or on the gentry of a single county such as Yorkshire. The debate encouraged historians to put the gentry in context, to see them not as members of a unified class but rather as individuals who were responsible for, and responsive to, their county communities.

The "storm over the gentry" had come to an end by the time G.E. MINGAY published his work. His book synthesized two decades of scholarship, and it remains to date the most coherent work on the subject. Mingay traced the emergence of the gentry in the late Middle Ages, its increasing power under Tudor and Stuart monarchs, and its decline in the late 19th century. He described, briefly, the agricultural context of the gentleman's estate, economic issues surrounding marriage, and the relationship of the gentry to local communities, as well as the group's culture, education, and sport.

In the 1960s and 1970s, many historians of the early Stuart period began to make a case for the fundamental conservatism of the English gentry. They saw the gentry no longer as a "rising" or "falling" class but as a group that sought to preserve the political status quo. This argument appears in works by Alan Everitt, Anthony Fletcher, John Morrill, and David Underdown, among others. The new fashion for "revisionism", or narrative political history, caused many historians to turn away from the study of economic and social origins of the civil wars.

STONE & STONE remained interested in the social and economic status of the gentry; they found far less upward mobility into the landed gentry than had previously been thought. Many lawyers, businessmen, members of the armed forces, and wealthy colonial elites could not make it past the social barriers erected by those with substantial country estates and, often, seats in parliament. However, the value of Stone & Stone's work was questioned by SPRING, who suggested that the Stones had knocked over a straw man – social mobility – but had not replaced it with a theory explaining the remarkable survival of the English landed classes.

The question remained: Were the gentry forward-thinking leaders of the Industrial Revolution? Or were they fundamentally conservative in their attitudes towards social change? JENKINS took the former position, arguing that the late 17th and early 18th centuries saw the creation of a sophisticated ruling class, "one so modern in political and economic outlook that the state it governed would dominate the politics of the world for over a century". In his study of the gentry of Glamorganshire he found that in the 1760s there emerged a new community of gentlemen who were more English than Welsh and more closely allied to the central government through careers in the military, commerce, or the professions than to their county community. ROSENHEIM drew similar conclusions. He traced two generations of a Norfolk family, the Townshends of Raynham, and explained the political circumstances which shaped the career of Charles, "Turnip" Townshend, a leading proponent of agricultural reform. Historians of the 18th century, including John Cannon, J.V. Beckett, and H.J. Habakkuk, support the idea that a powerful landed elite emerged in this period.

HEAL & HOLMES, in their more recent book, do not address questions about the gentry's relative social standing or its modernizing impulses. Instead, using rich evidence drawn largely from archival sources, they describe the "experience" of being a gentleman or gentlewoman in early modern England and Wales. The gentry is portrayed as a cultural group which shared common definitions of honour, charity, civility, and hospitality. In general, the authors adopt a sensible approach to their subject, suggesting that the gentry's survival was due to its ability to adapt and change. Their book includes notes and bibliography, and it provides a useful guide for further work in the field.

MOLLY McCLAIN

Social Structure: Rural Working Families

Hill, Bridget, *Women, Work, and Sexual Politics in Eighteenth-Century England*, Oxford and Cambridge, Massachusetts: Blackwell, 1989; Montreal and Kingston, Ontario: McGill-Queen's University Press, 1994

Howkins, Alun, *Reshaping Rural England: A Social History, 1850–1925*, London and New York: HarperCollins, 1991

Howkins, Alun, "Social, Cultural, and Domestic Life" in *The Agrarian History of England and Wales*, vol. 7, 1850–1914 (Part 2), edited by E.J.T. Collins, Cambridge: Cambridge University Press, 2000

Newby, Howard, *The Deferential Worker: A Study of Farm Workers in East Anglia*, London: Allen Lane, 1977; Madison: University of Wisconsin Press, 1979

Reay, Barry, *Microhistories: Demography, Society, and Culture in Rural England, 1800–1930*, Cambridge and New York: Cambridge University Press, 1996

Robin, Jean, *Elmdon: Continuity and Change in a North-West Essex Village, 1861–1964*, Cambridge and New York: Cambridge University Press, 1980

Samuel, Raphael, "'Quarry Roughs': Life and Labour in Headington Quarry – An Essay in Oral History" in *Village Life and Labour*, edited by Raphael Samuel, London: Routledge and Kegan Paul, 1975

Snell, K.D.M., *Annals of the Labouring Poor: Social Change and Agrarian England, 1600–1900*, Cambridge and New York: Cambridge University Press, 1985

Strathern, Marilyn, *Kinship at the Core: An Anthropology of Elmdon – A Village in North-West Essex in the Nineteen-Sixties*, Cambridge and New York: Cambridge University Press, 1981

This essay primarily addresses the history of non-landowning workers and their families in rural England during the 19th century, which was the greatest period of transition in agriculture. Historians have used different terms for the rural working family, including "rural working class", "labouring poor", and "rural poor". It is important to acknowledge that such people have not, historically, formed a homogeneous body because of the significant regional, occupational, and, consequently, economic and social distinctions between them. It is also essential to note whether the geographic focus of any research is on northern or southern England, given their differing agricultural histories. For example, from about 1750 to 1914 a noteworthy, albeit stereotypical, division can be made between farm servants who lived on northern farms for a transitional period before marrying or finding other employment, and southern day labourers on farms who lived in nearby villages.

Until the 1970s agricultural historians were principally concerned with the economic implications of technological and structural changes, such as those arising from the parliamentary enclosure of land c.1760–1850. Additionally, research into the family unit in Britain had normally concentrated on industrial, urban, and elite communities, partly because better documentary evidence was available for these groups. Even when rural families were studied systematically, they were usually from the landowning elite; the best example of this genre is F.M.L. Thompson's *English Landed Society in the Nineteenth Century*. Up to about 1900, "others" living in the countryside left relatively few written records about themselves and were the section of rural society least likely to be written about by contemporaries. SAMUEL's essay marked a shift from the established historiography in terms of both methodology and which sections of village society were being investigated. Samuel uses oral histories taken from villagers living at Headington Quarry near Oxford to underpin his research into their distinctive economic, social, and physical environment, from c.1860 to 1925. He illustrates the multiple occupations, secondary economies (e.g. pig-keeping, gardening, laundering, poaching), and kinship links that families took up as part of their strategy against poverty exacerbated by irregular and seasonal work.

HOWKINS's stimulating general history (1991) scrutinizes the gradual changes in English rural society between 1850 and 1925. Howkins warns that to stress the centrality of the nuclear family hides the complex life cycle of changing social and economic relationships experienced by family members, such as those involving the extended family. Further, until the new Poor Law of 1834 penalized illegitimacy, betrothal was more important than marriage in founding a family. Howkins also observes that after c.1865 the diminution of the "family unit as a workforce, among the labourers at least, saw a rise in its importance as a unit of socialisation".

SNELL utilizes a striking fusion of quantitative analysis and literary sources to assess the changing quality of life of rural labourers in Wales as well as southern England. He studies the agricultural family not in isolation but as an "intermediary between economic change and its qualitatively experienced effects" and considers how the family was affected by enclosure, the sexual division of labour, and the reduction of living-in servants in husbandry. After 1700 the effects included the following: children left home at an older age, social mobility declined as the new Poor Law made obtaining legal settlement difficult, live-in servants were no longer considered an "integral" part of the family they served, and the age of marriage decreased. However, across the whole period 1700-1900 Snell found no general disposition by agricultural families to use kinship networks for maintenance.

The incisiveness of Snell's work is matched by REAY, who uses total (family) reconstitution and oral history to investigate the Blean area of Kent. Reay discovered, by tracing families across the censuses of 1841-91, that "at least as many households in the area went through an extended phase as experienced only the simple [nuclear] family structure". Moreover, in 1851, 74 per cent of labouring households had kinship links with other households in the area, and qualitative evidence suggests that these links were not ignored at times of need. These findings challenge suggestions of loose kinship ties and the dominance of the nuclear family structure in rural areas, at least during the 19th century.

HOWKINS (2000) presents a helpful outline of the social histories of the main classes in English and Welsh rural areas from 1850 to 1914, particularly in the context of regional disparities. He again stresses that although for the majority of the labouring poor the nuclear family was the "basic unit of family life", there were local deviations from this norm, with relatively high rates of illegitimacy in some parishes, widows as heads of households, and extended families living together. He also emphasizes that before the 1870s most members of poorer rural families, including children over age seven, had to work to maintain the family as a viable economic entity. The outwork (e.g. gloving, making lace, and plaiting straw) undertaken by women and girls remained a critical part of the family economy until at least the Edwardian era.

With regard to women's work, following Ann Kussmaul's *Servants in Husbandry in Early Modern England*, HILL has produced a critical synopsis, contributing to our understanding of the slow decline through the 18th century of employment opportunities for female servants in husbandry. The decline was caused by a greater sexual division of labour, changing social sensitivities, and the development of more capitalistic agricultural systems, which devalued the use of women fieldworkers and increased the demand for (mostly) male day labourers.

A few studies principally analyse the rural working family from an anthropological or sociological perspective, while thoughtfully placing it in a historical context. NEWBY's work, on Suffolk, is pre-eminent in demonstrating the value of this approach to the examination of social relationships in the countryside and remains an important introductory text for the study of rural workers. One of the most successful studies at the village level was carried out in Elmdon, Essex, during the 1960s. The resulting books by ROBIN and STRATHERN are companion volumes, the first taking a historical viewpoint and the second an anthropological one.

MARK HATHAWAY

See also Enclosure and Land Use; Farming: Agricultural Depression; Farming: Agricultural Revolutions

Social Structure: Urban Artisan and Working-Class Families

Anderson, Gregory, *Victorian Clerks*, Manchester: Manchester University Press, 1976

Benson, John (editor), *The Working Class in England, 1875-1914*, London and Dover, New Hampshire: Croom Helm, 1985

Chesney, Kellow, *The Victorian Underworld*, London: Maurice Temple, 1970; New York: Schocken Books, 1972

Foster, John, *Class Struggle and the Industrial Revolution: Early Industrial Capitalism in Three English Towns*, London: Weidenfeld and Nicolson, 1974; New York: St Martin's Press, 1975

Houlbrooke, Ralph A., *The English Family, 1450-1700*, London and New York: Longman, 1984

Humphries, Stephen, *Hooligans or Rebels? An Oral History of Working-Class Childhood and Youth, 1889-1939*, Oxford: Blackwell, 1981

Kirk, Neville, *The Growth of Working Class Reformism in Mid-Victorian England*, London: Croom Helm, and Urbana: University of Illinois Press, 1985

Lewis, Jane (editor), *Labour and Love: Women's Experience of Home and Family, 1890-1940*, Oxford: Blackwell, 1986; Oxford and New York: Blackwell, 1987

Neale, R.S., *Class in English History 1680-1850*, Oxford: Blackwell, and Totowa, New Jersey: Barnes and Noble, 1981

Roberts, Robert, *The Classic Slum: Salford Life in the First Quarter Century*, Manchester: Manchester University Press, 1971

Smelser, Neil J., *Social Change in the Industrial Revolution: An Application of Theory to the Lancashire Cotton Industry 1770-1840*, London: Routledge and Kegan Paul, 1959; as *Social Change in the Industrial Revolution: An Application of Theory to the British Cotton Industry 1770-1840*, Chicago: University of Chicago Press, 1959

Smith, Dennis, *Conflict and Compromise: Class Formation in English Society, 1830–1914: A Comparative Study of Birmingham and Sheffield*, London and Boston: Routledge and Kegan Paul, 1982

Stedman, Jones Gareth, *Outcast London: A Study in the Relationship between Classes in Victorian Society*, Oxford: Clarendon Press, 1971; Harmondsworth and Baltimore, Maryland: Penguin, 1976

Tebbutt, Melanie, *Making Ends Meet: Pawnbroking and Working-Class Credit*, Leicester: Leicester University Press, and New York: St Martin's Press, 1983

NEALE comments that social history must concentrate on the family, described as the smallest and most intimate group; at the other extreme lie expanding urban environments where individuals have made their homes. Thus Neale mediates between SMELSER, to whom industrialization causes a disequilibrium in the working-class family, and FOSTER: "In his view serious – that is revolutionary – protest is the product not of the break up of the family consequent upon new technology but arises from the creation of a community in which family is a part". Robert ROBERTS talks of "ideas and views repeated in family, street, factory and shop" before going on to state unequivocally: "No view of the English working class in the first quarter of this century would be accurate if that class were shown merely as a great amalgam of artisan and labouring groups united by a common aim and culture".

Discussion of the family is important in the medieval and early modern periods. However, HOULBROOKE, like Michael Anderson and Lawrence Stone, covers the ground in general terms of love and marriage. Michael Anderson discusses two approaches – "sentiment" and household economics – whereas Houlbrooke covers kindred, marriage, infancy and childhood, adolescence, widowhood, and inheritance but not work per se.

It is only when one concentrates on the 19th century and the first half of the 20th century that the full complexity of the topic is revealed, covering the world of the artisan, the semi- and unskilled, the woman, and the child. In this discussion the importance of respectability and skill are fundamental. Concerning the artisan, SMITH and KIRK are of great importance. Smith, in a well-written and closely argued book which is founded in contemporary literature and statistical evidence, warns against generalizations in discussing Sheffield and Birmingham: "Sheffield had a strong and solidary working class, confronted . . . by a weak and anomic bourgeoisie. . . . Birmingham had a working class whose structural defences . . . were relatively weak . . . faced by a bourgeoisie which was well organised and confident". He points out that the combination of parental and workplace authority over the young in Sheffield's artisan society produced "exceptionally strong control by the local community over its members".

Writers such as Geoffrey Crossick, R.Q. Gray, Charles More, Takao Matsamura, and E.J. Hobsbawm discuss the concepts of labour aristocracy and respectability. The best way to access this debate is Kirk's long fifth chapter, "Respectability". Starting with the question "Was respectability the sole or main preserve of an 'aristocratic' elite of workers, or did it cast its net wider?" he proceeds to give a detailed, and clear exposition of the debate, analysing a wide range of writers and providing an exhaustive bibliography. In BENSON, Elizabeth Roberts, writing on "The Family", offers another authoritative introduction to respectability. She concentrates on the socialization of children and young people and the interaction in their lives of home, school, and work. Though there is no bibliography the exhaustive references provide a good way of following up the topic.

Elizabeth Roberts refers to the "use of a 'runner' who, for a small fee, took several families' bundles, thus saving them the embarrassment, or even disgrace of being seen entering the pawnbroker's". This is a good introduction to TEBBUTT's discussion of the fundamental importance of the topic for a deeper understanding of respectability and family finances in the working class. Tebbutt gives a clear, well-directed account which underlines that such methods of finance were logical in their own context. In this regard, Robert ROBERTS discusses how his mother, who ran a corner shop, used respectability as a guide to creditworthiness. Tebbutt is also important because she vividly illustrates women's loneliness, embarrassment, and struggle as the emergence of capitalism separated home and workplace.

LEWIS's edited book represents an important feminist contribution to the understanding of the urban artisan or working-class family; each article concludes with useful bibliographic notes. Jane Lewis's essay "The Working Class Wife and Mother and State Intervention, 1870–1918" takes as a starting-point the fact that a wife's not working was a badge of respectability among artisans. Lynn Jameson discusses "Working Class Mothers and Daughters in Urban Scotland", Ellen Ross covers London's working-class mothers, and Elizabeth A.M. Roberts covers "Women's Strategies, 1890–1940".

The consideration of childhood and youth is deepened by HUMPHRIES's detailed and humane account. Humphries discusses the "resistance of working class youth to powerful attempts to inculcate" respectability. This work, with its concise, excellent bibliography, is a good introduction to theoretical discussions about youth, crime, and social structure theory in general. STEDMAN moves down the social scale to the world of the unskilled, the casual labourer, and the "residuum". The casual labour market is painstakingly and thoroughly explored in Part 1 of Jones's book, and there are valuable insights into such concepts as "the residuum" and urban degeneration theory. In Part 2 environmental aspects, particularly housing, are covered thoughtfully and in detail, with a good selection of photographs. Part 3 is a scholarly exposition of the problems "not so much in the form in which they actually existed as in the form in which the middle and upper classes conceived them to exist". This world can be further explored in CHESNEY.

Some writers – for example, Elizabeth Roberts in Benson; Smith; and of course most notably Humphries – discuss the artisan and working-class view of the importance, or unimportance, of education. An area of the utmost importance to social structure, the family, and respectability, with notable political and electoral consequences down to the present day, is the emergence from the middle of the 19th century onwards of the lower middle class, among others of office workers and elementary school teachers. This trend was fundamental in the entry of women into larger areas of the job market and can be followed up in some detail in Gregory ANDERSON.

RAY GRACE

See also Industrial Revolution

Social Structure: Urban Commercial Families

Anderson, Gregory, *Victorian Clerks*, Manchester: Manchester University Press, 1976

Bagwell, Philip, *The Railway Clearing House in the British Economy 1842–1922*, London: Allen and Unwin, 1968

Brenner, Robert, *Merchants and Revolution: Commercial Change, Political Conflict, and London's Overseas Traders 1550–1653*, Princeton, New Jersey: Princeton University Press, 1993

Crossick, Geoffrey, *An Artisan Elite in Victorian Society: Kentish London, 1840–1880*, London: Croom Helm, and Totowa, New Jersey: Rowman and Littlefield, 1978

Crossick, Geoffrey and Heinz-Gerhard Haupt (editors), *Shopkeepers and Master Artisans in Nineteenth-Century Europe*, London and New York: Methuen, 1984

Crossick, Geoffrey and Heinz-Gerhard Haupt, *The Petite Bourgeoisie in Europe 1780–1914: Enterprise, Family, and Independence*, London and New York: Routledge, 1995

Garrard, John, *Leadership and Power in Victorian Industrial Towns, 1830–1880*, Manchester and Dover, New Hampshire: Manchester University Press, 1983

Grassby, Richard, *The Business Community of Seventeenth-Century England*, Cambridge and New York: Cambridge University Press, 1995

Mui, Hoh-cheung and Lorna H. Mui, *Shops and Shopkeeping in Eighteenth-Century England*, Montreal and Kingston, Ontario: McGill-Queen's University Press, and London: Routledge, 1989

Power, Eileen, *Medieval People*, London: Methuen, and Boston: Houghton Mifflin, 1924

Prothero, I.J., *Artisans and Politics in Early Nineteenth-Century London: John Gast and His Times*, Folkestone, Kent: Dawson, 1979

Rappaport, Steve, *Worlds within Worlds: Structures of Life in Sixteenth-Century London*, Cambridge and New York: Cambridge University Press, 1989

Smith, Dennis, *Conflict and Compromise: Class Formation in English Society, 1830–1914: A Comparative Study of Birmingham and Sheffield*, London and Boston: Routledge and Kegan Paul, 1982

Thrupp, Sylvia L., *The Merchant Class of Medieval London, 1300–1500*, Chicago: University of Chicago Press, 1948

Earlier studies tend to concentrate on merchant families; but shopkeepers and master artisans become more central from the 18th century, and the 19th century added the commercially important lower middle class. These families' lifestyles, connections, and social mores lead to wider considerations in the literature, such as industrialization, politics, and notions of respectability.

GRASSBY, taking a different perspective from Harold Perkin and other proponents of the aristocracy and gentry in the trend towards industrialization, concludes that "it was the businessman who made the pre-industrial economy work and who ultimately changed the rules of the game". CROSSICK & HAUPT (1995), unlike such writers as Robert Gellately, consider the shopkeepers and master artisans to have been relatively cohesive; Crossick and Haupt also cross swords with R.J. Morris on

the issue of how closely the petite bourgeoisie identified with the "labouring classes". RAPPAPORT takes issue with a long list of historians, including Phythian Adams, Dyer, and Palliser, concluding that whatever the social problems in Tudor London may have been, "chronic instability cannot be counted among them".

Writers covering the medieval and early modern periods tend to give pride of place to the urban merchant. A key discussion in THRUPP (a readable, clearly expressed book deeply grounded in original sources, in which social structure is a central theme), concerns the relationship between successful urban merchants and the more gentle ranks of society; this is vitally important to Harold Perkin's discussion of industrialization in the 18th century. As parliament emerged in England, merchant and gentry did not form separate estates: Thrupp demonstrates that the merchant families' lifestyle helped the merchant achieve a "recognized place of honor in any nobleman's hall", while "the net effect of parliamentary experience was to encourage people to associate the merchants and gentry together" as a significant middle social stratum. Merchants' family life is vividly depicted in POWER's polished chapters on Thomas Betson and Thomas Paycocke. Grassby covers business as a career, politics, lifestyles, and family structure, giving these topics the same centrality they have in other books. BRENNER sets out to show the decisive and opposing roles, from 1640 on, of the great London company merchants and the new colonial merchants, who had different commercial interests and political affiliations.

Rappaport, in a closely researched, closely argued, and persuasive study, reconstitutes the careers of 1,000 men from Tudor London, concentrating on a more petit-bourgeois "middling sort" of person – "brewers and butchers, carpenters and coopers . . . and indirectly their wives and children, apprentices and servants". These people's satisfaction with the degree of social mobility available to them in Tudor London "established a consensual basis for the stratification system and thus played an important role in preserving stability in sixteenth-century London".

These sections of urban society come more into their own in studies covering the 18th century and beyond, with increasing emphasis on the "shopocracy". MUI & MUI dispute the generalization that shops and shopkeepers did not become widely important until the 19th century; their book is a thorough, exhaustive, scholarly work which deals with its material in depth. They conclude that "the petty shopkeeper, so frequently ignored by contemporary social enumerators and later historians, was an important cog in this 'wheel whereon the inland trade turns'". CROSSICK & HAUPT (1984) provide a well-produced and delightful collection of high-quality essays. They discuss "Shopkeepers, Master Artisans, and the Historian: The Petite Bourgeoisie in Nineteenth Century Britain" and "Shopkeepers and the State in Britain, 1870–1914"; Clive Behagg discusses "Masters and Manufacturers: Social Values and the Smaller Unit of Production in Birmingham, 1800–1850". The first of these essays is an important discussion of the overall debates; Behagg introduces us to important writings on a series of northern English towns.

Crossick & Haupt (1995) comment that "urban society cannot be understood without the petite bourgeoisie, nor the petite bourgeoisie without the setting of the town". Clive Behagg, taking up Birmingham in Crossick & Haupt (1984), on the basis of a good, concise methodological and definitional discussion, refuses to identify the urban petite bourgeoisie after 1800 with the traditional master artisan sector of earlier society. He contributes to a number of important studies based on individual northern English towns – Birmingham, Sheffield, Salford, Bolton, Rochdale, Leeds. SMITH looks at Birmingham and Sheffield as urbanization proceeds, and at the role of the commercially-oriented artisanate and "shopocracy", taking a point of view that contrasts with Behagg's. Smith's book, which is vivid and well-researched, reminds us that broad generalizations in this topic can often be extremely misleading. Birmingham and Sheffield underwent widely different experiences. In Birmingham after 1860 "competing segments of [the] bourgeoisie allied with each of the two wings of the pre-industrial order: the rural aristocracy . . . and . . . the emerging social circles of the petit-bourgeois 'shopocracy' and the artisanry". In Sheffield, however, "the urban bourgeoisie threw its weight into the balance with the aristocracy, and overwhelmed the parochial networks of craftsmen and petty traders". GARRARD, in a clearly written and clearly argued work based on considerable detail, views the bourgeoisie of the towns he examines (Salford, Bolton, and Rochdale) as more cohesive than that of Birmingham, and as more cooperative with the petite bourgeoisie than that of Sheffield. This view confirms Crossick in Crossick & Haupt (1984): "Crucial to the bourgeois domination in Victorian Britain was the ability of the liberal bourgeoisie to integrate (the petite bourgeoisie) into the political and ideological framework of liberal society". CROSSICK (1978), in his chapter "Elites and the Community", includes a study of the local political importance of master artisans and shopkeepers; thus he links up with Rappaport but does not see eye to eye with Behagg or with such writers as PROTHERO, who emphasizes the distance between master and artisan.

The central importance of respectability in the urban and commercial family is shown in much of the literature described above. Once we add the increasingly large and important lower middle class of Mr Pooters – outlined in ANDERSON and detailed in BAGWELL – we are well on the way to the psephological calculations of Margaret Thatcher and Tony Blair.

RAY GRACE

See also Industrial Revolution

Socialism

Beckett, Francis, *Enemy Within: The Rise and Fall of the British Communist Party*, London: John Murray, 1995
Crosland, Anthony, *The Future of Socialism*, London: Jonathan Cape, 1956; New York: Macmillan, 1957
Hyams, Edward, *The Millennium Postponed: Socialism from Sir Thomas More to Mao Tse-Tung*, London: Secker and Warburg, 1973; New York: Taplinger, 1974
Laybourn, Keith, *The Rise of Socialism in Britain, c.1881–1951*, Stroud, Gloucestershire: Sutton, 1997
Laybourn, Keith, *A Century of Labor: A History of the Labour Party*, Stroud, Gloucestershire: Sutton, 2001
Marquand, David, *The Progressive Dilemma*, London: Heinemann, 1991; 2nd edition, as *The Progressive Dilemma: From Lloyd George to Blair*, London: Phoenix Giant, 1999
Miliband, Ralph, *Parliamentary Socialism: A Study in the Politics of Labour*, London: Allen and Unwin, 1961; New York: Monthly Review Press, 1964; 2nd edition, London: Merlin Press, 1972
Miliband, Ralph, *Socialism for a Sceptical Age*, Cambridge: Polity Press, 1994; New York: Verso, 1995
Minkin, Lewis, *The Contentious Alliance: Trade Unions and the Labour Party*, Edinburgh: Edinburgh University Press, 1991
Radice, Giles (editor), *What Needs to Change: New Visions for Britain*, with introduction by Tony Blair, London: HarperCollins, 1996
Sassoon, Donald, *One Hundred Years of Socialism: The West European Left in the Twentieth Century*, London: I.B. Tauris, and New York: New Press, 1996
Shore, Peter, *Leading the Left*, London: Weidenfeld and Nicolson, 1993
Weinbren, David, *Generating Socialism: Recollections of Life in the Labour Party*, Stroud, Gloucestershire: Sutton, 1997
Wright, Anthony, *R.H. Tawney*, Manchester: Manchester University Press, 1987

Socialism is the most durable and broadly based of the political doctrines and has roots in the Old and New Testament, in Greek philosophy, and in Utopian literature.

HYAMS describes the prominent theorists, from the early Continental social scientists to the scientific socialists Karl Marx and Friedrich Engels, who spent most of their adult life in England; the libertarian socialists; the rise of the social democrats, anarchists, and syndicalists; and how these diverse ideas influenced socialism in the 20th century. Hyams comes to the conclusion that classical socialism will never be implemented, for we as human beings are more interested in a higher standard of living than we are in "noble visions".

Hyams had a valid point in 1973. But within two decades the Communist Party of Great Britain, formed in 1920, had disintegrated, as well as the whole communist structure in eastern Europe and the Soviet Union. BECKETT tells the full story: of the communists who fought Mosley's fascists in the 1930s, organized hunger marches, recruited volunteers for the Spanish Civil War, and played a leading role in the trade union movement; of how the Soviet invasions of Hungary and Czechoslovakia destroyed the communists' credibility in Britain; of the vicious in-fighting between the party's factions throughout the Thatcher years; and of the party's final collapse in 1991 and the relaunching of its rump as the Democratic Left.

The Labour Party, which by tradition also propagates socialism in its literature, retreated from Clause 4 of its constitution – a clause drafted by Sidney Webb in 1918 and revised in 1926 that embraced public ownership as a basic aim. In the early 1900s most socialists believed that socialism was within grasp, and after 1945 they saw it in the nationalization of key industries. For the Left, Clause 4 was a symbol of socialism; but modernizers saw it as an albatross tying the party to nationalization. In 1995 Tony Blair persuaded a special conference to replace Clause 4 with a new "statement of aims and values". This meant that socialism in Britain – as LAYBOURN (2001) indicates – was very different at the end of the 20th century from what it had been at the beginning. LAYBOURN (1997) gives a great deal of emphasis to Clause 4 as a response to Bolshevism in Britain, to the Russian revolution, and to the declining fortunes of the Independent Labour Party formed in 1893. Ramsay MacDonald felt that it could accommodate and conceal many different socialist interests and be acceptable to the trade unionists. Laybourn examines why the Communist Party formed in 1920 failed to become the mass party of the working classes in Britain and why the Labour Party failed to become the party of socialism. Between 1920 and 1945 Labour in Britain was wedded to the trade union movement. MINKIN substantiates Laybourn's thesis, arguing that during World War II a number of socialists felt the Labour Party's commitment to socialism was being held back by the trade unions but that Labour's landslide victory in the general election of 1945 buried such thoughts for at least three decades. The weaknesses of the Labour Left, in its hard and soft forms, have been blamed for the failure of Attlee's administration to implement the kind of socialist measures that were introduced in Sweden.

MILIBAND (1961) is one of the most critical accounts. It is a detailed and scholarly record of the failure of the Labour Party from 1900 until Harold Wilson's governments (1964–70) to introduce classical socialism through parliament. Miliband ignores what has been called "gas and water socialism", perfected by Herbert Morrison as leader of the London County Council, and how after 1945 most of the municipal services were transferred to the state. He mentions in one sentence the creation of the National Health Service by Aneurin Bevan and the contribution of the rank-and-file socialists in their communities. Raymond Williams, the literary and cultural critic, argued that "Socialists in the Labour Party have been afraid, for too long, of describing it as it is".

WEINBREN, with the assistance of the Labour Oral History Project, proved otherwise in *Generating Socialism*, which presents the experiences of grass-roots activists. This book persuades us that the ideology still has a great deal to offer. Vi Willis of Ilford reminded her interviewer that recruitment should be a priority to ensure that the "torch of socialism is handed over to another generation of socialists". But that is the difficulty. Of the 88 people interviewed, the youngest was at least 60 years old. Most were in their late seventies. Socialism has to adapt not only to every country but to every generation.

SASSOON's book is a remarkable work of historical analysis, a comparative history of socialist parties in countries as diverse as Britain, Germany, Italy, Greece, Denmark, Finland, Austria, and Sweden. Sassoon discusses the constraints they faced from capitalist development, the nation-state, the international system, dominant ideologies, the past, and in particular the electorate. In many ways the most relevant section of this majestic work is Part 3, "Towards Revisionism 1950–1960", particularly the review of Anthony CROSLAND's influential book. Crosland, writing as a politician of the Labour Party, felt a need to distance socialism from Marxism by listing no fewer than 11 other socialist doctrines. Sassoon is critical of Crosland's Marxian scholarship, arguing that it was based on "ill-digested secondary sources" and also that most of what Crosland wrote was not very original. According to Sassoon, the most important pages of Crosland's book were not the first 517 but the last dozen, where Crosland saw politicians like himself having to deal with issues regarding the environment, human rights, civil questions, and new concerns for socialism.

Many of Crosland's disciples were unable, in the controversies with Tony Benn and the Bennite Left after the defeat of Callaghan's government of 1979, to remain within the Labour Party. A new party, the Social Democratic Party (SDP), was launched on 16 March 1981 by the "Gang of Four" – former Labour cabinet ministers. Among those who played a leading part in the creation of the SDP was the Labourite David Marquand. After the amalgamation of SDP and the Liberal Party after the general election of 1987, Marquand returned to his first career as a professor of politics. MARQUAND (1999) gives useful insights into the socialism of leading Labour politicians, such as Ernest Bevin, Hugh Dalton, Aneurin Bevan, Hugh Gaitskell, Richard Crossman, Harold Wilson, and David Owen, who became one of the "Gang of Four". Marquand's answer to the central paradox of British democracy – that is, the failure of the Left to become the national governing group – was the formation of a new progressive coalition, based on the values of community and citizenship.

MILIBAND (1995) disagrees vehemently with the right-wing Marquand, especially with Marquand's prescription. Miliband, a Marxian socialist, identifies three equally important, interrelated, and interdependent themes as defining contemporary socialism: democracy, egalitarianism, and the creation of an economy under democratic control. According to Miliband, socialism has to be understood as part of an age-old struggle for a more just society; he believes that socialism will in time come to command a majority, even in general elections – a view not endorsed by Marquand.

Miliband's vision was in tune with New Labour, and after the overwhelming victory in the general election of 1997 it could be implemented. The victory in 1997 had followed disappointment in the general election of 1992. Then, despite a vigorous campaign at the hustings and Neil Kinnock's success in destroying the Militant Tendency – a Trotskyist movement (a "party within a party") – and modernizing Labour's organization, the party won only 35 per cent of the popular vote. A former cabinet minister, Peter SHORE, saw a dilemma in the enduring conflict between the socialist minority and the labourist majority, the continual dissent on foreign aid and defence policies, and the strong internal opposition that every leader from George Lansbury to John Smith had to face.

Shore makes good reading, with a plea for more modernization. The sudden death of John Smith brought a new leader, Tony Blair, in 1994. Blair quickly implemented what Shore had called for, rewriting the constitution, changing the relationship with the trade unions, and renewing the democratic structure. RADICE spells out the new socialism. WRIGHT is the latest biography of R.H. Tawney, who embodied British socialism of the 20th century. Michael Foot stated that Tawney's books were read and loved, the greatest influence on a generation of socialists. A combination of Tawney's equality of opportunity – with a personal computer for every adolescent – and the battle cry "education, education, education" was one possible definition of socialism for New Labour in the year 2000. Or, as Peter Hennessy, one of Radice's authors, puts it, Tawney + Windows = New Labour.

D. BEN REES

See also Economic Theory: Post-Mercantilist; Fabian Society; Hardie; Labour Party; Marxism

Solway Moss, Battle of

see "Rough Wooing"

Somerset, Edward Seymour, 1st Duke of *c.*1500–1552

Soldier, politician, and lord protector of Edward VI

Bush, Michael Laccohee, *The Government Policy of Protector Somerset*, London: Edward Arnold, and Montreal: McGill-Queens University Press, 1975

Davies, Clifford Stephen Lloyd, "Slavery and Protector Somerset: The Vagrancy Act of 1547", *Economic History Review*, 2nd series, 19 (1966): 533–59

Elton, Sir Geoffrey Rudolph, *Studies in Tudor and Stuart Politics and Government*, 4 vols, Cambridge and New York: Cambridge University Press, 1974–92

Hoak, Dale Eugene, *The King's Council in the Reign of Edward VI*, Cambridge and New York: Cambridge University Press, 1976

Jordan, Wilbur Kirchener, *Edward VI: The Young King – The Protectorship of the Duke of Somerset*, London: Allen and Unwin, 1968; Cambridge, Massachusetts: Belknap Press of Harvard University Press, 1971

King, John Norman, *English Reformation Literature: The Tudor Origins of the Protestant Tradition*, Princeton, New Jersey: Princeton University Press, 1982

Loach, Susan Jennifer, *Protector Somerset: A Reassessment*, Bangor: Headstart History, 1994

Loach, Susan Jennifer, *Edward VI*, New Haven, Connecticut, and London: Yale University Press, 1999

Pollard, Albert Frederick, *England under Protector Somerset: An Essay*, London: Kegan Paul, Trench and Trubner, 1900; reprinted, New York: Russell and Russell, 1966

Seymour, William, *Ordeal by Ambition: An English Family in the Shadow of the Tudors*, London: Sidgwick and Jackson, 1972; New York: St Martin's Press, 1973

Shagan, Ethan M., "Protector Somerset and the 1549 Rebellions: New Sources and New Perspectives", *English Historical Review* 114 (1999): 34–63; and debate *infra*, 115 (2000): 103–33

There is no published life of Somerset, who as lord protector headed the government during the first two and a half years of the reign of his nephew Edward VI. His personal history is given by SEYMOUR in a book which also deals with Somerset's sister, Henry VIII's third queen; and with his wayward brother Thomas, Lord Seymour of Sudeley. William Seymour's account of his forebears is not overlaid with family piety, and it competently handles the printed and some manuscript sources. It predates the recent re-evaluation of Somerset's public career and private interests.

The debate begins with POLLARD, who portrayed the duke as an enlightened ruler, a proponent of modest reform in the church, a patron of education, and a beloved guardian of the poorer classes – the very ideal, in fact, of an aristocratic Victorian philanthropist. His downfall was attributed to his unwillingness, in 1549, to act harshly against the rebellious common people, with whose grievances he supposedly sympathized. This assessment was ostensibly supported by solid scholarship; but as Sir Geoffrey ELTON was to observe, Pollard's competence as an historian was circumscribed by his reliance on printed calendars and was conditioned by the English Liberal political tradition to which he adhered. Pollard's view of Somerset nevertheless held sway for 75 years. Some doubts were raised: for example, in 1966 DAVIES, examining the draconian legislation to curb employment introduced in 1547, questioned Somerset's credentials as a social reformer. Davies's conclusion – that the policy was inept rather than specially malevolent – did not redound much to Somerset's credit. Pollard's orthodoxy was, however, about to receive heavy reinforcement from JORDAN in the first of his two substantial volumes on Edward's reign. This work has been criticized for its inaccuracies of fact and interpretation, for its ponderous style, and above all for its perpetuation of the image of Somerset as the "good duke" (and that of his successor Northumberland as the bad one). Elton articulated these objections with characteristic force. Jordan has nevertheless provided a solid narrative history, of a kind unfashionable even when it was published and now unlikely to be replaced. In consequence Somerset's protectorate is among the best-chronicled periods in the Tudor century.

Pollard and Jordan's interpretation was wholly rejected by BUSH in his analysis (with authoritative sources) of the protector's administration. Bush's earlier work had revealed Somerset as a landlord of uncompromisingly aggressive tendencies, unencumbered by a social conscience, whose chief skill was in war. Bush argued that the military strategy which, as protector, Somerset deployed to secure peace with Scotland became an obsession, fatally impairing his political judgement. Following his successful rout of the Scots at Pinkie in 1547, Somerset set up a chain of garrisons along the border and deep into Scotland. He refused to abandon this scheme despite changing circumstances and mounting costs, and all other policies were conditioned by it. In this light, Somerset's supposed concern for the welfare of the peasantry was seen to be a need for able-bodied troops. Bush also highlighted Somerset's dictatorial use of proclamations and his inability to cooperate amicably with his colleagues. HOAK's work on the Privy Council (appearing after Bush had published his monograph) further demonstrated Somerset's poor control of the machinery of government – as well as Somerset's intolerance and rudeness, which alienated even those who were disposed to support his regime. His overthrow in 1549 appears to be simply the result of a coalition of divergent interests in the council temporarily united in exasperation at his megalomania and mismanagement.

Bush's thesis was warmly received by Elton, who incorporated it in his own later work. It has not, however, been universally accepted; the issue of the garrison, in particular, is regarded by some as Bush's own obsession. More generally there are those, unconvinced by evidence that Somerset was a conventionally hard-headed (if incompetent) politician, who persist in seeing him as a benign patron of education and intellectual freedom. Pollard's good duke, though pronounced clinically dead by Bush and Elton, survives on a life-support system operated chiefly by KING. King adduces many books that were dedicated to the protector, and the modest literary efforts for which Somerset's imprisonment gave him leisure.

LOACH, in her brief but thorough review of recent literature on Somerset (1994) and in her biography of Edward VI (1999), finds all this unconvincing. She notes that the dedications to Somerset began only when he came to power and proved no more than his having raised a certain amount of expectation among the intelligentsia. She also doubts that Somerset's interest in educational reform extended beyond the need to train men for government service. G.T.R. Parry had already demonstrated that one ostensibly contemporary piece of evidence – a speech by Somerset in praise of learning, much quoted by his modern admirers – was an invention of the Elizabethan writer William Harrison. More recently, SHAGAN has drawn attention to letters in which, he believes, Somerset offered authentic concessions to the rebels of 1549; this may be further evidence that Somerset's regime was spinning out of control. Loach dismisses King's remarkable suggestion that Somerset's execution made him a martyr to the protestant cause, though she accepts that his religious policy was probably genuinely based in the reformed faith.

But Somerset should not be judged on his intellectual compass or his spiritual purity. He was a soldier and governor, and he has to be assessed by his record in the saddle and at the council table. Inevitably he is compared mostly with Northumberland, whose reputation has risen as Somerset's has fallen. The archives assist this reversal; more state papers survive from Northumberland's regime, and he therefore appears as a good administrator, working in the system. By contrast Somerset seems more arbitrary, or just disorganized. Had William Cecil (whose public career began in Somerset's service) not destroyed most of his office papers when the protectorate collapsed, we might have had a more balanced picture of Somerset's rule.

C.S. KNIGHTON

See also Edward VI; Northumberland; Protestant Revolution; "Rough Wooing"

South Africa, Relations with

Atmore, A. and Shula Marks, "The Imperial Factor in South Africa in the Nineteenth Century: Towards a Reassessment", *Journal of Imperial and Commonwealth History*, 3/1 (1974): 105–39

Galbraith, John S., *Reluctant Empire: British Policy on the South African Frontier, 1834–1854*, California: Publisher, 1963

Macmillan, William Miller, *Bantu, Boer, and Briton: The Making of the South African Native Problem*, London: Faber and Gwyer, 1929; revised edition, Oxford: Clarendon Press, 1963

Marks, Shula and Stanley Trapido, "Lord Milner and the South African State Reconsidered", *History Workshop Journal 2*, (1979): 50–80

Nasson, Bill, *The South African War, 1899–1902*, London: Arnold, and New York: Oxford University Press, 1999

Peires, J.B., "The British and the Cape, 1814–1834" in *The Shaping of South African Society, 1652–1840*, edited by Richard Elphick and Hermann Giliomee, 2nd edition,

Cape Town: Maskew Miller Longman, and Middletown, Connecticut: Wesleyan University Press, 1989

Porter, A.N., *The Origins of the South African War: Joseph Chanberlain and the Diplomacy of Imperialism, 1895–1899*, Manchester: Manchester University Press, and New York: St Martin's Press, 1980

Robinson, Ronald and John Gallagher, with Alice Denny, *Africa and the Victorians: The Official Mind of Imperialism*, London: Macmillan, and New York: St Martin's Press, 1961; 2nd edition, London: Macmillan, 1981

Van Jaarsveld, F.A., *The Awakening of Afrikaner Nationalism 1868–1881*, translated from the Afrikaans by F.R. Metrowich, Cape Town: Human and Rousseau, 1961

Wilson, Monica and Leonard Thompson (editors), *The Oxford History of South Africa*, vol. 2, *South Africa 1870–1966*, Oxford and New York: Oxford University Press, 1971

Britain first seized control of the Dutch East India Company's Cape Colony during the French revolutionary wars in 1795. The French conquest of the Low Countries and declaration of the "Batavian Republic" had made control of the Cape of major strategic significance to the British shipping route to India. The Cape was handed back to the Batavian Republic during a lull in the fighting in 1803, but the British victory over the Napoleonic navy in 1805 enabled Britain to re-seize the Cape, this time permanently, in 1806. British possession was confirmed by treaty in 1814.

The strategic significance of the Cape to the British empire dominated historians' thinking on British South African history until at least the 1970s. ROBINSON & GALLAGHER (1961) synthesized this thinking in their influential work. They drew their inspiration from a detailed study of the case of Egypt, which the British had seized in 1882 for the same strategic purpose of protecting the sea route to India, following the opening of the Suez Canal in 1869. Robinson & Gallagher inferred, from less firm evidence, that the same strategic impulse drove the whole British participation in the "scramble for Africa", and in particular the increasingly aggressive extension of British control over most of southern Africa.

Robinson & Gallagher's seminal article "The Imperialism of Free Trade" (*Economic History Review*, 2nd series, 4/1, 1953) had already had considerable influence on historians' approaches to South Africa. Their concept – a minimal empire that was compatible with Britain's continued freedom to trade – was most forcefully argued by GALBRAITH (1963), whose interpretation of Colonial Office documents led him to conclude that during 1834–54 Britain had no real interest in the interior of South Africa, so long as its colony of the Cape was secure from foreign interference and "native wars". This was the period when 16,000 Boers (soon to call themselves Afrikaners) left the Cape Colony and trekked into the interior to set up their own colonies ("republics") free of British control.

The Afrikaner version of the Boers' exodus from the eastern districts of the Cape Colony had become the stuff of myth by the end of the 19th century. Glorified as the "Great Trek", the defining event of Afrikaner identity, it is best epitomized by VAN JAARSVELD (1961). In this interpretation, the defining feature of South African history from 1795 until the declaration of the Republic of South Africa in 1961 was the struggle between the British and Afrikaners for control of South Africa. During this heroic struggle, ultimately won by the Afrikaner, Africans were the backdrop, victory over whom proved the higher civilization of Afrikanerdom. The British betrayed white civilization by using the cloak of humanitarianism to champion African interests where these interests undermined those of the Afrikaners.

British "liberal" historiography in the same period tended to follow a similar trajectory, though hitting a different target. MACMILLAN (1963) championed the cause of the British missionaries who held that educated and Christian Africans should be treated with respect and entrusted with the same rights as other British citizens. The rural Afrikaner was strongly criticized for his brutal treatment of the African labour force. This liberal historiography reached its apogee in WILSON & THOMPSON's *Oxford History of South Africa* (1971), the most balanced survey to that date of the dichotomy between the British and Afrikaners regarding South African historiography. Africans were still primarily a backdrop to the "real story" of the making of South Africa.

A new historiographical approach to South Africa began to emerge during the 1960s; it was stimulated by the academic recovery of "African" history north of the Limpopo, and its foundations were then consolidated by a seminal article by ATMORE & MARKS (1974). In a review of the historiography to date, Atmore & Marks challenged the former focus on the apparent political conflict between "Boer and Briton". Whereas the African majority had been relegated to the background, Atmore & Marks placed it in the forefront of South African history, dramatically shifting the focus from the "white" political to the socio-economic.

This approach has allowed a reinterpretation of most aspects of South African history. It has, for instance, made possible a reinterpretation of the Boers' "Great Trek" of the late 1830s. In refusing to take the trekkers' word at face value, PEIRES (1989) has shown that there was far more to the northward migration than a mere general dissatisfaction with British rule. For a start, only about half the Boers of the eastern province left the colony at this time, and the majority of those who did leave had very specific economic reasons for doing so. Their primary concern was Britain's insistence on freeing up African labour, particularly the abolition of slavery in 1834.

Atmore & Marks theorized that the Boers' trek was not the turning-point of 19th-century South African history. Rather, what made South Africa distinct from the rest of the continent in this period was a "mineral revolution" that began with discoveries of diamonds at Kimberley in 1870 and continued with the even more dramatic and significant discoveries of gold at Johannesburg in 1886. The bones of this thesis have been fleshed out in numerous works, largely led by two collections of essays edited by Marks in collaboration with Atmore (*Economy and Society in Pre-Industrial South Africa*, 1980) and Rathbone (*Industrialisation and Social Change in South Africa: African Class Formation, Culture, and Consciousness 1870–1930*, 1982).

Marks followed up her reinterpretation with another challenge to perceived orthodoxy, this time in collaboration with Trapido (MARKS & TRAPIDO, 1979), with specific reference to the origins and aftermath of the South African War (Boer War or Anglo-Boer War) of 1899–1902. Liberal historians of earlier decades had rejected Hobson's contemporary study *Imperialism* (1902) as too uncomfortable. Hobson had placed the blame for the war firmly on the shoulders of the gold-mining capitalists of the Witwatersrand, who wished to free their mining interests from Boer republican restrictions and called upon their ally, the British imperial government, for assistance. Liberal historians had preferred the safer ground of the bellicose personalities of the British governor, Lord Milner, and the republican president, Paul Kruger, combined with some background assumptions about the importance of Robinson & Gallagher's strategic sea route. Apart from the point that the Suez Canal had greatly reduced the significance of the sea route since 1869, Marks & Trapido returned the focus to the economic imperatives first noted by Hobson. Although critics of Marks & Trapido, led by PORTER (1980), insist that there is no evidence in the official record that gold had anything to do with British motives for the war, the general thrust of the thesis still holds. In order to hang onto its precarious position as the world's premier trading nation, at a time when international trade had almost universally gone over to the gold standard, Britain needed to assert its influence, and if necessary its control, over what had by the late 1890s been shown to be the largest single source of gold in the world. This imperative, Marks & Trapido argue, is so obvious as to need no mention in the official record. What could be more strategically important about South Africa than the massive gold reserves of its interior hinterland?

The argument over origins rolls on, however. The best synthesis of these and other arguments and of the war itself is the centenary publication by NASSON (1999). In particular, Nasson considers the all-encompassing nature of the war in South Africa – seen no longer simply as a war between the white races but as a war also fought by and crucially affecting Africans. Nasson shows that it was in all respects a truly "South African war", fought over the nature of 20th-century South Africa.

The postwar reconstruction, which in 1910 culminated in the formation of the Union of South Africa, independent within the British empire, in effect ended Britain's direct involvement in the affairs of South Africa. According to the theme of Atmore, Marks, and Trapido, Britain now had local colonial collaborators, Afrikaner and British, who would together ensure the ultimate security of British capital investment in the region. South Africa's 20th-century history was to show that, despite the Afrikaner nationalists' technical break from Britain in 1961, the real struggle in South Africa was over class and colour rather than between Boer and Briton.

KEVIN SHILLINGTON

See also Africa I: British Interests to 1895; Africa II: British Imperialism; Asia and Africa: Second British Empire; Commonwealth of Nations; Decolonization; Rhodes

South African War

see **Ango-Boer Wars**

In 1869, GARDINER first showed his keen interest in the Spanish marriage planned by James I for his son Charles and the king of Spain's daughter Maria; during that one year he published three books about it: two volumes concerning the political developments of 1617–23; and a translation for the Camden Society, vol. 101, of a unique manuscript history of the events from the viewpoint of a Spanish Catholic – a court preacher of Philip IV. Fifteen years later Gardiner gave his final views in his *History*, vol. 4, chapters 41 and 42; and vol. 5, chapters 43–47. Although his interpretations of the parliaments of 1621 and 1624 have been challenged by revisionists, his polished narrative of the complex negotiations for the match includes valuable quotations from manuscripts.

Because the courtier commissioned to achieve James's plans for the marriage was the controversial duke of Buckingham, LOCKYER's biography has been welcomed as a revision of previous views. Using his wide research in manuscripts, Lockyer presents Buckingham as hard-working, ambitious, and "not exceptional", by the standards of the day, in enriching himself. In chapters 5 and 6, which describe Buckingham's journey to Spain and its aftermath, Lockyer maintains that Buckingham became convinced that James's policy "was not only unsound but positively dangerous", as it assured the Habsburgs' hegemony on the continent. For this reason, Buckingham and Prince Charles countered James's policy by all means possible. Reviewers have noted that Lockyer glosses over some of the duke's failings: a monopoly of royal patronage to others, his inexperience in foreign affairs as seen in France and Spain, and his miscalculation of parliament's financial support for a policy of war after 1624.

In a close analysis of the court and parliament in 1624, COGSWELL unravels a complex enigma – James's reluctance to change his mind on the Spanish match. After recalling the frustrations of Charles in Madrid, Cogswell's Part 1 shows how influential courtiers first successfully opposed the prince and the duke's "patriot" coalition against Spain. Part 2 explains how the two created a momentum towards war in the House of Commons, which for the puritans was a "blessed revolution" away from James's habitual Hispanophile policy. Part 3 points to mounting anti-Spanish sentiments in printed works supporting the prince and the duke.

Although written earlier, LAKE's study of Thomas Scott's tracts portrays the militant English Calvinist opposition cited by Cogswell. Scott, a prolific pamphleteer, considered the Spanish match a serious threat to England's "laws, liberties, lands, . . . and religion". Giving numerous examples, Lake points out that Scott's anti-papal rhetoric had a political bias, whereby the secular equal of the pope was the Spanish king, a new Antichrist. The corruption of James's court was to be seen in its Hispanophile courtiers, who encouraged the king to allow the recusancy laws to be ignored and to rule without a parliament. Scott saluted the prince and the duke in 1624 as an answer to the petitions of the godly.

However, RUSSELL has raised doubts about the depth of this anti-Spanish consensus in parliament. He samples the views of Thomas Wentworth at this session and suggests that Cogswell seemed to ignore certain members who either spoke out against the termination of the marriage or whose silence during a debate need not have signified support of one position alone. Because Wentworth, with several others, spoke against a war with Spain

in 1624, Russell maintains that it is rash to declare a "majority for one side or the other", or to declare that the English "nation" had a uniformly Hispanophobe viewpoint. He cites catholics, church papists, conservative protestants, and other interests who supported James's original policy in 1623–24.

The rationale of James I's policy towards Philip IV of Spain, or the Dutch republic, in 1621 is a vital insight into his hopes for the outcome of the negotiations. ADAMS has noted that after 1603 – contrary to the tradition of Elizabeth, who supported the protestant cause at all times on the Continent – James looked on a "confessional" alliance as a disaster. In effect, James ignored religion in seeking the advantage of a Habsburg connection, for with the death of Henry IV the French monarchy became unstable, and he resented the tactics of the Dutch republic in commerce and fishing, along with other grievances. Therefore, he remained Hispanophile throughout the last decade of his life, even though the Palatinate crisis after 1618 reduced public support in England for a Spanish marriage.

Clearly, there were misconceptions about Spain at Whitehall that ELLIOTT's highly praised biography of the duke of Olivares, Philip's main adviser, can remove. In chapters 2 and 6, Spain's priorities in northern Europe are assessed as of 1621, when Philip, at age 16, inherited not only an empire but a war against the Dutch, which his council of state had earlier voted to renew. During Charles's visit to Spain in 1623, Olivares knew that the emperor and the Spanish strategists of the land war were convinced that they had to control the Palatinate. Since the final articles of the marriage treaty were not certain, his real problem was "how to break free of the English commitment without involving Spain in another war". Ironically, Olivares and James expected diplomacy to resolve the crisis ultimately, while Charles and the duke wanted war.

The high stakes involved in Spain's renewal of its war against the Dutch in 1621 are very clear in chapters 2 and 3 of ISRAEL's fully documented history. Contrary to some misconceptions, Philip's forces were not fighting the "heretics"; rather, they wanted to force the Dutch republic to end its restrictions on Spanish commerce on the Scheldt and the pillaging of Spanish possessions in the Far East, and thereby restore the "reputation" of a tarnished crown. Unfortunately for James, the demands of this continental war had a higher priority than his ambitious dynastic marriage negotiations in Madrid.

ALBERT J. LOOMIE

See also Buckingham; Charles I

Spanish Succession, War of 1702–1713

Atkinson, C.T., *Marlborough and the Rise of the British Army*, London and New York: Putnam, 1921
Brewer, John, *The Sinews of Power: War, Money, and the English State 1688–1783*, London: Unwin Hyman, and New York: Knopf, 1989
Burton, Ivor F., *The Captain General: The Career of John Churchill Duke of Marlborough from 1702–1711*, London: Constable, 1968
Chandler, David, *Marlborough as Military Commander*, New York: Scribner, and London: Batsford, 1973

Chandler, David, *The Art of Warfare in the Age of Marlborough*, London: Batsford, and New York: Hippocrene, 1976

Chandler, David, (editor), *Military Memoirs of Marlborough's Campaigns, 1702–1712*, London: Greenhill, and Mechanicsburg, Philadelphia: Stackpole Books, 1998

Churchill, Winston, *Marlborough: His Life and Times*, 4 vols, London: Harrap, 1933–39; 6 vols, New York: Scribner, 1933–38

Coxe, William (editor), *Memoirs of the Duke of Marlborough, with His Original Correspondence*, revised by John Wade, 3 vols, London: Bohn, 1847–48; New York and London: Bell, 1885

Dickinson, Calvin and Eloise R. Hitchcock (editors), *The War of the Spanish Succession 1702–1713: A Selected Bibliography*, Westport, Connecticut: Greenwood Press, 1996

Francis, A. David, *The First Peninsular War 1702–1713*, London: Benn, and New York: St Martin's Press, 1975

Frey, Linda and Marsha Frey (editors), *The Treaties of the War of the Spanish Succession: An Historical and Critical Dictionary*, Westport, Connecticut: Greenwood Press, 1995

Hattendorf, John B., *England in the War of the Spanish Succession: A Study of the English View and Conduct of Grand Strategy, 1702–1712*, New York: Garland, 1987

Hugill, J.A.C., *No Peace without Spain*, Oxford: Kensal Press, 1991

Jones, D.W., *War and Economy in the Age of William II and Marlborough*, Oxford and New York: Blackwell, 1988

Jones, J.R., *Marlborough*, Cambridge and New York: Cambridge University Press, 1993

Kamen, Henry, *The War of Succession in Spain 1700–1715*, Bloomington: Indiana University Press, and London: Weidenfeld and Nicolson, 1969

Lynn, John A., *Giant of the Grand Siècle: The French Army, 1610–1715*, Cambridge and New York: Cambridge University Press, 1997

Lynn, John A., *The Wars of Louis XIV, 1667–1714*, London and New York: Longman, 1999

Ostwald, Jamel, "The 'Decisive' Battle of Ramillies, 1706: Prerequisites for Decisiveness in Early Modern Warfare", *Journal of Military History*, 64/3 (July 2000): 649–77

Owen, J.E., *War at Sea under Queen Anne*, Cambridge: Cambridge University Press, 1938

Scouller, R. (Raibert) E., *The Armies of Queen Anne*, Oxford: Clarendon Press, 1966

The War of the Spanish Succession (1702–13) is generally recognized as a turning-point in European history, marking the decline of Spain, the erosion of France's economic and military might, and, more importantly, Britain's ascendancy as an imperial and military power. Britain provided substantial financial and political leadership to a major alliance system comprising the Dutch, the Austrian Hapsburgs, most German principalities, and several smaller states, while Louis XIV's allies included Spain and Bavaria. Theatres of conflict consisted of Flanders, Spain – the bane of British involvement – the high seas, and limited engagements in Germany, Provence, the Savoy region, and North America.

No comprehensive modern single-volume study of the war exists in English or any other language. Most 20th-century scholars writing in English have either integrated a discussion of its diplomatic origins and military conduct into political histories of Queen Anne's reign or examined British involvement by referring to biographical narratives. Assessments of Britain's armies are inextricably linked to their commander, John Churchill, Duke of Marlborough, who is often lauded as the greatest British commander before Wellington. Recent research on military history analyses tactics and operations and reflects this biographical predilection; thus the study of military aspects of the War of the Spanish Succession has been surprisingly bereft of substantial areas of contention. Most of the detailed accounts of military operations by British authors are constructed around narratives of Marlborough's career and devote disproportionate attention to the Flanders theatre where he commanded.

The first systematic use of Marlborough's massive papers was by COXE. His detailed and sympathetic account reproduced a substantial number of Marlborough's most important letters and endeavoured to place Marlborough in the diplomatic and political contexts of Anne's reign. Coxe influenced G.M. Trevelyan's Whiggishly moralistic general study (1930–34) and largely shaped almost all later biographies of Marlborough.

Despite CHURCHILL's blatant and defiantly unrepentant favouritism, no research on the War of the Spanish Succession can afford to ignore his monumental biography of his ancestor. Its importance is underscored by Churchill's extensive consultation of primary sources and foreign archival materials, his comprehensive scope, and his discussion of complex diplomatic and political machinations of the period, which by 1710 had undermined the domestic war effort and affected Marlborough's political future as well as British war aims. Nevertheless, Churchill's predictable bias and irritating polemics frequently distort the truth, as in his constant efforts to explain away Marlborough's culpability for unsuccessful strategic decisions, omnipresent avarice, and, especially, decades of overtures to exiled Stuart pretenders. J.R. JONES, in a more balanced brief biography, astutely observes that readers must remember the historical circumstances of Churchill's magisterial work, which was written during his political exile and at a time when prospects of a Nazi-dominated Europe loomed; Churchill often reveals his phobia of fascism, portraying Marlborough as a European saviour (not unlike Churchill's own image after 1945).

ATKINSON's shorter and reasonably judicious discussion of Marlborough's military career and impact on the development of the British army emphasizes his innovative appreciation for combined arms and naval power, his aristocratic politeness, and his compassion for his troops. Atkinson, the author of dozens of journal articles on aspects of the war, portrays Marlborough in more human terms but also succumbs to occasional hero-worship.

More popular scholars echoing Churchill's endorsements include Corelli Barnett (*Marlborough*, 1974) and Maurice Ashley (*Marlborough*, 1939), who is more critical. Frank Taylor (*The Wars of Marlborough*, 1921), Hillaire Belloc (*The Tactics and Strategy of the Great Duke of Marlborough*, 1933), Frederick Maycock (*Outline of Marlborough's Campaign*, 1913), and others direct attention more specifically towards military lessons available from studying Marlborough's campaigns.

SCOULLER's analysis of the administration of Anne's army remains the most accessible and authoritative. BURTON integrates a discussion of Marlborough's victories into a learned exposition of the political implications of army policy. D.W. JONES and BREWER both provide important studies of financial and governmental innovations necessary for British involvement in such a prolonged conflict. OWEN's remains the best available full-length study of naval operations.

Whereas contemporary British accounts by subordinates and common soldiers tend to eulogize, first-hand accounts still provide insights to military operations and illustrate Marlborough's exalted reputation during his lifetime. These accounts include, among others, those by Thomas Broderick (1713), Thomas Lediard (1736), John Blackader (1824), and John Marshall Deane (1984, edited by Chandler). CHANDLER (1998) combines recollections of a British officer and a Flemish count on the French side.

CHANDLER (1976) places Marlborough's military innovations and army conduct during the Spanish succession conflict in a broader European context. CHANDLER (1973) is a prominent example of a study of military operations written in English that invariably reflects Marlborough's prominence and the perceived importance of the campaigns in Flanders to the exclusion of other theatres; its chapters are organized primarily around analyses of the annual role of the British army in operations in the Low Countries. This is the most detailed recent analysis (it was reprinted in the 1990s), although it is marred by the occasional incorrect reference and limited archival work. The influential Chandler epitomizes the tendency to praise Marlborough excessively as a vigorous, decisive commander who consistently sought battle in an age when limited, more positional siege warfare prevailed, yet was frustrated by forces (meddlesome Dutch field deputies) beyond his control. Hardly novel, such Churchillian views have been widely endorsed recently. Better-balanced perspectives, incorporating foreign evidence that Marlborough's limitations can be attributed more to physical and logistical deficiencies than to the time-worn excuse that the allies' leaders consistently restrained Marlborough's foolproof initiatives, are overdue.

Only international perspectives gleaned from non-English sources can allow historians to comprehend an international conflict adequately. Contributing towards that objective, OSTWALD highlights this long-standing historiographical problem; he concludes that even Marlborough's "decisive" victories produced only limited results because of the prevalence of fortified towns, lengthy sieges, and the potential threat posed by garrisoned fortresses which were bypassed. New research could clarify the significance of siege warfare; the impact of the War of the Spanish Succession on the larger scheme of the much-debated early modern military revolution; and areas such as naval warfare, logistics, partisan activities, localized economic effects, and military culture in the period.

Although most English-speaking authors usually focused their attention on Marlborough's career in Flanders, other works have begun to rectify this deficiency. HATTENDORF rejects the traditional view that the Flanders theatre was overwhelmingly important, arguing that British objectives in both Whig and Tory ministries reflected a "decentralized" strategy designed around waging a war of attrition on multiple fronts and diffusing French power, diverting French policy, and safeguarding the protestant succession. One unsatisfactory aspect of this argument is its failure to attribute the development of strategy to any single group or set of individuals and therefore minimizes the role of leading politicians such as Bolingbroke, who was instrumental in concluding a separate peace with France. Moreover, Hattendorf's portrayal of British strategy as monolithic and static ultimately fails to convince, as it utterly disallows any possibility of change; Hattendorf refuses to acknowledge the effects of internal political strife, manifestations of public opinion (for example, reaction to Malplaquet), changes in the number of claimants to the Spanish throne, etc. Still, Hattendorf's work is one of the few recent studies to place the conflict in its larger context; his views are summarized in David French's collection *The British Way of Warfare* (1990). The work of J.W. Wijn, in Dutch, offers deep insights into political, operational, and administrative aspects from a different viewpoint among the allies. Biographies of Prince Eugene of Savoy, Marlborough's often overshadowed subordinate, by Nicholas Henderson (1964) and Derek McKay (1977) also provide useful perspectives.

Lynn's recent and valuable work bridges a gap in scholarship on France's armies for readers who are not fluent in French. LYNN (1997) is a mammoth analysis of the 17th-century French army that traces its institutional development up to 1715 and will probably remain a standard work for many years; the title *Giant* is very appropriate. LYNN (1999) analyses Louis XIV as military commander and concludes with a long examination of campaigns for the Spanish succession. Arguing forcefully for the different character of war aims during this period as opposed to the Napoleonic era, Lynn demonstrates how war contributed to a nascent French national identity.

The economic and financial implications of the conflict in Spain have been debated. In contrast to the traditional view of the destructive impact of the war, KAMEN (1969) concludes that the conflict was localized and that the overwhelming majority of foreign troops engaged effectively limited its negative consequences. In this definitive study, drawn from Spanish archives, Kamen argues persuasively that war and concomitant dynastic change may have contributed to limited economic and industrial stimulation.

Relevant diplomacy, military operations, and strategy as perceived by British and Spanish ministers and generals have also been detailed by FRANCIS and more recently by HUGILL, largely supplanting a more dated study by Arthur Parnell (*The War of the Succession in Spain*, 1888). Two recent offerings facilitate further research on the War of the Spanish Succession, although neither is wholly satisfactory. DICKINSON & HITCHCOCK's compilation of the first detailed bibliography specifically dealing with the conflict published in over 50 years is hampered by its focus, mainly on printed sources; by its dated descriptions; by its haphazard and usually negative annotations; and by serious gaps in the assessment of journal literature. FREY & FREY supply rich bibliographical information; their work – which greatly exceeds the implications of its title – includes a long introduction summarizing the issues that provoked the war and the results of the treaty of Utrecht. However, this work's rather puzzling omission of pertinent topics is compounded by a decided deficiency in its treatment of contextual and thematic issues.

LAWRENCE B. SMITH

See also George II; Godolphin; Harley; Marlborough, 1st Duke of

Speenhamland Poor Relief System

from 1795

Blaug, Mark, "The Myth of the Old Poor Law and the Making of the New", *Journal of Economic History*, 23/2 (1963): 151–84

Hampson, E.M., *The Treatment of Poverty in Cambridgeshire, 1597–1834*, Cambridge: Cambridge University Press, 1934

Himmelfarb, Gertrude, *The Idea of Poverty: England in the Early Industrial Age*, London: Faber, and New York: Knopf, 1984

Hitchcock, Tim, Peter King and Pamela Sharpe (editors), *Chronicling Poverty: The Voices and Strategies of the English Poor, 1640–1840*, London: Macmillan, and New York: St Martin's Press, 1997

Lees, Lynn Hollen, *The Solidarities of Strangers: The English Poor Laws and the People, 1700–1948*, Cambridge and New York: Cambridge University Press, 1998

Neuman, Mark, *The Speenhamland County: Poverty and the Poor Laws in Berkshire, 1782–1834*, New York and London: Garland, 1982

Snell, K.D.M., *Annals of the Labouring Poor: Social Change and Agrarian England, 1660–1900*, Cambridge and New York: Cambridge University Press, 1985

Taylor, James Stephen, *Poverty, Migration, and Settlement in the Industrial Revolution: Sojourners' Narratives*, Palo Alto, California: Society for the Promotion of Science and Scholarship, 1989

Webb, Sidney and Beatrice Webb, *English Poor Law History*, Part 1: *The Old Poor Law*, London and New York: Longmans Green, 1927

The word "Speenhamland", meaning the land of the people of Speen, a parish in south-central Berkshire, is found as early as 1220 (Margaret Gelling, *The Place Names of Berkshire*, English Place Name Society XLIX, Cambridge: University Press, 1973, p. 259). At the Pelican Inn in Speen, on 6 May 1795, a number of Berkshire magistrates and distinguished guests adopted an allowance system for the poor, the amount regulated by family size and the price of a gallon loaf of wheaten second bread. This local initiative attracted attention and imitation, and it came to symbolize the English and Welsh relief system from 1795 until the Poor Law Amendment Act of 1834. However, the original meaning gave way to systematic relief given to the able-bodied poor out of an institutional setting, especially allowances in aid of wages in southern agrarian England. The act of 1834 was designed to end the practice by relieving the able-bodied in union workhouses and by providing a more centralized administration. Yet allowances continued to be given by recalcitrant local officers, and the poor law would go through many changes before its reconfiguration in the 20th century.

WEBB & WEBB provide the indispensable overview of the English poor law, with a wealth of detail and citations reflecting the view, preceding 1834, that allowances in aid of wages were a calamitous policy. This was the generally accepted interpretation until 1963, when BLAUG labelled it a "myth", arguing that there was an economic rationale for the allowances and that this form of relief was in any case declining in importance in the early 19th century.

No brief essay can do justice to the enormous outpouring of scholarly studies that followed, enriched by graduate theses focused on the parish, the county, or some dimension of the "Old Poor Law", and enlivened by both ideological convictions and presumed relevance to current social welfare policies. Much of the debate is quite specific, appearing in journal articles, especially in *Economic History Review*, *Continuity and Change*, and *Past & Present*. Three approaches figure: (1) the ideas, (2) local practices, and (3) efforts to combine the two. HIMMELFARB provides a synthesis of the first, though her work ranges well beyond 1834. Regarding the second, one of the earliest (before Blaug) and best is HAMPSON's, though like all worthwhile local studies it is informed by a wider vision. The third approach, involving grand themes and local illustrations, is benefited but also burdened by the tons of poor law records archivists have gathered and partially organized in county record offices. Diversity of practice bedevils synthesis, but one thing is clear: there never was a Speenhamland "system", not even in Speen, as NEUMAN has shown. However, giving partial relief to the underemployed was common in the rural south and the industrial north before and after 1795. Among the best studies of the south is SNELL's; its principal concern is the quality of life of the poor. Snell sees "Speenhamland" as a reaction to deep-seated poverty and unemployment, not their cause. Debates have arisen, however, over the degree to which the poor laws were instruments of social control as well as of social welfare.

Recent scholarship has also examined allowances in aid of wages in light of the settlement laws determining which parish or township was responsible for providing relief. TAYLOR has suggested that the laws contributed to industrial development through non-resident allowances provided by rural authorities to inveigle their urban counterparts into keeping the temporarily unemployed instead of removing them to their rural places of settlement. Debate has centred on the extent to which this and other settlement provisions were either economically repressive or stimulating.

Few areas of contemporary research have been more enriched by studies "from the bottom up". In the essays edited by HITCHCOCK, KING, & SHARPE, paupers' own words and strategies are explored. Using primary sources, such as settlement and bastardy examinations, pauper letters and inventories, and legal records, these essays emphasize the human dimension. Historians who have gone to documentary evidence sometimes end by talking past each other, and there is always a gulf between historians of ideas and opinions and those of practice. Indeed, so many pamphlets, treatises, and parliamentary papers were generated by the poor laws that it is a challenge to bridge the gap between this material and local research. A recent effort to do so is LEES's synthesis of English policies towards the poor and the specific impact of those policies at the local level.

The so-called Speenhamland system, like many other historical constructs, is a *non sequitur*, but behind the myth there is the reality that the administration of poor relief mattered more to more British subjects (the Irish and Scottish were deeply if indirectly affected as well) than any other aspect of government in the period 1795–1834. Precisely how it mattered will continue to occupy the attention of historians.

JAMES STEPHEN TAYLOR

Spencer, Herbert 1820–1903

Philosopher and sociologist

Brinton, Crane, "Spencer" in his *English Political Thought in the Nineteenth Century*, London: Benn, 1933; 2nd edition, London: Benn, and Cambridge, Massachusetts: Harvard University Press, 1949

Duncan, David, *The Life and Letters of Herbert Spencer*, London: Methuen, 1908; 2 vols, New York: Appleton, 1908

Gray, Tim S., *The Political Philosophy of Herbert Spencer: Individualism and Organicism*, Aldershot, Hampshire; and Brookfield, Vermont: Avebury, 1996

Kennedy, James G., *Herbert Spencer*, Boston: Twayne, 1978

Paxton, Nancy, *George Eliot and Herbert Spencer: Feminism, Evolutionism, and the Reconstruction of Gender*, Princeton, New Jersey: Princeton University Press, 1991

Peel, J.D.Y., *Herbert Spencer: The Evolution of a Sociologist*, London: Heinemann, and New York: Basic Books, 1971

Perrin, Robert G., *Herbert Spencer: A Primary and Secondary Bibliography*, New York and London: Garland, 1993

Riley, Jonathan, "Mill's Utilitarianism" in his *Liberal Utilitarianism: Social Choice Theory and J.S. Mill's Philosophy*, Cambridge and New York: Cambridge University Press, 1988

Taylor, M.W., *Men versus the State: Herbert Spencer and Late Victorian Individualism*, Oxford: Clarendon Press, and New York: Oxford University Press, 1992

Weinstein, D., *Equal Freedom and Utility: Herbert Spencer's Liberal Utilitarianism*, Cambridge and New York: Cambridge University Press, 1998

Wiltshire, David, *The Social and Political Thought of Herbert Spencer*, Oxford and New York: Oxford University Press, 1978

The multifaceted character of Spencer's oeuvre has led to numerous attempts to construct distinctive subcategories of Spencerian thought, despite Spencer's own claim to have constructed a "synthetic" philosophy that universalized a theory of "progress" through "evolution" – "a reaching of more and more complex products through successive increments of modification" (Spencer, quoted in DUNCAN). For example, PERRIN, in his monumental bibliography, arranged 1,760 secondary sources with reference to Spencerian philosophy, religion, ethics, biology, psychology, politics and political science, sociology and social thought, education, art, literature, style, and music as well as listing biographical and general studies and works on miscellaneous topics. This was clearly a result of an attempt to achieve "total coverage", whereas KENNEDY's more modest critical study distinguished Spencer's metaphysics from his philosophy of mind and concentrated on the disciplines of ethics, biology, sociology, economics, and political philosophy.

The encyclopedic character of Duncan's book may have deterred 20th-century scholars from attempting to produce full-fledged biographies of "Xhaustive Spencer" (the nickname Herbert acquired among fellow Victorian scientists). As Spencer's protégé, moreover, Duncan did not attempt to prioritize any one aspect of his mentor's "Synthetic Philosophy" over the others, preferring to describe it as "the fullest and grandest generalization of the knowledge of his day". By the 1930s,

however, Spencer's reputation had fallen to its nadir, and BRINTON (1933) is often cited as the archetypal intellectual obituary.

In the 1970s interest in Spencer was rekindled by PEEL; but his text was explicitly framed as a work in the fields of what Peel called "history of sociology" and "sociology of knowledge", so its significance will not be assessed immediately.

More akin to traditional biography was WILTSHIRE's treatment of Spencer's "Biographical and Intellectual Development" (approximately half of a 70,000-word study). Wiltshire offered a ground-breaking interpretation of the relative importance of the different aspects of the Synthetic Philosophy, claiming that Spencer was "an individualist liberal first and an evolutionist second". Although Wiltshire tended to conflate the evolutionist and organicist aspects of Spencer's theory, he acknowledged correctly that Spencer's ideas had "retained considerable force and become widely diffused" in Victorian Britain and America. Moreover, he concluded that "the political and scientific components of Spencerism were not compatible" – a claim that was allegedly half-recognized by Spencer himself through his "renunciation of universal suffrage, land nationalization and natural rights" in his final years. In the second part of his book, Wiltshire argued that:

> Liberalism posits the harmonization of the interests of free individuals. Social evolution tends inexorably towards the hegemony of the centralized state, and perpetuates aggression. In this irreconcilable contradiction lies the main flaw of Spencerian social and political theory.

This perspective reversed Peel's view that Spencerian functionalism and organicism were compatible with methodological individualism and laissez-faire liberalism, although Peel and Wiltshire agreed that social evolutionism was unsustainable as a purely sociological theory. Hence, both writers were obliged to explain Spencer's undoubted popularity among his contemporaries by the appropriateness of his "errors" to his own time, rather than by the logical force of the arguments found in his texts. Peel argued that "Spencer's assumptions and outlook belonged to provincial Dissent, whose traditions, albeit in a rather secularized form, had shaped him" and that this in turn made him a particularly suitable ideologist for "England at the close of the heroic period of her industrialization"; a similar case was made by Wiltshire.

Kennedy shared Wiltshire's concern that Spencerian sociology was excessively deterministic (and thereby endangered human freedom and creativity); but the tone of Kennedy's volume even more explicitly debunking: "One goes to Spencer not expecting to find what is right, but rather to review errors that were plausible a century ago". Hence, despite its wide-range, this work seems out of step with the more "empathic" fashion of contemporary historiography. In contrast, Perrin's introductory essay, "Remembering Spencer", was enthusiastic about its subject (though not sycophantic); it identified "individual liberty" as the predominant theme of Spencer's social science and "the successive evolution and dissolution of all existences" as the organizing hypothesis of his natural science. (A newcomer to Spencer should read Kennedy as a corrective supplement to Perrin's essay and may use Duncan's well-indexed work to follow up specific questions.)

TAYLOR's major contribution has been to situate Spencer's later work in the context of a strand of late-Victorian laissez-faire liberalism known to its proponents as "individualism". Taylor shared with Perrin a tendency to "disaggregate" the Synthetic Philosophy, but Taylor's approach was less sympathetic. For example, Taylor held that for Spencer biological theories of evolution were simply special cases of *cosmic* evolution, and so Spencerian references to Darwin in a *political* context were characterized as "tactical" – in other words, opportunistic. As Wiltshire put it, "a close survey" of Spencer's writings "reveals a 'primacy of politics'".

Of course such a formula is compatible with feminist scholarship which treats the "personal" as "political". Spencer played a distinctly minor role relative to George Eliot in PAXTON's literary study, but the notes and bibliography offer a gateway to general literature on "evolutionism" while the text itself provides some justification for the claim that Spencer played a significant role in "establishing evolutionary science as a master discourse defining sexuality, knowledge, and power in the second half of the nineteenth century".

Finally, the reader should be aware that recent debates in political philosophy have led GRAY and WEINSTEIN to reconstruct distinctive (but slightly abstract) versions of Spencerian liberalism. (Gray's chapter "International Relations Theory" is useful to historians as a reminder of Spencer's ambiguous contribution to the debate about imperialism, but this was not the thrust of Gray's argument.) Viewed as a whole, Gray's text took Spencer's objections to Benthamism at face value and contended that, within Spencerian ethics and politics, justice and individual liberty were significantly higher priorities than personal felicity. In contrast, Weinstein extracted certain themes from contemporary debates about utilitarianism (see RILEY) and argued that Spencer's personal friendship with J.S. Mill was paralleled by an intellectual concern to promote utility *indirectly* by promoting the concept of "strong moral rights".

Nearly all of the texts cited pay lip-service to the debate on whether Spencer was more significant as a political theorist or as an exponent of a *Naturphilosophie*. However, this debate indicates an instrumental concern to know if Spencer is still significant to "us". What type of intellectual Spencer was, what type of scientist he was, and what role he played in Victorian society are questions that have still to be effectively answered by historians.

CLIVE E. HILL

See also Biological Sciences; Mill

Sport: Professional Team Games

Birley, Derek, *A Social History of English Cricket*, London: Aurum Press, 1999
Collins, Tony, *Rugby's Great Split: Class, Culture, and the Origins of Rugby League Football*, London and Portland, Oregon: Cass, 1998
Conn, David, *The Football Business: Fair Game in the '90s?* Edinburgh: Mainstream, 1997; revised edition, 1998
Holt, Richard, *Sport and the British: A Modern History*, Oxford: Clarendon Press, and New York: Oxford University Press, 1989
Holt, Richard and Tony Mason, *Sport in Britain, 1945–2000*, Oxford and Cambridge, Massachusetts: Blackwell, 2000
Mason, Tony, *Association Football and English Society 1863–1915*, Brighton, East Sussex: Harvester Press, and Atlantic Highlands, New Jersey: Humanities Press, 1980
Moorhouse, Geoffrey, *A People's Game: The Centenary History of Rugby League Football 1895–1995*, London: Hodder and Stoughton, 1995; revised edition, 1996
Russell, Dave, *Football and the English: A Social History of Association Football in England, 1863–1995*, Preston: Carnegie, 1997
Taylor, Rogan and Andrew Ward, *Kicking and Screaming: An Oral History of Football in England*, London: Robson Books, 1995
Tranter, Neil, *Sport, Economy, and Society in Britain, 1750–1914*, Cambridge and New York: Cambridge University Press, 1998
Vamplew, Wray, *Pay Up and Play the Game: Professional Sport in Britain, 1875–1914*, Cambridge and New York: Cambridge University Press, 1988

Scholarly interest in the history of British sport has increased markedly since 1980, initially encouraged by a general expansion in the study of social and cultural history that occurred during the 1970s. The subject is now established in its own right with a robust historiography, although this needs better coverage of the roles of women and spectators, some less prominent sports and their participants, regional diversity, and the economic history of sport. Three major professional team games are played in Britain: cricket, rugby football (or rugby), and association football (or soccer, to distinguish it from rugby football). These activities have quite distinct histories, but also many similarities, since they have all experienced cycles of popularity, albeit at different times and in varying localities. Of fundamental importance is how and why these sports moved, within their higher echelons, from having predominately amateur players to the professional status they all enjoy today.

HOLT is indispensable for an understanding of the historical contexts through which British sport has evolved; his work is now the standard text. Holt manages both to entertain and to stimulate, explaining the evolution through the impact of cultural, social, and political developments since 1800. Holt demonstrates that particular facets of sport – such as hooliganism, or the role of sport in forging national and community identities – have long histories and are not merely modern manifestations.

Subsequent publications have complemented Holt. TRANTER's succinct survey provides a useful critical bibliography of British sport and an analysis of the most important influences shaping it up to 1914. HOLT & MASON focus on the period after 1945; they helpfully emphasize the transformation of British sport from "an amateur past to a free-market future", with the media as the major catalyst for this change. They also consider the growing involvement of the state and the rise of the cult of personality that surrounds the principal players.

Among the general histories, VAMPLEW's provides informative insights into what moulded the major professional sports emerging at the end of the 19th century. Vamplew finds that workers in cities with more time and better wages "created a market which sports entrepreneurs responded to", and "an observable pattern of the emergence of commercialisation injecting more money into sport, which in turn intensified the importance of winning and stimulated corruption, sharp practice and the like".

BIRLEY's superlative book has the virtues of the best sports history writing, blending meticulous respect for the subtleties of cricket with a comprehensive regard for the forces that altered it over time, especially its administrative arrangements. Birley details how cricket "was snatched from rustic obscurity by gentlemanly gamblers and in the late eighteenth century became the latest metropolitan fashion". During the succeeding century cricket "became a symbol of the ideals of the new model public schools which undertook the task of training the leaders of Church and State as Britain took on the responsibilities – and the emotional trappings – of imperialism". The top domestic cricketers were organized into competing county sides by about 1860, and England's teams were undertaking overseas tours from 1859 on. The so-called "golden age" of cricket – supposedly the time of the gentleman amateur during the late Victorian and the Edwardian eras – masked a different, more abrasive reality. Remarkable personalities (including W.G. Grace, Wilfred Rhodes, and C.B. Fry) were certainly playing the game at this time, but by the late 1880s the "shamateur" had already evolved: the gentleman who earned his living from cricket. Until the 1950s there was continued tension between the status and privileges of the "gentleman" amateur compared with the professional "player", which became a metaphor for class divisions in English society. Birley's epilogue, in which he studies the current state of village cricket in order to explore the importance of cricket in defining Englishness, is particularly apt and perceptive.

Many books about association football (soccer) are published in Britain every year. However most focus on individual clubs, players, and managers or are basically photographic essays. An early, noteworthy exception to this trend is MASON (1980). It must be stressed that association football differs considerably in Scotland, England, Wales, and Northern Ireland, each country having its own league structure and national side. RUSSELL provides a concise introduction to the history of English football from the pre-industrial versions of the game played in the countryside to its current quasi-religious role in society, tracing the influence of Victorian public schools (particularly on the codification of rules) and the emergence of football by 1900 as a mass, predominantly male spectator sport, closely identified with urban working-class communities. Russell's broad periodization allows him to address the impact of later developments, such as the abolition of the minimum wage for players in 1961, racism, and crowd disasters during the 1980s.

TAYLOR & WARD's study is extremely informative. The material is presented as a chronicle of the progress of English football from the 1900s to the early 1990s through a series of thoughtful interviews with administrators, male and female supporters, players, managers, and coaches. CONN's treatment of his subject, although essentially journalistic, provides one of the more valuable insights into the transformation of football during the 1990s, including the commercial renovation of teams such as Manchester United and Tottenham Hotspur, the effect of television, and the formation of a new Premier League of the leading sides in 1992.

Rugby football has two separate codes in England: rugby union and rugby league (each having a different number of players). Rugby union has traditionally been linked to private schools and rugby league to the northern working class; rugby league is usually played in international matches. Fundamentally, only amateurs played union until 1995, but professional players have always formed the foremost league sides. MOORHOUSE provides an accessible introduction to the sport, written as an official centenary history marking the foundation of the league in 1895, when the Northern Rugby Football Union of clubs broke away from its southern counterparts, becoming the Rugby Football League in 1922. COLLINS's work is a model of excellent research, using contemporary local newspapers to compensate for the paucity of official records. He eschews a thematic structure and adopts a narrative approach to describe the complexities of class and commercialism that produced the break.

MARK HATHAWAY

See also Leisure and Recreation

Sport and Society

Brailsford, Dennis, *Sport, Time, and Society: The British at Play*, London and New York: Routledge, 1991
Hargreaves, Jennifer, *Sporting Females: Critical Issues in the History and Sociology of Women's Sports*, London and New York: Routledge, 1994
Holt, Richard, *Sport and the British: A Modern History*, Oxford: Clarendon Press, and New York: Oxford University Press, 1989
Lowerson, John, *Sport and the English Middle Classes, 1870–1914*, Manchester and New York: Manchester University Press, 1993
McCrone, Kathleen E., *Sport and the Physical Emancipation of English Women, 1870–1914*, London: Routledge, 1988; as *Playing the Game: Sport and the Physical Emancipation of English Women, 1870–1914*, Lexington: University Press of Kentucky, 1988
Mangan, J.A., *Athleticism in the Victorian and Edwardian Public School: The Emergence and Consolidation of an Educational Ideology*, Cambridge and New York: Cambridge University Press, 1981
Mason, Tony (editor), *Sport in Britain: A Social History*, Cambridge and New York: Cambridge University Press, 1989
Polley, Martin, *Moving the Goalposts: A History of Sport and Society since 1945*, London and New York: Routledge, 1998
Tranter, Neil, *Sport, Economy, and Society in Britain, 1750–1914*, Cambridge and New York: Cambridge University Press, 1998
Vamplew, Wray, *Pay Up and Play the Game: Professional Sport in Britain, 1875–1914*, Cambridge and New York: Cambridge University Press, 1988

HOLT's book is exceptionally well informed and ambitious, serving both as an excellent introduction to the topic as a whole and as a sustained interpretive essay. The reader is offered discussions on such central issues as the survival or destruction of "traditional" sports, the impact of urbanization, the vexed question of amateurism, the relationship of newer sports to nationalism and imperialism, and the growth and characteristics of commercialism. Holt also offers an analysis of violence on and off the field over time, largely with reference to soccer (football). Holt places particular emphasis on sport and territoriality at a local level and makes an effective case for seeing passionate loyalty to local clubs as a development reflecting a long-established need for what amounts to tribal loyalty, despite people's displacement to new environments. As an historian Holt is cautious about efforts to create models to explain change over time, but he does introduce readers to some of the more influential theories, notably modernization. Inevitably, given that he covers so many sports, readers with specialized knowledge of any one activity will find errors in this work, but Holt's book is, and is likely to remain, of central importance to those interested in sport and society in Britain.

POLLEY offers a narrower chronological focus than Holt's; but, like Holt, he uses a thematic approach to good effect, although he too can be faulted for errors of detail. Polley's thematic concerns include gender, ethnicity, social class and status, sponsorship, and commerce. He also examines the relationship between sport and the state. In addition, he offers a short essay on the growing – recently, rapidly growing – coverage and analysis of sport by academic historians. The thematic approach inevitably fractures the narrative of how major sports have developed in Britain since World War II, but it does provide a workable approach, giving the reader a sense of the links between societal change and changes in sport. Again like Holt, Polley is brave enough to admit some of the irrationality that often manifests itself in the way many people view sport. He is also aware of the aesthetic dimension in how sport is viewed, a reality that presents great analytical problems.

TRANTER's short work, in the New Studies in Economic and Social History Series, is unusually helpful for the period covered. The reader is provided with cogent summaries of the work of many writers. In particular, Tranter makes good use of pertinent articles in and contributions to collections of works by multiple authors. He also offers an annotated bibliography. Tranter utilizes his own detailed research in Scottish sport, as well as suggesting some topics which would benefit from further research. Indeed, his central point that more, difficult research needs to be done on intensely local sports teams and organizations reflects the emphasis of his own work.

MASON's book is a collaborative project. The contributors have provided chapter-length discussions on angling, athletics, boxing, cricket, football, golf, horse-racing, lawn tennis, rowing, and rugby union. Mason offers a characteristically trenchant introduction and afterword and has himself written the chapter on football (soccer). He is the most distinguished academic writer on this game, and so his chapter is a particularly strong one. Perhaps unsurprisingly, the quality is uneven elsewhere, but readers can be confident that with, say, Lowerson on golf and angling, Williams on cricket, and particularly G. Williams on rugby union and Vamplew on horse-racing, they are reading authoritative summaries. Certainly this well-edited volume provides a useful reminder that the great spectator sports are not the be-all and end-all of the story, angling being

a striking example of a mass participatory sport with enthusiasts in all sections of society. Mason's own focus in his afterword is very different; he notes how professional sport, even by the late 1980s, was becoming ever more removed from those activities in which the great majority of people participate. Like others, Mason has a jaundiced view of the role of the media in this process.

With the obvious exception of Polley, most of the work noted so far emphasizes the period 1860–1914. This is seen as the time when "modern" sport emerged and Britain, after becoming the first industrial country, became the first sporting nation. The British – largely but not entirely English – public schools were an essential force in this process. MANGAN (1981), like much of his other writing, is a seminal work. Indeed, Mangan has gone on to describe and analyse how important such institutions were in the British empire as a whole in the diffusion of sport and a sporting ethos. In his work of 1981 Mangan offers a study of the "games cult" in elite Victorian schools. He has much to say about individual headmasters and also more lowly staff members. What they shared, for the most part, was a clear sense of the moral worth of team games and the practical usefulness of games in creating school spirit. Manliness and Christianity could both be aided by involvement in organized games. It was often through the enthusiastic proselytizing of alumni that some of these games became hugely popular among people far distant from the increasingly well-maintained playing fields of the great and not so great public schools. Games which were increasingly seen as the pre-eminent method for the developing a boy's character in the confines of a public school became widely and often controversially popular.

VAMPLEW and LOWERSON also focus on the Victorian and Edwardian periods, offering usefully contrasting focuses. Vamplew argues that whereas many economic historians have been critical of the performance of British industry and enterprise in the late Victorian and Edwardian periods, the emerging mass sports industry was an economic success story. It is very difficult to offer satisfactory evidence of the impact of this new industry on the economy as a whole. Indeed, a critical response could be that this new industry may have encouraged investment which could more usefully have gone into more productive technologies. As Vamplew makes clear, in some sports – cricket being perhaps an extreme example – "normal" economics did not apply. Grandees such as Lord Harris in Kent and the Duke of Devonshire in Derbyshire subsidized the country cricket clubs. Even in soccer (football), profit was not the chief motivation of those who ran the new Football League clubs. Perhaps horse-racing, a topic on which Vamplew has unrivalled scholarly knowledge, provides the most convincing example of an old sport becoming ever more industrialized.

LOWERSON is also interested in the economic consequences of the growth of sporting activities. He offers a very wide-ranging discussion of the development of middle-class sport, and so provides obvious links to other works already cited such as Mangan's and Vamplew's. Lowerson places considerable emphasis on the formation of clubs as a characteristic of the class he is studying. Golf, on which he is unusually well qualified to speak, is a striking example. Clubs offer excellent examples of the questions which surrounded participation in sport. There were problems of availability of space as well as how "popular" the membership was to be. The English answer anyway tended towards the exclusive, although contrasts with Scotland are important here. Exclusivity and the Lawn Tennis Club came to be seen as natural partners.

All the writers mentioned so far are aware of issues of gender, and some of them (such as Polley) offer specific analyses. Broadly, while noting the involvement of women in sport, they see sport as an important modern force emphasizing masculinity and the separateness of men's and women's activities. McCRONE and HARGREAVES offer specific treatments of women in sport. McCrone, like Lowerson, focuses on the middle classes. In the late Victorian era, pupils at girls' public schools were often encouraged to play the game, and McCrone's extensively researched book details the growing interest in sport and recreation among some middle-class women. They were given the space and facilities for sport – as working-class women of the time rarely were. Hargreaves offers a wide-ranging discussion of relevant issues in the sociology as well as the history of women's sports. She gives useful summaries of various theoretical approaches including popular ideas about sport and hegemonic theory. She herself is sympathetic to the hegemonic approach. She notes that the sexualization of the female athlete's body has become ever more characteristic of much sports coverage. She puts such discussion in an historical context, arguing persuasively that ideas about what women should look like and, therefore, about what sports they should and should not be involved in are long-standing realities. Hargreaves, like McCrone, is in no doubt that many women found physical activity within a sporting framework liberating. Both authors note the constraints that a male-dominated sporting culture placed on women, a significant minority of whom chose separatism, in terms of organization, as the best answer to the problem.

BRAILSFORD is unusual in that he was writing, as an academic, about the history of sport long before it became usual to do so. His own early work was on the 17th century; this too distinguishes him from the great bulk of students of this topic, who have focused on the 19th and 20th centuries. Like most other scholars, Brailsford is intrigued by economic modernization and how the games people play were affected by that process. He, however, is interested in a longer time span for change than many other writers. Indeed, "time" itself appears in his title. He is elucidating a process whereby sporting pastimes became a more central, or at least a more predictable, recurring, and organized part of people's lives in Britain. Some of the pastimes, as everyone notes, became businesses.

STEVE ICKRINGILL

See also Leisure and Recreation

Stamford Bridge, Battle of 1066

Adam, R.J., *A Conquest of England: The Coming of the Normans*, London: Hodder and Stoughton, 1965

Barclay, C.N., *Battle 1066*, London: Dent, and Princeton, New Jersey: Van Nostrand, 1966

Barlow, Frank, *The Feudal Kingdom of England, 1042–1216*, London and New York: Longmans Green, 1955

Furneaux, Rupert, *Conquest 1066*, London: Secker and Warburg, 1966; as *Invasion 1066*, Englewood Cliffs, New Jersey: Prentice Hall, 1966

Green, John Richard, *The Conquest of England*, London: Macmillan, 1883; New York: Harper, 1884

Hollister, C. Warren, *Anglo-Saxon Military Institutions on the Eve of the Norman Conquest*, Oxford: Clarendon Press, 1962

Howarth, David, *1066: The Year of the Conquest*, London: Collins, 1977; New York: Viking Press, 1978

Lloyd, Alan, *The Year of the Conqueror*, London: Longman, 1966; as *The Making of the King, 1066*, New York: Holt Rinehart and Winston, 1966

Loyn, Henry, *The Vikings in Britain*, New York: St Martin's Press, 1977; revised edition, Oxford: Blackwell, 1994; Oxford and Cambridge, Massachusetts: Blackwell, 1995

When William the Conqueror defeated Harold Godwineson at the battle of Hastings, he not only gained the kingdom of England but established the year 1066 as one of the key dates in British history. Historians have placed such emphasis upon the events of this single year that it is arguably the most studied year in the history of the British Isles. However, despite this attention, the battle of Stamford Bridge – which is viewed as "one of the most significant and illustrious of English victories" – has been relatively ignored and remains in the shadow of Hastings.

Historians are in general agreement regarding the significance of the battle of Stamford Bridge, yet few have gone beyond a cursory examination of it, discussion often being limited to a few pages in a much larger work on the events of 1066. Two points have dominated the discussions: the effect this northern conflict had upon the English army (did it weaken them for Hastings?) and whether or not the victory made Harold Godwineson overconfident, ultimately leading him to rush into battle at Hastings ill-prepared. BARLOW'S classic work is a case in point: little space is devoted to Stamford Bridge, despite the author's recognition that it has "to be considered one of the decisive battles of English history". GREEN gives very little attention to Stamford Bridge in the rush to Hastings; and HOWARTH, writing 70 years later, provides a brief narrative of the events surrounding Stamford Bridge but offers little else. LLOYD'S account is longer, but it is general and gives limited context or analysis of the significance of Stamford Bridge.

For Barlow the importance of Stamford Bridge is the effect it might have had upon Harold Godwineson and his army. Barlow contends that Godwineson, flushed with victory over the Scandinavian Harold Hardrada, may have rushed headlong into battle against William of Normandy. BARCLAY agrees with this assessment, suggesting that the importance of Stamford Bridge was that it established Godwineson as an exceptional leader and perhaps led him to overconfidence. Lloyd also agrees, arguing that the loss of his housecarls, and the exertion of the forced march south soon after, had a devastating impact upon the effectiveness of the English army at Hastings.

ADAM's analysis of Godwineson's actions offers a new twist on earlier theories. He agrees that Godwineson rushed things as he raced to meet the Norman threat; but, unlike earlier scholars who have found fault in this action, Adam concludes that Godwineson's hasty march south was hardly a mistake. He points out that Godwineson had been preparing for a Norman invasion all summer and would therefore have wanted to return to London as soon as possible. He argues that Godwineson would have gained little by waiting at York, a course of action which would not have replenished his fallen housecarls or supplied northern reinforcements. Harold was, in Adam's view, already on the way south when news arrived that the Normans had landed and therefore did not rush headlong to Hastings as is so often said.

In part, the lack of interest in Stamford Bridge stems from the scarcity of reliable sources, yet several writers have shown that if cautiously used, the evidence of Stamford Bridge offers important insight into Anglo-Saxon military practices. Adam notes that it is hard to establish details surrounding Stamford Bridge, as most information is based upon Icelandic tradition. Anecdotes that have an epic quality, such as Hardrada falling from his horse before the battle or Godwineson offering him seven feet of English soil, suggest that caution is required in using Snorri Sturlason's account. HOLLISTER does not accept Snorri's account as fact, but he does not dismiss it either. He uses it to argue effectively for the existence of an English cavalry and the use of archers. Hollister then uses Stamford Bridge to argue that the old assumption that the English army was inferior to the Norman army is inaccurate, and that the English force which lost at Hastings was equal to the Norman force but was in a weakened state and not up to strength. FURNEAUX is in agreement and, like Hollister, concludes that the evidence of Stamford Bridge points to an effective Anglo-Saxon army which occasionally fought on horseback and used archers in the same fashion as the Normans at Hastings.

Scholars themselves, as most would have us believe of Harold Godwineson, have rushed from Stamford Bridge in their haste to get to Hastings. Although they recognize the obvious significance of Stamford Bridge, few have given this battle the attention which is needed. Adam emphasizes that the long-term significance of Stamford Bridge is that it ended Norse attacks upon England; LOYN also makes this connection. Loyn provides a very limited discussion of the battle but does place it within the broader involvement of Scandinavian dynasties in England. To Loyn, Stamford Bridge represents a further example of Scandinavian activity and interest in the British Isles and, more significantly, marked the end of the Viking age. For this reason alone the battle of Stamford Bridge deserves much greater attention than it has received.

Scott A. McLean

See also Harold II; Hastings, Battle of

Standard, Battle of the 1138

Bradbury, James, "Battles in England and Normandy, 1066–1154" in *Anglo-Norman Warfare: Studies in Late Anglo-Saxon and Anglo-Norman Military Organization and Warfare*, edited by Matthew Strickland, Woodbridge, Suffolk; and Rochester, New York: Boydell and Brewer, 1992
Davis, R.H.C., *King Stephen, 1135–1154*, 3rd edition, London and New York: Longman, 1990 (1st edition, 1967)
Strickland, Matthew, *War and Chivalry: The Conduct and Perception of War in England and Normandy, 1066–1217*, Cambridge and New York: Cambridge University Press, 1996
Stringer, Keith J., *The Reign of Stephen: Kingship, Warfare, and Government in Twelfth-Century England*, London and New York: Routledge, 1993

In a brief and tactically decisive battle in 1138, a force of northern English earls led by Archbishop Thurstan of York stood around a mast taken from a ship and adorned with relics and banners of saints and a consecrated host – all mounted on a carriage and constituting the "standard" that gave the battle its name – and defeated an invading army of Scots under King David I. The course and the key events of the Battle of the Standard have never been in dispute. It opened with a charge on foot by unarmoured men from Galloway, who were slaughtered by the dismounted mailed knights of the English army; this foolishly brave attack by "naked Picts" has been the foundation of the battle's limited historiographical fame. Although the Battle of the Standard has not been the subject of any independent studies, it shows up as an example in many discussions of 12th-century warfare and as a representative episode in analyses of medieval Anglo-Scottish relations.

BRADBURY, for example, discusses this battle in the context of other battles fought in England and Normandy between 1066 and 1154. He correctly takes the dismounting of the English knights at the Standard as part of a pattern of dismounting by Anglo-Norman knights throughout this period, a pattern that reflected both the Anglo-Norman kings' appreciation of the tactical value of heavy infantry, especially on the defensive, and their ability to create such infantry, in part by exercising control over the tactics of their mounted retainers.

DAVIS, on the other hand, focuses on the immediate political context and consequences of the battle. King David was Empress Matilda's uncle, and his invasion was an early move in the civil war between the empress and her supporters on one side and King Stephen on the other. Davis sees the battle as one of a series of setbacks suffered by Matilda's side in 1138, from which recovery did not come until the next year. The effectiveness of David's position as a supporter of Matilda was seriously compromised by a widespread perception among the English that he wanted to invade anyway; the presence in his army of large numbers of unarmoured "barbarians" from the highlands and their plundering during the campaign reinforced this view.

STRINGER puts a different spin on the political context by considering the broader patterns of Anglo-Scottish relations and King David's position within the political class of England as Earl of Huntingdon. The battle itself may have been a temporary setback, Stringer argues, but the fact that it took place so far into England and that the English army was unable to follow up its battlefield victory in any way, simply emphasized the difficult position Stephen was in as he tried to defend northern England when his major preoccupations were elsewhere.

In his analysis of Anglo-Scottish warfare, Stringer largely follows STRICKLAND, whose superb study must be central to understanding the larger cultural contexts of the battle. Though Strickland does not discuss the battle at great length, he refers to it repeatedly, as it represents a number of his key themes.

He shows how ravaging and plundering by the Scottish army contributed to its reputation for godlessness and for failing to heed the "laws of war" despite the fact that such ravaging was central to much medieval warfare. His careful analysis of the components of class, ethnicity, religion, and culture that went into the evolution of notions of chivalry and honourable conduct is crucial for understanding the dynamics of the Battle of the Standard – which, in turn, beautifully illustrates those same themes.

STEPHEN MORILLO

Stanley, Sir Henry Morton 1841–1904
Explorer, imperialist, and journalist

Anstruther, Ian, *I Presume: Stanley's Triumph and Disaster*, London: Bles, 1956; as *Dr. Livingstone, I Presume?* New York: Dutton, 1956

Bennett, Norman R. (editor), *Stanley's Despatches to the New York Herald 1871–1872, 1874–1877*, Boston: Boston University Press, 1970

Bierman, John, *Dark Safari: The Life behind the Legend of Henry Morton Stanley*, New York: Knopf, 1990; London: Hodder and Stoughton, 1991

Casada, James A., *Dr David Livingstone and Sir Henry Morton Stanley: An Annotated Bibliography*, New York: Garland Publishing, 1976

Hall, Richard, *Stanley: An Adventurer Explored*, London: Collins 1974; Boston: Houghton Mifflin, 1975

Halladay, Eric, "Henry Morton Stanley: The Opening Up of the Congo Basin" in *Africa and Its Explorers: Motives, Methods, and Impact*, edited by Robert I. Rotberg, Cambridge, Massachusetts: Harvard University Press, 1970

Hird, Frank, *H.M. Stanley: The Authorized Life*, London: Stanley Paul, 1935

McLynn, Frank, *Stanley: The Making of an African Explorer*, London: Constable, 1989; Chelsea, Michigan: Scarborough House, 1990

McLynn, Frank, *Stanley: Sorcerer's Apprentice*, London: Constable, 1991

Maurice, Albert (editor), *H.M. Stanley: Unpublished Letters*, London: Chambers, and New York: Philosophical Library, 1957 (original French edition, 1955)

Riffenburgh, Beau, *The Myth of the Explorer: The Press, Sensationalism, and Geographical Discovery*, London and New York: Belhaven Press, and Cambridge: University of Cambridge, Scott Polar Research Institute, 1993

Smith, Iain R., *The Emin Pasha Relief Expedition, 1886–1890*, Oxford: Clarendon Press, 1972

Stanley, Richard and Alan Neame (editors), *The Exploration Diaries of H.M. Stanley: Now First Published from the Original Manuscript*, London: Kimber, and New York: Vanguard Press, 1961

Youngs, Tim, *Travellers in Africa: British Travelogues, 1850–1900*, Manchester and New York: Manchester University Press, 1994

Henry Morton Stanley bridged the gap between exploration and annexationist imperialism in Africa. In important ways, he influenced perceptions of the continent and actual British activities there. One of the most famous men of his day, he was honoured by the queen, became a member of parliament, and was given a knighthood. Yet he was never fully accepted by the establishment – a fact symbolized by the refusal to accord him burial beside Livingstone in Westminster Abbey. Controversies about Stanley have continued in the years since his death, fuelled by the appearance of several large biographies. These have tended to centre on his personal life and character rather than his wider historical significance.

Access to Stanley's papers, which are at Tervuren in Belgium, is difficult, although some copies are in the collections of the British Museum. Recent biographies include lists of known papers and contain good bibliographies. Nevertheless, the annotated bibliography produced in 1976 by CASADA remains an indispensable guide to Stanley's own papers and publications and to the literature existing on him up to that year; about a thousand items are listed. Published editions of any of Stanley's papers have been few and generally unsatisfactory. MAURICE in 1955 was concerned to show Stanley as the heroic founder of civilization in the Congo Free State by printing some of his reports of 1881–82; it is difficult to tell how selective the editor was. Stanley's greatest purely exploratory feat was the expedition of 1874–77, and the appearance of STANLEY & NEAME's edition of the diaries relating to that trip ought to have been a major event. However, again, it is unclear what was excluded, and the editorial input was meagre and largely unsatisfactory. Even so, this volume served to demonstrate how, in his books, Stanley, an accomplished journalist, produced "written up" versions of what he claimed to have seen and done.

Stanley's own books had not concealed his frequent ruthlessness towards Africans, and this occasioned hostile comment in Britain from the 1870s onwards. In addition, jealousy was aroused by his "finding" the nation's hero, Livingstone, in 1871. Snide comments were made about Stanley's origins in a Welsh workhouse and his American and journalistic background. Controversy was later exacerbated by Stanley's treatment of his companions during the Emin Pasha relief expedition of 1886–90. All this has provided ample scope for biographers. Following Lady Stanley's attempt to sanitize her husband's life by completing his *Autobiography*, HIRD, in 1935, described a man who ranked with Columbus as a discoverer, brought about the (necessary) partition of Africa, and had been unfairly misrepresented by his critics. The historical judgement at issue was, essentially, whether the ends justified the often dubious means which Stanley had used to achieve his exploratory and imperialist ends. As time went on, the end itself – the creation of empire, especially Leopold's Congo Free State – also seemed dubious, and so debate tended to become concerned less with historical circumstances and more with Stanley's personality as an explanation for his behaviour. ANSTRUTHER sought to show how the "difficult, lonely and exceptional young man" had been haunted by the words he had used at the famous meeting with Livingstone. Yet analyses of Stanley's character could not be convincing until the appearance of HALL's biography, which revealed the true details of Stanley's origins and early experiences together with much else about his personal life. Providing a balanced view of Stanley and showing more understanding of Africa than most other biographies, Hall's remains the best of the reasonably recent popular studies. The two works by McLYNN build on Hall; but McLynn goes much further in attempting to explain Stanley's background and its relation to his psyche. McLynn is an accomplished writer who has consulted an enormous amount of material on Stanley and the historical circumstances in which he operated. Arguably, not all this material is properly understood, but in any case McLynn's ultimate aim is to produce psychobiography, not history. Stanley's concealments and lies, his sexual ambivalence, and his admiration yet resentment of the British upper classes provide much material for such an approach. BIERMAN goes over much the same ground and reaches similar conclusions about Stanley's personality while remaining somewhat more tolerant of his failings than McLynn.

The task remaining, despite the existence of these major biographies, is to show Stanley in the context of the exploration, particularly the British exploration, of Africa from the 1850s to the 1870s; to explain his part in the development of British interests, both official and unofficial, in Africa in the 1880s and 1890s; and to see the significance throughout both periods of his interaction with Africa and Africans. HALLADAY made a useful preliminary attempt to tackle the last of these tasks, but two other works are especially notable. On the assumption that, compared with his books, Stanley's newspaper despatches were a more immediate and possibly more accurate record of his expeditions of 1871 and 1874, BENNETT reproduced these materials with a helpful introduction and full annotations on the people, places, and situations mentioned by Stanley. This was an important piece of scholarship. For the Emin Pasha expedition, there is the ground-breaking work of SMITH. Although Smith takes account of the arguments and jealousy among the European members of the expedition, his principal aim is to explain the significance of the expedition for Africa and for imperialism. Its leader's personality is not a preoccupation; rather, he is seen as the central actor in a complex series of developments which need to be unravelled and explained.

The task of obtaining a true estimate of Stanley's importance will be aided by the work of RIFFENBURGH, who explains much about the new role of newspapers in British and American life and, naturally, refers often to Stanley and to Stanley's employers. Notable also is the work on British travelogues by YOUNGS. Unconcerned about Stanley's veracity or lack of it, Youngs takes a postmodernist approach which allows him to show how Stanley's discourses "commodified" narrative about Africa and so served the needs of capitalist imperialism.

Since Stanley seems to have invented and popularized the idea of the "dark continent", his literary approach certainly ought be scrutinized. Yet to assume that we cannot learn from Stanley's writings any independent facts about the man himself, about imperialism in Africa, or about Africans seems a counsel of despair. It is to be hoped that a new generation of historians will look at Stanley with the benefit but not the undue influence of the works that have appeared about this remarkable man during the past hundred years.

ROY BRIDGES

See also Exploration: Since the 18th Century; Livingstone

Staple, Company of the

Bolton, J.L., *The Medieval English Economy, 1150–1500*, London: Dent, and Totowa, New Jersey: Rowman and Littlefield, 1980

Bowden, Peter J. *The Wool Trade in Tudor and Stuart England*, London: Macmillan, and New York: St Martin's Press, 1962

Hanham, Alison, *The Celys and Their World: An English Merchant Family of the Fifteenth Century*, Cambridge and New York: Cambridge University Press, 1985

Lloyd, T.H., *The English Wool Trade in the Middle Ages*, Cambridge and New York: Cambridge University Press, 1977

Munro, John H.A., *Wool, Cloth, and Gold: The Struggle for Bullion in Anglo-Burgundian Trade 1340–1478*, Toronto: University of Toronto Press, and Brussels: Éditions de l'Université de Bruxelles, 1972

Nightingale, Pamela, *A Medieval Mercantile Community: The Grocers' Company and the Politics and Trade of London 1000–1485*, New Haven, Connecticut and London: Yale University Press, 1995

Power, Eileen, *The Wool Trade in English Medieval History*, London and New York: Oxford University Press, 1941

Power, Eileen and M.M. Postan, *Studies in English Trade in the Fifteenth Century*, London: Routledge, 1933; New York: Barnes and Noble, 1966

Rich, E.E., "Introduction" in *The Ordinance Book of the Merchants of the Staple*, Cambridge: Cambridge University Press, 1937

The Ordinance and Statute of the Staple, which legally established the Fellowship of the Staple (Merchants of the Staple, Company of the Staple), was passed in 1353. The company finally wound itself up in 1928, by which time it had become, in RICH's words, a "family party" leaving as a reminder of its existence only a fund for prizes for the best fleece exhibited at the Royal Agricultural Society's show. In the introduction to his edition of the ordinance book of this monopolistic trading company, Rich sets out its history, pointing to the loss of the company's own records (most disappeared when the French took Calais in 1558) as a reason for the lack of information about its internal. In its heyday, it controlled much of the export trade in English wool and was vitally important to the crown as a source of loan finance. The years of its decline in the 16th and 17th centuries are also examined; Rich makes the point that by the 1580s the company's members had largely become wool brokers, an activity from which they were technically barred.

BOLTON's general history of the English economy from 1150 to 1500 sets out the background to the establishment of the company in the context of the development of English overseas trade. Bolton sees the process as full of "extraordinary twists and turns" but driven largely by the need of the crown to raise loans, particularly in time of war, which could be secured on the customs on wool. He also points out the links between the advance of the trade in cloth and the decline of the trade in wool.

POWER (1941) – her Ford lectures – contains a valuable study of the taxation of wool and a full consideration of the rationale for the staple system. POWER & POSTAN (1933) contains a superficially similar article by Power on the operation of the staple system as a whole, but here Power places greater emphasis on links with royal finance and the problem of the evasion of the staple in Calais whether by royal licences or by smuggling. Haward's article in the same collection, "The Financial Transactions between Lancastrian Government and the Merchants of the Staple from 1449 to 1461", not only discusses the merchants' loans to the king in this period but also their role in the financing of the Calais garrison. This culminated in the Act of Retainer of 1466, which placed the responsibility for paying the garrison on the shoulders of the merchant staplers. Haward also points out the hostility between the staplers and Italian merchants aroused by what was seen as the crown's overgenerous grant to them of licences to bypass the staple.

NIGHTINGALE, whose book is of much wider interest than might be guessed from its title, looks at the anti-alien movements in London and Southampton in the later 1450s, in which the staplers were strongly implicated. Another aspect of the close involvement of the Merchants of the Staple in matters of public policy emerges from MUNRO's work on bullionism and its effect on relations between England and Burgundy. The merchants supported the crown's policy, since the result of this was to strengthen their monopoly of the export trade in wool. Munro's work is of particular value because it is largely based on sources in Belgian archives and thus provides a different perspective on the staplers, placing their activities in a wider European context.

HANHAM's book on the Celys takes as its main source the family's voluminous correspondence. This not only allows a much closer look at the complexities of the staplers' trading activities but also provides an intimate portrait of a family of merchants whose prosperity depended on the wool trade and the vagaries of the Company of the Staple. Hanham also comments from an English point of view on bullionism and exchange problems and the difficulties of managing the company with authority split between the "Place" (the company's headquarters in Calais) and the Mayor of the Staple in London.

LLOYD's concern is not primarily with the staple system but with all aspects of the trade in wool over the period from c.1297 to the end of the 15th century. He does, however, offer valuable comments on Munro's and Postan's work, seeing the staple as relatively ineffective in advancing England's trade but necessary as a means of providing for the defence of Calais.

BOWDEN deals with a period when both the wool trade and the company were in decline and, in his opinion, the company had little to offer in return for the large admission fines charged to would-be new members. The company could offer no privileges in either the wool or the cloth trade. Even so, staplers had elbowed their way into the cloth trade by mid-century to such an extent that they were happy to see the ban on the export of raw wool, introduced in 1614, continued. The Merchants of the Staple, however, had no future as a monopoly company, despite this apparent victory over their rivals the Merchant Adventurers; and Bowden draws a line under the activities of both mercantile groups.

SUSAN ROSE

See also Antwerp; Calais; Cloth Industry, Medieval; Guilds and Lay Fraternities; Merchant Adventurers; Merchant Guilds

Statute Law

Baker, J.H., *An Introduction to English Legal History*, 3rd edition, London and Boston: Butterworths, 1990

Brock, Michael, *The Great Reform Act*, London: Hutchinson, 1973

Clifford, Frederick H., *A History of Private Bill Legislation*, 2 vols, London: Butterworth, 1885–87; reprinted, New York: Kelley, 1972

Dean, David, *Law-Making and Society in Late Elizabethan England: The Parliament of England, 1584–1601*, Cambridge and New York: Cambridge University Press, 1996

Edwards, J. Goronwy, *Historians and the Medieval English Parliament*, Glasgow: University of Glasgow, 1960

Elton, G.R. (editor), *The Tudor Constitution: Documents and Commentary*, Cambridge: Cambridge University Press, 1960; 2nd edition, Cambridge and New York: Cambridge University Press, 1982

Elton, G.R., *The Parliament of England, 1559–1581*, Cambridge and New York: Cambridge University Press, 1986

Galloway, Bruce, *The Union of England and Scotland, 1603–1608*, Edinburgh: John Donald, 1986

Jones, Norman, *God and the Moneylenders: Usury and Law in Early Modern England*, Oxford and Cambridge, Massachusetts: Blackwell, 1989

Lambert, Sheila, *Bills and Acts: Legislative Procedure in Eighteenth-Century England*, Cambridge: Cambridge University Press, 1971

Luders, Alexander *et al.* (editors), *The Statutes of the Realm 1253–1713*, London: Eyre and Strahan, 1810–22

McIlwain, Charles Howard, *The High Court of Parliament and Its Supremacy: An Historical Essay on the Boundaries between Legislation and Adjudication in England*, New Haven, Connecticut: Yale University Press, and London: Oxford University Press, 1910

Plucknett, Theodore F.T., *Statutes and Their Interpretation in the First Half of the Fourteenth Century*, Cambridge: Cambridge University Press, 1922; Buffalo, New York: Hein, 1980

Pollard, A.F., *The Evolution of Parliament*, London and New York: Longmans Green, 1920; revised edition, 1926

Richardson, H.G. and G.O. Sayles, *The English Parliament in the Middle Ages*, London: Hambledon Press, 1981

Roskell, J.S., *Parliament and Politics in Late Medieval England*, vol. 1, London: Hambledon Press, 1981

Thompson, E.P., *Whigs and Hunters: The Origin of the Black Act*, New York: Pantheon, and London: Allen Lane, 1975

Black's Law Dictionary defines a statute as a "law passed by a legislative body". However, according to William M. Lile *et al.* (*Brief Making and the Use of Law Books*, 3rd edition, 1914):

We are not justified in limiting the statutory law to those rules only which are promulgated by what we commonly call legislatures. Any positive enactment to which the state gives the force of a law is a "statute" whether it has gone through the usual stages of legislative proceedings, or has been adopted in other modes of expressing the will of the people or other sovereign power of the state. In an absolute monarchy, an edict of the ruling sovereign is statutory law.

These two contrasting definitions sum up much of the debate over what a statute comprises. It seems to have been settled in the medieval period that the earliest statute was the expanded confirmation of Magna Carta in 1225; but when the official *Statutes of the Realm* were compiled by LUDERS *et al.* and published in the early 19th century, the 13th-century legislation included charters, writs, ordinances, and "statutes", starting with the "provisions" of Merton in 1236. Furthermore, many of the pieces of legislation included were enacted by the king alone or in collaboration with his council or, as with the statute of Westminster II (1285), by "the Lord King in his Parliament at Westminster".

This confusion over what was included as a statute has led to a lively historical debate over the early statutes and the role of parliament. According to William Blackstone, the *lex scriptae* were the "statutes, acts or edicts, made by the King's majesty, by and with the advice and consent of the lords spiritual and temporal and commons in parliament assembled". But this definition is widely considered too narrow. The problem which modern scholars have faced is that the terms "statute" and "ordinance" seem to be interchangeable; and, as PLUCKNETT pointed out, in the reign of Edward I a statute "simply means something established by royal authority: whether it is established by the King in Council, or a Parliament of nobles and commons as well, is completely immaterial. It is equally immaterial what form the statute takes, whether it be a charter or a statute enrolled and proclaimed, or merely an administrative expression of the royal will". The core of Plucknett's argument is that we must look more to what contemporaries regarded as a statute than to any theoretical definition made centuries later. In this Plucknett was challenging the view of MCILWAIN, who emphasized the role of parliament as a judicial court rather than a statute-making body. In this view, parliament was a place which did not make statute law but merely declared it. McIlwain's view also found support in the early 20th century from POLLARD, whose monumental work, *The Evolution of Parliament*, enjoyed widespread credence despite its contorted prose style. However, most scholars in the second half of the 20th century, with the notable exception of RICHARDSON & SAYLES, have tended to follow Plucknett's lead, albeit with some modifications. This later reaction against McIlwain, Richardson, and Sayles has come through the work of ROSKELL and EDWARDS, who clearly stated that the role of parliament (and thus the place of statute) "consisted in being unspecific". Furthermore, as ELTON (1986) noted, "if medieval Parliaments did not legislate, much in the *Rolls of Parliament* becomes incomprehensible; and so does the further development of legislative functions in the sixteenth century".

For the remaining centuries, historical reflection on statute law has tended to concern either statutory interpretation (the relationship between the statute, its drafters in parliament, and the judges interpreting it) or, more usually, important discussions of individual acts. Thus no general history of statute law has been written, nor has statute law formed a major part of the various controversies over historical methodologies. This lack of development of the subject in part reflects the late development of modern legal history as a discipline; it also reflects the fact that historians have remained firmly fixated on the workings of parliament rather than its legislative output or on statute law as a reaction to calls for political, social, and economic reform. Nor has the impact of statute law been widely studied in the communities which it affected. However, BAKER has provided a clear and effective starting-point, and studies of legislation in Tudor England by ELTON (1960) and DEAN have illustrated the importance of statute law in the broader historical context of representation and the role of parliament. Elton, in particular, has emphasized the role of parliament as a legislative institution and noted its development in the 1530s to a situation in which it made statute law that "extended the operation of statute law virtually to omnicompetence". The process of statute-making in the 18th century has also been examined by LAMBERT. In these works – in the debates on the role of parliament, legislative intention, and the relationship between the monarch and the House of Commons and Lords – the groundwork has been laid for future studies of the concept and practice of statute law. For private bills, a useful although now outdated study by CLIFFORD discusses the rise of some categories of non-public statutes. This can be further developed, as studies of individual acts have done much to enlighten us regarding statutory process and the impact of legislation. Although it would be impossible to list all such works, those by JONES on usury, GALLOWAY on the union with Scotland, THOMPSON on the Black Act, and BROCK on the reform acts have shown how statute law can be interpreted and applied to the study of political and social history.

CHRIS R. KYLE

See also Constitutional Law

Steel Industry

Aylen, Jonathan, "Innovation in the British Steel Industry" in *Technical Innovation and British Economic Performance*, edited by Keith Pavitt, London: Macmillan, 1980

Aylen, Jonathan, "Privatization of the British Steel Corporation", *Fiscal Studies*, 9/3 (1988): 1–25

Beauman, Christopher, "The British Steel Case: How History Determines Strategy" in *The Steel Industry in the New Millennium*, vol. 2, *Institutions, Privatisation, and Social Dimensions*, edited by R. Ranieri and E. Gibellieri, London: IOM Communications, 1998

Burn, Duncan L., *The Economic History of Steelmaking, 1867–1939: A Study in Competition*, Cambridge: Cambridge University Press, 1940

Burn, Duncan L., *The Steel Industry, 1939–1959: A Study in Competition and Planning*, Cambridge: Cambridge University Press, 1961

Elbaum, Bernard, "The Steel Industry before World War I" in *The Decline of the British Economy*, edited by Elbaum and William Lazonick, New York: Oxford University Press, and Oxford: Clarendon Press, 1986

Keeling, B.S. and A.E.G. Wright, *The Development of the Modern British Steel Industry*, London: Longmans, 1964

McCloskey, Donald N., *Economic Maturity and Entrepreneurial Decline: British Iron and Steel, 1870–1913*, Cambridge, Massachusetts: Harvard University Press, 1973

Owen, Geoffrey, *From Empire to Europe: The Decline and Revival of British Industry since the Second World War*, London: HarperCollins, 1999

Ranieri, Ruggero, "Steel and the State in Italy and the UK: The Public Sector of the Steel Industry in Comparative Perspective (1945–1996)", *European Yearbook of Business History*, 2 (1999): 125–54

Temin, Peter, "The Relative Decline of the British Steel Industry, 1880–1913" in *Industrialization in Two Systems: Essays in Honour of Alexander Gerschenkron*, edited by Henry Rosovsky, New York: Wiley, 1966

Tolliday, Steven, *Business, Banking, and Politics: The Case of British Steel, 1918–1939*, Cambridge, Massachusetts: Harvard University Press, 1987

Tolliday, Steven, "Competition and Maturity in the British Steel Industry, 1870–1914" in *Changing Patterns of International Rivalry: Some Lessons from the Steel Industry*, edited by Etsuo Abe and Yoshitaka Suzuki, Tokyo: University of Tokyo Press, 1991

Tweedale, Geoffrey, *Sheffield Steel and America: A Century of Commercial and Technological Interdependence, 1830–1930*, Cambridge and New York: Cambridge University Press, 1987

Vaizey, John, *The History of British Steel*, London: Weidenfeld and Nicolson, 1974

Wengenroth, Ulrich, *Enterprise and Technology: The German and British Steel Industries 1865–1895*, translated by Sarah Hanbury Tenison, Cambridge and New York: Cambridge University Press, 1994 (German edition, 1986)

Wurm, Clemens A., *Business, Politics, and International Relations: Steel, Cotton, and International Cartels in British Politics, 1924–1939*, translated by Patrick Salmon, Cambridge and New York: Cambridge University Press, 1993 (German edition, 1988)

Between 1870 and 1914 Britain's share of world steel output declined dramatically. British exports ceased to dominate international markets, and foreign imports penetrated the UK market. In the interwar period the trend continued, despite a creditable performance during the late 1930s. Nor did the British steel industry succeed in regaining international prominence after 1945. Along with the issue of decline, a much debated topic is intervention by the state. During the 1930s the industry was shielded by tariff protection and formed a national cartel under government supervision; in 1949 it was nationalized, but from 1952 on it was gradually brought back into private ownership. In 1967 all the existing large steel companies were nationalized and amalgamated into the British Steel Corporation (BSC). In 1987 BSC was privatized by the Thatcher government. How did these changes reflect on the industry's performance?

BURN (1940) pinpoints failures in technological innovation, in entrepreneurial leadership, and in the ability to promote structural change. In particular he stresses a failure to take advantage of the basic process to exploit domestic iron ores in the east Midlands. Cheap basic Bessemer production would have resulted in low-cost, competitive steel, to match Germany's success in the Ruhr. Burn argues that this opportunity was not taken until the 1930s, when the industry was already lagging seriously behind.

McCLOSKEY argues that the case for decline is unproven: British entrepreneurs behaved rationally; Burn's alternatives would have been economically irrational. There was no gap in British and US total factory productivity.

TEMIN takes an intermediate path. He challenges the notion of entrepreneurial failure. The relative loss of world pre-eminence was due to factors largely outside Britain's control, especially the dynamic growth of German and American production behind protective barriers. The slower growth of British output necessarily brought with it a slower rate of investment and technological innovation.

The case for relative decline is restated by ELBAUM, who bases his argument mainly on a comparison of British and American practice between 1890 and 1914. The industry's performance was marked by fragmented organization, low plant and labour productivity, failure to achieve economies of scale by vertical concentration, and lags in technological innovation. This was not due to entrepreneurial failures; rather, it should be blamed on a fragmented, regionally diverse, sophisticated, and mature industrial structure; on the lack of a protectionist policy; and on a wage system encouraging high costs and low productivity.

TOLLIDAY (1991) and WENGENROTH conclusively demolish Burn's thesis. Burn, they argue, overlooked fundamental metallurgical obstacles to the development of a low-cost basic steel industry using east Midlands ores. Tolliday finds no evidence either of technical conservatism or of metallurgical inadequacy. He takes a positive view of the British industry's reaction to adverse circumstances regarding supplies of raw material (e.g., the growing relative costs of hematite ores) as well as to unfavourable market conditions in the late 19th century. By concentrating on higher-quality products, as opposed to the cheaper low-quality varieties produced on the Continent, the industry maintained a strong position. Sheffield retained world technological leadership in special steels in the face of a strong challenge from the United States, a point explored in detail by TWEEDALE.

In his technically proficient, detailed comparison of British and German companies between 1870 and 1890 Wengenroth maps the different technological paths of the two industries. There was no German superiority, only a concentration by German firms on cheaper, basic Bessemer steels. British firms remained market leaders in higher-quality open-hearth steels. The Germans, however, made capital out of their inferiority by managing tight, aggressive cartels wedded to export dumping, against which British firms were unable to react.

In a detailed investigation of steel companies' strategy between the wars, TOLLIDAY (1987) highlights how family ownership, regional monopolies, and market fragmentation posed serious obstacles to rationalization. While the industry managed to muddle through, its key problems remained unresolved. Protracted but largely misdirected attempts by the Bank of England also failed to bring about amalgamation and reorganization. The government was prepared to grant the industry a tariff and to establish a regulatory body in the form of the Import Duties Advisory Committee (IDAC). As WURM shows,

the government also supported the industry in successful negotiations with the European Steel Cartel. It was unable, however,
to impose a set of investment priorities, preferring to back
industrial self-government for the sake of market stability and
a regulated market.

Developments between 1940 and 1960 are covered in detail
by BURN (1961). Burn's account is complemented by those
of VAIZEY and KEELING & WRIGHT. The industry, Burn
argues, did not break away from its chequered pre-1939 record.
There was a lack of rationalization and no clear strategy aimed
at closing the productivity gap in order to catch up with the
United States and Germany. The British industry got the worst
of both worlds: nationalization was misconceived and ideological; return to private ownership meant more cartel-like behaviour under slack government supervision. Relations with the
European Coal and Steel Community (ECSC) were fraught with
difficulties. Refusal to join ECSC succeeded only in shielding the
British industry from competitive pressure.

AYLEN (1980) presents evidence of a failure in innovation
and of comparative decline in the 1960s. However, AYLEN
(1988) describes a buoyant industry as of 1987. The story of
this remarkable turn-around, against the backdrop of the competing performance of French and German steel, is well told by
OWEN. He argues that nationalization in 1967 was a mistake:
the industry should have been left to its own devices, as in
Germany. RANIERI compares the UK with Italy and finds that
in both countries success depended on giving technocratic management a free hand; this argument puts BSC in a better light.
During the 1970s, despite attempts at political meddling and a
serious economic downturn, BSC's management went ahead
with restructuring. There is some agreement that a turning-point
was reached in 1980, when BSC's management successfully
challenged union resistance to decentralized bargaining and to
a radical programme of closures. A more problematic view of
the industry's performance is given by BEAUMAN, who claims
that the industry's turn-around predates the Thatcher government and that privatization, although successful in the short
run, did not solve the industry's long-term structural problems.
Among these problems, relations with continental Europe
remain a critical issue.

RUGGERO RANIERI

See also Bessemer; Industry, Heavy: Decline; Nationalization
and Denationalization

Stephen c.1100–1154
King of England and Duke of Normandy

Chibnall, Marjorie, *The Empress Matilda: Queen Consort,
Queen Mother, and Lady of the English*, Oxford and
Cambridge, Massachusetts: Blackwell, 1992
Cronne, H.A., *The Reign of Stephen 1135–1154: Anarchy
in England*, London: Weidenfeld and Nicolson,
1970
Dalton, Paul, *Conquest, Anarchy, and Lordship: Yorkshire,
1066–1154*, Cambridge and New York: Cambridge
University Press, 1994
Davis, R.H.C., *King Stephen 1135–1154*, London: Longman,
and Berkeley, California: University of California Press,
1967; 3rd edition, London and New York: Longman,
1990
King, Edmund (editor), *The Anarchy of King Stephen's Reign*,
Oxford: Clarendon Press, and New York: Oxford
University Press, 1994
Round, J.H., *Geoffrey de Mandeville: A Study of the Anarchy*,
London: Longmans Green, 1892; New York: Franklin,
1960
Warren, W.L., *The Governance of Norman and Angevin
England 1086–1272*, London: Arnold, and Stanford,
California: Stanford University Press, 1987

The "anarchy" of Stephen's reign (1135–54) was invented
almost contemporaneously by the chroniclers who either lived
through or witnessed from a safe distance the events of those
19 long years. It is a concept that remains strong, as the title
of KING's collection suggests. In the mind of that anonymous
monk who wrote the relevant part of the *Anglo-Saxon
Chronicle*, probably in the mid-1150s, the disputed succession
between Stephen and his cousin Empress Matilda, which
resulted in civil war and the collapse of central government, was
a judgement for sin – not just the sins of the protagonists but
general sin, spinning out of control while "Christ and his saints
were asleep". At the end of the 19th century, ROUND asserted
that the anarchy was less a tragedy played out by devils and
sinners than a constitutional breakdown caused by irresponsible barons seeking to exploit an immediate opportunity for gain
instead of endeavouring to maintain the stability which the
Anglo-Norman monarchy had created.

Recent scholarship has maintained its interest in this
"anarchy", and its social, political, and constitutional consequences. From a study of Stephen's coinage and an examination
of local archives, historians have created a picture that dramatically modifies the chaos depicted by Round. The mechanisms
of royal government created by Henry I are now thought to have
survived, at least during the early years of the reign; and the civil
war itself caused much less devastation than was once believed.
However, historians remain divided over the underlying causes
as well as the extent of the breakdown.

DAVIS sees a gentle man and an excellent warrior, but an
incompetent king, who made a series of mistakes from the
beginning of his reign. In Davis's view, Stephen unwisely punished some of his subjects who, although they had at first been
half-hearted in supporting his claim, had accepted him willingly
after his early success. Stephen alienated Roger of Salisbury and
Roger's three nephews, whose support he needed to maintain
the smooth operation of the central administration. He even
alienated his own brother, Henry of Blois, Bishop of Winchester,
by failing to support Henry's bid for the archbishopric of
Canterbury; and this in spite of the fact that Henry had orchestrated the consensus which resulted in Stephen's coronation.
During his conflict with Matilda in the 1140s, Stephen made
further disastrous mistakes and drove more of his potential
supporters into his enemy's camp. As a result he was left surrounded by ruthless warriors and ineffectual administrators.
Overall, Davis argues that the king's incompetence, together
with a certain lack of integrity, was responsible for the whole
tragedy.

Davis complements the work of CRONNE, whose emphasis is less on Stephen's self-destructive personality than on the socio-political circumstances in which monarchy was evolving all over Europe in the 11th and 12th centuries. The conflict between the king and the empress, and the private wars between the English magnates, were not initiated by Stephen, intentionally or otherwise, but driven principally by the territorial ambitions of the warring parties. Stephen's difficulties with his prelates were caused not by his bad faith but by his lack of dexterity in simultaneously making concessions to the church and maintaining control over it. The greatest weakness of his government was its inability to moderate the centrifugal tendencies of feudalism. Sub-infeudation turned many tenants-in-chief into mesne tenants and vassals of other lords, creating many subvassals with multiple allegiances. As a result, conflicts between lords created total confusion, and anarchy was the outcome.

WARREN was not satisfied with the charges of incompetence levelled by Davis, or with the impersonality of Cronne's analysis. He argued forcefully that the anarchy of Stephen's reign was an inevitable consequence of the king's deliberate policy of decentralization. Stephen dismissed royal servants, both at the centre and in localities, without replacing them with men of equal talent, knowledge, and authority. He created earldoms for virtually every shire, and he endowed the earls with powers which should have belonged only to the king. These policies deeply divided local communities, and the private wars which subsequently erupted all over England did more than the disputed succession to undermine his kingship. Warren concluded that Stephen's rejection of the trend towards centralization and bureaucracy reflected his preference for an alternative concept of government through local control, as was practised in many parts of contemporary Europe.

Although in the writing of history it is always difficult to analyse human motivation, the governments envisaged by Stephen and his successor Henry II, who is generally credited with restoring law and order after the anarchy, will continue to attract interpretation and speculation. However, CHIBNALL, in her biography of Empress Matilda, shifts the focus of academic discussion from the confusion of England's domestic politics to the interactions between England, Normandy, and Anjou, and the empress's personal crusade in pursuit of her hereditary right. Matilda's objectives were at least as much to maintain the Anglo-Norman empire, restore peace among warring feudatories in France, and prepare her son Henry for his role in England as to secure her own title. Chibnall's comprehensive and thorough analysis demonstrates convincingly that the 19 turbulent years of Stephen's reign must be surveyed from many different angles.

Those years represent far more than a temporary setback in the constitutional development of medieval England. They show a continual testing of delicate and precarious balances between ruler and subject at all levels, between centre and locality, between church and state, and between England and its neighbours, as well as complex interactions among social forces, where interests sometimes coalesced and sometimes conflicted.

WENXI LIU

REVIEWED BY DAVID LOADES

See also David I; Henry I; Matilda

Stephenson, George 1781–1848
Engineer and railway pioneer

Beckett, Derrick, *Stephenson's Britain*, Newton Abbot, Devon: David and Charles, 1984

Davies, Hunter, *A Biographical Study of the Father of Railways, George Stephenson, on the Occasion of the 150th Anniversary of the Opening of the World's First Public Railway, the Stockton and Darlington, 1825–1975, Including an Account of Railway Mania and a Consideration of Stephensonia Today*, London: Weidenfeld and Nicolson, 1975

Jarvis, Adrian, "The Story of the Story of the Life of George Stephenson" in *Perceptions of Great Engineers: Fact and Fantasy*, edited by Denis Smith, London: Science Museum, 1994

Rolt, L.T.C., *George and Robert Stephenson: The Railway Revolution*, London: Longmans, 1960; New York: St Martin's Press, 1962

Skeat, William O., *George Stephenson: The Engineer and His Letters*, London: Institution of Mechanical Engineers, 1973

Smiles, Samuel, *The Life of George Stephenson, Railway Engineer*, London: John Murray, 1857; Columbus, Ohio: Follett Foster, 1859

Smiles, Samuel, *The Lives of George and Robert Stephenson*, London: Folio Society, 1975 (facsimile reprint of 1874 edition with introduction by Eric de Maré)

Our idea of Victorian civil and railway engineers in general, and George Stephenson in particular, has been shaped, over a century and a half, by the writings of one man – Samuel SMILES, a journalist working in Leeds who was their contemporary and went on to be their main champion in dozens of books that ran to many editions. Smiles met Stephenson a few years before the latter's death and later worked in the railway industry. Much of his information was gathered from people who knew his subjects, and his books are vivid and characterized by frequent citations of actual (or purported) dialogue between his subjects and others. At the time when Smiles was writing, Stephenson's life and achievements were already surrounded by myths. Although Smiles exploded some, he repeated and intensified others and generally portrayed Stephenson as a true hero. Smiles was also the author of *Self-Help* (1859) an early classic on the virtues of entrepreneurism and "self improvement" (reprinted during 1980s, the Thatcher years in Britain), and George Stephenson was his prime exemplar. All Smiles's biographies were written in this vein, offering models to inspire young men. Failings in the subject's character – such as Stephenson's propensity to fall out with colleagues – were conveniently overlooked. Nevertheless, Smiles's account was largely accurate; for instance, Smiles did *not* credit Stephenson with being the inventor of the railway locomotive or the designer of the locomotive *Rocket* (who was George's son Robert). However, the myth was ultimately too powerful; by the end of the century everyone "knew" that these achievements were George Stephenson's.

All subsequent biographies have drawn more or less heavily on Smiles's *Life of George Stephenson* and the later, more widely available biography of George and his equally eminent son Robert. Several popular biographies of Stephenson in the mid-20th century have been based on little else, including a charming retelling of Stephenson's exemplary life as a children's story (*Railway Engineer: The Story of George Stephenson*, by Clara Ingram Judson, New York: Charles Scribner's Sons, 1941).

ROLT was the first author to take a more modern historical approach to Stephenson. He disentangles much fiction from fact in Smiles's hagiography and presents a highly readable yet thorough account of both George and Robert – who, he argues, cannot really be separated, as their lives were intertwined and interdependent. Rolt's book is rich in detail and deftly places the subjects in their setting: engineering, economic, and social. Rolt helps the reader understand in modern terms the different activities of father and son. George was a steam engine mechanic who formed a company building the permanent way for railways and later became a consulting civil engineer; Robert was a well-educated mechanical engineer whose firm designed and made locomotives before he became a consulting mechanical engineer. However, Rolt is also the last author of the old era, for he was still firmly attached to the glory and romance of the steam age, when George Stephenson was "the most famous engineer who ever lived".

SKEAT continues the task of dispelling myth by going back to Stephenson's considerable correspondence to gain a better impression of his character and of how he made, and often nearly did not make, his gigantic achievements. Most of all, Skeat brings out what were perhaps Stephenson's greatest attributes – his vision of a national rail network, his supreme confidence in steam locomotion, and his ability to win over his backers in the face of considerable scepticism and ridicule by many eminent contemporary engineers.

The sesquicentenary of the Stockton-Darlington railway in 1975 brought a reprint of Smiles's dual biography of George and Robert Stephenson, introduced by a thoughtful commentary on his approach to biography by Eric de Maré, and a new biography of George by DAVIES. Davies's work was the first to be more objective about George Stephenson's character and achievements and was written from the broader perspective of engineering history rather than the rather adulatory perspective of a railway historian. The result captures the thrill of railway mania rather more dramatically than other books, and Davies is able to focus more carefully on the railway routes that George opened up, their commercial context, and their social and everyday consequences for the population of Britain.

Although BECKETT concentrates mainly on the work of Robert Stephenson in mid-century, his first chapter surveys George's life and, specifically, the engineering innovations in rail track, bridge, and locomotive design that George and his firm used, especially on the Stockton-Darlington and Liverpool-Manchester lines. This study brings out the way George helped others in his firm to develop and exploit the best engineering ideas and innovations in order to achieve the greater aim of an entire railway rather than merely its individual components.

With so many good biographies of George Stephenson, at least one of which has been in print since it first appeared in 1857, there is hardly a need for another. As with biographies of Shakespeare, the more pertinent task at present is to review what others have written, search for errors and omissions, dispel myth, filter out the prejudices and *Zeitgeist* of earlier authors,

place Stephenson's achievements in the broader context of economic and engineering histories, and distinguish what he achieved that was of historical significance in his field of technical and commercial activity. JARVIS has made a good start in all these directions. He begins by tracing four falsehoods through the literature on Stephenson and the extensive literature on railways: that he (1) invented the blast pipe, (2) designed or built the *Rocket*, (3) invented the method of crossing Chat Moss bog on the Liverpool-Manchester line, and (4) he exhibited a "truly noble and manly character". Jarvis correctly points out that Smiles did not orginate 1, 2, or 3; the mistaken attributions mostly arose in popular tributes to George when he died, and from the natural propensity of non-experts to create errors in the process of simplifying complex stories. Stephenson was a folk hero – even George Eliot declared that she had read Smiles's account of the two Stephensons with "real profit and pleasure" – and his story was talked about and repeated in every corner of the land. And, as Jarvis points out, much that was written in the 19th century about railways, and by or about railway men, was done with a commercial purpose – promoting one company's interests or denigrating another's.

BILL ADDIS

See also Engineering entries; Railways

Stigand c.1000–1072
Bishop of Winchester and Archbishop of Canterbury

Barlow, Frank, *The English Church, 1000–1066: A Constitutional History*, London: Longman, and Hamden, Connecticut: Archon, 1963; as *The English Church, 1000–1066: A History of the Later Anglo-Saxon Church*, London and New York: Longman, 1979

Brooks, Nicholas, *The Early History of the Church of Canterbury: Christ Church from 597 to 1066*, Leicester: Leicester University Press, 1984

Loyn, H.R., *The English Church 940–1154*, London and New York: Longman, 2000

Smith, Mary Frances, "Archbishop Stigand and the Eye of the Needle" in *Anglo-Norman Studies*, 16 (1994) 199–219

Stafford, Pauline, *Queen Emma and Queen Edith: Queenship and Women's Power in Eleventh-Century England*, Oxford and Cambridge, Massachusetts: Blackwell, 1997

Stenton, F.M., *Anglo-Saxon England*, Oxford: Clarendon Press, 1943; 2nd edition, 1947; 3rd edition, 1971; reprinted, Oxford and New York: Oxford University Press, 1990

Unlike his two successors as archbishop of Canterbury, Lanfranc and Anselm, Stigand has found no biographer. No book has been written about him, and the only extended treatment of his life and career appears to be the article by SMITH. Stigand is not an appealing figure and has generally received a bad press. The views of 12th-century writers, such as John of Worcester and William of Malmesbury, who disapproved of Stigand's ecclesiastical irregularities, were distinctly critical. His final failure and deposition have tended to obscure the achievements of his career as a churchman and magnate over 50 years.

All writers agree on some basic facts about Stigand. He grew up in a wealthy landowning family in East Anglia. His first ecclesiastical appointment was as royal priest at Ashingdon in 1020. By 1043 he was Bishop of Elmham. In 1047, probably with the support of the queen mother, Emma, he became Bishop of Winchester. In 1052, following the row over the appointment of Robert of Jumièges and his subsequent removal, Stigand also became Archbishop of Canterbury. He did not undertake archiepiscopal functions until he had received the *pallium* from Pope Benedict X in 1058. Unfortunately for Stigand, this pope was deposed the following year and subsequent popes refused to recognize his position as Archbishop of Canterbury. Although Stigand initially resisted the acceptance of Duke William as king in 1066, he wisely submitted and appeared to have gained the confidence of the new king. Then in 1070 he was deposed at a council by papal legates, no doubt with the king's approval. He then lived in Winchester until his death two years later.

Most modern accounts of Stigand have followed the early writers in stressing his ecclesiastical irregularities and his great appetite for acquiring land and power. There has been a tendency to judge him against the standards of the reformed papacy, which had little influence in England before 1070. Clearly Stigand was no saint, perhaps not even an attractive figure, but there is no evidence on which either his character or his spirituality can be assessed. Many historians of the later Anglo-Saxon period have warmed to the ideas of the 10th-century monastic reformers; however, it should be remembered that these were not accepted uniformly throughout the late Anglo-Saxon church. In Stigand's native East Anglia there were no more than two such establishments before 1066; it is not surprising that he did not share the ideals of monastic reformers.

In attempting to evaluate Stigand's life and career we should note that 12th-century writers, critical though they were of Stigand, did not attack his private life. Any hint of scandal would surely have been included in their accounts. Stigand clearly held the confidence of kings as different as Cnut (Canute) and Edward the Confessor and was a close adviser of Queen Emma. Certainly, according to canon law, Stigand should not have taken on the see of Canterbury in Robert's lifetime. However, there was a *de facto* vacancy and it was not entirely irresponsible of him to fill the gap. The fact that Pope Benedict X, who gave Stigand the *pallium*, was deposed the following year can be seen as a misfortune rather than a deliberate flouting of proper church order. Smith rightly draws attention to Stigand's skill as a survivor in the tangled politics of England during the early and middle 11th-century. His achievements were substantial, and James Campbell (*The Anglo-Saxon State*, 2000) has guessed that Stigand may have been running the government for King Edward up to the time of the king's death early in 1066.

In reading about Stigand, a start should be made with BROOKS's judicious discussion of Stigand as Archbishop of Canterbury. Brooks gives references to sources from the late 11th century and the 12th-century sources which mention Stigand. A fuller picture of Stigand can be gained from BARLOW, who discusses his earlier career as well as his time as archbishop. Barlow addresses questions and discusses them fairly, yet his conclusion, "Clearly Stigand was neither a good bishop [nor] a satisfactory metropolitan", does not convincingly sum up Stigand's long, successful ecclesiastical and political career.

In accordance with the scale of his book, LOYN covers Stigand more briefly; however, he does provide an illuminating comparison between Stigand and Ealdred, Archbishop of York, noting that "the similarities in their career patterns are striking". STAFFORD deals with Stigand's relationships with the two queens who are the subject of her book. She writes: "In this case, association with the queen, or a role in the royal chapel close to her, proved the route to the highest 11th century offices, though at one point it was almost his undoing". This is a fair point in the context of Stafford's book, but Stigand's personal and political skills may not have received sufficient recognition here. STENTON'S great work is also worth consulting for this and other aspects of Anglo-Saxon history.

Finally, Smith's article should be read. Her reassessment of Stigand's life and career is well balanced and convincing. She does not deny his shortcomings but does see him as a survivor in difficult times, with notable achievements to his credit. Her analysis of Stigand's landholdings shows that he acquired about a third from monasteries, notably Bury St Edmunds, Ely, and Peterborough, adding them to his already large personal holdings. There can be no doubt that he was a shrewd businessman, perhaps even unscrupulous. On the other hand, it is clear that he maintained an abbey's interests at the highest levels in difficult times. Smith suggests that only after Stigand's did abbeys claim that he had taken land unlawfully, so that they could then have it back. Stigand's protection was well worth having, as is shown by the fact that more than a thousand thegns in East Anglia chose him as their lord. As well as driving hard bargains, Stigand could be generous to monastic houses when he chose. He made gifts of crosses to the abbeys of Bury St Edmunds, Ely, and St Augustine's, Canterbury. At St Augustine's he was remembered with gratitude. William Thorne, writing in the late 14th century, described this cross as "very beautiful and a perpetual reminder of him".

Stigand's career was outwardly highly successful, and any assessment should recognize this. The ecclesiastical irregularities cannot be ignored, but they should not dominate our thinking about a man of great ability in both church and politics. The sources do not allow us any sure insight into his character, motivation, or spirituality. It was only with the coming of Anselm that such insights became possible. Stigand's life and achievements, notable as they were in many ways, remain enigmatic.

RICHARD EMMS

See also Edward "the Confessor"

Stillingfleet, Edward 1635–1699
Clergyman, Bishop of Worcester, and theologian

Carroll, Robert Todd, *The Common-Sense Philosophy of Religion of Bishop Edward Stillingfleet, 1635–1699*, The Hague: Nijhoff, 1975

Chappell, Vere, "Stillingfleet" in *Dictionary of Eighteenth-Century British Philosophers*, edited by John W. Yolton, John Valdimir Price, and John Stephens, Bristol: Thoemmes Press, 1999

Hutton, Sarah, "Science, Philosophy, and Atheism: Edward Stillingfleet's Defence of Religion" in *Scepticism and*

Irreligion in the Seventeenth and Eighteenth Centuries,
edited by Richard H. Popkin and Arjo Vanderjagt, Leiden
and New York: E.J. Brill, 1993

Hutton, William Holden, "Stillingfleet" in *Dictionary of
National Biography*, edited by Leslie Stephen and Sidney
Lee, 66 vols, London: Smith Elder, and New York:
Macmillan, 1885–1901

Popkin, Richard H., "The Philosophy of Bishop Stillingfleet",
Journal of the History of Philosophy, 9 (1971): 303–19

Yolton, John W., *John Locke and the Way of Ideas*, London:
Oxford University Press, 1956

Edward Stillingfleet was born in Cranborne, Dorset, in 1653.
He became a fellow of St John's College, Cambridge, then vicar
of Sutton in Bedfordshire, chaplain to Charles II, dean of
St Paul's, and in 1689 Bishop of Worcester. He was the author
of *Irenicum* (1659, 2nd edition 1662), *Origines sacrae* (1662),
Rational Account of the Grounds of Protestant Religion (1665),
Origines Britannicae (1685), *A Discourse in Vindication of the
Doctrine of the Trinity* (1696), and numerous other works.
Stillingfleet was perhaps the pre-eminent theologian in England
in the late 17th century. HUTTON aptly remarked, "No bishop
of his day was more prominent or more famous than Stillingfleet;
but the reputation which his remarkable industry, wide knowledge, and popular gifts gave him among contemporaries was
not enduring". It is true that after Stillingfleet's death in 1699,
his *Works* were gathered together by Richard Bentley in an
impressive six-volume edition (1707–10). Timothy Goodwin (or
Godwin) was the likely author of a *Life* of Stillingfleet which
was included in the *Works* but also published separately in 1710.
And Stillingfleet's published criticisms of John Locke's "new way
of ideas" aroused much interest in the early 18th century and
found their way into many contemporary books and periodicals. But in the second half of the 18th century and in the 19th
century (with a few exceptions, such as Richard Watson, Bishop
of Llandaff) there appear to have been far fewer extended discussions of Stillingfleet's thought. In the 20th century as well,
Stillingfleet was not the subject of much sustained scholarly
attention. Modern scholars who have focused on him, however,
increasingly have tried to see him in the context of his times.
They have also argued about Stillingfleet's orientation to the
"new science" and about his debate with Locke.

When Stillingfleet is remembered today, it is primarily for
his writings against Locke. YOLTON, for instance, in a well-received book that aimed to locate Locke's thought in the
context of its impact on his English contemporaries, devoted
considerable space to Stillingfleet's position in the debate with
Locke. Yolton rightly exposed inconsistencies in Stillingfleet's
argument, but he thought that Stillingfleet had "discerned
crucial theoretical fissures" in Locke's "doctrine of substance".
On the whole Yolton considered Stillingfleet's argument a
cogent one which Locke clearly took seriously.

In an important essay POPKIN convincingly argued that
Stillingfleet offered historians a glimpse of "what the intellectual world looked like to a sophisticated man at the very beginning of modern empiricism". Stillingfleet "was not a simple
moss-back, a religious reactionary, fighting progressive theories
like Locke's" but was "trying to maintain some basis for religious belief in the face of the intellectual upheavals in the
seventeenth century". Popkin held that Stillingfleet was opposed
to the mechanistic philosophy of René Descartes (which, by
implication, left no room for God) but that he embraced the
"new science" and "experimental philosophy" of Robert Boyle
and Isaac Newton, especially as it was pursued by the Royal
Society (which did leave room for God). According to Popkin,
Stillingfleet was keenly aware of the implications of Locke's
empiricist philosophy and opposed it for that reason: "Without
having to wait until Berkeley and Hume pushed Locke's theory
to its logical conclusion, Stillingfleet perceived that a kind of
scepticism was already involved. . . . Locke's world was reduced
to Hume's at the very outset, without any further intellectual
development being involved".

In an intellectual biography divided into six chapters,
CARROLL provided the most involved modern study of
Stillingfleet's thought. Chapter 1 places Stillingfleet within an
Anglican common-sense tradition that owed a good deal to
William Chillingworth. Chapter 2 outlines Stillingfleet's career
and examines his views on church and state, toleration, and revolution. Chapter 3 outlines Stillingfleet's common-sense defence
of religion and discusses Stillingfleet's anti-catholic writings; his
dialogue *Several Conferences between a Romish Priest, a
Fanatick-Chaplain, and a Divine of the Church of England*; and
his defence of miracles. Chapter 4 deals with Stillingfleet's
defence of the reasonableness of Christianity and provides a
section on his arguments with John Toland and Locke. Chapter
5 illuminates Stillingfleet's defence of natural religion. In
Chapter 6 Carroll argued that the "*via media* which Stillingfleet
wished to follow" was essentially negative. Stillingfleet aimed
"to make Christianity reasonable to the man of common sense
through the appeal, in great part, to the inadequacies of positions or theories which opposed Christianity". Carroll also
provides two short appendices ("An Essay on Biography" and
"Stillingfleet's Influence"), as well as bibliographies of Stillingfleet's works and relevant secondary sources.

Hutton also aimed to resurrect Stillingfleet's philosophical
reputation. It is, she claimed, "unfair" that Stillingfleet "has
gone down in the history of philosophy as the man who did
not understand Locke". Hutton reminds us that Stillingfleet
had something of a reputation for philosophical debate before
he took on Locke in 1696, and that Stillingfleet "understood
Locke's drift very well". Comparing the two versions of
Stillingfleet's *Origines sacrae*, Hutton found that the second version was less concerned with "ancient opinion" and more concerned with incorporating the scientific thought of Boyle, Robert
Hooke, and Newton. "Far from being a closed mind, Stillingfleet
was extraordinarily receptive to new currents of thought".

CHAPPELL's entry – curiously, appearing in a dictionary of
18th-century philosophers – is informative but adds little that
is new. It gives equal space to a concise summary of Stillingfleet's
life and writings and to the debate with Locke. Chappell concluded that Stillingfleet "scored some solid points against
Locke" but that Locke also "had no trouble demonstrating that
Stillingfleet was often careless in reading and reporting on
Locke's text, that he was apt to write and argue loosely, and that
his own positions were sometimes ill thought out or worse". In
fine, the "consensus, in their time as in ours, is that Locke was
the clear winner of the contest between them".

MARK G. SPENCER

See also Anglican Doctrine and Worship; Locke

Stopes, Marie 1880–1958

Pioneer of birth control

Briant, Keith, *Marie Stopes: A Biography*, London: Hogarth Press, 1962

Hall, Ruth, *Marie Stopes: A Biography*, London: André Deutsch, 1977; as *Passionate Crusader: The Life of Marie Stopes*, New York: Harcourt Brace, 1977

Maude, Aylmer, *Marie Stopes: Her Work and Play*, London: Davies, and New York: Putnam, 1933

Rose, June, *Marie Stopes and the Sexual Revolution*, London and Boston: Faber, 1992

Marie Stopes began her career as a botanist but became famous worldwide through her pioneering book *Married Love* (1918), which endorsed sexual fulfilment for women. She opened Britain's first birth control clinic three years after its publication. Throughout her life, the outspoken Stopes was concerned with controlling her public image. Her first two biographers were both intimate friends, and subsequent scholars have devoted much effort to revising their early portrayals. Stopes's biographers have suggested different motives for her work, but most point to her personal life: ironically, she had an unhappy childhood and two unhappy marriages, alienated her only son, and set impossibly idealistic goals.

MAUDE published his study in 1933 at Stopes's request, as a counterbalance to negative publicity after she lost a libel case. According to HALL, Stopes financed and even wrote much of Maude's book and forbade Maude to reveal her age. Maude presents Stopes as an innocent intelligent woman cruelly victimized, first by her impotent first husband and later by the "pertinacious and unfair opposition" of the catholic church, the medical profession, and the press. He endorses her claim that her work on sexual relations was stimulated by her discovery, five years after her first marriage, that the marriage had never been consummated. While he admits that public charges of egomania and neurosis have been made in relation to Stopes's strong-mindedness, he points out that she considered herself a prophet and a revolutionary trying to achieve happiness for others. He himself feels that "her crusade is a necessary one", meriting "respect" and "gratitude". Throughout the book, Maude offers lengthy excerpts from Stopes's own writings and speeches, as well as other people's comments about her, and an appendix provides a list of her published work. While this book offers interesting details, the reader must use it with caution. Although Maude acknowledges that Stopes is a friend, he does not mention that he lived with her and that they maintained a romantic, if platonic, relationship for some years. This and other omissions undermined the book even at the time of its publication.

BRIANT's biography, published 29 years after Maude's, also suffers from partiality. Like Maude, Briant had a romantic relationship with Stopes, and although his book was published after her death, it had been approved first by her family. Nevertheless, Briant claims to have sought "the truth" and not to have omitted anything that "considerably affects" the biography, and his work is somewhat more impartial than Maude's. Like Maude, Briant is a great admirer of Stopes, calling her a "distinguished scientist" and a "Renaissance character" and arguing that her work "revolutionized and enriched the lives of millions". But Briant compares Stopes's life to a Victorian melodrama, arguing that the personal tragedies and personality flaws which drove her to achieve paradoxically prevented her from obtaining happiness herself. He concedes that she exhibited "megalomania and sexual vanity" later in life, and was "morbidly self-conscious" of criticism. Briant's work also suffers from his name-dropping: he runs on for several chapters about Stopes's encounters with well-known writers, regardless of their relevance to an understanding of her life. The book includes a number of photos and long excerpts from Stopes's writings and speeches.

Hall's is the first biography of Stopes by someone outside her circle, and the first based on extensive research, using Stopes's many personal papers. Hall points out numerous deliberate inaccuracies in Maude's and Briant's work. In addition to greater objectivity, Hall provides much clearer explanations of Stopes's personal and legal crises. In contrast to Maude and Briant, Hall shows little personal sympathy with Stopes, noting that the "aura of saintly altruism" Stopes cultivated was "suffused with a large and equally genuine self-esteem", and that she refused to tolerate criticism. Hall does, however, argue that Stopes was a revolutionary figure, that her struggles were greater than those of the women's movement of the 1970s, and that she changed public opinion about sex. Hall does much more than previous biographers to show that birth control was, for Stopes, part of a larger commitment to the class- and race-based eugenics movement. Like Briant, Hall uses the idea of paradox to explain Stopes's personal and professional life, "the ideals of love she believed in and advocated for others perpetually eluding her own grasp". While Hall stresses the impact of *Married Love* and helps readers appreciate the context in which it was published, she also notes that it had little original content. Stopes was not so much an innovative thinker as a courageous and skilful popularizer. And while Stopes's goal of government-sponsored birth control services became reality in Britain, her larger goal of racial improvement through eugenics has become almost unmentionable.

ROSE's study is influenced by psychoanalytic theory; Stopes's actions are repeatedly traced back to childhood events and circumstances: a distant mother, a schoolgirl crush on a teacher, and a lifelong lack of self-esteem. Rose's writing style is very clear, almost simplistic, and her book is less detailed than the others, although it includes more photos. Rose stresses gender relationships in Stopes's life and has found some new archival evidence about their role. Most dramatically, Rose suggests that Stopes's claim to have begun her campaign after discovering that she was still a virgin five years after marriage – the claim which was made in *Married Love* to give her respectability and was accepted by her first three biographers – may have been false. She also notes that Stopes's public commitment to equality in relationships failed on a personal level, since Stopes insisted on dominating every relationship she ever had, often with disastrous results. Rose attributes Stopes's personal unhappiness to an unrealistic ideal of marriage and her professional obstacles to an inability to work with others. Like the other biographers, Rose concludes that Stopes's success in helping other women came at the price of personal unhappiness.

NAN H. DREHER

See also Childbirth, Gynaecology, and Family Planning; Marriage

Strafford, Thomas Wentworth, 1st Earl of 1593–1641

Politician and Lord Deputy of Ireland

Burghclere, Lady, *Strafford*, 2 vols, London: Macmillan, 1931

Kearney, Hugh, *Strafford in Ireland, 1633–1641: A Study in Absolutism*, Manchester: Manchester University Press, 1959, and Cambridge and New York: Cambridge University Press, 1989

Merritt, J.F. (editor), *The Political World of Thomas Wentworth, Earl of Strafford, 1621–1641*, Cambridge and New York: Cambridge University Press, 1996

Pogson, Fiona, "Making and Maintaining Political Alliances during the Personal Rule of Charles I: Wentworth's Associations with Laud and Cottington", *History*, 84/273 (1999): 52–73

Ranger, Terence, "Strafford in Ireland: A Revaluation" in *Crisis in Europe 1560–1660: Essays from Past and Present*, edited by Trevor Aston, London: Routledge and Kegan Paul, and New York: Basic Books, 1965

Salt, S.P., "Sir Thomas Wentworth and the Parliamentary Representation of Yorkshire, 1614–1628", *Northern History*, 16 (1980): 130–68

Wedgwood, C.V., *Strafford, 1593–1641*, London: Jonathan Cape, 1935, and Westport, Connecticut: Greenwood, 1970; as *Thomas Wentworth, First Earl of Strafford, 1593–1641: A Revaluation*, London: Jonathan Cape, 1961; New York: Macmillan, 1962

Zagorin, Perez, "Did Strafford Change Sides?" *English Historical Review*, 101/398 (1986): 149–63

The career of Thomas Wentworth, Earl of Strafford, has drawn widely differing interpretations from historians. His work in local, regional, and central government, in particular his deputyship of Ireland, in the years before the outbreak of rebellion and civil war in Charles I's kingdoms, explains his prominent place in historical work on this period. His surviving correspondence – impressive in size and scope – has been and continues to be a source of inspiration to historians.

The most useful early biography is BURGHCLERE's two-volume work, now dated in style and interpretation, but valuable because of its extensive and revealing quotations from Strafford's papers. Strafford's government of Ireland forms the central concern of the work, and, while the lord deputy is not treated wholly uncritically, his opponents are described in overwhelmingly negative terms. Burghclere's sympathetic portrayal of Strafford as a strong, talented man tragically destroyed by unscrupulous and self-serving enemies draws on the earl's own justificatory accounts.

WEDGWOOD's biography was revised by the author in 1961 after a more scholarly examination of the Strafford Papers, made possible when the archive was opened to professional historians. Wedgwood gives a less admiring account, recognizing Strafford's poor political skills and his habit of practising what he condemned in others, particularly with regard to his personal wealth. Yet this biography remains a largely sympathetic discussion of the earl's career; as in Burghclere's work, those who opposed him are treated unflatteringly. Although rightly

regarded as the standard biography, it is an unbalanced discussion of Strafford's career: nearly a quarter of the length is devoted to the last six months of his life. His relationships with the Yorkshire gentry and his English parliamentary career require greater attention.

KEARNEY's important study of Strafford's Irish government first appeared in 1959 and was reprinted in 1989 with a new introduction. In his knowledgeable account, Kearney takes issue with the traditional view of Strafford as an initiator, arguing that in most aspects of government his policies represented a continuation of earlier work. Strafford's religious policy and financial administration are exceptions, but "the real novelty of Strafford's deputyship lay elsewhere. It was, in the first place, an attempt by a prominent member of the English privy council at direct colonial administration of the whole island". Kearney sees the lord deputy's work as a source of increased tension in Ireland: supported by the king, he *did* much more than his predecessors, and the result was discontent on a large scale. This critical examination of Strafford's work is highly regarded, but Kearney's argument has not gone unchallenged. In 1961, RANGER disputed the claim that Strafford implemented a colonial policy towards Ireland, arguing that this cannot explain the significance of his deputyship in English politics. Ranger finds that regarding the reasons for the failure of Strafford's ambitious programme, the similarities between Ireland and England reveal more than the differences. Convinced that his manipulation of the law was necessary and justified, Strafford took on the powerful New English families, and his willingness to set aside legal and social convention earned him an exceptional degree of hatred. Ranger sees Strafford as an odd man who tried to do the impossible: "he was more than an exceptionally energetic and self-deluded seventeenth-century politician".

Strafford's active role in all but one of the parliaments of the 1620s and his "change of sides" in 1628 explain his attraction for historians attempting to understand political developments in this period. SALT adopts the revisionist argument that parliament was of limited usefulness for an ambitious man such as Strafford, who understood the prime importance of political developments at Whitehall and whose promotion of local concerns in parliament should be seen in many cases as a "tactical device" rather than as a straightforward response to the demands of the electorate. Salt thinks that in assessing Strafford's conduct during the 1620s, it is necesary to appreciate the importance of interacting court and country politics. This idea is dismissed by ZAGORIN, in an attempt to resurrect the traditional hostile view of Strafford's "change of sides". Strafford was allegedly willing to become Buckingham's "creature" – a move that resulted in a breach with former allies, cited by Zagorin as decisive proof that defined that "sides" existed in early Stuart politics.

MERRITT's excellent collection of essays offers insight into past and current debate on Strafford's career and, more widely, on the early Stuart period as a whole. This important book features work originally read at a conference in Sheffield in 1994, timed to coincide with the completion of new microfilming of the Strafford Papers, as well as additional essays including a substantial and very informative historiographical introduction. Some of the contributions focus on particular aspects of Strafford's career in England and Ireland and include a fresh approach to the vexed matter of his "change of sides"; others draw on his correspondence to look more broadly at his political world. POGSON also examines an aspect of this: the nature and function of Strafford's associations with arguably the most important of his allies, made and maintained to protect his Irish administration and his interests in England. Pogson, whose paper is intended to add to the rich tradition of scholarship on this important figure, argues that Strafford's experience reflects the fluid character of court politics during the personal rule of Charles I.

FIONA POGSON

See also Buckingham; Long Parliament; Pym; "Spanish Marriage"

Strathclyde, Gododdin, Rheged, "Kingdoms" of

Duncan, Archibald A.M, *Scotland: The Making of the Kingdom*, Edinburgh: Oliver and Boyd, and New York: Barnes and Noble, 1975-

Koch, John Thomas, *The Gododdin of Aneirin: Text and Context from Dark-Age North Britain*, Cardiff: University of Wales Press, 1997

Macquarrie, Alan, "The Kings of Strathclyde, *c.*400–1018" in *Medieval Scotland: Crown, Lordship, and Community – Essays Presented to G.W.S. Barrow*, edited by Alexander Grant and Keith J. Stringer, Edinburgh: Edinburgh University Press, 1993

Smyth, Alfred P., *Warlords and Holy Men: Scotland* AD *80–1000*, London and Baltimore: Arnold, 1984; Edinburgh: Edinburgh University Press, 1989

Thomas, Charles, *The Early Christian Archaeology of North Britain*, London and New York: Oxford University Press, 1971

The history of the sub-Roman northern British "kingdoms" of Strathclyde, Gododdin, and Rheged is shadowy at best, and more obscure still are such associated regions as Manaw, Berneich, and Nouant. Scraps of well-known evidence do exist and have been important in informing a number of long-standing debates among historians of early medieval Britain and Ireland, and ongoing archaeological and other work continues to add, if slowly, to our understanding. It has traditionally been the lot of historians of Scotland, the modern borders of which include them, to frame the early medieval history of the British territories that lay "between the walls". The problematic nature of the evidence means that with few exceptions the various interpretations advanced by the historians, archaeologists, and other scholars whose works are considered here have tended to be (necessarily) speculative and (consequently) controversial. Indeed, general agreement is elusive on even such basic questions as the names and locations of these "kingdoms", and whether or not some of them ever existed anywhere other than the poetic mind.

DUNCAN's important survey of early medieval Scotland continues to be the ideal place to begin, although Duncan is interested primarily in the Picts and the Dalriada and affords limited space to the British population that lived south of them. In undertaking the monumental task of summarizing and synthesizing the historical, archaeological, and onomastic scholarship of the previous century, Duncan establishes the basis for subsequent debate, enunciates the evidenciary difficulties involved, and, in disjointed sections, sketches in general terms the political, social, and ecclesiastical history of the intermural British "kingdoms" from their emergence from *Romanitas* to their disappearance. A fine supplement to Duncan (where it figures as a source) is THOMAS's detailed archaeological survey, still the best of its kind for sub-Roman north Britain. Here one of the most highly regarded recent archaeologists of the region has collected evidence from excavations spanning more than a century, presenting sensible conclusions with due caution and a sense of historical responsibility that is sometimes lacking in works of this nature. Thomas has built upon this work in a number of more recent syntheses, but this remains the most valuable of his books for students of the intermural British "kingdoms", even if it may prove challenging reading to the introductory reader or non-specialist. It should be noted that Stephen Driscoll's forthcoming work, provisionally entitled *Scotland in the Early Middle Ages*, should supplant Thomas as the most useful survey of the archaeological landscape of the region.

Less useful than Duncan, especially for the introductory reader, but a landmark in the study of the intermural British "kingdoms", is the more recent survey of early medieval Scotland conducted by SMYTH. Assigned a shorter and more manageable epoch by his series editor, Smyth is able to devote an unprecedented amount of space and thought to the northern British. In dealing with the sub-Roman period, he presents thoughtful considerations of the disappearances of the individual "kingdoms" of Rheged and Gododdin but otherwise offers much the same spectrum of evidence found in Duncan. The real value of the work is its sequence of important challenges to positions taken by Duncan and Thomas. Particular areas of divergence include the extent of the romanization process in north Britain (Smyth arguing for Celtic continuity and a limited Roman influence in north Briton), the origin of the various sub-Roman "kingdoms" of north Britain (Duncan speculating that they may represent established British bishoprics, Smyth suggesting that they reflect the Romans' attempts to sunder established British tribes into isolated smaller ones), and the importance of Strathclyde in northern affairs after the disappearance of the other "kingdoms" (Smyth suggesting that they dominated the Picts). While Smyth's work is unquestionably valuable, its contrariness with Duncan is sometimes forced, while the author's Celtic sympathies in dealing with the expansion of the English are unconstrained. The book is also frustratingly under-referenced (in fact, unreferenced; its editor must take responsibility for this), and so must be read as very much supplementary to Duncan's superior and more sober survey.

Smyth's greatest service to the study of the intermural British "kingdoms" has been to inspire a surge of interest among historians and other scholars. In his important essay MACQUARRIE has expanded the frontiers of the discussion by taking issue with Duncan and Smyth in dating the "fall" of Strathclyde – the only sub-Roman "kingdom" that survived into the later historical period – to the early 11th century (rather than the end of the 9th). He also places the "royal" pedigree of Strathclyde, a cavalcade of personal names that may confuse some readers, in an historical context, although in so doing he follows Smyth in the problematic assumption that each figure was a king. More ground-breaking is the extensive introduction to KOCH's controversial *textus restitutus* of the *Gododdin*, in which the author puts the famous poem into various historical contexts, using literary and philological evidence to cast new light upon the history of the intermural British "kingdoms" and to provoke further debate. In particular, Koch rightly stresses the impropriety of the convention of speaking of the sub-Roman "kingdoms" in the mono-ethnic or "ethnically pure" terms of the established surveys, showing that the royal kindreds of north Britain routinely formed "mixed", multi-ethnic war bands in which Anglo-Saxon, British, Pictish, and Irish warriors might be found working together. As befits its *raison d'être*, the introduction contains some difficult sections for readers who are not philologists or are unfamiliar with the textual history of the poem or the language of textual analysis.

Once relegated to peripheral treatment within the "national" historical traditions of England, Scotland, and Wales, the study of the intermural British population in the sub-Roman period has only recently begun to attract the attention it deserves. Koch has finally given us our first viable historical monograph on the subject, and his work, along with that of Macquarrie and the forthcoming work of Driscoll, is symptomatic of a flowering scholarly interest in the early medieval "kingdoms" of north Britain that promises to bear much fruit.

JAMES E. FRASER

See also Picts and Scots

Stuart Britain   from 1603

Ellis, Steven G. and Sarah Barber (editors), *Conquest and Union: Fashioning a British State, 1485–1725*, London and New York: Longman, 1995

Fitzpatrick, Brendan, *Seventeenth-Century Ireland: The War of Religions*, Dublin: Gill and Macmillan, 1988; Totowa, New Jersey: Barnes and Noble Books, 1989

Hirst, Derek, *England in Conflict 1603–1660: Kingdom, Community, Commonwealth*, London: Arnold, and New York: Oxford University Press, 1999

Jenkins, Gervaint H., *The Foundations of Modern Wales: Wales, 1642–1780*, Oxford and New York: Clarendon Press, 1987

Mitchison, Rosalind, *Lordship to Patronage: Scotland 1603–1745*, Edinburgh: Edinburgh University Press, and London and Baltimore: Arnold, 1983

Smith, David L., *A History of the Modern British Isles 1603–1707: The Double Crown*, Oxford and Malden, Massachusetts: Blackwell, 1998

Smith, David L., *The Stuart Parliaments, 1603–1689*, London and New York: Arnold, 1999

Williams, Glanmor, *Recovery, Reorientation, and Reformation: Wales, 1415–1642*, Oxford and New York: Clarendon Press, 1987; as *Renewal and Reformation: Wales 1415–1642*, Oxford and New York: Oxford University Press, 1993

HIRST (1999) is a major reworking of an earlier book, *Authority and Conflict: England 1603–1658* (London: Arnold,

1986), which quickly became a standard introductory text for students of the period. Its successor will probably become equally well used for studies firmly centred upon England. Even so, this book demonstrates that it is impossible to see England as an isolated unit; Hirst sets England within the context of the British Isles at several points, notably the reign of James VI and I and the Civil War period, which is dealt with in several chapters.

SMITH unapologetically uses broader brush strokes in *The Double Crown* (1998); in most of the sections, he examines the internal politics of each of the four nations and the relationships between them. This book opens with the accession of James VI of Scotland to the English and Irish thrones and discusses the political, social, and cultural developments pertinent to the "union" of 1603. The book highlights – at the beginning and again at the end – the complex relationship between England and Wales, which was at once more familiar to the English than either of the other two nations while at the same time still foreign and thus deceptively close. In SMITH (1999) the concentration is once again on England; here, Smith attempts an analysis of the structures of the parliamentary system throughout most of the 17th century.

ELLIS & BARBER (1995) is a very useful collection of essays which combine to throw light upon the complexity of relationships within the British Isles. It includes a series of essays embracing the Stuart period, such as Barber's astute analysis of the Commonwealth in Scotland and Ireland and Toby Barnard's examination of Scotland and Ireland under the later Stuarts. Keith Brown analyses the nature of "British" aristocracy, and Allan Macinnes explores the Gaelic reaction to the Reformation. The book is a highly important attempt not only to examine the development of a "British" state in the early modern period but also to explore the writing of "new British history".

In terms of new work on the Stuart period, Wales is very much the poor relation; studies of Wales consistently run behind studies of the other three nations. This is problematic, given what Smith rightly points out in *The Double Kingdom*: that Wales was close to England while still quite distinct. Two works in the Oxford History of Wales cover the Stuart period, and they are both formidable analyses of research and ideas. WILLIAMS (1987) provides an astute analysis of how Wales was brought under the political sway of England; thus this book helps readers develop an understanding of Smith's approach to the apparently contradictory familiarity and strangeness of Wales. Williams suggests that the Welsh took on aspects of Englishness which served their purpose; in much the same way, MITCHISON (1983) sees the Scots as having adapted to similar opportunities. JENKINS (1987) likewise clearly demonstrates the current level of understanding of Wales's part in the civil wars and how this relates to the context of the mid-17th century. This provides a valuable starting-point for analysing Wales's position in the war, given the assertion made by some historians that the war in Wales can be interpreted as if Wales were a region of England.

FITZPATRICK (1988) has a subtitle – *The War of Religions* – that sets the tone of the book. Fitzpatrick's preoccupation in this book is clearly the political-religious struggle of the protestant colonists from Scotland and England to establish various versions of protestantism in Ireland, and the resistance of the native catholic population to this imposition. The book is heavily weighted towards the early part of the century;

four-fifths of it looks at the period up to and including the "Cromwellian settlement". The chief argument is of course that the nation saw the crucial defeat of catholic politics, with a gradual if steadily enhanced erosion of political power at the beginning of the century radically transformed by the defeat of the Catholic Confederation of Kilkenny during the war. Fitzpatrick's approach does have the effect of creating a context for this defeat.

Mitchison's book is a valuable overview of an important period in Scottish history (1603–1745), which was also important in shaping the future of the British Isles. Even if Scotland's political ambitions in the end became almost subordinate to England's, in 1603 and again in 1637 it was Scotland which set the agenda. Moreover, Mitchison argues, Scotland was able to retain a distinctive quality, which saw Englishness or participation in English ambitions as an adjunct, not a substitute, for Scottishness. The book opens with a discussion of the country James VI left behind when he went to England in 1603 and continues with the effect that his departure and residence south of the border had on government in Scotland. Of course, this effect in turn had an impact during the reign of the absentee monarch, Charles I, when alienation was personal, cultural, and – critically – religious. The Civil War period is integrated into this perceptive discussion, and the Restoration is shown to have minimized Scottish influence in British affairs, as was underlined in 1688, and in 1700 when England decided, without consulting Scotland, that the throne would pass to the heirs of the electress Sophia.

MARTYN BENNETT

Stuart, Charles Edward 1720–1788
Pretender to the British throne and Jacobite leader

Bongie, L.L., *The Love of a Prince: Bonnie Prince Charlie in France, 1744–1748*, Vancouver: University of British Columbia Press, 1986

Daiches, David, *Charles Edward Stuart: The Life and Times of Bonnie Prince Charlie*, London: Thames and Hudson, 1973; as *The Last Stuart: The Life and Times of Bonnie Prince Charlie*, New York: Putnam, 1973

Forster, Margaret, *The Rash Adventurer: The Rise and Fall of Charles Edward Stuart*, London: Secker and Warburg, 1973; New York: Stein and Day, 1974

Maclean, Fitzroy, *Bonnie Prince Charlie*, London: Weidenfeld and Nicolson, 1988; New York: Atheneum, 1989

Woosnam-Savage, Robert C. (editor), *1745: Charles Edward Stuart and the Jacobites*, Edinburgh: HMSO, 1995

Youngson, A.J., *The Prince and the Pretender: A Study in the Writing of History*, London: Croom Helm, 1985; Edinburgh: Mercat Press, 1996

Charles Edward Stuart has emerged as one of the most interesting figures in Scottish history. Most writers agree that his catholicism worked against him in his attempt to restore a Stuart monarchy. Many also agree that some form of Scottish nationalism brought about most of his support in the rising of 1745. However, the impact of Charles's character and personality on the "'45" is still under debate.

DAICHES, one of Charles's more sympathetic biographers, asserts that Charles was very much aware of his ability to focus Scottish nationalism in the Jacobite movement, in spite of the Scots' traditional fear and hatred of catholicism. Earlier Jacobite leaders had been unable to comprehend the full force of Scottish anti-union sentiment or the importance of the split between the Lowlands and Highlands, but Charles, despite his flaws, was able to portray himself and his ancestors as kings who truly understood the Scottish political system, a mixture of conflicting clan and feudal traditions. He had many flaws, including immaturity and shallowness, but these were outweighed by his perceptiveness, his ambition, and his energy. He adeptly created a public image and lived up to it. Unfortunately, he relied almost entirely on other people to form his own self-image. When the public image he had forged was challenged, he reacted very badly – with petulance and rashness in his youth, and with drunkenness and abusive behaviour in his old age.

FORSTER, author of a popular biography of Charles, presents another sympathetic view. She is most interested in understanding Charles's character and how his failure affected him. Charles was groomed to regain his family's throne and convinced from an early age that this was his mission in life. He created an image of himself as a dashing young prince destined for greatness and had little depth of character beyond that image. When he was fulfilling that role, he was happy, energetic, and inspiring. When he faced opposition, he was cranky and restless. Charles's inability to deal with his failure, combined with his recognition of the futility of further attempts to regain his family's throne, explains his decline after 1746.

BONGIE presents the most romantic view of Charles. Bongie's book is not a traditional biography but rather a study of Charles's relationship with his cousin Louise, the Duchesse de Montbazon, who Bongie believes – on the basis of a little-known collection of Louise's letters – was Charles's first and greatest love. Bongie sees in Charles qualities of religious devotion, self-sacrifice, and passion rarely attributed to him by other authors. Charles emerges in this book as an idealistic, dutiful prince, willing to sacrifice himself in order to restore his family to its ancestral throne. He drowns his sorrows in alcoholism and despair after he is betrayed by his people, his family, and his French allies. Bongie concentrates on Charles's personal and social relationships rather than his political or cultural significance.

MACLEAN, in a readable narrative of Charles's life and the events of the '45, also argues that Charles was the only Stuart to recognize the importance of Scotland in an attempted Jacobite restoration. The '45 was, in his estimation, a succession of "unacceptable risks" that should not have paid off, but did. The Jacobites failed by refusing to take one more risk and advance on London from Derby. They had no reason not to do so, after having already risked so much, and the retreat led to frustration and conflicts between Charles and his advisers. Charles's strengths were his charm and his determination; his weaknesses were his stubbornness and his inability to assert his authority over the clan chiefs. His inability to contemplate defeat, let alone accept it, led to his personal decline after the rebellion failed.

The collection of essays edited by WOOSNAM-SAVAGE analyses Charles's symbolic value in Scottish history. It examines both the sources and the significance of Charles's support in Scotland during the '45 and his image as a cultural icon. The bulk of Charles's support came from episcopalians, not catholics. He gained some further support from Scottish presbyterians dissatisfied with Scotland's lack of representation in the union. These essays discount the idea that Charles relied on resurgent Celtic nationalism; the writers argue instead that he relied on thoroughly modern Scots who wanted a say in their country's government. After the failure of the '45 Charles became a folk hero in Scottish culture until the late 20th century, when he began to be seen as a symbol of failure and his rashness and alcoholism were emphasized.

One of the most fascinating studies of Charles Edward Stuart is the dual biography written by YOUNGSON. Interested in illustrating how perception affects history, Youngson wrote two short biographies of Charles, one from a Jacobite and one from a Hanoverian point of view. He was careful to include all the relevant information and to base his arguments on primary sources, but he came up with two very different pictures of Charles, thus illustrating how historians' attitudes and interests affect how they understand and write history. In the Hanoverian version of Charles's life, the '45 is presented in the context of the 18th-century European wars. Charles was a spoiled, self-absorbed, unrealistic adventurer who was used as a tool by France and Spain to gain an advantage over Britain. The '45 achieved its early successes only because the British government was preoccupied with European conflicts. In the Jacobite version, the '45 is presented as part of the history of the Stuarts and Scotland. European conflicts and the influence of the French and Spanish are secondary; in this view, the '45 was primarily a British affair. It was the last in a series of conflicts about religion and royal versus parliamentary power.

There remains much disagreement about whether Charles was primarily a romantic hero or a selfish man who sacrificed his country's interests to his own, but there is a growing consensus about the basic narrative of his life and several aspects of his personality.

KRISTEN ROBINSON

See also George II; Jacobite Rebellions; Jacobitism; Monarchy: Great Britain since 1603; Murray

Stuart Claimants 1689–1746

Lenman, Bruce, *The Jacobite Cause*, Glasgow: Drew/National Trust for Scotland, 1986
McLynn, Frank, *The Jacobites*, London and Boston: Routledge and Kegan Paul, 1985
Petrie, Charles, *The Jacobite Movement*, London: Eyre and Spottiswoode, 1932; as *The Stuart Pretenders: A History of the Jacobite Movement, 1688–1807*, Boston: Houghton Mifflin, 1935
Schwoerer, Lois G. (editor), *The Revolution of 1688–1689: Changing Perspectives*, Cambridge and New York: Cambridge University Press, 1992
Scott-Moncrieff, Lesley (editor), *The '45: To Gather an Image Whole*, Edinburgh: Mercat, 1988
Speck, W.A., *Reluctant Revolutionaries: Englishmen and the Revolution of 1688*, Oxford and New York: Oxford University Press, 1988
Szechi, Daniel, *The Jacobites: Britain and Europe, 1688–1788*, Manchester and New York: Manchester University Press, 1994

The loss of the throne by James II and the failure of attempts to regain it by his son James Francis Edward Stuart (1688–1766) and grandson Charles Edward Stuart (1720–88) have usually been blamed on their own personal weaknesses. The Stuarts are frequently portrayed as rigid and absolutist, a reputation that is somewhat, but not entirely, deserved. Historians approach the Stuarts with varying degrees of sympathy, but most agree that the Stuarts brought their fate upon themselves.

An early scholar of Jacobitism, PETRIE, argues that the Stuarts' failure to regain the British throne was primarily a result of personal flaws and misjudgements. James II was a bad judge of character who misinterpreted his situation following the Glorious Revolution, believing that eventually he would be called back to the throne. His son, James Francis Edward, recognized that this was improbable but failed to see the connection between his catholicism and his exile. According to Petrie, James Francis Edward was just and moderate and would have made a good king, but he lacked the "driving-force" necessary to restore his line to the throne. The third in the line, Charles Edward, finally grasped that in order to be restored to the throne he needed to unite the nation behind the idea of a Stuart monarchy, but he came to that conclusion and converted to protestantism far too late.

McLYNN essentially agrees with Petrie's analysis. He argues that James II and his son were both poor judges of character. James II vastly overestimated the British people's attachment to him in 1688. His catholicism and his gaffes in religious policy thoroughly alienated the British public. James II lacked his brother's realism, subtlety, and political skill and paid the price when he was removed from the throne. James Francis Edward had "great powers of realism and skills as a diplomat", but these were offset by his "lacklustre personal qualities", and he was unable to judge people's skills or affections accurately. McLynn holds that James Francis Edward would have made a "well-above average monarch" but was particularly ill-suited to lead a revolution owing to his lack of charisma. Charles Edward was an "individual of much sterner stuff" than his "attractive but ineffectual" father. McLynn argues that Charles Edward is frequently underestimated by historians. He maintains that in starting a rebellion in 1745, Charles Edward took the only available course. Without an actual rising, France would never have aided the Stuarts, and so Charles Edward tried to force their hand by creating a rising in Scotland.

LENMAN agrees with these assessments of the Stuarts' personalities but is more sympathetic to many of the Stuarts' actions and ideas. James II had an "unappealing public manner" and was "rigid" and "deeply self-centered"; however, he was not as bad a king as his opponents portrayed him to be. His policies were moderate and might eventually have ended the penal laws against catholics had James been a more able ruler. His autocratic tendencies and his public devotion to catholicism, however, disturbed the British public. Lenman argues that James Francis Edward had a "sensible, moderate temperament" and debunks the myth that he was illegitimate (the story of the warming-pan) by pointing out both his striking physical resemblance to James II and the birth of a sister. In his youth, Charles Edward had a "charismatic personality" and a great deal of energy to devote to a Stuart restoration, but he was unable fully to comprehend the problems he faced.

SZECHI asserts that the Stuarts were basically honest; James II and James Francis Edward, in particular, believed in keeping their word once they gave it. James II, however, was inflexible and self-centred. As time passed and the memory of James II's reign became more distant, many Jacobite supporters began to romanticize James Francis Edward and Charles Edward. They became charismatic legendary figures who would restore social harmony to Britain if they regained their family's throne. Charles Edward's logic in beginning the rebellion of '45 was unimpeachable, Szechi believes, but he argues that Charles Edward overestimated his own and Britain's importance by forgetting to consider France's commitments on the Continent.

The collection of essays edited by SCOTT-MONCRIEFF looks at the Stuarts, especially Charles Edward, in a more specifically Scottish context. This collection tries to link Charles Edward to his family's history. The Stuarts are portrayed as a group, a family of "undoubted genius" that consistently failed. The Stuarts were inextricably tied to a sense of Scottish identity and history. They were often presented in a "messianic light" by Gaelic writers, as embodying Scotland. Charles Edward shared many of his family's traits. His own personality had good and bad aspects: he was courageous and personable but also impious and impatient.

In SPECK's study of the Glorious Revolution, James II is the only Stuart claimant considered. Speck gives a detailed analysis of James's character, personality, and effect on Britain. Speck argues that James II, a devoted absolutist, showed "mental instability" in 1688. James could not believe that William would turn against him. Speck argues that James's problem came from the choices he confronted. He had to reject either his religious conviction or his Tory political allies – a choice he was unwilling to make. The essays in the collection edited by SCHWO-ERER present a similar picture of James II, adding that his foreign policy suffered from his preoccupation with domestic problems, especially his attempts to extend toleration of catholics. James II's policies alienated many of his natural supporters among the Tories. In the late 17th century, a British monarch's ability to rule depended on his ability to use charisma and personality to manipulate his subjects' attitudes. James II lacked that ability, and this, combined with his dedication to autocratic government and his catholicism, brought about his downfall.

The Stuarts have received little sympathy from historians, although many more recent authors have pointed out that they were not as bad as their reputation. While historians agree that the Stuarts had many flaws, many writers are now arguing that their flaws need not have been fatal.

KRISTEN ROBINSON

See also Jacobite Rebellions; Jacobitism; Monarchy: Great Britain since 1603

Suez Canal Purchase 1875

Avram, Benno, *The Evolution of the Suez Canal Status from 1869 up to 1956: A Historico-Juridical Study*, Geneva: Droz, 1958

Buckle, George Earle, *The Life of Benjamin Disraeli, Earl of Beaconsfield*, vol. 5, *1868–1876*, London: John Murray, and New York: Macmillan, 1920; revised edition, 2 vols, 1929

Cain, P.J. and A.G. Hopkins, *British Imperialism: Innovation and Expansion, 1688–1914*, London and New York: Longman, 1993

Eldridge, C.C., *Disraeli and the Rise of a New Imperialism*, Cardiff: University of Wales Press, 1996

Farnie, D.A., *East and West of Suez: The Suez Canal in History 1854–1956*, Oxford: Clarendon Press, 1969

Hallberg, Charles W., *The Suez Canal: Its History and Diplomatic Importance*, New York: Columbia University Press, and London: King, 1931

Robinson, Ronald and John Gallagher, *Africa and the Victorians: The Official Mind of Imperialism*, London: Macmillan, and New York: St Martin's Press, 1961; 2nd edition, 1981

Wilson, Arnold T., *The Suez Canal: Its Past, Present, and Future*, London: Oxford University Press, 1933; 2nd edition, London and New York: Oxford University Press, 1939

In November 1875, Disraeli purchased for the British government the 44 per cent stake of the khedive of Egypt (who was bankrupt) in the Suez Canal Company. The purchase delighted Queen Victoria and excited the nation; but this acquisition of 176,602 shares, with a loan of £4 million from the Rothschilds, also caused an ongoing debate among historians. Together with the subsequent British occupation of Egypt in 1882, it has formed a central part of recent imperial historiography.

The first detailed scholarly investigation of the purchase is in BUCKLE's standard biography of Disraeli, where he is presented as an ardent imperialist and the acquisition of a stake in the canal as the consummation of imperialist policy. Buckle traces Disraeli's growing concern, as early as April 1874, over the danger that British shipping might be prevented from using the canal, and charts in meticulous detail the complex negotiations for the purchase the following year. Disraeli declared himself a champion of imperial expansion, and Buckle is somewhat over-inclined to take him at his word; still, this account remains an invaluable source. It also conveys something of the reckless side of Disraeli's character. Writing to a confidante shortly before the news broke, he said, "We have had all the gamblers, capitalists, financiers of the world, . . . bands of plunderers, arrayed against us . . . and have baffled them all. . . . I have rarely been thro' such a week".

HALLBERG's substantial study, originally a doctoral thesis, is one of the first to make extensive use of the British and French diplomatic papers then available. It includes a long discussion of the background of Anglo-French rivalry in Egypt and early plans for the canal, and considerable detail on the purchase of the shares and the events leading to the British occupation. Hallberg tends towards a sceptical view of Britain's actions; he argues, "The repeated assertions of de Lesseps [the French construction engineer] that the canal was an international undertaking designed to serve the shipping of all nations without discrimination, did not sound convincing in English ears".

The study by WILSON is valuable primarily for the wealth of statistical material presented but is still useful to historians of the Suez Canal. Unlike Hallberg, Wilson adopts a rather pro-British tone and talks of the "arrogance of the [French] Suez Canal officials", against which "Monsieur de Lesseps was . . . in a state of half-veiled rebellion". Wilson suggests that de Lesseps tried, without success, to persuade Gladstone's administration in Britain to assume control over the canal, a year before Disraeli became prime minister.

Another revised doctoral thesis, by AVRAM, surveys the complex legal history of the canal, from the vantage point of the abortive Franco-British Suez action of 1956. Avram argues that Disraeli "spared no efforts to acquire Egypt's shares, and even went to the length of exceeding his constitutional powers". Avram also implies that Britain's control over the canal was probably less secure in international law than was supposed at the time, particularly if the Ottoman sultanate, Egypt's suzerain, had sided with Britain's enemies in time of war.

All previous studies of the canal's history have been eclipsed by the authoritative and massively documented book by FARNIE, which includes an exhaustive bibliography. This will undoubtedly remain the standard account for a long time. Farnie takes a stimulating approach to the decision to buy the shares. He argues that during 1875 "the reputation of Disraeli's Ministry was declining steadily . . . in an accumulation of embarrassments" and needed to restore its fortunes; a "means of deliverance was opportunely provided by the re-emergence of the Eastern Question" and the threat that a French syndicate was planning to buy the khedive's shares. Farnie also demonstrates that public opinion swung rapidly from surprise to elation, at what was presented as a master-stroke of diplomacy, "an emphatic assertion of British power to the states of the Continent". Jingoistic celebrations followed; they included illustrated lectures, dioramas, and the first performance in London of Verdi's *Aida* – all arguably helping to prepare public opinion for the British occupation of Egypt within seven years. Farnie also points out that the acquisition of the shares stimulated fresh commercial activity via the canal route into the Indian Ocean, by merchants like William Mackinnon, and so was retrospectively justified.

In their classic study of Victorian imperialism, ROBINSON & GALLAGHER place considerable emphasis on the British occupation of Egypt in 1882, which soured Anglo-French relations and triggered the most hectic phase of African partition. En route, they argue that Disraeli's purchase was not a bid for supremacy in Egypt; it was merely intended to forestall the establishment of an exclusive interest against Britain. Disraeli, and Salisbury at the Foreign Office, desired no more than to continue the Palmerstonian mode of informal influence, and a reasonably robust Anglo-French entente. Notably, Robinson & Gallagher also downplay the role of economic factors in general in determining British policy towards Egypt between 1875 and 1882.

In contrast, a recent major revisionist work by CAIN & HOPKINS places great weight on economic considerations in moulding British policy towards Egypt and the canal, under both Disraeli and Gladstone. In particular, these authors argue

that the purchase of shares in 1875 greatly increased Britain's financial stake in Egypt and thus made Britain the principal creditor when the khedive once again subsided into bankruptcy in 1876, in turn setting in train the events leading to rising Egyptian nationalism, outsiders' perception of the regime as unstable, and the eventual British intervention.

ELDRIDGE, in his recent survey of Disraeli's imperialist credentials, includes an accessible and stimulating perspective on the purchase of the shares. In a succinct critique of scholars like Buckle, Eldridge shows that "the more Disraeli's record in the 1874–80 ministry was probed, the quicker his reputation as an imperialist seemed to evaporate". The shares were obtained, according to recent scholarship, more as "one of those sudden diplomatic and personal coups in which Disraeli revelled". Eldridge argues that Disraeli bought the shares not as part of some grand scheme to advance the British presence in Egypt but merely, as Robinson & Gallagher suggest, to prevent France from "stealing a march" in the region. The dramatic presentation of the coup to Queen Victoria – "You have it, Madam" – may indeed hold more of a clue to Disraeli's immediate motives than any coldly considered analysis of his ideas about a forward imperial policy.

CHRISTOPHER SCHMITZ

See also Disraeli; "Eastern Question": The Dardanelles; Egypt, British Intervention in; Rothschild

Suez Crisis 1956

Eden, Anthony, *Full Circle: The Memoirs of the Rt Hon. Sir Anthony Eden*, London: Cassell, and Boston: Houghton Mifflin, 1960

Kyle, Keith, *Suez*, London: Weidenfeld and Nicolson, 1990; New York: St Martin's Press, 1991

Lloyd, Selwyn, *Suez 1956: A Personal Account*, London: Jonathan Cape, and New York: Mayflower Books, 1978

Love, Kennett, *Suez: The Twice-Fought War: A History*, New York: McGraw Hill, 1969; London: Longman, 1970

Lucas, W. Scott, *Divided We Stand: Britain, the US, and the Suez Crisis*, London: Hodder and Stoughton, 1991

Nutting, Anthony, *No End of a Lesson: The Story of Suez*, London: Constable, and New York: Potter, 1967

Ovendale, Ritchie, *Britain, the United States, and the Transfer of Power in the Middle East, 1945–1962*, London: Leicester University Press, 1996

Thomas, Hugh, *The Suez Affair*, London: Weidenfeld and Nicolson, 1967

The origins of the Suez crisis of 1956 lie partly in a mythology, current in the West in the 1950s, of Neville Chamberlain's policy for the appeasement of Europe and in the perhaps dangerous and inaccurate idea that history can repeat itself – that historical analogy should determine political policy. Anthony EDEN records in his memoirs that as prime minister, he viewed the events of the 1950s through the spectacles of the 1930s. Not only did Gamal Abdul Nasser's nationalization of the Suez Canal threaten Britain's national economy, which depended on supplies of oil from the Middle East, but Eden saw the Egyptian leader as another Mussolini. Eden felt that this time, the "dictator" should not be appeased but should be stopped before he went any further. President Dwight Eisenhower of the United States wanted to play for time and instructed his secretary of state, John Foster Dulles, accordingly: he could hardly run for re-election as a proponent of peace if Washington's two main allies were fighting what Americans might perceive as an old-style colonial war. London and Washington concluded that Moscow had opened up another front in the cold war by agreeing to supply the Egyptians with arms. Where they differed was in their diagnosis of how to deal with the Arabs over this.

The early debate on the Suez crisis focused on Britain's "collusion" with the French and Israelis to attack Egypt. Eden, in his memoirs, showed that even before the outbreak of the Suez crisis Britain was initiating a foreign and defence policy in line with its straitened financial circumstances, and with regard to the collusion maintained the silence agreed on by the parties concerned. By the mid-1960s conversations and unattributed sources had resulted in partial accounts of the collusion: one of the fullest, based on interviews with members of Eden's government, was by THOMAS. In 1967 NUTTING – who had resigned as minister of state for foreign affairs in October 1956 over the Suez landings – published his account; he not only gave details of the collusion but claimed that there was a breach in the relationship with the United States and a bitter personal battle between Eden and Dulles. LLOYD, who was foreign secretary at the time, published an account in 1978, just before his death; it was based on the cabinet material. Lloyd exposed inaccuracies in Nutting's book and argued that it was natural for nations facing a common threat to make plans in concert, and that it would be absurd for them to do this in public and expose their plans to the enemy. These accounts were supplemented by others: by Christian Pineau on the French side and Moshe Dayan on the Israeli side.

In 1970 a classic study by LOVE, an American journalist, appeared in Britain. This book encouraged debate in a wider context: it pointed to joint intelligence operations by the American Central Intelligence Agency and MI6, British external intelligence, to dispose of Nasser; it also offered a sympathetic diagnosis of Nasser and Egypt's relations with Britain, and Cairo's attempts to secure aid from in the West rather than from the Soviet Union to build the Aswan Dam. The British documents on the Suez affair became available before the American documents and provided material for two academic studies which appeared in the early 1990s, those by KYLE and LUCAS. Kyle, relying mainly on British sources, concludes that "Eden made a series of misjudgements fatal for a man in his exposed situation" (p. 557). Lucas, who also made extensive use of American sources, considers the evolution of British and American politics in the context of the politics of the Middle East and efforts to secure an Arab-Israeli peace settlement.

OVENDALE suggests that the Suez crisis was not a breach in the special relationship between Britain and the United States. For one thing, Eisenhower, when he assumed office, had demoted Britain to one among a number of allies. For another, Ovendale shows that Eden offered Dulles details of Britain's military plans and emphasizes the extent to which these two statesmen cooperated. The American sources reveal that Harold Macmillan, the chancellor of the exchequer, concealed the significance of the American presidential election from the British cabinet, and Ovendale speculates as to whether Macmillan saw an opportunity to become prime minister. Ovendale also argues that Eisenhower was not disturbed by the British operation until the results of the congressional election came through and that he then took his revenge on Britain by blocking its drawing rights on the International Monetary Fund, but that Macmillan's allegations of heavy selling of sterling in New York were unfounded and that the figures Macmillan gave the cabinet about the drop in the reserves were also untrue – information which led to the withdrawal of British forces from the Canal Zone. Ovendale considers the Suez crisis in the context of the transfer of power in the Middle East and of the Arab-Israeli wars and suggests that myths have obscured reality. Suez was not the "lion's last roar". Britain was already retreating from empire. Suez did not force Britain to turn to Europe: Macmillan decided on that only after South Africa's exclusion from the Commonwealth in 1961. Suez led to the revival of the "special relationship" with the United States on the old terms. Eisenhower's policy during the Suez crisis of 1956 meant, as Henry Kissinger later observed, that the United States would have to take over Britain's burdens in the Middle East.

RITCHIE OVENDALE

See also Colonial Wars and Counter-Insurgency; Decolonization; Eden; Macmillan; Palestine, Israel, and the Middle East

Suffragettes

see **Fawcett; Pankhursts; Women's Suffrage Movement**

Sugar Trade   17th–19th centuries

Batie, Robert Carlyle, "Why Sugar? Economic Cycles and the Changing of Staples on the English and French Antilles, 1624–1654", *Journal of Caribbean History*, 8/1 (1976): 1–41

Davies, K.G., "The Origins of the Commission System in the West India Trade", *Transactions of the Royal Historical Society*, 5th series, 2/1 (1952): 89–107

Deerr, Noël, *The History of Sugar*, 2 vols, London: Chapman and Hall, 1949–50

Drescher, Seymour, *Econocide: British Slavery in the Era of Abolition*, Pittsburgh, Pennsylvania: University of Pittsburgh Press, 1977

Dunn, Richard S., *Sugar and Slaves: The Rise of the Planter Class in the English West Indies, 1624–1713*, Chapel Hill: University of North Carolina Press, and London: Jonathan Cape, 1972

Edel, Matthew, "The Brazilian Sugar Cycle of the Seventeenth Century and the Rise of West Indian Competition", *Caribbean Studies*, 9/1 (1969): 24–44

McCusker, John J., *Rum and the American Revolution: The Rum Trade and the Balance of Payments of the Thirteen Continental Colonies*, New York: Garland, 1989

McCusker, John J., "Growth, Stagnation, or Decline? The Economy of the British West Indies, 1763–1790" in *The Economy of Early America: The Revolutionary Period, 1763–1789*, edited by Ronald Hoffman, John J. McCusker, and Russell R. Menard, Charlottesville, Virginia: University Press of Virginia for the United States Capitol Historical Society, 1988

Mintz, Sidney W., *Sweetness and Power: The Place of Sugar in Modern History*, New York: Viking, 1985; New York and London: Penguin, 1986

Pares, Richard, "The London Sugar Market, 1740–1769", *Economic History Review*, series 2, 9/2 (1956): 254–70

Pares, Richard, *A West-India Fortune*, London and New York: Longmans Green, 1950

Ragatz, Lowell J., *The Fall of the Planter Class in the British Caribbean, 1763–1833: A Study in Social and Economic History*, New York and London: The Century, 1928; reprinted, New York: Octagon Books, 1963

Richardson, David, "The Slave Trade, Sugar, and British Economic Growth, 1748–1776", *Journal of Interdisciplinary History*, 17/4 (1987): 139ff

Sheridan, Richard B., *Sugar and Slavery: An Economic History of the British West Indies, 1623–1775*, Barbados: Caribbean University Press, and Baltimore: Johns Hopkins University Press, 1974

Ward, J.R., "The Profitability of Sugar Planting in the British West Indies, 1650–1834", *Economic History Review*, 2nd series, 31/2 (1978): 197–213

Ward, J.R., *British West Indian Slavery, 1750–1834: The Process of Amelioration*, Oxford: Clarendon Press, and New York: Oxford University Press, 1988

Williams, Eric, *Capitalism and Slavery*, London: André Deutsch, and Chapel Hill, University of North Carolina Press, 1944

Sugar cane was originally domesticated in New Guinea around 8000 BC, but the first documented experiments in sugar manufacture date only from the 4th century after Christ. The rise of mass production and trade in sugar occurred later still, when Genoese merchants pioneered the cultivation of cane in southern Portugal, north Africa, and the Atlantic islands of Madeira and the Canaries from the mid-15th century on. DEERR's encyclopaedic work is a mine of information on the early history of sugar, and the author's attention to technical detail reflects his background as a sugar engineer. Deerr provides an overview of the migration of comparative advantage in sugar cultivation to the tropical islands of Fernando Pó and São Tomé during the late 15th century, to Brazil during the mid-16th century, and to the Caribbean in the mid-17th century.

The introduction of sugar into the West Indies owed much to the outcome of the war between the Dutch and the Portuguese, which culminated in the flight of Dutch capital and the New Christian artisans from the Pernambuco region of Brazil in 1645. EDEL argues that market forces no less than political events propelled the relocation of sugar to a region where the large-scale plantation had greater potential to develop. His hypothesis receives support from BATIE, who analyses the course of crop prices on the Amsterdam exchange to explain why the early settlers in Barbados abandoned tobacco, indigo, and cotton for sugar, thereby replacing a diverse agricultural economy of smallholders with a virtual crop monoculture. Noting that sugar is capital-intensive, Batie also stresses the importance of military security and stable property rights in explaining why Barbados took an early lead in sugar cultivation over other West Indian colonies. As its title suggests, DUNN's work examines the social consequences of the sugar revolution and illustrates how the abandonment of the minor staples was accompanied by a dramatic increase in inequality, the exodus of large numbers of white settlers, and the introduction of black chattel slavery. Inequality, Dunn suggests, resulted from both a renewed wave of investment, as new planters arrived from England, and the rise of large landowners from among the ranks of the original colonists as estates were subdivided or consolidated during the first sugar boom.

Sugar planting remained profitable in the British West Indies throughout the period of slavery, as WARD's meticulous accounts (1978, 1988) indicate. The level of profitability, however, varied in different periods and between established and developing colonial regions. In broad terms sugar enjoyed a "golden age" in the Caribbean for several decades after 1640, and profits peaked again in a "silver age" from the mid-18th century until the outbreak of the American Revolution. The activities of merchants and planters during these periods have been admirably described in a number of studies. DAVIES analyses the displacement of the colonial merchants (including the decline of the Jewish communities of Barbados and Jamaica) by the metropolitan merchants of London and the outports to whom planters increasingly consigned their sugars on a commission basis. One of the principal factors underlying this system was the role of the British merchant as the provider of both working capital and investment capital. SHERIDAN's book is the leading study of all commercial aspects of the sugar trade, though critics of its title have noted that Sheridan has comparatively little to say on the relationship between sugar and slavery. His book builds on foundations laid by PARES, whose account of the London sugar market remains unrivalled and whose study of the Pinney family of Bristol and Nevis is both a beautifully written exercise in biography and a vital source for the understanding of the legal instruments that bound debtors and creditors. In discussing sugar, it is impossible to ignore its by-product, rum. The monumental work by McCUSKER (1989) integrates the two commodities. McCusker's thesis remains the most accurate source of data for sugar production, and he demonstrates that the political consequences of the Sugar Act of 1764 have led historians to exaggerate the effect of credits earned by North American merchants in the rum trade to offset deficits in the British trade on the continental colonies' balance of payments.

The fluctuating fortunes of sugar after American independence have attracted a great deal of scholarship, with most attention being devoted to the consequences of the abolition of the slave trade in 1807 and the motivations behind the emancipation of all slaves in British colonies between 1834 and 1838. In his pioneering account RAGATZ argued that the plantations were teetering on the brink of bankruptcy after the Seven Years' War (1756–63) and were no longer viable enterprises by the beginning of the 19th century. It should be noted that in his book (originally published in 1928) Ragatz makes several regrettable allusions to the alleged racial inferiority of black slaves. Ragatz's interpretation strongly influenced WILLIAMS, whose *Capitalism and Slavery* is dedicated to him. Williams develops the thesis that the campaign for emancipation succeeded because British mercantile interests no longer regarded the colonies as profitable possessions, while some of the planters began to look for a way of extricating themselves from the slave system. Ragatz and Williams's interpretation has been the target of much criticism. In establishing his case Ragatz relied heavily on the British colonial archives which record the often exaggerated complaints of planters, expressed after increases in duties or the admission of new colonies to the system of imperial preference. MCCUSKER (1988), reworking data on customs and prices, takes issue with Ragatz's pessimistic account of the years 1763 to 1790. DRESCHER views the abolition of the slave trade as driven by political and humanitarian considerations; he argues that it was enacted at a time when the output and market share of the British sugar islands were increasing. Another impressive work of revisionism spanning the last years of slavery is Ward's analysis (1988) of the economic consequences of the abolition of the slave trade and the introduction of amelioration legislation. Ward acknowledges the increased costs of cultivating sugar that resulted from these measures during a period when, as a trend, the price of sugar fell, notwithstanding years of high prices following the revolution on the French colony of St Domingue (today's Dominica) and in the wake of the Napoleonic wars. On the basis of surviving plantation accounts, Ward demonstrates that sugar producers made a positive response to these challenges and succeeded in improving their productivity, but he argues that it took a supreme effort to remain competitive in the face of such daunting odds.

Much of the literature on the sugar trade focuses on the supply side and details the activities of plantation owners and the sugar merchants. Recent contributions have redressed the balance somewhat by treating sugar consumption in greater depth. RICHARDSON writes in the context of Williams's thesis that the profits of sugar and slavery boosted Britain's economic growth; but his data suggest that the fortunes of sugar were tied to the dynamism of the British economy, since it was the home market which consumed the bulk of sugar exported from the British West Indies during the 18th century. An interesting alternative approach is taken by MINTZ, who introduces an anthropological perspective to the study of humans' sweet tooth – a craving that manifests itself from infancy on – and the mechanisms established for satisfying it. Mintz's primary concern, however, is to show how the sugar trade contributed to the rise of capitalism, and for this reason his book is vulnerable to the charge of failing to define or justify its underlying conceptual apparatus with sufficient rigour.

S.D. SMITH

See also Americas, Trade with

Sussex, Thomas Radcliffe, 3rd Earl of c.1525–1583
Soldier, courtier, and statesman

Cokayne, G.E., *The Complete Peerage of England, Scotland, Ireland, Great Britain, and the United Kingdom, Extant, Extinct, or Dormant*, London: Bell, 1887–98; revised and enlarged, London: St Catherine Press, 1910–59; reprinted, New York: St Martin's Press, 1984

Doran, Susan, "The Finances of an Elizabethan Nobleman and Royal Servant: A Case Study of Thomas Radcliffe, 3rd Earl of Sussex", *Historical Research*, 61/146 (1988): 286–300

MacCaffrey, Wallace T., *The Shaping of the Elizabethan Regime*, Princeton, New Jersey: Princeton University Press, 1968; London: Jonathan Cape, 1969

Moody, T.W., F.X. Martin, and F.J. Byrne, *A New History of Ireland*, vol. 3, *Early Modern Ireland, 1534–1691*, Oxford: Clarendon Press, and New York: Oxford University Press, 1976

Read, Conyers, *Mr Secretary Cecil and Queen Elizabeth*, London: Jonathan Cape, and New York: Knopf, 1955

Read, Conyers, *Lord Burghley and Queen Elizabeth*, London: Jonathan Cape, and New York: Knopf, 1960

Stone, Lawrence, *The Crisis of the Aristocracy, 1558–1641*, Oxford: Clarendon Press, 1965; abridged edition, London and New York: Oxford University Press, 1967

Virgoe, Roger, "Sussex" in *The House of Commons, Sussex 1509–1558*, edited by S.T. Bindoff, London: Secker and Warburg for History of Parliament Trust, 1982

Williams, Penry, *The Later Tudors: England 1547–1603*, Oxford: Clarendon Press, and New York: Oxford University Press, 1995

Thomas Radcliffe, Earl of Sussex, was among the most prominent members of the ancient nobility in the reigns of Mary I and Elizabeth I. A soldier, who served Henry VIII both in France and Scotland, and a courtier, he was first elected and then summoned to parliament in 1553 as Lord Fitzwalter even before his father's death in 1557. He was appointed a royal carver by Mary I and a gentleman of Philip II's privy chamber; he was an educated man who spoke Spanish. There followed an exceptional succession of high offices as deputy and lieutenant of Ireland (1556–65), president of the Council of the North (1568–72, covering the rising of the northern earls), privy councillor (1570), and lord chamberlain (1572–83). He was an independent voice at court and in council for the first 25 years of Elizabeth's reign. Although a member of the Howard faction and opposed to Robert Dudley, Earl of Leicester, in the 1560s, he was completely loyal and a key ally of William Cecil Lord Burghley.

The vital facts of Sussex's life are set out by COKAYNE. His early life and career are comprehensively examined by VIRGOE. Virgoe concludes that for the greater part of his education Sussex was not at Cambridge University but in the household of Stephen Gardiner, Bishop of Winchester. Sussex's first significant office, as captain of Portsmouth in 1549–51, was attributable to his father-in-law Thomas Wriothesley, Earl of Southampton. Following the fall of the Howards in 1546 and his father's consequent emergence as the leading East Anglian nobleman, Sussex was elected a member of parliament for Norfolk in 1553, perhaps to counterbalance Northumberland's son Robert. Sussex and his father supported Mary Tudor rather than Jane Grey and were quickly and substantially rewarded with promotions, pensions, and offices. Virgoe outlines Sussex's movements up to 1558 and, more briefly, his dealings with parliament up to his death.

MOODY, MARTIN, & BYRNE survey Sussex's rule in Ireland. Evidently he felt little sympathy towards the native population: "I have often wished [them] to be sunk into the sea". His policy was aggressive. He attacked Shane O'Neill in Ulster and other Irish chieftains in Shannon, planted English settlers in Leix and Offaly, and established a string of forts north and west of the Pale financed by the expropriation of Irish landowners. All this produced no lasting results; it merely increased commitments and expenses. Sussex had "exhausted the resources of violence" by 1561 when Queen Elizabeth I tried conciliation. She received O'Neill in England, thus undermining Sussex without restraining O'Neill; Sussex returned to England in 1564, but his policy continued. WILLIAMS considers that Sussex's policy ignored realities and united all parts of society in opposition. Moreover, he concludes, it was Sussex's government which "then began the process of repression and colonisation that brought to birth a hatred which has lasted four hundred years".

READ provides the fullest narrative of Elizabethan politics and Sussex's role. Sussex returned from Ireland before the end of his term as lieutenant and immediately became involved in court politics. As a member of the pre-Tudor nobility, Sussex was contemptuous of Robert Dudley, whom he dubbed the gypsy and whom he regarded as an unprincipled parvenu, the son of a traitor and grandson of a merchant. For his own part, Sussex, as the son of a Howard, aligned himself naturally with the 4th duke of Norfolk. He knew of Norfolk's desire to marry Mary Queen of Scots but remained loyal. "It was characteristic of Sussex that he stood by Norfolk to the last; characteristic of him also that, notwithstanding his affection, he never swerved in his devotion to the Queen's service". He even participated in Norfolk's trial. Sussex's close relations with Norfolk put him in a difficult position in the north, where a distrustful government forced him to act against his better judgement and precipitate the uprising, and also doubted his commitment and loyalty. Sussex sought first to prevent, then to oppose, and ultimately to defeat the movement. Read recounts how effective Sussex's measures were, how he was exonerated, and how his excessive aggression against the Scots prompted his recall. Thereafter he was a leading courtier and councillor, a nobleman of rectitude and fidelity, whose steadfast support was of great value to Burghley and whose death was a considerable blow to him.

MacCAFFREY adds little information to Read's account but provides a clearer interpretation. He demonstrates how Sussex supported Elizabeth's marriage to Archduke Charles in the 1560s and how he alone did not oppose the Alençon-Anjou marriage late in the 1570s. He identifies Sussex as a conservative in the 1560s; Sussex's services in 1569–70 were therefore doubly valuable. "Sussex's unshaken loyalty to the Crown and his vigorous prosecution of war against the rebels were of untold value to the government", when any wavering would have been disastrous. It was a personal interview with the queen that exonerated him and led directly to his final years on the privy council and at court. Sussex, MacCaffrey considers, was an old-fashioned nobleman who saw himself as a servant of the crown: his duty was to offer disinterested advice and to implement decisions loyally.

DORAN (1988) has published only one aspect of her doctoral thesis (London, 1977), which certainly gives the fullest and most up-to-date account of Sussex's career. STONE had cited Sussex as an example of the old nobility reduced to penury during this inflationary era, the "crisis of the aristocracy". Doran's article examines the evidence for this belief, which is largely attributable to Sussex's own utterances, and demonstrates them to be special pleading and to have been more than compensated for by royal favours. Sussex undoubtedly extended his estates, raised his rents, and increased his income. He lived free of financial difficulties – indeed, lavishly – although after his death his accumulated obligations to the crown threatened to overwhelm his heir. "It is therefore unjustified to use, as Stone does, the case of Sussex to support an aristocracy in economic decline".

MICHAEL HICKS

See also Elizabeth I; Ireland: The Pale; Ireland: Tudor Plantations; Ireland: Reformation

T

Talbot, Richard, 1st Earl of Tyrconnel 1630–1691

Soldier, Lord-Lieutenant of Ireland, later Jacobite leader

Berresford-Ellis, Peter, *The Boyne Water: The Battle of the Boyne, 1690*, London: Hamish Hamilton, 1976

Corish, Patrick J., *The Catholic Community in the Seventeenth and Eighteenth Centuries*, Dublin: Helicon, 1981

Doherty, Richard, *The Williamite War in Ireland, 1688–1691*, Dublin: Four Courts Press, 1998

Foster, R.F., *Modern Ireland, 1600–1972*, London: Allen Lane, 1988; New York: Penguin, 1989

McGuire, James, "Richard Talbot, Earl of Tyrconnel (1630–1691), and the Catholic Counter-Revolution" in *Worsted in the Game: Losers in Irish History*, edited by Ciaran Brady, Dublin: Lilliput Press / Radio Telefís Éireann, 1989

Shepherd, Robert, *Ireland's Fate: The Boyne and After*, London: Aurum Press, 1990

Simms, John, "The Restoration 1660–1685" in *A New History of Ireland*, vol. 3, *Early Modern Ireland, 1534–1691*, edited by T.W. Moody, F.X. Martin, and F.J. Byrne, Oxford: Clarendon Press, and New York: Oxford University Press, 1976

The 17th century in Ireland was marked, as CORISH shows, by a collapse of the power and influence of the catholic gentry, particularly among the "old English" descendants of pre-Reformation settlers. This group not only saw their landholdings diminished as a consequence of the Cromwellian confiscations but also lost control of the Irish parliament to the protestant "new English"; furthermore, they were faced with increasingly harsh and restrictive recusancy laws. Although sharing a religious faith with the Gaelic Irish, they considered themselves English. The two communities were antagonistic and failed to cooperate against the new immigrants.

As McGUIRE explains, Richard Talbot came from an "old English" family in Kildare; his father was a lawyer and landowner who had represented the county in the parliament of 1613. Richard was the youngest of eight sons. His eldest brother was already active in catholic politics by the 1640s, and another brother became a Jesuit and later catholic archbishop of Dublin.

By 1642 the "old English" had been forced into making common cause with their Gaelic co-religionists in an alliance that was distasteful but allowed resistance to an increasingly anti-catholic English parliament. By 1647 Richard Talbot was serving as a cavalry officer in the confederacy's Leinster army, commanded by the pro-royalist Thomas Preston; in 1649, while serving in the garrison at Drogheda, Talbot was badly wounded. With the collapse of the catholic-royalist cause in Ireland the young Talbot joined with those who left for Europe seeking employment in various Continental armies.

His brother Peter, the Jesuit, introduced him to James, Duke of York, younger brother of the exiled Charles II, and the two men became close friends. Talbot's influence over his royal patron appears to date from this period – an influence which he was to use for the rest of his life to further not only his own interests but also those of the "old English" in Ireland. At the Restoration Talbot accompanied the Duke of York to London as a member of his household. As SIMMS shows, in the 1670s Talbot emerged as a leading campaigner on the issue of catholic land claims in Ireland; and he was condemned by parliament in 1673 on the grounds he "has notoriously assumed to himself the title of agent of the Roman Catholics of Ireland". Charles, unwilling to risk a breach with parliament, stripped Talbot of office and sent him into exile in Ireland and later Europe.

As FOSTER and SHEPHERD show, Talbot's fortunes revived early in 1685 when Charles died and was succeeded by his brother James, a convert to the catholic faith. In June Talbot was created earl of Tyrconnel, and a year later he was appointed lieutenant general of the Irish army. He proceeded to purge the army of "disaffected" protestants, replacing them with catholics and thereby creating a force loyal to him and to James. Although Talbot was not sworn in as lord deputy until February 1687, he was effectively in control of the country long before then and began to replace protestant judges and government officials with catholic appointees. In June 1687, on his own initiative, he began issuing new charters to cities and corporate towns, effectively returning them to catholic control.

Understandably these developments in Ireland were viewed with considerable concern in London and were probably a factor in bringing about the overthrow of James II in the "Glorious Revolution" of 1688. Although essentially an English coup d'état instigated by English political leaders for English reasons, this shift in power left Tyrconnel's Irish policy in ruins. The isolated lord lieutenant now had two choices: seek a compromise with William to ensure some degree of protection for Ireland's catholics, or declare for the exiled James in the hope that he might regain his throne. In the end the promise of substantial support from the French influenced Talbot to support James and urge his patron to come to Ireland in person.

In response to Talbot's pleading and at the insistence of Louis XIV, James travelled to Ireland, arriving at Kinsale in March 1689 to begin a campaign whose main objective was the recovery of the English throne using Ireland as a base. Talbot and the other Irish leaders raised no objection to this, considering a catholic king in London critical to their plans. A parliament was called in Dublin to begin the process of dismantling the Cromwellian and Restoration land settlements. However, such plans were impractical until the Jacobites were able to defeat William's forces and establish control of the whole country. Given the resources available to the Jacobites, this was not likely to be achieved, as BERRESFORD-ELLIS and DOHERTY demonstrate in their studies of the military aspects of the Williamite war.

After the battle of the Boyne in July 1690 there was no hope of a Jacobite victory, but the Jacobites fought on, hoping to obtain better conditions, supported by a French monarch who viewed the war as a useful diversionary strategy. After the Boyne James fled to France, to be joined in September by Talbot, who was seeking military aid. Talbot returned in January 1691 to organize further resistence. He saw the desperate attempts to establish a defensive line along the Shannon collapse between June and July with the capture of Athlone and the battle of Aughrim, and sent word that unless significant help arrived at once from France the Irish must be allowed to seek terms. It is unlikely that he received a reply, as he died in Limerick following a stroke on 14 August.

With Talbot's death any hope of keeping the Irish army in the field vanished, as did any possibility of his long-cherished plan to reverse the land settlements. It is doubtful that, even had he lived, he could have motivated the Irish to fight for James and his French master any longer. His catholic counter-revolution was doomed.

JOHN LYNCH

See also Glorious Revolution; Ireland: Reformation; Jacobitism; James VII and II

Tariff Reform

see Fiscal Politics 1688–1939

Taxation: Parliamentary

Braddick, Michael J., *The Nerves of State: Taxation and the Financing of the English State, 1558–1714*, Manchester: Manchester University Press, and New York: distributed in the United States by St Martin's Press, 1996

Brewer, John, *The Sinews of Power: War, Money, and the English State, 1688–1783*, London: Unwin Hyman, and New York: Knopf, 1989

Chandaman, C.D., *The English Public Revenue, 1660–1688*, Oxford: Clarendon Press, 1975

Daunton, Martin, *Trusting Leviathan: The Politics of Taxation in Britain, 1799–1914*, Cambridge: Cambridge University Press, 2001

Dietz, Frederick C., *English Public Finance 1485–1641*, vol. 1, *English Government Finance 1485–1558*, Urbana: University of Illinois, 1920; reprinted, London: Cass, and New York: Barnes and Noble, 1964

Dietz, Frederick C., *English Public Finance 1485–1641*, vol. 2, *English Public Finance 1558–1641*, New York and London: Century, 1932; reprinted, London: Cass, and New York: Barnes and Noble, 1964

Douglas, R., *Taxation in Britain since 1600*, Basingstoke: Macmillan, and New York: St Martin's Press, 1999

Gras, Norman Scott Brien, *The Early English Customs System: A Documentary Study of the Institutional and Economic History of the Customs from the Thirteenth to the Sixteenth Century*, Cambridge, Massachusetts: Harvard University Press, and London: Milford/Oxford University Press, 1918

Harriss, G.L., *King, Parliament, and Public Finance in Medieval England to 1369*, Oxford: Clarendon Press, 1975

Hoyle, R.W., "Crown, Parliament, and Taxation in Sixteenth-Century England", *English Historical Review*, 109 (1994): 1174–96

Jurkowski, M., C.L. Smith, and D. Crook, *Lay Taxes in England and Wales, 1188–1688*, Kew, Surrey: Public Record Office Publications, 1998

Leys, C., *Politics in Britain: From Labourism to Thatcherism*, London: Heinemann, and Toronto: University of Toronto Press, 1983; revised edition, London and New York: Verso, 1989

O'Brien, Patrick and Philip A. Hunt, "England, 1485–1815" in *The Rise of the Fiscal State in Europe c.1200–1815*, edited by Richard Bonney, Oxford and New York: Oxford University Press, 1999

Ormrod, W.M., "England in the Middle Ages" in *The Rise of the Fiscal State in Europe c.1200–1815*, edited by Richard Bonney, Oxford and New York: Oxford University Press, 1999

A number of national financial obligations developed in the early and central Middle Ages, but the origins of parliamentary taxation are inevitably connected with the growth of parliament itself. In the centuries before the English civil wars of the 1600s parliamentary taxation remained a significant part, rather than the basis of, public finance; and discussion of the relative importance of parliamentary taxation to royal finances as a whole is often related to a discussion of the political importance of parliament. Therefore, much of the work of historians on parliamentary taxation before 1640 concentrates on these constitutional issues. In the constitutional revolution of 1640–42, however, many forms of royal revenue were abolished, and during the civil wars new forms of taxation were developed by parliament which supported a military effort on an unprecedented scale. These forms of taxation, granted by parliament, were retained in 1660 and provided the basis for public finances throughout the 18th century. Thereafter the politics of taxation increasingly revolved around issues of political economy, rather than constitutional propriety. Since all taxation was parliamentary and the politics of taxation was related to issues of political economy, the history of taxation in the 19th and 20th centuries is usually subsumed within more general political histories of particular periods or administrations.

JURKOWSKI, SMITH, & CROOK provide the best overall introduction to taxation of the laity for the five centuries up to 1688. Their book, published by the Public Record Office, is a guide to records of tax assessment. It describes all the main taxes raised in the period, explaining methods of assessment and the politics surrounding each grant. It also contains chronological lists of taxes raised and an up-to-date bibliography. It does not include the customs, which are covered by GRAS in an old but still valuable administrative study. HARRISS gives the principal analytical treatment of the political and administrative history of medieval taxation, offering a thorough and up-to-date discussion of the politics and administration of national taxation from its origins in the 12th century until the late 14th century. Quantitative issues are authoritatively addressed by ORMROD, who also includes an extensive bibliography. The most famous taxes of the medieval period – the poll taxes raised between 1377 and 1381 – feature in most accounts of the Peasants' Revolt of 1381.

DIETZ is much criticized for interpreting exchequer records inadequately; thus his quantitative data must be treated with caution. However, his two volumes still provide the best administrative and political overview of government finances. An excellent treatment of the subject, in the 1963 Cambridge doctoral thesis of R.S. Schofield "Parliamentary Lay Taxation, 1485–1547," has regrettably remained unpublished for forty years. G.R. Elton's claim that Thomas Cromwell's use of parliamentary taxation represented a new principle was related to his larger claim that Cromwell oversaw a revolution which modernized English government. Once again, then, the history of taxation in the pre-modern period is related to claims about constitutional development and state-building. Elton's arguments about taxation have been controversial (as has been the argument about the revolution in government), and the essay by HOYLE offers a sensible resolution as well as a guide to the course of that part of the debate relating to taxation.

From the late 16th century on, parliamentary taxation was resorted to with increasing frequency, and this has led to further emphasis on the constitutional significance of parliament. In particular, the argument that parliament increasingly claimed a right of redress before supply has been questioned – in other words, it has been asked whether the increasing use of parliamentary sources of revenue led to an increased political role for parliament. The idea that it did not was related to the "revisionist" critique of long-term explanations for the outbreak of the Civil War. Also, the idea that the political unpopularity of alternatives to parliamentary taxation gave parliament increased influence has been challenged by revisionist historians of parliamentary politics and political thought. It is now hotly debated whether or not parliaments in the 1620s were consciously seeking to use control over finances to exert a greater influence over policymaking. These issues can be followed in the standard political histories of the period.

BRADDICK, whose book is largely a synthesis of the findings of more specialized studies, argues that the experience of the civil wars transformed national revenues. Before 1640 national revenues consisted of a bewildering range of duties, raised by different authorities, administered in varying ways, and falling on a variety of sources of wealth. Among them parliamentary taxation may have been, in the early 17th century, of declining significance. After 1640 almost all revenue came through parliament, and historians discussing taxation are much less concerned with the relative importance of parliament. Particular sources of revenue are discussed by Braddick and, for the period after 1660, by CHANDAMAN. BREWER provides an excellent account of the politics of finance during the 18th century, paying particular attention to the excise. Braddick, Brewer, and DAUNTON all use taxation as a way of exploring larger issues of the relationship between the citizen or subject and the state, and of the legitimacy of the state. They deal, respectively, with the 17th, 18th, and 19th centuries.

The shift towards parliament as the main, and eventually sole, source of public revenue was associated with dramatically increased yields. The quantification of early modern revenues is an imprecise science, and there is room for further work. Although we might learn more details of the story, the findings reported by Braddick are likely to be borne out. It appears that revenues doubled in real terms in the 1640s and again in the 1690s. The next period of rapid change was that associated with the Napoleonic wars, and the introduction of an income tax under Pitt. In general, all these periods of rapid change were periods of warfare, and this fact has led to an emphasis in accounts of state development on military spending as the principal motor of change. These quantitive and administrative issues are laid out clearly by O'BRIEN & HUNT, who also give an extensive bibliography.

As the constitutional status of revenues was settled, and as their scale increased, political debate seems to have shifted towards the political economy of taxation. By the 1970s tax receipts represented a very substantial proportion of the gross national product and significantly affected patterns of production and consumption. Tax rates could also be manipulated deliberately as a means of economic management and in order to affect the distribution of wealth. Certainly, historians' treatment of taxation before 1640 is dominated, in various ways, by the issue of the rise of parliament; after 1660 it is dominated by issues relating to political economy. The great 19th-century debate centred on the trend from indirect taxation back towards direct taxation in order to establish free trade and to shift the burden of taxation away from the poor. Peel's budgets of 1842 and 1845 were landmarks in this process, and the budgets of Palmerston and Gladstone were made with these questions in mind. The political presumptions underpinning them form part of the discussion of the general political character of the regimes that produced them. Lloyd George's "people's budget" (1909) again reflected structural questions about the uses of taxation for redistributive purposes and about the fairness of tax burdens. After World War II there was a broad consensus that the use of taxation to redistribute wealth was a legitimate political measure. However, during the early 1980s, on both sides of the Atlantic, there was an attack on the use of taxation in this way, which was also associated with an attack on levels of government spending in general. DOUGLAS offers an overview of many of these issues, along with a guide to further reading. LEYS reviews these developments from the perspective of the British left. These moments of political debate reflect issues which were clear by the mid-19th century, and the history of taxation between these climacterics can be followed in the standard political histories of particular periods.

MICHAEL J. BRADDICK

See also Excise, Uses of; Fiscal Politics 1688–1939; Peasants' Revolt; Petition of Right; Purveyance; Revenue, Non-Parliamentary

Technological Invention and Development

Allen, J., "The Introduction of the Newcomen Engine from 1710–1733", *Transactions of the Newcomen Society*, 42 (1969): 169–90

Barnett, Correlli, *The Audit of War: The Illusion and Reality of Britain as a Great Nation*, London: Macmillan, 1986; as *The Pride and the Fall: The Dream and Illusion of Britain as a Great Nation*, New York: Free Press, 1987

Berg, Maxine, *The Age of Manufactures: Industry, Innovation, and Work in Britain, 1700–1820*, Oxford: Blackwell/Fontana, 1985; New York: Oxford University Press, 1986; revised edition, as *The Age of Manufactures, 1700–1820: Industry, Innovation, and Work in Britain*, London and New York: Routledge, 1994

Berg, Maxine and Kristine Bruland (editors), *Technological Revolutions in Europe: Historical Perspectives*, Cheltenham, Gloucestershire and Northampton, Massachusetts: Elgar, 1998

Buchanan, R.A., *The Engineers: A History of the Engineering Profession in Britain, 1750–1914*, London: Kingsley, 1989

Cannadine, David, "The Present and the Past in the English Industrial Revolution, 1780–1980", *Past & Present*, 103 (1984): 131–72

Cardwell, D.S.L., *From Watt to Clausius: The Rise of Thermodynamics in the Early Industrial Age*, Ithaca, New York: Cornell University Press, and London: Heinemann, 1971

Chapman, Allan, "Scientific Instruments and Industrial Innovation: The Achievement of Jesse Ramsden" in *Making Instruments Count: Essays on Historical Scientific Instruments Presented to Gerard L'Estrange Turner*, edited by R.G.W. Anderson, J.A. Bennett, and W.F. Ryan, Aldershot, Hampshire; and Brookfield, Vermont: Variorum, 1993

Clarkson, L.A., *The Pre-Industrial Economy in England, 1500–1750*, London: Batsford, 1971; New York: Schocken Books, 1972

Coleman, D.C., *Industry in Tudor and Stuart England*, London: Macmillan, 1975

Day, Lance and Ian McNeil (editors), *Biographical Dictionary of the History of Technology*, London and New York: Routledge, 1996

Edgerton, David, *Science, Technology, and the British Industrial "Decline", 1870–1970*, Cambridge and New York: Cambridge University Press, 1996

Feingold, Mordechai, *The Mathematicians' Apprenticeship: Science, Universities, and Society in England, 1560–1640*, Cambridge and New York: Cambridge University Press, 1984

Fox, Robert (editor), *Technological Change: Methods and Themes in the History of Technology*, Amsterdam: Harwood Academic, 1996

Fox, Robert and Anna Guagnini (editors), *Education, Technology, and Industrial Performance in Europe, 1850–1939*, Cambridge and New York: Cambridge University Press, and Paris: Maison des Sciences de l'Homme, 1993

Hadden, Richard W., *On the Shoulders of Merchants: Exchange and the Mathematical Conception of Nature in Early Modern Europe*, Albany, New York: State University of New York Press, 1994

Harris, J.R., *Industrial Espionage and Technology Transfer: Britain and France in the Eighteenth Century*, Aldershot, Hampshire; and Brookfield, Vermont: Ashgate, 1998

Hills, Richard L., *Power from Steam: A History of the Stationary Steam Engine*, Cambridge and New York: Cambridge University Press, 1989

Hills, Richard L., "James Watt, Mechanical Engineer", *History of Technology*, 18 (1996): 59–80

History of Technology (annual), 1976–

Inkster, Ian, *Scientific Culture and Urbanisation in Industrialising Britain*, Aldershot, Hampshire and Brookfield, Vermont: Ashgate, 1997

Isis Current Bibliography of the History of Science and Its Cultural Influences (annual), 1975–

Jacob, Margaret C., *Scientific Culture and the Making of the Industrial West*, Oxford and New York: Oxford University Press, 1997

Kargon, Robert H., *Science in Victorian Manchester: Enterprise and Expertise*, Manchester: Manchester University Press, and Baltimore: Johns Hopkins University Press, 1977

Keller, Alex, "Technological Aspirations and the Motivation of Natural Philosophy in Seventeenth-Century England", *History of Technology*, 15 (1993): 76–92

Landes, David S., *The Unbound Prometheus: Technological Change and Industrial Development in Western Europe from 1750 to the Present*, Cambridge: Cambridge University Press, 1969

Liebenau, Jonathan (editor), *The Challenge of New Technology: Innovation in British Business since 1850*, Aldershot, Hampshire and Brookfield, Vermont: Gower, 1988

MacLeod, Christine, *Inventing the Industrial Revolution: The English Patent System, 1660–1800*, Cambridge and New York: Cambridge University Press, 1988

MacLeod, Christine, "Strategies for Innovation: The Diffusion of New Technology in Nineteenth-Century British Industry", *Economic History Review*, 45/2 (1992): 285–307

MacLeod, Christine, "Concepts of Invention, and the Patent Controversy in Victorian Britain" in *Technological Change: Methods and Themes in the History of Technology*, edited by Robert Fox, Amsterdam: Harwood Academic, 1996

MacLeod, Christine, "James Watt, Heroic Invention, and the Idea of the Industrial Revolution" in *Technological Revolutions in Europe: Historical Perspectives*, edited by Maxine Berg and Kristine Bruland, Cheltenham, Gloucestershire; and Northampton, Massachusetts: Elgar, 1998

McConnell, Anita, "From Craft Workshop to Big Business: The London Scientific Instrument Trades' Response to Increasing Demand, 1750–1820", *London Journal*, 19/1 (1994): 36–53

Miller, David, "Puffing Jamie: The Commercial and Ideological Importance of Being a Philosopher in the Case of the Reputation of James Watt, 1736–1819", *History of Science*, 38 (2000): 1–24

Morrell, J.B., "Bourgeois Scientific Societies and Industrial Innovation, 1780–1850", *Journal of European Economic History*, 24/2 (1995): 311–32

Musson, A.E. and Eric Robinson, *Science and Technology in the Industrial Revolution*, Manchester: Manchester University Press, and Toronto: University of Toronto Press, 1969

O'Brien, Patrick, Trevor Griffiths, and Philip Hunt, "Technological Change during the First Industrial Revolution: The Paradigm Case of Textiles, 1688–1851" in *Technological Change: Methods and Themes in the History of Technology*, edited by Robert Fox, Amsterdam: Harwood Academic, 1996

Pollard, Sidney, *Britain's Prime and Britain's Decline: The British Economy, 1870–1914*, London and New York: Arnold, 1989

Rubinstein, W.D., *Capitalism, Culture, and Decline in Britain, 1750–1990*, London and New York: Routledge, 1993

Sanderson, Michael, *The Universities and British Industry, 1850–1970*, London: Routledge and Kegan Paul, 1972

Sanderson, Michael, "The English Civic Universities and 'the Industrial Spirit', 1870–1914", *Historical Research*, 61 (1988)

Schofield, Robert E., *The Lunar Society of Birmingham: A Social History of Provincial Science and Industry in Eighteenth-Century England*, Oxford: Clarendon Press, 1963

Singer, Charles *et al.* (editors), *A History of Technology*, 8 vols, Oxford: Clarendon Press, and New York: Oxford University Press, 1954–84 (vols 3 onwards)

Smith, Alan, "'Engines Moved by Fire and Water': The Contribution of Fellows of the Royal Society to the Development of Steam Power, 1675–1733", *Transactions of the Newcomen Society*, 66 (1994–95): 1–25

Stewart, Larry, *The Rise of Public Science: Rhetoric, Technology, and Natural Philosophy in Newtonian Britain, 1660–1750*, Cambridge and New York: Cambridge University Press, 1992

Stewart, Larry, "A Meaning for Machines: Modernity, Utility, and the Eighteenth-Century British Public", *Journal of Modern History*, 70/2 (1998): 259–94

Tann, Jennifer, *The Development of the Factory*, London: Cornmarket Press, 1970

Tann, Jennifer, "The Steam Engine on Tyneside in the Industrial Revolution", *Transactions of the Newcomen Society*, 64 (1992): 53–75

Tann, Jennifer, "Riches from Copper: The Adoption of the Boulton and Watt Engine by Cornish Mine Adventurers", *Transactions of the Newcomen Society*, 67 (1995–96): 27–51

Tann, Jennifer, "Two Knights in Pandemonium: A Worm's Eye View of Boulton and Watt & Company", *History of Technology*, 20 (1998): 47–72

Tweedale, Geoffrey, *Steel City: Entrepreneurship, Strategy, and Technology in Sheffield, 1743–1993*, Oxford: Clarendon Press, and New York: Oxford University Press, 1995

Von Tunzelmann, G.N., *Steam Power and British Industrialization to 1860*, Oxford: Clarendon Press, 1978

Von Tunzelmann, G.N., "Technological and Organizational Change in Industry during the Early Industrial Revolution" in *The Industrial Revolution and British Society*, edited by Patrick K. O'Brien and Roland Quinault, Cambridge and New York: Cambridge University Press, 1993

Von Tunzelmann, G.N., "Technical Progress, 1780–1860" in *The Economic History of Britain since 1700*, vol. 1, edited by Roderick Floud and Donald McCloskey, revised edition, 3 vols, Cambridge and New York: Cambridge University Press, 1994

Von Tunzelmann, G.N., "Time-Saving Technical Change: The Cotton Industry in the English Industrial Revolution", *Explorations in Economic History*, 32/1 (1995): 1–27

Wiener, Martin J., *English Culture and the Decline of the Industrial Spirit 1850–1980*, Cambridge and New York: Cambridge University Press, 1981

Wrigley, E.A., *Continuity, Chance, and Change: The Character of the Industrial Revolution in England*, Cambridge and New York: Cambridge University Press, 1988

Any guide to the history of "technological invention and development" faces three problems. The theme itself consists of an apparently transparent but in fact opaque combination of confusing terms whose connotations ramify outwards from the particulars of individual techniques to generic issues of cause and consequence which run virtually the entire economic, social, and cultural gamut. This means, first, that a great deal of the writing upon it is in article form, and frequently very specific even when it has larger implications: examples include the studies of the Newcomen engine by ALLEN and SMITH and TANN's studies of the Watt engine and its deployment. The second problem is the opposite: the very large conceptual questions raised by the changing meanings of "technology" itself, by the process of invention, by the different incentives which promote the actual deployment of innovation, and by the actual circumstances in which this takes place. The third problem is that while these issues are obviously too important to be left to one side without ending with something resembling a chronological catalogue of gadgets and their particular applications, they tend towards a level of abstraction which would be of limited effectiveness in a guide such as this. On these different aspects, consult SINGER *et al.* for compendious technical reference; *ISIS* for a comprehensive yearly listing of current literature; *HISTORY OF TECHNOLOGY* as the main journal on the subject; and for individuals, DAY & McNEIL. Meanwhile the different components of the subject must be kept in practical balance.

Consider MacLEOD (1988): the title says that the Industrial Revolution was not just a result of inventions but was itself invented. What follows, the history of the English patent system, is in fact quite specific. This exposes the pitfalls of trying to chart the course of "technological innovation and development" in 18th-century England simply by counting patents. At the same time, however, the system's own evolution from a general register of privileges issued by Chancery under the Great Seal into the legal expression of a "culture of invention" leads to the far-reaching proposition that by the end of the century, invention no longer meant simply and literally the "finding" of pre-existing facts benignly placed in nature for discovery and use by humans within limits ordained by the Superior Wisdom which had put them there. In other words, the greatest "invention" of the century was the way of invention itself. Whatever its metaphysical implications, this, once found, became both the agent and the potentially unlimited object of its own cultivation. In this sense, the Industrial Revolution was greater than the sum its parts. At least at the cultural and intellectual level, this reaffirms the revolutionary nature of the transformation against the gradualism preferred by most current accounts of English industrialization. MacLeod thus corroborates WRIGLEY's assertion that in the late 18th century England became the first human society to cross the threshold between an "advanced organic economy" ultimately dependent on human and animal effort, and thus on the caloric balance between vegetative production and consumption, and a "mineral-based energy economy" possessing the technology to convert inorganic sources of heat into mechanical work.

At the heart of this is the long-vexed question of causal connections between the "scientific" and "industrial" revolutions. For the most part, the direct answer has been negative. Before the convergence of theoretical thermodynamics with practical engineering in the development of high-pressure steam in the second quarter of the 19th century (CARDWELL) and the advent of professional specialization and systematic laboratory research, the conclusion has usually been that any connection between science and the industrious tinkering of nimble-fingered but untheoretical artisans was serendipitous at most. Recently, however, the basic issue has been reformulated. Prompted by contextual investigations of the origins of the scientific revolution itself, by SCHOFIELD's landmark provincial study, and by the basic work of MUSSON & ROBINSON, which produced a mass of social and cultural material even though its search for direct connections proved inconclusive, STEWART (1992) asks how a society riven as late as the 1720s by *odium theologicum*, and still very aware of the precariousness of its recently achieved stability, managed to convince itself that experimental natural philosophy was a vital constituent of the public interest in the first place, and not, as Jonathan Swift would have had it, its most subversive enemy. This redirects the question from the linear application of "science" to "industry" – anachronistic categories – to the prior emergence of an environment in which the equation of "true philosophy" (Newtonian philosophy, as construed by its popularizers) with material improvement could develop.

The colloquial understanding of technology as science put to human use was thus constructed in 18th-century culture before it became practice in 19th-century industry. This faces in two directions. On one hand, it points back to the previous two centuries (COLEMAN; CLARKSON), when the direction of empirical innovation in particular manufactures was still

predominantly inwards to Britain, rather than outwards as it later became (HARRIS). Then, the status of "technology" – or rather the corpus of particular trade practices and terminologies which the word then signified – remained ambiguous: a powerful influence on the development of natural philosophy itself (FEINGOLD; HADDEN; KELLER), but despite the Baconian project for its full incorporation not yet accorded the broader modern connotations of "science-based" improvement which it has subsequently acquired. Even more clearly, however, Stewart's account of the Newtonian transformation points forward. Its main vector was the network of stockjobbing projectors, improving landowners, and urban developers orchestrated by the business interests of the spectacular James Brydges, first Duke of Chandos, and the promotional public experimentalism of his technical agent and adviser J.-T. Desaguliers. Latent in this were not only the future links in general between landed capital, urban development, and industrial initiatives, but also the pattern of the classic partnership between inventor and entrepreneur in those intiatives. Indeed, STEWART's manifesto (1998) on the meanings and uses of machines in the 18th century, especially in the marriage of West End philosophy and East End mathematical mechanism among the London instrument men, implies a direct and vital connection after all between science and technological innovation, transmitted through the precision screw cutting and dividing techniques pioneered in the 1770s by Jesse Ramsden, to Henry Maudslay and the beginnings of machine tool engineering at the Woolwich Arsenal a generation later (CHAPMAN; McCONNELL). In the first instance, however, the broader implication is again social and cultural rather than immediately practical: the emergence of a new ideal type in the hybrid persona of the engineer as enlightened artisan. This is placed in broader comparative perspective by JACOB, for whom James Watt supplies the quintessential example.

Watt indeed continues to figure in the historiography as prominently as he always did, with regard not only to his achievement but also to his formation (HILLS 1996) and to the reasons why it was important to represent him posthumously as a heroic philosopher-scientist-engineer (MACLEOD 1996, 1998; MILLER). It almost seems that current writers are resurrecting a postmodern version of the engineer as Victorian folk-hero originally popularized in the biographies by Samuel Smiles. Lest it seem that the course of "technological invention and development" can thus be fully captured, this brief survey must therefore end by recognizing that innovation at large was in actuality affected not only by its own logic and momentum but equally by considerations beyond them. Those considerations so far exceed the nominal bounds of the subject itself that any guidance is bound to be rough-and-ready. CANNADINE contemplates the overall trajectory of the Industrial Revolution as an historical concept. Within this, the classic work on innovation as a whole is LANDES's, though it has been criticized for overstating British "decline" since 1870. Technological deployment is the subject of TANN (1970); LIEBENAU; and O'BRIEN, GRIFFITHS, & HUNT. The development of the stationary steam engine itself as the principal source of industrial power is the subject of HILLS (1989). KARGON and TWEEDALE put science and technology into the context of two of the cities (Manchester and Sheffield) most characterized by their union. MORRELL and INKSTER look more generally at the circumstances and groups in which they came together. VON TUNZELMANN (1978) gives an important economic historian's caveat against overestimating the real extent and effect of steam power before 1860, and this is echoed in his later contributions on the actual deployment and impact of technological change. It is notable that the last of these appears in a collection edited by BERG (1998), who has been a proponent of the gradualist version of socio-economic change (1994). FOX and FOX & GUAGNINI also relate the British experience to more general problems and themes, including technical education. Ostensible deficiencies in this underlie much of the politically laden thesis proposed by WIENER and BARNETT: Britain's unreversed industrial and technological decline between the 1870s and the 1980s. SANDERSON (1972) had in fact refuted the educational argument behind this on its main ground before it was made and has continued to do so (1988), supported in broader terms by POLLARD and by BUCHANAN's history of the engineering profession. The larger cultural inference that the matrix of technological invention documented by Stewart and proselytized by Jacob "lost" its "industrial spirit" and turned into the opposite in the later 19th century is attacked by RUBINSTEIN on the paradoxical ground that since its hegemonic elite consisted of "gentry capitalists", Britain never had a fully technocratic "industrial spirit" to begin with. The questions begged by this and other ramifications of "declinism" are incisively addressed by EDGERTON. Besides being a further guide to the literature on British technological and industrial performance in the past century, Edgerton's book also clarifies the confusions inherent in the theme of technology and development itself and effectively sorts out the different approaches which have been taken to its history.

JOHN MONEY

See also Engineering: General Surveys; Industrial Revolution

Technology and Employment 20th century

Fothergill, Stephen and Graham Gudgin, *Unequal Growth: Urban and Regional Employment Change in the UK*, London: Heinemann, 1982

Hudson, R., *Wrecking a Region: State Policies, Party Politics, and Regional Change in North East England*, London: Pion, 1989

McLoughlin, Ian and Jon Clark, *Technological Change at Work*, Milton Keynes, Buckinghamshire; and Philadelphia, Pennsylvania: Open University Press, 1988

Nichols, Theo, *The British Worker Question: A New Look at Workers and Productivity in Manufacturing*, London: Routledge and Kegan Paul, 1986

Phillips, G.A. and R.T. Maddock, *The Growth of the British Economy, 1918–1968*, London: Allen and Unwin, 1973

Pollard, Sidney, *The Development of the British Economy, 1914–1990*, London and New York: Arnold, 1992

Powell, David, *British Politics and the Labour Question, 1868–1990*, London: Macmillan, and New York: St Martin's Press, 1992

Rothwell, Roy and Walter Zegveld, *Technical Change and Employment*, London: Pinter, and New York: St Martin's Press, 1979

Rowe, Christopher and Jane Thompson, *People and Chips: The Human Implications of Information Technology*, 3rd edition, London and New York: McGraw Hill, 1996

Although technological change in Britain has long been associated with the loss of employment, PHILLIPS & MADDOCK argue that this condition is unique to Britain's geo-economic history. Part of a merchant rather than a corporate industrial nation, British firms have sought to expand by developing new markets rather than new products, and consequently there has never been the concentration of investment in innovation necessary to provide long-term stability to industry. Consequently, although Britain has been at the vanguard in the development of new technologies in electronics and computers, exposure to heavy global competition has hindered the development and survival of more mature industrial sectors. Technological change can be divided in this way into two sectors: innovative and mature. In innovative sectors, the financial markets of the United Kingdom provide extensive venture finance which engenders significant growth in employment; conversely, in mature sectors, manufacturing operations are rationalized, activities are subcontracted to cheaper locations overseas, and businesses concentrate on their most profitable areas. As an interesting anecdote, Phillips & Maddock posit that the rejuvenation of coal and steel after the slump of the 1930s was based on intense (and one-off) public-sector investment through wartime command conditions, a temporary if welcome aberration which provided the sectors with a two-decade respite.

The natural corollary of this argument is the emergence of a geographical divide between localities dominated by mature industries and those dominated by innovative industries. FOTHERGILL & GUDGIN argue that historical factors, particularly economic structure, determine regional economic performance and drove the emergence of an uneven geography of production in the United Kingdom in the 1980s. Under-investment in new technologies reduced the competitiveness of coal and steel, whose locations were determined by the presence of raw materials. Decline was politically managed through piecemeal run-down and eventual closure impelled by the government's concern with short-term employment levels. Those industries which became dependent on the government for subsidies (and, in the case of the nationalized industries, for investment) crowded out a more active technology-driven industrial policy for declining regions and localities. Fothergill & Gudgin were writing during the monetarist depression of the early 1980s, when output across all sectors was falling, and it is easy with the benefit of hindsight to attack their conclusion that all industries and hence regions would suffer a decline. However, the comparative work is of historical value in understanding the uneven geographical impacts of technological change.

HUDSON examines the aggregate geographical effect of this process in one region, the north-east of England, and produces a compelling narrative for how a series of short-term political exigencies can produce the systematic run-down of a region. Policies designed to support the Durham coalfield and steel industries in the immediate postwar period created full employment; this acted as a disincentive to the new electric engineering industries which (socially) required skilled male workers, and consequently new investment was limited to branch plants with a preponderance of unskilled female operators. Postwar austerity favoured operating subsidies over investment in new technologies, with the result that sectoral productivity and competitiveness collapsed. A change in the political climate in the 1960s favoured a rationalization of the industry; as mining atrophied, the branch plants could not provide a market for either the skills or the number of workers made redundant. In the 1980s, as the last remnants of coal mining disappeared, the government cynically appreciated that miners had little chance of working again, and so redundancy was replaced by invalidity retirement, removing miners from the politically sensitive numbers of unemployed but imposing the same socially destructive loss of identity, occupation, and income as formal unemployment.

ROTHWELL & ZEGVELD argue that it is necessary to understand technological change on a global scale in order to understand the peculiarities of Britain's situation. They wrote at a time when "jobless growth" was a particular concern of policy, and so they made three main points around which to develop a historical framework for understanding the macroscopic impacts of technological change on employment. First, they hold that technological change does result in loss of jobs; they use the example of the National Coal Board, which sustained its aggregate output during the restructuring of the 1960s as some 70,000 jobs were lost in the sector. Second, technological change entails changes in the distribution of skills; jobs were lost, but there was an increase in the level of operators' skills, and the creation of jobs in the machine-tools sector was stimulated. Third, and most important, is the comment that the greatest effect has been through the creation of new opportunities. Rothwell & Zegveld cite BT's digital trunk switching System X: although the number of operators required per switch compared with a manual exchange fell from 26 to one, the development, maintenance, and management of the network created significant new employment in scientific and professional rather than purely technical and craft areas and presaged the development of globally competitive network management firms such as Vodafone and BT Syntegra.

POLLARD develops this final point at some length in his extensive overview of the development of the British economy. Linking the two themes – technological change and loss of employment – he observes that the scientific advances of World War I had stimulated many industries, which, however were much less labour-intensive and fundamentally altered the nature of the existing industrial base. This pattern was further reinforced by World War II, in which the blurring of science, research, and production transformed the organization of a number of staple industries, particularly aerospace and chemicals. Pollard argues that a critical factor was the geographical dominance of mature sectors, which slowed down the movement into newer technological areas and ensured an uneven distribution of growth. Although coal and steel were the first industries to enter a decline, he notes that by the 1950s motor manufacturing, a growth sector in the 1930s, had begun to decline and slow the emergence of the business service sector in the Midlands. All together, this produced a geographical split between scientific-intensive and innovative activities in the south-east and a reliance in the northern and western regions on declining and vulnerable mature production.

Although a macroeconomic approach might stress the changes in the level, geography, and sectoral distribution of employment, it is clear that technology has also changed the experience of employment. MCLOUGHLIN & CLARK bring a sociological analysis to an historical interpretation of technological change. They begin with the premise that while employees have tended to be portrayed as reactionary and anti-technology, employers and managers have managed to cast themselves as forcing technological change by "acting in the economic interests of the nation as a whole". Managers have a range of reasons for introducing new technologies to production, and the reasons behind technological change have a great impact on the way employees experience it. For instance, technologies introduced to improve surveillance and control might increase apprehension and unease among workers, and they create a new class of sub-managerial employees – particularly in occupations calling for "human information-processing, problem-solving and decision-making skills" – whose acquiescence is necessary to run those systems. Technological change has been critical in segmenting the labour market; thus increasing flexibility and uncertainty in employment is not a result of a monolithic process of globalization but has been at least partially purposively driven by managerial decisions in each workplace.

ROWE & THOMPSON take a similar approach in their comprehensive and engaging study of the more recent impact of information technologies on the experience of work. They posit that both Utopian and pessimistic perspectives on such change can be advanced, and that each particular situation needs to be analysed on its micro-scale merits. They present a case study of office occupations, which have gone through three phases of organization; historically, there is a difference between pre-industrial and industrial offices, but in both there was a degree of interdependence between the traditionally female office staff and male management. Positively, IT has promoted the prestige of office managers and personal assistants – traditionally female roles – by increasing their control over that increasingly rare commodity, personal access to senior management. However, there are a multiplicity of negative developments, from the relatively mundane implications of computer layouts for posture and eyesight to job satisfaction and social relations when administrative tasks are subcontracted to clerical factories (such as call centres) or *in extremis* home-workers. They argue that information technology will transform labour along a range of dimensions, including labour displacement, opportunities for women, workplace size, employment contracts, payment systems, skills compositions, work timing, information, management, and control. Indeed, the whole thrust of the book is that IT is currently driving a process of social, cultural, and political change as radical as the creation of the factory system in the late 18th and early 19th centuries.

Concluding by way of an interesting political digression is the analysis of the once-popular vernacular notion (the "British worker question") that the organized labour movement has systematically hindered the adoption of technology and undermined Britain's competitiveness. NICHOLS seeks to deconstruct the argument that the laziness of British workers engendered poor economic performance by opposing technological investment, and the subsequent politically expedient conclusion that unemployed British workers deserve their plight. Both Nichols and POWELL argue that in 1960s and 1970s the problem of adopting new technology became conflated with wider questions of industrial relations and productivity. When industries faced collapse under the threat of foreign competitors, Powell notes, events in the workplace "mirrored and exacerbated the [national-scale] antagonism of management and unions". He and Nichols therefore arrive independently at the conclusion that although Britain has historically experienced more loss of employment and less growth arising from technological change than comparable developed countries, it is as much a governmental and managerial (union and business) failure as the fault of particular workers who have borne the brunt of those misguided policies and strategies.

PAUL S. BENNEWORTH

See also Computing Industry; Electronics Industry; Mining, Decline of; Relative Economic Decline

Telecommunications 19th and 20th centuries

Baldwin, F.G.C., *The History of the Telephone in the United Kingdom*, London: Chapman and Hall, 1925

Foreman-Peck, James and Robert Millward, *Public and Private Ownership of British Industry 1820–1990*, Oxford: Clarendon Press, and New York: Oxford University Press, 1994

Harlow, Chris, *Innovation and Productivity under Nationalisation: The First Thirty Years*, London: Political and Economic Planning, and Allen and Unwin, 1977

Hazlewood, Arthur, "The Origin of the State Telephone Service in Britain", *Oxford Economic Papers*, 5 (1953): 13–25

Kieve, Jeffrey, *The Electric Telegraph: A Social and Economic History*, Newton Abbot, Devon: David and Charles, 1973

Perry, Charles R., "The British Experience 1876–1912: The Impact of the Telephone during the Years of Delay" in *The Social Impact of the Telephone*, edited by Ithiel de Sola Pool, Cambridge, Massachusetts: MIT Press, 1977

Pitt, Douglas C., *The Telecommunications Function in the British Post Office: A Case Study of Bureaucratic Adaptation*, Farnborough, Hampshire: Saxon House, 1980

Robertson, J.H., *The Story of the Telephone: A History of the Telecommunications Industry of Britain*, London: Pitman, 1947

Most of the historical literature on telecommunications deals with the industry in the 19th century and the early years of the 20th century. The principal question addressed has been the slow development of the telephone in Britain in its early years, especially compared with the United States. Because parts of the telecommunications industry have moved between state control and the private sector, the relative merits of public and private ownership have also received attention. There is, as yet, little serious work by historians on telecommunications in the second half of the 20th century, or on important topics such as the social impact of the telephone.

BALDWIN represents the first attempt to write a comprehensive history of the development of the telephone in the United Kingdom. The author was an engineer, and the book contains a great deal of technical information on the development of switchboard systems, underground cables, and the like, as well as relatively brief excursions into the commercial history of the industry. As a general account it is out of date, but it may still be worth referring to on matters of detail.

ROBERTSON's book is a well-written popular history which successfully blends information on technical and administrative matters. It covers the early years of telephony briefly, and the interwar period in more detail. The story that emerges is one of technical and engineering dynamism stifled by the mandarins at the top of the Post Office and in the Treasury. The main problems were bureaucracy and inefficiency, and a lack of autonomy resulting from the government's tight grip on finance. This kept telephony short of development funds and prevented long-term planning. However, in the early 1930s, following a good deal of lobbying, reform did take place. Robertson reaches the remarkably optimistic conclusion that the reforms were fully implemented, and that the industry was able to reach maturity and a high level of efficiency.

KIEVE gives an account of the electric telegraph, concentrating mainly on the heroic phase of development in the 19th century. The telegraph was run by private enterprise until 1868, when it was nationalized and taken over by the Post Office. Kieve considers the weaknesses of competition that led to nationalization and describes the expansion of the service and the financial problems that occurred under the control of the Post Office. The Post Office's restrictive approach to telephony is also documented. The latter part of the book charts the inexorable decline of the telegraph in the 20th century, mainly because of competition from the telephone.

HAZLEWOOD provides a clear and concise account of the ownership of telephone companies from the beginnings in the 1870s through to nationalization in 1912. He contends that government policy towards the telephone service included a willingness to give private enterprise a chance and that there was no rush towards public ownership. In Hazlewood's view, the main objectives of policy were, first, to protect the government's telegraph revenue against the effects of competition from the burgeoning telephone; and, second, to encourage the development of a satisfactory telephone service.

PERRY also explores the slow development of telephone usage in Britain during the late 19th century. He defends the record of the Post Office and, in contrast to Kieve, attributes much of the blame to the Treasury. Perry adds some interesting information on the social impact of the telephone. He shows that in its early years the telephone was regarded as a luxury item because it was expensive – and that some people saw it as an intrusion into the privacy of the home. During this period the telephone was very largely an urban phenomenon and had its greatest use in business rather than domestic life.

PITT provides a scholarly analysis of the slow diffusion of the telephone in Britain. By carefully analysing a range of source material, he seeks to show that the chief villain in this saga, from the 19th century onwards, was the Treasury, which adopted a restrictive approach to funding. Pitt assesses the reforms of the 1930s in depth and concludes that Robertson's optimism about their effects was misguided. Many of the proposed reforms were never implemented or else were allowed to lapse once war broke out. Pitt argues that telecommunications continued to suffer from inadequate financing and far too much centralized control well into the postwar years.

HARLOW discusses technological change in public-sector industries, including a substantial analysis of the record of Post Office telecommunications from the 1940s to the 1970s. It emerges that the Post Office's attempt to introduce electronic switching systems was highly innovatory. However, the system chosen turned out to be unreliable and in need of further development, so that the Post Office was forced to resort to less sophisticated systems in an unplanned manner. The influence of the structure of telecommunications within a government department, its lack of control over its own finances, and the relations built up with equipment manufacturers are analysed.

FOREMAN-PECK & MILLWARD's book deals with the economic history of network industries and includes much discussion of telecommunications, especially in the 19th century. It is a thorough research monograph which applies sophisticated economic analysis to the utilities in order to develop a quantitative assessment of their efficiency. Two attractive features of this book are its widespread use of international comparisons and its engagement with broader debates about the relative strengths and weaknesses of state ownership versus regulation in the private sector. The authors also analyse the causes and consequences of privatization in the 1980s. The long-run historical analysis suggests that network industries, such as telecommunications, have characteristics which make it very difficult to regulate them in an efficient way, whether they are in the public or the private sector.

ANDREW JENKINS

See also Electronics Industry; Information Technology: E-Mail, Internet, and World Wide Web; Nationalization and Denationalization

Telford, Thomas   1757–1834

Engineer

Allen, Grant, "Thomas Telford, Stonemason", in his *Biographies of Working Men*, London: Society for Promoting Christian Knowledge, 1884

Bracegirdle, Brian and Patricia H. Miles, *Thomas Telford*, Newton Abbot, Devon: David and Charles, 1973

Ellis, Keith, *Thomas Telford: Father of Civil Engineering*, London: Priory Press, 1974

Gibb, Sir Alexander, *The Story of Telford: The Rise of Civil Engineering*, London: A. Maclehose, 1935

Hadfield, Charles, *Thomas Telford's Temptation: Telford and William Jessop's Reputation*, Cleobury Mortimer, Shropshire: Baldwin, 1993

Maclean, Allan, *Telford's Highland Churches: The Highland Churches and Manses of Thomas Telford*, Inverness: Society of West Highland and Island Historical Research, 1989

Pearce, Rhoda M., *Thomas Telford: An Illustrated Life of Thomas Telford, 1757–1834*, Aylesbury, Buckinghamshire: Shire, 1973

Penfold, Alastair (editor), *Thomas Telford, Engineer: Proceedings of a Seminar Held at the Coalport China Works Museum, Ironbridge, April 1979, under the* *Auspices of the Ironbridge Gorge Museum Trust and Telford Development Corporation*, London: Thomas Telford, 1980

Rolt, L.T.C., *Thomas Telford*, London and New York: Longmans Green, 1958

Smiles, Samuel, *The Life of Thomas Telford, Civil Engineer, with an Introductory History of Roads and Travelling in Great Britain*, London: John Murray, 1867

Thomas Telford had humble beginnings. He was born on 9 August 1757 on the banks of the Megget Water, north of Langholm in Dumfriesshire, Scotland, the son of an Eskdale shepherd. His father having died when Telford was an infant, he was raised by his mother in a thatched cottage. The young Telford rose from sheep herder to stonemason, poet (published in the *Edinburgh Magazine*), and architect, and reached fame as one of Britain's foremost bridge, canal, harbour, and road engineers. As his career peaked, Telford became a fellow of the Royal Societies of both Edinburgh and London, knight of the Royal Order of Vasa (in Sweden), and first president of the Institution of Civil Engineers. Less official statements of Telford's contemporary reputation are found in the equally telling words of his travelling companion and friend, the poet Robert Southey, who aptly dubbed Telford the "Colossus of Roads" and "Pontifex Maximus". When Telford died in 1834, he was buried in the nave of Westminster Abbey, a long way from the wandering course of the Esk. Telford's striking rise could not have been accomplished without a powerful intellect, but it is his industry and diligence that are legendary. "His constitution," says one modern historian, "like many of his works, must have been of iron". Telford's personal character, however, is a matter of historical debate.

Telford's impressive career was duly moralized and romanticized by his earliest biographers. ALLEN celebrates "Tam" Telford as a "working man" nourished in his early days with only "thin oatmeal porridge (with very little milk, we fear)". In Telford's success story, Allen finds inspiration for British youth: for "what lad could ever have started in the world under apparently more hopeless circumstances than widow Janet Telford's penniless orphan shepherd-boy Tam, in the bleakest and most remote of all the lonely border valleys of southern Scotland?" SMILES's 19th-century account is longer and more balanced (with an interesting chapter on Telford's Scottish harbours), but not always accurate in detail. Smiles's Telford was "diligent and conscientious", but also "happy-minded" and "cheerful". Smiles, like Allen, has been largely surpassed by more recent scholarship.

GIBB gave the first full-scale study of Telford, and his well-written book is still worth pursuing – as is his useful 30-page bibliographical listing of the "Principal Works with Which Telford Was Connected". Gibb (a great-grandson of Telford's companion of the same name) traced Telford's story alongside the "rise of civil engineering", as his subtitle indicates. Lamenting the paucity of Telford's surviving personal papers, Gibb nevertheless made use of a range of primary research material in order not only to illuminate "the part he played in the founding of a great profession, whose standards and ideals alike derive largely, if not mainly, from him", but also to "present some sort of picture of the man". Gibb's Telford, while self-confident, "had an unusual modesty and reticence".

ROLT, by most accounts, has provided the best all-around biography of Telford. Rolt aimed "to write a more detailed account than has been available hitherto of the major works with which [Telford] was most closely associated and at the same time to present a portrait of Telford the man". After exploring Telford's early years, Rolt's professionally researched volume devotes chapters to Telford's role in the Ellesmere, Caledonian, and Gotha canals, as well as to his road-building projects in England, Wales, and Scotland. Rolt describes Telford as an "improver" who actively pursued the 18th-century ideal of melding "literature and business". With regard to Telford's elusive inner character, Rolt says that although "he was never arrogant", he "was at heart a very proud man".

Telford's life has lent itself to inclusion in a number of thematic biography series. ELLIS's work on Telford for the series Pioneers of Science and Discovery and PEARCE's for the series Lifelines provide little that is new, but both offer concise, well-illustrated chronological accounts of Telford's life and works. BRACEGIRDLE & MILES's volume on Telford for the series Great Engineers and Their Works tells the story of Telford's projects through 112 annotated photographs and drawings.

In more recent scholarship Telford and his work have been the subject of increasingly specialized study. MACLEAN explored Telford as a Scottish highland improver in his brief study of the historical context, architectural design, details of construction, and subsequent history of the 32 Highland churches and 43 manses with which Telford was involved by way of the 1823 Act for Building Additional Places of Worship in the Highlands and Islands of Scotland. HADFIELD's is a revisionist account which calls into question Telford's self-proclaimed and historiographically perpetuated title as the "king" of iron canal aqueducts. Telford, argued Hadfield, had "engaged in a gentle but persistent process of character erosion" against his fellow canal builder William Jessop. "Though he became a great engineer", Hadfield wrote, Telford was over-ambitious: "it seems that he could not bear to feel that others might be his equals, indeed even his superiors".

In PENFOLD's book we have a collection of eight essays which came out of the Thomas Telford seminar held in 1979 at the Coalport China Works Museum. Written by engineers and historians, the essays in this well-rounded (but unindexed) volume take as their subjects various aspects of Telford's life and works: J.B. Lawson on Telford's days in Shrewsbury, A.R.K. Clayton on Telford's early involvement with the Shrewsbury Canal and his more considerable commitment to the Newport Canal; B. Trinder on Telford and the Holyhead Road; A.W. Skempton on Telford's design for a new London Bridge; R.A. Paxton on Telford's famous suspension bridge, the Menai; A. Dalgeleish on Telford and steam carriages; A. Penfold on the managerial organization on the Caledonian Canal; and J.R. Hume on Telford's Highland bridges. Taken together, this collection attempts to integrate Telford's life with the people and society around him. As N. Cossons points out in the foreword, the volume sheds "new light not only on Telford's engineering genius, but also on his contribution to the social and historical development of Britain during the 19th century which he did so much to nurture".

MARK G. SPENCER

See also Engineering entries; Railways; River and Canal Transport

Television

see **Broadcasting; Reith, John**

Tenchebrai, Battle of 1106

Bradbury, Jim, "Battles in England and Normandy, 1066–1154" in *Anglo-Norman Warfare: Studies in Late Anglo-Saxon and Anglo-Norman Military Organization and Warfare*, edited by Matthew Strickland, Woodbridge, Suffolk; and Rochester, New York: Boydell and Brewer, 1992

David, Charles Wendell, *Robert Curthose, Duke of Normandy*, Cambridge, Massachusetts: Harvard University Press, and London: Oxford University Press, 1920; reprinted, New York: AMS Press, 1982

Hollister, C. Warren, *The Military Organization of Norman England*, Oxford: Clarendon Press, 1965

Le Patourel, John, *The Norman Empire*, Oxford: Clarendon Press, 1976

Morillo, Stephen, *Warfare under the Anglo-Norman Kings, 1066–1135*, Woodbridge, Suffolk; and Rochester, New York: Boydell and Brewer, 1994

Oman, Sir Charles, *A History of the Art of War: The Middle Ages from the Fourth to the Fourteenth Century*, London: Methuen, 1898; enlarged edition, as *A History of the Art of War in the Middle Ages*, 2 vols, London: Methuen, Boston: Houghton Mifflin, and New York: B. Franklin, 1924; reprinted, London: Greenhill, and Mechanicsburg, Pennsylvania: Stackpole, 1998

The battle of Tenchebrai was the decisive event in a sort of Norman Conquest in reverse: Henry I's conquest of Normandy from his brother Robert Curthose. But it has aroused little of the passionate debate that surrounds the battle of Hastings 40 years earlier. The events of the battle of Tenchebrai are relatively clear: there are only four primary sources for it – one an official letter from Henry himself – and they are in agreement about its course. The battle itself was fairly short, lasting only perhaps an hour or so; and in that respect, at least, it was typical of medieval combat. Harold's defeat at Hastings stood in contrast to the successes of the rest of his career and so seems to require explanation; but the result of Tenchebrai seems simply to confirm Robert Curthose's reputation as the least capable of the Conqueror's sons, despite his military successes as a crusader, and so has generated little comment. The consequences of the battle likewise have seemed uncontroversial: Henry retook Normandy, reuniting it with England, and spent much of the rest of his reign defending it and attempting to secure it for his heirs against Robert's son William Clito, the French king, and the Angevin counts.

Two aspects of the context of the battle have therefore tended to dominate the discussions. The first, its political context in terms of the unity (or lack thereof) of the Anglo-Norman realm, refers to the battle only indirectly. The question is this: Were the ties between the two parts of the realm – England and Normandy – so strong, particularly at the level of the aristocrats and their cross-Channel landholdings, that conflict and ultimately conquest of one part by the other was inevitable? Or, given that the inheritance settlements arranged by the Conqueror allowed a division of the realm between Robert and William Rufus, a division that recurred at William's death, were the battle and its consequences the contingent result of Robert's weak leadership and Henry's ambition? LE PATOUREL makes the strongest case for a "unitary realm", a theory which has the advantage of helping to explain the rapidity of Henry's conquest of the duchy after the battle: Henry having established a clear advantage, the Norman aristocrats rushed to his side to secure their holdings in both parts of the realm. HOLLISTER, by focusing his study on England, implicitly adopts the opposite stance, and it is true that the concept of underlying unity entails a risk of reading the consequences of the battle teleologically. But the arguments about this aspect of the context have largely turned on emphasis, not fundamental disagreement.

The second aspect of the battle's context, military practice, has therefore generated the most detailed analyses of the battle. The essential starting-point for these analyses is OMAN's view of the medieval period as an "age of cavalry", dominated by armoured knights against whom no infantry force could stand – the central thesis of an undergraduate prize essay first published in the 1880s and later revised and expanded. At Tenchebrai, however, infantry forces dominated both armies. Not only did Henry and Robert both have large numbers of unmounted troops, but most of Henry's mounted knights and all of Robert's dismounted to fight the battle. Thus while a charge on the rear of Robert's army by a hidden troop of cavalry helped win the battle for Henry, the main fighting was between two solid lines of infantry. As a result, as early as 1920 DAVID pointed out, "What ever the theorists may hold, foot-soldiers did play an unusually large part in the battle of Tinchebrai". David's study places Tenchebrai in the larger context of Robert's career: his experiences in the Holy Land, where infantry forces played an important part in the success of the First Crusade, are taken to have influenced his generalship in Normandy.

Subsequent military history has taken up this problem in several ways. HOLLISTER discussed the battle in the context of English military institutions; his aim was to show the continuing influence of the Anglo-Saxon in the Anglo-Norman kingdom. Thus he pointed out that all the major Anglo-Norman battles, few in number though they were, saw Anglo-Norman knights dismounting for combat. Hollister took this as indicating an Anglo-Saxon influence on the Normans' tactics. That influence, he argued, resulted both from the impressive showing the Saxon army made at Hastings, which taught the Normans the value of a solid wall of infantry, and from the continued survival of the Saxon five-hide army (the fyrd) under the Norman kings and their use of it to raise substantial infantry forces. Dismounted knights then formed an elite front for English infantry.

BRADBURY, in an article devoted to a closer examination of the patterns of Anglo-Norman battles rather than their institutional context, challenged Hollister's interpretation, pointing out that Continental forces at other times in the medieval period also dismounted. He interpreted Tenchebrai in terms of a larger pattern of medieval commanders searching for effective answers to the power of the cavalry charge. This represented an implicit acceptance of the premise of Oman's "age of cavalry", but without an explanation of how it came about.

MORILLO places Tenchebrai in the contexts of both Anglo-Norman military institutions and the usual patterns of Anglo-Norman warfare, including not just battles but campaigns, sieges, and other sorts of military activity, including a detailed examination of the other major Anglo-Norman battles. He agrees with Hollister that there was an Anglo-Saxon influence in Anglo-Norman warfare, partly through the continued use of the fyrd, but more importantly through the institutional strength and wealth that Saxon governance bequeathed to the Normans. Combined with the institution of the military household, which provided the Norman kings with a core of full-time professional troops, Morillo argues, this institutional strength was what made for effective infantry tactics. He claims that the relationship between the strength of the government and the quality of the infantry more generally helps explain both Oman's "age of cavalry" – really an age of bad infantry – and the exceptions, such as Tenchebrai and many of the cases Bradbury cites.

STEPHEN MORILLO

See also Henry I

Test and Corporation Acts, Repeal of 1828

Bradley, James E., *Religion, Revolution, and English Radicalism: Nonconformity in Eighteenth-Century Politics and Society*, Cambridge: Cambridge University Press, 1990

Clark, J.C.D., "England's Ancien Regime as a Confessional State", *Albion*, 21/3 (1989): 450–74

Clark, J.C.D., *English Society, 1688–1832: Ideology, Social Structure, and Political Practice during the Ancien Regime*, Cambridge and New York: Cambridge University Press, 1985; revised edition, as *English Society, 1660–1832: Religion, Ideology, and Politics during the Ancien Regime*, Cambridge and New York: Cambridge University Press, 2000

Ditchfield, G.M., "The Parliamentary Struggle over the Repeal of the Test and Corporation Acts, 1787–1790", *English Historical Review*, 89 (1974): 551–77

Machin, G.I.T., "Resistance to Repeal of the Test and Corporation Acts, 1828", *Historical Journal*, 22/1 (1979): 115–39

Mather, F.C., *High Church Prophet: Bishop Samuel Horsley (1733–1806) and the Caroline Tradition in the Later Georgian Church*, Oxford: Clarendon Press, and New York: Oxford University Press, 1992

Watts, Michael R., *The Dissenters*, vol. 1, *From the Reformation to the French Revolution*, Oxford: Clarendon Press, 1978

Watts, Michael R., *The Dissenters*, vol. 2, *The Expansion of Evangelical Nonconformity, 1791–1859*, Oxford: Clarendon Press, 1995

Following the Restoration, the Corporation Act of 1661 was passed in order to exclude protestant dissenters, seen as obdurate supporters of the Cromwellian revolution, from municipal corporations. It stipulated that all corporations' mayors and officials should take the oaths of allegiance and supremacy and that in order to qualify for office they had to take holy communion according to the rites of the Church of England. Thus, supposedly, dissenters would henceforth be unable to influence either local administration or the choice of members of parliament in corporation boroughs. The first Test Act, passed in 1673, was directed principally against Roman catholics, but it also affected dissenters. It instituted as the qualification for state office, civil and military, taking oaths of allegiance and supremacy, making a declaration denying transubstantiation, and receiving the Anglican sacrament within three months of assuming a position. In 1828 parliament passed a bill, introduced by the Whigs, which abolished the sacramental test prescribed by the acts, in order to benefit dissenters. Catholics remained disabled under the other stipulations of the laws, but emancipation was granted in 1829. It is worth noting that under George I, Stanhope contemplated abrogating the acts, and that their repeal was debated, but defeated, in parliament in 1736, 1739, 1787, 1789, and 1790.

Historians have taken different views of the repeal of the Test and Corporation Acts. In the 19th century, the great Whig historian Macaulay saw repeal as yet another stage in the gradual but sure evolution of constitutional and religious liberties from medieval times to the 19th century. Writing of the Bill of Rights of 1689, he maintained:

The Declaration of Right, though it made nothing law which had not been law before, contained the germ of the law which gave religious freedom to the Dissenter, ... of the law which abolished the sacramental test, [and] of the law which relieved the Roman Catholics from civil disabilities. ...

Though a slowly changing intellectual climate among the elite was a precondition for repeal, this "Whiggish" approach is not entirely satisfying. Its sense of inevitability is suspect. DITCHFIELD has detailed how and why parliament refused to concede change between 1787 and 1790. MACHIN has described the resistance to repeal in 1828. His article also shows the importance of contingency: "[t]he sudden emergence and passage of a repeal bill in 1828 is explained more convincingly by political circumstances than by long-term social trends or the rapid growth of dissent". In particular, Machin explains why the Whigs, seeking a cause around which to rally, could champion repeal in that year. It was a propitious moment because the related issue, catholic emancipation – deeply controversial in the country at large and problematic among dissenters themselves – appeared shelved after Wellington became prime minister. "Whiggish" praise for the ultimate victors is, furthermore, one-sided. One can observe, in recent writing, a sympathetic appreciation of men who evinced a principled opposition to change. MATHER's study of Bishop Samuel Horsley (1733–1806) illustrates this.

It would, of course, be possible to write the history of the repeal of the acts from an overwhelmingly denominational perspective, focusing on the dissenters' lobbying and tactics. An approach that emphasizes the spiritual aspects of the issues can be a valuable one. WATTS, among others, has noted that the practice of occasional conformity – the infrequent taking of the sacrament by nonconformists in Anglican churches in order to

qualify for office – did not necessarily compromise orthodox dissenters' theological convictions (despite churchmen's charges of hypocrisy). Nonetheless, in recent years interest in the subject has centred on the significance of the acts and their repeal for the concept of the state. CLARK argues that during the "long 18th century", England was "an ancien-regime State, dominated politically, culturally and ideologically by the three pillars of an early-modern social order: monarchy, aristocracy, church". Moreover, for Clark, one of its chief defining characteristics was that it was a "confessional" state, in which political power lay in Anglican hands. Clark sees politics and religion as wholly interwoven. Anglican hegemony was a principal buttress of the old order. During the late 1780s and 1790s, dissent – and especially rational dissent (whose adherents abhorred the test) – spawned radical ideas; and in the campaign for the repeal of the Test and Corporation Acts, the dissenters were indeed, according to Clark, dangerously subversive: they sought to overthrow the old regime. Eventually, repeal and catholic emancipation marked the end of the old order as decisively as the Reform Act of 1832.

Clark's emphasis on the confessional nature of the English state in the "long 18th century" has attracted criticism. For dissenters, though not for catholics, it can be shown that during the 18th century practice belied the paper theory to a significant degree. From 1727 on, indemnity acts were passed almost annually, protecting from prosecution dissenters who served on corporations without taking the Anglican sacrament. BRADLEY has demonstrated the power of nonconformists in some towns. But Bradley agrees with Clark in stressing the radical characteristics of dissenting politics – though he treats these sympathetically. Certainly, Clark's view of the repeal of the Test and Corporation Acts, along with catholic emancipation, as a defining episode in English history rings true when one reads the words of leading opponents and proponents of abolishing the sacramental test. The Tory Lord Eldon maintained that "the Church of England, combined with the State, formed together the constitution of Great Britain, and that the Test and Corporation Acts were necessary to the preservation of that constitution". For the Whig Lord Holland, repeal "explodes the real Tory doctrine *that Church & State are indivisible*".

COLIN HAYDON

See also Protestant Dissent; Russell

Tettenhall, Battle of   909 or 910

Campbell, A. (editor), *The Chronicle of Æthelweard*, London and New York: Nelson, 1962
Gelling, Margaret, *The West Midlands in the Early Middle Ages*, Leicester and New York: Leicester University Press, 1992
Hill, David, *An Atlas of Anglo-Saxon England*, Oxford: Blackwell, and Toronto: University of Toronto Press, 1981
Stenton, F.M., *Anglo-Saxon England*, Oxford: Clarendon Press, 1943; 2nd edition, 1947; 3rd edition, 1971; reprinted, Oxford and New York: Oxford University Press, 1990 (*Oxford History of England*, vol. 2)

Wormald, Patrick, *The Making of English Law: King Alfred to the Twelfth Century*, vol. 1, *Legislation and Its Limits*, Oxford and Malden, Massachusetts: Blackwell, 1999

The great Danish army under Ingwar and Halfdan, sons of Ragnar Lothbrok, landed in East Anglia in 865 to begin a new phase of Scandinavian attacks on the Anglo-Saxons; this ended in 954 when Eadred, king of the West Saxons, completed the reconquest and unification of England by taking over the Scandinavian kingdom of York. Almost exactly halfway between those two events three versions of the *Anglo-Saxon Chronicle* record the defeat in 910 (or 909) of the Danes by an English force at Tettenhall in Staffordshire; the *Chronicle of Æthelweard* gives the place of the battle as Wodnesfelda (Wednesfield) and supplies the actual date (5 August; Æthelweard also specifies the year as 909) with important additional matter about the campaign of which this battle was the climax. An army of Northumbrian Danes ravaged as far as the Bristol Avon, apparently approaching from the north-east: they then crossed the Severn, presumably at Gloucester by ferry, and marched north through the country to the west of the river, gaining much more booty as they went, until at Cuatbrycge they turned eastwards and crossed the river by a bridge. This army was pursued by a force of Mercians and West Saxons sent by King Edward the Elder, which caught and defeated the raiders at Wednesfield, slaying there three kings and several nobles. No source says precisely that King Edward the Elder commanded the English force in person.

Æthelweard was a descendant of the West Saxon royal house through King Alfred's brother Æthelred I, and himself an ealdorman with experience of high matters. Æthelweard's modern editor, CAMPBELL, testifies to his reliability, and the ealdorman appears to have had access to annals not otherwise known.

In this account two topographical points require comment. First, Cuatbrycge, where the Danes crossed the Severn, was named as the site of both a *geweorc*, or fortification, set up by earlier Danish raiders in 895 (*Anglo-Saxon Chronicle*) and the bridge mentioned by Æthelweard in 910; it is taken to be the modern Bridgnorth, but there is no other linguistic evidence to connect one place with the other, though some boundaries of 1300 within Quatford, two miles south-east of Bridgnorth, mention the "hethenedich" (Eyton, *Antiquities of Shropshire*), and for the unforgetting English the heathen were primarily the Danes. That the Danes chose to turn east here, at the last crossing of the Severn before the complications of what later came to be called the Ironbridge Gorge and before the long miles until the next bridge at Shrewsbury would have considerably lengthened their homeward journey, says much for the good sense of the raiders, as also for the wisdom of Æthelfleda, Lady of the Mercians, when in 912 she chose Bridgnorth as the site of one of the new fortified English *burhs* which she and her royal brother planted over the years in the Midlands to restrict the Danes. Second, whether the battle was fought at Tettenhall or Wednesfield need not greatly worry us, however much those places now differ from each other: from Bridgnorth to Tettenhall is 12 miles, and Wednesfield is a further three. Wednesfield took its name from Woden and represents the western limit of this type of name.

To E.A. Freeman (*History of the Norman Conquest of England*, 1877), Edward the Elder was "one of the greatest rulers that England ever beheld", and his reign of 25 years was the "turning-point" in the 170 years from Egbert to Edgar during which the "kingdom of England" was built up. In the three editions of his *Anglo-Saxon England* STENTON followed a lucid summary of the events of 910 with a rather more pertinent generalization: "The battle of Tettenhall opened the way to the great expansion of the West Saxon kingdom which occurred in the following years". His argument was that the heavy losses incurred at Tettenhall by the Danes from Northumbria prevented them from intervening further south in the interests of Danes in Essex and the south-east Midlands as these were subverted in turn by attacks by Edward the Elder and his sister Æthelfleda. GELLING accepts Stenton's main point.

Edward the Elder was clearly a warrior who saw a need not only for ferocity in battle but for superiority before giving battle: a notable point in Æthelweard's account of the campaign of 910 is that Edward's army was both Mercian and West Saxon; Edward could use the resources of Mercia by reason of its political junction with Wessex, its ruler Æthelred being husband to Edward's sister. When this sister died in 918 Edward swiftly displaced her only child, his niece Ælfwynn, around whom it seemed possible that Mercian support might gather. (This is one of the few Anglo-Saxon court intrigues to figure in a novel.)

What makes a single battle decisive for the future? Lessons learnt from one battle may be applied by the same commander or a successor in another; but the conditions in which battles recur, even between similar antagonists, must vary in terms of terrain and numbers. In the 10th century the physical energy of kings was all-important: the *Anglo-Saxon Chronicle* shows that Edward the Elder (d. 924) – clearly a military organizer of considerable skill – was, after some relatively quiet years in the 910s, able to renew activity as a warrior in his final years. His sons Athelstan and Edmund defeated a strong coalition of opponents at Brunanburh (wherever that may have been) in 937; and Edmund's successor Eadred invaded Northumbria early on, briefly recovered York in 944, and finally recovered it 10 years later (he was to die the following year). The chances of heredity produced not only this line of (for the times) long-lived and intelligent warriors but also (after 902) an absence of rival princes such as Edward the Elder's nephew Æthelwold, who had disputed the throne and curbed royal activity in Edward's early years.

The progress of events can be followed in the maps in HILL. However, these cannot reveal what Stenton saw as a basic feature of the situation, the antipathy between Danes and Norsemen: the Norse who came from the ports of the eastern coasts of Ireland achieved lodgements on the north-west coast of England from the Wirral to the Solway Firth and challenged the Danes who were established across the Pennines. Moreover, the submission to the West Saxons of increasing numbers of Danes further south demonstrated to still independent Scandinavians that the West Saxons' rule was not intolerable. Above all, the detailed researches of WORMALD have shown that King Edgar (959–75) was ready to grant a measure of autonomy to his Danish subjects.

The battle of Tettenhall was decisive because the good luck of the West Saxon royal house continued for two more generations, and the capacity and inclination of the Danes for war had diminished.

JOHN F.A. MASON

See also Edward "the Elder"

Textiles

see Cloth Industry, Medieval; Industrial Revolution

Thatcher, Margaret, 1st Baroness of Kesteven b. 1925

Conservative politician, stateswoman, and prime minister

Evans, Eric J., *Thatcher and Thatcherism*, London and
    New York: Routledge, 1997
Harris, Kenneth, *Thatcher*, London: Weidenfeld and Nicolson,
    and Boston: Little Brown, 1988
Junor, Penny, *Margaret Thatcher: Wife, Mother, Politician*,
    London: Sidgwick and Jackson, 1983
Smith, Geoffrey, *Reagan and Thatcher*, London: Bodley Head,
    1990; New York: Norton, 1991
Thatcher, Margaret, *The Downing Street Years*, London and
    New York: HarperCollins, 1993
Young, Hugo, *One of Us: A Biography of Margaret Thatcher*,
    London: Macmillan, 1989; 2nd edition, 1991

Opinion in the literature on Margaret Thatcher is divided. Some argue that, during her premiership from 1979 to 1990, she transformed the image of Britain from the parasitic sick man of Europe to an industrious, thriving, patriotic nation with a seat at the great table of world politics – a seat which she personally had earned at the very least through her role in ending the cold war. From Pretoria to Beijing, regimes across the world have followed her belief in the free-enterprise economy, if not in the primacy of the individual. Renowned for her abolition of society, and for her conviction that there are only individual men and women and families, Margaret Thatcher, at the end of the 20th century, in the opinion of this school, represents the triumph of John Stuart Mill's 19th-century philosophy of economic and personal liberalism over totalitarianism, socialism, and Marxism-Leninism. But Thatcher has been scorned by an intellectual elite and the professional classes, many of whom have found her taste "low" and her personality loathsome and repulsive, and have criticized her leadership of a government that placed too much emphasis on monetarism and privatization and too little on charity.

JUNOR has written a sympathetic account of Thatcher's background and her rise to power in a world dominated by male politicians, offering interesting insights into her personality. Junor argues that Thatcher's fundamental failing is a lack of personal confidence, which is reflected in an inability to be real; to swear, laugh, or cry; to show warmth and emotion. HARRIS notes that Thatcher has been the only British prime minister to inspire an "ism", but he offers a critique of the moral criteria of Thatcherism and its emphasis on Victorian values: to build a national morality on the moral value of work could be seen as economically short-sighted and offensive to those who were unable to get a job.

In a detailed work, YOUNG depicts a leader convinced within herself that by the time of her third election she had carried Britain, by the only honest policies available, towards "the destiny her people desired and the world would strive to emulate". The working class was predominant in this Thatcherite nation, whose prime minister was an enthusiastic exponent of market liberalism and global economic conservatism and led one of the "most fearlessly ideological" governments of modern times, one that believed in the virtues of inequality both as an economic motivating force and as a way of distributing the fruits. Young points to right-wing criticism of Thatcher for overlooking the dangers of "bourgeois triumphalism", reflected in the vulgarity of the "yuppies". He argues that Thatcher, far from reducing the role of government, made it felt wherever she thought that the blessing of its superior wisdom should be experienced, particularly in curbing local democracy in local government, education, and housing: she emasculated or dismantled bodies that could rival the central state. In Young's view Thatcher changed the estimation of Britain: Britain's international reputation was enhanced by victory in the Falklands War; Britain's economic recovery, with the trade unions under control, meant that it was no longer a supplicant; and much of this improvement was achieved by Thatcher's visible leadership – her strength and her long political life excited admiration. One of Thatcher's main characteristics was dominance, and Young portrays a woman whose presence overshadowed the whole of public life and much of private conversation, whose appeal to righteousness went deeper than economic management, drove her on, and fed her energy and enthusiasm. Depicting Thatcher as a pragmatist, a populist, and someone determined to pursue the economics of sound housekeeping she had learnt from her father, Young suggests that there is little evidence that many people liked her, still less loved her.

SMITH suggests that both Ronald Reagan and Margaret Thatcher were elected to lead countries whose self-confidence had been severely damaged and that wanted to walk tall in the world again. His book offers insights into the nature and style of the relationship between the British prime minister and the American president: in the end it is Thatcher who emerges as the more powerful force. According to Smith, the prime minister's visit to Russia confirmed her as a star on the world stage; and whenever there was a choice, her heart lay across the Atlantic rather than across the English Channel.

When they were published, THATCHER's own memoirs were not thought to be as revealing as those of her predecessors. She offered the theme that democratic socialism had been a miserable failure in Britain and had accelerated rather than reversed Britain's slow decline relative to its main industrial competitors. The failure of the Suez expedition of 1956 – a result of political and economic weakness rather than military failure, when the Eden government had withdrawn a victorious force from the canal zone, forced by a "run on the pound" encouraged by Washington – had entered the British soul and distorted Britons' perspective of their country's place in the world. In her memoirs, Thatcher admits having had a conviction that she could save the country and that no one else could; she also notes that her father's background as a grocer, as well as his economic theories about the free market, formed the basis of her economic philosophy. According to her own account, she saw the job of government as establishing a framework of stability within which individual families and businesses would be free to pursue their own dreams and ambitions.

EVANS attempts a preliminary evaluation of Margaret Thatcher and the legacy of Thatcherism as a cultural construct and an economic creed. In a highly critical volume, he argues that Thatcher's "conviction politics" led her to destroy rather than create, that her narrow vision prevented her from seeing the medium- and long-term consequences of her policies, and that in "using the power of the state negatively – to resurrect as much unbridled capitalism as a decade of power in an elective dictatorship could encompass – Thatcherism morally impoverished and desensitized a nation".

RITCHIE OVENDALE

See also Cold War; Conservative Party; European Economic Community–European Union; Falklands War; Heath; Nationalization and Denationalization

Theodore *c.*602–690
Archbishop of Canterbury

Bischoff, Bernhard and Michael Lapidge (editors), *Biblical Commentaries from the Canterbury School of Theodore and Hadrian*, Cambridge and New York: Cambridge University Press, 1994

Dales, Douglas, *Light to the Isles: A Study of Missionary Theology in Celtic and Early Anglo-Saxon Britain*, Cambridge: Lutterworth Press, 1997

Lapidge, Michael (editor), *Archbishop Theodore: Commemorative Studies on His Life and Influence*, Cambridge and New York: Cambridge University Press, 1995

Mayr-Harting, Henry, *The Coming of Christianity to Anglo-Saxon England*, London: Batsford, 1972; as *The Coming of Christianity to England*, New York: Schocken Books, 1972

Orchard, Andy, *The Poetic Art of Aldhelm*, Cambridge and New York: Cambridge University Press, 1994

Stevenson, Jane, *The "Laterculus Malalianus" and the School of Archbishop Theodore*, Cambridge and New York: Cambridge University Press, 1995

Theodore of Tarsus was a figure of prime importance in the early Anglo-Saxon church. DALES summarizes his work and its context, stressing that Theodore's appointment as Archbishop of Canterbury by Pope Vitalian in 668 was unusual; Theodore was a Greek from Tarsus, who had been closely identified with the papacy in its struggle with the Byzantine emperor during the Monothelite controversy. Theodore came to England, accompanied by the African abbot Hadrian, and together they developed a strong centre of learning and education at Canterbury. Both Aldhelm and Bede, the two foremost scholars of the end of the 7th century, owed much to its influence. Theodore reorganized the English church, creating new bishops and also new dioceses. He presided over two important church councils, at Hertford in 672 and Hatfield in 679, and left a legacy of penitential teaching, which proved fundamental in England and on the Continent. Theodore's primacy was dogged by controversy with Wilfrid, who for a time was Bishop of York until he fell out with the king of Northumbria. Wilfrid challenged Theodore's attempts to divide his vast northern diocese and went into exile on several occasions to appeal to the pope in

Rome. The rich teaching that Theodore and Hadrian offered at Canterbury has been a subject of much recent research, despite the relative paucity of documentary evidence remaining.

MAYR-HARTING deals with Theodore's work and influence throughout his book, showing how Theodore accepted the tribal basis of episcopacy, which had been created by the first Roman and Irish missionaries, while trying to reform it into smaller and more practical dioceses, such as he had experienced in Asia Minor and in Italy. Theodore's great achievement was ensuring the unity of the English church under the leadership of the Archbishop of Canterbury. Mayr-Harting indicates the extent of cultural and religious influence from the eastern Mediterranean on the 7th-century Anglo-Saxon church, and how Theodore was guided by the pastoral teaching of St Gregory the Great. Mayr-Harting also vindicates Aldhelm's tribute to the wealth of learning available at Canterbury and shows how vestiges remain of the "Antiochene" approach to the exegesis of the Bible in some manuscripts associated with Theodore. This reveals precise knowledge of history, geography, and topography of the Middle East, which could have come only from first-hand experience. He confirms the essentially humane ethos of Theodore's penitential teaching. The value of Mayr-Harting's work is that he is able to reveal the intricate pattern of cultural contacts which helped form Anglo-Saxon Christianity during the 7th century; and in this Theodore's contribution was decisive and abiding.

LAPIDGE has produced a thorough survey of the likely background to Theodore's life and religious formation. He sketches in the state of learning in Byzantium and Athens at this time and also explores the strong presence of Greek monks in Rome in the 7th century. He discusses in some detail the impact of the Monothelite controversy upon the papacy – the sufferings of Pope Martin and of Maximus the Confessor, with whom Theodore was closely associated. He shows how Theodore remained an authority on this matter even while far away in England. All this is valuable general background, which, again, emphasizes the unusual nature of Theodore's appointment to rescue the Roman mission-church in England. But perforce, much of it is conjectural because so little remains to corroborate Theodore's career before he came to Canterbury.

BISCHOFF & LAPIDGE's collaboration produced a critical translation of some fragmentary commentaries on the Pentateuch and the Gospels, which contain glosses (the "Leiden glossaries") associated with Theodore's school at Canterbury. These reveal a pattern of preference for eastern church fathers, some knowledge of Syrian theology, a strong interest in historical detail, and little evidence of Latin traditions of biblical exegesis. This "Antiochene" approach is distinctive and rare in the western church at that time.

The same pattern may be more fully discerned in the "Laterculus Malalianus", which is critically examined by STEVENSON. This is a simple commentary on the life of Christ in the Gospels, with explanations that reveal a typical Semitic and typological approach to the text of the Bible. They contain much evidence of a philological interest, and knowledge about medicine, philosophy, rhetoric, metrology, and chronology. There are many first-hand references to geographical and topographical details in the lands of the Bible, and hints of these features may also be detected in the writing of Aldhelm and of Bede.

The wealth of teaching at Canterbury under Theodore's leadership is reflected also in the learning of Aldhelm, a scholar and bishop of south-western England, who went to Canterbury in his thirties and later paid glowing tribute to what he had received there. The examination of Aldhelms' Latin poetry by ORCHARD confirms what has already been established elsewhere by Lapidge and others, that Aldhelm was proficient in his grasp of the language and familiar with the work of his predecessors in Christian Latin poetry. His influence upon Anglo-Latin poetry remained profound throughout the Anglo-Saxon period. In chapter 4 of his book, Orchard shows in some detail the range of association that permeates Aldhelm's verse: his first-hand knowledge of Virgil, Sedulius, Prosper, and Symphosius and his familiarity with imagery drawn from many of the later Roman poets, as well as from the Christian Latin tradition. This picture confirms the testimony, in his letters, to the intellectual significance of Theodore and Hadrian as leaders of the English church, a judgement also confirmed by Bede himself, who was an indirect beneficiary of their learning and the resources that supported it.

DOUGLAS DALES

See also Anglo-Saxon England: Church Organization

Thomas, Cardinal Bourchier c.1410–1486

Clark, Linda S. "The Benefits and Burdens of Office: Henry Bourgchier (1408–83), Viscount Bourgchier and Earl of Essex, and the Treasurership of the Exchequer", in *Profit, Piety, and the Professions in Later Medieval England*, edited by Michael Hicks, Gloucester: Alan Sutton, 1989; Wolfeboro Falls, New Hampshire: Alan Sutton, 1990

Du Boulay, F.R.H. (editor), *Registrum Thome Bourgchier Cantuariensis Archiepiscopi, AD 1454–1486*, Canterbury and York Society 54, Oxford: Oxford University Press, 1957

Emden, A.B., entry on Bourchier in his *A Biographical Register of the University of Oxford to AD 1500*, vol. 1, Oxford: Clarendon Press, 1957

Hicks, Michael, *False, Fleeting, Perjur'd Clarence: George, Duke of Clarence, 1449–1478*, Stroud, Gloucestershire: Alan Sutton, 1980; revised edition, Bangor: Headstart History, 1992

Scofield, Cora L., *The Life and Reign of Edward the Fourth, King of England and France and Lord of Ireland*, 2 vols, London and New York: Longmans Green, 1923; reprinted, London: Frank Cass, and New York: Octagon Books, 1967

Storey, Robin L., "Episcopal Kingmakers in the Fifteeenth Century" in *The Church, Poltics, and Patronage in the Fifteenth Century*, edited by Barrie Dobson, Stroud, Gloucester: Alan Sutton, and New York: St Martin's Press, 1984

Thompson, A. Hamilton, *The English Clergy and Their Organization in the Later Middle Ages*, Oxford: Clarendon Press, 1947

Thomas, Cardinal Bourchier, was primate of England through all the crises of the Wars of the Roses and crowned the three usurpers Edward IV, Richard III, and Henry VII, yet historians are not agreed on the nature of his role or his significance in either church affairs or politics. His precocious advancement to bishop while still in his twenties, his promotion to the archbishopric of Canterbury, and eventually his cardinalate (1468) are all to be explained at least partly by the eminence of his birth. His parents (he was their younger son) were William Count of Eu and the only daughter of Edward III's fifth son; he was born into the blood royal and was the half-brother of Humphrey Stafford, Duke of Buckingham, who was among the most reliable of Henry VI's noblemen. On the marriage of his elder brother Henry Bourchier to Isabel Plantagenet, sister of Richard, Duke of York, Thomas became closely related to the magnate most critical of Henry VI's regime and ultimately the king's rival for the crown. Thomas was uncle to both Edward IV and Richard III and great-uncle of Edward V and his sister Elizabeth of York, queen to Henry VII. He was one of the select group of the greatest nobility who attained the highest positions in the late medieval English church.

As a younger son, he was early designated for a career in the church and educated accordingly at Oxford University. The fullest record of his early career, his education, and his ecclesiastical appointments before his elevation to the episcopate is now in EMDEN; however, Emden regrettably omits the names of Thomas's patrons and supplies little explanation. Thomas's contested appointment as Bishop of Worcester in 1433–35 is recounted most fully by THOMPSON. In 1443 Thomas became Bishop of Ely. His elevation to the archbishopric of Canterbury in 1454 occurred during the first protectorate of his brother-in-law Richard, Duke of York, and at Richard's behest; but it was King Henry VI himself who first appointed Thomas Chancellor of England in 1455, and Henry's queen Margaret of Anjou is usually blamed for Thomas's dismissal from the chancellorship, along with the dismissal of Thomas's brother Henry from the treasurership, in 1456.

DU BOULAY, the editor of Thomas Bourchier's archiepiscopal register, has retold his career and attempted a reappraisal. While conceding that Thomas's personality "remains in the shadow", Du Boulay found sufficient evidence to rebut the charge that Thomas was merely a "clever time-server" who avoided commitment during crises. Du Boulay found a recurring theme in Thomas's role as "confidant and arbitrator, probably by temperament and almost by preference", and presented him as loyal to Henry VI until loyalty was no longer possible. As archbishop, Thomas Bourchier opposed York's unexpected claim late in 1460, accepted the compromise offered by the Act of Accord, and committed himself definitively to Edward IV in 1461. Du Boulay points out that Thomas was one of the first to be named a councillor and to be granted a salary. Thomas remained loyal to Edward in 1470–71, when he was involved in the reconciliation of the king with his brother Clarence, and to Edward V in 1483, reputedly crowning Richard, Duke of Gloucester, as Richard III only with reluctance. Apparently Thomas did not suspect Richard's intentions: Richard was fortunate to be able to exploit the cardinal's eminence and acceptability to all to secure possession of the young Duke of York, whom he consigned with his brother Edward V to the Tower. Following Richard's death at Bosworth and in the absence of any other credible claimant, the venerable primate had no choice but to crown Henry VII. Thomas Bourchier's aristocratic tastes are best illustrated by the splendid palace of Knole that he built for himself at Sevenoaks in Kent and the genuineness of his loyalty as a cleric in making it a bequest to his see of Canterbury.

STOREY re-examines Thomas Bourchier as an "episcopal kingmaker", finding that the ecclesiastical and political roles combined by Archbishop Arundel in 1399 were separated in 1460–61, when George Neville took the political lead and Thomas only the ecclesiastical one. Thomas indeed sought to use the opportunity to obtain royal protection for clerical liberties from interference by common lawyers, but he secured only fine words from King Edward and no effective action.

Du Boulay's treatment of Thomas's political career under the Yorkists is very thin. Very little factual information has been added to that collected by SCOFIELD, but interpretations have moved on. The fullest consideration of the family as a whole, by Clark (née Woodger) – her DPhil thesis, "Henry Bourgchier, Earl of Essex (1408–83), and His Family" (Oxford University, 1974) – is regrettably unpublished. CLARK's paper (1990) on Henry Bourchier's role as lord treasurer for much of the Yorkist period casts light on the family as a whole. Without questioning the commitment of all the Bourchiers to the house of York, HICKS presents them as a moderating influence, separate from but on good terms with all the warring factions: the Nevilles and Wydevilles (Woodvilles) before 1470, Clarence and the king's favourites thereafter, Hastings and the Wydevilles in 1483.

Since Thomas Bourchier did not change history and is relatively poorly documented, he seems an unlikely candidate for reappraisal.

MICHAEL HICKS

See also Edward IV; Henry VI; Richard III

Tillett, Ben 1860–1943
Trade union leader and Labour politician

Clegg, H.A., A History of British Trade Unions since 1889, vol. 2, 1911–1933, Oxford: Clarendon Press, and New York: Oxford University Press, 1985
Clegg, H.A., Alan Fox, and A.F. Thompson, A History of British Trade Unions since 1889, vol. 1, 1889–1910, Oxford: Clarendon Press, and New York: Oxford University Press, 1964
Coates, Ken and Tony Topham, The Making of the Transport and General Workers' Union, vol. 1, The Emergence of the Labour Movement 1870–1922, Oxford and Cambridge, Massachusetts: Blackwell, 1991
Holton, Bob, British Syndicalism 1900–1914: Myths and Realities, London: Pluto Press, 1976
Light, George (editor), Ben Tillett: Fighter and Pioneer, London: Blandford Press, 1943
Lovell, John, Stevedores and Dockers: A Study of Trade Unionism in the Port of London, 1870–1914, London: Macmillan, and New York: Kelley, 1969
McCarthy, Terry (editor), The Great Dock Strike, 1889, London: Weidenfeld and Nicolson/Transport and General Workers' Union, 1988
Saville, John and A.J. Topham, entry on Tillett in Dictionary of Labour Biography (DNB), vol. 4, edited by Joyce M. Bellamy and John Saville, London: Macmillan, and Clifton, New Jersey: Kelley, 1977
Schneer, Jonathan, Ben Tillett: Portrait of a Labour Leader, London: Croom Helm, and Urbana: University of Illinois Press, 1982
Taylor, J.J., entry on Tillett in Dictionary of National Biography 1941–1950, edited by L.G. Wickham Legg and E.T. Williams, London: Oxford University Press, 1959
Tillett, Ben, Memories and Reflections, London: John Long, 1931

Ben Tillett suddenly achieved renown as one of the leaders of the "new unionism" of 1889, and for over 40 years thereafter he had a prominent if idiosyncratic career as a labour leader. He was, in the words of his principal biographer, SCHNEER, "one part eccentric, two parts egoist, three parts crusader". This assessment is carefully documented by Schneer, who concentrates on the important early phases of Tillett's career, notably the foundation and early fortunes of the Dockers' Union; Schneer also assesses Tillett's role as an ultra-patriotic supporter of World War I and as a Labour MP (in 1917–24 and 1929–31). Schneer shows, too, that Tillett believed he was pushed aside by Ernest Bevin during the amalgamation that created the Transport and General Workers' Union (TGWU) in 1922; Tillett wanted to become the union's president but had to be content with the newly created post of international and political secretary. In his preface, Schneer notes that his book is "not intended to be a full-length biography" but rather is a study focusing on Tillett's public career between 1887 and 1921. It is nevertheless unlikely that sufficient new material will emerge to justify the publication of a biography that would supersede Schneer's able study.

In 1931 TILLETT published his autobiography, an account enlivened by assessments of the men and movements with which he was associated, but revealing only the odd gesture of self-criticism (and asserting, on the matter of the presidency of the TGWU, "I did not press my claim"). Tillett remained active in trade unionism into his seventies, though by the time of his death he had embraced the ideas of Moral Rearmament, and it is on this connection that LIGHT focuses in a commemorative pamphlet published following Tillett's death. TAYLOR, in a short sketch in the DNB, also takes a sympathetic approach, noting for instance that Tillett "belonged to the evangelistic days of trade-unionism, when men spoke with natural oratory", without adding that his power as a speaker did not always compensate for inadequate administrative ability. A more rounded short assessment is offered by SAVILLE & TOPHAM, who also supply a list of Tillett's writings in an entry followed by a detailed bibliography of the new unionism of 1889–93. The authors of a standard history of trade unionism, CLEGG, FOX, & THOMPSON, are rather more critical. In comparing the leaders of the new unionism, for instance, they characterize Will Thorne and James Sexton as "sensible and competent", and Tom Mann as "a more likeable person" than Tillett, whom they describe in part by quoting William Collison, an opponent: "a demagogue, with the taste of a sybarite; a voluptuary with the hide of an agitator. . . . Ever grasping at the present shadow of fleeting popularity, he lost the substance of future greatness". In the second volume of this history, CLEGG makes several references to Tillett's shortcomings. There is a similar delineation in the authorized history of the TGWU by COATES & TOPHAM, who include among Tillett's weaknesses a habit of blaming others for defeats and antipathy towards both backsliding members of his own union and the leaders of other unions.

Other writers have tended to concentrate on Tillett's role during periods of trade union militancy. McCARTHY, in a book on the dock strike of 1889 published with the support of the TGWU, includes many quotations from contemporary reports and reproduces numerous illustrations. A monograph by LOVELL shows the part played by the small Tea Operatives and General Labourers' Association, which had been established in the London docks in 1887 with Tillett as its secretary; in this author's estimation Tillett "was a flamboyant character, a man of grand gestures, sweeping generalisations, extravagant denunciations and considerable vision". Lovell's book is also useful for its account of Tillett's role in the dock strikes of 1911 and 1912, although more quotations illustrating the syndicalist, "class war" rhetoric of his speeches appear in the study by HOLTON. Addressing strikers on 19 July 1912, for example, Tillett said:

> The Cabinet, Parliament and politicians had declared that they were slaves, and all of them bowed down to Lord Almighty Devonport [chairman of the Port of London Authority and subject of Tillett's infamous prayer, "God, strike Lord Devonport dead!"]. . . . If they did not understand what the brutality of the class war was, they were slaves indeed.

A little over two years later, Tillett assumed the role of the patriotic voice of the ordinary serviceman, declaring, "In a strike I am for my class right or wrong; in a war I am for my country right or wrong"; and in 1917, at his fifth attempt, he entered the parliament he had once described as a farce and a sham.

D.E. MARTIN

See also Bevin; Labour Party

Tilotson, John 1630–1694
Archbishop of Canterbury and advocate of comprehension

Birch, Thomas (editor), *The Works of Dr. John Tillotson . . . with the Life of the Author*, 10 vols, London: R. Priestley, 1820

Every, George, *The High Church Party, 1688–1718*, London: SPCK, 1956

Mitchell, W. Fraser, *English Pulpit Oratory from Andrewes to Tillotson: A Study of Its Literary Aspects*, New York: Macmillan, and London: SPCK, 1932

Straka, Gerald M., *Anglican Reaction to the Revolution of 1688*, Madison: State Historical Society of Wisconsin, 1962

Sykes, Norman, *Church and State in England in the XVIIIth Century*, Cambridge: Cambridge University Press, 1934; reprinted, Hamden, Connecticut: Archon Books, 1962

Sykes, Norman, *From Sheldon to Secker: Aspects of English Church History, 1660–1768*, Cambridge: Cambridge University Press, 1959

The Anglican tradition has been somewhat neglectful of its moderates, preferring the commitment and zeal of figures like Laud and Pusey. Thus the so-called latitudinarians often find themselves regarded as men of weak faith who do not measure up to the standard of their deeply religious colleagues. This may account for the fact that John Tilotson has yet to find a modern biographer, even though there is no doubt about his importance in a variety of capacities.

For example, Tilotson stands out as a great preacher. He and Bishop Lancelot Andrewes at the beginning of the 1600s rank as the two foremost sermon writers of the 17th century. In fact, according to MITCHELL's study of pulpit oratory, Tilotson set the model for sermons well into the 1700s. Mitchell, who notes Tilotson's puritan upbringing and education, describes his style as a combination of puritan plainness with a rational approach. Other suggested influences are William Chillingworth, John Hales, and the Cambridge Platonists. Contemporaries, like Bishop Burnet, waxed ecstatic over Tilotson's skill. As was said, he spoke of "the majesty of things" in "the simplicity of words". Some, such as Norman Sykes, saw a certain shallowness in Tilotson's preaching, but nonetheless, his virtuosity in the use of the form has been widely acknowledged.

Moreover, Tilotson is also very significant as a leading churchman in the period from the Restoration to the Glorious Revolution. EVERY and SYKES make a number of interesting points about him in their studies of the clergy. They see, as a guiding principle in Tilotson's life, recognition of the authority of secular power. Sykes notes, for instance, that as a chaplain to Lord Russell, who was sentenced to death for his republican views at the time of the Rye House plot, Tilotson advised the earl to defer to the power of the sovereign and made clear his abhorence for those that would challenge lawful authority. Likewise, Every suggests, Tilotson's decision to accept the appointment as Archbishop of Canterbury, at the behest of William III, came from this same principle and overcame his scruples about replacing the nonjuror William Sancroft.

Another aspect of Tilotson which scholars have noticed was his consistent devotion to the principle of comprehension, not only toleration. Tilotson had the object of broadening the Church of England to include a number of other protestant communions. Mitchell remarks on the Enlightenment character of Tilotoson's thinking and the small part that dogma played in his world-view: thus his willingness to entertain broad ideas of union.

Every and Sykes note the long career Tilotson devoted to this effort, beginning with his service at the Savoy conference at the time of the Restoration and continuing during the reign of Charles II. In the ensuing years he continued to make a vigorous effort to attain that goal. For instance, he was active in advising the seven bishops who, in their petition to King James II, offered a blueprint for a policy of inclusion within the Church of England.

At the time of the Glorious Revolution, as STRAKA has pointed out, Tilotson was among those who supported William of Orange. In addition, Tilotson remained committed to a policy of comprehension in the church. When it became clear that a parliamentary solution was unlikely, Sykes notes, Tilotson urged the new king to have the matter taken up by convocation to ensure there would be no objections that the clergy were not directly involved. Tilotson himself was named to study the issue, along with others, but both Sykes and Every see the death-knell of comprehension most dramatically expressed in Tilotson's failure to be elected prolocutor of the lower house of convocation. Sykes sees the failure of the commission's efforts as causing great harm to the church in the future.

It is clear that Tilotson's career deserves close study and that a modern reappraisal is needed. This has already started in the evaluation of the influence of his preaching and oratory. Likewise his role as a churchman in the late 17th century requires attention. This is especially true because of the complex series of events Tilotson was concerned with in 1688 and the years that followed. It is quite possible that what might be revealed is a man of generosity, courage, and character.

MARC L. SCHWARZ

See also Anglican Establishment; Charles II

Toleration and Comprehension 17th and 18th centuries

Champion, J.A.I., *The Pillars of Priestcraft Shaken: The Church of England and Its Enemies, 1660–1730*, Cambridge and New York: Cambridge University Press, 1992

Clark, J.C.D., *English Society, 1688–1832: Ideology, Social Structure, and Political Practice during the Ancien Regime*, Cambridge and New York: Cambridge University Press, 1985; revised as *English Society, 1660–1832: Religion, Ideology, and Politics during the Ancien Regime*, Cambridge and New York: Cambridge University Press, 2000

Grell, Ole Peter, Jonathan Israel, and Nicholas Tyacke (editors), *From Persecution to Toleration: The Glorious Revolution and Religion in England*, Oxford: Clarendon Press, and New York: Oxford University Press, 1991

Jones, J.R. (editor), *Liberty Secured? Britain before and after 1688*, Stanford, California: Stanford University Press, 1992

Jordan, W.K., *The Development of Religious Toleration in England*, 4 vols, London: Allen and Unwin, and Cambridge, Massachusetts: Harvard University Press, 1932–40; reprinted, Gloucester, Massachusetts: Peter Smith, 1965

Marshall, John, *John Locke: Resistance, Religion, and Responsibility*, Cambridge and New York: Cambridge University Press, 1994

Spellman, W.M., *John Locke*, Basingstoke: Macmillan, and New York: St Martin's Press, 1997

Spurr, John, "The Church of England, Comprehension, and the Toleration Act of 1689", *English Historical Review*, 104 (1989): 927–46

Concerns regarding toleration and comprehension – who ought to be tolerated by, and who ought to be comprehended within, the national church – emerged in the aftermath of the religious and political fragmentation of the mid-17th century. Thereafter, as the ecclesiastical establishment was captured successively by presbyterians and independents and then restored to Anglicans, doctrinal positions proliferated, and questions of toleration and comprehension occasioned public debate and hastened the formulation of a variety of political strategies. Scholarly debate on these matters has focused upon how and why toleration became a reality and comprehension little more than a deferred and discarded hope.

JORDAN emphasized the gradual realization of toleration in the Miltonic high tide of the mid-17th century, rendering the so-called Toleration Act of 1689 virtually a foregone culmination. Jordan's modernist assumptions regarding a gradually realized toleration have been modified, but not discarded, in the collection of essays edited by JONES. The primary value of these essays, even for those who do not agree with their gradualist interpretation, is that the logic of the interpretation carries the story of toleration forwards and backwards from the Toleration Act. It thus joins, in a long term of unintended consequences and realized expectations, the ambitions of Restoration religious sects resisting later Stuart penal laws with 18th-century latitudinarians and evangelicals aiming to practise toleration in law and in spirit. Such categorizations have been challenged, if not quite exploded, by CLARK's insistence upon the existence of Anglican hegemony in church and state during the 18th century, a contention which implies that toleration was a bare concession made by a confessional state in order to mollify trinitarian nonconformists and marginalize various forms of dissent.

Recent work has extended and refined the project of theological contextualization that Clark's work foretold. It has stressed the tactical nature of arguments about toleration and comprehension and has focused upon two points of departure: the short-term options presented by the "Glorious" Revolution of 1688–89 and the emancipatory thought of the political philosopher John Locke. SPURR's work contains a detailed account of the controversial measures of indulgence during the reigns of Charles II and James II. Spurr focuses upon why toleration did not include comprehension and concludes that Anglican clergy, faced with a choice, decided it was better to have "a schism without the church, than a faction within it". Thus toleration comes to look like a strategic concession of the moment rather than an intellectual victory won over many decades. Its realization, according to Spurr, was more bound up with the origins of Anglicanism than of a dissenting ideology, let alone modern sensibilities of tolerance and religious liberty.

Essays in the volume edited by GRELL, ISRAEL, & TYACKE highlight the role of the "Glorious Revolution" in changing established policy from persecution to toleration and thus offer a contrast to certain of Spurr's arguments. Contributors to this work, led by Tyacke's insights regarding the transformation of "puritanism" into "dissent", deal in detail with the causative and effective role played by each constituency to toleration, including, among others, protestant nonconformists, the Dutch community in England, and – not least important – the Anglican establishment.

Although scholars have acknowledged the importance of the Toleration Act, it has come to seem more a beginning than an end in recent studies. Nothing illustrates this preoccupation better than recent work on Locke which has reinstated the religious and indeed sectarian nature of his undertaking in his famous *Letter Concerning Toleration*. MARSHALL, in a painstaking recontextualization, emphasizes Locke's transformation from a doctrinally orthodox adherent of the Anglican establishment at the time of the restoration of Charles II to a heterodox (probably Arian) proponent of religious toleration and magisterial forbearance by the 1690s. As a result, Locke's views are seen to have been embalmed for the time being in contemporary controversy, and, as such, were relegated during the succeeding century to the status of periodic revivals and re-readings rather than ideas of uniform influence.

CHAMPION's densely written study situates the debate over church establishment more firmly in a series of polemical disputes arising in the later 17th century and thus tacitly devalues Locke's role as an agent of modernization. Champion argues that out of these disputes came advocacy of a civil, public religion that looked back to the analysis of the political philosopher James Harrington and forward, anticipating the freethinking of the *philosophes* who masterminded the European Enlightenment. "Desacralization" rather than toleration or comprehension thus assumes a pre-eminent position in Champion's scheme of religious development. SPELLMAN admirably sums up recent trends, by insisting that the 18th century internalized certain secularizing readings of toleration which formed an ironic afterthought to how Locke himself had conceptualized his project.

Recent historians have treated the "achievement" of toleration less as a gradualist victory for forces of modernity and more as a hard-won yet ephemeral triumph for particular and rather modest brands of dissenting heterodoxy. As Clark has, rather contentiously, suggested, Lockean heterodoxy could only during the course of the 18th century win the opportunistic and partly mistaken allegiance of nonconformists waging a long-deferred attempt to breach the repaired and reinforced walls of the political and religious establishment. Nevertheless, that achievement is not entirely explicable without a consideration of the long inheritance of dissent in puritanism as it is traced in Tyacke's work. If toleration and comprehension have come to seem less like the metaphysical ideas or modernizing processes envisioned by Jordan than like tactical concessions designed to undergird an establishment steeling itself for more formidable tensions of empire and commerce, that cannot detract from the consideration emphasized implicitly in Jones's volume and explicitly in Tyacke's work that Britain experienced a long Reformation.

MYRON C. NOONKESTER

See also Locke; Protestant Dissent

Tolpuddle Martyrs 1830s

Chase, Malcolm, *Early Trade Unionism: Fraternity, Skill, and the Politics of Labour*, Aldershot and Brookfield, Vermont: Ashgate, 2000
Citrine, Walter M. *et al.*, *The Book of the Martyrs of Tolpuddle, 1834–1934: The Story of the Dorsetshire Labourers Who Were Convicted and Sentenced to Seven Years' Transportation for Forming a Trade Union*, London: Trades Union Congress General Council, 1934
Griffiths, Clare, "Remembering Tolpuddle: Rural History and Commemoration in the Inter-War Labour Movement", *History Workshop Journal*, 44 (1997): 145–69
Malleson, Miles and H. Brooks, *Six Men of Dorset: A Play in Three Acts*, London: Gollancz, 1937
Marlow, Joyce, *The Tolpuddle Martyrs*, London: André Deutsche, 1971
Webb, Sidney and Beatrice Webb, *The History of Trade Unionism*, London and New York: Longmans Green, 1894; revised edition, 1920
Wells, Roger, "Tolpuddle in the Context of English Agrarian Labour History, 1780–1850" in *British Trade Unionism, 1750–1850: The Formative Years*, edited by John Rule, London and New York: Longman, 1988

Few episodes in British labour history have attracted as much attention as the Tolpuddle Martyrs, whose story has even been made into a film (*Comrades*, 1987) that was a box-office success. The transportation of these six farm workers from the Dorset village of Tolpuddle to penal colonies in Australia has exercised a powerful hold on the imagination of textbook authors and the labour movement alike. Their conviction in 1834 is still marked each July by the Trades Union Congress (TUC) with a rally in the village. As GRIFFITHS shows in a skilful excavation of the layers of political meaning adhering to the TUC's commemoration, the first of these rallies (initiated to mark the centenary in 1934) was not merely to remind contemporary activists of the labour movement's history. The centenary events were intended to boost morale, and even to console, in the years of uncertainty after 1931 when Labour's first prime minister, Ramsay MacDonald, had led his National Administration into a general election against the party. Griffiths quotes critics who scoffed at the TUC's wide-ranging centenary celebrations as representing the "secular canonization" of the Tolpuddle labourers, and the *Manchester Guardian*'s comment on MALLESON & BROOKS's drama: "Trade Unionism Now Has Its Miracle Play".

The now-habitual terminology of martyrdom stems from 1934: during the 19th century and later the case was simply known as the "Dorchester labourers". The centenary celebrations were accompanied by the publication of a compendious history whose galaxy of authors was led by the TUC's then secretary, Walter CITRINE. Its argument was plain enough. The Tolpuddle labourers, and even their leader George Loveless, were political innocents, convicted as a consequence of repressive government policy and to discourage the formation of trade unions by others. The union they sought to join was the Grand National Consolidated Trades Union (GNCTU), which, as its title conveys, was a general union seeking to unite workers of all occupations nationally. Since trade unions had been legalized in 1824, the actual charge was administering an illegal oath of loyalty to members. A handful of other trade unionists were prosecuted around that time for the same offence, but this had been forgotten by the time the WEBB & WEBB set the historiographical tone in their enduringly influential history of trade unionism. Habitual poverty had long kept farm workers "in a state of sullen despair". The prosecution of these "simple-minded Methodists" "was a scandalous perversion of the law". By the time of their contribution to the collection by Citrine *et al.* 40 years later, their view had hardened further: "The case of the Dorsetshire Labourers stands out in the record, alike in the gentle innocence of the victims, and in the ruthlessness of the determination of the governing class to strike down an organization which threatened to encroach upon the profits of capitalist industry". This is essentially MARLOW's stance; Marlow emphasizes particularly the gentle innocence, in an account that is chiefly of value for its narrative of the labourers' lives after the trial.

A substantial revision to the customary account was made by WELLS in a collection itself derived from a conference organized by the Society for the Study of Labour History to mark the 150th anniversary of Tolpuddle. Wells, who is rather stronger on the context than the detail of the labourers' activities, emphasizes the deep-rootedness of rural poverty while tracing its counterpoint in a tradition of agitation by agricultural labourers that stretched back to the 1790s. This reached its apogee in Captain Swing, the rural protest movement that swept southern England in 1830. Arguing that "unionist mentalities were central to Swing", Wells establishes its centrality to understanding Tolpuddle. One of the Loveless family had been arrested as a Swing rioter but managed to escape. George Loveless himself emerged as a spokesman for Dorset agricultural workers in ensuing wage negotiations in 1831-32. Wells argues that the Tolpuddle prosecutions stemmed not from a governmental initiative but from the determination of local magistrates to stamp out a trade union movement that was becoming widespread in south Dorset; the Home Office was at first lukewarm. Eventually, the Home Office endorsed the prosecutions as a means of curtailing the appeal of the GNCTU in rural areas, a move prompted by the extent of opposition in the southern countryside to the new poor law, the centrepiece of the government's socio-economic policy. But even so, the government restrained local magistrates from a lockout of all local agricultural trade unionists. Wells also suggests that the very scale of popular protest against the Tolpuddle sentences sealed the labourers' fate, making any remission of the sentences politically impossible.

In his detailed history of early British trade unionism, CHASE considers further the extent to which these labourers were consciously part of a wider movement, pointing out that the society they formed predated the formation of the GNCTU by some weeks. In George Loveless's possession when he was arrested was a printed address dated Leeds, 30 November 1832, one of several circulating in the southern textile districts and part of a burgeoning general unionist movement of which the GNCTU was only the final phase. The Tolpuddle society was almost certainly part of a Friendly Protective Agricultural Association which can be glimpsed elsewhere in England, and possibly even Scotland, in the years 1833-35. Once formed, the GNCTU intended Tolpuddle to be the organizational hub of a "grand lodge" with which unionists across the region would affiliate. Chase also gives added emphasis to the wider impact of the Tolpuddle prosecutions. Culturally, this was discernible in a rapid "de-sacramental process" by which both trade and friendly societies purged their procedures of the most overt religious rituals. Politically, it flowed directly into chartism, which, in part, might itself be seen as a form of general unionism.

MALCOLM CHASE

See also Melbourne

Topography: Coastal

Aberg, Alan and Carenza Lewis (editors), *The Rising Tide: Archaeology and Coastal Landscapes*, Oxford: Oxbow Books, 2000

Allen, J.R.L. *et al.*, "The Archaeological Resource: Chronological Overview" in *England's Coastal Heritage: A Survey for English Heritage and the RCHME*, edited by Michael Fulford, Timothy Champion, and Anthony Long, London: English Heritage, 1994

Fox, Harold, *The Evolution of the Fishing Village: Landscape and Society along the South Devon Coast, 1086-1550*, Oxford: Leopard's Head Press, 2001

Fulford, Michael, Timothy Champion, and Anthony Long (editors), *England's Coastal Heritage: A Survey for English Heritage and the RCHME*, London: English Heritage, 1997

Gale, Alison, *Britain's Historic Coast*, Stroud, Gloucestershire: Tempus, 2000

Rippon, Stephen, *The Transformation of Coastal Wetlands: Exploitation and Management of Marshland Landscapes in North West Europe during the Roman and Medieval Periods*, Oxford and New York: Oxford University Press, 2000

Steers, J.A., *The Coastline of England and Wales*, Cambridge: Cambridge University Press, 1946; 2nd revised edition, 1964; reprinted with additions, 1969

Thomas, Charles, *Exploration of a Drowned Landscape: Archaeology and History of the Isles of Scilly*, London: Batsford, 1985

Tyson, H.J. *et al.*, "1994: Survey and Recording in the Intertidal Zone" in *England's Coastal Heritage: A Survey for English Heritage and the RCHME*, edited by Michael Fulford, Timothy Champion, and Anthony Long, London: English Heritage, 1997

One feature defining the character of Britain is its long and varied coastline; no one lives more than 70 miles from the sea. STEERS describes that coast region by region, starting with the Solway estuary and moving anticlockwise around to Berwick. He stresses the importance of geology in determining the form of the coast and describes the wide variety of coastal features, such as cliffs, sand and shingle barriers, and marshland. In some places the coast is eroding, while elsewhere there is an accumulation of material in the form of mud-flats and salt-marshes. There is a need to think of a coastal *zone*, as opposed to a coast *line*, to include the intertidal area and extending a short distance inland to where both natural processes and human activity are strongly influenced by the sea.

It is important to remember that the coastline is far from static, and rates of erosion and deposition vary enormously. One example of the extent to which coastal topography has changed over the past few millennia is THOMAS's study of the Scilly Isles.

The history of human activity along England's coastline is reviewed in the volume edited by FULFORD, CHAMPION, & LONG. This highlights the importance of changes in sea level in shaping the coastline, and although this is poorly understood for the medieval period, RIPPON (2000) has since argued that following a marked fall in relative sea level during the early Roman period, there was a rise that continued into the medieval period, before the level stabilized or even fell in the late medieval period. In Fulford *et al.*, Bell goes on to review the wide range of environmental evidence that is preserved in coastal areas, notably owing to the waterlogged condition of many deposits. Coastal deposits are found to contain an excellent record of environmental change, whose value is increased by the association with evidence for human activity.

Because of the threat of erosion, there is a growing need to record the archaeological remains that are being lost, and the range of survey methods that can be used in the intertidal zone is considered by TYSON *et al*. Some of the archaeological evidence found within the intertidal zone derived from "dryland" sites that have been eroded away, but there is also a wide range of evidence relating to sites and structures that were in origin associated with the coast. ALLEN *et al*. give a chronological overview of how the coastline has been used from prehistory through to the present. For the medieval period, key themes include reclamation (sea defence and land drainage), extractive industry (e.g., salt production, quarrying, fishing), trade and communications (ports, quays, and landing-places), and military defence.

There are in reality very few stretches of coast entirely untouched by human activity, and the recent uses to which Britain's coastline has been put are described by GALE. The shoreline and the sea itself are a very important source of resources. Apart from fishing, whaling, kelp burning, salt production, the mining of minerals, and dredging for gravel have all left their mark. The coast is also valued as a leisure resource, though the paradox of its use for disposing of waste is not lost. The sea, as a means of communication and of military threat makes the coastline the interface between Britain and the world beyond, and the infrastructure of trade, military defence, and the welfare of seafarers has also left some impressive monuments.

Many of these themes are explored further in a series of case studies in a volume edited by ABERG & LEWIS. The diversity of features characteristic of the coastal zone is illustrated by Buckley for Essex, Daniels for Cleveland, Martin for Fife, and Rippon for the Severn and Thames estuaries. Several papers look at the wealth of evidence that survives low down in the intertidal zone: Ratcliffe and Straker describe recent research on the Isles of Scilly, Tomalin looks at the Isle of Wight, and Hale reviews the evidence from Scotland. Fontana *et al*. consider the Langstone Harbour project, stressing the value of computers, particularly geographical information systems, in integrating data from archaeological and historical research. The importance of shipping is studied in Fife by Oxley. Currie considers the use of sea ponds in the fishing industry.

Rippon has reviewed the growing intensity of fishing during the medieval period. This is reflected in the physical evidence for increasingly substantial fish weirs found in intertidal areas all around Britain, and documentary and archaeological evidence (in the form of fish bones) for the consumption of fish on inland settlements. Eventually, sufficient profits could be made from fishing for specialist fishing villages to emerge in many areas. FOX has investigated their history along the south Devon coast. Many began as small clusters of beach huts and boathouses (or "cellars") used by local farmers, and only at the very end of the medieval period were these occupied on a year-round basis as specialized fishing communities emerged.

STEPHEN RIPPON

See also Channel Islands; Man, Isle of

Topography: Lowland

Board of Agriculture, *The Agricultural State of the Kingdom, in February, March, and April, 1816*, London: Sherwood, Neely and Jones, 1816; reprinted, with introduction by Gordon E. Mingay, New York: Kelley, and Bath: Adams and Dart, 1970

Chandler, John (editor), *John Leland's Itinerary: Travels in Tudor England*, Stroud, Gloucestershire; and Dover, New Hampshire: Alan Sutton, 1993

Darby, H.C., *Domesday England*, Cambridge and New York: Cambridge University Press, 1977

Everitt, Alan, *Continuity and Colonization: The Evolution of Kentish Settlement*, Leicester: Leicester University Press, and Atlantic Highlands, New Jersey: Humanities Press, 1986

Hoskins, W.G., *The Making of the English Landscape*, London: Hodder and Stoughton, 1955

Rippon, Stephen, *The Severn Estuary: Landscape Evolution and Wetland Reclamation*, London: Leicester University Press, 1997

Stamp, L. Dudley (editor), *The Land of Britain: The Report of the Land Utilisation Survey of Britain*, London: Geographical Publications, 1936–45

Thirsk, Joan (editor), *The English Rural Landscape*, Oxford and New York: Oxford University Press, 2000

Owing to its varied geology and complex cultural history, the British landscape is remarkably varied in character. Modern intensive farming has created some degree of uniformity in certain of the flatter lowlands (notably the east Midlands, East Anglia, and Fenland); but as one travels around, it is the diversity in the appearance of the countryside that leaves the most lasting impression.

Although mass travel and tourism are recent phenomena, there is a long history of topographical writing in Britain. Two broad divisions within the landscape underlie most early writings and remain an important theme of scholarship today: (1) the upland-lowland divide and (2) the division within the medieval and early post-medieval landscape between the Midlands, where the landscape was structured around large open fields and nucleated villages – what early writers termed "champion" landscape – and the south-east and west, where fields were enclosed and settlement was more scattered and dispersed, the "woodland" landscape of early writers.

The origins of topographical writing in Britain date from the medieval period in the sense that chroniclers, such as Matthew Paris in the 13th century, made some astute observations regarding the landscape as they saw it. But British topographical writing really began during the 16th century. Leland – for whom CHANDLER has provided an excellent modern version – is the most important of the early writers. Leland's collection of topographical observations, known as the *Itinerary*, actually derived from at least five separate journeys which cover England in varying detail; the south-west, the Midlands, and parts of the north are best served. Chandler has edited these to make a series of county descriptions supported by a range of excellent maps and engravings.

The late 18th century saw a series of county histories, though these tended to concentrate upon manorial and ecclesiastical history. More objective description of the landscape itself began around the start of the 19th century when the Ordnance Survey started the first large-scale mapping of the country. At the same time, an important set of reports (each titled *General View of the Agriculture of the County of . . .*), produced around 1800 for the Board of Agriculture, contain the first comprehensive survey of the British agricultural landscape. These accounts reflect the trenchant observations of agricultural improvers, whose county-by-county reports reveal marked regional variation within the agrarian landscape of Britain; for an overview, see Mingay's introduction in BOARD OF AGRICULTURE. With this and the remarkable achievement of the Tithe surveys of *c.*1840, and STAMP's survey of farming regions during the 1930s, we have a series of insights into how the British landscape has changed over the past two centuries.

The modern approach to studying the landscape began with HOSKINS's seminal study exploring the complex relationships between human society and countryside. The subsequent series of county volumes, although never completed, marked a clear shift away from the manor and ecclesiastical history that so dominated earlier county histories. Hoskins and fellow historians such as Beresford and Finberg produced popular yet scholarly publications that were accessible to students and the public alike, and fostered a strongly interdisciplinary approach to "reading the landscape".

Hoskins and Finberg pioneered what was to become known as the "Leicester school" of English local history (since they had been based at the Department of English Local History at the University of Leicester). The key characteristics of the work of these scholars were their interdisciplinary approach, the embedding of local and landscape study within the wider debates of social and economic history, and the close interaction of people and their environment. This work led to the recognition of distinctive regions, or *pays* (e.g. EVERITT on Kent), expanding upon the crude division between *bocage* (woodland) and *champagne* (champion, or open field) countryside recognized by people like Leland.

A recent volume edited by THIRSK reveals the progress that has been made in understanding why so many regions look so different: downland, wolds, lowland vales, marshes, fenlands, and moorlands all have distinctly different characters. This book is broadly based on physically distinct regions, and each chapter clearly shows how human communities have created greatly different landscapes through balancing the exploitation and management of "natural" resources, such as wetlands and woodlands, with the demands of agriculture.

Other important contributions to the recognition of historical regions have come through the detailed examination of one particular set of data. A classic example is DARBY's exhaustive analysis of the Domesday Book. Regional variations in features such as population, plough teams, and woodland were mapped in a series of county studies that conclude with a summary of the character the *pays*, being brought together in *Domesday England*.

There is, indeed, increasing awareness that modern counties are not necessarily the best study areas within which to write about the landscape. RIPPON, for example, in his study of the Severn estuary, selected those parts of five counties whose common characteristics gave them unity and coherence. The estuary itself, which today is seen as a barrier to communication,

was in the past the unifying feature; this is an example of how our perceptions of landscape also change over time. This study also illustrates the remarkable local diversity in landscape, with areas having a settlement pattern of wholly nucleated villages, associated with open fields, in close proximity to areas having a settlement pattern characterized by scattered farmsteads set amid small enclosed fields.

STEPHEN RIPPON

Topography: Marshland

Cook, Hadrian and Tom Williamson (editors), *Water Management in the English Landscape: Field, Marsh, and Meadow*, Edinburgh: Edinburgh University Press, 1999

Darby, H.C., *The Changing Fenland*, Cambridge and New York: Cambridge University Press, 1983

Eddison, Jill, Mark Gardiner, and Antony Long (editors), *Romney Marsh: Environmental Change and Human Occupation in a Coastal Lowland*, Oxford: Oxford University Committee for Archaeology, 1998

Grady, Damian M., "Medieval and Post-Medieval Salt Extraction in North-East Lincolnshire" in *Lincolnshire's Archaeology from the Air*, edited by Robert H. Bewley, Lincoln: Society for Lincolnshire History and Archaeology, 1998

Hall, David and John Coles, *Fenland Survey: An Essay in Landscape and Persistence*, London: English Heritage, 1994

Owen, A.E.B. (editor), *The Records of a Commission of Sewers for Wiggenhall 1319–1324*, Norwich: Norfolk Record Society, 1981

Rippon, Stephen, *The Severn Estuary: Landscape Evolution and Wetland Reclamation*, London and Washington: Leicester University Press, 1997

Steers, J.A., *The Coastline of England and Wales*, Cambridge: Cambridge University Press, 1946; 2nd edition, 1964; reprinted with additions, 1969

STEERS's study is more concerned with marshland than might be supposed from its title, since in the course of following the coast anticlockwise from Solway to Tweed he examines not merely the coastline itself but the land behind. The interaction between sea and marsh has nearly everywhere and at all times been close, and Steers discusses in turn every stretch of marshland and its physical and historical development, enabling each to be seen in the context of the landscape as a whole. He thus goes beyond most studies of marshland which limit themselves to a single region. Though his earlier chapters, first published in 1946, remain unaltered, the work has been updated by nearly 200 additional pages, benefiting from the renewed interest in the coast prompted by the floods of 1953.

COOK & WILLIAMSON likewise did not restrict the studies they edited to a single region. Seeking to bridge an interdisciplinary gap, they obtained contributions from specialists, many with monographs on particular marshes already to their credit, on a wide range of topics linked in some way to historic water management. These include the relationship of soils to drainage, especially of arable land; drainage techniques in different periods and areas; wetland reclamation from the Romano-British period onwards; management of water meadows; and nature conservation in the Fens. As to the last, the editors do not shrink from describing the post-medieval conversion of the peat fenland to productive arable land as having "amounted to an environmental disaster on a grand scale". They emphasize that "waterlogged environments are an archaeological resource of immense importance"; surprisingly, though, their volume includes no separate essay on this theme.

HALL & COLES summarize, for a wider readership, the results of the Fenland Project of 1981–88, whose detailed findings appear separately in a series of monographs. This programme of survey and excavation (extended in 1990–93 to a further evaluation of selected sites) had an archaeological emphasis. Almost two-thirds of the text concerns the pre-Roman period, and field-walking figures largely throughout. A major discovery during the survey was the Roman site at Stonea, with implications for the status of the Roman fenland – imperial estate or not? The chapter on Saxon settlement embodies evidence that many sites on the silt fen were abandoned as it became progressively wetter. The chapter on the period from 1066 to c.1500, when the survey concludes, does little more than slot archaeological details into a documentary frame; DARBY, writing when the project had barely begun, seems more at ease than its author with that period. His own study, effectively replacing his two pioneering volumes of 1940 on the fenland (*The Draining of the Fens* and *The Medieval Fenland*), deserves to become, like them, a standard source on its history. Direct comparison with the volumes of 1940 is not easy. Much has been rewritten; the sections have been rearranged; the former lengthy footnotes have been embodied in the text; new material and air photographs have been added; and many new maps are provided. The original *Medieval Fenland* is condensed into a single chapter that omits much detail, e.g. Domesday entries and maps now to be sought in the author's series *Domesday Geography*. To compensate, there is an entirely new chapter on the 20th century.

Dugdale's *History of Imbanking and Draining* of 1662 continues to be cited for the terms of reference of medieval sewers commissions, but their actual *modus operandi* in regulating land drainage and sea defence has had little attention, simply for want of records. OWEN's edition of a little group of early 14th-century documents which have chanced to survive for Norfolk Marshland has sought to compensate for this lack. These documents confirm the accepted view of the commissioners as primarily concerned to activate, in an emergency, the local "custom of sewers", with only such innovations as circumstances required – in this instance, an improved method of assessment for works of sewers together with, seemingly, the introduction of officials called dike reeves, hitherto confined to Lincolnshire. But there is also evidence here of continuity of policy and administration from one commission to another, something the ad hoc nature of commissions had previously seemed to rule out.

EDDISON, GARDINER, & LONG's volume is the third in an interdisciplinary series reflecting the work of the Romney Marsh Research Trust, all three being edited wholly or jointly by Eddison. The Soil Survey's *Memoir* and map of the soils of the marsh by R.D. Green (1968) profoundly influenced subsequent research on local topics well beyond those linked to physical geography, as is clear from frequent citations in footnotes in all three volumes. The contributions to these range widely: geology, archaeology, settlement history, drainage, farming, and the incidence of malaria are just some of the subjects treated. The volumes' large format, awkward to shelve but increasingly favoured by archaeologists, shares with the output of the Fenland Project the benefits this confers on reproduction of maps, diagrams, and air photographs.

RIPPON has made a comprehensive survey of "landscape exploitation" on both sides of the Severn estuary, intended to redress an imbalance between the considerable research on the Somerset peatland and a relative neglect of the coastal alluvial wetlands and, while so doing, to place the latter in a regional and national context. Interesting himself especially in the Roman period, he sees "clear evidence" of military involvement, probably from the legionary fortress at Caerleon, in reclamation on the Welsh side of the estuary. He believes that Roman sea walls may have existed, and – a hypothesis developed more fully in his earlier study *The Gwent Levels: The Evolution of a Wetland Landscape* (1996) – that a planned Roman landscape is at one point still recognizable there today, a remarkable survival if this is true. As with many coastal marshes, salt was extracted locally from seawater, though the industry was apparently confined to the Somerset side. One area where that industry survived into the early 17th century, the marsh of north-east Lincolnshire, has been studied in detail by GRADY in conjunction with aerial photography carried out for the National Mapping Programme of the Royal Commission on Historical Monuments. Grady discusses techniques of extraction and the documentary evidence and seeks to relate what appears on air photographs to the local saltern mounds, which are often very prominent. He also explores the still uncertain historical relationship between the mounds, the earliest sea banks, and early settlement.

ARTHUR E.B. OWEN

Topography: Upland

Bryden, John M. and George Houston, *Agrarian Change in the Scottish Highlands*, London: Martin Robertson, 1976

Collins, Edward J.T., *The Economy of Upland Britain 1750–1950: An Illustrated Review*, Reading, Berkshire: Centre for Agricultural Strategy, University of Reading, 1978

Darling, F. Fraser, *West Highland Survey: An Essay in Human Ecology*, Oxford: Oxford University Press, 1955

Fox, Cyril, *The Personality of Britain: Its Influence on Inhabitant and Invader in Prehistoric and Early Historic Times*, Cardiff: National Museum of Wales, 1932; 4th edition, 1947; reprinted, New York: AMS Press, 1979

Haldane, A.R.B., *The Drove Roads of Scotland*, London and New York: Nelson, 1952; Edinburgh: Edinburgh University Press, 1968

Millward, Roy and Adrian Robinson, *Upland Britain*, Newton Abbot, Devon; and Pomfret, Vermont: David and Charles, 1980

Pearsall, William Harold, *Mountains and Moorlands*, London: Collins, 1950; revised by Winifred Pennington, 1971

Spratt, Don and Colin Burgess (editors), *Upland Settlement in Britain: The Second Millennium* BC *and After*, Oxford: British Archaeological Reports, 1985

Symon, J.A., *Scottish Farming: Past and Present*, Edinburgh: Oliver and Boyd, 1959

Tranter, R.B. (editor), *The Future of Upland Britain: Proceedings of Symposium Held at the University of Reading in September, 1977*, Reading, Berkshire: Centre for Agricultural Strategy, University of Reading, 1978

MILLWARD & ROBINSON see the uplands as comprising land above 1,000 feet or 300 metres, which includes most of Scotland and Wales along with much of northern England (the Lake District, Pennines, and Peak District) and the south-west. A line from the Tees to the Exe conveniently identifies the zone of transition "where the lowland basins and lines of gentle hills of the southeast gradually gave way to the harsher contours of mountains and high plateaux of the north and west": a treasure-house of scenic contrasts arises to a considerable degree from the varying relationship between sea and land. Upland Britain is in many ways synonymous with Atlantic Britain, and because of its great extent of latitude – more than 10 degrees separate Land's End from the most northerly point of the Shetland Islands – "this vast region of mountains, moorlands and the interpenetrating seas may be regarded as the bridge between northern and southern Europe". While the south-west is mild, northern Britain is often enveloped in air from more northerly sources. Moreover, the north-west Highlands of Scotland are part of the north Atlantic, sharing many of the topographic and cultural features of Scandinavia.

The uplands are relatively remote and marginal today, but SPRATT & BURGESS point out that "the remarkably well-preserved prehistoric landscapes and field monuments found in so many upland regions of Britain make a contribution unique in its scale and complexity to European prehistoric studies". There was some retreat of settlement in the first millennium: for example, on Dartmoor, where human occupation became just a shadow of what it had been in the Bronze Age. Differences in land organization emerge through great blocks and parallel reaves on Dartmoor and Swaledale, with evidence of piecemeal colonization elsewhere. Then there was another retreat at the end of the 13th century, which can be linked with climatic change. FOX contrasted the lowlands as a zone of cultural replacement with the more elevated regions showing "greater continuity of cultural character". Yet there are diverse cultural links, for early Scottish history reveals a strong Viking influence, whereas in the south relationships of land and peoples are with Brittany and Iberia.

According to COLLINS, improvement of the uplands involved a new evaluation of scenery as 18th-century tourists started "taking the waters", and there was growing interest in the picturesque as mass tourism followed the railway. The Scottish Highlands were popularized by Queen Victoria, who took the "Royal Route" to Inverness via the Great Glen. Motor cars gave unprecedented accessibility between the wars: in 1924, 60,000 climbed Snowdon, a mountain Defoe had described as a hill of "monstrous height" – the last refuge of the ancient Britons. Winter sports date from the late 1940s (especially the hard winter of 1947).

Millward & Robinson emphasize the surge of agricultural improvement evident through new roads and enclosures on Exmoor and Dartmoor. SYMON writes about consumption dykes in northern Scotland where Sir John Sinclair (1754–1835) thought that sheep could revolutionize the prospects for small-scale farming. While Sinclair tried to popularize this new enterprise in Caithness, Thomas Johnes set about transforming a damaged lead-mining landscape in mid-Wales into his idea of Arcadia: the result was a great house on the Hafod estate, where plantations and shelter belts were established between 1796 and 1813. However, Collins points out that upland farmers could not exploit new technical developments (the turnip and leguminous fodder crops) that were the basis of the agricultural revolution in the lowlands. They could not break the fodder bottleneck and set in motion a "virtuous cycle" of crops, stock, and farmyard dung. TRANTER (1978) emphasizes the relative shortness of the growing season to provide fodder – often with bad harvesting conditions – coupled with a winter feeding period of seven months or more.

The improvement period was problematic for upland industry. Collins thinks that the greatest opportunity for sustained economic growth in the upland zone occurred during the early phase of the Industrial Revolution, before the age of coal and iron and the establishment of a free-trade economy. Mining had been of historic importance, but there was little expansion after 1900, though in north Wales Richard Pennant used industrial interests to further upland colonization, rationalizing slate quarries and (as Lord Penrhyn) laying out a village of 60 cottages at Mynydd Llandygai close to Penrhyn quarry. Upland industry was marginalized by concentrations in the ports and coalfields – with coal the predominant energy source and an increasing scale of production. As railways tended to benefit lowland producers by widening the gap in distribution costs between the inner and outer regions, capital, labour, and entrepreneurship migrated away from the uplands.

Despite their declining demographic and economic importance, much thought is given to the future of the uplands. They are valued as "green lungs", and conservation interests cast doubt on water supply and hydropower projects. Meanwhile the obligation to support fragile farming communities raises the option of maximizing production from the land. PEARSALL advocated more food production, for "the history of sheep-rearing in the British uplands, particularly during the last hundred years, has been a deplorable one, and it has been mainly responsible for their present depopulation and run-down condition". Following the research on grasslands by Stapledon, Tranter describes the scope for fertilizer treatment: upland soils have low fertility, and acid soils need heavy lime applications, while silage is an important tool in intensive grassland management. Land improvement is possible by ploughing and reseeding, though in wet and stony areas surface treatment may be more effective. DARLING showed how agriculture on Highland crofts could be improved and went on to call for an improved habitat, backed by crops and grass, to modify a sheep-to-cattle ratio of 1.4 million : 100,000 by halving the one and doubling the other to get 700,000 : 200,000. BRYDEN & HOUSTON show how the Highlands and Islands Development

Board took up the issue of underuse but could not force landowners to intensify land use, despite land capability surveys. Finally, forestry was much supported in the early 20th century because of its employment potential, but opinions have changed as a result of controversies over mechanization and conservation.

DAVID TURNOCK

See also Farming: Pastoral Husbandry

Tories: To 1714

Colley, Linda, *In Defiance of Oligarchy: The Tory Party, 1714–1760*, Cambridge and New York: Cambridge University Press, 1982

Halliday, Paul D., *Dismembering the Body Politic: Partisan Politics in England's Towns, 1650–1730*, Cambridge and New York: Cambridge University Press, 1998

Harris, Tim, *London Crowds in the Reign of Charles II: Propaganda and Politics from the Restoration until the Exclusion Crisis*, Cambridge and New York: Cambridge University Press, 1987

Harris, Tim, "Party Turns? Or, Whigs and Tories Get Off Scott Free", *Albion*, 25/4 (1993a): 581–90

Harris, Tim, *Politics under the Later Stuarts: Party Conflict in a Divided Society, 1660–1715*, London and New York: Longman, 1993b

Holmes, Geoffrey, *British Politics in the Age of Anne*, revised edition, London: Macmillan, 1967; London and Ronceverte, West Virginia: Hambledon Press, 1987

Scott, Jonathan, "Restoration Process. Or, If This Isn't a Party We're Not Having a Good Time", *Albion*, 25/4 (1993): 619–37

Speck, W.A., *Tory and Whig: The Struggle in the Constituencies, 1701–1715*, London: Macmillan, and New York: St Martin's Press, 1970

"Tory", a term first applied to Irish bandits earlier in the 17th century, was borrowed and applied to successive generations of English partisans, starting with royalist insurrectionists in the 1650s. Its general use in political parlance came later, in the context of the "exclusion crisis" of 1679–81, though it was used directly in conjunction with the term "Whig" only after the crisis was officially over in the summer of 1681. In the 1680s the term was associated with a commitment to the legitimate succession (of James, Duke of York), the rule of law, and perhaps above all to the restored Church of England, as settled in 1662.

Traditionally the Tories have been seen as an elite group, having their origins in the court and to a lesser extent in parliament, being thrown into crisis by the events of James II's reign (1685–88) and the subsequent revolution, and recovering somewhat in the reign of Anne (1702–14), only to succumb to the crushing weight of the Whig oligarchy established under the Hanoverians after 1714. But in recent years almost every aspect of this view of the Tories' fortunes has been challenged.

Previously, it was assumed that only the Whigs managed in the first round of the party battle (1679–81) to appeal beyond parliament to people in the London streets and in the provinces. But HARRIS (1987) has shown that the Whigs' appeal to public opinion in London in these years was matched by the Tories' appeal, which also met with a response in terms of street demonstrations and other forms of activism. In his subsequent publications – (HARRIS 1993a, b) – he has sought to show that this popular appeal and propensity to partisan demonstrations extended into the provinces as well.

HALLIDAY has taken this argument one stage further and traced the origins of the Tories and of partisanship generally in this period to the borough corporations in England and Wales, where rival groups were constantly vying to monopolize power and where the relative status of protestant dissent and the Church of England was a highly contentious issue. Far from emanating from parliament, parties originated in the localities and finally pushed their way into the Commons.

Halliday takes his account to 1730 and suggests that Tories remained a vital force in the localities right to the end of that period, a view that fits well with COLLEY's work on the Tories as a movement that continued to exist (to use the title of her book) "in defiance of oligarchy" well beyond even that date.

Such views are congruent with the works of HOLMES and SPECK, who argue for the centrality of the Whig-Tory divide in English politics in the reign of Anne. This is in contrast to an older view which suggested that nationally at this time faction and interest were more important than partisan considerations. Speck's work is a study of the constituencies, where party identity and activism remained strong.

However, the reality of a two-party system, which seems so well established by 1700 in all recent writings, has not gone unquestioned for the two decades before that. In particular the first emergence of the Tories from 1679 on has come under the critical spotlight. SCOTT has seen "Whigs" and "Tories" in this period not as organized political parties but rather as stations on a political pilgrimage made by the propertied classes collectively between 1678 and 1681, as fears of a Roman catholic successor gave way to fears of civil war. Thus to a large extent and with some important exceptions, the "Whigs" of 1678 *were* the "Tories" of 1681. Evidence for party political organization for either side, in this earliest period at least, seems to be lacking. Harris (1993a) admits that the Whig and Tory parties of this period were defined more by ideological allegiance than by organization. But he points to the reality of partisan confrontation at the street level from early in the political crisis and its continuation after 1681, especially at the provincial level, when the Whigs faced a proscription similar to the one that overtook the Tories in 1714. In periods like the early 1680s, when one party (in this case the Tories) was clearly in the ascendant nationally, the institutions of local government themselves could provide a structure for partisan organization. And this was very much a feature of the period of Tory reaction 1681–85.

There are complex issues of ideological continuity across the period. Recent scholarship has noted how the Tories adapted themselves to the new political situation after 1688. But over the course of the 1690s, as Harris (1993b) describes, the Tories became increasingly associated with a "country", or anti-court, platform. Nevertheless, conservatism with regard to the succession and the status of the Church of England continued to be Tory hallmarks, despite the shocks of 1688 and although both issues produced internal divisions in the Tory party under Anne, as the appropriate responses to the house of Hanover and occasional conformity were thrashed out.

ANDREW M. COLEBY

See also Anne; Bolingbroke, Henry St John; James VII and II

Tories: 1714–1830

Brock, W.R., *Lord Liverpool and Liberal Toryism 1820 to 1827*, Cambridge: Cambridge University Press, 1941; 2nd edition, London: Frank Cass, and Hamden, Connecticut: Archon Books, 1967

Colley, Linda, *In Defiance of Oligarchy: The Tory Party 1714–1760*, Cambridge and New York: Cambridge University Press, 1982

Cookson, J.E., *Lord Liverpool's Administration: The Crucial Years 1815–1822*, Edinburgh: Scottish Academic Press, and Hamden, Connecticut: Archon, 1975

Cruickshanks, Eveline, *Political Untouchables: The Tories and the '45*, London: Duckworth, and New York: Holmes and Meier, 1979

Dickinson, H.T., *Bolingbroke*, London: Constable, 1970

Dickinson, H.T., *Liberty and Property: Political Ideology in Eighteenth-Century Britain*, London: Weidenfeld and Nicolson, and New York: Holmes and Meier, 1977

Feiling, Keith Grahame, *The Second Tory Party 1714–1832*, London: Macmillan, 1938; reprinted, New York: St Martin's Press, 1959

Gunn, J.A.W., *Beyond Liberty and Property: The Process of Self-Recognition in Eighteenth-Century Political Thought*, Kingston, Ontario, and Montreal: McGill-Queen's University Press, 1983

Hill, B.W., *The Growth of Parliamentary Parties 1689–1742*, London: Allen and Unwin, and Hamden, Connecticut: Archon Books, 1976

Hill, B.W., *British Parliamentary Parties, 1742–1832: From the Fall of Walpole to the First Reform Act*, London and Boston: Allen and Unwin, 1985

Hill, B.W., *Robert Harley: Speaker, Secretary of State, and Premier Minister*, New Haven, Connecticut: Yale University Press, 1988

Hilton, Boyd, *Corn, Cash, and Commerce: The Economic Policies of the Tory Governments 1815–1830*, Oxford and New York: Oxford University Press, 1977

Holmes, Geoffrey, *British Politics in the Age of Anne*, London: Macmillan, 1967; revised edition, London and Reconverte, West Virginia: Hambledon Press, 1987

Holmes, Geoffrey (editor), *Britain after the Glorious Revolution 1689–1714*, London: Macmillan, and New York: St Martin's Press, 1969

Jupp, Peter, *British Politics on the Eve of Reform: The Duke of Wellington's Administration, 1828–1830*, Basingstoke: Macmillan, and New York: St Martin's Press, 1998

O'Gorman, Frank, *The Emergence of the British Two-Party System 1760–1832*, London: Arnold, and New York: Holmes and Meier, 1982

Sack, James J., *From Jacobite to Conservative: Reaction and Orthodoxy in Britain, c.1760–1832*, Cambridge and New York: Cambridge University Press, 1993

Speck, W.A., *Tory and Whig: The Struggle in the Constituencies 1701–1715*, London: Macmillan, and New York: St Martin's Press, 1970

Stewart, Robert, *The Foundation of the Conservative Party 1830–1867*, London and New York: Longman, 1978

Walcott, Robert, *English Politics in the Early Eighteenth Century*, Oxford: Clarendon Press, and Cambridge, Massachusetts: Harvard University Press, 1956; reprinted, New York: Russell and Russell, 1972

In 1956 the American historian Robert WALCOTT denied the reality of party conflict in the reign of Queen Anne (1702–14) and sought to depict parliamentary politics in terms of ins and outs, factions and connections, and divisions between court and country. This interpretation never carried much conviction among other historians. It was subjected to much criticism and was eventually utterly demolished by HOLMES's magisterial study (1967). This magnificent work, persuasively argued, beautifully written, and based on prodigious research, clearly demonstrated the reality of party divisions during Anne's reign. It contains a great deal of value on all aspects of the Tory party in this period. SPECK's shorter but equally scholarly work has demonstrated the reality of party divisions among the electorate, in the constituencies, and in the frequent elections in Anne's reign.

The two most important leaders of the Tory party in Anne's reign, Harley and Bolingbroke, whose fierce rivalry did much to destroy the Tories as a party of government, have attracted considerable scholarly attention. The best biographies of them are by HILL (1988) and DICKINSON (1970).

While historians now agree that there was an organized Tory party during the reign of Queen Anne, they remain divided on what happened to it after 1714 and are even more divided on what connected the Tory party of the early 18th century with the Tory party of the early 19th century. Indeed, it can be argued that they are at a loss to explain the links, if any, between these parties, a century apart, which bore the same name.

Some historians have argued that the Tory party collapsed quite quickly after 1714 when the Hanoverian succession inaugurated decades of Whig dominance of government and parliament. Holmes contributed a fine essay along these lines to his own edited volume, HOLMES (1969). Some historians have accepted that the Tories remained an identifiable group during long years of opposition in parliament, but they maintain that the political propaganda and platform of the Tories were dominated by a country ideology which they shared with many opposition Whigs. See, for example, Dickinson (1970) and DICKINSON (1977). More recent researchers, however, have stressed that the Tories did retain some of their previous policies (on religion, for example) and certainly remained a distinct parliamentary party with leadership, organization, and support which were different from those of the opposition Whigs with whom they sometimes allied. This case has been advanced most fully and most successfully in the fine monograph by COLLEY. She insists, though, that the Tory party under the first two Georges was loyal to the Hanoverian succession and largely abandoned the Jacobite cause. CRUICKSHANKS, on the other hand, maintains that a high proportion of Tories remained committed to a Stuart restoration. Despite the considerable revival of interest in Jacobitism in recent years, this claim has not convinced most historians of the period.

All historians are agreed that the Tory party declined sharply in the late 1740s and 1750s and that it had ceased to be an organized party by 1760. The research of Sir Lewis Namier and his disciples, from the late 1920s to the early 1960s, has convinced all historians that there were no organized political parties in parliament between the late 1750s and the early 1780s. Even the Whigs ceased to be an identifiable party, and parliament was dominated by competing political connections, which all proclaimed Whiggish political views, or by independent backbenchers unattached to any particular group. A new Whig party began to appear in the 1780s, but historians have been unable to identify a new, "second" organized Tory party before the 1810s. Most historians would call Lord Liverpool's governments (1812–1827) "Tory", but little work has been published which explains the emergence of this second Tory party or links it with the first Tory party of the earlier 18th century. The Tories in both eras were more "conservative" than their Whig opponents and were more committed to the monarchy, the Church of England, and the established social hierarchy. These ideological links across the decades have been traced most fully and most successfully by SACK, and to a lesser extent by GUNN in his fine work.

Little, however, has been done to try to connect the second Tory party as a political organization (with a distinctive structure and support) with the first Tory party. This is hardly surprising, since the origins of the second Tory party owe much to the actions and policies of William Pitt the younger and his closest disciples. These men regarded themselves as independent or conservative or government Whigs, not as Tories. It was not until the 1810s that Pitt's political heirs reluctantly accepted the label "Tory" that was foisted on them by their political opponents who claimed sole ownership of the "Whig" inheritance. As a result, historians face considerable difficulty in trying to establish a continuous history of the Tory party that links the party of the earlier 18th century with the party bearing the same political label in the early 19th century. FEILING tried hard to establish some connection but had to confess that there were considerable differences between them. Although Feiling was a very good historian, this is probably his weakest book. It is at its best in trying to show how Pitt's government "party" and its successors gradually acquired the label "Tory".

HILL (1976, 1985) provides a much better guide to the history of British parliamentary parties between 1689 and 1832. He has absorbed the research of the Namierites and the work of post-Namierites who have researched the parties of the earlier 18th century and the early 19th. Hill attempts to trace the history of both the Whig and the Tory parties. In his work of 1976 he has good material on both parties; but for the years after 1714, he has more to say on the Whigs – not surprisingly, since they were the party of government. He does agree with Colley that the Tories were a distinct party which was largely Hanoverian rather than Jacobite. Hill's work of 1985 is far better on the Whigs than on the Tories. He admits that the first Tory party collapsed, and he accepts that a new Tory party did not appear until the 1810s, but he does not adequately explain the emergence of the latter or its connections, if any, with the

first Tory party, and he writes little about the organization, support, or ideology of this second Tory party.

O'GORMAN's short book is the only serious study at present that attempts to explain the emergence of, first, a second Whig party and then a second Tory party in the late 18th and early 19th centuries. This is a brave and intelligent attempt to tackle a major problem, but it only breaks the ground, and it is better on the emergence of the new Whig party (on which O'Gorman and others have done detailed research). The best works on the Tory party in the earlier 19th century are studies of the government of Lord Liverpool, who led an administration from 1812 to 1827 that is always labelled "Tory", even though his support within parliament and in the country at large also included a court party, the Grenville connection, and many independents of a "conservative" persuasion. COOKSON has provided a reliable and informative study of Liverpool's administration between 1815 and 1822. BROCK's book still has its uses, but it is a much older work and many of its central arguments have been challenged. HILTON's book is altogether more successful. It is a very fine study of the economic policies of Tory governments between 1815 and 1830. All three of these studies, however, concentrate on the Tories' government policy and make only limited attempts to understand the nature, structure, support, or ideology of this emerging Tory party. They offer little in the way of a detailed, analytical study of the second Tory party in these years. Some information on these aspects of the Tory party can be gleaned, however, from some of the excellent analytical chapters in JUPP and STEWART.

H.T. DICKINSON

See also George III; Pitt, William, "the Younger"

Tourism

see Aviation; Leisure and Recreation; Service Industries

Towton, Barnet, and Tewkesbury, Battles of 1461 and 1471

Blyth, J.D., "The Battle of Tewkesbury", *Transactions of the Bristol and Gloucestershire Archaeological Society*, 80 (1961): 99–120

Boardman, A.W., *The Battle of Towton*, Stroud, Gloucestershire; and Dover, New Hampshire: Alan Sutton, 1994

Burne, Alfred H., *The Battlefields of England*, London: Methuen, 1950; 2nd edition, London: Methuen, and New York: Barnes and Noble, 1973

Cass, F.C., "The Battle of Barnet", *Transactions of the London and Middlesex Archaeological Society*, 6 (1882): 1–52

Hammond, P.W., *The Battles of Barnet and Tewkesbury*, Stroud, Gloucestershire: Alan Sutton, and New York: St Martin's Press, 1990; revised edition, 1993

Leadman, Alex. D.H., "The Battle of Towton", *Yorkshire Archaeological and Topographical Journal*, 10 (1889): 287–302

Ransome, Cyril, "The Battle of Towton", *English Historical Review*, 4 (1889): 460–66

The battles of Towton (29 March 1461), Barnet (14 April 1471), and Tewkesbury (4 May 1471) were arguably the three most decisive battles of the Wars of the Roses. Towton crushed the hopes of the Lancastrian party and brought Edward of York to the throne as Edward IV; the other two battles restored Edward to the throne in 1471 after the astonishing "readeption" of Henry VI of Lancaster in the previous year. The general course of all three battles is reasonably clear (this is not always the case with 15th-century battles). In discussing the literature it is important to bear in mind that all general histories of the period – for example *Lancaster and York* (2 vols, 1892) by Sir James H. Ramsay and *The Life and Reign of Edward the Fourth* (2 vols, 1923) by Cora L. Scofield – discuss them in some detail. Both Towton and Tewkesbury are dealt with by Richard Brooke in *Visits to Fields of Battle in England* (1857, reprinted 1975), and although his accounts are not up to the standard of modern scholarship, they contain some useful topographical material.

The battle of Towton, said by contemporary chroniclers to have been particularly bloody, has been written about rather more than most battles of this period. No fewer than three articles appeared in 1889. RANSOME's article is short but deals particularly clearly with the main points, especially the topography of the battlefield. Ransome makes little attempt to place Towton in the context of previous events; nor does LEADMAN. Leadman, however, does use a very good range of sources and is good on the events after the battle. The third account published in 1889 was by Clements R. Markham; it appeared in the same volume of the *Yorkshire Archaeological and Topographical Association Journal* as Leadman's. Markham adds nothing to the previous two accounts, but his article is worth looking at for the biographical details of the leading participants in the battle.

The account by BURNE is succinct and to the point, as are all his descriptions of battles; it is based on a thorough study of all the sources, which he comments on in his bibliography. The account is informed throughout by Burne's doctrine of "inherent military probability", which could be described as common sense.

All these accounts contain maps of the battlefield but not of the countryside around, which played an important part in the events before the battle. BOARDMAN has a good map which shows this, and he gives a good description of the skirmishes at Ferrybridge and Dintingdale before the battle, which are glossed over by the other accounts. His account of the battlefield, of which there are several maps, is by a man who has thought deeply about the battle and knows the ground it was fought over very well, although the range of sources used is rather limited. Boardman is good on what medieval warfare meant to the participants. There is a thorough discussion of the controversial question of the numbers involved in the battle (as there is in Burne) – an important point in a battle that was said to have involved larger armies than any other in these wars, and more casualties than any other fought on British soil. Boardman's book is well illustrated with modern and contemporary pictures.

The battle of Barnet was fought about ten miles north of London between the Earl of Warwick (Richard Neville, known as Warwick the Kingmaker), supporting the Lancastrian party, and Edward IV of York. Warwick was trying to reach London to release Henry VI from prison, and Edward had advanced from London with his army to prevent this. The battle was confused because of fog but ended in a victory for the Yorkists, and Warwick's death. For such an important battle, Barnet has had few historians. The first separate account was that of CASS. Cass was the rector of Monken Hadley, just north of Barnet and the actual site of the battle. He thus had ample opportunity for studying the site (he had in fact grown up in the area). This makes his account of the battle particularly valuable, since he describes the topography as it was in the late 19th century, before it changed out of all recognition. There is a valuable map of the area, although unaccountably not of the position of troops, and Cass places the opposing armies in the positions now usually given to them, at the northern end of Hadley Green, just outside Barnet.

Burne's account of Barnet is succinct, as before. There is a good clear map of the battlefield showing the position of the opposing armies, and Burne brought forward good arguments that a hedge which still exists (or did exist until fairly recently) was the one mentioned in one of the sources. This played a part in the defences of the Lancastrian army and helps to settle their position.

The most recent comprehensive account of Barnet and the campaign which led up to it is by HAMMOND, who attempts a detailed discussion of all the events leading to and during the battle. This study contains a map of the battlefield and troop positions on both sides and is illustrated from contemporary and modern sources. There is an appendix, which discusses who was responsible for the death of Henry VI a few weeks after the battle.

The battle of Tewkesbury followed the battle of Barnet within two weeks. In this battle Edward IV crushed the Lancastrian forces that had been raised by Queen Margaret, wife of Henry VI. It took place in Gloucestershire on the banks of the river Severn, but its exact position has been a matter of some controversy. Bazeley, the first modern historian to write about the battle, was a canon of Gloucester cathedral and thus (like Cass) had the advantage of valuable local topographical knowledge. His account is a thorough and valuable one, placing the opposing armies in much the same position as recent scholars, across the main road along which Edward IV was expected to advance. It ends with the first discussion of the fate of Edward, Prince of Wales, the only child of Henry VI, who died during or soon after the battle. Burne's discussion of the battle is particularly valuable because it represents the first attempt to work out the long distances marched by the two armies in the three days beforehand.

The account by BLYTH is a thorough piece of work; the author examines all the sources, has some useful things to say about the topography of the site, and provides some interesting maps. Unfortunately, he spends a great deal of time trying to prove that the battle was fought around a small hill just outside Tewkesbury, with the Lancastrians sheltering in the ruins of a castle. Excavation has shown that the castle did not exist in this form in 1471, however, and Blyth's position is military nonsense without this.

Hammond, in a more recent account of the battle, gives an account of the recruitment of the armies and builds on Burne in a discussion of the marches to the battlefield. He uses a wide range of sources to give a rounded picture of the events of the years 1470–71, both before and after the battles, and attempts to make better sense of a crux in the battle which caused the Lancastrian defeat. There is an appendix discussing the fate of Edward, Prince of Wales, using all available sources.

PETER HAMMOND

See also Edward IV; Henry VI; Neville, Richard; Richard III

Toynbee, Arnold 1889–1975

Historian and scholar

Geyl, Pieter, *Debates with Historians*, Groningen: Wolters, The Hague: Nijhoff, and London: Batsford, 1955; New York: Philosophical Library, 1956; revised edition, New York: Meridian Books, 1958; London: Collins, 1962

McIntire, C.T. and Marvin Perry (editors), *Toynbee: Reappraisals*, Toronto and Buffalo, New York: University of Toronto Press, 1989

McNeill, William H., *Arnold J. Toynbee: A Life*, New York and Oxford: Oxford University Press, 1989

Montagu, M.F. Ashley (editor), *Toynbee and History: Critical Essays and Reviews*, Boston: Porter Sargent, 1956

Morton, S. Fiona, *A Bibliography of Arnold J. Toynbee*, Oxford and New York: Oxford University Press, 1980

Perry, Marvin, *Arnold Toynbee and the Crisis of the West*, Washington, DC: University Press of America, 1982

Stromberg, Roland N., *Arnold J. Toynbee: Historian for an Age in Crisis*, Carbondale: Southern Illinois University Press, 1972

Toynbee, Arnold J., *A Study of History*, abridged by D.C. Somervell, 2 vols, London and New York: Oxford University Press, 1946–57

Arguably, no historian has ever written as widely about humanity's past as Arnold Toynbee (1889–1975). Not only did Toynbee produce an unusually large number of books, essays, and articles about world history, but he was the first historian to attempt to analyse all principal civilizations comprehensively. Toynbee's earlier writings about Greek and Ottoman history were already wide-ranging, but it was his 12-volume *A Study of History* (1935–61) that established his reputation as the most famous historian of his day. In fact, it was on the strength of this massive work that Toynbee acquired a reputation rarely achieved by an academic, as he was regarded partly as an historian and partly as a prophet whose grasp of the past and future of civilizations gave him a unique ability to forecast the main directions of world history.

Toynbee understood that civilizations were inherently dynamic, and he connected their fate with the history of major religions (including the denigration of Hebrew religion as a "fossil" of Syriac religion). Toynbee famously argued that the development of civilizations required "challenge-response" – that is, a stimulus to force a minority within a given culture or community to become creative enough to bring about civilization. In addition, Toynbee held that in order to grow adequately civilizations then had to face another challenge which forced them into more elaborate development. *A Study of History* also offered an explanation of the fate of civilizations. Most civilizations were not conquered by external forces; rather, they committed suicide. Toynbee offered a typology for the patterns which make up the suicide of civilizations: They lost critical energy. They then endured a "time of troubles". These troubles were resolved by the development of a "universal state" which, however, itself was emblematic of stagnation (because it revealed a lack of creative power). The universal state was able to restore an "Indian summer" to the declining civilization, but since it was defined by an attempt to maintain the status quo, it did not possess the resources to meet subsequent challenges. The civilization then collapsed from the weight of its own inertia.

Toynbee's history was immense, but what served to make him an international figure was the combination of his own circumstances and his pronouncements regarding the fate of western civilization, which he understood to be in a crisis – possibly a "time of troubles". The larger question of the direction of civilization proved to be a popular theme with readers who had experienced the emergence of the Soviet Union, the rise of fascism, the triumphs of the Nazis, World War II, and the beginnings of the cold war. Toynbee's writings appeared at the right time; he was able to address larger, often forgotten, questions about the direction and meaning of history. However, the sheer scale of Toynbee's agenda and prolific production (MORTON lists over 2,900 works) virtually ensured that at first he would receive frequent and harsh criticism; that later he would be little read, and even less well understood; and that his reputation would survive as something of a caricature.

While the first six volumes *A Study of History* attracted nearly universal interest and won wide praise, Toynbee's work also began to receive severe criticism. GEYL, who proved to be one of Toynbee's harshest critics, assailed *A Study of History* on empirical grounds. Not only were some of the details of Toynbee's history suspect, but Toynbee had drawn together an unsound system of ideas. Geyl argued that Toynbee's view of civilization, although provocative, was based upon a significantly flawed systemization of ideas. Having attacked Toynbee's understanding of history, Geyl challenged his ability to predict the future by rejecting the idea that western civilization was headed for inevitable collapse. Finally, Geyl claimed that it was better to consider Toynbee a prophet than to consider him an historian, noting that his work was disconnected from historical realities. In fact, Toynbee's imposing historical structure reminded Geyl of a dreamworld – not unlike the one Alice walked through in Wonderland.

MONTAGU's *Toynbee and History* offers possibly the best collection of Toynbee's critics; it can also usefully be read as a historical document because it illustrates how *A Study of History* generated immense interest in the 1950s. In addition to Geyl, this work contains some of the historian's harshest critics. Hugh Trevor-Roper charged that Toynbee played "intellectual hanky-panky", as he omitted evidence to fit his theory of history. A.J.P. Taylor argued that Toynbee's method was a "lucky dip"; Toynbee had over-relied on the ancient world for his comparison of 21 civilizations and, equally unacceptably, had allowed religious motivations to colour his assessments of the past.

Finally, Abba Eban attacked Toynbee for his interpretation of Hebrew religion as a fossil of the "Syriac community".

More recent interpretations of *A Study of History* (and Toynbee's work more generally) have lacked the urgency of the critics of the 1950s. The books by PERRY and STROMBERG are of service to contemporary readers because they provide overviews of *A Study of History*. Even more striking, the essays which make up McINTIRE & PERRY's collection tend to focus on diverse aspects of Toynbee's *oeuvre* (his view of the United States and Russian history – as well as his "conscience"), but they contain neither the sharp-edged anger of Montagu's volume nor the attempts to refute the "system" of ideas central to *A Study of History*. Taken together, these volumes imply that Toynbee is no longer regarded as a significant historian and that his place in history now seems to be roughly equivalent to an increasingly remote literary figure.

Finally, McNEILL's biography deftly places Toynbee's life and thought in historical perspective by tracing his development and career. McNeill shows that a combination of Toynbee's early experiences and relationships – his father's religion and commitment to social welfare, financial insecurity, his own wide travels, his ability to avoid service in World War I (and his subsequent feeling of guilt about it), and the dynamics of his marriage – all contributed to his passion for writing about world history and, then, for capitalizing on his status as a celebrity. Toynbee also emerges as a figure particularly well placed for his times: the tumultuous events of the early and mid-20th century enabled him to write for a transatlantic audience which was avidly seeking to comprehend its own experience in light of larger questions about the fate of civilizations and the direction of history.

STEPHEN L. KECK

Tractarianism   1830s and 1840s

Baker, Joseph Ellis, *The Novel and the Oxford Movement*, Princeton, New Jersey: Princeton University Press, 1932

Battiscombe, Georgina, *John Keble: A Study in Limitations*, London: Constable, 1963; New York: Knopf, 1964

Chadwick, Owen (editor), *The Mind of the Oxford Movement*, London: Adam and Charles Black, and Stanford, California: Stanford University Press, 1960

Chadwick, Owen, *The Victorian Church*, 2 vols, New York: Oxford University Press, and London: A. and C. Black, 1966–70; 2nd edition, 1970

Church, R.W., *The Oxford Movement: Twelve Years, 1833–1845*, London and New York: Macmillan, 1891; new edition, edited by Geoffrey Best, Chicago: University of Chicago Press, 1970

Gilley, Sheridan, *Newman and His Age*, London: Darton Longman and Todd, 1990

Newsome, David, *The Parting of Friends: A Study of the Wilberforces and Henry Manning*, London: John Murray, 1966; reprinted, Grand Rapids, Michigan: Eerdmans, and Leominster, Herefordshire: Gracewing, 1993

Nockles, Peter Benedict, *The Oxford Movement in Context: Anglican High Churchmanship, 1760–1857*, Cambridge and New York: Cambridge University Press, 1994

For well over a century, the Oxford Movement, of which tractarianism represented the early stage, has been seen as central to the history of the Victorian Church of England. In this view, a handful of Oxford University dons (most notably John Henry Newman, John Keble, and Edward Bouverie Pusey) shook the church out of its 18th-century latitudinarian torpor. They proclaimed that Anglicanism was not merely a faith enacted by parliament but an apostolic and ancient church bearing authority from God and not the state. This view saw the movement as almost exclusively an academic one, centred on Oxford University, expressing its views in theological debate (and in college politics) and gaining national attention for its ideas by means of publications, especially *Tracts for the Times* (hence the name "tractarians"). The view was earliest and best expressed by CHURCH, himself a disciple of Newman's and a participant in the events he narrates (although he conceals his participation from the reader). Church saw tractarianism as a reaction against what he understood to have been the conditions of the times: the aridity of the High Church, the accommodation of evangelicalism to middle-class respectability, and the political parties' Erastian view of the church as being little more than another department of state. The movement began in 1833 when Keble denounced the state's suppression of some Irish bishoprics, but Newman was its prime leader and most interesting man of ideas. The movement's important events all happened at Oxford. When Newman converted to Roman catholicism in 1845 (Church calls this "the catastrophe"), the movement was effectively over. Although Church does write in his final paragraph that the movement continued, he stresses that what continued after mid-century happened elsewhere than at Oxford and involved a new cast of characters.

Church's master narrative dominated historical writing on tractarianism for the following 75 years. The centenary of the Oxford Movement in 1933 saw the publication of several studies. Most were character sketches rather than sustained narratives, and their authors remained bound by Church's chronology and analysis. Of these, the study by BAKER is of greatest interest, for he used once widely read Victorian novels to elucidate tractarianism. His argument – which reinforced Church – was that Newman's conversion represented a turning-point in the movement. Before 1845 tractarians had seen evangelicalism as their main enemy, but for a decade thereafter their battle was with Roman catholicism. Ritualism, which did not appear until the 1860s and 1870s, was essentially a new development.

The writing of church history changed during the 1960s as historians grew more interested in religion as social, political, and ideological experiences rather than as exclusively institutional and theological systems. CHADWICK (1960) led the way with *The Mind of the Oxford Movement*, an anthology of selected writings by Newman, Keble, and Pusey to which he wrote a substantial 54-page introduction that advanced the historical understanding of the movement. Chadwick follows Church's basic line of argument, save for three points. First, he centres the movement on Newman but explains Newman's conversion as a result of a search for the "ideal" church. Second, he emphasizes the importance of practical political issues (e.g., catholic emancipation in 1829 and the campaign for parliamentary reform of 1830–32) in sparking the movement. Third, he stresses that many leaders of the movement were not so much reacting against an evangelical threat from outside as transforming their own evangelical backgrounds.

Other nuanced treatments followed. BATTISCOMBE's biography of Keble showed that other figures besides Newman were important to understanding the development of tractarianism and that Newman's conversion did not necessarily spell its end. NEWSOME's collective biographical study attempts to break free of Church's chronological and interpretative constraints by focusing on Samuel, Robert, and Henry Wilberforce (sons of the slave emancipator William Wilberforce); their brother-in-law Henry Manning; and several other bright young men. These figures were outside Oxford during Church's "twelve years", 1833–45; most of them had been raised as evangelicals. Newsome argues that the tractarians can be interpreted as a group of young men, linked by ties of kinship and friendship. Furthermore, he suggests that their evangelical background, which stressed the necessity of undergoing a conversion experience, is crucial to understanding their conversion to Anglocatholicism and in some cases to Roman catholicism, for those who convert once may convert again.

CHADWICK (1966–70), *The Victorian Church*, is a major synthesis of work done to the end of the 1960s. Here Chadwick devotes more space to the Church of England than to nonconformity and Roman catholicism, and more to the Oxford Movement than to evangelical and liberal Anglicanism. He integrates political and constitutional issues into his account of the origins of tractarianism (but writes little of social and pastoral issues), places Newman squarely at the head of the movement, and holds that when Newman converted the tractarians "subsided and slithered towards ruin".

The sesquicentenary of the tractarian movement in 1983 occasioned a spate of books on the subject, but, as had been the case with those written for the centenary, none was an analytical, sustained narrative. Rather, the centenary of Newman's death in 1990 saw the results of the scholarship of the last third of the 20th century come together in a coherent interpretation. Of the many biographies of Newman, GILLEY's gives the most original interpretation of his years as an Anglican. Gilley brings out in compelling detail the extent to which Newman's evangelical background both prepared him for tractarianism and smoothed his way to Roman catholicism: although Newman discarded distinctive evangelical teachings, he remained intensely interested in prophecy and in the quest for personal holiness. Gilley also analyses Newman's activities as a tractarian leader, showing that much of the estrangement between tractarians and their non-tractarian mentors and colleagues at Oxford was Newman's own doing, and demonstrating that Newman left the Church of England because he chose to do so and not because attacks by Anglican leaders drove him out.

If Gilley revised the internal history of tractarianism, NOCKLES revised its prehistory. His study firmly and authoritatively fixes tractarianism in the contexts of both the early evangelical movement and 18th-century High-Churchmanship. Although many tractarians had grown up in evangelical homes, the doctrines that they espoused as adults had their roots in a vigorous High Church tradition that was more than mere Jacobite romanticism or anti-Jacobin reaction.

DENIS PAZ

See also Anglican Doctrine and Worship; Newman; Oxford Movement; Oxford, University of; Ritualism

Tractatus de legibus et consuetudinibus regni Angliae (Glanvill) 12th century

Hall, G.D.G. (editor), *The Treatise on the Laws and Customs of the Realm of England Commonly Called Glanvill*, London: Nelson, 1965; Holmes Beach, Florida: Gaunt, 1983; Oxford: Clarendon Press, and New York: Oxford University Press, 1993

Hudson, John, *Land, Law, and Lordship in Anglo-Norman England*, Oxford: Clarendon Press, and New York: Oxford University Press, 1994

Milsom, S.F.C., *The Legal Framework of English Feudalism: The Maitland Lectures Given in 1972*, Cambridge and New York: Cambridge University Press, 1976

Pollock, Frederick and Frederic William Maitland, *The History of English Law before the Time of Edward I*, 2nd edition, 2 vols, Cambridge: Cambridge University Press, 1898; Union, New Jersey: Lawbook Exchange, 1996

Tractatus de legibus et consuetudinibus regni Angliae [Treatise on the Laws and Customs of the Realm of England] is the first known Latin treatise in the history of the English common law. It used to be attributed to Ranulf de Glanvill (d. 1190), justiciar of Henry II from 1179 to 1189, after whom it is commonly known, but his personal responsibility is now thought unlikely. There is little doubt, however, that it derives from the judicial proceedings of Glanvill's justiciarship. The author focused exclusively on providing knowledge of the secular procedures (*causarum secularium genera*) operating in the *curia regis* of Henry II. His intention was not only to enhance the force of existing laws by reducing them to writing but also to systematize the legal institutions that had emerged from the innovative activities of the Anglo-Norman kings since the conquest in 1066.

The treatise is available in the edition by HALL. The core of the work demonstrates the rapid development of the *curia regis*, which had resulted from the evolution of a number of original writs drafted by the Chancery as instruments to initiate royal civil pleas concerning rights to land. The new legal remedies, designed to assist those who had lost their tenures during the anarchy of King Stephen's reign (1135–54), that is the assizes of *novel disseisin* (chapter 13, 33–39) and *mort d'ancestor* (chapter 13, 3–16), attracted an unprecedented amount of litigation to the royal court. Only there could seisin be restored, after a speedy jury trial. Meanwhile the invention of the grand assize (chapter 2, 6–20), where litigants could establish their greater right (*maius ius*) to title in court, avoiding trial by battle, and the routine use of writs of *praecipe* (which ordered sheriffs to carry out various judicial orders) further increased the business of the royal court. As a result, professional judges had to sit more regularly to deliver such judgements. These changes inspired the author of the treatise to invest the routine of royal justice with an intellectual coherence which it may not in fact have possessed. He vehemently advocated the principle, based on ancient custom, that "no one is bound to answer concerning any free tenement of his in the court of his lord, unless there is a writ from the lord king or his chief justice" (chapter 12, 2 and 25). Much of the author's energy was also devoted to organizing the operative writs on property into a theoretically coherent system. On the level of actual possession (*possesio*), the so-called petty assizes offered a quick and efficient means of redress to a plaintiff who had recently been disseised "unjustly and without judgement". A judgement in such a case was usually delivered after a jury trial. On the level of right (*proprietas*), ancient and sometimes obsolete titles were decided either by the traditional writ *breve de recto* (chapter 12, 3–5), where the judgement of God was delivered by the outcome of battle, or by the grand assize. In the latter case judgement was delivered after a scrutiny of the evidence, by a jury of 12 local knights, who had in turn been selected by four knights summoned by the sheriff. On several occasions the author made it clear that, whereas judgement in a proprietory action was final, judgement in a possessory action did not bar a future use of *breve de recto*.

Modern scholarship focuses mainly on the growth of royal justice out of the complicated operation of original writs during the "age of Glanvill" (the reforming years of Henry II), and how that should be interpreted legally, socially, and constitutionally. Maitland, in POLLOCK & MAITLAND, starting from a contrast between the anarchy of Stephen's reign and the restoration of order under Henry II, argued that Henry deliberately carried out a series of legal reforms designed to deprive his subjects of the seigneurial jurisdiction customarily exercised in their own courts. As a result, feudal lords gradually lost their competence to do justice to their own dependents by *breve de recto*, and the writ itself was eventually reduced to a means of transferring litigation over property from seigneurial courts to the royal court by compelling feudal lords to default on their own justice. Maitland believed that the so-called rule of *nemo tenetur respondere*, as a universal rule of law, played the most significant part in the constitutional shift of power to the central government.

MILSOM offers a totally different interpretation. Instead of seeing the royal court as undermining seigneurial jurisdiction, he portrays a truly "seigneurial world" in 12th-century England, in which only property rights were created, disciplined, and decided. Henry II's legal reforms were designed not to dissolve the traditional order but to restore the mechanism of the royal court. This court had become dysfunctional under Stephen, and it needed to work according to its original feudal logic. The profound transformation of the law and the gradual centralization of government which actually took place were therefore largely unintentional – a result of that "judicial accident" which saw litigants striving to get their cases heard in the king's court. It was this voluntary movement, rather than the king's intention, which disabled the judicial functions of the seigneurial courts.

For the past two decades Milsom's interpretation has generated a new wave of enthusiasm for research into the origins of the common law. While the *Tractatus* remains the primary source for the early common-law court and its proceedings, more and more original material relating to the judicial procedures of the canon-law courts, feudal courts, and local popular courts is being scrutinized and used in recent studies. Academic reconstruction of the history of 12th-century English law, as demonstrated by HUDSON and other scholars, has moved to take account of more than the active involvement of central authority.

WENXI LIU
REVIEWED BY DAVID LOADES

See also Constitutional Law; Feudal Law; Feudal Tenures; Feudum; Henry II; Jurisprudence

Trade Patterns: Early Modern

Chaudhuri, K.N., *The Trading World of Asia and the English East India Company 1660–1760*, Cambridge and New York: Cambridge University Press, 1978

Cullen, L.M., *Anglo-Irish Trade, 1660–1800*, Manchester: Manchester University Press, and New York: Kelley, 1968

Davies, K.G., *The Royal African Company*, London and New York: Longmans Green, 1957

Davis, Ralph, *The Rise of the English Shipping Industry in the Seventeenth and Eighteenth Centuries*, London: Macmillan, and New York: St Martin's Press, 1962

Davis, Ralph, *English Overseas Trade, 1500–1700*, London: Macmillan, 1973

Devine, T.M., *The Tobacco Lords: A Study of the Tobacco Merchants of Glasgow and Their Trading Activities, c.1740–1790*, Edinburgh: John Donald, 1975

Fisher, F.J., *London and the English Economy, 1500–1700*, edited by P.J. Corfield and N.B. Harte, London and Ronceverte, West Virginia: Hambledon Press, 1990

Hancock, David, *Citizens of the World: London Merchants and the Integration of the British Atlantic Community, 1735–1785*, Cambridge and New York: Cambridge University Press, 1995

McCusker, John J. and Kenneth Morgan (editors), *The Early Modern Atlantic Economy*, Cambridge and New York: Cambridge University Press, 2000

Minchinton, W.E. (editor), *The Growth of English Overseas Trade in the Seventeenth and Eighteenth Centuries*, London: Methuen, 1969

Morgan, Kenneth, *Bristol and the Atlantic Trade in the Eighteenth Century*, Cambridge and New York: Cambridge University Press, 1993

Price, Jacob M., *France and the Chesapeake: A History of the French Tobacco Monopoly, 1674–1791, and of Its Relationship to the British and American Tobacco Trades*, 2 vols, Ann Arbor: University of Michigan Press, 1973

Price, Jacob M., *Capital and Credit in British Overseas Trade: The View from the Chesapeake, 1700–1776*, Cambridge, Massachusetts: Harvard University Press, 1980

Ramsay, G.D., *English Overseas Trade during the Centuries of Emergence: Studies in Some Modern Origins of the English-Speaking World*, London: Macmillan, and New York: St Martin's Press, 1957

Sacks, David Harris, *The Widening Gate: Bristol and the Atlantic Economy, 1450–1700*, Berkeley: University of California Press, 1991

British overseas trade in the early modern era experienced much growth and change and contributed significantly to the overall development of the domestic economy. In the period 1500–1650 most of England's foreign commerce was conducted with Ireland and Europe. Woollens dominated exports. Imports comprised iron and timber from the Baltic; linen and woollen yarn from Ireland; wine, oil, and fruit from the Iberian peninsula; and linen from the Netherlands. From c.1650 to 1800, British foreign trade expanded its geographical scope and merchants traded in a wider range of commodities. Commerce with the world outside Europe burgeoned, notably with the growth of transatlantic trades to North America and the Caribbean, the development of the East India Company's commerce with Asia, and trade with the Levant. This was also the era of British slave-trading with Africa and the Americas: from 1662 to 1807, when the British abolished the trade, some 3.3 million slaves may have been taken from Africa by British ships (estimates of the figure vary).

British exports diversified by the mid-18th century to include a broader range of textiles, metalware, and hardware. Groceries from the colonies grew substantially among imports, a reflection of the increased domestic demand for sugar, tobacco, and tea. By the late 17th century a quarter of all manufacturing production and half of the output of woollen goods were exported and nearly a quarter of the home consumption was imported. By 1700 shipping and maritime labour were an important segment of the urban labour force. During the 18th century, significant increases in imports and exports made foreign trade a dynamic part of the late pre-industrial economy in Britain. Trade increased at an annual rate of 0.8 per cent between 1700 and 1740, by 1.7 per cent between 1740 and 1770, and by 2.6 per cent between 1770 and 1800 – a faster rate of growth than total output.

Many fine studies have analysed the changes in British foreign commerce from the 16th to the 18th centuries, but there is no up-to-date synthesis of the entire subject. DAVIS (1973) is an elegant, slim book that covers the main trends in English foreign trade in the period 1500–1700; though written more than a quarter-century ago, it is still a good introduction to the topic. RAMSAY's book is not often cited today, but it is a useful, if slightly old-fashioned, attempt to look at significant aspects of English overseas trade in the early modern era. Though it lacks statistical tables, it includes useful discussions of the Antwerp mart, the expansion of trade with the Mediterranean, the Baltic trade, the smugglers' trade, the rise of the western outports, and the growth of the British Atlantic community.

MINCHINTON's collection reprints a selection of important papers on English overseas trade in the early modern era. Ralph Davis's seminal articles on the development of English foreign trade in the periods 1660–1700 and 1700–1774 are included. Davis charts the main trends in the growth and commodity composition of exports and imports. His data point to a great expansion of trade with the colonies between the restoration of the Stuart monarchy and the late 18th century. F.J. Fisher's well-known paper dealing with London's export trade in the early 17th century is another contribution. Fisher finds some growth in this trade during the period and also some diversification into new products and expansion into new markets. This article is also reprinted in FISHER (1990), which includes the author's helpful "Commercial Trends and Policy in Sixteenth-Century England". Minchinton also includes papers dealing with aspects of English economic growth in the first half of the 18th century, trends in smuggling in the 18th century, and Anglo-Portuguese trade from 1700 to 1770. The editor's long introduction is a wide-ranging survey of the field covered in these readings.

Scotland and Ireland played a significant role in British overseas trade in the early modern era. CULLEN provides a thorough survey of Anglo-Irish trade from 1660 to 1800. He emphasizes the prosperity of Ireland in that period and investigates trade in linen, coal, provisions, and smuggling. In 1660 the Irish and English economies were competitive; by 1800 they were complementary. Cullen argues that Ireland lacked the

capital for maritime expansion largely because it had limited natural resources and a predominantly agrarian economy: Irish overseas trading therefore was not hampered greatly by absentee landlords or by the Navigation Acts. During the 18th century, Scottish overseas trade flourished and Glasgow rose to pre-eminence as a commercial city. DEVINE traces the partnership structures, capitalization, and conduct of the tobacco trade among Glasgow's merchants in the mid-18th century. He demonstrates how the entrepreneurial ability of the Scots in running close-knit firms and chains of stores in Virginia and Maryland enabled Glaswegians to make their fortunes from the marketing of tobacco to re-export markets in northern Europe.

PRICE (1980), another leading authority on the Glasgow tobacco trade, throws light on the mobilization of credit by British firms trading with the Chesapeake from 1700 to 1776. He shows that most merchants had limited fixed capital resources but relied on commercial credit, rather than borrowing on bond or from banks, to support their trading activities. His book also illuminates the role of large wholesale London warehousemen in supplying goods for exports. PRICE (1973) is a magisterial study of the French farmers-general, who operated a state monopoly on tobacco imports into France. This book also covers a broader field of enquiry. Here one can find detailed consideration of the changing role of British ports in the tobacco trade in the 18th century and of the commercial connections between merchants in Britain, America, and Europe. Much contextual information is included on customs procedures, institutional mechanisms, and business practices in early modern British trade.

The merchant community and overseas trade of early modern London have attracted relatively little study, though one can find some useful specialist articles in academic journals and collections of essays. Perhaps the scale and scope of the subject have proved too daunting for historians. HANCOCK, however, provides interesting material about the trade of the metropolis in his account of the global commercial outlook of 23 merchants based in London – the "citizens of the world" of the title – who spent the period c.1735–85 devoted to trade, shipping, finance, and landed improvement. The book explores avenues for profit in the first British empire and how these opportunities influenced mercantile enterprise. There are also discussions of merchants' counting-houses in London, oceanic shipping interests, plantation ownership in the British Caribbean and southern mainland American colonies, the running of a slave-trade castle in West Africa, government provisioning in the Seven Years' War, and financial investments. Hancock shows how his merchant associates integrated the British empire by "deepening its infrastructure, expanding its trade, peopling its shores and hinterlands, and spreading the new optimistic, experimental ideas of the Enlightenment".

Bristol, the second largest city and port in England for much of the early modern period, has been the subject of several monographs. SACKS covers the development of the port and its trades in the 16th and 17th centuries, tracing the transition of the city from a medieval trading centre to an Atlantic entrepôt. In 1450 Bristol's overseas trade concentrated on the exchange of English woollens for French wines at Bordeaux. By 1700, Bristol's commerce was conducted with most overseas markets and the port had become a hub of the Atlantic economy. Sacks's main contribution is to show how competition between the large overseas merchants of Bristol and the city's artisans and retail shopkeepers was an essential part of the transition to a capitalist economy in the city. MORGAN follows up this analysis by concentrating on the "golden age" of Bristol in the 18th century. He shows that the absolute growth of Bristol's Atlantic trade between 1700 and 1800 was concomitant with the relative decline of Bristol as a port. The main reasons for this decline were a lack of improvements to port facilities, increasing specialization among Bristol's merchant community, the impact of war on trade, and more skilful business acumen in trading in tobacco by Glasgow's merchants and in slaves by Liverpool's merchants.

DAVIS (1962) is the first port of call for information on the English shipping industry in the early modern era. Davis demonstrates that shipping was one of the fastest-growing English industries between 1560 and 1689. The tonnage of ships multiplied sevenfold at a time when the population only doubled. The manpower needed for shipping enterprise was probably greater than for any other industry apart from cloth-making and building. The shipping industry was also one of the country's greatest users of capital. Economies of labour and capital were achieved in the English shipping industry of the 18th century, but these gains in efficiency were not a vital part of English economic development. Davis concludes that "the shipping industry was an important part of the English economy both before and after the decisive decades of the Industrial Revolution, but it cannot be said to have made a contribution of a special character to the transition".

Most foreign trade was conducted by private merchant firms in the early modern period, but commerce was also pursued by joint-stock companies such as the Russia Company, Levant Company, Eastland Company, and Hudson's Bay Company. DAVIES provides an authoritative history of the leading joint-stock organization in the slave trade, the Royal African Company, which was chartered in 1672 and was based in London. It held a monopoly over trading to Africa until 1698, when the trade was thrown open to all English merchants. Davies traces the organization and capitalization of the company, the markets to which slaves were delivered, and the chronic debts that made it difficult for the company to maintain its forts and castles in West Africa and a sufficient supply of slaves to the Caribbean. The Royal African Company was no longer supplying slaves to British colonies by 1730, and it ceased to exist in 1752.

A longer-lived joint-stock trading organization was the English East India Company, which from the early 1600s until its charter was changed in 1813 held a monopoly over English trade with Asia. Contemporaries regarded the East India Company as one of the chief sources of Britain's power and commercial prosperity. CHAUDHURI, in one of several books by him on the topic, discusses the formal bureaucracy of the company and how it operated effectively during commercial crises. He also dissects the quantitative dimensions of the English East India Company's trade over the century from 1660 to 1760. His statistics chart the growth of the company's imports of textiles, tea, and spices from Asia as well as the drain of silver bullion from England to India to pay for these imports. The British government and the East India Company had a symbiotic relationship: the government provided privileges, support, and monopolies, and the company in return lent its capital to the government.

McCUSKER & MORGAN (2000) is a collection of essays devoted to the interlocking commercial relationships of the Atlantic trading world during the early modern era. The four themes covered in the book are (1) the role of merchants and their connections, (2) the development of trades, (3) imperial economies, and (4) colonial working societies. The essays included offer broad reflections on the interconnections between kinship, risk, and credit; the business networks that bound together the Anglo-American export trade c.1750–1800; the internal history of the port of London in the early 18th century; the comparative history of the French and British empires in the Americas before 1800; the consumption of plantation goods and distilled alcoholic beverages in the Atlantic world; and Britain's monetary policy and foreign commerce during the French revolutionary and Napoleonic wars. This book is probably the best starting-place for those wishing to learn about the current concerns of historians of early modern British trade.

KENNETH MORGAN

See also Exploration: To the 18th Century; New World, Perceptions of

Trade Patterns: 1800–c.1890

Anstey, Roger and P.E.H. Hair (editors), *Liverpool, the African Slave Trade, and Abolition*, Liverpool: Historic Society of Lancashire and Cheshire, 1976

Ashworth, William, *An Economic History of England, 1870–1939*, London: Methuen, 1960

Cairncross, A.K., *Home and Foreign Investment, 1870–1913: Studies in Capital Accumulation*, Cambridge: Cambridge University Press, 1953

Checkland, S.G., *The Rise of Industrial Society in England, 1815–1885*, London: Longman, 1964; New York: St Martin's Press, 1965

Clapham, J.H., *An Economic History of Modern Britain*, 3 vols, Cambridge: Cambridge University Press, 1926–38

Court, W.H.B., *A Concise Economic History of Britain: From 1750 to Recent Times*, Cambridge: Cambridge University Press, 1954

Crafts, N.F.R., *British Economic Growth during the Industrial Revolution*, Oxford: Clarendon Press, and New York: Oxford University Press, 1985

Crouzet, François, *The Victorian Economy*, translated by Anthony Forster, London: Methuen, and New York: Columbia University Press, 1982

Davis, R., *A Commercial Revolution: English Overseas Trade in the Seventeenth and Eighteenth Centuries*, Historical Association pamphlet, 1967

Farnie, D.A., *The English Cotton Industry and the World Market, 1815–1896*, Oxford: Clarendon Press, and New York: Oxford University Press, 1979

Fieldhouse, D.K. (editor), *The Theory of Capitalist Imperialism*, London: Longman, and New York: Barnes and Noble, 1967

Floud, Roderick and Donald McCloskey (editors), *The Economic History of Britain since 1700*, 2 vols, Cambridge and New York: Cambridge University Press, 1981

Hopkins, A.G., *An Economic History of West Africa*, New York: Columbia University Press, 1973

Hoppen, K. Theodore, *The Mid-Victorian Generation, 1846–1886*, Oxford: Clarendon Press, and New York: Oxford University Press, 1998

Hudson, Pat, *The Industrial Revolution*, London: Edward Arnold, 1992

Imlah, A.H., *Economic Elements in the Pax Britannica: Studies in British Foreign Trade in the Nineteenth Century*, Cambridge, Massachusetts: Harvard University Press, 1958

Mathias, Peter, *The First Industrial Nation: An Economic History of Britain, 1700–1914*, London: Methuen, 1969; 2nd edition, 1983

Saul, S.B., *Studies in British Overseas Trade, 1870–1914*, Liverpool: Liverpool University Press, 1960

By 1800 Britain's so-called Industrial Revolution was progressing steadily, and Britain was becoming the "first industrial nation", to use the title of MATHIAS's informative book. The growth of factory industry and the expansion of manufactures on an unprecedented scale led to an expansion of markets overseas and a search for new markets for manufactures and new sources of raw materials. As a result, for the first half of the 19th century Britain became the "workshop of the world", supplying the other regions of the world with the bulk of their manufactures. Overseas trade thus developed greater complexity and sophistication during the 19th century than it had possessed in the 18th.

Any economic historian who writes about overseas trade patterns has to contend with several issues. First, Britain's external trade patterns cannot be appreciated without considering the prevailing economic thought of the period, and it was during the 19th century that Britain moved from the protection offered by mercantilism to free trade. Second, these patterns can be fully understood only in the context of the dynamics of the Industrial Revolution as a whole. Third, statistical data for this period are notoriously unreliable until the final quarter of the century.

Early accounts of the Industrial Revolution by CLAPHAM, ASHWORTH, COURT, and CHECKLAND consider the importance of overseas trade. Although in many respects now out of date, Clapham's work remains a valuable source of information and ideas, and an indispensable tool. Ashworth, Court, and Checkland all provide useful accounts of the significance of overseas trade and its changing patterns. Taking more modern approaches, FLOUD & McCLOSKEY and HUDSON similarly consider the role of overseas trade in the process of industrialization, but they also look outside Britain, and even outside Europe, for factors that influenced trade. These historians give a much clearer picture than do the earlier writers of patterns of trade.

CROUZET discusses the factors behind the changing patterns of trade – changes which, he states, were only gradual during a century of relative stability. He points out that the 18th century and the French wars – especially Napoleon's "continental system" – had led to a change in direction of Britain's trade away from Europe towards America, at first to the Colonies, then to the independent United States, and later to Latin America, where markets opened up from 1808 on as a result of a weakening of Spanish control in the Peninsular War. Britain's mercantilist policies encouraged the expansion of Britain's overseas trade, because, as DAVIS explains, the protective customs duties of mercantilism, especially the Navigation Acts, had nurtured infant British industry. CRAFTS points out that during the early 19th century as much as 35 per cent of industrial output was exported. In particular, the growth of textile industries had been encouraged. A change in the pattern of export commodities came with the decline in the export of woollens and the tremendous increase in the export of cotton manufactures. These formed the bulk of Britain's exports during the century.

Hudson gives a clear indication of the complexity of studying patterns of Britain's overseas trade during this time. Changes in trading patterns became necessary after the end of the Napoleonic Wars when some European countries began to experience their own industrial revolutions. The old pattern involved Britain in a very profitable re-export trade through which it shipped colonial goods such as sugar, tobacco, rum, and spices to Europe and was enabled to buy products such as linen, timber, and naval supplies from the Continent. Hudson emphasizes Britain's need to search for new markets overseas after 1815, when European countries developed their own textile industries, as a deliberate policy to substitute imports aided by protective tariffs. Britain thus became a supplier of semi-finished textile manufactures to its European rivals and looked elsewhere to sell its textiles. FARNIE thoroughly examines the role of cotton exports in the changing pattern of trade between 1815 and 1896.

This search for new markets brought increasing demands from merchants for "free trade". This was almost achieved with the repeal of the Corn Laws in 1846, a reflection of the greater influence of the merchant community in British politics. But the other consequence was a greater imperialism. Hudson states that in some cases the development of trade in new areas could be achieved without force, but in other cases, especially in times of depression in Britain, political or naval power was brought to bear. She gives examples: the China war of 1839–41 during the depression of 1837–42 when chartism was at its height; and the free-trade agreements reached with the north-west frontier provinces of India in the 1830s, with Turkey in 1838, and with Egypt and Persia in 1841. Aden was occupied in 1839, and there was growing activity in South America. Perhaps the greatest trading opportunities of the 1830s, however, came with the control of India. So, from the second quarter of the 19th century, Hudson confirms, Britain was able to develop international trade to a phenomenal extent.

One aspect of overseas trade not mentioned so far, yet one that significantly influenced the pattern of trade, was the slave-trade. Hudson claims that this demonstrates the separate roles of West Africa, the West Indies, and North and South America in "determining England's trading patterns and policy". While Britain was not the only slave-trading nation, it dominated the trade, and the triangular route between England, West Africa, and the West Indies in the early 19th century (it was abolished in 1807) is an example of the development of multilateral trade. ANSTEY & HAIR analyse in depth the complexity of this trade from the port of Liverpool, which by 1800 handled some 85 per cent of the English trade. It was an expensive trade for merchants to be involved in, because of the cost of purchasing the specially adapted vessels for carrying the slaves. When there were calls in England for the trade to be abolished on the grounds of inhumanity, merchants were reluctant to abandon it until an equally profitable trade had been found. However, the actual profitability of the slave-trade has been a matter for debate among historians. It has been closely examined by Anstey & Hair, but is an issue that is unlikely to be resolved.

By the third quarter of the 19th century Britain's trading pattern was forced to change because of the pressures created by increasing competition from Western Europe and America. HOPPEN points out that the composition of Britain's overseas trade in the Victorian free-trading economy after 1846 could not continue unchanged indefinitely. Of particular concern was the fact not only that the import of manufactured goods rose from 4 per cent to 25 per cent between 1840 and 1900, but also that the destination of exports had changed. The proportion going to the industrialized countries of Germany and North America had fallen while those going to the relatively unsophisticated economies of Africa and Asia had increased, with India in particular becoming increasingly important as the century progressed. In the face of growing competition British entrepreneurs had faced a choice: either they switched their investments into new industries or they continued to manufacture their traditional commodities and look for new markets for them. The latter seems to have been the more appealing option.

Crouzet, FIELDHOUSE, and HOPKINS are among a number of historians to have considered the role of imperialism in Britain's search for new markets during the later part of the century. While the empire was a useful destination for British manufactures, Crouzet argues that if the main motive behind the acquisition of colonies at this time was economic, then the results were disappointing, for much of the area that was annexed, in west and central Africa especially, was desert or undeveloped land. Hopkins and Fieldhouse focus on the scramble for colonies in West Africa, which were undoubtedly important as markets for cotton textiles and various manufactures and as the source of primary products such as palm oil and timber. Nevertheless, Crouzet claims that India, the "brightest jewel in the English crown", was most important, in that it was the largest unprotected market for the British cotton industry from the middle of the century onwards.

The pattern of Britain's "invisible" trade during this period must also be considered. It involved the sale of services such as shipping, the carrying and re-export trade – especially of colonial produce such as tea, coffee, rubber, ivory, wool, and cotton destined for Europe – insurance and banking services, and the export of capital for investment abroad. This trade ensured Britain's position as a leading international trading nation at a time when the country was facing increasing competition from America and industrialized Europe in its domestic and foreign markets. One of the most informative works in this field is IMLAH (1958), although other historians, including CAIRN-CROSS and SAUL, have traced the changing pattern of this trade through the century. Europe and the Americas were the major recipients of capital exports during the first half of the century, especially when Britain invested heavily in, for example, the construction of railways. India, Latin America – especially Argentina – and Canada were also significant recipients. The need to find fresh outlets for Britain's surplus capital has been suggested as a reason for the extension of empire in the late 19th century; but although the new colonies did take some of the capital exports, Crouzet points out that the amount

was small in comparison with what other countries were importing. In total, however, income received from "invisible trade" was generally enough to cover Britain's growing deficit in visible trade during the second half of the century.

ROSALIND E. TIGWELL

See also Capitalism; Cobden; Great Exhibition; Imperial Preference; Merchant Navy: Since 1840; Palmerston

Trade Patterns: English early medieval period

Carus-Wilson, Eleanora, "The Medieval Trade of the Ports of the Wash", *Medieval Archaeology*, 6/7 (1962–63): 182–201

Hughes, Richard and Brian Hobley (editors), *The Rebirth of Towns in the West* A.D. 700–1059: A Review of Current Research into How, When, and Why There Was a Rebirth of Towns between 700 and 1050, London: Council for British Archaeology, 1988

Miller, Edward and John Hatcher, *Medieval England: Towns, Commerce, and Crafts, 1086–1348*, London and New York: Longman, 1995

Platt, Colin, *Medieval Southampton: The Port and Trading Community*, A.D. 1000–1600, London and Boston: Routledge and Kegan Paul, 1973

Salzman, L.F., *English Trade in the Middle Ages*, Oxford: Clarendon Press, 1931

Weiner, A., "Early Commercial Intercourse between England and Germany", *Economica*, 1 (1921): 127–48

It is widely accepted that the British Isles were first valued by the Phoenicians as the tin isles and that prior to Christ's birth the trade of the south-west predominated. This may well be true, but opinion concerning the pattern of English trade before 1260 for the most part depends upon unwritten evidence. The pattern also depends on geographical situation and the currents of the sea. Such patterns can be detected only through the channels that used them, and the linkage to different towns becomes important. Place names such as "wic" are useful to a point: Aldwych might well be the old trading centre of the Roman Londinium. However, a better starting-point is to consider the archaeological evidence from several individual centres.

HUGHES & HOBLEY present an overview of the trade of Saxon London, Ipswich, Hamwic (which was located near present-day Southampton), Chester, and York. London received its trading charter as early as 673–74, and the majority of trade into the port was controlled by Frisians. The first objective reference to trade links is an exchange of letters between Offa and Charlemagne, who made a complaint about the length of the *sagae* (military cloaks) being shipped out to him, to which the reply was a complaint concerning the quality of the black stone querns being shipped in. Archaeological evidence supports both. Accordingly Offa is said to have made Charlemagne a trade proposal which is probably the first commercial treaty in English history. The authors then concern themselves with the actual location of Lundenwic, the major port of the Anglo-Saxon kings, in the 8th century. The archaeological evidence is particularly fascinating in the consideration of finds from pottery and textiles. London then had a thriving trade whose goods William Fitzstephen once described as gold, gems, silk, olive oil, and furs.

The early trade and trade agreements between Anglo-Saxon Britain and Germany are discussed by WEINER. He shows how the pattern of trade with Cologne, Bremen, Tiel, and Ribe in Jutland was established. Henry II gave the men of Cologne permission to sell wine in open competition with French merchants. Richard I's wars with Philip Augustus and John's subsequent loss of Normandy did much to build the Germanic connections. By the early 13th century the City of London framed regulations to deal with foreign traders from Lorraine, Germany, Denmark, and Norway. Weiner's short but excellent survey ends with the rise of the Easterlings and the early arrival of the Hanseatic league in London.

Another very informative local study is provided by CARUS-WILSON, who discusses the growth of Boston and Lynn. By John's reign Boston was probably the second most important port in the country. Lynn in the early 13th century was shipping corn, malt, and ale to Berwick, Flanders, Zeeland, Brabant, Gascony, and Norway. Indeed Norway was extremely dependent on corn from Lynn. In 1189 King Sverre expressed his opinion of good feeling towards the English merchants who brought wheat, honey, flour, and cloth. Lindsey wool supported the looms of Ypres and Ghent. The Wash also attracted wool overland from Cheshire monasteries. Norway, Denmark, Germany, and the Low Countries depended on salt imported from the Wash.

Many ships coming in from Scandinavia brought fish and timber, candles, pitch, tar, and wood ash, as well as furs. Lynn and Boston became the mart for London skinners. Birds, particularly gerfalcons and goshawks, almost became a currency in Lincolnshire. Certainly the eastern seaboard fostered an international trade. Although no customs accounts are available until the 14th century, we can get some idea of earlier trade patterns. Such trade included Flemish cloth, linen, and canvas; Spanish goods such as figs, raisins, dates, olive oil, soap, cordovan leather, and occasionally wine; East Indian dyestuffs like brasil or redwood; litmus from Norway; woad from Picardy; copper and steel from the Baltic; and swords and helmets from Cologne.

There are many references to trade patterns in more general works. Some impressions are gleaned from SALZMAN (1931), which still remains a key work. Yet early references need to be quarried out of a more anecdotal approach. In his chapter on distribution by sea Salzman considers the types of ships used, their provisions, and the laws of Oléron which laid down English maritime custom from the 11th century on. He also covers the early rise of the Hanse in England. A good basic introduction can be found in MILLER & HATCHER (1995). In a single section these authors consider the general situation in about 1230 and project it earlier. They survey the trade of the east coast ports and the connections referred to above. They then make a short analysis of London's trade and show clear links with Italy, Gascony, and Bayonne. They move on to consider the south coast ports of Sandwich, Winchelsea, Romney, Seaford, and Shoreham which dealt with French and Flemish merchants as well as Spanish and Italians. Moving to Portsmouth and Southampton, they briefly examine the dominant Gascon wine trade. They then consider Scandinavia, the Low Countries, and Normandy. Throughout, they note that the

evidence is incomplete and inconclusive. Apparently wool, grain, and possibly cheese and fish were exported, but little is known about the imports – though these were probably silk and wine. There was also a southern dimension based on the wine trade with Anjou and Poitou which was later developed by the Cahorsins.

PLATT (1973) underpins much of what we know about the medieval town of Southampton. Like other studies, it was largely influenced by archaeological digs and reassessment of artefacts. However, the early part of Platt's study concentrates on the development of the merchant families who laid the basis for the great mercantile dynasties of the 13th century. Richard I's charter to Southampton clearly protected an existing trade. Platt describes this earlier trade as wine, exotic victuals, and building materials such as limestone, slate, and lead. As would be expected, most of Southampton's trade seems to have been dominated by the links to Normandy, Flanders, and the far north. In a later chapter there are some details of how Walter le Fleming and his two trading cogs traded with Normandy and the French Atlantic seaboard. Once again it is not until the 14th century that real detail allows us to get a concrete grasp of patterns of overseas English trade.

ROBIN R. MUNDILL

See also Hanseatic League; Loans and Credit Finance; Markets and Fairs; Merchant Adventurers; Merchant Navy: To 1650

Trade Patterns: Medieval Period

Beardwood, Alice, *Alien Merchants in England, 1350 to 1377: Their Legal and Economic Position*, Cambridge, Massachusetts: Mediaeval Academy of America, 1931

Bridbury, A.R., *England and the Salt Trade in the Later Middle Ages*, Oxford: Clarendon Press, 1955

Carus-Wilson, E.M., "The Iceland Trade" in *Studies in English Trade in the Fifteenth Century*, edited by Eileen Power and M.M. Postan, London: Routledge, 1933a; New York: Barnes and Noble, 1966

Carus-Wilson, E.M., "The Overseas Trade" in *Studies in English Trade in the Fifteenth Century*, edited by Eileen Power and M.M. Postan, London: Routledge, 1933b; New York: Barnes and Noble, 1966

Carus-Wilson, E.M. and Olive Coleman (editors), *England's Export Trade 1275–1547*, Oxford: Clarendon Press, 1963

Childs, Wendy R., *Anglo-Castilian Trade in the Later Middle Ages*, Totowa, New Jersey: Rowman and Littlefield, and Manchester: Manchester University Press, 1978

Colvin, Ian D., *The Germans in England 1066–1598*, National Review, 1915; reprinted, Port Washington, New York: Kennikat Press, 1971

Gras, Norman Scott Brien, *The Early English Customs System: A Documentary Study of the Institutional and Economic History of the Customs from the Thirteenth to the Sixteenth Century*, Cambridge, Massachusetts: Harvard University Press, and London: Oxford University Press, 1918

Gray, H.L., "English Foreign Trade from 1446 to 1482" in *Studies in English Trade in the Fifteenth Century*, edited by Eileen Power and M.M. Postan, London: Routledge, 1933; New York: Barnes and Noble, 1966

Hanham, Alison, *The Celys and Their World: An English Merchant Family of the Fifteenth Century*, Cambridge and New York: Cambridge University Press, 1985

Haward, W.I., "The Financial Transactions between the Lancastrian Government and the Merchants of the Staple from 1449 to 1461" in *Studies in English Trade in the Fifteenth Century*, edited by Eileen Power and M.M. Postan, London: Routledge, 1933; New York: Barnes and Noble, 1966

James, Margery Kirkbride, *Studies in the Medieval Wine Trade*, edited by Elspeth M. Veale, Oxford: Clarendon Press, 1971

Jenks, Stuart, *England, Die Hanse, und Preussen: Handel und Diplomatie 1377–1474*, Cologne: Böhlau, 1992

Kaeuper, Richard W., *Bankers to the Crown: The Riccardi of Lucca and Edward I*, Princeton, New Jersey: Princeton University Press, 1973

Kerling, Nelly J.M., *Commercial Relations of Holland and Zeeland with England from the Late 13th Century to the Close of the Middle Ages*, Leiden: E.J. Brill, 1954

Kermode, Jenny, *Medieval Merchants: York, Beverley, and Hull in the Later Middle Ages*, Cambridge and New York: Cambridge University Press, 1998

Lloyd, T.H., *The English Wool Trade in the Middle Ages*, Cambridge and New York: Cambridge University Press, 1977

Lloyd, T.H., *Alien Merchants in England in the High Middle Ages*, New York: St Martin's Press, and Brighton, East Sussex: Harvester Press, 1982

Lloyd, T.H., *England and the German Hanse, 1157–1611: A Study of Their Trade and Commercial Diplomacy*, Cambridge and New York: Cambridge University Press, 1991

Munro, John H.A., *Wool, Cloth, and Gold: The Struggle for Bullion in Anglo-Burgundian Trade, 1340–1478*, Toronto: University of Toronto Press, and Brussels: Éditions de l'Université de Bruxelles, 1972

Nightingale, Pamela, *A Medieval Mercantile Community: The Grocers' Company and the Politics and Trade of London, 1000–1485*, New Haven, Connecticut, and London: Yale University Press, 1995

Postan, M.M., "The Economic and Political Relations of England and the Hanse from 1400 to 1475" in *Studies in English Trade in the Fifteenth Century*, edited by Eileen Power and M.M. Postan, London: Routledge, 1933; reprinted, New York: Barnes and Noble, 1966

Power, Eileen, "The Wool Trade in the Fifteenth Century" in *Studies in English Trade in the Fifteenth Century*, edited by Power and M.M. Postan, London: Routledge, 1933; reprinted, New York: Barnes and Noble, 1966

Power, Eileen, *The Wool Trade in English Medieval History*, London: Oxford University Press, 1941; New York: Oxford University Press, 1942

Power, Eileen and M.M. Postan (editors), *Studies in English Trade in the Fifteenth Century*, London: Routledge, 1933; reprinted, New York: Barnes and Noble, 1966

Ruddock, Alwyn A., *Italian Merchants and Shipping in Southampton 1270–1600*, Southampton: University College, 1951

Schulz, Friedrich, *Die Hanse und England von Eduards III bis auf Heinrichs VIII Zeit*, Berlin: Curtius, 1911

Terry, Schuyler B., *The Financing of the Hundred Years' War, 1337–1360*, London: Constable, 1914

Thirsk, Joan, *Economic Policies and Projects: The Development of a Consumer Society in Early Modern England*, Oxford: Clarendon Press, 1978

As an island nation, England had commercial ties that provided important links with its European neighbours on several levels. Accordingly, scholarship dealing with this endeavour has incorporated much more than just commercial facts and figures. Rather, this activity influenced political, social, and economic relations between the English and the rest of Europe. In addition, domestic and foreign merchants gained valuable political and economic rewards for their willingness to lend their resources. This survey therefore examines sources that deal with sub-topics within the commercial framework, so that the reader will have the best view of scholarly trends.

TERRY analysed commercial activities between 1337 and 1360. In his model, events are organized in three stages. Period I (1337–40) saw competition among English, Lombard, and Hanse traders to support Edward III's activities financially. In Period II (1340–48), English merchants gained control over the wool trade and supported the military endeavours on the Continent. Period III (1348–61) experienced the fiscal havoc wrecked by the Black Death, Edward III's control over the wool trade, and the formation of the staple. In analysing these factors, Terry interwove fiscal policy with commercial activity.

GRAS studied the history of the customs system and its operations pertaining to overseas trade. He surveyed various customs, subsidies, compositions, and the customs officials' daily activities and then focused on the economic workings of the customs. Gras included valuable documentation supporting his earlier points.

BEARDWOOD detailed the lives of foreign merchants and financiers during Edward III's later reign, establishing these foreigners as a separate social class. She then dealt with issues faced by bankers and discussed the merchants' role in the wool and cloth trades. Beardwood looked at the general economic privileges and disadvantages of these people. Through this study, Beardwood provided her readers with an initial sketch of the alien merchants' lives within English society.

POWER & POSTAN (1933), an important edited work, explored the multifaceted overseas trade between later medieval England and its commercial partners. In this collection, GRAY analysed fluctuations in English foreign trade between 1446 and 1482; POWER discussed the wool trade during this period; POSTAN studied the complex Anglo-Hanse political and economic relations during the first three-quarters of the century; CARUS-WILSON wrote essays on Anglo-Icelandic trade (1933a) as well as the overseas trade from Bristol (1933b); and HAWARD summarized relations between the Lancastrians and the Calais staple merchants during the 1450s. These essays touched upon many topics and laid the groundwork for other scholarly endeavours.

POWER (1941) discussed various issues related to this important commercial activity. In this work Power followed the path wool took from the middlemen to the exporters. She noted how the state monopoly on wool drove the foreigners from their privileged position, giving domestic entrepreneurs such as the Drapers' Company a chance to participate in trade. However, many lost their money in speculation, and the middling classes were excluded altogether from it.

RUDDOCK gave a complete picture of the complexities within the Mediterranean commercial networks. After stressing the importance of the Italians to English commercial activities in this period, the author looked at how commercial ties developed between England and the Continent through the Flemings, Gascons, and the Spanish, followed by the Florentines and the other Italian city-states. Next, she focused on the history of Anglo-Italian trade pertaining to Southampton in 1350–1460. The trade's commodities also received attention here, as did the complex route from the east to Southampton. Ruddock examined the Italians' control over commerce as well as their fluctuating relations with the native English. Finally, in the 16th century, her study shifted to the successes of the English in penetrating former Italian commercial strongholds in the Mediterranean, as well as the background reasons for these accomplishments. Throughout this work, Ruddock drew an exquisite picture of the trading activities.

KERLING charted the development of English trade with the Low Countries. After giving her readers insight into the political and geographical background of the events, the author illustrated the fractured nature of Baltic trade in the late 13th century and how the growing influence of Count William, followed by the dukes of Burgundy, established the Low Countries as an industrial centre. In her second chapter Kerling examined the wool and cloth trades and the competition between the English and Low Countries in this regard. Next, she examined the miscellaneous items other than cloth involved in the trade. Kerling also discussed the activities of the English merchants and their counterparts. The work also tracked the development of trade and industrial ties between these regions. Like Terry's study, this text stressed the commercial, financial, political, and social connections between these regions.

BRIDBURY provided a look at one specific type of commercial activity. After establishing the sources of the salt trade – indigenous (English), French, Spanish, and Portuguese – he focused on the importance of the salt trade in Europe. After the salt industry declined in England in the late 14th century, the English looked to France, Spain, and Portugal for their own supply of salt. Bridbury's work established the viability of a specialized study of this topic.

CARUS-WILSON & COLEMAN (1963), as editors, achieved two notable goals. First, their narrative followed the developing English monarchical policies with respect to taxation, the wool trade, and the customs. As in Gras's work, tables and charts clearly illustrated these trends. Second, their historiographical essay tied together the earlier contributions, forming a cohesive scholarly body to which their own work was then added.

COLVIN's analysis of German merchants' activities in England established their importance in medieval English commerce. First, Colvin focused on Anglo-German connections during the Norman and Angevin periods. Then, the work charted the history surrounding Anglo-Hanse relations as well as the relations of the English with other German powers during this time.

JAMES analysed the role of the wine trade in English overseas commerce. In this series of essays, she detailed the fluctuations of the trade, the Gascon merchants' commercial activities, and connections between English and Gascon ports, in addition to factors affecting the trade. Like Bridbury's study, James's work revealed still more detail on medieval English commercial activities.

MUNRO detailed the role of bullionism in English overseas trade. The study began with a discussion of the interconnectivity of England and Burgundy during this period and the growing rivalries concerning the wool trade and cloth industries. Like Terry before him, Munro stressed the fiscal element of this activity. However, in this case, he showed how bullionist policies shaped the relations between English kings and merchants vis-à-vis their Burgundian counterparts. Other financial matters also received attention, including the staple, Anglo-Hanse economic problems, and the three Burgundian bans on English cloth.

KAEUPER discussed the control of the Riccardi over customs and the English wool trade. This work illustrated how Edward utilized customs and overall wool revenues as collateral against the loans for his military campaigns. Like Gras, Carus-Wilson, and Coleman, Kaueper detailed the inner workings of the customs, showing how the king farmed the proceeds to the bankers until he stopped this cash flow in the mid-1290s. This book revealed how foreign merchant bankers influenced policies through their monetary assistance and their control over commercial revenue.

Between 1977 and 1991, Lloyd produced several key works. For instance, LLOYD (1977) made some important contributions. After starting with a solid historiographical account, Lloyd traced the different commercial partners with whom England shared its wool. Then the study shifted to policies related to the Hundred Years' War, most notably the staple, and demonstrated how the war caused a decline in the wool trade. Following in Beardwood's footsteps, LLOYD (1982) added still more detail to our understanding of foreign merchants' rights, privileges, and obligations, differentiating between the various nationalities' respective social standing. LLOYD (1991) drew upon Colvin's earlier work to render the most complete picture of Anglo-Hanse relations on all levels up to that point. To this mix, Lloyd added the complex diplomatic relations between England, Scandinavia, Denmark, and Prussia. He even went so far as to scrutinize splits within the league's ranks in its relations with England. With these works Lloyd built on his predecessors' studies, revealing still more detail about these pieces of commercial history.

CHILDS followed Colvin's example in her treatment of England's commerce with the Iberian peninsula. In this work, she examined every detail of this commercial connection, including overall history, imports, exports, shipping supplies, operations, mercantile techniques, and practices as well as the merchants' overall influence.

SCHULZ provided another look at Anglo-Hanse relations against the backdrop of turbulent 14th- and 15th-century politics. Schulz focused on a shorter era than Lloyd, concentrating on economic and political treaties between England and the Hanse as well as Prussia.

HANHAM covered a well-known family of staple merchants in great detail. After examining the members of their social circle, the study moved to the Celys' involvement in the wool staple. Accordingly, their activities pertaining to finance and governance, in addition to their commercial transactions, received a great deal of attention. Utilizing her predecessors' detail concerning alien merchants, and other urban studies such as those by THIRSK and Pamela NIGHTINGALE, Hanham constructed a fascinating study of this important stapler family in Calais.

Following Lloyd's example, JENKS studied the interrelationship between three political entities. In his analysis, Jenks combined Lloyd's attention to detail with the commercial documentation provided by Gras, Carus-Wilson, and Carus-Wilson & Coleman. Then he expanded his work, incorporating every element related to these connections. As a result, Jenks's work represented the most in-depth study to date of Anglo-Hanse relations in the later medieval period.

Nightingale's treatment of the medieval London Grocers' Company contained several interesting points. First, she discussed the foreign merchants' commercial activities – specifically, those of the Genoese, other Italians, and the Hanse. Then she touched upon the rivalry between those financiers and their English counterparts. She noted which products held the highest value at certain points. Like Hanham, she examined how commercial activity helped these people control civic affairs within London.

KERMODE incorporated elements of earlier studies into her framework. First, she utilized the element of local history that was prevalent in Ruddock's work on Southampton. Then, she used the merchants' lives and activities to detail their commercial activity. She also borrowed Ruddock's careful analysis in her study of Hull's exports to Mediterranean, Atlantic, and Baltic ports. In addition, she included Munro's points on Anglo-Burgundian bullion issues. Finally, her work detailed the competition with the Hanse and how that activity led to Hull's downfall. This combination of factors makes Kermode's work an excellent study with which to conclude this survey.

DAVID J. DUNCAN

See also Antwerp; Loans and Credit Finance; Manorial Economy; Markets and Fairs; Merchant Adventurers; Merchant Navy: To 1650

Trade Patterns: Scottish before 1707

Grant, Alexander, *Independence and Nationhood: Scotland, 1306–1469*, London and Baltimore, Maryland: Arnold, 1984; Edinburgh: Edinburgh University Press, 1991

Guy, I., "The Scottish Export Trade, 1460–1559" in *Scotland and Europe, 1200–1850*, edited by T.C. Smout, Edinburgh: John Donald, 1986

Lythe, S.G.E., *The Economy of Scotland in Its European Setting, 1550–1625*, Edinburgh: Oliver and Boyd, 1960; reprinted, Westport, Connecticut: Greenwood Press, 1976

Lythe, S.G.E. and Butt, J., *An Economic History of Scotland, 1100–1939*, Glasgow: Blackie, 1975

Smout, T.C., *Scottish Trade on the Eve of Union, 1660–1707*, Edinburgh: Oliver and Boyd, 1963

Whyte, Ian D., *Scotland before the Industrial Revolution: An Economic and Social History, c.1050–c.1750*, London and New York: Longman, 1995

Historians usually seek to avoid teleological explanation, but this has proved singularly difficult for those who explore Scotland's trade before 1707. Views on the strengths and weaknesses of the country's economy before the Treaty of Union are intrinsic to the controversy over the Anglo-Scottish treaty with which this period ended. It is almost universally agreed that the Scots concluded the treaty in the expectation of securing substantial material benefits from the transaction – in effect sacrificing their historic political sovereignty for a share in England's burgeoning commercial wealth. Any evaluation of Scotland's earlier circumstances thus appears to be either an endorsement or a repudiation of the critical judgements about the country's trading position and future economic prospects formed by those native politicians who successfully pushed for political accommodation with England.

SMOUT (1963), though in some details superseded by later work, remains the fundamental modern study of Scottish trade in the key decades immediately before the union. The general thesis – that trade in the 17th century was not as underdeveloped as was long believed, but that towards 1700 short-term factors had nevertheless produced substantial difficulties – underlies most subsequent treatments of the subject. Attention is drawn to Scotland's prospering export sector, notably fish exported to the Baltic and textile goods to the Low Countries. These exports, however, fell victim to the crown's (i.e. England's) continental wars from the 1690s onwards. Trade with England was also crucial, so much so that threatening it through the Alien Act of 1705 actually provided London with vital leverage over the Scots parliament during the treaty negotiations. Moreover, the evident strengths meant that by the later 17th century Scotland's independent commercial activity was excessively reliant upon a small number of niche exports, particularly to the south and to those Continental countries with which England's continuing good relations were a critical consideration. Consequently, Scotland's economic position was vulnerable to political imperatives in London. At the same time the need to import grain to supplement the deficient yields of Scotland's domestic agrarian sector proved highly damaging: famine struck catastrophically as a result of poor harvests in the 1690s, adding to a growing sense that the nation's economy, like its political structures, urgently needed modernization.

An almost contemporary work, LYTHE (1960), has similarly stood the test of time. This monograph takes as its focus the period from the Reformation to the accession of Charles I and provides a longer-term background to the age which culminated in the Treaty of Union. Its conclusion, that the Scots enjoyed significant and increasing trading relations with many northern and western European nations, remains sound and has provided encouragement for most of the detailed further studies that have since been undertaken. The joint study by LYTHE & BUTT is hampered by an overambitious chronological span but still offers some useful insights into the early development of these overseas trading networks during the later medieval period.

A superior overview for this much longer time-scale is supplied by WHYTE's more recent study. It emphasizes Scotland's continuing reliance, deep into the 17th century, upon the export of primary products from agriculture, fishing, and mining, together with low-grade linen and woollen cloth manufacturing, in return for imported raw materials (notably Norwegian timber) and a wide variety of consumer goods (including French wine). Overall it tends to confirm the conclusion of other studies that before the union, and probably far back into the later medieval period, Scotland had had to struggle to avoid a balance-of-trade deficit with its commercial partners.

Detailed analysis of the pre-modern period in its own right has been less common, mainly, it has to be said, because of insufficient evidence. General accounts of Scotland's emerging trading activities have, however, appeared in influential surveys by medieval historians. An outstanding example is GRANT (1991). Grant describes the international commerce (above all in wool and hide exports) in which the Scots were becoming successfully involved by the early 14th century. Wool exports may have peaked at as much as 1.8 million sheepskins per year – a remarkable figure – in the early 1370s. Flanders and France were already the most important foci for both imports and exports, though neither the precise volume of total Scottish overseas trade nor even how far it was controlled by native rather than foreign merchants is really clear.

Also worth consulting is the important specialist article by GUY, who discusses the rather better evidence that becomes available by the end of the medieval period. This reveals that Scotland's earlier reliance upon wool as the export staple, which was clearly in relative decline by the end of the 15th century, was being overtaken by enforced diversification, involving particularly the export of fish (salmon and herring), coal, and salt.

It will be clear, therefore, that Scottish overseas trade before 1707 sets two challenges for future scholarship. The first is to try, however difficult that may be, to develop interpretations – indeed, to ask relevant questions – which take less account of the battle-lines drawn up over the perennially vexatious question of the Treaty of Union. The second, especially in relation to the later Middle Ages, is to continue to attempt the reconstruction of the history of overseas trade in a period for which the evidence remains fragmentary.

DAVID ALLAN

See also Merchant Navy: Before 1650

Trade Unionism and Women Workers

Bornat, Joanna, "Lost Leaders: Women, Trade Unionism, and the Case of the General Union of Textile Workers, 1875–1914" in *Unequal Opportunities: Women's Employment in England 1800–1918*, edited by Angela V. John, Oxford and Cambridge, Massachusetts: Blackwell, 1986
Boston, Sarah, *Women Workers and the Trade Union Movement*, London: Davis-Poynter, 1980; updated edition, London: Lawrence and Wishart, 1987
Drake, Barbara, *Women in Trade Unions*, London: Allen and Unwin, 1920; with new introduction by Noreen Branson, London: Virago Press, 1984
Lawrence, Elizabeth, *Gender and Trade Unions*, Bristol, Pennsylvania: Taylor and Francis, 1994
Lewenhak, Sheila, *Women and Trade Unions: An Outline History of Women in the British Trade Union Movement*, London: Benn, and New York: St Martin's Press, 1977
Middleton, Lucy (editor), *Women in the Labour Movement: The British Experience*, London: Croom Helm, and Totowa, New Jersey: Rowman and Littlefield, 1977
Munro, Anne, *Women, Work, and Trade Unions*, London and New York: Mansell, 1999
Reynolds, Sian, *Britannica's Typesetters: Women Compositors in Edwardian Edinburgh*, Edinburgh: Edinburgh University Press, 1989
Soldon, Norbert C., *Women in British Trade Unions 1874–1976*, Dublin: Gill and Macmillan, and Totowa, New Jersey: Rowman and Littlefield, 1978
Thom, Deborah, "The Bundle of Sticks: Women, Trade Unionists, and Collective Organisation before 1918" in *Unequal Opportunities: Women's Employment in England 1800–1918*, edited by Angela V. John, Oxford and Cambridge, Massachusetts: Blackwell, 1986
Wightman, Clare, *More than Munitions: Women, Work, and the Engineering Industries, 1900–1950*, London and New York: Longman, 1999

Despite the burgeoning interest in social, economic, and feminist history over the past three decades, historians have largely neglected the role of women workers within trade unions. Up to the 1970s students relied on DRAKE (1920, reissued by Virago in 1984). Drake produced a detailed work examining women's trade union history, which though reflecting the time when it was written (immediately after World War I) nevertheless is still of great value to the modern student. It resulted from an enquiry made by the joint committee of the Labour Research Department and the Fabian Women's Group. The first section deals with the history of the women's trade union movement from the 18th century to 1918. Following sections give a detailed account of the various industries and women's unions and an interesting discussion of the problems women encountered in organizing in trade unions. These included a lack of recognition by male trade unionists, low wages, a lack of training, the refusal of equal pay, and the impact of family demands on working patterns. "When women receive men's wages, then and not before, they will gain men's full strength in organisation". The statistical data on female membership of trade unions and the analysis of the principal unions are also valuable.

The 1970s brought works by LEWENHAK, SOLDON, and MIDDLETON, all of which cover broadly the same ground. Lewenhak and Soldon follow Drake in distinguishing between women in mixed unions, women-only craft unions, and women's federated unions. Both make the point that women's trade unionism was liable to break down unless it was backed by male trade union organization or male self-interest. Lewenhak is concerned to trace women's roles in labour organization and protest from the Middle Ages. While these works provide useful detailed narrative frameworks of events and identify the main issues – such as Should women organize by themselves or with men? and What is a fair rate for the job? – they have a number of deficiencies. The further reading and lists of sources they provide are limitied. There is no attempt to link social issues to trade union history, and discussion of early white-collar unionism is slight. Lewenhak is also closely tied to line of the Trades Union Congress (TUC), but she is quite use-ful when dealing with more contemporary times. Middleton's collection of essays, too, is curate's-eggish, though it does con-tain some useful material on the Women's Labour League, the Women's Co-operative Guild, and women's trade unionism, and it does try to put women's trade unionism into its context within the labour movement.

BOSTON provides a work similar to that of Lewenhak and Soldon, though the narrative begins later and continues till the 1970s when she points out that the existing structure "perpet-uates the second-class status of women within the trade union movement". Interestingly, Boston cites neither Lewenhak nor Soldon in her bibliography, which, like theirs, is rather limited.

Studies of individual women's trade unions are not plentiful, but both REYNOLDS and WIGHTMAN demonstrate what can be done. Reynolds's work is important in providing a useful case study of women compositors in Edwardian Edinburgh. In 1873 the all-male compositors' union had suffered a defeat. In Edinburgh – unlike the rest of Britain, where few women entered what was a highly skilled craft – printing firms then began to employ many women as cheap labour, attempting to undercut English printers. The union then fought a long campaign to exclude women from the job, and in 1910 the employers agreed to this. Reynolds deconstructs the highly masculine language and practices of the trade and the effect this had on women workers. Because women did not serve an apprenticeship, they were not regarded as skilled. This enabled the employers to pay women at a rate of 50 per cent less than men, on the ground that women were not involved in finishing procedures. Women compositors were better paid than most female workers, and they did become involved in trade unions after 1910.

Wightman has produced an excellent study of women's work-ing experiences in the engineering industries in 1900–50. This period was chosen deliberately so that she could cover the growth in women's participation while at the same time trying not to overemphasize the atypical contributions of World War I and World War II (cf. Thom below). Wightman stresses the com-plexity of engineering work: from small workshops to assembly lines. She examines the workforce in three "new" industries: rayon, food, and engineering. While women's participation rates increased during this period, their pay was still largely based on sex scales and did not represent their skill levels. The only times when this was not so were during the two world wars, when dilution allowed women to play a greater role. Indeed World War II with its registration of women workers and universal male conscription meant that women joined unions in greater numbers. This would seem to contradict Wightman's desire to play down the wars' significance. Nevertheless, Wightman's case is that women took what they wanted from unionism. In con-trast to the works of the 1970s, Wightman's study includes graphs and charts about membership rates and individual employment as well as a sound bibliography.

Interesting work can also be found in chapters such as THOM (1986) and BORNAT (1986). Thom is keen to point out that the history of women's trade unionism has been "dominated by the history of its leaders and thence by their ideology of the weakness of working women". She warns against overempha-sizing women's wartime experiences (1914–18), preferring to note that long-term changes in women's employment oppor-tunities and their own demands did more to emancipate them.

Thom's chapter also contains a good discussion of primary sources. In particular, Thom urges caution in using the Tuckwell Collection, since it represents merely the interests of one woman or organization and is therefore of limited usefulness. Bornat's analysis of the Grand Union of Textile Workers from 1875 to 1914 identifies factors which seemed to keep women from sus-tained union membership and from taking leadership roles: the paternalism of male union leaders, the structure of women's employment in the woollen and worsted trades, and the strength of the ideology of domesticity in defining women's economic position.

The more contemporary period has seen a number of studies based on aspects such as the ways in which working-class women's concerns are represented in trade unions. MUNRO has produced an interesting analysis of the workplace experiences of cleaners and catering workers in the health service over the past 16 years. This is not a narrow work. It is based on a thor-ough examination of the records of four local branches (two NUPE and two COHSE) and has a good bibliography. It demon-strates clearly that even by the late 20th century, when women had the right to form unions, their problems were not over. It posits two premises: (1) trade unions have an institutional bias which sets an "agenda", thereby excluding issues of particular significance to women; (2) the hierarchically organized labour market leads to differences of interest between women and men, and this structuring – which trade unions maintain and in which women are disadvantaged – precludes a full representation of women's interests. Even increased participation by women in unions does not automatically result in improved representation of women's interests. In the long run, challenges to this "agenda" have to come through alterations in workplace organization.

LAWRENCE is also concerned with the factors which affect women's involvement in trade unions and thus their access to official positions. She presents a case study of shop stewards and lay union officials in the Sheffield local government branch of NALGO. She shows that, just as in previous centuries, gendered organization processes disadvantage women.

The overall conclusions are depressing: the majority of women remain in low-paid jobs requiring little training and are poorly organized. As far as sources are concerned, biogra-phies of leading women can be found in the *Dictionary of Labour Biography* (edited by John Saville and Joyce Bellamy, 1974 and 1979). Primary sources are held by the TUC, which holds the Tuckwell Collection, and there is material in the Imperial War Museum (though this tends to overemphasize the effects of war).

FIONA A. MONTGOMERY

See also Feminism, Second-Wave; Labour Party; Trades Union Congress

Trades Union Congress founded 1868

Allen, V.L., "The Re-Organization of the Trades Union Congress, 1918–1927", *British Journal of Sociology*, 11/1 (1960): 24–43

Birch, Lionel (editor), *The History of the TUC 1868–1968: A Pictorial Survey of a Social Revolution*, London: Trades Union Congress, 1968

Clegg, Hugh Armstrong, *A History of British Trade Unions since 1889*, vol. 2, *1911–1933*, Oxford: Clarendon Press, and New York: Oxford University Press, 1985

Clegg, Hugh Armstrong, *A History of British Trade Unions since 1889*, vol. 3, *1934–1951*, Oxford: Clarendon Press, and New York: Oxford University Press, 1994

Clegg, Hugh Armstrong, Alan Fox, and A.F. Thompson, *A History of British Trade Unions since 1889*, vol. 1, *1889–1910*, Oxford: Clarendon Press, 1964

Davis, W.J., *The British Trades Union Congress: History and Recollections*, 2 vols, London: Co-Operative Printing Society, for the Trades Union Congress Parliamentary Committee, 1910–16; New York: Garland, 1984

Dorfman, Gerald A., *British Trade Unionism against the Trades Union Congress*, London: Macmillan, and Stanford, California: Hoover Institution Press, 1983

Duffield, Sarah and Richard Storey, *The Trade Union Congress Archive 1920–1960*, Coventry: University of Warwick Modern Records Centre, 1992

Griggs, Clive, *The Trades Union Congress and the Struggle for Education, 1868–1925*, Lewes: Falmer Press, 1983

Lovell, John and B.C. Roberts, *A Short History of the T.U.C.*, London: Macmillan, 1968

Martin, Ross M., *TUC: The Growth of a Pressure Group 1868–1976*, Oxford: Clarendon Press, and New York: Oxford University Press, 1980

Musson, A.E., *Trade Union and Social History*, London: Cass, 1974

Roberts, B.C., *The Trades Union Congress 1868–1921*, London: Allen and Unwin, and Cambridge, Massachusetts: Harvard University Press, 1958

Wrigley, Chris (editor), *British Trade Unions, 1945–1995*, Manchester and New York: Manchester University Press, 1997

The sometimes important and often ambivalent role played by the Trades Union Congress (TUC) in the economic and political history of Britain cannot be approached through a single volume. However, a number of sources cover the main features of the TUC since its foundation in 1868 (although this article does not cite a few publications dealing with specific events and some themes such as education, training, and international affairs).

Still of some interest for the period before 1914 is DAVIS (1910–16), a semi-autobiographical work. Davis was a prominent trade unionist who, for long periods between 1880 and 1920, was a member of the TUC's parliamentary committee (a body elected by affiliated unions, reorganized from 1921 as the general council). LOVELL & ROBERTS, in a short book published to coincide with the TUC's centenary, chart the organization's landmarks between 1868 and 1968, but without the usual scholarly apparatus: they provide very few footnote references and no bibliography. However, one of these authors, ROBERTS, in a monograph dealing with the first fifty years or so of the TUC, did adopt an academic approach. He chronicled the extent to which affiliated trade unions were liberal in politics and conciliatory towards employers in the 1870s and 1880s; and he discussed the impact of the "new unionism" of 1889 and the resolution, carried at the annual congress of 1899, that opened the way to the establishment in 1900 of the Labour Representation Committee, the forerunner of the Labour Party. Although his study included developments in the Edwardian years and World War I, it ended with the restructuring of the trade union movement after the war. An essay by ALLEN on the reorganization of the TUC in the 1920s emphasized the influence of Ernest Bevin and the already uncertain cooperation between the industrial wing of organized labour and the political wing, in the form of the Labour Party. A monograph by GRIGGS provides a case study of a TUC campaign – to improve education in the working class in the years before 1925 – as well as usefully tracing the educational background of trade union leaders during this period.

The TUC has drawn its authority from the strength of the trade unions that have affiliated with it, though this process has at the same time compromised its autonomy. The interplay between trade unions, the TUC, and elected government in the two decades before 1910 can be traced in the substantial book by CLEGG, FOX, & THOMPSON (1964). They put into a wider context than Roberts did the ways in which the trade unions representing large numbers of workers in the coal and cotton industries, together with the older craft societies, accommodated the growth of general workers' unions in the TUC. Two further volumes, by CLEGG (1985, 1994), carried the story to 1951. Although concerned with trade unions in general, they include many references to the TUC, especially at times when the unions needed a collective voice. The general strike of 1926 was one such occasion: the TUC played a central role, although its officials – especially Walter Citrine, the acting general secretary – were never comfortable in it. Similarly, at times when Labour governments have held office, the TUC has sought to represent the often differing views of its affiliated members while giving general support to Labour, a party that has close links with trade unions (although the TUC itself is not affiliated to the Labour Party). MARTIN has provided a detailed account of many of these themes over a lengthy period of time, as well as discussing the changing relationship with governments formed by the Labour and Conservative parties. However, his book stops short of one of the most critical phases, which culminated in what became known as the "winter of discontent" of 1978–79. The disputes of that winter are the subject of a short book by DORFMAN, the author of a number of studies of wages politics since 1945. For later events such as the miners' strike of 1984–85, when the TUC was rather ineffectual, political biographies and more general treatments of industrial relations are the best available sources. There is a good guide to recent literature in WRIGLEY.

Any study of the TUC ought to take account of sources emanating from within the organization itself. In 1955 the TUC published *The Congress of 1868*, a booklet by an academic historian, A.E. Musson, detailing the origins of the first congress, held in Manchester on 2–6 June 1868. This account, reprinted in a slightly revised form in MUSSON (1974), a collection of his essays, remains authoritative. Less satisfactory, for an academic readership, is the TUC's profusely illustrated and celebratory publication compiled by BIRCH to mark its centenary. For researchers, the annual reports of the TUC, which include, verbatim, the proceedings of congresses, give in copious detail the public concerns of affiliated unions and their members. Most of the surviving archives of the TUC are available for consultation in the Modern Records Centre of the University of Warwick, for which there is a useful guide compiled by DUFFIELD & STOREY. The TUC website (http://www.tuc.org.uk) provides information about such matters as affiliated trade unions, current campaigns, research, and publications.

D.E. MARTIN

See also Bevin; General Strike; Labour Party

Trafalgar, Battle of

see Napoleonic Wars: Trafalgar and the War at Sea

Transport

see Aviation; Bicycles and Bicycling; Coastal Transport; Freight Transport; Merchant Navy; Motor Industry; Public Transport; Railways; River and Canal Transport; Road Transport; Sea Travel in the 20th Century

Transport Development 18th and 19th centuries

Aldcroft, Derek H. and Michael J. Freeman (editors), *Transport in the Industrial Revolution*, Manchester and New York: Manchester University Press, 1983

Baxter, Bertram, *Stone Blocks and Iron Rails*, Newton Abbot, Devon: David and Charles, 1966; New York: Kelley, 1967

Bray, N.P., *Transport and Communications*, London: Weidenfeld and Nicolson, 1968

Dyos, H.J. and D.H. Aldcroft, *British Transport: An Economic Survey from the Seventeenth Century to the Twentieth*, Leicester: Leicester University Press, 1969

Haldane, A.R.B., *New Ways through the Glens*, London: Nelson, 1962; also, Colonsay: House of Lochar, 1995

Hennessey, R.A.S., *Transport*, London: Batsford, 1966

Jackman, W.T., *The Development of Transportation in Modern England*, Cambridge: Cambridge University Press, 1916; revised edition, with new introduction by W.H. Chaloner, London: Cass, 1962; New York: Kelley, 1965

Pratt, Edwin A., *A History of Inland Transport and Communication in England*, London: Kegan Paul Trench Trubner, and New York: Dutton, 1912

Ransom, P.J.G., *The Archaeology of Railways*, Tadworth, Surrey: World's Work, 1981

Rolt, L.T.C., *Transport and Communications*, with line drawings by Paul Sharp, London: Methuen, 1967

Simmons, Jack, *Transport*, London: Vista Books, 1962

Szostak, Rick, *The Role of Transportation in the Industrial Revolution: A Comparison of England and France*, Montreal and Kingston, Ontario: McGill-Queen's University Press, 1991

At the beginning of the modern period there was much thought about road improvements. SIMMONS explains that improved coaches with steel springs were operating over roads maintained by turnpike trusts under legislation dating back to 1663. From 1754 on, the London–Edinburgh journey was completed in 10 days in summer and 12 in winter. But better coaches needed better surfaces. Following union with Ireland, Telford surveyed a new road from London to Holyhead over 10 years (1815–25): it was straighter and better-graded, with good foundations and drainage and an elliptical surface of gravel or small stones. However, J.L. McAdam found a simpler solution that did not require a specially planned foundation. In the 1830s the turnpikes reached their peak of efficiency: the London–Manchester journey came down to 18 hours in 1837. However, tolls came to be much resented, especially in south Wales, where rioting broke out (the "Rebecca Riots") over the issue in the 1840s. Under the Local Government Act of 1888 the new county councils became road authorities and the turnpike trusts were wound up: the last toll was collected in 1895.

Meanwhile momentous changes were occurring through the construction of canals and railways as part of what ALDCROFT & FREEMAN see as "an almost uninterrupted sequence of responses to demand". Expansion impelled by demand in the context of a switch from animal and vegetable to mineral raw materials – canals (with coastal shipping) and then railways – provided high capacity along key routes around which the main markets were situated. This is comparable to local markets in a variety of locations requiring a multitude of routes. Although canals and railways followed separate alignments; the networks were remarkably similar in the early stages, with a grand cross comprising north-west to south-east and north-east to south-west routes intersecting in the Midlands, and London–Bristol and Liverpool–Leeds connections. BAXTER shows that the canal age included the construction of many feeder wagon-ways, but in the context of steam the railway was able to take a lead and reduce the canals to a subsidiary role.

Steam locomotives first emerged at a time when the cost of fodder for horses was high; but RANSOM explains how steam constituted a second revolution by providing power that could overcome the most powerful natural forces. Engineering practices changed, since steam traction could cope with adverse gradients; thus inclined planes of the kind used on public railways of the 1820s and early 1830s, such as the Cromford and High Peak and Stanhope and Tyne, were no longer necessary. However, canals were slow to introduce mechanical haulage. William Symington's paddle steamer on the Forth and Clyde Canal (1789) was followed by the *Charlotte Dundas* in 1802, but the proprietors were worried about damage by wash. The Duke of Bridgwater ordered eight vessels of this type. but he died in 1803 and the order was never fulfilled. Tugs appeared only slowly.

ROLT notes that there was opposition to railways based on the argument that the railway companies controlled the traffic, contrary to the principle that "the road should be open to all". But JACKMAN's monumental survey, covering all aspects of transport, shows that the railways were all the stronger for this reason. In the face of competition from the railways, the canals lacked unity of management. With a diversity of carriers and inconsistent charging, they failed to adapt. They were usually unable to carry passengers and were prone to disruption due to frost or drought. By the end of the century there was better coordination. The government, which had passed legislation in

1872 obliging railways to maintain the canals they owned in working order, later declined to support a recommendation by the royal commission of 1906, which wanted to develop four trunk waterways to compete with the railways.

Aldcroft & Freeman show that roads continued to be needed as feeders, especially in connection with the domestic textile industry (for travel on foot, or with packhorse or wagon). Indeed, the road was superior to the canal if speed was paramount. Road transport offered regularity and reliability while canals were cheaper, but the margin can be exaggerated. Roads might have been even more competitive, for Telford was keen on steam road vehicles and wanted to introduce steam coaches on the London–Holyhead road, but the trusts failed to welcome them as a possible answer to competition from the railways. In areas with no navigations or railways, roads were especially important, as in the Scottish Highlands, where HALDANE writes about the Commission for Highland Roads and Bridges.

Discussing urban transport, Simmons shows that horse tramways developed after 1870, with some use of steam from 1877 on; but statutory conditions in 1879 involved a top speed of 10 miles per hour and other limitations (no discharge of smoke, steam, or water). Cable haulage was used on Highgate Hill in 1884; but after electric traction was first demonstrated by Werner von Siemens in Berlin in 1879, there was a rapid expansion of electric trams during the 1890s, and the main cities had changed over to electricity by 1901. Electric street tramways reached the peak of their popularity in 1919–20, when 4.8 million passengers were carried over 2,624 route miles. But there was the clutter of overhead wires: "Eastbourne, a seaside resort under aristocratic control, very conscious of the value of preserving its elegant character, declined to have trams at all" and graduated directly to the motor bus in 1903 (five years after its first introduction in London).

Railway companies also went into buses, although development was irregular because of unreliability and the facilities needed for fuel, maintenance, and repair. Meanwhile electricity was used for the City and South London Railway, opened in 1890 (this was the precursor of today's Northern Line). The Central London (Central Line), and Baker Street and Waterloo (Bakerloo Line) followed soon after. The early development of the internal combustion engine for use in transport was a slow and hesitant business. A breakthough was achieved in the 1880s, although the Red Flag Act limited cars to 4 miles per hour until 1896, when the speed limit was raised to 12 miles per hour. This was a boost for F.W. Lanchester, who had begun producing cars in 1895. The limit moved up to 20 miles per hour under the Motor Cars Act of 1903, which also provided for registration. In the first year 18,000 vehicles were registered; in 1913 there were 123,000 cars, lorries, and taxis; in 1920, there were 363,000.

With regard to shipping, BRAY describes the two great innovations. John Wilkinson, the Staffordshire ironmaster, built an iron barge for use on the Severn in 1787, though most people considered iron unsuitable for building ships – too heavy and liable to corrosion. The use of steam began with Henry Bell's *Comet* on the Clyde in 1812; as a result, coastal shipping became quicker, safer, and more reliable. Use of steam power on the Atlantic route dates from the 1840s, with Samuel Cunard's famous Cunard Line. Brunel's *Great Britain*, launched in 1843, made regular Atlantic voyages; when it ran aground off Ireland

it lay stranded for almost a year, but the iron hull stood up to the battering by the sea. Also in the *Great Britain*, the screw propeller positioned underwater at the stern replaced paddle wheels. Meanwhile the route to the east was not feasible by steam until coaling stations were provided at (especially) Suez. Brunel's *Great Eastern*, launched in 1858 (with engines and sail), was intended to steam to Australia and back without refuelling. But the Australian trade was in decline by 1860, so the vessel was used on the Atlantic and laid the first cable in 1866. It was too big for the Suez Canal, which opened in 1869.

PRATT considers that "until convenient means of transport were afforded, England had to be considered less as a nation than as a collection of more or less isolated communities, with all the disadvantages – social and moral as well as economic – necessarily resulting". Good transport was a precondition for "national" as opposed to "local" industries, and also for the growth of large cities; and rural areas benefited because village shops could operate with small stocks, given the ease of delivery from wholesalers. DYOS & ALDCROFT endorse these sentiments, remarking that "at the beginning of the eighteenth century Britain was still quite literally an underdeveloped country. The land was sparsely and patchily populated by some seven million people, three-quarters of whom were still living and working on the land". SZOSTAK says that the history of the iron industry, which is usually seen as a story of technology, should emphasize changes induced by transport, especially the reduction in the price of coal: from 13 shillings to 7 shillings per ton in Birmingham when the canal from Wednesbury opened in 1767.

HENNESSEY reminds us that few people could travel for pleasure before the railway age. Then, travel became reasonably cheap at a penny per mile (especially by excursion train), as well as being fast and relatively comfortable. Thomas Cook first persuaded a local railway to take people from Leicester to Loughborough at a reduced rate. There was initial prejudice against Sunday excursions, but trips to seaside resorts and inland watering-places became extremely popular. Pleasure steamers were prominent on the Clyde, the Bristol Channel, and the Thames estuary as well as in north Wales and along the south coast. There were also motor charabancs, not to mention private cars and bicycles.

DAVID TURNOCK

See also Bicycles and Bicycling; Brunel; Engineering: Civil; Railways; River and Canal Transport

Troyes, Treaty of 1420

Allmand, Christopher T., *Lancastrian Normandy, 1415–1450: The History of a Medieval Occupation*, Oxford: Clarendon Press, and New York: Oxford University Press, 1983

Allmand, Christopher T., *Henry V*, London: Methuen, and Berkeley: University of California Press, 1992; revised edition, New Haven, Connecticut and London: Yale University Press, 1997

Armstrong, C.A.J., "La double monarchie France-Angleterre et la maison de Bourgogne (1420–1435): Le déclin d'une alliance" in his *England, France, and Burgundy in the Fifteenth Century*, London: Hambledon Press, 1983

Bonenfant, Paul, *Du meurtre de Montereau au Traité de Troyes*, Bruxelles: Paris des Académies, 1956

Curry, Anne, *The Hundred Years War*, Basingstoke: Macmillan and New York: St Martin's Press, 1993

Griffiths, Ralph A., *The Reign of King Henry VI: The Exercise of Royal Authority, 1422–1461*, London: Ernest Benn, and Berkeley: University of California Press, 1981; without subtitle, Stroud, Gloucestershire: Alan Sutton, 1998

Newhall, Richard Ager, *The English Conquest of Normandy 1416–1424: A Study in Fifteenth Century Warfare*, New Haven, Connecticut: Yale University Press, and London: Humphrey Milford/Oxford University Press, 1924

Pollard, A.J., *John Talbot and the War in France 1427–1453*, London: Royal Historical Society, and Atlantic Highlands, New Jersey: Humanities Press, 1983

The treaty of Troyes concluded in 1420 between Henry V and the envoys of the French crown set out the terms by which Henry became the legitimate heir to Charles VI of France, would marry Charles's daughter Catherine of Valois, and would rule France as regent because of the incapacity of his future father-in-law. CURRY presents a wide-ranging review of the historiography of the Hundred Years' War and sets out the context of the conflict from 1337 to 1453. In a special section on the treaty, she claims that it marked a "major turning point in Anglo-French relations" but "created as many problems as it solved". She draws attention to the uncertainty over the basis of Henry's right to the French crown. Did he, by the terms of the treaty, in fact give up his claim to be the true king of France by inheritance in favour of his recognition as the heir of Charles VI? There were similar ambiguities over the status of the English conquests in Normandy and England's long-standing possessions, Gascony and Calais. Finally, the obligation to continue the civil war against the supporters of the disinherited dauphin presented another series of difficulties which became increasingly obvious after Henry's death.

ALLMAND (1992) includes a full discussion of Henry as a soldier in France, looking in detail at his campaigns and the surrounding diplomatic negotiations. In Allmand's opinion the treaty had its origins in deep divisions within France which "had allowed (indeed encouraged)" the neighbouring king to invade the kingdom. He points out, however, that many in France regarded the treaty with horror, fearing that it would lead to a loss of French identity. BONENFANT (1956) brings out strongly the attitude of the Burgundian faction at the French court to events since the murder of John the Fearless at Montereau in 1419, and the negotiation and implementation of the treaty itself. His work also includes a documentary appendix and a full discussion of sources and historiography. In his view the Burgundians always had their suspicions about the true intentions of the English in France. The support of the English was highly useful against the Burgundians' rivals, the Armagnacs; but if circumstances should change, the alliance would be abandoned without regret.

Some of the tension and difficulties which led eventually to the collapse of the alliance and ultimately to the expulsion of the English from France are set out by ARMSTRONG. The alliance grew out of the hatred of the English and Burgundians for the dauphin and his supporters. Armstrong sees the reason for its continuance for some fifteen years on the part of the Burgundians in their military weakness. Support from the English allowed them to pursue the conquest of the county of Holland, achieved in 1428, but by 1435 this support no longer seemed so valuable.

English rule in Normandy is considered by ALLMAND (1983) and NEWHALL. Newhall is concerned almost exclusively with the details of the military campaign up to the battle of Verneuil. Allmand, as well as looking at the fighting which he characterizes after 1420 as the "defence of the Treaty of Troyes", also discusses the nature of the administration set up in Normandy by the English and the degree to which it incorporated French personnel and governmental bodies. He also addresses the question whether English rule in Normandy was seen as oppressive or accepted by many of the inhabitants. In England itself the view taken of events in France changed from a degree of euphoria at the initial successes to anger at the failures of the 1450s. The influence of this on English politics is made clear by GRIFFITHS. He not only discusses the military situation but also looks at the enormous propaganda deployed to convince opinion on both sides of the Channel of the legitimacy of Henry VI's claim to be king of France. Griffiths even argues that the entire sequence of public events between 1429 and 1432 in both Paris and London was a "gigantic propaganda exercise". He notes a mood of "national shame and despair" when France was lost. The possible effect of these emotions on popular unrest (the situation in France was among the complaints made by Jack Cade and his followers) and on the political scene in general before the outbreak of the Wars of the Roses is also discussed.

POLLARD's life of John Talbot, Earl of Shrewsbury, is largely concerned with his military activities but also seeks to take a critical view of Talbot as a commander and of English military organization in Normandy after the death of the Duke of Bedford in 1435. Talbot's death at Castillon in 1453, leading a body of English and Gascon soldiers against the massed artillery of a much larger French force, was undoubtedly gallant. It also serves well to typify the complete defeat of the aspirations of the English in France that had been set out in the Treaty of Troyes.

SUSAN ROSE

See also Henry V; Hundred Years' War

Tudor Kingdom

Elton, G.R., *England under the Tudors*, London and New York: Methuen, 1955; New York: Putnam, 1956; 2nd edition, 1974; 3rd edition, London and New York: Routledge, 1991

Elton, G.R., *Reform and Reformation: England, 1509–1558*, London: Arnold, and Cambridge, Massachusetts: Harvard University Press, 1977

Guy, John, *Tudor England*, Oxford and New York: Oxford University Press, 1988

MacCaffrey, Wallace T., *The Shaping of the Elizabethan Regime*, Princeton, New Jersey: Princeton University Press, 1968; London: Jonathan Cape, 1969

MacCaffrey, Wallace T., *Queen Elizabeth and the Making of Policy, 1572–1588*, Princeton, New Jersey: Princeton University Press, 1981

MacCaffrey, Wallace T., *Elizabeth I: War and Politics, 1588–1603*, Princeton, New Jersey: Princeton University Press, 1992; London and New York: Arnold, 1993

Scarisbrick, J.J., *Henry VIII*, London: Eyre and Spottiswoode, and Berkeley: University of California Press, 1968; 2nd revised edition, New Haven, Connecticut, and London: Yale University Press, 1997

Williams, Penry, *The Tudor Regime*, Oxford: Clarendon Press, and New York: Oxford University Press, 1979

Modern accounts of the Tudor period may be thought of as beginning with the detailed *History of England from the Fall of Wolsey to the Defeat of the Spanish Armada* by J.A. Froude (1818–94), published in 12 volumes beginning in 1856. Froude was a Victorian man of letters, not an academic historian. In fact, the academic study of English history hardly predates the 20th century. The first professional Tudor historian was A.F. Pollard (1868–1948), who wrote many of the entries on the Tudors period for the *Dictionary of National Biography* and was instrumental in founding the Institute of Historical Research at the University of London. He wrote the volume covering the years 1547 to 1603 for the Political History of England series, (edited by William Hunt and R.L. Poole, 1913), as well as popular biographies of Henry VIII (1902) and Wolsey (1929). His student Sir John Neale carried on his work at the institute and published a popular biography, *Queen Elizabeth*, in 1934.

These works are now period pieces. For the present-day study of the Tudor period the classic text is ELTON (1955), which had been written in 1953, the year when Elton's controversial monograph *The Tudor Revolution in Government* was published. The textbook of 1955 incorporated Elton's new interpretation of Thomas Cromwell's revolutionary role in modernizing the machinery of government under Henry VIII as well as the view that the 1530s marked the watershed between medieval and modern times in England. Although initially this account was criticized – Elton had said that it would be, because it was ahead of its time – it came to be accepted as the new orthodoxy and held sway as the standard account for 40 years. Even today it is the essential starting-point for students of the period. Although intellectual history was never one of Elton's chief interests, the volume does include a chapter on the Renaissance. It is surprisingly acute in its discussion of literature, though weak on architecture and music. Political thought and economic history are also areas of weakness in Elton's survey; but in his defence it must be said that most of the important work in economic history was done after he wrote. In 1974 Elton published a second edition, minimally revised. As he said, his views had changed little and real revision was hardly possible; had he wished to alter the book he would have had to start anew, with a different structure and tone.

However, ELTON (1977) was a fresh account of the period from 1509 to 1558. Since the reign of Henry VIII was the era Elton knew best, and since he was able to treat it here at greater length, the volume was useful. Although his general conception of the age did not change, Elton did incorporate new information based on his own research and that of his numerous students. But the book never achieved the popularity of its predecessor, perhaps because it did not cover the entire Tudor period and therefore was not suitable for adoption as a textbook for courses on Tudor history.

A different approach was attempted by WILLIAMS, whose volume provided a good analysis of the organization of the government and its impact on ordinary people. Because it lacked a general narrative, it was not ideally suited for use as a classroom text; Elton's *England under the Tudors* remained the standard until 1988, when GUY's account was published. Guy, a student of Elton's, did not offer a picture of the age that was markedly different from his mentor's, but his work was new and fresh, and since it was considerably longer than Elton's it could include the results of more recent research.

In addition to these surveys covering all or most of the Tudor period there are important accounts of the reigns of Henry VIII and Elizabeth I, making up roughly the first and second halves of the 16th century. For Henry's reign one can do no better than rely on the detailed and masterful biography by SCARISBRICK, another of Elton's students. Scarisbrick is more interested than Elton was in the king's private life and its influence on politics; and Scarisbirck (since he is a serious catholic) gives interpretations of religion that differ from those of Elton (an agnostic of Jewish descent, the son of the distinguished ancient historian Victor Ehrenberg). MACCAFFREY, recently retired from a long career at Harvard University, devoted most of his life to the study of Elizabeth I and her reign; his trilogy, written over nearly twenty-five years, is the finest detailed consideration of the Elizabethan era. Although the author describes it as essays on a series of themes, the chapters fit together in such a way as to offer a connected account of high politics. The volumes are meticulously researched and elegantly written, and they contain fresh insights on a variety of topics. MacCaffrey's work provides a fitting conclusion to a century's study of Tudor history – it is traditional political history, written as a narrative, carrying forward the efforts of Pollard, Neale, and Elton. Future accounts of the period are likely to be cast in a different mould and to reflect the growing importance of social history and women's studies among younger scholars.

STANFORD LEHMBERG

See also Tudor "Revolution in Government"

Tudor "Revolution in Government"

Coleman, Christopher and David Starkey (editors), *Revolution Reassessed: Revisions in the History of Tudor Government and Administration*, Oxford: Clarendon Press, and New York: Oxford University Press, 1986

Elton, G.R., *The Tudor Revolution in Government: Administrative Changes in the Reign of Henry VIII*, Cambridge: Cambridge University Press, 1953

Elton, G.R., *Reform and Reformation: England, 1509–1558*, London: Arnold, and Cambridge, Massachusetts: Harvard University Press, 1977

Gunn, S.J., *Early Tudor Government, 1485–1558*, Basingstoke: Macmillan, and New York: St Martin's Press, 1995

Guy, John, *Tudor England*, Oxford and New York: Oxford University Press, 1988

Harriss, Gerald L., "Medieval Government and Statecraft", *Past & Present*, 25 (1963): 8–38

Williams, Penry, "The Tudor State", *Past & Present*, 25 (1963): 39–58

Williams, Penry, *The Tudor Regime*, Oxford: Clarendon Press, and New York: Oxford University Press, 1979

With the publication of *The Tudor Revolution in Government*, ELTON (1953) sought to recast the history of early Tudor England, shifting the debate on the development of government from discussion of the Tudors' despotism towards an appreciation of the strengths and virtues of their central administration. In particular, he argued that the 1530s were marked by a revolution in government – the transformation of a medieval ad hoc administration, dominated by the king's household, into a modern bureaucratic system. The architect of this revolution was Thomas Cromwell, "a modern type of English statesman". Cromwell was the creator of the Tudor Privy Council, the instigator of a reorganization of the work of the royal secretaries, and an innovator in financial administration long dominated first by the exchequer and then by the Chamber. New structures were developed (such as the Court of Augmentations, to handle monastic land revenue), and the personnel and departments of the royal household were excluded from royal government. The subsequent influence of *The Tudor Revolution in Government* reflected both the boldness of Elton's thesis and the impressive archival scholarship upon which it was based.

One of the first significant challenges to the "revolution" thesis came with the publication of a pair of related articles by HARRISS (1963) and WILLIAMS (1963). Harriss, a medievalist, criticizes Elton for assuming that Lancastrian and Yorkist government had always been household government; Harriss argues instead that the period from 1450 until 1530 (the age of household government) was the exception to an earlier bureaucratic tradition (exemplified by the medieval exchequer), and that the decline of household government identified by Elton during the 1530s was nothing more than a return to normal medieval practice. Harriss also casts doubt upon Elton's portrayal of Cromwell as a modern, bureaucratic minister, since in practice he preserved considerable personal control over administration. This is a crucial weakness in the thesis, which Williams pursues further. Rejecting Elton's claim that a bureaucratic system was created, he instead stresses the extent to which Cromwell's administration and his accomplishments were personal. The minister regularly relied upon his own private staff (responsible to him alone), and through them he maintained close personal control over financial affairs. Finally, Williams questions the significance of the revolution by noting that many of the reforms did not survive Cromwell's fall in 1540.

WILLIAMS (1979) expanded and elaborated upon these criticisms of the revolution thesis, asserting that the machinery of central government remained relatively weak throughout the century, and its success was contingent upon the active cooperation of local elites. The true strength of Henrician government lay not in a precocious central bureaucracy crafted by the administrative genius Thomas Cromwell, but rather in the networks and personal loyalties which bound the crown to the local officials who actually enforced the king's writs in the shires. Williams's analysis of Tudor government stresses relationships rather than structures and successfully expands the discussion beyond the confines of central administration to encompass a broader understanding of the functions and challenges of Tudor government.

Having earlier agreed to disagree with Harriss and Williams, in *Reform and Reformation* ELTON (1977) does acknowledge some criticisms of the revolution thesis, especially concerning the rise of the Privy Chamber and the continued role (however limited) of the household in government administration. He nonetheless reiterates his central thesis, with only the most limited qualification: Cromwell's reforms completely transformed royal government during the 1530s "whether or not one wants to speak of a revolution" (p. 211). Conceding little of substance to his critics, Elton portrays Cromwell as the architect of a new polity, who aimed to exclude the royal household entirely from royal government. There is something fresh, however, for behind these plans for reform Elton identifies the crucial role of commonwealth ideas; this attention to the intellectual origins of the Tudor revolution in government represents his chief refinement of the original thesis.

The most sustained assault upon the revolution was produced by a group of Elton's former students, in a revisionist collection edited by COLEMAN & STARKEY. Whereas earlier criticism had challenged the novelty of changes during the 1530s, these essays (with one exception) consider the consequences of Cromwell's revolution in the mid-Tudor period, rather than discussing late medieval antecedents for his allegedly modern reforms. Starkey, seeing no decline in the importance of the household, argues that the Privy Chamber rose to prominence under Henry VIII and occupied a central place in government, including royal finances. Alsop's essay on financial administration is especially valuable, as it gives a salutary warning on the dangers for historians of imposing rigid categories upon the past. He notes that early modern government was characterized by an overlap of personal and bureaucratic administration. Moreover, even the labels "medieval" and "modern" must be applied with considerable caution.

In his synthesis, GUY provides a balanced treatment of the debate, carefully examining both Elton's thesis and the arguments of its more vehement opponents. He focuses upon one of the central elements of the Tudor revolution, the development of the Privy Council, which he argues conclusively was a product of the political crises of 1536 and of Cromwell's fall in 1540. He also endorses Williams's observation that the success of early Tudor government was contingent upon its support in the localities, as much as or more than upon reform of central administration. While Guy accepts that there was a revolution in Tudor government, he believes that it was a slow one (the rise of the Privy Council, for example, continued into the reign of Elizabeth).

In his more recent assessment of early Tudor government, GUNN implicitly challenges Cromwell's revolution by cautioning against exaggeration of the importance of individuals, whether monarchs or ministers. Rejecting the centrality of the 1530s, he argues that the judicial changes implemented by the Angevin kings, and the fiscal revolution of the later 17th century, overshadow any Tudor revolution in government. Finally, the absence of detailed discussion of Elton's thesis in a study such as Gunn's testifies to the fact that, although Elton's work stimulated a generation of scholars to study the evolution of Tudor government, his claims for the primacy of Thomas Cromwell and the revolution of the 1530s have not endured. The age of revolution has ended.

PATRICK CARTER

See also Cromwell, Thomas; Henry VIII; Kildare Rebellion; Privy (King's) Council of England

20th Century: Constitutional Issues

Amery, L.S., *Thoughts on the Constitution*, London and New York: Oxford University Press, 1947

Brazier, Rodney, *Constitutional Reform*, Oxford: Clarendon Press, and New York: Oxford University Press, 1991

Hennessy, Peter, *The Hidden Wiring: Unearthing the British Constitution*, London: Gollancz, 1995

Johnson, Nevil, *In Search of the Constitution: Reflections on State and Society in Britain*, Oxford and New York: Pergamon Press, 1977

Norton, Philip, *The Constitution in Flux*, Oxford: Robertson, 1982

Sedgemore, Brian, *The Secret Constitution: An Analysis of the Political Establishment*, London: Hodder and Stoughton, 1980

Stankiewicz, W.J. (editor), *British Government in an Era of Reform*, London: Collier Macmillan, 1976

One of the most revered 20th-century works on the British constitution is that of AMERY, for although he provides a highly sympathetic synopsis of the evolution and nature of that constitution, he also acknowledges – much more readily than many of his fellow Conservatives – its need for revision and reform. Amery simultaneously marvels at the incremental, organic development of the British constitution in accordance with changing circumstances and recognizes the need for some adjustment and innovation to ensure its continued relevance in the second half of the 20th century. One of Amery's most interesting proposals is for a quasi-corporatist Third House or "House of Industry" based on the functional representation of organized professional and economic interests.

It was not until the 1960s and 1970s, however, that concern over Britain's constitution became wider and deeper. JOHNSON argued that Britain's constitutional principles and practices no longer corresponded to the economic problems and political realities confronting the country. Indeed, he suggested that many of the socio-economic difficulties experienced by Britain during this time were themselves a consequence of inadequate and inappropriate constitutional and political arrangements, which had not kept pace with wider societal changes. He therefore urged constitutional reform as a partial prerequisite to securing more effective government and administration in Britain.

The collection of essays edited by STANKIEWICZ clearly reveals the degree of concern felt by many commentators and politicians during the 1970s regarding the effectiveness of Britain's political institutions and constitutional practices. In the context of declining electoral turnout, diminishing support for the two main political parties, increasing support for devolution

in Scotland and Wales, and greater recourse to political protest and extra-parliamentary action, the contributors to this volume urge a wide range of reforms to reverse the trend towards greater secrecy and centralization. Yet while important issues such as electoral reform, referendums, and greater redress for aggrieved citizens are sympathetically examined, other aspects, most notably reform of the House of Lords and devolution, receive only cursory consideration. It is also somewhat disappointing that no conclusion is provided in an attempt to "draw together" the wide-ranging debates and disparate proposals for constitutional reform.

NORTON provides a rather more coherent and systematic discussion of the constitutional questions which emerged during the 1960s and 1970s. He offers a judicious account of issues, criticism, and various proposals for constitutional reform. While Norton himself subscribes to a conservative and sceptical perspective on many of the issues discussed, he nonetheless provides a clear and balanced outline of the arguments for and against specific proposals for reform in each area and aspect of the constitution, at the same time displaying an impressive mastery of detail.

A particularly trenchant critique of constitutional principles and practices is provided by SEDGEMORE, who served as both a civil servant and a member of parliament. He declares that Britain's claim to be a mature and exemplary liberal democracy belies the alarming degree to which political power is concealed and concentrated. Britain's professed constitutional liberalism and parliamentary sovereignty, he argues, is an illusion fostered by the real wielders of power – ministers, senior civil servants, industrialists, and assorted other professional experts, who, among them, make most key decisions and determine most key policies. Thus in empirical reality the theoretical tenets of Britain's uncodified constitution, most notably the notion of a liberal democratic political system entailing an open and pluralist system of checks and balances, are deemed woefully deficient. Sedgemore adds his voice to those calling for Britain's "secret constitution" to be replaced by one which would provide genuinely open government, freedom of information, and more power for parliament and MPs against the executive branch of government.

HENNESSY, too, is concerned by the excessive secrecy and lack of accountability which characterize governance in Britain. Drawing upon a wealth of empirical and anecdotal evidence accrued during his time as an eminent Whitehall journalist, he provides a highly intelligent, incisive, and often wry exposition which debunks the myths of Britain's uncodified constitution. What has enabled these myths to prevail for so long, Hennessy explains, is a combination of public complacency and political complicity about Britain's constitutional arrangements. Apathy from below and antipathy from above effectively conspired to protect Britain's constitution from searching examination and serious reform during most of the 20th century, thereby enabling the concealed core of the political system to operate relatively untrammelled and untroubled by the constitutional charade of checks and balances, democratic accountability, and parliamentary sovereignty.

BRAZIER considers, among other issues, the extent to which these concerns informed the professed commitment of New Labour to constitutional reform. He insists that it is simplistic and misleading to view the Labour Party's relatively new commitment to constitutional reform primarily as a response to 18 years of Thatcherite Conservatism and the concomitant centralization of political power. Instead, he notes that proposals to reform the constitution have emanated from a plethora of organizations and left-leaning think-tanks since the late 1980s, thereby providing Labour with a congenial intellectual framework within to which to develop a more coherent and confident programme of constitutional reform during the 1990s. How much of this programme New Labour would subsequently implement remained to be seen.

PETER DOREY

See also Constitutional Law

20th Century: Economic Issues

Alford, B.W.E, *Britain in the World Economy since 1880*, London and New York: Longman, 1996

Crafts, N.F.R. and N.W.C. Woodward (editors), *The British Economy since 1945*, Oxford: Clarendon Press, and New York: Oxford University Press, 1991

Dintenfass, Michael, *The Decline of Industrial Britain, 1870–1980*, London and New York: Routledge, 1992

Floud, Roderick and Donald McCloskey (editors), *The Economic History of Britain since 1700*, 2nd edition, vol. 2, *1860–1939*, and vol. 3, *1939–1992*, Cambridge and New York: Cambridge University Press, 1994

Glynn, Sean and Alan Booth, *Modern Britain: An Economic and Social History*, London and New York: Routledge, 1996

Middleton, Roger, *Government versus the Market: The Growth of the Public Sector, Economic Management, and British Economic Performance c.1890–1979*, Cheltenham, Gloucestershire: Edward Elgar, 1996

Pollard, Sidney, *The Development of the British Economy 1914–1950*, London: Arnold, 1962; 4th edition, as *The Development of the British Economy 1914–1990*, 1992

Tomlinson, Jim, *Public Policy and the Economy since 1900*, Oxford: Clarendon Press, and New York: Oxford University Press, 1990

The major issues addressed in surveys of the 20th-century economy include economic growth, changes in the share of government expenditure, economic management by successive governments, Britain's falling share of world trade, the loss of empire, and the changing composition of the economy between manufacturing and services. The overriding theme has been decline, with scholars debating the reasons for the slow growth of the British economy relative to its major competitors during much, if not all, of the 20th century.

POLLARD (1962), one of the oldest textbooks on 20th-century economic history, is now in its fourth edition (1992). Its strengths include excellent discussions of productivity, the pattern of industrial change, trade unions and industrial relations, and the effects of war on the economy. In its analysis of Britain's poor relative economic growth since 1945, the role of government is strongly emphasized. Pollard sees the "stop-go"

policies of the Keynesian era as harmful to business and is particularly critical of the role of the Treasury, which he regards as having been subservient to financial interests in the City of London because of a lack of industrial and economic expertise in the civil service. Hence, in politics, international affairs were given primacy over the domestic economy.

GLYNN & BOOTH (1996) is an up-to-date, accessible introductory text covering the period since 1914. It provides a balanced discussion of all the main themes in recent economic history and is particularly good on economic policy, unemployment, poverty, and industrial change. The authors are sceptical that "stop-go" policies and the growth of government spending since 1945 contributed anything very significant to relative economic decline, and they analyse critically the effects of Thatcherite policies. They express concern about the decline of the industrial base and argue that it is unlikely that Britain can prosper from the service economy alone.

TOMLINSON (1990) analyses the development of British economic policy in the 20th century, focusing mainly on macroeconomic issues – including the exchange rate, budgetary policy, inflation, unemployment, and economic growth – and examining the role of agencies such as the Bank of England and the Treasury in shaping events. The book covers nearly all of the 20th century, but a good deal of space is devoted to the years 1945 to 1951, when much of the foundation of postwar policy was laid. Tomlinson's verdict on Attlee's government is very favourable: both macroeconomic management and industrial policy were highly successful, given the extremely difficult circumstances of the transition from a wartime to a peacetime economy. More generally, Tomlinson also argues that the Treasury has been less culpable in Britain's relative economic decline in the postwar period than some commentators have alleged.

MIDDLETON (1996) is an impressive guide to, and analysis of, recent historical literature on the 20th-century British economy. With the aid of an array of clearly presented graphs and statistical tables, the book tackles three large themes: the development of a managed economy, Britain's economic performance, and the growth of government. Middleton demonstrates that much of the growth of government expenditure occurred in the interwar years so that by 1950, as a share of national product, Britain had one of the largest public sectors in Europe. Thereafter, there was a convergence to the European average in terms of the proportion of government spending in economic activity. The detailed analysis of trends in public expenditure provides a convincing basis for rebutting the arguments of writers such as Barnett, Bacon, and Eltis who have put forward theories about big government as a burden on the British economy.

DINTENFASS (1992) is a succinct and elegantly written survey of recent work on the decline of British industry since the late 19th century. Part of the problem was that in some industries new techniques were adopted slowly. Dintenfass summarizes recent research which is critical of the idea that unproductive British workers or militant trade unions were the cause of the "British disease" and instead lays a good deal of the blame on management. There was often poor distribution and marketing of products, particularly overseas. Dintenfass is also critical of notions that there was a cultural bias against industry in Britain. Other important topics briefly analysed in this book include the education system and research and development.

ALFORD focuses on the role of Britain in the international economy since the late 19th century. Topics covered include a clear account of the gold standard system and consideration of the vexed question whether Victorian Britain invested too much abroad (Alford concludes that it probably did not). There is also a valuable overview of theories of imperialism and the economics of the British empire. The problems of Britain's adjustment to a new position in the world economy during the interwar years are also ably discussed. Alford is strongly critical of Britain's international economic policy in the years following World War II. He argues that the question of Europe received insufficient attention, and he detects a general lack of coherence in policy at that time.

There are differences of opinion among economic historians as to method. One group takes an eclectic interdisciplinary approach, drawing on a range of social sciences including economics and political theory and devoting much attention to the study of primary archive sources. A second group emphasizes the testing of economic theory using econometric techniques and makes more use of data analysis than archive-based study. The books discussed so far have tended to belong mainly to the first of these groups. The work edited by CRAFTS & WOODWARD is a leading textbook which draws on the alternative approach, applied economics. It addresses many key themes in postwar economic history, notably the poor long-run growth record of the British economy, and trends in inflation and unemployment. The aim is to reassess economic performance between 1945 and 1979 in the light of policy changes introduced by the Thatcher governments in the 1980s. A central argument is that the consensual policies pursued by governments in the 30 years after World War II failed to tackle the core problem of economic growth, and that the Conservative policies since 1979 – strengthening competitive pressures on firms and reforming industrial relations – were steps in the right direction.

The multivolume textbook edited by FLOUD & MC-CLOSKEY covers a longer time-span than Crafts & Woodward but adopts a similar methodological approach. Each chapter is written by a specialist. If a common theme can be discerned, it is a very optimistic assessment of Britain's economic performance over the long run. Pollard offers a relatively favourable analysis of British entrepreneurship in the late Victorian and Edwardian periods. Edelstein, an expert on 19th-century finance, argues that in the main the capital markets were not misallocating resources. Mackinnon emphasizes the rising living standards of the majority of the population in the late 19th century, rather than the large pockets of dire poverty which have usually caught the eye of other commentators. For the interwar years it is shown that Britain's experience of recession was comparable to recessions in other countries, and that alternative policies which would have cut unemployment would have been extremely difficult to implement. On the postwar period, Supple points out that Britain's relative decline may have been exaggerated, while Feinstein demonstrates that much of Britain's slow growth was an inevitable result of catching up and convergence.

ANDREW JENKINS

20th Century: Social Issues

Burnett, John, *A Social History of Housing, 1815–1970*, Newton Abbot, Devon: David and Charles, 1978; 2nd edition, as *A Social History of Housing 1815–1985*, London and New York: Methuen, 1986

Davie, Grace, *Religion in Britain since 1945: Believing without Belonging*, Oxford and Cambridge, Massachusetts: Blackwell, 1994

Finlayson, Geoffrey, *Citizen, State, and Social Welfare in Britain, 1830–1990*, Oxford: Clarendon Press, and New York: Oxford University Press, 1994

Goldthorpe, John H. with Catriona Llewellyn and Clive H. Payne, *Social Mobility and Class Structure in Modern Britain*, Oxford: Clarendon Press, and New York: Oxford University Press, 1980; 2nd edition, 1987

Goulbourne, Harry, *Race Relations in Britain since 1945*, Basingstoke: Macmillan, and New York: St Martin's Press, 1998

Green, Jeffrey, *Black Edwardians: Black People in Britain, 1901–1914*, London and Portland, Oregon: Cass, 1998

Lowe, Rodney, *The Welfare State in Britain since 1945*, Basingstoke: Macmillan, and New York: St Martin's Press, 1993; 2nd edition, 1999

Machin, G.I.T., *Churches and Social Issues in Twentieth-Century Britain*, Oxford: Clarendon Press, and New York: Oxford University Press, 1998

Marsh, David C., *The Changing Social Structure of England and Wales, 1871–1951*, London: Routledge and Kegan Paul, and New York: Humanities Press, 1958; revised edition, London: Routledge and Kegan Paul, 1965

McKibbin, Ross, *Classes and Cultures: England, 1918–1951*, Oxford and New York: Oxford University Press, 1998

McLeod, Hugh, *Class and Religion in the Late Victorian City*, London: Croom Helm, and Hamden, Connecticut: Archon Books, 1974

Soloway, Richard Allen, *Birth Control and the Population Question in England, 1877–1930*, Chapel Hill: University of North Carolina Press, 1982

Weeks, Jeffrey, *Sex, Politics, and Society: The Regulation of Sexuality since 1800*, London and New York: Longman, 1981

Social issues in 20th-century Britain may be broadly categorized as follows: the opportunity for and extent of social mobility; crime, poverty, housing, unemployment, education, and welfare benefits; birth control, abortion, and provisions for divorce; sexual deviation, interracial conflict, and toleration; the messages and influence of the media; the expansion of controversial types of leisure activity; and the extent of secularization. All these issues have now received academic attention, as well as a vast amount of ideologically or politically motivated rhetoric. Most of the issues are dealt with individually elsewhere in this volume, and this entry will deal only with academic works on some of the broad areas.

Changes in social structure and social behaviour in relation to the size and nature of different occupations, life expectancy, size of families, and crime rates are thoroughly explored, numerically, by MARSH for the period from 1871 to 1951. The extent and limitations of social mobility in the period from 1945 to the 1980s are very carefully examined, statistically and argumentatively, in GOLDTHORPE's objective and exhaustive study. Class experiences and differences in relation to employment and unemployment, education and social mobility, and religion and morality are closely examined by McKIBBIN for the years from 1918 to 1951.

MACHIN studies major social issues as a whole in connection with changing and declining religious influence – including government intervention and the welfare state, and personal and moral behaviour over questions such as contraception, abortion, and leisure pursuits. The welfare state since 1945 and the controversial matter of its expanding and contracting boundaries under different governments are admirably surveyed by LOWE. FINLAYSON presents a skilful and fascinating study of the competition, complementarity, and general interrelatedness of state-provided benefits and private philanthropy. He carefully examines the complex interactions of government, commerce, and individuals in relation to the provision of welfare. One major strand in social welfare and well-being, housing, is comprehensively covered by BURNETT in an account which examines all major factors – physical, economic, social, and political.

Questions of moral change as they have affected personal behaviour in regard to sexual and marital practices, birth control, and abortion are studied comprehensively by WEEKS. The development of the issue of birth control, which became dominant and intensely controversial in the 20th century, is covered extensively by SOLOWAY from the 1870s to 1930. McLEOD, using the findings of a detailed local investigation in south London, illuminates attitudes toward religion and the extent of churchgoing in the early 20th century; DAVIE effectively attempts a wide survey and analysis of these matters in the later half of the century.

Racial friction in British society did not occur very notably or continuously until the 1950s. But GREEN's study informs us that in the early 20th century non-white people were not so largely absent from Britain, or so closely confined to certain districts, as has tended to be assumed. On the highly controversial subject of race relations since 1945, GOULBOURNE provides a very competent account which includes a study of political activities among ethnic minorities. Diverse religious reactions to racial matters are indicated and illustrated by Machin.

IAN MACHIN

Tyndale, William 1494–1536
Religious reformer and Bible translator

Daniell, David, *William Tyndale: A Biography*, New Haven, Connecticut, and London: Yale University Press, 1994

Dickens, A.G, *The English Reformation*, London: Batsford, and New York: Schocken Books, 1964; revised edition, London: Collins, 1967; 2nd edition, London: Batsford, 1989; University Park: Pennsylvania State University Press, 1991

Duffy, Eamon, *The Stripping of the Altars: Traditional Religion in England c.1400–c.1580*, New Haven, Connecticut: Yale University Press, 1992

Greenslade, S.L., *The Work of William Tindale*, London: Blackie, 1938

Hammond, Gerald, *The Making of the English Bible*, Manchester: Carcanet Press, 1982; New York: Philosophical Library, 1983

Haigh, Christopher, *English Reformations: Religion, Politics, and Society under the Tudors*, Oxford: Clarendon Press, and New York: Oxford University Press, 1993

Lloyd Jones, G., *The Discovery of Hebrew in Tudor England: A Third Language*, Manchester: Manchester University Press, 1983

Mozley, J.F., *William Tyndale*, London: SPCK, and New York: Macmillan, 1937

Norton, David, *A History of the Bible as Literature*, vol.1, *From Antiquity to 1700*, Cambridge and New York: Cambridge University Press, 1993

Robinson, Ian, *The Establishment of Modern English Prose in the Reformation and the Enlightenment*, Cambridge and New York: Cambridge University Press, 1998

Williams, C.H., *William Tyndale*, London: Nelson, 1969

William Tyndale, the most significant figure in the popular English Reformation, has been unjustly neglected. He was England's (probably Europe's) greatest early modern scholar of biblical languages, a translator of genius, a fine theologian, and the maker of an English prose which is still a base for our best writing.

Tyndale was at Oxford from c.1508 to some years after he became a master of arts in 1515, and possibly at Cambridge shortly after Erasmus had been teaching Greek there. He was the first in England to grasp the importance of Erasmus's printing of the Greek New Testament in 1516. Tyndale's life's work, cruelly cut off, was to give English speakers, even "the boy that driveth the plough", pocket-size printed Bibles in English. Working in Germany and the Low Countries, alone and in poverty, continually under threat of arrest for the heresies of Lutheranism and putting the gospel into English, he translated the New Testament from the Greek twice and wrote powerful treatises of applied New Testament theology and against corruption in the church, among them *The Parable of the Wicked Mammon* and *The Obedience of a Christian Man*. These were both printed in Antwerp in 1528 and, like all his books, smuggled into England. His Pentateuch volumes of 1530 were the first translations ever made from Hebrew into English; they were followed by the Old Testament historical books. He was arrested before he could finish the Old Testament; and after 16 months in a cell in Vilvoorde Castle outside Brussels, in October 1536 he was, in a high public ceremony, taken out, strangled, and burned for heresy.

Thomas More variously and at enormous length attacked Tyndale. But in spite of early condemnations and burnings, Tyndale's biblical translations were soon absorbed into official Bibles – *verbatim* into "Matthew's Bible" as early as 1537, and as the basis of the "Great Bible" in 1539 and Geneva versions after 1560. Few of the many thousands of versions thereafter, even up to today, do not show his hand. His gift to the English language, a direct brevity, is still perceptible in the everyday life of the English-speaking world.

Edward Hall gives Tyndale an admiring half-page in his chronicle of 1548, which concludes with the remark of an enemy that Tyndale was "*homo doctus, pius et bonus*". Tyndale's life and martyrdom were more fully described in successive editions of John Foxe's *Acts and Monuments* (1559, 1563, 1570, and 1576). His non-biblical works were printed in 1572 by John Day with new material by Foxe. Thereafter, though he was always the foundation of biblical translations, he was pushed aside in the centuries-long adoration of the "King James Bible" ("Authorized Version") of 1611. Victorian protestants took up Tyndale's cause: Christopher Anderson (*The Annals of the English Bible*, 1845, revised 1862) devoted his first volume to Tyndale; and Tyndale's works, apart from the translations, were issued in three Parker Society volumes (1848–50) and are only now being superseded. Robert Demaus (*William Tyndale: A Biography*, 1871, revised 1886) found Tyndale, wrongly, in Wittenberg, Marburg, and Hamburg. The proper cataloguing of printed English Bibles from Tyndale's first New Testament by Darlow and Moule (1903), continued by Herbert until 1961 (1968), began to clarify his importance. Sixty years after Demaus, MOZLEY still found "a man who has never received his due, whose reputation has still been at the mercy of ignorance and partizanship". Though overfond of his discovery of "evidence" that Tyndale went to Wittenberg via Hamburg, Mozley gave a balanced and still useful account of Tyndale's life and work.

GREENSLADE sketched Tyndale's life and then helpfully drew new attention to Tyndale's thought and language, printing illustrative extracts and a fine essay on that language by Gavin Bone. WILLIAMS gave the same emphasis. Donald Smeeton's thesis of 1979 from the Catholic University of Leuven – that Tyndale was dependent on Lollard ideas rather than the New Testament itself, or Luther – lacks evidence. Protestant hagiographies continued which were, sadly, not historically reliable; the two volumes on Tyndale (1986–87) in Lewis Lupton's multi-volume *History of the Geneva Bible* are an example. In spite of Tyndale's own passionate and learned defence of Hebrew in his *Obedience*, there were hostile attempts to claim that his work on the Old Testament was dependent on Luther's German. These claims were countered by HAMMOND, supported by LLOYD JONES: both showed Tyndale's mastery of Hebrew.

To Yale University's Thomas More project are being added, now from Catholic University Press, all Tyndale's works other than his biblical translations, led by O'Donnell's edition of Tyndale's short *Answer to More* (2000). Recent lives of More (e.g. Ackroyd, 1998) dismiss Tyndale with brief inaccuracy. Seeing Tyndale as a satellite of More is not acceptable to most Tyndale scholars, including Tyndale's most recent biographer, DANIELL, who emphasizes Tyndale's greatness in biblical learning and his skill in ancient and modern languages. Daniell also edited Tyndale's Old and New Testaments and his *Obedience*.

Tyndale's translations of the Bible, constantly reprinted, became, though unacknowledged, the bulk of the celebrated King James Version (KJV, the "Authorized Version" of 1611). Including Tyndale's first New Testament in 1526 and KJV in 1611 there were eight new translations of the Bible into English, indicating a high religious and cultural profile. In the same period, there were over 300 distinct editions – not simply reprintings – of the Bible in English. In the reign of Elizabeth I, in a population of 5 million, half a million English Bibles were bought. In all these, Tyndale's pioneering work was dominant. These statistics do not include the circulation of Tyndale's theological writing. Among early modern historians current revisionism disparaging the standard survey by DICKENS has, it is most recently felt, gone too far in announcing that the English Reformation was a failure, or even denying its existence. Early modern history has been written, and students have often been directed, entirely from catholic material (DUFFY and HAIGH) with very little, or indeed no, mention of the English Bible. Thus Tyndale, according to the recently influential model, had been wiped out. The academic journal of the Tyndale Society, *Reformation* (founded 1996), adds to historical studies of the period 1450–1600 work on literature, biblical studies, translation theory, and art. Outside the world of the historians, new work has been done by NORTON, who shows Tyndale's significance in the development of literary ideas of the Bible; and, in linguistics, by ROBINSON, who breaks new technical ground in demonstrating Tyndale's pioneering skill in making modern English prose.

DAVID DANIELL

See also Foxe; Henry VIII; Languages, English: Influence of the Bible and Prayer Book; Literacy: Since Printing;

Tyrconnel, Earl of

see **Talbot, Richard, 1st Earl of Tyrconnel**

Tyrone Revolt

see **Nine Years' War**

Tyrone, 3rd Earl of

see **O'Neill, Hugh**

U

Ulster, Conflict in

see **Northern Ireland, Conflict in**

Unemployment

Alford, B.W.E., *Depression and Recovery? British Economic Growth, 1918–1939*, London: Macmillan, 1972

Brown, Kenneth D., *Labour and Unemployment, 1900–1914*, Newton Abbot, Devon: David and Charles, and Totowa, New Jersey: Rowman and Littlefield, 1971

Constantine, Stephen, *Unemployment in Britain between the Wars*, London: Longman, 1995

Floud, Roderick and Donald McCloskey, *The Economic History of Britain since 1700*, vol. 2, *1860s to the 1970s*, Cambridge and New York: Cambridge University Press, 1981

Gilbert, Bentley B., *The Evolution of National Insurance in Great Britain: The Origins of the Welfare State*, London: Michael Joseph, 1966

Gilbert, Bentley B., *British Social Policy, 1914–1939*, London: Batsford, and Ithaca, New York: Cornell University Press, 1970

Greenwood, W., *Love on the Dole: A Tale of Two Cities*, London: Jonathan Cape, 1933; New York: Doubleday, 1934

Harris, J.F., *Unemployment and Politics: A Study in English Social Policy, 1886–1914*, Oxford: Clarendon Press, 1972

Hay, J.R., *The Origins of the Liberal Welfare Reforms, 1906–1914*, London: Macmillan, 1975; revised edition, 1983

Marshall, J.D., *The Old Poor Law, 1795–1834*, 2nd edition, London: Macmillan, 1985

Mowat, C.L., *Britain between the Wars, 1918–1940*, London, 1968

Orwell, George, *The Road to Wigan Pier*, London: Gollancz, 1937; New York: Harcourt Brace, 1958

Rose, Michael E., *The Relief of Poverty, 1834–1914*, London: Macmillan, 1972; 2nd edition, 1986

Stevenson, John, *Social Conditions in Britain between the Wars*, Harmondsworth: Penguin, 1977

Stevenson, John and Chris Cook, *The Slump: Society and Politics during the Depression*, London: Jonathan Cape, 1977; revised edition, as *Britain in the Depression: Society and Politics, 1929–1939*, London and New York: Longman, 1994

Before 1860, unemployment in Britain was never considered a major problem. It was acknowledged that the industrial changes of the late 18th and early 19th centuries would lead to periods of temporary unemployment. MARSHALL points out that in pre-industrial England some people had worked in more than one domestic occupation to avoid the problem of under-employment. When industrialization allowed them to move to find factory employment, in search of more regular wages, they found that they were now dependent on one source of income only. Similarly, years of poor harvests brought unemployment to farm-hands with no alternative work to support them and their families. But such unemployment was assumed to be temporary, and any relief that was given was "poor relief". Economists of the day assumed that the natural state of the economy would always be "full employment", and if anything more than a basic payment was made, it would probably encourage idleness. The Old Poor Law granted out-relief to the temporarily unemployed, usually by making cash payments to assist able-bodied paupers until they found work. Long-term relief was the workhouse, an institution dreaded by all families especially after the harsh regimes imposed by the Poor Law Amendment Act of 1834.

ROSE claims that a turning-point in attitudes towards unemployment was reached in the early 1860s when thousands of factory operatives were thrown out of work as a consequence of the Lancashire "cotton famine" – a shortage of American cotton during the U.S. Civil War. He states that "the degradation of poor relief and the patronage of private charity" forced the government to intervene to create opportunities for employment by way of a public-works scheme. The Poor Law had clearly failed to deal with the problem of large-scale industrial unemployment. Consequently, the Public Works (Manufacturing Districts) Act of 1863 gave local authorities the power to apply for cheap loans from the Public Works Loan Commissioners to carry out local improvements. Although public works were unable to solve the "unemployment problem", by the end of the 19th century the poor-law system was moving towards greater specialization in the treatment of those in need. Certainly, according to HAY, from the 1880s on "unemployment was recognised as a chronic problem of the British economy" and a "root cause of crime, vagrancy, prostitution and poverty". By this stage, the development of a world economy had highlighted the uncertainties of employment in an industrial and trading nation that depended heavily on a narrow range of export manufactures and fluctuating foreign trade.

GILBERT discusses the worsening unemployment problem – especially in the areas of traditional industries, such as the north of England – and the labour unrest of the early 20th century as factors leading to the Unemployed Workmen Act of 1905. This required the establishment of "distress committees" in every large urban area in the country. Empowered to find employment for those in need, the committees were also allowed to set up labour exchanges and assist unemployed workmen to migrate or emigrate. Although the act effectively failed, Gilbert states that it was significant in marking the culmination of attempts to deal with unemployment by means of work relief.

Hay examines the origins of the Liberal government's welfare reforms of 1906–14. Although the party came to power with no particular commitment to tackle unemployment, it could not sustain that position for long, as unemployment in 1906 rose to its highest level since 1886. HARRIS points out that there was also increasing pressure from the group of Labour members in parliament agitating in support of the "right to work", and he details the development of official policy on unemployment. Demands by trade unions for action to relieve unemployment were also significant – an aspect considered by BROWN. The ultimate outcome was Lloyd George's National Insurance Act of 1911, which introduced a new system of dealing with the unemployed based on contributions from the employee, the employer, and the state. By the time of the outbreak of World War I, attention was still focused on ways of dealing with the unemployed. There was, as yet, no real understanding of the *nature* of industrial unemployment.

CONSTANTINE's study of unemployment in the interwar period demonstrates that although there were areas of progress during these years, the regional nature of mass unemployment in the old industrial areas of the north and in south Wales, and its duration, placed a heavy burden on British society. There is a clearer picture of the unemployment problem during this period because reasonably accurate statistics became available when the Unemployment Insurance Act of 1920 went into operation. For the period before World War I statistical information was notoriously unreliable, but figures for the interwar years enabled politicians and economists to identify the geographical areas – and industries – most seriously affected. Still, as Constantine notes, statistics can disguise the variety of economic and structural problems that account for unemployment, issues which he examines in some detail. ALFORD studies the depression of these years in light of the considerable progress that was made in the new industrial sectors and the higher standard of living enjoyed by those who were in work. He suggests that the latter factor was often underestimated in earlier historical accounts. But, Alford states, it is not just the existence of unemployment that warrants the attention of the historian; it is also the effectiveness of government policies in dealing with a problem at this time of "unprecedented severity".

The picture of unemployment between the wars is complicated by the fact that although the British economy was in the doldrums between 1920 and 1929 and there was high unemployment in the coal and cotton industries especially, Britain was not plunged into a great slump until the Wall Street crash of 1929 triggered a worldwide depression. STEVENSON & COOK discuss the economic complexities of these years and the government's reaction to the hunger marches, the threat of public disorder, the fascist challenge, and the fears of communism and revolution. MOWAT's work also provides a reliable interpretation of this perceived challenge to British politics.

What about the social consequences of unemployment? Various historians, including Alford and STEVENSON (1977), point out that it was during the 1930s that "long-term" unemployment was recognized as such. With the final abolition of the Poor Law as the official body providing relief for the unemployed, in 1929, came the setting up of the much-hated Public Assistance committees. From 1934 on, the Unemployment Assistance Board moved the country one step nearer to the foundation of the welfare state. Stevenson provides a useful historical account of social conditions and the public reactions to these new bodies, making use of some social enquiries of the period. GREENWOOD's novel is still one of the most perceptive accounts of the human consequences of unemployment in the interwar years. Similarly, ORWELL's classic novel gives great insight into the effects of unemployment at this time.

William Beveridge's report of 1942 and the subsequent welfare legislation, culminating in the National Assistance Act of 1948, took away some of the fear of unemployment by setting a national minimum of welfare standards to which all were entitled. The act did not, however, take away the perceived stigma of being unemployed. Since 1945 unemployment has continued to be an issue faced by all governments. FLOUD & McCLOSKEY have looked at some of the complexities involved and the ways in which governments have tried to control levels of unemployment through fiscal policies. The unemployed, now financed directly with government money, have become the responsibility of the state. Fluctuations in trade, Britain's entry into the European Economic Community, and prolonged inflation have all affected unemployment to some extent. For the foreseeable future, unemployment will continue to be a feature of British society, and success in keeping it under control will depend very much on government policy.

ROSALIND E. TIGWELL

See also Depression

Union, Act of 1707

Brown, Peter Hume, *The Legislative Union of England and Scotland: The Ford Lectures, Delivered in Hilary Term, 1914*, Oxford: Clarendon Press, 1914; Westport, Connecticut: Greenwood Press, 1971

Devine, T.M., "The Union of 1707 and Scottish Development", *Scottish Economic and Social History*, 5 (1985): 23–39

Ferguson, William, "The Making of the Treaty of Union of 1707", *Scottish Historical Review*, 43/136 (1964): 89–110

Ferguson, William, *Scotland's Relations with England: A Survey to 1707*, Edinburgh: John Donald, 1977

Levack, Brian P., *The Formation of the British State: England, Scotland, and the Union, 1603–1707*, Oxford: Clarendon Press, and New York: Oxford University Press, 1987

Mackinnon, James, *The Union of England and Scotland: A Study of International History*, London and New York: Longmans Green, 1896

Pryde, George S. (editor), *The Treaty of Union of Scotland and England, 1707*, London and New York: Nelson, 1950

Riley, P.W.J., *The Union of England and Scotland: A Study in Anglo-Scottish Politics of the Eighteenth Century*, Manchester: Manchester University Press, and Totowa, New Jersey: Rowman and Littlefield, 1978

Robertson, John (editor), *A Union for Empire: Political Thought and the British Union of 1707*, Cambridge and New York: Cambridge University Press, 1995

Scott, Paul H., *Andrew Fletcher and the Treaty of Union*, Edinburgh: John Donald, 1992

Smout, T.C., *Scottish Trade on the Eve of Union, 1660–1707*, Edinburgh: Oliver and Boyd, 1963

Whatley, Christopher A., "Economic Causes and Consequences of the Union of 1707: A Survey", *Scottish Historical Review*, 68 (1989): 150–81

Although the Act of Union of 1707 occasioned numerous contemporary pamphlets and accounts and received additional historical treatment in the 18th and early 19th centuries, the modern literature on the subject really begins with MACKINNON. While his work is now more than a century old, it remains a standard one, owing to its highly detailed and careful narrative of the union negotiations, its consideration of a wide variety of primary sources, and the author's judicious conclusion that the Act of Union represented a complex solution to a series of issues facing England and Scotland in the opening decade of the 18th century. Of particular interest to the student of the period is Mackinnon's broad survey of the pamphlet literature which emanated from the pro- and anti-union factions in both kingdoms, and his analysis of the impact of union during the first century of the United Kingdom.

Part of the ongoing appeal of Mackinnon's study is that he eschewed deterministic or teleological explanations for the formation of the United Kingdom. Unlike many high Victorians or Whig historians of the late 19th and early 20th centuries, Mackinnon refused to portray the union of 1707 as either an inevitable marriage, fated by providence, or simply the most progressive and logical solution to England's and Scotland's divisions over such questions as the Hanoverian succession, the ongoing Jacobite threat from supporters of the exiled Stuarts, the security of the British kingdoms, and Scotland's restricted access to English markets. Indeed, he continues to be widely praised for his insistence that the two kingdoms could have pursued other options in the face of their common problems.

The more deterministic explanations for the union are well summarized and represented by BROWN, one of Scotland's foremost historians during the early 20th century. He remains an accessible example of this earlier component of the historiography. In addition, it is interesting to note that his generally positive portrayal of the union stands in marked contrast to the works of his more recent Scottish colleagues, who tend to underscore its deficiencies and assert that Scotland surrendered too much in 1707. (It is unfortunate that the Act of Union has not received nearly as much attention from English historians, particularly since World War II. In many ways, the union has come to be dominated by Scottish historians alone, and they have naturally studied its impact on Scotland, giving little attention to its impact on England.) Among the postwar generations of historians, PRYDE offers the best instance of a scholar who

furthered the argument that the Act of Union must be seen as an inevitable development. He offers his readers a useful appendix so that they may consider the topic through a selection of primary documents, but he himself draws the clear conclusion that union represented a statesmanlike, if somewhat flawed, compromise for the two kingdoms.

Such deterministic interpretations were ultimately challenged, not least by FERGUSON (1964, 1977) – first in a seminal article and later in a sweeping survey of Anglo-Scottish relations to 1707. According to Ferguson, earlier studies of the union (with the exception of Mackinnon's) suffered from an inability to see the incorporation of Scotland into the United Kingdom as anything other than a positive and inevitable event. What was needed, he believed, was a more complete analysis of the range of issues that had traditionally marked Anglo-Scottish relations before the union, along with a more detailed consideration of the role played by the Scottish parliament in the debate over the union, especially during the key session of 1704. Ferguson was also among the first to demonstrate, through scholarly analysis, the extent to which political management in Scotland – featuring requisite dispensations of patronge and cash – was a factor in the eventual passage of the articles of union by the Scottish parliament. Ferguson concluded that that the Act of Union ought to be viewed as a "political job", orchestrated by self-interested power brokers in England and especially in Scotland.

That conclusion was built upon by RILEY, who analysed the motives of key members of Scotland's governing class by drawing largely on their political correspondence. From his examination of these sources, Riley concluded that personal greed, a desire to recoup losses suffered from the failed Darien colonial scheme, and a marked hunger for future political favours from London caused many prominent Scots to support a union that would ultimately be detrimental to Scotland. If Riley's work has suffered from one consistent criticism, it is that he overemphasized the importance of personal motives to the exclusion of wider issues, such as a desire for free trade with England. Nevertheless, Riley's argument about the basic self-interest shown by many members of the Scottish elite is essentially shared by SCOTT, in a biographical treatment of Andrew Fletcher of Saltoun. Tellingly, Scott argues that Fletcher's opposition to what he considered a flawed arrangement was inflamed by the terms Scotland accepted in the Act of Union, not by the abstract notion of Anglo-Scottish union as such.

That Scotland gave away too much in 1707, and that the Act of Union hampered the development of the Scottish state, is a harsh judgement, which might well lead interested readers to seek a longer perspective. Ferguson's book provides some useful background; but those who want to consider the impact of earlier events, such as the union of the English and Scottish crowns in 1603, and efforts and ideas in support of incorporating union during the remainder of the 17th century, will find LEVACK (1987) an invaluable introduction. This study of the political, religious, legal, and economic issues which occasioned unionist projects and writings between 1603 and 1707 demonstrates that the eventual Act of Union should not be viewed only as a product of contemporary crises and individuals. At the same time, Levack reminds his readers that union was almost always viewed in pragmatic terms, and that the earlier proposals and the eventual Act of Union were not particularly effective in fostering a sense of shared nationhood among the English, the

Welsh, and the Scots after 1707. Similarly, the essays presented by ROBERTSON survey contemporary notions of political union and demonstrate that the eventual British solution must be viewed in a wider European context. Indeed, they show that many definitions of unions and empires were present in early modern Europe, and that constitutionally the Act of Union failed to consider or define the relationships which possessions like Ireland or America would thereafter have with the new United Kingdom. As the United Kingdom began to implement devolution at the start of the 21st century, these works stood as timely reminders of other options which were once considered, and of the fact that the adoption of the Act of Union did not immediately ensure its acceptance or its survival.

Assessments of the costs and benefits which stemmed from the Act of Union, especially for Scotland, have often revolved around economic analysis. Indeed, many members of the Whig school, up to and including Pryde, have concluded that one principal benefit of the union was that it permitted Anglo-Scottish free trade and gave Scotland access to English colonial markets and ventures. SMOUT was among the first to challenge this view, arguing that Scotland was already becoming more closely connected with England economically from the Restoration period on. Not surprisingly, this general development heightened the crisis in Anglo-Scottish relations during the reign of William and Mary, when the Scottish economy began to suffer most from English foreign and trade policies. Smout concludes that the Act of Union was largely a success because it permitted Scotland's economy to continue growing in a natural direction, with the positive results being seen in accelerated economic growth from the middle of the 18th century onward. DEVINE is less sure about the economic impact of the Act of Union itself. While he allows that it provided broad opportunities, and that certain sectors of the Scottish economy were able to benefit from free trade with England and its overseas possessions, he believes that Scotland's later advances were really home-grown. In other words, existing strengths in sectors such as Scottish agriculture and in particular industries – not union with England – helped to produce economic growth in the later 18th century. Perhaps the most trenchant observation about the economic aspects of union is provided by WHATLEY, who decides in his useful historiographical survey that it is dangerous to form very precise conclusions about the impact of the Act of Union. Ultimately, he concludes that historians studying the Act of Union have been at their best when they have avoided absolutes and have considered it from the broadest possible perspectives.

ANDREW D. NICHOLLS

See also Identities, National: British; Monarchy: England to 1603; Monarchy: Great Britain since 1603; "Rough Wooing"

Union, Acts of 1536 and 1543

Edwards, J. Goronwy, *The Principality of Wales, 1267–1967: A Study in Constitutional History*, Caernarvon: Caernarvonshire Historical Society, 1969

Rees, James F., *Studies in Welsh History: Collected Papers, Lectures, and Reviews*, Cardiff: University of Wales Press, 1947

Rees, William, *The Union of England and Wales*, Cardiff: University of Wales Press, l948

Roberts, P.R., "The 'Act of Union' in Welsh History", *Transactions of the Honourable Society of Cymmrodorion*, 1972a

Roberts, P.R., "The Union with England and the Identity of 'Anglican' Wales", *Transactions of the Royal Historical Society*, 22 (1972b): 49–70

Roberts, P.R., "The 'Henry VIII Clause': Delegated Legislation and the Tudor Principality of Wales" in *Legend, Record, and Historical Reality*, edited by T.G. Watkin, London, 1989

Williams, David, *A History of Modern Wales*, London: John Murray, 1950; revised edition, 1965

Williams, Glanmore, *Recovery, Reorientation, and Reformation: Wales c.1415–1642*, Oxford: Clarendon Press, and Cardiff: University of Wales Press, 1987

Williams, Glanmor, *Wales and the Act of Union*, Bangor, Gwynedd: Headstart History, 1992

Williams, William Llewelyn, *The Making of Modern Wales: Studies in the Tudor Settlement of Wales*, London: Macmillan, 1919

Williams, William Ogwen, *Tudor Gwynedd*, Caernarvon: Caernarvonshire Historical Society, 1958

The legislation known as the Acts of Union – a phrase first coined by O.M. Edwards in 1901 – formed part of Henry VIII's policy to consolidate his realm when he was in the process of breaking relations with the papacy. According to a pioneering study by W. Ogwen WILLIAMS, the policy of assimilating Wales with England was engineered primarily by Thomas Cromwell. In 1534 Henry had created himself supreme head of the church, and it was in the last session of the Reformation parliament that the first of two statutes was passed, royal assent being given on 14 April 1536, the last day of the parliament.

Governing Wales and the Marches before 1536 had not been easy and posed a problem for Henry VIII at the time when he needed a united realm to strengthen his power. In the Middle Ages Wales was formed as two separate entities: the native principality, conquered in 1282–83 and joined to England in the Statute of Wales (1284); and the independent Marcher lordships which enjoyed their own private jurisdictions and customs, almost totally free of royal jurisdiction. In 1471 a council was established by Edward IV, later to be given judicial powers, to govern Wales and the Marches; and in 1534 Rowland Lee, the most ruthless of lord presidents, unremittingly suppressed criminals. It was evident to Cromwell, however, that a more conciliatory policy was needed, and he decided to engage the rising Welsh gentry, many of whom were already experienced in public affairs, in creating a new settlement which assimilated Wales with England. In the last session of parliament in 1536 justices of the peace (JPs) were introduced into Wales for the first time, and shortly afterwards the first Act of Union was passed. The preamble of the act revealed that the legislators had based it on Edward I's Statute of Wales (1284), an ordinance issued by the king's council at Rhuddlan. This interpretation was accepted by J. Goronwy EDWARDS and Glanmor WILLIAMS; their views differed from those of W. Llewelyn WILLIAMS, who interpreted the Act of Union in the context of British imperialism and the triumph of liberalism.

The Act of Union of 1536 granted the Welsh equality of status, imposed English law on Wales, dissolved the Marcher lordships, created five new shires, established a chancery and exchequer at Brecon and Denbigh to complement those which had already existed at Caernarfon and Carmarthen, granted parliamentary representation, and imposed English as the language of law and administration. The clause imposing the English language has caused considerable debate among recent historians concerning the degree to which it enticed the Welsh gentry away from their native culture. The special judicial status accorded to Monmouthshire also became a matter of debate among those who subsequently regarded it as an English, not a Welsh, shire.

This measure of 1536 was followed by another, more organized statute in 1543, but it was evident that the second was not a natural consequence of the first. In the intervening period, as P.R. ROBERTS has shown, Henry VIII was uncertain how to finalize his policy because before 1537 he was preoccupied with the problem of succession. In that year Henry's son Edward was born, and it is now generally considered that Henry wanted to create a principality for him (although he was not invested as Prince of Wales) in preparation for his accession to the throne. To this end proposals were put forward in 1540–41 called "A breviat of the effectes devised for Wales" to revive the principality for Prince Edward as a patrimony. If Henry VIII had survived longer, these proposals might have been revived. The intention was to abolish the Council in the Marches and replace it by a court of chancery with jurisdiction exercised by Prince Edward over the 12 shires of Wales. Although not all these proposals were adopted, the courts of Great Sessions were incorporated in the statute of 1543; the governmental machinery introduced in 1536 was functioning by 1543, as well as the courts of Great Sessions; and writs had been issued to sheriffs and borough officials for the election of members of parliament.

The statute of 1543 was passed in the second session of the parliament of 1542 (January to May 1543), which was attended by Welsh MPs. In that act the Council in the Marches was made statutory, and from its centre at Ludlow it continued to play a key role in the administration of Wales and the borderland. Royal officials, including JPs and sheriffs, coroners, escheators, and high constables, were introduced into the new shires, and English laws of inheritance were imposed, replacing the Welsh laws of partible inheritance. Roberts has cast new light on the significance of Henry VIII's direct relationship with Wales when Henry was forming his policy in the 1530s and 1540s; Roberts draws attention to another feature of the "breviat": the "enabling clause" (or "Henry VIII clause"), which gave Henry the right to change or alter any part or the whole of the statute, as well as "make laws and ordinances" for Wales. Such a clause, introduced into the Act of 1543, followed upon the "suspensive clause" in 1536, which allowed the king, within three years, to suspend or repeal the act and gave Henry, like Edward I in 1284, a special relationship with Wales. It allowed him greater freedom to change the settlement if he chose to entrust the principality to Prince Edward. By then Cromwell had been executed, and it is doubtful, as W. Ogwen Williams declared, whether he would have agreed with a policy which gave the extended principality a judicial and administrative structure separate from that of England.

The Acts of Union led to different views on the nature and significance of Tudor policy in Wales. Contemporaries, such as Rice Merrick and George Owen, were passionately in favour of it, as were Edmund Burke and O.M. Edwards. A more critical approach was adopted from the 1930s onwards, especially among "nationalist" historians and littérateurs, such as W. Ambrose Bebb, Saunders Lewis, and Gwynfor Evans, who deplored the cultural effects of the settlement; in their view, the settlement "anglicized" the Welsh gentry and deprived Wales of its natural leadership. Other historians, such as J.F. REES, Edwards, W. Ogwen Williams, and Glanmor Williams, have offered more balanced interpretations of Tudor policy. W. Ogden Williams viewed it as a means, in due course, of advancing religious change and – contrary to Rees – not as an essential step forward to expedite the break with Rome in Wales.

Although the acts brought to an end a long period of division and diversity in Wales, they cannot be said to have been the only reason for the "anglicization" of the gentry. Nor was the Tudor settlement entirely innovatory, as W. Ogwen Williams revealed. New features were introduced in three respects, as Edwards states: the imposition of English law, the creation of JPs, and the introduction of parliamentary representation. Edwards argued further that, since the principality was extended to cover its natural boundaries, Wales was "united within itself" and remained a distinct entity. Historians now agree that the legislation was a turning-point, not a starting-point, in the history of Wales, for in a broader context it extended what had already developed in law and administration. It also gave the Welsh gentry further opportunities to increase their power; strengthen their landed wealth; extend their influence and authority in Wales and beyond in public office, commerce, and trade; and develop social relationships. The Acts of Union, as Glanmor Williams has observed, welded together the monarchy, parliament, the law, and in due course the protestant church – the chief buttresses of unity and uniformity in the Tudor state.

J. GWYNFOR JONES

See also Cromwell, Thomas; Henry VIII; Identities, National: British

Union of the Crowns of England and Scotland 1603

Galloway, Bruce R. and Brian P. Levack (editors), *The Jacobean Union: Six Tracts of 1604*, Edinburgh: Scottish History Society, 1985

Galloway, Bruce, *The Union of England and Scotland, 1603–1608*, Edinburgh: John Donald, 1986

Head, D.M., "Henry VIII's Scottish Policy: A Reassessment", *Scottish Historical Review*, 61 (1982): 1–24

Levack, Brian P., *The Formation of the British State: England, Scotland, and the Union, 1603–1707*, Oxford: Clarendon Press, and New York: Oxford University Press, 1987

Mason, Roger A., "Scotching the Beast: Politics, History, and National Myth in Sixteenth Century Britain" in *Scotland and England, 1286–1815*, edited by Roger A. Mason, Edinburgh: John Donald, 1987

Mason, Roger A., *Kingship and the Commonweal: Political Thought in Renaissance and Reformation Scotland*, East Linton, East Lothian: Tuckwell Press, 1998

Murray, James A.H. (editor), *The Complaynt of Scotlande*, London: Trubner, 1872–73; reprinted, Millwood, New York: Kraus Reprint, 1981

Williamson, Arthur H., *Scottish National Consciousness in the Age of James VI: The Apocalypse, the Union, and the Shaping of Scotland's Public Culture*, Edinburgh: John Donald, 1979

Williamson, Arthur H., "Scotland, Antichrist, and the Invention of Great Britain" in *New Perspectives on the Politics and Culture of Early Modern Scotland*, edited by John Dwyer, Roger A. Mason, and Alexander Murdoch, Edinburgh: John Donald, 1982

Wormald, Jenny, "The Creation of Britain: Multiple Kingdoms or Core and Colonies?" *Transactions of the Royal Historical Society*, 6th series, 2 (1992): 175–94

The union of crowns which resulted when James VI of Scotland inherited the kingdom of England has never been particularly controversial. The historiography has consequently been descriptive and analytical rather than dialectic. James's succession raised barely a ripple of dissent on either side of the border, even though the Scottish line had been effectively debarred by Henry VIII's act of 1543, which had defined the succession down to that point. In 1603, it was not convenient for anyone on the English side to remember that; James was a protestant, and his impeccable hereditary claim was therefore acceptable. Only committed catholics, like Robert Persons, who believed that no heretic could wield lawful authority, argued for an alternative.

The idea of union, however, went back a long way, and it had been fiercely controversial in the past, not least because it had at first been expressed in claims to English overlordship. The marriage of Henry VII's daughter Margaret to James IV in 1503 had raised the possibility of the peaceful union which eventually took place a century later. However, Henry VIII had continued to use the arguments of overlordship when he was pressing for a marriage between his son Edward and the infant Queen Mary between 1542 and 1547. This "rough wooing", as it was called, produced a spate of propaganda tracts from the English side, several of which are printed in MURRAY, including "A Declaration, Containing the Just Causes . . . of This Present War with the Scots" (1542); an "Exhortation to the Scottes to Conform Themselves . . . to the Union" (1547); and an "Epistle, or Exhortation to Unitie . . . " (1548). Although some of these were written by Scots, the net effect was to drive the country into the arms of France, an effect examined (among other things) by HEAD. In the mid-16th century, Scottish national consciousness was still pretty much that articulated in 1320 in the declaration of Arbroath, as is clear from the collection of essays assembled by MASON (1987). However, the protestant Reformation wrought some change. The reformers gained power in Scotland in 1560, with assistance from the English; forced the catholic Mary to abdicate in 1567; and drove her into exile in 1568. Thereafter, as is clear from WILLIAMSON (1979, 1982), there was a significant change in Scottish national consciousness, which became less concerned with resisting the encroachments of English overlordship and more concerned with the Roman Antichrist as represented by France. Without becoming specifically anglophile, it was much less explicitly anglophobe than it had been at the time of Henry VIII's wars. There were qualms in Scotland in 1603, because England was both bigger and richer than Scotland, and there were those who saw Scotland's independence being lost by attrition; but there was no overt opposition to the Scottish king's assuming a larger responsibility. The Scots were keenly aware of their own distinctive tradition in political thinking, a tradition examined in depth by MASON (1998). This tradition had none of the common-law elements so strong in the English tradition, but by 1600 it had become stronger on the constraints of godliness. The Scottish monarchy was more absolute than the English in theory, but less so in practice because of the greater strength of both the nobility and the kirk.

James, however, was not content with a personal union of the crowns. Impelled by a mixture of idealism and personal ambition, he pressed for a full union of the kingdoms. This campaign was marked by a quantity of pro-union propaganda, some of which is presented in the collection edited by GALLOWAY & LEVACK (1985). The issues were hotly debated, particularly in England, where anti-Scottish xenophobia became strong; but it was Scotland that stood to lose from a fuller integration, at least in the short term. These issues are examined in detail both by GALLOWAY (1986) and by LEVACK (1987). The fear was that the English would use their greater resources of manpower and wealth to treat Scotland as a colony, as they were already treating Ireland, a theme examined relatively recently by WORMALD. Between resentment on the part of the English over Scots encroaching upon English offices, and fear on the part of the Scots of an economic bear hug, the campaign for union was lost at that time.

Eventually, economic rather than constitutional arguments were to prevail. By 1700 the contrast between English wealth and Scottish poverty was becoming painful, and it was Scots based in London who took the lead in finding a solution. Levack concludes his account of the search for union with its eventual accomplishment in 1707, but no such step could have been taken, in spite of all argument to the contrary, without the acceptance of the logic of hereditary succession in 1603.

DAVID LOADES

See also Elizabeth I; James VI and I; Monarchy England to 1603; Monarchy: Great Britain since 1603; "Rough Wooing"

United States, Relations with: The "Special Relationship" from *c*.1940

Baylis, John, *Anglo-American Defence Relations, 1939–1980: The Special Relationship*, London: Macmillan, and New York: St Martin's Press, 1981

Campbell, Duncan, *The Unsinkable Aircraft Carrier: American Military Power in Britain*, London: Michael Joseph, 1984; updated edition, London: Paladin Grafton, 1986

Dobson, Alan P., *The Politics of the Anglo-American Economic Special Relationship 1940–1987*, Brighton, Sussex: Wheatsheaf Books, and New York: St Martin's Press, 1988

Duke, Simon, *United States Defence Bases in the United Kingdom: A Matter for Joint Decision?*, London: Macmillan, and New York: St Martin's Press, 1987

Dumbrell, John, *A Special Relationship: Anglo-American Relations in the Cold War and After*, London: Macmillan, and New York: St Martin's Press, 2001

Hathaway, Robert M., *Great Britain and the United States: Special Relations since World War II*, Boston: Twayne, 1990

Louis, William Roger and Hedley Bull (editors), *The "Special Relationship": Anglo-American Relations since 1945*, Oxford: Clarendon Press, and New York: Oxford University Press, 1986

Neustadt, Richard E., *Alliance Politics*, New York: Columbia University Press, 1970

Nunnerley, David, *President Kennedy and Britain*, London: Bodley Head, and New York: St Martin's Press, 1972

Richardson, Louise, *When Allies Differ: Anglo-American Relations during the Suez and Falklands Crises*, New York: St Martin's Press, and London: Macmillan, 1996

Smith, Geoffrey, *Reagan and Thatcher*, London: Bodley Head, 1990; New York: Norton, 1991

Anglo-American relations continue to fascinate scholars, especially British scholars. Consequently, there is no shortage of academic texts focusing on all aspects of the "special relationship" and demonstrating areas of conflict as well as cooperation between Great Britain and the United States. The main areas of dispute still surround the nature of the "special relationship": was or is it an alliance of convenience based on shared interests, or was or is something more involved? Is David Watt right when he argues in LOUIS & BULL – the best collection of essays on Anglo-American relations post-1945 – that "the underlying basis of the Anglo-American relationship has always been interest and not, in the first place, emotion"? Such neo-realist views still tend to prevail, although few would underestimate the effect of a common language, a shared heritage and values, and similar political traditions in fostering intimacy between the two countries.

HATHAWAY provides the best general account of how the goals of British foreign policy became incorporated into American foreign policy, largely in response to the threat posed by the Soviet Union following World War II. The governments of Churchill and Attlee recognized the military and economic asymmetry in the newly forged "special relationship" and decided that Britain's best hope of maintaining international prestige was to exert influence on the United States. However, as Hathaway is keen to reiterate, the relationship between Britain and America became less exclusive and less intimate over time. Hathaway analyses the interpersonal relationships between British prime ministers and American presidents but concludes that there is little evidence to show their importance in the decision-making process.

Some studies – for example, those by NUNNERLY and SMITH – are transfixed by the issue of personality. Nunnerly provides an engaging account of Anglo-American relations during the Kennedy administration from 1961 to 1963, the last years of a truly intimate bond between Britain's and the United States' leaders and makers of foreign policy. Paying particular attention to the close relationship between Prime Minister Harold Macmillan and President Kennedy, and between Kennedy and the British ambassador in Washington, Sir David Ormsby-Gore, Nunnerley's work covers relations during the construction of the Berlin wall; the Cuban missile crisis; the controversy over a nuclear weapon, the Skybolt missile; and Britain's application for membership in the European Common Market. Nunnerly shows that the British praised Kennedy's leadership and vision for the future. He singles out Kennedy's decision to authorize the sale of Polaris missiles to Britain as being partly due to a personal fondness for Macmillan.

The high point in the personal relationship after the Kennedy-Macmillan years is examined by SMITH in his study of the Reagan-Thatcher years of the 1980s. Smith analyses the role of personality in international relations; largely on the basis of interviews with key actors, including the two leaders themselves, he demonstrates the intimacy and atmosphere of the times. According to Smith, the relationship between Reagan and Thatcher was ideologically closer than that between any previous prime minister and president, and their relationship stood the test of time. Moreover, Thatcher was able to use her friendship with Reagan to good effect, particularly during the Falklands crisis, when Reagan never let her down, despite pressure from factions of his cabinet to avoid publicly supporting the British.

BAYLIS describes the evolution of relations between Britain and America with regard to defence from their high point during World War II to the early 1980s. According to Baylis, bilateral cooperation for defence has been the one demonstrably preferential and intimate aspect of the special relationship, particularly before the late 1960s and early 1970s, and most noticeably in terms of nuclear and chemical warfare, intelligence, and laser technology. Overall, Baylis believes, defence has reflected trends in other areas of the relationship between the two countries, but Britain has probably gained the most from such close collaboration.

DUKE provides a comprehensive study of the postwar development of American defence bases in the United Kingdom. Although plans for a system of American defence bases originated with President Franklin Roosevelt's idea of an international police force, the cold war escalated the American presence in the UK and the speed with which it was installed. Duke gives a detailed account, including maps and tables, of the costs and benefits of these military bases to both Britain and the United States and reminds readers that Britain was prepared to approve a huge American military presence on the basis of nothing more than a "gentlemen's agreement".

CAMPBELL provides a forthright, provocative, and controversial work on the impact of the American military presence in Britain. He analyses the reasons for the growth of American bases in Britain beginning in 1950 (the US Air Force arrived in 1948) and assesses the dangers of the presence of troops and nuclear weapons – and the unease with which these were received by the general public. Campbell raises questions of national sovereignty and accountability, challenging Duke's ultimately positive view of the United States' military presence. He argues that the British government was indifferent and complacent in monitoring and regulating the American presence in Britain and repeats that Britain has virtually no control over American bases and personnel in British territory. He shows that public opinion in the early 1980s was firmly opposed to letting American forces alone have control of the firing of cruise missiles. He records numerous nuclear accidents, notes the repeated false alarms by the American early warning system, and describes the hazards associated with nuclear technology and the dangers that were posed by allowing American atomic bases in Great Britain – most obviously, Britain became a major target for an attack by the Soviet Union. Equally important, according to Campbell, are the collaboration between Britain and the United States in gathering intelligence and the secret surveillance systems set up by the United States to monitor internal as well as external subversion, such as the United States National Security Agency centre at Menwith Hill in North Yorkshire. He concludes that British politicians paid a high price for their special relationship with the Americans, especially in 1980 when the decision was made to allow the stationing of cruise missiles on British soil.

DOBSON deals with the economic imperatives shaping the postwar Anglo-American relationship. He describes the evolution of a special economic relationship beginning in 1941 with the lend-lease agreement and cemented in the Bretton Woods agreement of 1944. He goes on to show that economic rivalry and economic cooperation are a major explanation for the vibrancy and disputes in the special relationship until the 1970s. He shows how Britain repeatedly asserted its economic independence from the United States in matters of east-west trade policy, often seeking to relieve economic difficulties through increased trade with the Soviet bloc and the People's Republic of China. The best-known incident came in 1964, when the government of Prime Minister Home sold Leyland buses to Cuba, earning Britain more than $10 million, despite a personal plea from President Johnson and the loss of American military aid for failing to curtail trade with Cuba under the provisions of the Foreign Aid Act of 1963. Dobson convinces the reader that economic diplomacy is an exciting aspect of high politics which has been insufficiently studied.

Why allies as close as the United States and Great Britain mishandled two crises in their relationship – Suez in 1956 and the Skybolt affair in 1962 – is the subject of NEUSTADT's seminal study of Anglo-American relations. Neustadt argues that misunderstandings are much more likely between countries with a close, intimate relationship, and that differences are magnified during periods of tension because the allies expect more of each other. This is apparent in the behaviour of the British and American leaders at the time of Suez and Skybolt. To Neustadt, the story of these two crises is one of miscommunication. Assuming that they knew each other's position, on both occasions, London and Washington failed to ask probing questions at the right time.

RICHARDSON updates Neustadt's thesis through her examination of two crises: Suez and the Falklands. According to Richardson, both crises show the dangers that arise when competing bureaucratic interests are refereed by a weak or disengaged executive. She agrees that friendship played a part in the mismanagement of both conflicts and believes it led to the false expectation that neither ally would act to jeopardize the other's national interest; but she also believes that the problem was more than miscommunication. With regard to Suez, she notes that there was a constant flow of letters and cables between the two countries and argues that problems arose because, owing to differing interests in the region, neither side was able to persuade the other of the wisdom of its position. In 1982 the United States managed to become entrapped in the Falklands War because of a bureaucratic conflict between a State Department trying to avert a war, a Defense Department trying to avert a British defeat, and a UN mission trying desperately to avoid damaging America's ties with Latin America.

DUMBRELL covers a period that has been relatively neglected. Focusing on the years since 1960, he takes a fresh look at the Anglo-American relationship during and immediately after the cold war. He bucks the trend by arguing that the closeness between Britain and America in the postwar period has been sustained as much by shared culture as by shared interests, although he emphasizes that the cosiness and familiarity of transatlantic diplomacy should not be exaggerated. One noteworthy and creditable feature of his work is the chapter on Ireland. Dumbrell traces the "American dimension" of the troubles in Northern Ireland from 1960 to the late 1990s and shows how the Clinton administration, freed from the shackles of the "special relationship" of the cold war, was able to engage with the Irish problem in an attempt to capitalize on the "peace dividend".

SYLVIA ELLIS

See also Attlee; Cold War; Decolonization; Defence Capability; European Economic Community–European Union; Korean War

Universities, Rise of Middle Ages

Aston, T.H., Ralph Evans, and J.I. Catto (editors), *The History of the University of Oxford*, vol. 2, *Late Medieval Oxford*, Oxford: Clarendon Press, and New York: Oxford University Press, 1992

Bender, Thomas (editor), *The University and the City: From Medieval Origins to the Present*, Oxford and New York: Oxford University Press, 1988

Cobban, Alan B., *The King's Hall within the University of Cambridge in the Later Middle Ages*, Cambridge: Cambridge University Press, 1969

Cobban, Alan B., *The Medieval English Universities: Oxford and Cambridge to c.1500*, Berkeley: University of California Press, and Aldershot, Hampshire: Scolar Press, 1988

Cobban, Alan B., *English University Life in the Middle Ages*, Columbus: Ohio State University Press, and London: UCL Press, 1999

Courtenay, William J., *Schools and Scholars in Fourteenth-Century England*, Princeton, New Jersey: Princeton University Press, 1987

Kibre, Pearl, *Scholarly Privileges in the Middle Ages: The Rights, Privileges, and Immunities of Scholars and Universities at Bologna, Padua, Paris, and Oxford*, Cambridge, Massachusetts: Medieval Academy of America, 1962

Leff, Gordon, *Paris and Oxford Universities in the Thirteenth and Fourteenth Centuries: An Institutional and Intellectual History*, New York: Wiley, 1968

Pedersen, Olaf, *The First Universities: Studium Generale and the Origins of University Education in Europe*, Cambridge and New York: Cambridge University Press, 1997

Rashdall, Hastings, *The Universities of Europe in the Middle Ages*, 3 vols, revised and edited by F.M. Powicke and A.B. Emden, Oxford: Clarendon Press, 1936; reprinted, New York: Oxford University Press, 1987

Thorndike, Lynn, *University Records and Life in the Middle Ages*, New York: Columbia University Press, 1944

Few topics in the history of education or in medieval history have been researched as extensively as the medieval universities. Trying to cover the literature of the field is nearly impossible. However, several books and collections of documents stand out as truly important and will be covered here.

The beginnings of medieval universities are shrouded in myth. For example, Oxford claims Alfred the Great as its original founder when, like most other European universities, it was an outgrowth of religious institutions such as cathedrals and monasteries that formed schools which developed between the 6th and 12th centuries.

The earliest universities appeared in Italy in the early 12th century; Salerno was noted for its medical school and Bologna for law. Later in the 12th century the French cathedral schools around Paris coalesced on the left bank of the Seine and became the University of Paris. For an overview of the beginnings of the university, with background on its classical antecedents, PEDERSEN (1997) is a good starting-point which includes the origins of Oxford and Cambridge. Oxford, for example, begins to be noticed as a place of higher education around 1100; the records are scanty before 1209, but there was an exodus from Paris to Oxford in 1167, when John of Salisbury states that the French king expelled all foreign students. For a fuller picture of medieval universities, the reader can do no better than to begin with RASHDALL's comprehensive survey, which covers cover not only Bologna, Paris, and Oxford but the rest of Italy and France as well as Germany and Scotland. The second volume has essays by R.K. Hannay on the foundation of St Andrews in 1413 and Glasgow in 1450–51. Rashdall also includes the foundation of Aberdeen in 1494. The third volume concentrates on student life at English universities. The set is well indexed and is an outstanding resource.

Edinburgh University was not founded until 1582, when it received a royal charter authorizing the town council to establish colleges and schools. In the 18th century Edinburgh was reformed to become one of the leading schools for modern liberal arts and for medicine. See Nicholas Phillipson's essay "Commerce and Culture: Edinburgh, Edinburgh University, and the Scottish Enlightenment" in BENDER.

For the medieval history of Oxford and Cambridge the reader has the choice of two works by Alan Cobban. COBBAN (1988) is a comprehensive scholarly study that puts the English experience into its continental perspective, stressing the relative success of the two institutions in providing an intellectual atmosphere with the personnel to carry out the missions of a medieval university. COBBAN (1999) is intended to give a composite picture of different aspects of Oxford and Cambridge,

rather than taking the developmental approach of the earlier book. Both studies are valuable contributions to the field. Oxford University Press has a multi-volume series covering the history of Oxford University; the volume edited by ASTON, EVANS, & CATTO is a collection of informative articles by various specialists.

For the reader interested in primary sources, there are many choices. THORNDIKE (1944), a compilation of translated documents for the nonspecialist, continues to be valuable.

In addition to the comprehensive studies there are many notable books that deal with more specific aspects of the medieval university. Noteworthy among these are COURTENAY, COBBAN (1969), LEFF's very important study, and KIBRE.

Publications on the beginnings of the medieval university cover a vast range, but the works mentioned above help chart a path that the interested reader and scholar can continue to follow.

SHARON D. MICHALOVE

See also Cambridge; Oxford, University of

University Expansion and Polytechnics

20th century

Carswell, John, *Government and the Universities in Britain: Programme and Performance, 1960–1980*, Cambridge and New York: Cambridge University Press, 1985

Dyhouse, Carol, *No Distinction of Sex? Women in British Universities, 1870–1939*, London: UCL Press, 1995

Halsey, A.H., *Decline of Donnish Dominion: The British Academic Professions in the Twentieth Century*, Oxford: Clarendon Press, and New York: Oxford University Press, 1992

Hargreaves, John D. and Angela Forbes (editors), *Aberdeen University 1945–1981: Regional Roles and National Needs*, Aberdeen: University of Aberdeen Press, 1989

Harrop, Sylvia, *Decade of Change: University of Liverpool, 1981–1991*, Liverpool: Liverpool University Press, 1994

Lowe, Roy, *Education in the Post-War Years: A Social History*, London and New York: Routledge, 1988

Soares, Joseph A., *The Decline of Privilege: The Modernization of Oxford University*, Stanford: Stanford University Press, 1999

Stewart, W.A.C., *Higher Education in Postwar Britain*, London: Macmillan, 1989

The growth of British higher education in the 20th century, from an elite to a near-mass system, may be seen as part of the general history of social progress and widening prosperity, stimulated by the democratizing effects of the two world wars and related to the expansion of secondary schooling. However, modest expansion in the aftermath of World War I was not sustained, and the interwar years have attracted little historical attention. More has been written about expansion since 1945, but it inevitably suffers from the problems of all contemporary history: sources are only partly available, judgements are provisional, and many of the interesting works are by sociologists and political scientists rather than historians.

For facts and figures down to *c*.1988, STEWART and LOWE provide reliable guides. Stewart, a former vice-chancellor, gives a somewhat blandly meliorist view from within the liberal establishment. Lowe is more critical, insisting especially on how expansion was channelled into institutional forms which allowed the traditional mission of the older universities to be preserved intact. The relation between old and new universities and the promotion of technical colleges, first to polytechnics (1965) and later to full university status (1992), are central to the story. It was slightly different in Scotland (where the term "polytechnic" was not used), but even less so in Wales and Northern Ireland.

In the interwar years the universities underwent little change. Very few new institutions were founded, and in the 1930s numbers of students stagnated or even fell. Outside the universities technical education was given in local colleges with low prestige, much of it on a part-time basis. And as DYHOUSE shows, women's higher education, a significant area of growth before 1914, failed to maintain its momentum. The percentage of women students reached a peak in the late 1920s, and that peak was not regained until the 1960s. Most women graduates went into schoolteaching, and social attitudes within the universities remained discriminatory.

Although expansion after World War II is popularly associated with the Robbins committee, which reported in 1963, it really began much earlier. Plans were laid during the war years, with a special emphasis on the need for more state investment in science and technology. The move to "secondary education for all" in the Education Act of 1944 (and equivalent developments in Scotland) created pressure from below for more places, and the new universities of this period were nearly all planned before Robbins – and all reflected the prestige of the Oxbridge model by adopting residential campuses and intensive methods of teaching. Coupled with the introduction of national student funding in 1962, which removed the need to attend a local university, this created (so HALSEY and other critics have argued) an unnecessarily expensive university ideal, delaying the move towards greater participation.

In the postwar years the University Grants Committee (UGC), which had distributed state funds since 1919, took a more active role in making policy. An important source for this, and for the implementation of the Robbins report, is CARSWELL, a former secretary of the UGC. Carswell shows that the outcomes of expansion were not always those intended. The political case for expansion rested strongly on hopes for science and technology, seen in the light of international industrial competition; yet the actual expansion of places was much greater in the arts and social sciences, partly because they were cheaper and partly (Carswell argues) because there was no radical reform in the secondary school curriculum. One by-product, though this also had deeper roots in postwar social expectations, was a strong move towards equal participation by women.

In the aftermath of Robbins, colleges of advanced technology created in 1957 were given full university status, and promotion of this kind was originally envisaged as a continuing process. But it was checked by the designation of some 30 polytechnics in 1965, creating a "binary" system: polytechnics retained a more vocational emphasis than universities, with less priority given to research, and remained under the control of local authorities. This situation was later reversed as national funding replaced local control (1988) and polytechnics and some other colleges gained full university status (1992). The political and social pressures behind these decisions await fuller historical investigation.

Meanwhile we have some studies of the impact of national policies on individual universities. The volume edited by HARGREAVES & FORBES shows how at Aberdeen, a university with a strong regional character, the initial postwar expansion was accepted very reluctantly, and how the university suffered when state funding was cut in the 1980s. That is also the period covered by HARROP (whose book supplements the excellent general history of Liverpool University by Thomas Kelly); adaptation to the harsher climate of that decade, and to the more business-oriented ethos which politicians demanded, proved extremely painful. One underlying factor was that as the habit of attending the local university declined, the civic and regional roots which had once been a powerful source of strength withered away.

This did not apply to Oxford, which had always been a national university, but the sociologist SOARES provides a comparable study of its adaptation to postwar needs. The cause of science was embraced, and recruitment was widened sufficiently to satisfy the reforming politicians of the 1960s, even if misleading stereotypes of social privilege persisted. In the 1980s, however, the ethos of the university was resistant to new demands, and it suffered correspondingly. Soares sees this as symptomatic of a general breakdown of the formerly close relationship between universities and the political establishment. He also gives some clues as to how, drawing on a socially segmented school system, universities are inevitably sorted into hierarchies of prestige despite the formal unity of status and funding since 1992.

Lowe argues that the nature of British higher education, and especially its stratification, cannot be understood without examining its inheritance from the past, and there is room for reflection on whether older ideas of a liberal education can still be valid in the age of the mass university. There is no better starting-point for such questions than Halsey, whose book is based on a series of surveys of the academic profession, which themselves provide valuable source material, but also distils the results of a lifetime's sociological study of the British educational system.

R.D. ANDERSON

See also Cambridge; Education for Leisure; Oxford, University of

University Reform 19th century

Anderson, R.D., *Education and Opportunity in Victorian Scotland: Schools and Universities*, Oxford: Clarendon Press, 1983

Brock, M.G. and M.C. Curthoys (editors), *The History of the University of Oxford*, vols 6–7, *Nineteenth-Century Oxford*, Oxford: Clarendon Press, and New York: Oxford University Press, 1997–2000

Brooke, Christopher N.L., *A History of the University of Cambridge*, vol. 4, *1870–1990*, Cambridge and New York: Cambridge University Press, 1993

Jarausch, Konrad H. (editor), *The Transformation of Higher Learning, 1860–1930: Expansion, Diversification, Social Opening, and Professionalization in England, Germany, Russia, and the United States*, Chicago: University of Chicago Press, and Stuttgart: Klett-Cotta, 1983

Jones, David R., *The Origins of Civic Universities: Manchester, Leeds, and Liverpool*, London: Routledge, 1988

Moody, T.W. and J.C. Beckett, *Queen's, Belfast, 1845–1949: The History of a University*, 2 vols, London: Faber, 1959

Rothblatt, Sheldon, *The Revolution of the Dons: Cambridge and Society in Victorian England*, London: Faber, and New York: Basic Books, 1968

Sanderson, Michael, *The Universities and British Industry, 1850–1970*, London: Routledge and Kegan Paul, 1972

Searby, Peter, *A History of the University of Cambridge*, vol. 3, *1750–1870*, Cambridge and New York: Cambridge University Press, 1997

Williams, J. Gwynn, *The University Movement in Wales*, Cardiff: University of Wales Press, 1993

Williams, J. Gwynn, *The University of Wales, 1839–1939*, Cardiff: University of Wales Press, 1997

England, Scotland, Wales, and Ireland have had separate histories of university reform. In 1800 England had only two universities – Oxford and Cambridge ("Oxbridge") – and BROOKE, SEARBY, and BROCK & CURTHOYS are essential reading regarding them. The interpretation of university reform at Oxbridge was pioneered by ROTHBLATT, and there is now wide agreement on its general features. The reforms, concentrated between 1850 and 1880, were designed (1) to make university education more effective by introducing new subjects and through the examination system which had been developing since the beginning of the century and (2) to adapt university education to the needs of the new upper middle class, especially its professional and public service element; there was a close connection with the parallel reform of the public schools. Reform was promoted by politicians but carried out with the collaboration of internal reformers, one result being that radical professorial models of the university were rejected in favour of adaptation of the college system, with its concentration on individual tuition and an ideal of liberal education as pastoral and character-forming. For contemporaries, removal of the ancient universities from the Anglican grip was an essential aim, and the dons became educational professionals rather than a branch of the clergy. Brooke and Searby give a vivid picture of personalities and students' social life. Brock & Curthoys's study is notable for incorporating work on a massive computerized database of staff and students. Projects of this kind, inevitably expensive and involving a long time-scale, are a feature of current research on university history.

The work edited by JARAUSCH is valuable for putting England in a comparative context; it brings together essays by Rothblatt, Harold Perkin, Roy Lowe, and Arthur Engel. Lowe in particular argues that the successful reform of Oxbridge imposed a hierarchical pattern on English universities, meaning that the civic universities founded in the later 19th century failed to establish an alternative, more middle-class, more utilitarian ideal. Most writing about the new colleges and universities (in London as well as the "redbrick" colleges of the great industrial centres) is of an institutional kind and varies greatly in quality. Two general studies, however, are those by JONES and SANDERSON. Jones stresses the active participation of local elites in the foundation of the colleges and the way in which, at least in the early years, these colleges represented a consciously new, anti-metropolitan ethos, often but not always inspired by nonconformism. Sanderson argues that the civic universities were quite successful in serving local industrial needs. (In subsequent work, Sanderson developed this argument to criticize theories which blame education for the "decline of the industrial spirit" in Britain.) Down to 1914 at least, the new universities, though small and lacking in national prestige, retained a vigorous local and regional identity. Some achieved full university status through royal charters, but others remained university colleges, awarding London degrees. The federal or examining university, the first example being London in 1836, was a distinctive British development of the 19th century. And the contribution of London and the civic universities, from the 1870s on, offered a more thorough welcome than Oxbridge for the women's higher education movement.

The creation of university education in Wales is well covered by WILLIAMS. Colleges were founded at Aberystwyth in 1872 and at Cardiff and Bangor in the 1880s; the federal University of Wales followed in 1893. The motives were partly economic and social but also reflected the religious and cultural distinctiveness of Wales. Williams argues that the university was a success in this respect, and that it produced a new and distinctive intelligentsia expressing essentially cultural rather than political nationalism.

Religious and cultural distinctiveness within an unchallenged political union was also a theme of Scottish university history. The state was traditionally more active in education in Scotland than in England, and there was a complex history of university reform which included acts of parliament in 1858 and 1889. This is analysed by ANDERSON, who seeks to relate the story to broader themes of secularization and social change, and particularly to the demands of the expanding Scottish middle class. An already well-developed system, once attuned to the needs of the church in a largely agrarian society, was successfully modernized; it has often been claimed that anglicization reduced the democratic features of the traditional education system, but Anderson argues, relating university history to the evolution of the schools which fed them, that this was not so.

If university reform was largely divorced from political nationalism in Wales and Scotland, the same cannot be said of Ireland. University education there was originally limited to Trinity College, Dublin, which remained strongly Anglican in character despite the abolition of religious tests for students in 1794. The attempts of successive British governments to provide a university education which would satisfy all religious parties formed one of the most intractable aspects of the Irish question. The best general account remains that in MOODY & BECKETT's history of Queen's, Belfast. This was one of three non-denominational colleges founded in 1845, and provided with a federal body, the Queen's University, in 1850. Non-denominationalism satisfied presbyterians, and the Belfast college was successful. The others – at Cork and Galway – were less so, as the catholic ideal demanded education on a confessional basis; the Catholic University founded in Dublin in 1854 satisfied this need but also contributed to the identification of

Irish national aspirations with catholic culture. In 1878 the Queen's University was transformed into the Royal University, which examined candidates from all institutions impartially; this provided an interim compromise until 1908. The act of 1908 left Trinity College untouched, gave Belfast independence as the Queen's University, and grouped the former Catholic University with Cork and Galway in the National University of Ireland. This settlement was to be long-lasting, but as Moody & Beckett observed, it foreshadowed partition in accepting that a university structure embracing all of Ireland's cultural communities was unattainable.

University education in the early 20th century remained the privilege of a tiny percentage of the age cohort. There had been significant expansion of the number of students in higher education since around 1870 (see Lowe, in Jarausch, for figures), and access to professional positions from lower social strata was certainly wider in Scotland than elsewhere. But university reform remained a question of elite formation and culture.

R.D. ANDERSON

See also Anglican Establishment; Cambridge; Oxford, University of

Urban Development medieval period

Baker, Timothy, *Medieval London*, London: Cassell, and New York: Praeger, 1970

Holt, Richard and Gervase Rosser (editors), *The Medieval Town: A Reader in English Urban History, 1200–1540*, London and New York: Longman, 1990

Miller, Edward and John Hatcher, *Medieval England: Towns, Commerce, and Crafts, 1086–1348*, London and New York: Longman, 1995

Platt, Colin, *The English Medieval Town*, London: Secker and Warburg, and New York: David Mckay, 1976

Reynolds, Susan, *An Introduction to the History of English Medieval Towns*, Oxford: Clarendon Press 1977

Schofield, John and Alan Vince, *Medieval Towns*, London: Leicester University Press, and Madison, Wisconsin: Fairleigh Dickinson University Press, 1994

Swanson, Heather, *Medieval British Towns*, London: Macmillan, and New York: St Martin's Press, 1999

That the medieval period was one of rapid urban development is an area of close agreement among urban historians. Not until then did the essential elements of urban settlement in Britain re-emerge from a time of hibernation which had begun soon after the end of Roman administration. Of course, by the standards of the 20th century the growth rate of urban regions was slow, but so was the growth rate of the population as a whole. Because very few towns had written records before the 13th century, historians have gained an understanding of the extent and causes of this change only relatively recently.

It is difficult, if not impossible, to discuss urban development in England without examining the development of London. BAKER makes a creditable job of this. He provides a vivid picture of what day-to-day life was like for the medieval Londoner. His account begins with the first narrative of life in the city, by Fitz Stephen (c.1180). The weakness of this work is that Baker does not attempt to explain why London grew to be the city it became. This is a central question that any urban historian – seeking to add insight to description – must grapple with, and its omission from Baker's work is striking.

PLATT represents the last gasp of an older literature on medieval towns in England. The central question of urban history in this literature is definitional: exactly how does one define a medieval urban settlement? This contrasts with the focus of modern literature, which seeks to understand the causal factors behind the significant growth of urban areas. Platt, however, unlike this older literature, does not focus purely on the legal definition of medieval boroughs. He expands his study into the urban landscape, economy, society, and religion, presenting a broad array of interesting and important facts. Platt suffers from difficulties similar to Baker's, but like Baker he presents a clear portrait of everyday life, in this case throughout medieval urban England.

The first study that fits squarely within the modern conception of what "urban history" ought to be about is REYNOLDS's. The focus here is on the causes – not merely a description – of urban development. Other modern elements are the comparative nature of the central questions and the author's desire to generalize. Too often urban history is narrowly focused on one specific town or city, with no consideration of broader questions. Reynolds offers a pioneering new interpretation, seeking to clarify what is known and not known, as well as what big questions lack answers. Economic and social factors behind urban development are discussed. This study avoids the pitfall of positing a simple answer to a complex question.

In contrast to Reynolds, HOLT & ROSSER present a collection of "local" essays on many topics. One strength of this volume is the diversity of topics tackled in the essays: these include suburban growth, political dimensions, the role of craftsmen, and the eventual decline of medieval towns, among other topics. The authors note that the continued use of archaeological evidence is presumably the best path to progress. SCHOFIELD & VINCE certainly agree with that conclusion, given the lack of a significant stock of written records from towns before the 13th century. However, they offer a significantly different interpretation of the evidence on medieval towns. The focus here is on summarizing the recent archeological evidence in clearly divided chapters so that historians with little background in archaeology will be able to have a clear understanding.

MILLER & HATCHER explain urban development by looking at changes in the economy and in specific industries. In their view, growth of urban areas is driven by three interrelated changes. First, owing to an increase in trade, urban areas began to specialize in the industry with the greatest comparative advantage; this led to expansion. Second, a more powerful merchant class developed that was able to protect its interests. Third, the broadening of political power through the creation of an inclusive parliament was a positive political development. Significant urban growth begins before the Norman Conquest, with some established urban areas appearing in Domesday Book. The expansion of trade leads to improved productivity (through regional specialization) and expansion of the economy.

An excellent and up-to-date survey of the subject is given by SWANSON. The strength of this work is its broad generality. A novel and possibly unique element is that an attempt is made to integrate into the analysis evidence from towns outside England (but in the United Kingdom). Generally there is little literature on medieval urban development in Ireland or Scotland. Swanson makes the interesting point that most towns were essentially the same in 1200; however, by 1500 each town had a much more distinctive character. Medieval urban history has clearly moved in a promising direction in the past 25 years.

ALEXANDER T. WHALLEY

See also County Histories: England

Urban Societies

Beier, A.L. and Roger Finlay (editors), *London, 1500–1700: The Making of the Metropolis*, London and New York: Longman, 1986

Borsay, Peter, *The English Urban Renaissance: Culture and Society in the Provincial Town, 1660–1770*, Oxford: Clarendon Press, and New York: Oxford University Press, 1989

Brenner, Robert, *Merchants and Revolution: Commercial Change, Political Conflict, and London's Overseas Traders, 1550–1653*, Princeton, New Jersey: Princeton University Press, and Cambridge: Cambridge University Press, 1993

Briggs, Asa, *Victorian Cities*, London: Odhams, 1963; New York: Harper and Row, 1965

Burnett, John, *A Social History of Housing, 1815–1985*, London and New York: Methuen, 1986

Cannadine, David, *Lords and Landlords: The Aristocracy and the Towns, 1774–1967*, Leicester: Leicester University Press, 1980

Clark, Anna, *The Struggle for the Breeches: Gender and the Making of the British Working Class*, Berkeley: University of California Press, 1995

Clark, Peter (editor), *The Early Modern Town: A Reader*, London and New York: Longman, 1976

Clark, Peter and Paul Slack, *English Towns in Transition, 1500–1700*, Oxford and New York: Oxford University Press, 1976

Corfield, P.J., *The Impact of English Towns, 1700–1800*, Oxford and New York: Oxford University Press, 1982

Davidoff, Leonore and Catherine Hall, *Family Fortunes: Men and Women of the English Middle Class, 1780–1850*, Chicago: University of Chicago Press, and London: Hutchinson Education, 1987

Dennis, Richard, *English Industrial Cities of the Nineteenth Century: A Social Geography*, Cambridge and New York: Cambridge University Press, 1984

Earle, Peter, *The Making of the English Middle Class: Business, Society, and Family Life in London, 1660–1730*, London: Methuen, and Berkeley: University of California Press, 1989

Foster, John, *Class Struggle and the Industrial Revolution: Early Industrial Capitalism in Three English Towns*, London: Weidenfeld and Nicolson, 1974; New York: St Martin's Press, 1975

Fraser, Derek, *Urban Politics in Victorian England: The Structure of Politics in Victorian Cities*, Leicester: Leicester University Press, 1976

Fraser, Derek, *Power and Authority in the Victorian City*, Oxford: Blackwell, and New York: St Martin's Press, 1979

Hennock, E.P., *Fit and Proper Persons: Ideal and Reality in Nineteenth-Century Urban Government*, Montreal: McGill-Queen's University Press, and London: Arnold, 1973

Koditschek, Theodore, *Class Formation and Urban-Industrial Society: Bradford, 1750–1850*, Cambridge and New York: Cambridge University Press, 1990

Neale, R.S., *Bath, 1680–1850: A Social History, or A Valley of Pleasure, Yet a Sink of Iniquity*, London and Boston: Routledge and Kegan Paul, 1981

Phythian-Adams, Charles, "Urban Decay in Late Medieval England" in *Towns in Societies: Essays in Economic History and Historical Sociology*, edited by Philip Abrams and E.A. Wrigley, Cambridge and New York: Cambridge University Press, 1978

Platt, Colin, *The English Medieval Town*, London: Secker and Warburg, and New York: McKay, 1976

Sacks, David Harris, *The Widening Gate: Bristol and the Atlantic Economy, 1450–1700*, Berkeley: University of California Press, 1991

Smith, Dennis, *Conflict and Compromise: Class Formation in English Society, 1830–1914 – A Comparative Study of Birmingham and Sheffield*, London and Boston: Routledge and Kegan Paul, 1982

Stedman Jones, Gareth, *Outcast London: A Study in the Relationship between Classes in Victorian Society*, Oxford: Clarendon Press, 1971; Harmondsworth and Baltimore: Penguin, 1976

Thrupp, Sylvia L., *The Merchant Class of Medieval London, 1300–1500*, Chicago: University of Chicago Press, 1948

Waller, P.J., *Town, City, and Nation: England, 1850–1914*, Oxford and New York: Oxford University Press, 1983

Wohl, Anthony S., *Endangered Lives: Public Health in Victorian Britain*, London: Dent, and Cambridge, Massachusetts: Harvard University Press, 1983

Wrigley, E.A., "A Simple Model of London's Importance in Changing English Society and Economy, 1650–1750" in his *People, Cities, and Wealth: The Transformation of Traditional Society*, Oxford and Cambridge, Massachusetts: Blackwell, 1987

Before the 20th century, no nation urbanized more rapidly than Britain. Throughout the Middle Ages, Britain had no city anywhere near the size of Paris, Naples, Venice, or Milan. During the early modern period, London alone entered the ranks of great cities, rising by 1700 to the top position as measured by numbers and wealth. But with the rapid expansion of industrial cities in the late 18th and early 19th centuries, an irreversible dynamics of urbanization was set in motion that made England a predominantly urban country as early as 1851. In assessing the historiography of urban society, this contrast between the slow start before 1750 and the fast finish thereafter must be borne in mind.

The pre-industrial town was composed essentially of three broad groups: (1) a narrow but never entirely stable oligarchy of elite merchants who dominated local society and urban government; (2) a larger body of small masters and ordinary craft journeymen, whose position was precarious but whose status as freemen entitled them to certain privileges and protections; and (3) an indeterminate mass of semi-employed wage labourers who were excluded from the benefits of the guild system and were often compelled to live beyond the town walls. THRUPP's classic study of the merchants of medieval London offers an exemplary "top-down" analysis of how this tripartite social structure worked. More recent works on smaller medieval towns are surveyed by PLATT. PHYTHIAN-ADAMS examines the widespread decay of towns in the late Middle Ages.

The early modern town is well reviewed in the essays collected by P. CLARK (1976), as well as in the surveys by CLARK & SLACK (1976) and by CORFIELD. Early modern London is treated in BEIER & FINLAY's work, which can be supplemented by WRIGLEY's classic essay on the increasingly central role of London within the national economy. By the 17th century, London had become a city of many aspects – an entrepôt, a political capital, a financial headquarters, and a consumption centre. The increasingly complex social structure that developed from these many activities has generated an entire sub-genre of urban history. Especially important is BRENNER, who traces the emergence during the 17th century of a counter-elite of interloping colonial merchants. Challenging the hegemony of the established oligarchy, they added a new and dynamic element to the urban economy and society. During the 1640s, Brenner argues, it was they (in alliance with radical craftsmen) who transformed the English Civil War into a revolution by delivering the capital to the parliamentary side.

Looking at the middle class in London during the late 17th century from a different angle, EARLE sees this group as an important precursor of an urban domestic culture more commonly associated with the 19th-century bourgeoisie. The rise of provincial towns in the 18th century as centres of consumption is treated masterfully by BORSAY and, from another perspective, by NEALE. The rise of Bristol is superbly surveyed by SACKS.

The study of urban society in Britain reaches a critical mass, of course, with the explosion of northern and Midlands industrial centres c.1770–1870. Whereas the pre-industrial town contained a relatively fixed hierarchy of ascending orders, the industrial city revealed a bewildering array of shifting classes, occupations, and voluntary associations. The tone of scholarship was initially set by BRIGGS, who brought coherence to this vast diversity of materials by associating a different city with each period of urban industrial growth in the 19th century. Thus Manchester, with its runaway economic expansion and stark class divisions, became the "shock city" of the early industrial period. Around mid-century, it was succeeded by Birmingham and Leeds, whose more variegated social structures and more harmonious class relations best embodied the social stabilization of this "age of equipoise". Then Middleborough – a late starter – is introduced to epitomize the age of iron and steel. Finally Briggs returns to London, now the "world city" of Britain's *fin de siècle* – the glittering jewel in the crown of its high imperial age.

Briggs's survey is brilliantly conceived and masterfully executed, but his handling of the socio-economic diversity of urban industrial Britain raises more problems than it resolves. For the more ambitious among the next generation of urban historians, gauging the significance of the divergence between industrial

cities indicated a need to turn towards comparative history. HENNOCK (1973) and FRASER (1979) led the way with comparative studies of urban government, revealing how its character in different cities was the product of a subtle interplay between the structure of the local economy and its stage in the urbanization process. For FOSTER, a Marxist, the specific contours of political mobilization and class struggle were to be explained by the relationship of a given city to the dominant mode of production and to the framework of labour exploitation which prevailed locally. For SMITH, the relevant distinction lay neither in the local economy nor in the prevailing social structure but rather in the vicissitudes of urban development which led Sheffield down the road of class confrontation, whereas Birmingham maintained Briggs's pattern of political consensus and class compromise. CANNADINE considered the role of landlords in urbanization – a role which varied from place to place.

These comparative studies, conducted at a high level of conceptualization and research, elucidated many patterns of similarity and contrast. Nevertheless, there was often an air of artificiality and arbitrariness about these socio-historical "experiments" which purported to test the operation of a series of dependent variables, with other variables presumed to be constant and independent. The messiness of history rarely allows for such heuristic precision. Hence, a second wave of analytical studies returned to the format of the individual case study in order to offer implicit comparisons; or to treat particular cities as microcosms of the forces of urbanization, industrialization, proletarianization, and class formation operating in the society at large; or to do both. An early classic was STEDMAN JONES's study. Here the problems of proletarianization were refracted through the prism of the Victorian metropolis, then undergoing a somewhat belated and attenuated process of industrial development. Focusing on Bradford – a "shock city", like Manchester – KODITSCHEK traced the dialectic of class formation. Even in this highly unusual environment, he argued, all the social and political elements found in other Victorian cities were present. Because the process of development was highly concentrated and compressed, however, class division was more visible and class conflict was more volatile than in other locales where the process of capitalist development was less relentless and the pace of urbanization was less swift.

Whether because of changes in historiographical fashion or because the theme of urban industrial development was deemed to have been played out, the flood of case studies in urban history hs dwindled to a trickle during the past decade. The best works have tended to focus on the most neglected topics – the middle class and gender (DAVIDOFF & HALL), or the working class and gender (A. CLARK 1995). Perhaps this means that the time for synthesis has finally arrived. Today, the findings remain dispersed among a series of specialized studies. Early attempts at synthesis by WALLER (1983) and FRASER (1976) were useful but inevitably premature. To date, the most successful syntheses have concentrated on particular dimensions of the urbanizing experience; these include DENNIS's study of urban geography, BURNETT's study of urban housing, and WOHL's study of public health.

THEODORE KODITSCHEK

See also Industrial Revolution entries; Industry, Location of

Ussher, James 1581–1656

Scholar, churchman, and Primate of All Ireland

Abbott, William M., "James Ussher and 'Ussherian' Episcopacy, 1640–1656: The Primate and His *Reduction* Manuscript", *Albion*, 22/2 (1990): 237–59

Boran, Elizabethanne, "An Early Friendship Network of James Ussher, Archbishop of Armagh, 1626–1656" in *European Universities in the Age of Reformation and Counter Reformation*, edited by Helga Robinson-Hammerstein, Dublin and Portland, Oregon: Four Courts Press, 1998

Copern, Amanda L., "The Caroline Church: James Ussher and the Irish Dimension", *Historical Journal*, 39/1 (1996): 57–85

Ford, Alan, "James Ussher and the Creation of an Irish Protestant Identity" in *British Consciousness and Identity: The Making of Britain, 1533–1707*, edited by Brendan Bradshaw and Peter Roberts, Cambridge and New York: Cambridge University Press, 1998

Knox, R. Buick, *James Ussher, Archbishop of Armagh*, Cardiff: University of Wales Press, 1967

Trevor-Roper, Hugh, "James Ussher, Archbishop of Armagh" in his *Catholics, Anglicans, and Puritans: Seventeenth Century Essays*, London: Secker and Warburg, 1987; Chicago: University of Chicago Press, 1988

James Ussher was a figure of great renown, both because of his eminence as scholar and because he attained the primacy of the Church of Ireland in 1626. As with many contemporaries, his life and career were dominated by the turmoil of the reign of Charles I, and when Ussher died in 1656, adherents and opponents of Charles were equally quick to lay claim to his legacy. This historiographical tradition continued until the 20th century, with Whig and Tory historians vying to prove that Ussher had sympathized with their inclinations in the ecclesiastical disputes before the Civil Wars.

KNOX, the author of the standard modern biography, attempted to reconcile these competing traditions by arguing that Ussher's scholarly pursuits subsumed his political guile. Thus Ussher was often bewildered by the forces that swirled around him. Knox saw Ussher as a man consumed with attaining a compromise position in the affairs of the Church of Ireland. He could never achieve this, however, since he lacked clarity and his theological preferences were unfocused and vague. Knox believes that Ussher succeeded only in muddling through as he attempted to strike a balance between the observational preferences of most members of the Church of Ireland and the ever-increasing "Arminian" orders coming from the king and his Archbishop of Canterbury, William Laud, in England. The picture presented is of a primate who was lost and tentative in the face of strong dictates from London.

TREVOR-ROPER challenged this overall perception in an accessible essay dealing with all the important periods of Ussher's life. He argues not only that Ussher's intellectual views were consistent but that they had been shaped early on, when Ussher was being educated at Trinity College in Dublin. There, Ussher acquired a Ramist, humanistic world-view that inspired a lifelong belief in, for example, the evils of Roman catholicism

and the historical basis for the independence of the Church of Ireland. BORAN, who also focuses on Ussher's early career, supports the thrust of Trevor-Roper's thesis. She shows that Ussher's network of friends and acquaintances included many men whose religious views were seen as "puritan", and that he would have been strongly disposed towards the views of this party in any religious disputes.

With this intellectual background, Ussher embarked on parallel careers as a scholar and antiquarian on the one hand, and as a figure of rising importance in the Church of Ireland on the other. In this way, he was able to reconcile his anti-catholicism with intellectual pursuits, and he corresponded warmly with European catholics on historical and theological matters. According to Trevor-Roper, Ussher's purpose as a scholar was to prove the inherent purity of a native Irish form of Christianity. FORD echoes this idea and asserts that Ussher should be seen as a product of a "double" tradition: Irish on the one hand and protestant on the other. Therefore, Ussher's scholarship was directed toward establishing a new, protestant Irish profile within the British kingdoms. While James I reigned, this sort of scholarly pursuit by a member of the episcopacy was encouraged and rewarded; and, as Ford asserts, Ussher helped to define native Irish protestantism for the first time.

Charles I demanded more in the way of political allegiance, however, and after 1625 Ussher found himself caught between a desire to support and obey his sovereign and his strong concern with protecting the traditions of his church. Trevor-Roper argues that Ussher's solution was to try to use his scholarship as an ideological weapon, something he favoured over episcopal administration and politics. Ultimately, he would be frustrated, as Laud and Lord Deputy Thomas Wentworth (Earl of Strafford after 1640) pushed through the policies known as "Thorough", affecting everything in Ussher's world from the doctrines of the Church of Ireland to the staffing of Trinity College.

COPERN has reacted to the suggestion in recent revisionist work that the proposed innovations and interference with the Church of Ireland were really the policies of Charles I himself, and that Laud was only the king's agent. She asserts instead that Laud was indeed the moving force behind the inclusive inter-kingdom church policies of the 1630s, presents Ussher as a staunch defender of the rights and traditions of his church, and argues that many historians have been confused over the relationship between the Caroline English and Irish primates. Rather than seeing Ussher as a man bewildered by events, as Knox presented him, Copern suggests that Ussher's relative silence in ecclesiastical politics from the mid-1630s until the outbreak of the civil wars indicates a sense of defeat. The wars clarified this, Copern tells us, because "as a Euro-Calvinist [Ussher] doubted not for a moment that Charles and the Caroline church had been sabotaged by antichrist and his instrument – 'Arminianism'." Even so, as a committed royalist, Ussher could not and would not abandon his king in the face of rebellion. Therefore, while he tried – unsuccessfully – to be a mediator, his ultimate loyalty was to his sovereign.

ABBOTT examines the role Ussher might have played in achieving a religious compromise during the civil wars, particularly concerning the role of episcopacy, a thorny problem. Following Ussher's death in 1656, his short tract *The Reduction of Episcopacy unto the Form of Synodical Government* began to circulate. Over the next three decades, it came to be seen as a basis for some form of presbyterian-episcopal reconciliation, because it called for a continued yet limited role for bishops. Abbott argues that most historians who have examined this tract have wrongly assumed that it failed to win sufficient support when Ussher wrote it in 1641, particularly among reform-minded parliamentarians, and was therefore put aside. Abbott's persuasive essay asserts that Ussher himself repressed consideration of the *Reduction* because he believed that it would accelerate calls for the outright elimination of episcopacy; something he was not prepared to endorse.

ANDREW D. NICHOLLS

See also Arminianism; Charles I; Ireland: Reformation

Utilitarianism

Albee, Ernest, *A History of English Utilitarianism*, London: Swan Sonnenschein, and New York: Macmillan, 1902

Bonner, John, *Economic Efficiency and Social Justice: The Development of Utilitarian Ideas in Economics from Bentham to Edgeworth*, Aldershot, Hampshire; and Brookfield, Vermont: Edward Elgar, 1995

Claeys, Gregory, "William Thompson: From 'True Competition' to Equitable Exchange" in his *Machinery, Money, and the Millennium: From Moral Economy to Socialism, 1815–1860*, Cambridge: Polity Press, and Princeton, New Jersey: Princeton University Press, 1987

Halévy, Élie, *La formation du radicalisme philosophique*, 3 vols, Paris: Alcan, 1901–04; as *The Growth of Philosophic Radicalism*, London: Faber and Gwyer, 1928; reprinted, Clifton, New Jersey: Kelley, 1972

Keynes, John Maynard, "Edgeworth, Francis Ysidero, 1845–1926", *Economic Journal*, 36/141 (1926): 140–53

Keynes, John Maynard, "William Stanley Jevons 1835–1882: A Centenary Allocution on His Life and Work as Economist and Statistician", *Journal of the Royal Statistical Society*, 99/3 (1936): 516–48

LeMahieu, D.L., *The Mind of William Paley: A Philosopher and His Age*, Lincoln: University of Nebraska Press, 1976

Plamenatz, John, *The English Utilitarians*, Oxford: Blackwell, 1949; 2nd edition, 1958

Riley, Jonathan, "Mill's Utilitarianism" in his *Liberal Utilitarianism: Social Choice Theory and J.S. Mill's Philosophy*, Cambridge and New York: Cambridge University Press, 1988

Scarre, Geoffrey, *Utilitarianism*, London and New York: Routledge, 1995

Stansky, Peter (editor), *The Victorian Revolution: Government and Society in Victoria's Britain*, New York: New Viewpoints, 1973

Stephen, Leslie, *The English Utilitarians*, 3 vols, London: Duckworth, and New York: Putnam, 1900

Thomas, William, *The Philosophic Radicals: Nine Studies in Theory and Practice, 1817–1841*, Oxford: Clarendon Press, and New York: Oxford University Press, 1979

Utilitas: A Journal of Utilitarian Studies, 1989 –

The term "utilitarianism" was coined in the 1820s to refer to a moral doctrine that had become a popular, though minority, view among intellectuals ("men of letters") in the previous century and that can be loosely defined as hedonistic, consequentialist, and (formally) egalitarian. PLAMENATZ insisted that a key task for historians was "to define the doctrine so narrowly that only those thinkers who are usually called utilitarians deserve the name", but in fact a canon of utilitarian authors (whose respective doctrines were by no means fully consistent with each other) had already emerged at the turn of the 20th century. Most historical literature (including Plamenatz's own work) has respected the family resemblance between these writers, while recent contributions from the discipline of philosophy have added analytical rigour to certain historical discussions; for example, RILEY synthesized a variety of Millite views into a set of "testable"–"contestable" axioms.

The major British authors generally deemed to have contributed significantly to utilitarian doctrine between 1765 and 1914 are (alphabetically) Jeremy Bentham, Richard Edgeworth, William Godwin, William Jevons, James Mill, John Stuart Mill, William Paley, Joseph Priestley, and Henry Sidgwick. This consensus was established by 1940 (see below). The "three-text cluster" of STEPHEN, HALÉVY, and ALBEE was far from "value-free", however, for each writer seems to have been concerned to show that utilitarianism was outdated at the turn of a new century. Halévy contended that "philosophic radicalism" should be replaced by a more flexible and egalitarian political theory; Stephen and Albee argued that a static, atomistic worldview should be supplanted by more evolutionary and organicist concepts in both sociology (Stephen) and ethics (Albee). Stephen's three-volume opus was organized around the lives of Bentham and the two Mills; and Albee treated Paley and Sidgwick as figures requiring special consideration. Halévy underlined the importance of Godwin's use of utilitarian concepts to criticize luxury and advocate an anarchistic form of socialism as well as noting Priestley's contribution of the "principle of the artificial identification of interests". Finally, the additions to utilitarian thought made by Jevons and Edgeworth were commonly viewed as wholly economic until another famous liberal economist, KEYNES, drew attention to the wider implications of their writings for psychology, mathematics, statistics, and logic.

At the same time as they established a canon of modern utilitarian authors, early 20th-century scholars were also concerned to establish intellectual affiliations between those thinkers and various early modern figures who were defined either as "fully fledged" utilitarians or as authors of concepts which were important precursors of utilitarian theories. Thus, Albee's predominant concern, theoretical ethics, led him to identify Richard Cumberland, John Brown, and John Gay (not the poet) as "theological utilitarians", while Halévy and Stephen treated Adam Smith as a secular utilitarian (and viewed Bentham as his pupil). George Berkeley, Anthony Ashley Cooper (the third Earl of Shaftesbury), and Francis Hutcheson were identified as notable predecessors of utilitarianism by Albee; John Locke, David Hume, and Horne Tooke by Stephen; Isaac Newton, Bernard Mandeville, and David Hartley by Halévy. Moreover, the contributions of two European intellectuals, Claude-Adrien Helvétius and Cesare Beccaria (Marchese di Beccaria), were noted and evaluated in this literature.

Some scholars have found it useful to discuss certain quasi-utilitarian writers who made use of some (though not all) typical utilitarian concepts, and to identify writers who anticipated the ideas of the classical utilitarians. Plamenatz viewed Hume as not just a precursor but "the founder of utilitarianism" yet was perhaps at his most illuminating when he identified Edmund Burke and Thomas Paine as "second cousins" of the philosophical radicals, who used arguments regarding human happiness to justify their respective doctrines of prescription and democratic reform. (Albee anticipated a contemporary trend in intellectual history which identifies Spencer as another quasi-utilitarian).

The growth of specialist historiography in the late 20th century has ensured that the four general texts cited so far have no recent equivalents. SCARRE followed Albee when he defined his own "province" as "moral philosophy rather than political science or welfare economics", but only four of his eight chapters were historical in outlook and took account of primary texts as well as recent scholarship. Nevertheless, these historical sections are worthy of attention. As well as surveying the ideas of Hutcheson, Hume, Priestley, Paley, Godwin, Bentham, J.S. Mill, and Sidgwick, Scarre noted that the first theoretical displacement of hedonism by aestheticism (as the main component of a consequentialist welfarism) was undertaken in the Edwardian period by George Moore and Hastings Rashdall. An intelligent survey of so-called ideal utilitarianism indicated, but did not explore, parallels with Bloomsbury and other radical artistic movements.

Because their authors take very different approaches, the general texts do not pay equal attention to each subdivisions of the utilitarian family of theories. Hence some reference to specialist works is essential; for example, LEMAHIEU offers a useful exploration of the realm of "natural theology" and "theological utilitarianism" – the doctrine that self-interested (but social) men must take special note of future rewards and punishments (consequences) that have been divinely ordained for the afterlife – with special reference to Paley. BONNER included an intelligent commentary on the economic doctrines of Jevons and Edgeworth, as well as exploring the political economy of Bentham, the Mills, and Sidgwick and rebutting the earlier view that all the classical economists were also utilitarians. CLAEYS paid notable attention to a neglected contribution by a utilitarian thinker to the British socialist tradition, and THOMAS provided a useful discussion of a variety of "orthodoxly" (that is, liberal) Benthamites. Finally, Benthamism – to some extent a construct of yet another Edwardian historian, A.V. Dicey – was a subject that exercised many anglophone historians from the 1940s into the 1960s, and the essay collection edited by STANSKY indicated clearly how the assumed primacy of utilitarian ideas in "the Victorian revolution in government" was gradually supplanted by a more pluralistic view of the social forces at work.

To return to the present, contemporary scholarship on utilitarianism is intertwined with philosophical speculation regarding the overall merits of the numerous possible variants of the doctrine (as was noted with reference to Scarre). As a gateway to much recent thinking on the subject, the journal *UTILITAS* strikes a judicious balance between philosophical and historical articles and is essential reading for any historian of British utilitarianism.

CLIVE E. HILL

See also Bentham; Mill; Priestley

Utrecht, Treaty of 1476

Colvin, Ian D., *The Germans in England, 1066–1598*, London: National Review Office, 1915; reprinted, Port Washington, New York: Kennikat Press, 1971

Dollinger, Philippe, *The German Hansa*, translated and edited by D.S. Ault and S.H. Steinberg, London: Macmillan, and Stanford, California: Stanford University Press, 1970 (French edition, 1964)

Fudge, John D., *Cargoes, Embargoes, and Emissaries: The Commercial and Political Interaction of England and the German Hanse, 1450–1510*, Toronto: University of Toronto Press, 1995

Jacob, E.F., *The Fifteenth Century, 1399–1485* (vol. 6 of *Oxford History of England*), Oxford: Clarendon Press, 1961; Oxford and New York: Oxford University Press, 1993

Lloyd, T.H., *England and the German Hanse, 1157–1611: A Study of Their Trade and Commercial Diplomacy*, Cambridge and New York: Cambridge University Press, 1991

Postan, M.M., "The Economic and Political Relations of England and the Hanse from 1400 to 1475" in *Studies in English Trade in the Fifteenth Century*, edited by Eileen Power and M.M. Postan, London: Routledge, 1933; New York: Barnes and Noble, 1966

Ross, Charles, *Edward IV*, London: Eyre Methuen, and Berkeley: University of California Press, 1974; 2nd revised edition, New Haven, Connecticut, and London: Yale University Press, 1997

Scofield, Cora L., *The Life and Reign of Edward the Fourth, King of England and France and Lord of Ireland*, vol. 2, London and New York: Longmans Green, 1923; reprinted, London: Frank Cass, and New York: Octagon Books, 1967

The treaty of Utrecht was concluded between the German Hanseatic cities and the English government in 1474 but was not fully ratified by all parties until the city authorities of Danzig approved it in May 1476. Edward IV needed to end hostilities with the Hanse before he could concentrate his military energies in a renewed French war. The treaty essentially granted the German cities all their demands, and the Edward's orders to his ambassadors indicated his willingness to concede whatever was necessary to end the conflict. All Hanse commercial privileges in England were confirmed, including not being subject to the lord high admiral's court; an indemnity of £10,000 was paid by the English for seizures of Hanse goods in 1468; and Cologne, which had a special relationship with England that violated the league's protocols, was now excluded from the benefits of being in the Hanse until it submitted to the rules. The major historiographic issues have been, mostly, how humbling the treaty was for England, how much it revitalized and re-empowered the Hanse, and its overall effect on English trade with the Continent.

Early 20th-century interpretations of the treaty are summarized in COLVIN's work, written during World War I at the height of anti-German sentiment in England. Using the typical hyperbole of his time, Colvin called Utrecht the "most shameful treaty ever signed by an English king". He was most critical of the treaty for giving the German traders an extraordinary degree of autonomy and especially for exempting them from the regular English court system. Most disturbing for Colvin was Edward IV's willingness to grant the Hanse all the privileges in England without insisting on reciprocity. Colvin also believed that the king's betrayal of Cologne, a loyal ally, was disgraceful. Much of Colvin's analysis of the treaty is heavily coloured by issues, alliances, and national prejudices relative to the European war of his own day. Still, his overall interpretation that this treaty was very bad and shameful for England became a touchstone for most later historians.

Except for SCOFIELD's relatively balanced chronicle of the negotiations, little work in subsequent decades addressed this treaty with much additional specificity or analysis. At first, only those scholars who constituted a relatively isolated subfield of English economic history gave it much notice. One of these, POSTAN, de-emphasized the non-economic basis for the treaty, never mentioning preparations for a new French war as a cause. However, he did stress the connection between the Hanse and Edward's attempt to return to the throne in 1471, and he credited support by the Hanse as the main reason behind England's nearly complete surrender to the demands of the Hanseatic league at Utrecht. But Postan did not think the English were as compliant as earlier historians had suggested; rather, they took a strong stand at the conference for as long as they realistically could. Overall, Postan subscribed to the prevailing belief that the treaty gave the Hansards tremendous powers that would not be reduced significantly until the mid-1500s.

JACOB, who wrote the standard and still influential text on the 15th century, added little to our understanding of Utrecht but did put it into a larger political context as part of a series of "anti-alien measures". Scholars at this time were beginning to examine early English xenophobia, perhaps as a result of an influx of immigrants into Britain in the aftermath of World War II and the final dismantling of the empire. Jacob called attention particularly to English piracy and seizures of Hanse goods and property as background to the peace conference. The need to protect English interests as part of an "international mercantile system" was behind much of the nation's policy concerning whether to protect foreigners or to exclude them.

The first major study of the Hanse and its foreign relations appeared in DOLLINGER (1964). Dollinger held that assistance from Danzig was largely responsible for Edward's return to the English throne; and that his neglecting to fulfil his promise to support the city, in favour of Cologne, precipitated the conflict. Piracy was also a factor. At Utrecht, Danzig was most demanding, refusing to allow the English to re-establish rights in Prussia and not ratifying the final treaty until 1476. As a Frenchman, Dollinger was the first to note the "good relations between the Hanse and France" that also resulted from Utrecht. With the dissolution of Burgundy soon thereafter, the peace became "one of the great events in the history of the Hansa", strengthening its international status and its commercial position throughout Europe.

The most notable biography of Edward IV, by ROSS, relates the treaty to larger concerns of England's foreign policy, especially the desire to renew the French war. In the king's putting "political before commercial advantage" the English "saw their share of trade with Germany and the Baltic dwindle". If there was any success, it was ephemeral, as the subsequent invasion of France was not successful either. Ross played down the role of piracy in the conflict, though, noting that it decreased dramatically after 1471.

LLOYD questioned many of the assumptions that had guided earlier understandings of Utrecht. First, he does not believe that the English government at the time gave a high priority to economic and commercial issues, and thus he agreed that the French war was the major impetus for making peace. In fact, a main objective of the peace commission was to try to arrange a political alliance with the Duke of Burgundy. Neither does Lloyd believe, as past scholars did, that the treaty of Utrecht was a "diplomatic disaster" for England. The treaty rights in Prussia had never been enforced, and the English continued to press their claims for reciprocity even after the conference concluded, asserting that the treaty had guaranteed this to them. In another important revelation, Lloyd showed that parliament tied the king's hands in one respect by passing an act, at the time, reinstating the Hanse franchises which had been in existence before 1473.

A more recent work on the treaty is FUDGE's detailed examination. This was one of the first studies to benefit from the new sources that became available after the reunification of Germany in 1990. Fudge tells the story of the negotiations vividly, stressing the internal disunity of the Hanseatic towns and their consequent inability to preserve many of their gains at Utrecht by the end of the century. He blames both the English and the Hansards for the failure of the treaty to achieve lasting peace, and in this way posits a less Anglocentric perspective. Fudge profitably incorporates much of the current German-language scholarship of Stuart Jenks and Walter Stark.

BEN LOWE

See also Hanseatic League

V

Versailles, Treaty of

see World War I: Versailles and Other Treaties

Victoria 1819–1901

Queen of Great Britain and Ireland; empress of India

Benson, E.F., *Queen Victoria*, London and New York: Longmans Green, 1935; abridged edition, as *Queen Victoria: An Illustrated Biography*, London: Chatto and Windus, 1987

Hardie, Frank, *The Political Influence of Queen Victoria, 1861–1901*, London: Oxford University Press, 1935; 2nd edition, corrected, London and New York: Oxford University Press, 1938

Hibbert, Christopher, *Queen Victoria: A Personal History*, London: HarperCollins, and New York: Basic Books, 2000

Lee, Sidney, *Queen Victoria: A Biography*, London: Smith Elder, 1902; New York: Macmillan, 1903; revised edition, 1904

Longford, Elizabeth, *Queen Victoria, R.I.*, London: Weidenfeld and Nicolson, 1964; as *Queen Victoria: Born to Succeed*, New York: Harper and Row, 1965

Munich, Adrienne, *Queen Victoria's Secrets*, New York: Columbia University Press, 1996

St Aubyn, Giles, *Queen Victoria: A Portrait*, London: Sinclair-Stevenson, 1991; New York: Atheneum, 1992

Strachey, Lytton, *Queen Victoria*, London: Chatto and Windus, and New York: Harcourt Brace, 1921

Weintraub, Stanley, *Victoria: Biography of a Queen*, London: Allen and Unwin, 1987; as *Victoria: An Intimate Biography*, New York: Dutton, 1987; revised edition, London: John Murray, 1996

Woodham-Smith, Cecil, *Queen Victoria: Her Life and Times*, vol. 1, *1819–1861*, London: Hamish Hamilton, 1972; as *Queen Victoria: From Her Birth to the Death of the Prince Consort*, New York: Knopf, 1972

According to a compilation as of the year 2000, there existed at least 492 books devoted to the life and reign of Queen Victoria – a number larger than that for any other woman in history except for the Virgin Mary, Joan of Arc, and Jane Austen.

At the time of her death, it was widely taken for granted that Victoria had served as an altogether appropriate symbol of personal morality, bourgeois domesticity, and imperial grandeur, as well as royal longevity and societal continuity. At the same time, it was generally assumed that during her almost four decades of widowhood she had remained a non-partisan head of state who took less and less interest in day-to-day politics and participated erratically at best in the ceremonial life which had been central to her early years and which was to become the defining role of Britain's monarchy during the 20th century.

Such an approach is certainly reflected in LEE's biography, which was the outgrowth of the article he had contributed shortly before to the *Dictionary of National Biography*, a monument to late Victorian scholarship of which Lee was co-editor. Although Lee portrays the "public Victoria" very sympathetically, he is critical both of "her imperious and somewhat impatient temperament" and of her neglect of ceremonial responsibilities during her widowhood. Lee was able to flesh out his account of the queen's private life during the years before Albert's death in 1861 by drawing on numerous published memoirs – most significantly the Greville memoirs (the candid multi-volume diary of the clerk of the Privy Council) as well as the five-volume biography of the prince consort by Theodore Martin (to which Victoria had contributed numerous recollections and personal diary entries).

By the time that STRACHEY produced his life in 1921, he was also able to use Victoria's published diary (up to the time of her marriage) and the first three volumes of her letters. These focused on the period up to 1861, a fact that helps to explain why three-quarters of Strachey's biography, which has remained in print to this day, was devoted to the first half of the queen's life. One of Strachey's professed purposes was to re-establish the historian as an artist, converting raw grape juice into a "subtle and splendid wine" and replacing the stolid Victorian three-decker with a pointed pen-portrait. Strachey had applied this method to Cardinal Manning, Florence Nightingale, Thomas Arnold, and General Charles Gordon in *Eminent Victorians* (1918). In the process, he had also skewered the evangelical Christianity, earnestness, prudishness, and pomposity of the Victorians against which, as a key member of the Bloomsbury group, he was rebelling. In the case of Queen Victoria, however, Strachey (according to G.M. Trevelyan) "went out to curse and stayed to bless". In the words of Strachey's own biographer, "the astringent, incisive style has softened into a kindlier mood of mellow and affectionate nostalgia". The scholarship was solid, and yet the book read like a "consummately written romantic novel".

Although Strachey's work continues to cast its spell, his could hardly be the last word, and in 1935 BENSON made use of the six additional volumes of Victoria's letters that had been published in the interval as well as the queen's published correspondence with Willliam Ewart Gladstone. Benson devotes as much space to the years after Albert's death as to Victoria's earlier life, and he pays far greater heed to Victoria's behind-the-scenes political partisanship during her widowhood. HARDIE was the first scholar to focus on the (to him) surprising degree to which a supposedly ceremonial monarch had influenced political appointments and decisions during those same years. More recent historians have devoted articles but no further full-length books to Victoria's role in politics and diplomacy.

A new era in scholarship on the queen opened with the publication of LONGFORD's carefully documented work in 1964. It remains the most thorough and persuasive of the full-length biographies of Victoria. For the first time an experienced scholar had been given access to the wealth of unpublished manuscript material that remained in the royal archives, including the long excerpts from the queen's daily journal that had been copied (and at times edited) by her youngest daughter, Beatrice, before the originals were destroyed. It was during the 1960s also that biographers were first able to make use of the four-decade correspondence between Queen Victoria and her eldest daughter, also called Victoria; in those letters, the queen showed herself at her most candid, opinionated, and illuminating. WOODHAM-SMITH drew on the same materials for a more detailed account of the first half of Victoria's life.

Approaching the subject as a specialist in Anglo-American literature, WEINTRAUB – in a work only fitfully documented – draws on these materials and some others to paint a far more jaundiced portrait of the queen. He persuaded at least one reviewer, David Cannadine, that fundamentally the queen "was callous, insensitive, obstinate, outspoken, capricious and bigoted" as well as inordinately selfish. ST AUBYN focuses somewhat less than Weintraub on the queen's personal life, and his approach is admirably balanced. Unfortunately, his book lacks footnotes and endnotes altogether. St Aubyn concedes, moreover, that Longford's work remains "the envy and despair of those who venture to follow her". MUNICH is one of several feminist cultural theorists to deal with Victoria. Her book includes a valuable collection of contemporary cartoons and verses, and its disparate essays throw light on topics such as the queen's absorption with death and devotion to animals. At the same time the work is marred by numerous factual errors, and Munich prefers jargon-filled speculation to careful documentation. Among the authors of full-length studies of the queen, professional historians have been notable for their absence. HIBBERT, a prolific author, does not significantly alter the prevailing historiography, but he writes very well, and his documentation is better than Weintraub's or St Aubyn's.

WALTER L. ARNSTEIN

See also Albert

Victorian Era: General Surveys

Gilmour, Robin, *The Victorian Period: The Intellectual and Cultural Context of English Literature, 1830–1890*, London and New York: Longman, 1993
Guy, Josephine M., *The Victorian Age: An Anthology of Sources and Documents*, London and New York: Routledge, 1998
Hoppen, K. Theodore, *The Mid-Victorian Generation, 1846–1886*, Oxford: Clarendon Press, and New York: Oxford University Press, 1998
Matthew, Colin (editor), *The Nineteenth Century: The British Isles, 1815–1901*, Oxford and New York: Oxford University Press, 2000
Mitchell, Sally (editor), *Victorian Britain: An Encyclopedia*, Chicago and London: St James Press, and New York: Garland, 1988
Newsome, David, *The Victorian World Picture: Perceptions and Introspections in an Age of Change*, London: John Murray, and New Brunswick, New Jersey: Rutgers University Press, 1997
Victorian Studies (periodical), 1957–
Young, G.M., *Victorian England: Portrait of an Age*, London and New York: Oxford University Press, 1936; annotated edition, edited by George Kitson Clark, 1977

The explosion of documentary evidence which the Victorian age produced has helped make it the most intensively studied of any period of British history. As result, in a brief introduction of this sort, it is possible to consider only works which make some effort to encompass the period as a whole.

The Victorian period occupies a significant place in the national history curriculum in England and Wales and its equivalent in Scotland; thus we find a multitude of introductory texts aimed at readers of all ages. The most authoritative guide currently available is HOPPEN's, a volume in the New Oxford History of England, magisterial in judgement and monumental in size. Although it explicitly excludes the earliest years and the last decade and a half of Victoria's reign, this is as close as anything comes to an "official" history of the Victorian period, drawing together a huge range of recent scholarship to present a detailed picture of all aspects of the history of the British Isles. The four sections of the work provided almost book-length studies of social architecture, politics, economic and cultural history, and the empire.

If Hoppen's study has weaknesses, they are in its restricted survey of the cultural history of the period, and in the relative lack of attention to the ramifications of gender, a topic which has recently engaged much attention. Both deficiencies are met in the much less daunting introduction provided by MATTHEW's parallel volume from the Short Oxford History of the British Isles. This work has a focus that extends beyond the commencement of the Victorian period; nevertheless, it conceives of its subject as the "Victorian century". Its eight essays by leading scholars of the period provide a themed approach and give much greater coverage of cultural history.

Both these volumes explicitly avoid grand characterizations of the period, and in this they reflect recent fashion. Once the early-20th-century modernist reaction against the Victorians – dismissing their society as materialist, hypocritical, complacent, and ugly – had waned, scholars became so acutely aware of the complexity and diversity of the period that few have felt brave enough to attempt broad interpretative studies. This is not to say that there are few books offering the reader a Victorian vista, panorama, or pageant. But most do not have pretensions to comprehending the subtleties, shifts, and shadings of period; they provide a surface view but rarely grasp the inner essentials. The one outstanding exception is YOUNG's portrait, a polemical counterblast against the excesses of anti-Victorianism in the interwar years. Young's study managed both to deny the notion of a monolithic "Victorianism" and to provide a seductive interpretation in which tension between formative influences, such as evangelicalism and utilitarianism, and the contradictory pressures of progress and perplexity was itself installed as a defining Victorian characteristics.

Young's book is not necessarily a natural port of call for the novice. His style is dense and allusive. Explicit citations of sources are few, and – as a later editor was to find to his horror – many of the references were distorted or untraceable. Like many of his successors, Young was most comfortable in the "high Victorian" period of the 1840s to the 1870s, and – as he himself acknowledged in later editions – his coverage of the closing decades was more cursory and less assured. Nevertheless, it is not easy to find a substitute. The 1950s and early 1960s saw a clutch of interpretative studies by Jerome Buckley, Asa Briggs, Walter Houghton, George Kitson Clark, and W.L. Burn which, along with the journal Victorian Studies (from 1957 on) helped establish Victorian studies as a vibrant area of interdisciplinary scholarship. Thereafter, the supply dwindles.

The only recent attempt at a broad interpretative canvas is NEWSOME's. It clearly bears the impress of Young's example, perhaps too much so. Erudite and assured, this is a study of the Victorians as they saw themselves. It provides vivid insights into the world of Victorian letters and the preoccupations and anxieties of the articulate elites, but it carries all the limits of interpretation which reliance on the published record entails. It is also rooted in the scholarship and the scholarly preoccupations of the late 1950s and early 1960s. More satisfactory in many respects is GILMOUR's volume, generally acknowledged to be by far the most accomplished of the numerous texts whose primary function is to provide a context for comprehending the literature of the Victorians. Drawing on the scholarship of literary and intellectual historians, Gilmour provides a down-to-earth picture of the complex forces which shaped the Victorian mentality and the ways in which these beliefs and attitudes resonate in the literature – fiction and non-fiction – of the period.

The Victorian period is well served with published resource materials. A guide to many of these, slightly dated but still useful, can be found in MITCHELL (1988), which also offers nearly a thousand introductory essays on aspects of the period, each with a brief bibliography of key readings. The journal VICTORIAN STUDIES, in addition to publishing much of the best scholarship on the period, albeit with a markedly literary bias, also includes an exhaustive annual bibliography of publications. Most of the steady stream of collections of texts illustrative of the period, emanating from literary studies, has sought to illuminate genre or has attempted to provide "context" through a wide variety of short extracts. One of the most modern and perhaps the most useful of this group is GUY's collection. More substantial than many of its predecessors, it has the two-fold

advantage of allowing itself to present often very substantial chunks from carefully selected texts, arranged thematically, and of providing a series of substantial introductions to these key themes.

MARTIN HEWITT

Viking Seamanship

Andersen, Erik and Bent Andersen, Råsejlet – Dragens Vinge [The Square Sail – The Wing of the Dragon], Roskilde: Vikingeskibshallen, 1989

Andersen, Erik et al., Roar Ege: Skuldelev 3 skibet som arkæologisk eksperiment [Roar Ege: The Skuldelev 3 Ship as an Archaeological Experiment], Roskilde: Vikingeskibshallen, 1997

Bill, Jan, "Ships and Seamanship" in The Oxford Illustrated History of the Vikings, edited by Peter Sawyer, Oxford and New York: Oxford University Press 1997

Bill, Jan, Bjørn Poulsen, Flemming Rieck, and Ole Ventegodt, Dansk søfarts historie, vol. 1, Indtil 1588: Fra stammebåd til skib [Danish History of Seafaring, vol. 1, Until 1588: From Logboat to Ship], Copenhagen: Gyldendal, 1997

Brøgger, A.W. and Haakon Shetelig, Vikingeskipene: Deres forgjengere og etterfølgere, Oslo: Dreyers, 1950; as The Viking Ships: Their Ancestry and Evolution, translated from the Norwegian by Katherine John, Oslo: Dreyers, 1951; revised edition, Los Angeles and Mogensen, Oslo: Dreyer, and London: Stanford, 1953

Christensen, Arne E., "Ships and Navigation" in Vikings: The North Atlantic Saga, edited by William W. Fitzhugh and Elisabeth I. Ward, Washington, DC: Smithsonian Institution Press, 2000

Crumlin-Pedersen, Ole, Viking-Age Ships and Shipbuilding in Hedeby / Haithabu and Schleswig, Schleswig: Archäologisches Landesmuseum der Christian-Albrechts-Universität, and Roskilde: Viking Ship Museum, 1997

Crumlin-Pedersen, Ole, "Ships as Indicators of Trade in Northern Europe 600–1200" in Maritime Topography and the Medieval Town, edited by Jan Bill and Birthe L. Clausen, Copenhagen: National Museum of Denmark, 1999

Haywood, John, Dark Age Naval Power: A Reassessment of Frankish and Anglo-Saxon Seafaring Activity, London and New York: Routledge, 1991

Lund, Niels (editor), Ottar og Wulfstan: To rejsebeskrivelser fra vikingetiden, Roskilde: Vikingeskibshallen, 1983; as Two Voyagers at the Court of King Alfred: The Ventures of Ohthere and Wulfstan Together with the Description of Northern Europe from the Old English Orosius, translated by Christine E. Fell, York: Sessions, 1984

Malmros, Rikke, "Leding og Skjaldekvad: Det elvte århundredes nordiske krigsflåder, deres teknologi og organisation og deres placering i samfundet, belyst gennem den samtidige fyrstedigtning" [Leidang and Scaldic Poetry: The Nordic War Fleets of the 11th Century – Their Technology and Organization, and Their Placing in Society, Illuminated through the Contemporary Princely Poetry], Aarbøger for Nordisk Oldkyndighed og Historie, 1985 (1986): 89–139

McGrail, Seán, *Medieval Boat and Ship Timbers from Dublin*, Dublin: Royal Irish Academy, 1993

Olsen, Olaf and Ole Crumlin-Pedersen, "The Skuldelev Ships: A Report of the Final Underwater Excavation in 1959 and the Salvaging Operation in 1962", *Acta Archaeologica*, 38 (1968): 73–174

Schnall, Uwe, *Navigation der Wikinger: Nautische Probleme der Wikingerzeit im Spiegel der Schriftlichen Quellen*, Oldenburg: Gerhard Stalling, 1975

Sørenson, Anne C., *Ladby: A Danish Ship-Grave from the Viking Age*, Roskilde: Viking Ship Museum, 2001

Discussion of Viking seafaring and seamanship relies largely on a relatively small number of ship finds from the Scandinavian area, especially Norway, western Sweden, Denmark, and northern Germany. Most of the archaeological literature on the topic, and indeed part of the historical literature as well, is therefore written in Scandinavian languages, not easily accessible to English-speaking readers. Furthermore, some key finds have not yet or have only recently reached final publication; this situation has hampered the production of syntheses in English on Viking seamanship. In compiling this bibliography, some preference has been given to literature in English, without omitting key works in other languages.

Scholarly interest in the seamanship of the Vikings first took off after the excavation of the Tune and Gokstad ships in southern Norway in 1867 and 1880. Along with the excavation of the Oseberg ship in 1904 and written and pictorial sources, these finds formed the bulk of evidence available for scholars up to the end of the 1950s. BRØGGER & SHETELIG (1950) presents a synthesis of this material and has remained in common use as a textbook on seafaring in the early Viking age – partly owing to the publication of an English edition and partly owing to a lack of any qualified alternative. This book is, however, seriously outdated on a number of important issues and should be used mainly for its technical descriptions of the Norwegian finds. Its lack of proper bibliographic references also limits its usefulness.

The Ladby ship, excavated in 1934–37 in Denmark, is so far the only Viking-age ship grave excavated outside Norway which provides extensive information about ship construction. The find, dating from the early 10th century, has recently been thoroughly reanalysed by SØRENSEN (2001).

The finding and excavation of the Skuldelev ships in 1957–62, including the earliest finds of specialized Viking-age cargo vessels, provided for the first time an insight into shipbuilding in the late Viking age. The preliminary publication by OLSEN & CRUMLIN-PEDERSEN is a fundamental study in Viking ship construction and will remain fundamental until the planned final publication of the find by Ole Crumlin-Pedersen *et al.* in the series Ships and Boats of the North from the Viking Ship Museum in Roskilde. This publication by Olsen & Crumlin-Pedersen and the publication of the ship finds from Hedeby by CRUMLIN-PEDERSEN (1997) together present the major part of the archaeological material on ships that is available for the study of Viking seafaring during the late 10th century and the 11th century. An important attempt at a modern synthesis of developments in shipbuilding techniques during the Viking age is presented in CRUMLIN-PEDERSEN (1999); it is based on the relatively recent dendrochronological dating of, among others, the Gokstad, Oseberg, and Tune ships. This article discusses, among other things, the date of the introduction of specialized cargo vessels in Scandinavia.

Viking ship finds outside Scandinavia are sparse, but the individual ship timbers from Dublin, described by McGRAIL (1993), illustrate that Scandinavian settlers brought their shipbuilding traditions with them.

The archaeological finds by nature cast light upon the material side of Viking seafaring – ships, boathouses, and blockages of sea routes – and to a much lesser degree upon aspects like organization and navigation. These have been explored mainly on the basis of written sources, especially medieval Scandinavian sagas and poetry. MALMROS (1986) presents a fundamental critique of the previous use of these sources in the discussion of Viking-age seafaring; this article is a good starting-point for anyone who wants to use older studies that discuss the topic on the basis of these sources. Malmros also suggests the existence of fairly homogeneous Viking fleets in the late Viking age, on the basis of her analyses of, primarily, the poems. The article includes an extensive summary in English.

Viking-age navigation is a problem which has occupied many scholars and which can mainly be discussed on the basis of written and iconographic sources, even though there have been a few archaeological finds of sounding leads and other instruments. Although SCHNALL (1975) is no longer completely up to date, it is the entry point to this discussion today; Schnall efficiently debunks many of the ill-founded hypotheses that dominated the debate before 1975. LUND (1983; in English, 1984) is a valuable contribution to the study of Viking navigation; it includes expert commentary upon the travel reports by Ohthere and Wulfstan in King Alfred's *Orosius*.

A central and long-lasting discussion regarding Viking seafaring concerns the date of the introduction of the sail. On the basis of historical sources, HAYWOOD (1991) rejected the view held by many that the sail was introduced as late as the 7th century. BILL *et al.* (1997), on the basis of archaeological sources, defend a late entry date, emphasizing that pre-Viking Scandinavia may not have been very coherent in terms of shipbuilding traditions; their work also offers the most extensive update to Brøgger & Shetelig available, including themes such as Viking navigation and the transatlantic journeys. ANDERSEN & ANDERSEN (1989) present the most comprehensive attempt yet made to analyse and reconstruct sail and rigging on Viking ships.

Experimental archaeology has, during the past decades, provided much new knowledge about the building and sailing of Viking ships. ANDERSEN *et al.* have published the experience from the construction in 1982–84 and subsequent tests of a copy of the small cargo carrier Skuldelev 3 at the Viking Ship Museum in Roskilde. An extract of this was to appear in English in the publication of the Skuldelev find mentioned above.

Much of this literature is not easily accessible unless the reader has knowledge of both Scandinavian languages and ship terminology. For the reader who wants a quick, up-to-date overview in English, the two articles by BILL (1997) and CHRISTENSEN (2000) can be recommended.

JAN BILL

See also Orkney and Shetland Islands

Viking Settlement

Bailey, Richard N., *Viking Age Sculpture in Northern England*, London: Collins, 1980

Cameron, Kenneth (editor), *Place-Name Evidence for the Anglo-Saxon Invasion and Scandinavian Settlements: Eight Studies*, Nottingham: English Place-Name Society, 1975. (Collection of reprinted essays including three by Cameron himself on "Scandinavian Settlement in the Territory of the Five Boroughs Parts 1–3", previously printed 1965, 1970, 1971)

Crawford, Barbara (editor), *Scandinavian Settlement in Northern Britain: Thirteen Studies of Place-Names in Their Historical Context*, London and New York: Leicester University Press, 1995

Fellows-Jensen, Gillian, *Scandinavian Settlement Names in Yorkshire*, Copenhagen: Institut for Navneforskning / Kommission hos Akademisk Forlag, 1972

Fellows-Jensen, Gillian, *Scandinavian Settlement Names in the East Midlands*, Copenhagen: Institut for Navneforskning / Kommission hos Akademisk Forlag, 1978

Fellows-Jensen, Gillian, *Scandinavian Settlement Names in the North-West*, Copenhagen: Institut for Navneforskning / C.A. Reitzels Forlag, 1985

Fellows-Jensen, Gillian, "Vikings in the British Isles: The Place-Name Evidence" in *Vikings in the West*, edited by Steffen Stummann Hansen, special issue of *Acta Archaeologica*, supplementum 2, 71 (2000): 135–46

Graham-Campbell, James, "The Early Viking Age in the Irish Sea Area" in *Ireland and Scandinavia in the Early Viking Age*, edited by Howard B. Clarke, Máire Ní Mhaonaigh, and Raghnall Ó Floinn, Dublin: Four Courts Press, 1998

Graham-Campbell, James and Colleen E. Batey, *Vikings in Scotland: An Archaeological Survey*, Edinburgh: Edinburgh University Press, 1998

Hall, Richard, *English Heritage Book of Viking Age York*, London: Batsford, 1994

The *Anglo-Saxon Chronicle* records that there was organized Scandinavian settlement in eastern England in 876, 877, and 880. Other documentary sources record the settlement in Wirral of a fugitive band of Vikings who had been expelled from Dublin in 902 and that grants of land were made to Scandinavians in the eastern part of Durham in the late 9th and early 10th centuries. No contemporary or near-contemporary records of Scandinavian settlement exist for other parts of Britain, and it was once thought that settlement in Scotland might have begun as much as three-quarters of a century earlier than in England. GRAHAM-CAMPBELL, however, has argued convincingly that the initial phase of seasonal raiding in Scotland did not give way to permanent settlement until towards the middle of the 9th century, at about the same time as the establishment of the documented bases for raiding and trading across the Irish Sea in Ireland. Settlement in the Isle of Man would seem to have been contemporary with, or slightly later than, that in England. Such limited Scandinavian settlement as there was in north Wales would seem to belong to the early 10th century.

For knowledge of the distribution of Scandinavian settlement we are largely dependent on place-names and on a close analysis of these by scholars with the appropriate linguistic background.

Fifty years ago the available distribution maps of Scandinavian place-names could at best reveal areas of mainly Danish or mainly Norwegian settlement, with some indication of the density of settlement. Pioneering work on how place-names can be made to reveal much more about the interaction of the Danish settlers with the English was published by CAMERON in his studies of the names in the Five Boroughs (Leicester, Lincoln, Nottingham, Stamford, and Derby). His methods were applied and refined by FELLOWS-JENSEN in her studies of the names in Yorkshire (1972), the east Midlands (1978), and the north-west (1985). FELLOWS-JENSEN (2000) presents a convenient brief survey of the distribution of settlement in the eight main areas of settlement in England and Scotland, as well as in the Isle of Man and the restricted areas of settlement near the coasts in Wales and Ireland. The place-names of Scandinavian origin in Britain vary greatly, depending on whether they were coined by Danes or by Norwegians and on the number of, and language spoken by, those among whom they settled. Only in Shetland and Orkney, to judge from the place-names, would the Scandinavians seem largely to have driven out the previous inhabitants. A useful volume of essays on place-names and settlement in northern Britain, edited by CRAWFORD, presents specimen studies of eight areas in Scotland and four in England. These all concentrate on pointing out how views on the settlement have changed as a result of recent research.

The contribution that can be made by archaeological research towards determining the extent of Scandinavian settlement is small. GRAHAM-CAMPBELL & BATEY, however, discuss the Viking-period settlements in Scotland and show how these can be distinguished from late Norse settlements. No certain find of a Scandinavian farm site or village site has been made in England, probably because the rural sites are mostly still occupied. The excavations in York, however, offer much information about urban settlement. HALL describes the impressive work that has made it possible to distinguish between the several chronological layers of settlement in York and demonstrates what the finds have revealed about the buildings and streets, crafts and industries, food and clothing, life and death of the mixed Anglo-Scandinavian population of the city and about contacts with Dublin. The finds from Dublin, as well as finds from the trading centres or beach markets in north Wales, are touched on briefly by Graham-Campbell.

Scandinavian cultural influence on the settlements in Britain is reflected in the clothing, silver ornaments, personal equipment, and decorated weapons that have been found in excavated graves from the pagan period; these are discussed by Graham-Campbell, Graham-Campbell & Batey, and Hall. The Scandinavians also left their mark on the art of Viking-age Britain. BAILEY has shown how the stone-carving tradition of Christian Anglo-Saxon England combined with Scandinavian ornamental traditions to produce a wealth of Anglo-Scandinavian sculpture, both crosses and the so-called hogback tombstones, which would seem to have originated in northern Yorkshire and spread from there over much of northern England and south-western and eastern Scotland in the wake of settlers from the Danelaw. Bailey has taken care to point out, however, that a liking for Scandinavian art styles does not necessarily mean that a man is a Scandinavian or of Scandinavian descent. Bailey's comments were a major inspiration for Fellows-Jensen's realization that a similar comment can be made about the use of Scandinavian place-names. In some areas of Britain, certainly the central Lowlands of Scotland and the Cardiff area, and probably the Isle of Man, many of the Scandinavian place-names seem likely to have been bestowed after the Viking age by settlers from the Danelaw rather than by Scandinavians fresh from their homelands.

GILLIAN FELLOWS-JENSEN

See also Alfred the Great; Alfred–Guthrum Treaty; Brunanburh, Battle of; Cnut; Danelaw; Edington, Battle of; Eric Bloodaxe; Maldon, Battle of; Orkney and Shetland Islands

Villiers, George

see **Buckingham, George Villiers, 1st Duke of**

Wages and Rents   medieval period

Beveridge, W.H., "Wages in the Winchester Manors",
    Economic History Review, 1st series, 7 (1936): 22–44
Beveridge, W.H., "Westminster Wages in the Manorial Era",
    Economic History Review, 2nd series, 8 (1956): 18–35
Britnell, R.H., *The Commercialisation of English Society,
    1000–1500*, Cambridge and New York: Cambridge
    University Press, 1993
Brown, Henry Phelps and Sheila V. Hopkins, *A Perspective of
    Wages and Prices*, London and New York: Methuen, 1981
Farmer, David L., "Prices and Wages" in *The Agrarian
    History of England and Wales*, vol. 2, *1042–1350*, edited
    by H.E. Hallam, Cambridge and New York: Cambridge
    University Press, 1986
Farmer, David L., "Prices and Wages" in *The Agrarian
    History of England and Wales*, vol. 3, *1348–1500*, edited
    by Edward Miller, Cambridge and New York: Cambridge
    University Press, 1991
Hilton, R.H., "Rent and Capital Formation in Feudal Society"
    in *The English Peasantry in the Later Middle Ages: The
    Ford Lectures for 1973 and Related Studies*, Oxford:
    Clarendon Press, 1975; as *Proceedings of the Second
    International Conference of Economic History*, 1962
Kosminsky, E.A., "The Evolution of Feudal Rent in England
    from the XIth to the XVth Centuries", *Past & Present*, 7
    (1955): 12–36
Rigby, S.H., *English Society in the Later Middle Ages: Class,
    Status, and Gender*, Basingstoke: Macmillan, and New
    York: St Martin's Press, 1995
Rogers, James E. Thorold, *Six Centuries of Work and Wages:
    The History of English Labour*, 2 vols, London: Swan
    Sonnenschein, 1884; several reprints

Wages and rents in medieval England have often been studied separately: wages are often paired with prices in wage and price series, and rents are discussed as elements of the "feudal" economy or within studies of manors or landlords. Historical discussion of both, however, relies heavily on manorial sources before the 15th century.

Between 1866 and 1902 J.E. Thorold Rogers published a seven-volume wage and price series. *A History of Agriculture and Prices in England* includes a dated but comprehensive account of wages and prices for the medieval period. Rogers's figures must be treated with caution because he accepted wages at face value and assumed uniform measures; nevertheless, his series remains a starting-point for discussion of medieval prices and wages, and it served as a reference for others, such as Beveridge, Brown & Hopkins, and Farmer.

ROGERS (1884) is a narrative survey based on the early volumes of the series; it is influenced by 19th-century laissez-faire liberal economics. Rogers concludes that peasant labourers in the Middle Ages enjoyed a relatively advantageous position, but that c.1400 to 1525 was the "golden age of the English labourer" in terms of real wages. Higher agricultural wages around London and the eastern counties are also identified and are attributed to the influence of guilds, a higher cost of living, and competition from manufacturing. Rogers's "golden age" and his rejection of demographic factors in wage fluctuations have been much debated by subsequent historians, but, like his wage and price series, this work is worth reviewing as a reference point for subsequent studies.

A more sophisticated investigation into wages and prices by BEVERIDGE in the 1930s resulted in articles about wages on manors in Winchester (1936) and Westminster (1956) during the medieval period. Beveridge adds fresh data and takes a more cautious approach to analysis but generally confirms Rogers's broad picture of trends. The collection of essays by BROWN & HOPKINS includes their classic examination of seven centuries of building wages (from 1264 on) relative to prices of consumables, based on their own wage and price series (*Economica*, 23, November 1956). In general, Brown & Hopkins, like Beveridge, agree with Rogers's trends. Although Brown & Hopkins did not attempt to establish real wages in the modern sense, their work is still important as a systematic model for the study of wages and consumption, as well as for its contributions to later debate on costs of living.

FARMER seeks to reconcile and add to previous studies by Rogers, Beveridge, and Brown & Hopkins. His well-written and thorough chapters offer an overview of medieval wages. He presents a detailed study of wages of manorial servants and casual employees, tables of prices and wages by year, and discussion of methodological issues. He also briefly addresses the cost of living. Wage rates as calculated by Farmer are quite close to both Rogers's and Beveridge's series. Farmer is more negative than Rogers about the position of agrarian laborers before 1350 but does conclude that by the mid-15th century most wages purchased significantly more than previously. Farmer also notes, like Rogers, that in general wages in London appear appreciably higher throughout the medieval period.

Rents have a much less developed historiography than wages, but as with the study of wages, the sources are primarily agrarian before the 15th century. The manorial rents in these sources are combinations of labour services, rents in kind, and money. Peasants' rents have been investigated as part of a debate over the evolution of money rents and larger ideological issues, and in manorial case studies too numerous to identify here. The study of leases involving knights and the nobility, in contrast, has focused on military and legal aspects of their tenure.

KOSMINSKY (a historian in the Soviet Union) addressed the "problem of the evolution of feudal rent" as represented by extractions in labour, cash, and kind from peasants *c.*1066–1500. He contrasts interpretations of the "liberal-positivist school" (including Rogers) with revisionist interpretations offered by M.M. Postan (who emphasizes demographic factors) on the subject of labour services, villeinage, commutation, and money rents. Kosminsky offers a chronological scheme for fluctuation between feudal rents and money rents, culminating in "crisis of feudalism" in the 14th century and the abandonment of the demesne labour system. The classic essay by HILTON (an English Marxist) emphasizes the burdens of tenancy, including generally high levels of rents, in limiting capital formation by the peasantry. Hilton agrees with Rogers and Farmer that conditions after the mid-14th century, including lower rents and changes in land use, favoured tenants.

A number of works since the 1950s, particularly manorial case studies, extended the historical understanding of labour and tenancy. Additional works examined manorial leases and feudal tenures in some depth. Building on the sources, methodology, and interpretations presented in these studies, more recent syntheses have looked at wages and rents, along with other elements, in integrated contexts. BRITNELL presents wages and rents as part of a larger process of commercialization that transformed the economy and society in the medieval period. His study stresses innovative aspects of economic development, placing peasants' rents and manorial wages within the context of landlords' incomes and the increasing importance of cash transactions in the national economy. RIGBY places the examination of labour, wages, feudal rents, tenancy, and other elements within an interpretive framework – social closure theory. Rigby's text is for undergraduates and is based largely on secondary works; but it has some quite dense discussion of theoretical constructs, and Rigby offers valuable introductions to a number of alternative interpretations that have coloured investigation into wages and rents (as well as other socioeconomic elements) in medieval England. The work of Britnell, Rigby, and others represents a move away from the study of wages and rents in isolation, as well as movement towards the integration of rural and urban elements.

LORI A. GATES

See also Feudal Tenures; Manorial Economy

Wales before Union with England: Early Kingdoms

Dark, K.R., *Civitas to Kingdom: British Political Continuity, 300–800*, Leicester and New York: Leicester University Press, 1994

Davies, Wendy, *Wales in the Early Middle Ages*, Leicester: Leicester University Press, 1982

Dumville, David, "Sub-Roman Britain: History and Legend", *History*, new series, 62 (1977): 173–92

Lloyd, John Edward, *A History of Wales from the Earliest Times to the Edwardian Conquest*, 2 vols, London and New York: Longmans Green, 1911

Maund, Kari, *The Welsh Kings*, Stroud, Gloucestershire; and Charleston, South Carolina: Tempus, 2000

LLOYD's account of the kingdoms of medieval Wales remains a classic work of historiography; it is to a certain extent a period piece but is nevertheless an invigorating introduction to the period. The limitations of Lloyd's Edwardian perspective, however, are particularly prominent in his treatment of the early period, for which he put much faith in nebulous "tradition". For example, 9th-century sources say that a leader called Cunedda, with eight of his sons, came from Manaw of the Gododdin (south-east Scotland) to Wales and expelled the Irish who had settled there; Cunedda's sons are said to have given their names to Welsh kingdoms, subkingdoms, and *cantrefi*. Lloyd accepted an underlying historicity of some sort in this "tradition" and accepted the existence of an historical Cunedda, representing a Brittonic dynasty from the "Old North".

Lloyd's outlook, mediated through succeeding generations of historians, held the field for about 60 years, until DUMVILLE reformed our understanding of the early medieval evidence for the Welsh kingdoms, their dynasties, and their chronology. He has shown that Gildas's *De excidio Britanniae* was the starting-point for all medieval historiography. Magnus Maximus, as the only "British" emperor identifiable in early Wales and as a person of the greatest historical significance in Gildas's work, became the founding figure of independent Roman Britain. In 9th-century historiography he has developed an invented family through which Brittonic rulers claim descent from him. He appears both as the last Roman emperor in Britain and as the first ruler of an independent Britain, from whom all legitimate power flowed. From his death, therefore, begins the history of the independent Brittonic kingdoms. This view is attested to for three major Welsh kingdoms: for Gwynedd and Powys in the ninth-century records, and for Dyfed in a 10th-century text. We also see that the story of Cunedda, which seeks to justify the creation of the kingdoms of north and west Wales, presented a welcome parallel of an outside dynasty coming to power after the rise of the second dynasty of Gwynedd in 826.

DARK, who has provided the most recent interpretation of the origins of Welsh kingdoms, sees a continuity of political structures in western and northern Britain from late Roman times through the early Middle Ages. The origin of the dynasty of sub-Roman Gwynedd is to be sought in local civilian society rather than in northern Britain or Ireland, as the Cunedda legend suggests. The name Gwynedd (Venedotia) derives from a tribal name, Venii, which superseded that of the Ordovices, whose territory may have extended from Rhyd Orddwy in Flintshire to Cantref Orddwy in Merionethshire, with Cantref Orddwy as the heartland of early Gwynedd. Despite the shift in political focus, the kingdom of Gwynedd is still seen as a post-Roman manifestation of the pre-Roman Ordovices. Maelgwn, based on Anglesey, is seen as a subking who seized the overkingship of the Ordovices, based in Merioneth. Powys is the successor to the sub-Roman territory of the Cornovii, whose political centre was at Wroxeter and was later relocated to the hill-fort of the Wrekin. The name Powys, from Latin *pagenses*, "country dwellers", is explained as either propagandist manipulation to negate rural opposition to urban rule or, alternatively, as analogous to Dumnonia, "the people of the land". Dyfed and Brycheiniog, which later formed the essence of the kingdom of Deheubarth, are the only areas where dynastic origins may be explained in relation to migration from outside Roman Britain. In the case of Dyfed, this migration may have occurred within a Romano-British context, and before the establishment of the sub-Roman kingdom. The British kingdoms of Dyfed and Brycheiniog originated in Irish aristocratic, and perhaps folk, migrations into the areas. The *civitas* of the Demetae, Dyfed, was relatively unromanized, and internal disunity may have led to both the seemingly rapid and peaceful Roman conquest of the area in the 1st century and the apparently equally rapid and peaceful Irish colonization, establishing its sub-Roman dynasty. An approved Irish population group may have been introduced by late or sub-Roman authorities to protect the *civitas*: this would explain the continuity of elite sites and rapid integration. Brycheiniog was also apparently founded in the sub-Roman period, and it maintained an Irish identity, Brychan being an Irish name. The spread of dedications to St David may link it to the west as a Dimetian subgroup. Dark's interpretation is, in general, somewhat speculative but points a way forward for further work.

DAVIES provided the first serious replacement for the first volume of Lloyd's *History of Wales*. Lloyd's comprehensive account of the political geography of medieval Wales is based on the post-12th-century viewpoint of the Welsh law-books, which provides an unchanging framework; Davies, on the other hand, has rejected Lloyd's reliance on the Welsh laws, treating them as sources appropriate only to the 13th century. Davies provides a much clearer sense of chronological development, but he points to the continuity of Gwynedd and Dyfed as political units; and in both cases, dynastic change preceded expansion. In the 9th century, Powys was assimilated by Gwynedd and Ceredigion by Dyfed; thus kingdoms might be absorbed, but new units did not emerge.

MAUND has furnished a straightforward political history of medieval Wales, in contrast to Davies's more thematic approach. Maund's is the first detailed narrative history of the Welsh kings since Lloyd. Maund stresses the importance of lineage to the native Welsh princes, and the role of genealogy – often manipulated by pseudo-history and legend – in the dynastic struggles of the early Middle Ages. This approach rests on the contribution that historians like Dumville have made to the transformation of our understanding of the role of early medieval historiography and genealogy in political culture, and its relationship to our historical perceptions. It is also the first extensive account of Welsh political history to encompass this new comprehension of the sources for its early medieval past, and it adds detail to Davies's broad brush strokes.

JOHN REUBEN DAVIES

See also Gruffydd ap Llywelyn; Montgomery, Treaty of; Rhodri "the Great" and Hywel "the Good"; Rhys ap Gruffydd

Wales: Medieval Period

Carr, A.D., *Medieval Wales*, Basingstoke: Macmillan, and New York: St Martin's Press, 1995

Davies, R.R., *Conquest, Coexistence, and Change: Wales 1063–1415*, Oxford: Clarendon Press, and Cardiff: University of Wales Press, 1987; as *The Age of Conquest: Wales 1063–1415*, Oxford: Clarendon Press, and New York: Oxford University Press, 1992

Lloyd, John Edward, *A History of Wales from the Earliest Times to the Edwardian Conquest*, 2 vols, London and New York: Longmans Green, 1911

Walker, David, *Medieval Wales*, Cambridge and New York: Cambridge University Press, 1990

Williams, Glanmor, *Recovery, Reorientation, and Reformation: Wales c.1415–1642*, Oxford and New York: Clarendon Press, and Cardiff: University of Wales Press, 1987; as *Renewal and Reformation: Wales, c.1415–1642*, Oxford: Oxford University Press, 1993

The fact that so much basic research on the history of medieval Wales is still being done has meant that few general surveys of the subject, as opposed to monographs, have so far appeared. When LLOYD's two volumes appeared in 1911, they were greeted by T.F. Tout with the comment that "a book on such lines of such a type has never previously been written". This was the first substantial work on the history of Wales by a professional historian; everything previously written on medieval Wales had been based on David Powel's *Historie of Cambria*, first published in 1584. Lloyd's purpose was to provide a basic narrative account of the history of Wales down to the Edwardian conquest of 1282, based on every available chronicle source and on printed public records and making effective use of evidence from a rich corpus of court poetry. His study can fairly be described as Cambrocentric in its emphasis, rather than as setting events in Wales in the context of contemporary developments in England; it was also rooted in an extensive topographical knowledge and awareness. The first volume, which dealt with the period before the coming of the Normans, has been largely overtaken by later advances in our understanding of early medieval Wales and in archaeology, although a later edition (1939) included an introductory chapter summarizing advances since the book was first published. But the second volume has stood the test of time, and most scholars agree that it is still essential reading for anyone working in this field.

Lloyd took his account as far as 1282, although he did not attempt much discussion of the last 15 years of Welsh independence following the treaty of Montgomery of 1267. Several later historians contemplated a volume on the later Middle Ages, but they all came to the conclusion that a great deal of fundamental research had still to be done before such a work would be feasible. This research took the form of a wide range of articles, many by a small group of younger scholars, especially from about 1950 onwards; eventually a multi-volume history of Wales was planned as a joint venture by the Clarendon Press and the University of Wales Press. DAVIES's book, covering the period between the coming of the Normans and the end of the revolt of Owain Glyn Dŵr (Owen Glendower), appeared in 1987, to be followed shortly by a paperback edition. This is far more than a work of synthesis, as it incorporates much of the author's own research; and it is now generally regarded as the standard treatment of the subject. The title encapsulates the three main themes of the book; Davies sees the extinction of political independence as inevitable, given the vastly superior power of the English crown and state, the concentration of English power and political ambition within Britain after 1204, and the failure of Llywelyn ap Gruffydd's principality to develop the institutions necessary to sustain it. In his view Glyn Dŵr's revolt was the "massive protest of a conquered people", and the Acts of Union of 1536 and 1543 were the logical conclusion of the process of conquest. To Davies the keynote of the whole period is change. This includes the changes which followed the coming of the Normans; the political and institutional changes of the 13th century, coupled with the emergence of a sense of national identity as the princes of Gwynedd strove to create a single Welsh principality; and the social and economic changes of the later medieval period.

WILLIAMS's volume in the same series follows on from Davies's; both authors stress that the traditional benchmark, 1485, is irrelevant to the history of Wales, although Bosworth was perceived by many as a Welsh victory. The end of Glyn Dŵr's revolt is seen as marking the start of the early modern age in Wales, the period between this and the outbreak of the Civil War in 1642 having, in the Welsh context, a certain unity. Williams devotes the first half of his book to 1415–1536, examining in some detail the 15th century, which has on the whole received less attention from historians than the 14th. Like Davies, Williams draws on contemporary poetry, and he provides a brief explanation for the layperson of the Welsh poetic tradition. All the ground is covered, and his discussion of the impact of the revolt complements that provided by Davies in the preceding volume. These two works together provide an excellent and detailed general survey of a long-neglected field in which a few scholars are still engaged in a great deal of fundamental research; the works also include comprehensive bibliographies.

WALKER, as he notes, concentrates on the political history of medieval Wales in all its aspects; his object has been to provide a substantial introductory textbook for those approaching the subject. Unlike the other authors discussed here, he ventures into the pre-Norman period and begins his account with the construction of Offa's Dyke at the end of the 8th century. The emphasis here is on the period between the coming of the Normans and the Edwardian conquest, reflecting the author's own interests and expertise; particular attention is paid to the interplay between the Welsh and the Normans and to the impact of the latter on the Welsh church.

CARR's short book, in the Macmillan series British History in Perspective, is intended as a brief introduction, particularly for undergraduates and the general reader; it deals with period between the death of Gruffydd ap Llywelyn in 1064 and the execution of the Duke of Buckingham, the last of the marcher magnates, in 1521 – a date which Carr considers more significant than 1536. This work is, by its nature, more selective than the other works discussed here. It begins with a historiographical survey of the subject, from Geoffrey of Monmouth to the present day.

A.D. CARR

See also Owain Gwynedd; Union, Acts of, 1536 and 1543

Wales, Principality of

Edwards, J. Goronwy, *The Principality of Wales 1267–1967: A Study in Constitutional History*, Caernarvon: Caernarvonshire Historical Society, 1969

Griffiths, Ralph A. with Roger S. Thomas, *The Principality of Wales in the Later Middle Ages: The Structure and Personnel of Government*, vol. 1, *South Wales, 1277–1536*, Cardiff: University of Wales Press, 1972

Jones, Francis, *The Princes and Principality of Wales*, Cardiff: University of Wales Press, 1969

Roberts, Peter R., "The Union with England and The Identity of 'Anglican' Wales", *Transactions of the Royal Historical Society*, 5th series, vol. 22 (1972): 49–70

Roberts, Peter R., "Wales and England after the Tudor 'Union': Crown, Principality, and Parliament, 1543–1624" in *Law and Government under the Tudors: Essays Presented to Sir Geoffrey Elton*, edited by Claire Cross et al., Cambridge and New York: Cambridge University Press, 1988

Roberts, Peter R., "The English Crown, The Principality of Wales, and the Council in the Marches, 1536–1641" in *The British Problem, c.1534–1707: State Formation in the Atlantic Archipelago*, edited by Brendan Bradshaw and John Morrill, London: Macmillan, and New York: St Martin's Press, 1996

Smith, J. Beverley, *Llywelyn ap Gruffudd: Prince of Wales*, Cardiff: University of Wales Press, 1998

The region which constituted the kingdom of Gwynedd in north-west Wales, ruled over by the native princes of Gwynedd in the 13th century, had since the mid-12th century gradually become the focus of political unity in independent Wales outside the Marches. Owain Gwynedd (d.1170) held his own against Henry II, adopted the title Prince of Gwynedd in the 1150s, and subordinated other Welsh rulers to his overlordship. The policy was continued by his grandson, Llywelyn ap Iorwerth, who was recognized by native rulers in 1230 as Prince of Aberffraw and Lord of Snowdonia. Llywelyn ap Iorwerth's grandson, Llywelyn ap Gruffudd, after the Barons' War, was formally acknowledged by Henry III in the treaty of Montgomery in 1267 as Prince of Wales. He possessed an autonomous principality extending into strategically placed marcher lands which he had gained by conquest, and he ruled as a feudal intermediary between the lesser Welsh lords of *Pura Wallia* and the English crown. Although the treaty signified the height of Llywelyn ap Gruffudd's power, SMITH reveals that it contained many weaknesses, and subsequently Llywelyn's authority was severely curtailed after his first war against Edward I in 1277. Llywelyn died in 1282, during a second war against Edward; thereupon Edward took possession of the principality. In the Statute of Wales, an ordinance of the king's council issued at Rhuddlan in 1284, the principality was attached to the realm of England. In the Lincoln parliament of 1301, the lands were transferred to the heir apparent, Edward of Caernarfon (Caernarvon), who was created Prince of Wales in that year, thus continuing a custom, established by the native princes, that has survived to the present day. However, JONES has proved that two traditional stories are unfounded: the story that Edward I presented his son, born at Caernarfon, to the Welsh people as a prince who knew no English; and the story that the motto "Ich Dien" and the plume of three ostrich feathers were adopted by Edward the Black Prince as symbols of his status.

The Statute of Wales established the framework of government for the principality down to the Act of Union (1536), and Caernarfon and Carmarthen became the chief centres of administration – a theme which GRIFFITHS and EDWARDS have investigated from different angles. The medieval principality retained its identity concerning fiscal organization down to the 19th century, its revenues – fines and rents for the most part – being modest and forming part of the hereditary revenues of the crown. The princes' lands and revenues were always allowed by special royal grant, and sanctioned by act of parliament; the last medieval prince to receive them was Arthur, eldest son of Henry VII. In 1715, George I also granted them to his son and heir when this son was created Prince of Wales.

The medieval structure of government of the principality was entrusted to the justices of north and south Wales and the justice of Chester (who administered Cheshire, Flintshire, and the borderlands) together with two chamberlains, sheriffs, and other officials such as escheators, coroners, and bailiffs. This structure remained, and most heirs apparent to the throne were created Prince of Wales in the later Middle Ages. In 1471 Edward IV created the Council in the Marches to manage his eldest son's domains, including the principality, and in 1473 a separate household was set up for the son, supervised by Anthony, Lord Rivers; and John Alcock, Bishop of Rochester.

On the dissolution of the royal rights of marcher lordships in 1536, the principality was extended to cover the whole of the country. In the Act of Union of that year Wales was assimilated with England and, as ROBERTS has shown, the status of the traditional principality was changed. When there was no Prince of Wales (as, for example, from 1509 to 1610), it was governed as part of the crown lands, and the revenues were administered as if they had issued from those lands. According to Roberts, the birth of Henry VIII's son Edward in 1537 created a new interpretation of the principality, and at that time the position of the prince's patrimony was seriously reconsidered. In the proposals, known as "the effectes devised for Wales" (1540–41), the intention was to unify and enlarge the old principality in western Wales to cover the whole country and make it a patrimony for Edward. That, however, did not materialize; George Owen, the Pembrokeshire historian, believed that preparations had been made to invest Edward with the principality, but apparently Henry's death intervened. If Henry had survived longer, Roberts argues, the power which he had reserved for himself (in what is called the "enabling clause") in the Act of Union of 1543 to legislate independently of parliament for Wales might have been implemented.

From that time onwards "principality" became the title used for the whole of Wales. James I of England revived the title for his sons Henry and Charles, but they inherited neither the medieval patrimony nor the type of patrimony that had been envisaged for Edward in the 1540s. The 17th-century principality was chiefly "honorific", and although the revenues were used to maintain the princes' household, the Council in the Marches no longer functioned as the prince's council. Despite the change in status, the principality and the office of prince continued to be well-received by the Welsh people. There were some long periods when no prince existed – for example, the years

between the deposition of James II in 1688 and the investiture of George, later George II, in 1714. (For the Jacobites, this period would have lasted until 1715, when James II's son James, the "Old Pretender", was created Prince of Wales in exile.) Another gap was between 1820 and 1841.

All told, 21 princes of Wales have been invested, 12 of them in a formal ceremony. Albert Edward, heir apparent to Queen Victoria, was invested in 1841, an event warmly approved by the Welsh; a grand Eisteddfod was held at Caernarfon castle in August of that year to mark the occasion. This principate was the longest thus far, lasting until 1901, when Edward ascended the throne as Edward VII. Only two princes were invested in Wales: the first, Edward Albert (later Edward VIII), son of George V, at Caernarfon castle on 13 July 1911; and the second, Charles, eldest son of Elizabeth II, again at Caernarfon, on 1 July 1969. On the latter occasion there were strongly divided opinions about the event, on nationalist grounds. The Welsh Language Society firmly opposed it, but Plaid Cymru remained neutral.

J. GWYNFOR JONES

See also Marcher Lordships; Montgomery, Treaty of

Wales, Statute of

see **Rhuddlan (Wales), Statute of**

Wallace, William   1270–1305
Scottish leader

Ash, Marinell, "William Wallace and Robert the Bruce: The Life and Death of a National Myth" in *The Myths We Live By*, edited by Raphael Samuel and Paul Thompson, London and New York: Routledge, 1990

Barrow, G.W.S., *Robert Bruce and the Community of the Realm of Scotland*, London: Eyre and Spottiswoode, and Berkeley: University of California Press, 1965; Edinburgh: Edinburgh University Press, 1976; 3rd edition, 1988

Blind Harry, *Hary's Wallace (Vita Nobilissimi Defensoris Scotie Wilelmi Wallace Militis)*, edited by Matthew P. McDiarmid, 2 vols, Edinburgh: Blackwood for the Scottish Text Society, 1968–69

Blind Harry, *Blind Harry's Wallace by William Hamilton of Gilbertfield*, introduced by Elspeth King, Edinburgh: Lauth Press, 1998 (original translation, 1722)

Brown, J.T.T., "The Wallace and the Bruce Restudied" in *Bonner Beiträge zur Anglistik*, Bonn: P. Hanstein, 1900

Craigie, William Alexander (editor), *The Actis and Deidis of Schir William Wallace, 1570*, Edinburgh: Scottish Text Society, 1938; New York: Scholars' Facsimiles and Reprints, 1939

Dunbar, Sir Archibald H., *Scottish Kings: A Revised Chronology of Scottish History, 1005–1625, with Notices of the Principal Events, Tables of Regnal Years, Pedigrees, Calendars, etc.*, Edinburgh: D. Douglas, 1899; 2nd edition, 1906

Fisher, Andrew, *William Wallace*, Edinburgh: Donald, and Atlantic Highlands, New Jersey: Humanities Press, 1986

Gray, D.J., *William Wallace: The King's Enemy*, London: Hale, 1991

Miller, J.F., "Some Additions to the Bibliography of Blind Harry's *Wallace*", *Records of the Glasgow Bibliographical Society*, 6 (1920): 14–19

Morton, Graeme, *William Wallace: Man and Myth*, Stroud, Gloucestershire: Sutton, 2001

Rosebery, Lord, *Wallace, Burns, Stevenson: Appreciations by Lord Rosebery*, Stirling: Eneas Mackay, 1905

Watson, Fiona J., *Under the Hammer: Edward I and Scotland, 1286–1306*, East Linton, East Lothian: Tuckwell Press, 1998

What historians actually know about Sir William Wallace is remarkably scanty, although we do know a little: his victory over superior numbers in the battle of Stirling Bridge in 1297; his appointment as Guardian of Scotland thereafter; his defeat at the battle of Falkirk in 1298; his resignation from the guardianship; his visit to France; then, on his return to Scotland, his betrayal, capture, and execution. Such key events are accepted and can be cross-referenced, although doubts abound with regard to the impartiality of the sources and their place alongside long-standing folk memories. But only meagre details of Wallace's personal history are established. His exact year of birth is debated, as are many details about his family. There are no actual likenesses of Wallace; and because his body was quartered after his execution in 1305, we do not even know his size, although he was reputed to have been a large man. In fact, this lack of information became a basis for ROSEBERY's argument that Wallace must have been the greatest of heroes because, when so few facts are known, his imprint on Scottish national consciousness throughout the generations has nevertheless been so profound and the power of his story has been so enduring.

The key debate has surrounded the veracity of the most comprehensive and most influential account of his exploits by Henry, known as Blind Harry, whose epic verse of 11,861 lines has dominated both academic and popular debate. Harry was by reputation a blind wandering minstrel who had based his account on a "Latin Buk" by John Blair, a contemporary and friend of Wallace. The "Latin Buk", however, does not exist, and it is far from clear that Harry could have been blind at all; certainly, he cannot have been blind from birth, since he gives accurate topographical details of Scotland and shows stylistic debts to Chaucer, Wyntoun, and the *Scotichronicon* – see the discussion in CRAIGIE. The manuscript version of Harry's verse is dated to 1460, according to DUNBAR's evidence; McDiarmid (in BLIND HARRY, 1968–69), suggests 1478; both dates are more than 150 years after Wallace's execution. The first printed edition of the complete manuscript appeared in 1570; MILLER provides the best account of its subsequent publishing history until 1920. Harry's epic was translated into modern Scots by Hamilton of Gilbertfield in 1722; this translation proved remarkably popular, and there were a number of reprints. The last edition of Hamilton's text for nearly a century and a half was published in 1859; it was then reissued with an introduction by Elspeth King (BLIND HARRY, 1998).

Stories of valour and bloodshed can easily inspire the baser varieties of national sentiment; this has ensured a long life for the story of Wallace. Moreover, the paucity of evidence has enabled people of many different political and national outlooks to merge the story into their own heritage, a point argued by MORTON in his survey of the poetry, histories, and monuments celebrating Wallace's life which have appeared since the 18th century especially. Much of the academic work regarding Wallace's impact on Scottish identity in the modern period has concentrated on a comparison with Robert the Bruce. Bruce was also celebrated in epic verse (by Barbour), as BROWN explains best. The presentation of Wallace as a proletarian hero is a contrast with the aristocratic Bruce, who was well-known for his tendency towards political expediency to gain and maintain power. ASH (in an article published posthumously) explains the contrast well.

Popular histories are represented best by GRAY and FISHER, who offer accessible and straightforward accounts of Wallace's life based predominantly on the wide-ranging secondary literature. Modern historians of the medieval period have done impressive work, taking advantage of efforts in the 19th century to gather whatever primary sources survived from Wallace's time, notably the efforts by Joseph Stevenson for the bibliographical Maitland Club in 1841. The most expert use of evidence from primary sources is found first of all in BARROW (1965) – a seminal work, although it is based primarily Bruce's exploits. It should be followed up with the more recent work by WATSON on the period 1286–1307; Watson includes much on Wallace's political and military impact.

GRAEME MORTON

See also Edward I; John Balliol; Robert I, the Bruce

Wallingford or Winchester, Treaty of 1153

Amt, Emilie, *The Accession of Henry II in England: Royal Government Restored, 1149–1159*, Woodbridge, Suffolk; and Rochester, New York: Boydell Press, 1993

Crouch, David, *The Reign of King Stephen, 1135–1154*, Harlow: Longman, 2000

Davis, Ralph H.C., *King Stephen, 1135–1154*, Berkeley: University of California Press, and London: Longman, 1967; 3rd edition, London and New York: Longman, 1990

Holt, James C., "1153: The Treaty of Winchester" in *The Anarchy of King Stephen's Reign*, edited by Edmund King, Oxford: Clarendon Press, and New York: Oxford University Press, 1994

Hudson, John, *Land, Law, and Lordship in Anglo-Norman England*, Oxford: Clarendon Press, and New York: Oxford University Press, 1994

Hyams, Paul R., "Warranty and Good Lordship in Twelfth Century England", *Law and History Review*, 5 (1987): 437–503

Leedom, J.W., "The English Settlement of 1153", *History*, 65 (1980): 347–64

Milsom, S.F.C., *The Legal Framework of English Feudalism*, Cambridge and New York: Cambridge University Press, 1976

Palmer, R.C., "The Origins of Property in England", *Law and History Review*, 3 (1985): 1–50

Richardson, H.G. and G.O. Sayles, "Duke and King" in *The Governance of Mediaeval England from the Conquest to Magna Carta*, Edinburgh: Edinburgh University Press, 1963

Warren, W. Lewis, *Henry II*, London: Eyre Methuen, and Berkeley: University of California Press, 1973

White, Graeme J., "The End of Stephen's Reign", *History*, 75/243 (1990): 3–22

The treaty which brought to a close the civil war of Stephen's reign has been given various titles, helpfully summarized by HOLT. Those who favour the name "Wallingford" stress the importance of the occasion at the end of July or the beginning of August 1153, when the armies of King Stephen and his rival the future King Henry II met there, on opposite sides of the River Thames, and by their refusal to fight forced the protagonists into a truce and preliminary peace negotiations. The name "Winchester" places the emphasis on the formal assembly held in that city on 6 November 1153. Here Stephen recognized Henry as heir to the throne but was allowed to remain king for the rest of his life; pacification measures were also announced, such as the razing of castles and the restoration of lands to their former holders. The issue of a new coinage and other administrative reforms may also have been agreed to on this occasion. DAVIS uses the term "treaty of Westminster", a reference to Stephen's charter issued there in December 1153, setting out the terms previously agreed on for tenure and the succession to the throne, along with elaborate guarantees of their fulfilment.

Whatever the peace settlement is called, it was clearly a process conducted in stages through the second half of 1153. Most historians regard the unexpected death of Stephen's eldest son Eustace on about 17 August of that year as having facilitated the process, although the second son, William, still had to be compensated with grants and confirmations which made him the richest magnate in the kingdom. Of more significance are two debates among historians which centre upon the treaty itself: First, how important was it in ensuring Henry II's accession to the English throne by the close of 1154? Second, what part, if any, did it play in the development of land law in the following decades?

The consensus until recently was that Henry II's ultimate success was all but inevitable by the early 1150s; his military campaign in England during 1153 reached a triumphant conclusion with a settlement which guaranteed him the succession to the throne, and Stephen lived out his remaining months as king ruling, in Davis's words, "by the favour of Duke Henry". This is essentially the view of WARREN and especially of LEEDOM; the latter held that Stephen had been abandoned by most of the magnates by the summer of 1153, that Eustace's death was irrelevant, that by autumn "Henry had won", and that "the Treaty of Winchester marks, in effect, the end of Stephen's reign".

A very different interpretation was put forward by RICHARDSON & SAYLES, who saw Henry in 1153 as "struggling . . . desperately for his lawful inheritance" and "contemplating failure" and pointed out that, had Stephen lived and remained on the throne for several years after the settlement, circumstances might well have changed to Henry's disadvantage.

WHITE has argued in similar terms, seeing the barons as anxious for a compromise which would guarantee their tenures whatever their allegiances in the war, but stressing that Henry was thereby forced into a settlement which obliged him to wait for an indeterminate period with an uncertain outcome. In the event, Stephen died within a year, "too soon for the treaty of 1153 to lose its impact"; but while Stephen remained alive "Henry could never assume that the . . . prize would eventually be his". AMT also notes Henry's continuing vulnerability after the settlement: his "accession was far from assured". CROUCH, on the other hand, while acknowledging that the outcome of the campaign of 1153 was not a foregone conclusion, stresses the cooperation between king and duke following the settlement and Henry's confidence that he would eventually be Stephen's successor. Such comments may be compared with those of HUDSON, who as an authority on 12th-century land law was aware that life-grants (of the type made to Stephen) had frequently led in practice to hereditary succession and therefore permanent alienation; there was still a risk that the kingdom would pass not to Henry, as agreed, but to Stephen's surviving son; in the event, however, this was to be a treaty which, "aided by the rapid demise of the life-tenant Stephen, was an unusually successful example of a settlement involving a life-grant to a losing party".

Several ideas have been put forward on the broader significance of the treaty for the development of land law. Attention has focused on two chronicle accounts of the settlement at Winchester: according to Robert de Torigni, it was sworn that possessions seized by intruders were to be restored to the ancient lawful holders of Henry I's time, and the *Gesta Stephani* reported that the disinherited were to be restored to "their own". MILSOM suggested that the writ of right (whereby the king initiated pleading on title to land in a seigneurial court) developed early in Henry II's reign as a means to implement these provisions, but this view has not found favour, since surviving examples of such writs make no mention of the civil war or its settlement. PALMER saw the arrangements for the throne as providing a model for tenurial settlements in general, with the incumbent (Stephen) remaining in seisin – i.e. possession – for life but the rightful heir (Henry) succeeding thereafter. However, many local disputes of the civil war were clearly settled in other ways, and in any case the settlement gave Stephen the kingdom to hold by right, not merely in seisin. More convincingly, Holt has concluded that the settlement helped to establish the principle that, while inheritances derived from title enjoyed before Henry I's death in 1135 were to be respected, acquisitions made during the war – including those subsequently inherited – might be revoked. HYAMS has cautioned that this principle might have been developed gradually in the early part of Henry II's reign rather than introduced within the settlement of 1153; but whatever its origins, it came to figure prominently under Henry II as a means of resolving disputes, and it was often upheld by the royal courts.

Any interpretation of the treaty must reckon with the fact that the king died in October 1154, less than a year after it had finally been agreed on. In the last months of his life, Stephen extended the area under effective royal control and made some headway with promised reforms such as the destruction of castles and the resolution of tenurial disputes. Had he lived longer, the treaty might have come to be seen as heralding a significant new phase in the reign. On the other hand, peace between Stephen and Henry might not have been sustained, and the treaty might then have been superseded by events. As it was, the settlement of 1153 formed the basis for Henry II's peaceable accession to the throne of England in December 1154, and hence for the successful restoration of royal authority which followed.

GRAEME WHITE

See also Henry II; Matilda

Walpole, Sir Robert 1676–1745

Politician, statesman, and prime minister

Baskerville, Stephen W. (editor), *Walpole in Power 1720–1742*, Oxford: University of Oxford Delegacy of Local Examinations, 1985

Black, Jeremy (editor), *Britain in the Age of Walpole*, Basingstoke: Macmillan, and New York: St Martin's Press, 1984

Black, Jeremy, *British Foreign Policy in the Age of Walpole*, Edinburgh: John Donald, 1985

Black, Jeremy, *Robert Walpole and the Nature of Politics in Early Eighteenth-Century Britain*, Basingstoke: Macmillan, and New York: St Martin's Press, 1990

Coxe, William, *Memoirs of the Life and Administration of Sir Robert Walpole, Earl of Oxford*, 3 vols, London: Cadell and Davies, 1798

Dickinson, H.T., *Walpole and the Whig Supremacy*, London: English Universities Press, 1973

Fritz, Paul S., *The English Ministers and Jacobitism between the Rebellions of 1715 and 1745*, Toronto and Buffalo, New York: University of Toronto Press, 1975

Hill, Brian W., *Sir Robert Walpole: Sole and Prime Minister*, London: Hamish Hamilton, and New York: Penguin, 1989

Holmes, Geoffrey, *British Politics in the Age of Anne*, London: Macmillan, 1967; revised edition, London and Ronceverte, West Virginia: Hambledon Press, 1987

Kemp, Betty, *Sir Robert Walpole*, London: Weidenfeld and Nicolson, 1976

Langford, Paul, *The Excise Crisis: Society and Politics in the Age of Walpole*, Oxford: Oxford University Press, 1975

Plumb, J.H., *Sir Robert Walpole*, 2 vols, London: Cresset Press, 1956–60; Boston: Houghton Mifflin, 1956–61

Woodfine, Philip, *Britannia's Glories: The Walpole Ministry and the 1739 War with Spain*, Woodbridge, Suffolk; and Rochester, New York: Boydell Press, 1998

Walpole was one of the greatest politicians in British history. He played a significant role in sustaining the Whig party, safeguarding the Hanoverian succession, and defending the principles of the Glorious Revolution (1688). Brought to the head of the ministry in 1721 by the financial crisis of the South Sea Bubble, he dominated court and parliament for the next 21 years to such an extent that he is generally regarded as Britain's first (and longest-serving) prime minister. He established a stable political supremacy for the Whig party and taught succeeding ministers how best to establish an effective working relationship between crown and parliament. In view of his enormous achievements, it is surprising that there is no reliable, detailed, and fully researched biographical study of his whole career. This is partly because there is a shortage of extant manuscript sources relating directly to Walpole's wide-ranging activities, but also due to the fact that for decades other scholars waited for PLUMB to complete his trilogy. Since he did not do so, the most detailed study of Walpole's whole career, based on extensive research into the available manuscript sources, remains Archdeacon COXE.

When the first volume of Plumb's biography, which took Walpole's career to 1722, appeared, it made a considerable impact. Plumb had used all the available manuscript sources on Walpole, and the work was clearly organized and very well written and was excellent in its study of character. The volume also caused a considerable stir because it brought Walpole's crucial involvement in the South Sea Bubble disaster to a wide public for the first time (though other scholars had paved the way for Plumb's discoveries). Its reputation no longer stands so high. The initial chapters on the social and political structure of the age, once seen as a tour de force, are now regarded as decidedly old-fashioned, while our understanding of the politics of Anne's reign was later transformed by HOLMES's magisterial volume. Plumb's second volume, which took Walpole's career to the great Excise Bill crisis of 1733 and the results of the general election of 1734, was something of a disappointment. While well written, it seemed concerned to appeal more to the general reader than to the serious student. The result was an attractive chronological narrative that failed to address the really important aspects of Walpole's great career. There was, in particular, no serious analytical study of Walpole's skill as a political manager or of his abilities and achievements as a minister of finance. Thus, his two greatest accomplishments were ignored. The more critical reception of this volume may have dispirited Plumb, since he never got around to producing the final volume of his biography. So far no one else has tried to write the deeply researched and large-scale biography that is so clearly needed.

There are a number of shorter studies of Walpole's life and several more specialized studies of particular aspects of his career. KEMP's short biography is very disappointing. It examines only four aspects of Walpole's career: his personal qualities, his position as prime minister, his constitutional differences with Bolingbroke, and his attitude toward the balanced constitution. Nothing original is written about any of these, and the usefulness of this book is seriously weakened by numerous factual errors, major omissions, and dubious interpretations. BLACK (1990) also offers an analysis of only a few aspects of Walpole's career: his attempts to manage parliament and his relations with the monarch and the political nation, together with studies of the party politics of the period and England's relations with Scotland and Ireland. This book lacks coherence, shows signs of being a rushed production, and makes no original or significant point about Walpole. DICKINSON's study is longer than either Kemp's or Black's, though still of modest length. Having explained Walpole's rise to power in a narrative section, Dickinson then concentrates on analysing several of the most important facets of his career. This work remains the best study of Walpole's abilities as a political manager and as a finance minister, though it is has been superseded in some other areas, such as foreign policy, and its treatment of the Tory opposition is inadequate. HILL's biography is longer than any of the three just noted. It is much less useful than Dickinson's in explaining Walpole's achievements; however, it has the advantage of being organized as a chronological narrative and thus it is the most reliable, if limited, modern account of Walpole's whole life available at present.

Particular aspects of Walpole's career have been fully researched and have been treated with greater detail than in any of the biographical studies noted above. BLACK (1984), an edited volume, includes a number of valuable essays explaining particular aspects of Walpole's achievements and of the context in which he operated. There are essays on his political management, his foreign policy, and his economic policies; on the literary opposition and the press; on his relations with Ireland and Scotland; and on popular politics beyond court and Parliament. BLACK (1985) is a detailed and well organized book-length study of Walpole's foreign policy, discussing how this policy was devised and what impact it had as well as looking in detail at actual diplomatic negotiations. WOODFINE has written a very good, well researched study of the last years of Walpole's regime, when diplomatic relations with Spain finally broke down and a war resulted that eventually ended Walpole's long tenure of office. FRITZ has examined in detail how Walpole infiltrated the European-wide networks of Jacobite spies and agents and how he used the resulting evidence to smear many of his political opponents with the taint of Jacobite treason. LANGFORD has produced a brilliant account of how and why the excise crisis developed and what its consequences were for Walpole. For those seeking primary sources to use in a course on Walpole, BASKERVILLE has produced a very useful and wide-ranging collection, taken from manuscript and printed primary sources.

H.T. DICKINSON

See also George I; George II; Hanoverian Succession; Newcastle, 1st Duke of; Pitt, William, "the Elder"; Prime Minister: Emergence and Development of Office

Walsingham, Sir Francis c.1532–1590

Statesman and principal secretary to Elizabeth I

Adams, Simon, "Favourites and Factions at the Elizabethan Court", in *Princes, Patronage, and the Nobility: The Court at the Beginning of the Modern Age, c.1450–1650* edited by Ronald G. Asch and Adolf M. Birke, London: German Historical Institute, and Oxford and New York: Oxford University Press, 1991

Elton, G.R., *The Parliament of England, 1559–1581*, Cambridge and New York: Cambridge University Press, 1986

Graves, Michael A.R., *The Tudor Parliaments: Crown, Lords, and Commons, 1485–1603*, London and New York: Longman, 1985

Jones, Norman L., *Faith by Statute: Parliament and the Settlement of Religion 1559*, London: Royal Historical Society, and Atlantic Highlands, New Jersey: Humanities Press, 1982

MacCaffrey, Wallace T., *The Shaping of the Elizabethan Regime*, Princeton, New Jersey: Princeton University Press, 1968; London: Jonathan Cape, 1969

MacCaffrey, Wallace T., *Queen Elizabeth and the Making of Policy, 1572–1588*, Princeton, New Jersey: Princeton University Press, 1981

Neale, J.E., *Queen Elizabeth I*, London: Jonathan Cape, and New York: Harcourt Brace Jovanovich, 1934

Read, Conyers, *Mr Secretary Walsingham and the Policy of Queen Elizabeth*, 3 vols, Oxford: Clarendon Press, and Cambridge, Massachusetts: Harvard University Press, 1925

Wernham, R.B., *Before the Armada: The Growth of English Foreign Policy, 1485–1588*, London: Jonathan Cape, 1966; as *Before the Armada: The Emergence of the English Nation, 1485–1588*, New York: Harcourt Brace and World, 1966

Wernham, R.B., *The Making of Elizabethan Foreign Policy, 1558–1603*, Berkeley, California: University of California Press, 1980

Wilson, Charles, *Queen Elizabeth and the Revolt of the Netherlands*, London: Macmillan, and Berkeley, California: University of California Press, 1970

READ's monumental work on Sir Francis Walsingham is a study of policy as seen from the perspective of one of Elizabeth's great secretaries of state. It complements Read's later volumes on Sir William Cecil and NEALE's work on Elizabeth and her parliaments. Read's Walsingham was a fierce puritan, driven by a need to serve his faith by serving his queen. A Marian exile, Walsingham returned to join his fellows in forcing the queen to accept a more protestant religious settlement than she had wanted. Although Walsingham was always a puritan, Read showed that his experience as ambassador in Paris during the Saint Bartholomew massacre made him more militant than ever, causing him thereafter to see the dangers of catholicism everywhere. To foil this menace Walsingham joined a puritan faction championed by the Earl of Leicester (Robert Dudley); it was the clash between this faction and a moderate faction led by Burghley which Read and Neale saw as the key to understanding Elizabeth's rule. Walsingham and Leicester favoured an interventionist policy in the Netherlands and France, fearing that if the rebels failed in those countries the victors would turn on England. In Read's view Walsingham provided the ideas behind the partnership while Leicester used his courtier's skills to try to persuade the queen to adopt them. Walsingham's zeal also impelled him to set up a celebrated network of spies which ultimately led to the entrapment of Mary Queen of Scots in the Babington conspiracy. Walsingham left no personal papers; therefore, any life must centre on the public service which seemed to consume him, and modifications to Read and Neale's interpretation come from studies of the queen rather than studies of Walsingham.

JONES's study of the Elizabethan religious settlement modified the traditional interpretation by challenging the role played by the Marian exiles in the House of Commons. Jones demonstrated that they had not been united in their exile (indeed, Walsingham spent most of his time studying in catholic Padua), nor had they been plotting a return to power; and when they returned they did not unite to oppose the moderate Elizabeth.

Jones argued that the conservative House of Lords, dominated by the Marian bishops, posed the greatest threat to Elizabeth, and therefore the settlement reached was close to Elizabeth's wishes and not one forced upon her by staunch protestants like Walsingham.

What Jones discovered in Elizabeth's first parliament – that the queen was in agreement with her House of Commons in religious matters – GRAVES and ELTON found true for the rest. Neale had depicted an ongoing conflict between the queen and a House of Commons dominated by a "puritan choir", and although Walsingham could not openly oppose the queen as they did, he was related to some of its leaders and was sympathetic to their cause. In Neale's view Walsingham served as a conduit between the two sides. Graves and Elton denied the existence of a puritan choir or a puritan Commons perpetually at odds with the crown. They found that there was far more cooperation between the queen and parliament than Neale had suspected. Where there was conflict, it was led not by disaffected puritans but by councillors who had not persuaded Elizabeth to accept their views on such touchy subjects as her marriage and the threat posed by Mary Queen of Scots; frustrated in the council chamber, they turned to parliament to get Elizabeth to adopt their views.

That Elizabeth's court was split by intense factional rivalry is an interpretation of long standing. It was first used in contemporary tracts like *Leicester's Commonwealth* and was repeated by Naunton, who turned the libel around by acknowledging the dominance of factions but praising the queen's ability to manage the conflict to her own advantage. This view has been challenged by ADAMS in a series of important essays. Although Adams had a much higher opinion of Leicester's role in the partnership with Walsingham, his main contribution to the debate was to minimize the factional conflict discerned by Read and Neale. Adams noted that the drift to ideological conflict precipitated by the revolt of the northern earls in 1569 and the papal bull of deposition of 1570 led Elizabeth to appoint courtiers and councillors with distinct protestant leanings. Thus by the time Walsingham returned from France to take up his post as secretary of state and privy councillor, there was a high degree of political homogeneity in court and council. Walsingham might have disagreed with his old patron Burghley on how policy should be implemented, but they generally agreed on the important issues of the day. Instead of accepting the celebrated rivalry between Leicester and Burghley, Adams claimed that the council worked to maintain a united front against a queen unwilling to commit herself.

MacCAFFREY disagreed with Adams's analysis to the extent that he saw intense rivalry between Cecil and Dudley (Leicester) at the beginning of the reign, centred on Dudley's desire to marry the queen; but he held that this conflict died down in the 1570s and the two settled into a sort of partnership that lasted until Dudley's death in 1588. It was in this period that Walsingham dominated foreign affairs, and although he and the council did not get Elizabeth to accept his grand strategy of intervening on behalf of protestant rebels against catholic rulers, they were able to thwart her marriage negotiations.

Read became more critical of Walsingham's foreign policy as he shifted the focus of his study from Walsingham to Burghley, coming to appreciate Elizabeth's views of the costs and dangers of supporting rebels against legitimate authority; but WILSON, writing from the perspective of the Dutch rebels, contrasted Walsingham's keen understanding of continental politics and the need for decisiveness with Burghley's timidity.

Any evaluation of Walsingham must consider the fact that, although he was considered Elizabeth's expert in foreign affairs, she rarely seemed to follow his advice. For this reason Neale, MacCaffrey, and, in a thorough discussion of foreign policy, WERNHAM have minimized Walsingham's role as policy maker, seeing Burghley and the queen herself as the driving force in foreign affairs. Why, then, did she keep Walsingham on? The answer must include her appreciation of his intelligence network and his single-minded dedication to her service even when they disagreed.

Walsingham remains a man who evokes strong feelings. His enemies believed that he would stoop to any depth to achieve his ends, from manufacturing plots against the queen to doctoring the evidence against Mary Queen of Scots. The most that can be said is that he might have done so, but no one has been able to show that he did.

ROBERT C. BRADDOCK

See also Anti-Catholicism and the Test Acts; Cecil, William; Dudley, Robert; Elizabeth I; Nonsuch, Treaty of

Walter, Hubert   *c.*1140–1205
Courtier, Archbishop of Canterbury, and Chancellor

Cheney, Christopher R., *From Becket to Langton: English Church Government, 1170–1213*, Manchester: Manchester University Press, 1956

Cheney, Christopher R., *Hubert Walter*, London: Nelson, 1967

Cheney, Christopher R. and Eric John (editors), *English Episcopal Acta*, vol. 3, *Canterbury 1193–1205*, London: Oxford University Press, 1986

Clanchy, M.T., *From Memory to Written Record: England, 1066–1307*, London: Arnold, and Cambridge, Massachusetts: Harvard University Press, 1979

Kemp, Brian R. (editor), *English Episcopal Acta*, vol. 18, *Salisbury 1078–1217*, Oxford: Oxford University Press, 1999

Stenton, Doris M., *English Justice between the Norman Conquest and the Great Charter, 1066–1215*, Philadelphia: American Philosophical Society, 1964; London: Allen and Unwin, 1965

Stratford, Neil, Pamela Tudor-Craig, and Anna Maria Muthesius, "Archbishop Hubert Walter's Tomb and its Furnishings", *Medieval Art and Architecture at Canterbury before 1220*, London: British Archaeological Association and Kent Archaeological Society, 1982

West, Francis, *The Justiciarship in England, 1066–1232*, Cambridge: Cambridge University Press, 1966

Young, Charles R., *Hubert Walter, Lord of Canterbury and Lord of England*, Durham, North Carolina: Duke University Press, 1968

Viewed by 19th-century historians as a meddlesome courtier, in part responsible for the accession of the evil King John and on occasion scandalously at odds with the reforming impulses and monastic spirituality of his age, Hubert Walter has been transformed by his 20th-century biographers into one of the presiding geniuses of medieval church and state.

This transformation began with CHENEY (1956), the Ford Lectures, which for the first time set out to challenge the notion that only at times of crisis in its relations with the king, under Becket and then later under Stephen Langton, did the church in England show itself in a favourable light. On the contrary, Cheney demonstrated, in the 1180s and 1190s the administrative machinery of the church, its courts and synods, came to proper maturity, freed from the more colourful but essentially egotistical posturings that had characterized Becket's years of conflict. CHENEY (1967), a full-scale biography, followed up this lead. While not denying that Hubert Walter was a very secular sort of prelate, steeped in the traditions of the royal court and appointed for his administrative rather than his spiritual capacities, Cheney conclusively demonstrated that he was a great archbishop, as adroit in clerical councils and papal judge delegacies as in his conduct of the king's affairs. Reform, Cheney suggested, is the prerogative not so much of the saints of the church as of its sinners. Curial bishops such as Hubert Walter were as essential to the church as saints such as Anselm or scholars such as Langton. By an unfortunate coincidence, the appearance of Cheney's study coincided with and quite overshadowed the publication of a second biography, by YOUNG, which, although reaching much the same conclusions, contains details lacking in Cheney. Young's footnotes remain extremely useful, and his text has much to add to the broader themes that Cheney expounds so magisterially. Cheney's biography made considerable use of a doctoral thesis presented by Eric John, collecting Hubert Walter's charters and letters as Archbishop of Canterbury. These documentary sources have since been published under Cheney's guidance and with full commentary (CHENEY & JOHN, 1986), followed more recently by a comparable collection, by KEMP, of the letters and charters issued by Hubert as Bishop of Salisbury before his elevation to Canterbury.

Distinct from these studies of Hubert Walter as bishop and churchman, both WEST (1966) and STENTON (1965) are valuable studies devoted to his role as justiciar and law-maker. In particular, West and Stenton emphasize his impact on the recording as well as the administration of justice. This theme is most fruitfully explored by CLANCHY, as part of a wider study of literacy and record-keeping in medieval England. Here, Clanchy accepts the argument that it was Hubert Walter who in the 1190s first ordered the preservation of copies of decisions – final concords – reached in the king's court, and who later, as chancellor, ushered in the preservation of copies of much of the outgoing administrative correspondence of England's kings. This constituted a resource of quite staggering extent and significance, whose survival and publication enable historians of 13th-century England to approach their subject with a degree of detail and confidence unmatched elsewhere in medieval Europe. Finally, viewing Hubert Walter as patron not only of the archives but also of the arts, STRATFORD et al. have re-emphasized his impact, as founder of Lambeth palace and as patron of building work at Canterbury, upon the art and architecture of his day.

Although various details remain to be added to this picture, and although a full-scale study of Hubert Walter's often troubled relations with the monks of Canterbury remains to be written,

he, more than any other medieval archbishop of Canterbury, can claim to have been fortunate in his modern biographers, achieving a posthumous venerability that his contemporaries might have found extraordinary to contemplate.

NICHOLAS VINCENT

See also John

Warbeck Conspiracy 1490s

Arthurson, Ian, *The Perkin Warbeck Conspiracy 1491–1499*, Stroud, Gloucestershire; and Dover, New Hampshire: Alan Sutton, 1994

Ballard, Mark and Clifford Stephen Lloyd Davies, "Étienne Fryon: Burgundian Agent, English Royal Secretary, and 'Principal Counsellor' to Perkin Warbeck", *Historical Research*, 62/149 (1989): 245–58

Barbé, Louis Auguste, *Sidelights on the History, Industries, and Social Life of Scotland*, London: Blackie, 1919

Dunlop, David, "The 'Masked Comedian': Perkin Warbeck's Adventures in Scotland and England from 1495 to 1497", *Scottish Historical Review*, 70/2 (1991): 97–128

Kleyn, Diana M., *Richard of England*, Oxford: Kensal Press, 1990

Roth, Cecil, "Perkin Warbeck and His Jewish Master", *Transactions of the Jewish Historical Society of England*, 9 (1922): 143–62

Roth, Cecil, "Sir Edward Brampton: An Anglo-Jewish Adventurer during the Wars of the Roses", *Transactions of the Jewish Historical Society of England*, 16 (1945–51): 121–27

The Warbeck conspiracy was the second major dynastic threat to Henry VII's throne. Following the usurpation of Richard, Duke of Gloucester (Richard III), in 1483, the two sons of Edward IV, the elder of whom was heir to the throne, were placed in the Tower of London, from which they were never to emerge. Contempories widely believed that they had been murdered on the orders of Richard III, but their disappearance was never firmly explained. As a result, it was not easy to refute Perkin Warbeck's claim to be Richard, Duke of York, the younger of the two brothers. Indeed, to this day some people consider that Warbeck's identity has never been satisfactorily established. The Duke of York's claim to the throne would have been superior to that of Henry VII, and so Warbeck declared himself to be the rightful king. He was supported by Emperor Maximilian and by Margaret, dowager Duchess of Burgundy (sister of Edward IV); and at various times he enjoyed the support of France, Ireland, and Scotland. He was finally captured by Henry VII in 1497 and was executed, along with the Earl of Warwick, in 1499, amid rumours of a government "frame-up".

ARTHURSON's well researched, illustrated book is the most up-to-date account of the conspiracy. Arthurson examines the origins and inception of the affair, including a reappraisal of Sir Edward Brampton's apparent role, and looks at Warbeck's parentage and early life. Addressing the claims of those who believe that Warwick was Richard, Duke of York, Arthurson offers a psychological appraisal of Warbeck in an attempt to understand the elusive figure behind the consummate actor. With colourful and lively descriptions, he successfully puts the plot into its English and European context, and he consistently demonstrates the significance of the conspiracy with regard to Henry VII's foreign policy. He looks at the effect of Henry's unpopular policies and thoroughly examines the motives of those involved, including Sir William Stanley and Lord Fitzwater, revealing that the conspirators were not an incoherent group. Arthurson also analyses the motives behind the Cornish rising of 1497 and the events leading to Warbeck's execution, successfully challenging the long-held belief that Warbeck's plan to escape was masterminded by Henry in order to bring him to the block. This account, which includes a comprehensive list of suggested works on the topic, is essential reading.

KLEYN's aim is to demonstrate that Perkin Warbeck was indeed the Duke of York. Her work is a one-sided and, at times, rather novelistic version of the conspiracy; it must be read with caution and in conjunction with other studies. It contains some inaccuracies, and the author tends to deliver unproven theories as statements of fact and does not always give the full picture if doing so would weaken her case. The result is to undermine the effect of some valid points, including Polydore Vergil's comments about Margaret Beaufort (the mother of Henry VII) and Henry VII's apparent refusal to allow his wife (who was the sister of Richard, Duke of York) to "identify" Warbeck. However, Kleyn's book does have a role to play: it puts forward theories which lie outside the boundaries of conventional historical opinion but which many people hold to be true.

BALLARD & DAVIES's article discusses the idea that Margaret of Burgundy's involvement with Warbeck began earlier than 1492. Ballard and Davies attach more credibility to the official view of the English government; they construct a sensible argument that the conspiracy was actually prompted by Margaret and that Etienne Fryon may have been her agent. As such, while serving Charles VIII of France, Fryon was used to win Charles's support for Warbeck, culminating in Warbeck's invitation to France in 1491.

DUNLOP's well-researched article centres on Warbeck's sojourn at the Scottish court in 1495–97. Dunlop is by no means convinced that the king of Scotland, James IV, genuinely believed Warbeck to be the Duke of York. The affair is used to highlight James's lack of judgement and political inexperience at that time, Henry VII's desperation to obtain peace with Scotland and Warbeck's person, and the seriousness with which Henry regarded the affair. Dunlop also provides a useful account of Katherine Gordon's career and speculates upon whether she became Henry's mistress. He believes the importance of the Warbeck conspiracy was the role it played in facilitating the marriage between James IV and Margaret Tudor (Henry VII's daughter).

Two chapters of BARBÉ's book concern Perkin Warbeck's period in Scotland and the subsequent fate of Katherine Gordon. Revealing the possible involvement of Margaret of Burgundy as early as 1489, it is a well-written and detailed account which also provides two interesting appendices: Perkin Warbeck's supposed letter to Katherine Gordon and Katherine's will.

ROTH (1922) accepts without doubt that Warbeck was an imposter and casts Edward Brampton – possibly a key figure in the plot – as someone who was drawn into the affair mostly by accident. Although this article provides an interesting account of Brampton's life, its emphasis is on his contribution to Jewish history. ROTH (1945–51), taking advantage of newly discovered information, updates the story of Brampton. Here, Brampton's role in the Warbeck plot remains largely unchanged; however, Roth does accept that Brampton could have provided a link not only between Warbeck and Edward IV but also between Warbeck and Margaret of Burgundy.

Although opinions continue to be divided over aspects of this conspiracy, the works described above introduce what is currently known and under discussion.

HAZEL PIERCE

See also Henry VII

Warwick "the Kingmaker"

see Neville, Richard

Waterloo, Battle of

see Napoleonic Wars: Waterloo and the War on Land

Watt, James 1736–1819
Engineer and inventor

Arago, M., *Historical Eloge of James Watt*, translated from the French by James Patrick Muirhead, London: John Murray, 1839

Dickinson, H.W., *James Watt, Craftsman and Engineer*, Cambridge: Cambridge University Press, 1936; reprinted, New York: Kelley, 1967

Dickinson, H.W. and Rhys Jenkins, *James Watt and the Steam Engine*, Oxford: Clarendon Press, 1927

Dickinson, H.W. and H.P. Vowles, *James Watt and the Industrial Revolution*, London and New York: Longmans Green, 1943

Muirhead, James Patrick, *The Origin and Progress of the Mechanical Inventions of James Watt Illustrated by His Correspondence with His Friends and the Specifications of His Patents*, 3 vols, London: John Murray, 1854

Musson, A.E. and Eric Robinson, *Science and Technology in the Industrial Revolution*, Manchester: Manchester University Press, and Toronto: Toronto University Press, 1969

Robinson, Eric and Douglas McKie (editors), *Partners in Science: Letters of James Watt and Joseph Black*, London: Constable, and Cambridge, Massachusetts: Harvard University Press, 1970

Robinson, Eric and A.E. Musson, *James Watt and the Steam Revolution: A Documentary History*, London: Adams and Dart, and New York: Kelley, 1969

Smiles, Samuel, *Lives of the Engineers: The Steam-Engine –
Boulton and Watt*, revised edition, London: John Murray,
1878

Williamson, George, *Memorials of the Lineage, Early Life,
Education, and Development of the Genius of James Watt*,
London: Constable, 1856

James Watt's crucial improvements to the steam engine have
rightly dominated biographical works about him. The invention
for which he is best remembered is the addition of the separate
condenser to the Newcomen engine. Not only did this make
a much more powerful and economical engine, but it led to
his development of the steam engine from a machine that could
only pump water into one that could turn rotating machinery directly. Watt applied scientific principles to solve the
problems he faced, and so he may be said to be the originator
of scientific engineering.

One difficulty with the published sources on Watt is that their
focus on the steam engine has generally been to the exclusion
of most of his other inventions and discoveries. Another difficulty is that most authors have taken an adulatory slant and
have not examined Watt's work critically. This is certainly true
of ARAGO, who was writing at a time when the effects of Watt's
steam engine in increasing mill and mine productivity were
becoming more apparent, and when moves were afoot to create
various memorials to Watt. Ever since Arago, biographies of
Watt have been produced regularly every 20 or 30 years; a
number of these have essentially relied on information from
earlier publications, and few will therefore be discussed here.

One such derivative biography is by WILLIAMSON, who
concentrates on Watt's ancestors and his early life at Greenock.
It is now virtually impossible to check the veracity of
Williamson's stories, because few papers have survived from this
period of Watt's life. Similarly, MUIRHEAD gives a short introductory life followed by extracts of Watt's correspondence with
such people as John Roebuck, Small, and Matthew Boulton,
principally concerning the development of his steam engine in
Scotland and then in Birmingham. Together with the text of
Watt's patents, these volumes are a source of much important
material.

For the best general account of Watt's life, we must turn to
SMILES, who begins with Watt's early career in Scotland and
then covers the rest of his life in Birmingham together with that
of Matthew Boulton. Smiles had access to some of the mass
of Watt's papers, then still with the family but now available at
Birmingham's Central Library.

One problem for biographers was that access to the papers
held in Watt's house at Doldowlod was restricted for many
years. DICKINSON & JENKINS (1927), 70 years after Smiles,
had access to these papers and hence gave a much fuller, more
accurate account than earlier works. Their book starts with a
sketch of Watt's life in Scotland; it does not really tackle Watt's
development of his engine with the vital separate condenser, but
it gives instead a comprehensive treatment of the later developments, after Watt had moved to Birmingham in 1774, showing
the many improvements to the pumping engines, especially
those in Cornwall, and how Watt pioneered his rotative engines.
DICKINSON (1936) does describe other inventions, such as
Watt's perspective and copying machines, but perhaps inevitably
concentrates on the pumping and rotative engines. Dickinson

examined the correspondence in the Muirhead collection
between Watt, Boulton, and Roebuck over the separate condenser, but it seems unlikely that he was able to refer to other
papers in the Doldowlod archives, and he fails to explain the
problems Watt had with this invention. On the steam engine,
this work is not as detailed as Dickinson's earlier collaborative
work with Jenkins. DICKINSON & VOWLES (1943) set the
story against the background of other developments and inventions that were then helping to launch the Industrial Revolution.

Access to the crucial Doldowlod papers was given to ROBIN-
SON & MUSSON (1969), who published a small fraction of
them in celebration of the 200th anniversary of Watt's crucial
patent for the separate condenser of 1769. Much of the material
had already appeared in Muirhead, but this later book does
contain some new additions. For accounts of some of Watt's
scientific contributions and discoveries, we must turn to other
works by Robinson. ROBINSON & McKIE (1970) published
the correspondence between Watt and his mentor Professor
Joseph Black, who moved to Edinburgh from Glasgow in 1766
and died in 1799. There are also letters to and from Professor
John Robison, who was often involved in their scientific experiments; subjects covered include the steam engine, alkali from
sea salt, the copying press, chlorine bleaching, and many other
chemical and scientific topics. A more detailed examination of
some of these scientific inquiries can be found in MUSSON &
ROBINSON (1969), which covers in detail Watt's attempts in
both alkali and chlorine manufacture, as well as his interest
in dyeing. Their article "Training Captains of Industry"
describes the education of James Watt Jr.

In spite of all these publications, the challenge of writing an
adequate biography remains. The acquisition of the Doldowlod
papers for the public domain means that a more thorough
appraisal of Watt's career, as first a scientific instrument-maker
and then a civil engineer at Glasgow, can now be made, for it
was in these professions that he laid the foundations for his later
work on the steam engine.

RICHARD L. HILLS

Webb, Sidney, Baron Passfield 1859–1947
Webb, Beatrice 1858–1943
Social historians and socialist reformers

Beilharz, Peter and Chris Nyland (editors), *The Webbs,
Fabianism, and Feminism: Fabianism and the Political
Economy of Everyday Life*, Aldershot and Brookfield,
Vermont: Ashgate, 1998

Cole, Margaret (editor), *The Webbs and Their Work*, London:
Muller, 1949; reprinted, Brighton, Sussex: Harvester Press,
and New York: Barnes and Noble, 1974

Durbin, Elizabeth, "Fabian Socialism and Economic Science"
in *Fabian Essays in Socialist Thought*, edited by Ben
Pimlott, London: Heinemann, and Rutherford, New Jersey:
Fairleigh Dickinson University Press, 1984

Harrison, Royden J., *The Life and Times of Sidney and
Beatrice Webb: 1858–1905, The Formative Years*,
London: Macmillan, and New York: St Martin's Press,
2000

MacKenzie, Norman, *Socialism and Society: A New View of the Webb Partnership*, London: London School of Economics and Political Science, 1978

Radice, Lisanne, *Beatrice and Sidney Webb*, London: Macmillan, 1984

The Webbs formed, after their marriage in 1892, an intellectual partnership, which during the first half of the 20th century exercised a significant influence on British institutions, government, and policy. Not all their activities were shared. They served separately on various public inquiries. Sidney had a political career as one of the first London County Councillors, as a member of parliament for a brief period in the early 1920s before going to the House of Lords (with the title Lord Passfield), and as a minister in the first two Labour cabinets. The Webbs' influence, however, was essentially exercised through joint research, writing, and other activities. They helped make the Fabian Society and Fabian socialism a major intellectual force in British politics, helped found the London School of Economics, helped establish the *New Statesman* as an influential periodical, and as historians laid the foundations for the history of the modern labour movement. Above all, they influenced the Labour party, especially after 1911, when they become involved more closely than before in its affairs. The general nature of their achievement can be easily summarized; exactly how it is to be assessed has been a subject of differences of emphasis and some disagreement.

COLE (1949) is an attempt to summarize the remarkable influence and achievements of the Webbs. It appeared shortly after they died; most of its contributors had known them; and the editor (and her husband G.D.H. Cole) had had past differences of opinion with them over Labour and Fabian policy. Although it made no claim to be definitive, this work marks the real start of historical analysis and debate.

Since its appearance, there has been a stream of publications on policies and activities in which the Webbs were involved. RADICE (1984) is the only modern joint biography (the only complete one apart from Margaret Hamilton's *Beatrice and Sidney Webb*, which was published in 1933). HARRISON (2000) is the first volume of a joint biography commissioned more than 30 years previously by the Passfield Trustees (of the Webbs' copyright and private papers). Whereas Radice's work is relatively brief and general, Harrison's promises to be nearly definitive, if it is ever completed. MACKENZIE (1978) is a published lecture by someone who is probably the major academic authority; it was given to mark the publication of his three-volume edition of the Webbs' letters. With his wife as co-editor, MacKenzie has also published a four-volume edition of Beatrice's diary that supersedes earlier published versions.

There are several biographical and other studies of Beatrice alone. Although by no means all of these are written from a feminist perspective, her prominence in public life and the existence of her diary have made her a focus of attention for feminist writers and historians, despite her early refusal to be typecast as an expert on women's employment and her failure ever to become active in the feminist movement of her own day. BEILHARZ & NYLAND contribute to and discuss this feminist debate, which reflects preoccupations of the late 20th century rather than those of the Webbs' lifetime.

It has always been generally recognized that the Webbs, as partners, showed consistency of thinking and purpose. In old age they betrayed a mistaken admiration for the Stalinist Soviet Union, partly because they were misled and partly because – always having had faith in planning – they wanted to believe in the success of the five-year plans. As MacKenzie notes, "All their lives . . . the Webbs . . . believed in a middle-class, quasi-scientific, technocratic or managerial form of collectivism". Under the influence of Alfred Marshall and other economists who had revised classical theory, from the start they regarded the existing social and economic system as open to reform, and for them the road to socialism always lay through an expansion of central and local government and the provision and improvement of public services. Their thinking can be seen as lending permanent intellectual support to the moderation of 20th-century Labour governments, from MacDonald's to Callaghan's, and it did undoubtedly have some sort of diffuse influence. Radice, however, points out that Labour politicians and intellectuals after World War II tended to dismiss the Webbs as irrelevant and outdated. DURBIN (1984) is a detailed study of a major shift, if not a complete break, in Labour thinking on the economy and on social and economic planning, which started before the war and ended after it, and which provided a new basis for postwar socialist policy.

JOHN BROWN

See also Fabian Society; Socialism

Wedmore, Treaty of

see Alfred–Guthrum Treaty

Weights and Measures

Berriman, Algernon E., *Historical Metrology: A New Analysis of the Archaeological and the Historical Evidence Relating to Weights and Measures*, London: Dent, and New York: Dutton, 1953

Graham, J.T., *Weights and Measures: A Guide to Collecting*, Aylesbury: Shire, 1979; 2nd edition, revised by Maurice Stevenson, as *Weights and Measures and Their Marks: A Guide to Collecting*, 1987

Grierson, Philip, *English Linear Measures: An Essay in Origins*, Reading: University of Reading, 1972

Kula, Witold, *Measures and Men*, translated by R. Szreter, Princeton, New Jersey: Princeton University Press, 1986 (Polish edition, 1970)

Munby, Lionel, *How Much Is That Worth?* Chichester, Sussex: Phillimore, 1989

Prior, W.H., "Notes on the Weights and Measures of Medieval England", *Bulletin Du Cange*, 1 (1924): 77–97; 141–70

Idiomatic references to legal and illegal trading down the ages are sufficient to prove the importance of weights and measures to the historian. "Paying on the nail" (the appointed spot in the market-place) and buying a "pig in a poke" and then "letting the cat out of the bag" (finding that one was duped at the fair) as well as seeing the actual bargain of dry weight (grain) "struck" are all reminders of the fact that buying and selling were very localized until comparatively recently. Although the history of trade has received a lot of attention, the actual weights and measures which were utilized have remained museum pieces. Further complications arrived in 1971, with the change from pounds, shillings, and pence (£sd) to decimal currency units (£p) and subsequently with metrication. Whenever and wherever weights and measures are encountered in history, they can be extremely remote and unyielding to any reader.

Academic work falls into two categories: that which takes the whole-world view and that which makes more than passing reference to specifically British units. BERRIMAN (1953) remains a classic example of the former. Much of this book considers the ancients. In reading Berriman's work, be prepared to think mathematically and to be made to think about units. The weights of ancient India, Russia, and Babylon all receive treatment. Berriman also discusses Palestinian and biblical as well as Greek and Roman measurements. The most relevant chapter is "Historical Aspects of English Metrology". Here we are treated to descriptions of the standard pound and the Tower pound. We are introduced to the steelyard and balance, the Winchester bushel, the old wine gallon, and even the barrel of beer. There are also explanations of the pole, mile, and league. In conclusion, and of great interest, there is a table of weights and measures in current use when the book was written.

Although KULA (1986) is "international in character and world-wide in scope", there is much of more academic interest. The author provides an interesting survey of how measures have affected humankind throughout history. In his opening chapters he tries to get his reader to banish 20th-century attitudes and to understand the relationship between techniques of production and the appropriate measure: for iron, the pig; for wrought iron, the bar; for glass, the pane. Kula traces measuring back to Cain in biblical days. Although much of his discussion is centred on Poland and France, there is considerable recognizable material on simple weighing and measuring. Of great importance is Kula's survey of historical metrology as a branch of history.

PRIOR (1924) is the starting-point for any aspiring metrologist of medieval and early modern British history. The author tracks down the origins of the commonly used descriptions of weights and measure such as the scilling or solidus, the mark, the Tower pound, and the wheat grain or denier. He also sets out the arrival of the troy system. Prior has been thorough with regard to sources for the measurements he describes, utilizing sources from the Fleta to Pegolotti. He then moves on to consider how weights and measures were regulated and the arrival of the assizes and Magna Carta, finally reaching the centralization which took place under Henry VII. However, as he later observed, even in the 1920s there were still many different local variations of measure as well as some that have disappeared, like the wey. He describes the clove (7 lb) and points out the confusion it can cause in contemporary records. Prior also warns us that weights varied from commodity to commodity such as cheese, lead, and wool. The importance of weights becomes even more evident because measures of capacity were based on weight, and the dolium and tun are explained. In the second part of this pioneering article there is a discussion of linear measurement – the yardland and farthingland. Prior ends with a discussion of more obsolete measures, like the sextarius, which in the 13th century roughly 4 gallons; the amber or

mina; the strike; and the sarplar, commonly used in the wool trade. For numismatists his final chapter on exchange values of coinage is an important contribution, as is his glossary. Prior forms the basis for many dictionaries of weights and measures that were published subsequently.

In a short but very well-researched paper GRIERSON (1972) traces the origins of English linear measures. He dispels some myths, refers to existing and other accessible works, and traces developments chronologically. He provides a complete discussion of Richard I's assize of measures and points out that while it was one thing to provide standards it was quite another to induce people to use them. This, he argues, is represented in the references to weights and measures in Magna Carta. Much attention is paid to how the editors of statutes of the realm and subsequent historians derived their information on the assize of 1196. Grierson produces a convincing pattern for linear measures in the 13th century and also reconsiders Maitland's work and reminds us of the importance of the St Paul's foot – which was actually sculptured in the base of one of the old cathedral's columns. He show that our present-day system is derived from two quite different systems and has both Roman and Anglo-Saxon origins.

GRAHAM (1979) is a short but invaluable guide to British weights and measures principally for the collector. There is a brief explanation of how our systems started; then the author goes on to consider the various sizes and shapes of measures. He examines standardization and devotes a small section to wool weights. Liquid measures – mainly in pewter, copper, and pottery – are then discussed, and all of them are extremely well illustrated. The final section provides a very useful basic guide to verification marks, including town and county symbols and a list of official stamp numbers used by the Board of Trade.

As an adjunct, a useful book for anyone interested in domestic trade and weights and measures is MUNBY (1989). Munby examines currency in full detail and provides a useful conversion table. Much of his work considers how various indices of standards of living have been compiled, from the Phelps Brown (& Hopkins) index – of prices from 1264 to 1954 – up to 1970.

ROBIN R. MUNDILL

Welfare State since 1945

Barnett, Correlli, The Audit of War: The Illusion, and Reality of Britain as a Great Nation, London: Macmillan, 1986

Briggs, Asa, "The Welfare State in Historical Perspective", Archives Européennes de Sociologie, 2/2 (1961): 221–58

Fraser, Derek, The Evolution of the British Welfare State: A History of Social Policy since the Industrial Revolution, Basingstoke: Macmillan, 1973; 2nd edition, 1984

Glennerster, Howard, British Social Policy since 1945, Oxford and Cambridge, Massachusetts: Blackwell, 1995; 2nd edition, 2000

Glennerster, Howard and John Hills (editors), The State of Welfare: The Economics of Social Spending, Oxford and New York: Oxford University Press, 1998

Harris, José, "Enterprise and the Welfare State: A Comparative Perspective" in Britain since 1945, edited by T.R. Gourvish and Alan O'Day, London: Macmillan, 1991

Lowe, Rodney, *The Welfare State in Britain since 1945*, Basingstoke: Macmillan, and New York: St Martin's Press, 1993; 2nd edition, 1999

Stewart, John, "The Twentieth Century: An Overview" in *British Social Welfare in the Twentieth Century*, edited by Robert M. Page and Richard L. Silburn, Basingstoke: Macmillan, 1998; New York: St Martin's Press, 1999

Thane, Pat, *The Foundations of the Welfare State*, London and New York: Longman, 1982; 2nd edition, 1996

Timmins, Nicholas, *The Five Giants: A Biography of the Welfare State*, London: HarperCollins, 1995

The British "welfare state" has been a subject of intense scrutiny and debate not only by historians but also by other social scientists such as economists and social policy analysts. The general works by FRASER, GLENNERSTER (1995), THANE, and TIMMINS are therefore useful starting-points for those seeking broad historical interpretations of this complex institution, although each puts forward a rather different viewpoint from the others. Timmins, for instance, is a journalist rather than an academic and brings to his study an immediacy based on extensive use of materials such as interviews and newspaper reports. His title, incidentally, draws on an analogy that William Beveridge identified – "five giants" that had be slain on the road to what Beveridge considered necessary social reconstruction in the aftermath of World War II. It was Beveridge's famous report of 1942 which, so the argument goes, laid the foundations of the "welfare state". For an outstanding account of what has happened to state social welfare in Britain over the last 20 or so years, GLENNERSTER & HILLS (1998) is invaluable. This work gives particular attention to patterns of expenditure at a time when the "welfare state" appeared to be going through one of its admittedly recurrent crises; and when the post-1979 Conservative administration was, rhetorically at least, committed to pushing back the boundaries of the state. The various paradoxes and complexities associated with the "welfare state" are captured by the chapter by Glennerster in this volume, "New Beginnings and Old Continuities".

Despite the huge volume of academic endeavour, the origins, development, and nature of the "welfare state" remain highly problematic. Even how the "welfare state" is written about has varied significantly over time. The important article by BRIGGS, for example, raised to new levels the historical analysis of the provision of welfare. But we need to acknowledge that Briggs's generally positive evaluation of social reforms in Britain after World War II in itself reflected optimism about the nature of the postwar settlement which continued to characterize British society into the 1960s. Such a "Whiggish" approach to welfare history was rather harder to maintain in the late 20th century, when the very nature and ends of welfare were subjected to intense scrutiny and debate. This has reinforced the need for a more critical view of the origins and subsequent history of modern British social policy. As Thane suggests, at "a time when the post-war 'welfare state' is being actively dismantled there is perhaps an especial need to understand the forces which can oppose, promote or defend state measures to meet social needs".

What the term "welfare state" actually means is a matter of some debate. There is an extremely useful discussion of this in LOWE (1993); the author points out that "welfare state" originated as a pejorative expression in Germany under the Weimar republic and acquired its current, generally accepted meaning in Britain in the late 1940s – that is, when the postwar Labour governments introduced measures such as the National Health Service. As Lowe also points out, it is not a simple matter to say precisely what areas of social activity are embraced by the term "welfare state". For practical purposes, however, it helps to see the "core functions" of the welfare state as health, education, social security, housing, and personal social services. State provision in these areas is underpinned by notions of universalism and comprehensiveness, that is, the idea that each citizen has a right to minimum standards some degree above basic subsistence. In certain areas, most obviously health and education, these services were, originally at least, also to be provided free at the point of consumption. Once again, this raises important issues.

First, it is important to bear in mind that much welfare has historically been, and is at present, provided by agencies other than the state. These can be voluntary organizations, such as the philanthropic agencies that flourished in the 19th century, or even more significantly the family. The family has always been the single most important provider of welfare – a fact that has implications for women in particular. Second, as Glennerster (1995) remarks, the decision not to implement particular welfare schemes constitutes policy just as much as the decision to implement them. Governments may shape their welfare policies according to, for example, ideological considerations or economic constraints that in turn might lead them to limits on actual provision. For its entire history there has been a tension within the "welfare state" between demands for an expanding volume and range of services and the perceived need to restrict public expenditure.

Such problems are more than simply matters of academic pedantry. How the "welfare state" is envisaged and defined has implications for discussions of its origins and development. As the title of the work by Fraser suggests, it is possible to see the "welfare state" as evolving over a relatively long period, from the 19th century – with its factory, poor law, and public health legislation – through to the sweeping reforms of the Labour governments after 1945. Once again, this illustrates a rather "Whiggish" approach to welfare history that might be seen as anachronistic (an issue that Fraser himself acknowledges in the foreword to his second edition). Other scholars, for example Briggs, while recognizing that the origins of the "welfare state" have deep historical roots, nonetheless emphasize the impact of World War II in advancing the case for state-sponsored social reform.

Once created, Lowe and others have argued, the "welfare state" entered its "classic phase", which lasted from the 1940s to the crises of the 1970s. Some have claimed that it thus became a central part of the postwar "consensus" – that is, a general agreement by the major political parties over the need for state-sponsored social welfare running alongside a "mixed economy". Once again, however, the notion of "consensus" is highly contentious, and for at least some critics it implies too great an emphasis on political harmony at the expense of underlying tensions. These arguments are reviewed by STEWART.

The actual impact of the "welfare state" became a matter of considerable controversy as Britain entered a period of economic and social instability in the 1970s. BARNETT argued that the desire to create a "new Jerusalem" in the postwar era was an an "illusion" fostered by the "'enlightened' Establishment", prominent among whom was Beveridge. Britain's social reform and economic strategies after 1945 were fundamentally flawed. One consequence was, as he described it in a much-quoted passage, "a dark reality of a segregated, subliterate, unskilled, unhealthy and institutionalised proletariat hanging on the nipple of state maternalism". The "welfare state" had not freed the population; rather, it had impaired economic performance and engendered what came to be called "welfare dependency".

Arguments such as these had a profound effect on the "new right" in British politics, which was in any case ideologically disinclined to intervene in either society or the economy. Barnett's analysis therefore had an influence beyond the academia, and for this reason alone should be taken seriously. However, a number of his central premises have been challenged, most effectively by HARRIS. She notes, for instance, that Barnett appears to have misunderstood the wartime debates over social reconstruction; that British postwar welfare expenditure was not necessarily high by European standards; and that institutions such as the National Health Service have been found to be both relatively cheap and relatively efficient. Nonetheless Harris is careful not to dismiss Barnett out of hand. In a remark that should form the basis of all investigations of the welfare state, she argues that Barnett is:

[S]urely correct in suggesting that historians should investigate the welfare state, not simply as a series of episodes in high politics but as a complex of institutions and values that interact with the lives of citizens at many levels, on a par with churches or property-ownership in earlier epochs. If, for good or ill, particular welfare policies do encourage particular types of economic, moral or civic behaviour, then historians should not be too squeamish to acknowledge and enquire into this fact.

It is, of course, the very complexity of the institution that makes the "welfare state" such a stimulating, if demanding, subject of study.

JOHN STEWART

See also Attlee; Bevan; Beveridge; Consenus in the Postwar Period; Dalton; Labour Party; National Health Service; Poverty: Poverty and Deprivation, 19th and 20th Centuries; Relative Economic Decline

Wellington, Arthur Wellesley, 1st Duke of 1769–1852
Soldier, later prime minister

Gash, Norman (editor), *Wellington: Studies in the Military and Political Career of the First Duke of Wellington*, Manchester and New York: Manchester University Press, 1990
Hamilton-Williams, David, *Waterloo: New Perspectives – The Great Battle Reappraised*, London: Arms and Armour Press, 1993; New York: Wiley, 1994
Hibbert, Christopher, *Wellington: A Personal History*, London: HarperCollins, and Reading, Massachusetts: Addison-Wesley, 1997
Howard, Michael (editor), *Wellingtonian Studies: Essays on the First Duke of Wellington by Five Old Wellingtonian Historians*, Aldershot, Hampshire: Gale and Polden, 1959
James, Lawrence, *The Iron Duke: A Military Biography of Wellington*, London: Weidenfeld and Nicolson, 1992
Longford, Elizabeth, *Wellington: The Years of the Sword*, London: Weidenfeld and Nicolson, 1969; New York: Harper and Row, 1970
Longford, Elizabeth, *Wellington: Pillar of State*, London: Weidenfeld and Nicolson, 1972; New York: Harper and Row, 1973
Neillands, Robin, *Wellington and Napoleon: Clash of Arms, 1807–1815*, London: John Murray, 1994
Paget, Julian, *Wellington's Peninsular War: Battles and Battlefields*, London: Leo Cooper, 1990
Rathbone, Julian (editor), *Wellington's War: Or, "Atty, the Long-Nosed Bugger That Licks the French" – Peninsular Dispatches*, London: Michael Joseph, 1984
Roberts, Andrew, *Napoleon and Wellington*, London: Weidenfeld and Nicolson, 2001
Thompson, Neville, *Wellington after Waterloo*, London and New York: Routledge and Kegan Paul, 1986
Weller, Jac, *Wellington in India*, London: Longman, 1972

Soldier and statesman, Arthur Wellesley, first Duke of Wellington, is a pre-eminent figure in the history of 19th-century Great Britain and Ireland, as well as the military history of Europe and India. He was born in Ireland, the second son of the Earl of Mornington and brother of Richard, Governor-General of India. Wellington (as he will be referred to here) received his early military training in France, and his commission was purchased for him in 1787. Early in his career, he is alleged to have stated, "Since I have undertaken a profession, I had better try to understand it". Many historians claim that he was the first truly professional soldier in Britain.

The story of his career, which began in the politico-military milieu of Dublin castle, is told in LONGFORD (1969, 1972), a two-volume biography that was later condensed into a single volume (*Wellington*, 1992). Neatly divided into two periods – Wellington's public service before and after Waterloo – this is the standard work on the man who rose through every rank of the military and the peerage, acquiring princely titles on the way, to become prime minister in the years 1828 to 1830. Longford writes with elegant style and balance, giving an account of the circumstances and events of Wellington's extraordinary life.

Wellington's first experience of active service in 1794 in the Low Countries taught him much about how not to conduct operations. Two years later he sailed to India with his command, the 33rd Regiment. WELLER's account of his service in India during the next nine years covers military operations undertaken against native rulers to preserve the ascendancy of the British East India Company's interests. Weller writes idiosyncratically but captures the excitement of service in the east and the exotic flavour of the expatriates' and local inhabitants' life. He also describes Wellington's growing expertise and promotions. JAMES writes about the victory at Seringapatam in the Mysore war of 1799. In command of the Nizam of Hyderabad's forces,

Wellington was responsible for defeating the Mysore troops of the sultan Tipoo (or Tipu). James writes cogently about the battle, four years later, at Assaye. In this remarkable battle, where his force was outnumbered by at least six to one, Wellington's eye for the country and for a rapid concentration of force was first evident; later, it would become famous. One feels that his exploits at Assaye merit closer scrutiny and interpretation than they have received so far.

Following a busy period of political activity as a member of parliament, during which Wellington first held political office, he was despatched with a force of men to the Iberian Peninsula in 1809, to re-establish a British presence after the catastrophic retreat to La Coruña (Corunna). In due course he became commander-in-chief, and for the next four years he fought a number of major battles and sieges in the peninsula.

James can be consulted for an assessment of Wellington's growing mastery of strategic movement and timing. PAGET's and RATHBONE's coverage of the battles, illuminated with Wellington's own words, will assist the reader by providing details of his victories, from Vimeiro, Salamanca, and Vitoria to the crossing of the Nivelle and Toulouse. Wellington – who would soon become a viscount and later a marquis – was punctilious about informing the government in London of all details of the war. The transformation of the army under his command into the most efficient British fighting force since Marlborough's war is evident in Wellington's own plain-spoken words. His dispatches range from the acerbic to the restrained, but they are always honest. Accounts of the battles by witnesses, as well as modern authors, all verify Wellington's remarkable *coup d'oeil*, his personal mastery of the ground and the relative dispositions and movements of forces. He also recognized the importance of conserving forces. Better administration of the army was another of his achievements, requiring much careful thought, over a long period.

The battle of Waterloo, Wellington's most famous victory (with a coalition force, reinforced by a German contingent), has relatively recently undergone close scrutiny by HAMILTON-WILLIAMS. Earlier writers may have relied too heavily on faulty accounts. Napoleon, in his first and last encounter with Wellington, threw caution to the wind; Wellington did not. HIBBERT (who has written a twin volume on Admiral Lord Nelson) shows the reader the personal side of Wellington, with glimpses of his carefully controlled feelings. "The most desperate business I ever was in", Wellington wrote privately to his brother of Waterloo. Both ROBERTS and NEILLANDS have written intriguingly about the two opponents: Napoleon's character and approach to all military and political endeavours could not have been more different from Wellington's.

Longford (1972) and THOMPSON write of Wellington's later career. Fascinated by politics, he soon reached senior cabinet rank, serving in Lord Liverpool's cabinet as master general of the ordnance. Two major political movements haunted him, as a staunch defender of the existing order. Although he acquiesced over the Catholic Emancipation Act of 1829, his later resistance to the Great Reform Act of 1832 made him very unpopular for some years.

Recently the Wellington papers have been lodged with the University of Southampton. There has thus been an increasing volume of studies and publications, illuminating his military professionalism (although he would not have recognized the term), experience, and mastery in battle; his administration of armies; and the diplomacy required in forming and holding together coalition armies and concluding peace treaties. His political career has likewise received academic scrutiny.

Wellington's marriage to Kitty Pakenham was not happy. Most authors write of this and his later reputation as ladies' man, which is still cloaked in mystery. In his twilight years, he had the reputation of a very great man, even if his period in office as the army's commander-in-chief did not reflect his brilliance as a field commander 30 years earlier. Finally, HOWARD's gathering of assessments by historians of Wellington "the man", "the general", "the diplomat", "the statesman", and his contribution to "the British Army" brings a succinct and rounded judgement of one of the most remarkable men in British history, whose influence persisted long after his death in 1852.

PATRICK MILEHAM

See also Army: To 1855; Canning; Catholic Emancipation; Congress System; East India Company; George III; George IV; India: Conquest; London, Treaty of; Napoleonic Wars: Waterloo and the War on Land; O'Connell; Palmerston; Peel

Welsh Law (Native and Canon)

Charles-Edwards, T.M., *The Welsh Laws*, Cardiff: University of Wales Press, 1989

Charles-Edwards, T.M., *Early Irish and Welsh Kinship*, Oxford: Clarendon Press, and New York: Oxford University Press, 1993

Charles-Edwards, T.M., Morfydd E. Owen, and D.B. Walters (editors), *Lawyers and Laymen: Studies in the History of Law Presented to Professor Dafydd Jenkins on His Seventy-Fifth Birthday, Gwyl Ddewi, 1986*, Cardiff: University of Wales Press, 1986

Davies, R.R., "Law and National Identity in Medieval Wales" in *Welsh Society and Nationhood: Historical Essays Presented to Glanmor Williams*, edited by Davies *et al.*, Cardiff: University of Wales Press, 1984

Jenkins, Dafydd (editor), *Celtic Law Papers Introductory of Welsh Medieval Law and Government: Studies Presented to the International Commission for the History of Representative and Parliamentary Institutions 42*, Brussels: Éditions de la Librarie Encyclopédique, 1973

Jenkins, Dafydd (editor and translator), *The Law of Hywel Dda: Law Texts from Medieval Wales*, Llandysul, Dyfed: Gomer Press, 1986; corrected edition, 1990

Jenkins, Dafydd and Morfydd E. Owen (editors), *The Welsh Law of Women: Studies Presented to Professor Daniel A. Binchy on His Eightieth Birthday, 3 June 1980*, Cardiff: University of Wales Press, 1980

Pryce, Huw, "The Prologues to the Welsh Lawbooks", *Bulletin of the Board of Celtic Studies*, 33 (1986): 151–87

Pryce, Huw, *Native Law and the Church in Medieval Wales*, Oxford: Clarendon Press, and New York: Oxford University Press, 1993

Stacey, Robin Chapman, *The Road to Judgment: From Custom to Court in Medieval Ireland and Wales*, Philadelphia: University of Pennsylvania Press, 1994

Thirteenth-century Europe was a society fascinated by law. Written law-books appeared all over the European world: the *Sachsenspiegel* in Germany, *Glanvill* and *Bracton* in England, and the *Grágás* in Iceland are but a few of the better-known examples. One of the richest law-book traditions arose in Wales, where no fewer than 40 manuscripts of law were produced in Welsh and Latin between the 13th and the 16th centuries. These law-books were not commissioned by kings or princes; they were, rather, private compilations composed by and for the lawyers who used them. Like the early Irish laws, they are divided into short treatises on individual subjects known as tractates; the subjects covered range broadly, including suretyship and guarantee, theft, the value of animals, and women.

Much of the earliest work on the laws focused on editing the texts and determining the relationships between the many manuscripts in which they were contained. Perhaps the clearest account of this historical process is to be found in CHARLES-EDWARDS (1989). As Charles-Edwards points out, scholars now believe that the principal redactions of the laws all descend from a model law-book composed in the 12th century or earlier. How much earlier has been a central question. Whereas none of the existing manuscripts predates the 13th century, the corpus as a whole is referred to frequently in Welsh prose tradition as the "law of Hywel", after the Welsh king Hywel Dda, "the Good", who died in 949–50. For years the validity of the ascription to Hywel, which is attested to in the prologues of all the extant law-books, was simply taken for granted. Recently, however, some scholars have challenged this association. PRYCE (1986) painstakingly reconstructed the political orientation of the principal versions of the prologues, arguing that their contents and structure reflect concerns of the 12th and 13th centuries rather than events of Hywel's day. Hywel's connection in these prologues with the beginnings of the written legal tradition cannot, Pryce reasoned, be accepted at face value but must be taken instead as a myth reflecting princely politics in the post-Norman period. Pryce's view has not gone unchallenged. Both JENKINS and Charles-Edwards make a case for accepting the ink with Hywel, citing the royalist character of the law-books; the claims of these texts to authority over all of Wales, such as Hywel possessed; and the unlikelihood that later jurists would father a lawbook on this king without cause.

One of the reasons the debate over Hywel has been so lively is that it has larger implications for our understanding of the nature of the laws. It has long been recognized that certain passages in the law-books refer to practices that seem archaic or out of date by contemporary European standards. Some sections indeed have been shown to derive from early medieval models; others to have strong parallels in early Irish tradition. No one disputes the presence of earlier material in these texts. However, there are disagreements as to the balance of early and late. Should the law-books be viewed as standing at the end of a long tradition of written law, much of which is no longer extant? Or should they be understood as part and parcel of the general resurgence of interest in law in Europe during the 12th and 13th centuries? Are they texts that speak to conditions and customs of the early Middle Ages, or do they relate more to the high medieval period in which the legal manuscripts themselves were composed?

Answers to these questions have varied, and usually this is more a matter of emphasis than an outright denial of the inherent ambiguity of the issue. JENKINS & OWEN's important collection of essays on the tractate on women embraced both perspectives. Two articles in the collection look backwards to ancient Irish and Indo-European parallels to the practices outlined in the Welsh law-books, while others focus mainly on the contemporary context. A similar willingness to entertain both points of view characterizes the later collection by CHARLES-EDWARDS, OWEN, & WALTERS. There the division in approach is rendered explicit by the separation of the book into two halves, the first focused on "Celtic suretyship" and featuring articles and translations pertaining to early medieval Irish and Breton as well as Welsh practices, and the second focused on lawyers and judges in England and Wales from the 13th century on. Similarly, both CHARLES-EDWARDS (1993) in his study on kinship and STACEY in her examination of personal suretyship pair Welsh customs with early Irish cognates in an effort to understand not merely the prehistory of the institution they describe but the manner in which ancient practices were adapted to meet the needs of the 12th- and 13th-century world.

Other scholars place the emphasis more firmly on post-Norman tensions and concerns. PRYCE (1993), in an excellent study of the church, acknowledges the presence of "old-fashioned" elements in Welsh ecclesiastical practice but argues that in general the treatment of the church in the laws reflects both post-Gregorian religious priorities and the realities of Welsh political life in the 12th and 13th centuries. Similarly, DAVIES details the role played by the laws in helping to crystallize national identities and political affiliations in the age of the princes.

One useful historiographical development over the past two or three decades has been an attempt to render Welsh law accessible to non-specialists. Jenkins's highly readable translation (1986) of the Iorwerth redaction has been an important step in this direction, as has the production of article collections focusing on individual tractates. Future work will probably continue in this vein and will, as well, begin to explore the legal material known as *damweiniau* ("eventualities") and *cynghawsedd* ("pleadings") frequently appended to the principal law-book redactions.

ROBIN CHAPMAN STACEY

See also Law: Structures of Administration before 1536; Rhodri "the Great" and Hywel "the Good"; Rhuddlan (Wales), Statute of

Wentworth, Thomas

see Strafford, Thomas Wentworth, 1st Earl of

Wesley, John 1703–1791
Founder of methodism

Abelove, Henry, *The Evangelist of Desire: John Wesley and the Methodists*, Stanford, California: Stanford University Press, 1990

Ayling, Stanley, *John Wesley*, London: Collins, and Nashville, Tennessee: Abingdon, 1979

Baker, Frank, *John Wesley and the Church of England*,
    London: Epworth Press, and Nashville, Tennessee:
    Abingdon, 1970
Green, V.H.H., *The Young Mr. Wesley: A Study of John
    Wesley and Oxford*, London: Arnold, and New York:
    St Martin's Press, 1961
Green, V.H.H., *John Wesley*, London: Nelson, 1964
Heitzenrater, Richard P., *Wesley and the People Called
    Methodists*, Nashville, Tennessee: Abingdon Press,
    1995
Rack, Henry D., *Reasonable Enthusiast: John Wesley
    and the Rise of Methodism*, London: Epworth Press,
    and Philadelphia: Trinity Press International, 1989
Schmidt, Martin, *John Wesley: A Theological Biography*,
    translated from the German by Norman P. Goldhawk,
    2 vols, London: Epworth Press, and New York:
    Abingdon, 1962–73 (original German edition,
    1953–66)

As befits a major religious figure, John Wesley – the founder of methodism – has had many biographers. Detailed accounts of his life appeared soon after his death. Nineteenth-century biographical treatments usually accorded him several volumes. An extensive literature on his life and times continued to flow in the 20th century, stimulated partly by Wesley's fame and partly by his elusive personality.

GREEN (1961), an account of Wesley's early life, is the best book on his formative years. It covers Wesley's career at Christ Church and Lincoln College, Oxford, providing much useful background on the political and religious context of university life in the Walpolean era. Wesley's friendships, his family, and the rise of the Oxford "Holy Club" are all dealt with. Material from Wesley's Oxford diaries is deployed effectively to trace these themes. GREEN (1964) is a short life in which the conscientious Wesley is portrayed as a conventional High Churchman in outlook and theology whose evangelical mission and advocacy of Christian perfectionism gave him a distinctive position among religious reformers.

AYLING's biography is a useful corrective to the hagiographical treatment of Wesley by some Victorian methodist writers. Ayling does not hesitate to point out Wesley's foibles but also highlights his more attractive qualities. On the critical side, Wesley is portrayed as credulous, superstitious, dictatorial, self-justifying, humourless, and sometimes blunt, insensitive, and bigoted. His narrow views on literature and children's education are discussed. More positively, Ayling reminds us that Wesley had courage, unflagging energy, a sense of mission, great will-power, and force of character. He propagated methodism by evangelistic methods, pragmatic leadership, and effective organization. His unexclusive societies had a broad appeal, especially to laymen and -women in the lower ranks of society.

SCHMIDT, a German church historian, offers a theological biography. Such a focus is justified by Wesley's lifelong commitment to salvation. There is particular emphasis on Wesley's piety and his puritan heritage. Thematic chapters cover Wesley's role as preacher, theological writer, pastor, educationalist, and organizer. The opposition to Wesley is also discussed. Schmidt sees Wesley as a dominant, rather austere personality who was influenced far more by the Bible and by individual fathers of the church than by his contemporaries.

Wesley's complex relationship with the Church of England is discussed by BAKER. He shows that Wesley's irregularity in his dealings with the established church led him towards promoting methodism as an independent denomination in his old age. The break did not occur in his lifetime, but it happened only a few years after his death. Baker does not explore whether Wesley clung to his Anglican position for ecumenical reasons or in order to retain a certain social status. Nor does Baker consider whether Wesley's Anglican critics may have been sound in pointing to the potential for schism as a negative legacy of the early methodist movement. Nevertheless, he shows clearly how Wesley's personality was intertwined with the Anglican church in thought, habit, and atmosphere.

ABELOVE examines why so many long-standing followers were attracted to Wesleyan methodism. He attributes this partly to Wesley's personal charisma as a spontaneous preacher reaching out to a large flock, but he also argues that early methodist members and hearers were not merely passive recipients of Wesley's teaching. Wesley attracted support by going directly to the ground of the poor to let them hear him there. He provided ordinary people with medical care, without charge, and offered charity and free grace. But early methodists were vigorously independent; they disagreed strongly with some of Wesley's main ideas. They reacted against his stance in favor of celibacy. They discriminated among the rules for daily conduct that Wesley set down for them. "They heard what he said", Abelove notes, "but they heard it in ways that suited themselves mutually".

RACK considers that to evaluate Wesley's career, an understanding of the religious and social environment of Hanoverian Britain is crucially important. He describes Wesley as a "reasonable enthusiast" because Wesley was an ordained, precise, lifelong member of the Church of England who also proselytized to the lower orders with spontaneity and concern for their spiritual and pastoral care. Wesley created a shared sense of purpose among his preachers and followers, but the efforts of other early pioneers of revivalism were as important as Wesley's itinerant activity for the success of methodism. Early methodism captured a religious minority that might never have experienced organized religion; it established a national connection at a time when church life was localized. These remarkable achievements, however, were accompanied by splits, tension, and controversy over the structure and piety of the movement.

HEITZENRATER looks at Wesley in relation to the religious revival of the 1730s and 1740s and to the movement Wesley's leadership spawned. He discusses the development of classes and bands, societies and schools, conferences and clinics that nourished the "people called methodists". He refers to many early methodists who are not usually mentioned in studies of John Wesley. These obscure people were at the heart of what methodism hoped to achieve, and any understanding of Wesley's mission needs to give them a voice. Heitzenrater also discusses the theological, missionary, and organizational aspects of early methodism. He agrees with Rack and other scholars that Wesley's personality was complex, paradoxical, and difficult to pin down but sees a unifying focus in Wesley's life – a concern for spreading scriptural holiness. Still, the early methodist movement was not very unified, and in the 18th century it never had a large membership: its broader appeal came with the rise of industrialization. Neither Rack nor Heitzenrater provides a conventional biography, yet more can be learned from their books about Wesley's character and achievements and the changing context in which he lived than from most other recent book-length treatments.

KENNETH MORGAN

See also Methodism; Protestant Dissent

Westminster, Statutes of 1275–1290

André, Thomas J. Jr, "The Implied Remedies Doctrine and the Statute of Westminster II", *Tulane Law Review*, 54 (1980): 589–623

Bean, J.M.W., *The Decline of English Feudalism, 1215–1540*, Manchester: Manchester University Press, and New York: Barnes and Noble, 1968

Brand, Paul, "Legal Change in the Later Thirteenth Century: Statutory and Judicial Remodeling of the Action of Replevin", *American Journal of Legal History*, 31 (1987): 43–55

Brand, Paul, "Lordship and Distraint in Thirteenth-Century England" in his *The Making of the Common Law*, London and Rio Grande, Ohio: Hambledon Press, 1992

Jenks, Edward, *Edward Plantagenet (Edward I), The English Justinian; or, The Making of the Common Law*, London and New York: Putnam, 1901

Kiralfy, A.K.R., *The Action on the Case: An Historical Survey of the Development of the Action up to the Year 1700, in the Light of the Original Plea Rolls and Other Unpublished Sources, with an Excursus on the Doctrine of Consideration and a Note on Case in Inferior Courts*, London: Sweet and Maxwell, 1951

Plucknett, T.F.T., *Legislation of Edward I*, Oxford: Clarendon Press, 1949

Plucknett, T.F.T., "Case and the Statute of Westminster II" in his *Studies in English Legal History*, London: Hambledon Press, 1983

Post, J.B., "Ravishment of Women and the Statutes of Westminster" in *Legal Records and the Historian: Papers Presented to the Cambridge Legal History Conference, 7–10 July 1975, and in Lincoln's Inn Old Hall on 3 July 1974*, edited by J.H. Baker, London: Royal Historical Society, 1978

Simpson, A.W.B., *An Introduction to the History of the Land Law*, London: Oxford University Press, 1961

Sutherland, Donald W., "Mesne Process upon Personal Actions in the Early Common Law", *Law Quarterly Review*, 82 (1966): 482–96

Sutherland, Donald W., *The Assize of Novel Disseisin*, Oxford: Clarendon Press, 1973

There is no one single work that treats the three 13th-century Statutes of Westminster – Westminster I, 3 Edw. I (1275); Westminster II, 13 Edw. I (1285); and Westminster III (or *Quia emptores*), 18 Edw. I (1290) – either individually or collectively as social, economic, legal, or administrative phenomena. Discussions have, instead, turned on sections of these statutes, not the statutes as a whole, for purely legal or legal historical purposes, not for their social or economic effects on later medieval England.

For example, ANDRÉ discusses whether the doctrine of "implied remedies" – that a private remedy can be implied in a statute not expressly providing for such – originated in Westminster II ch. 50, as first enunciated by Lord Justice Coke in his *Institutes*. André asserts that it cannot, as ch. 50 was instituted merely to delay immediate implementation of the statute until the statute could be made widely known. Another study dealing with bits and pieces of these statutes is that by POST, who discusses the clauses on rape and ravishment found in Westminster I, ch. 13, which prohibited abduction or rape with or without consent; and Westminster II, ch. 34, which made rape with or without consent a capital offence (it also provided that if the victim refused to appeal the rapist, the crown could do so within 40 days). Both provisions were important as statutory pronouncement because, though the treatises known as "Glanvill" and "Bracton" both considered rape and abduction a capital offence, in practice the courts rarely convicted. However, despite Westminster I, the courts still refused to enforce the statute and instead found innumerable ways to nonsuit an appellant. Westminster II, ch. 34, seems to be aimed at stopping this practice, but the entire thrust of the clause suggests that it was added as an afterthought, not as part of the king's general efforts to curb crime and disorder. Instead, the law was aimed at "willful womenfolk" who sought to use ravishment as a means to force familial acceptance of an unsuitable match.

Brand provides two further studies dealing piecemeal with the statutes. BRAND (1987) examines Westminster II, ch. 2, as it relates to the old practice of replevin (the laws concerning the restoration of stolen goods). The problem addressed was, as the statute itself explained, an abuse of replevin by tenants in county courts to escape a lord's distraint (seizure of goods) against them for services. The statute allowed the lords to remove the matter into the king's courts, make it one of record, and use the action of right to recover the land involved. Besides an immediate increase of such actions in the king's courts after 1285, the statute also allowed lords to avow such a distraint whether or not they or their immediate ancestor held the land, as long as any one of their ancestors had held it after the limitation date (then the year 1242) for novel disseisin (i.e. recent dispossession of lands). This dramatically expanded the use of distraint for a much wider range of situations than had previously been allowed. BRAND (1992) notices two further subsections of this chapter: one prevented a tenant from disposing of animals distrained without a pledge; the other penalized the tenant for not prosecuting his plea of unjust replevin against the lord without a special judicial writ awarded by the court. Although court rolls do not show that either practice was a particular problem before Westminster II, both practices suddenly appear frequently in the records thereafter. As the statute gave the advantage to the lord against the tenant, presumably the sudden appearance of both practices in the records indicates that lords immediately used these provisions to press claims against their tenants.

SUTHERLAND (1966) elaborates the context for ch. 45 of Westminster I and ch. 39 of Westminster II, both of which concern distraints to enjoin the appearance of a defendant in a civil process. Short of outlawry, compelling appearance was a difficult and time-consuming procedure. Thus both of these sections provided for a summary process of immediate attachment and distraint of all the defendant's lands and chattels. In theory this should have worked well. In practice, however, it did not, foundering on the inability of sheriffs to pursue the statutory remedy consistently. SUTHERLAND (1973) notes that one purpose of the Statutes of Westminster was to provide speedy justice – something that was still a foreign idea. Thus in Westminster II, ch. 45, a process of *scire facias* (requiring persons to attend court) was instituted to cut through the old requirements and provide for quick and easy enforcement of the plaintiff's rights. Heavy penalties were also set forth for mendacious pleas designed to delay enforcement of the action in Westminster II, ch. 25, which also extended the assize to common rights of every kind, thus extending royal justice into matters previously handled by the local sheriff. A process of *elegit* – choosing to have the defendant's lands seized and taking the debt from the profits thereof instead of the older cumbersome process – was provided by Westminster II, ch. 18, which made debt collection quicker.

One of the few controversies arising from the Statutes of Westminster concerns the action of *Case* (from whence derives much of the law of contract, personal property, and tort). PLUCKNETT (1983) examines the long-held idea that *Case* derives from the *in consimili casu* clause of Westminster II, ch. 24. Despite its appearance in Blackstone as an age-old remedy, he found that it could not be traced back beyond 1591, when it was originated by the legal writer and printer William Lambarde. However, KIRALFY found that the Provisions of Oxford of 1258 had prohibited, as a check on overreaching royal justice, the issuance of writs for forms of action not already recognized in the common law. *In consimili casu* effectively gutted this provision, by allowing the issuance of writs for new forms of action as long as the facts complained of were similar to those contained in already recognized writs because, as the phrase states in both ch 24 and ch 50 of Westminster II, "that plaintiffs from henceforth shall not depart from the King's court without remedy though a like writ were never granted out of Chancery before". Thus, *in consimili casu* allowed the broad expansion of trespass into our modern forms of tort.

SIMPSON's explication of Westminster II, ch. 1, commonly known as *De donis*, is the most valuable part in this classic work. *De donis* sought to prevent the alienation of land by holders of conditional fees to the detriment of the reversioners, thus defeating the purpose of the gift. From this derives the modern conception of future estates, and the division of tenure into fee simple, fee tail, fee conditional, life estates, contingent remainders, reversions, and terms of years. JENKS deals with *De donis* at greater length. He notes its conservativeness, and that, happily for the landowning aristocracy, it soon became a dead letter owing to the legal fiction known as the "common recovery". He notes its favouring of legal procedure over violence, and its elaborate provisions against abuse by the king's officials, ranging from regulation of fees to incarceration for extortion.

BEAN concentrates on the political and social aspects which lay behind the promulgation of Westminster III (*Quia emptores*). The evidence of the crown in granting licenses to alienate shows that the statute could not have been intended to apply to tenants-in-chief. Westminster III as it stands must, given the evidence, have been the result of a compromise between the king and his barons, to which the barons acquiesced only because of the crown's nearly automatic willingness to grant licences to alienate.

PLUCKNETT (1949) is the only work to discuss all three Westminster statutes in detail. Plucknett concludes that the tenor of these laws is to uphold the age-old forms incident to the feudal relationships, though these age-old forms actually dated back less than a century. Nonetheless, the laws promoted legal and social change, in that the procedural remedies were revolutionary in nature even though they purported to promote a conservative substantive process. In part, this was due to the casual, if not disjointed, nature of their legislative draftsmanship. For example, Westminster I, ch. 17, concerned with executing writs of replevin, requires the sheriff to act, even in a liberty, and even if violence would ensue – though procedure and method were not spelled out. Ten years later, Westminster II, ch. 39, provides this method by splitting the procedure in two. First, to provide a check upon a sheriff who claims no service of writ because of the existence of a liberty, the Treasury was to maintain a list of such liberties. Second, if the claimed liberty was genuine, a new writ could be sent back to the sheriff ordering the summoning of a jury *non omittas*, and a writ of *scire facias* could be sent directly to the bailiff of the liberty which could show fraud or indolence on the part of the sheriff. (*Non omittas*, according to the sixth editon of *Black's Law Dictionary*, is a clause usually inserted in writs of execution in England, directing the sheriff "not to omit" to execute the writ by reason of any liberty, because there are many liberties or districts in which the sheriff has no power to execute process unless he has special authority.) All well and good. However, in practice, often a plaintiff was compelled to accept a jury chosen by his adversary because when the bailiff of the liberty, the sheriff, and the jury chosen by the sheriff under the *non omittas* writ all showed up on the same day, and the bailiff could prove fraud on the part of the sheriff, the jury was improperly empanelled, yet the justices were reluctant to send the jurors back home and take the time and expense to empanel a new jury.

Again, in Westminster I, ch. 16, upon a proper distraint held and kept in a castle or fortress, the sheriff was given power to take the *posse comitatus* to retrieve the distraint if he could. Westminster II, ch. 36, gave tenants the power to claim a malicious distraint and recover treble damages; and ch. 37 prohibits all but bailiffs known to the countryside from levying the distraint. While both provisions deal with the old procedure of distraint, they give new remedies favouring tenants over landlords and tipping the judicial balance against the latter. Most famously, Westminster II, ch. 1 (*De donis*), begins by enacting that the will of the donor, in a gift of land, is to be observed, but goes on to detach the gift after only a life in being, thereby defeating the dynastic principle upon which the statute is purportedly based. Thus, while the purpose was to keep land within the family, the remedy adopted freed the land for alienation after only the life of the first taker.

Finally, in Westminster III, to keep landlords from losing their feudal incidents (escheats, marriages, and wardships) – a conservative goal – the remedy was to provide for transfer of the land henceforth by substitution (the alienee replacing the alienor in the tenurial chain, assuming all the obligations and incidents), not subinfeudation (so that the alienee held directly of the alienor, not the landlord, with the chances of escheat and the other incidents accruing to the landlord thus becoming more and more remote). However, this remedy was revolutionary in effect, as it gradually yet inevitably decayed the nexus between landlord and tenant, preventing the creation of new tenants in the tenurial chain, as well as the incidents which, through distraint, kept control of tenants by landlords. In the end, then, while Edward I's statutes of Westminster seemed to intend a strengthening of the feudal relationship, the remedies provided for this strengthening had a revolutionary effect which, by the end of the medieval era, destroyed the feudal relationship and paved the way for our modern landholding system.

JEROME S. ARKENBERG

See also Edward I; Feudal Law

Whigs: 1670s to 1714

Ashcraft, Richard, *Revolutionary Politics and Locke's Two Treatises of Government*, Princeton, New Jersey: Princeton University Press, 1986

Greaves, Richard L., *Secrets of the Kingdom: British Radicals from the Popish Plot to the Revolution of 1688–1689*, Stanford, California: Stanford University Press, 1992

Harris, Tim, *Politics under the Later Stuarts: Party Conflict in a Divided Society, 1660–1715*, London and New York: Longman, 1993

Jones, J.R., *The First Whigs: The Politics of the Exclusion Crisis, 1678–1683*, London and New York: Oxford University Press, 1961; revised edition, 1970

Kenyon, J.P., *Revolution Principles: The Politics of Party, 1689–1720*, Cambridge and New York: Cambridge University Press, 1977

Sachse, William L., *Lord Somers: A Political Portrait*, Manchester: Manchester University Press, and Madison: University of Wisconsin Press, 1975

Scott, Jonathan, *Algernon Sidney and the Restoration Crisis, 1677–1683*, Cambridge and New York: Cambridge University Press, 1991

Zook, Melinda S., *Radical Whigs and Conspiratorial Politics in Late Stuart England*, University Park: Pennsylvania State University Press, 1999

JONES set the agenda for modern studies of the emergence of what became the Whig party in the late 1670s. Jones's principal concern was defending the late 17th century from the extension of Namierite models of 18th-century English politics, based on factions and aristocratic connection rather than party struggles over political issues. In a Whiggish history of the Whigs, Jones describes them as an ideologically coherent and ideologically driven political grouping, under the overall leadership of the Earl of Shaftesbury. The programme of Shaftesbury and the party generally was the exclusion of the catholic James, Duke of York, the king's brother and heir, from the succession to the throne – hence the term "exclusion crisis" for the period 1679–81.

SCOTT (1991), the second volume of a two-volume study of Algernon Sidney, is based on much more extensive archival research than Jones's work; and an attack on Jones's thesis is a central feature of this book, which resembles Sidney himself in its pugnaciousness. Revealing the slimness of much of Jones's

evidence, Scott denies nearly every major aspect of Jones's picture of the early Whigs. The first Whigs constituted not a political party but an intellectual position that people moved into and out of at different times. Shaftesbury was not the leader of the Whigs, or even the most important Whig politician, but one of several sometimes cooperating and sometimes competing leaders, including most notably Sidney. Exclusion was not the central issue for the Whigs; it played a minor role for most of the period, subordinate to the Whigs' fear of "popery and arbitrary government". Like other recent writers, Scott avoids the term "exclusion crisis" entirely, preferring "restoration crisis". He puts this crisis in the context of the 17th century, when the Whigs were essentially reiterating the positions of Civil War parliamentarians – indeed, they were often (as in Sidney's case) the same people. Scott's influential work has provoked a great deal of debate in studies of the early Whigs, although most subsequent scholars have not followed him in denying that the Whigs constituted a party.

The ideology of the early Whigs has been mostly studied by American scholars interested in the more extreme Whigs and seeking the origins of liberalism in such allegedly Whig ideas as government by the consent of the governed, contract theory, and the right of revolution. ASHCRAFT's massive work, a combined study of the ideas of John Locke and radical Whig politics, basically accepts Jones's model of the Whig party. Ashcraft historically situates Locke, Shaftesbury's physician, as a Shaftesbury Whig, rather than as a timeless political thinker, and identifies the Whigs with proto-democratic thinking and political contract theory. Ashcraft's primary concern is Locke rather than Whiggism, and read in isolation his book gives a view of Whiggism which is unduly Locke-centric.

ZOOK, despite the reference to conspiracy in her title, offers primarily a study of the thought of five radical Whig activists and propagandists: William Atwood, Thomas Hunt, the Reverend Samuel Johnson, Robert Ferguson "the Plotter", and James Tyrell. She argues that these, and not Locke (or Sidney), were the intellectual leaders of the radical Whigs, in addition to being much bolder politicians and thinkers than Locke. Zook de-emphasizes the role of religion in Whig ideology, claiming the radical Whigs as ancestors of modern liberalism. She also attempts to include Whig women, often but not always printers and booksellers, in her picture of early Whiggism – a difficult task, owing to gaps in the historical record. The book contains a useful list of radical Whigs and their careers, and material on the formation of the Whig legend.

GREAVES (1992) is the final volume in a trilogy on Restoration radicalism. The author is less interested in ideology than Ashcraft or Zook and more interested in Whig activism and conspiracy and in religion. He puts English Whiggism in a British context, with extensive coverage of Scotland and Ireland as well as the British exile communities on the Continent. His detailed narrative is a vivid guide to the shadowy radical Whig underground of the 1680s and its myriad of plots and cabals. He emphasizes the contributions of the surviving radicals to the Revolution of 1688 and the Revolution settlement.

The radical Whigs have perhaps received attention disproportionate to their importance in their own time (whatever their importance for the liberal tradition). KENYON balances the scales with a history of Whig (and Tory) ideology which puts at the centre mainstream moderate Whig thought and its relation to national politics and the actions of parliamentary Whig leaders. He finds a continuous story of moral degeneration, particularly after the trial of Henry Sacheverell in 1710 made Whig leaders aware of their unpopularity. After the Whigs supported the Occasional Conformity Bill in 1711 and the Septennial Act in 1716, Whiggism lost what little revolutionary quality remained to it and became the ideology of a corrupt ruling class.

Surprisingly little has been written on the Whig parliamentary party during the reigns of King William and Queen Anne, particularly in comparison with the oceans of ink spilled for the Tories. One reason is that the Junto Whig leaders, who dominated the party, left few personal or political papers. SACHSE's biography of one Junto leader, Lord Keeper Somers, is scholarly, although perhaps overly favourable to Somers and not very sparkling. It focuses on the public life of a man who left a record of little else, and gives a Junto's-eye view of the high politics of the reigns of William and Anne. HARRIS synthesizes central government and local party politics from the Restoration to the Hanoverian succession in a series of analytical chapters. He sees the Whigs as fundamentally a religious party, emphasizing (contrary to Scott) the party organization of the first Whigs and (contrary to the liberal school) the Tory nature of the Revolution settlement. Harris complements Kenyon's analysis in the field of ideas with an analysis based on political practice; he argues that the Whigs slowly metamorphosed into a court party during the reigns of William and Anne, setting the stage for the Whig oligarchy of Sir Robert Walpole and the "Old Corps".

WILLIAM E. BURNS

See also Anne; Danby; James VII and II

Whigs: 1714 to *c.*1760

Browning, Reed, *The Duke of Newcastle*, New Haven, Connecticut: Yale University Press, 1975

Browning, Reed, *Political and Constitutional Ideas of the Court Whigs*, Baton Rouge: Louisiana State University Press, 1982

Cannon, John (editor), *The Whig Ascendancy: Colloquies on Hanoverian England*, London: Arnold, and New York: St Martin's Press, 1981

Dickinson, H.T., *Walpole and the Whig Supremacy*, London: English Universities Press, 1973

Dickinson, H.T., *Liberty and Property: Political Ideology in Eighteenth-Century Britain*, London: Weidenfeld and Nicolson, and New York: Holmes and Meier 1977

Hill, B.W., *The Growth of Parliamentary Parties, 1689–1742*, London: Allen and Unwin, and Hamden, Connecticut: Archon Books, 1976

Hill, B.W., *British Parliamentary Parties, 1742–1832: From the Fall of Walpole to the First Reform Act*, London and Boston: Allen and Unwin, 1985

Kenyon, John P., *Revolution Principles: The Politics of Party, 1689–1720*, Cambridge and New York: Cambridge University Press, 1977

Owen, John B., *The Rise of the Pelhams*, London: Methuen, 1957; New York: Barnes and Noble, 1971

Plumb, J.H., *Sir Robert Walpole*, 2 vols, London: Cresset Press, 1956–60

Sedgwick, Romney, *The House of Commons, 1715–1754*, 2 vols, London: HMSO, and New York: Oxford University Press, 1970

Wilkes, John W., *A Whig in Power: The Political Career of Henry Pelham*, Evanston, Illinois: Northwestern University Press, 1964

The fortunes of the Whigs were transformed by the Hanoverian succession in 1714, which ushered in decades of Whig political domination after the years of William and Anne when non-party and Tory men had been preferred. The Whigs had always been committed to the protestant succession, and they had striven hard for the accession of George I. By contrast, the Tories were ambivalent at best and hostile at worst. Not surprisingly, the first two Hanoverian monarchs believed that they owed their throne to the Whigs. The result was decades of Whig power and the slow but steady disintegration of the Tory party.

The leading Whig politicians who dominated the ministries of the first two Georges – particularly Robert Walpole, Henry Pelham, and the Duke of Newcastle – and the disciplined party that gave them their clear majorities in parliament were known as the "Old Corps Whigs", both by their contemporaries and by modern historians. They were opposed by the declining Tory party and by some disaffected Whigs. By 1760, when George III came to the throne, almost everyone in parliament was a "Whig" of some description and there was no organized Tory opposition. However, given the deep hostility of George III to the "Old Corps", this disciplined group rapidly disintegrated and parliament and the ministries were now dominated by a range of smaller Whig factions and connections.

The long supremacy of the Old Corps Whigs under the first two Georges had led them to abandon the more radical principles of their predecessors. As men of wealth, status, and power, they found it easier to accept the power of the crown and exploit royal patronage to their own political advantage. Not surprisingly, this allowed their opponents to charge them with betraying their principles and holding on to power by corrupt means. While there is some justice in this accusation, it goes too far. The Old Corps Whigs had never claimed to be radical democrats eager to give power to the common people, and they remained loyal to their most important political principles. They were staunch supporters of the Hanoverian succession and defeated the Jacobites' efforts to effect a Stuart restoration. They accepted and safeguarded the main achievements and consequences of the revolution settlement: limited monarchy, regular sessions of parliament, the national debt, toleration for protestant dissenters, the right to petition, a free press, and the rule of law.

There are, perhaps surprisingly, no studies devoted solely to a history of the Whig party after the Glorious Revolution. To trace the aims and activities of the Whigs in the reigns of William III and Queen Anne, see Tim Harris, *Politics under the Later Stuarts: Party Conflicts in a Divided Society, 1660–1715* (1993), a useful introductory overview for the student that deals with much more than the Whig party; William L. Sachse, *Lord Somers: A Political Portrait* (1975), a scholarly, reliable, though rather dull study of the greatest Whig leader; and Geoffrey Holmes's magisterial study *British Politics in the Age of Anne* (2nd edn, 1987).

No one has attempted a study devoted exclusively to the fortunes of the Old Corps Whigs in the reigns of George I and George II. However, much can be gleaned about them from the two volumes on parliamentary parties by HILL (1976, 1985). These studies are well researched, clearly written, and persuasively argued, though they do not focus on the Old Corps in particular. Much can also be learned about the Old Corps from useful biographical studies of its most important leaders. DICKINSON (1973) explains Walpole's political success and his Whig support in and out of parliament; see also PLUMB (1956–60). For other notable individuals, see WILKES on Henry Pelham and BROWNING (1975) on the Duke of Newcastle. A vast amount can be gleaned, but only by determined effort, from the short biographical studies of all the Old Corps members of parliament to be found in SEDGWICK. While there is no study devoted solely to the Old Corps under Walpole, there is a brilliant monograph by OWEN devoted to Pelham's and Newcastle's successful efforts to hold the Old Corps Whigs together after Walpole fell in 1742.

There are some excellent specialist studies devoted to the Whigs' political principles and ideology. KENYON provides much the best study of the shifting ideologies of the Whigs (and Tories) between 1689 and 1720. BROWNING (1982) is the fullest treatment of court Whig ideology under the first two Georges. There is a useful chapter by DICKINSON (1977), who has also attempted to explain the Whigs' programme and beliefs in an essay in CANNON's collection.

H.T. DICKINSON

See also George I; George II; George III; Hanoverian Succession

Whigs: *c.*1760–*c.*1860

Brock, Michael, *The Great Reform Act*, London: Hutchinson, 1973; reprinted, Aldershot, Hampshire: Gregg Revivals, 1993

Derry, John W., *The Regency Crisis and the Whigs 1788–1789*, Cambridge: Cambridge University Press, 1963

Elofson, W.M., *The Rockingham Connection and the Second Founding of the Whig Party, 1768–1773*, Montreal and Kingston, Ontario: McGill-Queen's University Press, 1996

Guttridge, G.H., *English Whiggism and the American Revolution*, Berkeley: University of California Press, 1942

Mandler, Peter, *Aristocratic Government in the Age of Reform: Whigs and Liberals, 1830–1852*, Oxford: Clarendon Press, and New York: Oxford University Press, 1990

Mitchell, Austin, *The Whigs in Opposition 1815–1830*, Oxford: Clarendon Press, 1967

Mitchell, L.G., *Charles James Fox and the Disintegration of the Whig Party 1782–1794*, Oxford: Oxford University Press, 1971

Namier, Lewis, *England in the Age of the American Revolution*, London: Macmillan, 1930; 2nd edition, London: Macmillan, and New York: St Martin's Press, 1961

O'Gorman, Frank, *The Whig Party and the French Revolution*, London: Macmillan, and New York: St Martin's Press, 1967

O'Gorman, Frank, *The Rise of Party in England: The Rockingham Whigs 1760–1782*, London: Allen and Unwin, 1975

Roberts, Michael, *The Whig Party 1807–1812*, London: Macmillan, 1939; reprinted, New York: Barnes and Noble, 1965

Southgate, Donald, *The Passing of the Whigs 1832–1886*, London: Macmillan, and New York: St Martin's Press, 1962

Vincent, John, *The Formation of the Liberal Party, 1857–1868*, London: Constable, 1966; 2nd edition, Hassocks, East Sussex: Harvester Press, 1976

The first Whig party had done most to secure the Glorious Revolution of 1688–89 and to safeguard the Hanoverian succession in 1714. The party's reward had been decades of political dominance throughout the reigns of the first two Georges. Throughout the period 1714–60 these two monarchs relied on the "Old Corps" Whigs to form their administrations and to support their policies. This situation came to a dramatic end with the accession of George III in 1760. This young, British-born monarch was determined to escape from the political clutches of the leading Whigs who had been in power for so long. He soon undermined the powerful Whig administration of Newcastle and Pitt and removed many second-rank Whigs from court and Treasury appointments. This so-called "massacre of the Pelhamite innocents" in 1761 (Pelham was the Duke of Newcastle's family name) effectively destroyed the Whig party that could trace its descent from the exclusion crisis of the late 1670s. For more than two decades George III made and remade ministries without thinking primarily of the party allegiance of those who composed or supported these administrations. There were no "party" governments at this time. And yet, ironically, since the first Tory party had already disappeared from the political scene by the 1750s, all leading politicians would have described themselves as "Whigs" because they all accepted the Glorious Revolution, the Hanoverian succession, the prevailing constitution, and the existing social hierarchy.

Party discipline and ideological differences were not to reappear as major forces in parliamentary and constituency politics until new issues arose that fundamentally divided both the political elite and the electorate on how best to respond to them. The most important issues were the American Revolution (the War of Independence), the French Revolution, and the profound social and economic problems created by rapid and unprecedented industrialization. On these issues the more liberal politicians began to take a line which resisted executive decisions, attacked the crown's patronage, defended civil and religious liberties, and advocated modest parliamentary reform. These men claimed to be the "true heirs" of the old Whig tradition; and as they developed organization, discipline, coherence, and policies, a second Whig party was born. By at least 1815 a new Whig party was clearly in existence (as was a new Tory party, arising largely from the deeply conservative Whigs). The Whigs were a minority in parliament on their first appearance in the 1780s and did not secure a clear majority until 1830, but they were the better organized and more ideologically coherent party. This second Whig party passed the Great Reform Act of 1832 and dominated British politics for the next two decades. In the 1850s and 1860s it gradually fused with more radical and middle-class forces, and with the remnants of the Peelites, to form the new Liberal party of the later 19th century. Thereafter, the Whigs quite quickly withered and disappeared as an organized party or even a section of a party.

NAMIER (1930) did much to demolish the idea of a survival of the Whig and Tory parties across the middle decades of the 18th century, and he established the reality that the political world was dominated by a number of factions or connections and by the independent back-benchers, all with a loose adherence to Whiggish ideas. While some of Namier's work has not stood the test of time, this particular work remains essential reading for any student of parliamentary and constituency politics in the 1760s.

GUTTRIDGE was the first scholar to study how the crisis of the American Revolution helped forge the Rockingham connection into a coherent group which claimed to be the true heirs of the Whig tradition and which began to acquire some of the discipline, organization, and ideological commitment expected of a "party". O'GORMAN (1975) is a massive, close, and detailed study of the Rockinghams as they developed into the second Whig party. O'Gorman, too, paid close attention to the impact of the American crisis on this particular connection, but he explored, in addition, the Rockinghams' attitude towards George III, crown patronage, and economic reform, and Edmund Burke's developing notions of "party". ELOFSON (1996) is less detailed, though it covers a narrower chronological span. Elofson concentrates on how the Rockingham connection was governed by a coherent set of constitutional ideals and saw "party" as a vehicle for public-spirited men to advance the right political principles.

L.G. MITCHELL (1971), a scholarly study, starts in 1782, where O'Gorman's study ends. Mitchell demonstrates how the intellectual and organizational bases of the new Whig party were developed under the leadership of Charles James Fox. He reveals the growing cohesion of the Whigs in the 1780s, and their growing organizational strength, but he also explores the severe strains the party faced in dealing with the problems created by the regency crisis of 1788–89 and by the French Revolution in the early 1790s (which irrevocably split the party in 1794). DERRY provides a more detailed and very valuable study of the Whigs' reaction to the regency crisis. O'GORMAN (1967), however, provides the best and most detailed study of how the Whig party was divided and all but destroyed by the end of 1793 through its inability to appreciate the threat that the French Revolution posed to the British constitution and ruling elite – a threat that drove the vast majority of the political nation into William Pitt's more conservative camp.

There is very little good work on the Whig party between its nadir in the mid-1790s and its slow revival up to 1815. ROBERTS has provided a scholarly study of the party during the middle years of this period. He concentrates on the party's attitude towards the catholic question, the war against Napoleon, and the question of reform, and on its internal disputes about how it should be led and where it should find allies. Roberts's work is narrowly focused, and much of value lies in its detailed treatment of these issues. For this period of the history of the second Whig party, the best studies are not

histories of the party as a whole but biographies of its leading men, particularly modern biographies of Charles James Fox and Charles, Earl Grey. For the years in opposition between 1815 and 1830 there is the fine analytical study by Austin MITCHELL (1967). This study examines the party's principles, its organization, and its attitude towards repression and reform. The author also provides a detailed narrative of the party's fluctuating fortunes until it found itself in office at last in 1830. On the basis of impressive research, he presents a very clear thesis about the reality of party and about the nature of Whiggism in this period.

BROCK rather neglects popular politics, but he does offer an excellent study of the events within court and parliament and the role of the Whigs in particular in passing the Great Reform Act of 1832, which did so much to allow the Whig party to dominate the next two decades. MANDLER's magisterial and invaluable study analyses the nature of aristocratic Whiggism and the development of a distinct liberalism in 1830–1852 and provides an excellent study of the Whigs in government and in opposition during these two decades. Mandler maintains that the aristocratic Whigs had ceased to be the dominant element in their coalition with the Liberals by 1852, as the Liberals took on a more pronounced middle-class character, particularly in the constituencies. In his view the idea of an aristocratic party posing as the people's trustees had become an anachronism by 1850. SOUTHGATE, on the other hand, sees a distinct Whig element surviving in the Liberal Party up to 1886. His older, though still useful, study is strongest on the period covered by Mandler's book. In the early chapters, Southgate analyses the Whig party's attitude towards the landed interest, the Corn Law crisis, the colonies, and Ireland. While he admits that the Whigs could not survive as an independent party after the early 1850s, he does see them as part of a coalition within the Liberal Party for another quarter of a century. VINCENT, in his classic work, regards the Whigs as one element in the political coalition which made up the mid-Victorian Liberal party.

H.T. DICKINSON

See also Fox, Charles James; Grey; Liberal Party; Pitt, William, "the Younger"; Rockingham

Whitgift, John 1532–1604
Archbishop of Canterbury

Ayre, John (editor), *The Works of John Whitgift D.D.*, 3 vols, Cambridge: Cambridge University Press, 1851–53; reprinted, New York: Johnson Reprint, 1968

Collinson, Patrick, "The 'Nott Conformytye' of the Young John Whitgift", *Journal of Ecclesiastical History*, 15 (1964): 192–200

Dawley, Powel Mills, *John Whitgift and the English Reformation*, New York: Scribner, 1954; London: A. and C. Black, 1955

Lake, Peter, *Anglicans and Puritans? Presbyterianism and English Conformist Thought from Whitgift to Hooker*, London and Boston: Unwin Hyman, 1988

McGinn, Donald Joseph, *The Admonition Controversy*, New Brunswick, New Jersey: Rutgers University Press, 1949

Porter, H.C., "The Anglicanism of Archbishop Whitgift", *Historical Magazine of the Protestant Episcopal Church*, 31 (1962): 127–41

Strype, John, *The Life and Acts of the Most Reverend Father in God, John Whitgift*, 2 vols, London: Horne, 1718; 2nd edition, as *The Life and Acts of John Whitgift, D.D.*, 3 vols, Oxford: Clarendon Press, 1822

John Whitgift began his long career at Cambridge in 1550. By 1567 he was master of Trinity College, and in 1570 he became vice-chancellor of the university. In 1572 he wrote against the presbyterian programme outlined in the "Admonition to the Parliament", and in 1574 he took up his pen against one of its most able champions, Thomas Cartwright. Whitgift left Cambridge in 1577 when he was made Bishop of Worcester, and on the death of Edmund Grindal in 1583 he became Archbishop of Canterbury. His reputation has fluctuated according to the confessional allegiances of his biographers.

Although Whitgift figures prominently in all histories of the Elizabethan church, he has not been the subject of a modern scholarly biography (a biography of Whitgift projected by P.M. Dawley in 1954 was never published). Consequently, we are obliged to rely on the narratives of earlier authors. The earliest of these is an attractive sketch by Whitgift's secretary, George Paule, which was published in 1612. Paule's account preserves many intimate details, but it remains a eulogy by a grateful dependent. STRYPE (1718) is still the best available account; at over 1,100 pages it may well have served to discourage successors. Strype's work is also valuable because most of the texts he edits have yet to receive the attentions of modern editors. However, Strype exaggerates the degree of consensus among Whitgift's conforming contemporaries.

In 1572 Whitgift published a refutation of the presbyterian position described in the "Admonition to the Parliament". Following the publication of Thomas Cartwright's response, Whitgift produced 1574 "The Defense of the Answere to the Admonition against the Replie of T.C." (1574). Strype has identified Whitgift's characteristic virtue as "invincible patience", and it is nowhere more apparent than in this vast compilation in which Whitgift quotes and refutes the arguments for presbyterianism line by line. This work is available in the accurate edition of AYRE.

Those who have not time to digest the confrontation in its entirety may sample it in McGINN's well-organized anthology. Here, the positions of the parties on each point are summarized through carefully chosen citations. McGinn also provides a provocative preface. He surveys earlier historiography which is critical of Whitgift's role in the controversy, and presents his own analysis as a corrective to those historians who have admired Cartwright the godly rebel: "only too often is the contribution of the Puritans to freedom of worship permitted to overshadow their fanatical intolerance". Whitgift's tolerance emerges here as his most laudable virtue. In an age of religious fanaticism, McGinn argues, Whitgift was less intolerant than his enemies; if he was oppressive, he might have been more so. To this end, McGinn exposes Cartwright's inconsistencies in detail and questions both Cartwright's scholarship and his honesty. McGinn does not, however, recognize that Whitgift's modesty is also a polemical device.

The polemical context of Whitgift's work is analysed by LAKE, who devotes his attention to conformists' contributions to the debate. He examines Whitgift's strategies, details their strengths and weaknesses, and indicates some of the arguments which grew out of them. He shows that although Whitgift and Cartwright shared many doctrinal positions, they had radically different conceptions of the role of the church in salvation. Lake stresses the part that polemical considerations play in the formation of new theological positions. Thus he argues that it was the pressure of Cartwright's attacks which obliged Whitgift to formulate a theory of monarchy. Of particular importance is Lake's observation that Whitgift's defensive stance supplied no spiritual alternative to puritan zeal. Although his position was intellectually coherent, devout conformists had to look to other writers for inspiration.

DAWLEY's detailed survey of Whitgift's activities has been supplemented by three writers. First, COLLINSON's brief essay clarifies Whitgift's position in the controversy of 1565–66 over clerical vestments. Dawley notes that the future archbishop had refused to wear the surplice but subsequently conformed, in the belief that it was a lesser evil than deprivation. Collinson's account shows why in the late 1560s conservative churchmen could still regard Whitgift with some suspicion, and why he could be reproached by puritan opponents as a traitor to their cause. Second, Lake evaluates the different emphases in Whitgift's position on the authority of the episcopate. Dawley suggests that Whitgift's position on episcopacy hardened during his last years. During the controversy with the presbyterians Whitgift had argued that it was an administrative convenience and the will of the sovereign in a matter otherwise indifferent. Later, according to Dawley, Whitgift maintained that the English episcopate was of apostolic foundation and divine inspiration. Lake prefers to define the boundaries of Whitgift's position on the episcopate, while arguing that Whitgift exploited a number of tactical advantages in the ambiguities of this position. Third, PORTER reconsiders Whitgift's role in the Cambridge controversy of 1595 which culminated in the "Lambeth Articles". Dawley, while correcting several earlier misreadings, believes that Whitgift attempted an administrative solution to a theological problem he did not fully understand. Porter, narrowing the debate to the nature of Christian assurance, emphasizes Whitgift's theological subtlety. Most interesting is his argument that the queen misinterpreted Whitgift's intentions in the matter, and that later historians have followed her interpretation.

Whitgift's important administrative reforms fall into two related categories. First, he attempted to ensure that benefices were occupied by well-educated ministers. The shortage of well-educated clergy was a particular embarrassment to the archbishop at a time when he was depriving able ministers who refused to subscribe. Dawley provides an account of Whitgift's measures to improve the education of the clergy. Second, arguing that inadequate livings did not attract educated men to the ministry, Whitgift resisted secular attempts to appropriate the wealth of the church. Later churchmen found this aspect of his administration congenial. In 1665 Izaak Walton's biography of Richard Hooker represented Whitgift as speaking boldly to the queen against the alienation of church property; this unlikely speech is successful because of her respect for her archbishop. Walton uses Whitgift as an example of an archbishop whose good relationship with his sovereign permits the church to maintain its ancient privileges. The tension in this relationship has not been closely studied.

PAUL BOTLEY

See also Cartwright; Elizabeth I; Hampton Court Conference; James VI and I

Wilberforce, William 1759–1833

Politician, philanthropist, and campaigner against the slave trade

Anstey, Roger, *The Atlantic Slave Trade and British Abolition, 1760–1810*, London: Macmillan, and Atlantic Highlands, New Jersey: Humanities Press, 1975

Bebbington, D.W., *Evangelicalism in Modern Britain: A History from the 1730s to the 1980s*, London and Boston: Unwin Hyman, 1989

Bradley, Ian, *Call to Seriousness: The Evangelical Impact on the Victorians*, London: Jonathan Cape, and New York: Macmillan, 1976

Brown, Ford K., *Fathers of the Victorians: The Age of Wilberforce*, Cambridge: Cambridge University Press, 1961

Cormack, Patrick, *Wilberforce: The Nation's Conscience*, London: Pickering, 1983

Coupland, Reginald, *Wilberforce: A Narrative*, 1st edition, Oxford: Clarendon Press, 1923; reprinted, New York: Negro Universities Press, 1968

Furneaux, Robin, *William Wilberforce*, London: Hamish Hamilton, 1974

Hempton, David, "Evangelicalism and Reform c.1780–1832" in *Evangelical Faith and Public Zeal: Evangelicals and Society in Britain 1780–1980*, edited by John Wolffe, London: Society for Promoting Christian Knowledge, 1995

Hilton, Boyd, *The Age of Atonement: The Influence of Evangelicalism on Social and Economic Thought 1785–1865*, Oxford: Clarendon Press, and New York: Oxford University Press, 1988

Howse, Ernest Marshall, *Saints in Politics: The "Clapham Sect" and the Growth of Freedom*, Toronto: University of Toronto Press, 1952; London: Allen and Unwin, 1953

Lean, Garth, *God's Politician: William Wilberforce's Struggle*, London: Darton, Longman and Todd, 1980; Colorado Springs: Helmers and Howard, 1987

Newsome, David, *The Parting of Friends: A Study of the Wilberforces and Henry Manning*, London: John Murray, 1966; as *The Wilberforces and Henry Manning: The Parting of Friends*, Cambridge, Massachusetts: Harvard University Press, 1966

Pollock, John, *Wilberforce*, London: Constable, 1977; New York: St Martin's Press, 1978

Walvin, James, *England, Slaves, and Freedom, 1776–1838*, London: Macmillan, and Jackson: University Press of Mississippi, 1986

Warner, Oliver, *William Wilberforce and His Times*, London: Batsford, 1962; New York: Arco, 1963

Wilberforce, Robert Isaac and Samuel Wilberforce, *The Life of William Wilberforce*, 5 vols, London: John Murray, 1838; reprinted, Freeport, New York: Books for Libraries Press, 1972

Wilberforce, Robert Isaac and Samuel Wilberforce (editors), *The Correspondence of William Wilberforce*, 2 vols, London: John Murray, 1840; revised and enlarged edition, Philadelphia: Perkins, and Boston: Ives and Dennet, 1841; 1st edition reprinted, Miami: Mnemosyne, 1969

Williams, Eric, *Capitalism and Slavery*, Chapel Hill: University of North Carolina, 1944; London: André Deutsch, 1964; with new introduction by Colin A. Palmer, Chapel Hill: University of North Carolina Press, 1994

The Yorkshire politician William Wilberforce was born in Hull on 24 August 1759 and died in London on 29 July 1833. He gained his great reputation when he was converted through an evangelical minister, forewent a promising political career, and became a leader in the campaign to abolish the slave trade and then the institution of slavery itself. He persisted in this, linked with the "Clapham sect", until his death in 1833.

All studies of Wilberforce start with Robert & Samuel WILBERFORCE (1838), a work by his sons which quoted extensively from his diaries, now held at the Bodleian Library at the University of Oxford. It was condensed by Samuel into a single volume in 1862. The dutiful sons also prepared an edition of Wilberforce's correspondence (1840), but this work of filial piety did little to advance understanding of his role.

Twentieth-century studies began with the work by COUPLAND (1923), a professor of colonial history at Oxford. This is still a very influential biography, drawing on major documentary resources. Coupland's emphasis was political; he focused on the abolition of the slave trade as a great event in the history of human freedom. His book was notable – well balanced and sensitive – although he was not interested in Wilberforce's religious values. The focus of HOWSE'S work was on the moral factors in the evangelical campaign. Beginning with the conversion of Wilberforce, Howse traced the impact of the associates in the Clapham sect. Subsequent writers have regarded that approach as somewhat naive: see V. Kiernan, "Evangelicalism and the French Revolution", *Past & Present*, 1 (February 1952); and D. Spring, "The Clapham Sect: Some Social and Political Aspects", *Victorian Studies*, 5 (1961–62).

The fascination with the Clapham sect as a moralizing reform campaign which contributed much to the tone of "Victorianism" reached its apogee with BROWN's account of evangelicalism. This massive (569-page) book expressed a bitter disdain for evangelicalism, reflecting the establishment in mid-century. Brown ridiculed the evangelicals as interfering do-gooders and made much of their innumerable campaigns and their self-righteousness. The overall depiction is of a middle-class movement determined to moralize and thus to silence the legitimate interests of the poor. Brown little understood the variety of evangelical styles and backgrounds, and in making Wilberforce the centre of his portrait he tended to emphasize Wilberforce's wealth, worldly wisdom, and deep political conservatism. There was much truth in the picture of the numerous philanthropic activities which Wilberforce patronized, but Brown simplified the alliances which also gave rise to genuinely radical solutions. Brown alleges, as well, that Wilberforce drifted towards a High Church position in his later life, a point rejected by NEWSOME.

Much was wrong with this approach to the story, and several aspects have been explored by subsequent writers. First, it was important to understand Wilberforce's religion. Second, the way that politics and religion intermeshed in the story required serious re-evaluation. Third, the real significance of reform campaigns in the transformation of old England has been subject to harsh questions.

The re-examination of Wilberforce's religion began with a work that was more about his sons than about Wilberforce himself. This was Newsome's evocative study of the drift of Wilberforce's sons and another prominent Anglican evangelical, Henry Manning, towards the Roman catholic church. Newsome sensitively portrays the inner values of the church evangelicals and traces the attitudes of the Wilberforce sons back to their father's churchly orientation. A series of discussions of early evangelicalism has developed a recent fine historiography epitomized in BEBBINGTON's work, although the best work on Wilberforce's religion is a chapter in ANSTEY's book on the slave trade.

Further discussion has focused on Wilberforce's place within the evangelical community, and more generally on the significance of his associates in the Clapham sect. Few terms could be more misleading than "sect" for this small group of liberal-minded evangelicals, who were willing to cooperate with the Whigs in the interests of social and moral reform. In this they differed sharply from many evangelicals, as BRADLEY showed in his study of evangelicals in parliament. Debate has continued on this point, and the sensitive account by HEMPTON suggests the shaping of Wilberforce's politics. From a different angle, HILTON presents an economic outlook; his perceptive work placed Wilberforce's thought in the context of the emergence of social and economic liberalism and laissez-faire views.

Meanwhile, much debate has focused on going beyond the "great heroes" approach to history and exploring whether humanitarianism was in fact responsible for the abolition of the slave trade or whether, as WILLIAMS alleged, economic motives were involved. The issue remains open, as WALVIN indicated.

The tradition of literary and popular accounts, partly directed towards an evangelical audience, continues. The best of these, by POLLOCK, is well-researched, literary, sensitive, and strongly sympathetic to Wilberforce's religion. CORMACK (1983) is a work by a contemporary politician.

PETER LINEHAM

See also Evangelicalism

Wilfrid *c.634–c.709*
Northumbrian bishop and saint

Colgrave, Bertram (editor and translator), *The Life of Bishop Wilfrid by Eddius Stephanus*, Cambridge: Cambridge University Press, 1927; Cambridge and New York: Cambridge University Press, 1985
Cubitt, C., "Wilfrid's 'Usurping Bishops': Episcopal Elections in Anglo-Saxon England c.600–800," *Northern History*, 25 (1989): 18–38
Foley, William Trent, *Images of Sanctity in Eddius Stephanus's Life of Bishop Wilfrid: An Early English Saint's Life*, Lewiston, New York and Lampeter, Dyfed: Edwin Mellen Press, 1992
Goffart, Walter, *The Narrators of Barbarian History (AD 550–800): Jordanes, Gregory of Tours, Bede, and Paul the Deacon*, Princeton, New Jersey: Princeton University Press, 1988
Gibbs, M., "The Decrees of Agatho and the Gregorian Plan for York", *Speculum*, 48 (1973): 213–46
Kirby, D.P. (editor), *Saint Wilfrid at Hexham*, Newcastle-upon-Tyne: Oriel Press, 1974
Kirby, D.P., "Bede, Eddius Stephanus, and the Life of Wilfrid", *English Historical Review*, 98 (1983): 101–14
Mayr-Harting, Henry, *The Coming of Christianity to Anglo-Saxon England*, London: Batsford, 1972; University Park: Pennsylvania State University Press, 1991 (see chapter 9)
Wormald, Patrick, "Bede, Beowulf, and the Conversion of the Anglo-Saxon Aristocracy" in *Bede and Anglo-Saxon England*, edited by Robert T. Farrell, London: British Archaeological Reports, 1978
Wood, Ian, "Ripon, Francia, and the Franks Casket in the Early Middle Ages", *Northern History*, 26 (1990): 1–19

The turbulent life and career of Wilfrid, a Northumbrian nobleman who exercised considerable power as a bishop in Northumbria and ruled a vast ecclesiastical diocese and federation of *monasteria*, are recounted in two major 8th-century narratives: Bede's *Ecclesiastical History* and the highly polemical *Vita Wilfridi*, which was edited and translated by COLGRAVE. Wilfrid was deprived of his see three times (664–69, 678–86, 691–706). His wanderings and persecutions had a profound effect upon the character and organization of the early English church, involving him in the conversion of the South Saxons, missionary work in Frisia, close contact with Francia, and – most important – appeals to Rome, where he twice sought restoration to his see despite the hostility of Archbishop Theodore and Northumbrian rulers. He was a spokesman for the Roman party at the synod of Whitby (664), was credited with introducing the Rule of Saint Benedict into Northumbria, and was an ambitious builder responsible for the great churches at Ripon and Hexham, of which the 7th-century crypts still survive. MAYR-HARTING provides the best introduction to his career.

Vita Wilfridi, believed to have been composed sometime in the period 710–20, shortly after Wilfrid's death, is directed at his supporters, for whom the saint was said to have worked posthumous miracles; it incorporates papal documents in a chronological narrative. It survives in only two manuscripts. Scholarly investigation has largely focused on establishing the historicity of its account, while recognizing that as a work of hagiography the text is highly tendentious and concerned to build up a particular image of Wilfrid and his episcopate. The identification of the author of *Vita Wilfridi* with a singing-master, Aedde, said to have been brought to Northumbria by Wilfrid has been disputed in KIRBY (1983); Kirby argues that some of the later chapters are interpolations and that *Vita Wilfridi* thus reflects a number of differing traditions about the saint preserved at his communities of Ripon and Hexham. The composite nature of the text is said to reflect ongoing tension surrounding the impact of Wilfrid on the early 8th-century Northumbrian church. This view is taken considerably further by GOFFART, who sees the text and Wilfrid's turbulent career as a catalyst in the prolific production of Northumbrian hagiographical and historical writing during this period. In Goffart's analysis, Bede's lukewarm attitude towards Wilfrid's career reflects political and ecclesiastical conflict between two opposed views of sanctity and church organization, Wilfrid's conception of the role of the holy man contrasting significantly with the asceticism of Cuthbert, who was more sympathetic to the ideals of the Irish church. Goffart considers that Bede had to rewrite Cuthbert's *Life* in order to rescue his cult from the denigration it had suffered at Wilfrid's hands. The tension between these differing ideals of holiness is also explored by FOLEY, who sees them as a product more of different theological traditions than ecclesiastical politics. Foley charts Stephanus's presentation of Wilfrid as a persecuted apostle-like figure whose allegiance to the pope and loyalty to his followers led him into conflict with secular powers.

Wilfrid's career as a bishop and the circumstances surrounding his expulsion are explored by Mayr-Harting, the various essays in CUBITT, GIBBS, and KIRBY (1974). Gibbs postulates that Wilfrid's struggles revolved around his desire to revive Gregory the Great's plan to accord York status as a metropolitan see and that this brought him into conflict with Archbishop Theodore, who sought to create smaller, more manageable Northumbrian dioceses. Gibbs's view has not been widely accepted, although Goffart suggests that those who commissioned *Vita Wilfridi* in the 8th century, rather than Wilfrid himself, were interested in the metropolitan status of York. Cubitt, in an analysis of episcopal succession, argues that Wilfrid was hostile towards Theodore's plan because the men chosen to occupy Theodore's new sees were not associated with his own federation of *monasteria*. Wilfrid's devotion to canonical procedure led him to refuse Theodore's offer of the see of Canterbury and to call for submitting the matter to an ecclesiastical council.

Wilfrid's ambitious building programmes, the romanizing architecture of his churches, and the growth and consolidation of his vast landholdings are covered in the essays in Kirby's edited volume. Wilfrid's life had "much of the flavour of the Germanic warlord" because of his command of a group of followers closely resembling an aristocratic war band, his wealth in treasure and land, and his interest in feasting and purchasing the "friendship of kings and bishops". WORMALD's analysis of the aristocratic environment of early Anglo-Saxon Christianity serves as a helpful contextualization of Wilfrid's career and a useful corrective to Bede's portrayal of the English church. Wilfrid's attachment to the secular values of the English aristocracy and the time he spent as a Continental traveller and exile are revealed through WOOD's suggestion that his community at Ripon may have been the original home for the "Franks casket", a whalebone casket found in Francia that has carved scenes juxtaposing Christian and pagan themes. Mayr-Harting, however, balances the worldly image of Wilfrid by providing evidence that he was not wholly immune to ascetic influences; that he had a strong interest in learning, revealed through his close friendship with Bishop Acca of Hexham, who was an important patron of Bede's biblical commentaries; and that he was eager to promote the religious life for women.

SIMON COATES

See also Anglo-Saxon England: Church Organization; Bede's *Ecclesiastical History*; Biscop; Cuthbert; Hagiography; Hild; Monasticism: Early; Northumbria; Religious Orders: Conventual; Theodore

Wilkes, John 1725–1797
Politician and radical campaigner

Brewer, John, *Party Ideology and Popular Politics at the Accession of George III*, Cambridge and New York: Cambridge University Press, 1976

Brewer, John, "The Wilkites and the Law 1763–1774: A Study of Radical Notions of Governance" in *An Ungovernable People: The English and Their Law in the Seventeenth and Eighteenth Centuries*, edited by John Brewer and John Styles, London: Hutchinson, and New Brunswick, New Jersey: Rutgers University Press, 1980

Christie, Ian R., *Wilkes, Wyvill, and Reform: The Parliamentary Reform Movement in British Politics, 1760–1785*, London: Macmillan, and New York: St Martin's Press, 1962

Donald, Diana, *The Age of Caricature: Satirical Prints in the Reign of George III*, New Haven, Connecticut: Yale University Press for the Paul Mellon Centre for Studies in British Art, 1996 (see chapter 2, "Wit and Emblem: The Language of Political Prints")

Rudé, George, *Wilkes and Liberty: A Social Study of 1763 to 1774*, London: Clarendon Press, 1962

Sainsbury, John, "John Wilkes, Debt and Patriotism", *Journal of British Studies*, 34/2 (1995): 165–95

Sainsbury, John, "'Cool Courage Should Always Mark Me': Politics and Eighteenth-Century Concepts of Class and Gender – John Wilkes and Duelling", *Journal of the Canadian Historical Association/ Revue de la Societé Historique du Canada*, 7 (1997): 19–33

Thomas, Peter D.G., *John Wilkes: A Friend to Liberty*, Oxford and New York: Clarendon Press, 1996

Wilson, Kathleen, *The Sense of the People: Politics, Culture, and Imperialism in England, 1715–1785*, Cambridge and New York: Cambridge University Press, 1995

THOMAS has written the only academic biography of Wilkes, superseding some half-dozen older accounts by historical popularizers. Building on a lifetime's work charting the high politics of these decades, Thomas has produced a well-researched, readable, and thoughtful study – strikingly sympathetic to its provocative central character. Thomas argues that Wilkes must have been essentially sincere in his radicalism. It did, after all, earn him two spells of imprisonment and a period in exile, and did little to advance his career, other than in a setting in the City of London too bourgeois to be Wilkes's natural habitat. This study is strong on the formal political context but has little to say about the world of popular, extra-institutional politics where most of Wilkes's supporters operated.

RUDÉ's study represents a pioneering attempt to penetrate that extra-institutional political world. Rudé directed his research efforts chiefly towards trying to identify the social status and occupations of Wilkes's supporters – including those who several times elected him a member of parliament for Middlesex; the gentry and middle classes who attended county and town meetings and signed petitions; and the shopkeepers, artisans, sailors, and labourers who were arrested amid crowds protesting about political or economic issues. Rudé argued that although the years of excitement over Wilkism also saw much economic unrest, the two forms of protest should not be conflated; Wilkes did enjoy grass-roots support, but socio-economic protests mobilized particular subgroups of the population and were not primarily presented in political terms. Though embodying much solid research, Rudé's attempt to determine the meaning of popular political activity by establishing the social status of actors, rather than by attending to ideas and images, now appears limited.

Brewer played a crucial part in reorienting the study of popular politics towards ideology and symbolism. BREWER (1976) argues that the 1760s saw the emergence of an "alternative structure" of politics – a lively extra-parliamentary political world with its own forms of articulation and modes of action – which "Old Corps" Whig politicians, marginalized by the accession of George III, learned to exploit for their own ends. Here, Brewer focused attention on the interaction between Wilkes and his followers, stressing the popular appeal of Wilkes's rascally persona. Brewer also called attention to the ritualized form of many demonstrations in Wilkes's support: the number 45 – issue number of the journal which first got Wilkes into serious trouble – acquired talismanic status. Brewer noted, as well, the commercial exploitation of Wilkism by manufacturers of printed pottery, medals, and other such memorabilia. BREWER (1980) further extended the range of the study of Wilkism, calling attention to the fact that "Wilkite" arguments were concerned as much with legal as political rights, and showing how they exploited law and the courts for propagandistic effect.

SAINSBURY's articles (1995, 1997) have extended and deepened our understanding of the interaction between Wilkes and his supporters. Sainsbury explores the irony that the high-living, rakish Wilkes should have become a hero to so many bourgeois and petty bourgeois Britons. Wilkes's lifestyle clearly did have a wider appeal, yet Sainsbury argues that this appeal was more contingent and limited than Brewer suggested.

DONALD's splendidly illustrated study further probes the iconography of Wilkite politics. She argues that the eruption of popular sentiment into the world of high politics is reflected in the revival, in Wilkite political prints, of forms of emblematic representation which had gone out of fashion among political cartoonists but which had retained their power and appeal in a more popular setting.

CHRISTIE's account – now somewhat dated, but still informative – sets Wilkism in a longer chronological context, treating it as a prelude to the better organized and more formidable parliamentary reform movement of the 1780s. Christie is at pains to stress the limited appeal of these movements, even at their peak. He also stresses the extent to which the movements were shaped by elite politicians for their own ends.

WILSON's more recent study is the first to chart the development of popular politics from the decades before Wilkism to the decades afterwards. As an episode, Wilkism appears less novel in Wilson's account than one might suppose from reading Christie or Brewer; Wilson argues, however, that high political realignments of the period did help to promote the growth of more autonomous forms of popular politics. She includes detailed case studies of the changing face of popular politics in Norwich and Newcastle. In exploring the ideology of Wilkism,

she also introduces a gender dimension absent from earlier accounts, stressing the rambunctious masculinity attributed to Wilkes.

JOANNA INNES

See also American Colonies: Loss of; Paine; Radicalism in Politics; Republicanism in the 19th Century

William I, the Conqueror   *c.*1028–1087
Duke of Normandy and King of England

Bates, David, *Normandy before 1066*, London and New York: Longman, 1982

Bates, David, *William the Conqueror*, London: Philip, 1989

Brown, R. Allen, *The Normans and the Norman Conquest*, New York: Crowell, and London: Constable, 1969; second edition, Woodbridge, Suffolk; and Dover, New Hampshire: Boydell, 1985; reprinted, Woodbridge, Suffolk; and Rochester, New York: Boydell and Brewer, 1994

Douglas, David C., *William the Conqueror: The Norman Impact upon England*, London: Eyre Methuen, and Berkeley: University of California Press, 1964

Gillingham, John, "William the Bastard at War" in *Anglo-Norman Warfare: Studies in Late Anglo-Saxon and Anglo-Norman Military Organization and Warfare*, edited by Matthew Strickland, Woodbridge, Suffolk; and Rochester, New York: Boydell and Brewer, 1992

Morillo, Stephen, *Warfare under the Anglo-Norman Kings, 1066–1135*, Woodbridge, Suffolk; and Rochester, New York: Boydell and Brewer, 1994

Searle, Eleanor, *Predatory Kinship and the Creation of Norman Power, 840–1066*, Berkeley: University of California Press, 1988

William the Conqueror has drawn the attention of as many historians, historical novelists, and romance writers as any king of England. It is therefore sometimes difficult to separate the "real" William from his myth and his many images. His obvious significance, furthermore, as the creator of the fusion of Anglo-Saxon and Norman worlds that shaped English history, especially its constitutional development, for so many centuries has stoked the fires of historical debate. William's achievement stands at the heart of debates about, for example, continuity versus discontinuity between the Anglo-Saxon and Anglo-Norman realms, and raises important historiographical issues concerning the role of "great men" in history.

DOUGLAS is the modern starting-point for studying William. Douglas's mastery of sources from both sides of the English Channel and his lucid writing style made for a ground-breaking biography and study of the Norman impact on England, still worth reading today. While his narrative of the William's life remains a standard reference point, however, his central interpretive stance now sounds somewhat outdated. Douglas sees William's Normandy as a model "feudal" society, and thus William's impact on England as built around his importation of feudalism to the island kingdom; this perspective has been somewhat superseded by recent scholarship calling into question the usefulness of the concept of feudalism, as well as by studies indicating that Norman society was less than fully formed before 1066. Still, if this issue is set aside, Douglas's emphasis on William's greatness as a leader remains intact.

Similarly, BROWN's work, first published in 1968 and reissued with some revisions and updated apparatus in 1985, focuses on feudalism as central to the Norman impact. Lively, opinionated, at times infuriating, Brown is virtually a hagiographer of the Normans and of William himself. For Brown, all things good in English history flowed from the benefits William brought with his conquest, above all the "up-to-date" feudalism that superseded a decadent, divided, and outmoded Anglo-Saxon government. Utterly unreliable on the Anglo-Saxons, Brown is nevertheless worth reading for William's Norman background and heritage and his qualities as a leader, and as the ultimate modern historiographic statement of what has come to be called the "Norman myth". The revisions in the second edition conceded little to the critics of either the concept of feudalism or the Norman myth.

The best deconstruction of the myth and reconsideration of the background from which William emerged is BATES (1982), a book with which Brown fundamentally disagreed. For good reason: Bates sets out to show, through a careful comparative examination of early Norman history with other areas of Viking conquest and with other provinces of the Frankish realm, that there was nothing exceptional about the Normans. Rather, they were in part typical northern French rulers, especially in being heirs to Carolingian administrative mechanisms, and in part lucky, with no particular claim to special abilities as conquerors or rulers. Above all, their much-vaunted expansionism did not emerge, according to Bates, before the reign of William as Duke of Normandy in the 1050s.

BATES (1989) extends this interpretation. This work is based on Bates's complete re-editing of William's charters; it offers a somewhat less detailed narrative of William's life than Douglas, but a more recent interpretive framework. This shows up in his assessment of William's impact on England after 1066. Bates, in line with most recent Anglo-Saxon scholarship, thinks the English kingdom was far from decadent, and in many ways minimizes the differences between Anglo-Saxon and Norman social structures, a natural corollary of his view of the Normans as unexceptional. While William still appears as a fine commander and ruler, the transformation he wrought on England, though still revolutionary, thus appears more synthetic with Anglo-Saxon contributions to governance than in either Douglas or Brown. This biography is the best starting-point for modern students of William.

SEARLE is a counterpoint to Bates on William's background. Her examination of early Norman history reinterprets rather than deconstructs the Norman myth. For her, there was little continuity with Carolingian practice in the foundations of Norman power; instead, the predatory practices of their Viking heritage gave to their entire history an expansionism and dynamism that made them stand out from their neighbours. In this context, William appears less a turning-point in Norman history, as he is for Bates, than a culmination of a long trend. Searle's model of predatory kinship allows her to bring to light some neglected aspects of William's abilities as a politician, above all his skilful "pruning of the family tree".

With regard to early Norman history, it is difficult to decide between Bates and Searle, not least because the sources are so few and problematic. But there is less argument than there appears to be about William's own reign and role. Ironically, Bates's convincing reappraisal of the Norman myth and Searle's reinterpretation of it agree on and reinforce the role of William as skilful political and military leader. William's military skills have therefore come in for more recent analysis. GILLINGHAM places William's career as a general in the context of common patterns of 11th-century warfare and concludes that his strategies and tactics were typical of the time. William generally avoided battle: Hastings was the first major engagement in which he commanded, and his strategy of seeking battle in 1066 stands out in contrast to the rest of his career before and after. Nor does Gillingham find anything exceptional about William's tactical conduct of battle. Gillingham acknowledges the skill with which William conducted his campaigns but concludes that his success was as much a matter of good fortune as of skill – and feels that his nickname should be "William the Lucky Bastard".

MORILLO similarly places William in the context of the warfare of the period, and devotes a section of his book to assessing William's generalship. Though placing somewhat more emphasis than Gillingham on William's skill, especially at moving armies rapidly from one theatre to another as needed, Morillo's conclusions are not at odds with Gillingham's. William was both lucky and good. And it was perhaps the good fortune that placed his conquest at the heart of an era of flux which accounts for much his subsequent reputation – for no matter how lucky and good he was as both military and political leader, the long-term consequences that flowed from his conquest were contingent and largely unpredictable.

STEPHEN MORILLO

See also Domesday Book; Edgar the Ætheling; Edward "the Confessor"; Harold II; Hastings, Battle of; Lanfranc; Malcolm III

William I, "the Lion" 1143–1214
King of Scotland

Barrow, G.W.S. (editor), *The Acts of William I, King of Scots, 1165–1214*, Edinburgh: Edinburgh University Press, 1971
Barrow, G.W.S., "The Reign of William the Lion" in *Scotland and Its Neighbours in the Middle Ages*, London and Rio Grande, Ohio: Hambledon Press, 1992
Crawford, B., "The Earldom of Caithness and the Kingdom of Scotland, 1150–1266" in *Essays on the Nobility of Medieval Scotland*, edited by K.J. Stringer, Edinburgh: John Donald, 1985
Duncan, Archibald A.M., *Scotland: The Making of the Kingdom*, Edinburgh: Oliver and Boyd, and New York: Barnes and Noble, 1975
Duncan, Archibald A.M. "John King of England and the Kings of Scots" in *King John: New Interpretations*, edited by S.D. Church, Woodbridge, Suffolk; and Rochester, New York: Boydell, 1999
McDonald, R. Andrew, "'Treachery in the Remotest Territories of Scotland': Northern Resistance to the Canmore Dynasty, 1130–1230", *Canadian Journal of History*, 34/2 (August 1999): 161–92

Owen, D.D.R., *William the Lion, 1143–1214: Kingship and Culture*, East Linton, East Lothian: Tuckwell Press, 1997

Stringer, K.J., *Earl David of Huntingdon, 1152–1219: A Study in Anglo-Scottish History*, Edinburgh: Edinburgh University Press, 1985

William "the Lion", also correctly known as William I of Scotland, second son of Earl Henry, son of David I, succeeded his brother Malcolm IV as King of Scots in 1165 at the age of 22. He died in 1214 in his 72nd year, after a remarkable reign of 49 years. William was Scotland's longest-reigning king before the union. His reign saw the extension of royal authority inside Scotland, but it was also characterized by often turbulent Anglo-Scottish relations and domestic unrest. William's reign was also a period when foreign – particularly Anglo-French – influences still flowed into Scotland. The epithet "the Lion" is not attested to in contemporary accounts, although one later chronicler called William the "Lion of Justice"; it is presumably from this that "the Lion" was derived, although a claim is often made that William adopted the lion rampant as the royal arms of Scotland.

Of the 12th-century Scottish monarchs, William is the best served by modern treatments; indeed, his long reign has attracted much scholarly attention since the 1970s. The essential starting-point is BARROW (1971), an edition of William's acts with a fine in-depth introduction to his reign; BARROW (1992), an article, is also valuable. Beyond these works, the best scholarly treatment remains the relevant chapter in DUNCAN (1975), but OWEN has provided a refreshing recent synthesis with a strong emphasis on the culture of the period. As might be expected, there is also much of value – particularly family background and contemporary political events – in STRINGER's study of King William's younger brother, Earl David of Huntingdon (d. 1219). Essays by CRAWFORD, DUNCAN (1999), and McDONALD address narrower thematic aspects of the reign, sometimes in a larger context.

Anglo-Scottish relations during William's reign have been covered in depth by Barrow (1971) and Duncan (1975) and synthesized in Owen's treatment. The capture of William at Alnwick in 1174, after he became involved in a rebellion against Henry II led by the Young Henry in 1173, was without doubt a turning-point in the reign; for Barrow (1971), William's capture and the subsequent treaty of Falaise mark "the most humiliating period of the reign, the fifteen years of English overlordship". Not until 1189 did the Quitclaim of Canterbury cancel the treaty of Falaise and restore Anglo-Scottish relations to what they had been during the reign of Malcolm IV.

The events of 1174 had domestic repercussions as well. Almost immediately after the king's capture, Galloway in the south-west erupted into rebellion; and in the late 1170s or early 1180s William had to deal with a dynastic rival operating in Moray and Ross, Donald MacWilliam. Duncan provides a good overview of these events and the various campaigns against these foes; Barrow (1971, 1992) and McDonald offer more detailed analysis of the MacWilliam threat.

By 1190, with Anglo-Scottish relations stabilized and the domestic scene returning to normality, William was at the zenith of his power. The next 20 years were prosperous and stable. The defeat of MacWilliam in 1187 led to a further extension of royal authority into the rest of the northern mainland and brought about conflicts with the powerful Earl of Orkney-Caithness, Harald Madaddsson, in the 1190s. Duncan (1975) provides a good overview of these events, while Crawford offers more detail on relations between the earls of Orkney-Caithness and the crown. Elsewhere in Scotland, particularly north of the Forth and the Tay, lands continued to be granted to newcomers in what Duncan (1975) calls a "rapid colonisation which showed the continuing vigour of Anglo-French feudal society in Scotland" – an important theme in the history of William's reign. Both Duncan (1975) and Barrow (1971) have also shown that the king was active in the patronage of burghs and merchants during this period, thereby both stimulating the economy and further consolidating royal authority.

The last years of the reign, from 1209 to 1214, form a distinct period; according to Barrow (1971), its dominant characteristics were the king's advancing age and increasing ill-health, the growing power and ruthlessness of King John in England, and the youth and inexperience of William's son Alexander. Duncan (1999) has done a masterful job of demonstrating how Anglo-Scottish relations, concern for the succession, and domestic threats (in the form of a further rebellion by MacWilliam), all entwined in the period from 1210 to 1212.

An early 13th-century English chronicler, writing in William's lifetime, famously remarked that "more recent kings of Scots profess themselves to be rather Frenchmen, both in race and in manner, language, and culture." Modern historians, however, have shown surprisingly little interest in cultural developments in William's Scotland, beyond noting the attachment of the ruling dynasty to French culture or remarking on the ongoing process of colonization in William's reign. Recently, however, Owen has provided a refreshing look at the "atmosphere of the society in which [William] moved", using as a point of entry a relatively obscure but nevertheless significant Anglo-French poem, the *Romance of Fergus* ("a milestone in the history of Scottish culture"), composed in William's lifetime by Guillaume le Clerc (possibly William Malveisin, Bishop of St Andrews). Through careful study of the poem, Owen contributes much to our understanding of William's reign; he argues that William presided over "the emergence of a distinct Franco-Scottish culture which for a brief period made its own individual contribution to that of Europe as a whole".

R. ANDREW McDONALD

See also Henry II; John; Malcolm IV; Richard I, "the Lionheart"

William II, Rufus c.1060–1100
King of England and Duke of Normandy

Barlow, Frank, *William Rufus*, London: Methuen, and Berkeley: University of California Press, 1983

Freeman, Edward A., *The Reign of William Rufus and the Accession of Henry the First*, Oxford: Clarendon Press, 1882; reprinted, New York: AMS Press, 1970

Hollister, C. Warren, "The Strange Death of William Rufus" in his *Monarchy, Magnates, and Institutions in the Anglo-Norman World*, London and Ronceverte, West Virginia: Hambledon Press, 1986

Morillo, Stephen, *Warfare under the Anglo-Norman Kings, 1066–1135*, Woodbridge, Suffolk; and Rochester, New York: Boydell and Brewer, 1994

Vaughn, Sally N., *Anselm of Bec and Robert of Meulan: The Innocence of the Dove and the Wisdom of the Serpent*, Berkeley: University of California Press, 1987

The bright light of historical inquiry cast on the reigns of William I, the justly famous Conqueror, and Henry I, the long-reigning state-builder, has tended to leave the intervening reign of Henry's brother William II in relative darkness. A colourful, flamboyant character, nicknamed Rufus for both fiery colouring and personality, William was famous in his own time (infamous to some, especially in the church) as a generous lord, a successful warrior, and as leader of a scandalous court. But after his untimely death his historical reputation suffered from the very flamboyance that had earned him fame, as it made him appear weaker and less serious than his father and younger brother. As a result, the historical literature focused directly on the second Norman king is somewhat scant.

Fortunately, the one major exception to this neglect is the masterful definitive biography by BARLOW, who approaches his controversial subject with both sympathy and a vast knowledge of the period. He shows that underneath the king's sometimes clowning style lay serious purpose and a clear understanding of the requirements of kingship: Rufus weathered an early rebellion and went on to confirm the strong royal powers his father had built from a combination of Norman military might and Anglo-Saxon administrative expertise, then reunified the Anglo-Norman realm by lending his older brother Robert money to go on crusade in exchange for control of Normandy. Barlow gives sensitive historical treatment to the king's reputation for homosexuality, licentiousness, and irreligion, putting each subject in the context of 11th-century attitudes and recognizing the bias of the mostly clerical sources for the reign. In short, Barlow presents a fascinating figure, interesting in his own right even if his most significant contribution was to prevent his brother Robert from becoming king, thus allowing Henry to reach the throne.

An intriguing historiographical contrast is presented by by the eminent Victorian historian FREEMAN (1882) in the only other full-length biographical study of Rufus. This biography, first published a century before Barlow's, is a work of moral condemnation rather than historical understanding. The king's private morals – the "sodomy" that pervaded his court, his irreligious oaths, and his long conflict with Archbishop Anselm – naturally draw Freeman's opprobrium, and are often passed over in little detail. Equally, Freeman blames the king for furthering the imposition of oppressive Norman feudalism (a word Barlow never uses) on the formerly free English nation. A better example of Victorian history would be hard to find.

Outside of biographies of the king, modern historians have focused on particular aspects of Rufus's reign. VAUGHN analyses the religious and administrative aspects of the reign through a dual biography of two of the great men of the kingdom: Anselm, Archbishop of Canterbury; and Robert of Meulan, the king's chief adviser. These two were principal players in the central political-religious issue of Rufus's reign, the investiture controversy; and Vaughn casts light on the personal dynamics of Anglo-Norman politics through her examination of their intertwined lives. The result offers a deeper understanding of the dynamics of royal and church government under the Norman kings.

MORILLO looks at Rufus's military campaigns as part of the larger patterns of Anglo-Norman warfare and offers an assessment of the king's generalship. The king is often neglected as a military leader, despite his high reputation among his contemporaries, because he fought no major battles. Nonetheless, Morillo argues that Rufus skillfully used his reputation and his money to achieve most of his military goals without battle – he was certainly a more successful leader than his more famous crusading brother Robert, and Rufus's methods tell us much about the foundations of the Anglo-Norman military system and its success.

Finally, Rufus is probably best known for his death. He was shot by a hunting companion in the New Forest, and ever since it has been an open question whether the incident was an accident or part of a plot engineered by William's younger brother Henry. HOLLISTER goes over all the evidence with care and deep scholarship and considers the three explanations offered through the centuries: witchcraft, murder, and accident. His conclusion is that the third is much the most likely. Accident is, as Hollister admits, neither the most appealing nor the most romantic end for the Red King, terror of the church, but his judgement has been widely accepted.

STEPHEN MORILLO

See also Anselm; Edgar the Ætheling; Henry I; Lanfranc; Malcolm III

William III 1650–1702
King of England, Scotland (William II), Ireland; Prince of Orange

Mary II 1662–1694
Queen of England, Scotland, and Ireland; consort of William

Baxter, Stephen B., *William III*, London: Longmans, 1966; as *William III and the Defense of European Liberty, 1650–1702*, New York: Harcourt, Brace and World, 1966

Claydon, Tony, *William III and the Godly Revolution*, Cambridge and New York: Cambridge University Press, 1996

Hamilton, Elizabeth, *William's Mary: A Biography of Mary II*, London: Hamilton, and New York: Taplinger, 1972

Horwitz, Henry, *Parliament, Policy, and Politics in the Reign of William III*, Manchester: Manchester University Press, and Newark: University of Delaware Press, 1977

Japikse, Nicolas, *Prins Willem III: De Stadhouder–Koning* [Prince William: The Stateholder King], 2 vols, Amsterdam: Meulenhoff, 1930–33

Ogg, David, *William III*, London: Collins, and New York: Macmillan, 1956

Riley, P.W.J., *King William and the Scottish Politicians*, Edinburgh: Donald, 1979

Rose, Craig, *England in the 1690s: Revolution, Religion, and War*, Oxford and Malden, Massachusetts: Blackwell, 1999

Frustratingly for British historians, for at least part of the 20th century the best biography of William III, by JAPIKSE, was in Dutch. Furthermore, over two-thirds of it deals with William's life before he became king of England and Scotland, and even the rest is strongest on his military and diplomatic activities. Japiske has provided a scholarly and sympathetic biography and does much to delineate William's character and explain his preoccupations, but this study has not been well integrated into British historiography.

In many ways, OGG (1956) is the opposite of Japikse. A much shorter work, it devotes only one of its six chapters to William's life before 1688 and adopts a distinctively English perspective. Largely a study of William's public life and reign, it emphasizes his political and constitutional achievements. In this respect, Ogg epitomizes the influential Whig view of William as the great deliverer who "saved England from the male Stuarts". William's intervention in 1688 and his "moderate use of the prerogative" helped provide England with a comparatively enlightened and stable constitution and polity. Ogg also praises William's resistance to French territorial ambitions but regards him as less effective as a military leader. This book concludes that owing to William, "the England of 1702 was a greater, a more united and even a more humane nation than that of 1689".

BAXTER (1966) – a product of massive research in French, Dutch, and British archives – is the definitive biography of William. This book has the virtue of treating William holistically as a major European figure with concurrent concerns in Britain, in the Netherlands, and in the larger Continent. As the subtitle of the American edition suggests, Baxter's main theme is William's lifelong and (for Baxter) noble struggle against Louis XIV's France. Baxter rates William much higher as a military leader than Ogg does, emphasizing especially his organizational abilities. Baxter argues that William refashioned the English army into an effective military force, thereby making possible Marlborough's successes. William also receives great praise as an administrator who, among other achievements, put England's finances on a solid footing. Baxter's William is an altogether heroic figure. At the same time, his adversaries and critics, foreign and domestic, are often disparaged, sometimes unfairly, as petty-minded or worse.

Given Baxter's one-sidedness, it is somewhat surprising that there has not been a good scholarly biography of William since his. However, some insights into William's kingship can be gained from more recent studies of his reign. The best of these is HORWITZ (1977). A comprehensive, if sometimes dense, study of parliamentary politics, it provides a more balanced treatment than Baxter's of the myriad motives and activities of English politicians. Horwitz sees William's unfamiliarity with English politics as the cause of at least some of his early problems with parliament and shows that William's reign witnessed a significant increase in the power and importance of parliament – not because William wanted to reduce the prerogative but because the exigencies of conducting and financing a major European war required him to yield greater authority to parliament. Horwitz sees William acting as his own first minister and, while crediting him with working hard, does not believe he was altogether successful in coordinating the work of the various administrative departments.

RILEY is harder on William, characterizing his rule in Scotland as marked by "misgovernment, indecision, and sheer administrative inertia". He attributes this in part to William's neglect of Scottish affairs and to his use of poor advisers. But Riley is so unremittingly cynical about the selfishness of Scottish politicians of all stripes that it is difficult to see from his account how even an attentive William, or any other monarch for that matter, could have governed Scotland successfully.

Two recent studies of the 1690s reflect the interest of scholars of the 1990s in studying perceptions and modes of discourse. CLAYDON (1996) examines "Williamite" propagandistic rhetoric and finds that it relied heavily on a religious theme: William and Mary as providentially sent by God to rescue England from popery and cleanse it of sin. But this book rarely penetrates behind the rhetoric to the actual beliefs and behaviour of the monarchs. Claydon concludes that the court, through this propaganda, "shaped the events of the 1690s". This is a difficult thesis to maintain, partly because, as Claydon himself concedes, the effects of propaganda are difficult to measure, but also because it assumes a broad consensus in support of William's regime that the book fails to demonstrate.

ROSE's examination of contemporary opinion presents a picture of a more deeply divided society. Rose views William as a "conqueror" who got what he wanted in 1689. But he sees William's reign as less successful, concluding that its hopes were "unfulfilled" and its fears "unallayed". Rose usefully surveys a wide variety of contemporary opinion, but his focus on perceptions leaves the actual William and Mary somewhat shadowy figures.

None of these works devotes much attention to Mary. Yet all broadly agree in seeing her as a supportive wife, quite willing to play second fiddle to William. Some of the authors, like Horwitz, contend that, when given the chance in William's absence, she proved a capable administrator. Others note her piety. Claydon, in an interesting few pages, describes how Mary actively promoted "godly reformation". Rose makes the important point that Mary's piety and personal warmth were valuable in gaining support for the joint monarchy, especially given William's perceived aloofness.

Mary has been the subject of several biographies, but most are more popular than scholarly and focus more on her private and personal life than on her public life. HAMILTON (1972), one of the more recent and detailed biographies, quotes liberally from Mary's memoirs and letters, thereby providing a window into her personality. But it adds little, other than detail, to the basic picture of Mary drawn by previous biographers and by the works cited above – that of a loving and dutiful wife and a pious and unassuming queen.

ROBERT J. FRANKLE

See also Glorious Revolution; Harley; James VII and II; Limerick, Treaty of; Marlborough, 1st Duke of; Nonjurors

William IV 1765–1837
King of Great Britain, Ireland, and Hanover

Brock, Michael, *The Great Reform Act*, London: Hutchinson, 1973
Fulford, Roger, *Hanover to Windsor*, London: Batsford, 1960

Gash, Norman, *Politics in the Age of Peel: A Study in the Technique of Parliamentary Representation, 1830–1850*, London and New York: Longmans Green, 1953

Gash, Norman, *Reaction and Reconstruction in English Politics, 1832–1852*, Oxford: Clarendon Press, 1965

Newbould, Ian, *Whiggery and Reform, 1830–1841: The Politics of Government*, London: Macmillan, and Stanford, California: Stanford University Press, 1990

Woodward, E. Llewellyn, *The Age of Reform, 1815–1870*, 2nd edition, Oxford: Clarendon Press, 1962

Ziegler, Philip, *King William IV*, New York: Harper and Row, 1973; London: Collins, 1971

William IV's reputation for most of the 20th century was that of "Silly Billy", a pear-headed, pear-bodied object of ridicule. WOODWARD depicts William as little more than a nuisance. Because royal support still mattered to a ministry's life, politicians had to cater to the king's "personal likes and dislikes", which thus had a political effect, wasted valuable ministerial time, and fostered petty intrigue. Woodward calls William "an eccentric, simple, kindly man, less troublesome . . . than was George IV". But his narrative of events describes a capricious, purposeless ruler. During the Reform Bill crisis of 1831–32, William at first refused and then agreed to dissolve parliament. He agreed to create enough peers to get the measure through the House of Lords, quibbled over the number to be created, and ultimately agreed to create as many peers as necessary. In a fit of pique, he refused to announce in person the royal assent to the bill. Woodward's account of the dismissal of Lord Melbourne's Whig government in 1834 also illustrates this point. Blind to the facts of party enmity, William wanted a Whig-Tory coalition. When Melbourne told the king he doubted that the ministry could survive the loss of Lord Althorp's leadership in the Commons, and offered to resign, William accepted. "It is not unlikely", Woodward adds, "that Melbourne wanted the king to come to this decision".

FULFORD recasts William as the saviour of the monarchy. He grants that William was "strange, explosive, unpolitical and not clever" but considers him a capable and commonsensical king. Yet Fulford's narrative describes a silly, selfish, stupid king. William asked the Whig Earl Grey to form a government when Wellington's Tory ministry fell in 1830; but during the Reform Bill crisis, according to Fulford, William withdrew his support from Grey, resisted promising to create peers, refused to make them when Grey asked for them, accepted Grey's resignation "with tears", and then eventually had to take Grey back. The king revenged himself against the Whigs in 1834 by sacking "his tormentors". How, then, did he save the monarchy? "By existing at that particular moment", Fulford maintains. In other words, William lived long enough for Princess Victoria, the heiress presumptive, to turn 18, thereby sparing Britain a regency. Fulford concludes by commenting that George IV had bequeathed to his brother a crown with enhanced political authority, but William's struggles diminished that authority.

Fulford's idiosyncratic account does not reflect the change in the writing of early 19th-century political history attributable to Norman Gash. GASH (1953) reoriented the study of political history in two ways. First, he insisted that historians must take into account the politician's daily working world, how elections were conducted, and the practical constraints that limited politicians' scope of action. In explaining political events, these are more decisive factors than constitutional theory or ideological goals. Second, he argued that the Reform Act of 1832 changed the political scene less than historians had thought. Gash devotes a chapter to the court's influence in constituencies where it had a significant economic presence. The crown's influence generally went to candidates who pledged to support the sitting government, and William was active in deciding whom to put forward. It was his successor, Victoria, who ceased exercising the crown's influence in these constituencies.

GASH (1965) addresses William's role more directly. First, he contrasts George IV, "a highly constitutional King" whose influence on government was peripheral, and William IV, "a cauldron of energy" who twice dismissed a ministry, twice dissolved parliament for political reasons, thrice asked his ministers to form a coalition with their political adversaries, and once attempted to influence a critical vote in the Lords independently of his advisers. Second, Gash identifies William's policy as that of an "Old Whig": one who accepted that some measure of limited parliamentary reform was necessary but denied that anything else needed reform. William therefore rapidly became disenchanted with the Whigs. When Grey retired from office in July 1834, William asked Melbourne to form a coalition with Peel, Stanley, and the Duke of Wellington. When Althorp succeeded to the House of Lords in November 1834, he sacked Melbourne and asked the Tories under Peel to form a ministry. During Peel's short first ministry of 1834–35, the king tried to engineer a coalition between Peel and Stanley; urged the prime minister to approach moderate Conservatives on both sides of the party divide; when Peel's government fell, tried to persuade Grey to come out of retirement; and when that persuasion failed, asked Melbourne to form a moderate Conservative coalition. Gash argues that the long-term consequences of the king's action were to make Peel the leader of the Conservative Party, rally the forces of the right, and facilitate the Tamworth manifesto, which defined moderate Conservatism in a reforming age.

Gash's approach influenced major studies from the 1970s on. ZIEGLER's accounts of the Reform Bill crisis and the dismissal of Melbourne's ministry in 1834 stress William's moderate conservatism, his desire for a cross-party moderate-Conservative coalition, and his attempts to preserve (and exercise) the royal prerogative. BROCK's detailed day-by-day account of the vicissitudes of the bill strengthens Gash's interpretation and underscores William's independent role and moderate Conservative agenda. NEWBOULD seeks "to develop a comprehensive view of the Whigs during the age of reform far different from that of those . . . who have studied the Whigs through the eyes of Peelite or Conservative opponents". He largely succeeds in his goal, by means of a close analysis of the daily doings of Whig politics, legislation, and administration (not unlike Gash's emphasis on the politicians' daily world and the practical constraints on their actions). Along the way, Newbould addresses William's influence on the Reform Bill, Irish legislation, and the formation of ministries. The picture that Newbould draws is not unlike that of Gash.

DENIS PAZ

See also Grey; Hanoverian Britain: Later Years; Melbourne; Parliamentary Reform: Reform Acts of 1832–1885; Peel

Williamite War

see James VII and II; Limerick, Treaty of; William III and Mary; Ireland: 1688–1800

Willibrord c.658–739

Northumbrian-born monk and apostle of the Netherlands

Goetzinger, Nikolaus (editor), *Willibrordus: Echternacher Festschrift zur XII. Jahrhundertfeier des Todes des Heiligen Willibrord* [Willibrord: Echternach *Festschrift* for the 12th Centenary of the Death of St Willibrord], Luxembourg: St Paul, 1940

Kiesel, Georges and Jean Schroeder (editors), *Willibrord: Apostel der Niederlande, Gründer der Abtei Echternach* [Willibrord: Apostle of the Netherlands, Founder of the Abbey at Echternach], Luxembourg: St Paul, 1989

Krier, J., "Echternach und das Kloster des hl. Willibrord" [Echternach and the Monastery of St Willibrord] in *Die Franken: Wegbereiter Europas – vor 1500 Jahren, König Chlodwig und seine Erben*, exhibition catalogue, 2 vols, Mainz: Philipp von Zabern, 1996

Levison, Wilhelm, *England and the Continent in the Eighth Century*, Oxford: Clarendon Press, 1946

Netzer, Nancy, "Willibrord's Scriptorium at Echternach and Its Relationship to Ireland and Lindisfarne" in *St. Cuthbert: His Cult and His Community to AD 1200*, edited by Gerald Bonner, David Rollason, and Clare Stancliffe, Woodbridge: Boydell, and Wolfeboro, New Hampshire: Boydell and Brewer, 1989

Netzer, Nancy, *Cultural Interplay in the Eighth Century: The Trier Gospels and the Making of a Scriptorium at Echternach*, Cambridge and New York: Cambridge University Press, 1994

Parsons, D., "England and the Low Countries at the Time of St Willibrord" in *Utrecht, Britain, and the Continent: Archaeology, Art, and Architecture*, edited by Elisabeth de Bièvre, London: British Archaeological Association, 1996

Parsons, D., "Willibrord's 'Frisian' Mission and the Early Churches in Utrecht" in *Northumbria's Golden Age*, edited by Jane Hawkes and Susan Mills, Stroud, Gloucestershire: Sutton, 1999

Van Vlierden, Marieke, *Willibrord en het Begin van Nederland* [Willibrord and the Beginning of the Netherlands], Utrecht: Clavis, 1995

Weiler, A.G., *Willibrords Missie: Christendom en Cultuur in de Zevende en Achtste Eeuw* [Willibrord's Mission: Christianity and Culture in the 7th and 8th Centuries], Hilversum: Gooi & Sticht, 1989

The early career of the Northumbrian-born St Willibrord (Clement) was both undistinguished and largely undocumented; he did not become a historical figure of importance until AD 690, when he left the Irish monastery of Rath Melsigi (an expatriate monastic colony whose exact location is unknown) for the mission field in the Low Countries. His continued activity in the Low Countries until his death in 739 and his subsequent recognition as apostle of the Netherlands have resulted in a mainly Dutch-language literature, with some contributions in German.

Publications since 1953 are listed by P. Bange in WEILER's straightforward and descriptive textbook account of the saint and his activity in a broad historical context. There is little biography or historical analysis in the English language, but titles include the seminal work by LEVISON, in which the section on Willibrord largely repeats his article of 1940 in the *Durham University Journal*. Levison summarizes the little that is known of Willibrord's life and activities as recorded in Bede's *Ecclesiastical History* and Alcuin's *Life* (English version in C.H. Talbot, *The Anglo-Saxon Missionaries in Germany*, London: Sheed and Ward, 1954), and witnessed by charters and other contemporary documents. Willibrord's mission to the Frisians is seen against the background of *peregrinatio*, first practised by the Irish and later adopted by Anglo-Saxon monks, some of whom, like Willibrord, had spent time in "exile" in Rath Melsigi. Levison's account, which has not been superseded in 60 years, makes clear the limited success of Willibrord's mission. Practising Christianity and preaching to the unconverted were safe only in that part of the Low Countries under the control of the Frankish rulers. It is a commonplace of the literature on missionary activity in early medieval Europe that evangelism went hand in hand with military conquest, and that the process of Christianization was an integral part of the acculturation of vanquished peoples. Among the unconquered, the arrival of Christian missionaries would be seen as having a political agenda, irrespective of their actual motives. The hostility of the Frisian rulers, principally Radbod, to Willibrord and his associates should be seen in this light. In practical terms this meant that Willibrord's activity had to be restricted to the area south and west of the Rhine delta: the effective frontier was still the former Roman *limes*. The cautious approach of Willibrord and his companions to missionary activity is emphasized by their use in the early days of Antwerp in Belgium as their base – well away from the border between the Frankish empire and the unconquered Frisians – and by their continued use of Willibrord's own monastery at Echternach in Luxembourg as a safe haven and fall-back position. The murder of Willibrord's younger contemporary, St Boniface, in 754 at Dokkum in the north of Frisia indicates that the area beyond the *limes* remained a dangerous mission field well into the 8th century.

A review of the evidence for early church foundations in the Low Countries undertaken by PARSONS (1999) serves to reinforce Levison's conclusion. Documentary evidence suggests that many of the early churches were founded before the arrival of Willibrord and were largely concentrated in Belgium; archaeological evidence extends the distribution as far as the Rhine, with important churches established by Willibrord in the old Roman fort at Utrecht, where an earlier Frankish church had evidently been destroyed. No more than three churches can be detected beyond the Rhine in North Holland. This distribution confirms Willibrord's activity as consolidation rather than pioneering.

PARSONS (1996) sets the mission against a background of the long-standing trade and political relations between Anglo-Saxon England and the Franks in the Low Countries, for which there is historical and, more particularly, archaeological evidence, such as pottery, glass vessels, and coins. Some of this material is illustrated and discussed in VAN VLIERDEN's excellent exhibition catalogue, which also includes ecclesiastical artefacts more directly related to the activities of the Anglo-Saxon missionaries and their successors in what is now Benelux. It remains one of Willibrord's most important contributions to the cultural life of the area that his mission was responsible for the importation of artefacts from Anglo-Saxon England into the area and for the training of craftsmen in the English tradition. Thus Anglo-Saxon influence can be seen in such rarities as the embroidery panels now at Maaseik and the more common illuminated manuscripts. Many of the latter were produced in the famous scriptorium of the Echternach monastery, which has recently been the subject of research, especially by NETZER (1989, 1994). Following earlier work by Ó Crónín, she has argued for Irish, rather than Anglo-Saxon, origins for the earliest Echternach manuscripts. This is not surprising in view of the relatively long time spent by Willibrord in Ireland at Rath Melsigi. Later manuscripts, however, seem to show a Northumbrian influence, particularly from the Lindisfarne scriptorium.

Willibrord's monastery at Echternach stands out, then, as an insular cultural centre in an area where the saint himself made little impact; it has been the subject of both historical and archaeological investigation reported in GOETZINGER (1940), KIESEL & SCHROEDER (1989), and KRIER (1996).

DAVID PARSONS

See also Hagiography; Monasticism: Early

Wilson, (James) Harold, 1st Baron Wilson 1916–1995
Labour politician and prime minister

Morgan, Austen, *Harold Wilson*, London: Pluto Press, 1992
Pimlott, Ben, *Harold Wilson*, London: HarperCollins, 1992
Roth, Andrew, *Sir Harold Wilson: Yorkshire Walter Mitty*, London: Macdonald and Jane's, 1977
Wilson, Harold, *The Labour Government 1964–1970: A Personal Record*, London: Weidenfeld and Nicolson/Michael Joseph, 1971; as *A Personal Record: The Labour Government, 1964–1970*, Boston: Little Brown, 1971
Wilson, Harold, *The Governance of Britain*, London: Weidenfeld and Nicolson/Michael Joseph, and New York: Harper and Row, 1976
Wilson, Harold, *A Prime Minister on Prime Ministers*, London: Weidenfeld and Nicolson/Michael Joseph, and New York: Summit, 1977
Wilson, Harold, *Final Term: The Labour Government 1974–1976*, London: Weidenfeld and Nicolson/Michael Joseph, 1979
Ziegler, Philip, *Wilson: The Authorised Life of Lord Wilson of Rievaulx*, London: Weidenfeld and Nicolson, 1993

The long anticipation of Harold Wilson's death stimulated historical interest and added to a literature notable for the extent to which the subject was himself a chronicler. Paradoxically, Wilson's propensity to write about his own actions served to shroud his motives even further, and his reputation sank very low in the 1980s. Until recently, Wilson, the most enigmatic of postwar prime ministers (1964–70 and 1974–76), remained a largely spectral presence in the literature.

Few leading statesmen of the 20th century have added much to the sum of historical knowledge through their own pens. Wilson, though he did not write a full autobiography, detailed much of his professional life and interests himself. Unfortunately, unlike many of his cabinet colleagues, he did so in a consistently underwhelming way; this was why the relative abundance of interest during his final years was so welcome.

Wilson's early publications were frequent; by the time he became prime minister in 1964 there had been a lengthy series of tracts which were often recycled speeches: *New Deal for Coal* (1945), *In Place of Dollars* (1952), *The War on World Poverty* (1953), *The Relevance of British Socialism* (1964), *Purpose in Politics* (1964), *The New Britain* (1964), and *Purpose in Power* (1966). These werre undistinguished, even by the standards of politicians' writings, but all of them nevertheless served to reinforce the public's and the party's perception of Wilson as a modern, busy, productive prophet of governance, an objective of which the Labour Party has too often appeared unaware.

Office, when it came to Wilson, stimulated the usual spasm of journalistic potboilers: Leslie Smith's *Harold Wilson: The Authentic Portrait*; Dudley Smith's *Harold Wilson: A Critical Biography*; Gerard Noel's *Harold Wilson and the New Britain*; Ernest Kay's *Pragmatic Premier: An Intimate Portrait of Harold Wilson*. All appeared between 1964 and 1967 and are rarely to be found today. *The Politics of Harold Wilson*, by Paul Foot, was a highly critical, popular, and influential Penguin Special of 1968.

Wilson's decision to write an account of his first administration immediately after its fall in 1970 was surprising, and this intense effort remains unlikely to be repeated by a party leader. The author would probably not have been afforded much perspective after a wholly unexpected defeat, and *The Labour Government 1964–1970* is little more than an – apparently – comprehensive chronicle. It might have been even more comprehensive, since Wilson originally envisaged a three-volume work.

A similarly unexpected victory in 1974 provided Wilson with more material for writing. He resigned in 1976 and began *The Governance of Britain* two days later. This was followed by *A Prime Minister on Prime Ministers*, a disappointingly insubstantial coffee-table book culled from a television series; and by the second, and lesser, record of his governments, *Final Term*. In 1981 Wilson published the more auspicious *The Chariot of Israel: Britain, America, and the State of Israel*. Its principal significance lay in the fact that it was written at all: the area was not notably one in which Wilson was interested. Though suffering from the author's industry, these books are not without moments of insight and interest.

A year after Wilson's resignation the parliamentary journalist ROTH (1977) published an account that was, despite its unpromising title, insightful. Concerned with motive rather than action, Roth's was a hazardous enterprise, but his book remains the most valuable to be published on Wilson during the subject's active life. This may or may not be attested to by the fact that Wilson successfully sued the author over some of the book's contents.

Wilson began suffering from what was probably Alzheimer's disease in the late 1970s, and in the last 10 years of his life was seldom seen or heard of. His final publication, *Memoirs* (1986), covered the years before he became prime minister; it is underpowered and strewn with errors, in part because it was ghostwritten by Brian Connell. Wilson had long been revered for the calibre of his memory, so it was particularly upsetting that this was the quality which had most deteriorated.

Notwithstanding his own contributions, Wilson's name was continually raised in political and academic circles in a seemingly endless stream of diaries and memoirs by his ministerial colleagues, with the effect that he appeared a figure perpetually at the margins. After additional revelations of various spies and traitors throughout the period, he was burdened with a reputation for having harboured notions of being overthrown or undermined – an accusation which a man who was never slow to discern plotting did not really need.

Then, in a very short period of time, three substantial and long-awaited biographies appeared. PIMLOTT had a solid reputation as a scholar of the labour movement, and he exploited his connections fully for his comprehensive and exhaustively researched biography. ZIEGLER's work, as befitted a biographer of royalty, was the authorized life, and it benefited and suffered in consequence. MORGAN, unfortunately and quite unfairly, was at something of a disadvantage in the light of this sudden competition. Also, his mildly critical biography is not helped by not having a bibliography. The three reach broadly similar conclusions: Wilson was a deeply flawed but decent prime minister. Pimlott's is generally accepted as being the standard work, while Ziegler's is the more digestible for the layperson.

Wilson remains a highly contentious figure despite having been, by all accounts, a thoroughly congenial person. His conduct of policy as a politician and his assiduous erection of literary landmarks are consistent with a man perhaps preoccupied with position. There are few in the labour movement who do not regard his governments as having missed opportunities, a sense he no doubt sought to arrest by being the first to write of them. His own works remain those of a man blessed with an eye for detail, but with little sense of direction or of colour. Only scholars concerned with Wilson himself will gain anything from, or indeed consult, his own voluminous writings, which did nothing for his reputation.

Harold Wilson – for so long written about too little, the ghostly vision of Ruskin Spear's portrait which adorns the cover of Pimlott's biography – has finally been adequately served, and his governments more than adequately served, by the literature.

MARTIN FARR

See also Callaghan; Labour Party

Winchester, Treaty of

see **Wallingford or Winchester, Treaty of** (1153)

Witchcraft

Capp, Bernard, *Astrology and the Popular Press: English Almanacs, 1500–1800*, London and Boston: Faber, 1979

Geneva, Ann, *Astrology and the Seventeenth Century Mind: William Lilly and the Language of the Stars*, Manchester and New York: Manchester University Press, 1995

Gibson, Marion, *Reading Witchcraft: Stories of Early English Witches*, London and New York: Routledge, 1999

Hester, Marianne, *Lewd Women and Wicked Witches: A Study of the Dynamics of Male Domination*, London and New York: Routledge, 1992

Larner, Christina, *Enemies of God: The Witch-Hunt in Scotland*, London: Chatto and Windus, and Baltimore: Johns Hopkins University Press, 1981

Macfarlane, Alan, *Witchcraft in Tudor and Stuart England: A Regional and Comparative Study*, London: Routledge and Kegan Paul, and New York: Harper and Row, 1970

Sharpe, James, *Instruments of Darkness: Witchcraft in England 1550–1750*, London: Hamish Hamilton, 1996, and New York: Penguin, 1997

Summers, Montague, *The History of Witchcraft and Demonology*, London: Kegan Paul, Trench, Trubner, and New York: Knopf, 1926; facsimile as *The History of Witchcraft*, London: Senate, 1994

Thomas, Keith, *Religion and the Decline of Magic: Studies in Popular Beliefs in Sixteenth and Seventeenth Century England*, London: Weidenfeld and Nicolson, and New York: Scribner, 1971

Willis, Deborah, *Malevolent Nurture: Witch-Hunting and Maternal Power in Early Modern England*, Ithaca, New York: Cornell University Press, 1995

Most assessments of early modern witchcraft treat the phenomenon as a product of specific intellectual and social conditions that allowed irrational beliefs to flourish. SUMMERS is set apart from these in giving those beliefs credence. Summers's general history provides an excellent bibliography of contemporary sources, reflecting his valuable work on the translation of many witchcraft texts into English. However, his historical interpretation is severely hampered by an insistence that witches were, as their contemporaries claimed, a channel for satanic power.

More useful to the modern scholar is the work of Macfarlane and Thomas. Both reject a view of belief in witchcraft as evidence of ignorance and bigotry, demonstrating rather that it coexisted with religion and science within the specific intellectual context of early modern England. MACFARLANE's study places accusations of witchcraft in the context of community relations and popular belief systems of the period; he finds that these accusations often came from the populace rather than – as had been presumed – from the elites. Macfarlane finds witchcraft popularly used as an explanation for misfortune and local troubles, and he uncovers a number of "good witches" who operated as healers and fortune-tellers.

THOMAS (1971), published a year later than Macfarlane's study, is widely acknowledged as the seminal text on popular belief in early modern England. It is broader in scope than Macfarlane's book, though with some common ground. Thomas uncovers a world in which magic, astrology, divination, ghosts, and prophesying all stood harmoniously alongside the teachings of the Christian church. He also shows how early scientific endeavours were fuelled by an interest in astrology and numerology. He attempts to account for the decline in belief in witchcraft, refusing to attribute it simply to rationalism brought by the expanding sciences. Instead, he points to a complex model of social and intellectual change in which a number of factors contributed to a gradual decline of beliefs involving the supernatural. The work of Thomas and Macfarlane marks a turning-point in witchcraft studies, in that both accept the beliefs as credible within the specific social and philosophical context of early modern society at all intellectual levels, not merely the level of the uneducated. Thomas's book in particular is invaluable, with a breadth of material that makes it an excellent introductory text and a useful bibliographic guide to contemporary sources on religion, science, and supernatural beliefs.

Though many histories of witchcraft stress our distance from such beliefs, it is interesting that SHARPE emphasizes how witchcraft has been "repackaged" for successive generations (including our own). Stressing survival as well as decline, Sharpe explores the factors that affected early modern representations of the witch. He suggests that the persecution of witches may have owed as much to misogyny and local rivalries as to fear of malefic influence, and his work is a rich and highly readable foray into the intellectual world of early modern England.

LARNER (1981) similarly stresses the importance of locality. This is an excellent example of a localized study of society, culture, and belief. Systematically dissecting records of Scottish witch-hunts and relating legal proceedings to localized social conditions, Larner demonstrates that beliefs regarding witchcraft beliefs were flexible, so that they reflected local values and tension. She sees the witch-hunts themselves as being led by the social elites, reflecting the concerns of lawyers and clergymen – an interesting reversal of Macfarlane's argument. Larner also argues that historians should address the predominance of female defendants in witchcraft trials, though she warns against using misogyny as an all-encompassing explanation for the witch-hunt.

Misogyny has been emphasized more in the work of scholars seeking a feminist interpretation of the witch craze. HESTER explores early modern beliefs in the light of modern psychological studies and is specifically concerned with the issue of male violence against women in the context of the witch-hunts. Hester's book is an interesting contribution to the debate, but its credibility depends on an acceptance of Hester's application of modern psychological and social theory to past events. In contrast, WILLIS, challenging the assumption that men were mainly responsible for the persecution of women as witches, explores the active role of women in accusations of witchcraft. She finds that accusers were often female and that witchcraft trials were frequently bound up with local politics; she concludes that witchcraft trials reflect the struggles of women (both as accusers and as accused) for survival and power in a patriarchal culture. Notably, Willis emphasizes an aspect of the witchcraft trials that, ironically, is often overlooked – the experiences of the women involved. She also provides an interesting account of the popular presentation of the figure of the witch and relates this to contemporary views of female sexuality and motherhood. Thus her work is a useful contribution to gender history as well as to the history of witchcraft.

More recently, GIBSON has challenged the assumption by Macfarlane, Thomas, and Sharpe that in rejecting the supernatural elements of witchcraft narratives, it is still possible to accept other parts of those narratives as "real". Gibson explores the factors that shaped the presentation of certain generic witchcraft stories in print (in trial records, newsbooks, pamphlets, and personal accounts of witchcraft trials). Her approach is characteristic of a late 20th-century move towards deconstructionist history, displaying an interest in the figuring of historical accounts and an unease with the labels "truth" and "fiction". Though dealing with some complex literary methodology, her work is accessible to the non-specialist and may mark another turning-point in the history of witchcraft.

For those interested in other forms of supernatural belief, valuable work on astrology has been done by CAPP and GENEVA. Looking at the popular almanac, which disseminated scientific progress and medical learning to the masses along with astrological prognostications, Capp emphasizes the extent to which astrology was a part of everyday life. His work includes an exhaustive bibliography of English almanacs to 1700 and is a valuable reference text; it may may stand alongside Thomas in opening up the debate over popular belief. Though Geneva's scope is smaller than Capp's, her book is an excellent guide to the complex workings of astrology as a system.

SARAH A. TODD

Wollstonecraft, Mary 1759–1797

Prose writer and novelist

Ferguson, Moira and Janet Todd, *Mary Wollstonecraft*, Boston: Twayne, 1984

Kelly, Gary, *Revolutionary Feminism: The Mind and Career of Mary Wollstonecraft*, London: Macmillan, and New York: St Martin's Press, 1992

Lorch, Jennifer, *Mary Wollstonecraft: The Making of a Radical Feminist*, Oxford: Berg, and New York: St Martin's Press, 1990

Maurer, Shawn Lisa, "The Female (as) Reader: Sex, Sensibility, and the Maternal in Wollstonecraft's Fictions" in *Essays in Literature*, 19/1 (1992): 36–54

Poovey, Mary, *The Proper Lady and the Woman Writer: Ideology as Style in the Works of Mary Wollstonecraft, Mary Shelley, and Jane Austen*, Chicago: University of Chicago Press, 1984

Todd, Janet (editor), *A Wollstonecraft Anthology*, Bloomington: Indiana University Press, 1977; Cambridge: Polity Press, 1989

Todd, Janet, *Mary Wollstonecraft: A Revolutionary Life*, New York: Columbia University Press, 2000

Tomalin, Claire, *The Life and Death of Mary Wollstonecraft*, London: Weidenfeld and Nicolson, and New York: Harcourt Brace Jovanovich, 1974; revised edition, Harmondsworth: Penguin, 1992

The revival of interest in Mary Wollstonecraft began in the 1960s, as the women's liberation movement achieved social and cultural prominence. Scholars were greatly interested in recovering texts by women writers and seeking out works by – in the words of FERGUSON AND TODD (1984) – "pioneer theorists of feminism". Thus Wollstonecraft, whose writings include *Thoughts on the Education of Daughters* (1786) and *A Vindication of the Rights of Woman* (1792), was a rediscovery of great value. A look at Wollstonecraft criticism reveals that those writing about her tend to be equally interested in her life and her work. Typically, the revivalist trend in Wollstonecraft scholarship can be traced from a new edition of *A Vindication of the Rights of Woman* published in the late 1960s through numerous biographies written in the 1970s to more current feminist and new-historicist assessments of her life and works. Fascination with Wollstonecraft shows no sign of abating. There has even been a "bodice-ripper" fictionalized account of her life: *Vindication*, by Frances Sherwood (1993). Scholarly interest in Wollstonecraft's works also continues: new considerations of her views on colonization and slavery and of her place in women's literary history appear frequently.

TODD (1977) is an anthology; in her introduction, Todd presents Wollstonecraft's works chronologically while discussing background information on her personal life and political views. In synthesizing these elements, Todd argues that "clearly, Wollstonecraft came to her ideas on women's sorry situation from her own experiences as a dependent and independent woman". Todd's book is a good starting-point for the scholar new to Wollstonecraft: it covers a broad selection of Wollstonecraft's writings, some as excerpts, and includes a useful bibliography.

TOMALIN's biography reconstructs Wollstonecraft's life in an engaging manner, with lively depictions of Wollstonecraft, her family, and the colourful political and literary circles in which she moved. Tomalin emphasizes biographical influences on Wollstonecraft's writing, discussing the works throughout her text. The book also includes several pages of portraits of Wollstonecraft and many signficant figures in her life.

FERGUSON & TODD's study is an introduction to Wollstonecraft, acquainting the reader with her personal life, family history, and major works. Ferguson and Todd trace the development of her philosophy through her career, noting the influence of John Locke, William Cowper, Richard Price, and many others, as well as her opposition to the ideas of Edmund Burke and Jean-Jacques Rousseau. Additionally, they provide historical background on the state of women's writing and publishing at the time.

KELLY argues that "in her life and writing, Mary Wollstonecraft addressed the problematic relation of subjectivity and society, 'mind' and the state, ideology and culture, especially for women", and, in doing so, created a feminism for her age. Kelly presents his book as a reading of Wollstonecraft's "mind" and career "in relation to the cultural revolution that founded the modern state in late eighteenth-century Britain", and he explores how the atmosphere and tenets of revolution in general affected and inspired Wollstonecraft's theories. He rebuts the view of her writing as incompetent and inartistic, suggesting that it may simply *appear* so because it challenges the traditional "gendered order of writing". Kelly's book is especially valuable for its assessment of the history of revolutionary feminism and Wollstonecraft's place in the movement.

LORCH's short book takes a dual approach to Wollstonecraft's biography and works. Part 1 traces Wollstonecraft's life from her experience in Bath as a lady's companion to her death in childbirth 19 years later. This portion of the narrative is organized around the motifs of Wollstonecraft's "search for independence and her yearning for wholeness or integrity". Part 2 traces the development of her thought from "a prim radicalism" in her early writings to a combination of "feminism and proto-socialism" in *Maria, or The Wrongs of Woman*. Additionally, Lorch pays homage to Ralph Wardle, citing his work with Wollstonecraft's letters (*Collected Letters*, 1979; *Godwin and Mary: Letters*, 1967) as an invaluable resource for her own analysis of Wollstonecraft's complex character. The book also contains a useful select bibliography, which includes Wollstonecraft's works published during her lifetime, facsimile reproductions, and later editions, along with secondary sources on her life and works.

POOVEY explores the cultural, political, and social background with regard to women in the 18th century and devotes two chapters specifically to Wollstonecraft: "Man's Discourse, Woman's Heart: Mary Wollstonecraft's Two Vindications" and "Love's Skirmishes and the Triumph of Ideology". Poovey argues that Wollstonecraft "tried to confront directly and aggressively the political inequalities perpetuated in the name of propriety"; she illustrates this idea by showing how Wollstonecraft's works raise "the questions that late eighteenth-century intellectuals implicitly posed to the normative definition of woman". Poovey suggests that the early stage of Wollstonecraft's life and writing is "characterized by the persistence of two conflicting desires": the traditional emotional rewards for women of "love, gratitude, and a sense of being necessary to someone else's happiness", and "a fierce determination to be independent" – a dichotomy she analyzes in *A Vindication of the Rights of Men* and *A Vindication of the Rights of Woman*. Next, Poovey turns to the *Letters Written during a Short Residence in Sweden, Norway, and Denmark* and discusses them in comparison with *Maria, or, the Wrongs of Woman*, suggesting that in these later works Wollstonecraft "grants subjectivity and personal experiences the authority she had previously reserved for the objective 'clear truths' of reason". Poovey's essays provide a valuable comparative analysis of Wollstonecraft's early and later works.

MAURER posits that "Wollstonecraft promotes the expression of female subjectivity through and within motherhood because she recognizes that the conditions of her society" militate against "the possibility of rational and reciprocal relations between women and men". Maurer pursues this thesis through a comparative study of the unfinished novel *Maria, or, The Wrongs of Woman* and *Mary, A Fiction*, suggesting that although the two works are driven by relationships between mothers and daughters, they differ significantly "in each heroine's enactment of the maternal role". She also discusses *Thoughts on the Education of Daughters* and *A Vindication of the Rights of Woman* in relation to Wollstonecraft's fiction and provides an overview of current criticism.

TODD (2000) is the most authoritative biography to date. Todd carefully contextualizes Wollstonecraft's life, times, and writing and also provides several black-and-white illustrations showing portraits of Wollstonecraft and important people in her life. The bibliography is an excellent resource for scholars.

JULIE D. CAMPBELL

Wolseley, Garnet, 1st Viscount Wolseley

1833–1913

Soldier and army reformer

Hamer, W.S., *The British Army: Civil-Military Relations, 1885–1905*, Oxford: Clarendon Press, 1970

Kochanski, Halik, *Sir Garnet Wolseley: Victorian Hero*, London and Rio Grande, Ohio: Hambledon Press, 2000

Lehmann, Joseph H., *All Sir Garnet: A Life of Field-Marshall Lord Wolseley*, London: Jonathan Cape, 1964; as *The Model Major-General: A Biography of Field-Marshall Lord Wolseley*, Boston: Houghton Mifflin, 1964

MacKenzie, John M. (editor), *Popular Imperialism and the Military, 1850–1950*, Manchester and New York: Manchester University Press, 1992

Major, E., *Lord Wolseley*, London: James Nisbet, 1913

Maurice, F. and George Arthur, *The Life of Lord Wolseley*, London: Heinemann, and New York: Doubleday, 1924

Maxwell, Leigh, *The Ashanti Ring: Sir Garnet Wolseley's Campaigns, 1870–1882*, London: Cooper/Secker and Warburg, 1985

Wolseley, Garnet J., *The Story of a Soldier's Life*, 2 vols, London: Constable, and New York: Scribner, 1903

Of all the military officers whose careers flourished in tandem with the expanding British empire in the later 19th century, few achieved as much popular fame as Garnet Wolseley. A string of dazzling military successes in Canada, West Africa, and Egypt between the 1860s and early 1880s, and his pivotal role in modernizing the British army, ensured that for the queen and the country he was "our only general"; and to his men the expression "all Sir Garnet" conveyed a sense of confident efficiency.

Like the "lives" of other contemporary soldier heroes, the earliest biographies of Wolseley tend to be hagiographic. The one by MAJOR is among the more substantial and still has value for the historian in demonstrating the place men like Wolseley held in the Victorian imperial imagination. Major's style is inspirational and was probably intended at least in part for a younger audience; his book portrays "a man of unswerving devotion to duty and of fine loyalty to his friends . . . gallant in danger and modest in success". The book also betrays some of the prejudices inherent in the colonial conquests of the era: for example, discussing the origins of Wolseley's West African campaign in 1873–74, Major suggests, "Little by little there had grown up in the minds of the Ashanti rulers an idea that they could defy the English with impunity."

A densely detailed autobiography by WOLSELEY takes his career only to the end of the Ashanti expedition but nevertheless is valuable for insights into his own attitudes. He demonstrates his impatience with civilian interference in army affairs: "We are never ready for war . . . ye iconoclastic civilian officials who meddle and muddle in Army matters. . . . Leave the management of our fighting men to soldiers of experience". Wolseley reflects that he has "set down nought in malice", but the vitriol in his private journals is apparent to modern scholars; there, he bitterly scorns fellow officers and politicians alike: the Duke of Cambridge is repeatedly described as "cowardly flesh", and Michael Hicks-Beach is called "Sir Hitch-Bitch".

MAURICE & ARTHUR (1924) is a solid and admiring biography by two army officers, unable quite to distance themselves from Wolseley's aura. For their authorized account they were able to draw on private papers; and although they did not have access to sources more recently opened to scholars, this book remains an indispensable study. Maurice & Arthur gloss over Wolseley's one significant campaign failure – the Gordon relief expedition of 1884–85 – and his devastating senility during his last decade; but they do illustrate, although without reference to the sarcasm in his journals, his frequent impatience with politicians and administrators (for example, with Sir Bartle Frere in South Africa, in the wake of the Zulu conflict of 1879).

The biography by LEHMANN provides a narrative that is accessible and reasonably well researched (Lehmann has used a wide range of sources). It includes a clear account of Wolseley's major campaigns, although his career after 1885 is rather sketchily covered and Lehmann makes no reference to Wolseley's acid comments about colleagues and says little about other negative traits. Like Maurice & Arthur, Lehmann also largely fails to place Wolseley in a broader context of imperial or military history, and there is little explicit discussion of the evolution of or influences on, Wolseley's military thinking. Nevertheless, this remains a useful starting-point for an assessment off Wolseley the soldier.

The detailed, scholarly study by HAMER is particularly valuable, as it addresses many of the issues not fully considered by previous authors, and Hamer succeeds in placing Wolseley's achievements as an army reformer in a wider context of military and political change. In addition to an extensive discussion of Wolseley's role in evolving civil-military relations, Hamer supplies some sharp insights into Wolseley's background and character. Wolseley, a "staunch Irish Protestant", is depicted as seeing his career as "moulded by the hand of God", and while "in later life this idea was to cloud his mind with a dark fatalism . . . undoubtedly in his early years it encouraged his already keen ambitions". Hamer confirms that Wolseley held politicians in low esteem and shows how, under his leadership, "a group of progressive-minded officers . . . urged the necessity and logic of reforming the army if Britain's far-flung Empire was to be successfully defended". Hamer also believes that Wolseley "ruined his health in the struggle to overcome conservative habits in the army". The primary achievement was the Cardwell reform programme of 1870–71, but Hamer makes it clear that much remained which angered Wolseley, right through to the South African War of 1899–1902. Generally, Hamer is not concerned with the darker side of Wolseley's character, and he feels able to conclude that his subject "represented a new spirit in the British army. . . . He was a political general as well as a leader of rare ability".

MAXWELL's volume is a popular account of Wolseley's career as a campaigner, up to his victory over the Egyptians at Tel-el-Kebir in 1882. This is by no means a scholarly work; it has no footnotes and is based entirely on secondary sources. Also, it says nothing of substance about Wolseley's life before 1873, or about his role in army reform. The tone is generally uncritical: Wolseley is regarded as one of the best commanders in the history of the army. Nevertheless, this work is of some value for the background it provides on tension between the "African Ring" – the army officers' faction most closely associated with Wolseley – and the rival "Indian Ring" surrounding Lord Roberts.

The valuable collection edited by MacKENZIE is broader in scope, examining the cult of the soldier-hero as it evolved during the heyday of the British empire and providing a yardstick against which Wolseley's career and reputation can be measured. It suggests that in an era of "small" colonial wars, the image of soldiers in general and officers like Wolseley in particular was recast in a heroic mould as a Christian-militaristic exemplar for society, especially for young men. MacKenzie concludes that such heroic myths "were vital to the British sense of moral purpose" in the imperial context, "because they provided a range of justifications for state power and expansion".

A well-researched and wide-ranging biography by KOCHANSKI provides many insights into Wolseley as a soldier and as a reformer. Although it perhaps does not delve as deeply into his private life as the surviving sources might allow, and although it has a rather large number of typographical errors, this book undoubtedly supersedes all the previous studies and should become the standard work.

CHRISTOPHER SCHMITZ

See also Army: Since 1855; Buller; Cardwell; Egypt, British Intervention in; Gordon

Wolsey, Thomas c.1473–1530
Minister to Henry VIII and cardinal

Elton, G.R., *Studies in Tudor and Stuart Politics and Government: Papers and Reviews 1946–1972*, vol. 1, Cambridge and New York: Cambridge University Press, 1974

Gunn, S.J. and P.G. Lindley (editors), *Cardinal Wolsey: Church, State, and Art*, Cambridge and New York: Cambridge University Press, 1991

Guy, J.A. *The Cardinal's Court: The Impact of Thomas Wolsey in Star Chamber*, Hassocks, Sussex: Harvester Press, and Totowa, New Jersey: Rowman and Littlefield, 1977

Gwyn, Peter, *The King's Cardinal: The Rise and Fall of Thomas Wolsey*, London: Barrie and Jenkins, 1990

Pollard, A.F., *Wolsey*, London and New York: Longmans Green, 1929; illustrated and corrected edition, 1953; Westport, Connecticut: Greenwood Press, 1978

Scarisbrick, J.J., *Henry VIII*, London: Eyre and Spottiswoode, and Berkeley, California: University of California Press, 1968; revised edition, New Haven, Connecticut, and London: Yale University Press, 1997

Walker, Greg, *John Skelton and the Politics of the 1520s*, Cambridge and New York: Cambridge University Press, 1988

Thomas Cardinal Wolsey has not received much respect from historians. Foxe, the protestant martyrologist, thought that Wolsey's pride, avarice, and ostentation were typical of what was wrong with the old church; Harpsfield, the Marian persecutor of heretics, held Wolsey responsible for Henry VIII's divorce from Catherine of Aragon, the break with Rome, and the evils that followed. Although Wolsey's personal servant Cavendish attempted to clear his master's memory, only in the 19th century did Wolsey come to be seen as one of England's great statesmen.

POLLARD brought an end to this brief rehabilitation in his biography, which continued themes he had developed in an earlier study of Henry VIII. Since Pollard considered the king to have been a statesman of great vision, anyone who served him would consequently be diminished. In Pollard's view, Wolsey carried out policy but did not create it and was a failure when left on his own. In foreign policy Wolsey selfishly subordinated English national interests to those of the papacy, hoping that by so doing he would one day be pope himself. In domestic matters Wolsey mishandled the economy, and although he had good ideas for reforming the judicial and tax systems, he did not carry them out. For the church, his rule had even more serious consequences. As papal legate he had full power to reform an institution which desperately needed reform, but he was too busy with secular affairs to accomplish much, and his use of *praemunire* set a dangerous precedent for him personally as well as for the church he served. Moreover, by taking away the independent powers of the bishops and convocation he weakened the church and rendered it unable to withstand the attack that followed his own fall. Only as an administrator did Wolsey earn Pollard's grudging praise. As lord chancellor he brought justice to the poor and powerless in the courts of the Star Chamber and Requests, but he did so at the expense of common law. In short, to Pollard, Wolsey subverted the constitution by reducing parliament to insignificance and by his autocratic leadership of the council and the church.

ELTON continued the assault on Wolsey's reputation from at least two directions. First, he denied Pollard's view of the king as a statesman who had a clear vision of the constitution. Second, Elton concluded – after contrasting Wolsey with his former protégé Thomas Cromwell – that Wolsey had no such vision either. Where Wolsey had subverted parliament, Cromwell exalted it; and unlike Cromwell, Wolsey had no vision of government and left behind no reforms or even lasting solutions to pressing problems. He was an improvisor reacting to events, not an innovator.

SCARISBRICK, however, challenged Pollard's and Elton's negative view of Wolsey. Scarisbrick's interpretation of Wolsey, like Pollard's, was inversely related to his assessment of the king; but to Scarisbrick – unlike Pollard – Wolsey was the statesman with a clear vision and the king was the one who merely reacted to events. According to Scarisbrick, Wolsey's foreign policy was driven by a desire for peace, not personal advancement. If it appeared, as it appeared to Pollard, that Wolsey always followed the pope's lead, this was because the way to peace, England's national interest, and the pope's interest happened to coincide.

Pollard had argued that Wolsey's greed and ambition to rise in the church motivated a foreign policy which was not in England's interest; Scarisbrick countered by shifting the responsibility. Wolsey did not aspire to the papacy – the idea was that of King Henry, who fancied having his man in Rome. In domestic matters the story was the same. Instead of an arrogant, greedy churchman, Scarisbrick portrayed a humane chancellor who tried to solve pressing economic and social issues.

Scarisbrick's coverage of the issues of canon law surrounding the king's divorce is particularly strong. Unlike Pollard and most of Henry's other biographers, Scarisbrick thought Wolsey had a strategy for gaining the divorce that would have succeeded, but the inept king, who never understood the legal situation, kept interfering and forced the cardinal to adopt a case which was doomed from the beginning.

GUY continued this rehabilitation of Wolsey in his detailed study of the Court of Star Chamber. Elton had held that "Wolsey the great judge is almost certainly a myth", but Guy demonstrated that Wolsey – not the statute of 1487 and not Thomas Cromwell – was the true creator of the court. Whatever Star Chamber was to become under the Stuarts, it was not an instrument of royal despotism under Henry VIII, and it did not subvert common law. Although Guy found that the number of suits between private parties increased dramatically while Wolsey was chancellor, he could find only nine official prosecutions. True, on two notorious occasions Wolsey used the court to pursue his enemies, but in those cases Speaker Sheffield and Bishop Standish were, arguably, not so much Wolsey's personal enemies as enemies of the clerical estate for which Wolsey as papal legate was also responsible. In one respect, though, Guy found Wolsey's leadership inadequate: Wolsey failed to appreciate human nature and thus failed to stem the large number of relatively trivial suits that clogged the court and frustrated his good intentions.

WALKER's detailed monograph attacked another long-held myth: that Wolsey, the son of a butcher in Ipswich, was jealous of aristocrats and therefore seized every opportunity to put them down. Walker maintained that Wolsey's celebrated expulsion of the "king's minions" in 1519 should be seen as an attempt to keep the peace at court, and that by and large it was supported by the nobility who had no desire to return to the instability of the previous century. Aside from Skelton's bitter satire, there is no evidence that Wolsey was responsible for the Duke of Buckingham's downfall; and Walker concluded that Skelton's attack should not be taken literally, for a few years later Skelton was praising the cardinal in hopes of preferment.

The 11 essays in GUNN & LINDLEY attempt to assess Wolsey not only as a statesman and papal legate but also as a patron of the arts. Political historians generally overlook the topic of Wolsey and the arts, but this area of his life bore the brunt of attacks by his enemies because his projects were so large and so expensive. The authors' premise is that since Wolsey left no personal papers, examining the projects he chose to support will bring us as close as we can get to discovering his personality. They conclude that Wolsey's desire to be a patron of the English Renaissance mirrors his desire to pursue a "humanist quest for peace", but their essays also reinforce Pollard's image of an unimaginative and avaricious cleric who built as he lived, on a royal scale.

GWYN's large biography took issue with Pollard as well as with most contemporary authorities, especially over the matter of faction as the driving force in political life. Instead of a man impelled by insatiable ambition, Gwynn presented a minister anxious only to serve his king; instead of a cleric motivated by a desire for a universal Christian peace, or to become pope, Gwynn presented a man working selflessly to make his master the arbiter of Europe. Indeed, Gwynn portrays Wolsey as the first among equals of the king's councillors, not the *alter rex*.

ROBERT C. BRADDOCK

See also Boleyn, Anne; Catherine of Aragon; Cromwell, Thomas; Henry VIII; Henry VIII: Divorce from Catherine; Norfolk; Privy (King's) Council of England

Women and Employment: To 1914

Davidoff, Leonore and Catherine Hall, *Family Fortunes: Men and Women of the English Middle Classes, 1780–1850,* London: Hutchinson, and Chicago: University of Chicago Press, 1987

Davidson, Caroline, *"A Woman's Work Is Never Done": A History of Housework in the British Isles, 1650–1950,* London: Chatto and Windus, 1982

Gordon, Eleanor, *Women and the Labour Movement in Scotland, 1850–1914,* Oxford: Clarendon Press, and New York: Oxford University Press, 1991

Hanawalt, Barbara A. (editor), *Women and Work in Preindustrial Europe,* Bloomington: Indiana University Press, 1986

Higgs, Edward, "Women, Occupations, and Work in the Nineteenth-Century Censuses", *History Workshop Journal,* 23/1 (1987): 59–80

Hill, Bridget, *Women, Work, and Sexual Politics in Eighteenth-Century England,* Oxford and New York: Blackwell, 1989

Hunt, Margaret R., *The Middling Sort: Commerce, Gender, and the Family in England, 1680–1780,* Berkeley: University of California Press, 1996

John, Angela V., *By the Sweat of Their Brow: Women Workers at Victorian Coal Mines,* London: Croom Helm, 1980; reprinted, London and Boston: Routledge and Kegan Paul, 1984

John, Angela V. (editor), *Unequal Opportunities: Women's Employment in England 1800–1918,* Oxford and New York: Blackwell, 1986

Rendall, Jane, *Women in an Industrializing Society: England 1750–1880,* Oxford and Cambridge, Massachusetts: Blackwell, 1991

Sharpe, Pamela, *Adapting to Capitalism: Working Women in the English Economy, 1700–1850,* Basingstoke: Macmillan, and New York: St Martin's Press, 1996

Snell, K.D.M., *Annals of the Labouring Poor: Social Change and Agrarian England, 1600–1900,* Cambridge and New York: Cambridge University Press, 1985

No matter what time period is examined, similar questions are raised in the historical debate over the participation of women in the workforce and the family economy. What exactly was "women's work"? Did women have an economic role outside the family? If so, did this role bring independence and freedom, or did it simply impose different but equally restrictive limits on women's choices? Scholars have approached these basic questions in a variety of ways; and through the imaginative approaches of many historians, and a creative use of sources, the reader can begin to understand the continuity and change in examining the long history of women's work.

The essays in HANAWALT address these issues by considering a range of stations in life. The authors discuss the labour of urban and rural women, servants, widows, and midwives. Although circumstances and details vary widely, some conclusions are reached about women's work from the 13th to the 16th centuries. Household and domestic production was the dominant feature of women's work in pre-industrial times; the family economy was seen as the basic unit. Earlier female historians had emphasized the strengths and options of medieval women, perhaps because these historians themselves were seeking to establish new options and roles for women. Hanawalt and the essayists in her volume view the same evidence in a different light. They find that the domestic framework was restrictive: women were unable to step out of their space and their sphere and were bound by the supervision and control that the family-based economy imposed.

HILL presents a slightly different construction of the possibilities open to women. She argues that in the first half of 18th century women worked in wide range of trades, some of which later became the monopoly of men. Gradually, certain types of work came to be seen as unsuitable, as unfeminine, or as encouraging immoral habits. The 18th century witnessed a much clearer demarcation of working roles of men and women than previous centuries, according to Hill's evidence. Women were gradually pushed into unskilled and poorly paid work.

According to HUNT, the 18th century was a time of transition for the "middling sort" in commerce as well as for the lower orders. Commerical middling families experienced a continual sense of vulnerability because of frequent insolvency, imprisonment for debt, and the unavailability of capital. These fears contributed to new ways of organizing work and the family which gradually restricted the participation of women.

DAVIDOFF & HALL take a different position in their examination of the middle classes of a century later. They emphasize the importance of women in establishing and running family businesses. Clearly, these women did not have complete economic autonomy, but Davidoff & Hall stress that they were crucial to the success of a business concern and that, in the main, their contributions were recognized and valued. This book corrects the facile notion of a rigidly separate sphere for females, since these middle-class women contributed strongly to the economic well-being of their families.

In contrast to Hunt and Davidoff & Hall, SHARPE argues that the ordinary boundary between pre-industrial and industrial influences is not always helpful to an appreciation of women's work. Sharpe finds that there was both continuity and change; some trends began before industrialization in certain areas but not in others. Local customs and political culture affected the availability and type of work deemed acceptable for females. The position of the female worker must be examined in context: it depended on and interacted with male employment and the availability of male labourers.

Even though separate domestic and public worlds were a middle-class construct, this idea may have been mirrored in the world of work by a clear division of labour considered appropriate for men and women. SNELL suggests that enclosures in the late 18th century accelerated the trend towards sexual specialization in farm work. For centuries women had relied on common land for tending livestock and had cultivated kitchen gardens on small plots; when this work was swept away, women gravitated toward casual paid work which depened on the availability of male labour. Thus increasing specialization in farm labour brought a much sharper division of jobs into what was thought appropriate for each sex.

Snell's study included men as well as women, but many works focus solely on female work in a particular industry or occupation and examine women's experience as opposed to men's. Among many interesting and valuable studies, JOHN (1980)

provides invaluable details of the gruelling work in coal mines and also makes important connections with concepts of gender separation and labour combinations. John finds that certain types of mining employment were considered suitable for females and that this resulted in limited opportunities and lower pay and complicated the legislation regarding coal mining.

The difficulties of gaining acceptance in male-dominated unions is an important aspect of women's work that has been too little studied. In JOHN (1986), three essays address women's union activity in various industries and find that animosity between male and female workers generally overrode the desire to join forces against employers.

Although RENDALL's volume is not completely based on original historical research, it is valuable addition to this list. Because of the plethora of works on how the industrial period affected women's work, and because of their widely disparate approaches, it is useful to have a clear summary and restatement of the current historical debate. Rendall provides this admirably and succinctly and also comes to conclusions about the period based on the evidence she presents. Rendall finds it useful to widen traditional historical time periods in order to let historians examine more gradual patterns of change. She warns the reader against dividing all women of the industrial age into the three simplistic categories "angel in the house", factory girl, and domestic servant. The image which tended to dominate thinking about working women in industrialized Britain is that of the factory girl; and in the past there was an overemphasis on the effects of industrialization on working women, in terms of lax morality and destruction of family ties. This view probably reflects the middle-class values of parliamentary reformers and Victorian novelists, Rendall notes. The profound differences between classes and between different regions must be considered if the debate is to be deepened significantly.

Housework is an occupation so central to virtually all females that it is often overlooked. In a creative study of this occupation, DAVIDSON finds that cleaning increasingly became a focus of housework after the mid-17th century. The wide use of coal in urban areas created grime and smoke, and the affordable new goods which cluttered the homes of all classes had to be regularly washed or blackleaded. Through careful use of domestic sources, Davidson reveals that women whose labour was restricted to the domestic hearth found these demands increasing, for a wide variety of reasons.

Most of the recent historical efforts have been concerned with England, but there are some examinations of other areas of Britain. GORDON offers a fine examinaton of regional differences in Scotland, although she concentrates on working-class occupations rather than attempting to consider all levels.

Because an abundance of evidence is available for the 19th century, this period tends to be over-represented in studies; also, there are inherent dangers in using sources uncritically. HIGGS warns of pitfalls in taking early census figures on trust as an accurate representation of the number of women who worked outside the home. He notes that part-time workers were not included, nor were temporarily unemployed females. He also finds a class bias which virtually eliminates the use of census figures in determining middle-class female employment.

To return to the questions posed at the beginning of this essay, historians agree that there was a definite concept of "women's work"; but they disagree as to when this concept developed, and some scholars have noted that different industries defined female labour in ways that gave male workers an advantage. Working-class women of course had an economic role outside the family during the industrial period, but once again there is no consensus as to when this occurred. In addition, there is disagreement over the independence of middle-class women. As the historical debate has developed, historians seem to emphasize continuity rather than change between the pre-industrial and industrial periods in that there is some agreement that work did not bring independence and freedom – work simply imposed different but equally restrictive limits on women's choices. An increasing movement towards regional and specialized studies has developed to give a more complex and sophisticated picture of the lives of all working women.

CYNTHIA CURRAN

See also Prostitution

Women and Employment: 20th century

Arnold, Erik, *et al.*, *Microelectronics and Women's Employment in Britain*, Brighton, Sussex: Science Policy Research Unit, University of Sussex, 1982

Bradley, Harriet, *Men's Work, Women's Work: A Sociological History of the Sexual Division of Labour in Employment*, Cambridge: Polity Press, and Minneapolis: University of Minnesota Press, 1989

Hakim, Catherine, *Key Issues in Women's Work: Female Heterogeneity and the Polarisation of Women's Employment*, London: Athlone Press, 1996

Pennington, Shelley and Belinda Westover, *A Hidden Workforce: Homeworkers in England, 1850–1985*, London: Macmillan Education, 1989

Roberts, Elizabeth, *Women's Work 1840–1940*, London: Macmillan, 1988; Cambridge and New York: Cambridge University Press, 1995

Stubbs, Cherrie and Jane Wheelock, *A Woman's Work in the Changing Local Economy*, Aldershot, Hampshire; and Brookfield, Vermont: Avebury, 1990

Summerfield, Penny, *Women Workers in the Second World War: Production and Patriarchy in Conflict*, London and Dover, New Hampshire: Croom Helm, 1984

Walby, Sylvia, *Gender Transformations*, London and New York: Routledge, 1997

A Whiggish interpretation of the relationship between employment and women stresses women's increasing rates of participation across industrial sectors, as mechanization has reduced the hazards of manufacturing and the service economy has increased employment opportunities for women. However, feminists argue that to understand this change, we need to appreciate the changes within family life as well as in the experience of employment.

SUMMERFIELD emphasizes this distinction between public and private. She argues that World War II gave women an opportunity to move into the public sphere; and unlike World War I, it transformed the private (domestic) sphere, making these changes more enduring. Because of its duration, the war not only required the government to encourage and coerce women to enter the public domain but also required it to assume some responsibility for meeting the private needs of female workers. Initially, this took the form of exemptions for married women, but during the course of the war the state began to provide, directly, some of the services hidden within the private domestic sphere of production and reproduction. One consequence was that a conceptual foundation was laid for the postwar welfare state, because it was proved that such interventions did not entail social collapse. Another consequence was that because women's work was monetized and hence valorized, the "box" of the domestic sphere was opened, and proof was offered that gender was no barrier to adequate performance at work.

ROBERTS notes that the period 1840–1940 heralded no uniform transformation of conditions of employment, or indeed of social assumptions about female labour. She also notes the importance of this early industrial period for creating a gendered distinction between public and private spheres of employment – a common theme of feminist histories. World War I was an important period of change; the government, employers, and (organized, masculine) workers were forced to find ways to incorporate female labour without undermining the reproduction of households and the implicit subsidy of male employment. As an aside, Roberts includes a "bibliographic appendix" in which she provides a short review essay which complements the present essay rather well.

Roberts describes home-workers as the most exploited class of female workers during the pre-war period, and it is to this subject that PENNINGTON & WESTOVER turn. Their book makes it clear that interpreting the phenomenon of home-working requires a detailed understanding of the social context of the Industrial Revolution. Pennington & Westover provide a political background to the situation after 1914, in particular the Select Committee on the Sweating System and Booth's and Rowntree's studies of urban poverty studies, all in the 1880s. They make the point that defending poorer female workers from exploitation entailed a division of labor which was gendered and which distinguished between public and private; this division was enhanced through measures designed to improve the protection of working men. Although World War I brought women into the public sphere of production, the accompanying strategic rhetoric of patriotism and increased production actually served to further depress the wages and conditions of those women still involved in home-working during the war. In the words of an issue of *Women's Dreadnought* (1914), "Strange patriotism this, that allows the Government contractors who are making money out of this war to sweat the women workers in this disgraceful fashion". Pennington & Westover are pessimistic concerning the degree to which technological change has actually improved the women's position in the labour market. They argue that many women had junior positions as operators of machinery (rather than being engineers or technicians); as a result, women bore the brunt of redundancy in the recession of the early 1980s.

ARNOLD, *et al.* deal with this point at some length, although the argument is undermined to a degree by technocentrism. The book examines the historical impact of technological change on employment, particularly in sectors which are deemed female-dominated, such as electronic assembly; but the analysis stresses the effects of deskilling, making the argument that automation will benefit male employees. This inevitably leads to a tremendously negative reading of the changes, overlooking the potential benefits of automation, casting women as subaltern actors forced to react to change and unable to shape the social introduction of new technologies into particular workplaces. This text is quite weak, but from it can be inferred the critical point: that the changes must be seen in the round: studies which examine what they class as female employment overlook the most important elements of the transformation of the labour process in the 20th century – the political processes through which women have sought to redefine and renegotiate the terms on which they engage with the labour market – and their broader social, economic, and political effects.

In deducing socio-cultural changes from analyses of particular events and phenomena, Arnold *et al.* all allow the inference that the changes in the material practices of businesses are merely part of a wider socio-political shift. BRADLEY begins from the observation that the predominant shift in female employment since 1914 is best explained in terms of a socially constructed redefinition of male and female occupations. Bradley's text develops a long argument which spans a narrative of debates concerning gendered divisions of labour in prehistoric societies to a comprehensive analysis of the redefinition of genders associated with 10 industrial sectors, covering primary, secondary, and tertiary employment. According to Bradley, a concentration on changes since 1914 overlooks the fact that "in the majority of industrial societies . . . agriculture, fishing and mining, in all of which women have in the past performed essential tasks, are now marked . . . by a near total absence of women". Although this occurred in agriculture, mining, and fishing through a moral redefinition of the appropriateness of female involvement, in manufacturing female employment was associated with cost-reduction strategies while trade unions fought very effectively for several decades to protect their (male) members. This enforcement used an ingenious set of tools (e.g. the "marriage bar") to force women into more flexible (less protected) areas of the labour market. Bradley weaves an interesting narrative about how these social rules were continually reinterpreted in new industries to assign gender-specificity to particular occupational classes.

WALBY devotes her text to a dual argument. In the first half of her book she presents compelling empirical and statistical evidence that the nature of female employment changed greatly in the 20th century. These empirical chapters make the case that changes in the gendered division of labour are particular manifestations of changes more usually referred to in the abstract; Walby notes, for example, the relationship between increasing female participation in the labour market and the increase in the rhetoric of flexible labour practices. However, the historically more interesting theses are advanced in the second part of the book. Walby takes a more structural approach to explaining changes in the labour market in terms of the history of feminism, and the way in which a series of political and social movements laid down the antecedents both for feminism and for later changes in the labour market. A key element of the thesis is that feminism alone has not transformed employment; rather, there has been a continual struggle in which the state, businesses, and organized labour have sought to diminish the material benefits of feminist political action, creating tension that in turn drives the dynamics of change.

HAKIM specifically seeks to attack the feminist position espoused by, inter alia, WALBY as received wisdom, noting that growing female employment has not overturned the essential reliance of female workers on supplementary sources of income, from a spouse or the state. Thus the transformation in the material conditions of employment has not overcome the patriarchal problem of financial dependence. The argument is forcefully advanced that because the labour market in the period after 1914 was dominated by men, the so-called demasculinization of labour has been accompanied by a parallel though less visible process of defeminization. This is evinced in the death of much of the personal service economy (domestic service, personal tailoring, etc.) and its replacement with gender-neutral and indeed degendered occupations. An interesting point is that as women have made advances in areas with high media profiles – including the media themselves – the vernacular discourse has become dominated by these few positive but unrepresentative voices.

STUBBS & WHEELOCK use a feminist framework to analyse the changing nature of female employment in one locality suffering industrial decline: Sunderland in north-eastern England. What is most compelling about this work is the argument that the social purpose of female employment has changed since 1914, and that for the most deprived communities female employment has once more become associated with family survival. The authors examine more than one dimension of change in female employment. In the formal sector women have had to deal with the structural problems of social discrimination in parallel with the problems of all workers seeking employment during a severe recession. Informally, women's skills and actions have provided important social cohesion for these socially excluded communities in a way that formal statistics cannot capture. Women have had some success in starting new businesses, although there are significant barriers to female entrepreneurship, particularly in terms of gender-biased viability assessments requiring particular forms of experience. In this analysis it therefore becomes necessary to assign a gender dimension to interpretations of regional industrial decline, noting the centrality of equality to social justice.

PAUL S. BENNEWORTH

Women Writers since 17th century

Gilbert, Sandra M. and Susan Gubar, *No Man's Land: The Place of the Woman Writer in the Twentieth Century*, 3 vols, New Haven, Connecticut and London: Yale University Press, 1988–94

Gilbert, Sandra M. and Susan Gubar, *The Madwoman in the Attic: The Woman Writer and the Nineteenth-Century Literary Imagination*, New Haven, Connecticut and London: Yale University Press, 1979; 2nd edition, 2000

Goulianos, Joan (editor), *By a Woman Writt: Literature from Six Centuries by and about Women*, Indianapolis: Bobbs-Merrill, 1973; London: New English Library, 1974

Hanscombe, Gillian and Virginia L. Smyers, *Writing for Their Lives: The Modernist Women 1910–1940*, London: Women's Press, 1987; Boston, Massachusetts: Northeastern University Press, 1988

Harrison, Elizabeth Jane and Shirley Peterson (editors), *Unmanning Modernism: Gendered Re-Readings*, Knoxville: University of Tennessee Press, 1997

Lawrence, Karen R., *Penelope Voyages: Women and Travel in the British Literary Tradition*, Ithaca, New York: Cornell University Press, 1994

Michie, Elsie B., *Outside the Pale: Cultural Exclusion, Gender Difference, and the Victorian Woman Writer*, Ithaca, New York: Cornell University Press, 1993

Showalter, Elaine, *A Literature of Their Own: British Women Novelists from Brontë to Lessing*, Princeton, New Jersey: Princeton University Press, 1977; revised edition, London: Virago, 1982; revised and expanded edition, Princeton, New Jersey: Princeton University Press, 1998 and London: Virago, 1999

Spencer, Jane, *The Rise of the Woman Novelist: From Aphra Behn to Jane Austen*, Oxford and Cambridge, Massachusetts: Blackwell, 1986

Spender, Dale and Janet Todd (editors), *Anthology of British Women Writers*, London: Pandora Press, 1989; as *British Women Writers: An Anthology from the Fourteenth Century to the Present*, New York: Bedrick Books, 1989; as *Anthology of British Women Writers from the Middle Ages to the Present Day*, London: Pandora, 1990

Recent studies have indicated how crucial women's writing and reading were to the development of the novel, and literary scholars now look not only at "forgotten" women writers but at how literature is affected by gender. Whenever women were writing, from the 17th century through the 20th, it seems clear that their themes and concerns typically varied from those of male writers, and women have used literature to explore and escape their marginalized societal status.

GOULIANOS (1973) represents one of the earliest attempts to uncover women's writings since the Middle Ages. Selections from diaries, letters, protest tracts, poetry, plays, novels, and autobiographies allow women from the past to speak about their lives. Common themes include childbirth, housework, female friendship, marriage, and women's roles as daughters, wives, mothers, widows, and workers. The anthology excludes more famous writers such as Austen, Woolf, and Eliot in order to introduce readers to lesser-known authors. Though the collection does not provide a sufficient historical context for the excerpts, it does present writings from women throughout Europe. Despite geographical boundaries, women writers shared similar problems and experienced similar discrimination in patriarchal societies.

SPENDER & TODD trace the origins of women's writing from the 14th century to the present, focusing solely on Britain. From Julian of Norwich to Angela Carter, the "evolutionary and interconnecting patterns in British women's writing" are explored. Diary and journal entries help provide commentary on women's relationship to writing and their notions of self-expression. The excerpts from Margaret Cavendish, the Duchess of Newcastle, Eliza Haywood, Lady Mary Wortley Montagu, and others all discuss women's education and the desire for independence and literary legitimacy. Whereas Goulianos stresses the similarity of women's writings, Spender & Todd also point out diversity among women writers, particularly since the flourishing of the novel in the 18th and 19th centuries.

SPENCER explores the rise of women novelists since the 18th century. Considering the novel within the larger context of other writings (periodicals, letters, essays, conduct books), she exposes society's often hostile attitude toward women writers. Using such writers as Eliza Haywood, Fanny Burney, and Jane Austen, Spencer demonstrates women's shifting position as authors. In the 18th century, women's writing was expected to be marked by femininity, but by Austen's time women writers had shifted from simple romances to social satires and a demand for women's rights. Linking changes in women's writing to changes in the ideology of womanhood, Spencer also shows how women saw themselves within the cultural and social climate. She reminds us of an important point: that "women's writing is not the same thing as women's rights" and that by the 19th century, as women writers became more socially acceptable, the link between writing and feminism tended to weaken.

SHOWALTER continues the analysis where Spencer leaves off. Showalter's study of 200 women novelists from 1800 to 1980 suggests that they "lived in a different country from men" and had a "literature of their own". This study – now a classic – provides a lively discussion of the social and literary history of women's writing and represents an early feminist attempt to save women writers from the trivial category of "lady novelists". Showalter argues that the growth of a female consciousness helped shape the novel. Looking at each woman novelist "against the backdrop of the women of her time" as well as in relation to other writers in history, Showalter concludes that "women have constituted a subculture within the framework of a larger society and have been unified by values, conventions, experiences, and behaviors impinging on each individual". Rejecting the notion of an innate female sexual attitude, Showalter does, however, recognize the self-awareness of the woman writer that has translated itself into a literary form.

GILBERT & GUBAR (1979), like Showalter, examine women writers in the 19th century and find that a disturbing image – the "madwoman in the attic" – emerges from these women's work. They argue that images of enclosure, escape, lunacy, and disease dominate the novels of Jane Austen, Mary Shelley, the Brontë sisters, and George Eliot; that close readings of these texts highlight the anxieties which produced such a literary tradition; that the literal and figurative confinement of women is reflected in these writings; and that the writings show a shared "strength in agony".

MICHIE expands Gilbert and Gubar's thesis but relies more on a theoretical analysis. Using the work of Teresa de Lauretis, Mary Poovey, Catherine Gallagher, and Homi Bhabha, Michie offers a rereading of familiar Victorian novels to illuminate political, social, and economic issues of the 19th century. Images of monsters, menstruation, and fallen women, she holds, really refer to larger debates on suffrage, prostitution, feminism, and women's access to higher education. Michie also points out that not only gender but also race and class shaped the writing of the novel.

Other familiar tropes of women's writing, according to LAWRENCE, have been movement, wandering, and exile. Writing was a form of travel for women who wanted to escape cultural constraints and become free agents. Lawrence uses feminist theory to analyse the textual strategies and rhetorical devices of writers from Fanny Burney and Margaret Cavendish to Mary Wollstonecraft, Mary Kingsley, and Virginia Woolf to post-modern writers such as Christine Brooke-Rose and Brigid Brophy. As an outsider looking in, the woman writer was at last able to achieve the privileged position of observer.

GILBERT & GUBAR (1988–94), a three-volume study of women writers, continues the project of feminist analysis but focuses primarily on the 20th century. Volume 1 provides an overview of the social, literary, and linguistic interactions between men and women from the mid-19th century to the present, and of modernism as differentiated by gender. This volume discusses the ongoing battle of the sexes, the rise of feminism, the fall of Victorian concepts of "femininity", and the emergence of literary modernism. Volume 2 explores the impact of World War I on modernism and the emergence of a lesbian literary tradition. Volume 3 looks at the works of Virginia Woolf, H.D. (Hilda Doolittle), and others in relation to such hostile male contemporaries as Ezra Pound, James Joyce, and Wyndham Lewis.

Gilbert and Gubar's thesis about the impact of the sexual struggle on literature and about writing as a gendered process has been expanded by HANSCOMBE & SMYERS, who argue that the personal lives and friendships of such female modernists as H.D., Dorothy Richardson, Amy Lowell, and Djuna Barnes affected what they wrote and their rejection of "heterosexism". Placing these writers alongside their male counterparts, Hanscombe and Smyers conclude that female modernists were just as avant-garde and influential but have remained ignored by most scholars.

HARRISON & PETERSON also reclaim the lives and works of important female modernists, offering theoretical and feminist readings of the works of Gertrude Stein, Woolf, Radclyffe Hall, H.D., and Rebecca West. The essays in this collection examine such themes as lesbianism, maternity, and the misogyny directed at the women writers by their male colleagues.

Each of these works provides valuable information on women at particular moments in history. Women's concerns in the 17th century may have differed from those in the 20th, but most of the writers discussed shared a tradition of oppression and exclusion from the literary mainstream. Their writings reflect the impact of gender as well as that of the cultural, social, and political milieu on their lives and their art.

JULIE ANNE TADDEO

See also Fiction entries

Women's Education

Bennett, Daphne, *Emily Davies and the Liberation of Women 1830–1921*, London: Deutsch, 1990

Copelman, Dina M., *London's Women Teachers: Gender, Class, and Feminism, 1870–1930*, London and New York: Routledge, 1996

Dyhouse, Carol, *No Distinction of Sex? Women in British Universities 1870–1939*, London: University College London (UCL) Press, 1995

Hunt, Felicity (editor), *Lessons for Life: The Schooling of Girls and Women 1850–1950*, Oxford and New York: Blackwell, 1987

Jordan, Ellen, "'Making Good Wives and Mothers'? The Transformation of Middle-Class Girls' Education in Nineteenth-Century Britain", *History of Education Quarterly*, 31/4 (1991): 439–62

Kamm, Josephine, *Hope Deferred: Girls' Education in English History*, London: Methuen, 1965

Oram, Alison, *Women Teachers and Feminist Politics, 1900–39*, Manchester and New York: Manchester University Press, 1996

Purvis, June, *Hard Lessons: The Lives and Education of Working-Class Women in Nineteenth-Century England*, Cambridge: Polity Press, and Minneapolis: University of Minnesota Press, 1989

Purvis, June, *A History of Women's Education in England*, Milton Keynes, Buckinghamshire, and Philadelphia: Open University Press, 1991

Spender, Dale (editor), *The Education Papers: Women's Quest for Equality in Britain, 1850–1912*, London and New York: Routledge and Kegan Paul, 1987

As PURVIS (1989) has pointed out, interest in women's education in 19th-century England has "tended to concentrate overwhelmingly upon the experiences of middle-class girls and women, and, in particular, upon the struggle by a minority of middle-class women to enter higher education". Older work such as KAMM (1965), however, is useful in tracing the progress of popular education and the work of leading figures who fought to bring girls' education up to the level of boys'. Kamm's sections on charity schools, the bluestockings, and those opposed to any type of academic education for girls provide a concise analysis of the forces which aided and retarded education for both middle- and working-class girls. From the 1780s on, evangelicalism led to an expansion in the education available to the poor in the form of charity and Sunday schools. The main impetus, however, was to enable girls to read the Bible and to become good wives, mothers, and servants. Religious motivations also led to the foundation of two voluntary societies: the National Society (Church of England) in 1811 and the British and Foreign School Society (Nonconformist) in 1814. In practice, though, these represented little advance on the education provided by charity schools. The particular strength of Kamm's book is its use of primary sources.

The education of working-class girls is considered further by Purvis. The focus of PURVIS (1989) is an investigation of women's adult education in the mechanics' institutes and working men's and women's colleges, but there is also an excellent discussion of the elementary education received by working-class girls. Purvis explains that these girls were more likely to be found in dame-schools, which had a low status and – because of the pupils' domestic responsibilities, such as the care of younger siblings – a higher rate of absenteeism. It is hardly surprising that working-class women had difficulty gaining access to study.

PURVIS (1991) takes a socialist feminist perspective, in order to move away from educational histories focusing on "great men". Here Purvis examines how social class and gender differentiation affected the form and context of women's education in England from 1800 to 1914. There are four central chapters on the education of working-class girls, working-class women, middle-class girls, and middle-class women. Girls' education was not on a par with that of boys, and for the first half of the 19th century working-class girls received, in practice, an education superior to that of much of the middle class (though the middle classes considered theirs "prestigious"). Domestic ideology permeated both working- and middle-class education. The working-class girl was to be educated to be a good wife and mother; and middle-class girls were not expected to engage in paid employment – part of the hallmark of being a lady was to be supported – and therefore their education centred on accomplishments designed to enable them to attract husbands. These themes are ably dealt with by JORDAN.

Despite attempts to put education on a more academic footing (e.g. by Miss Buss at the North London Collegiate School and Miss Beale at Cheltenham Ladies College), it was not until the Taunton Commission (1866–68) that the widespread inadequacies of existing education were exposed. BENNETT describes how Emily Davies virtually compelled the Taunton Commission to include girls' schools in its inquiry and thus challenged women's ordained roles and the dominant ideology. Gradually, as a result of further campaigns by Davies and others, women were admitted to all British universities.

Gaining the right to higher education, however, did not mean that the battle for equality had been won. Because of the forces of conservatism and the establishment – the traditional masculine values of the university world coupled with a continuing lack of resources for women's education – there was no commitment to equal opportunities, and women were not fully accepted (for instance, they did not become full members of Cambridge till 1948).

DYHOUSE, a feminist scholar, demonstrates the "gendered dimension" of history. Even in the universities which claimed to make "no distinction of sex", women were segregated from men and were subjected to petty rules and moral supervision, including chaperonage. Women's accommodations were poorer, and women certainly did not have equal access to scholarship or research funds. Dyhouse questions the idea that single-sex communities were liberating for women. Higher education was opened up through women's own efforts: through women's educational associations, individual donations, and their own professional association, the British Federation of University Women, founded in 1907.

Recent work has considered the role of women teachers and their politicization. Distinctions of sex applied not only to students but also to dons and teachers. Using a mix of oral history, autobiography, biography, institutional records, and photographs, COPELMAN gives a voice to London's women teachers and shows the importance of gender and class in structuring identity. Teachers in London – like teachers elsewhere – came from the labour aristocracy and the lower middle classes. This put them in an anomalous position: the working classes saw them as agents of the state while the middle classes considered them rather rough and unladylike. Copelman sees the school as a site of conflict and demolishes the notion that women teachers formed a harmonious sisterhood. Teachers may have been part of a gendered community, but this did not necessarily mean that they cooperated with one another. Copelman also produces evidence that the idea that all women teachers resigned when they married is not true.

The question of women teachers' politicization is dealt with by ORAM. She claims that women teachers in the state sector (both primary and secondary) were involved in ongoing political activity: before 1914 they campaigned for suffrage and equal pay; in the 1920s and 1930s they campaigned for better promotion prospects and the removal of the marriage bar. Oram's study demonstrates how examination of what was a female-dominated profession – in this case, teaching – can illuminate feminism in general. Her aim is to show how these women "saw themselves as women and as teachers, how they made sense of their own lives and the different ways in which they understood and managed the contradictory tensions in their experience".

What education actually meant for girls and their teachers in the period 1850–1950 is explored in some depth in the series of articles edited by HUNT. Finally, useful collections of source material are to be found in SPENDER.

FIONA A. MONTGOMERY

Women's Legal Status

Bennett, Judith M. *et al.* (editors), *Sisters and Workers in the Middle Ages*, Chicago and London: University of Chicago Press, 1989

Erickson, Amy Louise, *Women and Property in Early Modern England*, London and New York: Routledge, 1993

Erler, Mary and Maryanne Kowaleski (editors), *Women and Power in the Middle Ages*, Athens: University of Georgia Press, 1988

Holcombe, Lee, *Wives and Property: Reform of the Married Women's Property Law in Nineteenth-Century England*, Oxford: Robertson, and Toronto: University of Toronto Press, 1983

Ingram, Martin, *Church Courts, Sex, and Marriage in England 1570–1640*, Cambridge and New York: Cambridge University Press, 1987

Kennedy Helena, *Eve Was Framed: Women and British Justice*, London: Chatto and Windus, 1992

Kermode, Jenny and Garthine Walker (editors), *Women, Crime, and the Courts in Early Modern England*, Chapel Hill: University of North Carolina Press, and London: University College London Press, 1994

Staves, Susan, *Married Woman's Separate Property in England 1660–1833*, Cambridge, Massachusetts: Harvard University Press, 1990

ERLER & KOWALESKI's book provides a sound background for women's position in Europe from AD 500 to 1500, showing how women's legal, economic, and political statuses were intertwined, and how their restricted legal status hampered their public and economic roles. Both common and customary law prohibited women from holding land on an equal basis with men. Women were also prevented from running for public office and excluded from the guilds. Using wide-ranging sources – such as English manorial court rolls and legal statutes on inheritance and wills – the studies presented by Erler and Kowaleski outline women's changing legal status within a broader setting of family, politics, and work, and provide examples of how women managed to exploit their position within the structures of male authority.

The essays edited by BENNETT *et al.* survey the development of laws within a social and economic context during the Middle Ages. Some laws were made to protect women's work against foreign competition, as seen in the study of women silk-workers in London during the 15th century. Other laws were introduced in order to prevent women from working in certain increasingly male preserves – for example, the attempts to preclude women from practicing medicine in Britain and elsewhere in Europe. Two articles in this book examine prostitution as seen in medieval canon law and the regulation of brothels in medieval London. This is a comprehensive collection of articles, which gives a broad understanding of how women's legal status affected their social and economic life.

During the early modern period common law, equity, manorial law, and ecclesiastical law operated jointly as a workable, though complex, system. A sound guide to the ecclesiastical courts can be found in INGRAM's survey of patterns of prosecutions within the church jurisdiction *c.*1570–1640. In a thorough investigation of various aspects of sexual behaviour, Ingram uses the diocesan records of Ely, Leicester, Norwich, Salisbury, and Chichester to uncover implications of prenuptial fornication, bridal pregnancy, incest, adultery, and sexual slander. His research is augmented by local archives such as wills, manorial records, tax lists, and parish registers. The broad scope of ecclesiastical justice, which meted out punishment for a wide range of sins, gradually gave way to the increasing encroachment of common law. This work provides an understanding of the importance of church courts in regulating sexual behaviour and their public control over marriage, while placing disputes within a social context and giving faces to people who were involved in the courts.

Women were not always passive victims; some were lawbreakers and some manipulated situations to suit themselves. KERMODE & WALKER (1994) is an authoritative collection of essays, covering 1550–1700 and assessing the extent of female criminal activity and the relationship between women's legal position and their role in the legal process. Ordinary women are portrayed as they stood before the criminal courts as plaintiffs, defendants, and witnesses in cases ranging from slander and scolding to theft and witchcraft. In this book, defamation cases, criminal court records, accusations of witchcraft, and trials are used to reveal the complexity of women's relationship with the law.

ERICKSON (1993) is a pioneering work on women and property, covering the period 1580–1720. Erickson explores probate documents and records of lawsuits over marriage settlements; considers the tripartite division of women's lives as maids, wives, and widows; and compares the transmission of property with regard to males and to females. As a result, she questions the premise that the inheritance laws automatically disfavoured women. In her observation of ordinary families, daughters were not necessarily at a disadvantage compared with sons but often inherited on a relatively equitable basis; and despite the laws of coverture, wives had their own property, and widows, on regaining their legal identity after the death of their husbands, made their own wills based on their own choices. On the whole, though, Erickson finds that women were more likely to receive personal property than land, and that they remained subordinate in the legal system.

STAVES offers a feminist, critical legal history of the period 1660–1833, incorporating an analysis of the ideology behind changing laws governing married women's property. She examines several aspects of women's property – dower, jointure, pin money, and a wife's separate property. During a brief period in the mid-18th century, contract law was applied to women's rights, enabling women to own and dispose of property; but the results were considered socially intolerable, and the courts quickly retreated to the old patriarchal structure.

HOLCOMBE's survey of the legislative reforms of the 19th century starts with the introduction of the Dower Act in 1833 and then traces the battle for women's rights through to the reform of the married women's property law. Holcombe admirably describes the prominent women who helped to bring about legal changes and laid the foundations for the feminist movement. The introduction gives a good outline of the different courts in operation at the beginning of the 19th century. Overall the book describes women's lot under common law and equity whereby married women during the Victorian era were deprived of power and citizens' rights, with the law regarding a woman and her chattels as the property of her husband. When a marriage broke down, the woman had no right to a divorce and no jurisdiction over her children. Sweeping measures brought dramatic changes for women, transferring the jurisdiction of the ecclesiastical courts in marital matters to newly created secular courts – the Court of Divorce and Matrimonial Causes and the Court of Probate. Caroline Sheridan Norton is described as instrumental in the call for reform that resulted in the Infant Custody Bill of 1839 and the Married Women's Property Act of 1870.

KENNEDY brings us up to date with a broad assessment of women's position under the current legal system. Although her book is a polemic describing discrimination against women, rather than an academic exercise, it is an admirable discussion of problems within the legal hierarchy. Tracing the cases of Ruth Ellis and Myra Hindley through to comments made about his wife in Jeffrey Archer's libel case, she reveals that in the 20th century, courts still invoked the double standard. She raises important questions about a legal system which can permit men being tried for rape to argue that their female victims "asked for it", and in which blacks are twice as likely as whites to be apprehended on the street. This is an admirable and eminently readable book which addresses problems of British justice in its dealings with women.

JULIE PEAKMAN

See also Class; Divorce Law Reform; Gender and Power; Inheritance, Patterns of; Marriage

Women's Movements 20th Century

Banks, Olive, *The Politics of British Feminism, 1918–1970*, Aldershot, Hampshire; and Brookfield, Vermont: Elgar, 1993
Caine, Barbara, *English Feminism, 1780–1980*, Oxford and New York: Oxford University Press, 1997
Coote, Anna and Beatrix Campbell, *Sweet Freedom: The Struggle for Women's Liberation*, Oxford and Cambridge, Massachusetts: Blackwell, 1982; 2nd edition, 1987

Harrison, Brian, *Prudent Revolutionaries: Portraits of British Feminists between the Wars*, Oxford: Clarendon Press, and New York: Oxford University Press, 1987

Lovell, Terry (editor), *British Feminist Thought: A Reader*, Oxford and Cambridge, Massachusetts: Blackwell, 1990

Lovenduski, Joni and Vicky Randall (editors), *Contemporary Feminist Politics: Women and Power in Britain*, Oxford and New York: Oxford University Press, 1993

Mirza, Heidi Safia (editor), *Black British Feminism: A Reader*, London and New York: Routledge, 1997

Neustatter, Angela, *Hyenas in Petticoats: A Look at Twenty Years of Feminism*, London: Harrap, 1989

Pugh, Martin, *Women and the Women's Movement in Britain 1914–1959*, Basingstoke: Macmillan, 1992; New York: Paragon House, 1993; revised edition, as *Women and the Women's Movement in Britain 1914–1999*, London: Macmillan, and New York: St Martin's Press, 2000

Rowbotham, Sheila, *The Past Is before Us: Feminism in Action since the 1960s*, London: Pandora, and Boston: Beacon Press, 1989

Smith, Harold (editor), *British Feminism in the Twentieth Century*, Amherst: University of Massachusetts Press, and Aldershot, Hampshire: Elgar, 1990

Spender, Dale, *There's Always Been a Women's Movement This Century*, London and Boston: Pandora Press, 1983

Dale SPENDER once asked Mary Stott (b. 1907) about her activities in the mid-20th century, when presumably no women's movement existed. Stott, a lifelong activist for women's equality, swiftly replied, "There's always been a women's movement this century!" – providing Spender with the title for a book (1983) and unwittingly opening a scholarly debate about the nature, extent, and complexity of the women's movement after suffrage had been won. Spender argues that feminist activism did not disappear between the campaign for suffrage in the 1910s and the movement for women's liberation in the 1970s. Her book profiles Stott and four other feminist activists: Hazel Hunkins Hallinan, Rebecca West, Dora Russell, and Constance Rover. These women worked within an array of organizations, weathered changing political tides, and overcame fragmented leadership but always interpreted their activism as part of a wider movement for the equality of women.

Since Spender's book appeared, a considerable amount of research has illuminated continuity and changes in issues, organizations, and personnel in the women's movement from the achievement of (partial) suffrage in 1918 to the present. Most studies are fairly specialized, concentrating on a particular decade or group, but several surveys provide a valuable starting-place.

In the most comprehensive account to date, PUGH sets the changing fortunes of organized feminism in Britain against a backdrop of wider economic, social, and political trends in women's lives. Pugh is less concerned with feminist ideology than with political strategies; his study is strongest when he is assessing the inroads women have made (or not made) into the British political establishment. Pugh argues that few of the legislative gains in the 1920s (on divorce and custody rights, for example) were due to feminists' campaigning. A lack of consensus among feminists in the 1920s and 1930s on such issues as birth control and family allowances hampered the development of a distinct feminist voice in politics and prevented the formation of a "women's party". Often the movement reflected the generally conservative attitudes of British women. Their entrance into the workforce in greater numbers after World War II was driven more by a desire for the new consumer items than by zeal for emancipation. They planned smaller families, but thanks to a proliferation of home and fashion magazines in the 1950s and 1960s, they remained under the influence of domestic ideology. In assessing the women's liberation movement (WLM) of the late 1960s and 1970s, Pugh is less impressed by radical feminism than by the new approaches of the 1980s, when the onset of a conservative political climate helped feminists to realign "along a more structured and politically oriented strategy".

In contrast to Pugh, CAINE emphasizes the shifting terms and applications of feminist ideology rather than organizational or political strategies. Caine provides a sympathetic analysis of the new conceptualizations of feminism that emerged in response to the attainment of the vote. Searching for relevance to the average woman, the "new feminists" of the 1920s and 1930s paid less attention to legal and political rights and focused increasingly on economic and cultural questions. For example, Eleanor Rathbone, a member of parliament and author of *The Disinherited Family* (1924), talked about women's specific needs, such as birth control and family endowments. Other feminists continued the classic liberal approach, focusing on legal and political equality and joining such organizations as the Six Point Group and the Open Door Council. But by the 1930s even these organizations focused less on achieving legal equality and more on such economic issues as the elimination of marriage bars and equal opportunity in the civil service. Caine traces developments in feminist theory through the 1950s and 1960s, when many activists voluntarily subordinated their goals to children's needs and interests, and into the 1970s and 1980s, when feminism became associated less with political and economic emancipation and more with personal liberation and consciousness-raising. Complementing Pugh, who provides ample statistics about trends in employment, voting, and fertility during the 1980s and 1990s, Caine's consideration of the most recent periods explores the proliferation of "feminisms" and the rise of identity politics.

In addition to these surveys, there are a number of more specialized studies. The interwar period in particular has received attention from historians, who debate the impact of women's enfranchisement on the feminist agenda. In her article in SMITH's volume, Susan Kingsley Kent argues that in the 1920s, after the cataclysm of World War I, perceptions of gender – among feminists and in society at large – took a decidedly conservative turn. Whereas pre-war feminists opposed the notion of separate spheres and traditional concepts of femininity, postwar feminists tended to espouse traditional gender roles and essentialist theories of sexual difference. In contrast, HARRISON argues that moderate feminism after 1918 was a much-needed change from the militant suffragism of the pre-war period. Harrison traces the postwar activism of 16 individuals, some formerly involved in the suffrage movement, others emerging as leaders after World War I. Contrasting the strategy of "prudent realism" (of Millicent Fawcett, for example) with "impatient idealism" (of the Pankhursts and Billington-Greig, among others), Harrison argues that the prudent approach was more effective in the interwar context. Like Kent, BANKS is also critical of the postwar "new feminism", arguing that it trapped women within the doctrine of domesticity and buttressed anti-feminist ideology through the 1950s.

While most historians agree that the movement never actually disappeared in mid-century, it did enter a period of relative quiescence. After the legislative victories in the 1920s on equal suffrage, widows' pensions, and equal guardianship, for instance, women had to wait until the 1960s for the next legislative revolution. Arising in response to labour unrest, youth protests, and international developments in feminism, the so-called second wave focused on economic power and body politics. Feminists demanded equal pay, equal access to jobs, state-supported childcare, and abortion on demand. Rallying around the slogans "the personal is political" and "sisterhood is powerful", women stormed beauty pageants, organized sit-ins, published magazines, and formed consciousness-raising groups to increase individual awareness of women's oppression.

A handful of books outline organizational and strategic developments in the women's liberation movement of the 1970s and 1980s. Because of the nature of recent events, the historiographical debates have yet to take identifiable shape; nevertheless, a methodological and ideological range is evident in the existing literature. COOTE & CAMPBELL, who are both journalists, provide an accessible yet scholarly narrative of the basic issues, strategies, and legislation. Defining the movement broadly, they include discussions of gay liberation, the anti-nuclear movement, and trade-union activism. Two political scientists, LOVENDUSKI & RANDALL, have written a definitive account of the movement in the 1980s and 1990s, analysing the intertwining of feminist activism, traditional politics, legal developments, institutional change, theory, and history. Implicitly advancing a critique of Thatcherism, these authors use issues and cases to sketch a history of a movement continually progressing, fragmenting, and reinventing itself.

Several participants in the women's liberation movement provide more personal perspectives. ROWBOTHAM, a veteran of the movement and the author of classic studies including *Hidden from History* (1973), has supplemented her experience with archival research and produced a kind of collective memoir and conceptual reflection on the issues, ideas, and assumptions of women involved in the movement. NEUSTATTER, a journalist, has brought together the stories of dozens of ordinary women, representing a broad demographic cross-section, who were active in and "reactive" towards the movement. Avoiding discussions of organization and policy, Neustatter considers the impact of liberation on women's sexuality, the experience of motherhood, perceptions of beauty, and opportunities for self-expression in literature, the visual arts, and theatre.

Finally, the development of 20th-century British feminist theory has been explored in several edited volumes. There is as yet no single survey of the whole century, but LOVELL has compiled selections from key texts of the second wave. Acknowledging internal divisions as well as international influences, Lovell identifies a distinct national feminist tradition, most visible in the critical engagement between feminism and socialist theory and practice. Lovell's volume also includes pieces that probe feminism and race, psychoanalysis, the family, sexuality, nationalism, and cultural studies. MIRZA's collection represents the range of feminist ideas expressed by British women of colour over the past 20 years. Mirza includes Hazel Carby's classic article calling into question the applicability of white feminist theory to black women's lives and exploring how black women tend to understand such concepts as the family, patriarchy, and work differently because of their historical experience with racism.

JACQUELINE deVRIES

See also Birth Control and Abortion; Divorce Law Reform; Feminism, Second-Wave; Marriage; Pankhurst entry; Patriarchy

Women's Roles and Authority

Bennett, Judith, "'History That Stands Still': Women's Work in the European Past", *Feminist Studies*, 14/2 (1988): 269–83

Breitenbach, Esther and Eleanor Gordon (editors), *Out of Bounds: Women in Scottish Society, 1800–1945*, Edinburgh: Edinburgh University Press, 1992

Clark, Alice, *Working Life of Women in the Seventeenth Century*, London: Routledge, and New York: Dutton, 1919; with introduction by Amy Louise Erickson, London and New York: Routledge, 1992

Davidoff, Leonore, and Catherine Hall, *Family Fortunes: Men and Women of the English Middle Class, 1780–1850*, London: Hutchinson, and Chicago: University of Chicago Press, 1987

Hollis, Patricia, *Ladies Elect: Women in English Local Government, 1865–1914*, Oxford: Clarendon Press, and New York: Oxford University Press, 1987

Jones, Helen, *Women in British Public Life, 1914–1950: Gender, Power, and Social Policy*, London and New York: Longman, 2000

Leyser, Henrietta, *Medieval Women: A Social History of Women in England, 450–1500*, London: Weidenfeld and Nicolson, and New York: St Martin's Press, 1995

Marshall, Rosalind K., *Virgins and Viragos: A History of Women in Scotland from 1080 to 1980*, London: Collins, and Chicago: Academy Chicago, 1983

Mendelson, Sara, and Patricia Crawford, *Women in Early Modern England, 1550–1720*, Oxford: Clarendon Press, 1998

Stenton, Doris Mary, *The English Woman in History*, London: Allen and Unwin, and New York: Macmillan, 1957; with introduction by Louise A. Tilly, New York: Schocken Books, 1977

Valenze, Deborah, *The First Industrial Woman*, Oxford and New York: Oxford University Press, 1995

Vickery, Amanda, "Golden Age to Separate Spheres? A Review of the Categories and Chronology of English Women's History", *Historical Journal*, 36/2 (1993): 383–414

Few single works attempt to survey women's history from the Middle Ages to the 20th century, and none covers the whole of Britain. A large quantity of work has been done on women in particular periods, areas, industries, and roles, making any general review only the tip of an iceberg, but the works here have been selected for the insight they give into the general themes and debates which have been considered important. The main focus is on continuity and change in women's history: some historians argue that there has been little or no fundamental change in women's roles over many centuries, and others identify particular periods as times of progress or of setbacks for women.

MARSHALL's survey of Scottish women's history is built around an assumption of gradual progress towards "freedom" for women in the late 20th century. She also argues, however, that there has been little change in women's fundamental roles as wives and mothers; even industrialization has had little real impact. This book is full of interesting details and vivid accounts of personalities, but it is based largely on evidence concerning women who are members of elites and on works of prescription and social criticism, which recent historians widely consider an unreliable basis for generalization.

STENTON's long-range survey is similarly based on evidence predominantly about upper-class women. Stenton, who pioneered the study of medieval women in England, argued that the Norman Conquest was a defeat for women – that under feudalism women lost the property rights and political influence they had enjoyed in Anglo-Saxon times. As far as later centuries are concerned, the 16th and 17th centuries are seen as a period of progress for women, industrialization is almost completely ignored, and the role of feminism in improving women's status is summarily dismissed on the grounds that its origins were tainted with socialism and its later leaders were elite women who did not themselves "suffer" from oppression. This agenda of opposition to previous feminist histories modifies the work's usefulness as a survey.

LEYSER brings the history of women in medieval England up to date, providing a balanced account of the main issues, with a selection of extracts from primary sources appended. She rejects Stenton's view of the Norman Conquest, on the grounds that Anglo-Saxon queens were insecure and only occasionally powerful, and upper-class women depended on their husbands for the maintenance and defence of their property both before and after 1066. Medieval women had much informal power in their homes and communities, though they were formally subordinate to men. The Middle Ages were nevertheless no golden age for women, whose economic position was deteriorating at the end of the period. Women are shown, however, to have played a strong part in culture and spirituality, and literary images of women to be more than a matter of crude male misogyny.

CLARK's work has been of lasting importance in popularizing the idea that women had wider and more highly regarded economic roles in the Middle Ages than in later centuries, though her extensive original research was confined to the 17th century, and she openly confessed to speculating about earlier centuries. In pre-capitalist society, she argued, the household was the basic productive unit in town and country, and women regularly participated as partners in production; but with the rise of capitalism, by the late 17th century they were increasingly excluded from crafts and confined to low-paid wage-earning such as spinning and domestic work. Clark's book is rich in examples drawn from primary sources, and Clark is concerned with a far wider social range than Marshall or Stenton;

but she is still vulnerable to the criticism that individual examples do not amount to much if they represent only a small minority of women – and this continues to be debated, as the introductions to successive editions make clear.

BENNETT, a medieval historian, represents one pole of the debate, and her review article (1988) in particular has had enormous influence. In this article she argues not only that the Middle Ages were no golden age for women, who already suffered many of the disadvantages attributed by Clark and others to the rise of capitalism, but that women's roles show a remarkable continuity over succeeding centuries up to and including the 20th. Bennett prioritizes some features of women's position, such as the gap between males' and females' wages and the allocation of housework to women, and dismisses others, such as structural changes in employment and in the social context of work itself; she concludes that continuity points to patriarchy, rather than capitalism or industrialization, as being responsible for women's subordination.

MENDELSON & CRAWFORD show the positive result of decades of debate about the history of early modern women, in a wide-ranging and admirably thorough study of many aspects of their roles, including property ownership, work, motherhood, culture, and politics. These authors find a rich variety of experience rather than an "average woman" whose fate could resolve the debate. Particularly interesting is their investigation of women's public roles, from the four queens regnant of the period to local office holders and radical petitioners, showing the "vital interest and active engagement" of women in politics despite a theoretically increasing exclusion from this arena.

DAVIDOFF & HALL focus on the formation of an ideology of a "domestic sphere" for middle-class women and their exclusion from the "public sphere" of business as well as politics. These authors regard 1780–1850 as the crucial period for these changes in women's prescribed roles, which were linked to the formation of a new middle class in English society, a class with an emerging consciousness and sense of mission – including evangelical religion, moral reform, and resistance to the threat of revolution – which they defined in gendered terms. Though the range of occupations for middle-class women narrowed, such women's contribution to their families' property and prosperity still constituted an important "hidden investment", and many women actively supported the domestic ideal and its wider dissemination among the upper and lower classes.

This view of change in women's roles and its timing has also come under attack in the name of continuity. VICKERY accuses these and other historians of contrasting their findings for a later period with a "pre-capitalist utopia" of egalitarianism and gender partnership which never existed. Doubt is cast on all "turning-points" in the marginalization of women by the fact that historians tend to find such points in whichever period they are studying. Instead, it is suggested that women's public presence was increasing in this period – through religious associations, moral campaigns, and organized charity – and that arguments for women's domesticity may have been a conservative reaction against this widening of female roles. The concept of slow but continuous evolutionary improvement underlying Stenton's and Marshall's accounts thus seems to have gained a new lease of life.

Discussion about the changing roles of working-class women in this period, which centres on the advent of modern industries (especially textiles), has been complex and voluminous, but VALENZE's book usefully bridges several aspects of female roles. Valenze's main focus is on the transformation of the image of labouring women's work between 1750 and 1850, from a necessary and valuable national resource to a morally dubious anomaly, as their traditional occupations in agriculture and domestic industry were reallocated to men or downgraded, and the domestic ideal of the dependent housewife was extended to the working class even though many women were in fact "hidden breadwinners". Meanwhile, the charitable activities of middle-class women, on which many historians have commented, led to their assuming moral and institutional authority over the poor as they followed the philanthropists' call to promote the re-education of "good wives for working men".

HOLLIS shows how the philanthropic activities of upper- and middle-class women grew into a public and openly political role as social intervention by the state expanded in the late 19th century and women ratepayers acquired local voting rights and became eligible for election as poor-law guardians, school board members, and eventually town councillors. The poor law, board schools, public health measures, and "municipal housekeeping" such as water supplies and the provision of housing enabled many women not only to participate in the public sphere but to influence policy, particularly in the transformation of poor-law institutions into public education and health care for the poor, by gaining acceptance for their "feminine" perspective. In these ways they publicly assumed authority over the poor, especially women and children – an authority which was not always welcomed. Women's influence declined in the early 20th century, however, as municipal councils and the party politics involved in them made access to local power, and effective use of it, more difficult for women.

BREITENBACH & GORDON's useful collection examines women's developing public roles in Scotland from 1800 onwards, including the role of women in promoting domestic education for working-class schoolgirls; gentlewomen "childsavers" and the street girls they encountered; and Scotswomen's participation in religion, suffrage campaigns, and the British parliament (this last being assessed as only the beginning of a "long, slow march" to equal involvement in politics). In common with many historians of women's public role in 19th-century England, the editors argue that involvement in these wider concerns subverted and often contradicted the prevailing ideology of women's confinement to the private sphere.

JONES examines the impact of women's eventual enfranchisement on policy making in Britain and comes to pessimistic conclusions. Though enfranchisement (like the experience of local power before 1900) raised high hopes that women would influence state policies, the processes of policy making worked systematically to exclude women, whose campaigns were often frustrated by the civil service bureaucracy as well as the by the overwhelming male domination of parliament. The differential impact of poverty on women and children was especially important to such campaigns, in which Jones does not find the contradiction between "rights feminism" and "welfare feminism" that other historians have suggested. Women also organized campaigns on international issues such as refugees and anti-fascism, with even less impact on government policies. The changes in family and welfare law which did take place owed little to women's campaigns and much to the pressures of party politics and wartime strategies. Paradoxes and ambiguities in women's widening public role persist, and it remains to be seen how women's roles in the second half of the 20th century will be assessed and debated.

NORAH CARLIN

See also Class; Gender and Power; Marriage; Prostitution

Women's Suffrage Movement later 19th century to 1918

Fletcher, Ian Christopher, Laura E. Nym Mayhall, and Philippa Levine (editors), *Women's Suffrage in the British Empire: Citizenship, Nation, and Race*, London and New York: Routledge, 2000

Holton, Sandra Stanley, *Feminism and Democracy: Women's Suffrage and Reform Politics in Britain, 1900–1918*, Cambridge and New York: Cambridge University Press, 1986

John, Angela V. and Claire Eustance (editors), *The Men's Share? Masculinities, Male Support, and Women's Suffrage in Britain, 1890–1920*, London and New York: Routledge, 1997

Kent, Susan Kingsley, *Sex and Suffrage in Britain, 1860–1914*, Princeton, New Jersey: Princeton University Press, 1987

Leneman, Leah, *A Guid Cause: The Women's Suffrage Movement in Scotland*, Aberdeen: Aberdeen University Press, 1991; revised edition, Edinburgh: Mercat Press, 1995

Liddington, Jill and Jill Norris, *One Hand Tied behind Us: The Rise of the Women's Suffrage Movement*, London: Virago, 1978

Murphy, Cliona, *The Women's Suffrage Movement and Irish Society*, Brighton, Sussex: Harvester Press, 1988; as *The Women's Suffrage Movement and Irish Society in the Early Twentieth Century*, Philadelphia: Temple University Press, 1989

Pugh, Martin, *The March of the Women: A Revisionist Analysis of the Campaign for Women's Suffrage, 1866–1914*, Oxford and New York: Oxford University Press, 2000

Rover, Constance, *Women's Suffrage and Party Politics in Britain, 1866–1914*, London: Routledge and Kegan Paul, and Toronto: University of Toronto Press, 1967

Strachey, Ray, *The Cause: A Short History of the Women's Movement in Great Britain*, London: Bell, 1928; Port Washington, New York: Kennikat Press, 1969

Tickner, Lisa, *The Spectacle of Women: Imagery of the Suffrage Campaign, 1907–1914*, London: Chatto and Windus, 1987; Chicago: University of Chicago Press, 1988

Vicinus, Martha, "Male Space, Women's Bodies: The Suffragette Movement" in her *Independent Women: Work and Community for Single Women, 1850–1920*, London: Virago, and Chicago: University of Chicago Press, 1985

Few topics in British women's history have received more attention than the suffrage movement. The first accounts appeared shortly after the vote was won, and by the 1970s suffrage had become a main focus of research in the emerging field of women's history. In recent years, scholars of the suffrage movement have applied ever more sophisticated interpretative frameworks to illuminate and enliven what now may seem like a familiar subject.

STRACHEY (herself a suffragette) published the first comprehensive account of the movement, which together with Sylvia Pankhurst's *The Suffragette Movement* (1931) fundamentally shaped interpretations of the suffrage campaign for the next 30 years. Their hagiographic account centred on the Pankhurst family – the mother, Emmeline; and her daughters Christabel and Sylvia – who founded the Women's Franchise League (WFL) in 1889 and the Women's Social and Political Union (WSPU) in 1903, and introduced the slogan "deeds not words". These "suffragettes" adopted a strategy of direct action (in contrast to the lobbying of the "suffragists") and, after 1905, militant protest, which by 1911 resulted in widespread arson and window-breaking, mass arrests, hunger strikes in prison, and in response the government's unpopular force-feeding.

In the early 21st century the suffragettes remain a popular focus, but recently historians have offered more analytical, less theatrical accounts and have thoroughly debated the meanings of militancy and its effectiveness as a strategy for political reform. VICINUS offers a probing analysis of the political idealism, millenarian spirituality, and military discipline that helped propel respectable women into the political fray. TICKNER's account of the movement's visual propaganda – the banners, posters, costumes, and choreographed mass demonstrations – highlights the creativity and ingenuity displayed by suffrage activists in their attempts to capture the nation's attention and exert pressure on parliament.

Although much publicized, the militant suffragettes were only a small proportion of the suffrage movement. Since the late 1960s and early 1970s, when new interest in women's past accomplishments led to more comprehensive and less self-absorbed accounts, historians have given more attention to the non-militant branch of the movement. ROVER redirected the historical gaze away from the Pankhursts and emphasized the movement's 19th-century origins. Her account reveals political continuity between the "Ladies of Langham Place", a London-based group of radical women who in 1866 gathered 1,499 signatures on the first petition for women's suffrage, and the 20th-century movement.

In her study of suffrage and reform party politics in the early 20th century, HOLTON, a prolific scholar of the movement, argues that the distinction between militants and non-militants is misleading: many militants did not stage public demonstrations whereas some non-militants did. A more fundamental difference among suffrage workers involved political strategy. By the 1910s, the WSPU had rejected its Labour Party origins and openly opposed the Liberal Party for being ambivalent toward suffrage, leaving itself in an unlikely collaboration with the Conservatives. Meanwhile, the National Union of Women's Suffrage Societies (NUWSS) pursued an alliance with the Labour Party, which, PUGH argues, ensured the movement's eventual success.

Class divisions in the movement, which figure prominently in Holton's work, were first examined by LIDDINGTON & NORRIS in their ground-breaking work on radical suffragists in Lancashire. These suffragists struggled to mobilize working-class women and educate their male counterparts in the Independent Labour Party and Labour Party on the issue of suffrage. Liddington & Norris's research illuminated the social contexts of the movement, revealing how the campaign was shaped by labour politics, patterns of women's employment in the textile factories, and links to local trade unions and the Women's Co-Operative Guild. Their work made social class a permanent category of analysis in suffrage historiography and shifted attention to local and regional variations in the movement.

Other historians have further explored the influence of regional cultures and identities on the movement. In her analysis of Scottish suffragists, LENEMAN shows that most organizing in Scotland was done through local branches of the nationally based WSPU, NUWSS, and WFL, but suffrage workers personalized their campaign by drawing upon Scottish history and folklore in an effort to equate the vote with Scottish democratic traditions. In a similar pattern, Welsh suffrage campaigners worked with national suffrage organizations but also formed their own Cymric Suffrage Union to demonstrate the compatibility of feminism and Welshness. In contrast, Irish suffragists formed their own separate organizations – representing various religious, regional, and political identities – and they cooperated infrequently with the British organizations. According to MURPHY, nationalism and the Home Rule campaign created a precarious situation in which suffragists constantly confronted an unpatriotic, irreligious image.

While a social-history framework has dominated suffrage historiography in recent decades, some of the most provocative work represents a cultural approach and explores the historical construction of gender roles and identities. In her Foucauldian reading of the discourse on suffrage, KENT makes a strong argument that the movement aimed at no less than rejecting the ideology of "separate spheres" and bringing about a transformation of women's lives. To its sheltered, Victorian middle-class participants, the vote symbolized the possibility of a free, emancipated, sexually autonomous woman. While many of the essays in JOHN & EUSTANCE (1997) reconstruct the social contexts of men's participation in the struggle for suffrage, a few analyse how the movement destabilized gender boundaries and fostered new conceptions of masculinity. Finally, the essays in FLETCHER, MAYHALL, & LEVINE (2000) represent a confluence of new analytical frameworks. Questioning Britain's place as the "storm-centre" of feminism in the British empire, the essays probe the intersection of gender politics with issues of nationalism, imperialism, and national identity.

JACQUELINE deVRIES

See also Asquith; Fawcett; Lloyd George; Pankhurst entry; Parliament: House of Commons; Parliament: Representation and Suffrage; Proportional Representation

World War I: Home Front 1914–1918

Bond, Brian (editor), *The First World War and British Military History*, Oxford: Clarendon Press, and New York: Oxford University Press, 1991

Fussell, Paul, *The Great War and Modern Memory*, New York: Oxford University Press, 1975; London: Oxford University Press, 1977

Higonnet, Margaret Randolph *et al.* (editors), *Behind the Lines: Gender and the Two World Wars,* New Haven, Connecticut, and London: Yale University Press, 1987

Liddell Hart, Basil H., *The Real War, 1914–1918*, London: Faber, and Boston: Little Brown, 1930; enlarged edition as *A History of the World War, 1914–1918*, London: Faber, 1934; Boston: Little Brown, 1935; reprinted as *History of the First World War*, London: Cassell, 1970

Marwick, Arthur, *The Deluge: British Society and the First World War,* London: Bodley Head, 1965; Boston: Little Brown, 1966

Turner, John, *British Politics and the Great War: Coalition and Conflict, 1915–1918*, New Haven, Connecticut, and London: Yale University Press, 1992

Wilson, Trevor, *The Myriad Faces of War: Britain and the Great War, 1914–1918*, Oxford and New York: Blackwell, and Cambridge: Polity Press, 1986

Winter, J.M., *The Great War and the British People*, London: Macmillan, 1985; Cambridge, Massachusetts: Harvard University Press, 1986

Early histories of the Great War concentrated on the reputations of "soldiers and statesmen", assuming a fundamental conflict over the primacy of the western front and the civilian leadership of the war effort. With official documents sealed until the 1960s, the memoirs of those with personal access to relevant documents, reputations to defend, and positions to advance (in politics most notably Beaverbrook, Churchill, and Lloyd George) dominated. Biographies sustain this often controversial element of the war's history.

As far as military issues are concerned, the foremost author during the interwar period was LIDDELL HART. His was the prevailing influence in creating the predominant and persistent characterization of attrition and trench fighting as an exercise in futility led by unimaginative "plodders" (personified by Douglas Haig). Although he simplified the war largely to matters of strategy, he set the parameters for a highly critical interpretation of British generalship. The essays edited by BOND offer an extensive and perceptive analysis of the ongoing debate over the military aspects of the war, beginning with its foundations and covering the "battle of the memoirs" during the 1920s and 1930s through the contentious wave of "bunking" and debunking of military leadership in the 1960s, and going on to more recent attempts to place military events in their full context. The section "Indirect Approaches" seeks to redress a lingering preoccupation with the western front. Peter Simkin's chapter, "Everyman at War: Recent Interpretations of the Front Line Experience", discusses the important influence of social and cultural history in the past few decades in turning attention towards "Tommy's" war.

The opening of state papers and renewed popular interest associated with the 50th anniversary of the war led to a resurgence and broadening of scholarship. Much of this literature centred on the war's social, economic, and political impact as historians discussed to what extent the conditions of war created or merely occasioned change, the degree to which the war shattered or maintained structures, and whether change that did occur could be defined as progress. Focusing on the working class, new cultural attitudes, and the collectivist approach to social improvement and state control, MARWICK laid the

groundwork by claiming that the scale, duration, and intensity of modern industrial warfare forced a social and political revolution in British history. Extreme sacrifice required extensive political and social concessions. Along with other scholars, Marwick, in his ongoing work, asserted that the war was a catalyst for reform.

In his study of the demographic impact of World War I, WINTER supports the thesis that the war forced significant change by reducing social inequality. His work is also illustrative of a trend among historians of World War I to incorporate theories and methods from the social sciences. Relying on statistical analysis, Winter asserts that wartime conditions provided the labouring classes with better nutrition and health care, higher wages, full employment, and greater social welfare benefits. Consequently, there was a substantial improvement in civilians' life expectancy, especially among women and children. Economic, physiological, and demographic advances for the working class more than compensated for massive military losses, which disproportionately affected the elite. For Winter this is the "central paradox" of the war: "wastage" actually saved lives. The end result: progress.

While some historians specializing in various aspects of the war have found revolutions and watersheds, others have doubted that the war produced fundamental change, let alone progress. For example, feminist scholars have disputed Marwick's optimistic appraisal of the war as having liberated women; according to the feminists' findings, women rarely received equal pay, were repeatedly reminded that their industrial advances were temporary, and remained secondary in status as labourers and citizens. Furthermore, war reinforced patriarchal structures by identifying women primarily as noncombatants and mothers. The influential theoretical approach to war and gender in HIGONNET *et al.* (1987) has shifted this debate away from a binary concept (watershed or no watershed) towards a "discourse of war" which reveals the intertwined relationship of the genders. Many have taken up the challenge of Higonnet *et al.* to study how the war altered or reinforced social constructions. Much of this work is sceptical about the supposed transformative effect of war; the writers often argue that the changes which did occur did not represent a real shift in power or resources.

Cultural history has been particularly productive and influential in expanding the scope of the historiography of World War I. In a widely praised seminal study, FUSSELL argued that in terms of cultural expression the war created a dramatic rupture: between 1914 and 1918 Britain rejected traditional forms, and "modernity" emerged. Relying on the writings of educated soldiers who served on the western front, Fussell described the creation of a new ironic mode characterized by pessimism and destruction which he asserts became the predominant form. Although primarily literary in approach, Fussell's work inspired an enormous historical response, and a rich discussion of how culture is defined, how war is remembered, and what meaning is attached to remembrance.

Volumes have been written on the extent to which the war transformed politics and political attitudes – particularly with regard to volunteerism and collectivism – and whether changes that did occur can be traced to the pre-war era or not. Debate has centred on a number of related issues including the decline of liberalism (both as an ideology and as a political expression), changes in class attitudes and structures, and interventionist policies concerning control of the economy (especially in regard to the allocation of manpower). TURNER offers a solid synthesis of high politics, party structure, and government policy which allows students to grasp the historiographic landscape of this immense topic. His work is also representative of scholars who pragmatically urge that interpretation of the war be directed away from embattled paradigms: Turner suggests that rather than seeing wartime politics as a struggle between individuals or political philosophies, historians focus on the dispute over strategy between those hoping to minimize the war's social and economic consequences and those who sought a rapid victory.

In response to the proliferation and increasing specialization of scholarship, a counter-trend towards "total history" that explores interactions between the home front and the battle front has emerged. WILSON (1986) is the most noted of several ambitious attempts to create a one-volume history of Britain between 1914 and 1918 that integrates social, cultural, political, and military history in a detailed narrative. Wilson holds that the war created its own momentum owing to industrial developments and military technology. Thus politicians and generals, as well as soldiers and civilians, were victims rather than perpetrators of conflict. This diminishment of human agency allows for both a sympathetic portrayal of wartime leaders and an empathic view of the common Briton. While many scholars have been dubious about the war's purpose and conduct, Wilson argues that the war made sense for the British government and people: the challenge from Germany could not be disregarded, nor did most people want it to be.

ANNE AIRTH-KINDREE KELSCH

World War I: Naval and Air Operations 1914–1918

Cole, Christopher (editor), *Royal Air Force, 1918*, London: Kimber, 1968

Cooper, Malcolm, *The Birth of Independent Air Power: British Air Policy in the First World War*, London and Boston: Allen and Unwin, 1986

Corbett, Julian S. and Henry Newbolt, *Naval Operations*, vols 1–5 of *History of the Great War Based on Official Documents*, London and New York: Longmans Green, 1920–31

Frothingham, Thomas G., *The Naval History of the World War*, 3 vols, Cambridge, Massachusetts: Harvard University Press, 1924–26

Halpern, Paul G., *A Naval History of World War I*, Annapolis, Maryland: Naval Institute Press, and London: UCL Press, 1994

Marder, Arthur J., *From the Dreadnought to Scapa Flow: The Royal Navy in the Fisher Era, 1904–1919*, vols 2–5, London and New York: Oxford University Press, 1965–70

Powers, Barry D., *Strategy without Slide-Rule: British Air Strategy, 1914–1939*, London: Croom Helm, 1976

Raleigh, Walter Alexander and H.A. Jones, *The War in the Air, Being the Story of the Part Played in the Great War by the Royal Air Force*, 7 vols, Oxford: Clarendon Press, 1922–37

The historiography of naval and air operations in World War I is so voluminous that the reader is advised to lay a foundation by consulting the official war histories before proceeding to more critically analytical works addressing particular aspects of the war. Three such histories provide a chronological narrative that can serve as a baseline for understanding: CORBETT & NEWBOLT (1930–31), FROTHINGHAM (1924–26), and RALEIGH & JONES (1922–37). All are multivolume works with extensive indexes and appropriate maps and diagrams and can be used as encyclopedic reference sources for specific operational aspects and events. While they address associated issues of economics, domestic politics, societal concerns, and so forth only minimally – as is typical of more current works – it must be remembered that the authors' purpose was to chronicle operational events, a necessary first step for any subsequent analytical treatment. Some readers may find the official histories stylistically antiquated; however, the more formal style popular among historians of the 1920s and 1930s does not diminish the value of the works for an understanding of operational events.

Corbett & Newbolt provide the most comprehensive chronological treatment available of British naval operations. In 1916, in a speech to parliament, the prime minister stated that the public would demand an "authentic account" of the war; as a result, work on an official history began immediately following the armistice. Sir Julian Corbett, the premier British naval historian of the day, brought the endeavor validity and prestige. Although some documents of the Allied and Central powers were used, the authors primarily consulted British naval, military, and political official documents. Corbett strove to produce, in narrative format, a reference "free from technicalities" that would offer the public "an intelligible view not only of the operations themselves but of their mutual connection and meaning, the policy which dictated them, [and] their relation to military and diplomatic action". After Corbett's untimely death in 1922, Newbolt completed the project, using the same methodology while adding more peripheral operations outside the North Sea and North Atlantic.

Frothingham provides a less detailed but no less useful reference source for British naval operations from a distinctly American viewpoint. His sources are primarily documents provided by the Historical Section of the United States Navy; however, considerable information was also obtained from British official sources. Readers might find Frothingham's work less cumbersome in terms of details while still maintaining historical integrity and offering sufficient depth for most purposes. Additionally, some footnotes referring to official documents are provided, whereas Corbett & Newbolt's work has no notes.

Raleigh & Jones wrote the official history of World War I British air operations using sources from the historical section of the Air Ministry; their work is analogous to the official naval history. Since they were writing for the general public, Raleigh & Jones avoided distinctly military jargon. Additionally, to ensure accuracy, they consulted actual witnesses to events. Like Corbett, Raleigh died before his project was completed; Jones finished the task, applying the same methodology of superimposing air operations on a "framework of naval and military operations".

From the baseline established by the official naval histories written during the interwar years, the reader should consult the two best treatments of British naval operations currently available: MARDER (1965–70) and HALPERN (1994). Marder analyses and summarizes using a "considerable body of fresh material" including German documents, diaries, personal memoirs, and biographies of primary participants. He addresses only the more important engagements and specific themes; thus some peripheral subjects, such as the submarine war in the Baltic and the activities of the Royal Naval Air Service, are not covered. Marder is far more concerned than Corbett & Newbolt with the formulation of naval policy; and since he was writing years after the principals had died, he is less concerned with criticizing personalities or wartime actions and decisions.

Most naval histories of World War I take up only the actions of the Royal Navy in the North Sea and British home waters (along with mentions of significant peripheral events such as Coronel and the Falklands). Halpern broadens the historiographical focus by addressing secondary campaigns conducted by other Allied and Central powers. In addition to major operations of the Royal Navy, Halpern analyses naval events in regions including the Mediterranean, Mesopotamia, north Russia, the Adriatic, the Danube, and the east coast of North America.

Building upon the narrative foundation established in the interwar years, COOPER (1986) and POWERS (1976) analyse Britain's air policy and strategy in the development of an independent air force during and after the war, incorporating German documents, memoirs, and personal papers not available to Raleigh & Jones. Cooper addresses air power as a valuable tactical adjunct to ground operations on the western front, as well as the conflict between personalities and policy that hampered air commanders. He also addresses the political imperatives driving the creation of an independent air service.

Powers explores two aspects of British air history that are typically ignored: the interaction of factors including popular opinion, the media, and politics in conjunction with purely military concerns on the development of air policy; and the "extremely close interconnections between defensive concerns and offensive planning". In so doing, he examines the roots of British air power and the evolution of air strategy during World War I and the interwar years based on public, political, and military perceptions of air warfare, and the impact of technological advances.

Often, the best sense of the nature of military operations is gained from the dairies and memoirs of participants. COLE (1968) provides an edited version of the Royal Air Force (RAF) communiqués written by the headquarters staff as derived from pilots' combat reports and additional sources. The communiqués were a "hastily-produced digest, primarily for internal consumption"; nonetheless, they provide a testament to the harrowing nature of air combat from the participants' viewpoint.

STANLEY D.M. CARPENTER

See also Navy: Modern

World War I: Other Fronts 1914–1918

Aldington, Richard, *Lawrence of Arabia: A Biographical Enquiry*, London: Collins, and Chicago: Regnery, 1955
Bean, C.E.W., *The Official History of Australia in the War of 1914–1918*, vols 1–2: *The Story of Anzac*, Sydney: Angus and Robertson, 1921–24; St Lucia and New York: University of Queensland Press, 1981

Bond, Brian (editor), *The First World War and British Military History*, Oxford: Clarendon Press, and New York: Oxford University Press, 1991
Churchill, Winston S., *The World Crisis*, 6 vols, London: Thornton Butterworth, 1923–31; New York: Scribner, 1923–37; revised and abridged edition, London: Butterworth, 1931
Garsia, Clive, *A Key to Victory: A Study in War Planning*, London: Eyre and Spottiswoode, 1940
Graves, Robert, *Lawrence and the Arabs*, London: Jonathan Cape, 1927; as *Lawrence and the Arabian Adventure*, New York: Doubleday Doran, 1928
Hughes, Matthew, *Allenby and British Strategy in the Middle East, 1917–1919*, London and Portland, Oregon: Frank Cass, 1999
James, Robert Rhodes, *Gallipoli*, London: Batsford, and New York: Macmillan, 1965
Lawrence, T.E., *Seven Pillars of Wisdom: A Triumph*, London: Jonathan Cape, and New York: Doubleday Doran, 1935 (privately published, 1922)
Liddell Hart, Basil, *T.E. Lawrence in Arabia and After*, London: Jonathan Cape, 1934; as *Colonel Lawrence: The Man behind the Legend*, New York: Dodd Mead, 1934; revised edition, 1935
Marder, Arthur J., *From the Dreadnought to Scapa Flow: The Royal Navy in the Fisher Era, 1904–1919*, 5 vols, London and New York: Oxford University Press, 1961–70; revised and enlarged edition, 1978
North, John, *Gallipoli: The Fading Vision*, London: Faber, 1936
Till, Geoffrey, "Brothers in Arms: The British Army and Navy at the Dardanelles" in *Facing Armageddon: The First World War Experienced*, edited by Hugh Cecil and Peter H. Liddle, London: Cooper, 1996
Wallin, Jeffrey D., *By Ships Alone: Churchill and the Dardanelles*, Durham, North Carolina: Carolina Academic Press, 1981
Wavell, A.P., *Allenby: Soldier and Statesman*, London: Harrap, 1946; London and New York: White Lion, 1974
Wilson, Jeremy, *Lawrence of Arabia: The Authorised Biography*, London: Heinemann, 1989; New York: Atheneum, 1990
Winter, Denis, *25 April 1915: The Inevitable Tragedy*, St Lucia: University of Queensland Press, 1994

One of the persistent debates over strategy during World War I concerned the primacy of the western front, which stretched from the English Channel across France to Switzerland. Those who believed that Germany was the key to the Central Powers and that victory could be won only by crushing Germany in Europe were called "Westerners". The most important members of this group were generals, including both of the commanders of the British Expeditionary Force (British troops in France), Field Marshal Sir John French and later Field Marshal Sir Douglas Haig and Field Marshal Sir William Robertson, for most of the war chief of the Imperial General Staff. As the fighting in France developed into a stalemate and the casualty lists began to grow, questions about the "Western" strategy also began to grow. Since there was no flank to turn in Europe, perhaps the war could be taken to the enemy in another theatre. Those who took this view were called "Easterners". Pre-eminent among this group was Winston Churchill, whose political star was significantly dimmed when the Dardanelles campaign failed. David Lloyd George, the prime minister after 1916, also favoured the "Eastern" view, but he was much too wily to be trapped in any unescapable advocacy. He argued for change and conceded to the generals when he was unable to control them.

Although there was a campaign in Africa, for the British the "other fronts" were on the Gallipoli peninsula as part of a campaign to take the Dardanelles and Constantinople and force Turkey out of the war; and in the Middle East, where the strategic goals were quite varied. Protection of the Suez Canal was an obvious necessity. Because the Middle East was, at least technically, still part of the Ottoman empire, it offered a means of reducing Turkish power and weakening one of the Central Powers. Finally, with biblical themes still common and powerful, the possibility of victories in the Middle East offered an emotional counter to the failure to win practical victories in France. In the end, although the canal was protected and there were victories that provided useful propaganda, the other fronts made little difference to the outcome of the war. The people involved, two of whom – Churchill and T.E. Lawrence – ultimately became larger-than-life British national heroes, drew much more historical attention than the actual results merited.

The other fronts make up a full section in BOND (1991), with essays by Edward Spiers, Jonathan Newell, and Brian Holden Reid. These trace the historical arguments over Gallipoli, the Middle East campaign and General Edmund Allenby, and the Arab revolt inspired by T.E. Lawrence. The quality of the essays and the large number of works on the topics make this an essential reference for studying any of them.

The Dardanelles campaign was intended to take the straits and force Turkey from the war (as noted above), and to open a supply route to Russia. This campaign was precipitated by a request from St Petersburg for help at the beginning of 1915. It was advocated by Winston Churchill, then first lord of the Admiralty. When the secretary for war, Lord Kitchener, said no troops were available, Churchill argued that the navy could win through on its own. Initial bombardments seemed promising but may have warned the Turks to prepare, and the navy ultimately failed. Then troops were sent, both to help the Russians and to prevent the appearance of a loss to a Muslim foe and potential ill consequences in the empire. The initial invasion, in April 1915, bogged down, and a subsequent amphibious landing at Suvla Bay behind Turkish lines was also contained.

Early accounts of the Dardanelles campaign tended to take the Westerners' view and condemn the strategy and its tactical implementation. In the first volumes of the Australian official history, BEAN damned the British for attempting the campaign with insufficient means and emphasized the heroism of the Australian and New Zealand (Anzac) troops, which he contrasted with the less effective English. Although this "Anzac myth" has often been criticized, it was recently renewed by WINTER. The publication of CHURCHILL's wonderfully written account changed the tenor of the discussion. As criticism of the Western strategy became dominant, blame for the failure at the Dardanelles was attributed, for example by NORTH and MARDER, to the military's handling of the campaign and to the politicians who had failed to provide adequate men and *matériel*. New critics emerged; and in the work of JAMES Churchill once again emerges as the villain, using his eloquence to manipulate his colleagues and England's allies into an unrealistic plan. Winter carried the critique to the extreme of suggesting that nothing about the campaign – from plan to tactics to support to personnel – was even reasonable. Critics did not hold the field unchallenged, however. WALLIN has argued that the naval attack had the potential for success; and TILL (expressing a theme common among revisionists of the war in France), believes that the campaign was a success in that it was part of the learning process necessary for the military to comprehend modern war.

The derring-do of Lawrence of Arabia on the Middle Eastern front has captured the popular imagination, but in this arena the capture of Jerusalem in December 1917 and the Megiddo campaign of 1918 were more important. The man associated with both was General Edmund "The Bull" Allenby, who has received exaggerated praise in much of the literature since the war. The best-known of his supporters is WAVELL, who was something of a protégé of Allenby's. In such accounts, Allenby is credited with infusing energy into a flagging campaign and designing tactics based on a brilliant understanding of the use of cavalry. He did get the job done, and the taking of Jerusalem was quite a lift in the month after the less than successful effort at the third battle of Ypres in 1917. There have been some critics, however. GARSIA argues that Allenby had a chance to crush the Turks at the third battle of Gaza and end the Middle Eastern campaign, possibly with a total surrender by the Turks, in 1917. Recently, HUGHES has suggested that the entire campaign was poorly organized and often mishandled and that it had little effect on the outcome of the war.

LAWRENCE began the romanticization of the Arab revolt with his book *The Seven Pillars of Wisdom*, which remains the best-known account. GRAVES and LIDDELL HART then set the tone for historiography until the 1950s. In their version, an otherworldly, almost saintly, Lawrence – through personal leadership, suffering, and bravery – persuades and inspires the sometimes childlike Arab tribes to mount a revolt against the Turks, cutting the Turkish lines of communication and ultimately achieving strategically significant success. This was an interpretation that pleased the critics of the Westerners, for it suggested that victory might have been achieved outside France. In the mid-1950s, ALDINGTON launched a savage attack on Lawrence, suggesting that he had not only exaggerated the importance of the campaign but had also misrepresented his own activities. In fact, Aldington actually called Lawrence a "liar". Although Aldington was himself severely criticized by reviewers, his work did crack the image of romantic heroism that had been built around Lawrence. Some thirty years later, WILSON, in the authorized biography, managed to produce a balanced account, exposing some of the myths that had developed but giving Lawrence due credit for his efforts and accomplishments.

FRED R. VAN HARTESVELDT

See also Lawrence, T.E.

World War I: Versailles and Other Treaties 1919–1923

Bennett, G.H., *British Foreign Policy during the Curzon Period, 1919–1924*, Basingstoke: Macmillan–King's College, and New York: St Martin's Press, 1995

Busch, Briton Cooper, *Britain, India, and the Arabs, 1914–1921*, Berkeley: University of California Press, 1971

Busch, Briton Cooper, *Mudros to Lausanne: Britain's Frontier in West Asia, 1918–1923*, Albany: State University of New York Press, 1976

Calder, Kenneth J., *Britain and the Origins of the New Europe 1914–1918*, Cambridge and New York: Cambridge University Press, 1976

Dockrill, Michael L. and J. Douglas Goold, *Peace without Promise: Britain and the Peace Conferences, 1919–1923*, London: Batsford, and Hamden, Connecticut: Archon Books, 1981

Egerton, George W.W., *Great Britain and the Creation of the League of Nations: Strategy, Politics, and International Organization, 1914–1919*, Chapel Hill: University of North Carolina Press, 1978; London: Scolar Press, 1979

Fromkin, David, *A Peace to End All Peace: Creating the Modern Middle East 1914–1922*, London: André Deutsch, and New York: Holt, 1989

Goldstein, Erik, *Winning the Peace: British Diplomatic Strategy, Peace Planning, and the Paris Peace Conference, 1916–1920*, Oxford: Clarendon Press, and New York: Oxford University Press, 1991

Henig, Ruth, *Versailles and After, 1919–1933*, London and New York: Methuen, 1984; 2nd edition, London and New York: Routledge, 1995

Kedourie, Elie, *England and the Middle East: The Destruction of the Ottoman Empire, 1914–1921*, London: Bowes and Bowes, 1956; reprinted, London: Mansell, and Boulder, Colorado: Westview Press, 1987

Keynes, John Maynard, *The Economic Consequences of the Peace*, London: Macmillan, 1919; New York: Harcourt, Brace and Howe, 1920

Lentin, A., *Lloyd George, Woodrow Wilson, and the Guilt of Germany: An Essay in the Pre-History of Appeasement*, Leicester: Leicester University Press, and Baton Rouge: Louisiana State University Press, 1984; as *Guilt at Versailles: Lloyd George and the Pre-History of Appeasement*, London: Methuen, 1985

Orde, Anne, *British Policy and European Reconstruction after the First World War*, Cambridge and New York: Cambridge University Press, 1990

Sharp, Alan, *Versailles Settlement: Peacemaking in Paris, 1919*, New York: St Martin's Press, 1991

Silverman, Dan P., *Reconstructing Europe after the Great War*, Cambridge, Massachusetts: Harvard University Press, 1982

Temperley, H.W.V. (editor), *A History of the Peace Conference of Paris*, 6 vols, London: Frowde/Hodder and Stoughton, 1920–24

The peace settlement at the end of World War I has generated a steady stream of scholarly publications since 1919. The international literature on this important and controversial subject is vast; and even if the reader limits enquiries to Britain's role in framing the peace settlement, there is still a large volume of material which needs to be read. KEYNES's attack (1919) appeared within a year of the Paris Peace Conference, and within five years TEMPERLEY had concluded a six-volume study of the conference.

The most useful all-round modern text on the subject remains the one by DOCKRILL & GOOLD. Although these authors concentrate on the role of Britain, they survey all the postwar peace treaties from Versailles to the treaties dealing with eastern Europe, concluding with the Treaty of Lausanne (1923) which constituted the peace settlement with Turkey. The chapters are clear, concise, and wide-ranging, incorporating considerable research on original documents as well as on the voluminous secondary sources which have appeared since 1919. Of particular importance to an understanding of the postwar settlement are the six well-drawn maps which appear at the start of the book. Dockrill & Goold's analysis conforms to the title of their book – *Peace without Promise* – which expresses the consensus about the postwar settlement. However, they show how the difficulties facing the peacemakers made it difficult to arrive at anything else. They also show how the pressures facing the statesmen continually changed, making the task of drawing up a viable settlement ever more complex.

Alongside Dockrill & Goold's study, the books by BENNETT and ORDE might be read. Both Bennett and Orde show the changing pressures on British statesmen which meant that there was a lack of will and energy to enforce and adapt the peace treaties after they had been signed. Bennett argues that the failure to evolve the peace settlement at a fast enough rate was just as significant a cause of its ultimate failure as the unsatisfactory nature of what was originally drawn up.

Of the more narrowly focused monographs, GOLDSTEIN's book is particularly useful, since it gives much of the background of British planning for the Paris conference and thoroughly revises and updates the work of earlier scholars. SHARP's study (published in the same year as Goldstein's) draws upon recent scholarship and constitutes the best single-volume study of the peace conference from an international, as opposed to a purely British, perspective. Sharp, like Dockrill & Goold, considers that the task of forging a long-lasting European peace was simply beyond the peacemakers in 1919. He does a particularly good job of showing how seriously the interests and aspirations of the victorious powers conflicted in Paris.

A considerable number of short texts on the treaty of Versailles are aimed at the "A" level and first-year undergraduate markets. About the best are those by LENTIN and HENIG. Both authors set Versailles against the background of the origins of World War II. Henig in particular views the treaty of Versailles as a source of the antagonisms which dogged western Europe after 1919. She sees the difficulty of revising the treaty – rather than the inevitably flawed nature of the version that was signed – as the Achilles heel of the peace settlement. According to Lentin, the British government was so dissatisfied with the treaty that it set out on a path which culminated in Neville Chamberlain's policy of appeasement; thus Versailles and Munich were intrinsically linked.

Since the publication of Keynes's study in 1919, the financial aspects of the treaty of Versailles have long been regarded as a key feature of the peace settlement. SILVERMAN provides a modern up-to-date analysis of the financial aspects of international relations after World War I. He shows how the war produced a financial crisis all across Europe and resulted in grave doubts about contemporary financial and monetary theories. He also shows the complex links between war debts and reparations created by the peace treaties that were to dog international relations until the 1930s.

Beyond the treaty of Versailles there has been comparatively little written in English on the eastern European settlement. The work by CALDER, which is a product of sound research and is well written, helps to fill this gap. However, the eastern European settlement remains under-researched in comparison with the plethora of books which have appeared on the treaty of Versailles.

The Middle Eastern settlement has been a subject of considerable work by scholars from a variety of backgrounds. It remains politically contentious, and this has tended to show through in some of the scholarship. Of the earlier texts, KEDOURIE's is particularly interesting because the author is acutely aware of the sensitive nature of his subject. BUSCH's studies (1971 and 1976) reflect the author's mastery of archives, his attention to the details of policy, and his painstaking approach to understanding how British policy regarding a Middle Eastern settlement evolved; these books are required reading on the settlement in Asia Minor. However, the most modern full monograph on the Middle Eastern settlement is FROMKIN (1989), a product of massive research on the available primary and secondary sources; Fromkin's chapters update some of the conclusions drawn by Busch.

One aspect of the postwar settlement that has become a separate area of research is the formation and history of the League of Nations. Some historians believe that the failure of this body allowed World War II to break out in 1939. In the conventional narrative, the League of Nations was doomed because of the mistakes that were made in setting it up. One mistake was to link the League to the treaty of Versailles, so that revisionist statesmen in Germany could not help rejecting one with the other. A further problem concerned the fact that many people saw the ostensible purpose of the League as overseeing the workings of the peace treaties. The failure of the League to contribute to their revision was thus another severe handicap. The problems encountered in setting up the League, and the mistakes that contributed to the eventual failure of the peace settlement, are explored by EGERTON. Although other works deal with the establishment of the League, Egerton's book is particularly useful because it concentrates on the development of the idea of having an international organization to the point where the idea became a reality.

In addition to the very large number of books on this subject, there is a still larger number of journal articles. Whereas the books produced so far tend to concentrate on the broad issues of peacemaking, the academic journals contain a wealth of analysis and detail on many of the rather narrower aspects of the postwar treaties.

The peace treaties signed after World War I remain a subject of continuing importance and interest. While most of the postwar treaties are defunct, the Treaty of Lausanne remains, with some revision, the international foundation-stone of modern Turkey. The repercussions of the postwar settlement were massive, and World War I consequently helped generate a second global conflict. Thus the flow of literature on this subject shows no signs of abating.

G.H. BENNETT

See also Mandated Territories

World War I: Western Front 1914–1918

Griffith, Paddy, *Battle Tactics of the Western Front: The British Army's Art of Attack, 1916–1918*, New Haven, Connecticut, and London: Yale University Press, 1994

Johnson, Hubert C., *Breakthrough! Tactics, Technology, and the Search for Victory on the Western Front in World War I*, Novato, California: Presidio Press, 1994

Johnson, J.H., *Stalemate! The Great Trench Warfare Battles of 1915–1917*, London: Arms and Armour Press, 1995

Keegan, John, *The First World War*, London: Hutchinson, 1998; New York: Knopf, 1999

Liddell Hart, Basil H., *The Real War, 1914–1918*, London: Faber, and Boston: Little Brown, 1930; enlarged edition, as *A History of the World War 1914–1918*, London: Faber, 1935; Boston: Little Brown, 1936; reprinted as *History of the First World War*, London: Cassell, 1970

Liddle, Peter H., *The 1916 Battle of the Somme: A Reappraisal*, London: Leo Cooper, 1992

Middlebrook, Martin, *The First Day on the Somme, 1 July 1916*, London: Allen Lane, 1971; New York: Norton, 1972

Prior, Robin and Trevor Wilson, *Command on the Western Front: The Military Career of Sir Henry Rawlinson, 1914–18*, Oxford and Cambridge, Massachusetts: Blackwell, 1992

Terraine, John, *Douglas Haig: The Educated Soldier*, London: Hutchinson, 1963; as *Ordeal of Victory*, Philadelphia: J.B. Lippincott, 1963

Although there are many disputes about the western front, the most substantial one concerns generalship and the enormous numbers of casualties suffered by the armies fighting there. The traditional school of thought represented and in many ways dominated by LIDDELL HART is that the generals, particularly Sir Douglas Haig, were ignorant, old-fashioned, and unable to see the need for change. The traditional view was that battles were won by attacking. Unfortunately, the typical tactical method used on the western front was a frontal assault. For this school of thought, the results of such generalship were summed up by 1 July 1916, the first day of the battle of the Somme, when the British suffered nearly 60,000 casualties. Liddell Hart wrote extensively on this theme and made real efforts to stop attempts at revisionism. A more recent exponent of Liddell Hart's school is MIDDLEBROOK, who concentrates on the first day of the Somme – a focus that critics have argued is misleading.

TERRAINE has argued over the course of his career, and in many books, that Liddell Hart is wrong. Terraine's view is that World War I was a unique situation. No general could reasonably have been expected to know how to handle a situation dominated by modern defensive weaponry. A process of learning had to occur before soldiers understood what to do. The horrific bloodshed, however regrettable, was an inevitable result of the struggle to learn. LIDDLE has extended this argument by pointing out, for instance, that the Somme was not over in a day and that if the casualties suffered by the British over the entire six months of the offensive are averaged the rate is not unusual for modern war. The revisionists expanded the argument in the latter part of the 20th century.

GRIFFITH argues that the British army was actually at the forefront of tactical innovation during World War I. Frequently, the Germans have been credited with leading the way to tactical change that made possible the breaking of the stalemate on the western front. Griffith, although he faults British generalship and technology, especially in the early years of the conflict, argues that the small-unit tactics of the British Expeditionary Force did improve. By 1918 the British army had the skills and adequate tools to increase mobility and turn the tables on the Germans. Despite the high price, he regards the evolution of military techniques as a British triumph.

PRIOR & WILSON think it is necessary to focus on the tactical commander; they highlight the command of Sir Henry Rawlinson. These authors have brought logistics and the technical aspects of artillery into the debate. The importance of artillery bombardment is undisputed, but Prior & Wilson have shown that the percentage of shells which hit a particular target was much lower than had been thought. They look at the evolution of artillery doctrine and suggest that Rawlinson and others were learning how to make the most effective use of their guns. This study offers a different perspective on the necessity of learning that resulted in victory for the Allies.

J.H. JOHNSON examines the British attacks in the middle of the war and attempts to analyse the factors that made them unsuccessful. Although he is also critical of the generalship involved, his focus is more on the training and preparation of the troops. He argues that the British failed to consider the potential for changes in the enemy's tactics as they sought to draw lessons from their experiences. His is yet another perspective on the effort to learn that resulted in ultimate victory.

Hubert C. JOHNSON, although he picks up a number of the themes of other historians, focuses his analysis more on technology. He sees the initial stalemate as resulting from the dominance of defensive weapons, and he believes that the key to the return of mobility in 1918 was the evolution of war machines – especially tanks, artillery, and aeroplanes – which allowed the forces on the western front to break the siege-style struggle that had frustrated them for four years. Thus to him the problem was less a matter of learning than of technical innovation.

KEEGAN, in one of the best survey histories of World War I, provides a moderate overview incorporating the various positions that have been argued. Although in the past he has been more inclined to the views of Liddell Hart's school, he now gives much more credit to the revisionist arguments, but ultimately he asserts that real command was simply impossible on the western front. Communication technology was not adequate to inform the generals behind the lines of the shifting tactical situation. Wireless contact was not available, and telephone lines were quickly cut. Runners were slow and were often killed before reaching their destinations. The result was that artillery fire could not be directed after an attack began, and

reinforcements could not be directed as needed. Commanders, even at the battalion level, were left in utter ignorance of what their attacking forces were doing. In the end, attacks tended to collapse into confusion and become targets for enemy counter-attacks, which if pressed very far in turn bogged down. Victory, as the generals had concluded by 1915, came down to a matter of wearing out the enemy.

FRED R. van HARTESVELDT

World War I: Women's Roles 1914–1918

Braybon, Gail, *Women Workers in the First World War: The British Experience*, London: Croom Helm, and Totowa, New Jersey: Barnes and Noble, 1981; reprinted, London and New York: Routledge, 1989
Braybon, Gail and Penny Summerfield, *Out of the Cage: Women's Experiences in Two World Wars*, London and New York: Pandora Press, 1987
Kent, Susan Kingsley, *Making Peace: The Reconstruction of Gender in Interwar Britain*, Princeton, New Jersey: Princeton University Press, 1993
Marwick, Arthur, *Women at War 1914–1918*, London: Croom Helm, 1977; 1st edition, Fontana
Mitchell, David, *Monstrous Regiment: The Story of the Women of the First World War*, New York: Macmillan, 1965; as *Women on the Warpath: The Story of the Women of the First World War*, London: Jonathan Cape, 1966
Wiltsher, Anne, *Most Dangerous Women: Feminist Peace Campaigners of the Great War*, London and Boston: Pandora Press, 1985
Woollacott, Angela, *On Her Their Lives Depend: Munitions Workers in the Great War*, Berkeley: University of California Press, 1994

One of the main debates in the recent historiography of World War I concerns the impact of the conflict on women's lives and social status and the extent, nature, and stability of any transformation. MITCHELL's study reflects the established view, during the 1960s, that the war had liberated and emancipated women. He argued that through their novel roles and important achievements in the munitions factories, military hospitals, auxiliary corps, and farming corps, British women demonstrated that their abilities were equal to men's and thus earned their enfranchisement. Although his argument was all-embracing, Mitchell focused exclusively on the leaders of this "social revolution". On the basis of the diaries and memoirs of a few dozen suffrage activists, professional and leisured women, he described how their charitable and franchise work before the war prepared them for their wartime roles in organizing medical units, relief efforts, and women's military, police, and factory work. This biographical approach from a top-down perspective results in an uncritical celebration of exceptional individuals, but Mitchell does provide a wealth of information about their activities.

MARWICK also regarded World War I as a watershed in the history of women's emancipation. However, he argued that women's inferior status derived from social conventions and prejudices as much as from legal discrimination, and he undertook a comprehensive analysis of women's war experience to examine how all these disadvantages diminished. Thus his study surveys conditions in a wide range of war occupations as well as developments which influenced women's domestic life, sexual behaviour, and recreation. Marwick contended that movement into men's jobs was the single most important factor in advancing women's position. Besides obtaining the vote for women by reducing social prejudices about their abilities, it provided women with higher wages and a new consciousness, enabling them to enjoy greater social freedom and more equal sexual relations. Marwick's book includes many contemporary photographs and a great deal of documentary evidence; it gives a good introduction to the various sources on the subject but leaves the reader with an impressionistic view of women's war experience.

During the 1980s, feminist scholarship challenged the causal relationship between World War I and women's emancipation, arguing that changes in women's conditions were both limited and temporary. BRAYBON (1981), a study of the impact of the conflict on working-class women, is an example of this revisionist school. It is written from a socialist-feminist standpoint: working women's oppression is attributed to capitalism and patriarchy. Braybon focuses on the attitudes of male employers, workers, unions, and government officials' toward women's proper role in society and examines the effects of these views on female workers' job prospects. Braybon contends that despite the wartime labour shortage, there was no change in the dominant belief that women should not work outside the home, because their first duty was to their family. As a result, most female workers were confined to monotonous and unskilled jobs for lower wages than men received and were dismissed from their positions at the earliest opportunity. Moreover, in the postwar period women's perceived wartime gains generated a powerful antifeminist backlash which made female workers' industrial position worse than it had been before the war. Thus, instead of improving women's job opportunities, the war actually intensified the sexual division of labour.

Feminist critics of this interpretation argued that concentrating on public attitudes and official policies led to a depiction of women as passive victims controlled by powerful male institutions. Instead, these critics wanted to discover women's historical agency by exploring how women utilized wartime opportunities to their advantage and resisted or negotiated with the controlling forces. Inspired by this shifting perspective and by an ongoing protest against the installation of cruise missiles at the U.S. Air Force base at Greenham Common in the 1980s, pacifist authors discussed women's role in the wartime peace movement. WILTSHER challenged the dominant view that most suffrage activists supported the war in the hope of enfranchisement; she claimed that half of the leaders of the suffrage movement saw their duty as feminists in opposing the fighting. On the basis of these women's papers and memoirs, Wiltsher recounted how they organized a peace conference with fellow suffragists from Europe and America, adopted a plan for a negotiated settlement, and sent envoys to leading politicians to lobby in favour of the scheme. Wiltsher considered these activities worthwhile, despite their failure to stop the war. She argued that the resolutions of feminist activists influenced the principles of the League of Nations and that their pacifist agitation generated a new consciousness which inspired women's peace campaigns throughout the century. This study provides a good summary of

feminist antiwar opposition, but it exaggerates the extent of pacifism among British suffragists and fails to point out the theoretical problems of linking feminism with the promotion of peace.

Early feminist scholarship also advocated exploring women's historical agency through personal testimony. BRAYBON & SUMMERFIELD were influenced by this trend; they draw on oral histories (interviews) and autobiographical accounts. Seeking to uncover women's own perceptions of their participation in the war, Braybon & Summerfield examined women's motives in taking up war work; their views about working conditions, co-workers, and recreation; and their feelings about their demobilization and postwar employment options. Surveying the narratives of women workers of all classes, Braybon & Summerfield stressed that experiences varied greatly, depending on social background; nevertheless, they saw these women's statements as expressing a widespread belief that women had benefited from filling the new war jobs by leaving behind restrictive families and occupations, learning new skills, earning better wages, and, as a result, gaining a sense of independence, freedom, and self-discovery. The accounts also revealed that women felt proud of their contribution and left their war jobs regretfully, but with little bitterness. Despite these findings, Braybon & Summerfield emphasized the persistence of hostile attitudes toward women's outside employment over the next half century and concluded that the war had not produced significant or lasting changes for female workers.

In the late 1980s, feminist critics abandoned the focus on women's war experience because this perspective was unable to explain why women's novel roles had failed to transform their subordinate position. Instead, they urged historians to analyse how symbolic representations of gender in dominant discourses give meaning to male and female identities and roles and thus constitute unequal relations between men and women. KENT's cultural explanation of why the feminist movement could not capitalize on women's wartime gains exemplifies this approach. Kent argues that the postwar re-establishment of traditional gender norms, manifesting itself in renewed emphasis on sexual difference and the need for separate spheres, marked a decline of feminism as a distinct political force, as most of its leaders embraced these ideas, contrary to their prewar beliefs. Kent attributed these developments to the trauma of the war, which fundamentally transformed perceptions of gender relations. To understand how this shift occurred, she analysed the language and images through which feminists and other commentators portrayed gender and sexuality in their published writings. She argued that representations of the war as a sexual conflict made any confrontation between the sexes look like a return to war itself, prompting contemporaries to seek peace in traditional gender relations after the upheavals of the fighting. Despite contributing to this discursive identification, feminists became its victims as well. Fearing a recurrence of sexual antagonism if they persisted in their egalitarian demands, they accepted the dominant gender discourse and pursued maternalist campaigns on women's behalf in the interwar period.

WOOLLACOTT made a conscious attempt to redefine the terms of the debate in several ways. Whereas previous accounts viewed women's work in the war industries as an aberration in the pattern of female employment, she regarded it as women's active participation in the war effort, the female equivalent of soldiering. Therefore, abandoning the broad perspective of earlier studies, she focused on munitions workers, whose job involved them directly in the waging of the war. Finally, instead of analysing how dominant discourses limited women's opportunities after the conflict, she concentrated on how female workers responded to wartime changes and thereby reconstituted their identity and their understanding of their position in relation to others. Woollacott examined all aspects of munitions workers' experience. She discussed how they entered the factories, travelled to work, coped with long hours and dangerous and restrictive working conditions, and spent their time and higher earnings after their shifts. She argued that through their patriotic skilled work, financial autonomy, and strong collective identity, munitions workers developed greater gender consciousness in terms of self-esteem, assertiveness, and ambitions. These changes elevated their expectations and ability to resist servile working conditions and invested their new role as voters with added meaning in the postwar period.

KRISZTINA ROBERT

World War II: Air Operations 1939–1945

Air Ministry Historical Branch, *Works: The Second World War, 1939–1945, Royal Air Force*, London: Air Ministry, 1956; reprinted, with new introduction, as *The Royal Air Force Builds for War: A History of Design and Construction in the RAF, 1935–1945*, London: Stationery Office, 1997

Bowyer, Michael J.F., *2 Group RAF: A Complete History, 1936–1945*, London: Faber, 1974

Bowyer, Michael J.F., *Aircraft for the Few: The RAF's Fighters and Bombers of 1940*, Sparkford, Somerset: Patrick Stephens, 1991

Bowyer, Michael J.F., *Aircraft for the Many: A Detailed Survey of the RAF's Aircraft in June 1944*, Sparkford, Somerset: Patrick Stephens, 1995

Collier, Basil, *The Defence of the United Kingdom*, London: HMSO, 1957

Dempster, Derek and Derek Wood, *The Narrow Margin: The Battle of Britain and the Rise of Air Power 1930–1940*, London: Hutchinson, and New York: McGraw Hill, 1961

Dowding, Hugh C.T., *The Battle of Britain*, London: HMSO, 1946

Frankland, Noble and Charles K. Webster, *The Strategic Air Offensive against Germany, 1939–1945*, 4 vols, London: HMSO, 1961

Harris, Arthur Travers, *Bomber Offensive*, London: Collins, and New York: Macmillan, 1947

Richards, Denis and Hilary St George Saunders, *Royal Air Force 1939–1945*, 3 vols, London: HMSO, 1953–54; revised edition, 1974–75

Roskill, S.W., *The War at Sea 1939–1945*, 3 vols, London: HMSO, 1954–61; new edition, London: Imperial War Museum/Battery Press, 1994

Wright, Lawrence, *The Wooden Sword*, London: Elek, 1967

British air operations in World War II fell into four main categories: (1) protection of the United Kingdom and coastal shipping, (2) a strategic bombing offensive, (3) maritime support or attack, and, in a repeat of earlier tactics, (4) close support of ground forces, particularly overseas. The official series "History of the Second World War" (HMSO) offers the most reliable accounts of these, and the extensive records upon which the accounts were based are now available for research in the Public Record Office, Kew.

A helpful starting-point for any study is the three-volume history by RICHARDS & SAUNDERS summarizing the war effort of the Royal Air Force (RAF). Their Volume 1 traces the expansion of the RAF during the 1930s; but the rebuilding of Britain's air defences in the 1920s to face a perceived threat from France is dealt with by COLLIER. Pre-war aerodrome design and wartime construction at home and abroad are featured in detail in AIR MINISTRY HISTORICAL BRANCH (1956), a history compiled originally for internal use.

Richards & Saunders deal well with the first year of the air war in their Volume 1, showing how the crippling losses suffered by Wellingtons of the Bomber Command operating in daylight forced the switch to difficult night operations. Also recalled are the Scandinavian misadventure and the terrible hammering the tactical bomber force received in France during 1940. More detailed accounts of the latter appear in BOWYER (1974).

Lord DOWDING's report on the battle of Britain provides an excellent basis for study; also, Dowding considers aspects that others do not generally recount, such as the part played by anti-aircraft weapons and balloons. DEMPSTER & WOOD catalogue the main aspects of each day's fighting from July to October 1940 after recalling the build-up to the campaign, whereas Collier deals more with the policy behind the battle. Both sources have ample statistics relevant to the fighting, and Collier also surveys plans to thwart any invasion of Britain. Collier goes on to describe the changing nature of air attacks on the British Isles in later years and the responses directed against them. BOWYER (1991), unusually, includes daily summaries of operational activity by other RAF home commands during the summer of 1940.

Collier outlines the night blitz on Britain during 1940–41, part of an attempt to blockade the United Kingdom by air and U-boat action. Richards & Saunders deal with the war at sea particularly in their Volume 2, which also summarizes the RAF's part in debacle in the Far East during 1941–42.

Throughout 1941 the Bomber Command was hampered by a lack of aids to find targets accurately, a failing described in FRANKLAND & WEBSTER's Volumes 1 and 2. Important changes were under way when, in February 1942, HARRIS became commander-in-chief of the Bomber Command; in his personal account he explains the changes he introduced and recalls the stunning effect of his "thousand-bomber raids" during the summer of 1942. Friction between him and his political masters is evident in his account, along with his strong faith in the bomber as a weapon. He pays heartfelt tribute, at length, to the courage of those under his command who carried out operations his political masters orderd him to undertake.

Richard & Saunders, in their Volume 2, describe how an effective combined operations team – army and RAF – emerged from the north African desert war; this was the basis for the operations of the Allied Expeditionary Air Force in 1944. This volume also discusses the invasions of Sicily and the involvement of glider-borne forces, whose origin and operations are fascinatingly dealt with in WRIGHT's history. The large-scale, very effective derivatives which were part of the assault on Normandy in 1944 are also featured in Richards & Saunders's Volume 2. Extensive details of air operations, their organization, and the aircraft used on 5–6 June 1944 appear in BOWYER (1995).

From the mid-1930s on, the air staff promoted a strategic bombing campaign as the best means of defeating Germany. Frankland & Webster provide an all-embracing account of the course of the bomber offensive, the backbone of the RAF's wartime operations. The war cabinet's policy, the air ministry's directives, command operations, and their effectiveness are all considered. Volume 3 recalls the famous raid on the Ruhr dams. Volume 4 contains detailed appendices.

June 1944 saw the beginning of the era of cruise missiles. Collier describes the difficulties involved in defeating the unmanned jet-propelled "flying bombs". He shows that the V2 long-range rockets could be beaten only by preventing them from being launched; interestingly, this was still the case with the Scud missiles in the Gulf conflict in 1991.

Difficulties in rebuilding an effective air force in south-east Asia, and its operations, are described by Richards & Saunders in their volume 3.

There has never been a detailed account entirely devoted to the complex air war at sea, although there are references in Richards & Saunders's volumes to operations against supply vessels, large warships, and particularly U-boats. The three volumes by ROSKILL deal to some extent with the topic and provide coverage of the varied operations of the Fleet Air Arm (FAA); Roskill also includes U-boat sinkings.

MICHAEL J.F. BOWYER

See also Harris; Royal Air Force

World War II: Far East 1941–1945

Ministry of Information, South-East Asian Command Film Units, *Burma Victory*, London: Imperial War Museum, 1945 (film)
Hickey, Michael, *The Unforgettable Army: Slim's XIVth Army in Burma*, Staplehurst, Kent: Spellmount, 1992
Kirby, S. Woodburn with C.T. Addis, *The War against Japan*, 5 vols, London: HMSO, 1957–69
Owen, Frank, *The Fall of Singapore*, London: Michael Joseph, 1960
Rooney, David, *Burma Victory: Imphal, Kohima, and the Chindit Issue, March 1944 to May 1945*, London: Arms and Armour Press, 1992
Rooney, David, *Wingate and the Chindits: Redressing the Balance*, London: Arms and Armour Press, 1994
Slim, William, *Defeat into Victory*, London: Cassell, 1956; reprinted, New York: Cooper Square Press, 2000
Tsuji, Masanobu, *Singapore: The Japanese Version*, edited by H.V. Howe, translated by Margaret E. Lake, Sydney: Smith, 1960; as *Japan's Greatest Victory, Britain's Worst Defeat*, New York: Sarpedon, 1993; Staplehurst, Kent: Spellmount, 1997
Wood, Derek (editor), *The RAF and the Far East War, 1941–1945: A Symposium on the Far East War, 24 March 1995*, Bracknell, Berkshire: Royal Air Force Historical Society, 1995

The attack on the American naval base at Pearl Harbor on 7 December 1941 by aircraft from a Japanese task force was followed, only hours later, by attacks on a number of British colonies in the Far East. This transformed what had been, since 1939, an essentially European conflict into a world war and opened up a vast new theatre of operations for the already over-stretched British armed forces.

The Japanese invasions of Hong Kong and Malaya found the British unprepared. In Hong Kong the defenders, outnumbered and with little hope of support, surrendered on Christmas night 1941. In Malaya, the Japanese landed in the north and quickly pushed south. Since the 1930s, British strategy for the defence of the region had been based upon naval power. Thus Singapore was intended as the base for a powerful Far Eastern fleet that would prevent Japanese expansion towards Australia and New Zealand. However, because of the demands of the European and North African theatres, the naval forces at Singapore were woefully under strength. The British had also gambled that any attack on Malaya would come from the sea at Singapore itself, not from in the north. The Japanese easily wrested command of the air from Royal Air Force units in Malaya, which were also under strength, as Lieutenant-General A.E. Percival's 10th Army was outmanoeuvered and outfought and forced back on Singapore. Percival, despite a numerical advantage, finally surrendered his whole command on 15 February 1942. In what Winston Churchill called "one of the worst military disasters in the history of the British Army", some 130,000 British and Commonwealth troops became prisoners of war. Percival's decision to surrender has been hotly debated by historians but can be partly explained by years of neglect of the defences of Singapore, a lack of air cover, and the overwhelming panic that arose when it was realized that the Japanese army was not the incompetent, racially inferior foe which most British soldiers had envisioned. KIRBY provides the most detailed picture of these tragic events, albeit with a somewhat defensive tone. OWEN examines the fall of Singapore more critically in a popular, highly readable, and well-researched account. Colonel Masanobu TSUJI, the director of planning and operations for the invading 25th Army, explores events in detail from the Japanese perspective. His account was first published in English in 1965; the latest edition has been extensively revised.

With the conquest of Malaya complete, the Japanese turned their attention to Burma, which they had invaded in late January. Advancing into north and central Burma, they soon took Rangoon and threatened northern India and the Burma Road – the only overland supply route from India to nationalist China. The British fought a desperate rearguard action but were forced to evacuate most of the country. Over the next 12 months or so they reorganized and built up their strength. The Japanese adopted an equally defensive strategy until 1944, when they began a major offensive in the north which was aimed at gaining a foothold in north-east India and which led to the battles at Kohima and Imphal. A recent detailed examination of these bloody, decisive battles is ROONEY (1992). In the autumn of 1943, Lieutenant-General Sir William Slim was appointed commander of the newly formed 14th Army, which later began a counter-offensive that finally culminated in the surrender of the surviving Japanese forces in Burma in May 1945. Kirby again provides the most detailed narrative of operations in Burma. HICKEY, in a more recent work on the campaign, places greater emphasis on the Commonwealth contingents in the 14th Army, particularly the Indian and African units, and analyses why the Japanese were such formidable opponents in jungle warfare.

Despite Mountbatten's claim that Slim was the "finest general the Second World War produced", Slim and his 14th Army were largely overshadowed by contemporaries who fought in Europe and North Africa and whose campaigns received far more attention at the time and in the later literature of the war. Yet Slim's achievements were considerable; he built up the 14th Army, sustained morale during one of the most vicious and unpleasant campaigns of the war, and established the strong-point strategy around Kohima and Imphal, which guarded the route into India and against which the Japanese 15th Army virtually destroyed itself in 1944–45. SLIM's own account – one of the most readable memoirs of the period – provides considerable insight into his strategy and his tactful handling of his American counterpart General Joseph "Vinegar Joe" Stilwell (commander of American forces for the India-Burma-China theater) and of his own subordinate Orde Wingate. Wingate, an unorthodox soldier responsible for airborne offensives deep into enemy-occupied territory, remains a controversial figure. He was virtually dismissed as a maverick in the official histories, but ROONEY (1994) offers a careful reassessment of Wingate and the "Chindits", the British and Commonwealth units under his command. Given the nature of the terrain, extensive military operations in Burma, particularly the deep-penetration attacks by the Chindits, were possible only because land forces could be supplied from the air. The Allies had virtually gained air supremacy in the region by 1944, and the 14th Army developed a remarkable degree of cooperation with the British and American air forces. The essays in WOOD, some by participants in the events, explore the role of the Royal Air Force in the Far Eastern Theatre, from the early failures in Malaya and Java to the vital part played by air power in the reconquest of Burma.

An excellent introduction to the Burma campaign is MINISTRY OF INFORMATION (1945), a documentary filmed for the minstry by cameramen of Mountbatten's South East Asia Command to inform the public about the achievements of the "forgotten army". This film provides a useful narrative of the military events, accompanied by dramatic combat footage that offers considerable insight into the nature of jungle warfare.

MICHAEL PARIS

See also East Asia, Relations with (1930s to Korean War); Mountbatten

World War II: Home Front 1939–1945

Addison, Paul, *The Road to 1945: British Politics and the Second World War*, London: Jonathan Cape, 1975; London and New York: Quartet Books, 1977; revised edition, London: Pimlico, 1994

Brooke, Stephen, *Labour's War: The Labour Party during the Second World War*, Oxford: Clarendon Press, and New York: Oxford University Press, 1992
Calder, Angus, *The People's War: Britain, 1939–1945*, London: Jonathan Cape, and New York: Pantheon, 1969; 2nd edition, London: Pimlico, 1992
Lant, Antonia, *Blackout: Reinventing Women for Wartime British Cinema*, Princeton, New Jersey: Princeton University Press, 1991
Mackenzie, S.P., *The Home Guard: A Military and Political History*, Oxford and New York: Oxford University Press, 1995
McLaine, Ian, *Ministry of Morale: Home Front Morale and the Ministry of Information in World War II*, London and Boston: Allen and Unwin, 1979
Marwick, Arthur, *The Home Front: The British and the Second World War*, London: Thames and Hudson, 1976
Morgan, David and Mary Evans, *The Battle for Britain: Citizenship and Ideology in the Second World War*, London and New York: Routledge, 1993
Pelling, Henry, *Britain and the Second World War*, London and Glasgow: Collins, 1970

PELLING presents one of the better overviews of Britain in World War II produced during the 1970s. Writing in narrative style, he examines how Britain got into the war; leftist, rightist, and centrist attitudes toward war in British politics; how the war proceeded, including an assessment of Britain's wartime relations with various parts of the empire and with its principal ally, the United States; how the public viewed the war and changes within British society effected by the war; and the impact of the war on the concept of state power and realities of the British economy. He concludes that World War II had much less impact than World War I on the outlook of Britons.

The Home Guard, which was highly popular but not particularly well understood, is the subject of MACKENZIE's excellent study. The Home Guard included many influential men and women with backgrounds in the military, business, politics, and academia, such as the Oxford historian A.J.P. Taylor. Many more were locals, whose apparent patriotism, it is argued here, appealed to Winston Churchill's romantic and historic sentiments. Both elements gave the Home Guard an impressive amount of political influence which enabled its members to pressure the War Office into giving it adequate arms and equipment, and status. The author places the Home Guard in the British "amateur tradition" which emphasized locally controlled volunteers. This book is thoroughly researched, though MacKenzie does not contend that it is a definitive history of the subject.

CALDER wrote a brilliant if cynical book which was the first to challenge virtually every existing assumption about how the war affected civilian life in Britain. He brought to this aspect of the war an element of reality that was either missing or played down in studies which tended to glorify or romanticize ordinary citizens' attitudes and roles. Calder debunks a notion, popular in the 1950s, that by paving the way for a Labour government, the war actually liberated the British from the pre-war dominance of wealth, bureaucracy, and privilege; also, noting the expansion of the power of the Soviet Union and the United States after 1945, he challenges the postwar view that the war was a generally liberating experience around the world.

MARWICK takes an illuminating yet cautious look at the effect of war at home. His study of the home front is well illustrated with photographs of everything from pre-war hunger marchers to ballet performed outdoors in Bethnal Green, and along the way he gives space to conscientious objectors. He reflects an increasingly popular theme in war histories of the 1970s: the effect of propaganda and its various channels, such as film and broadcasting, on the civilian population. Marwick takes a middle-of-the-road view of the extent to which the war prepared the way for significant social change in Britain. This book is an excellent place to begin gaining an understanding of the effect of the war on the British home front.

ADDISON argues persuasively that, whether or not the war genuinely affected social change for the better, power was in the hands of those who believed society could be improved for everyone. His describes the shift of popular opinion to the side of Labour as the party seeking dramatic social reform, and he concludes that this shift came about in large part because of the effect of the war on political and social life. Addison was one of the first scholars to have full access to a wide range of government documents from the war period.

BROOKE takes a revisionist view of the degree to which Labour put its ideology aside in order to cooperate with Conservatives in the wartime coalition government. He claims that most historians were wrong about wartime politics and argues instead that leftist Labour leaders such as Harold Laski and Aneurin Bevan represented a radical alternative to Conservatives and were the essential force in forming Labour views on education, health, and nationalization. Brooke claims that these views, far too radical for Conservatives or Liberals, were those around which Labour united to win a parliamentary majority in 1945.

MORGAN & EVANS take issue with the idea of unity and resolution among Britons during the war. They argue that conflict and disunity were as common as camaraderie: evacuees from London slums were shunned by their more affluent rural hosts; women in the forces or wartime industry were discriminated against; and many areas of wartime manufacturing saw poor management, shoddy workmanship, absenteeism, and strikes more than quality and dedication to the war effort.

LANT adds to a significant collection of works on women in wartime with her excellent study of how the role British women were expected to play in the war was conveyed through propaganda films, and to a lesser extent through posters, cartoons, advertising, and other media. Women were encouraged to put aside any preference for marriage and motherhood in order to do their duty. When the war was winding down, film also was used to prepare women to return to their peacetime roles as housewives and mothers. This study also makes the point that the war was the only time British film held its own against Hollywood; the war had effectively created for Britain a national film culture.

McLAINE wrote the first major work on British war propaganda on the home front and set the stage for a number of significant studies that analysed British war propaganda directed at enemy, enemy-occupied, neutral, and allied countries. McLaine's was the first study of British propaganda in the war to draw upon the official records of the Ministry of Information (MOI), and the author uses these sources to good affect, detailing MOI's planning and execution, relationships and conflicts, and successes and failures. This is a positive work; McLaine concludes that morale was successfully maintained on the home front because British propagandists recognized that their audience was intelligent, and that victory depended on an openly acknowledged partnership between government and citizenry.

ROBERT COLE

See also Chamberlain, Neville; Elizabeth; Morrison

World War II: Naval Operations

1939–1945

Creswell, John, *Sea Warfare, 1939–1945*, London and New York: Longmans Green, 1950; revised edition, Berkeley: University of California Press, 1967

Gray, Edwyn, *Operation Pacific: The Royal Navy's War against Japan, 1941–1945*, London: Cooper, and Annapolis, Maryland: Naval Institute Press, 1990

Hough, Richard, *Former Naval Person: Churchill and the Wars at Sea*, London: Weidenfeld and Nicolson, 1985

March, Edgar J., *British Destroyers: A History of Development, 1892–1953*, London: Seeley Service, 1966

Middlebrook, Martin, *Convoy: The Battle for Convoys S.C.122 and H.X.229*, London: Allen Lane, 1976; New York: William Morrow, 1977

Raven, Alan and John Roberts, *British Cruisers of World War Two*, London: Arms and Armour Press, and Annapolis, Maryland: Naval Institute Press, 1980

Roskill, S.W., *The War at Sea, 1939–1945*, vols 1–3, parts 1 and 2, London: HMSO, 1954–61

Roskill, S.W., *White Ensign: The British Navy at War, 1939–1945*, Annapolis, Maryland: Naval Institute Press, 1960

The historiography of British naval operations in World War II is so voluminous that before proceeding to more analytical works addressing particular aspects of the war, readers are advised to lay a foundation by consulting the official war history: ROSKILL (1954–61, part of the History of the Second World War, United Kingdom Military series edited by J.R.M. Butler). In this multivolume work, Roskill (Captain, DSC, RN) provides a chronological narrative that can serve as a baseline for an understanding of the strategic and operational naval and maritime aspects of World War II. Roskill's history primarily reflects the standpoint of "those responsible for the central direction of the maritime war", but Roskill did not write solely from the naval viewpoint; he also incorporated events of air and land warfare that "markedly influenced our maritime strategy and operations". Current historical conflict analysis typically views military operations from a "joint" or multi-service perspective; however, this is a rather recent phenomenon. The guidelines established by parliament in 1946 for official war histories called for a "broad survey of events from an inter-Service point of view", whereas previous official war histories had each addressed only a single service. Roskill's work was one of the first to take an inter-service approach to naval and maritime operations, and it remains one of the most useful and complete histories of World War II.

ROSKILL (1960) is single-volume work published in the United States and aimed at both British and American audiences. It grew out of the author's recognition of a need for a more concise naval history to reach a broader readership than the official history. Here, with regard to the participation of the United States Navy, he integrates the operational histories of the Allied naval forces to offer a total picture. In particular, he addresses the the impact of strictly American operations on the derivation of strategy and planning by Britain and the Commonwealth, while still writing from a British historical viewpoint.

CRESWELL (1950), which was originally published before the official history, presents the war at sea from a distinctly Allied perspective. Creswell gives a broad outline of the maritime struggle but advises the reader to await the anticipated operational histories for more in-depth and specific narratives. In the revised edition (1967), Creswell incorporates much of the intervening historiography, an analysis of the interwar naval strategic outlook of the major belligerents, and brief biographical sketches of the principal participants.

The war in the Atlantic against German submarines (U-boats) represented a critical and resource-intensive theatre for the Royal Navy. To safeguard Britain's oceanic lifeline to both North America and the empire, the Admiralty reinstituted the merchant convoy system, which had proved its usefulness in World War I. MIDDLEBROOK tells the story of two such transatlantic convoys to illustrate the dynamics as well as the perils of the convoy system. Throughout this narrative the reader learns about the ships, aircraft, equipment, and tactics of the Allied navies and merchant marine as well as those of the Kriegsmarine U-boats and gains an understanding of the character of the men on each side.

Most of the history of Britain's naval war against Japan in the Pacific theatre dwells on the early disasters: the sinking of HMS Prince of Wales and HMS Repulse, the destruction of Force Z in the Indian Ocean, or the crushing battle of the Java Sea. Little is said of the operational successes, particularly the participation of British and Commonwealth forces in the western Pacific and China–Burma–India theatre during 1944–45, when the Japanese empire was rolled back. GRAY, an accomplished naval historian and novelist, helps to fill this historiographical void. He provides a highly analytical yet engaging history of the Royal Navy's war against Japan – a "sombre narrative of tragedy and defeat" that nevertheless ended in victory and vindication.

Winston Churchill, although he was a former army officer, developed an intimate relationship with the Royal Navy and its senior officers during his terms as first lord of the Admiralty in both world wars and as prime minister in the second. By the nature of the coalition against the Axis powers, Churchill also had a close relationship with President Franklin Roosevelt of the United States (a former political naval leader as undersecretary of the navy in World War I). HOUGH analyses Churchill's dual relationship with his own naval service and with Roosevelt, and, by extension, with the United States Navy. In terms of the wartime operations, Hough's work provides a political and diplomatic context for understanding the resultant strategic and ultimately operational aspects of the period 1939–45.

Any student of naval operations in World War II will benefit from a well-crafted reference guide that lays out technical specifications of particular vessels or general classes of warships.

This is provided by RAVEN & ROBERTS (1980), a work on British cruisers (and their similar reference work on battleships); and by MARCH (1966), a work on destroyers that covers a much broader period than World War II. Numerous drawings and photographs of vessels illustrate the evolution of British warship design up to the end of the war in 1945; and both books, as thorough encyclopedias, give precise specifications and details of armament, displacement and tonnage, procurement, manning, electronic capabilities, construction, propulsion systems, and so forth. In this respect they are a very useful complement to any reading on the operational aspects of the naval and maritime history of World War II.

STANLEY CARPENTER

See also Mountbatten; Navy: Modern

World War II: North Africa 1939–1945

Anglo-American Film Units for the Ministry of Information, Tunisian Victory: From the Invasion of North Africa to the Fall of Tunis, London: Imperial War Museum, 1944 (film)
Army Field and Photographic Unit for the Ministry of Information, Desert Victory, London: Imperial War Museum, 1943 (film)
Barnett, Correlli, The Desert Generals, London: Kimber, 1960; New York: Viking Press, 1961
Brooks, Stephen (editor), Montgomery and the Eighth Army, London: Bodley Head, 1991
Doherty, Richard, A Noble Crusade: The History of the Eighth Army, 1941 to 1945, Staplehurst, Kent: Spellmount, 1999
Gilbert, Adrian (editor), The Imperial War Museum Book of the Desert War, London: Sidgwick and Jackson, 1992
Hamilton, Nigel, Monty: Master of the Battlefield, 1942–1944, London: Hamish Hamilton, 1983; as Master of the Battlefield: Monty's War Years, 1942–1944, New York: McGraw-Hill, 1983
Playfair, I.S.O., The Mediterranean and Middle East, vols 3–4 of the "History of the Second World War" series, London: HMSO, 1960–66
Turner, Adrian, Alamein to Tunis: The Eighth Army's North Africa, London: Combined University Press, 1999

On 10 June 1940 Italy declared war on Britain and France. Mussolini, envious of the success of his German allies in western Europe, saw the fall of France and the subsequent isolation of Britain as a perfect opportunity to extend his African empire by conquering Egypt and by seizing the strategically important Suez Canal. The campaign in North African began on 13 September 1940, when the Italian 10th Army crossed the Libyan frontier into Egypt and attacked the under-strength, poorly equipped British troops of Middle East Command under General Sir Archibald Wavell. It ended in May 1943 with the capture of Tunisia by Anglo-American forces and the complete destruction of Axis power in North Africa. For almost the first two years of the war in North Africa the conflict was little more than a series of bitterly fought offensives and counter-offensives which see-sawed across the Western Desert as both sides attempted to gain a decisive advantage. Then, at the second battle of El Alamein in October 1942, the 8th Army under the command of General Bernard Law Montgomery started the final offensive, which began to push the Axis forces back into Libya. As a result of the Anglo-American landings in Algeria in November 1942 (Operation Torch), a second force squeezed the enemy from the west. Between these two well-equipped Allied armies, the Italians and the German Afrika Korps under Field Marshall Erwin Rommel fought a losing battle until, starved of equipment and with their supply routes from Europe virtually severed, the remnants of their forces surrendered outside Tunis.

The most comprehensive account of the desert campaign is PLAYFAIR's two-volume official history. While now somewhat dated, it still offers the most detailed examination of British military operations between September 1940 and the collapse of Axis power in 1943. A useful visual overview of the North African campaign can be gained from two films: ARMY FIELD AND PHOTOGRAPHIC UNIT FOR THE MINISTRY OF INFORMATION (1943) and ANGLO-AMERICAN FILM UNITS FOR THE MINISTRY OF INFORMATION (1944). The former, *Desert Victory* – arguably one of the finest documentaries of World War II – was made by army and Royal Air Force (RAF) film units during the campaign and covers events from the battle of El Alamein to the capture of Tripoli. It clearly explains Montgomery's successful strategy and provides a dynamic visual record not only of the Allies' military achievements but equally of the logistical backing from the home front and the contribution of Commonwealth contingents. Although several scenes were reconstructed, this film powerfully evokes the feel of the war in the desert. *Tunisian Victory*, which is only slightly less interesting, opens with the Allies' landings in Algeria and details the final stages of the campaign and the major contribution of American forces to victory.

The events of the North African campaign from the perspective of the 8th Army are detailed by both DOHERTY and TURNER. In what will probably become the standard history of the 8th Army for some time to come, Doherty, using official records and personal accounts, describes military operations beginning with the Italian invasion of Egypt and, unlike other works on the topic, takes the story of perhaps the best-known British army of World War II through to the conclusion of the Italian campaign in 1945. Turner offers a history of operations in North Africa but also examines the achievements of Rommel, who, gradually forced to retreat into Libya after El Alamein by the better-equipped and numerically superior Allied armies, still managed to fight all the way back to Tunis. Unlike many German commanders, Rommel was held in considerable esteem by the men of the Allied armies. GILBERT, using the vast resources of the Imperial War Museum's document and oral history archives, focuses on several important aspects of the desert campaign. Instead of a straightforward narrative history of operations, the author explores, for example, the contribution of Commonwealth troops, who played a vital role within the 8th Army; the Royal Navy's coastal operations, which helped starve the Italian army and the Afrika Korps of supplies; and the effort made by the Desert Air Force, which gained air supremacy over North Africa and developed a tactical doctrine of air power that did much to ensure the success of Montgomery's ground operations.

Much of the historiography of the North African campaign has focused on the personalities of the commanders, and in particular on Montgomery. Volume 2 of HAMILTON's biography, based on Montgomery's own papers and diaries, carefully covers the general's leadership of the 8th Army from August 1942 on. While Hamilton's study is highly detailed and painstakingly researched, the author is perhaps too sympathetic toward Montgomery's foibles and his sometimes unfounded criticism of his fellow generals. A useful corrective is the well-balanced collection of Montgomery's papers edited by BROOKS. This work never underrates the achievements of Montgomery – who raised the morale of the desert army after a long series of defeats and forged a superb fighting machine – but it does provide the documentation for a more balanced view of his abilities and ideas. Although BARNETT's book is now somewhat dated, it usefully reminds us that Montgomery was not the only British general in North Africa. Earlier desert commanders like Wavell and Auchinleck are sometimes criticized, but Barnett emphasizes the valuable contribution they made to the final victory by holding the initial Axis advance into Egypt and by helping to mould the desert army into the instrument which Montgomery fine-tuned and led to Tunis. Barnett also focuses attention on less well-known figures like Ritchie and O'Connor, who have to some extent been overshadowed by Montgomery but who played an important role in the success achieved in North Africa. This was the first decisive defeat for the German war machine in World War II, and it paved the way for subsequent success in the Mediterranean theatre.

MICHAEL PARIS

See also Montgomery, Bernard

World War II: Teheran, Yalta, and Potsdam Conferences 1943–1945

Alperovitz, Gar, *Atomic Diplomacy: Hiroshima and Potsdam: The Use of the Atomic Bomb and the American Confrontation with Soviet Power*, New York: Simon and Schuster, 1965; London: Secker and Warburg, 1966; revised edition, Harmondsworth and New York: Penguin, 1985

Feis, Herbert, *Between War and Peace: The Potsdam Conference*, Princeton, New Jersey: Princeton University Press, and London: Oxford University Press, 1960

Fenno, Richard F., Jr (editor), *The Yalta Conference*, Boston: Heath, 1955

Gaddis, John Lewis, *The United States and the Origins of the Cold War, 1941–1947*, New York: Columbia University Press, 1972

Gormly, James L., *From Potsdam to the Cold War: Big Three Diplomacy, 1945–1947*, Wilmington, Delaware: SR Books, 1990

Kolko, Gabriel, *The Politics of War: The World and United States Foreign Policy, 1943–1945*, New York: Random House, 1968; London: Weidenfeld and Nicolson, 1969

Mee, Charles L., *Meeting at Potsdam*, London: André Deutsch, and New York: Evans, 1975

Morray, Joseph P., *From Yalta to Disarmament: Cold War Debate*, New York: Monthly Review Press, 1961; London: Merlin, 1962

Ulam, Adam B., *Expansion and Coexistence: The History of Soviet Foreign Policy, 1917–1967*, London: Secker and Warburg, and New York: Praeger, 1968; extended edition, New York: Praeger, 1974

The best-known wartime conferences of the Allies – at Yalta in February 1945 and Potsdam in July 1945 – and the arguably less well-known meeting at Teheran (Tehran) in December 1943 tend to have taken their places in the history of the cold war rather than attracting discussion in their own right. They are featured as a starting-point for all historical analyses of relations between the superpowers (the United States and Soviet Union) during the cold war and are therefore discussed in the early accounts of many such studies. Their significance, rather than their content, tends to dominate the historiography of the period. Within this historiography there is a division between the traditional view, popular in the 1940s and 1950s, that expansionism on the part of the Soviet Union led to the cold war; and the revisionist view of the 1960s and 1970s, which maintained that the real cause was expansionism on the part of the United States, coupled with its persistent misreading of the Soviet Union's intentions. Another important dimension of the historiography of the cold war has emerged since 1989: an ability to study the cold war *as history* rather than as an ongoing state of affairs. This has resulted in the publication of a great deal of new work. The release of a significant amount of material from the archives of the Soviet Union has meant that a more balanced view of events can now be taken. Many of the later studies also emphasize the role of Britain in the evolution of the cold war.

GADDIS traces the origins of the cold war back to 1941 and thus includes the Teheran conference. When the three wartime leaders – Roosevelt, Churchill, and Stalin – met for the first time, military issues predominated. Although there was some discussion of the future control of Germany, and Roosevelt sounded Stalin out on a United Nations organization, the main emphasis was on cooperation in finishing the war with Germany and Japan, and on opening a second front against Germany. Stalin made it clear that he would expect political compensation for military support against Japan, although he did not make specific demands until December 1944. Gaddis describes the private conversations in Teheran between Roosevelt and Stalin over the question of eastern Europe, which give a revealing insight into Roosevelt's thinking. This contrasts sharply with the position the Americans adopted when they accused Stalin of bad faith over the Yalta agreements in early 1945. In Teheran, Roosevelt asked that Stalin leave the question of Poland to one side; while he recognized Stalin's position over Poland, Roosevelt would soon be faced with an election in which he did not wish to lose the votes of 6 or 7 million Polish-Americans. This applied equally to the Baltic states, Lithuania, Latvia, and Estonia. Roosevelt was happy to accept Stalin's desire for control in these areas but did not wish to make his agreement public. He also tacitly accepted that Churchill, for his part, had agreed to the Soviet Union's influence in these areas, at an earlier meeting with Stalin.

The significance of the Teheran conference lies in the fact that in effect it underpinned agreements made later at Yalta, and many historians date the real beginning of the cold war from Yalta. The main topics discussed at Yalta were the postwar organization of Europe and the Far East, where many territorial concessions were made to Stalin, and, again, the United Nations. An excellent example of the traditional view of the origins of the cold war is the short volume edited by FENNO, which contains a series of essays by the policy-making elite of the time, including Churchill, James F. Byrnes, Averell Harriman, and Harry Hopkins. Their attitude is consistent: the Soviet Union's expansionism was fuelled by the concessions which Roosevelt made at Yalta. Fenno does suggest that students of the period should ask *why* Roosevelt made these concessions and whether they would have made any difference in the face of Stalin's determined ambition, but there is no question that Stalin is to blame for the onset of the cold war.

MORRAY saw the cold war as a contest between ideologies and maintained that "the Communists have deliberately chosen to fight with ideological weapons, and the American government must respond at peril of losing this battle by default". His first chapter, "The Spirit of Yalta", provides a detailed analysis of the correspondence between Stalin, Roosevelt, and Churchill which took place after the conference. It is interesting that, after Roosevelt's death on 12 April 1945, Churchill took over the detailed interpretation of the Yalta agreements with Stalin, and Churchill was responsible for much of the difference of opinion which arose. Morray accepts that it was unreasonable of the west to expect Stalin to agree to a Polish government which consisted purely of anti-communists, and that this was not the spirit in which agreement had been reached at Yalta.

ULAM, like many of the later revisionists, looks at the question of Yalta from the perspective of the Soviet Union: "the interests of the Soviet Union, her ability to rebuild her shattered economy and to avoid any threat to her western regions . . . required complete Russian dominance of Eastern Europe and preponderance on the Continent". He brings out one major reason why Roosevelt, in fact, made concessions to Stalin. It was not merely that Roosevelt wanted Stalin's agreement to the formation of the new United Nations, but also that America desperately needed military support from the Soviet Union in order to defeat Japan. This point was not, of course, brought out in Roosevelt's communication of events; it would be difficult to admit publicly that America was incapable of crushing Japan without assistance. Roosevelt also went to some lengths to exclude Churchill from discussions at Yalta, anxious to convince Stalin that Britain and America were not trying to form an alliance against him – a point which makes Stalin's somewhat negative reactions to Churchill's later strictures perhaps more easily understood.

KOLKO points out that the aid from the Soviet Union was also vital in ensuring military victory over Germany; Churchill "half pleaded" with Stalin to provide "distracting relief" from German pressure in the west. Yalta was not, therefore, a one-way event; concessions were asked for, and received, on both sides.

The conference at Potsdam in July 1945, at which the main points of discussion were Germany and the question of reparations, is also the subject of much debate. Traditionalists maintain that Truman did not reverse Roosevelt's policy of cooperation with and conciliation of Stalin; Truman merely expressed himself in a more brusque and assertive manner. Revisionists argue strongly against this contention. Of those who look at both sides, and give Potsdam equal status with Yalta and Teheran, MEE has produced an extremely readable analysis of the two weeks "that changed the world for all time". He looks at Potsdam from the perspectives of the three men who shaped the cold war world and asks how it was possible to rescue discord from the threatened outbreak of peace. Permeating the conference halls of Potsdam was, of course, the United States's successful testing of the atomic bomb, and Mee describes in vivid detail Truman's quandary regarding when, and how, to tell Stalin the momentous news. The overriding question for Truman was how the timing of the announcement would affect Stalin's position toward Japan; at all costs, the Soviet Union must now have none of the glory of defeating Japan.

FEIS has also produced a monograph on the Potsdam conference, rather than building it into an analysis of the cold war. He concludes that the reason why Potsdam was seen as a failure rather than a success similar to Yalta is that at Yalta the Allies "were under a bond of mutual military dependence to get along with one another" and they could "submerge or postpone issues that might estrange them"; at Potsdam they were not and could not.

ALPEROVITZ categorically maintains that it was the existence of the atomic bomb, tested just the day before the Potsdam conference began, which gave Truman the confidence to demand severe modifications to Roosevelt's perceived concessions. He quotes Byrne, Truman's secretary of state-designate, who said that the bomb was used "to make Russia more manageable", and takes these words as evidence that the bomb was a "master-card" in American postwar diplomacy. Once the United States had the bomb, it no longer needed help from the Soviet Union in order to defeat Japan; and the reason for bombing Hiroshima and Nagasaki was not to end the war in Japan but to eliminate any need for the involvement of the Soviet Union, as well as to demonstrate American superiority. GORMLY looks at the Potsdam conference as a starting-point for the cold war and also emphasizes the importance of the bomb as a factor in Truman's diplomacy. He holds that to support their diplomacy, Byrnes and Truman "counted on their skill at negotiation with Stalin, the postwar economic power of the United States, and the atomic bomb".

CAROLYN J. KITCHING

World War II: Western Front 1939–1945

Addison, Paul and Jeremy A. Crang (editors), *The Burning Blue: A New History of the Battle of Britain*, London: Pimlico, 2000

Brickhill, Paul, *The Dam Busters*, foreword by Lord Tedder, London: Evans, 1951; revised edition, London: Pan, 1999

Calvocoressi, Peter and Guy Wint, *Total War: Causes and Courses of the Second World War*, London: Allen Lane, 1972; as *Total War: The Story of World War II*, New York: Pantheon, 1972; revised edition, also by John Pritchard, vol. 1, *The Western Hemisphere*, London and New York: Viking Penguin, 1989

Carell, Paul, *Sie kommen!: Der deutsche Bericht über die Invasion und die 80tägige Schlacht um Frankreich*, Oldenburg: Stalling, 1960; as *Invasion – They're Coming! The German Account of the Allied Landings and the 80 Days' Battle for France*, translated by E. Osers, London: Harrap, 1962; New York: Dutton, 1963

Churchill, Winston S., *The Second World War*, 6 vols, London: Cassell, and Boston: Houghton Mifflin, 1948–54

Deighton, Len, *Blood, Tears, and Folly: In the Darkest Hour of World War II*, London: Jonathan Cape, 1993; as *Blood, Tears, and Folly: An Objective Look at World War II*, New York: HarperCollins, 1993

Lawlor, Sheila, *Churchill and the Politics of War, 1940–1941*, Cambridge and New York: Cambridge University Press, 1995

Liddell Hart, Basil H., *History of the Second World War*, London: Cassell, and New York: Putnam, 1970

Mordal, Jacques, *Les Canadiens à Dieppe*, Paris: Presses de la Cité, 1962; as *Dieppe: The Dawn of Decision*, translated by Mervyn Savill, London: Souvenir Press, 1963

Overy, Richard, *Why The Allies Won*, London: Jonathan Cape, 1995; New York: Norton, 1996

Sainsbury, Keith, *Churchill and Roosevelt at War: The War They Fought and the Peace They Hoped to Make*, London: Macmillan, and New York: New York University Press, 1994

Spears, Edward, *Assignment to Catastrophe*, 2 vols, London: Heinemann, and New York: Wyn, 1954

Though World War II has often been popularly described as "the good war", there is still no agreement among historians on the objectives, action, or achievements of British forces in the major phases of the war in the west. Controversy still surrounds the "phoney war" (1939–40); the battle of France (1940); the battle of Britain (1940); the discussions of a second front and the associated operations in occupied Europe and Germany, like the Dieppe raid (1942) or the air attacks by the Bomber Command on civilian targets; and the final campaign in north-west Europe (1944–45). The disagreements revolve around the strategic, political, and (a more recent development) ethical aspects of the British role in the war in Europe and the Mediterranean. In the past, while all commentators agreed that the American war effort had been decisive in the Pacific theatre, many, like CHURCHILL, insisted that Britain had been central in the European theatre, notably on the western front. Nowadays, historians – including British historians such as OVERY – tend to reduce the importance of Britain even in the west, compared with the United States; moreover, since the end of the cold war they have also argued increasingly that the western European theatre was a sideshow, or at least that the Anglo-American victory there would have been impossible if the bulk of German armour and aviation had not been engaged primarily in a desperate struggle on the eastern front with Soviet Russia.

It can be said (although this is an oversimplification) that Britain's strategic choices are now criticized in terms of cost-efficiency, the best example being the decision to give priority to landings in Italy (in 1943) rather than the French coastline. These choices, not unexpectedly, are explained and justified by Churchill, in a magisterial and magnificently readable exposition of all the important phases of the war. They had to be made, of course, in consultation with Britain's major ally in the west, and they are the subject of SAINSBURY's book, which is representative of recent critiques. According to this school of thought, by persuading a reluctant Roosevelt to align himself with Britain's choices Churchill won a "Pyrrhic victory" (in Sainsbury's words), for at least two reasons: first, because relations with the Soviet Union immediately deteriorated when Stalin realized that the relief he could have expected from the opening of a second front in the west would be further delayed; and second, because the United States never again followed the advice of the British on grand strategy. The purely military operations of, in LIDDELL HART's phrase, "re-entry into Europe through Sicily" are fully covered by CALVOCORESSI & WINT, by Churchill, and by Liddell Hart himself. The Dieppe raid – the failed rehearsal for D-Day, which made Churchill wary of a frontal attack on the French coastline – receives dispassionate treatment from MORDAL, who tries to strike a balance between those who argue that the death of so many Canadians served the useful purpose of showing the Allies how powerful German defences were and what action would be needed to overwhelm them, and those who believe this was too dear a price to pay.

Britain's western strategy had already been criticized as having entailed infelicitous choices in 1939–40. Few authors defend the "Sitzkrieg" strategy reluctantly and disastrously abandoned for the Norway campaign of 1940: Churchill, who was largely in charge, tries to give a factual account, while DEIGHTON adopts a caustic tone. The "battle of France", as Churchill immediately called it, has been at the centre of controversy from the start, given the seemingly inextricable links between foreign policy, home politics, and military strategy. German propagandists and Vichy France attributed the defeat of the Anglo-French in May-June 1940 to Britain's refusal to commit the Royal Air Force fully to the defence of France. Churchill, supported by Calvocoressi & Wint, argues that the decision was justified because the interests of France in the long run would be best served by an unconquered United Kingdom defended by an intact fighter command. Deighton finds another angle of attack, suggesting that the chiefs of the British Expeditionary Force were defeatist from the start, quite apart from the obvious inadequacy of British armoured forces due to their neglect by the "guilty men" of the Chamberlain era. For a complement to Churchill's comprehensive account of these events, including the evacuation from Dunkirk, one can recommend SPEARS, who, as a liaison with the French authorities on the spot, was an eyewitness. Spears's day-by-day narrative of the fast-deteriorating military and psychological situation in June 1940 as seen from the high command remains a primary source of the first importance.

Arguably, therefore, the opening phases of the war on the western front immediately showed that it was a highly political war. LAWLOR concentrates on the interface between political and military issues, especially on the way Britain's major strategic choices were made over Norway, France, and Greece. This in fact provides the dimension of "high politics" of the important military decisions taken in the early stages of the war, notably what one author has called the "decision to fight on in 1940". Likewise, the British intervention in Greece in 1941 is set in the context of international rivalries: Churchill probably believed that Greece was lost anyway, but as he told the defence

committee, Britain had to show that it stood by its friends. The battle of Britain, exceptionally, seems to have been "apolitical"; but some of the essays in ADDISON & CRANG (2000), which are based on recent international evaluations of the battle, adopt a definitely revisionist tone as to its central position in the defence of the west, as exemplified by such titles as Overy's "How Significant was the Battle?" Overy suggests in his own book that the Bomber Command rather than the Fighter Command won the war in the west. Popular accounts like BRICKHILL (1951), whose continued presence on booksellers' shelves today testifies to its success with the public, never had any doubt. Brickhill's story of the "dam busters" and the exploits of Squadron 617 in bombing Germany and German-occupied Europe, finally sinking the *Tirpitz*, has all the ingredients of a "good read", with few "politically correct" qualms over the civilians and Russians who were drowned when the dams yielded:

> There was a moral price to pay too; there always is. 1,294 people drowned in the floods, and most were civilians. Most were not German: there were 749 slaves and prisoners among the dead. There had been a Russian P.O.W. camp in the valley below the Eder.

Some authors have remarked that the Fighter Command has all the heroes while the Bomber Command is now seen (despite its own many dead) as an ethical embarrassment because of operations like the bombing of Dresden in 1945; other authors continue to have doubts about the effectiveness of "saturation bombing". But Overy's final argument on the matter seems hard to counter: "There has always seemed something fundamentally implausible about the contention of bombing's critics that dropping almost 2.5 million tons of bombs on tautly-stretched industrial systems and war-weary urban populations would not seriously weaken them."

The final campaign in the west from June 1944 onwards receives full treatment, with maps, from Calvocoressi & Wint and from Liddell Hart. Anyone interested in the Germans' perception of the "invasion" should turn to CARELL, who describes a struggle that the German troops saw as unequal owing to the Allies' absolute command of the air; Carell ends his narrative when the 21st Army Group crosses the Seine in August 1944. Churchill gives the most complete details of the planning and operations associated with "Overlord" and the conquest of Germany but also insists on the political dimension, notably on the conferences of the Grand Alliance over the future map of Continental Europe: Yalta and Potsdam. As he concludes on the eve of VE-Day, "Britain, though still very powerful, could not act decisively alone"; and Overy, who argues that this incapacity was in fact revealed by the events of 1940 in the west, attempts to draw the consequences for the postwar period:

> Britain and France, the key actors in 1919, found their postwar international position fatally weakened by their inability to stop Germany in 1940. Without allies there would have been no way that Britain could secure her empire, let alone defeat her enemies, once the French army was out of the contest. After 1945 Britain and France became powers of the second rank. Their evident weakness during the war encouraged nationalist struggles in . . . the British and French empires, and within a

generation the empires were mostly gone. Of the western Allies, Britain lost most from the war: the old balance of power, the empire and a dominant role in the world's economy.

It is therefore clear that the triumphant tones characteristic of Brickhill and still found in most films and television series are increasingly remote from the re-evaluations by academic historians, who are no longer sure that, even on the western front, World War II was a "good war" from the British point of view.

ANTOINE CAPET

See also World War II: Teheran, Yalta, and Potsdam Conferences

Wulfstan *c.*1008–1095
Bishop of Worcester and saint

Barrow, J., "How the Twelfth-Century Monks of Worcester Perceived Their Past" in *The Perception of the Past in Twelfth-Century Europe*, edited by Paul Magdalino, London and Rio Grande, Ohio: Hambledon Press, 1992

Brooks, Nicholas and Catherine Cubitt (editors), *St Oswald of Worcester: Life and Influence*, Leicester: Leicester University Press, 1996

Darlington, Reginald R. (editor), *The Vita Wulfstani of William of Malmesbury*, London: Royal Historical Society, 1928

Gem, R.D.H., "Bishop Wulfstan II and the Romanesque Cathedral Church of Worcester" in *Medieval Art and Architecture at Worcester Cathedral*, edited by Glenys Popper, London: British Archaeological Association, 1978

Ker, N.R., "Hemming's Cartulary: A Description of the Two Worcester Cartularies in Cotton Tiberius A.XIII" in *Studies in Medieval History Presented to Frederick Maurice Powicke*, edited by R.W. Hunt, W.A. Pantin, and R.W. Southern, Oxford: Clarendon Press, 1948; Westport, Connecticut: Greenwood Press, 1979

Mason, E., "Change and Continuity in Eleventh-Century Mercia: The Experience of St Wulfstan of Worcester" in *Anglo-Norman Studies VIII: Proceedings of the Battle Conference 1985*, edited by R. Allen Brown, Woodbridge, Suffolk and Dover, New Hampshire: Boydell, 1986

Mason, Emma, *Saint Wulfstan of Worcester, c.1008–1095*, Oxford and Cambridge, Massachusetts: Blackwell, 1990

Swanton, Michael (translator and editor), *Three Lives of the Last Englishmen*, New York: Garland, 1984

Williams, A., "The Spoilation of Worcester" in *Anglo-Norman Studies XIX: Proceedings of the Battle Conference, 1996*, edited by Christopher Harper-Bill, Woodbridge, Suffolk and Rochester, New York: Boydell, 1997

Williams, Ann, *The English and the Norman Conquest*, Woodbridge, Suffolk and Rochester, New York: Boydell, 1995

Wormald, Patrick, "Lordship and Justice in the Early English Kingdom: Oswaldslow Revisited" in *Property and Power in the Early Middle Ages*, edited by Wendy Davies and Paul Fouracre, Cambridge and New York: Cambridge University Press, 1995

Wulfstan's career is of particular interest to historians of the late Anglo-Saxon and early Norman polity because, as bishop of Worcester from 1062 to 1095, Wulfstan lived through tumultuous times and before he died was the last surviving Anglo-Saxon member of the episcopate.

The fullest attempt at a biography was undertaken by MASON (1990). Mason's book has a two-fold purpose: to reconstruct the life of Wulfstan, largely through reference to William of Malmesbury's *Vita*; and, more broadly, to contextualize his career by examining his impact on the English church after the Conquest and the extent to which he encapsulated the preservation of English values in the Anglo-Norman world. An appendix to this book deals with the main sources for Wulfstan's life and career. These consist of a number of late chronicles; charters (some of which were composed in Wulfstan's name), and William of Malmesbury's *Vita* (DARLINGTON, 1928; SWANTON, 1984), which serves as a Latin translation of a lost Old English *Life* by Coleman. The cartulary composed by the monk Hemming was intended to record Worcester's title deeds and contains a short biography of Wulfstan. Its concern with safeguarding monastic land forms a focus of a number of studies of Wulfstan's career. Full details of Hemming's text can be found in KER.

In reconstructing an outline of Wulfstan's career, Mason is inclined to accept William of Malmesbury's *Vita* too readily as a factual account and seems insufficiently aware of the role, structure, and function of hagiography as a genre. She establishes that Wulfstan was probably the son of a priest and attempts to rationalize certain elements in the *Vita*. Thus the account of how Wulfstan fled into some bushes to avoid being tempted by a seductive young woman is taken as indicating that his monastic upbringing may have rendered him frigid and, quite possibly, homosexual, without any acknowledgment that such incidents are a common hagiographical topos. The incident also had wider repercussions for Wulfstan's career, leading him to campaign against married clergy in later life. Mason's work contains much reflection upon the reporting of miracles associated with Wulfstan, attempting to rationalize such incidents with the aid of psychological and anthropological theory and to explain the natural processes behind many of Wulfstan's alleged miracles of healing. This concern, at times, consists of almost verbatim retelling of miracle stories, making the book read like another *Vita*. Moreover, the concern with Wulfstan's career and miracles entails an account of the development of his cult, and the book closes with this aspect of Wulfstan's life as it considers the growth of his cult in the 12th and 13th centuries.

MASON (1986) is a contextualization of Wulfstan's career and his impact after the Norman Conquest; this is the element in Mason's work which has aroused the fullest historiographical debate. Some of the key sources for Wulfstan's career have recently been subjected to criticism. BARROW scrutinizes several texts associated with 10th- and 11th-century Worcester and concludes that a synodal document presumably of 1092 bearing Wulfstan's name was actually the result of a 12th-century forgery. Barrow argues that the monks of Worcester sought to invent the history of their community so as to imply that monks had rapidly replaced secular clerks. These arguments are further expounded in Mason's essay in BROOKS & CUBITT, which shows that the cathedral community could have become monastic at any time between the beginning of the 11th century and

Wulfstan's own episcopate. This essay also shows how, from the mid-11th century onwards, Worcester became more self-consciously Benedictine and began to acquire a number of monastic texts, including the Old English version of *Regularis concordia*, while remaining an important pastoral foundation.

WORMALD (1995) and this author's essay in Brooks & Cubitt are companion pieces. Wormald shows how the triple-hundred of Oswaldslow, held by the church of St Mary, Worcester, and granting the right to exclude royal judicial officers, was cited three times in Hemming as a judicial immunity as a result of local political collaboration between Wulfstan and the Domesday commissioners. There is no evidence for judicial immunities before 1066, since Wulfstan was in no need of a judicial immunity before the Conquest, owing to his ability to act as a local power-broker. After 1066, however, he faced renewed onslaughts on Worcester's property from Abbot Æthelwig of Evesham and the sheriff, Urse d'Abetot, creating a need to assert the liberties assigned to Oswaldslow.

The issue of assaults on the property of Worcester is analyzed by WILLIAMS (1997). In this article, Williams rearranges Hemming chronologically rather than geographically and tabulates Worcester's secular enemies from the Danish wars of Æthelred II until the Domesday Book. The lengthy dispute between Worcester and Evesham over land at Bengeworth and Hampton is discussed here as well as by Wormald. Wulfstan's continuing need to assert the freedom of Worcester from the see of York, which claimed Worcester as its suffragan see, is dealt with thoroughly in Mason (1990). Mason's article in Brooks & Cubitt is also of use, since it makes some notable comparisons between Wulfstan and the 10th-century reformer Oswald, showing how Wulfstan was similarly concerned about issues of reform and about building a confraternity league of monasteries to uphold *Regularis concordia*. GEM surveys the building of the Romanesque cathedral, begun under Wulfstan c.1084, and details how his building programme was influenced by Christ Church and St Augustine's, Canterbury. Gem also notes Wulfstan's concern to translate the relies of Saint Oswald into the new church of St Mary begun around 1092.

Finally, an overview of the conquest and its impact on the native English can be found in WILLIAMS (1995).

SIMON COATES

See also Anglo-Saxon England: Law; Cnut; Edward "the Confessor"; Eric Bloodaxe

Wyclif(fe), John   c.1329–1384
English theologian and founder of the lollards

Catto, J.I., "Wyclif and Wycliffism at Oxford 1356–1430" in *The History of the University of Oxford*, vol. 2: *Late Medieval Oxford*, edited by J.I. Catto and Ralph Evans, Oxford and New York: Oxford University Press, 1992
Hudson, Anne, *The Premature Reformation: Wycliffite Texts and Lollard History*, Oxford: Clarendon Press, and New York: Oxford University Press, 1988
Hudson, Anne and Michael Wilks (editors), *From Ockham to Wyclif*, Oxford: Blackwell for the Ecclesiastical History Society, 1987
Kenny, Anthony, *Wyclif*, Oxford and New York: Oxford University Press, 1985
Kenny, Anthony (editor), *Wyclif in His Times*, Oxford: Clarendon Press, and New York: Oxford University Press, 1986
Leff, Gordon, *Heresy in the Later Middle Ages: The Relation of Heterodoxy to Dissent, c.1250–c.1450*, 2 vols, Manchester: Manchester University Press, and New York: Barnes and Noble, 1967
McFarlane, Kenneth B., *John Wycliffe and the Beginnings of English Nonconformity*, London: English Universities Press, 1952; New York: Macmillan, 1953; as *The Origins of Religious Dissent in England*, New York: Collier Books, 1966; as *Wycliffe and English Nonconformity*, Harmondsworth and New York: Penguin, 1972
Workman, Herbert B., *John Wyclif: A Study of the English Medieval Church*, 2 vols, Oxford: Clarendon Press, 1926; reprinted, Hamden, Connecticut: Archon Books, 1966

John Wyclif, the 14th-century Oxford theologian and philosopher, founded the only full-scale English heretical movement of the Middle Ages, the lollards. Although he inspired numerous 19th-century biographies, there is no satisfactory modern life of Wyclif. During the mid-20th century, historians were eager to demolish the portrait of Wyclif as a proto-protestant hero and to minimize his influence both on late 14th-century Oxford and on the lollards. The most recent scholarship has, to some extent, reinstated Wyclif at the centre of academic life in the late 14th century and as the conscious leader of a heretical movement with a coherent programme for reform.

Protestant martyrologists of the 16th century like John Bale and John Foxe propagated a view of Wyclif as the "morning star" of the Reformation – the founder of an order of "poor preachers" to evangelize the population, the sole translator of the Bible into English, and an exemplar of an authentically English tradition of protestantism predating by more than a century the introduction of Luther's ideas. Champions of Low Church Anglicanism in the 19th century embraced this portrait, and Wyclif became a powerful symbol of a particular view of the English protestant tradition. WORKMAN's biography (1926), still in many ways the most complete life of Wyclif, eschews the more fanciful aspects of this 19th-century view of Wyclif but nonetheless falls largely into that school. Although Workman remarked that Wyclif could be inconsistent – not practising what he preached – and that ultimately his revolt against the religious system of his day was "too negative", this life of Wyclif tends towards apologetics. For Workman, Wyclif was both a typical man of his age and a harbinger of modernity, the last of the schoolmen and the first of the reformers, his political and religious ideas "hopelessly in advance of his age". Workman's biography is still used for the wealth of information it provides on certain aspects of Wyclif's life and world; but many of Workman's assumptions are no longer widely accepted, including Wyclif's composition of English works, his authorship or at least management of the first Wycliffite translation of the Bible, and his organization of a Franciscan-type order of preachers.

Perhaps the most widely influential biography of Wyclif in the 20th century was McFARLANE's (1952). McFarlane sought, explicitly, to counter the prevailing protestant view; he portrayed Wyclif as an ivory-tower academic motivated primarily by frustrated ambition. According to McFarlane, Wyclif's influence inspired, somewhat accidentally, a ragtag band of religious rebels, whose only lasting effect on English religious life was to impede real church reform for a century and a half. McFarlane's biography was part of "Teach Yourself History", a series for a popular audience, but it nonetheless has had a considerable impact on the scholarly world, both because of its author's manifest learning and because of its strong and rather contrary viewpoint. McFarlane incorporated considerable cynicism in his study of a man whom he evidently found unattractive – in his prologue he described Wyclif as "learned, subtle, ingenious, opinionated, tirelessly argumentative, and rather humourless". He saw himself as an "impartial biographer" and his goal as to "free his subject from a great deal of ignorant repainting and several layers of rich brown protestant varnish". Recent scholars argue that McFarlane's lack of sympathy with Wyclif, and his ignorance of large bodies of source material relevant to the early years of the lollard movement, led him to underestimate the coherence of Wyclif's thought as well as Wyclif's influence on those who pursued his ideas, first at Oxford and then outside the academic world.

In the past several decades there has been significant reassessment both of Wyclif and of the importance of the early lollard movement. Scholars have more closely examined Wyclif's role in the intellectual development of late medieval scholasticism and more particularly in the Oxford of his day. LEFF provides the most comprehensive picture of Wyclif's place in 14th-century political, theological, and philosophical thought, although, like McFarlane, he sees the lollards as having moved away from Wyclif's ideas and as having had little lasting influence on English religious life. KENNY (1985), a short biography in the "Oxford Past Masters" series, focuses primarily on Wyclif as a philosopher – as the "evening star" of late medieval English scholasticism – and examines how his realism influenced his subsequent theological thought. CATTO studies Wyclif's career in the context of the history of Oxford in the 14th century, noting that although Wyclif fell into a tradition of academic controversy at the university, he was unique in conceiving of ambitious projects for applying philosophical and theological insights to contemporary religious and political life. Contributions to two important essay collections – KENNY (1985) and HUDSON & WILKS – further elucidate various aspects of Wyclif's thought, his importance in his own day, and his impact on the lollard movement.

The most important reassessment of Wyclif and the lollard movement in the past several decades has been HUDSON's. Especially, Hudson has done extensive work with the English writings produced by Wyclif's early followers (a source that had previously been largely ignored, especially after Wyclif's own authorship of the works was disproved). She has argued for making more connections between Wyclif's ideas and the subsequent lollard movement, for attributing more influence to Wyclif and his followers at Oxford in the late 14th and early 15th centuries, and for seeing greater coherence in the lollard movement as a whole. Hudson considers the lollard writings direct ideological inheritors of Wyclif's own theology, and although there are divergences, there is "a coherent development . . . from positions traceable in Wyclif himself" rather than oversimplification or bastardization. Using a metaphor first applied by Workman, she hypothesizes that Wyclif and his followers had a reasoned programme for reform, even if the reformation they envisaged could only be premature in the world of the late 14th century.

SHANNON McSHEFFREY

See also Grosseteste; Lollardy; Oldcastle

Y

York

Armstrong, Alan, *Stability and Change in an English County Town: A Social Study of York 1801–1851*, Cambridge and New York: Cambridge University Press, 1974

Attreed, Lorraine, *The King's Towns: Identity and Survival in Late Medieval English Boroughs*, New York: Peter Lang, 2001

Aylmer, G.E. and Reginald Cant (editors), *A History of York Minster*, Oxford: Clarendon Press, 1977

Borthwick Papers (formerly *St Anthony's Hall Publications*), York: University of York, since 1951

Hall, Richard, *English Heritage Book of Viking Age York*, London: Batsford for English Heritage, 1994

Murray, Hugh, *Dr Evelyn's York: The Life and Work of a Pioneer of Conservation of the City between 1891 and 1935*, York: Ebor Press, 1983

Palliser, D.M., *Tudor York*, Oxford and New York: Oxford University Press, 1979

Tillot, P.M. (editor), *A History of Yorkshire: The City of York*, London: Oxford University Press, 1961

Throughout its history, York has been recognized as the second city of the realm, an ecclesiastical and administrative capital with a cloth industry that flourished until the late 14th century, a regional communications centre and vibrant market town in all periods, and a palimpsest of preserved monuments for today's visitors. Its Roman, Viking, and medieval periods have attracted the most attention from historians, but the post-Reformation period has also received significant study.

TILLOT provides the fullest narrative and topical treatment of the city's history, from the Roman period to the mid-20th century. Although monographs have supplemented our knowledge and archaeological findings have expanded the very questions we ask about the past, the individual chapters in Tillot's volume remain fundamental statements about York's history, economy, political structure, and relations with the rest of the realm. The extensive references note the contributions of earlier local historians and antiquarians as well, ranging from Francis Drake in the 18th century to George Benson and Charles Knight early in the 20th.

York began life as Eboracum, the site of a Roman legionary fortress established in AD 71. By the 3rd century, the *colonia* that had developed outside the fort became the capital of Britannia Inferior, and both the extensive monumental remains and the excavated items from modest households have provided archaeologists with details about the living conditions of those early residents. Rescue archaeology deserves the credit for the equally important finds related to Viking Jorvik, the 9th- and 10th-century period of Scandinavian dominance. HALL has written extensively on the discovery, excavation, and presentation of artefacts from the Coppergate site, but the volume listed above (1994) deserves particular praise for its clear narrative, drawings of reconstructed buildings, and detailed explanation of environmental archaeology.

Apart from Edward Miller's chapter on medieval York in Tillot, there is no general narrative study of a period that ranges from the heights of Anglo-Saxon learning which fostered Alcuin in the 8th century to the close, responsible relationship between city and monarchy expressed during the brief reign of Richard III in the 15th century. Important monographs have examined particular aspects of York's medieval government, economy, and cultural life, including studies of the city's municipal charters, its cycle of mystery plays, and the role of women in the workforce. With due respect continuing to be given to Tillot, (ATTREED 2001) on the constitutional, economic, and social development of towns from the 14th century to the eve of the Reformation, with a particular focus on York, is the most recent and comprehensive as of this writing.

York during the turbulent 16th century provides the focus for PALLISER's study, but this is far more than a narrow study of religious experience during the Reformation. Chapters on civic governance, economic structure, and demographic patterns illuminate a period marked by population decline and financial problems continuing since the late 14th century. While economic recovery began gradually in the 1560s, resurgence coincided with religious challenges. Palliser examines the "lukewarm protestantism" of that period as city governors strove to accommodate the prevailing government but resided within a culture of still-vibrant catholicism.

York's role as the ecclesiastical centre of northern England has been studied from various perspectives. AYLMER & CANT's well-illustrated volume deals not only with York minster as an historical monument but with its corporate life and continuing function as a place of worship. This collection of essays by leading authorities begins with an overview of Christianity during the Roman and Anglo-Saxon periods and the building of the first minster in 627, and continues through the Middle Ages and the challenges of the Reformation. Narrative chapters carry the story of the role of the minster in urban society through to 1975. There are additional chapters on the minster's stained glass, music, monuments, and library. Independent, nonconformist preachers reached York during the 1670s. Few dominated the economic life of the city as much as the Society of Friends, although the city also was a host to baptists, several groups of methodists, Moravians, Sandemanians, and Roman catholics. The experiences of these groups, as well as those of the Church of England, are best studied in the pamphlet-length monographs published as the BORTHWICK PAPERS.

Just as religious houses surrounded the city during the Middle Ages, country houses like Middlethorpe Hall and Castle Howard proliferated during the 18th century, and their wealthy inhabitants turned York into a centre of culture and fashion. The Palladian Assembly Rooms, opened in 1732, provided a venue for entertainment within a building that was extremely influential in the history of architecture. During the 18th century York had hoped that the expansion of the canal system would bring major industry to the city, but the traffic flow, trade, and the water itself went elsewhere. Hope was renewed in the 19th century during the years of railway construction. Today, the railway strikes visitors as a means to visit York, and its history is well-displayed in the city's National Railway Museum. ARMSTRONG studies the social and economic impact of early 19th-century railways on an established county town, in a ground-breaking work of demographic and urban history. His main focus is on the early Victorian period, but he also uses later material, particularly a classic study by B.S. Rowntree of poverty in York (1902). Although – like the canals – the new means of transport and the economic climate in general failed to attract modern, large-scale, progressive industry, York remained an active market town, a hub of communications, and a distribution centre for the rural hinterland. The reputation of its cattle market, flour mills, and confectionery firms remained strong well into the 20th century.

York without its historical character and active preservation movement is almost impossible to contemplate, but respect for ancient monuments did not always characterize its officials or citizenry. MURRAY's study of the York physician William Arthur Evelyn (1860–1935) traces the career of a pioneer of conservation whose efforts preserved many of the walls and buildings that grace the city today. Illustrated with photos from Evelyn's extensive collection of lantern slides, this book reveals an early 20th-century city physically more medieval than modern, poised on the brink of appreciating its past as well as utilizing its heritage for both cultural and economic benefits.

LORRAINE ATTREED

See also Eric Bloodaxe

Youth Culture since 1945

Cohen, Stanley, *Folk Devils and Moral Panics: The Creation of the Mods and Rockers*, London: MacGibbon and Kee, 1972; New York: St Martin's Press, 1980
Hall, Stuart and Tony Jefferson (editors), *Resistance through Rituals: Youth Subcultures in Post-War Britain*, Birmingham: Centre for Contemporary Culture Studies, University of Birmingham, 1975
Hebdige, Dick, *Subculture: The Meaning of Style*, London: Methuen, 1979; London and New York: Routledge, 1988
McRobbie, Angela, *Feminism and Youth Culture: From "Jackie" to "Just Seventeen"*, London: Macmillan, and Boston: Unwin Hyman, 1991; 2nd edition, as *Feminism and Youth Culture*, Basingstoke: Macmillan, and New York: Routledge, 2000
Nelson, Elizabeth, *The British Counter-Culture, 1966–1973: A Study of the Underground Press*, London: Macmillan, and New York: St Martin's Press, 1989
Osgerby, Bill, *Youth in Britain since 1945*, Oxford and Malden, Massachusetts: Blackwell, 1998
Rock, Paul and Stanley Cohen, "The Teddy Boy" in *The Age of Affluence, 1951–1964*, edited by Vernon Bogdanor and Robert Skidelsky, London: Macmillan, 1970
Thornton, Sarah, *Club Cultures: Music, Media, and Subcultural Capital*, Cambridge: Polity Press, 1995; Hanover, New Hampshire: University Press of New England, 1996

Deviant youth subcultures, while representing a only minority of their age group, were a focus of public discussions of the "youth problem" and have tended to dominate subsequent scholarship on adolescence. Policing the behaviour of working-class adolescents was a public concern long before the 20th century; however, the postwar period represents a significant change. One reason was that adolescence was increasingly perceived as a unique phase of life. Structurally, adolescence was first defined as the years between leaving school at age 15 and national service at 18. Postwar prosperity provided this demographic group with disposable income unknown to earlier generations, resulting in the growth of a youth-oriented entertainment industry. The surge in the birth rate during and immediately after the war increased the number of people in this age group. At the same time, the establishment of the welfare state made deviance among young people an increasing concern for psychologists, sociologists, and social workers. Television and other mass media played a major part in the spread of youth culture.

The first working-class deviants to come to light after the war were the Teddy boys of the 1950s, named for their Edwardian-style clothes. In adopting an instantly recognizable uniform, the Teddy boys established a pattern followed by subsequent youth groups. They also created an association in the media between youth, rock music, and violence that would carry through to other subcultures. ROCK & COHEN give the best description of the Teds.

At the beginning of the 1960s, the Teddy boys were supplanted by the mods and the rockers. These groups' different attitudes were reflected in their hairstyles, clothes, music, and use of drugs and led to an adversarial relationship. The mods and the rockers came to national attention through a series of fights at seaside resorts during bank holidays beginning in 1964. As COHEN describes, these fights became the focal point of a debate on the "youth problem" that represented a confluence of rebellion by youth, exaggeration by the media, and overreaction by the public. Cohen's book remains the key text on portrayals of deviant youth culture in the media.

The mid-1960s saw the rise of the "underground" or counter-culture. This group was markedly different from other youth movements. It was overtly political, with roots in the earlier Campaign for Nuclear Disarmament. While many people from the working class participated in the counterculture, its interest in avant-garde music and literature was distinctly middle-class. With the lapse of national service, the definition of "youth" expanded to include people in their twenties, and many former public school and university students took part in the counterculture.

The counterculture was also more articulate than previous groups and published a variety of underground newspapers to disseminate its ideas. While it had no well-defined social or political agenda, it was generally libertarian in outlook. Scholars of youth culture have tended to celebrate the collectivist resistance they read into working-class youth groups; as a result, there is scant work on the counterculture, whose ideology reflected middle-class individualism. NELSON's work is the best in this small field.

The skinheads of the 1960s were proudly working-class and the sartorial opposite of the counterculture. Their hair was closely cropped, and their "uniform" consisted of working boots and braces. The skinhead movement was also the youth group most associated with violence, which included "Paki-bashing" (attacks on immigrants) and hooliganism at football matches.

In the mid-1970s the punk movement emerged. The fashion included dyed hair, ripped clothing, bondage gear, and other accessories calculated to shock. The punk aesthetic also blurred gender lines and allowed much greater participation by girls and women. Originally nihilistic, punk eventually developed some degree of political involvement, challenging racism, poverty, and Thatcherism.

The majority of the work on youth culture has been by sociologists, and the field has been dominated by the "cultural studies" approach advocated by the Centre for Contemporary Cultural Studies (CCCS). The key to this approach is to decode the meaning of fashion, behaviour, and taste to find hidden meanings or sites of resistance to the dominant culture. The collection edited by HALL & JEFFERSON is the best introduction to this school of thought; it includes the early work of those who would go on to define the field, including Dick Hebdige and Angela McRobbie.

HEBDIGE (1988) not only tries to interpret the significance of subcultural style but also looks at the development of youth culture through the relationship between working-class whites and black immigrants. From the racialist violence of the Teddy boys and skinheads to the mods' aspirations to black "hipness" and the punks' appreciation for Rastafarian politics and music, Hebdige illustrates how white working-class youth culture cannot be understood in isolation from issues of race that arose with postwar immigration.

McROBBIE (1991) looks at the experiences of adolescent women in youth culture. Most analysts of youth groups have looked at the male experience, as policing male violence has always been a central issue of policing adolescent behaviour. Because of this, the experiences of women in youth cultures have frequently been undervalued. McRobbie considers the cultural expectations of young women, the roles they created for themselves, and how these were reflected in the media.

While the punk subculture was not particularly violent or politically threatening, it succeeded in outraging public opinion to a degree unmatched by subsequent youth groups. New movements have continued to emerge, but the process of accommodation and marketing has accelerated and now begins as soon as a new youth movement is identified. Although post-punk youth cultures continue to be studied, the arguments are often about authenticity and consumerism rather than resistance. An example is THORNTON's work on the subcultures that grew up around dance clubs in the 1990s. Thornton is especially good at describing the construction of hierarchies within subcultures and the interactions between youth and consumer cultures.

OSGERBY provides a good overview of the history and historiography of postwar youth culture. He also discusses related topics such as race relations, popular music, consumerism, and agencies of social control. His bibliography is an excellent starting-place for those interested in exploring the field further.

CHAD MARTIN

See also Childhood; Consumerism; Music: Popular

Z

Zoological Evolution and Classification

Bowler, Peter J., *The Eclipse of Darwinism: Anti-Darwinian Evolution Theories in the Decades around 1900*, Baltimore: Johns Hopkins University Press, 1983

Bowler, Peter J., *Life's Splendid Drama: Evolutionary Biology and the Reconstruction of Life's Ancestry, 1860–1940*, Chicago: University of Chicago Press, 1996

Desmond, Adrian, *Archetypes and Ancestors: Palaeontology in Victorian London, 1850–1875*, London: Blond and Briggs, 1982; Chicago: University of Chicago Press, 1984

Di Gregorio, Mario A., *T.H. Huxley's Place in Natural Science*, New Haven, Connecticut: Yale University Press, 1984

Gillispie, Charles Coulston, *Genesis and Geology: A Study in the Relations of Scientific Thought, Natural Theology, and Social Opinion in Great Britain, 1790–1850*, Cambridge, Massachusetts: Harvard University Press, 1951

Provine, William B., *The Origins of Theoretical Population Genetics*, Chicago: University of Chicago Press, 1971

Rehbock, Philip F., *The Philosophical Naturalists: Themes in Early Nineteenth-Century British Biology*, Madison, Wisconsin: University of Wisconsin Press, 1983

Winsor, Mary P., *Starfish, Jellyfish, and the Order of Life: Issues in Nineteenth Century Science*, New Haven, Connecticut: Yale University Press, 1976

To some extent the theory of evolution grew out of earlier efforts to classify the relationships between the various forms of life. The modern system of classification had been pioneered by Linnaeus in the mid-18th century, and much effort was devoted to making the system more "natural" by taking all characteristics of an organism into account.

By the early 19th century the French biologist Georges Cuvier had focused on the internal structure of organisms as the best indication of their relationships and had identified four main "types" of animals: vertebrates, molluscs, articulates, and radiates. But for Cuvier each species within a type was a distinct creation, and each was adapted to a particular way of life. The situation was made more complex as worldwide discoveries revealed a host of new creatures, including some which did not fit into accepted categories (the duckbilled platypus has fur but lays eggs). Cuvier also studied fossils, revealing a sequence of populations in geological time. His British followers explained the diversity and the history of life in terms of natural theology, the idea that each species is a divine creation and that each fills its place in the divine plan. Many noted that there was a progress in the fossil record from the simplest animals up to humans, but this was seen as part of the divine plan, not as evidence of evolution.

The conventional view adopted by historians of science was that this image of a divinely planned universe dominated natural history until it was suddenly overthrown by Darwin's more materialistic theory in the 1860s. For Darwin, the similarities between related species are a sign of descent from a common ancestor, and his theory of natural selection was introduced to explain the process of adaptation by which a single original form could diversify into a group of distinct species. Modern historical studies have shown, however, that the transition from the old model of a divinely created universe to the modern Darwinian theory was extremely complex. Natural theology could be made more sophisticated to accommodate the later discoveries. Darwin's was not the first theory of evolution to be widely discussed, and some of the earlier ideas focused on different principles – portraying evolution more as an ascent up a ladder than as a branching tree. *On the Origin of Species*, published in 1859, converted the scientific world to evolutionism; but few accepted the complete theory of natural selection, and alternative explanations continued to flourish into the early 20th century.

A good example of the older view of the pre-Darwinian situation is that offered by GILLISPIE, who focuses on resistance to change on the part of natural theology and its adherents. Later studies have revealed that radical alternatives flourished outside the ranks of respectable Oxbridge naturalists. In particular, the theory of evolution of the French naturalist J.-B. Lamarck was hailed by anatomists such as Robert Grant as the foundation for a materialist world-view. DESMOND explores the debates between conservative and radical accounts of the fossil record, showing how the radicals were held in check until after Darwin published. In part the conservatives suceeded because they could modernize the idea of design to include more sophisticated models of creation. REHBOCK provides an account of the "philosophical naturalists" who did this, but he also includes some who wanted to find explanations in natural terms without sinking into complete materialism. Much technical work was done in the area of classification without introducing the theory of evolution, and the book by WINSOR on invertebrate taxonomy provides an insight into these developments. Desmond also notes a popular book by Robert Chambers, *Vestiges of Creation* (1844), which made an influential attempt to interest the middle class in the idea of progressive evolution.

T.H. Huxley, soon to become one of Darwin's leading supporters, was deeply involved in these debates and was at first hostile to evolutionism. DI GREGORIO explores how Huxley gradually accommodated the theory to his biological work and notes how this work constrained Huxkey's support for Darwin. Huxley never accepted the selection theory wholeheartedly and continued to believe that evolution took place by sudden jumps or saltations. BOWLER (1983) has shown that the majority of naturalists in the late 19th-century preferred non-Darwinian explanations of evolution, including saltationism, Lamarck's theory of the inheritance of acquired characteristics, and orthogenesis (evolution in straight lines). These theories did not necessarily support Darwin's view of branching adaptive evolution and often portayed the history of life as a complex bush with many branches advancing in parallel. The complexity of the resulting debates in classification and palaeontology is highlighted in the later chapters of Desmond's book and in BOWLER (1996). Both authors describe how many of the theories were intended to show that evolution was a more directed and more purposeful process than natural selection would allow, thus preserving some elements of the old teleological view of creation.

Darwin's *Origin of Species* thus had a more limited effect than historians used to imagine. It converted the world to evolutionism but left the mechanism of change open to debate because few accepted Darwin's claim that natural selection was the main process involved. This has often been overlooked because of the subsequent success of the selection theory in the 20th century. At the time there were many debates over the plausibility of selection and alternatives such as Lamarckism, described in Bowler (1983). Eventually a group of biologists opposed to Lamarckism began to explore the idea that heredity works by transmitting unit characters from one generation to the next. This was originally inspired by saltationism, and almost all the founders of Mendelian genetics in the early years of the 20th century were originally saltationists. There is a vast literature on the origins of genetics and the process by which the theory was eventually synthesized with Darwinism in the 1920s and 1930s. Perhaps the best general survey is still the book by PROVINE, who shows how the modern theory of natural selection was created by the development of population genetics.

PETER J. BOWLER

See also Biological Sciences; Darwin; Evolution Controversy

NOTES ON CONTRIBUTORS

Adams, R.J.Q. Texas A & M University.

Adams, Simon. Reader in History, University of Strathclyde. Author of *Leicester and the Court: Essays on Elizabethan Politics* (2002). Editor of *Household Accounts and Disbursement Books of Robert Dudley, Earl of Leicester* (1995). Coeditor (with M.J. Rodríguez-Salgado) of *England, Spain, and the Gran Armada 1585–1604* (1991). Contributor to *The Oxford Illustrated History of Tudor and Stuart Britain*, edited by John Morrill (1996); and *The Sixteenth Century, 1485–1603* (The Short Oxford History of the British Isles), edited by Patrick Collinson (2001). Also contributed articles to *English Historical Review, Scottish Historical Review*, and *Archives*.

Addis, Bill. Lecturer, Department of Construction Management and Engineering, University of Reading. Author of *Structural Engineering: The Nature of Theory and Design* (1990). Coauthor (with Derek Walker) of *Happold: The Confidence to Build* (1997). Editor of *Structural and Civil Engineering Design* (1999). Contributor to *Structure and Style*, edited by Michael Stratton (1997). Also contributed articles to *Journal of the International Association for Shell and Spatial Structures, Structural Engineering, International Journal of Engineering Education*, and *History of Technology*, among others.

Albala, Ken. Associate Professor and Chair of the History Department, University of the Pacific, Stockton, California. Author of *Eating Right in the Renaissance* (2002) and *Food in Early Modern Europe* (2003). Contributor to *The Cambridge World History of Food*, edited by Kenneth F. Kiple and Kriemhild Coneè Ornelas (2000). Series Editor of *Food Culture around the Globe* (forthcoming).

Allan, David. Lecturer in Scottish History, University of St Andrews. Author of *Virtue, Learning, and the Scottish Enlightenment* (1993); *Philosophy and Politics in Later Stuart Scotland* (2000); and *Scotland in the Eighteenth Century* (2002). Also contributed articles to *Historical Journal, Journal of Ecclesiastical History, History of European Ideas*, and *Scottish Historical Review*, among others.

Allen, Rick. Principal Lecturer in English and Director of Studies in Humanities and Arts, Anglia Polytechnic University, Cambridge. Author of *The Moving Pageant: A Literary Sourcebook on London Street-Life, 1700–1914* (1998). Also

contributed articles to *Victorian Studies, Journal of Victorian Culture*, and *Dickens Quarterly*, among others.

Almond, Richard. Senior Tutor, Darlington College of Technology. Author of *Medieval Hunting* (2003). Contributor of articles to *Past and Present, Medieval History, Medieval Life*, and *Deer*.

Anderson, R.D. Professor of Modern History, University of Edinburgh. Author of *Education and Opportunity in Victorian Scotland* (1983), *The Student Community at Aberdeen 1860–1939* (1988), *Universities and Elites in Britain since 1800* (1992), *Education and the Scottish People 1750–1918* (1995), and numerous similar articles. Currently working on a history of European universities from the Enlightenment to 1914.

Archer, John E. Reader in History, Edge Hill College of Higher Education in Lancashire. Author of *"By a Flash and a Scare": Arson, Animal Maiming, and Poaching in East Anglia 1815–1870* (1990); and *Social Unrest and Popular Protest in England 1780–1840* (2000). Contributed chapters to *The Unquiet Countryside*, edited by G.E. Mingay (1989); *Crime, Protest, and Police in Modern British Society*, edited by D.W. Howell and K.O. Morgan (1999); and two volumes on violence edited by E. Stanko (2002 and 2003). Journal articles have also appeared in *Agricultural History Review, Economic History Review*, and *British Journal of Criminology*.

Arkenberg, Jerome S. Lecturer, Department of History, California State University, Fullerton. Editor of *The Naked Past: Revealing Records of Human History* (1999) and *The Medieval Ecumene: A Comparative Florilegium* (1998). Contributor to *The Historical Dictionary of Late Medieval England 1272–1485*, edited by Ronald H. Fritze (forthcoming); and *The Late Medieval Age of Crisis and Renewal, 1300–1500*, edited by Clayton J. Drees (2001). Also contributed articles to *Historia, Harvard Library Bulletin*, and *ORB*.

Armstrong, John. Professor of Business History, Thames Valley University, London. Author of *Business Documents: Their Origins, Sources, and Uses in Historical Research* (1987). Coeditor (with Stephanie Jones) of *Coastal and Short Sea Shipping* (1996), and *Journal of Transport History 1990–2001*. Also contributed articles to *Business History, International Journal of Maritime History, London Journal*, and *Mariner's*

Mirror, among others. Research interests include business and transport history from the 18th to the 20th centuries.

Arnstein, Walter L. Professor of History Emeritus, University of Illinois at Urbana-Champaign. Author of numerous books and articles including *The Bradlaugh Case* (1965), *Protestant versus Catholic in Mid-Victorian England* (1982), *Britain Yesterday and Today: 1830 to The Present* (8th ed., 2001), and *Queen Victoria* (2003). Also contributed articles to the journals *Historical Research, Victorian Studies,* and *Albion,* among others.

Aster, Sidney. Professor of History, University of Toronto, Ontario. Author of *1939: The Making of the Second World War* (1973), and *Anthony Eden: A Biography* (1976). Editor of *The "X"Documents by A.P. Young: The Secret History of Foreign Office Contacts with the German Resistance, 1937–1939* (1974); *The Second World War as a National Experience* (1981); *A.P. Young, Die X-Dokumente: Die geheimen Kontakte Carl Goerdelers mit der britischen Regierung, 1938–1939* (1989); and *British Foreign Policy, 1918–1945: A Guide to Research and Research Materials* (1991). Contributor to *Lloyd George: Twelve Essays,* edited by A.J.P. Taylor (1971); *Paths to War: New Essays on the Origins of the Second World War,* edited by Robert Boyce and Esmonde M. Robertson (1989); *Power, Personalities, and Policies,* edited by Michael Graham Fry (1992); *Diplomatic Documents and Their Users,* edited by John Hilliker and Mary Halloran (1995); *Military Planning and the Origins of the Second World War,* edited by B.J.C. McKercher and Roch Legault (2000); *All Souls and Appeasement: A Portrait with Documents, 1937–1939* (forthcoming); and *Leadership and Responsibility in the Second World War,* edited by Brian Farrell (forthcoming). Also a contributor to the journal *Diplomacy and Statecraft.*

Aston, Nigel. Lecturer in Early Modern History, University of Leicester. Author of *The End of an Elite: The French Bishops and the Coming of Revolution* (1992), *Christianity and Revolutionary Europe 1750–1830* (2002), and *Christianity after the Reformation: From Public Culture to Private Belief* (forthcoming). Editor of *Religious Change in Europe, 1650–1914* (1997).

Attreed, Lorraine. Associate Professor of History, College of the Holy Cross, Worcester, Massachusetts. Author of *The King's Towns: Identity and Survival in Late Medieval English Boroughs* (2001). Editor of *The York House Books, 1461–1490* (1991). Contributor to *Perspectives on Audiovisuals in the Teaching of History,* edited by Susan Gillespie (1999); and *American Historical Association's Guide to Historical Literature,* edited by Mary Beth Norton (3rd ed., 1995). Also contributed articles to *Journal of Interdisciplinary History, Speculum, Journal of British Studies,* and *Mediterranean Studies.*

Balch-Lindsay, V. Suzanne. Associate Professor, Department of History, Eastern New Mexico University.

Barton, Patricia S. Honorary Research Fellow, University of Strathclyde, Glasgow. Contributor to *Britain in the Hanoverian Age, 1714–1837: An Encyclopedia,* edited by Gerald Newman (1997).

Bayer, Gerd. Lecturer, Department of Modern Languages and Literatures, Case Western Reserve University, Cleveland, Ohio. Doctoral candidate, Department of English, Friedrich-Alexander-Universität, Erlangen-Nürnberg, Germany. Research interests include 20th-century literature and postcolonial discourse studies. Contributed articles to the journals *Arachne, Journal of Popular Culture,* and *Journal of Cultural Studies.*

Beal, Joan Christine. Director of the National Centre for English Cultural Tradition, University of Sheffield. Author of *English Pronunciation in the Eighteenth Century: Thomas Spence's "Grand Repository of the English Language"* (1999). Contributor to *The Edinburgh History of the Scots Language,* edited by Charles Jones (1997); and *Real English: The Grammar of English Dialects in the British Isles,* edited by James and Lesley Milroy (1993). Also contributed articles to the journals *English Language and Literature, Language and Style,* and *Transactions of the Philological Society.*

Beam, Aki Chandra Li. Doctoral candidate, Department of History, McMaster University, Hamilton, Ontario. Dissertation in progress on women and old age in early modern England.

Beaven, Brad. Senior Lecturer in Social History, University of Portsmouth. Author of *The Pleasure Seekers: Working-Class Male Leisure, 1850–1945* (forthcoming). Contributor to *Popular Culture and the Motor Car in the Twentieth Century Car,* edited by David Thomas *et al.* (1998). Also contributed articles to the journals *Midland History, Northern History, Business Archives,* and *Urban History,* among others.

Beckett, Ian F.W. Major-General Matthew C. Horner Distinguished Professor of Military Theory, U.S. Marine Corps University, Virginia. Chairman of the Army Records Society (U.K.). Author of *The Great War, 1914–18* (2001) and *Modern Insurgencies and Counter-Insurgencies* (2001). Coeditor (with David Chandler) of *The Oxford History of the British Army* (1996).

Bennett, G.H. Lecturer in History, University of Plymouth. Author of *British Foreign Policy during the Curzon Period, 1919–24* (1995) and coauthor (with R. Bennett) of *Survivors: British Merchant Seamen in the Second World War* (1999).

Bennett, Martyn. Reader in History and Director of the School of Graduate Studies Research, Faculty of Humanities, Nottingham Trent University. Research interests include formation of a "united kingdom" (1590–1720), early modern wars and civil wars in Britain and Ireland, and local government and administration. Publications include *The Civil Wars Experienced* (2000), *The Civil Wars of Britain and Ireland 1637–1651,* (1997) and *A Nottinghamshire Village in War and Peace: The Accounts of the Constables of Upton 1640–1666,* (1995). Currently writing a biography of Oliver Cromwell for Routledge.

Benneworth, Paul Stephen. ESRC Postdoctoral Research Fellow at the Centre for Urban and Regional Development Studies, University of Newcastle upon Tyne. Author of *Regional Development Agencies: The Early Years* (2001). Also contributed articles to *Regional Studies, Enterprise and Innovation Management Studies, Local Economy, European Planning Studies,* and *Journal of Environment Planning and Management.*

Bill, Jan. Senior researcher at the Centre for Maritime Archaeology at the National Museum of Denmark, Roskilde. External lecturer at University of Aarhus. One of several authors of *Danish History of Seafaring.* Research interests include the Viking age, medieval seafaring, and maritime aspects of medieval society in general.

Botley, Paul. Independent scholar based in Farnborough, Hampshire.

Bowler, Peter J. Professor of the History of Science, Queen's University, Belfast. Author of *Evolution: The History of an Idea* (1983), *Charles Darwin: The Man and His Influence* (1990), and numerous other books on the history of evolution theory and related topics.

Bowyer, Michael J. F. Independent writer on aviation. Author of *The Battle of Britain: 50 Years On* (1990); *2 Group RAF: A Complete History, 1936–1945* (1974); *The Stirling Bomber* (1980); and *Action Stations* (1979). Coauthor (with C. Martin Sharp) of *"Mosquito"* (1967). Contributor of numerous articles to aviation journals and magazines.

Boyd, Kelly. Senior Lecturer in History and American Studies, Middlesex University, London. Author of *Manliness and the Boys' Story Paper in Britain: A Cultural History, 1855–1940* (2003). Editor of the *Encyclopedia of Historians and Historical Writing* (1999).

Braddick, Michael J. Professor of History, University of Sheffield. Author of *Parliamentary Taxation in Seventeenth Century England* (1994), *The Nerves of State* (1996), and *State Formation in Early Modern England* (2000). Editor (with John Walter) of *Negotiating Power in Early Modern Society* (2001) and (with David Armitage) of *The British Atlantic World, 1500–1800* (2002). Contributor to *The Origins of Empire: British Overseas Enterprise to the Close of the Seventeenth Century,* edited by Nicholas Canny (Oxford History of the British Empire, vol. 1, 1998). Also contributed articles to the journals *Social History, Historical Journal, Comparative Studies in Society and History, Northern History,* and *Huntington Library Quarterly.*

Braddock, Robert C. Professor of History, Saginaw Valley State University, University Center, Michigan. Contributor to *Recent Historians of Great Britain,* edited by Walter L. Arnstein (1990); *Historical Dictionary of Tudor England, 1485–1603,* edited by Ronald H. Fritze (1991); and *Oxford Dictionary of National Biography* (forthcoming). Also contributed articles and reviews to the journals *Albion, Journal of British Studies, Renaissance Quarterly,* and *Sixteenth Century Journal.*

Brand, Paul. Senior Research Fellow, All Souls College, University of Oxford. Author of *The Making of the Common Law* (1992) and *The Origins of the English Legal Profession* (1992). Editor of *The Earliest English Law Reports,* vols 1 and 2 (1995–56). Also contributed articles to *Irish Jurist, Irish Historical Studies, Historical Research, English Historical Review, Law and History,* and *American Journal of Legal History,* among others.

Braun, Lindsay Frederick. Doctoral candidate, Department of History, Rutgers University, New Brunswick, New Jersey. Research interests include British imperial science and technology and its application during the nineteenth century, with special reference to geography and cartography in southern and central Africa.

Breslow, Boyd. Associate Professor of History, Florida Atlantic University, Boca Raton. Author of *Social and Economic Interests of Richer de Refham, Lord Mayor of London, The Ambiguities of Political Loyalties in Edwardian England,* and *London Merchants and the Origins of the House of Commons.*

Brett, Peter. Senior Lecturer in History, St Martin's College, Carlisle, U.K. Author of *The Grey Monument in Newcastle upon Tyne* (University of Teesside, 2001). Contributed articles on early 19th-century popular politics to the journals *History, Northern History,* and *Southern History.*

Breuninger, Scott. C. Doctoral candidate, University of Wisconsin, Madison.

Bridges, Roy. Emeritus Professor of History, University of Aberdeen and President of the Hakluyt Society. Author of *People and Places in Newmachar Past and Present* (2001). Editor of and contributor to *Compassing the Vaste Globe of the Earth* (1996) and *Imperialism, Decolonization, and Africa* (2000).

Brown, Anthony E. Reader Emeritus, University of Leicester, formerly Staff Tutor in Archaeology, Department of Adult Education. Author of *Fieldwork for Archaeologists and Local Historians* (1987), *Early Daventry: A Study in Early Landscape Planning* (1991), co-author (with Glenn Foard) of *The Making of a County History: John Bridges' Northamptonshire* (1994). Also editor of several volumes of essays and author of numerous papers on archaeological topics and of a number of entries in the *New Dictionary of National Biography* (forthcoming).

Brown, John. Senior Lecturer in History, University of Edinburgh. Author of *The British Welfare State: A Critical History* (1995). Contributed articles to *Scottish Historical Review, Economic History Review,* and *Bulletin of the Institute of Historical Research,* among others.

Brunsman, Denver Alexander. Doctoral candidate, Department of History, Princeton University, New Jersey. Research interests include British naval *impressment,* 18th-century Anglo-American crowds, and early American political and social development.

Buchanan, Carl Jay. Assistant Professor of English, University of Tennessee, Martin. Author of *Ripper!, A Book of Poems* (1999). Published poems in over one hundred journals.

Contributor to *A Century Less Than a Dream,* edited by Scott Connors (forthcoming). Also contributed articles to both print and online journals on contemporary poets, the H.P. Lovecraft circle, science fiction, and other topics.

Buckley, John. Senior Lecturer in History and War Studies, University of Wolverhampton. Author of several books on air power, including *Air Power in the Age of Total War* (1999).

Burns, William Earl. Historian based in Washington, D.C. Author of *An Age of Wonders: Prodigies, Providence, and Politics in England, 1657–1727* (2002) and *The Scientific Revolution: An Encyclopedia* (2001). Also contributed articles to the journals *Albion, Harvard Theological Review, The Seventeenth Century, The Sixteenth Century Journal,* and *Eighteenth-Century Women* and several articles to the *New Dictionary of National Biography,* edited by Brian Harrison.

Butt, John J. Professor of History, James Madison University, Harrisonburg, Virginia. Author of *Daily Life in the Age of Charlemagne* (forthcoming). Research interests include medieval and early modern European agricultural and economic development.

Calkins, Susanna. Assistant Professor, University of Louisville, Kentucky. Contributor to *New Dictionary of National Biography,* edited by Brian Harrison (forthcoming); and *Twentieth Century World Leaders* (1999).

Campbell, Julie D. Assistant Professor of English, Eastern Illinois University, Charleston. Contributed to *Critical Approaches to English Prose Fiction, 1520–1640,* edited by Donald Beecher (1998). Also contributed articles to the journals *Biography, Women's Writing,* and *Shakespeare Yearbook.*

Campbell-Kease, John. Independent writer on heraldry. Fellow of the Society of Antiquaries of Scotland. Author of *A Companion to Local History Research* (1989) and *Aspects of Heraldry* (2001). Contributor to *A New Dictionary of Heraldry,* edited by Stephen Friar (1987). Contributor to *New Dictionary of National Biography,* edited by Brian Harrison (forthcoming). Author of numerous articles in the journals *Double Treasure* and *Coat of Arms;* was for many years Managing Editor of the latter.

Capet, Antoine. Fellow of the Royal Historical Society, Professor of British Civilization, University of Rouen. Author of *Le poids des années de guerre: Les classes dirigeantes britanniques et la réforme sociale, 1931–1951* (1992). Also contributed articles and chapters on Britain in World War II to French journals and books. Edited several collections of essays on contemporary Britain. Editor of "Britian since 1914" in *Annual Bibliography of the Royal Historical Society* and *Revue Française de Civilisation Britannique.*

Carlin, Norah. Principal Lecturer in History, Middlesex University, London. Author of *The Causes of the English Civil War* (1999). Contributor to *Representing Ireland: Literature and the Origins of Conflict, 1534–1660,* edited by Brendan

Bradshaw *et al.* (1993); and to *Tolerance and Intolerance in the European Reformation,* edited by and Ole P. Grell and Bob Scribner (1996). Also contributed articles to *Historical Journal.*

Carpenter, Stanley D.M. Professor of Strategy and Policy, U.S. Naval War College, Newport, Rhode Island. Author of *"The Genius of This Age": Military Leadership in the British Civil Wars, 1642–1651* (forthcoming). Also contributed articles to *New Dictionary of National Biography,* edited by Brian Harrison (forthcoming); *Blackwell's Companion to the Eighteenth Century; Encyclopedia of Warfare; Encyclopedia of World War II; Encyclopedia of World War I; History of Late Medieval England, 1258–1485; Encyclopedia of the War of 1812,* edited by David S. and Jeanne T. Heidler (1997); *Britain in the Hanoverian Age, 1714–1837,* edited by Gerald Newman (1997); and *Historical Dictionary of Stuart Britain, 1603–1689* (1996).

Carr, Antony David. Professor of Medieval Welsh History, University of Wales, Bangor. Author of *Medieval Anglesey* (1982), *Owen of Wales: The End of the House of Gwynedd* (1991), and *Medieval Wales* (1995). Contributor to several edited collections and to various journals, including *Welsh History Review* and *Transactions of the Honourable Society of Cymmrodorion.*

Carroll, Francis M. Senior Scholar, St John's College, University of Manitoba, Winnipeg. Author of *American Opinion and the Irish Question, 1910–1923* (1978) and coauthor (with Franklin R. Raiter) of *The Fires of Autumn* (1990). Editor of *American Commission on Irish Independence, 1919* (1985). Contributor to *Crossroads in Time: A History of Carlton County, Minnesota* (1987).

Carter, P.R.N. Teaches history at Appleby College, Oakville, Canada. An authority on the Reformation in early modern England. Completed a PhD at Cambridge University and has held teaching and research posts at McMaster University (Hamilton, Canada) and the University of St Andrews (Scotland). He is the author of a number of published articles on royal taxation, government administration, and the English church.

Chamberlain, Muriel E. Professor Emeritus, University of Wales, Swansea. Author of *Britain and India: The Interaction of Two Peoples* (1974); *The Scramble for Africa* (1974); *British Foreign Policy in the Age of Palmerston* (1980); *Lord Aberdeen: A Political Biography* (1983); *Pax Britannica? British Foreign Policy, 1789–1914* (1988); and (with others) *Longman Companion to European Decolonisation in the Twentieth Century* (1998), among other works. Associate Editor of *New Dictionary of National Biography* (forthcoming), joint Editor of *Historical Association Studies* series, and Editor of *Historian.*

Chase, Malcolm. Reader in Labour History, School of Continuing Education, University of Leeds. Author of *"The People's Farm": English Radical Agrarianism, 1775–1840* (1988), and *Early Trade Unionism: Fraternity, Skill, and the Politics of Labour* (2000). Also contributed articles to the journals *English Historical Review, Labour History Review, Oral*

History, and *Past and Present.* Current research interests include writing a narrative history of the Chartist movement.

Chinn, Carl. Senior Lecturer in Modern History and Community Historian, University of Birmingham. Author of *They Worked All Their Lives: Women of the Urban Poor in England 1880–1939* (1988); *Better Betting with a Decent Feller: Bookmakers, Betting, and the British Working Class 1750–1990* (1991); and *Poverty amidst Prosperity: The Urban Poor in England 1840–1914* (1995).

Clark, James G. Lecturer in History, Department of Historical Studies, University of Bristol. Research focuses on monastic life and learning in the later Middle Ages. Publications include articles in the *English Historical Review* and *Speculum.* Editor of *The Religious Orders in Pre-Reformation England* (2002). Author of *Monastic Learning in Late Medieval England* (forthcoming from Oxford University Press).

Clayton, David William. Lecturer, Department of History, University of York. Author of *Imperialism Revisited: Political and Economic Relations between Britain and China, 1950–1954* (1997). Contributor to *Asia Pacific Dynamism, 1550–2000,* edited by A.J.H. Latham and Heita Kawakatsu (2000).

Coakley, Jean. Associate Professor of English, Miami University, Oxford, Ohio. Research focuses on Arthurian legend and the social, political, religious, prophetic, and marketing contexts of four early medieval Gawain romances composed near Carlisle and their relationship to St Mary's Cathedral.

Coates, Simon. House of Commons Library. Formerly British Academy Postdoctoral Research Fellow, King's College London. Research interests are the cultural and ecclesiastical history of early medieval Europe. Published articles on the episcopate, saints' cults, monasticism, and gender in Anglo-Saxon England and Merovingian Gaul. Also a contributor to numerous historical dictionaries and atlases.

Cohen, Michèle. Professor of Humanities, Richmond College, American International University, London. Author of *Fashioning Masculinity: National Identity and Language in the Eighteenth Century* (1996). Editor (with Tim Hitchcock) of and contributor to *English Masculinities 1660– 1800* (1999). Contributor to *Failing Boys? Issues in Gender and Achievement,* edited by Debbie Epstein *et al.* (1998); and *Private and Public: Studies in the History of Knowledge and of Education,* edited by Richard Aldrich, (forthcoming 2003). Also contributed articles to the journals *History of Education* and *Changing English.*

Cole, Robert C. Professor of History, Utah State University, Logan. Author of *Britain and the War of Words in Neutral Europe, 1939–1945: The Art of the Possible* (1990), *A.J.P. Taylor: The Traitor within the Gates* (1993), and *Propaganda in Twentieth Century War and Politics: An Annotated Bibliography* (1996). Also contributed articles to the journals *Eire-Ireland, Albion,* and *Historical Journal of Film, Radio, and Television.* Research interests include modern British political history, 20th-century war and political propaganda, and propaganda and Anglo-American relations with neutral Ireland in World War II.

Coleby, Andrew M. Priest-in-Charge, All Saints', Didcot. Fellow of the Royal Historical Society. Author of *Central Government and the Localities: Hampshire 1649–1689* (1987). Contributor of articles to *Historical Journal* and *Christianity and History.*

Connolly, Margaret. Lecturer, Department of English, University College Cork. Author of *Contemplations of the Dread and Love of God* (1994) and *John Shirley: Book Production and the Noble Household in Fifteenth-Century England* (1998). Contributor of articles to the journals *Notes and Queries, Scottish Historical Review, British Library Journal,* and *Trivium,* among others.

Corrigan, Karen P. Lecturer, Centre for Research in Linguistics, University of Newcastle. Contributor to *Dàn do Oide,* edited by A. Ahlquist and V. D. Čapková (1997). Also contributor to the journals *Irish University Review* and *English World-Wide.*

Cosgrove, Richard. University Distinguished Professor of History and Department Head, University of Arizona, Tucson. Author of *The Rule of Law: Albert Venn Dicey, Victorian Jurist* (1980); *Our Lady the Common Law: An Anglo-American Legal Community, 1870–1930* (1987); and *Scholars of the Law: English Jurisprudence from Blackstone to Hart* (1996).

Coupland, Philip M. Completed a PhD in the Department of History at the University of Warwick in 2000 and is currently working on the project "The Churches and European Integration" at the University of Glasgow. Contributor of articles on contemporary British political history to *Journal of Contemporary History, Twentieth Century British History,* and other publications.

Cowie, Evelyn. Formerly at King's College London. Author of *Examining the Evidence: Nineteenth Century England and Education* (1973) and (with Leonard Cowie) *"That One Idea": Nathaniel Woodard and His Schools* (1991). Also a contributor to the journal *History of Education.*

Cowie, Leonard. Formerly at King's College London. Author of *Seventeenth-Century Europe* (1960), *Eighteenth-Century Europe* (1963), *Hanoverian England* (1967), *The Reformation* (1973), and *Sixteenth-Century Europe* (1977).

Cox, D.C. Lecturer in History, University of Keele. Author of *The Battle of Evesham: A New Account* (1988). Editor of *Sir Stephen Glynne's Church Notes for Shropshire* (1997). Contributor to the journal *Victorian History of Shropshire.*

Croft, Pauline. Reader, Early Modern History, Royal Holloway, University of London. Editor of *Patronage, Culture, and Power: The Early Cecils 1558–1612* (2002) and of Robert Cecil's confidential treatises to James I (Royal Historical Society Camden Miscellany 1990). Also contributed articles on Robert Cecil to *Economic History Review, History Journal,* and *TRHS.*

Cunningham, Hugh. Professor of Social History, University of Kent at Canterbury. Author of *The Children of the Poor: Representations of Childhood since the Seventeenth Century* (1991) and *Children and Childhood in Western Society since*

1500 (1995). Editor (with Pier Paolo Viazzo) of *Child Labour in Historical Perspective 1800–1985: Case Studies from Europe, Japan, and Colombia* (1996). Contributor to *Child Labour: Policy Options,* edited by Kristoffel Lieten and Ben White (2001). Also contributed articles to *Past and Present, American Historical Review,* and *Economic History Review.*

Curran, Cynthia. Associate Professor of History, College of St Benedict/St John's University, St Joseph, Minnesota. Author of *When First I Began My Life Anew: Middle-Class Widows in 19th-Century Britain* (2000). Contributor to *Encyclopedia of Colonialism* and *Encyclopedia of the Victorian Era* (both forthcoming); contributor of articles and reviews for *Albion.*

Dales, D.J. Chaplain and Head of Religious Studies, Marlborough College, Wiltshire. Author of *Dunstan: Saint and Statesman* (1988) and *Light to the Isles: Missionary Theology in Celtic and Anglo-Saxon Britain* (1997).

Daniell, David. Emeritus Professor, University of London. Author of *The Critics Debate: The Tempest* (1989), Introduction to *Tyndale's New Testament 1536* (1989), Introduction to *Tyndale's Old Testament* (1992), *William Tyndale: A Biography* (1994), and *Julius Caesar: The Arden Shakespeare* (1998). Editor of and wrote the introduction to William Tyndale's *The Obedience of a Christian Man* (2000), among others. Formerly Editor of *The Year's Work in English Studies* and *Reformation I and II.*

Davies, John Reuben. North East Wales Institute of Higher Education, Wrexham. Author of *The Book of Llandaf and the Norman Church in Wales* (2003). Contributor to *Local Saints and Local Churches in the Early Medieval West,* edited by A.T. Thacker and R. Sharpe (2002).

de Chadarevian, Soraya. Senior Research Associate and Affiliated Lecturer, Department of History and Philosophy of Science, University of Cambridge. Author of *Zwischen den Diskursen. Merleau-Ponty und die Wissenschaften* (1990), *Designs for Life: Molecular Biology after World War II* (2002), and (with Harmke Kamminga) *Representations of the Double Helix* (exhibition catalogue, 2002). Coeditor (with Harmke Kamminga) of *Molecularizing Biology and Medicine: New Strategies and Alliances, 1910s–1970s* (1998) and (with Nick Hopwood) of *Models: The Third Dimension of Science* (in press). Contributor to numerous volumes and journals. Associate editor of *Studies in History and Philosophy of Biological and Biomedical Sciences.*

Deacon, Bernard. Lecturer in Cornish Studies, Institute of Cornish Studies, University of Exeter. Author (with Garry Tregidga and Dick Cole) of *MK and Cornish Nationalism* (2003). Coeditor (with Michelle Winslow) of *Family and Community History.* Has published widely in the field of Cornish Studies and recently contributed articles to *Rural History* and *Cornish Studies.*

deVries, Jacqueline R. Associate Professor of History and Women's Studies, Augsburg College, Minneapolis, Minnesota. Contributor to *Women Preachers and Prophets through Two Millennia of Christianity,* edited by Beverly Mayne Kienzle and Pamela J. Walker (1998); and *Borderlines: Genders and Identities in War and Peace, 1870–1930,* edited by Billie Melman (1998). Author of numerous book reviews.

Dewey, Peter. Reader in Economic History, Royal Holloway, University of London. Author of *British Agriculture in the First World War* (1989) and *War and Progress: Britain 1914–1945* (1997). Research interests include the history of the British agricultural engineering industry.

Dickinson, H.T. Richard Lodge Professor of British History, University of Edinburgh. Author and editor of many books, including *Bolingbroke* (1970), *Liberty and Property: Political Ideology in Eighteenth-Century Britain* (1977), and *The Politics of the People in Eighteenth-Century Britain* (1995). Contributor to numerous books and journals, and formerly editor of the journal *History.*

Ditchfield, G.M. Reader in Eighteenth-Century History, University of Kent at Canterbury. Author of *The Evangelical Revival* (1998) and *George III: An Essay in Monarchy* (2002). Coeditor (with David Hayton and Clyve Jones) of *British Parliamentary Lists 1660–1800* (1995). Also contributed many articles on 18-century British history to books and journals.

DiVanna, Joseph A. Author, management consultant, independent writer, and researcher whose interests include medieval architecture, medieval history, and the evolution of technology. Director of the research project on the construction of the fan vaulting of King's College Chapel, Cambridge, England. Contributing author to the INSCRIPTION database of the Forum on Information Standards in Heritage (FISH) maintained by the Museum Documentation Association.

Donnachie, Ian. Senior Lecturer in History and Staff Tutor Arts, The Open University in Scotland, Edinburgh. Author (with George Hewitt) of *Historic New Lanark* (1993) and *Robert Owen: Owen of New Lanark and New Harmony* (2000), among other works. Contributed articles to *Economic History Review, Explorations in Entrepreneurial History, Scottish Economic and Social History, Scottish Historical Review,* and many other publications on 18th- and 19th-century social and economic history.

Dorey, Peter. Senior Lecturer in Politics, Cardiff University. Author of *British Politics since 1945* (1995), *The Conservative Party and the Trade Unions* (1995), *Wage Politics in Britain: The Rise and Fall of Incomes Policies since 1945* (2001), *The Labour Party and Constitutional Reform* (2003), and *Policy-Making in Britain* (forthcoming, 2004). Editor of *The Major Premiership: Politics and Policies under John Major* (1999) and *The 1964–1970 Labour Governments* (forthcoming, 2004).

Doyle, Barry M. Reader in History, School of Arts and Media, University of Teesside. Author of a forthcoming book on the social history of 20-century Britain. Contributor to *Cambridge Urban History of Britain, 1840–1950,* vol. 3, edited by Martin Daunton (2000). Also contributed articles to the journals *Historical Journal, Urban History,* and *Historical Journal of*

Film, Radio, and Television. Book review editor of *Urban History.*

Dreher, Nan H. Upper-school history teacher, Holton-Arms School for Girls, Bethesda, Maryland. Author of articles published in *World History Bulletin* (2000), *Albion* (1997), and *Victorian Periodicals Review* (1993), as well as various book reviews and encyclopedia articles.

Dudley, Martin R. Rector of the Priory Church of St Bartholomew the Great, City of London. Author of numerous books including *A Herald Voice: The Word of God in Advent and Christmas* (2000) and *The Collect in Anglican Liturgy: Texts and Sources 1549–1989* (1994). Contributor to *Unity and Diversity in the Church,* edited by Robert Swanson (1996); and *The Liturgy of the Medieval Church,* edited by E. Ann Matter and Thomas Heffernan (2001).

Duncan, David J. Reference Librarian, Humanities; and Assistant Professor, University Libraries, Wichita State University, Wichita, Kansas. Has contributed articles to *Arab Studies Quarterly* and *Bulletin of Bibliography.* Research interests include the history of books and printing and cross-cultural connections within the medieval world.

Dunn, Richard. Editor, *The British Museum.* Research interests include Elizabethan astrology and the history of British globes.

Edgington, Susan B. Lecturer in Further, Higher, and Adult Education, and Research Associate at the Open University, Milton Keynes. Author of *The First Crusade* (1996); coauthor and cotranslator (with Thomas S. Asbridge) of *Walter the Chancellor's The Antiochene Wars* (1999); and coeditor (with Sarah Lambert) of *Gendering the Crusades* (2001); has also written many essays and articles. Main research interests include the Crusades and medieval medicine.

Ellenberger, Nancy W. Professor of History, U.S. Naval Academy, Annapolis, Maryland. Contributed articles on the late Victorian aristocracy to *Albion, Victorian Studies,* and *Journal of British Studies.*

Ellis, Sylvia. Senior Lecturer, Department of History, University of Northumbria, Newcastle upon Tyne. Author of *Britain, America, and Vietnam* (forthcoming). Contributor to *The Insular Dream,* edited by Kristiaan Versluys (1995); *Student Protest: The Sixties and After,* edited by Gerard J. DeGroot (1998); and *Twentieth Century Anglo-American Relations,* edited by Jonathan Hollowell (2001).

Elston, Timothy G. Doctoral candidate, Department of History, University of Nebraska, Lincoln. Contributor to *High and Mighty Queens of Early Modern England: Representations and Realities,* edited by Carole Levin, Jo Eldridge Carney, and Debra Barrett-Graves (2003). Research interests are gender and the religious and educational history of late medieval and early modern England.

Emms, Richard. Retired schoolteacher based in Norfolk. Contributor to *Canterbury and the Norman Conquest,* edited by Richard Eales and Richard Sharpe (1995); and *St Augustine and the Conversion of England,* edited by Richard Gameson (1999). Also contributed articles to the journals *Anglo-Saxon England, Studies in Church History,* and *Transactions of the Cambridge Bibliographical Society.*

Evans, Robert C. Professor of English, Auburn University, Montgomery, Alabama. Author of *Ben Jonson and the Poetics of Patronage* (1989) and other books and essays on Jonson and other Renaissance writers. An editor of *Ben Jonson Journal* and *Comparative Drama.*

Evans, Stephen. Associate Lecturer in Politics, University of Wales, Cardiff. Contributed articles to the journals *History* and *Parliamentary Affairs.*

Fair, John D. Professor of History, Georgia College and State University, Milledgeville. Author of *British Interparty Conferences: A Study of the Procedure of Conciliation in British Politics, 1867–1921* (1980) and *Harold Temperley: A Scholar and Romantic in the Public Realm, 1879–1939* (1992). Also contributed articles to *English Historical Review, Albion, Journal of British Studies,* and *Victorian Studies.*

Farnsworth, Susan H. Professor of History, Trinity College, Washington, D.C. Author of *The Evolution of British Imperial Policy during the Mid-Nineteenth Century: A Study of the Peelite Contribution, 1846–1874* (1992). Contributor to *The Encyclopedia of Colonialism* (forthcoming) and to *Biographical Dictionary of Literary Influences: The Nineteenth Century, 1800–1914,* edited by John Powell (2001). Research areas include Victorian political and imperial history and the intellectual impact of Darwinian ideas, both in Britain and in the United States.

Farr, Martin. Lecturer, School of Historical Studies, University of Newcastle, since 2000. Author of *Reginald McKenna 1863–1943: A Life* (forthcoming). Has contributed articles to *War in History* and *BBC History.* Currently preparing *The Personnel of Armageddon,* a monograph dealing with the fate of the members of the Liberal government of 1906. Research interests include political biography and British party politics.

Faulkner, Thomas E. Senior Lecturer in the History of Architecture and Design at the University of Northumbria, Newcastle upon Tyne. Author (with Phoebe Lowery) of *Lost Houses of Newcastle and Northumberland* (1996) and (with Andrew Greg) of *John Dobson: Architect of the North East* (2001). Editor of *Northumbrian Panorama: Studies in the History and Culture of North East England* (1996). Chairman of the Northern Architectural History Society. Fellow of the Society of Antiquaries of London. Has a particular interest in the architecture of north-east England.

Fellows-Jensen, Gillian. Formerly reader in name studies at the Institute of Name Research, University of Copenhagen. Author of several books and many articles on Scandinavian personal names and place-names in the British Isles and Normandy. Arranger (with Peter Springborg) of eight international seminars on Care and Conservation of Manuscripts and editor (with Peter

Springborg) of the proceedings of the first seven of these (1995–2003). Editor of *Denmark and Scotland: The Cultural and Environmental Resources of Small Nations,* Royal Danish Academy of Sciences and Letters (2001).

Ferrell, Lori Anne. Professor of Religion and Reformation Studies, Claremont School of Theology and Claremont Graduate University, Claremont, California. Author of *Government by Polemic* (1998). Editor (with David Cressy) of *Religion and Society in Early Modern England* (1996) and (with Peter McCullough) *The English Sermon Revised* (2000).

Fleming, Peter. Principal Lecturer, Faculty of Humanities, Social Science, and Languages, University of the West of England, Bristol. Author of *Family and Household in Medieval England* (2001). Author (with Michael Wood) of *Gloucestershire's Forgotten Battle: Nibley Green, 1470* (2003). Author (with Kieran Costello) of *Discovering Cabot's Bristol* (1998). Editor (with Anthony Gross and J.R. Lander) of and contributor to *Regionalism and Revision: The Crown and Its Provinces in England, 1250–1650* (1998). Contributor to *Gentry Culture in Late Medieval England,* edited by Raluca Radulescu and Alison Truelove (forthcoming); and to *The Making of Modern Bristol,* edited by Madge Dresser and Philip Ollerenshaw (1996). Research interests include later medieval urban, gender, and cultural history.

Foot, M.R.D. Formerly professor of modern history at Manchester University. Original editor of the Gladstone diaries. Author of *SOE in France* (1966) and *SOE: An Outline History of the Special Operations Executive, 1940–1946* (1984). Consulting editor for *Oxford Companion to World War II,* edited by I.C.B. Dear (2nd ed., 2001).

Frankle, Robert J. Associate Professor of History, University of Memphis, Tennessee. Research interests include late Stuart parliamentary and constitutional history. Contributed articles to *Historical Journal* and *Parliamentary History Yearbook.*

Frantzen, Allen J. Professor of English Literature, Loyola University, Chicago, Illinois. Author of *The Literature of Penance in Anglo-Saxon England* (1983); *Desire for Origins: Old English, New Language, and Teaching the Tradition* (1990); *Troilus and Criseyde: The Poem and the Frame* (1993); and *Before the Closet: Same-Sex Love from "Beowulf" to "Angels in America"* (1998). Editor of *Speaking Two Languages: Traditional Disciplines and Contemporary Theory in Medieval Studies* (1990) and (with John D. Niles) *Anglo-Saxonism and the Construction of Social Identity* (1997).

Fraser, James E. Lecturer in Early Scottish History and Culture, School of History and Classics and School of Literatures, Languages, and Cultures, University of Edinburgh. Author of *The Battle of Dunnichen 685* (2002). Also contributed articles to the journals *Innes Review* and *Scottish Historical Review.*

Fraser, W. Hamish. Professor of Modern History, University of Strathclyde, Glasgow. Author of *Trade Unions and Society 1850–1880* (1974); *The Coming of the Mass Market* (1981); *Conflict and Class: Scottish Workers, 1700–1838* (1988); *A*

History of Trade Unionism, 1700–1998 (1999); and *Scottish Popular Politics* (2000). Editor (with I. Maver) of *Glasgow 1830–1919* (1996) and (with C.H. Lee) of *Aberdeen 1800–2000* (2000).

Frazer, Heather T. Professor of History, Florida Atlantic University, Boca Raton. Author (with John O'Sullivan) of *We Have Just Begun to Not Fight: An Oral History of Conscientious Objectors in Civilian Public Service during World War II* (1996). Contributor to *Language and Society in Modern India,* edited by Robert I. Crane and Bradford Spangenberg (1981). Also contributed articles on India to *Southeast Review of Asian Studies* and *Journal of Third World Studies,* among other publications.

Galgano, Michael James. Professor of History, James Madison University, Harrisonburg, Virginia. Contributor to *The Portrayal of Life Stages in English Literature, 1500–1800,* edited by Jeanie Watson and Philip McM. Pittman (1989); and *The World of William Penn,* edited by Richard S. Dunn and Mary Maples Dunn (1986). Also contributed articles to *American Benedictine Review, Recusant History,* and *History Microcomputer Review,* among other publications.

Gates, Lori A. Independent scholar based in Springfield, Oregon; formerly at Missouri Valley College, Marshall. Research interests include women's history and medieval agrarian, social, and economic history. Contributor of articles and reviews to the journals *Albion* and *Journal of Economic History.*

Ghosh, Ishita. Assistant Professor of History, Winthrop University, Rock Hill, South Carolina. Research interests include decolonization and race relations and immigration in post-imperial Britain.

Gill, Louise. Honorary Research Associate, Department of History and Classics, University of Tasmania. Author of *Richard III and Buckingham's Rebellion* (1999). Also contributed an article to the journal *English Historical Review.*

Gillespie, Stuart. Reader in English Literature, University of Glasgow. Author of *Shakespeare's Books: A Dictionary of Shakespeare Sources* (2001) and *The Poets on the Classics: An Anthology* (1988). Editor of the journal *Translation and Literature* and joint general editor of *Oxford History of Literary Translation in English* (forthcoming).

Glassey, Lionel K.J. Senior Lecturer in Modern History, University of Glasgow. Author of *Politics and the Appointment of Justices of the Peace, 1675–1720* (1979). Editor of *The Reigns of Charles II and James VII and II* (1997). Also contributed articles to *Bulletin of the Institute of Historical Research* (with Norma Landau), *Transactions of the Lancashire and Cheshire Antiquarian Society, Transactions of the Historic Society of Lancashire and Cheshire,* and *Records of the Scottish Church History Society,* among others. Currently engaged on a new edition of Gilbert Burnet's *History of His Own Time.*

Goodall, Francis. Honorary Research Fellow, Centre for Business History, Manchester Metropolitan University. Author of *Burning to Serve: Selling Gas in Competitive Markets* (1999) and *A Bibliography of British Business Histories* (1987). Editor (with Terry Gourvish and Steven Tolliday) of *International Bibliography of Business History* (1997). Contributor to *Dictionary of Business Biography*, edited by David J. Jeremy (1984–86); and *New Dictionary of National Biography*, edited by Brian Harrison (forthcoming). Also a contributor to the journal *Economic History Review*.

Goodman, Anthony. Professor of Medieval and Renaissance History, University of Edinburgh. Author of *The Loyal Conspiracy* (1971), *A History of England from Edward II to James I* (1977), *The Wars of the Roses* (1981), and *John of Gaunt* (1992). Previously review editor of *History*.

Gordon Jr., John L. Professor of History and International Studies, University of Richmond, Virginia. Contributor to *Imperial Canada, 1867–1917*, edited by Colin M. Coates (1997); *Historical Dictionary of the British Empire*, edited by James S. Olson and Robert Shadle (1996); *Boswell's Children: The Art of the Biographer*, edited by R.B. Fleming (1993); *Research Guide to European Historical Biography*, edited by James A. Moncure (1992); *Biographical Dictionary of Modern British Radicals*, edited by Joseph O. Baylen and Norbert J. Gossman (1984, 1988); and various journals.

Gorman, Daniel. Instructor, Department of History, McMaster University, Hamilton, Ontario. Contributed to *Dictionary of American History*, edited by Stanley Kutler (forthcoming); and *Industrialization and Imperialism, 1800–1914: A Biographical Dictionary*, edited by Jeffrey Bell (2002). Also contributed articles to *Journal of Colonialism and Colonial History* and *Australasian Victorian Studies Journal*. Research interests include imperial politics, Britain's presence in Africa, British conservatism, and the history of citizenship.

Grace, Ray. Senior Lecturer in Social History, University of Northumbria at Newcastle. Author of *Small Town Industrialization in the North of England, 1750 to the Present Day* (forthcoming). Contributor to *Essays in Tyneside Labour History*, edited by Norman McCord (1977). Compiler and editor for BBC Radio: *Social Life on Tyneside* (1981 and 1983), two series based on oral history covering the 1920s and 1930s. Feature-length programmes on "Cholera on Tyneside, 1847–1856" and "Northumberland Street: Tyneside shopping, 1850–1950" (1986).

Grieve, Neil F. Lecturer in European Urban Conservation, Department of Town and Regional Planning, University of Dundee. Also Director, Tayside Building Preservation Trust, and Director of Scottish Urban Archaeological Trust. Author of *An Appraisal of the Character of Mdina: Ancient Capital of Malta*, *Conservation Study of Dundee Docks* (1999), and *Conservation Glossary* (forthcoming).

Hale, Amy. Exeter University.

Hall, Mark Edward. Curator, Niigata Prefectural Museum of History, Nagaoka. Contributor of articles to *American Journal of Archaeology, Journal of the Royal Society of Antiquaries of Ireland*, and *Speculum*, among other publications.

Hall-Witt, Jennifer L. Independent scholar based in Denison, Ohio; formerly at Denison University. Contributor to *Music and British Culture 1785–1914*, edited by Christina Bashford and Leanne Langley (2000).

Halliwell, Martin. Senior Lecturer in English and American Studies, University of Leicester. Author of *Romantic Science and the Experience of Self* (1999), *Modernism and Morality* (2001), and *Images of Idiocy* (2003). Coauthor of *Critical Humanisms* (2003). Also contributed to *American Quarterly, Borderlines*, and *Journal of American Studies*.

Hammond, Peter. Independent scholar. Author of *The Battles of Barnet and Tewkesbury* (1990) and *Food and Feast in Medieval England* (1993). Editor (with Anne F. Sutton) of *Richard III: The Road to Bosworth Field* (1985) and *The Coronation of Richard III: The Extant Documents* (1983); editor (with Rosemary Horrox) of *British Library Harleian Manuscript 433 (1979–1982)*. Editor of *The Complete Peerage, or a History of the House of Lords and all its Members from the Earliest Times*, vol. 14 (1998).

Harding, Richard. Professor of Organizational History, University of Westminster, London. Author of *Amphibious Warfare in the Eighteenth Century* (1991), *The Evolution of the Sailing Navy* (1995), and *Seapower and Naval Warfare, 1650–1830* (1999). Coeditor (with Peter Le Fevre) of *The Precursors of Nelson: British Admirals of the Eighteenth Century* (2000). Also contributed articles to *Journal of Imperial and Commonwealth History, Historical Research, Historical Journal, Parliamentary History*, and *Mariner's Mirror*.

Harris, Bernard J. Senior Lecturer in Social Policy, Department of Sociology and Social Policy, University of Southampton. Author of *The Health of the Schoolchild: A History of the School Medical Service in England and Wales* (1995). Editor (with Waltraud Ernst) of *Race, Science, and Medicine, 1700–1960* (1999). Also contributed articles to *Contemporary Record, Social History of Medicine, Ageing and Society*, and other publications. Current interests include anthropometric history, the history of public health, and the development of British social policy.

Harris, Jonathan. Lecturer in Byzantine History, Royal Holloway, University of London. Author of *Greek Emigrés in the West, 1400–1520* (1995); editor (with Philip Schofield) of *Legislator of the World: Writings on Codification, Law, and Education* (Collected Works of Jeremy Bentham, 1998). Contributed articles to *London Journal, Journal of Medieval History*, and *Journal of Ecclesiastical History*.

Harris, Kathryn. Retired teacher. Contributor to *Robert Grosseteste and His Works of Greek Translation: Studies in Church History*, edited by D. Baker (1976).

Hart, Cyril. Stilton, Cambridge, U.K.

Hathaway, Mark. Doctoral candidate, Kellogg College, University of Oxford. Contributor to *The Encyclopedia of British Sport*, edited by Richard Cox et al. (2000); and *The*

Encyclopedia of British Traditional Sports, edited by Wray Vamplew (2003). Research interests include British rural society since 1750 and leisure and sport in Britain, including sporting art.

Haydon, Colin. Reader in Early Modern History, King Alfred's College, Winchester. Author of *Anti-Catholicism in Eighteenth-Century England* (1994). Editor (with John Walsh and Stephen Taylor) of *The Church of England, c. 1689–1833: From Toleration to Tractarianism* (1993) and (with William Doyle) of *Robespierre* (1999).

Hessenbruch, Arne. Researcher, Project on History of Recent Science and Technology on the Web, Dibner Institute, Massachusetts Institute of Technology, Cambridge. Editor of *Reader's Guide to the History of Science* (2000). Contributed articles to *British Journal for the History of Science, Social Studies of Science,* and *Archives for the Exact Sciences,* among others.

Hewitt, Martin. Professor of Victorian Studies, Trinity and All Saints, University of Leeds, and Director of the Leeds Centre for Victorian Studies. Author of *The Emergence of Stability in the Industrial City: Manchester 1832–1867* (1996) and editor of *An Age of Equipoise? Reassessing Mid-Victorian Britain* (2000). Has also contributed to *Historical Journal, Historical Research, Urban History, Journal of Victorian Culture,* and *Nineteenth Century Prose.*

Hickerson-Carey, Megan. Doctoral candidate, Syracuse University, Syracuse, New York. Editorial Assistant, *Journal of the Institute of Romance Studies.*

Hicks, Michael. Professor of Medieval History and Head of History, King Alfred's College, Winchester. Author of *Who's Who in English History 1272–1485* (1991), *Bastard Feudalism* (1995), *Warwick the Kingmaker* (1998), *Richard III* (2000), and *English Political Culture in the Fifteenth Century* (2002). Editor of *Revolution and Consumption in Fifteenth Century England* (2001). Also contributed articles to *English Historical Review, History,* and *Northern History and Southern History,* among other publications.

Hill, Clive E. Associate Teacher, Royal Holloway, University of London. Author of *Understanding the "Fabian Essays in Socialism"—1889* (1996) and *A Bibliography of the Writings of W.A. Robson* (1986). Editor of *Intellectuals, Identities, and Popular Movements* (2000). Also a contributor to *Reader's Guide to the Social Sciences,* edited by Jonathan Michie (2000); and to the journals *History of Political Thought* and *Shaw.*

Hill, L.M. Professor of History, University of California, Irvine. Author of *The Ancient State, Authoritie and Proceedings in the Court of Requests by Sir Julius Caesar* (1975) and *Bench and Bureaucracy: The Public Career of Sir Julius Caesar* (1988). Contributor to *State, Sovereigns, and Society in Early Modern Europe,* edited by C. Carlton *et al.* (1998). Also contributed articles to *Historical Journal, Bulletin of the Institute of Historical Research, Albion,* and *Sixteenth Century Journal,* among other publications.

Hill, Richard. Author of *Lewin of Greenwich* (2000), *War at Sea in the Ironclad Age* (2000), *The Prizes of War* (1998), *Arms Control at Sea* (1988), *Air Defence at Sea* (1988), *Maritime Strategy for Medium Powers* (1986), *British Sea Power in the 1980s* (1985), *Anti-Submarine Warfare* (1984), and *The Royal Navy Today and Tomorrow* (1981). Editor of *Oxford Illustrated History of the Royal Navy* (1995). Contributed numerous articles to *Naval Review* (editor, 1983–2002), *Survival, Defense and Diplomacy, Naval Forces,* and *Navy International;* has written conference papers on maritime strategy and arms control.

Hoffman, Steven M. Professor of Political Science and Director of Environmental Studies, University of St Thomas, St Paul, Minnesota; and Adjunct Research Professor, Center for Energy and Environmental Policy, University of Delaware. Coeditor (with John Byrne) of *Governing the Atom: The Politics of Risk* (1996). Contributor to *Environmental Justice: Discourses in International Political Economy,* edited by John Byrne *et al.* (2002). Coeditor of and contributor to special issues of *Energy Sources* and *Bulletin of Science, Technology, and Society,* among others.

Holt, Patrick J. Assistant Dean, Fordham University, Tarrytown, New York. Moderator of the H-Catholic Listserv. Contributor to *Medieval Sermon Studies* and *Journal of the American Association for History and Computing,* among others. Research interests include late medieval religion and society, early modern Ireland, and the history of education.

Hopper, Andrew J. Independent writer based in Norfolk. Contributor to the journals *Midland History, Northern History,* and *Recusant History.*

Houlbrooke, Ralph. Professor of Early Modern History, University of Reading. Author of *Church Courts and the People during the English Reformation* (1979); *The English Family, 1450–1700* (1984); *English Family Life, 1576–1716* (1988); and *Death, Religion, and the Family in England, 1480–1750* (1998). Editor of *Death, Ritual, and Bereavement* (1989). Chairman, Berkshire Record Society.

Houliston, Victor. Associate Professor of English, University of the Witwatersrand, Johannesburg. Editor of *The Silkewormes and Their Flies* by Thomas Moffet (1989) and *The Christian Directory* by Robert Persons (1998). Also contributed articles to *Renaissance Studies, Sixteenth-Century Journal,* and *English Studies in Africa,* among other publications.

Howell, David W. Reader in History, University of Wales, Swansea. Author of *Land and People in Nineteenth-Century Wales* (1978) and *Patriarchs and Parasites: The Gentry of South-West Wales in the Eighteenth-Century* (1986).

Hudson, Benjamin. Associate Professor of History and Medieval Studies, Pennsylvania State University, University Park. Author of *Kings of Celtic Scotland* (1994) and *Prophecy of Berchan* (1996). Contributor to *Britain and Ireland 900–1300,* edited by Brendan Smith (1999); *Last Things: Death and the Apocalypse in the Middle Ages,* edited by Caroline Walker Bynum and Paul Freedman (2000); and *Ogma: Essays in Celtic Studies,* edited by

Michael Richter and Jean-Michel Picard (2002). Also contributed articles to *English Historical Review*, *Medium AEvum*, *Irish Historical Studies*, *Scottish Historical Review*, and *Welsh History Review*, among other publications.

Hunter, Michael. Professor of History at Birkbeck College, University of London. Principal editor of the definitive edition of *The Works of Robert Boyle*, 14 vols (1999–2000); and *The Correspondence of Robert Boyle*, 6 vols (2001). Author or editor of many books on science and its milieu in late 17th-century England.

Ickringill, S.J.S. Senior Lecturer in History, University of Ulster, Coleraine. Editor (with S.L. Hilton) of *European Perceptions of the Spanish-American War* (1999). Contributor to *Sport, Culture, and Politics*, edited by John C. Binfield and John Stevenson (1993); and *The Insular Dream*, edited by K. Versluys (1995). Editor of three volumes in the series *European Contributions to American Studies*. Member of the Editorial Board of *Sports Historian*.

Innes, Joanna. Fellow and Tutor in Modern History, Somerville College Oxford. Coeditor of journal *Past and Present* 1990–2000. Author of numerous articles on British government and social policy in the 18th and early 19th centuries; currently preparing a collection of her articles for publication.

Ives, Eric W. University of Birmingham.

Jaffe, James A. Professor of History, University of Wisconsin, Whitewater. Author of *The Struggle for Market Power* (1991) and *Striking a Bargain* (2000). Also contributed articles to *Journal of British Studies*, *History of Political Economy*, *Journal of Ecclesiastical History*, *Historical Studies in Industrial Relations*, *Law and History Review*, and other journals.

James, Frank A.J.L. Reader in the History of Science at the Royal Institution, London. His main research concentrates on the physical sciences in the 19th century and how they relate to other areas of society and cultures—for example, art, religion, technology, and the military. Editor of the *Correspondence of Michael Faraday* (1991–), of which four (of six) volumes have so far been published. He recently published *The Common Purposes of Life*, a series of essays on the history of the Royal Institution.

Janes, Dominic. Director of Academic Programs, Foundation for International Education, London. Author of *God and Gold in Late Antiquity* (1998) and *Romans and Christians* (forthcoming).

Jarvis, Adrian. Curator of Port History, Merseyside Maritime Museum, Liverpool. Author of *Liverpool Central Docks 1799–1905* (1991), *The Liverpool Dock Engineers* (1996), *Samuel Smiles and the Construction of Victorian Values* (1997), and *The Liverpool Overhead Railway* (1997). Editor of *Port and Harbour Engineering* (1998). Area coeditor for *Oxford Encyclopedia of Maritime History*; member of the editorial board of *The Northern Mariner*.

Jenkins, Andrew. Research Officer, Centre for the Economics of Education, Institute of Education, University of London. Editor

of *Bread and the British Economy c.1770–1870* (1995). Also contributed articles to *Journal of Industrial History* and other journals. Current research interests include nationalization and privatization of utility industries, the economics of education, and lifelong learning.

Jewell, Helen M. Formerly Senior Lecturer, School of History, University of Liverpool. Author of *English Local Administration in the Middle Ages* (1972), *Court Rolls of the Manor of Wakefield 1348–50* (1982), *The North-South Divide: The Origins of Northern Consciousness in England* (1994), *Women in Medieval England* (1996), and *Education in Early Modern England* (1998). Section editor, *Constitutional, Administrative, and Legal History, 1050–1500, Royal Historical Society Bibliography on CD-ROM* (1998), available (from 2002) online as *Royal Historical Society Bibliography of British and Irish History*.

Johnman, Lewis. Principal Lecturer in History, University of Westminster, London. Coauthor (with Anthony Gorst) of *The Suez Crisis* (1997) and (with Ian Johnston and Iain Mackenzie) of *Down the River* (2001). Also contributed articles to *International Journal of Maritime History*, among other publications.

Johns, Cathy. Independent author and editor. Assistant Librarian, Royal College of Art, London. Contributed essays to *Dictionary of Artists' Models*, edited by Jill Berk Jiminez (2001) and texts on British painting for the Tate (London) public website. Has also contributed articles to *World Book Encyclopedia*.

Johnson, Gaynor. Lecturer in History, Bolton Institute. Publications include *The Berlin Embassy of Lord D'Abernon, 1920–1926* (2002); (editor) *Locarno Diplomacy Revisted: European Diplomacy 1920–1929* (2003); and a number of articles on British foreign policy and international history in the 1920s. Currently editing the Berlin diary of Sir Eric Phipps (1933–1937) for Brasseys and writing a biography of Viscount Cecil of Chelwood.

Jones, J. Gwynfor. Professor of Welsh History, University of Cardiff. Specialist in 16th- and 17th-century social, administrative, cultural, and religious history. Author of (among many other works) *Concepts of Order and Gentility in Wales, 1540–1640* (1992); *Early Modern Wales, c.1526–1640* (1994); *Law, Order, and Government in Caernarfonshire, 1558–1640* (1996); *The Welsh Gentry, 1536–1640: Images of Status, Honour, and Authority* (1998); and *Conflict, Continuity, and Change in Wales c.1500–1603* (2000).

Kadane, Matthew. Doctoral candidate, Department of History, Brown University, Providence, Rhode Island. Research interests include the early phase of industrialization, spiritual journals, economic thought, and radical religion. Recently contributed an article to *Bulletin de la Société de l'Histoire du Protestantisme Français*.

Keck, Stephen L. Assistant Professor of History, National University of Singapore. Contributor to *An Age of Equipoise? Reassessing Mid-Victorian Britain*, edited by Martin Hewitt

(2000). Also a contributor to *Proceedings of the South Carolina Historical Association, A Journal of Ideas and Culture,* among other publications.

Keenan, Jerry. Independent writer and scholar, specializing in American and Irish military history. Author of *Encyclopedia of the American Indian Wars, 1492–1890* (1997); *Wilson's Cavalry Corps: Union Campaigns in the Western Theater, October 1864 through Spring 1876* (1998); *The Wagon Box Fight* (2000); and *Encyclopedia of the Spanish-American and Philippine-American Wars* (2001).

Kelsch, Anne Airth-Kindree. Assistant Professor of History, University of North Dakota, Grand Forks. Research interests include World War I, gender, and pedagogy.

Kelsey, Sean. Author of *Inventing a Republic: The Political Culture of the English Commonwealth, 1649–1653* (1997). Has recently contributed articles on the trial and death of Charles I to *English Historical Review* and *Historical Journal.*

Kettle, Ann. Senior Lecturer in Medieval History, University of St Andrews. Contributor to *Victoria County Histories of Cheshire, Shropshire, and Staffordshire*; and to volumes of the *Staffordshire Record Society.* Author of articles on the history of women in the Middle Ages.

Kidd, Alan J. Professor of History, Manchester Metropolitan University. Author of *Manchester* (3rd ed., 2002) and *State, Society, and the Poor in Nineteenth Century England* (1999). Editor (with Ken Roberts) of *City, Class, and Culture: Studies of Social Policy, Cultural Production in Victorian Manchester* (1985); and (with David Nicholls) *The Making of the Middle Class? Studies of Regional and Cultural Diversity since the Eighteenth Century* (1998) and *Gender, Civic Culture, and Consumerism: Middle Class Identity in Britain 1800–1940* (1999). Founding coeditor (with Terry Wyke and Ken Roberts) of *Manchester Region History Review* (1987–present). Also contributed articles to *Economic History Review, Social History, International Review of Social History, Twentieth Century British History, Journal of Historical Sociology,* and several other journals.

Kinealy, Christine. Senior Lecturer, Department of Historical and Critical Studies, University of Central Lancashire, Preston. Author of *A Disunited Kingdom: England, Ireland, Scotland, and Wales 1800–1949* (1999); *A Death-Dealing Famine: The Great Hunger in Ireland* (1997); and *The Great Calamity: The Irish Famine 1845–52* (1994).

Kitching, Carolyn J. Senior Lecturer in Modern History, University of Teesside, Middlesbrough. Author of *Britain and the Problem of International Disarmament, 1919–34* (1999); *Britain and the Geneva Disarmament Conference, 1932–1934* (forthcoming); and (with Dick Richardson) *A History of Disarmament and Arms Control* (forthcoming). Contributor to *Anglo-French Relations in the Twentieth Century,* edited by Alan Sharp and Glyn Stone (2000); and to *Locarno Revisited: European Diplomacy 1920–1929,* edited by Gaynor Johnson (forthcoming)

Kitching, Christopher. Head of the Historical Manuscripts Commission, National Archives, London. Author of *Archives: The Very Essence of Our Heritage* (1996) and *Surveys of Historical Manuscripts in the United Kingdom: A Select Bibliography* (3rd ed., 1997; and electronic updates). Compiler of *Archives at the Millennium* (1999). Has written many other articles and reviews on archives for (among others) *Journal of the Society of Archivists, Archives,* and *Gazette des Archives.*

Knighton, C.S. Editorial Staff, Public Record Office, London. Editor of *Calendar of State Papers, Domestic Series: Edward VI* (1992); *Acts of the Dean and Chapter of Westminster 1543–1609,* 2 vols (1997–99); and *Calendar of State Papers, Domestic Series, Mary I* (1998). Coeditor (with D. Marcombe) of *Close Encounters: English Cathedrals and Society since 1540* (1991). Deputy Editor of *Catalogue of the Pepys Library at Magdalene College, Cambridge.* Compiler of *Catalogue of the Pepys Library at Magdalene College, Cambridge,* 5/2 (1981).

Knowles, James. Reader in English, University of Stirling. Author (with Jenny Richards) of *Shakespeare's Late Plays* (1999) and (with Gene Giddens) of *The Roaring Girl and Other Plays.* Contributor to *Re-Presenting Ben Jonson,* edited by Martin Butler (1999). Has written on Jacobean and Caroline masque, and especially on Jonson's scurrilous political verse, sexuality, apes on the early modern stage, modern gay fiction, and Shakespeare.

Koditschek, Theodore. Associate Professor, Department of History, University of Missouri, Columbia. Author of *Class Formation and Urban, Industrial Society: Bradford, 1750–1850* (1989), which received the Schuyler and Adams Prizes from the American Historical Associations. More recent articles appear in *Victorian Studies, Gender and History,* and various edited collections. Research interests include modern British social history, social theory, and the history of imperialism.

Kriegel, Abraham D. Professor of History, University of Memphis, Tennessee. Editor of *The Holland House Diaries, 1831–1840* (1977). Has also contributed articles to *Journal of British Studies, Journal of Modern History, Albion,* and *English Historical Review.*

Kyle, Chris R. Associate Professor of the Humanities, History Department, Syracuse University, Syracuse, New York. Editor of *Parliaments, Politics, and Elections, 1604–1648* (2001). Editor (with Jason Peacey) of *Parliament at Work* (2002). Has also contributed articles to *Historical Journal, Parliamentary History, Journal of Legal History,* and *Parliament, Estates, and Representation.*

Laing, Lloyd. Senior Lecturer in Archaeology, Nottingham University, Nottingham. Author of many books, monographs, and papers. Recent titles include (with Jennifer Laing) *Early English Art and Architecture* (1996), (with J. Laing) *Art of the Celts* (1992), and *A Catalogue of Celtic Ornamental Metalwork in the British Isles, c. AD 400–1200* (1993). Main research interests relate to the art and archaeology of early historic Britain (pre-1066), particularly early medieval Celts and Saxons.

Lambert, Andrew David. Laughton Professor of Naval History, Department of War Studies, King's College London. Author of *The Crimean War: British Grand Strategy against Russia, 1853–1856* (1990); *The Foundations of Naval History: John Laughton, the Royal Navy, and the Historical Profession* (1998); *War at Sea in the Age of Sail* (2000); and several other books and articles on naval history, technology, and strategy. Fellow of the Royal Historical Society and Honorary Secretary of the Navy Records Society.

LaRocca, John J. Professor, History Department, Xavier University, Cincinnati, Ohio. Translator and editor of *Jacobean Recusant Rolls for Middlesex* (1997). Contributor to *The Reckoned Expense: Edmund Campion and the Early Jesuits*, edited by Thomas M. McCoog (1996). Has also contributed articles to *Recusant History, Albion*, and *Journal of British Studies*.

Lavelle, Ryan. Doctoral candidate. King Alfred's College, Winchester. Contributor to *Peace and Negotiation*, edited by Diane Wolfthal (2000).

Laybourn, Keith. Professor of History, University of Huddersfield. Author of *Britain on the Breadline* (1990), *The Evolution of Social Policy and the Welfare State* (1995), *A Century of Labour* (2000), and *Unemployment and Employment in Relation to Women, c. 1900–1951* (forthcoming), among other works. Coeditor (with others) of *The Centennial: History of the Independent Labour Party* (1992). Editor of *Annual Bulletin of Historical Literature*.

Lee, Clive H. Professor of Historical Economics and Head of Department of Economics, University of Aberdeen. Author of several studies on modern economic development including *Scotland and the United Kingdom: The Economy and the Union in the Twentieth Century* (1995) and *The British Economy since 1700: A Macroeconomic Perspective* (1986).

Lee, Simon David. Lecturer in Politics, Department of Politics and International Studies, Hull University. Author of *Blair's Third Way* (forthcoming) and (with Andrew Cox and Joe Sanderson) *The Political Economy of Modern Britain* (1997). Editor (with Maurice Mullard) of *The Politics of Social Policy in Europe* (1997). Contributor of articles to *New Political Economy* and *Public Policy and Administration*, among other publications.

Leech, Melisé L. Doctoral student, Department of History, University of Nevada, Las Vegas. Research interests include 18th-century British cultural history, scepticism, and gender, and the Scottish Enlightenment.

Lehmberg, Stanford. Professor of History Emeritus, University of Minnesota, Minneapolis. Author of *Sir Thomas Elyot, Tudor Humanist* (1960); *Sir Walter Mildmay and Tudor Government* (1964); *The Reformation Parliament, 1529–1536* (1970); *The Later Parliaments of Henry VIII* (1977); *The Reformation of Cathedrals* (1988); and *Cathedrals under Siege* (1996). Member of the Editorial Board for *Oxford Encyclopedia of the Reformation*, edited by Hans J. Hillerbrand (1996); and for *Encyclopedia of the Renaissance*, edited by Paul F. Grendler (1999).

Lenman, Bruce P. Professor of Modern History, University of St Andrews. Coauthor of *Dundee and Its Textile Industry* (1969), *From Esk to Tweed* (1975), *An Economic History of Modern Scotland 1660–1976* (1977), *Jacobite Risings in Britain 1689–1746* (1980), *Integration and Enlightenment* (2nd ed., 1992), *The Jacobite Threat: A Source Book* (1990), and *The Eclipse of Parliament* (1992).

Lentin, Antony. Professor of History, Open University, Milton Keynes; barrister. Author of *Guilt at Versailles: Lloyd George and the Pre-History of Appeasement* (1984) and *Lloyd George and the Lost Peace* (2001). Contributor to *The Treaty of Versailles: A Reassessment after 75 Years*, edited by Manfred F. Boemeke *et al.* (1998). Editor of *Peter the Great: His Law on the Imperial Succession in Russia, 1722* (1996). Author of other books and articles on 18th-century Russia and Europe. Author of entries on eminent lawyers for *New Dictionary of National Biography*, edited by Brian Harrison (forthcoming).

Lester, V. Markham. Associate Professor of History, Birmingham-Southern College, Birmingham, Alabama. Author of *Victorian Insolvency: Bankruptcy, Imprisonment for Debt, and Company Winding-Up in Nineteenth-Century England* (1995). Has also contributed articles and reviews to *Historical Journal* and *Albion*.

Levin, Carole. Willa Cather Professor and Professor of History, University of Nebraska, Lincoln. Author of *The Reign of Elizabeth I* (2002), *The Heart and Stomach of a King: Elizabeth I and the Politics of Sex and Power* (1994), and *Propaganda in the English Reformation: Heroic and Villainous Images of King John* (1988), as well as editor or coeditor of four collections. Has also contributed articles to *Sixteenth Century Journal, Albion*, and *Quidditas*, among other publications.

Lineham, Peter. Associate Professor of History in the School of Social and Cultural Studies, Massey University, Auckland. Author of *There We Found Brethren* (1977), *No Ordinary Union* (1980), *New Zealanders and the Methodist Evangel* (1983), *Religious History of New Zealand: A bibliography* (1984, and subsequent editions to 1999), *Bible and Society* (1996), with (Allan K. Davidson) *Transplanted Christianity* (4th ed., 1997), and numerous articles on the religious history of New Zealand and on 18th-century Methodism and sectarianism in England.

Liu, Wenxi. Associate Professor of History, Miami University, Florida. Contributor to *Anglo-American Law Review*.

Loades, David. Honorary Research Professor, University of Sheffield. Director of the British Academy John Foxe Project. Author of *Two Tudor Conspiracies* (1965, 1991); *The Oxford Martyrs* (1970, 1992); *Politics and the Nation, 1450–1660* (1974, 5th ed. 1999); *The Reign of Mary Tudor* (1979, 1991); *The Tudor Court* (1986); *Mary Tudor: A Life* (1989); *The Tudor Navy* (1992); *The Mid-Tudor Crisis* (1992); *Henry VIII and His Queens* (1994); *John Dudley: Duke of Northumberland* (1996);

Power in Tudor England (1997); *Tudor Government* (1997); *England's Maritime Empire* (2000); and *Elizabeth I* (2003).

Loades, Judith. Burford, Oxfordshire, U.K.

Lobban, Michael. Reader in Law, Queen Mary and Westfield College, University of London. Author of *The Common Law and English Jurisprudence, 1760–1850* (1991) and *White Man's Justice: South African Political Trials in the Black Consciousness Era* (1996). Has also contributed articles to *Oxford Journal of Legal Studies* and *English Historical Review*. Associate Editor of *New Dictionary of National Biography*, edited by Brian Harrison (forthcoming).

Locherbie-Cameron, Margaret. Head of Department of English, University of Wales, Bangor. Contributor to *The Battle of Maldon, AD 991*, edited by Donald Scragg (1991). Has also contributed articles to *Medium AEvum, Medieval History, Parergon*, and *Poetica*, among other publications.

Loomie, Albert J. Professor Emeritus of History, Fordham University, New York. Author of *The Spanish Elizabethans: English Exiles at the Court of Philip II* (1963) and *Spain and the Early Stuarts, 1585–1655, Collected Studies* (1996). Editor of *Spain and the Jacobean Catholics*, 2 vols (1973, 1978) and *Ceremonies of Charles I* (1987).

LoPatin-Lummis, Nancy. Professor of History, University of Wisconsin, Stevens Point. Author of *Political Unions, Popular Politics, and the Great Reform Act of 1832* (1999). Has also contributed articles to *Parliamentary History, Midland History, Victorian Periodicals Review*, and *Journal of Victorian Cultural*, among other publications.

Lowe, Ben. Associate Professor of History, Florida Atlantic University, Boca Raton. Author of *Imagining Peace: A History of Early Pacifist Ideas, 1340–1560* (1997). Has also contributed articles to *Albion, Sixteenth Century Journal*, and *Fides et Historia*, among other publications, and has contributed essays to a number of books. Research interests include Tudor political culture, early Reformation England, and mid-Tudor social ideas and policies.

Lynch, John M. Lecturer, Barrett Honors College at Arizona State University, Tempe. Editor of *Vestiges and the Debate before Darwin* (2000); *Darwin's Theory of Natural Selection, British Responses, 1859–1871* (2001); and *Creationism and Scriptural Geology* (2002). Contributing editor to *Dictionary of Nineteenth Century British Scientists* (forthcoming). Research interests include interactions between science and religion in the works of Adam Sedgwick and St George Jackson Mivart.

Lynch, John P. Institute of Continuing Education, Queen's University, Belfast. Author of *A Tale of Three Cities* (1998) and *For King and Parliament* (1999). Also a contributor to *Doing Irish Local History*, edited by Myrtle Hill and Raymond Gillespie (1998).

Mac Giolla Chriost, Diarmait. Lecturer, Department of History, Trinity College, Carmarthen. Contributor to *Literature and Politics in the Celtic World*, edited by J. Wooding and P. James (forthcoming) and (with J. W. Aitchison and H. Carter) to *National Identities* (forthcoming). Has also contributed articles to *Irish Studies Review, Current Issues in Language and Society, Area*, and *Welsh Internationalist*.

MacFarlane, Leslie J. Honorary Reader, Department of History, University of Aberdeen. Author of *William Elphinstone and the Kingdom of Scotland: The Struggle for Order* (2nd ed., 1995). Contributor to *Dictionary of Scottish Church History and Theology*, edited by N. Cameron (1993); and *Freedom and Authority: Scotland c. 1050–1650*, edited by Terry Brotherstone and David Ditchburn (2000). Also a contributor to the journals *Innes Review* and *Northern Scotland*. Formerly Chairman, Consultative Committee, Calendars of Entries in the Papal Registers relating to Britain and Ireland.

Machin, Ian. Professor of British History, University of Dundee. Author of *The Catholic Question in English Politics, 1820 to 1830* (1964); *Politics and the Churches in Great Britain, 1832 to 1868* (1977); *Politics and the Churches in Great Britain, 1869 to 1921* (1987); *The Liberal Governments, 1905–1915* (1991); *Disraeli* (1995); and *Churches and Social Issues in Twentieth-Century Britain* (1998).

MacKinnon, Dolly. Fellow, Department of History, University of Melbourne, Victoria. Author of *Women and Music in the British Isles 1500–1800* (forthcoming). Editor (with Catharine Coleborne) of *Madness: History, Heritage, and Asylums in Australia* (2003). Has also contributed articles to *Essex Archaeology and History, Local Historian, Context*, and *Parergon*. Research interests include early modern social history, women and music, and medical history.

Manning, Martin J. Librarian, U.S. Department of State, Washington D.C. Contributor to *Encyclopedia of Gardens*, edited by Candice Shoemaker (forthcoming); *Encyclopedia of Radio*, edited by Christopher H. Sterling (forthcoming); and *American National Biography*, edited by John A. Garraty and Mark C. Carnes (1999).

Martin, Anthony. Associate Professor, School of Literature, Waseda University, Tokyo. Contributor to *John Foxe and His World*, edited by Christopher Highley and John N. King (2002); and *Anatomy of Tudor Literature*, edited by Mike Pincombe (2001). Also a contributor to the journals *Shakespeare Studies* and *Studies in Philology*.

Martin, Chad. Lecturer, Department of History, Stanford University, Stanford, California. Research interests include radical politics, bohemian and youth cultures, and censorship in Great Britain and the United States from the late 19th century to the present.

Martin, David E. Senior Lecturer in History, University of Sheffield. Coauthor (with Donald R. MacRaild) of *Labour in British Society 1830–1914* (2000). Coeditor (with David Rubinstein) of *Ideology and the Labour Movement* (1979) and (with others) of *The History of the City of Sheffield 1843–1993* (3 vols, 1993). Contributor to *Dictionary of Labour Biography*, edited by Joyce M. Bellamy and John Saville (10 vols, 1972–2000); *Biographical Dictionary of European Labor Leaders,* edited by A. Thomas Lane (2 vols, 1995); *Oxford Companion to 20th-Century British Politics,* edited by John Ramsden (2002); and *New Dictionary of National Biography,* edited by Brian Harrison (forthcoming).

Maslen, R.W. Senior Lecturer in English Literature at the University of Glasgow. Author of *Elizabethan Fictions* (1997). Editor of Philip Sidney's *Apology for Poetry* (2002). Contributor to *Shakespeare's Ovid,* edited by A.B. Taylor (2000). Has also contributed articles to *Studies in Philology, Translation and Literature,* and *Foundation: The Review of Science Fiction,* among other publications.

Mason, John F.A. Formerly Fellow and Tutor of Christ Church College, University of Oxford. Author (with E.G.W. Bill) of *Christ Church and Reform 1850–67* (1970). Contributed (with J. Cook) to *Salisbury: The Man and His Policies,* edited by R. Blake and H. Cecil (1987). Has also contributed articles to *New Dictionary of National Biography,* edited by Brian Harrison (forthcoming); *History of the University of Oxford,* edited by T.H. Aston (1984–94); and journals such as *Economic History Review.*

Masschaele, James. Associate Professor of History, Rutgers University, New Brunswick, New Jersey. Author of *Peasants, Merchants, and Markets: Inland Trade in Medieval England, 1150–1350* (1997). Has also contributed articles to the journals *English Historical Review, Economic History Review, Journal of Historical Geography,* and *Speculum,* among others.

Maunder, Andrew. Lecturer in English Literature, University of Hertfordshire, Hatfield. Editor of *The Mill on the Floss* and *Silas Marner* (forthcoming) and *East Lynne* (2000). Has also contributed articles to *Victorian Periodicals Review, Études Anglaises,* and *Journal of Pre-Raphaelite Studies,* among other publications.

McClain, Molly. Associate Professor, Department of History, University of San Diego, California. Author of *Beaufort: The Duke and His Duchess, 1657–1715* (2001) and coauthor (with Jacqueline D. Roth) of *Schaum's Quick Guide to Writing Great Essays* (1998). Contributor to *Political Culture and Cultural Politics in Early Modern England,* edited by Susan D. Amussen and Mark A. Kishlansky (1995); and to the journal *Welsh History Review.*

McDonald, R. Andrew. Assistant Professor of History, Brock University, St Catharines, Canada. Author of *The Kingdom of the Isles: Scotland's Western Seaboard c.1100–c.1336* (1997). Editor (with E.J. Cowan) of *Alba: Celtic Scotland in the Middle Ages* (2000) and of *History, Literature, and Music in Scotland 500–1560* (2002). Contributor to *Britain and Ireland 900–1300,* edited by Brendan Smith (1999); and *New History of the Isle of Man,* edited by S. Duffy (forthcoming). Has also contributed articles to *Journal of Medieval History, Scottish Historical Review,* and *Albion.*

McKean, Charles A. Professor of Scottish Architectural History, University of Dundee. Author of *The Scottish Château* (2001),

The Making of the Museum of Scotland (2000), *The Scottish Thirties* (1987), and other works. Founder and series editor of the RIAS/Landmark Trust *Illustrated Architectural Guides to Scotland* (28 vols). Also a contributor to *Architectural History, Architectural Heritage, Journal of Architectural Conservation, Architect's Journal,* and *New Dictionary of National Biography,* edited by Brian Harrison (forthcoming).

McLean, Scott Alan. Lecturer, Queen's University International Study Centre, Herstmonceux Castle, East Sussex. Author of *From Lochnaw to Manitoulin: A Highland Soldier's Tour through Upper Canada* (2000) and *The Cheap Literature Movement in Scotland, 1768–1845* (forthcoming). Has also published articles on medieval and modern Scotland. Research interests include the Scottish periodical press, Scottish migration, and popular culture.

McLoughlin, John. Alumni Officer, King's College London. Contributor to *England in the Twelfth Century,* edited by Daniel Williams (1990); *Faith and Identity: Christian Political Experience,* edited by David Loades and Katharine Walsh (1990); and *Persecution and Toleration,* edited by W.J. Sheils (1984).

McNeill, John. Lecturer, Faculty of Continuing Education, Birkbeck College, London. Honorary Secretary of the British Archaeological Association. Author of *Blue Guide: Normandy* (1993) and *Blue Guide: The Loire Valley* (1995). Jointly edited *Anjou: Medieval Art, Architecture, and Archaeology* (2003).

McSheffrey, Shannon. Associate Professor of History, Concordia University, Montreal, Quebec. Author of *Gender and Heresy: Women and Men in Lollard Communities, 1420–1530* (1995) and *Love and Marriage in Late Medieval London* (1995). Editor (with Norman Tanner) of *Lollards of Coventry, 1486–1522* (forthcoming). Contributor to *Conflicted Identities and Multiple Masculinities: Men in the Medieval West,* edited by Jacqueline Murray (1999); *Women, Marriage, and Family in Medieval Christendom,* edited by Joel T. Rosenthal and Constance M. Rousseau (1998); and *Women, the Book and the Godly,* edited by Jane H.M. Taylor and Lesley Smith (1995). Has also contributed articles to *Journal of British History* and *Canadian Journal of History.*

Michalove, Sharon. Associate Director of Undergraduate Studies, Department of History and Adjunct Assistant Professor, Department of Educational Policy Studies, University of Illinois at Urbana-Champaign. Editor (with A. Compton Reeves) of *Estrangement, Enterprise, and Education in Fifteenth-Century England* (1998) and (with Douglas Biggs and A. Compton Reeves) of *Traditions and Transformations in Late Medieval England* (2002). Contributor to *Women's Education in Early Modern Europe,* edited by Barbara J. Whitehead (1999).

Mileham, Patrick. Reader of Corporate Management and Governor of the University of Paisley, Scotland. Author of *The Yeomanry Regiments* (2nd ed., 1994), *The Scottish Regiments* (2nd ed., 1996), *Fighting Highlanders: A History of the Argyll and Sutherland Highlanders* (1993), and *Difficulties Be*

Damned: A History of the King's Regiment, City Regiment of Manchester and Liverpool (2000). Also contributes to numerous journals on military professionalism and ethics.

Miller, Karen E. Doctoral candidate, School of History and History of Art, University of Aberdeen. Research interests include the medieval church, medieval Ireland, medieval Scotland, and secular-ecclesiastical relations.

Moir, Scott. University of Guelph, Ontario, Canada.

Money, John. Associate Professor, Department of History, University of Victoria, British Columbia. Author of *Experience and Identity: Birmingham and the West Midlands 1760–1800* (1977). Contributor to *Transformation of Political Culture in Late Eighteenth Century England and Germany,* edited by Eckhart Hellmuth (1990); and *Consumption and Culture: The 15th to 18th Centuries* (1993). Has also contributed articles to the journals *Albion, Historical Journal, Midland History, Canadian Journal of History, Enlightenment and Dissent,* and *Journal of British Studies,* among others. On the Editorial Board of *Albion.*

Montgomery, Fiona A. Head of School of Historical and Cultural Studies, Bath Spa University College, Bath. Author of *Edge Hill University College: A History, 1885–1997* (1997). Editor (with Christine Collette) of *The European Women's History Reader* (2002) and *Into the Melting Pot* (1997). Contributor to *Gender Roles and Sexuality in Victorian Literature,* edited by Christopher Parker (1995); and *Biographical Dictionary of Modern British Radicals,* edited by Joseph O. Baylen and Norbert J. Gossmann (1984). Has also contributed articles to the journals *History, Scottish Historical Review,* and *Teaching in Higher Education,* among others.

Morgan, Gwenda. Reader in History and American Studies, University of Sunderland. Author of *The Hegemony of the Law: Richmond County Virginia 1692–1776* (1989). Coauthor (with Peter Rushton) of *Rogues, Thieves, and the Rule of Law* (1998). Coeditor (with Peter Rushton) of *The Justicing Notebook of Edmund Tew* (2000).

Morgan, Kenneth. Professor of History, Brunel University, Middlesex. Author of *Bristol and the Atlantic Trade in the Eighteenth Century* (1993) and *The Birth of Industrial Britain: Economic Change, 1750–1850* (1999). Editor of *An American Quaker in the British Isles: The Travel Journals of Jabez Maud Fisher, 1775–1779* (1991).

Mori, Jennifer. Associate Professor of History, University of Toronto, Ontario. Author of *William Pitt and the French Revolution 1785–1795* (1997) and *Britain in the Age of the French Revolution 1785–1820* (2000). Has also contributed articles to *Historical Journal, English Historical Review,* and *Historical Research.*

Morillo, Stephen. Associate Professor of History, Wabash College, Crawfordsville, Indiana. Author of *Warfare under the Anglo-Norman Kings, 1066–1135* (1994). Editor of *The Battle of Hastings: Sources and Interpretations* (1996). Contributor to

The Normans and Their Adversaries at War, edited by Richard Abels and Bernard S. Bachrach (2001); and *The Circle of War,* edited by Donald Kagay and Andrew Villalon (1999). Has also contributed articles to *Journal of World History, Haskins Society Journal, Medieval History Journal,* and *Res Militaria,* among other publications.

Morrill, John. Professor of British and Irish History at the University of Cambridge and Deputy Director of the Centre for Research in the Arts, Social Sciences and Humanities in the University of Cambridge. He is a Fellow and currently Vice President of the British Academy. Author of *Revolt in the Provinces: The English People and the Tragedies of War* (1999) and editor of *The Oxford Illustrated History of Tudor and Stuart Britain* (1996), among other works. Current research interests include state formation in early modern Britain and Ireland, and Oliver Cromwell and the Bible.

Morrow, Mary Jane. Visiting Assistant Professor, Duke University, Durham, North Carolina. Contributor to *Voices in Dialogue: New Problems in Reading Women's Cultural History,* edited by Linda Olson and Katherine Kerby-Fulton (forthcoming).

Morton, Graeme. Lecturer in Economic and Social History, University of Edinburgh. Author of *William Wallace: Man and Myth* (2001); *Unionist-Nationalism: Governing Urban Scotland, 1830–1860* (1999); and (with A. Morris) *Locality, Community, and Nation* (1998). Contributor to *The New Penguin History of Scotland,* edited by R.A. Houston and W.W.J. Knox (2001); *The Challenge to Westminster: Sovereignty, Devolution, and Independence,* edited by H.T. Dickinson and Michael Lynch (2000); and *Image and Identity: The Making and Re-Making of Scotland through the Ages,* edited by Dauvit Broun *et al.* (1998). Has also contributed articles to *Scottish Historical Review, Urban History, Nations and Nationalism,* and *History and Computing.*

Mulhearn, Rachel. Curator of Maritime Collections, National Museums and Galleries on Merseyside, Liverpool. Contributor to *International Journal of Maritime History* and (with Kenneth Smith and Graham Tonks) to *Transit Sheds in Liverpool Docks in Albert Dock Trade and Technology,* edited by Adrian Jarvis and Kenneth Smith (1999).

Mulholland, Marc. Lecturer in History, Hertford College, Oxford. Author of *To Care Always: A History of Holywell Mental Hospital 1898–1998* (1998) and *Northern Ireland at the Crossroads: Ulster Unionism in the O'Neill Years* (2000).

Mullan, David George. Professor of History and Religious Studies, University College of Cape Breton, Nova Scotia. Author of *Episcopacy in Scotland: The History of an Idea, 1560–1638* (1986) and *Scottish Puritanism, 1590–1638* (2000). Editor of *Religious Pluralism in the West* (1998) and *Religious Controversy in Scotland, 1625–1639* (1998). Forthcoming works include a collection of early modern Scottish women's religious narratives and a study of Scottish religious narrative: *Lively Memories and Useful Lives—Scottish Religious Self-Writing, 1670–1730.*

Mullett, Michael A. Professor of Cultural and Religious History, University of Lancaster. Author of *Radical Religious Movements in Early Modern Europe* (1980); *Popular Culture and Popular Protest in Late Medieval and Early Modern Europe* (1987); *Calvin* (1989); *Sources for the History of English Nonconformity, 1660–1829* (1991); and *James II in English Politics* (1994). Editor of *New Light on George Fox, 1624–1691* (1994); *John Bunyan in Context* (1996); *Catholics in Britain and Ireland, 1558–1829* (1998); and *The Catholic Reformation* (1999). Has also contributed articles to journals of English regional history and journals of religious studies, as well as essays in edited collections.

Mumm, Susan. Senior Lecturer in Religious Studies, Open University, Milton Keynes. Author of *Stolen Daughters, Virgin Mothers: Anglican Sisterhoods in Victorian Britain* (1999) and *All Saints Sisters of the Poor: An Anglican Sisterhood in the Nineteenth Century* (2001). Editor of *Religion Today: A Reader* (2002) and author of a number of articles on Victorian purity movements and related subjects.

Mundill, Robin R. Head of History, Glenalmond College, Perth, U.K. Author of *England's Jewish Solution: Experiment and Expulsion, 1262–1290* (1998 and 2002). Contributor to *Credit and Debt in Medieval England c.1180–c.1350*, edited by P.R. Schofield and N.J. Mayhew (2002); and *The Jews in Medieval Britain*, edited by P. Skinner (2003). Has also contributed articles to *Jewish Historical Studies, Jewish Quarterly Review, Jewish Culture and History, Aschkenas, Journal of the Pewter Society*, and *Family History*, among other publications; and to BBC2 Timewatch documentary (1990) and BBC Radio 4 (2001).

Murphy, B. Keith. Associate Professor of English and Foreign Languages, Fort Valley State University, Fort Valley, Georgia. Contributor to *Theorizing Fandom*, edited by Cheryl Harris and Alison Alexander (1998); *Popular Musicians*, edited by Steve Hochman (1999); and *Magill's Guide to Military History*, edited by John Powell (2001). Has also contributed articles to journals such as *Studies in Popular Culture* and *Journal of the Georgia Association of Historians*. Received (in 2002) a National Endowment for the Humanities Faculty Research Grant to study comic strips in African-American newspapers.

Murray, Mary. Senior Lecturer in Sociology and Women's Studies, Massey University, Palmerston North. Author of *The Law of The Father? Patriarchy in the Transition from Feudalism to Capitalism* (1995). Research interests include death and dying, emotion and society, and relationships between humans and animals.

Neushul, Peter. Visiting Researcher, University of California, Santa Barbara. Contributor to *Magill's Survey of Science*, edited by Frank N. Magill (1989); *Seaweed Cultivation for Renewable Resources*, edited by K.T. Bird and P.H. Benson (1987); *Great Events from History*, edited by Frank N. Magill (1991); and *Magill's Survey of Science*, edited by Frank K. Magill (1993–98). Contributor to the journals *Technology and Culture* and *Discovery*.

Neville, Peter. Senior Lecturer in Twentieth Century European History, University of Wolverhampton. Author of *Appeasing Hitler: The Diplomacy of Sir Neville Henderson 1937–39* (1999) and *The Holocaust* (1999). Contributor to *Munich Crisis 1938: The Prelude to World War II*, edited by Igor Lukes and Erik Goldstein (1999); and to *Journal of Contemporary History*.

Newman, Christine M. Assistant Editor, Victoria County History of Durham, University of Durham. Author of *Late Medieval Northallerton: A Small Market Town and Its Hinterland, c. 1470–1540* (1999). Also a contributor of articles in *Studies in Church History, Archives, Northern History*, and *Continuity and Change*, among other publications.

Nicholls, Andrew D. Assistant Professor of History, Buffalo State College, Buffalo, New York. Author of *The Jacobean Union: A Reconsideration of British Civil Policies under the Early Stuarts* (1999) and coauthor (with Paul J. Delaney) of *After the Fire: Sainte Marie among the Hurons since 1649* (1988). Has also contributed articles to *Scottish Tradition* (*Journal of the Canadian Association for Scottish Studies*) and *Inland Seas* (*Quarterly Journal of the Great Lakes Historical Association*).

Nicholls, David. Professor of History and Head of Department at Manchester Metropolitan University. Author of *The Lost Prime Minister: A Life of Sir Charles Dilke* (1995) and of several essays on the British middle class and on 19th-century radicalism.

Noonkester, Myron C. Dean of Arts and Sciences, William Carey College, Hattiesburg, Mississippi. Co-Director, Center for Study of Life and Work of William Carey. Contributor to *Historical Dictionary of Stuart England*, edited by Ronald Fritze and W.B. Robison (1996); *A Global Encyclopedia of Historical Writing*, edited by Daniel Woolf (1998); *Encyclopedia of Historians and Historical Writing*, edited by Kelly Boyd (1999); and *Magill's Guide to Military History*, edited by John Powell (2001). Has contributed articles to *English Language Notes, Explicator, Harvard Theological Review, Historical Research, Journal of British Studies, New England Quarterly, Notes and Queries*, and *Sixteenth Century Journal*.

O'Brien, Matthew J. Assistant Professor of History, Franciscan University of Steubenville, Ohio. Contributor to *Proceedings of the Irish and Polish Migration in Comparative Perspective Conference*, edited by John Belchem and Claus Tenfeld (2002); and *The New Irish American History* (forthcoming). Has also contributed an article to *Eire–Ireland*. Research interests are Irish migration, British immigration, and American ethnicity.

O'Day, Alan. Visiting Fellow, Rothermere American Institute, University of Oxford, and Fellow in Modern History at Greyfriars. Has served as Senior Visiting Fellow, Institute of Irish Studies, Queen's University Belfast (2001–2). Author of *The English Face of Irish Nationalism* (1977), *Parnell and the First Home Rule Episode* (1986), *Irish Home Rule 1867–1921* (1998), and *Charles Stewart Parnell* (1998), among other works.

O'Donnell. Tracey L. Independent scholar based in Richmond, Virginia.

O'Donovan, Perry. Cambridge University Library.

Onslow, Barbara. Lecturer, School of English, University of Reading. Author of *Women of the Press in Nineteenth Century Britain* (2000). Contributor of articles and reviews to *Victorian Poetry, Victorian Periodicals Review, Media History, Journal of Modern History,* and *Nineteenth Century Prose.* Has also contributed to *Reader's Guide to Literature in English,* edited by Mark Hawkins-Dady (1996); *Encyclopedia of Life Writing,* edited by Margaretta Jolly (2001); and *Encyclopedia of the Written and Printed Word* (forthcoming). Research interests lie in the field of 19th-century periodicals, with a specialty in women's journalism.

Orbell, John. Vice President, ING Barings, London. Head of Record Services, including historical archives and art collection. Business archivist and historian. Author (with Alison Turton) of *British Banking: A Guide to Historical Archives* (2001), and of other monographs and articles in the areas of business archives and business history.

Ovendale, Ritchie. Formerly Professor of International Politics, University of Wales, Aberystwyth. Author of *"Appeasement" and the English Speaking World* (1975); *The English-Speaking Alliance: Britain, the United States, the Dominions, and the Cold War, 1945–51* (1985); *Britain, the United States, and the End of the Palestine Mandate, 1942–1948* (1989); *Britain, the United States, and the Transfer of Power in the Middle East, 1945–1962* (1996); *Anglo-American Relations in the Twentieth Century* (1998); *The Longman Companion to the Middle East since 1914* (2nd ed., 1998); and *The Origins of the Arab-Israeli Wars* (3rd ed, 1999). Editor of *The Foreign Policy of the British Labour Governments 1945–1951* (1984) and *British Defence Policy since 1945: Documents in Contemporary History* (1994).

Owen, Arthur E.B. Formerly Keeper of Manuscripts, Cambridge University Library. Author of *Cambridge University Library: Summary Guide to Accessions of MSS since 1867* (1996). Editor of *Records of the Commissioners of Sewers in the Parts of Holland (Lincs), 1547–1603* (1977), among other works. Contributor to *Local Maps and Plans from Medieval England,* edited by R.A. Skelton and P.D.A. Harvey (1986); and *Names, Places, and People,* edited by Alexander R. Rumble and A.D. Mills (1997). Formerly editor of *Archives.*

Palgrave, Derek A. Historian, chartered chemist, freelance lecturer in chemical technology and history, tutor in local history at Cambridge University Institute of Continuing Education. Compiler and editor of *Fluid Fertilizer Science and Technology* (1991). Author of articles in *Industrial Archaeology Review, Journal of the Science of Food and Agriculture, Journal of Agricultural Engineering Research,* and many other publications. Current interests include onomastics, semiotics, and demography.

Paris, Michael. Reader in Modern History at University of Central Lancashire and Fellow of the Royal Historical Society. Author of *Winged Warfare* (1992), *From the Wright Brothers to Top Gun* (1995), *The First World War and Popular Cinema* (1999), and *Warrior Nation* (2000).

Parsons, David. University Fellow in the Centre for English Local History and Emeritus Reader in Church Archaeology at the University of Leicester. Formerly Head of the Department of Adult Education. Sometime Honorary Editor of *Archaelogical Journal.* Editor of *Tenth-Century Studies* (1975) and author of articles on the archaeology of the Anglo-Saxon missions to the Continent. Research interests include the architecture of Anglo-Saxon England and Carolingian Europe.

Patterson, Catherine F. Associate Professor of History, University of Houston, Texas. Author of *Urban Patronage in Early Modern England: Corporate Boroughs, the Landed Elite, and the Crown, 1580–1640* (1999). Contributor to the journals *History, Journal of British Studies,* and *Midland History.*

Paz, Denis. Professor of History, University of North Texas, Denton. Author of *The Politics of Working-Class Education in Britain, 1830–50* (1980); *The Priesthoods and Apostasies of Pierce Connelly: A Study of Victorian Conversion and Anticatholicism* (1986); and *Popular Anti-Catholicism in Mid-Victorian England* (1992). Editor of *Nineteenth-Century English Religious Traditions: Retrospect and Prospect* (1995). Has also contributed articles to the journals *Albion, Journal of British Studies, Historical Research, History of Education,* and *Historian,* among others.

Peakman, Julie. Visiting lecturer at Oxford Brookes University and Fellow of Wellcome Institute for the History of Medicine. Author of *Mighty Lewd Books: The Development of Pornography in Eighteenth-Century England* (2003) and *Sexual Behaviour in Eighteenth England* (under commission from Atlantic, London). Contributor to *The Encyclopedia of Erotic Literature* (forthcoming); *This Launch into the Wide World: Essays on Fanny Hill,* edited by Patsy Fowler and Alan Jackson (forthcoming); *From Physico-Theology to Bio-Technology,* edited by Kurt Bayertz and Roy Porter (1998), and *Voltaire Studies.*

Pearson, M.J. Tutor in Medieval History, University of Wales, Bangor. Author of *Fasti Ecclesiae Anglicanae, 1066–1300: The Welsh Dioceses* (forthcoming). Has also contributed articles to *Welsh History Review* and *Cambrian Medieval Celtic Studies.* Research interests are medieval Wales, Anglo-Norman politics, the Wars of the Roses, and the medieval Near East.

Pelteret, David A.E. Senior Research Fellow, Department of History, King's College London. Author of *Slavery in Early Medieval England* (1995) and *Catalogue of English Post-Conquest Vernacular Documents* (1990). Editor of *Anglo-Saxon History: Basic Readings* (2000) and (with J. Douglas Woods) *The Anglo-Saxons: Synthesis and Achievement* (1985). Contributor to various books and reference works. Has also contributed articles to *Anglo-Saxon England* and *Mediaeval Studies.*

Phillips, Ann Marie. Also a contributor to *Reader's Guide to Women's Studies.*

Pierce, Hazel. Business Development Manager, University of Wales, Bangor and independent writer. Author of *Margaret Pole, Countess of Salisbury, 1473–1541: Loyalty, Lineage, and Leadership* (forthcoming).

Pirie, Gordon. Lecturer in Human Geography, University of Salford, Manchester. Author of *Civil Aviation and British Imperialism, 1919–1939* (forthcoming). Has also contributed articles to *Journal of Contemporary History, Journal of Transport History,* and *Journal of Historical Geography.*

Pogson, Fiona. Senior Lecturer in History, Liverpool Hope University College. Contributor to *Government, Religion, and Society in Northern England, 1000–1700,* edited by John C. Appleby and Paul Dalton (1997); and *New Dictionary of National Biography,* edited by Brian Harrison (forthcoming). Has also contributed to the journals *History, Northern History,* and *Recusant History.*

Pollard, Anthony James. Professor of History, University of Teesside, Middlebrough. Author of *The Wars of the Roses* (2nd ed., 2001), *Richard III and the Princes in the Tower* (1993), and *Late-Medieval England, 1400–1529* (2000). Also the editor of several collections of essays on fifteenth-century history and a contributor to various historical journals.

Pratt, David. Fellow and Director of Studies in History, Downing College, University of Cambridge. Research interests include Anglo-Saxon kingship, early medieval political thought and court culture, and the reign of King Alfred the Great.

Prior, Charles W.A. Teaching Fellow, Department of History, Queen's University at Kingston, Ontario. Editor of *Mandeville and Augustan Ideas: New Essays* (2000). Has contributed reviews to *History of Political Thought, Eighteenth-Century Studies,* and *Scriblerian,* among other publications.

Pritchard, Jane. Archivist, Rambert Dance Company, London. Contributor to *Les Ballets, 1933,* edited by S. Tobin (1987); *Dance History: An Introduction,* edited by Janet Lansdale and June Layson (2nd ed., 1994); *The Royal Swedish Ballet 1773–1998,* edited by George Dorris (1999); and *One Hundred Years of British Dance* (2000). Also has written numerous articles on dance and ballet for *Dancing Times, Dance Research, Dance Chronicle, Dance Theatre Journal,* and *Ballet Review,* among other publications.

Proctor, Tammy M. Associate Professor and Chair of History, Wittenberg University at Springfield, Ohio. Author of *On My Honour: Guides and Scouts in Interwar Britain* (2002) and *Female Intelligence: Women Spies and the Great War* (forthcoming). Has also contributed articles to *History Workshop Journal* and *Comparative Studies in Society and History.*

Pryke, Sam. Lecturer in Sociology, Liverpool Hope University College. Contributed articles to *Social History, Nations and Nationalism, Sexualities,* and *Sociology.*

Purdue, A.W. Senior Lecturer in History, Open University, Milton Keynes. Author of *The Second World War* (1999) and *Merchants and Gentry in North East England* (1999). Coauthor (with J. M. Golby) of *The Civilization of the Crowd* (1984), *The Making of the Modern Christmas* (1986), and *The Monarchy and the British People* (1988).

Quilley, Geoffrey. Formerly at University of Leicester.

Ranger, Paul. Independent writer and director, based in Oxford. Author of *Experiments in Drama* (1970); *The Lost Theatres of Winchester* (1976); *A Masterguide to She Stoops to Conquer* (1985); *A Masterguide to The School for Scandal* (1986); *Terror and Pity Reign in Every Breast* (1991); *Form, Meaning, and Performance* (1995); and *The Playwright in the City and the Poet in the Country* (1996), among other works. Has also contributed articles to *Theatre Notebook, Speech and Drama, Hatcher Review,* and *Oxoniensia,* among other publications. Editor of *Speech and Drama.*

Ranieri, Ruggero. Senior Lecturer and Jean Monnet Professor in History at the University of Manchester. Editor of *The Steel Industry in the New Millennium* (1988). Publications on the history of European integration, the development of the European steel industry after 1945, and the European Coal and Steel Community.

Rees, D. Ben. Professor of Ecclesiastical History, University of Potchestfrore, South Africa. Author of *Wales, the Cultural Heritage* (1981); *Preparation for Crisis: Adult Education 1945–1980* (1982); *The Life and Work of Owen Thomas: A Welsh Preacher in Liverpool* (1991); and *Violence and Virtue in the Social and Political Life of Liverpool 1800–1911* (2000). Coeditor (with R. Merfyn Jones) of *Liverpool Welsh and Their Religion* (1984). Formerly editor of *Reconciliation Quarterly* and currently coeditor of *Peace and Reconciliation.*

Rees, Emma L.E. Senior Lecturer in English and Programme Leader, Literature and Film, University College Chester. Author of *Gender, Genre, Exile: Margaret Cavendish's Writings of the 1650s* (2003). Contributor to *Consuming Narratives: Gender and Monstrous Appetite in the Middle Ages and the Renaissance,* edited by Liz McAvoy and Teresa Walters (2002); *A Princely Brave Woman: Collected Essays on Margaret Cavendish, Duchess of Newcastle,* edited by Stephen Clucas (2003); and *Authorial Conquests: Essays on Genre and Poetics in the Writings of Margaret Cavendish,* edited by Line Cottegnies and Nancy S. Weitz (2003). Contributed articles to *In-Between: Essays and Studies in Literary Criticism* (2000); *The Guinness Encyclopedia of Popular Music,* edited by Colin Larkin (1991); *A Reader's Guide to Literature in English,* edited by Mark Hawkins-Dady (1996); *Encyclopedia of Feminist Literary Theory,* edited by Elizabeth Kowaleski-Wallace (1997); *The Cambridge Guide to Women's Writing in English,* edited by Lorna Sage (1999); and *Women's Writing.* Author of the introduction to Margaret Cavendish's *Nature's Pictures* for Brown University's Women Writers Electronic Publications project, *Renaissance Women Online* (1997).

Rex, Richard. Senior University Lecturer in Church History, University of Cambridge. Tutor and Director of Studies in History, Queens' College, Cambridge. Author of *The Theology of John Fisher* (1991), *Henry VIII and the English Reformation* (1993), *The Lollards* (2002), and *The Tudors* (2002). Editor of *A Reformation Rhetoric: Thomas Swynnerton's Tropes and Figures of Scripture* (1999). Contributor to *Humanism, Reform, and the Reformation,* edited by Brendan Bradshaw and Eamon

Duffy (1989); *The Education of a Christian Society,* edited by N. Scott Amos *et al.* (1999); and *The Beginnings of English Protestantism,* edited by Peter Marshall and Alec Ryrie (2002). Has also contributed articles to *Journal of Ecclesiastical History, Historical Journal,* and *Analecta Bollandiana,* among other publications.

Richardson, R.C. Professor of History at King Alfred's College, Winchester, U.K. Publications include *The Changing Face of English Local History* (2000), *The Study of History: A Bibliographical guide* (2nd ed., 2000), *The Debate on the English Revolution* (3rd ed., 1998), *Images of Oliver Cromwell* (1993), *Town and Countryside in the English Revolution* (1992), and *Freedom and the English Revolution* (1986). He is coeditor of the international journal *Literature and History.*

Rippon, Stephen John. Reader in Landscape Archaeology, University of Exeter. Author of *The Gwent Levels* (1996), *The Severn Estuary* (1997), and *The Transformation of Coastal Wetlands* (2000). Editor of *Estuarine Archaeology* (2001). Research interests include wetland and landscape archaeology of the Roman and medieval periods in northwest Europe.

Ritschel, Daniel. Associate Professor of History, University of Maryland, Baltimore County, Baltimore. Author of *The Politics of Planning: The Debate on Economic Planning in Britain in the 1930s* (1997). Contributor to *Modern Thinkers on Welfare,* edited by Robert Page and Vic George (1995). Has also contributed articles to *English Historical Review* and *Twentieth Century British History,* among other publications.

Robert, Krisztina. Independent historian and author of various articles on women's military service and the social and cultural history of war.

Robinson, Kristen. St Joseph, Michigan. Independent scholar focusing on 18th-century Britain.

Robison, William B. Professor of History and Head of the Department of History and Political Science, Southeastern Louisiana University, Hammond. Coeditor (with Ronald H. Fritze) of *Historical Dictionary of Stuart England, 1603–1689* (1996) and *Historical Dictionary of Late Medieval England, 1272–1485* (2002). Contributor most recently to (among other works) *From Polis to Empire: The Ancient World c.800 B.C.–A.D. 500: A Biographical Dictionary,* edited by Andrew Traver (2002); *The Rise of the Medieval World, 500–1300: A Biographical Dictionary,* edited by Jana Schulman (2002); *The Late Medieval Age of Crisis and Renewal, 1300–1500: A Biographical Dictionary,* edited by Clayton Drees (2001); *Renaissance and Reformation, 1500–1620: A Biographical Dictionary,* edited by Jo Eldridge Carney (2001); *Absolutism and the Scientific Evolution, 1600–1720: A Biographical Dictionary,* edited by Christopher Baker (2002); *Enlightenment and Revolution, 1690–1815: A Biographical Dictionary,* edited by Kevin E. Dodson (forthcoming); *The Modern Age, 1914–2000: A Biographical Dictionary,* edited by Joseph E. Nordgren (forthcoming); and *New Dictionary of National Biography,* edited by Brian Harrison (forthcoming). Has also contributed articles to the journals *Criminal Justice History,*

Historical Journal, and *Lamar Journal of the Humanities,* among others.

Roe, (Owen) Michael. Formerly at the University of Tasmania. Fellow of the Australian Academy of the Humanities. His publication record spans 50 years, in the subject areas of Australian, imperial, and British affairs.

Roos, Anna Marie E. Assistant Professor, Department of History, University of Minnesota Duluth. Author of *Luminaries in the Natural World: Perceptions of the Sun and Moon in England, 1400–1720* (2001). Contributor to *Expertise Constructed: Didactic Literature in the British Atlantic World* (2003) and *Looking Up: Science and Observation in the Early Modern Period* (2002). Has also contributed articles to *Bulletin of the History of Medicine* and *Ambix.*

Rose, Jonathan. Professor of History, Drew University, Madison, New Jersey. Author of *The Intellectual Life of the British Working Classes* (2001) and *The Edwardian Temperament 1895–1919* (1986). Editor of *The Holocaust and the Book* (2001) and *The Revised Orwell* (1992). Editor (with Patricia Anderson) of *British Literary Publishing Houses 1820–1965* (1991). Editor (with Ezra Greenspan) of *Book History* (journal). Has also contributed articles to *Albion, Journal of the History of Ideas, Journal of British Studies, Leipziger Jahrbuch zur Buchgeschichte, Victorian Periodicals Review,* and other journals.

Rose, Susan. Senior Lecturer in History, School of Humanities and Cultural Studies, University of Surrey, Roehampton. Director of the Hearth Tax Research Centre. Editor of *The Navy of the Lancastrian Kings; The Accounts of William Soper, Clerk of the King's Ships, 1421–27* (1982); *Southampton and the Navy in the Reign of Henry V* (1998); and *Medieval Naval Warfare 1000–1500* (2002). Computing editor of *The Hearth Tax for Kent* (2000) and the *Hearth Tax for Cambridgeshire* (2000). Has also contributed articles to *Mariner's Mirror, Journal of Military History,* and other journals.

Ross, Andrew C. Honorary Fellow, School of Divinity, University of Edinburgh. Author of *John Philip: Missions, Race and Politics in South Africa* (1986), *A Vision Betrayed: the Jesuits in Japan and China, 1542–1742* (1994), *Blantyre Mission and the Making of Modern Malawi* (1996) and *David Livingstone: Mission and Empire* (2002).

Ross, David R. Independent writer and broadcaster, based in Scotland. Author of *On the Trail of William Wallace* (1999), *On the Trail of Robert the Bruce* (1999), *On the Trail of Bonnie Prince Charlie* (2000), *Wallace and Bruce* (2001), and *A Passion for Scotland* (2002). Contributor to *Scotland's Story.*

Rossi, John P. Professor of History, La Salle University, Philadelphia, Pennsylvania. Author of *The Transformation of the British Liberal Party: A Study in the Tactics of the Liberal Opposition, 1874–1880* (1978); *A Whole New Game: Off the Field Changes in Baseball, 1946–1960* (1999); and *The National Game: Baseball and American Culture* (2000). Contributed articles to *Irish Historical Studies, Canadian Journal of History,*

Church Studies, Proceedings of the American Philosophical Society, and *Catholic Historical Review.*

Roth, Christine. Assistant Professor of English, University of Wisconsin, Oshkosh. Author of *Cult of the Little Girl Narratives in Late-Victorian Britain* (forthcoming). Contributed articles to *ELT: English Literature in Transition* and *Contemporary Novelists,* edited by Neil Schaler and Josh Laurer (7th ed., 2001). Research interests include 19th-century literature, art, and culture.

Rubinstein, Hilary. Part-time Lecturer in Modern Jewish History, University of Wales, Lampeter. Author of *The Jews in Victoria, 1835–1985* (1986); *Chosen: The Jews in Australia* (1987); and *The Jews in Australia: A Thematic History,* vol. 1, *1788–1945* (1991). Coauthor (with William D. Rubinstein) of *Philosemitism: Admiration and Support in the English-Speaking World for Jews, 1840–1939* (1999). Contributor of many articles in Jewish historical journals. Formerly on the Editorial Board, *Australian Journal of Jewish Studies.*

Rubinstein, William D. Professor of Modern History, University of Wales, Aberystwyth. Author of *Men of Property: The Very Wealthy in Britain since the Industrial Revolution* (1981); *Capitalism, Culture, and Decline in Britain, 1750–1990* (1993); *Elites and the Wealthy in Modern British History* (1997); and *Britain's Century: Political and Social History, 1815–1905* (1998). Formerly editor of *Australian Jewish Historical Society Journal.*

Rule, John. Emeritus Professor of History, University of Southampton. Author of *The Vital Century: England's Developing Economy 1714–1815* (1992); *Albion's People: English Society, 1714–1815* (1992); *The Labouring Classes in Early Industrial England 1750–1850* (1986); and numerous articles on social and labour history. Coauthor (with Roger Wells) of *Crime, Protest, and Popular Politics in Southern England* (1997). Formerly editor of *Southern History.*

Rushton, Neil S. Archaeology Officer, North Hertfordshire District Council. Contributor to *Historical Atlas of Sussex,* edited by Kim Leslie and Brian Short (1999); and *Purbeck Papers,* edited by David Hinton (2002). Author of *Baldock: Excavations of the Iron Age and Romano-British Settlement and Cemeteries 1979–1995* (forthcoming). Has also contributed articles to *Journal of Interdisciplinary History, Continuity and Change,* and *Architectural History,* and to the county archaeological journals for Hampshire, Sussex, and Herefordshire.

Sampson, Joyce E. Associate Professor of Strategy and Policy, U.S. Naval War College, Newport, Rhode Island. Contributed articles to the *Historical Dictionary of Late Medieval England 1272–1485,* edited by Ronald H. Fritze and William B. Robison (2002); *New Dictionary of National Biography,* edited by Brian Harrison (forthcoming); and *Dictionary of Irish Biography* (forthcoming).

Schaffer, Simon. Cambridge University.

Schmitz, Christopher J. Lecturer in Modern History, University of St Andrews. Author of *The Growth of Big Business in the United States and Western Europe, 1850–1939* (1993). Editor of *Big Business in Mining and Petroleum: Critical Writings in Business History* (1995). Contributor to *A Soldier and a Woman: Sexual Integration in the Military,* edited by Gerard DeGroot and Corinna Peniston-Bird (2000). Has also contributed articles to *Economic History Review, Business History, Journal of European Economic History,* and *German History,* among other publications.

Schulenburg, Alexander Hugo. Research Officer, Corporation of London. Formerly Lecturer in Social Anthropology, University of Sussex. Research interests include the spatial history of London, the East India Company, and the British empire. Has contributed articles to *Journal of Historical Geography, Notes and Queries,* and *Local Historian,* among other publications. Author of *Transient Observations: The Textualizing of St Helena through Five Hundred Years of Colonial Discourse* (forthcoming).

Schwarz, Marc L. Associate Professor of History, University of New Hampshire, Durham. Research interests include early modern English political and ecclesiastical history. Contributor to *Journal of British Studies, Albion,* and *Quaker History.*

Shillington, Kevin. Independent scholar based in London. Editor of *The Encyclopedia of African History* (forthcoming). Author of *History of Africa* (revised ed., 1995), *A History of Southern Africa* (revised ed., 2002), *The Colonisation of the Southern Tswana* (1985), *Jugnauth: Prime Minister of Mauritius* (1991), *An African Adventure: A Brief Life of Cecil Rhodes* (1993), *Ghana and the Rawlings Factor* (1992), and *The Causes and Consequences of Independence in Africa* (1997). Editor (with Elizabeth Kanyogonya) of *Sowing the Mustard Seed: The Autobiography of Yoweri Museveni, President of Uganda* (1997). Contributor to *Encarta Encyclopedia.* Book reviewer for *Journal of African History, Journal of Southern African Studies,* and *African Studies Review.*

Smith, Brendan. Senior Lecturer in History, University of Bristol. Author of *Colonisation and Conquest in Medieval Ireland: The English in Louth, 1170–1330* (1999). Editor of *Britain and Ireland 900–1300* (1999). Has also contributed articles to *English Historical Review, Peritia,* and *Thirteenth Century England,* among other publications.

Smith, Lawrence B. Assistant Professor of History, University of Mobile, Mobile, Alabama. Editor of annotated edition of *The Diary of a Scottish Officer in Marlborough's Army* (2001). Contributor to *New Dictionary of National Biography,* edited by Brian Harrison (forthcoming). Also a contributor to *Journal of the Society for Army Historical Research* and book reviewer for *Albion* and *History.*

Smith, S.D. Lecturer in History, Department of History, University of York. Author of *An Exact and Industrious Tradesman: The Letter Book of Joseph Symson of Kendal, 1711–1720* (forthcoming). Has also contributed articles to *Business History, Economic History Review, Journal of Interdisciplinary History, Journal of Plantation Societies in the Americas, Social History of Medicine,* and *Slavery and Abolition.*

Snyder, Christopher A. Associate Professor of History and Chair, Department of History and Politics, Marymount University, Arlington, Virginia. Author of *An Age of Tyrants: Britain and the Britons, AD 400–600* (1998); *The World of King Arthur* (2000); and *The Britons* (2003).

Sommers, Susan Mitchell. Associate Professor of History, St Vincent College, Latrobe, Pennsylvania. Author of *Parliamentary Politics of a County and Its Town: Suffolk and Ipswich in the Eighteenth Century* (2002). Has also contributed articles to *Parliamentary History, 1650–1850: Ideas, Inquiry, and Aesthetics in the Early Modern Era* and to the Suffolk Institute of Archaeology and History. Research interests include 18th-century British electoral politics and Catholic emancipation.

Sommerville, C. John. Professor of History, Department of History, University of Florida, Gainesville. Author of *Popular Religion in Restoration England* (1977), *The Secularization of Early Modern England* (1992), *The News Revolution in England* (1996), and other works. Has also contributed articles to *Church History, Religion, Journal of Interdisciplinary History, Past and Present, Albion, History Today, Journal of Religious History, Social Science History, Library, Journal of the History of Ideas,* and *Journal of British Studies,* among other publications.

Sorrenson, Richard. Indiana University, Bloomington.

Sparkes, Ivan G. Formerly curator of Wycombe Chair Museum. Author of *The English Country Chair* (1973), *English Domestic Furniture: 1100–1837* (1980), *Four-Poster and Tester Beds* (1990), *The English Windsor Chair* (2000), and *Dictionary of Group Terms and Collective Nouns* (2nd ed., 1985). Has also contributed to the journals *Regional Furniture* and *Furniture History,* among others.

Speck, W.A. Emeritus Professor of Modern History, University of Leeds. Author of *James II* (2002) and (with Mary K. Geiter) *Colonial America from Jamestown to Yorktown* (forthcoming), among other works.

Spencer, Mark G. Postdoctoral Research Fellow, University of Toronto, St Michael's College. Author of *Hume and Eighteenth-Century America* (forthcoming). Editor of *Hume's Reception in Early America* (2 vols, 2002). Has contributed articles and reviews on American and British topics to many journals including *Eighteenth-Century Studies, Hume Studies, Scottish Historical Review,* and *William and Mary Quarterly.*

Spensley, Ronald Mason. Former Research Fellow at the University of Leeds, Further Education Lecturer, and Senior Education Officer. Author of articles on, among other topics, medieval French literature and English 18th- and 19th-century social history, with particular reference to country house studies.

Spivack, Charlotte. University of Massachusetts, Amherst.

Sprey, Ilicia J. Assistant Professor, Department of History, Saint Joseph's College, Rensselear, Indiana. Contributor to *Historical Dictionary of Late Medieval England, 1272–1485,* edited by

Ronald H. Fritze and William B. Robison (2002); *Revue d'Histoire Ecclésiastique;* and *Sixteenth Century Journal.*

Stacey, Robin Chapman. Associate Professor of History and Adjunct Associate Professor of Women Studies, University of Washington, Seattle. Author of *The Road to Judgment: From Custom to Court in Medieval Ireland and Wales* (1994). Contributor to *Ireland and Europe in the Early Middle Ages: Texts and Transmission,* edited by Proinséas Ní Chatáin and Michael Richter (2002); *The Welsh King and His Court,* edited by T.M. Charles-Edwards *et al.* (2000); *Crossed Paths: Methodological Approaches to the Celtic Aspect of the European Middle Ages,* edited by Benjamin Hudson and Vickie Ziegler (1991); and *Lawyers and Laymen,* edited by T.M. Charles-Edwards, M. Owen, and D. Walters (1986). Has also contributed articles to *Cambridge Medieval Celtic Studies.*

Stearn, Roger T. Research Editor, *New Dictionary of National Biography,* Oxford. Contributor to *Popular Imperialism and the Military,* edited by J.M. MacKenzie (1992); *Journal of Imperial and Commonwealth History;* and *Journal for the Society for Army Historical Research.* Editor of and contributor to *Soldiers of the Queen.*

Stewart, John. Director, Centre for Health, Medicine, and Society: Past and Present, Oxford Brookes University. Author of *"The Battle for Health": A Political History of the Socialist Medical Association* (1999) and of numerous articles for journals such as *Scottish Historical Review, Journal of Policy History, Annals of Science, Medical History,* and *Twentieth Century British History.*

Stollery, Martin. Southampton Institute.

Strahorn, Eric A. Assistant Professor of History, Florida Gulf Coast University, Fort Myers. Contributed articles to *Selected Annual Proceedings of the Florida Conference of Historians* and *The Encyclopedia of Modern Asian History.*

Taddeo, Julie Anne. Visiting Scholar, University of California at Berkeley. Author of *Lytton Strachey and the Search for Modern Sexual Identity: The Last Eminent Victorian* (2002). Contributor to *Journal of the History of Sexuality, Clues: A Journal of Detection,* and anthologies on women's history, travel literature, and modernism and sexuality.

Tanner, Norman. University Research Lecturer, University of Oxford. Author of *The Church in Late Medieval Norwich, 1370–1532* (1984); *The Councils of the Church: A Short History* (2001); and *Is the Church Too Asian? Reflections on the Ecumenical Councils* (2002). Coauthor of vol. 4 (1999) of *Storia del concilio Vaticano II,* edited by G. Alberigo. Editor of *Heresy Trials in the Diocese of Norwich 1428–1431* (1977); *Decrees of the Ecumenical Councils* (2 vols, 1990); *Kent Heresy Proceedings 1511–1512* (1997); and (with Shannon McSheffrey) *Lollards of Coventry 1486–1522* (2003).

Taylor, Antony. Senior Lecturer in History, School of Cultural Studies, Sheffield Hallam University. Author of *"Down with the Crown": British Anti-Monarchism and Debates about Royalty*

since 1790 (1999). Contributor to *Re-Reading the Constitution: New Narratives in the Political History of England's Long Nineteenth Century,* edited by James Vernon (1996). Coeditor with David Nash of *Republicanism in Victorian Britain* (2000) and with John Breuilly and Gottfried Niedhart of *The Era of the Reform League: English Labour and Radical Politics 1857–1872: Documents Selected by Gustav Mayer* (1995). Contributor to *Historical Journal, Historical Research, History Today, International Review of Social History, Journal of British Studies, Parliamentary History,* and *Social History.*

Taylor, James Stephen. Emeritus Professor of History, State University of West Georgia, Carrollton. Author of *Jonas Hanway* (1985) and *Poverty, Migration, and Settlement in the Industrial Revolution* (1989). Contributor to *Comparative Development in Social Welfare,* edited by E.W. Martin (1972); and *Chronicling Poverty,* edited by Tim Hitchcock *et al.* (1997). Has also contributed articles to *Journal of Economic History, Past and Present, Eighteenth-Century Studies,* and *Journal of British Studies,* among other publications.

Thompson, Bruce. Lecturer in History, University of California, Santa Cruz. Editor of *The Literal Imagination: Selected Essays by Ian Watt* (forthcoming). Contributor to *Stanford Humanities Review; Judaism: A Quarterly Journal of Jewish Life and Thought;* and *Encyclopedia of Historians and Historical Writing,* edited by Kelly Boyd (1999).

Thompson, Helen. Assistant Professor of English, University of Louisiana at Lafayette. Editor (with Caitriona Moloney) of *Irish Women Writers Speak Out: Voices from the Field* (2003). Editor (with Caitriona Moloney and Frederick Sanders) of Special Irish Issue of *Journal of Commonwealth and Postcolonial Studies* (2000).

Thompson, Michael James. Clerk in Holy Orders, Rector of St Mary and St Martin, Stamford, Lincolnshire. Administrator of the Armagh Cathedral Choir Appeal and Secretary of the Alcuin Club for the Study of Liturgy. Research interests include Irish ecclesiastical history, cathedral constitutions, worship and music, and the liturgy. Contributor to *New SCM Dictionary of Liturgy and Worship* (2002).

Thompson, Noel. Professor, Department of History, University of Wales, Swansea. Author of *The People's Science: The Popular Political Economy of Exploitation and Crises, 1816–1834* (1984); *The Market and Its Critics: Socialist Political Economy in Nineteenth Century Britain* (1988); *John Strachey: An Intellectual Biography* (1993); *Political Economy and the Labour Party: The Economics of Democratic Socialism, 1884–1995* (1996); *The Real Rights of Man: Political Economics for the Working Class* (1998); and *Left in the Wilderness: The Political Economy of British Democratic Socialism since 1979* (2002).

Thomson, William P.L. Formerly Rector of Kirkwall Grammar School, Orkney. Author of *The Little General and the Rousay Crofters* (1981), *Kelp-Making in Orkney* (1984), *History of Orkney* (1987), *Lord Henry Sinclair's 1492 Rental of Orkney* (1996), and *New History of Orkney* (2001). Has also con-

tributed articles to *Scottish Geographical Magazine, Northern Studies, Northern Scotland,* and *New Orkney Antiquarian Journal,* among other publications, and to books dealing with the social and economic history of Orkney and Shetland.

Thornton, Tim. Principal Lecturer and Head of History, School of Music and Humanities, University of Huddersfield. Author of *Cheshire and the Tudor State, 1480–1560* (2000). Editor of *Social Attitudes and Political Structures in the Fifteenth Century* (2000) and (with Bertrand Taithe) *Prophecy: The Power of Inspired Language in History, 1300–2000* (1997); *War: Identities in Conflicts, 1400–2000* (1998); and *Propaganda: Political Rhetoric and Identity, 1300–2000* (1999). Contributor to *Courts, Counties, and the Capital in the Later Middle Ages,* edited by Diana Dunn (1996); *Crises, Revolutions, and Self-Sustained Growth: Essays in European Fiscal History, 1130–1830,* edited by W.M. Ormrod *et al.* (1999); *The Reign of Richard II,* edited by Gwilym Dodd (2000); and *Authority and Consent in Tudor England,* edited by George Bernard and Steven Gunn (2002). Has also contributed articles to *Northern History, History Today, Historical Research, Scottish Historical Review, Bulletin of the John Rylands University Library of Manchester, Welsh History Review, New Medieval Literatures,* and *Transactions of the Royal Historical Society.*

Thorpe, Nick. Senior Lecturer in Archaeology, King Alfred's College, Winchester. Author of *The Origins of Agriculture in Europe* (1996); coauthor (with Peter James) of *Centuries of Darkness* (1991), *Ancient Inventions* (1994) and *Ancient Mysteries* (1999). Has also contributed articles to *Neolithic Enclosures in Northwest Atlantic Europe,* edited by Timothy Darvill and Julian Thomas (2001); and the journals *Antiquity* and *Cambridge Archaeological Journal,* among others.

Tigwell, Rosalind Elizabeth. Formerly Senior Lecturer in Social, Economic, and Local History, Bolton Institute. Author of *Cheshire in the 20th Century* (1985). Coauthor of *The Thomas Risley Church* (1980). Research interests include local history, history of the family, west African economic history, and British imperialism in the 19th century.

Till, Geoffrey. Dean of academic studies and head of the Defence Studies Department, (King's College London), Joint Services Command and Staff College, Watchfield, Swindon, Wiltshire. Visiting professor in maritime studies, Department of War Studies, King's College London. Author of a number of books, including *Air Power and the Royal Navy* (1979), *Maritime Strategy and the Nuclear Age* (2nd ed., 1984), and *Modern Sea Power* (1987). Coauthor (with Bryan Ranft) of *The Sea in Soviet Strategy* (2nd ed., 1989). Editor of *Coastal Forces* (1994), *Sea Power: Theory and Practice* (1994), and *Seapower at the Millennium* (2001).

Todd, Andy. Assistant Master, Harrow School, Harrow, Middlesex. Research interests include Anglo-Saxon England, especially King Offa of Mercia; and Matthew Paris and the St Albans view of the Anglo-Saxon past. Also a contributor to *New Dictionary of National Biography,* edited by Brian Harrison (forthcoming).

Todd, Sarah. Independent historian. Research interests include ballad literature of the 17th century and the history of the cultural presentation of violence.

Tomkins, Alannah. Lecturer, School of History, Keele University, Staffordshire. Editor (with Steven King) of *The Poor in England 1700–1850: An Economy of Makeshifts* (2003). Has also contributed articles to *Medical History, the Shropshire Records Series* (concerning a Shropshire man-midwife); *Midland History*; *History and Computing*; and *Women's History Notebooks*.

Tonge, Jonathan. Professor of Politics, University of Salford. Author of *Northern Ireland: Conflict and Change* (2nd ed., 2002). Co-author (with Gerard Murray) of *The SDLP and Sinn Fein 1970–2001* (2002). Coeditor (with Chris Gilligan) of *Peace or War? Understanding the Peace Process in Northern Ireland* (1997). Contributor to various journals with articles on Northern Ireland politics.

Treharne, Elaine M. Professor of Medieval Literature and Head of the Department of English, University of Leicester. Author of *Old and Middle English: An Anthology* (2000). Coeditor (with Mary Swan) of *Rewriting Old English in the Twelfth Century* (2000) and (with Phillip Pulsiano) *A Companion to Anglo-Saxon Literature* (2001). Author of numerous articles in her main research area, late Old English prose, and manuscript studies. Chair of the English Association, Chair of the Research Group into Post-Conquest Old English Manuscripts, and Second Vice-President of the International Society of Anglo-Saxonists.

Trentmann, Frank. Senior Lecturer, School of History, Classics, and Archaeology, Birkbeck College, University of London. Director of Cultures of Consumption, an Economic and Social Reserarch Council-Arts and Humanities Research Board research programme. Editor of *Paradoxes of Civil Society* (2000) and (with Mark Bevir) *Critiques of Capital in Modern Britain and America: Transatlantic Exchanges, 1800 to the Present Day* (2002). Contributor to *The Politics of Consumption*, edited by Martin Daunton and Matthew Hilton (2001); *The Political Economy of British Historical Experience, 1688–1914*, edited by Patrick O'Brien and Donald Winch (2002); and *Citizenship and Community*, edited by Eugenio Biagini (1996). Also a contributor to *Historical Journal, Journal of Contemporary History*, and *Review of International Political Economy*, among other publications.

Turnock, David. Reader in Geography, University of Leicester. Author of *The Human Geography of East Central Europe* (2002). Editor (with F.W. Carter) of *Environmental Problems of East Central Europe* (2002). Has contributed articles to *European Spatial Research and Policy, GeoJournal, Journal of Transport Geography, Land Use Policy*, and *Rural History*.

Van Hartesveldt, Fred R. Professor of History, Fort Valley State University, Fort Valley, Georgia. Author of *The Battles of the Somme, 1916: Historiography and Bibliography* (1996); *The Dardanelles Campaign, 1915: Historiography and Bibliography* (1997); *The Boer War*, edited by Asa Briggs (2000); and *The Boer War: Historiography and Bibliography* (2000). Editor of *The 1918–1919 Pandemic of Influenza: The Urban Impact in the Western World* (1992). Has also contributed articles to *Journal of the Georgia Association of Historians, Phylon, Maryland Historian,* and *Teaching History.*

Van Vugt, William E. Professor of History at Calvin College, Grand Rapids, Michigan (teaches courses in English and American history). Author and editor (with G. Daan Cloete) of *Race and Reconciliation in South Africa: A Multicultural Dialogue in Comparative Perspective* (2000). Author of *Britain to America: Mid-Nineteenth Century Immigrants to the United States* (1999); *British Buckeyes: The English, Scots, and Welsh in Ohio, 1750–1920* (forthcoming from Kent State University Press); and numerous scholarly articles and chapters in books on migration and the economic history of the North Atlantic.

Vincent, Julien. Doctoral Candidate, University of Paris-1 (Panthéon-Sorbonne) and Institut d'Histoire Moderne et Contemporaine (École Normale Supérieure). Research interests include late 19th-century economic and political thought.

Vincent, Nicholas. Professor of Medieval History, Christ Church College, Canterbury. Author of *Peter des Roches* (1996), *English Episcopal Acts IX* (1994), *The Letters of the Legate Guala Bicchieri* (1996), *The Holy Blood* (2000), and numerous articles. Editor and Director of the British Academy's Plantagenet Acts project.

Walker, Sue Sheridan. Emeritus Professor of History, Northeastern Illinois University, Chicago. Editor of *Wife and Widow in Medieval England* (1993) and *The Court Rolls of the Manor of Wakefield 1331–1333* (1983). Contributor to *The Life of the Law*, edited by Peter Birks (1993); *Journal of Medieval History*; *Journal of Legal History*; and *American Journal of Legal History*.

Walsh, Frances. Emeritus Fellow, Harris Manchester College, University of Oxford.

Walsh, George. Chicago and London.

Ward, Matthew C. University of Dundee.

Warne, Vanessa. Assistant Professor of English Literature, University of Manitoba. Research interests include Victorian print culture and gender theory.

Webster, Bruce. Honorary Senior Research Fellow, University of Kent at Canterbury. Author of *Scotland from the Eleventh Century to 1603* (1975); *The Acts of David II, King of Scots* (1982); *Medieval Scotland: The Making of an Identity* (1997); and *The Wars of the Roses* (1998). Also a contributor to the journals *Antiquarian Society, English Historical Review, Medieval History,* and *Scottish Historical Review,* among others.

Webster, Eve. Formby, Liverpool.

Webster, Wendy. Senior Lecturer in History, University of Central Lancashire. Author of *Imagining Home: Gender, "Race", and National Identity, 1945–1964* (1998). Contributor to *Women in Twentieth-Century Britain*, edited by Ina Zweiniger-Bargielowska (2001); and *Re-Presenting the Past: Women, History, and Representation*, edited by Ann-Marie Gallagher (2001). Has also contributed articles to *Historical Journal of Film, Radio, and Television*; *Journal of British Studies*; and *Women's History Review*.

Wells, Lynn. Assistant Professor of English, University of Regina, Saskatchewan. Author of *Allegories of Telling: Self-Referential Narrative in Contemporary British Fiction* (forthcoming). Contributor to *Iconoclastic Departures: Mary Shelley after "Frankenstein"*, edited by Syndy M. Conger *et al.* (1997); and *Reading Matters: Narratives in the New Media Ecology*, edited by Joseph Tabbi and Michael Wutz (1997). Has also contributed articles to *Modern Fiction Studies* and *Cyclopedia of Literary Places*, among other publications.

West, Francis. Emeritus Professor of History and Government, Deakin University, Victoria, Australia. Publications include *Political Advancement in the South Pacific* (1961, reprinted 1984); *The Justiciarship in England, 1066–1232* (1966); *Hubert Murray: The Australian Pro-Consul* (1968); (as editor) *Selected Letters of Hubert Murray* (1970); *Biography as History* (1973); *Gilbert Murray: A Life* (1984); and *From Alamein to Scarlet Beach* (1989). Has contributed articles to journals such as *Historical Studies, Speculum, Pacific Historical Review, Pacific Affairs, Foreign Affairs, History, Journal of Commonwealth and Imperial History*, and *Journal of Southeast Asian History*; and to *Encyclopaedia Britannica*.

Westfall, Richard. Indiana University, Bloomington.

Whalley, Alexander. Doctoral student in economics, University of Maryland, College Park, Maryland.

White, Graeme J. Head of History and Professor of History in the Community, Chester College of Higher Education. Author of *Restoration and Reform, 1153–1165: Recovery from Civil War in England* (2000). Contributor to *The Anarchy of King Stephen's Reign*, edited by Edmund King (1994); *Government, Religion, and Society in Northern England, 1000–1700*, edited by John C. Appleby and Paul Dalton (1997); and *War and Society in Medieval and Early Modern Britain*, edited by Diana Dunn (2000). Has also contributed articles to *Anglo-Norman Studies* and the journals *English Historical Review, History*, and *Midland History*, among others.

Williams, Carolyn D. University of Reading, Berkshire.

Williams, Chris. Professor and Director, Centre for Modern and Contemporary Wales, University of Glamorgan. Author of *Democratic Rhondda: Politics and Society, 1885–1951* (1996); *Capitalism, Community, and Conflict: The South Wales Coalfield, 1898–1947* (1998); (with Bill Jones) *B. L. Coombes* (1999); and an introduction to a new edition of *B. L. Coombes, These Poor Hands: The Autobiography of a Miner Working in South Wales* (2002). Coeditor (with Duncan Tanner and Deian Hopkin) of *The Labour Party in Wales, 1900–2000* (2000); and (with Bill Jones) of *With Dust Still in His Throat: A B.L. Coombes Anthology* (1999). Editor of *A Companion to Nineteenth-Century Britain* (2003).

Williams, Jack. Reader in Cultural History, Liverpool John Moores University. Author of *Cricket and England: A Cultural and Social History of the Inter-War Years* (1999) and *Cricket and Race* (2001). Editor (with Jeffrey Hill) of *Sport and Identity in the North of England* (1996). Contributor to *Sport in Britain: A Social History*, edited by Tony Mason (1989); *Sport and the Working Class in Modern Britain*, edited by Richard Holt (1990); and *Social Conditions, Status, and Community*, edited by Keith Laybourn (1997). Has also contributed articles to *Local Historian, Sports Historian*, and *Sporting Traditions*.

Williamson, Philip. Professor of History, University of Durham. Author of *National Crisis and National Government: British Politics, the Economy, and Empire 1926–1932* (1992); and *Stanley Baldwin: Conservative Leadership and National Values* (1999). Contributor to *English Historical Review, Historical Journal, Parliamentary History*, and other journals.

Wilson, Peter H. Professor of Early Modern History, University of Sunderland. Author of several books and articles, including *War, State, and Society in Württemberg, 1677–1793* (1995); *German Armies: War and German Politics 1648–1806* (1998); *The Holy Roman Empire 1495–1806* (1999); and *Absolutism in Central Europe* (2000).

Winstanley, Michael. Senior Lecturer in History, University of Lancaster. Author of *The Shopkeepers' World, 1830–1914* (1983); and *Ireland and the Land Question, 1800–1922* (1984). Contributor to *Business Enterprise in Modern Britain*, edited by M.B. Rose and M.W. Kirby (1994); and *The English Urban Landscape*, edited by P.J. Waller (2000), among other works.

Wordie, J.R. Lecturer in History, Reading University. Author of *Estate Management in Eighteenth-Century England* (1982) and *Enclosure in Berkshire, 1485–1885* (2000). Editor (with C.W. Chalklin) of *Town and Countryside: The English Landowner in the National Economy, 1660–1860* (1989); and *Agriculture and Politics in England, 1815–1939* (2000). Contributor to *Past and Present, Research in Economic History*, and *Economic History Review*.

Yates, Nigel. Honorary Fellow in Church History, University of Wales, Lampeter. Author of *Buildings, Faith, and Worship: The Liturgical Arrangements of Anglican Churches 1600–1900* (2nd ed., 2000), and *Anglican Ritualism in Victorian Britain 1830–1910* (1999). Formerly Review Editor of *Southern History* and currently General Editor, Kent History Project.

Yorke, Edmund. Senior lecturer in defence and international affairs, Royal Military Academy Sandhurst, Surrey. Author of *Rorke's Drift, 1879: Anatomy of an Epic Zulu War Siege* (2001). Co-author (with Malcolm Flower-Smith) of *Mafeking: Story of a Great Boer War Siege* (2000). Coeditor (with F.H. Toase) of *The New South Africa: Prospects for Domestic and*

International Security (1998). Contributed articles to *Aspects of Peacekeeping*, edited by D. S. Gordon and F. H. Toase (2000); and *Diplomacy at the Highest Level*, edited by David Dunn (1996). Research interests include colonial war studies and contemporary African peacekeeping.

Young, John R. Senior Lecturer in History, University of Strathclyde, Glasgow. Author of *The Scottish Parliament* *1639–1661: A Political and Constitutional Analysis* (1996). Editor of *Celtic Dimensions of the British Civil Wars* (1997). Coeditor (with T. M. Devine) of *Eighteenth Century Scotland: New Perspectives* (1999). Contributor to *Scotland and the Thirty Years' War*, edited by Steve Murdoch (2001). National Convenor of the United Kingdom section of the International Commission for the History of Representative and Parliamentary Institutions.

INDEXES

BOOKLIST INDEX

Works and articles discussed in the entries are listed here under the name of the author/editor. The page numbers refer to the lists themselves, where full publication information is given.

Donaldson, Gordon, *Scots Overseas*, 455

Donaldson, Gordon, Scottish Bishops' Sees before the Reign of David I, 378

Donaldson, Gordon, *Scottish Church History*, 44

Donaldson, Gordon, *Scottish Kings*, 49, 722, 1126, 1128

Donaldson, Gordon, *Scottish Reformation*, 172, 464

Donaldson, Peter Samuel, Bishop Gardiner, Machiavellian, 556

Donaldson, Peter Samuel, *Machiavellian Treatise*, 556

Donkin, Ellen, *Women and Playwriting in Nineteenth-Century Britain*, 402

Donkin, R.A., *Cistercians*, 495, 1107

Donnachie, Ian, *Historic New Lanark*, 946, 987

Donnachie, Ian, *Industrial Archaeology in the British Isles*, 63

Donnachie, Ian, *Robert Owen*, 987

Donnan, Hastings, *Borders*, 1176

Donnelly, James S., Jr., chapters 12–19 in *New History of Ireland*, vol 5, 585

Donnelly, James S., Jr., *Land and the People of Nineteenth-Century Cork*, 706

Donnelly, Tom, *Coventry Motor Industry*, 915

Donnison, Jean, *Midwives and Medical Men*, 254

Donoghue, Emma, *Passions between Women*, 648, 1180

Donoughue, Bernard, *Herbert Morrison*, 911

Donoughue, Bernard, *Prime Minister*, 213

Doody, Margaret Anne, *Daring Muse*, 1051

Doody, Margaret Anne, *True Story of the Novel*, 508

Doran, Patrick Francis, *Andrew Mitchell and Anglo-Prussian Diplomatic Relations during the Seven Years War*, 1179

Doran, Susan, Finances of an Elizabethan Nobleman and Royal Servant, 1250

Doran, Susan, *Monarchy and Matrimony*, 450

Doran, Susan, *Princes, Pastors and People*, 90

Dore, R.N., *Civil Wars in Cheshire*, 371

Dorey, Peter, Labour Party and the Problems of Creating a 'Reprsentative' House of Lords, 1017

Dorfman, Gerald A., *British Trade Unionism against the Trades Union Congress*, 1295

Dorman, Bernard E., *Story of Ely and Its Cathedral*, 361

Dorril, Stephen, *MI6*, 286

Dorsten, J.A. van, *Leicester's Triumph*, 958

Doubleday, H.A., *History of Hampshire and the Isle of Wight*, vol 2, 364

Douglas, David C., *English Historical Documents*, 187

Douglas, David C., *English Historical Documents, 1040–1189*, 187, 271

Douglas, David C., *English Monarchs: William the Conqueror*, 192

Douglas, David C., *Norman Achievement, 1050–1100*, 429

Douglas, David C., *William the Conqueror*, 609, 762, 1361

Douglas, David Charles, *English Scholars*, 506

Douglas, R., *Taxation in Britain since 1600*, 1252

Douglas, Roy, *History of the Liberal Party, 1895–1970*, 806

Douglas-Hume, Charles, *Dignified & Efficient*, 566

Dow, F.D., *Cromwellian Scotland, 1651–1660*, 194, 907

Dowding, Hugh C.T., *Battle of Britain*, 1395

Dowling, Linda, *Hellenism and Homosexuality in Victorian Oxford*, 648, 991

Dowling, Maria, *Fisher of Men*, 530

Downie, J.A., *Robert Harley and the Press*, 608

Dowse, Robert E., *Left in the Centre*, 677

D'Oyley, George, *Life of William Sancroft, Archbishop of Canterbury*, 1156

Drake, Barbara, *Women in Trade Unions*, 1293

Draper, Derek, *Blair's First Hundred Days*, 302

Drees, Clayton J., *Authority and Dissent in the English Church*, 364

Drescher, Seymour, *Capitalism and Antislavery*, 673, 1188

Drescher, Seymour, *Econocide*, 1189, 1247

Dresser, Madge, *Making of Modern Bristol*, 186

Drewett, Perter, *South-East to AD 1000*, 360, 363

Drewry, Gavin, *Law and Parliament*, 299

Driver, Cecil, *Tory Radical*, 484

Driver, Christopher, *British at Table, 1940–1980*, 534

Drower, George M.F., *Kinnock*, 753

Drower, George M.F., *Neil Kinnock*, 753

Drummond, Andrew L., *Scottish Church, 1688–1843*, 260, 464

Drummond, J.C., *Englishman's Food*, 534

DuBois, Armand Budington, *English Business Company after the Bubble Act, 1720–1800*, 1215

Du Boulay, F.R.H., Fifteenth Century, 1000

Du Boulay, F.R.H., *Registrum Thome Bourgchier Cantuariensis Archiepiscopi, AD 1454–1486*, 1267

Duckham, Baron F., Canals and River Navigations, 1123

Dudley, Donald R., *Rebellion of Boudicca*, 176

Dudley, Edmund, *Tree of Commonwealth*, 628

Dudley-Smith, Timothy, *John Stott*, 548

Duffield, Sarah, *Trade Union Congress Archive, 1920–1960*, 1295

Duffy, A.E.P., Differing Policies and Personal Rivalries in the Origins of the Independent Labour Party, 677

Duffy, Eamon, *Humanism, Reform, and the Reformation*, 530

Duffy, Eamon, *Stripping of the Altars*, 233, 235, 385, 813, 1003, 1032, 1058, 1076, 1095, 1304

Duffy, John, Anglo-American Reaction to Obstetrical Anesthesia, 877

Duffy, Michael, *New Maritime History of Devon*, vol 1, 882

Duffy, Michael, *Profiles in Power: The Younger Pitt*, 192

Duffy, Michael, *Soldiers, Sugar, and Seapower*, 545

Duffy, Michael, World Wide War, 1793–1815, 545

Duffy, Seán, *Ireland in the Middle Ages*, 697, 699

Duffy, Sean, Irishmen and Islesmen in the Kingdoms of Dublin and Man, 1052–1171, 847

Dugdale, Blanche E.C., *Arthur James Balfour, First Earl of Balfour*, 122

Duiker, William J., *Cultures in Collision*, 178

Duke, Simon, *US Defence Bases in the United Kingdom*, 1313

Dukes, Paul, Leslie Family in the Swedish Period (1630–1635) of the Thirty Years' War, 804

Dumbrell, John, *Special Relationship*, 1313

Duminy, Andrew, *Anglo-Zulu War*, 743

Dumville, David, *Gildas*, 570

Dumville, David, 'Six' Sons of Rhodri Mawr, 1114

Dumville, David, Sub-Roman Britain, 570, 1332

Dumville, David N., *Æthling*, 421

Dumville, David N., *English Caroline Script and Monastic History*, 171

Dumville, David N., *Historia Brittonum*, vol 3, 636

Dumville, David N., *Histories and Pseudo-Histories of the Insular Middle Ages*, 636

Dumville, David N., *Liturgy and the Ecclesiastical History of Late Anglo-Saxon England*, 811

Dumville, David N., *Saint Patrick, AD 493–1993*, 1022

Dumville, David N., Terminology of Overkingship in Early Anglo-Saxon England, 442, 985

Dumville, David N., Treaty of Alfred and Guthrum, 18

Dunbar, Sir Archibald H., *Scottish Kings*, 1335

Duncan, A.A.M., Community of the Realm in Scotland and Robert Bruce, 1125

Duncan, Archibald A.M., Battle of Carham, 1018, 841

Duncan, Archibald A.M., Early Parliaments of Scotland, 1013

GENERAL INDEX

Page numbers in **boldface** indicate a subject with its own entry.

anti-Catholicism, **54–55**, 657, 659, 1183, 1197
  evangelicalism and, 468
  Exclusion crisis and, 474
  in Ireland, 1321
  Methodism and, 890
  in Scotland, 1243
  "Spanish Marriage" and, 1219
anticlericalism, 631, 1174
anticolonialism. *See* decolonization; nationalism
Anti-Corn Law League, **56–57**
  Bright and, 185
  Cobden and, 283
  free trade and, 527, 528
Anti-Parliamentary Communist Federation, 864
antiquarianism, 122, 206, 344, 640, 777
anti-Semitism, 733–34
  of Baden-Powell, 119
  Disraeli and, 385
  fascism and, 499, 500, 914–15
  Toynbee and, 1281, 1282
antisepsis, 875, 878, 892
anti-slavery movement, **1189–90**, 1287–88, 1358–59, 1371
Anti-State Church Association, 990
Antonine Wall, 1131, 1133
Antonio, Prior of Crato, 393
Antonius Pius, Emperor, 1133
Antrim, County, 271
Antwerp, **57–59**, 821, 880, 958, 1285, 1304, 1367
ANZAC, 949–50, 1390
Aoife of Leinster, 338, 349, 350
apartheid, 1113, 1114
Apollo missions, 1216
Apostles (University of Cambridge), 216, 749
apostolic succession, 1004
apothecaries, 876, 877
Apothecaries' Company (London), 175
appeasement
  Neville Chamberlain and, 244–45, 1246, 1391
  Winston Churchill and, 263
  Cripps and, 319
  Eden and, 419
  Hoare and, 647
  Lloyd George and, 818
  Macmillan and, 838
  Suez crisis and, 1246–47
apprenticeship, **59–60**, 82, 257, 549, 1209
  factory reform and, 484, 1160
Apuleius, 509
Aquinas, Thomas, 531, 559, 937
Aquitaine, 32, 622, 735
Arab Revolt in Palestine (1936–39), 289
Arabi, Ahmad, 443
Arabia, 796, 997, 1173, 1390
arable husbandry, 494–95, 496, 497, 1178
Arbroath, Declaration of, **60–61**, 1126
archaeology, **61–68**
  Anglo-Saxon Britain, 134, 158, 170, 258, 326, 409, 916–17, 1178–79

architecture influenced by, 76
bibliographical studies of, 146, 150
in Birmingham, 155–56
of bronze industry, 889
in Carlisle, 370
of castles, 72–73
in Dublin, 405
of farming, 495, 496, 497
in Germany, 170
historiography of, **61–63**
industrial, **63–64**
of industrial revolution, 460
in Ireland, 312, 696
in London, 824
in Low Countries, 1367
in Manchester, 849
maritime, **64–65**, 1191, 1328
in marshlands, 1275
of Merovingian monasteries, 291
in Northumbria, 966
in Norwich, 967
prehistoric, 62, **65–66**, 135
of Roman Britain, 177, 1132, 1133, 1134, 1136
of Rose Theatre, 395
Scandinavian settlement sites, 1329
in Scotland, 1039, 1241
in Sussex, 310
in Syria, 796
techniques and methods, **66–68**
topography and, 1273
urban, 1318
in Wales, 664, 1333
of Whitby Abbey, 636
in York, 1407
Archer, Jeffrey, 1381
Archer-Shee case, 227
archery, 599, 600, 893
Arches, Court of, 861
architecture, **68–81**
  Anglo-Saxon, **68–69**, 170, 1360
  of Belfast, 135
  Blenheim Palace, 858
  chivalry and, 315
  Cistercian, 1103, 1107
  classical culture's influence on, 275–76
  of Cornwall, 665
  of country houses, 1204, 1408
  Crystal Palace, 584
  of Dublin, 405–6
  Duchy of Cornwall and, 307
  of Edinburgh, 423
  English Renaissance, **73–74**
  food history and, 536
  George IV and, 566
  late Georgian and neoclassical, **75–76**
  in London, 826, 827
  of market halls, 1111
  medieval ecclesiastical, 62, **70–71**
  medieval military, **71–73**
  in Roman Britain, 1135
  twentieth-century, **77–78**
  vernacular, **78–81**
  Victorian and Gothic Revival, **76–77**
  in York, 1408

archives, **81–89**
  of Chester Palatinate, 578
  company and society, **81–82**
  of Conservative Party, 298
  European, 88–89
  genealogical resources in, 488
  of Hanover, 563
  institutional and academic, **82–83**
  local and municipal, **83–84**, 1274
  national, **85–86**
  private and family, **86–87**
  of royal family in Windsor Castle, 729
  state papers, **87–89**
  War Office, 599
Archives of Contemporary Scientists, 87
Arctic, 478, 547
Ardfert, diocese of, 375
ard-ri, 184, 696, 697
Areley Kings, 259
Arfast of Thetford, 363
Argentina, 127, 151, 346, 487, 1288
Argyll, diocese of, 379
Argyll, dukes of, 1203
Argyll, John Campbell, 2nd Duke of, 719
Argyll, Synod of (1639–61), 304–5
aristocracy. *See* aristocratic affinity; barons; Lords, House of; nobility
aristocratic affinity, **89–90**. *See also* patronage
  Buckingham and, 1219
  Edward III and, 436
  Henry I and, 620
  Tudor kingdom and, 1300
Aristotle
  economic theory derived from, 416
  Grosseteste and, 590
  John of Salisbury and, 739
  rediscovery of, 276
  on women, 559
Arklow, 697
Arkwright, Richard, 64, 946
Arles, Council of (314), 372
Arlington, Sir Henry Bennet, 1st Earl of, 330
Arliss, Leslie, 520
Armada, 21, 65, 659, **1217–18**
  Frobisher in defence against, 547
  Hawkins and, 616
Armagh, Archbishopric of, 373–74, 376, 377
Armagnac, 1298
Armes Prydein (poem), 111
Arminianism, **90–91**, 1321
  Anglicanism and, 35
  Cecil and, 238
  Laud and, 228, 779
  Methodism and, 890
  Pym and, 1083
  in Scotland, 464
Arminius, Jacobus, 35, 90
Armistead, Elizabeth, 539
Armitage, Ella, 72
arms and armour. *See* weaponry
arms, coats of. *See* heraldry
Armstrong (company), 448
Armstrong-Siddeley aircraft, 5
Armstrong-Whitworth aircraft, 5

bastard feudalism, 89, 507, 1047, 1197, 1201
Bastian, Henry Charlton, 154
Batavia, 476
Batavian Republic, 1213
Bates, David, 638
Bath, 401, 421, 916–17
Bath Abbey, 373, 427
Bath and Wells, diocese of, 372–73
Batten, Jean, 5
battery farming, 499
Battle Abbey, 132, 334
Battle of Brunanburh, The, 41, 198, 426, 466
Battle of Maldon, The, 7, 198, 1048
Baugh, Daniel A., 929
Bauhaus, 553
Bavaria, 170
Baxter, Richard, **129–30**, 589
Bayeux Tapestry, 72, 610–11, 613
Bayonne, 32
BBC. *See* British Broadcasting Company; British Broadcasting Corporation
Beaconsfield, Benjamin Disraeli, 1st Earl of. *See* Disraeli, Benjamin
Beagle, HMS, 333
Bean, J. M. W., 1046
Beatles, 923
Beaton, David, Cardinal, 464, 1140
Beatrice, Princess, 1326
Beatty, David, 940
Beaufort dukes of Somerset, 131
Beaufort family, 625
Beaufort, Henry, Cardinal, **130–31**, 576, 577
Beaufort, John, Earl of Somerset and Marquis of Dorset, 625
Beaufort, Lady Margaret, **131–32**, 182, 628, 629, 1342
Beaumaris Castle, 72
Beaumont, Francis, 396–97
Beaver, Patrick, 458
Beaverbrook, Sir Maxwell Aitken, 1st Baron, 537, 1387
Bebb, W. Ambrose, 1311
Bec, Abbey of, 52, 762
Beccaria, Cesare, 1029, 1322
Bechuanaland. *See* Botswana
Becket, Thomas, **132–33**, 1341
    Clarendon Constitutions and, 271–72
    clerks of, 172
    Foliot and, 534
    Henry II and, 623, 1047
    John of Salisbury and, 738
    on London, 362
    martyrdom of, 1156
    Owain Gwynedd and, 987
Beckett, J. C., 709
Beckett, J. V., 1206
Beckett, Samuel, 404, 406, 518
Beckford, William (1760–1844), 649
Beddoe, Thomas Lovell, 1053
Beddoes, Thomas, 337
Bede, **133–34**, 258, 668, 1178, 1266
    on Aidan, 12
    on Augustine on Canterbury, 114

on Battle of Mount Badon, 916–17
on Bertha of Kent, 140, 141
on Biscop, 157
on British conversion to Christianity, 257, 258
on church councils, 43
church learning and, 43, 906, 926
Cuthbert of Lindisfarne and, 325–26
on Gildas, 571
on Hild(a) of Whitby, 635, 636
on Ninian, 378
North of England and, 669
on Northumbrian Kingdom, 965, 966, 985, 986
on Theodore, 1267
on Wilfrid, 1359, 1360
on Willibrord, 1367
Bedford, 430
Bedford, Francis Russell, 4th Earl of, 1082, 1083
Bedford, Francis Russell, 5th duke of, 979
Bedford, John, Duke of (1389–1435), 577, 1191, 1298
Bedfordshire, 203, 310, 331, 368
Bedingfeld, Henry, 633
beds. *See* furniture
Beeching, H. C., 111
beer, 285, 473
Beer, George Louis, 24
Behagg, Clive, 1209–10
Behan, Brendan, 517
Behn, Aphra, 509
Bekynton, Thomas, 276
Belfast, **134–36**, 773
Belgium, 9, 829–30, 850
Belgrano, 487
Bell, Andrew, 1159, 1160
Bell, Clive, 162–63
Bell, Henry, 1297
Bell, Vanessa, 100, 162–63, 529
Belloc, Hilaire, 109, 1220
Bell-the-Cat. *See* Drummond, John, 1st Baron Drummond
Belmeis, Richard de, 362
Beloff, Max, 837
Bemont, Charles, 340
Benedict X, Pope, 1237
Benedict XII, Pope, 1001
Benedict Bisco. *See* Biscop, Benedict
Benedict of Nursia, 597, 1102
Benedictinism, 906, 1100, 1102, 1103, 1107
    Ælfric and, 3
    Biscop and, 158
    in Chester, 371
    in Coventry, 365
    cult of Dunstan and, 409
    David cult and, 334
    in Durham, 965
    Edgar I and, 420, 421
    Edmund I and, 426, 427
    in Ely, 361
    English Catholicism after 1560 and, 1101
    in Gloucester, 366
    in Northumbria, 1359–60
    in Norwich, 363
    nunneries and, 1104

at Saint Albans, 1151–52
at Westminster Abbey, 232
Wulfstan and, 1404–5
Benedictional of Æthelwold, 410
benefices, 1001, 1003
Bengal
    Clive and, 277–78
    conquest of, 678, 679
    Curzon and, 324–25
    dual government in, 103–4
    East India Company and, 413–14
    Hastings and, 614
    masculinities in, 871
    partition (1905) of, 682
    Rawdon-Hastings and, 1093
Benn, Tony, 303, 1211
Bennett, Arnold, 512
Bennett, D. C. T., 117
Bennett, Louise, 10
Bennett, Michael, 253
Benson, George, 1407
Bentham, Jeremy, **136–37**, 240, 740–41, 785, 1029, 1322, 1323
Bentham, Thomas, 367
Benthamism, 241, 681, 1224, 1323
Bentinck, Lord William (1774–1839), 328, 681, 682
Bentinck, William Cavendish, 3rd Duke of Portland. *See under* Portland
Bentley, Richard, 1238
Beornred, 974
Beornwulf, King of Mercia, 366, 442
Beowulf, 1048–49
Berehaven, 712
Beresford, Lord Charles, 441
Bergen, 606
Berger, John, 102
Berkeley, George, **137–39**, 208, 375, 1322
Berkeley, John, 27
Berkshire, 310, 364, 369, 1222
Berlin, Conference of (1884–85), 9, 104
Berlin, Congress of (1878), **139–40**, 415
Bernal, J. D., 1037
Bernard of Clairvaux, 335, 374, 738, 1103
Bernard of St David's, 384
Bernard, Thomas, 1145
Bernardino of Siena, 1106
Berneich, 1241
Berners, Sir Gerald Tyrwhitt-Wilson, 14th Baron, 125
Berners-Lee, Tim, 694
Bernicia, Kingdom of
    Aidan and, 12
    bisected by modern Borders, 664
    Hild(a) of Whitby and, 636
    as part of Northumbrian Kingdom, 966, 985
    Scots English and, 775
Berry, H. F., 405
Bertha, Queen of Kent, **140–41**
Berwick, 1289
Berwick, bishopric of, 372
Berwick, Treaty of (1560), 424
Berwick-upon-Tweed, 599
    Borders and, 664
    Edward IV and, 438

Churchill, Winston (*continued*)
  Cold War and, 287–88
  Conservative Party and, 299
  on Dalton, 328
  Eden and, 419
  espionage and, 1173
  father and, 261–62
  George VI and, 567, 568
  Hoare and, 646
  Lawrence and, 796
  Macmillan and, 838
  Middle East and, 997
  Morrison and, 912
  Mountbatten and, 918
  Reith and, 1098
  Rosebery and, 1137, 1138
  Teheran, Yalta, and Potsdam
    Conferences and, 1401–2
  United States and, 1313
  World War I and, 1387, 1390
  World War II and, 1396, 1397, 1399,
    1403
Churchman, Joan. *See* Hooker, Joan
churchwardens, 488
Cicero, 276
Cináed mac Ailpín. *See* Kenneth I, mac
  Alpin
cinnamon, 683
Cinque Ports, 479
circuit courts, 479, 480
circumnavigations of the Earth, 53–54, 476
Cistercianism, 1102, 1103, 1107
  architecture and, 71
  farming and, 496
  Gilbert of Sempringham and, 570
  nunneries and, 1104
  in Wales, 1177
Citrine, Walter, 1st Baron Citrine, **263–64**,
  1295
City and South London Railway, 1297
City livery companies. *See* livery companies
  (London)
City of London, 824, 826, 827
  archives in, 81–82
  banking in, 126–27
  British intervention in Egypt and,
    443
  Civil Wars and, 266
  East India Company and, 414
  economic decline and, 1099
  electronics industry and, 448
  financial services in, 521–22, 1176
  free trade and, 528
  Hawkins and, 615
  imperialism and, 674, 675
  Jews in, 733, 1139
  taxation and, 527
  trade policies of, 1289
  Treasury and, 1302
  Whigs and, 204
  Wilkes and, 1360
civil aviation. *See* aviation (civil)
civil engineering, **458–59**, 460
Civil Pleas, 480
Civil Rights Association (Northern Ireland),
  351

Civil Service
  taxation and, 526, 527
  women and, 1382
Civil Wars, **264–71**
  aristocratic affinity and, 89
  armies in, 92
  Blake and, 160–61
  Boyle and, 180
  British Republic and, 194
  Bunyan and, 203
  Canterbury diocese and, 360
  causes of, 1253
  Charles I and, 247–48
  Charles II and lessons of, 249
  Chester diocese and, 371
  constitutional issues, **264–66**
  defeat and fall of Charles I, **266–67**
  Duchy of Cornwall and, 306–7
  education and, 1159
  English gentry and, 1205
  excise during, 472
  Exeter during, 475
  Fairfax and, 485, 486
  general surveys of, **267–68**
  Gloucester during, 366
  Hereford Cathedral during, 367
  James VI and I and origins of, 728
  Kent and, 311
  Laud and, 1156
  Leslie and, 804
  Lilburne and, 808, 809
  Lincoln in, 810
  Long Parliament and, 831
  merchant class and, 1320
  millenarianism and, 130
  Navy during, 942
  Newcastle upon Tyne and, 951
  Norwich diocese and, 363
  Oxford University and, 992
  pamphlet literature of, 463–64
  Parliament of Scotland during, 1014
  political patronage and origins of, 1024
  Presbyterianism within, 173
  Pym and, 1082
  religious issues of, **268–70**, 1075
  religious radicals and, 897–98
  Rochester Cathedral during, 364
  Saint David's Cathedral during, 384
  Scotland and, 1167
  Shaftesbury and, 1182
  social issues of, **270–71**
  Stuarts and, 1242, 1243
  taxation and, 1252
  Warwickshire and, 311
  Welsh context of, 1334
  women in, 503
  Worcester during, 369
civil wars (other). *See* Irish Civil War;
  United States
Clanmer, David, 743
clans (Scottish), 662, 667, 1166, 1203, 1243
Clapham, John, 959
Clapham, Sir John, 126, 693
Clapham Sect, 1189, 1358–59
Clare (Cambridgeshire), 1105
Clare, County, 202, 710

Clare, Isabel de, 338
Clare, John Fitzgibbon, Earl of, 1093
Clare, Richard de. *See* de Clare, Richard
Claremont Landscape Garden (556), 556
Clarence, George Plantagenet, Duke of
  (1449–78), 438, 1189, 1267, 1268
Clarence, Thomas, Duke of (1388–1421),
  625
Clarendon, Constitutions of (1164), 133,
  271–72, 623
Clarendon, Edward Hyde, 1st Earl of,
  272–73
  Burnet and, 206
  Charles II and, 249, 1110
  as historiographer, 639, 640
  on Monck, 907
Clarendon, George William Frederick, 4th
  Earl of, 1
Clarendon Laboratories (University of
  Oxford), 1036
Clarion (newspaper), 161, 800
Clark, George Kitson, 1327
Clark, Kenneth, Lord Clark, 76
Clarke, B., 76
Clarke, J. S., 729
Clarke, Samuel, 207
Clarke, William, 1074, 1082
class, **273–75**. *See also* social structure
  BBC and, 196
  in Bristol, 187
  Burke and, 204
  capitalism and, 220–21, 1193
  Chartism and, 251
  childhood and, 257
  Civil Wars and, 270
  consumerism and, 301–2
  counterculture and, 1409
  Dissenters and, 1076
  in Edinburgh, 423–24
  evangelicalism and, 469
  factory reform and, 485
  feminism and, 502, 503
  fiction-writing and, 1378
  film depictions of, 520
  in Hanoverian Britain, 603, 604
  heavy industry's decline and, 690
  imprisonment and, 1029
  Indian caste system, 328
  industrialization and, 689
  Irish Home Rule movement, 710
  land enclosure and, 457
  leisure and recreation and, 799–801
  in Liverpool, 815
  in London, 689, 826
  marriage and, 861, 862
  masculinity and, 871
  in Northern Ireland, 135, 350
  patriarchy and, 1021
  politeness and, 1057
  political radicalism and, 1360–61
  politics and, 186
  prostitution and, 1073
  in Scotland, 1165
  in Scottish Highlands, 668
  slave-owning societies and, 1189
  social conflict and, 1195, 1198, 1199

cows, 496, 499
CPGB. *See* Communist Party of Great
   Britain
Crabbe, George, 1052
craft guilds, 59, 221, **315–16**, 549, 593–94,
   1295, 1318, 1319–20
   in Edinburgh, 423
   in London, 881
Craig, Gordon, 263
Craig, Hardin, 393
Craig, James, 227, 583, 588
Craigie, Jill, 537
Craigie, Robert, 411, 423
Cramp, Rosemary, 69, 134, 966
Cranmer, George, 651
Cranmer, Thomas, **316–18**
   Edward VI and, 964
   Henry VIII and, 631
   Kentish opposition to, 557
   liturgies and, 814, 1077
   martyrdom of, 1156
Crawford, O. G. S., 63
Crawford, Virginia, 359, 360
Crealock, Henry Hope, 743
Crécy, Battle of (1346), 436
credit, 692, 693. *See also* loans and credit
   finance
Crediton, 170
Crediton, diocese of, 108, 373
Creeks, 21
Creighton, Mandell, 362, 368
Cremin, Cornelius, 712
Crespin, Jean, 542
Crete, Battle of (1941), 918
Crick, Francis, 153, 1037
cricket, 10, 1224–25, 1226
crime. *see also* heresy; homicide; law; police;
      prisons; prostitution; regicide; sodomy
   among Scottish elite, 1203
   in early modern period, 1195, 1196
   law enforcement and, 786–95, 891
   in medieval England, 1197, 1351–53
   in twentieth century, 1303–4
Crimea, 318–19, 581
Crimean War, **318–19**
   Lord Aberdeen and, 1–2
   Army and, 92, 93, 95–96
   Bright and, 185
   Eastern Question and, 415
   Nightingale and, 955, 956
   nursing in, 10
   Palmerston and, 998
   Rothschild and, 1139
   steel manufacture and, 141
criminal justice, 115, 456, 783–84, 786–95
Crínán, 408
Cripps, Sir Stafford, 113, **319–20**, 329
Cristin of Gwynedd, 987
critical reviews (18th and 19th centuries).
      See periodical press and critical reviews
Croft, Herbert, 369
crofting, 634, 635, 667, 668, 1276
Croke, Thomas, 707
Crome, Edward, 105
Cromer, Evelyn Baring, 1st Earl of, 755
Crompton, R. E. B., 446

Cromwell, Oliver, **320–21**
   Baxter and, 130
   Blake and, 160
   Cooper's portrait of, 98
   espionage and, 1173
   Fairfax compared with, 486
   Fox and, 540
   Ireland and, 267
   Irish campaign of, 194, 1243, 1251
   Jews and, 733
   Long Parliament and, 831, 832
   Monck and, 907
   Protectorate of, 1074–75
   Putney Debates and, 1082
   on Ralegh, 1092
   religious issues and, 269
   Shaftesbury and, 1182
   Sharp and, 464
Cromwell, Richard, 130, 1074
Cromwell, Thomas, 122, 182, **321–22**,
   1299
   Acts of Union and, 1310–11
   William Cecil compared with, 240
   creation of new dioceses and, 368, 369
   dissolution of religious houses and
      chantries and, 1107, 1108
   Duchy of Lancaster and, 761, 762
   government reorganization and, 1300,
      1301
   Henry VIII and, 630, 631–32
   Kildare Rebellion and, 750
   Norfolk (3rd Duke of) and, 960
   Pilgrimage of Grace and, 1040
   Privy Council and, 1070
   Scotland and, 1140
   State Papers and, 88
   taxation and, 1253
   Wolsey and, 1373, 1374
crop rotation, 493, 494–95
Crosfield, Joseph, 1059
Crosland, Anthony, 328
Crossick, Geoffrey, 1208
Crossman, Richard, 1017–18, 1211
Crouchback, Edmund. *See* Edmund
      "Crouchback"
Crowe, Dame Sylvia, 556
Crowland Abbey, 496
crown jewels, 131
Crowther, Geoffrey, Baron Crowther, 428
Crowther Report (1959), 60
Croydon, 360
Cruickshanks, Eveline, 563, 721
cruise missiles, 1314, 1394, 1396
Crumlin-Pederson, Ole, 1328
Crusades, 315, **323–24**, 893, 1103–4, 1118,
   1262, 1364
Crutched Friars, 1105
cryptography, 344
Crystal Palace, 552, 584
Cuatbrycge, 1264
Cuba, 1188, 1190, 1313, 1314
Cúchulainn, 669
Cudworth, Ralph, 207
Cullen, Paul, Cardinal, 1059
Culloden, Battle of (1746), 605, 720
Cumann na nGaedheal, 307, 308

Cumberland, 833
   Borders and, 664
   Chester diocese and, 371
   county history of, 311
   Grindal and, 589
   Jacobitism in, 721
Cumberland, Richard, 1322
Cumberland, William Augustus, 3rd Duke
   of, 720
Cumbria
   Athelstan and, 110
   Borders and, 664
   Edmund I and, 427
   iron ore from, 545
   origins of, 370
Cumming, Sir Mansfield, 1173
Cunard (shipping line), 815
Cunard Line, 1297
Cunard, Samuel, 1297
Cunedda, 1332
Cunedda ap Cadwallon, 987
Curthose, Robert. *See* Robert II,
      "Curthose," Duke of Normandy
Curtis, Lionel, 109, 293
Curzon, George Nathaniel, 1st Marquis
   Curzon of Kedleston, **324–25**, 567,
   682, 755
Curzon, Mary, Marchioness Curzon of
   Kedleston, 325
Cust, Henry, 501
custodes pacis, 788
Custom House, Exeter, 475
customary law, 49, 271–72, 543, 854, 1289,
   1380–81
customs duties, 58, 313, 883, 1287, 1290,
   1291
Cuthbert of Lindisfarne, 361
   Aidan and, 12
   Bede on, 134
   as Bishop, 371
   Northumbrian Kingdom and, 257, 965
   Wilfrid and, 1360
Cuthbert's Gospel, 172
Cuvier, Georges, 1411
Cymric Suffrage Union, 1386
Cynan ap Iago, 592, 593
Cynegils, King of Wessex, 985
Cynethryth, Queen of Mercia, 367
Cyngen, King of Powys, 1114
Cyprus, 289, 292, 1026
Cyprus Convention (1878), 140
Czechoslovakia, 244, 1210

Dafydd ab Owain Gruffydd, 1117
Dafydd ap Gruffydd, 820
Dafydd ap Gwilym, 777
Dafydd ap Llywelyn, 819
Dafydd Nanmor, 777
Dáil Éireann, First (1919–21), 342, 588
Daily Citizen, 912
Daily Herald, 778
Dai'r Cantwr. *See* Davies, David
dairy farming, 492, 950
Dal gCais dynasty of Munster, 184–85
Dál Riáta. *See* Dalriada
Dale, David, 946

French Revolution (*continued*)
  social conflict and, 1199
  trade during, 1286, 1287
  Whigs and, 1355, 1356
French Revolutionary Wars
  Britain and, **545–46**, 929–30
  Fox during, 539
  military technology in, 894–95
  Navy during, 929–30, 942
  Pitt the Younger and, 1044, 1045
  taxation and, 526
Frere, Sir Bartle, 1372
Frere, W. H., 1004
Fresh Force, Assize of, 479
Freud, Lucian, 101
Freudianism. *See* psychoanalysis
Friar, Stephen, 633
friars, 236, 1101, 1105
Friars Minor. *See* Franciscanism
Friars of the Cross, 1105
Friars of the Sack, 1105
Friars Preachers. *See* Dominicanism
Friendly Protective Agricultural Association,
  1272
Friends of the Earth, 969
Friends of the People, 587
Friern Barnet, 695
Frise, L. G., 5
Frisia, 170, 1359, 1367
Frith, William, 100
Frithegod, 973
Frobisher, Sir Martin, 246, **546–47**
Froissart, Jean de, 259, 436
Frost, Terry, 101
Froude, J. A., 407, 1157, 1299
Froude, Richard Hurrell, 989
fruit growing, 492
Fry, C. B., 1225
Fry, Roger, 101, 162–63
Fryon, Etienne, 1342
Fujitsu, 294
Fulham, 362, 695
Fulk Nerra, Count of Anjou, 32
Fuller, Thomas, 310, 323
Fullmer, June, 491
fundamentalism, Christian, **548–49**
Furness Abbey, 370
furniture, **549–53**
Furniture Society, 553
furs, 476, 607
Fury biplane, 5

Gabor, Dennis, 1037
Gaelic languages. *See* Irish; Manx; Scots
  Gaelic
Gaelic League (Ireland). *See* Conradh na
  Gaeilge
Gagnan, Émile, 65
Gahan, Daniel, 710
Gaillard, Château, 72
Gainsborough Studios, 520
Gainsborough, Thomas, 99
Gaitskell, Hugh, 142
  Citrine and, 264
  Dalton and, 328
  Fabian Society and, 484

Morrison and, 912
National Health Service and, 143
postwar consensus and, 303
socialism and, 1211
Galapagos Islands, 333
Galashiels, 666
Galbraith, V. H., 171
Galen, 876
Gallagher, Catherine, 1378
Gallipoli, 893–94, 949–50, 1390
Galloway, 15, 173, 197, 844, 1228, 1363
Galloway, diocese of, 379, 380, 381, 464
Galloway, Patrick, 601
Galsworthy, John, 403, 404, 512
Galway, 809, 1317
Galway, diocese of, 377, 378
Gambia, 9
gambling, 801
Gandhi, Mohandas, 588, 679, 680–81
Gandon, James, 405
Gang of Four, 1211
gangster films, 520
Garda Siochána, 308
gardening and garden design, **555–56**
Gardiner, A. G., 608
Gardiner, Samuel R., 640, 728, 831
Gardiner, Stephen, **556–57**, 814, 1249
Garnet, Henry, 594, 732
Garrick, David, 401
Garsdale, 692
Garter, Order of the, 436
gas industry, **557–58**, 574
  coal industry and, 281, 544, 545
Gas Light & Coke Co. (GLCC), 558
Gascony, 32, 1289, 1298
Gaskell, Elizabeth, 669
Gasquet, Francis Aidan, 386
Gates, David, 92, 930
Gauden, John, 369
Gaul, 257, 291, 696
  Biscop in, 157, 158
gavelkind, 695
Gaveston, Piers, 128, 434, 435, 983
Gay, John (philosopher), 1322
Gay, John (poet), 920
Gay Liberation Front, 650
gay men. *See* homosexuality
Gay-Lussac, Joseph-Louis, 337
Gearoid Mor. *See* Fitzgerald, Gerald, 8th
  Earl of Kildare
Gearoid Óg. *See* Fitzgerald, Gerald, 9th Earl
  of Kildare
GEC. *See* General Electric Company
Geddes, Sir Eric, 117
Geddes, Jane, 889
Gelasius, 271
Gellately, Robert, 1209
Gellilyfdy, 777
Gelling, Margaret, 155
gender. *See also* feminism; masculinities;
    women
  BBC and, 196
  childhood and, 257
  class and, 275, 1195
  employment and, 1257–58, 1377, 1382
  family planning and, 255

historical studies of, 640–42
labour divisions and, 1207
literature and, 1378
patriarchy and, 1021–22
poetry and, 1051
politeness and gentility and, 1057
power and, **559–60**, 1095, 1384–85
Salvation Army and, 1155
sexuality and, 1181–82
urban societies and, 1320
witches and, 1370
genealogy, 310, **488–89**, 632. *See also*
  family history
general election. *See* election, general
General Electric Company (GEC), 294, 446,
  448
General Labourers' Association, 1269
General Post Office. *See* Post Office
General Strike (1926), **560–61**, 795, 1295
  Baldwin and, 121
  BBC and, 195
  George V and, 567
General Synod of the Church of England,
  304
genetics, 332, **388–89**, 471. *See also* DNA
  and genetics
Geneva, 756
Geneva Conference on Indochina (1954),
  412
Genoa, 1190
gentility. *See* politeness and gentility
gentlemen's clubs. *See* clubs, gentlemen's
gentry, British, 1311
  capitalism and, 221
  county government and, 309–10
  crime and, 789
  land enclosure and, 457
  social hierarchy and, 1195
gentry, English
  Cade Rebellion and, 212
  Catholicism among, 233, 594, 595
  in Cornwall, 306
  in Devon, 748
  food and nutrition and, 536
  Henry VII and, 629
  Lollardy among, 823
  Palatinate of Chester and, 253
  Peasants' Revolt and, 1027
  political radicalism and, 1360–61
  Puritanism and, 601
  in Salisbury diocese, 365
  social structure of, 1205–6
  Wars of the Roses and, 1047
  in Yorkshire, 1240
Geoffrey, Count of Anjou (1113–51), 32,
  622, 872, 1047
Geoffrey, Duke of Brittany (1158–86), 622
Geoffrey of Monmouth, 259, 1334
  Arthurian legend and, 916
  Gildas and, 571
  Historia Brittonum's influence on, 637
  influence of, 62, 926
geography, 456–57, 824, 938–39, 1107,
  1177
  employment and, 1257–58
geology, 456–57, 471

Hicks, Michael, 639
Hicks-Beach, Sir Michael, 1372
Higden, Ranulf, 434
High Church "party" in Church of
England, 304, 573, 1122
High Court of Justice (1649), 267
High Court of Parliament, **1005–6**
Higham, Charles Watson-Wentworth,
Viscount. *See* Rockingham, Charles
Watson-
highland Britain, 456–57, 496
Highland Games, 668
Highlands and Islands Development,
1276–77
Highlands of Scotland
churches built by Telford, 1261
clans in, 1166, 1203
Clearances of, **634–35**, 667
emigration from, 635
famine in, 1046
Jacobitism in, 719, 720, 1243
under John Balliol, 736
regional identities and, 664, 666–67
roads in, 1297
Scottish national identity and, 662
topography of, 1276
high-tech architecture, 78
Hild(a) of Whitby, 12, 361, **635–36**
Hill, Abigail. *See* Masham, Abigail, Lady
Masham
Hill, Christopher, 270, 273, 643, 644, 897
Hill, Joyce, 3
Hill, Peter, 639
Hill, Rowland 1st Viscount Hill, 94
Hill, Thomas D., 1048
Hilliard, Nicholas, 98, 451, 731
Hilton, Rodney H., 497, 643, 644
Hilton, Walter, 740
Himalayas, 478
Hinchliff, Peter, 36
Hindley, Myra, 1381
Hinduism, 679, 680
Hines, Barry, 517
Hingston Down, Battle of (838), 442
Hinkley C power station, 969
Hinsley, Arthur, Cardinal, 234
Hiroshima, 1402
Hirst, Damien, 101, 102
Hispaniola, 321
Historia Brittonum, **636–37**, 916
Historic Scotland, 662
historical dictionaries and reference works,
637–39
Historical Manuscripts, Royal Commission
on, 82, 84, 85, 87, 147
country houses and, 267
Hatfield House collection, 238
Historical Monuments of England, Royal
Commission on, 67, 70
historicism, 642–43
historiography, **639–46**
of archaeology, 61–63
of botanical sciences, 175–76
British history, 187–94
Burnet and, 205
capitalism and, 220

chronicles and, 258–60
of Civil Wars, 267–68, 269–70
Clarendon and, 273
class and, 274–75
empirical, **639–40**
feminist, **640–42**
historicist, **642–43**
Marxist, **643–44**
perception and, 1244
religious and sectarian, **644–46**
of science, 153, 154
Toynbee and, 1281–82
of Tudor kingdom, 1299
History of the War in South Africa, 37
Hitler, Adolf, 109
Chamberlain and, 245
Churchill and, 262
Lloyd George and, 818
Hlobane, Battle of, 202
Hoadly, Benjamin, 304
Hoare, Sir Samuel, Viscount Templewood,
117, **646–47**
Hoare-Laval Pact (1935), 646
Hobbes, Thomas, 207, 463, **647–48**, 937,
1057
Boyle and, 180
Clarendon and, 273
Hobkirk's Hill, Battle of (1781), 1093
Hobsbawm, Eric, 643, 644, 692, 1208
Hobson, J. A., 283, 444
Hockney, David, 101
Hoddom, 378
Hodges, William, 306
Hodgson, William, 1159–60
Hofmeister, Wilhelm, 175
Hofuðlausn, 466
Hogarth, William, 98–99, 560, 1142
Hogg, James, 512
Holbein, Hans, 98, 322
Holderness, B. A., 692
Holiday Association, 800
Holinshed, Raphael, 165, 177
Holkham Hall, 555
Holland, Henry Fox, 3rd Baron
(1773–1840), 200
Holland, Henry Richard, 3rd Baron,
1263
Holland House, 540
Holland, Peter, 398
Holland, Province of (Netherlands), 39
Holland, Sir Thomas Erskine, 741
Holles, Denzil, 1st Baron Holles, 266
Holmby, 808
Holmes, Cilve, 270
Holmes, Geoffrey, 1354
Holmes, P. J., 868
Holmes, Peter, 639
Holt (shipping line), 815
Holtby, Winifred, 993
Holy Alliance (1815–30), 295
Holy League (1511–13), 726
Holy Roman Empire, 624, 725, 1001
Holyoake, George Jacob, 988
Home Counties, 663, 666
Home Guard, 93, 1397
Home, John, 1166

Home Office, 247, 254, 793, 879, 1095,
1272
Home Rule. *See* devolution; Irish Home
Rule
Homer, 276
Homer, R. F., 889
homicide, 480, 752, 756, 787, 788, 789,
832, 841, 1166, 1189, 1364
Homildon Hill, Battle of (1402), 1128
homilies, 235
homosexuality, **648–50**, 870–72, 1051,
1181, 1182. *See also* lesbianism
Baden-Powell and, 119
Bloomsbury group and, 162, 163
Castlereagh and, 229
classical culture and, 276
Dictionary of National Biography
treatment of, 358
in early modern period, 560
of Edward II, 434
gay liberation and, 1383
Gordon and, 581, 582
Keynes and, 749
Kitchener and, 755
at Oxford University, 992
William II and, 1364
Honest Toun Fetival, 314
Hong Kong, 412, 413, 771, 840, 841,
1396
Honiton, 1155
Honorius of Canterbury, 363
Honourable Society of Cymmrodorion,
777
Hooke, Robert, 1036, 1238
Hooker, Joan, 651
Hooker, Joseph, 478
Hooker, Richard, 228, **650–51**, 733,
1147, 1357
hooliganism, 1224–25, 1409
Hooper, John, 366, 439, 757
Hooper, Nicholas, 613
Hope, David, 363
Hopkins, Gerard Manley, 1054
Hopkins, Harry, 1401
Horace, 276
Horner, Francis, 1031
Hornsey, 695
horror fiction, 519
horses
in farming, 493, 496, 497, 498
in racing, 301, 449, 799, 800, 1226
trade in, 683
in transport, 544, 1079, 1125, 1296,
1297
in warfare, 892, 894, 1262
Horsley, Samuel, 1263
Hoskins, W. G., 64
hospitals, medieval, 1061
hospitals, modern, 255, 874–75, 876,
1393
in National Health Service, 933, 934
Nightingale and, 955–56
Hotham, Sir John, 486
Hotol, 1217
Hottentot Rebellion, 816
Houghton, Walter, 1327

International Computers Limited. *See* ICL
International Genealogical Index, 84
International Labour organization, 145
International Military Tribunal for the Far
    East, 412
International Monetary Fund, 214
International Research & Development
    (company), 449
internationalism, 120, 283, 284
    European Community/Union and, 466–68
    Great Exhibition and, 584
internet, 694, 795
Interregnum (1649–60). *See* British
    Republic; Commonwealth; Protectorate
Inter-Varsity Fellowsip, 548
investiture controversy, 52–53, 621
investment. *See also* banking; financial
        services
    capitalism and, 221, 1202
    in computing industry, 294
    economic decline and, 1099
    heavy industry's decline and, 690, 691
    Industrial Revolution and, 686
    management of, 521–23
    South Sea Bubble and, 1215–16
    trade and, 31, 1248
Iolo Goch, 383, 777
Iolo Morganwg, 777
Iona, 12, 290, 696
Ipswich, 401, 845, 1288
IRA. *See* Irish Republican Army
Iraq, 796, 850, 851
IRB. *See* Irish Republican Brotherhood
Ireland, 696–713. *See also* Irish Free State;
        Irish Republic; Northern Ireland;
        specific cities and regions
    Anglicanism in, 36, 37
    Anglo-Norman kingdom and, 337–38,
        349–50
    archaeology of, 62
    architecture in, 76, 80
    Balfour's policies toward, 123–24
    Battle of Clontarf and, 184–85
    bibliographical studies of, 146–47, 148,
        149
    Bright and, 185
    British national identity and, 659
    Buckingham and, 201
    Buller and, 202
    Burke and, 204, 205
    Butt and, 208–9
    Campbell-Bannerman and, 216
    Carnarvon and, 224–25
    Carson and, 227
    Castlereagh and, 230
    cathedrals in, 230
    Catholic Emancipation in, 234
    Celtic Church in, 44, 257
    Joseph Chamberlain and, 243
    Chartism and, 251
    church councils in, 42
    church learning in, 44
    Civil Wars (1642–51) and, 267–68,
        270–71
    classical culture and, 275
    Columba and, 290

Corn Laws and, 56
county histories of, 270–71, 311–12
Cromwell and, 320
Oliver Cromwell and, 1074
David cult in, 333
decolonization and, 343, 1310
Dermot MacMurrough and, 349–50
diary-writing practices in, 357
dictionaries and reference works on,
    638–39
emigration to America from, 24, 27,
    455–56
English language in, 771–74
evangelicalism's impact in, 469
farming in, 493
Fenian movement and, 504–5
Fitzgerald earls of Kildare and, 531–32
franchises in, 312
French Revolutionary Wars and, 546
furniture of, 550
genealogical resources for, 488
George III and, 565
Gerald of Wales on, 569
Gladstone and, 573
Glorious Revolution and, 576
Grattan and, 583
Griffith and, 588
hagiography in, 597, 598
Harold II and, 610
Henry II and, 622
Henry VII and, 629
hermits and anchorites in, 634
Historia Brittonum on, 637
historical surveys of, 188–91
illuminated manuscripts produced in, 97
Isle of Man and, 847
Jacobitism in, 605, 720
James VII and II and, 729
Jesuits in, 731, 732, 1096
Kilmainham "Treaty" and, 752–53
Leslie and, 805
Limerick Treaty and, 809–10
loss of American colonies and, 26
Manx language origins and, 765
medieval urban development in, 1319
metalwork in, 888
Methodism in, 641, 890
monasticism in, 291, 1101, 1102, 1103,
    1367
music in, 920, 921–22, 924
national identity in, 657, 658, 659–60
Nine Years' War and, 956–57
Olafr Gothfrithsson and, 198–99
Papacy and, 1001
Parnell and, 1019–20
as part of Angevin empire, 32
as part of British Republic, 194
partition of, 124, 135, 350, 351, 712
Patrick and, 1022, 1023
plague (1640s) in, 271
police in, 136, 791, 793, 891, 1199
poor relief in, 1222
popular religion in, 1059
Poynings's Law and, 1066–67
Ralegh in, 1092
Richard de Clare and, 338

Rockingham and, 1130
Russell and, 1148
science in, 154
Scotland and, 379, 380
Scottish campaign in, 198
soldiers in continental armies from, 704,
    719, 1251
Strafford and, 1240
suffragists in, 1386
Sussex and, 1249, 1250
Talbot and, 1251–52
trade with, 1284–85
United States and, 1314
university reform in, 1317–18
Viking settlement in, 1329
Walpole and, 1338, 1339
Whigs and, 1356
William IV and, 1366
Ireton, Henry, 1082
Irish annals, **713–14**
Irish Church Temporalities Act (1833), 37,
    374, 377, 1148
Irish Civil War, 710, 711
Irish community in Great Britain, 646, 659,
    671, 1087
    Catholicism and, 233, 234
    Glasgow and, 574
    industrialization and, 688
    Leeds and, 798
Irish Famine. *See* Great Irish Famine
Irish Free State, 227, 712–13
    Commonwealth of Nations and, 292–93
    Cosgrave and, 307–8
    de Valera and, 341–42
    Griffith and, 588
Irish Guards, 94–95
Irish Home Rule Bill (1886), 300
Irish Home Rule Bill (1912), 567, 670
Irish Home Rule movement, **708–10**
    Bonar Law and, 167–68
    Bright and, 185
    Butt and, 208
    Carnarvon and, 225
    Carson and, 227
    Joseph Chamberlain and, 243
    Randolph Churchill and, 262
    Devonshire (9th Duke) and, 354
    in Dublin, 406
    English national identity and, 659
    Fawcett and, 501
    Fenian movement and, 504
    Gladstone and, 216, 224, 573
    Irish Question and, 716
    Liberal Party and, 807
    Rosebery and, 1138
    suffragists and, 1386
Irish Land Act (1881), 752–53
Irish Land League. *See* Land League
    (Ireland)
Irish language, 772, 773, **774–75**
    de Valera and, 341
    historiography of Ireland and, 697, 699
    in Irish Free State, 307–8, 712
    Irish national identity and, 659–60
    Irish Reformation's hostility toward, 702
    poetry in, 271

MacDonald, Sir Hector, 358
MacDonald, Malcolm, 837
Macdonald of Glengarry, Alexander. *See under* Macdonell
MacDonald, Ramsay, 142, **836–37**, 1211
    Blair compared with, 303
    Citrine and, 264
    Great Depression and, 347
    Hardie and, 607, 608
    Independent Labour Party and, 677, 678
    Morrison and, 912
    Snowden and, 1194
    Tolpuddle martyrs and, 1271
    World War I and, 618
MacDonalds of Keppoch, 720
Macdonell of Glengarry, Alexander, 720
Macdougall, Norman, 723
MacGregor, Ian, 794, 795
Machiavelli, Niccolò, 167, 276
MacHugh, Roger J., 583
Macinnes, Allan, 1242
Mackendrick, Alexander ("Sandy"), 520
Mackenzie, Compton, 262
Mackinder, Sir Halford, 1170
Mackinnon, Sir William, 8, 1246
Mackintosh, Charles Rennie, 552–53, 575
Macknight, Thomas, 166
MacManus, Terence, 505
Macmerry Aerodrome, 314
Macmillan Committee (1930), 145
Macmillan, Harold, 1st Earl of Stockton, 9–10, 299, **837–39**, 912, 1247, 1313
Macmurray, John, 159
MacMurrough, Maurice, 532
Macnab, Henry, 947
MacNeill, Eoin, 698
Macpherson, James, 1052
Macquarrie, Alan, 43
Macready, William, 402
MacWilliam, Donald, 1363
Madeira, 1248
madness. *See* mental illness
Madras, 1093
Máel Sechnaill II, King of Tara, 697
Maelgwn, 1332
Maeshowe, 984
Mafeking, 37, 119
Magdalen College, Oxford, 541
Magdalen Islands, 476
Magdeburg, 805
Magee, William, 368
magic, 344–45, 398, 877, 938, 1369–70
Magiscan system, 294
Magna Carta, **839–40**, 1232
    English national identity and, 658
    feudal law and, 506, 507
    Forest Charter compared wit, 538
    Henry III's reissue of, 339
    John and, 735, 990–91, 1010
    Langton and, 764
    Llywelyn ab Iorwerth and, 819
    weights and measurers in, 1345
magnetism, 1036
Magnus, King of Norway, 803
Magnus of Orkney, 382
Magonsaetan, Kingdom of the, 44, 47

Magrath, Milo, 375
Maguire, Hugh, 956
Mahan, Alfred T., 929
Mahdism, 581
Mahdist state, 8
Maine (France)
    Henry I and, 621
    heraldry in, 632
    Humphrey, Duke of Gloucester and, 577
    as part of Angevin empire, 32
Maine, Sir Henry, 741
Mainz, 171
Mair, John, 1166
Maitland earls/dukes of Lauderdale. *See under* Lauderdale
Maitland, Frederic, 18, 390, 529, 639, 851
Maitland of Lethington, William, 424
Maitland, S. R., 542
Major Generals, rule of (1655–56), 1074
Major, John, 168, 298, 302–3
Majuba, 37
Makepeace, John, 553
Makwanpur, 1093
Malachy of Armagh, 374, 376
Malawi, 8, 900
Malaya, 289, 346, **840–41**
    decolonization and, 343–44, 412
    in World War II, 1396, 1397
Malaysia, 289, 412, 771, 841
Malcolm I, King of Scots, 427
Malcolm II, King of Scots, 408, 775, 835, 836, **841–42**
Malcolm III, "Canmore," King of Scots, 14, 335, 408, 422, **842–43**
Malcolm IV, King of Scots, 335, **843–44**, 1363
Malcolm, Sir John, 1093
Maldon, 198
Maldon, Battle of (991), 430, **844–46**
Maldred, 408
Malory, Sir Thomas, 102, 103, 237
Malthus, Thomas Robert, 255, 333, **846–47**, 1118
Malthusianism, 274, 1046
Malton, Charles Watson-Wentworth, Earl of. *See* Rockingham, Charles Watson-Wentworth, 2nd Marquis of
Malvern Priory, 369
Man, Isle of, **847–48**
    Battle of Clontarf and, 184
    Christianization of, 370
    Manx language and, 765
    medieval sculpture in, 69
    Northumbria and, 669
    Viking settlement in, 1329, 1330
management, 690, 691, 1141
Manaw, 1241
Manchester, **848–50**
    art patronage in, 100
    boundaries of, 309
    canals for, 544
    Chester diocese and, 371
    Cobden and, 283
    Edward the Elder and, 431
    engineering in, 460, 1256
    factory reform in, 988

Fenian movement in, 504
    hospitals in, 875
    India and, 328
    industrialization and, 688, 1320
    Jacobite rebellion (1745) and, 720
    Peterloo Massacre in, 1033–34
    policing of, 793
    railways and, 459
    Salvation Army in, 1155
Manchester Anti-Corn Law Association, 56, 57
Manchester, Duchess of, 354
Manchester long-range bombers, 5
Manchester Mercury, 666
Manchester School, 283–84, 528, 849
Manchester Ship Canal, 850
Manchester Times, 56
Manchester United, 1225
Manchester, University of, 82, 1037
Manchurian crisis (1931–33), 411
Mancini, Dominico, 1121
Mandated Territories, **850–51**, 1392
Mandelson, Peter, 159, 302
Mandeville, Bernard, 207, 1057, 1143, 1322
Manley, Delarivier, 509
Mann, Horace, 1160
Mann, Tom, 1268
mannerism, 98
manners. *See* politeness and gentility
Mannheim, Hermann, 1029
Manning, Brian, 644, 897
Manning, Henry, Cardinal, 952, 989, 1283, 1359
Mannyng of Brunne, Robert, 259
manorial economy, **851–52**, 857–58, 1331–32
Manorial Society, 1218
manors, 457
    in Anglo-Saxon England, 49
    in Domesday Book, 390
    Duchy of Cornwall and, 306–7
    in feudalism, 508, 543
    inheritance and, 695
Mansfield, William Murray, 1st Earl of, 785
manufacturing, 313, 693, 815, 1287, 1288, 1398. *See also specific industries*
    in Glasgow, 575
    in London, 826
    motor industry, 915–16
    unemployment and, 1307
    weights and measures and, 1345
    women's employment and, 1376
manuscripts, 845. *See also* illuminated manuscripts
    Caxton and, 236
    Cnut and, 280
    copied at Monkwearmouth–Jarrow, 158
    Iona production of, 290
    Lindisfarne production of, 326
    medieval production of, 171–72
    of music, 921
Manx language, **765–66**
Maori people, 949
Map, Walter, **852–53**, 1117
Mappa Mundi, 476

Moore, G. E., 749, 750
Moore, George, 512, 1323
Moore, Henry, 101
Moore, Mark, 401
Moral Rearmament, 1268
morality plays, 393
Moravians, 21, 1408
Moray, 408, 836
Moray, diocese of, 379
Moray, James Stewart, Earl of (1531–70), 869
Morcar, Earl, 422
More, Charles, 1208
More, Hannah, 163–64, 1057
More, Thomas, **910–11**, 1304
    Catherine of Aragon and, 232
    classical culture and, 276
    Henry VIII and, 630
    as historiographer, 639
    as source on Richard III, 1121
More, Thomas de la. *See* de la More, Thomas
Morgan Grenfell, 522
Morgan, Kenneth O., 664, 1094
Morgan of Morgannwg, 111
Morgan, Philip, 253
Morgan, William, 383, 777
Morgenau of Saint David's, 384
Morland, George, 99
Morley, George, 273, 1110
Morley, John, 320
Mormons, 488
Morocco, 9, 461, 462
Morrell, David, 934
Morrill, John, 191, 1205
Morris (motor company), 915
Morris & Company, 552
Morris, Christopher D., 966
Morris Jones, Sir John, 777
Morris, R. J., 1209
Morris, W. A., 901
Morris, William, 161, 777
    furniture design and, 552
    Marxism and, 865
    medievalism and, 100
Morris, William, 1st Viscount Nuffield. *See under* Nuffield
Morrison, Herbert, 329, **911–12**, 1211
Mortain, 32
mortality rates, 1078, 1195
Mortimer family, 625
Mortimer, Roger, 1st Earl of March, 434, 435, 470
Mortmain, Statute of (1279), 1197
Morton, A. L., 644
Morton, Andrew, 250
Morton, John, 182, 183, **912–13**
Moslems. *See* Islam
Mosley, Sir Oswald, 499, 500, **913–15**
Motor Cars Act (1903), 1297
motor industry, 691, **915–16**, 1258. *See also* road transport
motorways, 545
Mount Badon, Battle of, 102, 571, **916–17**
mountaineering, 801, 1276

Mountbatten family, 452
Mountbatten, Louis, 1st Earl Mountbatten of Burma, 1397
    Charles, Prince of Wales and, 250, **917–18**
    India and, 293, 680, 681, 682
    papers of, 83
Mountbatten-Windsor families, 452
Mountjoy, Charles Blount, Lord, 957, 978
Mousehold, 748
Mowbray, Sir Philip, 127
Mozambique, 9
Mozart, Wolfgang Amadeus, 980
Much Wenlock, 804
Muckelroy, Keith, 64
Muggleton, Lodowick, 897
Muggletonians, 897–98
Mughal empire, 678, 679, 680, 683, 895
Muirchú, 1022
Mulcahy, Richard, 588
Mulling, Book of, 97
Mun, Thomas, 416
municipal archives, 83–84
Municipal Corporations Act (1835), 84, 308
Munro, Sir Thomas, 1093
Munster, 669
    Battle of Clontarf and, 184
    Civil Wars and, 271
    dioceses in, 374–75
    medieval, 696, 697, 698
    Nine Years' War and, 957
    Tudor "plantation" of, 701
murage tax, 73
murder. *See* homicide
Murdoch, Iris, 517
Murphy, Seán, 712
Murray, Lord George, 720, **918–19**
Muscovy, 245–46, 683, 805, 865
Muscovy Company, 246, 730
Museum of Labour History (Manchester), 537
Museum of Welsh Life, 981
Musgrave, Thomas, 304
Mushet, Robert, 142
music, **919–25**. *See also* opera
    archives related to, 87
    for ballet and dance, 125
    broadcasts of, 196, 197
    consumption of, 301, 800, 801
    under James V, King of Scots, 727
    John of Gaunt and, 737
    in late Hanoverian Britain, 604
    popular, **922–24**, 1408, 1409
music halls, 403, 674, 799, 801
Muslim League (India), 680
Muslims. *See* Islam
Musselburgh, 314
Mussolini, Benito, 1399
Musson, A. E., 1295
Mutiny Act (1766), 1129
Myers, A. R., 189
Mynydd Carn, Battle of (1081), 691
Mysore War (1799), 1347–48
mysteries (medieval dramas), 393–94, 1407
mystery novels, 519

Mytens, Daniel, 98
myths of origin, **925–27**

nabobs, 679
Nagasaki, 1402
naifty, 543
Namibia, 771, 850
Namier, Sir Lewis, 26, 166, 640, 644, 951, 1279, 1353
Nanking (or Nanjing), Treaty of (1842), 981
Napier, Sir Charles, 358
Naples, 943, 944
Napoleon I, Emperor of the French, 277, 443, 551, 552, 880, 1348
Napoleon III, Emperor of the French, 415, 830
Napoleonic Wars, **929–31**
    Bank of England during, 126
    Cape Colony and, 1213
    Congress of Vienna and, 217–18, 229, 295
    diplomacy during, 546
    George III and, 565
    inflation during, 693
    logistics and, 884
    military technology in, 894–95
    Navy during, 942
    slave trade and, 1189
    sugar trade and, 1249
    taxation and, 1253
    trade during, 1286, 1287
    Wellington and, 1348
    Whigs and, 1356
Naseby, Battle of (1645), 486
Nash, Paul, 101
Nashe, Thomas, 731
Nasser, Gamal Abdul, 1246–47
Natal, 202
National Aeronautics and Space Administration, 1216
national archives, 85–87
National Archives of Scotland, 86, 87
National Assembly of Wales (from 1999), 353, 663, 1071, 1072
National Assistance Act (1948), 1308
National Bus Company, 1079
National Coal Board, 794, 795, 898, 1258
National Council for Civil Liberties, 795
National Council of Girls' Clubs, 428
National Covenant (1638), 260, **931–32**, 1203. *See also* Covenanters
National Debt (Irish Free State), 307
National Debt (United Kingdom), 126, 1354
National Defence League, 120
National Education League, 1160
National Enterprise Board, 294, 448
National Evangelical Anglican Congresses, 549
National Front, 499, 500, 1088
National Government (1931–35)
    Attlee on, 113
    Baldwin and, 121
    George V and, 567
    Great Depression and, 347–48
    Lansbury and, 778
    MacDonald and, 836
National Government (1935–40), 121

planning (continued)
  in Birmingham, 155
  in Cardiff, 222
  in Edinburgh, 423, 424
  in Exeter, 475
  in London, 826, 827, 912
  Roman concepts of, 158
Plantagenet, Geoffrey. See Geoffrey, Count
    of Anjou
Plantagenet, Isabel, 1267
Plantagenet Kingdom, **1046–48**. See also
    specific rulers
Plassey, Battle of (1757), 277
Plato, 276, 650
Plautus, 276
Plegmund of Canterbury, 372
Plot, Robert, 310
ploughs, 493
Plumb, J. H., 189, 643
Plummer, C., 41
Plummer, Charles, 17, 133
Plunkett, Sir Horace, 708
Plunkett, Oliver, 374
Plutarch, 276, 738, 1132
Plymouth, 373, 393
Plymouth Brethren, 548
Plymouth colony, 28
Pneumatic Institute (Clifton), 337
Pocock, J. G. A., 167, 191–92
Poe, Edgar Allan, 519
poetry, **1048–56**
  Anglo-French, 1363
  Columbanus and, 291
  courtly love and, 315
  in Irish, 271
  Latin Christian, 1267
  of Map, 853
  medieval Scandinavian, 1328
  in Middle English, **1049–50**
  in Modern English, **1050–56**
  in Old English, 258, 635, **1048–49**
  Renaissance, **1050–51**
  Restoration and eighteenth-century,
    1051–52
  Romantic era, **1052–53**
  in Scots English, **1049**
  in Scots Gaelic, 271
  since 1914, **1055–56**
  Victorian and Edwardian, **1053–55**
  in Welsh, 776–77, 1333, 1334
Pointblank, Operation, 611
Poitiers, Battle of (1356), 436
Poitou, 32, 445, 446, 839, 1289
Poland, 278, 287, 314, 415, 1401
Pole, Margaret, 232
Pole, Reginald, Cardinal, 235, 453
Pole, Sir Richard, 89
Poles, de la (earls/dukes of Suffolk). See
    under de la Pole
police, 791, 792–95, 1199
  Chadwick and, 241
  in Channel Islands, 246
  in Ireland, 136, 891
  in Irish Free State, 308
  in Lancashire, 309
  in London, 784, 891–92

  in Norfolk, 309
  in Northern Ireland, 136, 351
  Seven Years' War and, 1179
Police Act (1805), 423
politeness and gentility, 285, 536, **1056–58**,
    1164
  Burke on, 205
  English aristocracy and, 1202
Political Register, 282
political thought
  of Alfred the Great, 17–18, 20
  of Bale, 122
  of Baxter, 130
  of Bentham, 137, 1323
  of Bolingbroke, 166–67
  of Burke, 204, 298
  of Butt, 208
  classical influences on, 276
  of Cobbett, 282
  Conservative Party and, 298
  of Disraeli, 385
  in eighteenth-century Ireland, 704
  Glorious Revolution and, 575
  of Hobbes, 647, 648
  of Hooker, 651
  of John of Salisbury, 738
  of Knox, 756, 757
  Labour Party and, 760
  of Locke, 822, 937, 1021, 1089, 1183,
    1270–71, 1353
  of Mills, 1323
  of More, 910, 911
  natural law and, 937, 938
  of Paine, 995, 996
  Putney Debates and, 1081
  in Scotland, 1312
  of Sidgwick, 1323
politics, contemporary. See contemporary
    politics
poll tax, 1027, 1253
Pollard, A. F., 640, 1299
Pollen, Allen, 940
Pollock, Sir Frederick, 741
pollution control, 2
Polybius, 276
Polynesia, 305–6
polyphony, 921–22
polytechnics, 428, 460, 1315–16
Pontefract, 761
Poitiers, Battle of, 436 — [no]
Poor Law, 488, 875, **1060–65**, 1199, 1385
  public health and, 1078
  relief system and, 1222, 1307, 1308
Poor Law Amendment Act (1834), 241,
    1064, 1207, 1307
Poor Law Commission (administrative),
    240, 1064
Poor Laws, Royal Commission on the
    (investigative), 240
Poore, Herbert, 365
Poore, Richard, 365
Poovey, Mary, 1378
Pop Art, 101, 102
Pope, Alexander, 138, 167, 555, 1051, 1052
Popish Plot (1678), 55, 731, 1101, 1183
Popular Front movement, 319, 678
popular music, 922–24, 1408, 1409

Popular "party" in Church of Scotland, 261
popular religion, **1058–59**, 1155–56
population. See also demography; settlement
  Agricultural Revolution and, 494
  early distribution of, 1178–79
  inflation in sixteenth and seventeenth
    centuries and, 693
  Irish Famine and, 585, 586
  land ownership and, 457
  of London, 825
  Malthusianism and, 846–47
  manorial economy and, 852
  marriage and, 861
  prostitution and, 1072
  in Scotland, 1165
  social conflict and, 1195
pornography, 573, 1073, 1181
porphyria, 564, 565
Port Sunlight, 264, **1059–60**
Portal, Sir Charles, 611
Porter, Brian, 412
Porter, George, 1144, 1145
Portland Bill, 547, 616
Portland, William Cavendish Bentick, 3rd
    Duke of, 539, 1129
ports, 281, 544
Portsmouth, 64, 1289
Portugal, 218
  Africa and, 9
  contact with, 476
  Dominicans in, 1101
  Drake and, 393
  Eden and, 419
  Howard, Earl of Nottingham and, 652
  in Peninsular Wars, 931
  trade with, 1291
Post Office, 294, 328, 446, 447, 1259–60
Postan, M. M., 1045, 1332
Post-Impressionist Exhibition (1910), 162
postmodernism, 78
potatoes, 499, 585, 586, 706
Potsdam Conference (1945), **1400–1402**,
    1403
Potter, Beatrice. See Webb, Beatrice
Potteries district, 544
pottery, 301, 1132, 1178, 1179, 1289
poultry, 492, 499
Pound, Ezra, 516, 1054, 1055, 1379
Pounds, N. J. G., 691
poverty, **1060–65**
  in Belfast, 135
  Bentham's views on, 137
  in Bristol, 187
  childhood and, 256–57
  emigration and, 455
  of farm workers, 1271–72
  Franciscans and, 1106
  during Great Depressin, 347
  in Ireland, 585
  in Liverpool, 815
  medicine and, 876, 877
  mortality rates and, 1078
  old age and, 976
  railways and, 459
  Rowntree and, 1141
  in Scotland, 313, 634–35

royal succession. *See* Hanoverian succession; succession, royal
royal supremacy, **1147**
 Cartwright and, 228
 Thomas Cromwell and, 322
 Elizabeth I and, 453
 Henry VIII and, 630
 impact of Catholic Restoration, 236
 Llywelyn ab Iorwerth and, 819
Royal Tank Corps, 796
Royal University, Belfast, 1318
Ruaraidh (or Ruaidrí) Uí Conchobar. *See* Rory O'Connor
rubber, 683, 840, 1288
Rudé, George, 644
Rufus, Richard, 590
Rufus, William. *See* William II
rugby, 1224–25, 1226
rum trade, 1248, 1286, 1287
Rumford, Benjamin Thompson, Count, 337, 1144, 1145
Rump Parliament, 160, 677, 831, 832
Runciman, Sir Steven, 422
Runcorn, 431, 544
Runnymede, 839, 1119
Rupert, Prince, Count Palatine of the Rhine, Duke of Bavaria, Duke of Cumberland, and Earl of Holderness, 486
Rural Constabulatory Act (1839), 241
Rushdie, Salman, 518
Ruskin, John, 77, 100, 992
Russell, Bertrand, 162
Russell, Conrad, 191, 201
Russell, Dora, 1382
Russell, Francis, 4th Earl of Bedford. *See under* Bedford
Russell, Gordon, 552
Russell, J. C., 1045
Russell, Lord John, later 1st Earl Russell, 327, 584, **1147–49**
Russell, William Russell, Lord, 1269
Russia Company, 1286
Russian empire. *See also* Muscovy
 Belgium and, 830
 Congress of Berlin and, 139–40
 Congress system and, 295
 Crimean War and, 318
 Eastern Question and, 415
 feminism in, 503
 Great Game and, 478
 Hoare and, 647
 pre–World War I rapprochement with, 462
 Rothschild and, 1139
Russian Federation (since 1991), 757, 758
Russian Revolutions (1917), 711, 999
Russo-Japanese War (1904–5), 415, 462
Russo-Turkish War (1828–29), 415
Russo-Turkish War (1877–78), 225, 415
Rutherford, Samuel, 260, 269
Rutland, 311, 368, 666
Ruxburghe, dukes of, 313
Rwanda, 850
Ryan, Butterfield, 287
Ryder, Henry, 367

Rye House Plot, 822, 1269
Rymer, Thomas, 909

Sabah, 840
Sacheverell, Henry, 111, 112, 579, 859, 1354
Sachs, Julius, 175
Sackville-West, Vita, 162
sacramentalism, 90
Sadler Committee (1832), 485
Sadler, Michael Thomas, 484, 485
Sadlers Wells Theatre (London), 124
Safeway (British retail chain), 1111
sailing ships, 281, 544, 545
Sainsbury's (retail chain), 1111
Saint Albans, 1135
Saint Albans, Abbey of, 259, 334, 1002, **1151–52**
Saint Albans, archdeaconry of, 368
Saint Albans, diocese of, 362
Saint Andrews, Archbishopric of, 379, 464, 746
Saint Andrews Cathedral, 379, 380
Saint Andrews, University of, 745, 1315
Saint Asaph Cathedral, 230
Saint Asaph, diocese of, 382, 383
Saint Augustine's Abbey, Canterbury, 41, 68, 1237, 1405
 Augustine and, 114
 David cult at, 334
 Gildas manuscript at, 571
Saint Bartholomew's, Smithfield (London), 1105
Saint Cross, hospital of, 131
Saint Cuthbert, liberty of, 832
Saint David's Cathedral, 230, 334, 384
Saint David's, diocese of, 383–84
Saint David's Monastery, 107, 108, 334, 569
Saint Edmund, College of, Salisbury, 231
Saint George's Chapel, Windsor, 182, 231, 232, 436
Saint Germain, 721
Saint Gildas de Rhuys, Monastery of (Brittany), 571
Saint Helens, 815
Saint Ives (Cambridgeshire), 1061
Saint Ives (Cornwall), 101
Saint John, Oliver, 601
Saint John the Baptist, Coventry, 231
Saint John's College, Cambridge, 530
Saint Magnus, Cathedral of, Kirkwall, 379, 382
Saint Mark's Hospital, London, 875
Saint Mary the Great, Church of, Cambridge, 361
Saint Mary's Hospital (Paddington, London), 533
Saint Nicholas's Priory, Exeter, 475
Saint Omer, 376, 732
Saint Patrick's Cathedral, Dublin, 376
Saint Paul's Cathedral, London, 230, 826
Saint Peter and Saint Paul, collegiate church of, Heytesbury, 231
Saint Peter, College of, Wolverhampton, 231–32

Saint Peter, Collegiate Church of. *See* Westminster Abbey
Saint Salvator's College, Saint Andrews, 746
Saint Stephen's Chapel, Westminster, 231, 1008
Saint Thomas's (Devon), 475
sake and soke, 832, 833
Salesbury, William, 777
Salford, 1210
Salisbury, 231, 279
Salisbury Cathedral, 205–6, 230, 231, 364, 365
Salisbury, diocese of, 364, 365, 369, 373, 733, 1381
Salisbury, Oaths of (1086), 662, **1152–53**
Salisbury, Robert Cecil, 1st Earl of. *See under* Cecil
Salisbury, Robert Gascoyne-Cecil, 3rd Marquis of, 944, **1153–55**
 Balfour and, 123
 Randolph Churchill and, 261
 Conservative Party and, 298
 county councils and, 308
 Devonshire (9th Duke) and, 354
 Kitchener and, 755
 Suez Canal and, 1246
 waning influence of, 461
Sallust, 61
Salmon, Nathaniel, 310
salmonella, 499
salt, 473, 544, 815, 1273, 1289, 1291, 1293
Saltaire, 1059
Saltmarsh, J. A., 1046
Salvation Army, **1155–56**
Salzman, L. F., 889
Samoa, 850
Samuel, Herbert, 1st Viscount Samuel of Mount Carmel and Toxteth, 561
Samuel Memorandum (1926), 561
Samuel, Raphael, 982
San Felipe (ship), 393
San Juan d'Ulloa, 615
San Rosario (ship), 547
San Stefano, Treaty of (1878), 139, 140
Sancroft, William, **1156**
sanctuary, right of, 833
Sandemanianism, 490, 1408
Sander(s), Nicholas, 165, 166, 317, **1157–58**
Sandon, Lord, 1160
Sandwich, 845, 1289
Sandys, Sir Edwin, 29–30, 651
Sanitary Commission, 956
sanitary reform, 240–41, 955–56, 1078
Sankey Commission, 1191, 1192
Sanquhar, Declaration of (1680), 464
Sant, King of Ceredigion, 334
Santiago de Compostela, 744
São Tomé, 1248
Sarawak, 840–41
Sargant, William Lucas, 988
Sargent, John Singer, 99
Saro Princess flying boats, 5
Sarrail, Maurice, 850

Sarsfield, Patrick, 810
Sarum, 334, 364, 365. *See also* Salisbury
Sarum Primer, 235
Sarum, Use of (liturgy), 369, 814
satellite technology, 1217
Saul, Nigel, 737
Savile, Sir George, 1129
Saville, John, 644
Savoy, 1220
Savoy, Eugene, Prince of, 1221
Sawtre, William, 363–64
Sawyer, P. H., 965
Sawyer, Peter, 966
Saxe-Coburg-Gotha, House of, 905
Saxon Shore, 1133
Saxonism, 926–27
Saxons, 48, 1178, 1262, 1275
Saxton, Christopher, 310, 730
Saye and Sele, William Fiennes, 1st
        Viscount, 601
Sayers, Dorothy L., 993
SBAC. *See* Society of British Aerospace
        Companies
Scandinavia. *See also* Denmark; Norway;
        Sweden; Vikings
    Cnut and, 280
    Crusades and, 323
    Danelaw and, 331
    Godwine and, 580
    Malcolm II and, 842
    trade with, 1289, 1291
Scapa Flow, 985
Scapula, Ostorius, 1131, 1137
Scarborough, 1027
Scargill, Arthur, 561
Scarisbrick, Jack, 247
scarlet fever, 1078
Schalby, John de, 368
Schaller, Dieter, 291
Schapera, I., 816
schiltron, 127–28
Schoenbein, Christian Friedrich, 490
Scholastic Registration Association, 1159
Scholasticism, 416–17, 590, 1406
schooling. *See* education
schools. *See also* education; universities
    boarding, 1205
    botany in, 175
    cathedral, 1161
    Catholic Church and, 233
    chantry, 1162
    charity, 1159, 1379
    child labour and, 254
    Church of England and, 123
    classical influences in, 275–76
    furniture of, 550
    grammar, 1161, 1162
    impact of dissolution of religious houses
        and chantries on, 387
    in Lancashire, 309
    leaving age for, 530
    literacy and, 813, 1159
    in New Lanark, 947
    in Northern Ireland, 351
    polytechnics, 1316
    in Scotland, 313

song, 1159, 1161
    vocational, 60
    women and, 1385
Schroders (merchant bank), 522
Schumpeter, Joseph, 674
science, 137. *See also* biological sciences;
        chemistry; evolution; natural philoso-
        phy; technology
    archives of, 83, 87
    bacteriological, 532–33
    biological, 153–54
    botanical, 175–76
    chemistry, 179–81
    coffee house culture and, 285
    computing industry and, 294
    Darwinism and, 332–33
    Davy and, 337
    Dee and, 345
    Great Exhibition and, 584
    Hobbes and, 647, 648
    Huxley and, 655–56
    missionary movements and, 900
    natural philosophy and, 938
    Newton and, 954–55
    Matthew Paris and, 1152
    Priestley and, 1067–68
    Ralegh and, 1092
    Royal Society of London and, 1145–46,
        1162–64
    schools for, 1316
    secularization and, 1175
    sexual mores and, 1181
    space technology and exploration and,
        1216–17
    technology and, 1256
    Watt and, 1343
    witchcraft and, 1370
    zoological classification, 1411–12
science fiction, 519
Science Museum (London), 152
Scientific Survey of Air Warfare, Committee
        for the, 968
Scilly Isles, 307, 373, 1272, 1273
Scofield, Cora L., 1280
Scofield, Paul, 911
Scone, 14, 747
Scone Palace, 556
Scotichronicon, 1336
Scotland. *See also* Highlands of Scotland;
        Lowlands of Scotland; *specific cities
        and regions*
    Act of Union and, 1309–10
    Queen Anne and, 51, 52
    Arbroath Declaration and, 60–61
    archaeology of, 64
    archives in, 84, 85, 86, 87
    Athelstan and, 110
    banking in, 522
    Battle of Brunanburh and, 198–99
    Battle of the Standard and, 1228–29
    bibliographical studies of, 146–47, 148,
        149–51
    Books of Discipline in history of, 173
    botany in, 176
    Edward Bruce and, 197
    castles in, 72

Celtic church in, 44
Charles I and, 248
child labour in, 254
Civil Wars (1642–51) and, 266, 268,
        270, 271
Cnut and, 280
coastal topography of, 1273
Columba and, 290
Conservative Party in, 380
constitutional law and, 300
county councils in, 308
county histories of, 270, 271, 312–14
Crusades and, 323–24
Darien scheme and, 331–32
David cult in, 334
devolution in, 302, 351–52, 1301
diary-writing practices in, 357
dictionaries and reference works on,
        638–39
divorce law in, 387–88
early medieval Ireland and, 379
early modern, **1165–67**
Edgar the Ætheling and, 422
Edward I and, 127, 736, 945
Edward II and, 127–28, 435
Edward III and, 336, 436, 945, 946
Edward IV and, 438
eighteenth-century, 603
electronics industry in, 448
emigration to America from, 24, 455
emigration to Australia from, 455
English language in, 775–76
Episcopalianism in, 464–65
Eric Bloodaxe and, 465
European Community/Union and, 467
evangelicalism in, 469
farming in, 455
Fenian movement in, 505
film industry and, 520
football (soccer) in, 1225
Franciscans in, 1106
French Revolutionary Wars and, 546
furniture of, 550
genealogical resources, 488
Glorious Revolution and, 576
Godolphin and, 579
Gunpowder Plot and, 594
Halidon Hill battle and, 599
Hardie and, 608
Henry I and, 621
Henry II and, 622
Henry VII and, 629
Henry VIII and, 50–51
heraldry in, 632, 633
hermits and anchorites in, 634
historical surveys of, 188–91
impact of Highland Clearances on, 635
Irish immigration to, 380, 660
iron industry in, 459
Isle of Man and, 848
Jacobitism in, 605, 719, 720, 1243–45
James VI and I and, 728
James VII and II and, 729
Jesuits in, 731, 732, 1096
Labour Party in, 380
land ownership in, 456–57

espionage and, 1173
George V and, 567
Girl Guide movement during, 572
Great Depression's origins in, 347
Haig and, 598–99
Hardie and, 607
Henderson and, 618
Hoare and, 647
home front in, **1386–88**
Kitchener and, 755–56
Lloyd George and, 818
Merseyside and, 264
naval and air operations, **1388–89**
Navy and, 941
New Zealand and, 949–50
other fronts, **1389–90**
Parliament and, 1011
shipbuilding during, 1185
Smillies's opposition to, 1192
Snowden and, 1193
taxation and, 527
treaties, **1391–92**
western front, **1392–93**
women and, 358, 501, 1294, 1376,
1393–95
World War II, **1395–1404**
air operations, **1395–96**
Army and, 93, 94
Australia and, 116
Baldwin and, 120
Bank of England and, 126
BBC in, 196
Bevin and, 144
British-American relations during,
1313
Neville Chamberlain and, 245
Channel Islands during, 246–47
Winston Churchill and, 262–63
coastal transport and, 281
Cold War origins and, 287
Cripps and, 319–20
Eden and, 420
Elizabeth the Queen Mother and, 449,
450
espionage and, 1174
Exeter during, 475
Far East in, **1396–97**, 1399
food and nutrition during, 535
George VI and, 567, 568
Hanover bombed during, 563
Harris and, 611–12
historiography and, 1281
home front, **1397–98**
Irish Free State during, 341–42, 712,
713
League of Nations and, 1392
Merchant Navy and, 886
Montgomery and, 908–9
naval operations, **1398–99**
Navy and, 941
New Zealand and, 949
North Africa campaign, **1399–1400**
Pacific front, 411
Polish airmen in, 314
postwar consensus and, 296–97
Rochester diocese during, 364

Royal Air Force in, 1143, 1144
shipbuilding during, 1186
Teheran, Yalta, and Potsdam Conferences,
1400–1402
western front, **1402–4**
women and, 1294, 1376
World Wide Web, 694
Worms, Concordat of (1122), 53
Wrekin, 1333
Wren, Sir Christopher, 826
Wright, Dickson, 873
Wright, Frank Lloyd, 552
Wright, Neil, 291
Wright, Stephen, 639
Wrightson, Keith, 1165
Wrigley, E. A., 643
Wriothesley, Sir Thomas, 1st Baron
Wriothesley of Titchfield and Earl of
Southampton, 105, 1249
Wroth, Mary, 509
Wroughton, 442
Wroxeter, 67, 1332
WSPU. *See* Women's Social and Political
Union
Wulfhere of Wiltshire, 426
Wulfred of Canterbury, 42, 442, 443
Wulfric of Haselbury, 633
Wulfron (or Wulfruna), Lady, 231
Wulfstan of Worcester, 369, **1404–5**
Wulfstan of York, 973
church organization and, 42
Danelaw and, 330
on kingship, 420
law codes and, 49
Northumbrian Kingdom and, 465–66
Wulfstan the Dane, 1328
Würzburg, University of, 175
Wyatt, George, 1157
Wyatt, James, 76
Wyatt, Sir Thomas, 165
Wyatt's rebellion, 451
Wycherley, William, 399–400
Wyclif(fe), John, 977, **1405–6**
Grosseteste's influence on, 590
John of Gaunt and, 737
Lollardy and, 823, 824
Wyke, Terry, 849
Wynne, Ellis, 777
Wyvill, Christopher, 1089

xenophobia, 178–79
Xhosas, 743

Yahuda, Abraham, 955
Yalta Conference (1945), 287, 838,
1400–1402, 1403
Yardley, Edward, 384
Yates, Joseph Brooks, 253
Yearsley, Ann, 164
Yeatman, R. J., 716
Yeats, W. B., 406, 515, 1054, 1055
Yeavering, 966
Yellow Ford, Battle of the (1598), 957
Yelverton's Act (1782), 1066
Yemen. *See* Aden
Yeu, Ile d', 1093

Yihe Quan. *See* Boxer Rising
York, **1407–8**
archives of, 84
Carlisle and, 370
church learning in, 43
cloth industry in, 278
craft guilds in, 316
Dublin and, 405
Merchant Adventurers of, 880
music in, 925
Olafr Gothfrithsson and, 426, 427
Peasants' Revolt and, 1027
poverty in Victorian, 1064
prostitution in, 1073
public transport in early modern, 1079
in Roman era, 1135
Rowntree and, 1141
as trading center, 1288
Vikings in, 1329
York, Anne, Duchess of (1637–71). *See*
Hyde, Anne
York, Archbishopric of, 42, 43
provincial councils and, 304
Scottish dioceses and, 14, 379, 380, 381,
464
York, Convocation of, 304
York Cycle of plays, 394
York, diocese of, 360, 371–72, 1405
Grindal and, 589
hermits and anchorites in, 634
Wilfrid and, 1360
York Gospels, 97
York, Kingdom of
Athelstan and, 110–11, 198, 199
Eadred and, 1264
Edward the Elder and, 430
Eric Bloodaxe and, 465, 466
York Minster, 230, 231, 1032–33,
1407–8
York Primer, 235
York Retreat, 875
York, Richard, Duke of (1411–60), 1047,
1189, 1267
Cade Rebellion and, 211
Calais and, 213
Henry VI and, 627, 628
York, Richard, Duke of (1473–83?), 1120,
1267, 1341–42
York, Sarah, Duchess of, 452, 905
Yorkshire. *See also* East Riding; North
Riding; West Riding
Catholicism in, 233
chantries in, 387
Chester diocese and, 371
Civil Wars and, 270
cloth industry in, 278–79
Danby and, 329–30
Danelaw and, 331
dioceses and, 372
emigration to American colonies from,
28
eyres in, 479, 1086
Fairfax and, 485, 486
gentry in, 1205
hermits and anchorites in, 633
Independent Labour Party in, 678

For Reference

Not to be taken from this room